IFIP Advances in Information and Communication Technology

488

Editor-in-Chief

Kai Rannenberg, Goethe University Frankfurt, Germany

Editorial Board

IFIP – The International Federation for Information Processing

IFIP was founded in 1960 under the auspices of UNESCO, following the first World Computer Congress held in Paris the previous year. A federation for societies working in information processing, IFIP's aim is two-fold: to support information processing in the countries of its members and to encourage technology transfer to developing nations. As its mission statement clearly states:

IFIP is the global non-profit federation of societies of ICT professionals that aims at achieving a worldwide professional and socially responsible development and application of information and communication technologies.

IFIP is a non-profit-making organization, run almost solely by 2500 volunteers. It operates through a number of technical committees and working groups, which organize events and publications. IFIP's events range from large international open conferences to working conferences and local seminars.

The flagship event is the IFIP World Computer Congress, at which both invited and contributed papers are presented. Contributed papers are rigorously refereed and the rejection rate is high.

As with the Congress, participation in the open conferences is open to all and papers may be invited or submitted. Again, submitted papers are stringently refereed.

The working conferences are structured differently. They are usually run by a working group and attendance is generally smaller and occasionally by invitation only. Their purpose is to create an atmosphere conducive to innovation and development. Refereeing is also rigorous and papers are subjected to extensive group discussion.

Publications arising from IFIP events vary. The papers presented at the IFIP World Computer Congress and at open conferences are published as conference proceedings, while the results of the working conferences are often published as collections of selected and edited papers.

IFIP distinguishes three types of institutional membership: Country Representative Members, Members at Large, and Associate Members. The type of organization that can apply for membership is a wide variety and includes national or international societies of individual computer scientists/ICT professionals, associations or federations of such societies, government institutions/government related organizations, national or international research institutes or consortia, universities, academies of sciences, companies, national or international associations or federations of companies.

More information about this series at http://www.springer.com/series/6102

Irenilza Nääs · Oduvaldo Vendrametto
João Mendes Reis · Rodrigo Franco Gonçalves
Márcia Terra Silva · Gregor von Cieminski
Dimitris Kiritsis (Eds.)

Advances in Production Management Systems

Initiatives for a Sustainable World

IFIP WG 5.7 International Conference, APMS 2016
Iguassu Falls, Brazil, September 3–7, 2016
Revised Selected Papers

 Springer

Editors
Irenilza Nääs
Paulista University
São Paulo
Brazil

Oduvaldo Vendrametto
Paulista University
São Paulo
Brazil

João Mendes Reis
Paulista University
São Paulo
Brazil

Rodrigo Franco Gonçalves
Paulista University
São Paulo
Brazil

Márcia Terra Silva
Paulista University
São Paulo
Brazil

Gregor von Cieminski
ZF Friedrichshafen AG
Friedrichshafen
Germany

Dimitris Kiritsis
EPFL
Lausanne
Switzerland

ISSN 1868-4238   ISSN 1868-422X   (electronic)
IFIP Advances in Information and Communication Technology
ISBN 978-3-319-84576-0   ISBN 978-3-319-51133-7   (eBook)
DOI 10.1007/978-3-319-51133-7

Printed on acid-free paper

This Springer imprint is published by Springer Nature
The registered company is Springer International Publishing AG
The registered company address is: Gewerbestrasse 11, 6330 Cham, Switzerland

Preface

The APMS has been the official conference of the IFIP Working Group 5.7 on Advances in Production Management Systems, bringing together leading experts from academia, research, and industry.

The first conference was in Helsinki in 1990, and since then the conference has become an important annual event. The conference has been hosted in various parts of the world including Cernobbio (Italy, 2010), Stavanger (Norway, 2011), Rhodes (Greece, 2012), State College (USA, 2013), Ajaccio (France, 2014), and Tokyo (Japan, 2015). For the first time, the conference was held in Latin America at Iguassu Falls (Brazil, 2016). The overall organization was supported by Paulista University/UNIP with the financial grant of Itaipu Binacional. The topics of APMS 2016 were similar to those of the IFIP WG 5.7. They cover all the aspects of the systems of production of goods and services. For the 2016 issue, the theme selected was "Production Management Initiatives for a Sustainable World."

A total of 112 papers from 18 countries were accepted for oral presentation based on blind peer-review. The main review criteria were the paper quality and contributions to science and production management processes. The Scientific Committee consisted of 78 researchers, most of them active members of the IFIP WG 5.7. Accepted papers of registered participants are included in this volume. This year, ten special sessions and one Research Workshop were planned consistent with the main theme of the conference. Following the tradition of past APMS conferences, the 9th APMS Doctoral Workshop offered seven PhD students the opportunity to present, discuss, receive feedback, and exchange comments and views on their doctoral research from the academic and the IFIP WG 5.7 community.

Three honors were awarded during APMS 2016: the Burbidge Award for best paper, the Burbidge Award for best presentation, and the Doctoral Workshop Award.

We hope that the contents of this volume will be of interest to researchers and practitioners alike.

October 2016

Irenilza A. Nääs
Oduvaldo Vendrametto
João Mendes Reis
Rodrigo Franco Gonçalves
Márcia Terra Silva
Dimitris Kiritsis
Gregor von Cieminski

Organization

APMS 2016 was organized by the Postgraduate Program in Production Engineering of Paulista University and IFIP workgroup WG5.7.

Conference Chair

Irenilza de Alencar Nääs	UNIP, Brazil

Co-chairs

Dimitris Kiritsis	EPFL, Switzerland
Oduvaldo Vendrametto	UNIP, Brazil
Gregor Von Cieminski	ZF Friedrichshafen AG, Germany

International Scientific Committee

Chairs

Pedro Luiz Costa Neto	UNIP, Brazil
Cecilia Villas Boas	UNIP, Brazil

Members

Erry Yulian Triblas Adesta	Kulliyyah Department of Engineering, Malaysia
Erlend Alfnes	Norwegian University of Science and Technology, Norway
Thecle Alix	IUT Bordeaux Montesquieu, France
Susanne Altendorfer-Kaiser	Montanuniversität Leoben, Austria
Farhad Ameri	Texas State University, USA
Bjørn Andersen	Norwegian University of Science and Technology, Norway
Eiji Arai	Osaka University, Japan
Frédérique Biennier	INSA de Lyon Department Informatique, France
Umit S. Bititci	Heriot Watt University, UK
Magali Bosch-Mauchand	Université de Technologie de Compiègne, France
Abdelaziz Bouras	Qatar University, Qatar
Jim Browne	CIM Research Unit University College, Ireland
Alfred Büchel	Switzerland
Luis Camarinha-Matos	Universidade Nova de Lisboa, Portugal
Allan S. Carrie	University of Strathclyde, UK
Sergio Cavalieri	University of Bergamo, Italy
Stephen Childe	University of Plymouth, UK
Hyunbo Cho	Pohang University of Science and Technology, Korea

Byoung-Kyu Choi	KAIST Faculty, Korea
Adolfo Crespo Marquez	University of Seville, Spain
Catherine Da Cunha	Ecole Centrale de Nantes, France
Irenilza de Alencar Naas	Paulista University, Brazil
Frédéric Demoly	Université de Technologie de Belfort-Montbéliard, France
Shengchun Deng	Harbin Institute of Technology, China
Alexandre Dolgui	Ecole Nationale Supérieure des Mines de Saint-Etienne, France
Slavko Dolinšek	University of Ljubljana Institute for Innovation and Development, Slovenia
Guy Doumeingts	BPM Expert ADELIOR France GFI Group, France
Heidi C. Dreyer	Norwegian University of Science and Technology, Norway
Eero Eloranta	Helsinki University of Technology, Finland
Christos Emmanouilidis	Innovation Centre in Knowledge, Communication and Information Technologies, Greece
Peter Falster	Technical University of Denmark, Denmark
Jan Frick	Stavanger University, Norway
Susumu Fujii	Kobe University, Japan
Paolo Gaiardelli	University of Bergamo, Italy
Marco Garetti	Politecnico di Milano, Italy
Samuel Gomes	Université de Technologie de Belfort-Montbéliard, France
Bernard Grabot	ENIT, France
Robert W. Grubbström	Linköping Institute of Technology, Sweden
Gerhard Gudergan	FIR Research Institute for Operations Management, Germany
Thomas R. Gulledge Jr.	George Mason University, USA
Gideon Halevi	Hal Tech Ltd., Israel
Bernd Hamacher	University of Bremen, Germany
Hironori Hibino	Technical Research Institute, Japan
Bernd E. Hirsch	University of Bremen, Germany
Hans-Henrik Hvolby	Aalborg University, Denmark
Ichiro Inoue	Kyoto Sangyo University, Japan
Christopher Irgens	University of Strathclyde, UK
Harinder Jagdev	National University of Ireland, Ireland
John Johansen	Aalborg University, Denmark
Toshiya Kaihara	Kobe University, Japan
Tomasz Koch	Wroclaw University of Technology, Poland
Ashok K. Kochhar	Aston University, UK
Boonserm Kulvatunyou	National Institute of Standards and Technology, USA
Thomas R. Kurfess	Clemson University, USA
A. Kusiak	University of Iowa Industrial Engineering, USA
Andrew Kusiak	University of Iowa, USA
Lenka Landryova	Technical University of Ostrava, Czech Republic

Sponsoring Institutions

Itaipu Binacional

Contents

Modelling of Business and Operational Processes

Collaborative Systems

Innovation and Collaborative Networks

Agrifood Supply Chains

Production Economics

Lean Manufacturing

Sustainable Production Management - Which Approaches Work in Practice?

Operations Management in Engineer-to-Order Manufacturing

Computational Intelligence in Production Managements

Determination of Operating Parameters and Performance Analysis of Computer Networks with Paraconsistent Annotated Evidential Logic Eτ

Avelino Palma Pimenta Junior[(✉)], Jair Minoro Abe,
and Genivaldo Carlos Silva

Graduate Program in Production Engineering, Paulista University,
R. Dr. Bacelar 1212, São Paulo 04026-002, Brazil
appimenta@gmail.com, jairabe@uol.com.br,
gcsilva@ig.com.br

Abstract. Computer networks have two important characteristics: the vast diversity of connecting devices and a great variability of the physical distribution of equipments. Therefore, the performance analysis of a specific network based on absolute references or third parties may not be applicable in all circumstances, especially in highly complex and heterogeneous networks. Indeed, it carries a high degree of uncertainty, and the classical logic may not be appropriate to deal it. This paper aims to parameterize and evaluate the operating elements of heterogeneous networks, from the analysis of representative attributes, based on concepts of Paraconsistent Annotated Evidential Logic Eτ.

Keywords: Paraconsistent logic · Computer networks · Network parameterization · Pattern recognition

1 Introduction

Computer networks are currently used in most companies, and represent an important means of interoperability and data communication. As the World Wide Web and users are explicating at a very rapid rate, the performance of World Wide Web systems become rapidly high [1]. Since its inception, the foundation for the deployment of networks pointed to a variety of devices from different manufacturers and architectures, and often operates at varying speeds. The different links in the local area network can operate at different speeds and can run at different medias, such as 1 Gbps or 100 Mbps, copper or fiber [2]. The copper-based communications encode data via electrical impulses, unlike the optical fiber that uses light signals for this purpose. The existence of these two physical means of data communication, in varying degrees of use, must be rendered compatible. However, the communication of heterogeneous systems is not always an easy task, and it is not always possible to obtain optimal and predictable results.

A computer network consists of several connected hosts, which can be represented by a desktop, a laptop, a smartphone, among others. In such an heterogeneous client

I. Nääs et al. (Eds.): APMS 2016, IFIP AICT 488, pp. 3–11, 2016.
DOI: 10.1007/978-3-319-51133-7_1

environment, efficient content adaptation and delivery services are becoming a major requirement for the new Internet service infrastructure [3]. However, many of these equipments may have different architectures, and also use different operating systems and applications.

All the previous elements are part of computer networks, but also constitute as conflict elements, which makes it even more difficult to measure the performance of a network. Typical evaluation methods, such as benchmark performance, however, are limited in applicability. Often they are not representative of the traffic characteristics of any customer facility [4]. The issue of uncertainty, therefore, should be considered. A possible solution could be the analysis of experts in the field of computer networks. This approach may not be suitable for all cases, since not always the professional knows profoundly the network to be analyzed. Moreover, although differences exist, some elements are common in network communications. For the establishment of network communication, there must always be a request from the side of the "client". It is a typical protocol of request-response, which controls the data transfer between server and client (such as a web browser) [5].

This request, when answered by the side of the "server" – typically a proxy, produces a corresponding response. Proxy servers are designed with three goals: decrease network traffic, reduce user (client) perceived lag, and reduce loads on the origin servers [6].

Every request from the client passes through the proxy server, which in turn may or may not modify the client request based on its implementation mechanism [7]. This response is accompanied by several attributes that can be used to analyze network performance. The most representative attributes may be used as a means of determining the network operating parameters. This work aims to analyze and detect problems in a computer network from a public university with about two hundred hosts, divided into two different departments (academic and administrative) with the aid of Paraconsistent Logic. In the academic department, there are six computer labs with twenty hosts each, plus two coordination rooms, with the total of ten hosts each. In the administrative department, five operating rooms, with approximately fifty hosts, as well as servers, routers and switches, all connected by copper or fiber optic links, and operating for fifteen hours a day, five days a week. Each department has different needs and use different services and applications. Therefore, it is clear the high degree of hetero-geneity and uncertainty of the analyzed scenario, which makes it appropriate to use a non-classical logic, the subject of this paper.

2 Methodology

Responsive service plays a critical role in determining end-user satisfaction. In fact a customer who experiences a large delay after placing a request at a business's web server often switches to a competitor who provides faster service [8]. Network infrastructure needs to be constantly improving to satisfy QoS (Quality of Service) users demand, including both technology aspects (e.g. fastest links, proxies and servers) and related software [9].

To parameterize the operation of the network, a day of operation shall be monitored, during 15 h, divided into 30-minute intervals. Some of the most significant attributes shall be used, such as:

- Total network packets (bytes).
- Total response time (ms).
- Average speed (bytes/ms).
- Number of requests.
- Number of zero bytes responses.

From the network logs, it is possible to extract the values of the attributes, shown in Table 1:

The first attribute is used to analyze the response time (in milliseconds) related to the conducted requests. The second attribute is related to the volume of data (in bytes) that was requested in a given interval. At first, one might think that the higher the value, the more efficient the network operation. However, this attribute is loaded of uncertainty, considering that it can also denote network congestion. The third attribute range is calculated based on the first two, by simple arithmetic average, to calculate the use of network bandwidth. The fourth attribute is the number of requests that occurred in a given interval. This attribute itself is not enough to determine the level of the network quality. A network with many requests may indicate either a good performance or a high rate of retransmissions, which is considered undesirable. The fifth attribute is especially important when considered in conjunction with the fourth attribute, as it allows differentiating situations where there is large number of retransmissions. The obtained values of the attributes are then tabulated and normalized in the range from 0 to 1. For a contextualized view, the image of Fig. 1 can give a good idea of network operation from two significant parameters: average speed and number of zero bytes responses:

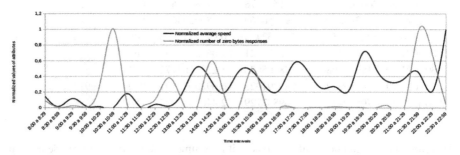

Fig. 1. Comparison between average speed and number of zero bytes responses

With the values obtained, it is possible to analyze specific scenarios in the operation of a network, through the development of a ranking of the evidence (favorable or unfavorable) using the Paraconsistent Annotated Evidential Logic Eτ.

The concepts of Paraconsistent Logic Eτ will be used from this point. According to Abe [10]: "The atomic formulas of the logic Eτ are of the type p(μ, λ), where (μ, λ) ∈ [0, 1]^2 and [0, 1] is the real unitary interval (p denotes a propositional variable)".

Table 1. Atributes values obtained from a day operation of a computer network

Hour interval	Total network packets (bytes)	Total response time (ms)	Average speed (bytes/ms)	Number of requests	Number of zero bytes responses
8:00 a 8:29	101550313	186703410	0,5439124706	3311	779
8:30 a 8:59	101317599	384871739	0,2632502954	4515	32
9:00 a 9:29	144107833	296218480	0,4864917037	5020	201
9:30 a 9:59	149058945	558951986	0,2666757588	10348	84
10:00 a 10:29	153643549	603540143	0,2545705547	13126	2705
10:30 a 10-59	129625661	535538428	0,2420473569	18442	8644
11:00 a 11:29	113215036	181009325	0,6254652129	6829	296
11:30 a 11:59	98916878	429472435	0,2303218319	2671	40
12:00 a 12:29	89950808	281068865	0,3200312066	5051	894
12:30 a 12:59	93957712	348408989	0,2696764864	6844	3304
13:00 a 13:29	40352244	60526974	0,6666819987	1489	568
13:30 a 13:59	34759397	25246230	1,3768153503	1786	7
14:00 a 14:29	82984378	82816003	1,0020331215	8493	5147
14:30 a 14:59	103544699	156568116	0,6613396242	5180	1180
15:00 a 15:29	97323535	77590646	1,2543204628	4090	19
15:30 a 15:59	111349090	88934444	1,2520356005	9973	4345
16:00 a 16:29	116516110	148779326	0,7831471827	8299	59
16:30 a 16:59	134981701	177338304	0,7611536704	9268	43
17:00 a 17:29	101774848	98992388	1,0281078177	6730	36
17:30 a 17:59	84745862	67398212	1,2573903593	3868	28
18:00 a 18:29	63605693	81593640	0,7795422903	5449	38
18:30 a 18:59	92411148	113160272	0,8166395005	5153	109
19:00 a 19:29	91532492	124104104	0,7375460525	2359	55
19:30 a 19:59	200608215	111540378	1,798525508	4727	37
20:00 a 20:29	255225540	199250269	1,2809294626	5517	49
20:30 a 20:59	184581912	194732439	0,9478744936	4061	44
21:00 a 21:29	159659251	150403821	1,0615371999	3676	146
21:30 a 21:59	119997798	98105026	1,2231564772	12739	8554
22:00 a 22:29	126283972	180791028	0,6985079591	10007	5917
22:30 a 22:59	170579432	69887729	2,4407636997	4500	398

Therefore, $p(\mu, \lambda)$ can be intuitively read: "It is assumed that p's favorable evidence is μ and unfavorable evidence is λ.". This will lead to the following conclusion:

- $p_{(1.0, \ 0.0)}$ can be read as a true proposition,
- $p_{(0.0, \ 1.0)}$ as false,
- $p_{(1.0, \ 1.0)}$ as inconsistent,
- $p_{(0.0, \ 0.0)}$ as paracomplete, and
- $p_{(0.5, \ 0.5)}$ as an indefinite proposition.

To determine the uncertainty and certainty degrees, the formulas are [11]:

- Uncertainty degree: $G_{un}(\mu, \lambda) = \mu + \lambda - 1$ $(0 \leq \mu, \lambda \leq 1)$;
- Certainty degree: $G_{ce}(\mu, \lambda) = \mu - \lambda$ $(0 \leq \mu, \lambda \leq 1)$;

An order relation is defined on $[0, 1]^2$: $(\mu_1, \lambda_1) \leq (\mu_2, \lambda_2) \Leftrightarrow \mu_1 \leq \mu_2$ and $\lambda_2 \leq \lambda_1$, constituting a lattice that will be symbolized by τ.

With the uncertainty and certainty degrees, it is possible to manage the following 12 output states, showed in the Table 2.

Table 2. Extreme and non-extreme states

Extreme states	Symbol	Non-extreme states	Symbol
True	V	Quasi-true tending to Inconsistent	QV→T
False	F	Quasi-true tending to Paracomplete	QV→⊥
Inconsistent	T	Quasi-false tending to Inconsistent	QF→ T
Paracomplete	⊥	Quasi-false tending to Paracomplete	QF→⊥
		Quasi-inconsistent tending to True	QT→V
		Quasi-inconsistent tending to False	QT→F
		Quasi-paracomplete tending to True	Q⊥→V
		Quasi-paracomplete tending to False	Q⊥→F

All states are represented in Fig. 2:

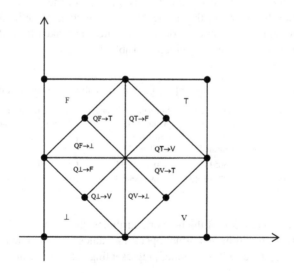

Fig. 2. Decision-making states of lattice τ

Based on the values of the attributes, obtained from one day operation of the computer network, two different scenarios from two time intervals on another day of operation will be analyzed in order to verify the operation of the network.

In the selected intervals, the following values were obtained, as shown in Table 3:

Table 3. Network attributes from two assessed scenarios

Scenarios	Total network packets (bytes)	Total response time (ms)	Average speed (bytes/ms)	Number of requests	Number of zero bytes responses
Scenario1	99646060	228119138	0,4368158712	4086	40
Scenario2	126428976	76538921	1,6518259514	11238	5532

A computer network that is operating at high speeds within its parameters is taken as favorable evidence. Therefore the average speed attribute can be considered a directly proportional greatness. This argument can also be applied to the number of requests attribute, since it indicates that the network has been operated in full working capacity to meet the user demands. In what concerns the zero byte responses attribute, the opposite occurs, as a network with high non responses indicates that the searched resources could not be found, thus it can be considered an inversely proportional greatness.

In both evaluated scenarios, the attribute values shall be normalized based on the operating values of the computer network. These values shall be used as degrees of favorable evidence for the average speed and number of requests attributes, as directly proportional greatnesses. The opposite shall be applied to the number of zero bytes responses attribute. In this case, the favorable evidence shall be defined as its denial. The favorable (μ) and unfavorable (λ) degree evidences are taken from the normalized values of the attributes, and are presented in Table 4:

Table 4. Normalized values and favorable (μ) and unfavorable (λ) evidences of the attributes

Scenarios	Normalized average speed (attribute 1)	Normalized number of requests (attribute 2)	Normalized number of zero bytes responses (attribute 3)	Attribute 1 evidences		Attribute 2 evidences		Attribute 3 evidences	
				μ	λ	μ	λ	μ	λ
Scenario1	0,093417539	0,1565117821	0,0038207711	0,9	0.91	0,15	0,85	100	0
Scenario2	0,643085955	0,5875369132	0,3696885493	0,64	0,36	0,58	0,42	0,36	0,64

After the parameterization of the network attributes, the proposition "The computer network is functioning within its normal operating values?" shall be analyzed. For this purpose, the Para-analyzer will be applied, representing scenarios 1 and 2, respectively in Figs. 3 and 4:

The global analysis is calculated considering the favorable evidences (μ) multiplied by their respective weights (all equal, in both scenarios), and finally added. The same is done to the unfavorable evidence (λ) [11].

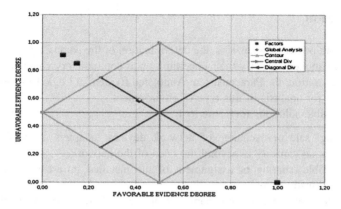

Fig. 3. Analysis of scenario 1 result by the Para-analyzer algorithm

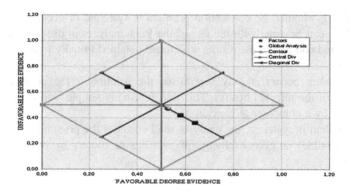

Fig. 4. Analysis of scenario 2 result by the Para-analyzer algorithm

3   Analysis of the Results

In scenario 1, the global analysis presents a quasi-false result tending to paracomplete and inconsistent to the normal network performance. Although the number of zero bytes responses attribute has high favorable evidence, this was not enough to represent a standard operation, since the other two attributes have not been sufficient to support the results. Diagnosis: the analyzed network in scenario 1 is not congested due to the low number of requests and is able to locate the searched resources. Abnormally, it still functions in low speed, which leads to the conclusion that the network is underutilized, or the network infrastructure project was oversized.

In scenario 2, the global analysis presents a quasi-true result, tending to paracomplete and inconsistent to the normal network performance. The high average speed and number of requests presents a situation of full use of the network capacity. However, it is observed that it begins to show clear signs of degradation due to the high number of zeros bytes responses. Diagnosis: the analyzed network in scenario 2 operates in a high degree of utilization, with early congestion signals and performance degradation.

4 Conclusion

As seen in both presented scenarios, the determination of the parameters in a computer network is a complex task. By their uncertainty and contradictory characteristics, and its dynamic operation, the Paraconsistent Annotated Evidential Logic Eτ emerges as an important tool for analysis of this type of environment.

Some possible solutions for scenario 1:

- Downsizing: sale or exchange of network devices (adapters, switches, routers) whose nominal capacity is beyond the need of the network.
- When possible, sharing or assignment of the installed infrastructure to another company or institution.
- Outsourcing services for companies that do not wish to have their own infrastructure.

Some possible solutions for scenario 2:

- Determining whether the congestion problem is systemic or occurs at only a few hosts. This can be done with the use of the Para-analyzer in different hosts of the network, and comparing the results with those obtained initially from the operating parameters.
- If the problem occurs at only few hosts, the solution is the physical or logic correction of the affected host(s). This task is usually simple, and its resolution is performed by a computer technician.
- If the problem is systemic, the analysis shall consider the possibility of upgrading (where possible) or even exchange of switches or routers by other with higher capacity.

References

1. Benadit, P.J., Francis, F.S.: ScienceDirect improving the performance of a proxy cache using very fast decision tree classifier. Procedia Comput. Sci. **48**, 304–312 (2015)
2. Kurose, J.F., Ross, K.W.: Computer Network: a Top-Down Approach, 6th edn. Addison-Wesley, Boston (2013)
3. Canali, C., Cardellini, V., Lancellotti, R.: Content adaptation architectures based on squid proxy server. World Wide Web **9**, 63–92 (2006)
4. Davison, B.D., Wu, B.: Implementing a web proxy evaluation architecture (2004)
5. Sysel, M., Doležal, O.: An educational HTTP proxy server. Procedia Eng. **69**, 128–132 (2014)
6. Romano, S., ElAarag, H.: A neural network proxy cache replacement strategy and its implementation in the squid proxy server. Neural Comput. Appl. **20**, 59–78 (2010)
7. Agarwal, T., Leonetti, M.A.: Design and Implementation of an IP based authentication mechanism for Open Source Proxy Servers in Interception Mode (2013)
8. Austin, I.B.M., Road, B., Tx, A., Rajamony, R., Elnozahy, M.: Measuring client-perceived response times on the WWW. In: 3rd Conference on USENIX Symposium on Internet Technologies Systems. 16 (2001)

9. Cárdenas, L.G., Sahuquillo, J., Pont, A., Gil, J.A.: The multikey web cache simulator: a platform for designing proxy cache management techniques. In: Proceedings of the 12th Euromicro Conference on Parallel, Distributed and Network-Based Processing, pp. 390–397 (2004)
10. Abe, J.M., Akama, S., Nakamatsu, K.: Introduction to Annotated Logics - Foundations for Paracomplete and Paraconsistent Reasoning. Springer, Heidelberg (2015)
11. Abe, J.M.: Paraconsistent logics and applications. In: 4th International Workshop on Soft Computing Applications, pp. 11–18. IEEE (2010)

Logical Decision-Making Method Relating to Innovation Management

Nélio F. dos Reis[1,2], Priscila Facciolli S.L. Tavares[1(✉)],
Cristina Oliveira[1], and Jair Minoro Abe[1]

[1] Paulista University, São Paulo, Brazil
neliojundiai@ig.com.br, pril979@gmail.com
[2] Federal Institute of Education,
Science and Technology of São Paulo, São Paulo, Brazil

Abstract. This paper is intended to serve as a support for decision in innovation management from the Eτ Logic. We intend to propose a new method for innovation management, based on technical and operational criteria in order to make decisions can be not only reliable but also operationally efficient. This research presents results that can serve to innovation managers.

Keywords: Innovation · Management · Paraconsistent annotated logic

1 Introduction

Many companies claim to be innovative, creative and be ahead of your competitors, despite the fact that they are not using appropriate metrics and methods to innovative processes and results.

The model for this purpose is built through an approach of Paraconsistent Logic Annotated Evidential Eτ (Eτ Logic), a technique that is gaining space and consideration in the various fields of research.

The main advantages of the use of Eτ Logic derived from one of the input parameters are set by the thought of evaluator's structure, consolidating a collective logic translated into mathematical terms.

De Bes and Kotler [1] claim that "without innovation companies end up." Innovation is the development and introduction of a new idea, making it a process, product or service. O'Sullivan [2], states that: "Innovation is the process by which the productive resources are developed and used to generate higher quality and/or lower cost products compared to the current available". According to Tidd and Bessant [3], innovation "is more than just having good ideas is the process of growing them".

1.1 Innovation

Sinsit [4], he distinguishes invention of innovation as follows: "invention is the creation of a new idea or concept. While innovation transforms the new concept in commercial success or general use. Ronan [5], explains innovation as "profitable

I. Nääs et al. (Eds.): APMS 2016, IFIP AICT 488, pp. 12–19, 2016.
DOI: 10.1007/978-3-319-51133-7_2

implementation of strategic creativity and which comprises four main components (1) creativity, (2) strategy (3) implementation and (4) profit".

Innovation is both a strategic factor for companies willing to remain competitive in the long term [6] and [7], as one of the least known aspects of business as states Takeuchi e Nonaka [8]. Due to increased competition, changes in demand and customer tastes, it seems extremely important for companies to manage innovation in a fast and flexible way in order to beat the competition and achieve a sustainable competitive advantage.

The scope of the innovation can be incremental or disruption [9]: "Incremental: typically performed to improve a product or service with a new feature that is easily integrated; and radical: usually associated with disruption for new steps and unpredictable uses for existing technology." Still according to Vacek [9], the common places of innovation are product, process, structure and market.

1.2   Innovation Models

Many companies claim to be innovative, creative and be ahead of their competitors, despite the fact that they are not using appropriate metrics and methods to innovative processes and results. "Innovation is a disorderly process: difficult to measure and difficult to manage [1]."

However, states that innovation is an art, not a science and it is therefore not possible to predict the success of an innovation until it is accepted by the respective market [10]. Since the 1950s there has been a proliferation of innovation models, each with the purpose of guiding the innovation process within companies, as summarized in Table 1.

Table 1. Development of innovation models (adapted from Hobday [11])

Model	Generation	Feature
Technological	1ª (1950–1960)	Emphasis on R&D. Innovation R&D
Market	2ª (1960–1970)	Market is the source of new ideas for R&D
Coupled	3ª (1970–1980)	Feedback link between market and R&D
Interactive	4ª (1980–1990)	Emphasis in marketing and R&D
Network	5ª (1990–2000)	Knowledge and systems integration
Open	6ª (2000–current)	Combined ideas for innovation

For each step, there are several tools and techniques that can be selected based on company structure, the target market or type of products or services. The decision-making method in Innovation Management is established not as a process of innovation, but through the interaction between six distinct phases: identification, intelligence, idealization, instrumentation, implementation and indicators. These phrases have been identified in the A-F models [1], who claim: "This model results from analysis of various companies that are consider innovative and have good results concerning the time and resources invested in innovation: Apple, Google, Netflix, 3 M,

Procter & Gamble, General Electric, BMW, Frito Lay, IBM, Toyota, Southwest Air-lines, Starbucks, Microsoft, Tesco, Royal Dutch/Shell, Walmart, Exxon, Ikea, Ericsson, Nokia and Corning were the main companies studied".

1.3 Eτ Logical

The Eτ logical allows to treat subjective data from the real worldinto accurate data with numerical outputs [12]. One of its advantages is to perform the translation of natural language (linguistic terms) used in daily communication in mathematical expressions. This is achieved by means of crosslinked annotation properties.

De Carvalho and Abe [13], states that: "In Eτ **logical** logical every *p* prepoitio associates, n commom sense, a pair (μ, λ), represented by Greek letters *mi* (μ) and *lambda* (λ), depicted in the following manner: $p(\mu; \lambda) \mu$ nd λ varies in the real closed interval [0, 1]. Therefore, the pair $\mu; \lambda$ belongs to the Cartesian product [0, 1] x [0, 1]. Intuitively, μ represents the degree of favorable evidence expressed in *p*, nd λ, the degree of contrary evidence expressed by *p*. The pair (μ, λ) It is called annotation constant or simply note. The atomic propositions of Eτ logical are $p(\mu, \lambda)$ type".

The advantages in the development of paraconsistent systems are: how quickly the building of system is carried out in relation to models based on logic "fuzzy" (common or Boolean) and make it unnecessary knowledge or the development of a mathematical model [13]. Innovation is important, but that executives lack confidence in their decisions [1].

The decision-making method in Innovation Management is established through six distinct phases, as follows [1]: (i) Identification: Expressed by X percentage of the population on the whole; (ii) Intelligence: Translated globally in size of the impact on the innovation site; (iii) Idealization: The Y amount, of ideas attributes, can be pre-sented as a comparison measurement with the average M attributes in available similar. (iv) Instrumentation: Can be represented by the average expenditure G function compared to similar available S; (v) Implementation: In period P to development and implantation measured as a function of C lifecycle; and (vi) Indicators: Investment I measured by the R expected return on the life cycle of innovation.

2 Methods

The methodology used was as follows: (1) Problem in the form of question: - How to make innovation management with contradictory data? (2) Elaborated hypothesis: - You can take decision in innovation management with logical data. (3) Literature review: - Theoretical research on innovation and Eτ Logic. (4) Data collection: - Expert systems, divided into three groups: - A: 03 (three) innovation experts; - B: 03 (three) management experts; and - C: 02 (two) risk investment experts. (5) Study object: - Extensive direct observation of experts.

The experts evaluated the Six I's factors for innovation in product, process and market. Initially the experts understood the model. After that, brainstorm sessions were conducted to identify the factors and building the logical proposition. The Six I's and the propositions are presented in Table 2.

Table 2. Six I's and propositions

Factors	Sections	Propositions	Description
Identification I1	S1	X > 70%	The population benefited X is greater than 70% of the whole
	S2	30% ≤ X ≤ 70%	The population benefited X is greater than or equal to 30% and less than or equal to 70% of the whole
	S3	X < 30%	The population benefited X is less than 30% of the whole
Intelligence I2	S1	Large	Major positive impact at the place of innovation
	S2	Medium	Medium positive impact on the local of innovation
	S3	Small	Small positive impact on the local of innovation
Idealization I3	S1	Y > 1,5 M	Y innovation attributes are 1.5 times higher than the average similar M
	S2	0,5 M ≤ Y ≤ 1,5 M	Y attributes of innovation are greater than or equal to 0.5 times and less than or equal to 1.5 times the similar average
	S3	Y < 0,5 M	Y attributes of innovation are greater than or equal to 0.5 times and less than or equal to 1.5 times the similar average
Instrumentalization I4	S1	G < 40%S	Average spending G innovation is less than 40% of similar S
	S2	70% S ≤ G ≤ 40%S	Average spent G of innovation is greater than or equal to 70% and less than or equal to 40% similar to S
	S3	G > 70%S	Average spent G of innovation is greater than 70% similar to S
Implementation I5	S1	P < 30%C	P deadline of development and deployment of innovation is less than 30% of the current life cycle
	S2	30% C ≤ P ≤ 70%C	P deadline of development and deployment of innovation is greater than or equal to 30% and less than or equal to 70% of the current life cycle
	S3	P > 70%C	P deadline of development and deployment of innovation is greater than 70% of the current life cycle
Indicators I6	S1	I < 30%R	Investment in innovation is less than 30% of the expected return in the life cycle
	S2	30% R ≤ I ≤ 70%R	Investment in innovation is greater than or equal to 30% and less than or equal to 70% of the expected return in the life cycle
	S3	I > 70%R	Investment in innovation is greater than 70% of the expected return in the life cycle

Were executed two (02) Delphi rounds that sought to: identify the certainty of the expert regarding the decision of each factor and the possible contradiction in relation to expert.

The consultation was conducted by form via email. The biggest difference between them is that in the second round, the answers to each of the first round proposals of all the experts had the result informed, giving the respondent an opportunity to review its earlier evidence, if desired.

3   Aplication

Regarding the factors, one should reason that they are independent of each other. Thus, the experts allocated their degree of favorable evidence (μ) and contrary evidence (λ) in each proposition, as shown in Fig. 1.

Factors	Sections	Group A						Group B						Group C			
		Experts 1		Experts 2		Experts 3		Experts 4		Experts 5		Experts 6		Experts 7		Experts 8	
		μ_1	λ_1	μ_2	λ_2	μ_3	λ_3	μ_4	λ_4	μ_5	λ_5	μ_6	λ_6	μ_7	λ_7	μ_8	λ_8
I1	S1	1,0	0,1	0,3	0,2	0,8	0,3	0,3	0,2	0,9	0,3	0,7	0,1	0,3	0,2	0,2	0,0
	S2	0,5	0,5	0,4	0,6	0,6	0,4	0,6	0,4	0,4	0,6	0,5	0,5	0,5	0,5	0,5	0,5
	S3	0,1	1,0	0,2	0,9	0,3	0,8	0,3	0,9	0,3	0,9	0,1	0,9	0,3	1,0	0,0	1,0
I2	S1	0,8	0,4	0,9	0,3	0,7	0,1	1,0	0,1	0,9	0,2	0,8	0,3	0,8	0,3	0,9	0,2
	S2	0,5	0,5	0,4	0,6	0,6	0,4	0,6	0,4	0,4	0,6	0,5	0,5	0,5	0,5	0,5	0,5
	S3	0,1	1,0	0,2	0,9	0,3	0,8	0,3	0,9	0,3	0,9	0,1	0,9	0,3	1,0	0,0	1,0
I3	S1	1,0	0,1	0,9	0,2	0,8	0,3	0,8	0,4	0,9	0,3	0,7	0,1	0,9	0,1	0,9	0,1
	S2	0,5	0,5	0,4	0,6	0,6	0,4	0,6	0,4	0,4	0,6	0,5	0,5	0,5	0,5	0,5	0,5
	S3	0,1	1,0	0,2	0,9	0,3	0,8	0,3	0,9	0,3	0,9	0,1	0,9	0,3	1,0	0,0	1,0
I4	S1	0,8	0,4	0,9	0,3	0,7	0,1	1,0	0,1	0,9	0,2	0,8	0,3	0,8	0,3	0,9	0,2
	S2	0,5	0,5	0,4	0,6	0,6	0,4	0,6	0,4	0,4	0,6	0,5	0,5	0,5	0,5	0,5	0,5
	S3	0,1	1,0	0,2	0,9	0,3	0,8	0,3	0,9	0,3	0,9	0,1	0,9	0,3	1,0	0,0	1,0
I5	S1	1,0	0,1	0,9	0,2	0,8	0,3	1,0	0,1	0,9	0,2	0,8	0,3	0,9	0,1	0,9	0,1
	S2	0,5	0,5	0,4	0,6	0,6	0,4	0,6	0,4	0,4	0,6	0,5	0,5	0,5	0,5	0,5	0,5
	S3	0,1	1,0	0,2	0,9	0,3	0,8	0,3	0,9	0,3	0,9	0,1	0,9	0,3	1,0	0,0	1,0
I6	S1	0,8	0,4	0,9	0,3	0,7	0,1	1,0	0,1	0,9	0,3	0,7	0,1	0,7	0,4	1,0	0,0
	S2	0,5	0,5	0,4	0,6	0,6	0,4	0,6	0,4	0,4	0,6	0,5	0,5	0,5	0,5	0,5	0,5
	S3	0,1	1,0	0,2	0,9	0,3	0,8	0,3	0,9	0,3	0,9	0,1	0,9	0,3	1,0	0,0	1,0

Fig. 1. Database of evidence from experts

With the Table 1 database, it emerges clearly the evidence of experts on the Six I's factors. They are shown in Table 3 with use of Maximum and Minimum rules.

3.1   Maximization (Max) and Minimization (Mini) Rules

The next step is to apply the maximization (Max) and minimizing (Min) rule to the evidence of the experts for each innovation factors.

Apply to the rules of maximization of favorable evidence within groups being connective (Max) the favorable evidence and connective (Min) in contrary evidence within each group and the minimization rule of favorable evidence among the groups, the connective (min) the favorable evidence, and connective (Max) in contrary evidence to the results obtained in the three groups (between groups), grouped as shown in Fig. 2:

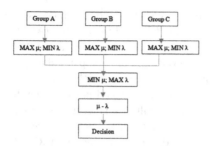

Fig. 2. Application of the scheme of MAX and MIN operators.

3.2 Analysis

There is favorable or contrary evidence of innovation acceptance, if there is a degree of certainty in magnitude equal to or greater than 0.6. This level of demand may change depending on the focus of innovation. However, in this study, the value after discussions with experts are as follows.

The Certainty is defined as follows: $G_{cert} = \mu - \lambda$

Summarizing, the division criterion is the following:

(a) $G_{cert} \geq 0,6 \rightarrow$ True (T), i.e., INNOVATE;
(b) $G_{cert} \leq -0,6 \rightarrow$ False (F), i.e., NOT INNOVATE; and
(c) $-0,6 < Gcert < 0,6 \rightarrow$ Area between Truth and False is DOUBT.

The database was treated with connective Max and Min and the results of the three themes are shown in Fig. 3.

Factors	Sections	Max and Mini A Group		Max and Mini B Group		Max and Mini C Group		Max and Mini between groups		Indicators: 18 Requirement level > 0,600 Conclusions	
		μ_{1A}	λ_{2A}	μ_{1B}	λ_{2B}	μ_{1C}	λ_{2C}	μ_{1R}	λ_{2R}	Gcert	Decision
I1	S1	1,0	0,1	0,9	0,1	1,0	0,0	0,9	0,1	0,8	INNOVATE
	S2	0,6	0,4	0,6	0,4	0,5	0,5	0,5	0,5	0,0	DOUBT
	S3	0,3	0,8	0,3	0,9	0,3	1,0	0,3	1,0	-0,7	NOT INNOVATE
I2	S1	0,9	0,1	1,0	0,1	0,9	0,2	0,9	0,2	0,7	INNOVATE
	S2	0,6	0,4	0,6	0,4	0,5	0,5	0,5	0,5	0,0	DOUBT
	S3	0,3	0,8	0,3	0,9	0,3	1,0	0,3	1,0	-0,7	NOT INNOVATE
I3	S1	1,0	0,1	0,9	0,1	0,9	0,1	0,9	0,1	0,8	INNOVATE
	S2	0,6	0,4	0,6	0,4	0,5	0,5	0,5	0,5	0,0	DOUBT
	S3	0,3	0,8	0,3	0,9	0,3	1,0	0,3	1,0	-0,7	NOT INNOVATE
I4	S1	0,9	0,1	1,0	0,1	0,9	0,2	0,9	0,2	0,7	INNOVATE
	S2	0,6	0,4	0,6	0,4	0,5	0,5	0,5	0,5	0,0	DOUBT
	S3	0,3	0,8	0,3	0,9	0,3	1,0	0,3	1,0	-0,7	NOT INNOVATE
I5	S1	1,0	0,1	1,0	0,1	0,9	0,1	0,9	0,1	0,8	INNOVATE
	S2	0,6	0,4	0,6	0,4	0,5	0,5	0,5	0,5	0,0	DOUBT
	S3	0,3	0,8	0,3	0,9	0,3	1,0	0,3	1,0	-0,7	NOT INNOVATE
I6	S1	0,9	0,1	0,9	0,1	1,0	0,0	0,9	0,1	0,8	INNOVATE
	S2	0,6	0,4	0,6	0,4	0,5	0,5	0,5	0,5	0,0	DOUBT
	S3	0,3	0,8	0,3	0,9	0,3	1,0	0,3	1,0	-0,7	NOT INNOVATE

Fig. 3. Evidence degrees resulting from the application of Max and Mini rules

Observing the degree of favorable and contrary evidence resulting from the application of maximizing rules (OR) and minimizing (AND) the evidence of experts, we note that the degree of certainty (Gcert) to S1 is above 0.6 as established the criteria for certainty in relation to innovation. For example, although experts E3, E4 and E7 in I1 S1 have given evidence (μ 0,2; λ 0,8) which is a statement of (F) Falsehood, so there's sure the statement is false and should not innovate, to take into account other evidence of other experts is the result (V) True, that is, this proposition is a condition for innovation. Anyway, you can tell which region he sure is. As shown in the figure is plotted on I1S1 factor (μ 0,9; λ 0,1) in the region of OPJC = (V) true. I1S2 already has its collective evidence in the area of ($\perp$) paracompleteza and is plotted in (μ 0,5; λ 0,5) in the central region, highlighting questions regarding innovate. I1S3 already has its collective evidence in the area of (F) is plotted on falsehood (μ 0,3; λ 1,0), i.e., the evidence of the expert is not innovate given this proposition. The I2S1 factor is plotted below the square unit of the Cartesian plane - QUPC, adapted from studies of De Carvalho and Abe [13]. The other results coincide with I1S1, I1S2, I1S3 and I2S1 as plotted in Fig. 4.

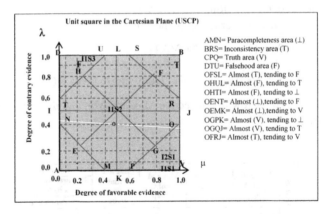

Fig. 4. Application of para-analizer device at USCP.

If there is need for a more stringent criterion for decision making, safer decision, more reliable, it is necessary to increase the level of demand, that is, one should approximate the PQ and TU lines of C and D, respectively, and also may use a larger number of experts, or even consider evidence assigned depending on the weight of each expert. You can still adjust and calibrate the data of propositions for a better result in decision-making.

4   Conclusion

If there is need for a more stringent criterion, i.e., more safe and reliable decision, it is necessary to increase the level of requirement, or use a larger number of experts, or even consider the evidence given depending on the weight of each expert. A major advantage of this method is its versatility. Experts can be influenced, but in general are not the same for everyone. Surely, at a time of latent conflict, the expert tends to discredit innovation more than believing and the opposite can happen in times of elation, joy, but hardly all specialists will be with the same feeling. Finally, virtually all problems in which uncertainty, ambiguity or natural language of human beings is relevant present favorable situations the application of Eτ Logic.

References

1. De Bes, F.T., Kotler, P.A.: Biblía da Inovação: Princípios Fundamentais para Levar a Cultura da Inovação Contínua às Organizaçoes. São Paulo, Leya (2011)
2. O'Sullivan, M.: The innovative enterprise and corporate governance. Camb. J. Econ. **24**(4), 393–416 (2000)
3. Tidd, J., Bessant, J.: Managing Innovation: Integrating Technological, Market and Organizational Change. Wiley Press, New York (2009)
4. Sinsit, Z.T., Vayvay, O., Ozturk, O.: An outline of innovation management process: building a framework for managers to implement innovation. Procedia – Soc. Behav. Sci. **150**, 690–699 (2014)
5. Ronan, D.: A Study of Innovation Measurement and Innovation Management at Irish Medical Device SME's. National University of Ireland (2009)
6. Prahalad, C.K., Hamel, G.: The core competence of the corporation. Harvard Bus. Rev. **68**(3), 79–91 (1990)
7. Gourville, J.T.: The Curse of Innovation: A Theory of Why Innovative New Products Fail in the Marketplace. Marketing Research Papers, 05–06 (2005)
8. Takeuchi, H., Nonaka, I.: The new product development game. Harvard Bus. Rev., 137–146 (1986)
9. Vacek, J.: Innovation Management. University of Washington Bothell (2009)
10. Poots, A.J., Woodcock, T.: Statistical process control for data without inherent order. BMC Med. Inform. Decis. Making **12**(1), 86 (2012)
11. Hobday, M.: Firm-level innovation models. Technol. Anal. Strateg. Manag. **17**(2), 121–145 (2005)
12. Reis, N.F.: Método Paraconsistente de Cenários Prospectivos. Universidade Paulista (2014)
13. De Carvalho, F.R., Abe, J.M.: Tomadas de Decisão com Ferramentas da Lógica Anotada. São Paulo, Blucher (2011)

IT Incident Management and Analysis Using Non-classical Logics

Priscila F. Tavaves[✉], Liliam Sakamoto, Genivaldo Carlos Silva,
Jair M. Abe, and Avelino P. Pimenta Jr.

Paulista University, São Paulo, Brazil
pril979@gmail.com

Abstract. The classification and the proper incident handling in an IT environment are strategic to remain competitive in corporations. Service Desk technicians with knowledge and expertise can often have conflicting beliefs in their analysis. This study aims to apply Paraconsistent Logic to treat contradictions directly in the classification of incidents in IT, helping managers to improve the quality of services they provide to users through the efficiency of the Service Desk in decision-making.

Keywords: Critical incident · ITIL · ISO 20000 · Quality in IT service · Paraconsistent logic

1 Introduction

Organizations currently rely increasingly on various IT (Information Technology) services for maintenance of their operations [1]. Proper management of these services is of paramount importance because in many cases the services are subject to incidents, which may be defined as unplanned events that have the potential to lead to an accident.

Although the concept of incidents seems to deal with faults that occurred or that may occur and/or may be foreseen by the IT team, in several areas as an example: telecommunications, infrastructure and defects in software.

Categorization and correct classification of incidents is of paramount importance, as they may cause stoppage of important services and result in financial losses and even cause impact on the organization's image. Classification of incidents is the act of identifying the exact kind of incident and what components are involved, as well as determining the incident priority, which is, for example, classifying it as critical or not.

However, big part of the technical support in IT is run by contracted companies that have no commitment with the organization's business and most importantly, are not properly prepared in what regards the correct classification of incidents.

The more precise the categorization and the classification are, the faster will the service for the requesting user be, and it can also help in referring it for more advanced support teams to resolve the issue.

Depending on the size of the operation, the Service Desk can have many technicians of level 1 (first contact with the user), and differences in classification of incidents

I. Nääs et al. (Eds.): APMS 2016, IFIP AICT 488, pp. 20–27, 2016.
DOI: 10.1007/978-3-319-51133-7_3

occur frequently, i.e. the same type of incident can be classified as critical by a technician and as not critical by the other. Therefore, classification is naturally subject to inconsistencies. On the other hand, it is well known that Classical Logic cannot deal with contradictions, at least directly. So we have to seek suitable logical systems.

The goal of this work is to use Paraconsistent Annotated Evidential Logic Eτ (Logic Eτ) [2] to address inconsistencies in the classification of IT Incidents, helping managers to maintain the quality of services used by the organization for the increase of the efficiency in the Service Desk area. We used the ITIL (*Information Technology Infrastructure Library*) as a management tool, which is a framework of better practices that deal with Incident Management in IT and the ISO/IEC 20000, which addresses this concept depicting Systems Certification of Services Management in IT.

2 Backgrounds

2.1 ITIL – Information Technology Infrastructure Library

ITIL describes a set of best practices for managing IT services, improving the relationship between the strategic management of the company's business to these services [3].

Incident Management focuses primarily on restoring the service as fast as possible, minimizing the negative impact on business. A workaround or quick fix, which allows the client to return to work and ensures that the highest levels of availability and quality of service, according to the service level agreements (SLA) [4].

The term incident [5] is any event that is not part of the standard operation of a service and that causes or may cause interruption or reduction of its quality.

The objectives of the Incident Management, according to ITIL, are:

- Re-establishing the IT services as soon as possible in accordance with the service level agreement;
- Establishing workaround solutions, while identifying the root of the problem;
- Reducing the impact of the incident on the operations of the business;
- Maintaining communication between IT and users about the state of the incident;
- Ensuring the highest level of quality of services rendered, according to the ANS.

2.2 ISO/IEC 20.000

ISO/IEC 20000-1:2011 defines the requirements for the IT services provider to manage its processes and delivered services with acceptable quality for its customers. It is divided into: Management Systems and Management Processes, where the former is aligned with ISO 9001:2000 and the latter, which is our focus, receives strong influence of ITIL, library of best IT services management practices, covering four macro-processes: delivery, resolution, control, release and relationship.

In this norm, there is a topic which addresses the resolution process specifically, visualizing the Incidents and Problems Management.

In the Incident Management, its goal is to restore the agreed services as soon as possible to the company, or to respond to requests of the services.

The norm also points out that it is appropriate that there are [6]:

- Receipt of the call, record, determination of the priority, classification;
- First level of resolution or referral;
- Consideration of security issues;
- Tracking and managing of the incident life cycle;
- Verification and closure of the incident;
- First level of contact with the customer;

2.3   Paraconsistent Annotated Evidential Logic Eτ

Roughly speaking, Paraconsistent logics are logics that can serve as underlying logic of theories in which there are formulas A and ¬A (the negation of A) both true without being trivial [2]. There are infinitely many paraconsistente systems. In this work we consider the Paraconsistent Annotated Evidential Logic Eτ.

The atomic formulas of the language of the Logic Eτ are of the type $p_{(\mu,\lambda)}$, in which p is a proposition and e $(\mu, \lambda) \in [0, 1]$ is the real unitary closed interval.

$p_{(\mu,\lambda)}$ can be intuitively read as: " The favorable evidence of p is μ and the contrary evidence is λ" [7]. For instance, $p(1.0, 0.0)$ can be read as a true proposition, $p(0.0, 1.0)$ as false, $p(1.0, 1.0)$ as inconsistent, $p(0.0, 0.0)$ as paracomplete, and $p(0.5, 0.5)$ as an indefinite proposition [8]. Also we introduce the following concepts: Uncertainty degree: $G_{un(\mu, \lambda)} = \mu + \lambda - 1$ $(0 \leq \mu, \lambda \leq 1)$ and Certainty degree: $G_{ce(\mu,\lambda)} = \mu - \lambda$ $(0 \leq \mu, \lambda \leq 1)$ [9].

An order relation is defined on [0, 1]: $(\mu_1, \lambda_1) \leq (\mu_2, \lambda_2) \Leftrightarrow \mu_1 \leq \mu_2$ and $\lambda_2 \leq \lambda_1$, constituting a lattice that will be symbolized by τ.

With the uncertainty and certainty degrees we can get the following 12 output states (Table 1): extreme states, and non-extreme states. It is worth observed that this division can be modified according to each application [10].

Table 1. Extreme and Non-extreme states

Extreme states	Symbol	Non-extreme states	Symbol
True	V	Quasi-true tending to Inconsistent	QV→T
False	F	Quasi-true tending to Paracomplete	QV→⊥
Inconsistent	T	Quasi-false tending to Inconsistent	QF→T
Paracomplete	⊥	Quasi-false tending to Paracomplete	Qf→⊥
		Quasi-inconsistent tending to True	QT→V
		Quasi-inconsistent tending to False	QT→F
		Quasi-paracomplete tending to True	Q⊥→V
		Quasi-paracomplete tending to False	Q⊥→F

Some additional control values are:

- V_{scct} = maximum value of uncertainty control = Ft_{un}
- V_{scc} = maximum value of certainty control = Ft_{ce}
- V_{icct} = minimum value of uncertainty control = $-Ft_{un}$
- V_{icc} = minimum value of certainty control = $-Ft_{ce}$

All states are represented in the next Figure (Fig. 1).

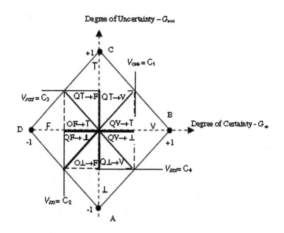

Fig. 1. Extreme and non-extreme states

3   Methodology

The methodology is as follows:

1. Research Problem: How to manage incidents with contradictory data?
2. Hypothesis: The resolution of incidents is more accurate with non-classical logic.
3. Literature review: Theoretical Review of ISO 20000, ITIL and Logic Eτ.
4. Proposition: There was critical incident;
5. Factors and Control Sections: We listed the Factors "F" and Sections "S", with influence of ISO 9126 [11], as it presents a set of characteristics that verify whether software can be considered "of good quality", on Table 2:

Table 2. Factors and sections source

Factors	Sections
F1- Is the slowness in a system a critical incident?	S1- In ERP systems
	S2- In supporting system
F2- Is the interruption of service a critical incident?	S1- ERP not available
	S2- Supporting system not available

6. Data collection: We have developed an online questionnaire to obtain quantitative data (see Table 2). Twenty seven IT professionals answered, where the mathematical average of the values found was calculated and grouped into: A: nine final users, B: nine Service Desk analysts and C: nine IT managers. The groups were chosen from the SLA according to ITIL.
7. Object of study: Extensive direct observation of experts.
8. Construction of database: Responses were collected between values of 0 and 1 Fig. 2:

   (i) From the data in Table 3, it was applied Eτ Logic and we obtained:

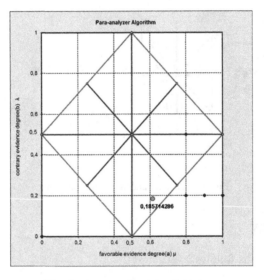

Fig. 2. Average factors and sections

Table 3. Data collection from experts

F	S	Group 1 - users						Group 2 - service desk analysts						Group 3 - IT mangers					
A	E																		
C	C																		
T	T																		
O	I																		
R	O																		
S	N	Expert 1		Expert 2		Expert 3		Expert 4		Expert 5		Expert 6		Expert 7		Expert 8		Expert 9	
	S	μ	λ	μ	λ	μ	λ	μ	λ	μ	λ	μ	λ	μ	λ	μ	λ	μ	λ
F1	S1	1	0,1	0,5	0,5	0,7	0,9	0	0,7	0,8	0,2	0,6	0,4	1	0,7	0,8	0,2	1	0,1
	S2	0,9	0,2	0,6	0,4	0,8	0,7	1	0,2	0,7	0,2	0,6	0,4	1	0,5	0,9	0,3	1	0,2
F2	S1	1	0,2	0,5	0,5	0,8	0,9	0,2	0,8	1	0,1	0,6	0,5	1	0,6	0,9	0,1	1	0,1
	S2	0,9	0,1	0,7	0,6	0,8	1	0,4	0,6	0,8	0,2	0,5	0,6	1	0,7	0,6	0,5	0,7	0,5

4   Analysis and Discussion

After analyzing the data employing the Logic Eτ it was concluded:

F1- Is the slowness in a system a critical incident?

F1-S1 - Slow ERP System: The result was found to be true, it can be considered a critical incident because the ERP is an integrated system and can be used throughout the organization and its unavailability is of high impact.

F1-S2 - Slow support system: The result is true, it can be considered a critical incident, since this system concentrates on the activities ERP does not perform, for example, specific customizations required by business line, sometimes referred to as ADD-ON.

F2 - Is the interruption of service a critical incident?

F2-S1 - Unavailability of ERP: The result found was true, it can be considered a critical incident, because the unavailability of an ERP system would damage one or more activities of the company and the impact would be immense: financial losses and low credibility with the users of the organization.

F2-S2 - Is the interruption of the support system services a critical incident? The response after analysis with the Eτ logic was true; it may be considered a critical incident. When we talk about legacy systems or customized systems, it can impact directly and negatively in the areas of business, as we have discussed in item F2-S1.

4.1   Comparisons with Real Data

We used information from a foreign trade company, here as "A", which has headquarters in Santos (São Paulo) and two branches, one in Vitória (Espírito Santo) and another one in Itajaí (Santa Catarina). This company uses ERP SAP/R3 system for Small Business, customized with a module ADD-ON of Foreign Trade and Electronic Invoice. Moreover, it used two Support Systems: A Legacy System used for Customs transaction of ports and another Logistic System for load control, in addition to other system developed internally for controlling suppliers contracts (customs brokers and carriers) and their respective SLA.

It has major MPLS links (Embratel) between headquarters and branch offices, and secondary radio links (WCS).

There are, on average, 100 employees, its capital is of family origin and it was requested that its name and period of analyzed data remained secret.

A survey about Critical Incidents in the analyzed period of 1 year was conducted, starting in March/x1 and finishing in February/x2. According to a chart that summarizes the total analyzed incidents Fig. 3.

We analyzed situations in which the ERP or Support System were unavailable or slow, as well as disconnection between headquarters and branches. We didn't observe a direct correlation between disconnection and slowness or unavailability of Systems (ERP or Support), as they didn't occur in the same months Fig. 4.

It was noticed that situations when the system is slowcan foresee a possible stop of their systems. The chart below represents this situation month by month.

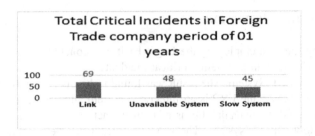

Fig. 3. Total of Critical Incidents - COMEX "A"

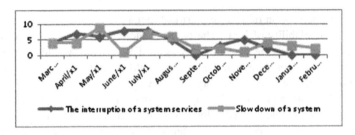

Fig. 4. Amount of occurrence of critical incident in the period of 1 year COMEX "A"

Analyzing the data of the critical incidents of company "A", it can be compared with the results presented in item 4 by logic Eτ, according to the items below:

- The critical incidents that are related to links won't always impact the whole company. In most cases they are related to specific problems, for example a particular server.
- The continued slowness of a given system can foresee a possible unavailability in the immediate or farther future.
- The unavailability of the company's "core" systems may be a potential trouble spot that causes loss of competitiveness in business, financial impacts and even negative impacts on the company's image.

5   Final Considerations

The Logic Eτ was a useful tool in this study because it is capable to analyse conflicting, imprecise, and paracomplete data directly, converging on a single type of central decision-making and is suitable for managers who need speed and accuracy when resolving critical incidents.

After analyzing the results from Logic Eτ and comparing with research of Company "A", we reached the conclusion that the tool based on Paraconsistent Logic presents coherent and effective front compared to real facts. The use of the data answered by the experts and the application were essential to validate this instrument study, reaching the proposed goal.

References

1. Laudon, K.C., Laudon, J.P.: Management Information Systems. PrenticeHall, Upper Saddle River (2014)
2. Abe, J.M., Akama, S., Nakamatsu, K. (eds.): Introduction to Annotated Logics - Foundations for Paracomplete and Paraconsistent Reasoning. ISRL, vol. 88. Springer, Heidelberg (2015)
3. ITIL®: Lifecycle Publication Suite — Books, United Kingdom's Cabinet Office, TSO (The Stationery Office) (2011)
4. IT Infrastructure Library: Service Support. OGC, London (2000)
5. Bon, J.V.: Foundations of IT Service Management based on ITIL. Van Haren Publishing, Lunteren-Holand (2005)
6. ISO/IEC 20000-1:2011: Information Technology – Service Management – Part 1: Service Management System Requirements, ISO (International Organization for Standardization) (2011)
7. Carvalho, F.R., Abe, J.M.: Tomadas de Decisão com Ferramentas da Lógica Paraconsistente Anotada. Blucher, São Paulo (2011)
8. Abe, J.M., et al.: Lógica Paraconsistente Anotada Evidential Eτ. Comunnicar Santos, pp. 38–39 (2011)
9. Carvalho, F.R., Brunstein, I., Abe, J.M.: Paraconsistent Annotated Logic in Analysis of Viability: in approach to product launching. In: Dubois, D.M. (ed.), vol. 718, pp. 282–291 (2011)
10. Dill, R.P., Da Costa Jr., N., Santos, A.A.P.: Corporate profitability analysis: a novel application for paraconsistent logic. Appl. Math. Sci. **8**, 1271–1288 (2014)
11. International Organization for Standardisation. ISO/IEC: 9126 Information Technology-Software Product Evaluation-Quality Characteristics and Guidelines for their use (1991)

Hierarchical Clustering Based on Reports Generated by Scriptlattes

Wonder A.L. Alves$^{(\boxtimes)}$, Saulo D. Santos, and Pedro H.T. Schimit

Universidade Nove de Julho, São Paulo, Brazil
{wonder,saulods,schimit}@uni9.pro.br

Abstract. Scriptlattes has been used as an important tool to analyze a curriculum database of Brazilian researchers (Lattes curriculum). Such analysis enables a user generating reports for specific research field, knowledge area, graduate courses, and so forth. However, when users need a report of a Graduate Program, for instance, it is necessary to create subsets of information in order to run the script. Since each report needs a subset, in this paper we propose a hierarchical clustering method to categorize reports generated by Scriptlattes. Finally, experimental results show hierarchical clustering of a higher education institution, and approaches to stress such clustering.

Keywords: Lattes curriculum · Sucupira platform · Scriptlattes · Clustering · Hierarchical clustering

1 Introduction

The growth of scientific community in the last decades created new issues to quantify the production, quality and innovation of research results. Besides the evaluation of researchers, institutes and countries concerning the research that has been done, keep a robust database of the activities and production is becoming crucial to manage the research properly. In this direction, several computational tools specific to the scientific community have been developed, including: social networks [1], institutional [2] and patents [3] repositories, curriculum platforms [4] and others [5,6].

In Brazil, it is practically mandatory that all researchers keep their Lattes curriculum updated. Created with effort from the National Counsel of Technological and Scientific Development (CNPq - *Conselho Nacional de Desenvolvimento Científico e Tecnológico*), Lattes platform allows that every curriculum is available online to public consultation [7,8]. Therefore, if a researcher wants to apply to a position in an University, sure his Lattes will be consulted previously by the University commission. According to CNPq, the Lattes Platform exceeds 3 million Lattes curriculum, being 6.35% of PhDs, 10.85% of masters 27.69% of graduates, 16.18% of specialists, 35.54% other levels and 3.39% of Lattes curriculum that do not have the information [9].

I. Nääs et al. (Eds.): APMS 2016, IFIP AICT 488, pp. 28–35, 2016.
DOI: 10.1007/978-3-319-51133-7_4

Although the public information is individually available for each researcher, automatic compilation of data to generate reports concerning scientific production of a certain research group is not an easy task, and it is not provided by Lattes plataform. Regarding this problem, ScriptLattes has been created as an open source tool to make the information extraction easier. Given a group of researchers registered in the Lattes platform, ScriptLattes downloads the curriculums in html format, extracts the information of interest, eliminates redundancies and create reports [8]. It is important to remember that the Scriptlattes has been widely used by various studies in Brazil and the results so far have been of great value as can be seen in [10–18].

Informations that can be collected by using ScriptLattes are, for instance, statistic descriptions and collaboration graphs. This collection of information of curriculums is performed globally for all dataset and then the Scriptlattes displays the report produced by HTML pages containing links between its pages. Further, Scriptlattes user can be interested in getting reports with different views of dataset, such as: specific research line, course, knowledge area and so forth. Each report needs a subset of the dataset (e.g., segmenting the curriculum by some criteria) and a execution of the subset.

From this limitation of Scriptlattes, this paper proposes a method that use Scriptlattes functionality to categorize reports generated by Scriptlattes. Precisely, this categorization is modeled by elements of graph theory in which is constructed a partially ordered set that induces a hierarchy based on a categorization of the data. Thus, the nodes represent subsets of curriculum grouped by some criteria that associates them. Finally, running a Scriptlattes for each node, user has different views of the dataset with its own settings (subsets of curriculum and customizations in general).

This paper is organized as follows: Sect. 2 has definitions and properties about hierarchical clustering. In Sect. 3, the proposed method is described. Results and applications of the hierarchical clustering of a higher education institution are in Sect. 4. Finally, Sect. 5 has conclusions and future works.

2   Theoretical Background

Consider Cv a set of Lattes curriculum. In machine learning, we say that $\mathbb{P}$ is a clustering (partition) on the dataset Cv if and only if $\mathbb{P}$ containing n groups (subsets) $S_1, S_2, ..., S_n$ of Cv such that the following conditions hold:

1. The clustering $\mathbb{P}$ does not contain the empty set, i.e.,

$$\emptyset \notin \mathbb{P}. \tag{1}$$

2. The union of the groups in $\mathbb{P}$ is equal to Cv, i.e.,

$$Cv = \bigcup_{S_i \in \mathbb{P}} S_i. \tag{2}$$

3. The intersection of any two distinct groups in $\mathbb{P}$ is empty.

$$\forall \mathcal{S}_i, \mathcal{S}_j \in \mathbb{P}, \mathcal{S}_i \neq \mathcal{S}_j \Rightarrow \mathcal{S}_i \cap \mathcal{S}_j = \emptyset. \tag{3}$$

In this paper, we denote that $\mathbb{P}(C)$ is the group $\mathcal{S}_i \in \mathbb{P}$ containing the Lattes curriculum C, i.e., $\mathbb{P}(C) = \mathcal{S}_i$ if and only if $C \in \mathcal{S}_i$. Thus, we define a binary relation *finer than* on the set of clusterings of Cv, as follows: for any two clustering $\mathbb{P}_i$ and $\mathbb{P}_j$ on Cv, we say that $\mathbb{P}_i$ is finer than $\mathbb{P}_j$ (and that $\mathbb{P}_j$ is coarser than $\mathbb{P}_i$) if and only if every group of $\mathbb{P}_i$ is a subset of some group of $\mathbb{P}_j$, i.e.,

$$\forall C \in \text{Cv}, \mathbb{P}_i(C) \subseteq \mathbb{P}_j(C). \tag{4}$$

In this case, we say that $\mathbb{P}_i$ is a refinement of a clustering $\mathbb{P}_j$ and written as $\mathbb{P}_i \preceq \mathbb{P}_j$. More details see in [19,20].

This relation $\preceq$ on a subset $\mathcal{T}$ of clusterings of Cv constitutes a partially ordered set (poset) and thus, we can run a scriptlattes for each clustering $\mathcal{T}_i \in \mathcal{T}$ and presents them in a manner categorized by a hierarchy based on the Hasse diagram of poset $(\mathcal{T}, \preceq)$. To illustrate this idea, consider the following example: let $\mathbb{P}_{\text{Area}}, \mathbb{P}_{\text{Course}}$ and $\mathbb{P}_{\text{ResearchLine}}$ partitions of Cv clustered by knowledge area, course and research line, respectively, in such a way to satisfy: $\text{Cv} \preceq \mathbb{P}_{\text{ResearchLine}} \preceq \mathbb{P}_{\text{Course}} \preceq \mathbb{P}_{\text{Area}} \preceq \{\text{Cv}\}$. Thus, we have:

- $\mathcal{S}_i \in \mathbb{P}_{\text{Area}}$ is the group of Cv belonging the knowledge area i;
- $\mathcal{S}_{ij} \in \mathbb{P}_{\text{Course}}$ is the group of $\mathcal{S}_i \subseteq \text{Cv}$ belonging the course j of the knowledge area i;
- $\mathcal{S}_{ijk} \in \mathbb{P}_{\text{ResearchLine}}$ is the group of $\mathcal{S}_{ij} \subseteq \mathcal{S}_i \subseteq \text{Cv}$ belonging the research line k of the course j of the knowledge area i.

Therefore, $\mathcal{T} = \mathbb{P}_{\text{Area}} \cup \mathbb{P}_{\text{Course}} \cup \mathbb{P}_{\text{ResearchLine}} \cup \text{Cv}$. Figure 1 shows part of a branch of the Hasse diagram $(\mathcal{T}, \preceq)$.

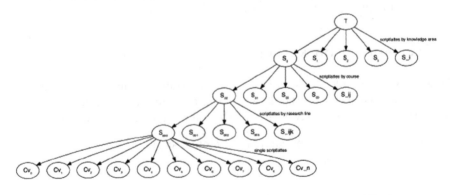

Fig. 1. Example of part of a branch of the Hasse diagram $(\mathcal{T}, \preceq)$.

To build the hierarchy of clusterings $\mathcal{T}$ is employed the technique traditional of machine learning, called hierarchical clustering [21,22], described in Sect. 2.1.

2.1 Hierarchical Clustering

Hierarchy of clustering can offer more information about the structure of the curriculums in the dataset. With a hierarchy, the cluster of curriculums can be seen at different levels, i.e., from the bottom level where each curriculum forms an independent cluster (singleton clusters) to the top level with only one cluster containing all the curriculums. The hierarchical clustering involves creating clusterings that have a predetermined ordering from top to bottom. There are two traditional approach for construction hierarchical clustering [21, 22], divisive and agglomerative:

- *Divisive*: In this method is assigned all of the curriculums to a single cluster and then partition the cluster to two least similar clusters. Finally, we proceed recursively on each cluster until there is one cluster for each curriculums.
- *Agglomerative*: Initially, the set of all curriculum is considered to be a single cluster and then, recursively, is calculated the similarity (e.g., distance) between each of the clusterings and join the two most similar clusterings.

In order to build the Hierarchy of clustering, it is required to determine the (dis)similarity between each pair of clusterings using a distance function. The main methods used to measure the distance between the clusters are [21, 22]:

1. *Single Linkage*: the distance between two clusters is defined as the shortest distance between two curriculum in each cluster, i.e.,

$$\forall \mathcal{T}_i, \mathcal{T}_j \in \mathcal{T}, D_{min}(\mathcal{T}_i, \mathcal{T}_j) = \min\{dist(C_i, C_j) : C_i \in \mathcal{T}_i, C_j \in \mathcal{T}_j\}. \quad (5)$$

2. *Complete Linkage*: the distance between two clusters is defined as the longest distance between two curriculum in each cluster, i.e.,

$$\forall \mathcal{T}_i, \mathcal{T}_j \in \mathcal{T}, D_{max}(\mathcal{T}_i, \mathcal{T}_j) = \max\{dist(C_i, C_j) : C_i \in \mathcal{T}_i, C_j \in \mathcal{T}_j\}. \quad (6)$$

3. *Average Linkage*: the distance between two clusters is defined as the average distance between each curriculum in one cluster to every curriculums in the other cluster.

$$\forall \mathcal{T}_i, \mathcal{T}_j \in \mathcal{T}, D_{avg}(\mathcal{T}_i, \mathcal{T}_j) = \frac{1}{|\mathcal{T}_i| \times |\mathcal{T}_j|} \sum_{C_i \in \mathcal{T}_i} \sum_{C_j \in \mathcal{T}_j} dist(C_i, C_j). \quad (7)$$

Note that, the distance functions between clusterings need of a distance function between curriculums that is defined in Sect. 3.

3 Proposed Method

Hierarchical clustering allows the creation of a cluster tree, as mentioned previously. The tree is not a single set of clusters, but rather a multilevel hierarchy, where clusters at one level are joined as clusters at the next level. This allows adjustment of the grouping level most suitable for our pretensions. Therefore, it is necessary to build a distance function between the curriculum, that is used in the kernel of hierarchical clustering algorithms.

Consider $\mathrm{Inf}_{\mathrm{Field}}(C)$ the function that represents the value associated in a given field on the Lattes curriculum $C \in \mathrm{Cv}$. For example, $\mathrm{Inf}_{\mathrm{Area}}(C)$ is the value associated the knowledge area of curriculum C. Thus, consider $\mathcal{F}$ a list of associated functions on the Lattes curriculums. Note that, $\mathcal{F}$ are informations that are associated in each row of dataset, which is built by using a file where each row contains: personal ID, name, list of associated informations. Table 1 has the structure of the dataset.

Table 1. Structure of the dataset

Dataset				
Personal ID	**Name**	**Inf$_{\mathrm{Area}}$**	**Inf$_{\mathrm{Course}}$**	**Inf$_{...}$**
Lattes ID of the person 1	person 1	ID of area 1	ID of course 1	...
Lattes ID of the person 2	person 2	ID of area 1	ID of course 1	...
Lattes ID of the person 3	person 3	ID of area 1	ID of course 2	...
Lattes ID of the person 4	person 4	ID of area 1	ID of course 2	...
Lattes ID of the person 5	person 5	ID of area 2	ID of course 3	...
Lattes ID of the person 6	person 6	ID of area 2	ID of course 4	...
Lattes ID of the person 7	person 7	ID of area 2	ID of course 4	...
Lattes ID of the person 8	person 8	ID of area 2	ID of course 4	...
Lattes ID of the person ...	person ...	ID of area ...	ID of course ...	

The distance function between curriculum is defined as following:

$$\forall C_i, C_j \in \mathrm{Cv}, dist(C_i, C_j) = \sum_{k \in \mathcal{F}} \omega_k |\mathrm{Inf}_k(C_i) - \mathrm{Inf}_k(C_j)|, \tag{8}$$

where ω_k is a weight associated the function $\mathrm{Inf}_k \in \mathcal{F}$.

For example, the hierarchy of clusterings shown in Fig. 1 can be built using single linkage as the distance function between clusterings and the functions associated $\mathrm{Inf}_{\mathrm{Area}}, \mathrm{Inf}_{\mathrm{Course}}$ and $\mathrm{Inf}_{\mathrm{ResearchLine}}$ also used to define the following distance function between curriculums:

$$\forall C_i, C_j \in \mathrm{Cv}, dist(C_i, C_j) = \omega_{\mathrm{ResearchLine}} |\mathrm{Inf}_{\mathrm{ResearchLine}}(C_i) - \mathrm{Inf}_{\mathrm{ResearchLine}}(C_j)| +$$
$$\omega_{\mathrm{Course}} |\mathrm{Inf}_{\mathrm{Course}}(C_i) - \mathrm{Inf}_{\mathrm{Course}}(C_j)| +$$
$$\omega_{\mathrm{Area}} |\mathrm{Inf}_{\mathrm{Area}}(C_i) - \mathrm{Inf}_{\mathrm{Area}}(C_j)|, \tag{9}$$

where $\omega_{\mathrm{ResearchLine}} = 1, \omega_{\mathrm{Course}} = \omega_{\mathrm{ResearchLine}} + \max\{\mathrm{Inf}_{\mathrm{ResearchLine}}(C) : C \in \mathrm{Cv}\}$ and $\omega_{\mathrm{Area}} = \omega_{\mathrm{Course}} + \max\{\mathrm{Inf}_{\mathrm{Course}}(C) : C \in \mathrm{Cv}\}$.

Once the hierarchy of clusterings $\mathcal{T}$ is build, we can visit the clusters $\mathcal{T}_i \in \mathcal{T}$ (see Fig. 2) and associate each cluster $\mathcal{S}_k \in \mathcal{T}_i$ the result of Scriptlattes. Moreover, depending on the cluster height in the hierarchy we can provide different settings for Scriptlattes, allowing different treatment to clusterings by knowledge areas, courses, research lines and single curriculum.

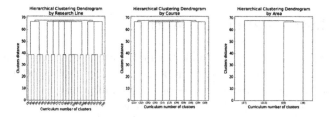

Fig. 2. Hierarchical clustering dendrograms.

A implementation in Python language for constructed the hierarchy of clusterings $\mathcal{T}$ can be acessed at link: https://goo.gl/9v6Wvw

4   Application: Data Extraction for Sucupira Platform

The Sucupira platform is a management tool used by the Coordination for the Improvement of Higher Education Personnel (CAPES - Coordenação de Aperfeiçoamento de Pessoal de Nível Superior). By using this platform, programs report their performance to the coordination annually and, at the end of each four-year period, while CAPES verify if they show minimum quality required for maintenance. Data is imported directly from the Lattes platform, and it refers to the scientific production of each of the professors belonging to the assessed course. After the import, we need to perform a manual checking, since many information regarding the registration of the professors data as well as the scientific productivity may still be incomplete [13].

For this purpose, we construct a sequence of hierarchies ($\mathcal{T}^{2013}$, $\mathcal{T}^{2014}$, $\mathcal{T}^{2015}$, $\mathcal{T}^{2016}$, $\mathcal{T}^{2013-2016}$), where each element of this sequence contains a hierarchy of clusterings configured to execute scriptlattes for a specific period. Moreover, the clusters formed by curriculums of a same course are configured with the Qualis of knowledge area. Once the hierarchies of clusterings ($\mathcal{T}^{2013}$, $\mathcal{T}^{2014}$, $\mathcal{T}^{2015}$, $\mathcal{T}^{2016}$, $\mathcal{T}^{2013-2016}$) are build, we can visit each hierarchy of clusterings $\mathcal{T}^{\text{Period}}$ and run a Scriptlattes for each level of them in $\mathcal{T}^{\text{Period}}$. Finally, the reports produced by Scriptlattes throughout hierarchies of clusterings are organized into a web page that can be accessed at link: https://db.tt/5JnRPH7e.

Note that it is possible to make a thorough checking of the information to be submitted to Sucupira platform by using the hierarchies of clusterings based on reports generated by scriptlattes. It is worth remembering that the preliminary check of scientific productivity of each professor permits the identification of those who may have not achieved the goals set by the program, determined by CAPES. With this result, managers can improve research strategies in order to improve their production during the period of quadrennial, avoiding any unfortunate surprises when assessing the course. A further hierarchy of clustering without period setting can be seen in this link: https://db.tt/ZOxTXHiP.

5   Conclusion and Future Works

In this paper, we proposed a method that makes use of the Scriptlattes to build a hierarchy of clusterings based on reports generated by scriptlattes. In this hierarchy, the nodes represent subsets of curriculum grouped by a criteria that associates them and Scriptlattes is executed for each node. The hierarchy of clusterings built provides more information about the structure of the curriculums in the dataset. Thereby, the cluster of curriculums can be seen at different levels, i.e., from the bottom level where each curriculum forms an independent cluster (singleton clusters) to the top level with only one cluster containing all the curriculums. It allows the Scriptlattes user to access different views on the reports generated from the dataset. Moreover, it has been presented a example of application for data extraction for Sucupira platform, which used the proposed hierarchy approach. As a future work, we intend to study the similarities between clustering on different hierarchies, and analyze the evolution of collaboration graph along the hierarchy of clusterings.

References

1. Kadriu, A.: Discovering value in academic social networks: a case study in ResearchGate. In: Proceedings of the ITI 2013 35th International Conference on Information Technology Interfaces, 57–62. IEEE (2013)
2. Lynch, C.A.: Institutional repositories: essential infrastructure for scholarship in the digital age. Libr. Acad. **3**, 327–336 (2003)
3. Ernst, H.: Patent information for strategic technology management. World Pat. Inf. **25**, 233–242 (2003)
4. Fernández-Breis, J.T., Castellanos-Nieves, D., Hernández-Franco, J., Soler-Segovia, C., del Carmen Robles-Redondo, M., González-Martínez, R., Prendes-Espinosa, M.P.: A semantic platform for the management of the educative curriculum. Expert Syst. Appl. **39**, 6011–6019 (2012)
5. Burns, C.S., Lana, A., Budd, J.: Institutional repositories: exploration of costs and value. D-Lib Mag. **19**, 1 (2013)
6. Edgar, B.D., Willinsky, J.: A survey of scholarly journals using open journal systems. Sch. Res. Commun. **1** (2010)
7. Lane, J.: Let's make science metrics more scientific. Nature **464**, 488–489 (2010)
8. Mena-Chalco, J.P., Junior, R.M.C.: ScriptLattes: an open-source knowledge extraction system from the lattes platform. J. Braz. Comput. Soc. **15**, 31–39 (2009). http://link.springer.com/10.1007/BF03194511
9. CNPq. http://estatico.cnpq.br/painelLattes/
10. Ferraz, R.R.N., Quoniam, L.: A Utilização da Ferramenta Computacional Scriptlattes para Avaliação das Competências em Pesquisa no Brasil. Revista Prisma. Com (21) (2014)

11. Ferraz, R.R.N., Quoniam, L.M., Maccari, E.A.: The use of scriptlattes tool for extraction and on-line availability of academic production from a department of stricto sensu in management. In: 11th International Conference on Information Systems and Technology Management-CONTECSI, vol. 17 (2014)
12. Giordano, D.M., Bruning, E., Bordin, A.S.: Uso do Scriptlattes e Gephi na Análise da Colaboração Científica. In: Anais do Computer on the Beach, pp. 239–248 (2015)
13. Nigro, C.A., Ferraz, R.R.N., Quoniam, L., Alves, W.A.L.: Strategic management of research productivity from graduate medicine program by the use of scriptsucupira computational tool. In: Proceedings of the 13th International Conference on Information Systems and Technology Management (2016)
14. Mena-Chalco, J., Cesar-Jr, R.: Bibliometria e Cientometria: Reflexões Teóricas e Interfaces. Pedro & João Editores, São Carlos (2013)
15. Mena-Chalco, J.P., Digiampietri, L.A., Lopes, F.M., Cesar, R.M.: Brazilian Bibliometric Coauthorship Networks. J. Assoc. Inf. Sci. Technol. 65, 1424–1445 (2014). http://dx.doi.org/10.1002/asi.23010
16. Mena-Chalco, J.P., Junior, R.M.C.: Towards automatic discovery of co-authorship networks in the Brazilian academic areas. In: IEEE Seventh International Conference on e-Science Workshops (eScienceW), pp. 53–60 (2011)
17. Perez-Cervantes, E., Mena-Chalco, J.P., Cesar-Jr, R.M.: Towards a quantitative academic internationalization assessment of Brazilian research groups. In: 2012 IEEE 8th International Conference on E-Science (e-Science), pp. 1–8 (2012)
18. Perez-Cervantes, E., Mena-Chalco, J.P., Oliveira, M., Cesar, R.M.: Using link prediction to estimate the collaborative influence of researchers. In: 2013 IEEE 9th International Conference on eScience (eScience), pp. 293–300 (2013)
19. Brualdi, R.: Introductory Combinatorics. Pearson Education, Pearson Education International, Upper Saddle River (2012)
20. Newman, M.H.A.: Elements of the Topology of Plane sets of Points. Dover Publications, Mineola (1992)
21. Duda, R.O., Hart, P.E., Stork, D.G.: Pattern Classification. Wiley, Hoboken (2012)
22. Friedman, J., Hastie, T., Tibshirani, R.: The Elements of Statistical Learning. Springer Series in Statistics, vol. 1. Springer, Berlin (2001)

Using Logic Concepts on Six Sigma

Caique Z. Kirilo$^{(\boxtimes)}$, Jair M. Abe, Luiz Lozano, Renato H. Parreira,
and Eduardo P. Dacorso

Paulista University, São Paulo, Brazil
{zaneti,luiz,renato}@paradecision.com

Abstract. Decision Making process is key to success. With this in mind, this paper discusses the implementation of Paraconsistent Logic to the Six Sigma concepts. It is known that the human factor can be risky, so it can benefit with the addition of some artificial intelligence such as Paraconsistent Logic. Applying the Paraconsistent Decision-Making Method can minimize the human factor risk, avoiding rework, as it eliminates any discrepancy among the opinions of the specialist involved on the decision making process.

Keywords: Decision-making · Six Sigma · Quality · Paraconsistent Annotated Evidential Logic Eτ

1 Introduction

This paper proposes an improvement on the Six Sigma concept by reducing the human factor risk causes by the misallocation of human resources for the execution of tasks or the misapplication of the DMAIC method. The proposed is a method based on an expert system Paraconsistent Annotated Evidential Logic Eτ. Such system identifies inconsistencies in the decisions taken by experts in the program, making possible to deal with these inconsistencies and, also to identify if the experts have the necessary knowledge to take the right decision. Six Sigma is a process based entirely on the human factor, so applying an artificial intelligence will minimize errors caused by it making Lean Six Sigma stronger and more efficient, empowering the process of quality improvement.

We can best exemplify the idea as follows: imagine many managers and employees participating in a brainstorm where the goal is to create a cause and effect diagram for a particular problem, in that meeting will be people from different hierarchies and influence, then if we want to get the most reliable results in this brainstorm we need to shield the environment so that factors such as appearance, influence or intimidation will not interfere in the decision-making process.

Integrating paraconsistent logic in the creation of this cause and effect diagram through software is a solution to make the environment that is happening brainstorm get as close as possible to neutrality. In that way participants will register their opinions transparently and totally focused on the problem, thus obtaining more accurate results.

© IFIP International Federation for Information Processing 2016
Published by Springer International Publishing AG 2016. All Rights Reserved
I. Nääs et al. (Eds.): APMS 2016, IFIP AICT 488, pp. 36–42, 2016.
DOI: 10.1007/978-3-319-51133-7_5

2   Six Sigma – Backgrounds

Based on studies of Werkema [1], Lean Six Sigma is a quantitative management strategy starting from the number of faults in the production or product process. It aims to improve them to increase customer satisfaction and generate a higher profit margin. It must be implemented "top-down" and all employees, regardless of their segment or hierarchy, should be part and have knowledge about the program. Each of them will have responsibilities and tasks in order to have a good Lean Six Sigma implementation. Each employee assumes a position and respective responsibilities described below:

- **Sponsor of Lean Six Sigma:** The person with the highest executive level in the company, responsible for defining all the factors necessary for the implementation of the program.
- **Sponsor Facilitator:** It is one of the company directors. It has the function of advising the Lean Six Sigma Sponsor in implementing the program.
- **Champions:** are directors or managers of the company who is responsible for supporting the projects and remove difficulties for its development.
- **Master Black Belts:** They are professionals who advise the Sponsors and Champions, which must have great ability to teach and act as mentors for Black Belts and Green Belts.
- **Black Belts:** They are team leaders, whose function is to coordinate projects. Must have a high technical knowledge and a number of qualities that characterize as being able to perform this function.
- **Green Belts:** They are members of teams led by Black Belts or leading teams in conducting functional designs.
- **Yellow Belts:** They are usually supervisors, properly educated and trained to understand the basics of the program. It has the function of supervising the program is well implemented across the organization and run projects focused on development.
- **White Belts:** They are professionals operating company level, properly educated and trained in the program. They have the function to support the Green Belts and Black Belts.

This hierarchy is respected when Paraconsistet Logic is applied to these concepts.

3   The DMAIC Method in Six Sigma

One of the Lean Six Sigma infrastructure elements is the establishment of teams to execute projects that strongly contribute to the achievement of strategic goals of the company. The development of these projects is carried out based on a method called DMAIC [2]. The DMAIC method consists of 5 steps, Define, Measure, Analyze, Improve and Control.

- **D** – **Define:** Define the precise scope of the project.
- **M** – **Measure:** Determine the location or focus of the problem.
- **A** – **Analyze:** To determine the causes of each priority problem.
- **I** – **Improve**: To develop, evaluate and implement solutions for each priority problem.
- **C** – **Control:** To ensure that the scope of the long-term goal is maintained.

4 Human Errors in Six Sigma

No doubt this is the most sensitive part of Six Sigma, the people who are responsible to make it work are the same that causes its fail. Weighing it [3] addressed this issue based on the studies of Schmidt [4] and the result was a list of most significant factors involving human error. The Paraconsistent Logic has the intention to minimize or eliminate the negative impacts caused by these factors.

Misinterpretation: To ensure uniform interpretation of the words is necessary to provide precise definitions, plus auxiliary tools such as checklists and examples. They should also be given detailed information and examples of how to calculate, summarize, record, etc. On critical issues, should provide formal training, along with tests to check the "capacity" of candidates for sensors on the process [3].

Inadvertent error: Inadvertent error is unintentional, unpredictable and often unconscious, that is, the person who makes the mistake is not, then, conscious of having committed it. The data produced by an inadvertent error has a random characteristic, which is useful for identifying errors of this type. The choice of solution for this type of error is somewhat limited because the root cause of inadvertent mistakes is an inherent weakness in the human been, so to say, the inability to keep an eye indefinitely [3].

Lack of technique: The error for lack of technique is the result of incomplete knowledge by the human sensor. Some people have developed a more skillful way - some kind of "trick", i.e. a small difference in the method that represents a big difference in the results. Those who know the "trick" get superior results; others, not. The solution in this case is to study the methods used both by those who have superior performance, as for those that have underperformed. These studies have identified the "tricks" that can then be transferred to all employees through training or embedded technology [3].

Conscious error: The conscious mistake is intentional. The person who made it is aware of that, and intends to continue, often as a form of defense against real or imagined injustices [3].

Dissimulation: Dissimulation is a deliberate alteration of data collected for a variety of usually selfish purposes: reducing workload, escape from unpleasant tasks, self-promotion, fear of being punished for delivering bad news. The reduction of dissimulation can be achieved in part by the establishment of an environment that adopts open communication, which requires leadership by example, senior management [3].

Distortion: Distortion and dissimulation are similar, but there are subtle differences. In dissimulation the human sensor knows the facts and alters consciously. The distortion is not necessarily consciously, the possible existence of interior forces influencing the human sensor response (e.g., fixed ideas due to the habit). The distortion can even be results from the human sensations and feelings. An example is the test conducted by a razor blade manufacturer, in which the reports of the employees who did the test were distorted because they knew the number of beards already made with the blade being tested [3].

Uselessness: The feeling of worthlessness is another source of conscious error. If the employees find out that their reports do not lead to anything, they stop making them. The situation is even worse if workers find that their reward for acting as sensors is an unjustified guilt [3].

5   An Expert System Based on Paraconsistent Logic

Studies based on [5], a synthesized form of PDM, a support method in the decision-making process based on Paraconsistent Logic, which uses the experts' experience to check the feasibility or unfeasibility of a given situation.

From an initial issue called proposition, factors that impact the feasibility or unfeasibility of the matter must be determined. These factors can be divided into sections that are analyzed in order to extract the most of the experience from the specialists.

To make a feasibility analysis of an enterprise for decision making, planning is under the coordination of a particular person (the entrepreneur himself, an engineer, a consultant etc.). This person works the data in a way to translate them for the language of Eτ logic. This will be called expert knowledge engineer (CE) [5].

According to [6] the Paracon-sistent Decision-Making Method has 8 steps:

1. To set the level of demand of the decision whether to take.
2. Select the most important factors and most influential in the decision.
3. Establish the sections for each of the factors, if necessary. The quantity of sections can be chosen depending on the desired granularity/precision.
4. Build the database, which consists of the weights assigned to the factors (When necessary to distinguish them by importance) and the values of favorable evidence (or degree of belief) (a) and contrary evidence (or degree of disbelief) (b) assigned to each factor-sections combination. The weights and the evidence values are assigned by experts chosen conveniently. The database may also be built with stored statistical data obtained from previous experience in performing similar undertakings.
5. Do field research (or data collection) to check, in this case, where section (condition) each factor is.
6. Get the value of the favorable evidence ($a_{i,R}$) and the value of the evidence against ($b_{i,R}$) resulting, with $1 \leq i \leq n$, for each of the factors (F_i) chosen. The sections found in the search (S_{pj}) by application of the techniques of maximization (operator MAX) and minimizing (MIN operator) of Eτ logic.

7. Get the degree of favorable evidence (a_w) and the unfavorable evidence (b_w) of global analysis of the points representing the factors chosen in the lattice τ.
8. Making the decision, applying the decision rule or algorithm para-analyzer.

6   Unifying Concepts

Unifying the concepts of Paraconsistent Logic with Six Sigma is relatively simple; it is possible to draw an equivalence between these two issues.

Paraconsistent Logic has a role of knowledge engineer, who will be responsible for assigning and coordinating the specialists' tasks. The Lean Six Sigma Sponsor will play that role. As he/she is the person who has the macro view of the company, however has access to and power over the micro views.

Other specialists will perform different tasks as described in Chap. 2 of this paper, these experts according to Paraconsistent Logic can have certain weight in decision-making, this weight is set according to the degree of experience that the expert has with the issue at hand. For example, a Green Belt can opine better on a particular issue than the Black Belt due to have more operational knowledge, as the Black Belt has more management experience.

The experts opine on predetermined tasks, stipulated by the Lean Six Sigma Sponsor. He/She will play the role of the knowledge engineer and will split the task on several factors, which will be investigated by all experts. Thus experience of all members will be utilized optimally. The contradictions will be canceled by PDM, making the whole process more effective. Following is illustrated the union of concepts.

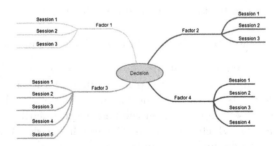

Fig. 1. The MPD concept

The decision is made upon certain factors, shown in Fig. 1. The factors are split into sections to better specify function the issue being dealt. That is, the issue to be addressed is thoroughly analyzed before being discussed, and when discussed will be extensively analyzed.

Figure 2 shows a fictitious example of how you deploy a part of the Six Sigma in paraconsistent logic. The program members will respond to certain factors with a percentage of certainty and uncertainty, and then the logic will do the calculations that will eliminate the contradictions.

Factor	Session	Group 1		Group 2				Group 3	
		Sponsor 1		Sponsor 2		Champion		Master Black Belt	
		favorable	adverse	favorable	adverse	favorable	adverse	favorable	adverse
F01	S1	100%	0%	90%	10%	100%	10%	90%	0%
	S2	70%	20%	80%	30%	60%	20%	70%	30%
	S3	50%	50%	60%	50%	60%	40%	50%	40%
F02	S1	100%	5%	95%	15%	100%	10%	85%	0%
	S2	75%	25%	85%	25%	85%	30%	73%	35%
	S3	55%	45%	55%	45%	65%	40%	45%	55%
F03	S1	92%	8%	98%	18%	88%	12%	82%	7%
	S2	67%	23%	83%	27%	77%	18%	63%	28%
	S3	52%	47%	57%	48%	62%	43%	52%	45%
	S4	17%	73%	24%	65%	37%	67%	33%	64%
	S5	100%	98%	17%	83%	18%	2%	21%	95%
F04	S1	92%	8%	98%	18%	88%	12%	82%	7%
	S2	67%	23%	83%	27%	77%	18%	63%	28%
	S3	52%	47%	57%	48%	62%	43%	52%	45%
	S4	100%	98%	17%	83%	18%	2%	21%	95%

continuation		Group 3		Group 4					
		Black Belt		Green Belt		Yellow Belt		White Belt	
		favorable	adverse	favorable	adverse	favorable	adverse	favorable	adverse
F01	S1	90%	0%	100%	10%	90%	0%	90%	0%
	S2	70%	30%	80%	20%	70%	30%	70%	30%
	S3	50%	40%	60%	40%	50%	40%	50%	40%
F02	S1	85%	0%	100%	10%	85%	0%	85%	0%
	S2	73%	35%	85%	30%	73%	35%	73%	35%
	S3	45%	55%	65%	40%	45%	55%	45%	55%
F03	S1	82%	7%	88%	12%	82%	7%	82%	7%
	S2	63%	28%	77%	18%	63%	28%	63%	28%
	S3	52%	45%	62%	43%	52%	45%	52%	45%
	S4	33%	64%	37%	67%	33%	64%	33%	64%
	S5	21%	95%	18%	2%	21%	95%	21%	95%
F04	S1	82%	7%	88%	12%	82%	7%	82%	7%
	S2	63%	28%	77%	18%	63%	28%	63%	28%
	S3	52%	45%	62%	43%	52%	45%	52%	45%
	S4	21%	95%	18%	2%	21%	95%	21%	95%

Fig. 2. The union of concepts

This way the human error causes can be eliminated as the tasks will be extensively treated during its course, so, before been executed. It is also possible to ensure that all program members effectively understand the importance of a particular task.

This system can be implemented at any time the progress of the Six Sigma program. There is a Decision Making Software developed by ParaDecision Company that simplifies the implementation of the PDM. There is a free version on the website www.paradecision.com.

Fig. 3. The specialist association

Figure 3 shows how it can be made the integration between the experts of Six Sigma and paraconsistent logic. The weights assigned to the experts will impact the decision-making, then in certain situations these weights can be changed according to the greater knowledge of the expert in question.

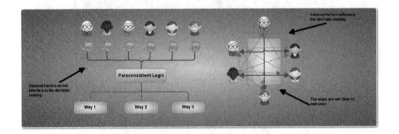

Fig. 4. Difference between two ways of making decisions

7   Conclusions

This paper, though bring a more superficial view of the subject, invites the reader to reflect on the use of paraconsistent logic as a way to improve the implementation of Six Sigma and mitigate their vulnerabilities.

It is possible with the use of an artificial intelligence minimize human errors that put at risk the program. The intention was never eliminated the human's deci-sion-making process; on the contrary, the intention is to improve the experience of the human being and makes it less susceptible to failures throughout the process.

References

1. Werkema, C.: Criando a Cultura Seis Sigma. Werkema Editora, Nova Lima (2004)
2. Werkema, C.: Métodos PDCA e Dmaic e Suas Ferramentas Analíticas, vol. 1. Elsevier Brasil, Rio de Janeiro (2013)
3. Werkema, C.: Perguntas e Respostas sobre o Lean Seis Sigma, 2nd edn. Elsevier Brasil, Rio de Janeiro (2011)
4. Schmidt, P., dos Santos, J.L., Arima, H.: Fundamentos de Auditoria de Sistemas. Atlas, Rio de Janeiro (2006)
5. de Carvalho, F.R.: Aplicação de Lógica Paraconsistente Anotada em Tomadas de Decisão na Engenharia de Produção. Ph.D. thesis, Universidade de São Paulo (2006)
6. Abe, J.M., Akama, S., Nakamatsu, K.: Introduction to Annotated Logics: Foundations for Paracomplete and Paraconsistent Reasoning, vol. 88. Springer, Heidelberg (2015)

Intelligent Manufacturing Systems

A Method Towards Modelling and Analysis of Semantically-Enriched Reconfigurable Manufacturing Systems

Damiano Nunzio Arena$^{(\boxtimes)}$ and Dimitris Kiritsis

École Politechnique Fédérale de Lausanne, Lausanne, Switzerland
{damiano.arena,dimitris.kiritsis}@epfl.ch

Abstract. Modelling and simulation are two relevant facets for thorough and effective analysis of industrial systems that nowadays have to cope with the evergrowing complexity of the industrial processes and the need of modelling flexibility and knowledge sharing. For all these reasons, the following work seeks to explore and combine together different methodologies by exploiting their best features. In particular, the current research aims to combine semantic technologies, such as ontologies, and high-level Petri nets to revamp the actual assembly systems. Thus, key research concepts are presented, explaining such potential integration and providing a short example of the dynamic configuration of an assembly system within a semantically enriched modelling environment.

Keywords: Reconfigurable manufacturing systems · Colored Petri net · Ontologies

1 Problem Statement

In today's manufacturing industry, staying in business is a life-and-death issue for many manufacturing companies. It is well-known that the one thing most surviving or winning manufacturing companies have in common is continuous improvement and adaptation of their manufacturing systems. During the last few decades, these have thoroughly evolved, from low volume, high variety job-shop production systems to more robust mid-volume and variety flexible manufacturing systems. Nonetheless, manufacturing systems still suffered from low responsiveness and large capital investment until the introduction of reconfigurable manufacturing systems. Reconfigurability can be defined as the ability to repeatedly change capacity and functionality in a cost-efficient way, in order to meet different demand situations in terms of variation in volume as well as in product characteristics [1]. This ability can be achieved at different enterprise levels, e.g. network, factory, segment, system, cell, workstation [2].

Though there is a substantial amount of research work available in the domain of reconfigurable systems, especially at system level [3], systems with full level

© IFIP International Federation for Information Processing 2016
Published by Springer International Publishing AG 2016. All Rights Reserved
I. Nääs et al. (Eds.): APMS 2016, IFIP AICT 488, pp. 45–52, 2016.
DOI: 10.1007/978-3-319-51133-7_6

of reconfigurability are still non-existent [4]. In particular, in the domain of developing Reconfigurable Manufacturing Systems (RMS), just limited research that incorporates its true dynamic, rapid nature and accurate decision making in complex systems is available.

Towards development of Reconfigurable Manufacturing Systems, several promising models have been proposed in the past two decades [5–8]. However, these models are only limited to control, physical and structural aspects that would support reconfiguration but lacked a rapid reconfigurability and decision making capabilities.

To summarize, our effort in this work focuses on the definition of a semantic-enriched modelling environment for Reconfigurable Manufacturing Systems taking full advantage of the dynamic properties of ontologies and Petri nets.

2   Proposed Approach

The objective of this research is to investigate and support the re-configurability of manufacturing systems by applying CPN modelling language and Knowledge Engineering (KE) methodologies, such as Ontologies. The rationale of this work is two-fold:

- Semantic extraction and modelling of Reconfigurable Manufacturing Systems.
- Integration of the aforementioned enabling technologies to support the dynamic design of Reconfigurable Manufacturing Systems.

The key feature of this approach resides with the integration of Semantic Techniques and Colored Petri Nets. This potential integration seeks to bridge the lack of interoperability between such methodologies by creating a Semantically Enriched Environment where a RMS can be (dynamically) instantiated.

CPNs are proven to be suitable for modelling the system structure and behavior, therefore, RMS concepts are mapped into CPN ones, and then transformed into CPN-oriented elements. The resulting CPN model can be, therefore, verified and simulated in order to explore and perform either quantitative or qualitative analysis of the system [16]. In particular, qualitative analysis searches for structural properties [17], such as:

- absence of deadlocks
- absence of overflows
- presence of certain mutual exclusions (in case of resource sharing)

Quantitative analysis, instead, looks for performance properties such as:

- throughput, average completion times
- average queue lengths
- utilization rates

The simulation outcomes can be, hence, reasoned in order to feedback the system and achieve continuous re-adaptation and improvement. Figure 1 shows the proposed (closed-loop) architecture together with an overview of the main system elements:

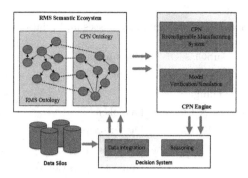

Fig. 1. System architecture

– *Data Silos*, manufacturing/assembly data that are a vital element for the RMS itself, which are either structured or unstructured;
– *DS*, decision system based on semantic technologies, that aims to provide data integration and reasoning features;
– *Semantic Ecosystem*, where domain-specific ontology elements are related to one another to enable CPN concepts inferring from RAS ones;
– CPN engine to perform the above-mentioned assessments.

A Reconfigurable Manufacturing System poses itself a modelling challenge because of its dynamic nature. On the other hand, Petri Net formalism, and in particular CPN, has a general-purpose nature and it is based on strong math foundations, which results very suitable for both modelling and analysis phases of reconfigurable systems.

3   Method Conceptualization

The backbone of this solution is represented by the semantic-enriched environment through which all the domain specific concepts are outlined and related each other. Particular emphasis has to be given to the non-trivial semantics of the selected modelling language (CPN), which extends the simple PN formalism by introducing some enriched features. In fact, the so-called CPN Ontology (see Fig. 2) should consists of basic PN concepts (place, transition, arc, and token) plus high-level ones (see Table 1).

The RMS Ontology, should consists, instead, of domain specific concepts, such as Equipment, Components, Worker roles, Work Station (see Fig. 3). However, some details about this ontology models have been omitted. As mentioned earlier, ontologies themselves do not provide simulable models. The introduction of PN-based concepts, hence, aims to bridge this lack of simulation through the translation of RMS elements into CPN ones. In this regards, Zhou et.al [18] suggest an interpretation of the simple PN elments such as Places, Transitions and directed Arcs (see Table 2), which can be, therefore, inferred through the semantic models. The proposed approach, in fact, aims to set inference rules

Table 1. CPN ontology classes and relations

Class	subClassOf	Class property	
		Name	Range
CPN_Element	Thing	-	-
Place	CPN_Element	hasTokens	Token
Transition	CPN_Element	hasTInscription	Inscription
Arc	CPN_Element	hasAInscription	Inscription
PTArc	Arc	connectsTransitionTo	Transition
TPArc	Arc	connectsPlaceTo	Place
Token	CPN_Element	hasInfo	TokenInfo
TokenInfo	Token	-	-
Inscription	CPN_Element	-	-
A_Inscription	Inscription	definesFlowRuleOn	Arc
T_Inscription	Inscription	definesExecutionRuleOn	Transition

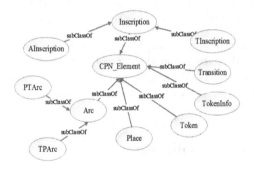

Fig. 2. CPN Ontology

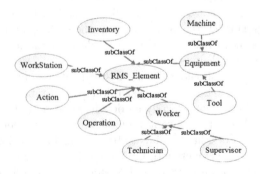

Fig. 3. RMS Ontology

to automatically perform the aforementioned concepts mapping and, then, provide a PN-based semantic-enriched description of the re-configurable assembly system. For example, using a human readable syntax, we can set the following rule:

```
hasMachine (?Activity, ?Machine) ∧
hasMachineStatus (?Machine, ?MachineStatus) ⇒
connectsPlaceTo (?PTArc, ?Transition) ∧
hasPTArc (?Place, ?PTArc)
```

Table 2. Interpretation of the PN elements

PN elements	Interpretation
Places	Resource status, operations and conditions
Transitions	Operations, processes, activities and events
Directed Arcs	Material, resource, information, and control flow direction

This is valid according to the assumption that an Activity is intepreted as a *Transition* and a *MachineStatus* as a *Place*. These can be then instantiated as shown in Fig. 4.

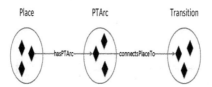

Fig. 4. PlacePTArcTransition inference-based instantiation

That said, the exploration of the system behavior through the Decision System aims at achieving continuous re-adaptation of the model according to specific goals. Let us consider the RMS as described in the PN model below (see Fig. 5). The system might be influenced by different conditions, for example:

- The sequence can be optimized (respecting the technological specifications)
- The work load of the assigned operator should be modified by splitting the execution of those steps among more operator, e.g. increasing the efficiency of the process.
- The expected output should be adapted to respond new customer requirements

Thus, starting from the initial configuration, the system will require some adjustments and consequence re-assessment. For instance, a small portion of

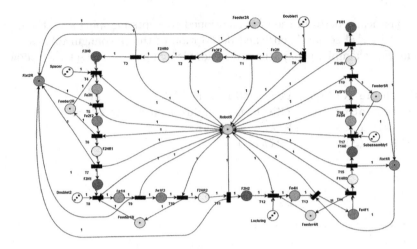

Fig. 5. RMS initial configuration

the model will be reconfigured (see Fig. 6) according to the new requirements revealed by the DS. In fact, once the system receives an input from the DS regarding the need of reconfiguring the system, the new Manufacturing System can be instantiated within the semantic framework, then, translated into Petri Net entities and finally transformed into a new CPN-based model that can be further verified and analyzed.

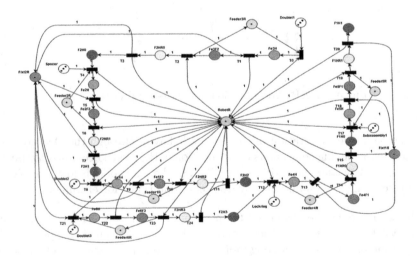

Fig. 6. Reconfigured manufacturing system

4   Conclusions

In the current research we focus on the conceptualization of a modelling framework for Reconfigurable Manufacturing Systems based on Colored Petri Nets and Knowledge Engineering technologies, such as Ontologies. The scope of the presented work is to provide an overview of the key concepts, modelling issues and potential solutions together with a short example of a reconfigurable assembly system. Petri nets are used to model the Manufacturing System while ontologies are exploited to achieve system interoperability, integration and reusability through semantics. However, the work is still at an early stage and requires some effort in terms of both analysis and implementation in order to explore more critical design facets and pinpoint eventual drawbacks, which might prevent the full interoperability among the system elements. In particular, future work will necessitate the formal assessment of design and deployment requirements (e.g. semantics integration, verification and simulation metrics), the selection of a suitable development environment, and the instantiation of a real case scenario. In this regard, the presented modelling approach has been applied to RMS example but it will be re-used and further tested in the context of Satis-Factory European research project in order to support the analysis and design of dynamically evolving shop floor operations.

References

1. Mehrabi, M.G., Ulsoy, A.G., Koren, Y.: Reconfigurable manufacturing systems: key to future manufacturing. J. Intell. Manuf. **11**(4), 403–419 (2000)
2. Wiendahl, H.P., ElMaraghy, H., Nyhuis, P., Zäh, M., Wiendahl, H.H., Duffie, N., Brieke, M.: Changeable manufacturing - classification, design and operation. CIRP Ann. Manuf. Technol. **56**(2), 783–809 (2007)
3. Andersen, A.L., Brunoe, T.D., Nielsen, K.: Reconfigurable manufacturing on multiple levels: literature review and research directions, pp. 266–273 (2015)
4. ElMaraghy, H.A.: Flexible and reconfigurable manufacturing systems paradigms. Int. J. Flex. Manuf. Syst. **17**(4), 261–276 (2005)
5. Rakesh, K., Jain, P., Mehta, N.: A framework for simultaneous recognition of part families and operation groups for driving a reconfigurable manufacturing system. Adv. Prod. Eng. Manag. J. **5**(1), 45–58 (2010)
6. Nourelfath, M., Ait-kadi, D., Issac Soro, W.: Availability modeling and optimization of reconfigurable manufacturing systems. J. Qual. Maint. Eng. **9**(3), 284–302 (2003)
7. da Silva, R.M., Bentez-Pina, I.F., Blos, M.F., Filho, D.J.S., Miyagi, P.E.: Modeling of reconfigurable distributed manufacturing control systems. IFAC PaperOnline **48**(3), 1284–1289 (2015)
8. Lohse, N., Ratchev, S., Valtchanov, G.: Towards web-enabled design of modular assembly systems. Assembly Autom. **24**(3), 270–279 (2004)
9. Shah, S.A., Bohez, E.L., Pisuchpen, R.: New modeling and performance evaluation of tool sharing control in FMS using colored Petri nets. Assembly Autom. **31**(2), 137–152 (2011)
10. Yu, J., Yin, Y., Sheng, X., Chen, Z.: Modelling strategies for reconfigurable assembly systems. Assembly Autom. **23**(3), 266–272 (2003)

11. Kuo, C.H., Huang, H.P., Wei, K.C., Tang, S.S.H.: System modeling and real-time simulator for highly model-mixed assembly systems. J. Manuf. Sci. Eng. **121**(2), 282 (1999)
12. Jensen, K.: Coloured Petri Nets: Basic Concepts, Analysis Methods and Practical Use, vol. 1. Springer, Heidelberg (2013)
13. Zhang, L.L.: Process platform-based production configuration for mass customization (2007)
14. Vidal, J.C., Lama, M., Bugarn, A.: OPENET: ontology-based engine for high-level Petri nets. Expert Syst. Appl. **37**(9), 6493–6509 (2010)
15. Zhang, F., Ma, Z.M., Ribaric, S.: Representation of Petri net With OWL DL Ontology, pp. 1396–1400. IEEE (2011)
16. Tüysüz, F., Kahraman, C.: Modeling a flexible manufacturing cell using stochastic petri nets with fuzzy parameters. Expert Syst. Appl. **37**(5), 3910–3920 (2010)
17. Kahraman, C., Tüysüz, F.: Manufacturing system modeling using Petri nets. In: Kahraman, C. (ed.) Production Engineering and Management Under Fuzziness, pp. 95–124. Springer, Heidelberg (2010)

Formal Information Model for Representing Production Resources

Niko Siltala$^{(\boxtimes)}$, Eeva Järvenpää, and Minna Lanz

Department of Mechanical Engineering and Industrial Systems,
Tampere University of Technology, Tampere, Finland
{niko.siltala,eeva.jarvenpaa,minna.lanz}@tut.fi

Abstract. This paper introduces a concept and associated descriptions to formally describe physical production resources for modular and reconfigurable production systems. These descriptions are source of formal information for (automatic) production system design and (re-) configuration. They can be further utilized during the system deployment and execution. The proposed concept and the underlying formal resource description model is composed of three different description levels, namely Abstract Resource Description (ARD), Resource Description (RD) and Resource Instance Description (RID), each having different scope and objectives. This paper discusses in details the content and differences between these description levels.

Keywords: Production resource model · Production resource description · Production system design · Reconfigurable manufacturing system · RMS · XML

1   Introduction

The requirements on production systems are continuously being shifted towards higher flexibility and adaptability. Increasing volatility in the economies, shortening innovation and product life cycles, and ever increasing number of variants, call for production systems, which comply with these changing demands. There is a need for rapidly responding production systems that can timely adjust to the required changes in processing functions and production capacity. System reconfiguration is required on three levels: physical, logical and parametric [1]. System reconfiguration is the enabler for re-use and sustainability of production resources.

Despite the high efforts towards reconfigurable production systems and standardization activities focusing on unification of mechanical as well as communication and control interfaces, reconfiguration of assembly systems is still rare in real factories. The usual business today, when the product model changes, is to scrap the existing resources and build a new assembly system from a scratch. This is due to high engineering, integration, and programming efforts and skills

© IFIP International Federation for Information Processing 2016
Published by Springer International Publishing AG 2016. All Rights Reserved
I. Nääs et al. (Eds.): APMS 2016, IFIP AICT 488, pp. 53–60, 2016.
DOI: 10.1007/978-3-319-51133-7_7

needed to re-configure the existing system, as well as uncertainties related to the needed effort. One of the main reasons for infeasibility of reconfiguration is the lack of sufficient and accurate information about the production resources, and their capabilities associated to the current system, its life cycle, and usage history [2]. In addition to Hardware (HW) and Software (SW) interfaces, efficient methodologies, tools and information models are needed to support planners and engineers in the reconfiguration process, and also to allow logical and parametric reconfiguration to take place autonomously while the system is running.

The European Commission funded project ReCaM [3], started in November 2015, aims to find solutions for the above mentioned issues. It targets to develop a set of integrated tools for rapid and autonomous reconfiguration of production systems, integrated with the existing production planning and scheduling tools - MES. The ReCaM approach is based on intelligent plug-and-produce capable self-describing Mechatronic Objects (MOs), which are able to auto-program and self-adjust to the required task. The formal resource descriptions are proposed to capture comprehensively and thoroughly the characteristics of a production devices, providing a foundation for rapid creation of new system configurations.

The objective of this paper is to open the insights of the resource description model and its formal resource descriptions. The paper is organized as follows: Sect. 2 discusses other existing resource description models. Section 3 represents the proposed three level resource description model. Finally, Sect. 4 discusses the future developments and concludes the paper.

2   Existing Production Resource Descriptions

There exist some device related descriptions, however having a slightly different focus. Electronic Device Description Language (EDDL) [4–6] and its continuation Field Device Integration (FDI) [7,8] are used to describe process automation components, having focus on lower level elementary components. The various fieldbus device descriptions for e.g. Prodibus/-Net, DeviceNet and EtherCAT, all fall into same category, having focus even lower level components and configurations for control systems.

Contrary, AutomationML [9–11] has focus in system integration and representation. The basic assumption of the AutomationML is that the templates of modules are injected to the system description, but they are always customised and modified extensively for the project's purposes. This means that the modules are not stable and reusable entities, but are engineered or customised over and over again. Furthermore, the concept requires that the internal design and implementation of a module is revealed extensively and completely for the system design. Nevertheless, the generality of the approach brings the expression power for this concept. It is more probable that the same concept can cover all unexpected situations arriving in realistic production system design landscape. In context of AutomationML, there exist some publications representing aspects of re-usable components like [12] with mechatronic units and [13,14] with Smart-Components. These both get close to objectives of the work reported in this paper, having the main difference on harmonisation of capabilities, not having abstraction layer present and encapsulation of resource's Intellectual Properties and implementation. This paper is refining and extending the earlier work reported in [15–17] and summarizes the core models from [18].

3 Proposed Production Resource Description Model

Resource description concept is a comprehensive XML-based digital representation of a technical entity. It integrates together information of a production resource related to functional, geometrical, mechanical, communication and control aspects. It allows giving a description of resources' functionality including capabilities; interfaces to other resources; parameters related to business, environment and technical characteristics; and life cycle related information. Resource description concept is a roof term and encapsulates detailed parts of descriptions, namely Abstract Resource Description (ARD), Resource Description (RD) and Resource Instance Description (RID), and their interrelations. Figure 1 describes the relation between the three main parts of the model (Resource Description Model part). In addition, figure shows the link to the Capability Model. The Capability Model, its application, and how it is combined with Resource Description Model are discussed more in details in [19]. Figure 3 provides more detailed view of different resource descriptions and their content.

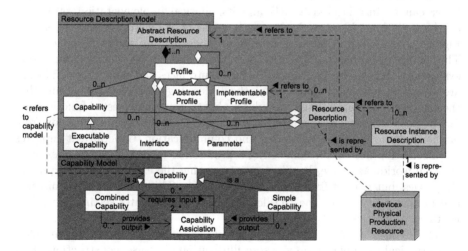

Fig. 1. Main parts of the resource description model and connection to capability model. A concrete production resource (device) is represented at right bottom.

3.1 Abstract Resource Description

Abstract Resource Description (ARD) is an abstraction and a reference model for production resources. It forms an abstract digital specification and generalisation for a collection of similar kind of production resources (e.g. grippers, feeders, glue dispensers, welding devices, etc.). In other words, ARD is a generalisation, which can be specialised as a physical production resource. The objective of ARD is to enable compatibility, interchangeability and connectivity between different production resources, through harmonisation and grouping of interfaces specifications across different types of resources. For example, the task of ARD is to ensure that a robot can be connected to a base, and that a gripper can be connected to a robot, and interchanged with another gripper. The purpose of ARD is to provide harmonisation over RDs and its content is controlled by a user group(s) or standardisation bodies.

ARD cannot be directly instantiated as a physical resource, but it is composed of one or more Profiles (See Fig. 1), which are reflecting production resources. Profile is an integral and inseparable part of ARD and cannot exist alone outside of ARD. Profile defines a reusable construction block of definitions, a structure which is used to specify the detailed section of an ARD. It includes information related to interfaces, capabilities, properties and other features that are composing the generalisation for a set of production resources. This way the information is defined only in one place, which then can be referenced and re-used in other parts of the descriptions. This improves the quality and consistency of the descriptions, as e.g. typing or mishaps related errors can be reduced, consistency of information can be increased, and the maintenance of descriptions is facilitated.

Two kinds of Profiles exist - *abstract* and *implementable* ones, but only the latter can be instantiated as RD and its physical implementation. A Profile can be built from N other Profiles with concepts of inheritance or referencing. Figure 2 provides an example of inheritance hierarchy in case of *Gripper* ARD. The content of Profile characterises the module, and can be used for comparison, evaluation, and selection purposes. Included interfaces and capability definitions are the enablers for mating and fitting the devices together, and making sure that the composition of production modules is able to provide requested functionality for the production task. The interfaces include comprehensive information from mechanical and electrical to service and communication. Generally, it captures all information needed for connecting a production module to other ones or to external world. As a rule, Profiles are introducing the existence and purpose of Properties, but not yet fixing the property values. This provides harmonisation and predictability across the RD definitions, which are later setting the values for these properties.

The *Gripper* ARD and its *Force controlled 2-finger gripper* Profile are used as a practical example. It provides an illustration of re-use, construction block behaviour (i.e. define only once), and use of the two types of Profiles. Figure 2 illustrates this example and aforementioned characteristics of Profiles. Each rectangle is a Profile entity. The rectangles with white background and italics are abstract Profiles, of which physical module cannot be created of, and ones with grey background are implementable Profiles, from which the production modules and corresponding RD can be created of. The implementable Profile of our

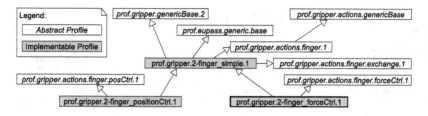

Fig. 2. Example of profile inheritance

interest is at bottom, highlighted with thicker boarder. The main advantage of Profile concept is coming from inheritance. The Profile *Force controlled 2-finger gripper* could define all its features within a single Profile, but instead it is inheriting features from totally seven other Profiles. Directly it inherits another implementable Profile *Simple 2-finger gripper* and one abstract Profile *prof.gripper.actions.finger.forceCtrl.1*. In turn, the Profile *Simple 2-finger gripper* is inheriting four other abstract Profiles, and so on. The effective advantages are gained when other Profiles are added, like *prof.gripper.2-finger_positionCtrl.1*.

3.2 Resource Description

Resource Description (RD) is a digital representation of a real, physical production resource. It is the main description in this model as it describes the details associated to a specific type of HW resource, used for production as a part of a production system. The description is common to all same kind of resources i.e. resources having the same vendor, model, type and version. It is defined and distributed by the module provider, and it serves both as advertisement and source of detailed information for system integration and resource usage.

RD represents the catalogue information and a bit more about the resource. First, it contains a reference to the ARD and Profile of which this resource claims to implement. This can be used for validation, interoperability and interchangeability purposes. Secondly, in contrast with ARD, RD provides values for the properties defined in ARD/Profiles. Furthermore, it provides the vendor information; functional description and related parameter values (i.e. relation to Capability Model); physical properties (mass, centre of gravity and energy consumption); technical, business and environmental properties; interface port information including type and gender, spatial location, force and torque limits, and kinematics; CAD models, manuals and documentation; and test and calibration routines. These are illustrated in Fig. 3, which provides a detailed view of the three different resource descriptions and their content.

The different RDs are intended to be available on-line, like the ARDs as well. Thus, a web service [20] is made available in order to demonstrate a solution to share and distribute these information, and make searches from it. The web service is discussed in [21].

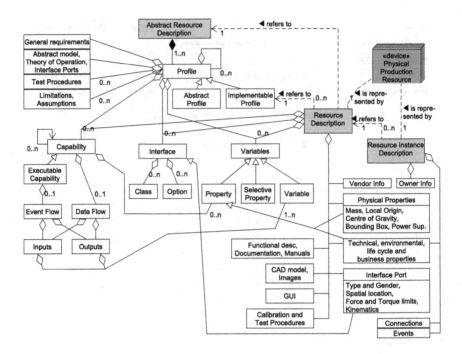

Fig. 3. Resource description model

3.3   Resource Instance Description

Condition and capabilities of the resources evolve during their individual life cycles and usages. Resource Instance Description (RID) is a digital representation of an individual physical instance of a resource. It carries the resources' current state and historical data events – it is an accumulating information storage. It appends the RD with information that cannot be generalised over all instances of the same resource type, but is specific to one instance only. For instance, if the capability or life cycle parameters (such as Mean Time Between Failure (MTBF) or tolerances) are changed during the resource life cycle, the RID will contain the updated information. The RID should travel all the time with the physical production resource.

3.4   Example Instances of Resource Description Model

Table 1 summarises the characteristics of different top level descriptions composing the Resource Description Model, by connecting these with compacted definition and an illustrative example of each description. ARD represents specific technologies such as grippers, axis-systems or feeders, and collect all associated Profiles together. Profile provides generalised specification of specific kind of entities, such as 2-finger grippers. These are the parts composing a single ARD. RD turns focus to the module providers (vendor V_A). They provide a detailed

Table 1. Comparison of main entities of production resource model

Entity	Definition	Example
ARD	is container for Profiles	Grippers ARD
Profile	is description of abstract module and part of ARD	Abstraction of a 2-finger gripper
RD	is digital representation of physical module. Derived from one Profile	2-finger gripper from vendor V_A w/ type: T1
RID	is digital representation of a specific module instance	Type: T1 gripper w/ serial: SN123

description of their module (third row in Table 1). This description respects the definitions made in aforementioned Profile and ARD. Finally, when vendor V_A produces physical entity of such gripper of type T1, they assign a serial number to this piece of HW and create a RID for it (fourth row in Table 1).

4 Discussion and Conclusions

This paper presented an overview of a three level model to describe production resources. This model and descriptions can be utilised in various phases of Reconfigurable Manufacturing System (RMS) production system design, reconfiguration and commissioning. How to apply these models is discussed in [18, Ch.7].

In the due course of the ReCaM project, there are already identified improvements and new requirements related to the production resource descriptions. These are: (a) further development, synchronisation, and tighter integration with the Capability model; (b) detailed definition of Executable Capability concept, i.e. interfaces for the controls and SW services; (c) improvements on mechanical interface description in relation to interfaces connecting the resource to the produced items; (d) including generalised Graphical User Interface (GUI) definitions into descriptions, from which resource specific GUIs can be generated automatically; and finally, (e) editors for creating and modifying the resource description files. These improvements are in progress. There is interest to research if this model, especially RD, could be translated to format of AutomationML. The presented models and proposed improvements will be validated during the ReCaM project.

Acknowledgement. This research has received funding from the European Union's Horizon 2020 research and innovation programme under grant agreement No. 680759 [3].

References

1. ElMaraghy, H.A.: Flexible and reconfigurable manufacturing systems paradigms. Int. J. Flex. Manuf. Syst. **17**, 261–276 (2005)

2. Järvenpää, E.: Capability-based adaptation of production systems in a changing environment. Ph.D. dissertation. Tampere University of Technology, 190 p. (2012)
3. ReCaM - Rapid reconfiguration of flexible production systems through capability-based adaptation, auto-configuration, integrated tools for production planning - project, EU Horizon 2020, GA No 680759. http://www.recam-project.eu
4. Merget, O.: FDT and EDDL: the electronic integration of field devices. Comput. Control Eng. **14**(5), 22–23 (2003). doi:10.1049/cce:20030504
5. IEC: IEC 61804-3: 2006. Function blocks (FB) for process control - Part 3: Electronic Device Description Language (EDDL) (2006)
6. FDI Cooperation: Electronic Device Description Language. http://www.eddl.org/
7. Neumann, P., Simon, R., Diedrich, C., Riedl, M.: Field device integration. In: 8th International Conference on Emerging Technologies and Factory Automation (ETFA 2001), Proceedings (Cat. No.01TH8597), pp. 63–68. IEEE (2001)
8. FDI Cooperation. http://www.fdi-cooperation.com
9. AutomationML/IEC.: IEC 62714-1: 2014 Engineering data exchange format for use in industrial automation systems engineering - automation markup language - Part 1: Architecture and General Requirements (2014)
10. AutomationML. http://www.automationml.org/
11. Lüder, A., Hundt, L., Keibel, A.: Description of manufacturing processes using AutomationML. In: 2010 IEEE 15th Conference on Emerging Technologies & Factory Automation (ETFA 2010), 8 p. (2010)
12. Lüder, A., Foehr, L.H.M., Wagner, T., Zaddach, J.-J., Holm, T.: Manufacturing system engineering with mechatronical units. In: IEEE 15th Conference on Emerging Technologies & Factory Automation (ETFA 2010), 8 p. Bilbao, Spain (2010)
13. Bartelt, M., Schyja, A., Kuhlenkötter, B.: More than a Mockup - SmartComponents: reusable fully functional virtual components from scratch. Prod. Eng. **8**, 727–735 (2014)
14. Schyja, A., Bartelt, M., Kuhlenkötter, B.: From conception phase up to virtual verification using AutomationML. Procedia CIRP. **23**, 171–177 (2014)
15. Siltala, N., Hofmann, A.F., Tuokko, R., Bretthauer, G.: Emplacement and blue print-an approach to handle and describe modules for evolvable assembly systems. In: Hideki, H. (ed.) Proceedings of 9th International Symposium on Robot Control (SYROCO 2009), pp. 86–91. IFAC, Gifu, Japan (2009)
16. Siltala, N., Tuokko, R.: Emplacement and blue print-electronic module description supporting evolvable assembly systems design, deployment and execution. In: Huang, G.Q., Mak, K.L., Maropoulos, P.G. (eds.) Proceedings of 6th CIRP-sponsored International Conference on Digital Enterprise Technology (DET), pp. 773–788. Springer, Heidelberg (2009)
17. Siltala, N., Tuokko, R.: Use of electronic module descriptions for modular and reconfigurable assembly systems. In: 2009 IEEE International Symposium on Assembly and Manufacturing, pp. 214–219. Suwon, Korea (2009)
18. Siltala, N.: Formal digital description of production equipment modules for supporting system design and deployment. Ph.D. dissertation. Tampere University of Technology, 211 p. (2016)
19. Järvenpää, E., Siltala, N., Lanz, M.: Formal resource and capability descriptions supporting rapid reconfiguration of assembly systems. In: 2016 IEEE International Symposium on Assembly and Manufacturing. USA, Texas (to be published)
20. Emplacement Web Service, http://resourcedescription.tut.fi/EmplacementWS/
21. Siltala, N., Tuokko, R.: A web tool supporting the management and use of electronic module descriptions for evolvable production systems. In: 2010 IEEE International Symposium on Industrial Electronics, pp. 2641–2646. Bari, Italy (2010)

A Communication Procedure Between Tactical and Operational Levels in Spare Parts Supply Chains

Matheus Cardoso Pires[1(✉)], Enzo Morosini Frazzon[1],
Ann-Kristin Cordes[2], and Bernd Hellingrath[2]

[1] Universidade Federal de Santa Catarina, Florianópolis, Brazil
matheus.pires@grad.ufsc.br, enzo.frazzon@ufsc.br
[2] Westfälische Wilhelms-Universität Münster, Münster, Germany
cordes@ercis.uni-muenster.de,
bernd.hellingrath@wi.uni-muenster.de

Abstract. Supply Chain Management has been an important issue for competitiveness in today's market. Different decision-support models focus on specific time horizons and goals. The most common way of structuring supply chain planning process is dividing it in three different levels: operational, tactical and strategic. However, the planning on one level generally does not communicate with the others, limiting its efficiency and feasibility. The present work proposes a communication procedure between tactical and operation support-decision models in order to coordinate both, thus improving their overall performance. The procedure will be applied to a test case comprising a Spare Parts Supply Chain (SPSC) problem for maintenance in production facilities with the concept of integrating spare parts supply chain and intelligent maintenance systems implemented.

Keywords: Supply chain · Planning · Management · Integrated planning · Operations research

1 Introduction

A Supply Chain (SC) can be defined as a network of organizations, flows, and processes where companies work to transform raw material in final products delivered to a customer. [1] Presents Supply Chain Management (SCM) as the study of resources of enterprises and human decisions in relation to cross-enterprise collaboration processes to transform and use these resources in the most rational way along the entire value chain, from customers up to raw material suppliers, based on functional and structural integration, cooperation, and coordination throughout. The author classifies SCM as the most popular strategy for improving organizational competitiveness in the twenty-first century.

Supply Chain planning can be seen as a set of goals, performance indicators and decisions to be taken in order to optimize the SC performance. The Supply Chain Planning comes in different levels of application, each one focusing in actions that fit its time horizon and goals. The Strategic Planning is on the top of the pyramid, and

© IFIP International Federation for Information Processing 2016
Published by Springer International Publishing AG 2016. All Rights Reserved
I. Nääs et al. (Eds.): APMS 2016, IFIP AICT 488, pp. 61–68, 2016.
DOI: 10.1007/978-3-319-51133-7_8

consists in long-term decision and goals, as desired service level and facilities location. In the middle of the pyramid is placed the Tactical Planning, working on mid-term decisions what includes the allocation of production and transports capacities, for example. At the bottom of the pyramid, the Operational Planning takes care of the daily decisions, as transport strategies and production scheduling.

All the levels of planning are necessary in SCs planning. However, these planning are usually built without communicating with the other, in despite of the fact that the efficiency and applicability of the output of each plan can decrease if the different levels of planning are considered in isolation of each other [2].

This research paper aims to develop a communication procedure between the operational planning and tactical planning of a spare parts supply chain. To reach this objective, a flowchart comprising the planning steps of each level as well as mutual feedbacks between the decision-support models will be proposed.

The paper is organized in three sections. In the Literature Review section, a brief contextualization about the state of the art of the studying will be presented, as well as a contextualization about the emerging concept of integration between spare parts supply chain and intelligent maintenance systems wherein the output of the paper is intended to be used. In the second section, the communication procedure will be proposed by means of a test case. In the last section, the results will be discussed and the work summarized.

2 Literature Review

2.1 Supply Chain Management

According to Christopher [3] Supply Chain Management (SCM) is the management of upstream and downstream relationships with suppliers and customers to deliver superior customer value as less cost to the supply chain as a whole. Therefore, SCM becomes an interesting object of study, widely addressed by numerous approaches, being needed in any product factoring and flow around the world.

Supply Chain Management seeks to link and coordinate processes from different entities (as customers and suppliers) and to organize them [3]. This add an enormous level of complexity in decision making, once each action should not just consider each company limitation and goals, but all limitations and requirements from other agents present in the SC.

According to [4] considerable work has been invested in developing decision methods for overcoming supply chain issues, which generally adopt conventional approaches as mathematical programming (optimization), simulation and heuristics. These models can be very helpful since they assist managers to overcome the dimensions of the mental models for Supply Chains and provide non-biased results, helping to deal with the high complexity of considering a big number of agents, limitation, goal and variables in the system.

According to [1] decision-supporting methods can be divided in optimization, simulation and heuristics, where the optimization has been very visible and influential for the operations management. However, there is a challenge in the optimization development that consists in developed a well detailed model that can represent the reality of the supply chain at the same time it keeps simple enough to be solved with a relative low processing cost. High computational costs could turn the planning, especially on an operational level, impracticable, since it could require too much time to be executed that its results become obsolete. Since the aggregation of both tactical and operational planning levels in a single model would probably require high computational power to be solved, the goal of the present work is to describe a procedure of communication between two models.

2.2 Spare Parts Supply Chain

Spare parts need to be available in the right place within the supply chain, to ensure the desired level of service. However, several aspects make this task complicated, such as: the high number of parts to be managed, high responsibility required due to customer downtime costs, and the risk of obsolete inventory. Among these problems, according to [5], "due to the high costs for spare parts and their sporadic demand, keeping inventories of all parts at all warehouses in the spare parts network are not economical". Also, SCs are thus characterized by distinct, yet mutually interdependent decision domains with in-dependent business objectives. This way, the capability of existing models for supporting an intelligent and flexible synchronization and coordination of the involved process is limited. Given this intertwined and complex aspects, management processes of spare parts supply chain (SPSC) cover different areas of knowledge, which, in turn, use various resources, methods, techniques for solving coordination problems.

Some features of SPSC can be highlighted in the literature. First, the demand for spare parts usually has an intermittent and/or erratic character, making more difficult the forecasting process by classical statistical methods and inventory control [6]. The second characteristic relates to high levels of required services. Components for maintenance need to be available as soon as a fault occurs, otherwise the productive systems may be unavailable, causing high costs for the production facility [7]. Another feature derives from the two previous characteristics, as there is a wide variation in demand and a network of well-lined stocks, distribution costs are high. In periods of low demand, inventories are still needed for high demand periods, implying more expensive distribution process [8].

Having seen these concepts, detailed planning of the spare parts supply chain is necessary in order to meet service levels while minimizing costs. Furthermore, not only the planning but also the coordination between different levels and actors can be seen as a relevant topic, considering the autonomy of the different actors involved in the supply chain coordination. The collaboration can be reached through exchanging relevant data from multiple individual planning domains (e.g. demand planning, master planning, production planning, etc.), aiming to design a collaborative planning concept (CP). But the applicability of existing CP approaches for coordinating the different autonomous actors in heterarchical SPSCs has not yet been investigated [5]. The portability of CP approaches to other scenarios is still an open research issue, especially to a SPSC scenario.

2.3 Integrating Intelligent Maintenance Systems and Spare Parts Supply Chain

The Integrating Intelligent Maintenance Systems and Spare Supply Chain (I2MS2C) concept is proposed to approach the challenge of simultaneously coping with the constraints and specificities of Intelligent Maintenance Systems (IMS) and Spare Parts Supply Chain (SPSC). The primary objective of the I2MS2C is the improvement of the effectiveness and efficiency of service management operations for complex technical systems. This will be achieved by integrating information provided by embedded IMS systems with planning and coordination methods and processes in the spare parts supply chain. On the other way around, maintenance operation benefits from an improved planning of the service operation synchronizing service demands with spare parts availability and servicing capacities.

From the technological perspective, the goal is to improve IMS capabilities in order to achieve more reliable estimations of maintenance needs. The use of intelligent maintenance technology will predict future failures in components allowing the operator to react directly on the component degradation. Besides, through techniques of mixed reality integrated into an Intelligent Maintenance System, we intend to bring relevant data about the components and machines aiding thus the provision of information to operators and service personnel.

To achieve these goals, the I2MS2C concept is divided into four main elements of the model. Research on IMS will in the following be related to the first element. Here, the concept aims at developing improved spare parts planning methods integrating IMS information and the coordination of the spare parts supply chain's actors. The focus relies on the extension and development of spare part-specific mid-term forecasting and planning methods in the domain of inventory and transportation planning. The IMS used in this project is based on the Watchdog Agent (WA), developed by the IMS center [9].

The second element of the I2MS2C concept aims to integrate the planning domains into a supply chain-wide coordination concept which also includes tactical production and maintenance service planning methods. Methods for planning short-term decisions of the supply chain actors as well as their coordination are developed in third element. Here, the interconnections to the tactical planning layer have to be regarded. The focus relies on short-term inventory planning, transportation and production scheduling. Both layers, tactical as well as operational planning, are restricted to the improvement of pro-active supply chain planning. In other words, this means that supply chain planning not include issues of reacting upon concrete machine breakdown alerts, i.e. only failure forecasts of the IMS are included. Also, the integration architecture of the overall research work was built upon a Service Oriented Architecture (SOA), and is a cloud-based system and each entity is built as a device, following the Device Profile for Web Services (DPWS) standard, and exposes a set of services.

Lastly, the fourth element of the I2MS2C concept works with solutions to integrate the results of the previously described elements and furthermore provided a simulation environment for the evaluation of the overall I2MS2C concept. Here, the challenge of integrating IMS with SPSC are analyzed using simulation-based computational experiments and is intended to be evaluated in real-world case studies. Also, in order to achieve a proof-of-concept and an evaluation of the proposed concept, regarding to necessity to align the extended/developed intra-organizational planning methods as well as the coordination process, this element deals with the integration by aligning and fixing the interfaces between the developed concepts of the other thematic areas. Finally, the last part of this area relies on the validate of I2MS2C concept applying the methods proposed in cases studies, especially from the domain of ship building and the oil industry which both show the characteristics of slow moving and expensive components.

The main contribution of the I2MS2C concept is the integration of three different sub-systems: a distributed and networked embedded diagnostic system able to assess the error degradation of machinery/equipment and forecast the need for spare parts. A distributed decision-making sub-system for spare parts supply chain planning and coordination, responsible for tactical spare parts inventory and distribution planning as well as maintenance service planning concepts. An operational planning and scheduling system that is based on the information provided by the other sub-systems optimizes the operational production, transportation and inventory processes. Therefore, two decision-support models are need for the optimization of the systems. In the present paper, a supply chain with the I2MS2C concept fully implemented will be considered as the test case, which implies great data exchange among supply chain participants and deterministic demand of spare parts for maintenance in industries as the final clients.

3 Communication Procedure Proposal

The study developed in this paper is based on the study of a real case of a reference company in the production and distribution of spare parts for electric actuators in Brazil, which will be described hereafter in this work.

The supply chain in which the communication procedure will be based was first presented in [8], and consists of a simplified spare parts supply chain having a production facility that produces three types of products and has to attend, as final destination, the five biggest markets. The final clients of this supply chain are industries that buy these products as spare parts for maintenance on their production machines. In this supply chain, intelligent maintenance systems are used, that makes the demand visible for each one of the fifteen following days. The supply chain scheme is represented in Fig. 1.

The communication procedure is shown on Fig. 2 and it was modeled base on the model proposed in [10]. In the first step, the tactical optimization model is solved, using as input the predefined service level (defined in a previous strategic plan), minimum and maximum capacities per transportation mode and the demand per region (deterministic in this case). As outcome, the support-decision model will provide the inventory level desired per item per facility location, the service level in each region, the transport capacities required per transport mode and region, the emergency shipments capacities per region, the service personnel capacities required per service center and the production capacities required per item. Based on this outputs, tactical strategies will be studied and implemented in order to attend the settled goals. An

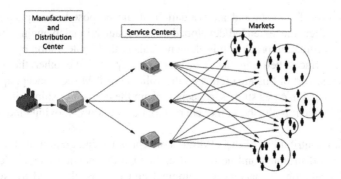

Fig. 1. Supply chain structure from a spare parts supply chain (Source: [8]).

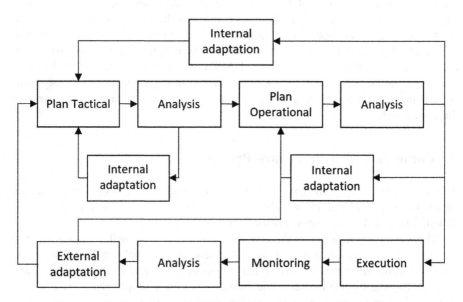

Fig. 2. Proposed communication procedure between tactical and operational decision-support models. (Source: author)

analysis of the result of the plan shall be done to verify its feasibility and applicability. Otherwise, a feedback shall be given to the model to implement an internal adaptation and the model solved again. Then, the results of the tactical model will be used as boundaries and limitations for the operational planning. The operational plan will consider the allocated capacities and demands and will optimize the scheduling of the production and distribution throughout the supply chain on a daily basis. The results must be analyzed, and in case of unfeasibility or improvement opportunity, the feedback must be given to the model for an internal adaptation and the planning process re-executed. Otherwise, the result can be used to feedback the tactical plan, to verify its feasibility. If the operational plan is unfeasible, the desired standards are too high, and the boundaries given by the plan are too demanding to be achieved, and the tactical plan must be reviewed. Otherwise, the plan must be executed, and the supply chain monitored in other to verify if the results of the plans are being achieved. Otherwise, a feedback must be given to the decision-support models, to implement an external adaptation.

The communication procedure is guided to synchronize the execution of two mixed-integer linear problem (MILP) models developed in order to manage the already introduced spare parts supply chain. Summarizing, the tactical decision-support model will provided the objectives to be reach by the operational level, which will be executed and analyzed its feasibility by simulation in order to forecast the behavior of the results implemented with stochastic characteristics. The last result will feedback the tactical planning. When both plans converge, the output can be implemented on the real case, which will be also analyzed in order to feedback both support-decision models.

4 Conclusion

In the present work it was elucidated the importance and necessity of decision-support models in decision taking in supply chains. These models are designed in three different levels of wideness. These models generally do not consider the other levels decision, concluding that there is a lack in today's approaches concerning in communication between planning levels.

The work also introduces the concept about integrating intelligent maintenance systems and spare parts supply chain. A concept that can be shortly summarized being the use of electronic sensors in order to predict spare parts demands in industries combined with mathematical optimization models, both for tactical and operational levels, in order to provide lower costs on the supply chain while delivering higher service level.

It was, as main objective of the paper, proposed a communication procedure between tactical and operational support-decision models in order to align different levels of planning. The procedure is recommended because no alignment between planning levels can reduce the efficiency and feasibility of the outcome plan, as well as a unique plan for more than one level could result in high computational cost. Using this procedure, it is possible to use more detailed optimization models in each planning level.

As future work directions it is recommended to develop support-decision models for each level in order to run a test application of the communication procedure. As well as an in-depth study about the possibility of including the strategic level in the procedure.

Acknowledgements. This research was supported by the German Research Foundation (DFG) and the Brazilian Federal Agency for the Support and Evaluation of Graduate Education (CAPES) as part of the BRAGECRIM project "Integrating Intelligent Maintenance Systems and Spare Parts Supply Chains (I2MS2C)" (BRAGECRIM 022/2012).

References

1. Ivanov, D.: An adaptive framework for aligning (re) planning decisions on supply chain strategy, design, tactics, and operations. Int. J. Prod. Res. **48**(13), 3999–4017 (2010)
2. Ivanov, D., Sokolov, B., Kaeschel, J.: A multi-structural framework for adaptive supply chain planning and operations control with structure dynamics considerations. Eur. J. Oper. Res. **200**(2), 409–420 (2010)
3. Christopher, M.: Logistics and Supply Chain Management: Creating Value-Added Networks. Pearson Education, Upper Saddle River (2005)
4. Narasimhan, R., Mahapatra, S.: Decision models in global supply chain management. Industr. Mark. Manag. **33**(1), 21–27 (2004)
5. Espíndola, D., Frazzon, E.M., Hellingrath, B., Pereira, C.E.: Integrating intelligent maintenance systems and spare parts supply chain. Inf. Control Prob. Manuf. **14**(1), 1017–1022 (2012)
6. Boylan, J.E., Syntetos, A.A.: Spare parts management: a review of forecasting research and extensions. IMA J. Manag. Math. **21**(3), 227–237 (2010)
7. Huiskonen, J.: Maintenance spare parts logistics: special characteristics and strategic choices. Int. J. Prod. Econ. **71**(1–3), 125–133 (2001)
8. Israel, E.F.: Planejamento Operacional de Cadeias de Suprimentos de Peças de Reposição Integrado com Sistemas Inteligentes de Manutenção. Federal University of Santa Catarina, Florianópolis (2014)
9. Djurdjanovic, D., Lee, J., Ni, J.: Watchdog agent-an infotronics-based prognostics approach for production performance degradation assessment and prediction. Adv. Eng. Inform. **17**(3–4), 109–125 (2003)
10. Ivanov, D., Dolgui, A., Sokolov, B.: Applicability of optimal control theory to adaptive supply chain planning and scheduling. Annu. Rev. Control **36**(1), 73–84 (2012)

Digital Factories for Capability Modeling and Visualization

Farhad Ameri[(⊠)] and Ramin Sabbagh

Texas State University, San Marcos, USA
{ameri, r_s343}@txstate.edu

Abstract. This paper introduces the concept of Digital Factory (DF) that can be used for representing the technological capabilities of manufacturing facilities. The DF, as the digital twin of physical facilities, replicates the facility in terms of installed machinery, material handling equipment, and layout. DF is supported by a formal ontology that describes the capabilities of the factory in a formal and machine-understandable fashion and enables capability quantification and visualization. Through exploring and querying the Digital Factories, companies can develop a deeper and more precise understanding of the technological capabilities of prospective suppliers, thus making more informed decisions when building supply chain partnerships. By creating their digital twins, small to medium-sized manufacturers can significantly improve their visibility in the virtual space. Digital Factories also enable automated supply chain formation. DF is introduced and discussed from a conceptual perspective in this paper. Also, a mathematical model for quantifying the processing capabilities of Digital Factories is introduced.

Keywords: Digital factory · Manufacturing capability · Service ontology

1 Introduction

To remain competitive in today's volatile economy, manufacturing companies need to be provided with the decision-support systems that enable them to manufacture products more efficiently, less expensively, and more quickly. One of the key decisions that has a profound impact on the agility and responsive of manufacturing companies is the sourcing decision [1]. Sourcing is defined as the process of finding, evaluating, and engaging suppliers for acquiring goods and services [2]. Sourcing process, in its traditional form, is a lengthy and time-consuming process because it often entails visiting suppliers' facility or launching trial production runs in order to evaluate suppliers' true qualifications, capabilities, and capacities. However, when there is a need for rapidly responding to fast-changing market trends, traditional sourcing methods fail in meeting the strict time constraints of such projects.

An alternative solution for collecting information about suppliers' qualifications is to explore their web-based profiles to learn about the technological capabilities of suppliers. However, the online profiles are oftentimes outdated and incomplete and cannot accurately reflect the true capabilities of suppliers [3]. Also, the sheer size of the returned set in web-based searches makes supplier evaluation a costly and lengthy

© IFIP International Federation for Information Processing 2016
Published by Springer International Publishing AG 2016. All Rights Reserved
I. Nääs et al. (Eds.): APMS 2016, IFIP AICT 488, pp. 69–78, 2016.
DOI: 10.1007/978-3-319-51133-7_9

process [4]. Consequently, in fast-track production projects with stringent time constraints, sourcing decisions are often made based on superficial insights into the qualifications of prospective suppliers. To improve the intelligence and effectiveness of sourcing decisions, when the Internet is the only medium for interaction with the prospective suppliers, companies need to gain real-time, dynamic, and accurate insight into the capabilities and capacities of prospective suppliers [5].

In this paper, the problem of capability modeling and representation is addressed through introducing the concept of Digital Factory. Digital Factory provides a virtual representation of a manufacturing facility. It replicates the facility in terms of installed machinery, material handling equipment, and layout. It provides both visual and textual representation of the facility. Digital Factories, as the digital twin of physical facilities, can enhance the visibility of small and medium-sized manufacturers in the virtual space. The novel feature of the Digital Factory is that it is annotated by a formal ontology that is used for representing the capability model of the factory. Through exploring and querying the capability model of digital factories, companies can develop a deeper and more precise understanding of the technological capabilities of prospective suppliers, thus making more informed decisions when building supply chains. Some of the attributes of technological capability that can be captured by the Digital Factory include achievable tolerances and surface finishes, acceptable stock sizes, and available primary and secondary processes. The proposed model of Digital Factory perfectly meets the needs of the factories of the future, as they will be reconfigurable, adaptive, and evolving [6]. A Digital Factory can be quickly updated to reflect the changing nature of its associated physical factory in real-time. Digital Factories are developed on a web-based platform referred to as the Digital Manufacturing Market (DMM) [7]. DMM provides user-friendly interfaces and machine libraries for capability visualization and virtual factory modeling. This paper provides a conceptual perspective about Digital Factory, its utilities, development environment, and information backbone.

The paper is organized as follows. The next section describes the system architecture of DMM through introducing its main functional modules. The underlying ontology of DMM is introduced in Sect. 3. In Sect. 4, an example for a Digital Factory for a hypothetical machine shop is provided. The paper ends with the concluding remarks.

2 System Architecture

Manufacturing companies can create Digital Factories for advertising their capabilities in the Digital Manufacturing Market. The Digital Manufacturing Market (DMM) is a web-based market platform designed based on a service-oriented architecture (SOA) and supported by a formal ontology [7]. In DMM, units of manufacturing capacity are represented as standard service modules. Manufacturing service capabilities are described in a semantically rich fashion using a formal ontology called Manufacturing Service Description Language (MSDL) [8]. More details on MSDL is provided in Sect. 3. In DMM, participating suppliers can create digital twins of their facilities, dynamically update their digital factory through adding and removing

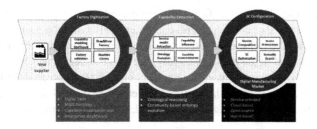

Fig. 1. The main modules of the proposed solution

machines and equipment to reflect the real conditions on the shop floor, and deploy software agents that represent them in the virtual space. Through building the digital factory, the service model associated with the factory is generated and published automatically. As can be seen in Fig. 1, the main functional modules of the DMM include Factory Digitization, Capability Extraction, and Supply Chain Configuration.

The service model is then used for capability quantification. DMM's functions and features enable manufacturing suppliers to: (i) Describe their technological capabilities in terms of manufacturing services in a machine-readable fashion using an open-source standard; (ii) Describe the parts produced in the past and the qualities achieved; (iii) Create a "digital twin" of their facility through selecting their installed equipment and machines from a given library of physical resources (*Drag & Drop Factory*); (iv) Update their capability model in real-time through updating the configuration and layout of the digital factory; (v) Find the right customers through using the automated matching utility provided by the platform; (vi) Evaluate their technological readiness and competencies based on the current demand through using the capability scoring utility provided by the platform.

DMM's functions and features enables manufacturing OEMs (customers) to: (i) Evaluate the technological capabilities of prospective suppliers through capability visualization and scoring utilities; (ii) Find the right suppliers through using the automated supplier search and evaluation tool; (iii) Deploy supply chains rapidly using the service composition and orchestration utility provided by the platform; (iv) Mitigate their risks through on-demand consumption of the pooled manufacturing capacities and capabilities available on the cloud.

2.1   Factory Digitization

Factory digitization entails creating the digital twin of the manufacturing facility owned by the supplier. Two user interfaces, namely, drag and drop factory and the capability modeling and visualization dashboard enables suppliers to interactively create the digital model of their facility and annotate it with explicit capability and capacity-related information. The user-friendly interface hides the complexities of the underlying knowledge models used in the platform's knowledge base. Also, it encourages rapid and regular update of the digital facility such that it accurately mirrors the physical facility. Any change in the digital facility will be reflected in the supplier's service and capability models in real-time. The digital factory is connected to a comprehensive library of manufacturing resources (machinery and equipment), allowing the user to populate the virtual facility with the right set of resources. The digital factory not only represents the type of resources used in the physical facility, but also it reflects the actual layout of the physical facility. The layout is used by the Capability Extraction module for inferring the system-level capabilities of the facility. System-level capabilities are characterized through properties such as throughput time, cycle time, and average in-process inventory level.

2.2   Capability Extraction

The Capability Extraction module builds the formal capability model of the digital factory coded in MSDL. It uses the explicit capability information provided by the supplier and expands upon it through discovering latent and implicit capability patterns. The extracted manufacturing capability is packaged as standard service units with well-defined input, output, and quality measures. Capability extraction is a knowledge-intensive process that capitalizes on the domain knowledge already encoded in the ontology. Capability extraction is a bottom-up process starting with device and machine-level capability model going up to supply chain level. The capability extraction module can create regional models of manufacturing capability and represent them through "capability heat map" thanks to the rigorous capability quantification algorithms embedded in this module (Fig. 2). This module also provides capability recommendation service which suggests new and supplementary capabilities to suppliers depending on the available work orders in the demand pool of the market.

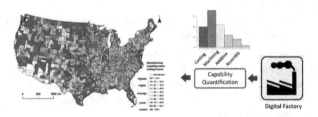

Fig. 2. The capability quantification techniques provided in this solution can be used for developing regional and national capability maps.

2.3   Supply Chain Configuration

Supply Chain configuration module provides the functionalities required for automated deployment of customized and short-lived supply chains for given work orders. In the Digital Manufacturing Market, supply and demand entities are translated into units of manufacturing service. Therefore, semantic matchmaking between requested services and provided services is one of the core functionalities of this module. The deployed supply chains are optimized in terms of the embedded capacity and capability in order to minimize underutilization of resources in the DMM. Suppliers and customers in the

DMM are represented by intelligent software agents with predefined goals and knowledge. One of the functions of a supplier agent in the DMM is to analyze the demand pool in order to identify the emerging trends and demand patterns in the market. This will enable manufacturing suppliers to gain insight into market conditions and react to changes in a timely manner through acquiring new capabilities and launching new services.

3 Manufacturing Service Ontology

In this section, the ontology of the digital factory is described and a method for quantifying the capabilities of the digital factories are described. The capability quantification method directly used the information that is provided by the service model of the factory that is represented ontologically.

3.1 Manufacturing Service Description Language (MSDL)

The recent advances in information technology, particularly in explicit knowledge representation using open-standards, provide a promising opportunity for enhancing the intelligence and automation capabilities of e-sourcing solutions through employing advanced knowledge modeling techniques for capability representation. In particular, creation of formal and standard ontologies for unambiguous description of manufacturing services can radically change the way manufacturing supply chains are configured and deployed [9]. Ontologies play a key role in any distributed intelligent system as they provide a shared, machine-understandable vocabulary for information exchange among dispersed agents [10]. A formal ontology with explicit semantics can provide the required building blocks for construction of a shared body of knowledge that can be understood and interpreted by all agents, machine or human, who subscribe to the ontology.

In the manufacturing domain, ontologies are at their early stage of development. Several ontologies have been proposed with the objective of facilitating knowledge management and information exchange across the extended enterprise. Most of the existing manufacturing domain ontologies are procedural in nature in a sense that they provide the required means for describing manufacturing transactions and operations within a manufacturing system. However, there are few ontologies that directly deal with declaration and characterization of a manufacturing system itself with respect to capabilities. Manufacturing Service Description Language (MSDL) is one of the few descriptive ontologies developed for representation of capabilities of manufacturing services. MSDL is used to build the ontological underpinning of DMM. MSDL decomposes the manufacturing capability into five levels of abstraction, namely, supplier-level, shop-level, machine-level, device-level, and process-level. The capabilities of every instance of the Digital Factory is formally described using MSDL ontology.

MSDL is based on Description Logic (DL) formalism that provides sufficient expressivity and extensibility for manufacturing knowledge modeling. A unique feature of MSDL is that it is built around a service-oriented paradigm, therefore, it can be used for representing a manufacturing system as a collection of manufacturing services. MSDL was initially designed to enable automated supplier discovery in distributed environments with focus on mechanical machining services. However, to address a wider range of services offered by small and medium-sized suppliers in contract manufacturing industry, the service ontology can always be extended systematically through active involvement of a community of ontology users. DMM contains an ontology evolution module that enables a wider range of stakeholders, including domain experts and ontology users, to contribute to extension of MSDL in various domains.

Web Ontology Language (OWL) is used as the ontology language of MSDL. OWL is recommended by the World Wide Web Consortium (W3C) as the ontology language of the Semantic Web. It uses XML as the syntax language, thus having enough portability, flexibility, and extensibility for web-scale applications. Furthermore, OWL is supported by the Semantic Web (SW), meaning that OWL-based Ontologies can be shared, parsed, and manipulated through open-source web-based tools and technologies. Figure 3 shows the Factory class diagram in together with the axiomatic description of End Milling process in MSDL.

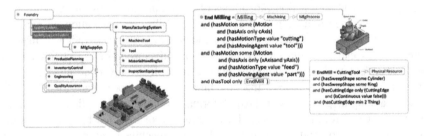

Fig. 3. MSDL describes different manufacturing processes and systems through ontological classes and logical axioms.

3.2 Capability Quantification

In the Digital Manufacturing Market, the capabilities of manufacturing companies can be objectively evaluated and quantified using the input provided by the ontological instances. Manufacturing capability is a multidimensional entity that depends on various factors such as production capacity, facilities, processing capabilities, quality, human resources, new product development systems, and production planning and inventory control techniques [11]. Since the Digital Factory mainly describes a manufacturing facility in terms of installed machinery and equipment, it can be used for assessing the processing capabilities of a manufacturing firm. For a Digital Factory composed of CNC machine tools, the attributes of processing capability include resolution, accuracy, surface finish, available machining power, part size, and part complexity. Every MSDL instance of the Digital Factory contains sufficient data for process capability measurement.

Table 1. Processing capability equations for machining process

Capability factor	Capability equation	Eq. number	Weight
Horsepower	$\frac{H}{H_{max}}$	1	W_H
Accuracy	$1 + \frac{1}{\log(A)}$	2	W_A
Resolution	$1 + \frac{1}{\log(R)}$	3	W_R
Automatic pallet changer	P	4	W_P
Number of axis	$\frac{X-3}{2}$	5	W_N
Working area	$\left(\frac{2}{Y_{max}^2}\right)(Y^2) + \left(\frac{-2}{Y_{max}}\right)(Y) + 1$	6	W_Y

Table 1 shows the equations that can be used for measuring the processing capability along different dimensions. In these equations, H = the machine horsepower for the CNC machine under study, Hmax = max horsepower provided by the CNC machines available in the market, A = machine accuracy, R = machine resolution, P is a boolean value indicating whether or not a machine has an automated pallet changer, X = number machining axes of the CNC machine, Y = size of the work area of the machine, Ymax = the largest work area available in the market. Each individual equation generates a capability score in [0, 1] range. For example, Eqs. 2 and 3 are formulated such that as the accuracy and the resolution of the machine improve, its capability scores along those dimensions increase exponentially. Equation 6, related to the working envelope of machine tool ensures that machine with very small or very large working envelop receive high score. The overall score of processing capability of the Digital Facility is the weighted average of the individual capability scores.

4   Digital Factory: Machine Shop Example

Consider a hypothetical machine shop (called Texas Precision Machining - TPM) that owns the machine tools shown in Table 2.

Because TPM is a member of the Digital Manufacturing Market, it needs to be represented digitally on DMM such that it can be discovered by potential customers. For this purpose, a TPM engineer uses the interfaces and libraries provided in DMM for replicating the physical machine shop on DMM. Out of five machine tools that TPM owns, four of them are directly available in the library. Using the drag & drop feature, the engineer adds those machines to the shop floor. The fifth machine, CNC

Table 2. The machines owned by TPM Company.

Machine type	Model	Quantity
Vertical machining center	Haas VF-5XT	1
Vertical turning center	Bridgeport Series 1	1
Precision grinder	Harig 612	1
Universal mill	Haas UMC-750	2
Swiss type lathe	Sprint 42	1

Swiss-type lathe, is not available in the machine library. Therefore, the engineer instantiates a generic CNC lathe class from the library and then adds the extra properties needed to create an instance of the specific Swiss-type lathe owned by TPM. A new class based on the newly created instance will be added to the DMM library such that other users can instantiate a similar machine if necessary in future. This is one of the methods used for extending DMM's underlying ontology. As the engineer adds new machines to the digital factory, the service and capability models of TPM are generated automatically in the backend. The score for the processing capabilities of each CNC machine owned by TPM can be calculated using the equations given in Table 1. For example, the processing capability score of the VF-5XT CNC machine is 0.73 as shown in Table 3.

Table 3. The processing capability score for VF-5XT milling center. The calculated score is based on $Y_{max} = 50,000$ cubic feet and $H_{max} = 100\,hp$

Capability factor	Value	Weights		Score	Weighted score
Horsepower (H)	30	W_h	5	0.3	1.5
Accuracy (A)	0.0001	W_a	12	0.75	9
Resolution (R)	0.001	W_r	13	0.66	8.66
Pallet changer (P)	1	W_p	5	1	5
Number of axis (X)	5	W_x	7	1	7
Working area (W)	39000	W_w	6	0.65	3.94
		Total machine score			= 0.73

Because each of the machines available in TPM's digital factory is described ontologically, the capability inference engine can infer the overall processing capabilities of the digital factory automatically. Figure 4 shows the inferred capabilities of TPM.

Once the processing capabilities are extracted, the work order suggestion module of the DMM produces a list of work orders that are within the range of capabilities of

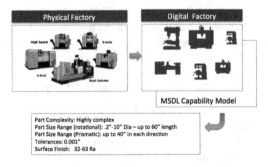

Fig. 4. The MSDL capability model of TPM is generated automatically based on the composition and types of machines available in the digital factory

TPM. Also, the system recommends TPM to acquire a new 5-axis milling center, because this machine tool would supplement and enhance the technological capabilities of TPM to a level that it can cover more than 75% of the parts available in the market. The supply chain configuration module recommends three potential supply chains in Central Texas for which TPM is a close match. Also, upon addition of TPM to DMM's supply pool, the capability model of Central Texas is updated to reflect the new capabilities introduced through TPM. The classification module of DMM classifies TPM as a high-complexity/high-precision/medium-production range supplier. Automated classification of suppliers improves the efficiency of the search process and also enhances the visibility of suppliers in the virtual space.

5 Conclusion

This paper presented a conceptual view of the Digital Factory in the context of the Digital Manufacturing Market. The DMM is a platform for building supply chain connections supported by semantic ontologies and data analytics tools and system. DMM create an ecosystem of manufacturing services that are formally described and can be discovered, evaluated, and integrated autonomously. Digital Factory, as a component of the DMM, is the virtual twin of a physical factory that is registered on DMM. There is no limit on the size and type of machines and equipment that can be included in a Digital Factory. Two models can be derived from the digital factory, namely, service model, and capability model. The service model described the primary and secondary manufacturing services that can be offered by a facility while the capability model describes the aggregate capabilities of the facility based on the available machinery and equipment. The main advantage of Digital Factory is real-time and accurate representation of the technological capabilities of manufacturing companies. Since Digital Factories are described semantically using MSDL ontology, they are amenable to automated search and reasoning. This will significantly enhance the intelligence of supply chain formation and sourcing tools in virtual space.

This research is part of an ongoing project in the broad area of intelligent supplier discovery. Some of the components of the described framework, such as the ontology, the search engine, and the agent based model, are already developed and validated in separate research projects [3, 7]. The Digital Factory is the next component that will be added to the DMM technology suite in near future. Also, the Digital Factories will be connected to MTConnect agents to collect operational information from the shop floor. This will enable further analysis and reasoning about operational capabilities of machine shops based on their actual production data. One limitation of the idea of Digital Factory is slow adoption rate particularly at the early stages of implementation. Since the envisioned users of this technology are mainly the SMEs that are accustomed to more traditional means of sourcing and marketing, they may exhibit resistance to migrating to the digital arena. To mitigate this risk and also learn about the behavior of manufacturing suppliers, the pilot implementation phase will involve a small number of select suppliers from Texas and Illinois who will voluntarily join the digital manufacturing market.

References

1. Kotula, M., Ho, W., Dey, P.K., Lee, C.K.M.: Strategic sourcing supplier selection misalignment with critical success factors: findings from multiple case studies in Germany and the United Kingdoms. Int. J. Prod. Econ. **166**, 238–247 (2015)
2. Liu, J., Liao, W., Guo, Y.: Sourcing configuration in global manufacturing based on double-link genetic algorithm. Chin. J. Mech. Eng. **44**(2), 189–195 (2008)
3. Ameri, F., Dutta, D.: Results of a survey on web-based approaches to global outsourcing in the manufacturing industry. In: Proceedings of International Conference on Manufacturing Science and Engineering, MSEC 2006, 8–11 October 2006. American Society of Mechanical Engineers (2006)
4. Barua, A., Ravindran, S., Whinston, A.B.: Efficient selection of suppliers over the internet. J. Manag. Inf. Syst. **13**(4), 117–137 (1997)
5. Richardson, C.M.: Sourcing in America: how will buyers find you? In: Proceedings of FABTECH 2013 Conference. Society of Manufacturing Engineers, Chicago (2013)
6. EFFRA, European Factories of the Future Association: Factories of the Future: Multi-annual Roadmap for the Contractual PPP Under Horizon 2020. Publications Office of the European Union, Luxembourg (2013)
7. Ameri, F., Patil, L.: Digital manufacturing market: a semantic web-based framework for agile supply chain deployment. J. Intell. Manuf. **23**(5), 1817–1832 (2012). doi:10.1007/s10845-010-049
8. Ameri, F., Dutta, D.: A matchmaking methodology for supply chain deployment in distributed manufacturing environments. ASME J. Comput. Inf. Sci. Eng. (Special Issue on Eng. Inform.) **8**(1), 011002 (2008)
9. Martins, J.C.C., Machado, R.J.: Ontologies for product and process traceability at manufacturing organizations: a software requirements approach. In: 8th International Conference on the Quality of Information and Communications Technology (QUATIC 2012), Piscataway, NJ, USA, 3–5 September 2012
10. Witherell, P., Grosse, I.R., Krishnamurty, S., Wileden, J.C.: AIERO: an algorithm for identifying engineering relationships in ontologies. Adv. Eng. Inform. **27**, 555–565 (2013). doi:10.1016/j.aei.2013.06.003
11. Jain, B., Adil, G.K., Ananthakumar, U.: Development of questionnaire to assess manufacturing capability along different decision areas. Int. J. Adv. Manuf. Technol. **71**(9–12), 2091–2105 (2014)

Learning Analytics Deployment at an University

Elisângela Mônaco de Moraes$^{(\boxtimes)}$ and Márcia Terra da Silva

Paulista University, São Paulo, Brazil
emonaco@unip.br

Abstract. This article presents the implementation of Learning Analytics in a University with the aim of testing the extraction of knowledge from databases of two systems used in distance education, aiming to provide support for the management of the distance education as a way to understand students' difficulties. Therefore, it was validated the applicability of literature reference model for the implementation the Learning Analytics. The data were extracted from the system of academic management and from the entrance exam to universities and were chosen the integration data, database and analytical tools. On the presented results, the model has been successfully applied, guiding the implementation of Learning Analytics at the University. The chosen tools facilitated the deployment and, brought benefits to University.

Keywords: Learning Analytics · Tools visualization · Distance Education

1 Introduction

The Distance Education is a type of education in expansion, which meets the new demands of a society oriented to information, as in new lifestyles and of consumption. We live in an interconnected world over the network, where more and more people study at home, as they can access from there, the information available online.

The distance education in Brazil is seen as a potential model to enable the demand for higher education in Brazil. EAD democratizes the entry to higher education, for the portion of the population that did not have undergraduate course offering in their localities. The expansion of this modality is clearly in higher education census conducted by INEP.

According to the technical summary of 2014 higher education census, published by the National Institute of Educational Studies Anisio Teixeira [1], which provides information on higher education in Brazil, the distance mode continues growing, with 1.34 million enrollment of higher education, representing 17.1% of total enrollment. Noteworthy the degree, where there were a total of 1,466,635 enrollments, with 540,693, or 36.9% of the distance mode. This figure shows an increase of 6.7% between 2013 and 2014.

This increase in the number of students in the distance education mode, and the characteristic of this type of education which is measured by Information and Communication Technology, results in an increasing volume of data produced,

© IFIP International Federation for Information Processing 2016
Published by Springer International Publishing AG 2016. All Rights Reserved
I. Nääs et al. (Eds.): APMS 2016, IFIP AICT 488, pp. 79–85, 2016.
DOI: 10.1007/978-3-319-51133-7_10

introducing the need to manipulation of various types of data in a fast way. Thus universities, seek ways to manage these data in order to transform them into information, and with that information, take faster decisions so they can be effective in their actions in the various organizational levels.

In this sense the objective of this study is to verify whether it is possible to extract knowledge from the two systems databases that are used in distance education, the main system that is the Academic Management and the Vestibular system. Therefore it will be validated the applicability of the reference model of Chatti et al. [2] chosen in the literature review of Moraes et al. [3] so that it is possible the extraction of knowledge from these two databases. Thus, provide support for the management of the Distance Education, in order to improve the targeting strategies for the achievement of goals, for example the evasion control.

2   Learning Analytics

Different definitions are assigned to the term learning analytics, being one of the most widely adopted in the literature: "the measurement, collection, analysis and reporting of data of students and its contexts, for the purpose of understanding and learning, optimizing the environment it occurs in"[4]. Another definition for Learning Analytics is that if applied in several organizational levels, where each level gives access to a different set of data and contexts, this process provides valuable information [5].

3   Methodology

This study used data obtained from the Information Systems used in Distance Education, specifically the Academic Management System and Vestibular system. The courses that will be analyzed in this research are technological undergraduate courses, both information and communication area, as follows: Course of Technology Analysis and Systems Development, whose mnemonic is DS, this course is offered in the distance model at the University since 2014 and now has 1,889 students; and the Course of Technology in Information Technology Management, whose mnemonic is IT, this course is offered in the distance model at the University since 2009 and today has 2,122 students. So that it is possible the realization of this work, the research was divided into distinct phases: research questions; collection and production of data; search results and conclusion.

3.1   Application Process of Learning Analytics

The reference model, proposed by Chatti et al. [2], divides the application of learning analytics in 04 dimensions: what? Why? Who? How?, thus facilitating and classifying the literature. Hence, using the model for the application of Learning Analytics, the following research questions will be addressed:

– RQ1 - How and what are the data to be analyzed?
– RQ2 - What are the aims of the analysis carried out and who will be presented?

4   Collection and Production Data

RQ1 - How and what are the data to be analyzed? Using the reference model Chatti et al. [2] were chosen tools and which systems used for this analysis. Thus, to achieve the goal of dimension How?, proposed in the model, the tools will be used the tools:

- Talend Open Studio - An open source solution for data integration and extraction, transform and load (ETL)
- Database HP Vertica - Database to streamline the handling of high volumes of data, its use is free up to 1TB of data, which, for this research is well above the need of analysis.
- Tableau - Data analysis tool, leader in the market, has a public version and is also free for teachers, easy to use. The choice of systems for the collection and analysis of data, thus meeting the dimension What? (Fig. 1), was carried out by the researcher, based on the analysis aim, namely:
- Academic Management System - Responsible for controlling the administrative processes and the academic management of the University
- Vestibular System - system responsible for the student, admission to the University.

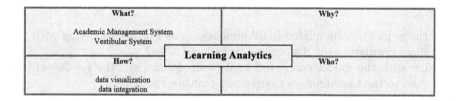

Fig. 1. Learning analytics (Source: Adapted from Chatti, and Dyckoff Thus)

The tools were chosen by the large volume of data, around 100 million records only in the Academic Management System, the variety of data and the speed required in the presentation of information. Each system uses a transactional database, but using a columnar database connected to a display tool, we obtain some benefits as: reduced time for consultations; ability to analyze faster the University data and thus consolidating the information into a single tool for use in the various levels of the organization (Fig. 2).

RQ2 - What are the aims of the analysis carried out and who will be presented? Using the reference model Chatti et al. [2], dimensions, Why? and Who? were filled with questions asked by the course coordinators, namely: How are the students distributed supported poles and what is the profile? What are the subjects that failed most? What is the number of students who pass the entrance exam? The managers of the University would like to know way online: How many people enrolled in the University entrance exam, by year, month, and day? What is the course that has the largest number of students enrolled? What is the profile of the student who seeks the IES, to take the entrance exam? This

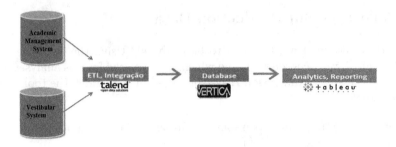

Fig. 2. Consolidating information

What?	Why?
Academic Management System Vestibular System	How are the students distributed supported poles and what is the profile? What are the subjects that failed most? What is the number of students who pass the entrance exam? How many people enrolled in the University entrance exam, by year, month, and day? What is the course that has the largest number of students enrolled? What is the profile of the student who seeks the IES, to take the entrance exam?
How?	**Learning Analytics**	**Who?**
data visualization data integration		Coordinators Course managers

Fig. 3. Learning analytics (Source: Adapted from Chatti, and Dyckoff Thus)

way, the model was completed in all dimensions, as Fig. 3, completing with the following information the dimensions, Why? and Who?

Now with the model completed in its four dimensions, the results will be presented to the Coordinators Course and managers of IES.

4.1 Results

In this section, it will be presented the results of analyzes, based on the questions raised, first by the coordinators and then by managers. For the data to be presented on online form to those involved, data integration tool was connected to transactional databases, data were extracted, transformed and loaded into columnar database and visualization tool connected on this data-base, so that it were developed the visualizations. Information is updated hourly and the involved people received access credentials.

For the coordinators the information's were presented, first answering the question: How are the students distributed at the support poles and what is the profile? (Fig. 4).

The information extracted for the coordinators of the two courses, show the highest concentration of students in the Southeast, the number of students per pole, the percentage of students by sex, being the male far superior, to DS course 88.06% are male and 11.94 are female, and for IT course are 13.62% female and 86.38% male. The number of enrolled students, distributed by age group for both courses, has the highest concentration in the range of 30 to 34 years.

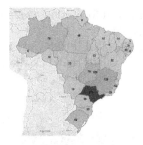

Fig. 4. Geographical distribution of students

In the visualization, the coordinators go through the information, interacting in a drill-down fashion, thus, down in the details as follows: in the student enrollment numbers information, you can click to go in the geographical distribution by state, clicking again appear the information by city and in the city, the presential support poles, in the poles appear the students and clicking in the student is possible to view the failed, approved, registered, exempt and locked disciplines.

For questions: What are the disciplines that most failed? What is the number of students who pass the entrance exam? The visualizations were presented as Figs. 5 and 6.

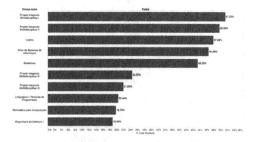

Fig. 5. Failed in the disciplines and exam

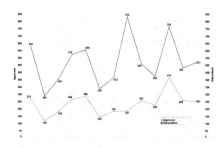

Fig. 6. Number of students who pass the entrance exam

The extracted data generated information to managers and the aim analysis were of objectives were presented.

The questions: How many enrolled in the University entrance exam by year, month, and day? What is the course that has the largest number of students enrolled? (Fig. 7). What is the profile of the student who seeks the IES, to take the entrance exam? (Fig. 8).

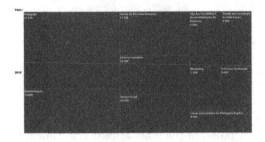

Fig. 7. Course that has the largest number of students enrolled

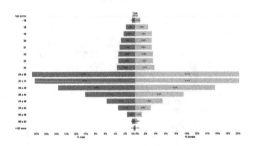

Fig. 8. Profile of the student

It were answered, so that you can check that the registered numbers in the college entrance is on the rise since 2011, the interaction with the tool enables the display of information per year, per month, per week, per day, per hour and even by minutes. The course with more enrolled people is Pedagogy, the age of the candidates are mostly between the groups: from 25 to 29 and 30 to 34.

5 Conclusion

The aim of this study was to verify the applicability of the reference model of Chatti et al. [2], chosen in Moraes et al. literature review, so that it is possible to extract knowledge from two databases. On the presented results, the model has been successfully applied, guiding the implementation of Learning Analytics at the University. The chosen tools facilitated the deployment and brought benefits to the University such as:

- Reduced time to check the number of entries in the vestibular system, because the data were processed at dawn and presented in spreadsheets, which with the deployment the information's are accessed online.
- The access to information from different systems, concentrated in a single tool.

By gaining the ability to analyze students from the extraction of knowledge, using the integration, database and visualization tools, the University gained a clearer profile of their student population. Managers and Coordinators of courses involved in this study evaluated that the information's presented are useful and relevant. Since the focus of this study was the implementation, from a model of learning analytics, and thus extracting knowledge from data, in the next studies are suggested the correlation of data from other systems. Additionally it is necessary expand to more departments of the higher education institution.

References

1. Instituto Nacional de Estudos e Pesquisas Anísio Teixeira. http://portal.inep.gov.br/basica-levantamentos-acessar
2. Chatti, M.A., Dyckhoff, A.L., Schroeder, U., Thüs, H.: A reference model for learning analytics. Int. J. Technol. Enhanced Learn. 4(5–6), 318–331 (2012)
3. Moraes, E., Silva, M., Souza, M.: Models to implement learning analytics: a literature review. In: 27th POMS Annual Conference, Orlando (2016)
4. Siemens, G., Long, P.: Penetrating the fog: analytics in learning and education. Educase Rev. 46(5), 30 (2011)
5. Shum, S.B., Crick, R.D.: Learning dispositions and transferable competencies: pedagogy, modelling and learning analytics. In: 2nd International Conference on Learning Analytics & Knowledge, British Columbia, Vancouver (2012)

Relationship Networks: Social Innovation and Earnings for Companies

Marcelo T. Okano[1(✉)], Oduvaldo Vendrametto[2],
Marcelo Eloy Fernandes[3], and Osmildo S. Dos Santos[4]

[1] Getulio Vargas Foundation, São Paulo, Brazil
marcelo.okano@fatec.sp.gov.br
[2] Paulista University, São Paulo, Brazil
[3] Fatec Barueri/Uninove, São Paulo, Brazil
[4] Universidade Potiguar, São Paulo, Brazil

Abstract. This study proposes an investigation to prove that when companies organize in networks and use social innovation in a productive system gets economic and social gain. The object of study is a case study of Milk Producers Association of Fartura, São Paulo. The object of study is a case study of Milk Producers Association of Fartura, São Paulo. This case study can be interpreted as a social innovation, as the association of producers brought social and economic benefits for a community; there has been new products and processes in order to innovate the marketing and production of lasting and sustainable milk.

Keywords: Social innovation · Network · Milk

1 Introduction

Innovation and its cycle can historically be divided into three stages: invention, present since the beginning of mankind; imitation or diffusion, common in markets whose economy was underpinned by the production and outsourcing of consumer products and innovation, strategy for economic sustainability of organizations in the twenty-first century, emerging after economic globalization and alternative to keep up with demand speed for new products, feature contemporary dynamics [1].

A new type of innovation begins to emerge; concerns about social issues begin to appear and to be important for organizations, called social innovation. According Juliani et al. [2], the mobilization around the theme stems from the lack of state capacity meet the needs of the population and the policies that direct public investment to increase competitiveness at the expense of social development.

Often these social changes begin mobilizing stakeholders to form a interorganizational network level, the companies operate in a network when there is cooperation and commitment in the relationship between them, providing not only economic gains, but also social.

This study proposes an investigation to prove that when companies organize in networks and use social innovation in a productive system gets economic and social gain. The object of study is a case study of Milk Producers Association of Fartura, São Paulo.

I. Nääs et al. (Eds.): APMS 2016, IFIP AICT 488, pp. 86–95, 2016.
DOI: 10.1007/978-3-319-51133-7_11

2 Conceptual Reference

2.1 Interorganizational Networks

Puffal and Puffal [3], consider based on research conducted on the evolution of inter-organizational networks studies field that the past 30 years the interest on interorganizational networks has grown significantly, and produced several studies and publications on the subject and the theme networks interorganizational is a fragmented field, multidisciplinary and his studies being conducted from various theories, from various points of view it is necessary to periodically analyze this field of study and to identify the most discussed topics and the light which theories it is being analyzed.

Companies operating in network when there is cooperation and commitment in the relationship between them. A growing use of information systems to interconnect companies - the so-called inter-organizational systems [4].

As a result, companies adopt new forms of work management, innovate in the concern to adjust to the global requirements and create collaborative strategies as a way to acquire skills that do not yet have, and corroborate DYER & SINGH [5].

Interorganizational networks are important in economic life, because facilitate the complex transactional and cooperative interdependence between organizations. Its importance is recognized from the point of theoretical saw, because it can be, and indeed are studied from different theoretical approaches. Thus, studies on networks provide a valuable basis of common interests and potential dialogue between the various branches of social science [7].

According to Baum and Ingram [8], inter-organizational networks can be divided into two classes analysis: horizontal and vertical networks. Figure 1 reflects the main divisions of studies on inter-organizational networks [6].

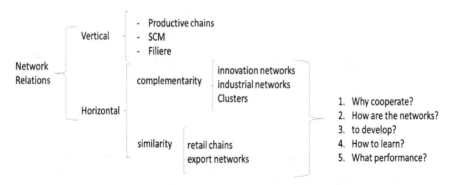

Fig. 1. Divisions of inter-organizational networks. Source: Pereira [6]

Among the types of networks, there are the so-called social networks, which have characteristics similar to the others, especially the line towards a common goal among the actors and decentralization in decision-making with the participation of individuals and organizations. Table 1 describes the main characteristics of the types of networks.

Table 1. Characteristics of the types of networks

Characteristics	Agglomerate	Cluster	Local productive arrangement	Social networks
Types of actors involved	Private and public organizations	Private and public organizations	Private, public, educational institutions, non-governmental organizations, associations, unions and the community in general	Private, public, educational institutions, non-governmental organizations, associations, unions and the community in general
Form of actors	Organizations	Organizations	Organizations	Organizations and individuals
Typology	Market	Market and communications	Market, communications and support	Support
Models	Vertical and horizontal	Vertical and horizontal	Vertical and horizontal	Horizontal
Organizations in a given geographical area	Concentrated	Concentrated	Concentrated	Concentrated
Types of organizations	Various sectors	A sector or activity	A sector or activity	One or more sectors or activities
Strategy level	Organizational	Organizational	Among all the local agents	Among all the local agents
Actions	Competitive	Competitive-cooperative	Competitive-cooperative	Cooperatives
Interaction form	Formal and informal	Formal	Formal	Informal
Essential factors of strengthening	Geographical proximity, similarity of market and regional competences	Geographical proximity, similarity of market, regional expertise and strong competition	Close geographic, similar market, regional expertise, strong competition and social cooperation	Trust, reputation and cooperation
Goal setting	Does not exist	Common goals between partners	Common objectives with all local actors	Common objectives with all local actors
Types of goals	Economics	Economics	Economics and socials	Economics and socials

2.2   Social Business

Organizations with unique view on offer and demand fluctuations have a short-time management, are closed to new markets generated by new demands. Consequently, closed to the innovative process and its vital contribution to growth [1].

According to Yunus et al. [9], in the capitalist system, two extreme types of corporate bodies can be distinguished. On the one hand, companies can be seen as profit-maximizing businesses, whose purpose is to create shareholder value. On the other, non-profit organizations exist to fulfil social objectives. In organizational structure, this new form of business is the same as profit-maximizing businesses: it is not a charity, but a business in every sense.

A social business is designed and operated just like a 'regular' business enterprise, with products, services, customers, markets, expenses and revenues. It is a no-loss, no-dividend, self-sustaining company that sells goods or services and repays investments to its owners, but whose primary purpose is to serve society and improve the lot of the poor. Here it differs from NGOs, most of which are not designed to recover their total costs from their operations, and are therefore obliged to devote part of their time and energy to raising money. As it seeks self-sustainability, a social business only relies on its investors at the beginning of a development project [9].

Business Models

(a) Conventional Business Model.

Yunus et al. [9] suggest that a business model has three components, as shown in Fig. 2:

- A value proposition, that is, the answer to the question: 'Who are our customers and what do we offer to them that they value?'
- A value constellation, that is, the answer to the question: 'How do we deliver this offer to our customers?' This involves not only the company's own value chain but also its value network with its suppliers and partners.
  These two components need to fit together like pieces of a puzzle in order to generate:
- A positive profit equation, which is the financial translation of the other two, and includes how value is captured from the revenues generated through the value proposition, and how costs are structured and capital employed in the value constellation.

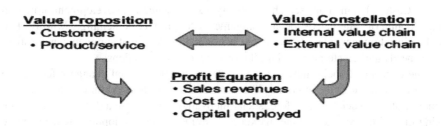

Fig. 2.   The three components of a conventional business model Source: Yunus et al. [9].

(b) Social Business Model.

To adapt the model to the social business, Yunus et al. [9] propose the following changes: The first change is the specification of targeted stakeholders, and the provision that the value proposition and constellation are not focused solely on the customer, but are expanded to encompass all stakeholders. The second is the definition of desired social profits through a comprehensive eco-system view, resulting in a social profit equation. The third is that the economic profit equation targets only full recovery of cost and of capital, and not financial profit maximization. Figure 3 illustrates these changes.

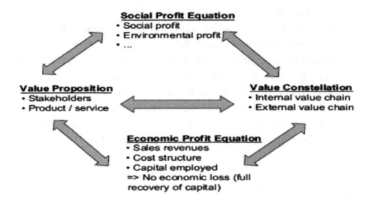

Fig. 3. The four components of a social business model. Source: Yunus et al. [9].

2.3   Social Innovation

The social innovation process produces the effect of reconstructing the social relations systems, as well as the structure of rules and resources that reproduce such systems. Therefore, according to the author, just it comes to social innovation "when the changes alter the processes and social relations, changing the pre-existing power structures" [10].

Already, Cloutier [11] considers social innovation as a new response, defined in the action and with lasting effect, to a social situation deemed unsatisfactory, that seeks the well-being of individuals and/or communities. To Bignetti [12], is the result of knowledge applied to social needs through the participation and cooperation of all stakeholders, creating new and lasting solutions to social groups, communities or society.

To Castor [13] include "search, discovery, experimentation, development, imitation and adoption of" alternative social arrangements "to produce something". Murray et al. [14] defines how new ideas (products, services and models) that simultaneously satisfy social needs and create new social relationships or collaborations.

The concept of social innovation in order to generate social change refers to the concern with the idea of improving living conditions, create opportunities and provide a more fraternal society. Therefore, social innovation arises from a desire or a need not being met by the State or by the market and are mainly in developing countries, more work space, the conditions of degradation of human life [15].

3   Method

To achieve the objective of this study an exploratory survey was conducted, qualitative, along with the milk producers of Fartura region, state of São Paulo. Gil [16], the exploratory research aims to provide greater awareness of the problem, in order to make it more explicit.

The qualitative approach presents a reality that cannot be quantified or measured and involves subjective items of reality research. It can work with data without specific statistical analysis, seeking the understanding of reality [17]. The research used the following methodologies:

1. Bibliographic Survey: Is the survey and review of all literature used for the theoretical foundation of the research.
2. Case Study: To accomplish the gathering of information, it was necessary to resort to the case study to evaluate the scenarios analyzed. The case study, according to Gil [16], need not be a hard road, closed.

4   Results

After a literature review, which served as a theoretical basis for the development of the survey instrument, selected the main features to prove the case of Fartura producers' association can be characterized as a social innovation.

4.1   Scenario Before the Producers' Association

The several visits and interviews in various dairy farms of Fartura region shown that the Interorganizational relationships were small and largely were limited to the sale of milk to cooperatives or dairy. These relationships were related just trade relations between the owner and the purchaser of milk. The buyer of milk just paid a fixed amount for a litter of milk, without any differentiation. There was an association of producers, cooperative or cluster, making it difficult to characterize an organizational inter network.

4.2   Formation of the Producers Association

A dairy company (Frutap) would launch a new product, a type of fermented milk, but need milk with a better quality. Quality milk production differs slightly from traditional definitions, therefore, are considered items such as protein, fat and total solids. To achieve improvement in milk, producers would have to improve production by investing in genetic control, artificial insemination, endemic controls, improved feeding and pastures adoption of strict inspection, handling, cleaning and disinfection.

In return the dairy company would pay more for better quality milk. The properties that adhered to change had a year to adapt the requirements. In this period, producers began meeting to create the association.

4.3 Scenario After the Formation of the Producers Association

In the city of Fartura, there is a group of 34 dairy farmers who have organized themselves into an association and provide for a dairy company with different prices according to the quality of the milk produced, as well as receive assistance and technical guidance, veterinary and institutions such as SEBRAE.

This group is characterized as a network level and second Balestrin and Vargas [18]. The characteristics of this network, as shown in Table 1 of the literature, is shown in Table 2.

Table 2. Network characteristics of producers association

Features	Producers association	Network types
Types of stakeholders	Milk producers association of producers, private enterprises, support institutions	Social networks or LPA
Way the actors	Organizations and individuals	Social networks
Network functions	Mercantile exchanges, information, knowledge, relationships, support and contacts	LPA or cluster
Type	In the market, support and communication	LPA
Network model	Horizontal	Social networks
Organizations in a given geographical area	Fartura/SP	Clusters, LPA or social networks
Types of organizations	Public, private and third sector	Clusters and social networks
Level of association	Strategies of producers and dairy farms	Social networks or LPA
Actions	Cooperative and competitive	Clusters or LPA
Interaction form	Formal and informal	Clusters or social network
Essential factors in establishing	Trust, reputation and cooperation	Social networks
Establishment of goals	Association with the owners	Social networks or LPA
Types of objectives	Economic objectives, social, environmental and political	LPA
Responsible for the actions	Association and the owners	Social networks or LPA
Supply chain	Unlinked	Clusters
Benefits	Economic, social and environmental	Social networks or LPA
Job type stimulated	Formal and informal	social networks or LPA

As for the theoretical framework of the Association of producers, there is the existence of mixed Social Networking features, prevalent, and the Local Productive Arrangement.

4.4 Business Models

We use models of conventional and social business of Yunus et al. [9] to analyze the scenes before and after formation of the association of producers, Table 3.

Table 3. Conventional and social business models applied to association of producers. Source: Prepared by the author and adapted from Yunus et al. [9].

		Scenario 1 - without association of producers	Scenario 2 - with the association of producers
Conventional business model	Value proposition	Sale of milk production to cooperative	
	Value constellation	The cooperative collects and commercializes milk	
	Profit equation	The cooperative pays a single value for a liter of milk, depending on the daily rate	
Social business model	Value proposition		Payment litter as differentiated by the qualify of milk
	Constellation value		Network of relationships between producers and the association
	Economic profit equation		The best-structured properties are privileged as the milk price setting criteria by industries
			Getting a better value for milk, the owners are able to maintain the association of producers
	Social profit equation		Bonus for productivity
			Access to consultants and professionals through the Casa da Agricultura and SEBRAE
			Relationships in other areas such as social, information exchange, knowledge and support
			Increasing productivity through improved farming conditions brought about by information and actions taken by the association of producers

5   Conclusion

The fact that the producers have organized themselves into a network level showed that social benefits are greater than the economic benefit, but the main benefit is that contributes to the evolution of the producers themselves.

This case study can be interpreted as a social innovation, as the association of producers brought social and economic benefits for a community; there has been new products and processes in order to innovate the marketing and production of lasting and sustainable milk.

References

1. Dos Santos, A.B., Fazion, C.B., de Meroe, G.P.: Innovation: a study on the evolution of the Schumpeter concept. Caderno de Administração. Revista da Faculdade de Administração da FEA (2011)
2. Juliani, D.P., Juliani, J.P., de Souza, J.A., Harger, E.M.: Social Innovation: Prospects and Challenges. Revista Espacios, **35**(5) (2014)
3. Puffal, D.D.P., Puffal, C.W.: A Evolução do Campo de Estudos de Redes Interorganizacionais: Uma Análise de Publicações Internacionais das Relações entre Empresas. Braz. J. Manag. Innov. **1**(3), 63–86 (2014)
4. Silveira, M.A.P., Trefiglio, R.P., Zambanini, M.E., Ceo, M.: Sistemas Interorganizacionais e Redes de Empresas no Setor Automobilístico: Indicadores e Relações. In: Anais do 7° CONTECSI, São Paulo (2009)
5. Dyer, J.H., Singh, H.: The relational view: cooperative strategy and sources of interorganizational competitive advantage. Acad. Manag. Rev. **23**(4), 660–679 (1998)
6. Pereira, B.A.D.: Structuring of horizontal relationships in networks. Thesis (Doctorate in Business Administration) – Universidade Federal do Rio Grande do Sul, Porto Alegre 219 f. (2005)
7. Balestrin, A., Vargas, L.M.: Evidências Teóricas para a Compreensão das Redes Interorganizacionais. ENEO, Encontro de Estudos Organizacionais, São Paulo (2002)
8. Baum, J.A.C., Ingram, P.: Interorganizational learning and network organization: toward a behavioral theory of the interfilm. In: March, J.G., Augier, M. (eds.) A Tribute to Richard M. Cyert. Edward Elgar, Aldershot (2000)
9. Yunus, M., Moingeon, B., Lehmann-Ortega, L.: Building social business models: lessons from the Grameen experience. Long Range Plan. **43**(2–3), 308–325 (2010)
10. Fleury, S.: Observatory on social innovation. In: Anais do Congreso Internacional del Clad Sobre la Reforma del Estado y de la Administración Pública, Buenos Aires, vol. 9 (2001)
11. Cloutier, J.: Qu'est-ce que l'innovation sociale? Crises (2003)
12. Bignetti, L.P.: Social innovations: a raid by ideas, trends and research focus. Ciências Sociais Unisinos **47**(1), 3–14 (2011)
13. Castor, B.V.J.: Social innovation and development. FIEP–Federação das Indústrias do Estado do Paraná (2007)
14. Murray, R., Caulier-Grice, J., Mulgan, G.: The Open Book of Social Innovation. National Endowment for Science, Technology and the Art, London (2010)
15. de Oliveira, N.D.A., da Silva, T.N.: Social innovation and sustainable social technologies inter-cooperatives relationships: an exploratory study. CREDITAG-RO. Revista de Administração da UFSM **5**(2), 277–295 (2012)

16. Gil, A.C.: How to design research projects. São Paulo, vol. 5, p. 61 (2002)
17. Costa, M.A.F., Costa, M.F.B.: Research Methodology-Concepts and Techniques. Inter-Ciência, Rio de Janeiro (2001)
18. Balestrin, A., Vargas, L.M.: Evidências Teóricas para a Compreensão das Redes Interorganizacionais. ENEO, São Paulo (2002)

Knowledge-Based PLM

Environmental Support for Dilution of Pollutants from Broiler Production and Aquaculture in Brazil

Silvia H. Bonilla[1(✉)], Helton R.O. Silva[1], Robson P. Faustino[1], Irenilza de Alencar Nääs[1], and Nilsa Duarte[2]

[1] University Paulista, São Paulo, Brazil
shbonilla@hotmail.com
[2] State University of Campinas, Campinas, Brazil

Abstract. Due to the rising demand for food, increasing intensive livestock production contributes significantly to the anthropogenic loading of the biosphere. Poultry and fish from intensive operations are a primary source for global human food consumption, and the contribution to air and water emissions. The environment can act as a sink of emissions by using it the capacity for diluting pollutants. In this way, the "support area" derived from the renewable resources supplied by region was quantified for both enterprises regarding emergy. Results suggest that poultry production seems to be a thousand times more "eco-efficient" than aquaculture as well as presenting a lower support area. Accounting for the environmental services required to dilute emissions is shown to be a necessary procedure towards the proper evaluation of long-term sustainability and quantification of externalities.

Keywords: Poultry · Aquaculture · Emergy · Environmental services

1 Introduction

Livestock production contributes significantly to the anthropogenic loading of the biosphere. As the world's demand for food increases, the increasing emissions to land, water and atmosphere from intensive livestock production is worthy of concern.

Poultry and fish from intensive operations are an important source for global human food consumption [1]. Aviaries are a source of ammonia emissions that are a function of NH_3 concentration inside the housing. It depends on flock density, litter, diet and ventilation systems. Some of these parameters and consequently the ammonia emission can be controlled through proper management [2]. On the other hand, concerns are expressed about the discharge of wastes, increasing the concentration of nutrients, pathogens and chemical such as drugs and pesticides from aquaculture operation [3].

The environment can act as a source of resources and a sink of emissions. This might be accomplished by taking advantage of the current cycles and processes of the biosphere, and free environmental services. In this context, emissions from production process would rely on an amount of available resources (land, water, air) which acting as a sink will, at least, dilute them down to the biosphere background. In this way, the

© IFIP International Federation for Information Processing 2016
Published by Springer International Publishing AG 2016. All Rights Reserved
I. Nääs et al. (Eds.): APMS 2016, IFIP AICT 488, pp. 99–105, 2016.
DOI: 10.1007/978-3-319-51133-7_12

"support area", would act as a buffered piece of land, with the capacity of providing the natural services necessary to dilute or abate emissions derived from any producer system. The problem arises with the establishment of the "support area" since natural services have to be quantified. The quantification of natural services taking into account their function and the involved support of the biosphere is not trivial, and the need for a well-established and well-sustained tool becomes evident.

This approach is provided by the emergy environmental accounting [4], an assessment framework that evaluates resources based on the environmental work required to generate them and make them available. The methodology, based on thermodynamics and systems theory, enables accounting for all natural and economic inputs entering a system in a common metric. It provides indices capable of quantifying environmental performance as well as monitoring improvements and it is a useful tool for decision making.

By quantifying the "work" of the biosphere involved in pollutants dilution (sun, wind, rain, deep heat, gravitational energy) in emergy terms, it is possible to make the conversion into the area of land demanded to supply those environmental services by the local renewable resources of the region [5, 6].

This paper addresses the use of emergy to explore the role of natural services from a land area to act as a sink for ammonia emissions from a poultry production housing and phosphorous from an aquaculture farm. The environmental work done by the biosphere intending to dilute the considered emissions is accounted regarding emergy and converted to the "support area" concept, the land demand responsible for acting as a buffer.

2 Methodology

2.1 Emergy Environmental Accounting

Emergy accounting methodology [4] was developed over the last decades as a tool for environmental policy and to evaluate quality and distribution of resources in the dynamics of complex systems. A complete assessment of the methodology cannot be provided here, but the reader may refer to published reports [4, 7]. Briefly, emergy is defined as the sum of all inputs of energy (directly or indirectly) required for a process to provide a given product, when inputs are expressed in the same form (or type) of energy, such as solar energy [4].

The emergy flows are classified into three categories of resources: R as renewable resources, N as non-renewable resources and the inputs provided by the economy, F. All three categories are fundamental to the emergy accounting and the understanding of the system interactions with the environment. R and N flows are provided by the environment and are economically free.

While renewable resources can be replaced at least at the same rate as they are consumed, the non-renewable resources are depleted faster than their ability of recuperation. The economic inputs, F, are provided by the market and are related to flows supplied by the economy.

Every input has to be inventoried and multiplied by its correspondent "transformity" to calculate the emergy flows. "Transformity" (expressed in seJ/J) is the factor to convert each kind of energy in emergy, and it represents all past environmental work necessary to obtain one joule of a given resource. When inputs are expressed in units others than energy ones (mass or money), the UEV (unit emergy value) is used to convert values into solar energy joules (seJ). To carry out the emergy flux determination, the planetary baseline of 15.83×10^{24} seJ/year was adopted [8]. The transformity values that were calculated using another baseline were corrected and properly informed during calculation.

2.2   Accounting for Environmental Services and Support Area

The energy system diagram is described in Fig. 1. Inputs directly required to develop livestock production are aggregated into types, classified as R_1, F and N, converging towards the inner frame. The outputs are food and waste by-products. The larger frame contains the environmental systems which act as the sink of the by-products also generated in the production system. The environmental services required to drive the dilution process are expressed as R_2. The following steps were adopted to account for the environmental services:

(a) Determination of mass of air required to dilute NH_3 and mass of water required to dilute phosphorous emissions for poultry production and tilapia aquaculture, respectively, up to acceptable concentration levels: (i) close to average values of NH_3 in the biosphere, and (ii) phosphorous concentration in water below the critical threshold of eutrophication.

(b) Determination of the emergy flow of the required environmental services (noted as R_2 in Fig. 1) by calculating the kinetic energy of the mass of dilution air (measured as the wind power needed to spread and dilute pollutants) and the chemical energy of the mass of dilution water (Gibbs energy necessary to dilute pollutants). Procedures were adopted from [5, 9], respectively.

(c) Calculation of the "support area" (As), known as the area of land necessary to balance the emergy of the environmental services (R_2), and calculated from the average annual flux of renewable emergy per year per unit area of landscape (Emd_R), As $= R_2/Emd_R$ [5]. The value of Emd_R was calculated from the results of the annually renewable emergy flows of Brazil, (extracted from [10]), divided by the Brazilian continental area and it accounts for 3.66×10^{11} seJ/m^2.

2.3   Systems Under Study

The present study was carried in broiler houses located inland Mato Grosso do Sul state and a tilapia farm inland São Paulo state, Brazil. Necessary data to accomplish the study for both production systems were extracted from [11, 12], respectively.

Average values of four commercial broiler houses (tunnel system ones) at Itaquiraí – MS county, were used to carry out the study. There were 25,200 broilers in each house from the Hubbard' genetic strain reared for 42 days until they reach the commercial weight of 2 kg.

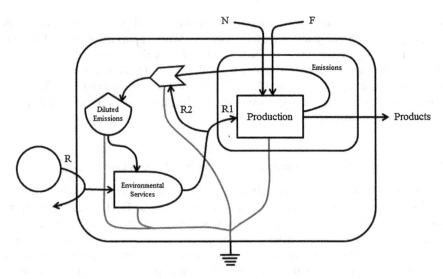

Fig. 1. -To drive production (poultry or aquaculture), flows of renewable (R_1), nonrenewable (N) and purchased resources (F) are needed (represented by -) emissions are diluted by nature through renewable services (R_2). Flows of energy dispersion is represented by -

The tilapia (Genomar Supreme Tilapia) farm is located in Iperó city, distant from São Paulo city 128 km. The installation is comprehensive of a total of 200 fish cages, 40 of 4 m^3 and 60 of 6 m^3 each. The pond where the cages are placed covers an area of 30 ha with an average depth of 2.10 m. The pond is fed by a water course which pours a water supply of 150 l/s in average. Fingerlings are placed into the cages and after a cycle of approximately 180 days, the fish reach 484 g. The proper chemical analysis shows no eutrophication of pond water. The annual production is 320,000 fishes. Ammonia emission values were obtained from the application of a predicting model confirmed by measurements in loco [11]. Phosphorous release due to fish metabolism was estimated according to the conversion factor in biomass and the content of phosphorus in the food. Additional data were retrieved from literature.

3   Results and Discussion

Table 1 shows the results of the environmental services involved in dilution of emissions accounted for both the enterprises.

The OECD (OECD-Organisation for economic cooperation and development) has called eco-efficiency "the efficiency with which ecological resources are used to meet human needs" and defines it as a ratio of an output (the value of products and services produced by a firm, sector, or economy as a whole) divided by the input (the sum of environmental pressures generated by the firm, the sector, or the economy)." [13]. The concept was reformulated in emergy terms, and it was expressed as units of mass produced by seJ of environmental services committed to dilute pollutants (kg/seJ). Values can be seen in Table 1, calculated as the inverse of the emergy flows

Table 1. -Mass of air required to dilute ammonia emissions from the poultry house and mass of water required to dilute phosphorous released from the tilapia farm, on a yearly basis; energy values and corresponding annual emergy flows of the environmental services R_2 expressed in seJ and seJ by kg of food produced.

	Poultry production	Tilapia aquaculture
Mass of air (g/y)	6.20×10^{14} (1)	
Mass of water (g/y)		2.23×10^{07} (5)
Energy (J/y)	7.75×10^{12} (2)	1.06×10^{14} (6)
Emergy from environmental services R_2 (seJ/y)	1.95×10^{16} (3)	1.17×10^{19} (7)
Emergy from environmental services R_2 by mass (seJ/kg y)	7.70×10^{10} (4)	7.50×10^{13} (8)
"Emergy eco-efficiency" (kg y/seJ 10−10)	1.3	0.0013

corresponding to the environmental services normalized by mass. At a first glance, poultry production seems to be a thousand times more "eco-efficient", according to the definition adopted here. However, although all the environmental services are accounted for by using a common metric, the present approach only takes into consideration dilution of pollutants in a simplified way. The inclusion of pollutants into biogenic cycles occurs, and kinetics of the diverse reaction should be considered. Even so, present results serve as a starting point to evidence that real efficiency of production systems are not adequately measured without taking into consideration the externalities caused by the use of resources, and release of by-products, even in compliance with legal threshold concentrations. Moreover, the degree of eco-efficiency attained is not just limited to an absolute value obtained by the index calculation but to a holistic enterprise management towards environmental improvement.

If it is assumed that the whole emergy required to dilute pollutants is derived from renewable resources supplied by region, the calculated "support area" will act as a sustainability predictor of long-term sustainability. Table 2 shows the values of "support area" and the ratio between them and the direct areas (real area of the enterprise being 1800 m^2 for poultry production and 30 ha for aquaculture farm).

Table 2. - The support area (As), the specific As (by mass) and the ratios between As and direct areas (DA), calculated for Poultry production and Tilapia aquaculture.

	Poultry production	Tilapia aquaculture
As (m^2)	5.30×10^{04}	32.0×10^{06}
As (m^2/kg)	0.21	206.5
As/DA	29	107

When As by mass produced is considered differences between both systems are evidenced. Each kilogram of tilapia produced relies on almost a thousand times more support area than poultry. According to emergy theory, transformity related to water capacity for diluting solutes are higher than transformity for the wind, the environmental service involved for ammonia dilution. The hierarchies of environmental processes that originate both services are different, and comparison should be made carefully. Even so, the As/DA ratio evidences that the direct area is not a good indicator to attain the real contribution of the biosphere when acting as source and sink of resources. In this way, areas 29 times and more than hundred times greater than the direct areas respectively are need to support the enterprises just from the emissions, without taking into account resources side (or inputs).

4 Concluding Remarks

Accounting for the environmental services required to dilute emissions is shown to be as a necessary procedure towards the proper evaluation of the sustainability of processes and quantification of externalities.

The challenge is to fit humans' production patterns to the biosphere's capacity to absorb waste by-products, without overload. For this purpose, services provided by natural capital have to be adequately evaluated and finally quantified in terms comparable with the economy.

References

1. Food and Agricultural Organization of the United Nations: Global Agriculture Towards. http://www.fao.org/fileadmin/templates/wsfs/docs/Issues_papers/HLEF2050_Global_ Agriculture.pdf
2. Gates, R.S., Xin, H., Casey, K.D., Liang, Y., Wheeler, E.F.: Method for measuring ammonia emissions from poultry houses. J. Appl. Poult. Res. **14**, 622–634 (2005)
3. Naylor, R., Burke, M.: Aquaculture and ocean resources: raising tigers of the sea. Annu. Rev. Environ. Resour. **30**, 185–218 (2005)
4. Odum, H.T.: Environmental Accounting: Emergy and Environmental Decision Making. Wiley, New York (1996)
5. Ulgiati, S., Brown, M.T.: Quantifying the environmental support for dilution and abatement of process emissions. J. Clean. Prod. **10**, 335–348 (2002)
6. Lou, B., Qiu, Y., Ulgiati, S.: Emergy-based indicators of regional environmental sustainability: a case study in Shanwei. Ecol. Ind. **57**, 514–524 (2015)
7. Brown, M.T., Ulgiati, S.: Emergy-based indices and ratios to evaluate sustainability: monitoring economies and technology toward environmentally sound innovation. Ecol. Eng. **9**, 51–69 (1997)
8. Odum, H.T., Brown, M.T., Brandt-Williams, S.: Introduction and Global Budgets, Folio #1. University of Florida, Gainesville (2000)
9. Odum, H.T.: Emergy Evaluation of Salmon Pen Culture. University of Florida Press, Gainesville (2001)
10. Demétrio, F.J.C., Giannetti, B.F., Bonilla, S.H., Almeida, C.M.V.B.: Emergy accounting of Brazilian states and regions. In: Brown, M.T., et al. (eds.), Emergy Synthesis 7: Theory and Applications of the Emergy Methodology. Gainesville, FL, pp. 413–418 (2013)

11. Lima, N., Garcia, R., Nääs, I., Caldara, F., Ponso, R.: Model-predicted ammonia emission from two broiler houses with different rearing systems. Scientia Agricola **72**(5), 393–399 (2015)
12. Pierobom, J.L.: Estudo da Sustentabilidade Ambiental em Diferentes Sistemas de Criação de Tilápias. Universidade Paulista, São Paulo (2009)
13. OECD: Eco-efficiency. http://www.oecdbookshop.org
14. Buenfil, A.A.: Emergy evaluation of water. University of Florida (2001)

Water Usage Charge in Brazil: Emergy Donor-Side Approach for Calculating Water Costs

Helton R.O. Silva and Silvia H. Bonilla(✉)

University Paulista, São Paulo, Brazil
shbonilla@hotmail.com

Abstract. The Federal Water Law 9433 enacted in 1997 gave the legal frame relative of the water usage charge. The aim of this paper is to interpret legal terms through the emergy environmental accounting approach in order to establish the donor-side costs related to water usage under the user-pays and polluter-pays principles. The procedure was performed for agricultural activities at the Jundiai-Mirim Basin, located at São Paulo State, Brazil. The proposed procedure resulted in costs comparable to those already implemented at the watershed under study by using other economical procedures.

Keywords: Water charges · Brazilian Law 9433 · Polluter-pays principle

1 Introduction

In Brazil, payment for water had been already foreseen by the first water resources management legislation, the Federal Water Code, enacted in 1934. But it was the Federal Water Law (FWL) 9433 enacted in 1997 [1] that gave the legal frame for water usage charge. The Law also defines that water is a scarce resource, which has economic value, and recognizes the existence of multiple water uses and user rights. Only users who exploit water with economic benefits are subjected to charges. Another essential characteristic given by this legal document is the legitimation of the River Basin Committee to arbitrate in the first instance level conflicts in the watersheds, to implement methodologies to establish water charge values and to propose those values to the National Agency (ANA).

Complementarily, the National Environmental Policy through the Law 6938/81 had already imposed "recuperation and/or compensation to polluters and predators for caused damages as well as payment to users for the environmental resources when used for economic purposes", reflecting the polluter-pay and the user-pay principles [2].

Some basins have already implemented the management instruments targeted at the Water Resource Management Policy (WRMP), including the fixation of the water usage charge. The PCJ basin (Piracicaba, Capivari, Jundiai basin) is an example of a basin that makes progress implementing all the necessary instruments for water managements. The PCJ basin adopted a weighted coefficients methodology to fix the usage charges. The objective of this work is not making a judgment on the criterion adopted

© IFIP International Federation for Information Processing 2016
Published by Springer International Publishing AG 2016. All Rights Reserved
I. Nääs et al. (Eds.): APMS 2016, IFIP AICT 488, pp. 106–112, 2016.
DOI: 10.1007/978-3-319-51133-7_13

but offering a proposal capable to unify criteria among the different basins with a background theory to sustain the accounting.

To capture the economical value of natural resources is not easy and some economical instruments have been proposed with more or less success [3]. Motta [4] recognized the difficulty of fixing natural resources market prices that properly reflect the value assigned to them. Furthermore, he emphasizes [4] that each analyst will assume different hypothesis according to the valuation object, data availability and knowledge of the ecological dynamic of the resource.

The emergy accounting, based on thermodynamics and systems theory provides an approach to evaluate natural resources contribution to society, by calculating the biosphere work directed to generate them and make them available. In this way, all type of natural resources can be evaluated and quantified with the same basis: biosphere cost in the form of solar energy. The state of water resources and the pressure exerted by human activities in Chinese cities [5], as well as the value of water resources in Chinese rivers [6] and Italian watershed [7] was studied using emergy. The methodology was proposed to capture the recovery cost for water usage within the Water Frame Directive (WFD) definitions [8]. Differently from the Brazilian water administration, the WFD provides a framework of definitions with the purpose of identifying the different kinds of water use costs (services, resources and environmental costs). Brazilian directive enables a broader interpretation of the terms involved since the extent of the use (UPP) and pollution-pays principle (PPP) is not completely defined. Kind of water usages subjected to charges include only those relative to water grant. Whether or not externalities should be included into the PPP or only direct pollution costs depends on the analyst expertise or interpretation, social interests or basin committee considerations, making difficult to propose a unified method to quantify charges. Different legal interpretations arise from the broad approach of the definitions and in order to establish a criterion, in the present work, the extent of the environmental effects due to usage included the externalities caused due to enterprises operation.

The aim of this paper is to make an interpretation of the WRMP in terms of the emergy theory in order to establish the costs related to water usage under the UPP and PPP. Since the scenarios of usage are diverse only the agricultural case is shown and discussed here. Quantification for the other scenarios is in advance. Data from Jundiai–Mirim basin are employed for calculation. Selection of the Jundiai-Mirim watershed, a management unit (unit n° 5) that belongs to the JPC basin, as a case study was done since the macro-basin has a well-organized system of usage charge.

2 Materials and Methods

2.1 Emergy Accounting

Emergy is defined as the available energy of one kind previously used up directly and indirectly to make a service or a product [9]. A complete assessment of the methodology cannot be provided here, but the reader can refer to published reports [9, 10].

In contrast to economic valuation, which has a user-side approach giving into account the users willingness-to-pay, emergy accounting provides a donor-side approach, quantifying the cost of nature to generate a service. From that cost quantification, the methodology can translate cost into currency flows, creating the interface with economy.

In order to calculate the emergy of a resource, the quantity expressed in units of energy is determined and multiplied by its correspondent "transformity". "Transformity", expressed in seJ/J, is the factor to convert energy inputs in emergy and it represents all past environmental work necessary to obtain one joule of a given resource. When inputs are expressed in mass or money, the specific emergy or the emergy-money-ratio (EMR) is used to convert values into solar energy joules (seJ), respectively. The emergy-money-ratio used in this study was calculated by dividing the annual emergy (in seJ/y) of the São Paulo state economy by its gross national product (R$/y). On the contrary, conversion of emergy to currency is accomplished by dividing emergy values by the EMR corresponding to the economy where the study is conducted. The units derived from the division are defined as emR$ (em-real, real is the Brazilian currency) and serve to make an analogy with currency.

The emergy flows are classified into three categories of resources: R as renewable resources, N as non-renewable resources and the inputs provided by the economy, F.

The theory In order to carry out emergy flux determination, the planetary baseline of 15.83×10^{24} seJ/year was adopted [11, 12]. The transformity values that were calculated using another baseline were corrected and properly informed during calculation.

2.2   Interpreting Law Terms Trough the Emergy Approach

When the emergy approach is used to interpret the terminology employed by the WRMP, two kinds of costs emerged, usage costs, related to the UPP and those derived by the PPP concept.

UPP-related costs of water correspond to the quantity of water diverted and used to carry out the enterprise, in this case, for agriculture production. Although it is true that a parcel of the diverted water is not directly used and returned to the water-body or infiltrates, it will suffer modification if compared to the initial conditions. The natural water cycle is the responsible of the water presence at the basin, so the emergy costs can be assimilated to the emergy of the water itself. Geopotential energy and chemical potential energy are the two main components of emergy, of water and derived from rainfall onto the watershed area. In this way, CUPP (expressed in seJ/m^3), the emergy usage cost, is defined as the emergy flow (Emrain) related to geopotential or chemical potential aspects of rain distributed through the whole volume of water (wrain) within the watershed, CUPP = Emrain/wrain. The division of CUPP by EMRSP converts emergy to equivalent monetary values, expressed in emR$.

PPP related costs of water are considered here as those related to alteration of the physical and biological aspects of water bodies due to human activities of water usage. The usage of water in agricultural activities directs not only water but also other inputs, nonrenewable resources and market goods that generate a load in the used land [13]. The excess of local emergy density created as a consequence of the load from water usage used is then distributed through superficial and ground water along the watershed causing interference of water bodies. Accounting of these effects are calculated by CPPP = EmN + F/wdisch, (expressed in seJ/m^3) being EmN + F the annual emergy flow of nonrenewable and purchased inputs involved in agricultural activities at the region and wdisch the volume of discharge water of the watershed (that portion of water that is not involved in evapotranspiration). The CPPP expression implies in the distribution of the load caused by the convergence of N and F inputs per area through the total volume of discharge water. Analogously, division of CPPP by EMRSP offers an emR$ value that can be considered as currency and compared to actual prices.

2.3   Calculation Considerations

For the emergy flow (Em_{rain}) calculations, the higher of the two flows from geopotential and chemical potential was selected in order to avoid double accounting according to the Emergy Theory-algebra [9]. In this case, chemical potential emergy flows were used.

Since no data about volume of groundwater in the watershed is available, for the w_{disch} estimation the hydro balance of the region was used by means of the specific discharge value of 10.0 l/s km^2 from [14].

The Em_{N+F} derives from the annual areal emergy intensity (expressed in seJ/ha y) of each kind of agricultural activity at the region multiplied by the area occupied by each activity (in ha). Two kinds of calculations were adopted in order to estimate the Em_{N+F} value. From these two calculations two values of cost will arise which could be considered as the upper and lower limits of the cost interval. It is difficult to evaluate the extent and intensity of the damages exerted by human activities to water bodies and nature in general. Also, to establish the area that has direct influence on damages and disturbance is not trivial. In order to establish an interval of influence, two regions were considered to carry out calculation: the activities occurring at the permanent protection areas (PPA) and activities at the whole watershed. Activities occurring in both regions considered generate load due to the intensity increase of nonrenewable resources. Although it seems that those occurring at the PPA will create more disturbance, activities at the whole watershed certainly will also contribute.

2.4   Jundiai-Mirim Micro-Watershed

The Jundiai-Mirim River watershed belongs to the São Paulo state, Brazil. It presents an area of 117.50 km^2 and is located within parallels 23° 00' and 23° 30'S and meridians 46° 30' and 47° 15'W. Jundiai-Mirim River has 16 km extension and is one of Jundiai River affluent. Diverse anthropogenic activities occur at the basin.

3   Results and Discussion

The evaluation of the UPP-related costs of the resource was performed by calculating the chemical potential energy in a yearly basis. Table 1 shows the C_{UPP} in emergy values and their conversion to currency.

Table 1. The chemical potential energy of water, transformity value, emergy UPP-related cost of water and the cost expressed in currency.

	Chem. pot. energy* (J/m^3)	Transformity (seJ/J)	C_{UPP} (seJ/m^3)	C_{UPP}/EMR_{SP}*** $(emR\$/m^3)$
Basin water	4.94E+06	3.106E+04**	1.53E+11	0.89

*From $V \times d \times G$, being $V = 1$ m^3, $d = 1.0E+06$ g/m^3 water density, G (Gibbs free energy) = 4.94 J/g, assuming rain water with 10 ppb of dissolved solids; **From [12]; ***EMR_{SP} = 1.7E+12 seJ/\$, from [15].

To estimate the PPP-related costs of water, the disturbance caused by the agricultural activities was calculated. Table 2 shows the upper and the lower values of the interval. The upper limit is almost 7 times greater than the lower load due to agricultural activities. To obtain CPPP, division by the discharge water (10 l/s $km^2 \times 117.5$ km^2) was done, as shown in Table 3. To convert these values into currency, they were multiplied by the EMRSP (1.7E+12 seJ/\$, from [15]), see Table 3.

Table 2. The Em_{N+F} (the annual emergy flow of nonrenewable and purchased inputs involved in agricultural activities) for the agricultural activities performed at the PPA and in the whole watershed.

Agricultural activity	Area PPA (ha)*	Total area (ha)*	Areal emergy intensity (seJ/ha y)**	PPA $EmEm_{N+F}$ (E15seJ/y)	Total $EmEm_{N+F}$ (E15seJ/y)
General agriculture	51.2	522.7	1.26E+15	64.5	658.6
Row crops	8.4	682.8	2.34E+15	19.7	1597.8
Pasture	574.1	2781	1.08E+15	620.0	3003.5
Tree plantation	295.8	1683.9	2.44E+15	721.8	4108.7
total				1426.0	9368.6

*Values are taken from [16]; **Values are taken from [17].

Table 3. The C_{PPP} values expressed in emergy and the value expressed in currency for the agricultural activities performed in the PPA (lower limit) and in the whole watershed (upper limit).

	Lower limit	Upper limit
C_{PPP} (E+09 seJ/m^3)*	38.4	252.5
C_{PPP}/EMR_{SP} ($emR\$/m^3$)**	0.022	0.146

*$C_{PPP} = Em_{N+F}/w_{disch}$ being water discharge estimated as (10 l/s $km^2 \times 117.5$ km^2); **EMR_{SP} = 1.7E+12 seJ/\$, from [15].

The values calculated here for water charging pricing are comprised within the interval 0.91 and 1.04 emR\$/m^3 for agricultural uses. They are computed as the sum of the two emergy costs after conversion to monetary values. Comparison with the results derived from the emergy approach performed for the Spanish basin [8], shows comparable but lower values for the present case study. On the other hand, the procedure already implemented at the PCJ committee, fixed basic unitary prices from of 0.01 to 0.10 R\$/m^3 for catching and organic load, respectively.

4 Concluding Remarks

The emergy approach offers a tool to aid in water usage charge estimation. It provided a systemic point of view that in the present case results in costs comparable to those already implemented at the whole PCJ macro-basin, when the Jundiai-Mirim micro-basin is located. Although the charge of water due to usage and pollution is still a controversial topic, the present work evidences that the whole biosphere contributes trough concentration of free natural resources to maintain the hydrological cycle and offer eco-services to anthropogenic activities.

Acknowledgments. Helton R.O. Silva wants to recognize the CAPES-PROSUP master degree scholarship.

References

1. Brazil. Law 9433. http://www.ana.gov.br/Legislacao/default2.asp
2. Brazil. Law 6938/81. http://www.planalto.gov.br/ccivil_03/Leis/L6938.htm
3. Cánepa, E.M., Pereira, J.S., Lanna, A.E.L.: A Política de Recursos Hídricos e o Principio Usuário-Pagador (PUP). Revista Brasileira de Recursos Hídricos **4**(1), 103–117 (1999)
4. Motta, R.S.: Valoração e Precificação Dos Recursos Ambientais Para Uma Economia Verde. Política Ambiental, Belo Horizonte (2011)
5. Lv, C., Wu, Z.: Emergy analysis of regional water ecological-economic system. Ecol. Eng. **32**, 703–7010 (2009)
6. Chen, D., Chen, J., Luo, Z., Lv, Z.: Emergy evaluation of the natural value of water resources in Chinese rivers. Environ. Manag. **44**, 288–297 (2009)
7. Pulselli, F.M., Patrizi, N., Focardi, S.: Calculation of the unit emergy value of water in a Italian watershed. Ecol. Model. **222**, 2929–2938 (2011)
8. Brown, M.T., Martínez, A., Uche, J.: Emergy analysis applied to the estimation of the recovery of costs for water services under the European water framework directive. Ecol. Model. **221**, 2123–2132 (2010)
9. Odum, H.T.: Environmental Accounting: Emergy and Environmental Decision Making. Wiley, New York (1996)
10. Brown, M.T., Ulgiati, S.: Emergy evaluation of the biosphere and natural capital and biosphere services. Ambio **28**(6), 486–493 (1999)
11. Odum, H.T., Brown, M.T., Brandt-Williams, S.: Introduction and Global Budgets, Folio #1. University of Florida, Gainesville (2000)

12. Odum, H.T.: Emergy of Global Processes, Folio #2. University of Florida, Gainesville (2000)
13. Brown, M.T., Vivas, B.: Landscape development intensity index. Environ. Monit. Assess. **221**(101), 289–309 (2005)
14. Giansante, A.E, Belli, P.: Medidas de Proteção da Bacia Hidrográfica do Rio Jundiaí. http://www.bvsde.paho.org/bvsAIDIS/PuertoRico29/giansante.pdf
15. Demétrio, F.J.C.: Avaliação de Sustentabilidade Ambiental do Brasil com a Contabilidade em Emergia. Tese de Doutorado, Universidade Paulista (2011)
16. Freitas, E.P.: Análise Integrada do Mapa de Uso e Ocupação das Terras da Microbacia do rio Jundiaí-Mirim para Fins de Gestão Ambiental. Tese de Doutorado, Instituto Agronômico de Campinas (2012)
17. Agostinho, F.D.R.: Estudo da Sustentabilidade dos Sistemas de Produção Agropecuários da Bacia Hidrográfica dos rios Mogi-Guaçú e Pardo Através da Análise Emergética. Tese de Doutorado, Universidade Estadual de Campinas (2009)

Combining Genetic Algorithm with Constructive and Refinement Heuristics for Solving the Capacitated Vehicle Routing Problem

Stanley Jefferson de Araujo Lima$^{(\boxtimes)}$, Renato Alessandro Rocha Santos, Sidnei Alves de Araujo, and Pedro Henrique Triguis Schimit

Universidade Nove de Julho, São Paulo, Brazil
stanley@winplace.com.br,
{alessandro3santos,saraujo,schimit}@uni9.pro.br

Abstract. This work presents a hybrid strategy for optimization of Capacitated Vehicle Routing Problem (CVRP) that employs Genetic Algorithms (GA) combined with the heuristics of Gillett & Miller (GM) and Hill Climbing (HC). The first heuristic is used to incorporate feasible solutions in the initial population of the GA while the second is responsible for the refinement of solutions after a certain number of generations without improvements. The computational experiments showed that the proposed strategy presented good results for the optimization of CVRP with respect to the quality of solutions well as the computational cost.

Keywords: Capacitated Vehicle Routing Problem · Heuristics · Genetic Algorithm · Gillett & Miller · Hill Climbing

1 Introduction

The optimization of production processes in the industrial environment has been an object of study and research in various areas of knowledge, such as business management, economics, logistics, among others, being most notably studied in production engineering [1,2]. In logistics, for example, the distribution of products and routing of vehicles are gaining space and becoming competitive advantages for companies. To reduce the delivery time, increasing the availability of products and inputs, it is mandatory to make deliveries respecting the deadlines. Nevertheless, the reduction of costs associated with the vehicles routing activity becomes an important tool for effective planning of products distribution.

The Vehicle Routing Problem (VRP) has attracted, in the last years, an increasing attention of researchers due to the great difficulty of its solution and its presence in many practical applications [3]. As consequence, there has been great effort to develop robust algorithms that can be modeled according to the scenario that describes a determined situation.

The Capacitated Vehicle Routing Problem is a variant of VRP and consists, basically, in determining the routes to be followed by a fleet of homogeneous

I. Nääs et al. (Eds.): APMS 2016, IFIP AICT 488, pp. 113–121, 2016.
DOI: 10.1007/978-3-319-51133-7_14

vehicles, to serve a given number of customers, without violating the capacities of the vehicles [4]. The CVRP belongs to the class of NP-hard problems, that is, problems whose the solution usually requires non-polynomial complexity time algorithms and because of this are usually solved with the use of heuristic and metaheuristics algorithms such as Gillett & Miller [5], Clarke and Wright [6,7], Tabu Search [6,8], Simulated Annealing [6] and Genetic Algorithms [9,10].

This work presents a strategy for CVRP optimization using Genetic Algorithms combined with two heuristics: Gillett & Miller and Hill Climbing. The first one is used to generate solutions that are included in the initial population of GA, starting it with some feasible solutions while the second is responsible for making a refinement of the solutions generated by the GA, after a certain number of generations without improvement. It is worth mentioning that among the works available in the literature, we did not find approaches using the constructive and refinement heuristics considered in this work combined with GA for solving CVPR.

The performed experiments showed that the proposed strategy presented good results for CVRP solution, confirming that the use of the employed heuristics helps the GA to converge on promising points in the search space with a smaller number of generations.

2   Theoretical Background

2.1   Capacitated Vehicle Routing Problem

The CVRP is the classic version of VRP in which all customers have their demands previously defined and that must be attended entirely by a only vehicle, the fleet is homogeneous, in other words, all vehicles are similar and run from only distribution center. In this problem, just the vehicle capacity restriction is imposed [6]. This restriction determines that the sum of the demand of all customers of a route does not exceed the capacity of vehicle used to execute that route.

Let $G = (V, A)$ be a graph in which $V = 0.....,n$ is the set of vertices that represent the customers and A the set of edges, representing the connections among the customers and the distribution center.

Each edge (v_i, v_j) is associated with a cost, C_{ij}, representing the cost of the connection between the vertices i and j. When $C_{ij} = C_{ji}$, the problem is recognized as symmetrical, otherwise the problem is identified as asymmetrical. A set of K identical vehicles with capacity cv is allocated to the distribution center. For each customer vi a demand di is associated, and for the distribution center is defined $d_0 = 0$.

In summary, the CVRP consists of finding a set of routes, where each route is traveled by a vehicle, with the objective of minimizing the total cost of the routes (tc), respecting the following restrictions: (i) Each route must start and finish at the distribution center; (ii) Each customer must be visited just only time and (iii) The sum of the customers' demands included in a route can not exceed the vehicle's capacity. The mathematical formulation of CVRP, adapted from Vieira [11], is expressed as follows:

Minimize

$$tc = \sum_{i=0}^{nc} \sum_{\substack{j=0 \\ j \neq i}}^{nc} \sum_{k=1}^{K} c_{ij} x_{ijk} \tag{1}$$

Subject to

$$\sum_{k=1}^{K} \sum_{j=1}^{nc} x_{0jk} \leq K \tag{2}$$

$$\sum_{j=1}^{nc} x_{0jk} = \sum_{j=1}^{nc} x_{j0k} = 1, \quad k = 1, ..., K \tag{3}$$

$$\sum_{k=1}^{K} \sum_{j=0}^{nc} x_{ijk} = 1, \quad i = 1, ..., nc \tag{4}$$

$$\sum_{j=0}^{nc} x_{ijk} - \sum_{j=0}^{nc} x_{ijk} = 0, \quad k = 1, ..., K \quad i = 1, ..., nc \tag{5}$$

$$\sum_{k=1}^{K} \sum_{i \in S} \sum_{j \in S} x_{ijk} \leq |S| - v(S), \quad \forall S \subseteq V \setminus \{0\}, \quad |S| \geq 2 \tag{6}$$

$$\sum_{i=1}^{nc} d_i \sum_{\substack{j=0 \\ j \neq i}}^{nc} x_{ijk} \leq cv, \quad k = 1, ..., K \tag{7}$$

$$x_{ijk} \in \{0, 1\}, \quad i = 1, ..., nc, \quad j = 1, ..., nc, \quad k = 1, ..., K \tag{8}$$

where: d_i: demand of customer i; k: vehicle; K: set of vehicles; S: Set of customers; nc: number of customers; v(S): Minimum number of vehicles to attend S; cv: Capacity of vehicles; c_{ij}: cost of the connection from vertex i to vertex j; tc: is the total cost of routes (Eq. 1); x_{ijk}: connection from the vertex i to vertex j with vehicle k;

Equation 2 ensures that K vehicles will be used starting from the distribution center, while the Eq. 3 guarantees that each route has its beginning and ending at the distribution center. Equation 4 defines that customers must be attended exactly one time and the Eq. 5 keeps the flow ensuring that the vehicle arrives at a customer and out of it, preventing that a route ends prematurely. The Eq. 6 prevents the formulation of routes which do not include the distribution center. In this restriction, v(S) represents the minimum number of vehicles required to attend a set of customers S.

To ensure that the number of vehicles used to attend the set customers of S is not less than v(S), the restriction 6 establishes, indirectly, that the capacity of the vehicle is not exceeded. However to let explicit, the Eq. 7 is used to formulate the capacity restriction. The Eq. 8 is related to the dimensions and allowed values of matrix x. The Eq. 9 is used to evaluate the solutions generated by the proposed strategy. It reflects the value of the objective function (OF) or fitness and involves the number of vehicles used in the solution, the violated restrictions (Eqs. 2 to 7) and the total cost of routes.

$$OF = fitness = (K * W_v) + (nr * W_r) + tc \qquad (9)$$

where: W_v is the weight assigned to the number of vehicles used in the solution; nr is the Number of violated restrictions and W_r is the weight given to the violated restrictions.

2.2 Heuristics and Metaheuristic Techniques Employed by Proposed Approach

Genetic Algorithms (GA) are probabilistic search methods that are based on the evolutionary process, in other words, based on the theory of species evolution proposed by Charles Darwin [10]. GA present the following operational steps: starts a population containing a predefined number of individuals, in which each individual represents a possible solution. For each individual is attributed a value of aptitude or fitness, in our case represented by Eq. 9, which indicates how good is the individual in relation to the population. Thereby, individuals are selected based on their aptitudes and pass their characteristics to the next generation. To this end, it is applied the crossover and mutation methods between individuals, aiming the development of a new generation with fittest individuals (best solutions). This iterative process is repeated until the stopping criterion is reached [9].

The algorithm of Gillett & Miller [5] is based on the notion of economies and is part of the group of two stages heuristics (or constructive heuristics). The strategy consists in dividing the problem in two steps to solve it. In the first step, the vertices (points of demands) are grouped according to some criterion of proximity. Then, the routes are obtained by solution of CVRP for each of the formed groups of vertices [12].

The Hill Climbing algorithm is a local search technique based on depth [13]. It adjusts the position of a candidate solution (state) only if the new position (neighbor) is better than the current state. In other words, the optimization of this algorithm occurs by evaluating neighboring solutions of current state, based on their objective function values. At each step, the solution generated by the current state is replaced by the solution represented by the best neighbor and the algorithm terminates when it reaches a peak (or a valley when it is trying to minimize a fitness function), that is, when it did not find better solution in the neighborhood [14]. Due to the characteristics of this algorithm, it has been used for refining of solutions generated by metaheuristics, in solving several problems. In additon, when this algorithm is applied in a minimization problem, as CVPR addressed in this work, it is also referred as "downhill".

3   Methodology

For development of proposed strategy, the programming language C/C++ and GAlib library[1] were used. The GAlib is a free library widely used in solving combinatorial optimization problems. To evaluate the strategy, experiments were performed and the results obtained were compared with the best results found in the literature, for the sets of instances from Christofides [15] and TSPLIB[2] with up to 30 customers. In the experiments, the following hardware configurations were used: Intel Celeron 2955U, 1.40 GHz processor; 4 GB of RAM; operating system Windows 7 Ultimate 32-bits.

4   Proposed Strategy for CVRP Optimization

In the proposed strategy (illustrated in Fig. 1), it was decided to represent the chromosome by a binary matrix with dimensions nc x nc x K, in which rows represent the number of customers to be visited, columns represent the order that customers will be visited and K, the number of vehicles (fleet). A chromosome is a solution contemplating customers information which will be attended by some vehicle, including customer visiting order. This representation facilitates the control of the restrictions imposed on the problem an also the execution of GA operations such as crossover and mutation.

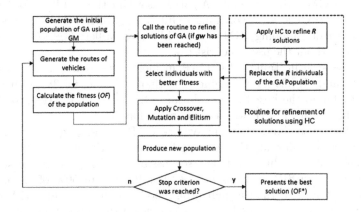

Fig. 1. Sequence of operations employed by the proposed strategy.

In the refinement process by HC algorithm, the neighborhood of a current state (solution) is generated by shifting the elements of chromosome's matrix in a circular manner along the two dimensions indicated by nc (rows/columns), considering four directions (up, down, left and right). The parameters used by GA were defined (empirically) as follows: Chromosome encoding = Binary Matrix;

---

[1] http://lancet.mit.edu/ga/dist/galibdoc.pdf.

[2] http://comopt.ifi.uni-heidelberg.de/software/TSPLIB95/vrp/.

Population Size = 1200; Population subset for refinement (R) = 1/3 of population; Number of generations without improvement (gw) = 30; Number of Generations (used as stop criterion) = 5000; Population rate of replacement = 80%; Elitism = 20%; Crossover = 80%; Selection Method = Roulette; Rate of Mutation = 1%; Type of Mutation = Flip Bit.

5   Results and Discussion

In the evaluation of the proposed strategy, we performed ten tests for each of 16 considered instances and the results obtained were compared with the best solutions in the literature. For instances of Christofides [15], the optimal solutions presented by Reinelt and Wenger [16] were considered and for TSPLIB instances, the optimal solutions indicated by Ralphs et al. [17] were adopted.

To evaluate the goodness of the solutions obtained, a measure known in the literature as GAP was used. In our case, GAP = (OF_Med - OF_Best) OF_Best, being OF_Med the average of the objective function (OF) values obtained in the 10 tests (using Eq. 9) and OF_best the OF value of the best solution found in the literature. In addition, the standard deviation of OF values (OF_σ), the execution time and the best solution (OF*) obtained by our strategy, for each instance, are presented in Table 1. Nevertheless, we present in Table 2 the results of proposed strategy evaluation, with and without the use of heuristics Gillett & Miller and Hill Climbing were performed in a combined way, as follows: GA + GM + HC = Genetic Algorithms + Gillett & Miller + Hill Climbing; GA + GM = Genetic Algorithms + Gillett & Miller; GA + HC = Genetic Algorithms + Hill Climbing; GM = only Gillett & Miller; GA = Only Genetic Algorithms (without the use of heuristics).

As can be seen in Table 1, the GAP in most cases (exception of instances "E-n13-k4", and "E-n23-k3") remained less than 10% and, for 38% of instances, the strategy found the best known solution (OF_Best). In addition, for 69% of instances the obtained GAP was less or equal than 5%.

The Table 1 also shows that the average GAP considering the 16 instances did not exceed 5%, showing the good performance of the strategy with respect to the quality of the solutions. It is also possible to observe that the standard deviation (OF_σ) in 81% of cases is less than 10 and, in 50% of the cases, it was obtained OF_σ less than 5, indicating good stability strategy with respect to the exploitation of the search space. Concerning the computational cost, the processing time ranges from 80 seconds to smaller instance (Eil7) to 250 seconds for larger instances (Eil30 and E-n30-k3). Thus, this strategy showed the relatively low computational cost. However, this processing time could be improved minimizing the sparsity of chromosome representation.

Table 2 shows a comparison of the results obtained by the proposed strategy with and without the application of considered heuristics (GM and HC). Note that, in general, the results are better when these heuristics are embedded in GA. These results suggest that the use of heuristics Gillett & Miller and Hill Climbing helps the GA to converge for promising points in the search space, creating solutions with good quality.

Table 1. Results of experiments with the proposed strategy.

Source	Instance	nc	K	OF_Best	Proposed strategy				
					OF*	OF_Med	GAP %	OF_σ	Time (s)
TSPLIB	Eil7	7	2	114	114	114	0	0	80
	Eil13	13	4	290	290	290	0	0	140
	Eil22	22	4	375	377	385	3	6	210
	Eil23	23	5	875	902	902	3	36	220
	Eil30	30	3	545	545	548	1	6	250
Christofides	P-n16-k8	16	8	450	450	464	3	8	150
	P-n19-k2	19	2	212	215	224	6	7	160
	P-n20-k2	20	2	216	220	226	5	2	190
	P-n21-k2	21	2	211	216	223	6	6	200
	P-n22-k2	22	2	216	220	235	9	11	210
	P-n22-k8	22	8	590	590	590	0	0	210
	P-n23-k8	23	8	529	529	544	3	3	220
	E-n13-k4	13	4	247	290	290	17	0	140
	E-n22-k4	22	4	375	387	390	4	4	200
	E-n23-k3	23	3	569	625	649	14	22	220
	E-n30-k3	30	3	534	545	549	3	4	250

Table 2. Results of the experimental strategy with and without the application of heuristics.

Source	Instance	OF_Best	GM	GA	GA + GM	GA + HC	GA + GM + HC
TSPLIB	Eil7	114	114	114	114	114	114
	Eil13	290	332	332	332	332	290
	Eil22	375	573	595	420	397	377
	Eil23	875	1039	1023	1003	984	902
	Eil30	545	795	979	548	617	545
Christofides	P-n16-k8	450	474	520	464	450	450
	P-n19-k2	212	296	284	224	222	215
	P-n20-k2	216	273	270	226	220	220
	P-n21-k2	211	271	229	223	223	216
	P-n22-k2	216	271	338	235	234	220
	P-n22-k8	590	635	722	614	610	590
	P-n23-k8	529	553	675	544	534	529
	E-n13-k4	247	332	315	312	290	290
	E-n22-k4	375	522	430	390	390	387
	E-n23-k3	569	762	828	673	655	625
	E-n30-k3	534	792	850	587	545	545
Average GAP			26,60%	31,60%	8,40%	6,80%	2,70%

6 Conclusions and Outlook

In this work, a hybrid strategy for solving the Capacitated Vehicle Routing Problem (CVRP) using Genetic Algorithms (GA) combined with the heuristics of Gillett & Miller (GM) and Hill Climbing (HC) was presented. From the computational experiments, it was possible to conclude that the proposed strategy achieved good results with re-spect to quality of solutions with low computational cost, considering the instances extracted from Christofides and TSPLIB libraries. The experiments also demonstrate that the use of heuristics Gillett & Miller and Hill Climbing helped the GA to converge on promising points in the search space with a smaller number of generations.

Acknowledgments. The authors would like to thank UNINOVE by financial support.

References

1. Kunnathur, A.S., Sundararaghavan, P., Sampath, S.: Dynamic rescheduling using a simulation-based expert system. J. Manufact. Technol. Manag. **15**(2), 199–212 (2004)
2. Heinonen, J., Pettersson, F.: Hybrid ant colony optimization and visibility studies applied to a job-shop scheduling problem. Appl. Math. Comput. **187**(2), 989–998 (2007)
3. Cordeau, J.F., Laporte, G., Potvin, J.Y., Savelsbergh, M.W.: Chapter 7 transportation on demand. In: Barnhart, C., Laporte, G. (eds.) Transportation, Handbooks in Operations Research and Management Science, vol. 14, pp. 429–466. Elsevier, Amsterdam (2007)
4. Xu, H., Chen, Z.L., Rajagopal, S., Arunapuram, S.: Solving a practical pickup and delivery problem. Transp. Sci. **37**(3), 347–364 (2003)
5. Gillett, B.E., Miller, L.R.: A heuristic algorithm for the vehicle-dispatch problem. Oper. Res. **22**(2), 340–349 (1974)
6. Laporte, G.: The vehicle routing problem: an overview of exact and approximate algorithms. Eur. J. Oper. Res. **59**(3), 345–358 (1992)
7. Laporte, G., Gendreau, M., Potvin, J.Y., Semet, F.: Classical and modern heuristics for the vehicle routing problem. Int. Trans. Oper. Res. **7**(4–5), 285–300 (2000)
8. Cordeau, J.F., Laporte, G.: Tabu Search Heuristics for the Vehicle Routing Problem. Technical report (2002)
9. Holland, J., Goldberg, D.: Genetic Algorithms in Search, Optimization and Machine Learning. Addison-Wesley, Reading (1989)
10. Bjarnadóttir, Á.S.: Solving the vehicle routing problem with genetic algorithms. Ph.D. thesis, Technical University of Denmark, DTU, DK-2800 Kgs. Lyngby, Denmark (2004)
11. Vieira, H.P.: Metaheurística para a Solução de Problemas de Roteamento de Veículos com Janela de Tempo. Ph.D. thesis, Instituto de Matemática, Estatística e Computação Científica, Universidade Estadual de Campinas (2008)
12. Goldbarg, M.C., Luna, H.P.L.: Otimização Combinatória e Programação Linear: Modelos e Algoritmos, vol. 2. Elsevier, Amsterdam (2005)

13. Engelbrecht, A.P.: Fundamentals of Computational Swarm Intelligence. Wiley, Hoboken (2006)
14. Russell, S., Norvig, P., Intelligence, A.: A Modern Approach: Artificial Intelligence. Prentice-Hall, Egnlewood Cliffs (1995)
15. Christofides, N.: Vehicle Routing. A Guided Tour of Combinatorial Optimization. Wiley, New York (1985)
16. Reinelt, G., Wenger, K.M.: Maximally violated mod-p cuts for the capacitated vehicle-routing problem. INFORMS J. Comput. **18**(4), 466–479 (2006)
17. Ralphs, T., Pulleyblank, W., Trotter Jr., L.: On capacitated vehicle routing. In: Problem, Mathematical Programming (1998)

Container Crane Controller with the Use of a NeuroFuzzy Network

Ricardo Pinto Ferreira[1], Andréa Martiniano[1(✉)], Arthur Ferreira[2],
Marcio Romero[1], and Renato Jose Sassi[1]

[1] Universidade Nove de Julho, UNINOVE, São Paulo, Brazil
andreia.martiniano@gmail.com
[2] Universidade de São Paulo, USP, São Paulo, Brazil

Abstract. A container crane has the function of transporting containers from one point to another point. The difficulty of this task lies in the fact that the container is connected to the bridge crane by cables, causing an opening angle while the container is being transported, interfering with the operation at high speeds due to oscillation that occurs at the end point, which could cause accidents. Fuzzy logic (FL) is a mathematical theory that aims to allow the modeling of approximate way of thinking, imitating the human ability to make decisions in uncertain and imprecise environments. The Artificial Neural Networks (ANN) models are made of simple processing units, called artificial neurons, which calculate mathematical functions. The aim of the paper was to present a container crane controller pre-project using an artificial neural network type Multilayer Perceptron (MLP) combined with FL, referred to as Neuro Fuzzy Network (NFN).

Keywords: Container crane · Artificial neural network · Fuzzy logic · Neuro Fuzzy Network

1 Introduction

The container crane is widely used to transfer heavy loads in ports and shipyards. This transfer is desirable that the container crane transport the loads to the desired position as quickly and as accurately as possible without colliding with any other equipment. This rapid movement naturally induces undesirable balance of the container, which could cause damage to the load and other types of hazards, also reducing the performance of the operation. Therefore, these oscillations in the track must be damped before another container come into operation. Thus, the performance transshipment loses the desired efficiency, increasing the cost involved in the operation and the risk of accidents with heavy loads that are transferred continuously throughout the operation.

Fuzzy Logic (FL) was developed in 1965 with the work of [1] to represent the uncertain, imprecise and vague knowledge. FL translates the ambiguous information, imprecise, uncertain, in numeric values and includes the human experience in intelligent systems, processed by computer, and versatile for solving real problems [2]. The use of FL has been growing in several areas of knowledge, as in the control of electromechanical systems, character recognition, robotics, elevator systems, landing aircraft, etc.

I. Nääs et al. (Eds.): APMS 2016, IFIP AICT 488, pp. 122–129, 2016.
DOI: 10.1007/978-3-319-51133-7_15

The growth in the use of FL is due to its great simplicity of implementation, and require little tired in its modeling, which provides both for the manufacturer, which reduces their costs, and the final consumer who acquires a more efficient product [3].

Artificial Neural Networks (ANNs) are a from the Artificial Intelligence technique based on simulation of the functioning of the brain by computer data structures, the great motivation of the use of this technique in performing tasks that require fault tolerance, flexibility, imprecision and parallelism [4]. The NeuroFuzzy Network (NFN) ANNs are applied in various fields such as modeling, time series analysis, pattern recognition, signal processing, control, image recognition and data mining [4–10]. The NFN is the combination of FL and ANNs, some techniques may be combined to generate the so-called hybrid systems, or hybrid architectures. The advantage of this type of system must be obtained by cooperation combination of techniques [11]. NFN is an alternative to the development of new studies seeking the possible applications in engineering problems. Several studies have been published to control the cranes containers, describing some recent work related to this study that bring interest [3, 12–17]. Cranes controller using fuzzy clustering techniques [18], parallel neural network for crane control [19], adaptive control crane [20]. The aim of the paper was to present a container crane controller pre-project using a NFN.

2   Theoretical Bases

2.1   Container Crane

Figure 1 illustrates a crane container with its basic elements: the cart, (responsible for the displacement), the opening angle (θ), the load (container), cable (support), the track and the direction of the force gravity.

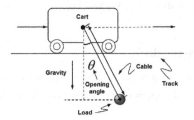

Fig. 1. Container crane (Source: Adapted from [17, 21, 22])

2.2   Fuzzy Logic

FL is a mathematical theory, which aims to model human reasoning, mimicking the human ability to make decisions in uncertain and imprecise environments, expressed by a set of linguistic variables [2, 9]. It uses the concept of FL as the mathematical tools in fuzzy sets [23]. In this case, we used the nomenclature of fuzzy sets defining them as a class of continuous variables objects. Those sets are characterized by membership functions, which indicate for each element a degree of relevance 0–1 [24]. For a wide range of physical phenomena it is difficult to clearly establish whether an element belongs or not a particular set. Thus, [1] proposed a broader characterization, such that membership function may assume continuous values between 0 (zero) and 1 (one). The concepts of intersection, union, complement, convexity, etc., are extended to those sets and various properties of these notions in the context of fuzzy sets are established in the work of [1]. The membership functions have various forms, depending on the concept you want to express and can be set from the user's needs, but it is common to use standard membership functions, such as: triangular function, trapezoidal and Gaussian, or even, through analytics.

The central question for consistency to model a system by FL is the determination of a rule base representing the satisfaction of its dynamics, that is, as the input variables are related to each other, what there are outputs and, from that, their corresponding associated errors are determined. Therefore, the accuracy of the model is directly proportional to the adhesion between the real dynamics of the system and the basic proposal rules to represent it [1]. Related systems some features where the application of FL is necessary or beneficial. Such complex systems are difficult to model, as an example we can mention: systems controlled by human experts, systems with inputs and complex and continuous outputs, systems which use the human observation, as starters or as the basis for rules, systems that are naturally inaccurate as the description systems is extremely complex [25]. The application of FL for predicting or monitoring for a given system is characterized by use of an inference engine. This feature makes it necessary that the events displayed in the entry must necessarily be classified in one of these rules [26]. The establishment of the inference engine that simulates a system involves two stages: the premises of all the rules are compared to the controlled inputs to determine which rules apply in a given situation, then the conclusions are established using the rules which have been determined. To represent the inference mechanisms in fuzzy sets, we used the concept of fuzzy relationship, which generalizes the concept of present relations in the Classic Set Theory and represent the degree of association between elements of two or more fuzzy sets [26].

2.3   Artificial Neural Networks

The ANNs are models inspired in brain structure aiming to simulate human behavior in processes such as learning, adaptation, association, fault tolerance, generalization and abstraction [4, 7, 26].

In the ANNs learning occurs through a set of simple processing units called artificial neurons. In Fig. 2 is shown a representation of the artificial neuron. the data is observed (data vectors) neuron input $(X_1,..., X_n)$, the neurons of the input layer $(W_{1J}..., W_{nj})$ with their respective weights, then immediately the additive junction or sum represented by the letter sigma, then the activation function (φ) and finally the output (y).

In a conventional computer system, if a failure part, in general the system as a whole deteriorates, while in an ANN, the fault tolerance is a part of architecture, due to its distributed nature processing. If a neuron fails, your erroneous output is overwritten by the correct output of its neighboring elements. So, at first, an ANN exhibits a soft performance degradation instead of presenting a catastrophic failure [4]. One of the first

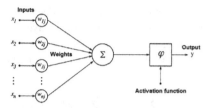

Fig. 2. Representation of the artificial neuron (Source: Adapted from [4])

ANNs, whose architecture is based on the biological neuron, has been proposed by [28] the Perceptron. The purpose of this network is to classify the inputs xi (or stimulus) into two classes by a hyperplane. For the simple case of a space in two dimensions, the hyperplane is reduced to a straight line whose equation is represented in Eq. 1.

$$\sum x_i w_i + w_0 \tag{1}$$

The activation is performed through artificial neuron activation function, which performs similar to the biological neuron synapse task, transmitting or blocking nerve impulses. In general, learning Perceptron networks is through the adjustment of synaptic weights. The value of the synaptic weight W (t + 1) at the instant t + 1, its will be determined on the basis of its value in the previous iteration wt, as in Eq. 2.

$$w_i^{t+1} = w_i^t + \Delta w_i^t \tag{2}$$

The updating of the weights depends on the algorithm, but generally is based on minimizing the error αi, between the values proposed by the network and outputs yi desired, as Eq. 3.

$$\varepsilon_i = \sum w_i x_i - y_i \tag{3}$$

Thus, the learning (or training) on an ANN is defined as the iterative adjustment of synaptic weights to minimize errors [4]. A general definition of what constitutes learning in an ANN can be expressed as a learning process by which the parameters are adjusted through a continued form in which the network is operating by particular way to the setting of the parameters occur. Several methods for learning have been developed and can be grouped into two main paradigms: supervised learning and unsupervised learning. In supervised learning, there is a prior knowledge of the values of xi yi inputs and their outputs. In this set of ordered pairs (x_i, y_i), that is known a priori gives the learning database name. The most widely used algorithm is the retro error propagation (error back-propagation) used by the MLP type ANN used in this work.

A Multilayer Perceptrons is one of the most used ANN in classification. The ANN architecture MLP typically consist of a specification of the number of layers, type of activation function of each unit and weights of connections between the different units should be established for the construction of the neural architecture [4].

The error back-propagation training algorithm works as follows: shows a pattern in input layer of the network, this pattern is processed, layer by layer, until the output provides the processed response, fMLP, calculated as shown below in Eq. 4. where vl and wlj are synaptic weights; bl0 and b0 are biases; and φ the activation function.

$$f_{MLP}(x) = \phi\left(\sum_{1}^{Non} v_l \cdot \phi\left(\sum w_{lj}x_l + b_{l0}\right) + b_0\right) \tag{4}$$

Learning an ANN, in most cases, it happens to a subset of examples (data vectors) which define the so-called training set and ANN testing is performed with another subset of examples (data vectors) which define the so-called test set.

The ANNs can be trained using random initial values for the weights of connections. The learning parameters are initialized and data vectors training patterns are presented to the ANN. Throughout the training progress the connections weights are adjusted and you can monitor the performance of ANN [4].

2.4   Neuro Fuzzy Network

Some techniques can be combined to generate the so-called hybrid or hybrid architectures systems [9]. The advantage of this type of system is due to the synergy obtained by combining two or more techniques. This synergism reflects in getting a more powerful system (in terms of interpretation, learning, estimation parameters, training, among others) and with fewer disabilities [2, 11]. The purpose of this combination is to get good ability to learn and adapt to the needs to solve real-world problems, ideal for applications such as identification, prediction, classification and control [2, 26]. NFN is the term used [28] for approaches that have the following properties: (i) Items are based on FL and are trained by a learning algorithm derived from one of ANNs. The learning procedure (heuristic) operates in local information, and causes only local changes in the foundation of NFN; (ii) Have three layers where the first layer is the input variables, the middle layer (hidden) represents the inference rules and the third layer is the output variables; (iii) Can always be interpreted as an inference engine. Since not all learning templates specify procedures for creation of fuzzy rules; (iv) The learning procedure of NFN transforms the semantic properties of a fuzzy system into a set of descriptions. This results in restrictions that may become relevant changes to system parameters, however, not all approaches in a NFN possess this property; (v) Near an n-dimensional function that is defined in part by training data.

3   Materials and Methods

An ANN Multilayer Perceptron (MLP) combined with FL forming a NFN was adopted. The MATLAB software was used to generate the 15 fuzzy rules, the inference model and the response surface. The hardware platform used in the experiments was a computer with Intel® Core ™ 2 Duo CPU T6600 2.20 GHz with 4.00 GB of memory,

1 TB hard drive. To model the fuzzy membership functions of the speed of moving container bridge we used three Gaussian functions: low, medium and high. To model the fuzzy membership functions with the angle of the crane container were used five Gaussian functions: large negative angle, small negative angle, angle zero, small positive angle and large positive angle. The tractive power was modeled in three functions of Gaussian relevance: low, medium and high [1].

The parameters used in ANN were: number of input neurons equal to 2 (the fuzzy inference to: speed and angle), the number of layers equal to 2, the number of neurons in the hidden layer equal to 10, the initial rate of learning equal to 0, 3 with decay 1% every 20 times, starting time factor of 0.3 to decay 1% every 25 times, stopping criterion was the maximum number of times equal to 150. the ANN training was sequential (online), and the processing time was 5 s. The output of the NFN was the tractive power. Figure 3 shows the hybrid topology of NFN used in the experiment.

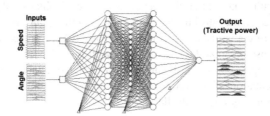

Fig. 3. Hybrid topology NeuroFuzzy used in the experiment.

4 Results of Computational Experiments

Figure 4(a) shows the fuzzy membership functions generated by the 15 rules (Speed, Angle and power), and Fig. 4(b) gives the response surface. Figure 5 shows the validation phase of NFN.

The results presented in the validation phase of NFN was satisfactory for the proposed model.

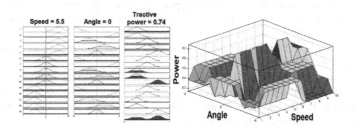

Fig. 4. (a) Fuzzy pertinence functions. (b) Response surface area modeled by the 15 fuzzy rules

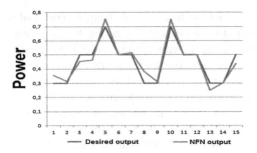

Fig. 5. Validation phase NFN

5 Conclusions

With the initial result is noted that the response surface 15 obtained through the fuzzy rules, allows pre-design a control mechanism, including the inputs and outputs required development system container crane controller. The NFN presented adherent experimental results the use of fuzzy logic associated with the ANN produced an inference engine capable of representing the dynamics of a crane container. The results recommend the implementation of the proposed NFN control. It contributes to the formulation of simple programming controllers.

References

1. Zadeh, L.A.: Fuzzy sets. Inf. Control **8**, 338–353 (1965)
2. Pacheco, M.A.C., Vellasco, M.M.B.R.: Sistemas Inteligentes de Apoio à Decisão: Análise Econômica de Projetos de Desenvolvimento de Campos de Petróleo Sob Incerteza. Interciência, Rio de Janeiro (2007)
3. Costa, H.C.: Aplicação de Técnicas de Modelagem e Controle em Sistemas Tipo Ponte Rolante. Dissertação de Mestrado, Instituto Militar de Engenharia, Rio de Janeiro (2010)
4. Haykin, S.: Redes Neurais – Princípios e Práticas. Bookman, Porto Alegre (2001)
5. Bigus, J.P.: Data Mining with Neural Network: Solving Business Problems from Applications Development to Decision Support. McGraw-Hill, New York (1996)
6. Maass, W., Bishop, C.M.: Pulsed Neural Networks. First MIT Press Paperback Edition, Cambridge (2001)
7. Silva, I.N., Spatti, D.H., Flauzino, R.A.: Redes Neurais Artificiais para Engenharia e Ciências Aplicadas. Artliber, São Paulo (2010)
8. Braga, A.P., Carvalho, A.C.P.L.F., Ludermir, T.B.: Redes Neurais Artificiais: Teoria e Aplicações. LTC, Rio de Janeiro (2011)
9. Goldschmidt, R., Passos, E., Bezerra, E.: Data Mining: Conceitos, Técnicas, Algoritmos, Orientações e Aplicações. Elsevier, Rio de Janeiro (2015)
10. Ferreira, R.P., Martiniano, A., Ferreira, A., Ferreira, A., Sassi, R.J.: Study on daily demand forecasting orders using artificial neural network. IEEE Latin Am. Trans. **14**(3), 1519–1525 (2016)
11. Sassi, R.J.: An hybrid architecture for clusters analysis: rough setstheory and self-organizing map artificial neural network. Pesqui. Oper. **32**(1), 139–164 (2012)

12. Mohammed, T., Hayajneh, S.M., Radaideh, I., Smadi, A.: Fuzzy logic controller for overhead cranes. Eng. Comput. **23**(1), 84–98 (2006)
13. Chang, C.Y.: Adaptive fuzzy controller of the overhead crane with nonlinear disturbances. IEEE Trans. Industr. Inf. **3**(2), 164–172 (2007)
14. Yu, W., Moreno-Armendariz, M.A., Rodriguez, F.O.: Stable adaptive compensation with fuzzy CMAC for an overhead crane. Inf. Sci. **181**, 4895–4907 (2011)
15. Zhao, Y., Gao, H.J.: Fuzzy-model-based control of an overhead crane with input delay and actuator saturation. IEEE Trans. Fuzzy Syst. **20**, 181–186 (2012)
16. Smoczek, J., Szpytko, J.: Evolutionary algorithm-based design of a fuzzy TBF predictive model and TSK fuzzy anti-sway crane control system. J. Eng. Appl. Artif. Intell. **28**, 190–200 (2014)
17. Qian, D., Tong, S., Lee, S.: Fuzzy-logic-based control of payloads subjected to double-pendulum motion in overhead cranes. J. Autom. Constr. **65**, 133–143 (2016)
18. Sadati, N., Hooshmand, A.: Design of again-scheduling anti-sway controller or tower cranes using fuzzy clustering techniques. In: Proceedings of the International Conference on Computational Intelligence for Modeling, Control and Automation, Sydney, Australia (2006)
19. Lee, L.H., Huang, P.H., Shih, Y.C., Chiang, T., Chang, C.: Parallel neural network combined with sliding mode control in overhead crane control system. J. Vib. Control **120**(5), 749–760 (2014)
20. Nguyen, Q.C., Ngo, H.Q.T., klin, W.H.: Nonlinear adaptive control of a 3D overhead crane. In: 15th International Conference on Control, Automation and Systems (ICCAS), Busan, Korea, pp. 41–47 (2015)
21. Smoczek, J.: Fuzzy crane control with sensor less payload deflection feedback for vibration reduction. J. Mech. Syst. Signal Process. **46**, 70–81 (2014)
22. Peng-Cheng, W., Yong-Chun, F., Zi-Ya, J.: A direct swing constraint-based trajectory planning method for underactuated overhead cranes. Acta Automatica Sinica **40**(11), 2414–2419 (2014)
23. Passino, K.M., Yurkovich, S.: Fuzzy Control. Addison Wesley Longman, Inc., Boston (1998)
24. Nicoletti, M.C., Camargo, H.A.: Fundamentos da Teoria de Conjuntos Fuzzy. Edusfscar, São Carlos (2004)
25. McNeill, F.M., Thro, E.: Fuzzy Logic: A Practical Approach. AP Professional/Academic Press, Boston (1994)
26. Simões, M.G., Shaw, I.S.: Controle E Modelagem Fuzzy. Blucher, São Paulo (2007)
27. Rosenblatt, M.: The perceptron: a probabilistic model for information storage and organization in the brain. Psychol. Rev. **65**(6), 386–408 (1958)
28. Mendel, J.M., Mclaren, R.W.: Reinforcement-learning control and pattern recognition systems. In: Adaptive, Learning and Pattern Recognition Systems, Cap. 8, pp. 287–318. Academic Press, New York e London (1970)

Agility Challenges in Finnish Manufacturing Companies – Manufacturing Operations Management Viewpoint

Eeva Järvenpää[✉], Minna Lanz, and Eemeli Lammervo

Department of Mechanical Engineering and Industrial Systems,
Tampere University of Technology, Tampere, Finland
{eeva.jarvenpaa,minna.lanz,eemeli.lammervo}@tut.fi

Abstract. This paper presents an analysis of the manufacturing operations management related challenges which hinder agility in Finnish manufacturing companies. Critical challenges were identified by performing cause-effect analysis between different challenges identified from the interview material collected from 25 manufacturing companies. The main output is a relationships graph which visualizes interconnections between 49 agility related challenges. The graph supports the identification and prioritization of the actions to be taken while seeking for better agility.

Keywords: Agile manufacturing · Manufacturing operations management · Agility challenges · Manufacturing IT systems

1 Introduction

Today's production environment is characterised by frequent changes in terms of high product variation, small batch sizes, high demand fluctuation as well as random unexpected disturbances on the factory floor. In order to prosper, the manufacturing companies and their production systems and networks need to rapidly adapt to these changing requirements. Thus, rapid responsiveness and agility has become a new strategic goal for manufacturing enterprises alongside with quality and costs [1]. Literature offers numerous definitions for agility. For instance Stamatis [2] defines agility as the *ability to thrive in a competitive environment of continuous and unanticipated change and to respond quickly to rapidly changing market driven by customer-specified products and services*. Christopher [3], on the other hand defines agility as the *ability of an organization to rapidly respond to changes in demand, both in terms of volume and variety*.

The objective of this paper is to analyse the manufacturing operations management (MOM) related challenges which affect negatively to agility in Finnish manufacturing companies. Second goal is to identify actions that could improve the situation. According to the ISA-95 standard [4], *the activities of manufacturing operations management are those activities of a manufacturing facility that coordinate the*

I. Nääs et al. (Eds.): APMS 2016, IFIP AICT 488, pp. 130–137, 2016.
DOI: 10.1007/978-3-319-51133-7_16

personnel, equipment, material and energy in the conversion of raw materials and/or parts into products. The analysis is based on interview study conducted during LeanMES-project among 25 Finnish manufacturing companies [5].

2 Research Method

The research was divided into three sub-objectives and associated methods:

(1) To investigate the enablers of agility by reviewing the existing literature in the field of agile manufacturing.
(2) To identify challenges that hinder agility in Finnish manufacturing companies. This objective was approached by comparing the existing interview material from 25 Finnish manufacturing companies against the identified agility enablers. The interviews were conducted during the fall 2013 and spring 2014 with the original goal to study the current challenges and practices regarding the manufacturing operations management [5].
(3) To find out the most critical challenges hindering agility, based on the interview material, and to propose actions for solving those challenges. This objective was approached by defining interconnections between the challenges with cause-effect analysis and drawing a relationship map. These interconnections were defined in several workshops with the research group.

3 Background – Enablers of Agility

Yusuf et al. [6] identified the core concepts of agile manufacturing as: Core competence management; Virtual enterprise; Capability for re-configuration; and Knowledge-driven enterprise. Gunasekaran [7] presented a framework, which divides different enablers of agile manufacturing under four major categories, namely Strategies, Technologies, Systems and People. Under the strategy he mentioned concurrent engineering, virtual enterprise and rapid partnership formation. As stated by Sanchez and Nagi [8] agile manufacturing requires resources that are beyond the reach of a single company, which means that sharing resources and technologies among companies is necessary. In virtual enterprise the core competencies of carefully chosen real organizations are integrated as temporary alliances are formed.

Under systems category Gunasekaran [7] included design systems and production planning and control systems, while under technologies he listed hardware, i.e. equipment and tools, as well as information technologies (IT). Reconfigurable and modular manufacturing resources enabling rapid changeover are examples of agile-enabled hardware technologies [9]. Fast and easy interchange of information in dynamic manufacturing environment requires IT systems that support and enable quick responds to changes. Gunasekaran [7] stated that IT has a fundamental role in integrating physically distributed manufacturing firms in today's global manufacturing environment. Avoiding human related errors in information exchange is one key issue which can be addressed by increasing the use of IT. Mondragon et al. [10] emphasized the importance of IT systems in supporting manufacturing, and stated that for instance real-time monitoring of manufacturing operations enhances manufacturing agility. According to Kletti [11], faster flow of information between every level in a manufacturing company enable problems and unplanned events to be detected faster, and thus allows rapid reaction. Wiendahl et al. [9] mentioned the adaptive production planning and control as a one important enabler of changeability.

Under the people category Gunasekaran [7] included flexible and motivated workforce, top management support and employee empowerment. An agile workforce should be multi-skilled and flexible, thus having a capability of shifting job functions and carry out other tasks rapidly, when a need occurs. Therefore, agile companies must be committed to continuous workforce training and education. Continuous learning, self-organising and reconfigurable teams are attributes of an agile workforce [12].

Yusuf et al. [6] listed 32 attributes of an agile organization. Those relating tightly to MOM-domain are summarised here: Concurrent execution of activities; Enterprise integration; Information accessible to employees; Empowered individuals working in cross-functional teams; Teams across company borders; Decentralized decision making; Skill and knowledge enhancing technologies; Flexible production technology; Continuous improvement; Rapid partnership formation; Close relationship with suppliers; Multi-skilled and flexible people; Continuous training and development.

4 Analysis of the Agility Challenges

4.1 Identified Challenges and Their Interconnections

The challenges Finnish manufacturing companies face with their current manufacturing operations management practices have been discussed in [5]. For this research, the challenges relating especially to the agility enablers were collected. Altogether 49 challenges affecting agility were identified from the interview material for further analysis [13]. These are shown in the relationship map in Fig. 1. This paper will summarise and further enrich the analysis presented in [13].

In summary, it can be said that in large OEM companies one of the biggest challenges was lack of information transparency between different departments and actors in the network. In supplier side the difficult forecasting and unexpected disturbances, e.g. rush orders or machine breakdowns, were causing the main uncertainties for the manufacturing operations management and thus set requirements for agile reaction. In general the identified challenges hindering agility were very similar in different company types. One of the most visible issue was that most of the companies didn't have proper IT systems for production planning and control, such as MES (Manufacturing Execution System) and APS (Advanced Planning and Scheduling), to support rapid reactions to changes. This issue is strongly reflected in the analysis.

Figure 1 presents the relationships map drawn to illustrate the cause-effect relations between the different agility challenges identified from the interviews. The relationships map is intended to serve two purposes: (1) To identify the most critical challenges, which are causing multiple other challenges; (2) To increase understanding on how different kind of challenges relate to each other in order to be able to identify what may be the reasons behind some challenges.

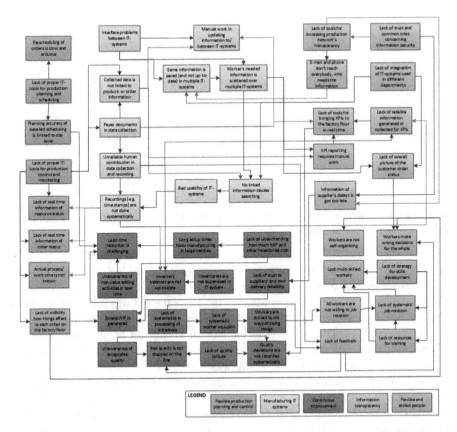

Fig. 1. Relationships map showing the identified interconnections between agility challenges (please see the digital version for colours).

4.2   Analysis of Critical Challenges

As the relationships map indicates, the amount of direct effects originating from an individual challenge is varying from zero to six. The higher the number, the more critical the challenge is assumed to be. However, it has to be mentioned that in some cases it was difficult to identify which is the cause and which is the effect (i.e. chicken-egg problem).

Few challenges having direct effect on six to four other challenges can be identified from the map. Based on this analysis those challenges are considered to be critical challenges hindering agility in Finnish manufacturing companies. In the following figures, these challenges and their effect chains are shown. Two "levels" of effects are included in these graphs. Figure 2 shows the effect chains for two connected challenges, namely "Lack of proper IT tools for production control and monitoring", and "Paper documents in data collection". It has to be noted that this analysis includes only those challenges and causes that came up during the interviews. Thus, there may be

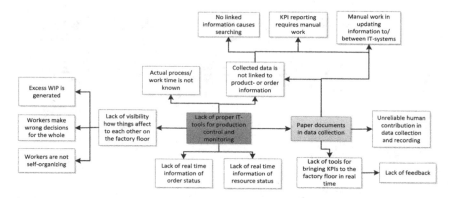

Fig. 2. Effect chains for challenges "Lack of proper IT-tools for production control and monitoring" and "Paper documents in data collection".

several reasons still behind the identified "root causes". E.g. the lack of proper IT tools may be caused by lack of resources – human, money or time – to implement such tools, lack of knowledge or interest, or reluctance to change the old ways of working. Each company may have their own reasons and therefore they are not analysed any further.

The first critical challenge refers to the lack of IT-support for production control and monitoring, i.e. lack of MES-functionality, which was a major challenge in most of the interviewed companies. As Fig. 2 indicates, it causes lack of visibility to the real time situation on the factory floor, e.g. the resource or order status. This hinders the worker's ability to self-organize and make good decisions for the whole. Lack of MES also makes the collection of history data cumbersome, requiring a lot of manual information inputting and updating, e.g. when the information is collected to various spreadsheets or paper documents. This also leads to the fact that the information is not linked to the product and order information in upper level management systems, which again means that information needs to be searched from, maintained and updated in multiple places.

Second critical challenge is the usage of paper documents in data collection. It slows down information flows, causes human errors and affect negatively to information management and transparency. They cause unnecessary manual typing of data to the IT systems. Furthermore, it hinders the real time calculation of Key Performance Indicators (KPIs), not to mention bringing feedback to the production workers through KPIs in real time.

Third critical challenge is "Unreliable human contribution in data collection and recording" (Fig. 3). Although the usage of paper documents has a direct effect to human contribution, this challenge may also exist without the previous. Elimination of paper documents from data collection does not remove the risk that human for instance forgets to make recordings to the IT system. In the same figure, another critical challenge "Recordings (e.g. time stamps) are not done systematically", is also analysed as it is direct effect of unreliable human contribution, and also direct cause for five other challenges. If the workers don't make the recordings systematically, no reliable history information e.g. relating to work phase duration is generated. Same applies to the

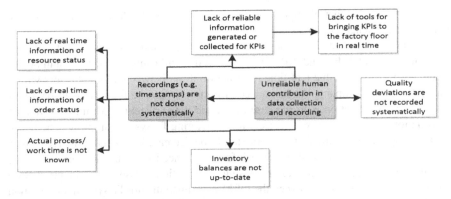

Fig. 3. Effect chains for challenges "Recordings (e.g. time stamps) are not done systematically" and "Unreliable human contribution in data collection and recording".

generation of reliable KPI information. Also, it makes it difficult to keep on track of the resource and order statuses. Faulty inventory balances can also be caused by human, if recordings are not done immediately when material is picked from the storage.

Other important critical challenge recognized from the relationship map was the "interface problems between IT systems". Since the IT systems used for different purposes lack capabilities to communicate with each other, information flow is non-existent. Information is often scattered over multiple IT systems and due to the interoperability issues, updating information in these multiple systems typically requires manual error prone typing. Scattered information causes a problem that the overall "big picture", e.g. of customer order status, is difficult to get. From the worker skills perspective an important challenge "Lack of strategy for skills development" was identified. It causes insufficient allocation of resources for training, lack of systematic job rotation and therefore the companies lack multi-skilled workers. From the continuous improvement perspective, the "Lack of quality culture" was regarded as an issue, since it caused lack of systematic quality reporting and the habit to let the low quality product travel through the whole production line.

4.3   Actions for Improving Agility

The presented relationship map helps to prioritize the actions that need to be taken while seeking for better agility. However, it has to be noted that the presented analysis didn't take into consideration the severity of each challenge, i.e. some of the challenges may be more severe than others, even they would be directly causing fewer other challenges. For example, the challenge *"lack of proper IT tools for production planning and scheduling"*, which refers to lack of APS systems, affects only two other challenges included in the map. However, implementing an APS system would enable faster and easier re-scheduling of orders, and allow increasing the planning accuracy of detailed scheduling, both of which are important factors for agility. This example indicates that the number of interconnections must be considered at some level, but the type of the challenge counts as well.

Based on the collected interview material and the conducted cause-effect analysis, implementation of MES and APS systems could significantly reduce the number of challenges by ensuring that real-time information flows between different actors within a manufacturing company. As human contribution should be minimized in data collection, a relevant action is to increase automatic data collection. Minimizing human contribution is made easier with correct manufacturing IT systems in place. The usage of paper documents on the factory floor should be decreased, especially the recordings should be made digitally and also the information needed by the worker should be presented in a digital form. For increasing information transparency in production network, better integration between the OEM and subcontractor IT system, or common portals would be needed. This would support digital information flow and reduce the need for manual inputting of information to order management systems based on the email and telephone communications.

For solving challenges related to quality issues, three actions are proposed. Firstly, a quality culture should be built throughout the company. It is of high importance that workers are engaged to report about quality problems immediately when they are noticed. Secondly, clear visualized instructions of acceptable quality should be provided to the workers. Thirdly, clear procedures for more systematic quality monitoring procedures should be created. Regarding multi-skilled workers, companies should first make sure that they have a clear strategy for skills development. It would make sure that enough resources are allocated for training and that job rotation is practiced systematically. Multi-skilled workers would contribute towards agility by allowing workers to rapidly change between workstations and tasks when need occurs.

For systematic lead time reduction, value stream analysis is suggested. It helps to identify the non-value adding activities and make them visible to everybody in the organization. Regarding the large inventories, due to the delivery reliability issues, companies may find it difficult to minimise the inventories. Implementing first the actions for solving quality related issues and improving production network's transparency will create certain readiness for companies to operate with smaller inventories. Through faster information flow in production network, delivery reliability can be improved, and less need for excess inventories exists. Furthermore, when quality issues are minimized, not so much buffer is needed to compensate them.

5 Conclusions

This paper focused on analysing the most critical challenges hindering agility in Finnish manufacturing companies from manufacturing operations management perspective, and proposing actions for solving these challenges. Interconnections between the identified challenges were defined with cause-effect analysis and the results were visualized in the relationships map. Cause-effect analysis helped to identify few critical challenges, which were considered as causes for several other challenges. These were: lack of proper manufacturing IT tools; usage of paper documents in data collection;

recordings are not done systematically; unreliable human contribution in data collection; interface problems between IT systems; lack of strategy for skills development.

As a main result, this paper presented a visual map, which can be utilized in identifying and prioritizing development activities while thriving towards higher agility. The relationships map increases the understanding on how problems may be generated and how they are connected to each other. An individual manufacturing company may use the map to find out what could be possible causes for certain challenges they encounter in their operations. However, the relationships map only presents the challenges that emerged during the interviews. Therefore, the map is unable to provide information of all possible challenges or reasons hindering agility among manufacturing companies. Instead, it presents challenges that are mostly related to manufacturing operations management, and highly concentrated to IT aspects.

Acknowledgements. This research was carried out as part of the Finnish Metals and Engineering Competence Cluster (FIMECC)'s MANU program in LeanMES-project.

References

1. Koren, Y., Shpitalni, M.: Design of reconfigurable manufacturing systems. J. Manufact. Syst. **29**(4), 130–141 (2010)
2. Stamatis, D.H.: TQM Engineering Handbook. Marcel Dekker, Inc., New York (1997)
3. Christopher, M.: The agile supply chain competing in volatile market. Ind. Mark. Manag. **29** (1), 37–44 (2000)
4. ANSI/ISA-95.00.03-2005, Enterprise-Control System Integration, Part 3: Models of Manufacturing Operations Management (2005)
5. Järvenpää, E., Lanz, M., Tokola, H., Salonen, T. and Koho, M.: Production planning and control in Finnish manufacturing companies – current state and challenges. In: Proceedings of the FAIM2 015, 23rd–26th June 2015, Wolverhampton, UK (2015)
6. Yusuf, Y.Y., Sarhadi, M., Gunasekaran, A.: Agile manufacturing: the drivers, concepts and attributes. Int. J. Prod. Econ. **62**, 33–43 (1999)
7. Gunasekaran, A.: Agile manufacturing: a framework for research and development. Int. J. Prod. Econ. **62**(1–2), 87–105 (1999)
8. Sanchez, L.M., Nagi, R.: A review of agile manufacturing systems. Int. J. Prod. Res. **39**(16), 3561–3600 (2001)
9. Wiendahl, H.-P., et al.: Changeable manufacturing - classification, design and operation. Ann. CIRP **56**(2), 783–809 (2007)
10. Mondragon, A., Lyons, A., Kehoe, D.: Assessing the value of information systems in supporting agility in high-tech manufacturing enterprises. Int. J. Oper. Prod. Manag. **24**(12), 1219–1246 (2004)
11. Kletti, J. (ed.): Manufacturing Execution Systems – MES, 272 p. Springer, Heidelberg (2007)
12. Jin-Hai, L., Anderson, A., Harrison, R.: The evolution of agile manufacturing. Bus. Process Manag. J. **9**(2), 170–189 (2003)
13. Lammervo, E.: A roadmap towards agility for Finnish manufacturing companies. MSc. thesis, Tampere University of Technology, 47 p. (2015)

Improving Process Management in a Water Treatment Plant Using Control Modelling

Cleber Gustavo Dias[1]([✉]), Fábio Cosme Rodrigues dos Santos[1,2],
André Felipe Henriques Librantz[1], Cristiano Morais de Sousa[1],
and Luiz Carlos da Silva[1]

[1] Nove de Julho University, São Paulo, Brazil
diascg@uni9.pro.br
[2] Companhia de Saneamento Básico do Estado de São Paulo, São Paulo, Brazil

Abstract. This work presents a modelling and a simulation of a pH control for process management in a drinking water treatment plant. A range of historical data, or knowledge base, was used to define the behavior of each input and disturbances of the process, using the MATLAB/Simulink software. The present pH control modelling has been simulated and compared to some experimental tests, thus contributing to achieve and identify operational scenarios in a real water treatment plant. Therefore, the present results allows to predict not only the present scenarios but also new operational conditions, in order to estimate the better process parameters and reduce some costs related to raw materials, such as the lime consumption, in water treatment plants.

Keywords: pH control · Water treatment plant · Modelling and simulation · Industrial process management

1 Introduction

The pH neutralization process, or the control of pH, is a crucial task in wide industrial applications, such as chemical, biotechnological engineering, wastewater and water treatment plants (WTP). The pH, as a definition, is the logarithmic value of hydrogen ion activity in an aqueous solution or a measure of the acidity or alkalinity of a solution [1]. In terms of numerical values, a solution with a pH equal to 7 is neutral and for an alkalinity solution, this value is greater than 7. In an acidic solution, the pH value is less than 7.

The control of a pH neutralization is one of the major problem in water treatment plants, particularly due to its highly nonlinear characteristics [2]. In the last years, many researchers have studied pH control strategies and methods to resolve or minimize this strong nonlinearity [2].

In some cases, an extended Kalman filter (EKF) and an unscented Kalman filter (UKF) were used to estimate some values in a nonlinear pH process [3,4]. In [5], double-control scheme for pH process was employed to obtain a good load rejection performance, particularly simultaneous change occurs in set point and

I. Nääs et al. (Eds.): APMS 2016, IFIP AICT 488, pp. 138–145, 2016.
DOI: 10.1007/978-3-319-51133-7_17

in disturbance inputs. This solution was proposed to overcome some drawbacks usually found in conventional PID (proportional-integral-derivative) systems, such as the robustness of the control.

In [6], a Wiener-Laguerre model was used to evaluate the pH neutralization process as a nonlinear model predictive control framework, based on the sequential quadratic programming algorithm. This solution was designed considering an operation of the pH process in distinct set points. A Wiener model identification and predictive control also was applied of a pH neutralization process in [7], but in this case in an effluent solution control.

A multi-model nonlinear predictive control scheme was applied in [8] to describe and handle the nonlinearities of a pH industry process. This approach included a parallel integral action in the controller to compensate unmeasured states.

In a WTP, for example, natural dissolved organic matter (DOM) is present and this kind of product may cause relevant problems for process control [9]. In this situation, a coagulation step should be applied to maximize the removal of DOM in water, but accordingly to [9], some coagulants are able to modify the final pH, especially after enhanced coagulation. In [10], a reset/hybrid control application was applied an in-line pH process, in order to test the performance of a reset controller for a non-linear system with disturbances.

In some cases, a pH process requires an online monitoring and control system due to its highly nonlinear aspects [11,12]. Other researches took into account the use of artificial intelligence techniques to improve pH control, in particular for predictive purposes and adaptive and/or optimization strategy [13–21].

As aforementioned, the pH control is a major issue in some industrial processes due to its nonlinear behavior, thus, in this context, the aim of this work consists in the modelling and simulating a pH closed-loop control of a real WTP, in order to better manage the process and reduce some costs related to the use of raw materials in a water treatment plant, for some operational scenarios, as well as identify the better parameters for this type of process.

2 Methodology

The present work has been applied for simulation purposes and some process variables were chosen by mathematical modelling. These variables were identified con-sidering their impact for pH control in a real drinking water treatment plant, located at São Paulo city, Brazil. The rated flow of this WTP is 33 m^3/s. In this context, this research has been performed in six steps, as follows:

1. Identify the process variables according to the desired pH behavior. Thus, considering the knowledge of the operators, some parameters were identified as relevant for pH control, such as, chlorine dosage and fluorine dosage at the end of the process treatment, raw water flow, treated water turbidity and the lime dosage;

2. Select a range of historical data stored in a Supervisory Control and Data Acquisition (SCADA system). This system is running at the local water plant and Fig. 1 shows a screen of the SCADA used for operating the WTP and lime dosage to control the pH of the drinking water. On this screen is possible to adjust the reference value for automatic controller or the lime pump frequency, as well as other parameters such as the lime flow, lime dosage and dosage pumps.

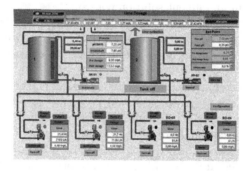

Fig. 1. A process screen in the SCADA system for pH monitoring and lime dosage

3. Identify a sample data wherein the pH process was being controlled in automatic mode. Table 1 shows a brief sample of the experimental data used for modelling and simulation.

Table 1. Some historical data selected from SCADA software

Data and time	Measured	Turbidity	Chlorine dosage	Fluorine dosage	Raw water flow
	pH	(UNT)	(mg/L)	(mg/L)	(m^3/s)
2015-10-06 03:39:08:117	7.93	0.42	1.74	0.64	13.82
2015-10-06 03:41:38:163	9.04	0.45	1.64	0.61	13.85
2015-10-06 03:44:08:147	8.96	0.46	1.66	0.63	13.86
2015-10-06 03:46:38:677	9.04	0.45	1.68	0.68	13.87
2015-10-06 03:49:08:177	8.70	0.45	1.67	0.73	13.86
2015-10-06 03:51:38:193	8.33	0.44	1.66	0.80	13.77
2015-10-06 03:54:08:803	8.34	0.45	1.69	0.60	13.81

4. Load these data in the MATLAB® software and execute some specific commands to determine the behavior (transfer function) of each input and respective output variable. In this case, the output variable is the measured pH. The following commands were used:

– Command "*iddata*": create a data object to encapsulate the input/output data and their properties (Eq. 1).

$$DAT = iddata(Y, U, Ts) \tag{1}$$

Where: Y = output, U = input and Ts = sampling interval

– Command "*tfest*": This MATLAB® function estimates a continuous-time transfer function, sys, using time- or frequency-domain data, DAT obtained from "*iddata*" command, and contains np poles, as follows Eq. 2:

$$sys = tfest(DAT, np) \tag{2}$$

5. Modelling each input/output variable and/or equipment in the MATLAB Simulink environment, in order to proceed to the operational scenarios simulation. Figure 2 shows an aerial view of the WTP used for modelling and experimental validation. Figure 3 shows a final model of each variable, i.e., chlorine dosage, treated turbidity and flow, as well as the equipment behavior, such as lime and fluorine pumps, after modelling step. Figure 3 also highlights a transfer function obtained for one disturb-ance, i.e., for chlorine dosage, using Eqs. 1 and 2. This function is a relation between the chlorine dosage and its influence in the pH value. Equations 1 and 2 also were used for determining the other disturbances, such as fluorine dosage, flow and turbidity influence.

Fig. 2. The water treatment plant used for modelling and simulation

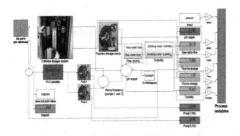

Fig. 3. The process modelling in the MATLAB/Simulink® software

6. The performance of the final model is measured by the mean absolute error (MAE), as shown in Eq. 3:

$$MAE = \frac{1}{N}\sum_{i=1}^{N} t_i - y_i \tag{3}$$

Where, t_i is desired value; y_i is value obtained from the mathematical model and N is number of existing samples. The next section shows the results and discussion about the simulation of three operational scenarios using the model depicted in Fig. 3.

3   Results and Discussion

This session shows the results and discussion about the simulation of three operational scenarios using the final mathematical model depicted in Fig. 3. In each case, the initial conditions were used to start the simulation and proceed with experimental validation.

– First scenario (initial conditions): in this case the initial parameters were defined as follows: chlorine dosage = 1.74 mg/l, fluorine dosage = 0.645 mg/l, raw water flow = 13.83 m³/s and treated turbidity = 0.422 NTU. Figure 4(a) and (b) show the lime pumps dosage, and the pH obtained in the experimental and simulated data (Fig. 4).

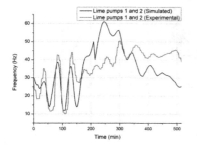
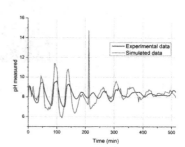

(a) Frequency of lime pumps 1 and 2   (b) pH measured for experimental and simulated data

Fig. 4. (a) Frequency of lime pumps 1 and 2 and (b) pH measured for experimental and simulated data

– Second scenario (initial conditions): in this case the initial conditions were defined as follows: chlorine dosage = 1.86 mg/L, fluorine dosage = 0.654 mg/L, raw water flow = 17.24 m³/s and turbidity = 0.33 NTU. Figures 5(a) and (b) show the lime pumps dosage and the pH obtained in the experimental and simulated data.

– Third scenario (initial conditions): in this case the initial conditions were defined as follows: chlorine dosage = 1.76 mg/L, fluorine dosage = 0.691 mg/L, raw water flow = 27.03 m³/s and turbidity = 0.272 NTU. Figures 6(a) and (b) show the lime pumps dosage and the pH obtained in the experimental and simulated data.

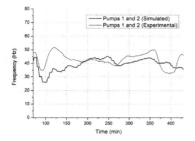
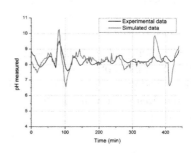

(a) Frequency of lime pumps 1 and 2   (b) pH measured for experimental and simulated data

Fig. 5. (a) Frequency of lime pumps 1 and 2 and (b) pH measured for experimental and simulated data

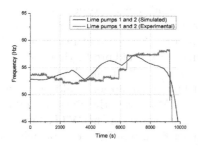
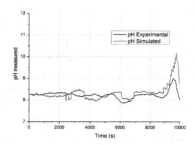

(a) Frequency of lime pumps 1 and 2   (b) pH measured for experimental and simulated data

Fig. 6. (a) Frequency of lime pumps 1 and 2 and (b) pH measured for experimental and simulated data

The results show a good approximation between the simulated and experimental data, even though some operational points should be better evaluated in each case. On the other hand, it should be noted that the results achieved in the scenario 3 are better than those obtained in other cases, as this last scenario have considered a data sampled time equal to 10 s from the knowledge base (SCADA system), while in the first and second cases were employed data sample time equal to 2.5 min. Table 2 shows the MAE values for each scenario.

Table 2. Values of MAEs scenarios

Scenario	Mean absolute Error (MAE) of the frequency of lime pumps	Mean absolute Error (MAE) of the pH value
1	9.28 Hz	0.573
2	5.69 Hz	0.334
3	2.06 Hz	0.192

The frequency of each lime pump is a relevant parameter capable of estimating the lime consumption in the WTP, since this parameter is useful to determine lime flow. Today, the pH control at the water plant used for experimental validation requires more than 15 tons of lime per day, when the raw water flow is near 33 m^3/s.

4   Conclusions

This work presented a model of a pH control for process management in a drinking water treatment plant. A data set obtained from a SCADA software was used to define the behavior of each input and disturbances of the process, using the MATLAB/Simulink® software. The results of the three operational scenarios show a good approximation between simulated and experimental data, thus, the present model can be used in other operational conditions, in order to estimate the lime pump frequency and the pH in the treated water, as well as improve the raw water quality and reduce the lime consumption. The current mathematical model can be a useful tool for a decision-making process and production management; particularly for estimating the daily chemical refills in the WTP, which is not an easy task. It should be mentioned that lime consumption could represent 15% of total operational costs in a WTP [22]. Moreover, the lime consumption could be better evaluated due to initial parameters of the WTP. Further investigations should be considered, using an artificial intelligence approach, to estimate the minimum dosage of the lime pumps, maintaining the quality of the treated water. That could lead to cost reduction in the water treatment process.

References

1. Hermansson, A.W., Syafiie, S.: Model predictive control of pH neutralization processes: a review. Control Eng. Practice **45**, 98–109 (2015)
2. Abdullah, N., Karsiti, M., Ibrahim, R.: A review of pH neutralization process control. In: 4th International Conference on Intelligent and Advanced Systems, vol. 2, pp. 594–598. IEEE (2012)
3. Barhoumi, A., Ladhari, T., M'sahli, F.: The extended Kalman filter for nonlinear system: application to system of waste water treatment. In: 15th International Conference on Sciences and Techniques of Automatic Control and Computer Engineering, pp. 445–450. IEEE (2014)

4. Romanenko, A., Santos, L.O., Afonso, P.A.: Unscented Kalman filtering of a simulated pH system. Industr. Eng. Chem. Res. **43**(23), 7531–7538 (2004)
5. Shobana, S., Panda, R.C.: Control of pH process using double-control scheme. Nonlinear Dyn. **67**(3), 2267–2277 (2012)
6. Mahmoodi, S., Poshtan, J., Jahed-Motlagh, M.R., Montazeri, A.: Nonlinear model predictive control of a pH neutralization process based on Wiener-Laguerre model. Chem. Eng. J. **146**(3), 328–337 (2009)
7. Gomez, J., Jutan, A., Baeyens, E.: Wiener model identification and predictive control of a pH neutralisation process. IEE Proc.-Control Theor. Appl. **151**(3), 329–338 (2004)
8. Hermansson, A.W., Syafiie, S.: Control of pH neutralization system using nonlinear model predictive control with I-controller. In: IEEE International Conference on Industrial Engineering and Engineering Management, pp. 853–857. IEEE (2014)
9. Xie, J., Wang, D., van Leeuwen, J., Zhao, Y., Xing, L., Chow, C.W.: pH modeling for maximum dissolved organic matter removal by enhanced coagulation. J. Environ. Sci. **24**(2), 276–283 (2012)
10. Carrasco, J., Baños, A.: Reset control of an industrial in-line pH process. IEEE Trans. Control Syst. Technol. **20**(4), 1100–1106 (2012)
11. Jacobs, O., Hewkin, P., While, C.: Online computer control of pH in an industrial process. In: IEE Proceedings D-Control Theory and Applications, vol. 127, pp. 161–168. IET (1980)
12. Aparna, V.: Development of automated pH monitoring & control system through usb data acquisition. In: 6th IEEE Power India International Conference, pp. 1–6. IEEE (2014)
13. Tan, W., Lu, F., Loh, A., Tan, K.C.: Modeling and control of a pilot pH plant using genetic algorithm. Eng. Appl. Artif. Intell. **18**(4), 485–494 (2005)
14. Menzl, S., Stühler, M., Benz, R.: A self adaptive computer-based pH measurement and fuzzy-control system. Water Res. **30**(4), 981–991 (1996)
15. Saji, K., Kumar, M.S.: Fuzzy sliding mode control for a pH process. In: IEEE International Conference on Communication Control and Computing Technologies, pp. 276–281. IEEE (2010)
16. Sabharwal, J., Chen, J.: Intelligent pH control using fuzzy linear invariant clustering. In: Proceedings of the Twenty-Eighth Southeastern Symposium on System Theory, pp. 514–518. IEEE (1996)
17. Mollov, S., Babuska, R., Abonyi, J., Verbruggen, H.B.: Effective optimization for fuzzy model predictive control. IEEE Trans. Fuzzy Syst. **12**(5), 661–675 (2004)
18. Xu, C., Shin, Y.C.: A multilevel fuzzy control design for a class of multi-input single-output systems. IEEE Trans. Industri. Electron. **59**(8), 3113–3123 (2012)
19. Loh, A., Looi, K., Fong, K.: Neural network modelling and control strategies for a pH process. J. Process Control **5**(6), 355–362 (1995)
20. Böling, J.M., Seborg, D.E., Hespanha, J.P.: Multi-model adaptive control of a simulated pH neutralization process. Control Eng. Pract. **15**(6), 663–672 (2007)
21. Navghare, S., Bodhe, G.: Design and implementation of real time neurofuzzy based pH controller. In: 2009 Second International Conference on Emerging Trends in Engineering & Technology, pp. 946–952. IEEE (2009)
22. Plappally, A.K., Lienhard, J.H.: Costs for water supply, treatment, end-use and reclamation. Desalin. Water Treat. **51**(1–3), 200–232 (2013)

An Integrative Model of Productivity and Logistic Objectives

Robert Glöckner$^{(\boxtimes)}$, Martin Benter, and Hermann Lödding

Hamburg University of Technology, Hamburg, Germany
{robert.gloeckner,m.benter,loedding}@tuhh.de

Abstract. Labor productivity as well as its influencing factors are closely linked to the logistic objectives. This linkage has been so far only described on a qualitative basis. Consequently a coordinated configuration of production planning and control and productivity management is missing. This paper presents an approach to link labor productivity and production planning and control on a quantitative level.

Keywords: Labor productivity · Logistic objectives · Production planning · Control

1 Introduction

Manufacturing companies compete in the target dimensions time, quality and cost. On the one hand models for production planning and control (PPC), such as Lödding's manufacturing control model [1] or the underlying funnel model [2], aim to explain and influence the time related logistic objectives. They determine to what extend a company can achieve short lead times and high delivery reliability. On the other hand the productivity determines the manufacturing costs. Thus productivity management tries to organize the use of manufacturing resources in the most effective way. Although a fair amount of research has been conducted in both disciplines, it is often difficult to put methods and knowledge into practice. A reason for these difficulties lays in the interdependencies between productivity and logistic objectives [1].

This paper presents an approach to model these interdependencies.

2 Productivity and Logistic Objectives

2.1 Labor Productivity

Productivity is generally defined as the ratio of input and output [3,4].

$$PRO = \frac{Output}{Input} \tag{1}$$

© IFIP International Federation for Information Processing 2016
Published by Springer International Publishing AG 2016. All Rights Reserved
I. Nääs et al. (Eds.): APMS 2016, IFIP AICT 488, pp. 146–153, 2016.
DOI: 10.1007/978-3-319-51133-7_18

There are several approaches to measure productivity. The output can be measured in pieces, target hours or monetary units. Depending on the specific productivity different inputs are considered. Common productivity figures are machine productivity and labor productivity [5].

This paper focusses on labor productivity, since labor costs are especially important in high wage countries. The labor productivity of a manufacturing system may thus be defined as the ratio of number of products produced (output) and payed working time (input) [5].

$$PRO_L = \frac{Output}{Paid\ working\ time} \tag{2}$$

According to Saito [6] several factors influence labor productivity. These factors are method, performance and utilization.

$$PRO = Method \cdot Performance \cdot Utilization \tag{3}$$

The utilization describes how much of the payed working time is actually used to perform the intended work task. This considers losses such as the sickness rate and idle times that result from maintenance or a lack of orders. The method describes how the working time spent on the task performance is transferred into actual output. The factor can be calculated as the inverse of the ideal cycle time. It maps losses resulting from a poor task design or wrong tooling. The performance determines how fast a certain task is performed by the worker compared to a standard time, such as provided by MTM [7].

2.2 Logistic Objectives and the Manufacturing Control Model

The manufacturing control model shows the tasks of production planning and control and its effects on logistic objectives via several actuating and control variables. Figure 1 shows the model. The presented logistic objectives are WIP, throughput time, schedule reliability and utilization. The WIP describes the number of orders at a workstation either in queue or in the process of completion. The time period from the release of a job until its completion is the throughput time. Schedule reliability is defined as the percentage of jobs that are completed within a certain due date tolerance before and/or after the planned date of completion. Utilization describes the ratio of maximum possible output rate and actual output rate of a workstation or worker. Losses in utilization occur due to a lack of orders [2]. The manufacturing control model further presents the control variables WIP, backlog and sequence deviation. Backlog is defined as the difference of the cumulated planned output and the cumulated actual output of a work station. Yu [8] describes the mean output lateness as the ratio of the mean backlog and the mean output rate. Therefore backlog directly influences the schedule reliability. Sequence deviations occur when the actual sequence deviates from the planned sequence [1]. Sequence deviations lead to an increase in the variance of the lateness and therefore cause a decrease of the schedule reliability. Besides its appearance as a logistic objective WIP functions as a control variable as well. It influences

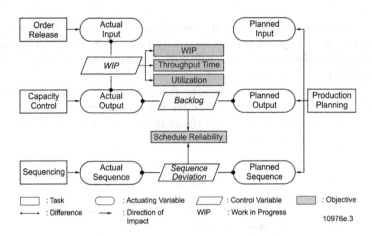

Fig. 1. Manufacturing control model [1]

the logistic objectives WIP, throughput time and utilization. A detailed analysis of the relationship between WIP and throughput time is given by the funnel formula [9] as well as by Little's Law [10].

3   Linking Capacity, Productivity and Output

The capacity of manufacturing systems can be defined as the capability of all resources in a system, such as workers or machines, in a certain reference period. Capacity is usually measured as a ratio of output and time and can thus be directly compared to an output rate, such as pieces per shop calendar day. On the contrary, capacity planning and control as capacity related tasks aim at influencing the amount of working time. In terms of labor this means the number of workers assigned to a work system, the number of shifts and the duration of the shifts including overtime and shortened work. Due to this, PPC related literature distinguishes several types of capacity. Nyhuis and Wiendahl [2] for example are using the terms theoretical capacity, available capacity and effective capacity. The working time as determined by capacity planning and control is considered as theoretical capacity. It can be calculated as shown in Eq. 4.

$$CAP_{theo} = NO_{work} \cdot NO_{shift} \cdot WT_p \tag{4}$$

CAP_{theo}: Theoretical capacity [hrs/SCD]
NO_{work}: Number of workers [-]
NO_{shift}: Number of shifts per SCD [-/SCD]
WT_p: Paid working time per shift and worker [hrs]

Due to illnesses, maintenance and other disturbances the available capacity is regularly somewhat lower than the theoretical capacity. The effective capacity describes the maximum output rate of a work system. It results from the available capacity and the degree of efficiency. The degree of efficiency is dependent on the work system's performance. The actual output rate of the work system again is determined by the effective capacity and the WIP-dependent utilization. Figure 2 shows the transformation of theoretical capacity towards output rate.

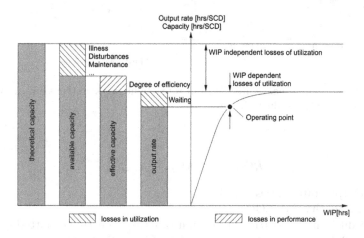

Fig. 2. Differentiation of the capacity and output rate, according to [2]

By examining the considerations that lead from the theoretical capacity or the working time of a work system towards its output rate one can see that the influences equal the factors utilization and performance of Saito's productivity model. The method factor is not represented in the figure, because the capacity here is given in planned hours.

As explained before, labor productivity describes to what extend an input of paid working time can be transformed into actual output. The working time as part of the labor productivity is directly related to the theoretical capacity in terms of capacity planning and control. Consequently the transformation from a work system's theoretical capacity to its output rate can be described by its productivity.

To illustrate this, the relations between capacity, productivity, output rate and output are shown in Fig. 3. The complete working time in a reference period is shown in Fig. 3 Left. It is calculated as the product of theoretical capacity and the duration of the reference period.

$$WT = CAP_{theo} \cdot PE \tag{5}$$

WT: Working time [hrs]

CAP_{theo}: Theoretical capacity [hrs/SCD]

PE: Reference Period (time) [SCD]. Based on the observations above, a work system's output rate can be calculated as the product of the system's theoretical capacity and its productivity (Eq. 6).

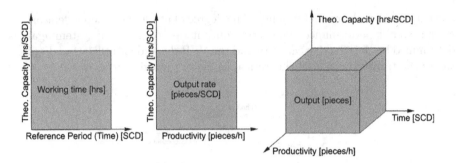

Fig. 3. Left: Working time; Center: Output rate; Right: work system's output as product of theo. capacity, productivity and time

$$ROUT = CAP_{theo} \cdot PRO \qquad (6)$$

ROUT: Output rate [pieces/SCD]

CAP_{theo}: Capacity [hrs/SCD]

PRO: Productivity [pieces/h]. The output rate therefore can be plotted as shown in Fig. 3 Center. The cuboid shown in Fig. 3 Right represents the work system's output depending on the amount of capacity in the work system, its productivity and the duration of the reference period.

$$OUT = CAP_{theo} \cdot PRO \cdot PE \qquad (7)$$

OUT: Output of the work system [pieces]

CAP_{theo}: Theoretical capacity [hrs/SCD]

PRO: Productivity [pieces/h]

PE: Reference period [SCD]. To better understand the influence of productivity on the output rate, logistic operating curves were observed. It can be seen from Fig. 4 that the influence of productivity on the output rate is only partly dependent on the WIP. Productivity losses such as a high sickness rate or a poorly designed work task reduce the maximum possible productivity to the maximum WIP dependent productivity. WIP dependent productivity losses result from to low WIP levels. The mechanics behind that are therefore the same as described by logistic operating curves. It must be noted that Fig. 4 shows an operating point in the underload operating zone to demonstrate the effect of WIP on productivity. Usually an operating point with higher WIP would be chosen and thus WIP dependent productivity losses would be much lower. Therefore a much lower effect of WIP on productivity has to be expected.

Productivity improvement actions usually aim at improving WIP independent productivity e.g. by improving ergonomic conditions, reducing non-value-adding processes, etc.

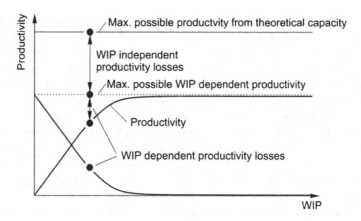

Fig. 4. Interdependencies of WIP, productivity and output rate

4   Integrating Productivity into the Manufacturing Control Model

According to the findings of Sect. 2.3, capacity control as well as capacity planning are not able to directly influence the actual or planned output of a manufacturing system. They rather determine the actual or planned working time. To this aim, the planned and actual working time is introduced. Figure 5 shows the adapted manufacturing control model. To reduce complexity, the task of sequencing and the related actuating variables actual sequence and planed sequence as well as the control variable sequence deviation are omitted. The focus of the adapted model lies on the newly included objectives actual and planned productivity.

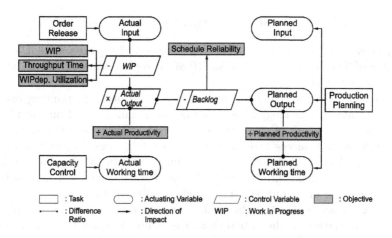

Fig. 5. Adapted manufacturing control model

The planned productivity results from the ratio of planned output and planned working time. Production planning is a hierarchical process that, in the beginning, determines the planned output based on the expected customer demand. In further steps the planned working time is determined on the basis of the planned productivity. The planned productivity is thus an important objective. On the one hand it should be aligned with the productivity targets for the actual productivity. On the other hand it is used to calculate the required working time for a given planned output. From a planning perspective, planned productivity needs to reflect the possible productivity of a work system precisely, in order to enable realistic planning. From a productivity perspective, the planned productivity should be raised in a way that enables productivity improvement.

The actual productivity results from the ratio of actual output and actual working time. This ratio is influenced by the objective utilization. The actual working time is determined by the task of capacity control. Based on the actual productivity, a certain actual output results from the product of actual working time and actual productivity. For this reason the actual output is not considered as an independent actuating variable, but as a control variable.

5   Interaction of Productivity and Logistic Objectives

To illustrate the several effects caused by the interaction of productivity and logistic objectives a simple scenario is examined. The scenario is based on a simple assembly work system with two operators working an 8 h shift. The planned output rate of the work system is 32 pieces/SCD with a planned productivity of 2 pieces/h.

As an example we assume a lower actual productivity (due to ambitious productivity targets) of 1.8 pieces/h leading to an actual output rate of 28.8 pieces/SCD (Eq. 7).

$$ROUT = 16[hrs/SCD] \cdot 1,8[pieces/h] = 28.8[pieces/SCD] \tag{8}$$

This deviation would lead to a backlog increase of 3.2 pieces per SCD causing a backlog of 32 pieces after two weeks (10 SCD) representing an output lateness of roughly one SCD.

We further assume that overtime is used to reduce the resulting backlog. To compensate the backlog, 16 h overtime are planned based on the planned output rate. As a result of the lower actual productivity, these 16 h would raise the output by 28.8 pieces leaving a backlog of 3.2 pieces. Capacity adaptions are therefore depending on precise productivity data. In case the backlog is the result of a lower actual productivity, the capacity increase will not lead to a sufficient increase of output and some backlog will remain.

If order release is based on the planned output rate (actual input = planned output), a deviation of the actual from the planned productivity will as well cause a changing WIP increase. In the example stated above, the lower actual productivity would lead to a WIP of 16 pieces per week. If the work system is not already working at maximum utilization, this could lead to a (most likely modest) increase in productivity. The growing WIP level would also lead to an increasing throughput time. Based on the actual productivity and output rate, throughput time will have increased by roughly one SCD after two weeks.

6 Summary

This paper presents an approach to model the interrelations between productivity and the logistic objectives as presented in Lödding's manufacturing control model. As an outcome, the enhanced manufacturing control model offers the following advantages:

- Better understanding of capacity control: Considering actual productivity allows a better adjustment of capacity control (especially when overtime is applied).
- Better understanding of production planning: The understanding of the effect of production planning on the planned productivity exposes the need for productivity considerations in production planning.

Acknowledgement. The Authors would like to thank Deutsche Forschungsgesellschaft (DFG) for funding the project "Development of an overall model for labor productivity and the logistic objectives" (LO 858/12-1).

References

1. Lödding, H.: A manufacturing control model. Int. J. Prod. Res. **50**(22), 6311–6328 (2012)
2. Nyhuis, P., Wiendahl, H.P.: Logistische Kennlinien: Grundlagen, Werkzeuge und Anwendungen. Springer-Verlag, Heidelberg (2012)
3. Bokranz, R., Landau, K., Deutsche, M.: Produktivitätsmanagement von Arbeitssystemen: MTM-Handbuch. Schäffer-Poeschel, Stuttgart (2006)
4. Sumanth, D.J.: Productivity Engineering and Management: Productivity Measurement, Evaluation, Planning, and Improvement in Manufacturing and Service Organizations. McGraw-Hill College, New York (1984)
5. Weber, H.: Rentabilität, Produktivität und Liquidität: Grö\s sen zur Beurteilung und Steuerung von Unternehmen. Springer, Heidelberg (1998)
6. Saito, S.: Reducing labor costs using industrial engineering techniques. In: Zandin, K. (ed.) Maynard's Industrial Engineering Handbook. McGraw-Hill, New York (2001)
7. Almström, P.: Productivity measurement and improvements: a theoretical model and applications from the manufacturing industry. In: Emmanouilidis, C., Taisch, M., Kiritsis, D. (eds.) APMS 2012. IAICT, vol. 398, pp. 297–304. Springer, Heidelberg (2013). doi:10.1007/978-3-642-40361-3_38
8. Yu, K.: Terminkennlinie: Eine Beschreibungsmethodik für die Terminabweichung im Produktionsbereich. Eine Beschreibungsmethodik für die Terminabweichung im Produktionsbereich. VDI Progress Reports, Series 2 (2001)
9. Bechte, W.: Steuerung der Durchlaufzeit durch Belastungsorientierte Auftragsfreigabe bei Werkstattfertigung. VDI-Verlag, Düsseldorf (1984)
10. Little, J.D.C.: A proof for the queuing formula: $L = \lambda W$. Oper. Res. **9**(3), 383–387 (1961)

Pursuit of Responsiveness in SMEs Through Dynamic Allocation of Flexible Workers: A Simulation Study

Sayyed Shoaib-ul-Hasan[1,2(✉)], Marco Macchi[1], and Alessandro Pozzetti[1]

[1] Politecnico di Milano, Milan, Italy
{sayyed.shoaibulhasan,marco.macchi,alessandro.pozzetti}@polimi.it
[2] Universidad Politécnica de Madrid, Madrid, Spain

Abstract. The aim of this research is to study production responsiveness in Small and Medium Enterprises (SMEs) in Italy. Responsiveness is considered as the ability of a production system to achieve its goals in the presence of disturbances. The main issue this research tries to address is "how responsiveness can be achieved in production environments facing recurring uncertain disturbances in demand?" This research is particularly focused on the "worker flexibility" as a lever to achieve responsiveness. In this regard, alternative control logics for decision-making, regarding use of workers with varying levels of flexibility, have been evaluated through simulation for their potential impact on production responsiveness. It is found that, contrary to general belief, higher flexibility does not always guarantee higher responsiveness; it is the right level of flexibility combined with the proper decision-making logic which leads to higher production performance in the face of recurring uncertain disturbances.

Keywords: Responsiveness · Simulation · Demand variability · SMEs · Flexibility

1 Introduction

Mass customization has emerged as a new business strategy to respond to customers' demand for high product variety. It has brought many challenges for manufacturing industry, particularly for small and medium-sized enterprises (SMEs) operating in global market. Mass customization is characterized by high demand variability, which adversely impacts production performance [4]. In fact, mass customization production companies face swings in demand and thus vary in their capacity utilization [2,5]. Demand variability has been recognized as having the broadest negative impact on plant performance and it represents a pure measure of dynamic complexity [11]. If not properly and timely addressed, demand variability may cause productivity loss as well as human errors with negative impacts on production performance [10]. Furthermore, uncertain demand disturbances cause snow-ball effects such as delays on customer orders, logistics errors and high level of work-in-progress inventories [7].

© IFIP International Federation for Information Processing 2016
Published by Springer International Publishing AG 2016. All Rights Reserved
I. Nääs et al. (Eds.): APMS 2016, IFIP AICT 488, pp. 154–161, 2016.
DOI: 10.1007/978-3-319-51133-7_19

However, in order to compete in the global market, companies need to respond to such uncertain disturbances in demand quickly and effectively. Therefore, many companies are pursuing responsiveness as one of their main performance priorities and are looking for ways to achieve higher responsiveness in their production environments [3].

In line with contingency theory, the required level of responsiveness that every company needs is different and depends on their individual business strategies [1, 8]. Hence, the basis for competitiveness must be designed individually according to the company's own particular circumstances [3] which may vary according to country, industry, company size and/or other contingencies. In this regard, this research particularly focuses on uncertain demand disturbances in SMEs and the use of "worker flexibility" as a lever to achieve responsiveness. Thus, the paper tries to answer the following question: How SMEs can properly use their worker flexibility to achieve responsiveness to recurring uncertain disturbances in demand?

In this regard, to evaluate the impact of different alternative control logics regarding use of worker flexibility, a simulation study has been designed in collaboration with an Italian SME. For simulation purposes "Plant Simulation" software is used. Simulation is performed based on real production data and with real system constraints. Performance for alternative control logics is measured based on their ability to meet the average monthly demand across different product models. Simulation results for alternative control logics are analyzed and compared to identify the best solution for adaptive decision-making in the face of recurring uncertain disturbances in demand.

2 Worker Flexibility

The purpose of this study is to investigate the use of worker flexibility to address demand variability in a production layout made of assembly cells. Previously, in literature, different terms have been used to conceptualize "worker flexibility", such as multi-tasking [13] and multi-functionality [9]. This conceptualization of worker flexibility implies that the workers have the capacity to perform more than one task. However, researchers in group technology argue that multi-tasking alone is not enough, in fact workers should be able to perform different tasks in different areas (or call it cells) according to the needs. In this regard [12], for example, argues that "labor flexibility is the ability to assign varying number of operators as needed to perform different tasks. This requires training of operators to perform various tasks as well as their flexible assignment between different cells". In a similar vein [6] argued that "the presence of worker flexibility is characterized by cross-trained workers and the ability of workers to move between cells". Therefore, we can conclude that worker flexibility has two dimensions: (i) capacity to perform more than one task, i.e. multi-tasking (ii) dynamic allocation between tasks, i.e. flexible assignment. In this research, these dimensions are conceptualized as following: multitasking (worker characteristic) is the capacity of workers to carry out tasks within their assembly cell as well as tasks required in other cells; dynamic (re)allocation between tasks (system characteristic) is the possibility, by the system management, to be able to (re)allocate workers among different cells according to needed tasks, thanks to their capacity of multitasking.

3   Case Company

This research has been performed in collaboration with an Italian SME. The company produces slicers and offers more than 55 different models of slicers. These slicers are divided into two macro families which are (i) vertical slicers, and (ii) inclined slicers. This division arises from the fact that the assembly operation of a vertical blade differs from that of an inclined blade (which is a critical operation and requires different skill set). These macro families have further sub families (micro families). In total there are 8 micro families of slicers each consisting of different product models. Figure 1 shows the product family tree and how different products belong to the micro and macro families.

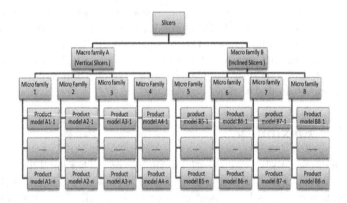

Fig. 1. Product family tree

The company organizes production according to assemble-to-order (ATO) strategy where individual components are produced and stocked beforehand. Final assembly is performed only when the actual orders arrive. The assembly of all slicers consists of five phases which are (1) Preassembly operations on the motor; (2) Preassembly operations on the blade; (3) Assembly of the motor and related components on the base; (4) Assembly of the blade on the base and its fitting with the motor; (5) Calibration of blade. The precedence of assembly phases is shown in Fig. 2. Phase 1 and 2 consist of pre-assembly operations and are performed by low skill workers (LSW). LSW are workers with no specialization and they lack skills to perform final assembly phases. Therefore, the final assembly phases 3, 4 and 5 are performed only by the high skill workers (HSW) who are well trained and experienced. However, workers can perform assembly operations only within their own macro family. This constraint is put by the management to achieve high quality in assembly as assembly of both macro families require different skill set and experience. This constraint is particularly important for this study as we try to understand its impacts on responsiveness when evaluating different alternatives. The sub division of high skill and low skill workers in an assembly cell is given as in Table 1.

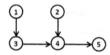

Fig. 2. Precedence of assembly phases

Table 1. Subdivision of workers within a cell

Total number of workers in a cell	Number of LSW	Number of HSW
2	1	1
3	1	2
4	2	2
5	2	3

Company uses 8 different assembly cells, where each cell is dedicated to a particular micro-family. The demand for different product models varies during the year and company needs to make some adjustments in its existing configuration at shop floor to meet the new demand. Company is looking for other better ways and capabilities to achieve a quick and effective reconfiguration in response to recurring uncertain disturbances in demand. In this regard, different alternative control logics for adaptive decision-making regarding reconfiguration are being considered which are discussed in next section.

4   Control Logics for Adaptive Decision-Making and Simulation Design

Control logics for adaptive decision-making are built on dynamic allocation and multi-tasking. Regarding dynamic allocation, the company has two options: shift the product/workload from mother-cell to a host-cell or move the workers from an offering-cell to a cell-in-need to meet the demand in that cell. Furthermore, regarding mul-titasking there are also two options: train workers to perform assembly operations within one macro-family (basic level multi-tasking) or train workers to perform assembly operations on both macro families (high level multi-tasking). Thus, there are four alternatives that can be evaluated through simulation as shown in Fig. 3. Correspondingly, two are the decisions that will be compared: (i) the dynamic allocation of workers versus the dynamic allocation of workload between the cells; (ii) the level of worker flexibility, with the purpose to understand if capacity to perform tasks on both macro families is actually better or not, despite this would lead to a loss of efficiency due to less experience of workers on some tasks. The efficiency value for worker is 100% if he performs assembly operation within his family, 90% when he performs operation on other family but within the same macro family, and 80% if he performs operations on family outside his own macro family. These values are validated by the company manager who collaborated in this research. He has served for several departments before assuming his current position.

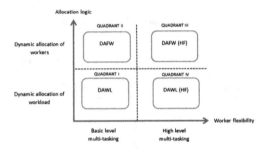

Fig. 3. Alternative control logics

From Fig. 3, it is apparent that there are four quadrants and each quadrant has its own control logic which is designed according to the requirements of the production context in SMEs: it should be easily and quickly manageable. To verify the effect on performances, the models for all control logics are developed. Because of space constraint in this paper, we discuss in detail only the control logic and the model for dynamic allocation of workers with basic level multi-tasking (DAFW). In order to develop such logic, the following procedure is adopted at the end of every week: (a) calculate the current amount of workload present in each cell (workload as a function of number of slicers allocated to each cell); (b) calculate the production capacity as function of the number of high skill and low skill workers currently working within each cell; (c) calculate the remaining number of working days from the current moment till the end of the month; (d) with the information provided by 'b' and 'c', calculate the number of slicers that can be assembled by the end of the month in each cell; (e) if this quantity calculated in step 'd' is greater than that specified in step 'a', start an iterative process from step 'b' and calculate the production capacity with one worker less than the previous condition; (f) after second iteration, for any cell, if the quantity calculated in step 'd' is still greater than that specified in step 'a', that cell becomes an offering-cell and makes available its worker to the whole macro-family, i.e. worker can be used to meet the capacity requirement of a cell-in-need within the same macro-family. In fact, if a cell is generating a delay of one week with respect to the end of the month (it is the cell-in-need), then it can receive a worker from another cell (depending on availability of worker) to increase its production capacity.

Overall, it is worth pointing out that when a cell has a worker to offer to the system, the worker leaves only in the case when there is need in another cell. Similarly, if a cell is expected to mature late delivery and one or more of its workers are allocated to other cells-in-need, the cell will get its workers back regardless of the situation in host cells. With these constraints the quality and workers performance loss (due to inefficiency when working outside of their micro-family) becomes less influential, while the cells with delayed delivery can get extra workers from offering-cells to increase their production capacity. In order develop a mathematical model for the control logic explained so far, we need to calculate the total number of needed hours, based on current workload for both HSW and LSW, in each cell, then comparing it with total number of remaining hours, both for HSW and LSW, in each cell till the end of month. In this regard, following indexes are used:

Xi: the total number of slicers of micro-family i currently present in the cell
Ti: the total average time for the production of a slicer of the micro-family i
αi: the share of total average time spent by the final assembly operations
1-αi: the share of total average time spent by the pre-assembly operations
glr: the remaining number of working days until the end of month
nli: the number of low skill workers present in cell belonging to micro-family i
nhi: the number of high skill workers present in cell belonging to micro-family i
xhi: the number of remaining working hours for HSW till the end of month
xli: the number of remaining working hours for LSW till the end of month
wh: number of daily working hours available for both HSW and LSW

We can calculate the number of hours needed by HSW and LSW in a cell to complete the current workload of micro-family i by following equations:

$$h\_HS_i = X_i * T_i * \alpha_i \tag{1}$$

$$h\_LS_i = X_i * T_i * (1 - \alpha_i) \tag{2}$$

h_HS and h_LS are used as benchmarks that allow system to figure out if a cell is able to yield a worker or is in need of a worker by comparing it with the total number of hours remaining, for both HSW and LSW in a cell till the end of the month. Remaining working hours can be calculated by the following equations respectively:

$$xh_i = nh_i * wh * glr \tag{3}$$

$$xl_i = nl_i * wh * glr \tag{4}$$

xhi and xli are the total working hours calculated by adding up the hours that each worker can work from the current moment till the end of the month. If xhi $> h\_HS_i$ and/or xli $> h\_LS_i$, the Eqs. 3 and 4 are executed again with one less worker. After second iteration again if xhi $> h\_HS_i$ and/or xli $> h\_LS_i$, then the cell yields, respectively, a HSW or LSW that can be used in a cell where xhi $< h\_HS_i$ and/or xli $< h\_LS_i$ (provided delay is more than one week, otherwise no action is required).

5   Simulation, Analysis and Results

Simulation is performed for all four control logics, where, monthly throughput is measured for each micro-family. All control logics used same resources and same types of demand patterns. In fact, simulation is performed using real production data and with real system constraints. Summary of findings is shown in Table 2 where alternative control logics for adaptive decision-making are compared for their ability to meet monthly demand of each micro-family (calculated as the ratio between average monthly throughput and average monthly demand for each micro-family). It can be seen from the table that without any allocation logic the production system can meet only less than 90% of the monthly demand of micro-families 7 and 8; while with dynamic allocation of flexible workers (DAFW) the production system can meet more than 99% of the overall demand for each micro-family with same resources. Overall, DAFW with basic level multi-tasking yields the highest performance when compared with other control logics. Interestingly, our results show that, with high flexibility (i.e. by high level multitasking) the overall performance is decreased due to worker efficiency losses when performing operations on products other than their own macro-family.

Table 2. Comparative results for different control logics

	DAFW	DAFW (HF)	DAWL	DAWL (HF)	No allocation
Family 1	99.96%	99.95%	97.90%	98.94%	97.41%
Family 2	99.91%	99.36%	97.49%	98.95%	93.52%
Family 3	99.55%	99.94%	98.97%	99.88%	98.97%
Family 4	99.89%	99.94%	99.92%	100.00%	99.92%
Family 5	99.80%	99.91%	99.01%	99.64%	98.76%
Family 6	99.84%	99.86%	98.57%	**94.35%**	92.69%
Family 7	99.87%	99.78%	99.33%	99.48%	**89.60%**
Family 8	98.58%	98.58%	**94.41%**	98.05%	**89.67%**
Overall	**99.68%**	99.66%	98.20%	98.66%	95.07%

6   Conclusion

This paper addressed uncertain demand disturbances and the achievement of production responsiveness in an environment made of assembly cells with workers as main resource. In this paper, simulation is used to evaluate alternative control logics for decision-making regarding recurring uncertain disturbances in demand. These control logics include (i) dynamic allocation between cells (workload versus workers), (ii) different levels of worker flexibility (basic versus high level multitasking). Our simulation study shows that dynamic allocation of flexible workers leads to higher responsiveness to disturbances in demand when compared with dynamic allocation of workload. Furthermore, we found that higher flexibility does not always guarantee higher performance. In fact, it is the right level of flexibility combined with the proper decision-making logic which leads to higher performance. Therefore, a careful analysis of requisite flexibility and the proper decision logic is important to achieve higher responsiveness. Our results are clearly contingent to type of production environment and the type and nature of disturbance; therefore, in the future it will be interesting to study variants of such type of control logics in different environments subject to different demand patterns.

Acknowledgments. This paper is produced as part of the EMJD Programme European Doctorate in Industrial Management (EDIM) funded by the European Commission, Erasmus Mundus Action 1.

References

1. Gunasekaran, A., Reichhart, A., Holweg, M.: Creating the customer-responsive supply chain: a reconciliation of concepts. Int. J. Oper. Prod. Manag. **27**(11), 1144–1172 (2007)
2. Holweg, M., Pil, F.K.: Successful build-to-order strategies start with the customer. MIT Sloan Manag. Rev. **43**(1), 74 (2001)
3. Pil, F.K., Holweg, M.: Linking product variety to order-fulfillment strategies. Interfaces **34**(5), 394–403 (2004)
4. Bozarth, C.C., Warsing, D.P., Flynn, B.B., Flynn, E.J.: The impact of supply chain complexity on manufacturing plant performance. J. Oper. Manag. **27**(1), 78–93 (2009)
5. Hu, S., Zhu, X.W., Wang, H., Koren, Y.: Product variety and manufacturing complexity in assembly systems and supply chains. CIRP Ann.-Manuf. Technol. **57**(1), 45–48 (2008)
6. Zhong, R.Y., Dai, Q., Qu, T., Hu, G., Huang, G.Q.: RFID-enabled real-time manufacturing execution system for mass-customization production. Robot. Comput.-Integr. Manuf. **29**(2), 283–292 (2013)
7. Jimenez, C.H.O., Machuca, J.A., Garrido-Vega, P., Filippini, R.: The pursuit of responsiveness in production environments: from flexibility to reconfigurability. Int. J. Prod. Econ. **163**, 157–172 (2015)
8. Roh, J., Hong, P., Min, H.: Implementation of a responsive supply chain strategy in global complexity. Int. J. Prod. Econ. **147**, 198–210 (2014)
9. Uskonen, J., Tenhiälä, A.: The price of responsiveness: cost analysis of change orders in make-to-order manufacturing. Int. J. Prod. Econ. **135**(1), 420–429 (2012)
10. Norman, B.A., Tharmmaphornphilas, W., Needy, K.L., Bidanda, B., Warner, R.C.: Worker assignment in cellular manufacturing considering technical and human skills. Int. J. Prod. Res. **40**(6), 1479–1492 (2002)
11. Molleman, E., Slomp, J.: Functional flexibility and team performance. Int. J. Prod. Res. **37**(8), 1837–1858 (1999)
12. Julie Yazici, H.: Influence of flexibilities on manufacturing cells for faster delivery using simulation. J. Manuf. Technol. Manag. **16**(8), 825–841 (2005)
13. Ruiz-Torres, A., Mahmoodi, F.: Impact of worker and shop flexibility on assembly cells. Int. J. Prod. Res. **45**(6), 1369–1388 (2007)

Effectiveness of Production Planning and Control (PPC) in a Baby Fashion Cluster, Under the Prism of Paraconsistent Logic

Elizangela Maria Menegassi de Lima[1,2(✉)], Fabio Papalardo[2],
Jose B. Sacomano[2], Priscila Facciolli Tavares[2],
and Esdras Jorge Santos Barboza[2]

[1] Paranaense University, Umuarama, Brazil
menegassi@unipar.br
[2] Paulista University, Sao Paulo, Brazil

Abstract. This research aimed at understanding relevant aspects of production planning and control of a baby wear cluster in Terra Roxa, Paraná State, Brazil, employing the Paraconsistent Logic as an analysis. In the methodology, a descriptive approach with quantitative and qualitative procedures has been opted for, making use of data collection tools such as survey, which is appropriate for this kind of approach. Results show that the effectiveness of Production Planning Control in the Cluster is viable under the Prism of Paraconsistent Logic.

Keywords: Cluster · Production planning and control · Paraconsistent Logic · Competition · Baby Fashion

1 Introduction

Production management comprehends the activities involved in the transformation process of products or services, corresponding to the set of actions of planning, management and control of operational activities. For the adequacy and longevity of a company or process in the economically profitable and efficient market it is necessary to provide basic conditions for the introduction in current concepts [1,2]. In an intense and competitive scenario, the products and services depend on the quality of the organizational operation [2,3].

Reuter and Brambring [4] state that excellence in production planning and control (PPC) is the main pre-requirement for the managing of the production system.

In that sense, the productive process has to offer flexibility, in the process of solutions and alternative adapted to the needs of the company. The management of operations is responsible for the planning and control of the use of production resources to develop products with excellence, enabling the company's competition and longevity in the market [5].

I. Nääs et al. (Eds.): APMS 2016, IFIP AICT 488, pp. 162–169, 2016.
DOI: 10.1007/978-3-319-51133-7_20

The study of operations and production control seeks to define and employ the tools, methods and instruments viable to the generation of positive results in organizational life development. The generation of results derives from consumer's (i.e. end user's), satisfaction and loyalty.

This planning reflects on the production costs and deadlines. The more efficient and effective the planning is, the better the cluster PPC development will be. The knowledge of the elements of the production, as for providing information for the many areas of the organizations manufacturing system aid the operations for the achievement of excellence and desirable finished products [5,6].

Therefore, the main objective of this study is understand the relevant aspects of the PPC in a Baby Fashion cluster, making use of Paraconsistent Logic with analysis tools. This tools is essential for the efficiency of the planning and control in the cluster enabling the achievement of goals with shorter deadlines and smaller costs.

2 Literature Review

2.1 Production Planning, Programation and Control

The PPC is one of the most important administrative operations from the perspective of productive activities. Planning and subsequently control, as the name implies, is not an easy task, but rather a very complex one, because it takes into consideration a relevant number of variables [1,5].

One of the biggest PPC difficulties, rather than planning, is controlling production because disturbances and incidents common in a production process, can hamper the original program, causing delays and additional costs. In order to make this PPC viable it is necessary to study its evolution along the time and the causes which triggered the changes. Such causes will indicate the influence of all the sectors involved in the production process, and how these sectors interact [1].

PPC is considered an operation which involves areas of a company or a project to achieve the organizations productive goals, which seek to systematize its processes considering the effectiveness and efficiency aspects, that is to say, PPC has as its essence the carrying on a program of coordinate actions in order to obtain the smallest cost within the shortest possible deadline in the making of a product or performing a service, and subsequently, control those actions so that it sticks to the original program as much as possible [1,5].

As time passes by, according to technological developments, the concept of PPC has been changing, also. The most important aspect of the development and maintenance context of a production control and planning system may be the Constant change in its competitive environment, and such changes vary from technological to the strategic and legal fields [7].

With the constant technological development and a great set of market strategies and legislation variation due to globalization, the Production planning becomes more and more complex, with a number of variables which increases systemically, being some of those variables are unchanging or imponderable [8].

Regardless of the kind of manufacturing, or manufacturing system, the Planning is an essential factor for the task to succeed. Traditional planning systems such as ERP among others, are no more sufficient for a safe and assertive planning [9].

2.2   Paraconsistent Logic Annotated

The paraconsistent logic is capable of manipulating inconsistent information systems without running the risk of trivialization. In the paraconsistent logic there are formulas A such that from A and ¬ A no formula B comes, that is to say, there is a formula B of a set of all the sentences such that B is not the theorem of the theory. Subrahmanian, in the 1980s, made use of paraconsistent logic in logic programation [10].

The employing of Evidential Paraconsistent Logic Annotated Eτ (Eτ Logic{XE"Lógica Eτ" \t"- Lógica Paraconsistente Anotada Evidencial Eτ"}) has as its main objective implementing computerized systems which allow the handling of uncertain knowledge which can also be inconsistent [11]. The Eτ Logic treats the premises as partial evidences and presents characteristics of an Evidential Logic where the notes are considered as positive degree of evidence or negative degree of evidence and the analyses take into consideration the value of the information produced by real and uncertain sources [10].

The Eτ Logic owns a Eτ language and the atomic propositions are the type p (μ, λ) where p is a proposition and $\mu, \lambda \in [0.1]$ (closed real unitary interval). For each proposition P the value of μ is associated, which indicates the degree of positive evidence of p, and λ, which indicates the degree of negative evidence of p. The values μ, λ depend on the applications and can undergo changes where μ can be the degree of positive belief and λ can be the degree of negative evidence of the proposition p; also, μ can indicate the probability of p to occur and λ the improbability of p to occur [10].

The Logic atomic propositions p (μ, λ) can be read as: I believe in p with the positive degree of belief μ and the negative degree of belief λ, or the positive evidence degree p(μ) and the negative evidence degree p(λ) [10]. It is possible to calculate the Degree of Certainty (Gc) from the equation: Gc $= \mu - \lambda$. This degree can also vary from -1 to $+1$, and its value corresponds to the distance from the intersection point between the Degrees of Evidence to the line which connects the point D $= (0.0)$, Paracomplete, to the point C $= (1.1)$, Inconsistent, according to the Fig. 1.

The degree of certainty chosen for this work has been H $= 0.7$, which corresponds to a certainty of 95.5%, and this is considered good for a planning. Lower degrees lessen PPC certainty safety whereas higher degrees become expensive from when it comes to investments to optimize performance. It can be verified that the area inside the certainty zone is the area of the triangle, in that case $= 0.3 \times 0.3/2$ which results in a surface of area 0.045, the total area of the graph is the surface of a square $= 1 \times 1$ which results in a surface of area 1. The percentage of certainty area in relation to the total surface is $= 1 - (0.045/1) = 0.955$, which gives a 95.5% certainty, considered to be a good number for a planning.

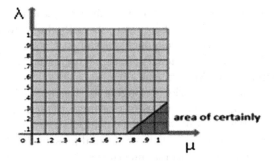

Fig. 1. Region of certainty in a Cartesian graph where $0 \leq \mu \leq 1$ and $0 \leq \lambda \leq 1$.

It goes without saying that for stricter values above 0.70 the costs for the intra-organizational network can be equally higher.

2.3 Competitive Clusters

Globalization has contributed to increase more and more competitivity in the market, making viable a great concentration of efforts in the development of businesses in small companies. It is certain that the isolated performance in this market will hardly ever have a globalized reach, with competitive advantages and competition chances [2,3].

In that context, the formation of regional clusters and local productive systems are relevant strategies for the geographic concentration of companies and institutions interconnected on a specific level, involving suppliers, machines, services and infrastructure which make competition viable for the companies [2,12,13].

Clusters are concentration of interconnected companies of a specific sector, encompassing arrangements of related companies and other entities important for competition, including, for instance, specialized raw material suppliers, such as components, machines, services and specialized infrastructure suppliers [13,14].

2.4 Baby Fashion Cluster

In Brazilian territory, textile national industry involves about 30 thousand apparels, creating 1.65 million Jobs in all its production chain in the sectors of apparel production with an annual US \$21 billion profit [15].

The demand for children's products is among the segment which can be explored. More specifically the city of Terra Roxa, the baby wear cluster is still developing, favoring business in the city and in the region.

For its dynamics in the children fashion Field, Terra Roxa has characteristics related to its economical and population dynamics, which needs more attention. The modernization in the rural areas made viable the culture of soy and wheat, using the room which was once used for coffee culture. The failure in agricultural activities forced economic players to look for new products and services [16].

The replacement of rural workforce with mechanization contribute to the advent of clusters in the sector of apparel, specially baby wear, as a viable alternative for the economical development of the city, considerably impacting competition, with the creation of new Professional opportunities and Jobs in the companies participating in this segment [16].

The children fashion industries belonging to the studied cluster have an annual production of 3,500,000 articles of clothing, attracting consumers from the Northeastern, northern, southeastern, central western and southern regions of Brazil and Mercosul, creating 1,203 direct formal jobs until 2016. This segment consists of 19 companies acting as manufacturers.

Among them, 16 children fashion producers, seven factions, two service providers, coming to 28 companies, including 250 micro entrepreneurs acting on their own.

3 Methodology

The research took place in the cluster of children fashion in Terra Roxa, Paraná, Brazil, which amount to 16 companies totally, characterized by 26% micro enterprises, 53% small enterprises and 21% medium to big enterprises.

From the objective of the work, a descriptive approach has been opted for, with quantitative and qualitative procedures [17] making use of data collection tools such as survey, which is appropriate for this kind of approach [17,18].

Structure interviews were used, with specialists in the management and production from 16 companies belonging to the cluster. Data were gathered personally in the second semester of 2015 and each specialist answered the quantitative and qualitative questions from a pattern $(\mu;\lambda)$ to determine the level of beliefs and disbeliefs assigned. The data collected were organized in form of tables. The results obtained from the specialists from the same area were considered using disjunction criteria $(\vee)$, where $p1(\mu1;\lambda1) \vee p2(\mu2;\lambda2)\rightarrow$ p1 or 2 $(\mu max;\lambda min)$. For results from obtained from specialists from different areas, junction criteria was used $(\wedge)$, where $p1(\mu1;\lambda1) \wedge p2(\mu2;\lambda2)\rightarrow$ p1 or 2 $\mu min;\lambda max)$ [11].

The level of certainty chosen for this work was H = 0.7, considered a good number for a planning. It is important to consider that for more restrict values above 0.7, the costs for the intraorganizational network operations can be high.

4 Results and Discussion

4.1 Planning Premises

Elements used as premise in the PPC duties were analyzed, as it can be verified in Fig. 2.

The analysis from specialists shows that the average or center of gravity of the premises network revealed a 0.85 positive index and 0.15 negative index, resulting in 0.71 index of certainty for this analysis.

In your opinion, what are the most important and fundamental elements for your company's manufacturing system?	μ	λ
Time	0.91	0.09
Quality	0.96	0.04
Delivery Deadline	0.95	0.05
Price	0.81	0.19
Product Change	0.72	0.28
Quantity	0.77	0.23
	0.85	0.15
	H=	0.71

Fig. 2. Planning premises and production control

4.2 Considerations on Intraorganizational Network

The Fig. 3 shows the relations of the Intraorganizational Network of all the productive sectors considered in the PPC.

Considering the different sectors of your company, how would you evaluate their ellaboration and management of the PPC in your company?	μ	λ
Purchases	0.93	0.07
Sales	0.97	0.03
Quality	0.93	0.07
Project of new products	0.88	0.12
Industrial Engineering	0.79	0.21
Logistics	0.81	0.19
Production	0.95	0.05
Guaranteed Quality	0.92	0.08
Finances	0.95	0.05
	0.90	0.10
	H= 0.81	

Fig. 3. Considerations of intraorganizational network *versus*PPC

The average of Center of gravity of the Intraorganizational Network has a 0.90 positive index and a 0.10 negative index, resulting in a 0.81 index of certainty for this analysis.

4.3 Planning Functions

The PPC encompasses many functions in order to consider all the resources, time/equipment/staff, which bring the PPC result. The Fig. 4 illustrates the performance of each function.

According to the analysis, it can be verified that the average or center of gravity of the PPC has a 0.79 positive index and a 0.21 negative index, resulting in a 0.58 index of certainty for this analysis, which, individually, is not a good index of certainty. However, these functions combined with the considerations of premises and of the intraorganizational network result in a global index of certainty which will determine the effectiveness of the PPC.

4.4 Intersectional Factors

The Fig. 5 reveals the global result among the three individual analyses.

Considering the many steps in PPC, evaluate the importance of the functions in the production planning and control?	μ	λ
Sales forecasting	0.85	0.15
Product project ellaboration	0.80	0.20
Productive process planning	0.84	0.16
Production programming	0.88	0.12
Finished product storage	0.55	0.45
Demand planning	0.72	0.28
Capacity planning	0.79	0.21
Information flow for the PPC	0.75	0.25
Material Management	0.83	0.17
Production control	0.84	0.16
Finished products stock control	0.84	0.16
	0.79	0.21
	H= 0.58	

Fig. 4. PPC functions

	μ	λ
Premises	0.85	0.15
Intra Network	0.90	0.10
Planning	0.79	0.21
	0.85	0.15
	H= 0.69	

Fig. 5. Influences combined among premises/intraorganizational network/planning

5   Conclusions

The composition of factors reveals a 0.69 index of certainty, which is close to the objective "0.70". That means that the Effectiveness of PPC in the Cluster is consistent, under the prism of Paraconsistent Logic. As a suggestion for the Planning, the item: "Finished Products Storage" should be improved, because it has $\mu = 0.55$ e $\lambda = 0.45$ becoming $\mu = 0.80$ e $\lambda = 0.20$. This means a better planning for finished products storage. A new scenario will be had according to Fig. 6.

	μ	λ
Premises	0.85	0.15
Intra Network	0.90	0.10
Planning	0.81	0.19
	0.85	0.15
	H= 0.71	

Fig. 6. New efficiency scenario of the PPC

If so, in spite of the functions of the PPC having a low index of certainty individually, 0.58 in that case; the general result of 0.69 is closer enough to the desired 0.70. Which by itself would show the consistency of the PPC effectiveness. In order to be stricter, a sole item belonging to the PPC should improve, which is finished products storage. This simple improvement can lead the general situation to a 0.70 effectiveness, which according to what was previously mentioned, can provide a 95.5% guarantee.

References

1. Slack, N., Chambers, S., Johnston, R.: Administração da Produção. Atlas (2009)
2. Porter, M.E.: Location, competition, and economic development: local clusters in a global economy. Econ. Dev. Q. **14**(1), 15–34 (2000)
3. Tilahun, N., Fan, Y.: Transit and job accessibility: an empirical study of access to competitive clusters and regional growth strategies for enhancing transit accessibility. Transp. Policy **33**, 17–25 (2014)
4. Reuter, C., Brambring, F.: Improving data consistency in production control. Procedia CIRP **41**, 51–56 (2016)
5. Costa Neto, P.L.O., Canuto, S.A.: Administraçao com Qualidade: Conhecimentos Necessários para a Gestao Moderna. Blucher, São Paulo (2010)
6. Cichos, D., Aurich, J.C.: Support of engineering changes in manufacturing systems by production planning and control methods. Procedia CIRP **41**, 165–170 (2016)
7. Volllmann, T., Berry, W., Whybark, D., Jacobs, F.: Sistemas de Planejamento e Controle da Produção. Bookman, Porto Alegre (2006)
8. Mourtzis, D., Doukas, M., Psarommatis, F.: A toolbox for the design, planning and operation of manufacturing networks in a mass customisation environment. J. Manuf. Syst. **36**, 274–286 (2015)
9. Behboudi, A.M., Khalilzadeh, A., Youshanlouei, H.R., Mood, M.M.: Identifying and ranking the effective factors on selecting enterprise resource planning (ERP) system using the combined Delphi and Shannon entropy approach. Procedia-Soc. Behav. Sci. **41**, 513–520 (2012)
10. Abe, J.M., Lopes, H.F.S., Nakamatsu, K.: Paraconsistent artificial neural networks and delta, theta, alpha, and beta bands detection. In: Kountchev, R., Nakamatsu, K. (eds.) Advances in Reasoning-Based Image Processing Intelligent Systems, pp. 331–364. Springer, Heidelberg (2012)
11. de Carvalho, F.R., Abe, J.M.: A simplified version of the fuzzy decision method and its comparison with the paraconsistent decision method. In: Ninth International Conference on Computing Anticipatory Systems, CASYS 2009, vol. 1303, pp. 216–235. AIP Publishing (2010)
12. Reis, J.G.M., Neto, M.M., Vendrametto, O., Costa Neto, P.L.O.: Qualidade em Redes de Suprimentos: A Qualidade Aplicada ao Suplly Chain Management. Atlas (2015)
13. Amato Neto, J.: Gestão de Sistemas Locais de Produção e Inovação (Clusters/APLS): um Modelo de Referencia. Atlas (2009)
14. Söylemezoğlu, E., Doruk, Ö.T.: Are clusters efficient for the relation between milk production and value added per capita in regional level? An empirical assessment. Procedia-Soc. Behav. Sci **150**, 1277–1286 (2014)
15. IBGE: Instituto Brasileiro de Geografia e Estatísticas: Demografia das Empresas. IBGE (2016)
16. Willers, E.M., Lima, J., Staduto, J.A.R.: Desenvolvimento Local, Empreendedorismo e Capital Social: O Caso de Terra Roxa no Estado do Paraná. Interações **9**(1), 45–54 (2008)
17. Collis, J.: Pesquisa em Administração: Um Guia Pratico para Alunos de Graduaçã Pos-graduacao. Bookman, Porto Alegre (2005)
18. Hahn, M.H., Lee, K.C., Lee, D.S.: Network structure, organizational learning culture, and employee creativity in system integration companies: the mediating effects of exploitation and exploration. Comput. Hum. Behav. **42**, 167–175 (2015)

Dynamic Seed Genetic Algorithm to Solve Job Shop Scheduling Problems

Flávio Grassi, Pedro Henrique Triguis Schimit[✉],
and Fabio Henrique Pereira

Universidade Nove de Julho, São Paulo, Brazil
{schimit, fabiohp}@uninove.br

Abstract. This paper proposes a simple implementation of genetic algorithm with dynamic seed to solve deterministic job shop scheduling problems. The proposed methodology relies on a simple indirect binary representation of the chromosome and simple genetic operators (one-point crossover and bit-flip mutation), and it works by changing a seed that generates a solution from time to time, initially defined by the original sequencing of the problem addressed, and then adopting the best individual from the past runs of the GA as the seed for the next runs. The methodology was compared to three different approaches found in recent researches, and its results demonstrate that despite not finding the best results, the methodology, while being easy to be implemented, has its value and can be a starting point to more researches, combining it with other heuristics methods that rely in GA and other evolutionary algorithms as well.

Keywords: Genetic Algorithms · Job shop · Scheduling · Dynamic seed

1 Introduction

Scheduling is the process of assigning one or more resources to perform certain activities whose processing will require a certain amount of time [1]. These resources in an industrial environment may be associated with machines, and the activities that will be processed in a machine are known as operations or tasks. Thus, a job is a set of one or more tasks.

The scheduling problems in scenarios of job shop (JSSP) is a NP-hard problem which has been studied by using exact methods, such as the Branch and Bound [2] and the Shifting Bottleneck [3]. It consists of scheduling a set of tasks in different machines; known as jobs, where the precedence of each task must be obeyed. Each job can be processed in one machine at a time, and the task started in a certain machine must be completed before this resource starts a new process, i.e., no pre-emption is allowed. The time need for each task to be proceeded is known in advance for deterministic problems, and finally, all the jobs are available in the time zero [1]. Usually, researchers consider the minimization of the makespan as the goal, where makespan refers to the total time needed to process all operations of all the jobs in the machines.

In recent years, the metaheuristic methods have been widely used in solving this type of problem. Among these methods, those with greater emphasis for solving JSSP

© IFIP International Federation for Information Processing 2016
Published by Springer International Publishing AG 2016. All Rights Reserved
I. Nääs et al. (Eds.): APMS 2016, IFIP AICT 488, pp. 170–177, 2016.
DOI: 10.1007/978-3-319-51133-7_21

are Tabu Search [4], Simulated Annealing [5], Genetic Algorithms [6, 7], and Ant Colony Optimization [8].

This paper presents a different methodology to solve JSSP using genetic algorithms. A genetic algorithm (GA) is as a class of metaheuristic techniques that is aimed at finding solutions based on the mechanisms of natural selection and genetics. From an initial population, each individual is evaluated by a fitness function which depends on the purpose. Crossover and mutation operators are used for new generation of individuals in order to ensure a better access to the search space.

The paper is organized as follows. The detailed presentation of the JSSP is provided in Sect. 2. Section 3 provides the experimental results to solve a set of deterministic JSSP in comparison with different works that have been currently referenced. Section 4 presents the conclusions and suggests some aspects that could be subject to further researches.

2 Proposed Methodology

The proposed methodology suggests a simple indirect representation based on a binary matrix and, therefore, the use of simple genetic operators, such as the one-point crossover and bit-flip mutation. Despite its simplicity, it proved powerful enough by its association with the dynamic seed, which is based on the inheritance of the previous seed that generated the best solution within a certain number of generations and its best individual, as further explained in the next sections.

In order to evaluate the simulation code developed, 10 different sequences for the FT06 problem, generated from LISA [9], were presented to the simulation code. LISA is an open-source software developed by a group of researchers at Otto-von-Guericke University (under the supervision of Prof. Dr. Frank Werner) for creating, editing and troubleshooting deterministic scheduling problems, which has a useful graphical interface.

2.1 Representation Mechanism

The representation adopted in this work is based on a binary matrix of dimension $m \times (n - 1)$, where m is the number of the machines and n is the number of jobs. Since this representation does not allow a direct interpretation of a solution for the problem, Figs. 1 and 2 are used in order to clarify the process of decoding, considering a specific instance of JSSP known as FT06, available at the OR-Library [10].

First, the matrix of routes (Fig. 1a), which is given by the problem, is converted into a sequence of jobs per machine, according to the natural order of arrival of jobs, which is the seed for the solutions (Fig. 1b). To that end, the initial matrix is read by columns, from left to right, for each machine, in ascending order of jobs. This process is executed just once within GA, at the first run of the optimization process.

Thus, reading the first column in the matrix of routes, job 1 comes first in the machine 3, followed by jobs 3, 5, and jobs 2, 4 and 6 from the columns 2, 3 and 6 in the

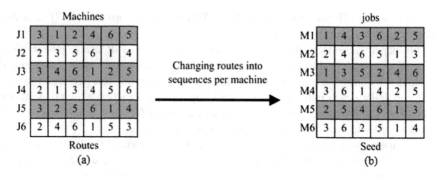

Fig. 1. Generation of the seed (b) based on the routes (a)

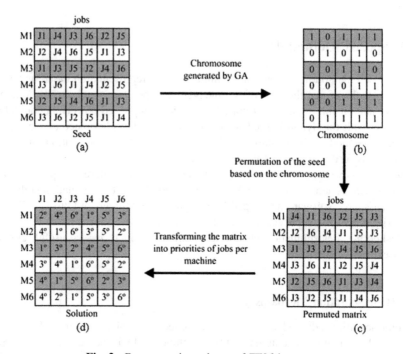

Fig. 2. Representation schema of FT06 instance

matrix of routes, respectively; thereby generating the third row of the seed (Fig. 1b). Then, the process is repeated for all other machines.

The GA generates a binary matrix (Fig. 2b), which is the chromosome. After the first generation, the genetic operators act over this matrix. A reading of this matrix by rows is performed, from top to bottom, and where the value 1 is identified, a permutation in the seed is accomplished. The permutation occurs between the element in the same position where the value 1 in the chromosome was found, and its successor.

Therefore, as the value of first element of the chromosome (in Fig. 2b) is 1, a permutation between the values 1 and 4 in the seed occurs (Fig. 2a), generating the first element of the new array of sequences (Fig. 2c), which is the job 4, and the second element, that is the job 1. Until this moment, the job 1 is temporarily in the position 2, since his stay in that position depends upon the value of the second element in the chromosome.

As the value of the second position in the chromosome is 0, there will be not swapping between the second and third element of the original sequence. Thus, the first two elements of the new matrix are really the jobs 4 and 1, respectively. This process is repeated with all the elements of the first row of the seed, and then all the elements of the second row, and so forth. The reason to have just five elements in the rows of the chromosome is because the swapping occurs between the element in the current position and its successor, which means a value of 1 in the fifth position already generates permutation between the fifth and sixth elements of the original seed, and therefore is not necessary to have a sixth column (considering the problem FT06).

Finally, the new matrix generated through the permutation is turned into a matrix of priority of the jobs per machine (Fig. 2d), which is the way that the simulation code interprets the sequences. Analyzing the first three jobs in the first row of the permuted matrix is clear to see that job 4 should be scheduled first in the machine 1, followed by jobs 1 and 6, respectively. Therefore, in the matrix of the priorities (which is the representation of the solution itself), these are the jobs that receive priority values 1, 2, and 3, respectively. This process is conducted on all elements of the new matrix, called a solution (Fig. 2d).

2.2 Dynamic Seed Genetic Algorithm

The proposed approach, called Dynamic Seed Genetic Algorithm (DSGA), applies the classical GA as an inner level in which the candidate solutions are generated through permutations of the seed based on chromosomes, according to Fig. 2. Additionally, an external level is created in order to update the seed dynamically. After some generations of the classic GA in the inner level, a defined number of best solutions are chosen and a local search is performed in each of them, related to the original route of the problem addressed, thus generating new seeds. Specifically, the local search permutes the predecessor and successor of a chosen job that its delay will directly cause a delay that affects the whole system (i.e. a job that belongs to the so called critical path). Then, the best current solution and the corresponding permuted seed are used to update the seed from the previous step and a new set of generations in the inner level takes place.

3 Experiments

To prove the effectiveness of the proposed approach, a set of JSSP instances was taken from OR-Library, which is used by several researchers to compare their results against different methods and techniques. The instances set range from LA01 to LA10, due to Lawrence [11]. This set of problems deals with the classical deterministic job shop problem, which does not take into account the dynamic and stochastic behavior that can reflect more appropriately real-world industry situations. However, GA presents peculiar aspects in relation to other optimization methods and it is simple, flexible, robust and particularly useful in solving problems where other optimization techniques facing difficulties. Especially in relation to the fitness function, that may be a mathematical function, an experiment, a simulation model or a metamodel.

So, the proposed approach can be easily integrated with a simulation model in order to deal with a dynamic job shop scheduling problem that can take into account factors like, for example, random release and processing times, setup times, random machine breakdowns, and create more robust scheduling with regard to the stochastic and dynamically changes in the real manufacturing environment [12].

For each instance the proposed approach was run 10 times, in order to allow statistical references. The implementation was made through GAlib, which is a library of GA written in C++ by Matthew Wall, from the Massachusetts Institute of Technology [13]. Parameters adopted in GA are summarized in Table 1.

Table 1. Parameters of the GA adopted in the experiments

Parameter	Adopted value	Reason
Chromosome representation	Binary, matrix of dimension $m \times (n-1)$	Proposed methodology
Selection	Steady state	[14]
Replacement rate	90%	Experiments
Population size	10	Experiments
Crossover	One-point	Proposed methodology
Crossover rate	10%	Experiments
Mutation	Bit-flip	Proposed methodology
Mutation rate	1%	Experiments
Total number of generations	20,000 (50 internal plus 400 external)	Experiments
Stop criteria	Number of generations	[15]
Fitness Function	Simulation code	Proposed methodology

3.1   Performance Related to the Quality of the Solution

Unlike to run the total number of iterations once with elitism, which is largely used in the classic GA, in addition to inherit the best individual, the proposed approach also copies to the next generations the generator seed that was associated with that better individual. So, the seed is updated and used to create new candidate solutions in the following inner level, which contributes to the convergence process.

This approach allows the GA to route new and possibly better paths, as the initial population after each external loop is based on the best seed from previous generations in the inner level (i.e., a classic GA). By route better paths we mean to create a larger number of feasible solutions during the evolution process of the genetic algorithm in relation to the classical elitism approach, as it can be seen in Table 2.

The results of the proposed approach were also compared to three different methodologies found in the current researches. The Memetic Algorithm approach

Table 2. Feasible solutions of LA01 problem: classic GA vs. DSGA

Classic GA (with elitism)			DSGA		
Run	Feasible solutions	Non-feasible solutions	Run	Feasible solutions	Non-feasible solutions
1	103377	21623	1	115866	9134
2	102310	22690	2	116068	8932
3	101788	23212	3	114116	10884
4	101450	23550	4	115649	9351
5	102594	22406	5	114525	10475
6	103293	21707	6	118684	6316
7	104061	20939	7	118174	6826
8	102746	22254	8	115275	9725
9	101706	23294	9	116231	8769
10	103665	21335	10	116218	8782
Average	82.16%	17.84%	Average	92.86%	7.14%

(MA) is due to [16], while the Differential Algorithm with Sub-Group (DE) is due to [17] and the Hybrid Genetic Algorithm (HGA) is due to [7].

In order to ease compare the approaches, Table 3 summarize the makespan values obtained from the proposed methodology and those reported from other recent methodologies used to compare with. It is important highlight that the approaches DE, MA and HGA are not based only on the AG and can therefore be even more difficult to program and use.

Table 3. Makespan values obtained from the different methodologies (BKS = Best Known Solution, Avg. = Average)

			Methodology							
			MA		DE		HGA		DSGA	
Instance	Size ($n \times m$)	BKS	Best	Avg.	Best	Avg.	Best	Avg.	Best	Avg.
LA01	10 × 5	666	666	NA	666	666.0	666	NA	666	672.6
LA02	10 × 5	655	655	NA	655	663.6	655	NA	660	680.8
LA03	10 × 5	597	597	NA	597	610.4	597	NA	616	619.2
LA04	10 × 5	590	590	NA	590	597.3	590	NA	607	619.8
LA05	10 × 5	593	593	NA	593	593.0	593	NA	593	593.0
LA06	15 × 5	926	926	NA	926	926.0	926	NA	926	926.0
LA07	15 × 5	890	890	NA	890	890.0	890	NA	890	890.0
LA08	15 × 5	863	863	NA	863	863.0	863	NA	863	863.0
LA09	15 × 5	951	951	NA	951	951.0	951	NA	951	951.0
LA10	15 × 5	958	958	NA	958	958.0	958	NA	958	958.0

4 Conclusions and Suggestions

This paper presented a different methodology to solve Job Shop scheduling problems using Genetic Algorithms, which the authors called DSGA. The methodology works by using a simple indirect binary representation as the chromosome and simple genetic operators (one-point crossover and bit-flip mutation), and change the seed that generates a solution from time to time, initially defined by the original sequencing of the problem addressed, and then adopting the best individual from the past runs of the GA as the seed for the next runs.

The proposed methodology is easy to implement and, despite not finding the optimal solution for all instances, the simple proposed approach fails in problems in which the convergence to the optimal makespan is harder in all the different approaches, even for more sophisticated techniques which is especially true for square problems that are admittedly more difficult problems. Moreover, the proposed approach allows the GA to go through new and possibly better paths, which means to create a larger number of feasible solutions during the evolution process of the genetic algorithm in relation to the classical elitism approach.

As a continuity of this work, it is suggested to implement the proposed methodology in stochastic problems, with randomly processing times, obeying a probability distribution.

Acknowledgements. The authors would like to thank grant #2014/08688-4, São Paulo Research Foundation (FAPESP), for their funding of this research.

References

1. Pinedo, M.L.: Scheduling: Theory, Algorithms and Systems. Springer, New York (2008)
2. Jamili, A.: Robust job shop scheduling problem: mathematical models, exact and heuristic algorithms. Expert Syst. Appl. **55**(15), 341–350 (2016)
3. Braune, R., Zäpfel, G.: Shifting bottleneck scheduling for total weighted tardiness minimization—a computational evaluation of subproblem and reoptimization heuristics. Comput. Oper. Res. **66**, 130–140 (2016)
4. Bo, P., Zhipeng, L., Cheng, T.C.E.: A tabu search/path relinking algorithm to solve the job shop scheduling problem. Comput. Oper. Res. **53**, 154–164 (2015)
5. Faccio, M., Ries, J., Saggioro, N.: Simulated annealing approach to solve dual resource constrained job shop scheduling problems: layout impact analysis on solution quality. Int. J. Math. Oper. Res. **7**(6), 609–629 (2015)
6. Kurdi, M.: An effective New Island model genetic algorithm for job shop scheduling problem. Comput. Oper. Res. **67**, 132–142 (2016)
7. Qing-Dao-Er-Ji, R., Wang, Y.: A new hybrid genetic algorithm for job shop scheduling problem. Comput. Oper. Res. **39**(10), 2291–2299 (2012)
8. Huang, R., Yang, C.-L., Cheng, W.-C.: Flexible job shop scheduling with due window—a two-pheromone ant colony approach. Int. J. Prod. Econ. **141**(2), 685–697 (2013)
9. LISA: A Library of Scheduling Algorithms. http://www.math.ovgu.de/Lisa.html
10. Beasley, J.E.: OR-Library (2003). http://people.brunel.ac.uk/~mastjjb/jeb/orlib/files/jobshop1.txt

11. Lawrence, S.: Resource constrained project scheduling: an experimental investigation of heuristic scheduling techniques (supplement). Ph.D. dissertation, Carnegie-Mellon University (1984)
12. Menezes, F.M., Blanco, G.T., Rodriguez, P.C., Pereira, F.H.: Application of simulation and optimization for dynamic job shop scheduling under stochastic demand variability. In: Proceedings of 7th International Conference on Management of Computational and Collective Intelligence in Digital EcoSystems (MEDES 2015), vol. 1, pp. 1–8 (2015)
13. GAlib: A C++ Library of Genetic Algorithm Components. http://lancet.mit.edu/ga/dist/. Accessed 19 Nov 2014
14. Yamada, T.: Studies on metaheuristics for jobshop and flowshop scheduling problems. Ph.D. dissertation, Kyoto University (2003)
15. Mitchell, T.M.: Machine Learning. McGraw-Hill, New York (1997)
16. Gao, L., Zhang, G., Zhang, L., Li, X.: An efficient memetic algorithm for solving the job shop scheduling problem. Comput. Industr. Eng. **60**(4), 699–705 (2011)
17. Wisittipanich, W., Kachitvichyanukul, V.: Two enhanced differential evolution algorithms for job shop scheduling problems. Int. J. Prod. Res. **50**(10), 2757–2773 (2012)

An Improved Computer-Aided Process Planning Method Considering Production Scheduling

Eiji Morinaga$^{(\boxtimes)}$, Nattapoom Charoenlarpkul, Hidefumi Wakamatsu,
and Eiji Arai

Graduate School of Engineering, Osaka University, Suita, Japan
{morinaga,c.nattapoom,wakamatu,arai}@mapse.eng.osaka-u.ac.jp

Abstract. Process planning is essential for achieving a sophisticated manufacturing system, and computer-aided process planning (CAPP) have been discussed. Considering recent requirements for realizing agile manufacturing, a set of flexible CAPP methods have been developed, in which process planning for one product using one machine is dealt with. In actual manufacturing, multiple workpieces are usually machined with multiple machine tools in the same period, and pursuing optimality for each product independently may result in poor productivity. For this reason, integration of process planning and production scheduling was performed by formulating the integrated problem as a 0–1 integer programming problem. However, this formulation involves huge computational load. This paper provides an improved method where the integrated problem is formulated as a mixed integer programming problem.

1 Introduction

In order to convert product design data into a real product, it is necessary to perform process planning, that is, to select manufacturing processes and determine the sequence in which they are carried out. Because it plays an important role as a bridge between product design and manufacturing, numerous works on computer-aided process planning (CAPP) have been actively conducted [1].

Recent diversified and changeable customers' needs have increased a need to realize agile manufacturing [2] that is capable of immediately adapting to changes in the manufacturing situation, and flexibility has been a keyword in recent manufacturing. This need is also being addressed in research related to CAPP [3]. This research aimed at developing autonomous machine tools that require no NC programming and can flexibly adapt to changes in the manufacturing situation, and a flexible process planning method for rough milling was proposed. This method consists of four main steps—(i) decomposing the total removal volume (TRV) through the application of decomposition rules to transform it into sets of machining primitive shapes (MPSs), (ii) converting each of the MPS sets to a set of machining features (MFs) by determining a machining sequence for

I. Nääs et al. (Eds.): APMS 2016, IFIP AICT 488, pp. 178–186, 2016.
DOI: 10.1007/978-3-319-51133-7_22

each set of MPSs and recognizing each MPS as an MF, (iii) executing rough operation planning by applying a tool selection rule and a case-based reasoning system for cutting condition decisions, and (iv) extracting the optimal set of MFs to achieve the shortest machining time with information on the machining sequence and the utilized tools as the optimal process plan. With this method, process plans are generated and then the optimal plan is selected. Therefore, when the manufacturing situation changes, it is possible to quickly provide a new optimal plan by executing steps (iii) and (iv). Several enhancements have been made to this method for enabling extraction of a better set of MFs [4], for taking multi-axis milling into account and reducing computational complexity [5], and for improving computational efficiency [6].

These methods deal with process planning to create one product using one milling machine. In actual manufacturing, multiple workpieces are usually machined with multiple machine tools in the same period, and pursuing the optimal plan without consideration of total production may result in poor productivity. Considering this point, selection of the optimal process plan in the flexible CAPP methods and production scheduling (PS) were integrated, and selection of a set of the optimal process plans for multiple workpieces from the point of view of total productivity was formulated as a 0–1 integer programming problem [7]. However, this formulation needs a huge number of 0–1 variables, since it is necessary to define the variables for each sub-period defined by dividing the whole period, and therefore this method involves large computational load.

In this paper, this method is improved by formulating the integrated problem as a mixed integer programming (MIP) problem. In the next section, the flexible CAPP method [6] is outlined, and then the problem of the conventional integrated method [7] based on this CAPP method is explained. Section 3 provides formulation of the integrated problem of selection of the optimal process plans for multiple products and PS as an MIP problem. This improved method is applied to an example in Sect. 4, and Sect. 5 presents our conclusion.

2 Overview of Conventional Method

This section provides an outline of the conventional CAPP method [5,6], which was improved considering integration with PS [7] and will be also improved further in Sect. 3. In this method, which is for rough milling, it is assumed all surfaces of the workpiece and the product are parallel to the xy, yz or zx plane of an orthogonal coordinate system and the tool approaches the workpiece along one of these axes (Fig. 1). Process planning is performed by the following steps:

1. TRV extraction
   The total removal volume (TRV), which is the volume to be eliminated from a workpiece to obtain the product shape, is calculated by subtracting the product shape from the workpiece shape (Fig. 2).

2. Concavity-based division
   A cutting plane is generated at a concave part of the TRV contour by extending a surface, and then the TRV is divided by it. This process is repeated until the division has been executed at all concave parts, and the TRV is converted into a set of machining primitive shapes (MPSs). Since type of the MPS set depends on the generation direction and sequence of the cutting planes, multiple MPS sets can be produced from one TRV (Fig. 3).
3. Machining sequence and direction assignment
   For each MPS set, the machining direction (Fig. 1) for each MPS and the machining sequence for those MPSs are considered.
4. MF recognition
   The machining directions and sequence assignment enables recognizing an MPS as a machining feature (MF) based on the number of its "open faces" and the relationship among its vertices and edges. For each MPS set, multiple MF sets are generated depending on the direction and sequence (Fig. 4).
5. Process plan generation
   For each MF set, a tool used for each MF is chosen from available tools by applying a given rule, and the machining condition for the MF is decided by a case-based reasoning system [8]. This operation generates, for each MPS set, MF sets including information about the machining sequence, the machining directions, and the tools to be used—that is, a process plans is generated.
6. Evaluation
   For each process plan of each MPS set, the total machining time is estimated. The plan that achieves the shortest total machining time is selected as the optimal process plan for the MPS set by the full search [5] or mathematical optimization framework [6]. After performing this operation for all MPS sets, the estimated total machining times for the optimal plans are compared with each other. The optimal plan for which the estimated total machining time is the shortest is ultimately output as the optimal process plan for the TRV.

In actual manufacturing, multiple workpieces are usually machined by using multiple machines in the same period. If this method is applied to those workpieces, the optimal plan is generated for each of them independently. Those plans would not be optimal from the point of view of manufacturing systems, since a machine tool can machine only one workpiece at a time. It is desirable to integrate process planning by this method with PS, and the integrated problem was formulated as a 0–1 integer programming problem where 0–1 variables are defined for each sub-period defined by dividing the whole period [7]. Since machining requires long time generally, the number of those variables are huge and therefore the integrated method involves a very large computational load.

3   Improved Integrated Method of CAPP and PS

This section provides formulation of the integrated problem of the optimal plan selection and PS as an MIP. Two kinds of 0–1 variables $x_{avS_1\cdots S_N dt}$, $y_{a,i,b,j}$ and

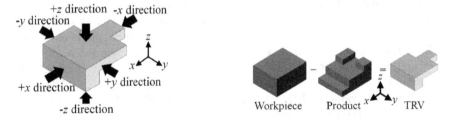

Fig. 1. Definition of machining directions [7].

Fig. 2. TRV extraction [7].

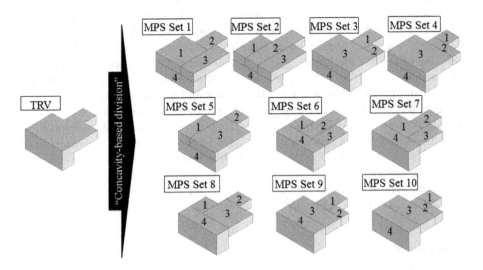

Fig. 3. Sets of MPSs extracted from the TRV. The numbers in each set are the identification numbers for the MPSs [7].

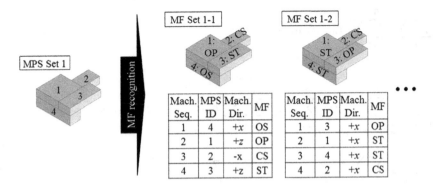

Fig. 4. MF recognition for an MPS set. Strings in each set stand for feature types ("CS", "OS", "OP", and "ST" stand for "closed slot", "open slot", "open pocket", and "step", respectively) [7].

three kinds of real variables $s_{a,i}^m$, $f_{a,i}^m$, C_{max} are introduced, where $a, b \in \mathcal{R} := \{1, \ldots, R\}$ and $v \in \mathcal{V} := \{1, \ldots V\}$ stand for the ID number of product and its MPS set, respectively, and N is the total number of the MPSs. (It is assumed that the total numbers of MPS sets and MPSs in the set are same for any product and any MPS set.) S_k is the ID number of the MPS that is machined after machining other $k - 1$ MPSs. S_1 takes a value in $\mathcal{N} := \{1, \ldots, N\}$, and S_k, $k \geq 2$ takes a value in $\{0\} \cup \mathcal{N}$, $k \geq 2$. $S_{\tilde{k}} = 0$, $\forall \tilde{k} > k$ means only the first k MPSs has been machined. $d \in \mathcal{D} := \{1, \ldots 6\}$ is machining direction ($1 : +x$; $2 : -x$; $\cdots 6 : -z$). $t \in \mathcal{T} := \{1, \ldots T\}$ and $m \in \mathcal{M} := \{1, \ldots, M\}$ are the ID number of the utilized tool and machine. $i, j \in \mathcal{N}$ are the operation number. $x_{avS_1 \cdots S_{k-1} S_k 0 \cdots 0 dt} = 1$ means that the MPS S_k of the MPS set v for the product a is machined in the direction d with the tool t after machining MPS S_1, S_2, \ldots, S_{k-1} in this order, and the time required for this machining is $P_{avS_1 \cdots S_{k-1} S_k 0 \cdots 0 dt}$, which has been calculated in advance and set to an negative value for unfeasible machining. $y_{a,i,b,j} = 1$ means the i-th operation of product a is executed after the j-th operation of product b. $s_{a,i}^m$ and $f_{a,i}^m$ stand for the starting and finishing times of the i-th operation of product a. C_{max} is the time at which all operations are completed. Let $\tau_{a,i}^m$ is the required time for the i-th operation of product a by machine m, T_m is the set of tools implemented on machine m and $\overline{M}$ is a positive value that is large enough, then the problem of finding the optimal plans for the products which achieve the smallest makespan C_{max} is described as an MIP by the following equations and inequalities. (1–12) are same as those in the conventional method, (14–20) are for formulation of PS problem as an MIP, and Eq. (13) integrates CAPP and PS.

minimize: C_{max} $\hfill$ (1)

subject to:

$$P_{avS_1 \cdots S_i 0 \cdots 0 dt} \cdot x_{avS_1 \cdots S_i 0 \cdots 0 dt} \geq 0,$$
$$\forall a \in \mathcal{R}, \ \forall v \in \mathcal{V}, \ \forall S_1, \ldots, S_i \in \mathcal{N}, \ i \in \mathcal{N}, \ d \in \mathcal{D}, \ \forall t \in \mathcal{T} \quad (2)$$

$$\sum_{v=1}^{V} \sum_{S_1=1}^{N} \sum_{d=1}^{6} \sum_{t=1}^{T} x_{avS_1 0 \cdots 0 dt} = 1, \ \forall a \in \mathcal{R} \quad (3)$$

$$\vdots$$

$$\sum_{v=1}^{V} \sum_{\substack{S_N=1 \\ S_N \neq S_{N-1}, \cdots S_1}}^{N} \cdots \sum_{\substack{S_2=1 \\ S_2 \neq S_1}}^{N} \sum_{S_1=1}^{N} \sum_{d=1}^{6} \sum_{t=1}^{T} x_{avS_1 S_2 \cdots S_N dt} = 1, \ \forall a \in \mathcal{R} \quad (4)$$

$$\sum_{v=1}^{V} \sum_{S_1=1}^{N} \sum_{d=1}^{6} \sum_{t=1}^{T} x_{avS_1 0 \cdots 0 dt} \leq 1, \ \forall a \in \mathcal{R} \quad (5)$$

$$\vdots$$

$$\sum_{v=1}^{V}\sum_{S_N=1}^{N}\cdots\sum_{S_2=1}^{N}\sum_{S_1=1}^{N}\sum_{d=1}^{6}\sum_{t=1}^{T} x_{avS_1S_2\cdots S_N dt} \leq 1, \ \forall a \in \mathcal{R} \tag{6}$$

$$\sum_{d=1}^{6}\sum_{t=1}^{T}\left(x_{avS_10\cdots0dt} + \sum_{S_k=1}^{N}\cdots\sum_{\substack{\tilde{S}_1=1\\\tilde{S}_1\neq S_1}}^{N} x_{av\tilde{S}_1\cdots S_k0\cdots0dt} \right) \leq 1,$$

$$\forall k \in \mathcal{N}\setminus\{1\}, \ \forall a \in \mathcal{R}, \ \forall v \in \mathcal{V}, \ \forall S_1 \in \mathcal{N} \tag{7}$$

$$\sum_{S_1=1}^{N}\sum_{d=1}^{6}\sum_{t=1}^{T}\left(x_{avS_1S_20\cdots0dt} + \sum_{S_k=1}^{N}\cdots\sum_{\substack{\tilde{S}_2=1\\\tilde{S}_2\neq S_2}}^{N} x_{avS_1\tilde{S}_2\cdots S_k0\cdots0dt} \right) \leq 1,$$

$$\forall k \in \mathcal{N}\setminus\{1,2\}, \ \forall a \in \mathcal{R}, \ \forall v \in \mathcal{V}, \ \forall S_2 \in \mathcal{N} \tag{8}$$

$$\vdots$$

$$\sum_{S_{N-2}=1}^{N}\cdots\sum_{S_1=1}^{N}\sum_{d=1}^{6}\sum_{t=1}^{T}\left(x_{avS_1\cdots S_{N-1}0dt} + \sum_{S_N=1}^{N}\sum_{\substack{\tilde{S}_{N-1}=1\\\tilde{S}_{N-1}\neq S_{N-1}}}^{N} x_{avS_1\cdots\tilde{S}_{N-1}S_N dt} \right)$$

$$\leq 1, \ \forall a \in \mathcal{R}, \ \forall v \in \mathcal{V}, \ \forall S_{N-1} \in \mathcal{N} \tag{9}$$

$$\sum_{S_1=1}^{N}\sum_{d=1}^{6}\sum_{t=1}^{T}\left(x_{avS_10\cdots0dt} + \sum_{\substack{\tilde{v}=1\\\tilde{v}\neq v}}^{V}\sum_{S_2=1}^{N} x_{a\tilde{v}S_1S_20\cdots0dt} \right) \leq 1, \ \forall a \in \mathcal{R}, \ \forall v \in \mathcal{V} \tag{10}$$

$$\sum_{S_1=1}^{N}\sum_{d=1}^{6}\sum_{t=1}^{T}\left(x_{avS_10\cdots0dt} + \sum_{\substack{\tilde{v}=1\\\tilde{v}\neq v}}^{V}\sum_{S_3=1}^{N}\sum_{S_2=1}^{N} x_{a\tilde{v}S_1S_2S_30\cdots0dt} \right) \leq 1,$$

$$\forall a \in \mathcal{R}, \ \forall v \in \mathcal{V} \tag{11}$$

$$\vdots$$

$$\sum_{S_1=1}^{N}\sum_{d=1}^{6}\sum_{t=1}^{T}\left(x_{avS_10\cdots0dt} + \sum_{\substack{\tilde{v}=1\\\tilde{v}\neq v}}^{V}\sum_{S_N=1}^{N}\cdots\sum_{S_2=1}^{N} x_{a\tilde{v}S_1S_2\cdots S_N dt} \right) \leq 1,$$

$$\forall a \in \mathcal{R}, \ \forall v \in \mathcal{V} \tag{12}$$

$$\tau_{a,i}^{m} = \sum_{v=1}^{V}\sum_{S_i=1}^{N}\cdots\sum_{S_1=1}^{N}\sum_{d=1}^{6}\sum_{t\in T_m} P_{avS_1\cdots S_i0\cdots0dt} \cdot x_{avS_1\cdots S_i0\cdots0dt},$$

$$\forall a \in \mathcal{R},\ \forall i \in \mathcal{N},\ \forall m \in \mathcal{M} \tag{13}$$

$$C_{max} \geq f_{a,i}^m,\ \forall a \in \mathcal{R},\ \forall m \in \mathcal{M},\ \forall i \in \mathcal{N} \tag{14}$$

$$f_{a,i}^m = \tau_{a,i}^m + s_{a,i}^m,\ \forall a \in \mathcal{R},\ \forall m \in \mathcal{M},\ \forall i \in \mathcal{N} \tag{15}$$

$$s_{a,i}^m \geq -1 \cdot \left(1 - \sum_{v=1}^{V} \sum_{S_i=1}^{N} \cdots \sum_{S_1=1}^{N} \sum_{d=1}^{6} \sum_{t \in T_m} x_{avS_1 \cdots S_i 0 \cdots 0 dt} \right),$$
$$\forall a \in \mathcal{R},\ \forall m \in \mathcal{M},\ \forall i \in \mathcal{N} \tag{16}$$

$$s_{a,i}^m - \overline{M} \cdot \sum_{v=1}^{V} \sum_{S_i=1}^{N} \cdots \sum_{S_1=1}^{N} \sum_{d=1}^{6} \sum_{t \in T_m} x_{avS_1 \cdots S_i 0 \cdots 0 dt} \leq -1,$$
$$\forall a \in \mathcal{R},\ \forall m \in \mathcal{M},\ \forall i \in \mathcal{N} \tag{17}$$

$$s_{a,i+1}^{\tilde{m}} + \overline{M} \cdot \left(1 - \sum_{v=1}^{V} \sum_{S_{i+1}=1}^{N} \cdots \sum_{S_1=1}^{N} \sum_{d=1}^{6} \sum_{t \in T_m} x_{avS_1 \cdots S_{i+1} 0 \cdots 0 dt} \right) > f_{a,i}^m,$$
$$\forall a \in \mathcal{R},\ \forall m, \tilde{m} \in \mathcal{M},\ \forall i \in \mathcal{N} \setminus \{N\} \tag{18}$$

$$s_{a,i}^m + \overline{M} \cdot \left(1 - \sum_{v=1}^{V} \sum_{S_i=1}^{N} \cdots \sum_{S_1=1}^{N} \sum_{d=1}^{6} \sum_{t \in T_m} x_{avS_1 \cdots S_i 0 \cdots 0 dt} \right)$$
$$\geq f_{b,j}^m - \overline{M} \cdot y_{a,i,b,j} - \overline{M} \cdot \left(1 - \sum_{v=1}^{V} \sum_{S_j=1}^{N} \cdots \sum_{S_1=1}^{N} \sum_{d=1}^{6} \sum_{t \in T_m} x_{bvS_1 \cdots S_j 0 \cdots 0 dt} \right),$$
$$\forall a, b \in \mathcal{R},\ a \neq b,\ \forall m \in \mathcal{M},\ \forall i, j \in \mathcal{N} \tag{19}$$

$$s_{b,j}^m + \overline{M} \cdot \left(1 - \sum_{v=1}^{V} \sum_{S_j=1}^{N} \cdots \sum_{S_1=1}^{N} \sum_{d=1}^{6} \sum_{t \in T_m} x_{bvS_1 \cdots S_j 0 \cdots 0 dt} \right)$$
$$\geq f_{a,i}^m - \overline{M} \cdot (1 - y_{a,i,b,j}) - \overline{M} \cdot \left(1 - \sum_{v=1}^{V} \sum_{S_i=1}^{N} \cdots \sum_{S_1=1}^{N} \sum_{d=1}^{6} \sum_{t \in T_m} x_{avS_1 \cdots S_i 0 \cdots 0 dt} \right),$$
$$\forall a, b \in \mathcal{R},\ a \neq b,\ \forall m \in \mathcal{M},\ \forall i, j \in \mathcal{N} \tag{20}$$

4 Case Study

The proposed method was applied to an example of $R = 3, V = 4, N = 4, M = 2, T = 8, T_1 = T_2 = 4$ (Fig. 5 and Table 1). The calculation was performed with a workstation (Intel Core i7-6700K 4.00 GHz, 8 GB RAM) and a commercial solver (IBM ILOG CPLEX Optimization Studio 12.6.2). The result shown in Table 2 and Figs. 6 and 7 was obtained after computing about 8 h, though it was impossible to solve the problem by the conventional method.

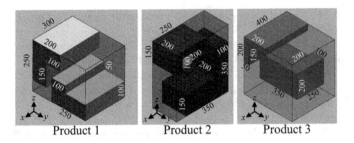

Fig. 5. TRVs (the blue/brown/green volumes) and their dimensions (in mm). (Color figure online)

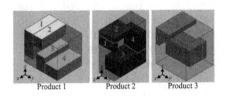

Fig. 6. MPS set of the optimal plans.

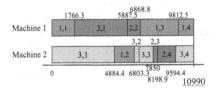

Fig. 7. Gantt chart.

Table 1. Available tools. "F" and "E" stand for facemill and endmill.

Tool ID	1	2	3	4	5	6	7	8
Tool type	F	F	E	E	F	F	E	E
Diameter [mm]	3	8	4	6	4	7	5	9
The number of teeth	4	4	4	4	4	4	4	4
Machine ID	1	1	1	1	2	2	2	2

Table 2. Machining sequence in the optimal process plan. "X, Y, Z" stands for MPS ID, direction and Tool ID.

Product	1	2	3
1st	4, 3, 2	3, 6, 2	3, 3, 8
2nd	3, 1, 8	2, 1, 2	4, 2, 8
3rd	1, 5, 2	1, 1, 8	2, 1, 8
4th	2, 5, 2	4, 2, 8	1, 1, 8

5 Conclusion

The integrated method of flexible CAPP and PS has been improved by formulating the integrated problem as an MIP. It has become possible to obtain solutions for larger problems. Further improvement is still required for actual machining.

Acknowledgement. We thank MAZAK Foundation for its support and Prof. Rei Hino, Nagoya University, Japan, for his advice.

References

1. Isnaini, M.M., Shirase, K.: Review of computer-aided process planning systems for machining operation – future development of a computer-aided process planning system –. Int. J. Autom. Technol. **8**, 317–332 (2014)

2. Sanchez, L.M., Nagi, R.: A review of agile manufacturing systems. Int. J. Prod. Res. **39**, 3561–3600 (2001)
3. Nakamoto, K., Shirase, K., et al.: Automatic production planning system to achieve flexible direct machining. JSME Int. J. Ser. C **47**, 136–143 (2004)
4. Hang, G., Koike, M., et al.: Flexible process planning system considering design intentions and disturbance in production process. In: Arai, E., Arai, T. (eds.) Mechatronics for Safety, Security and Dependability in a New Era, pp. 113–118. Elsevier, Amsterdam (2007)
5. Morinaga, E., Yamada, M., et al.: Flexible process planning for milling. Int. J. Autom. Technol. **5**, 700–707 (2011)
6. Morinaga, E., Hara, T., et al.: Improvement of computational efficiency in flexible computer-aided process planning. Int. J. Autom. Technol. **8**, 396–405 (2011)
7. Morinaga, E., Joko, H., Wakamatsu, H., Arai, E.: A computer-aided process planning method considering production scheduling. In: Umeda, S., Nakano, M., Mizuyama, H., Hibino, H., Kiritsis, D., Cieminski, G. (eds.) APMS 2015. IAICT, vol. 459, pp. 348–355. Springer, Heidelberg (2015). doi:10.1007/978-3-319-22756-6_43
8. Nagano, T., Shirase, K., et al.: Expert system based on case-based reasoning to select cutting conditions. J. JSPE **67**, 1485–1489 (2001). (in Japanese)

Modelling of Business and Operational Processes

Strategic Portfolios for the Integral Design of Value-Added Networks

Paul Schönsleben[1,2(✉)] and Manuel Rippel[1]

[1] BWI Center for Industrial Management, ETH Zürich, Zurich, Switzerland
pschoensleben@ethz.ch
[2] Chairman of the Board of the A. Vogel / Bioforce Group, Roggwil, Switzerland

Abstract. An adequate decision method plays an important role in strategic location planning, especially for physical goods. After a breakdown of the value-added network into its natural components, this paper uses strategic portfolios for determining the different network designs (e.g. production, transport, distribution, service). The portfolios depend on generic market, product and service features and fit together. The combination of the single portfolios represents the design options of the integral value-added network in a comprehensive way.

Keywords: Strategic management · Value-added network design · Portfolios

1 Importance of Portfolios for Strategic Planning

In practice, managers in firms like to base their strategic decisions on simple approaches that provide intuitive transparency and allow assessment of the robustness of the solution. Portfolios correspond to such an approach. In fact, most human beings intuitively understand logical relations if these are expressed in two dimensions, e.g. on a piece of paper, where both the horizontal and the vertical dimension stand for features that characterize the issue of the management task. Thus, people within and across companies can obtain a mutual understanding that can entail a successful cooperation.

Decisions to invest in value-added networks are strategic, owing to the high financial commitment and the long lead time until the facilities enter into operation. By using the portfolio approach, [1–3] introduce centralized and decentralized production concepts. The adequate concept may differ for each product family. To be feasible in practice, such a decision also involves the determination of the suitable transport, distribution and service concepts. Though, in general, authors of qualitative methods limit their discussion on one type of concept. This paper proposes a portfolio-based approach that allows an *integrated* determination of value-added networks. It builds on methods for designing production networks in [2,4], distribution networks in [5], and retail, service and transport networks in [6]. The approach first breaks down the network into its natural components. Then, by looking at the properties of the market, the product or the

© IFIP International Federation for Information Processing 2016
Published by Springer International Publishing AG 2016. All Rights Reserved
I. Nääs et al. (Eds.): APMS 2016, IFIP AICT 488, pp. 189–197, 2016.
DOI: 10.1007/978-3-319-51133-7_23

service as *generic features*, it is possible to combine the *values* of these features to get a set of portfolios of the design options for the production, transport, distribution and service network. This set mutually fits, that is, the combination of the single portfolios represents the design options of the integral value-added network.

2   Modelling of the Value-Added Network at the Strategic Level

At the strategic level, the value-added network of the vendor has to fulfill the requirements of the consumer. This is true for any kind of product or service, be it for typical consumer goods such as furniture and cars or for investments goods such as machine tool. The Fig. 1 shows the typical life-cycle phases of a product at the consumer's site and the classical, natural breakdown into *areas* of the value-added network of the vendor for the complementing life-cycle phases of the product.

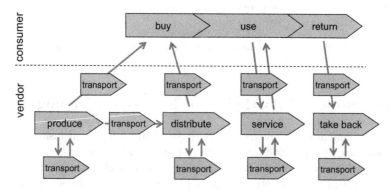

Fig. 1. Breakdown in areas of the value-added network of the vendor in function of the life-cycle phases of the product at the consumer's site.

After design, a product is produced by the vendor or his suppliers. A number of transport processes link the different value-added steps during this life-cycle phase of the product. Subsequently, the product is either transported directly to the consumer or to a distribution network that finally delivers the product to the consumer via a number of echelons and warehouses. Decentralized distribution can include a retail network. Thereby, it is not important whether the vendor possesses the different networks or mandates 3rd party providers for the respective tasks. During the use phase, a service network maintains the product, then called "service object". For this, owned or mandated transport networks pick up and later bring the service object at/to the customer or a collection point. If the product is used up, an adequate network will take back the product from the consumer. As a service network generally can take back products at the end of their use phase, there is no need for a separate network for this task.

3 Portfolios for the Network Design in Different Areas

For each area, we explain the strategic portfolio of design options and the underlying conflict of aims by presenting the generic features. Due to space restriction, the section on service network design had to be omitted. The reader is referred to [6].

3.1 Production Network Design

As a point of departure, and in order to introduce terminology, Fig. 2, copied from [2] (see also the adaption in [3]), shows more centralized or decentralized design options between two (conflicting) dimensions, taking the example of a product with four operations (or production levels) and subsequent distribution.

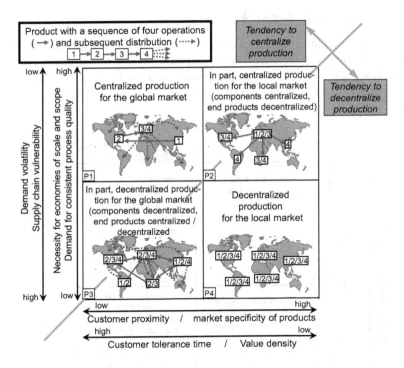

Fig. 2. Features of and design options for production networks (adapted from [2,4])

Figure 2 shows two times four generic features for designing production networks. In the x-axis, these are (a) *Customer proximity*: To sell a product it can be necessary to locate the value-adding processes close to the customers; (b) *Market specificity of products*: Adapting to the market is essential for functional requirements or for the appearance; (c) *Customer tolerance time*: After [7], this is the time span the customer will (or can) tolerate from the date of the order release to delivery of the product; (d) *Value density*, defined as item costs per kilo or cubic meter: Transport costs are of greater consequence if value density is low than if value density is high.

In the y-axis, the four features are (a) *Demand volatility*: Items have high demand volatility if many periods with no or very little demand are interrupted by few periods with large demand, for example ten times higher, often without recognizable regularity; (b) *Supply chain vulnerability*: Disruptions can arise from either the supply chain partners or the macro-economic environment; (c) *Necessity for economies of scale*: Are the manufacturing costs of the product low enough? (d) *Demand for consistent process quality*: Can customer needs be satisfied despite differing process quality? For more detailed discussion of Fig. 2, as well as for industrial examples for the four sectors P1, P2, P3 and P4, see [2, 4].

3.2   Transportation Network Design

Figure 3, copied from [6], shows, in addition to the two classical designs (direct or indirect transport) two possible mixed designs for the transport between two locations L1 and L2. The four possible designs lie in a two-dimensional space, spanned by the dimensions that correspond to two (conflicting) groups of features.

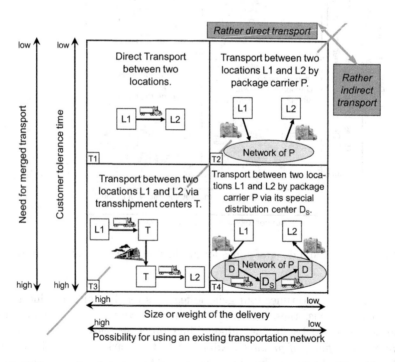

Fig. 3. Features of and design options for transportation networks (taken from [6])

Figure 3 shows two times two generic features for designing transport networks. In the x-axis, these are (a) *Size or weight of the delivery* in kilos or cubic meters: How do the suitable means of transport match up to this? (b) *Possibility of using an existing transport network*: Can the delivery specify a means of transport that is already carrying deliveries between the point of dispatch and the recipient, that is not yet at full capacity, and that has a known and fitting timetable. In the y-axis, the two features are (a) *Customer tolerance time*, as defined in Sect. 3.1; (b) *Need for merged transport*: To which extent delivery will be made together with products from another manufacturer? In the case of returns, to what extent must several products or parts thereof be sent back to a number of manufacturers at the same time? For detailed discussion of Fig. 3, and for industrial examples for the four sectors T1, T2, T3 and T4, see [6].

3.3 Distribution Network Design

Based on an idea in [5] and copied from [6], the portfolio in Fig. 4 shows, in addition to the two classical designs (centralized or decentralized distribution) two possible mixed designs. The four possible designs lie in a two-dimensional space, spanned by the dimensions that correspond to the two (conflicting) groups of features.

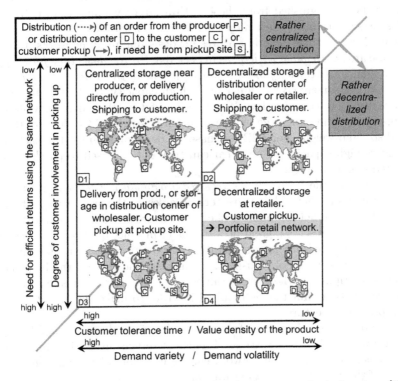

Fig. 4. Features of and design options for distribution networks (taken from [6]).

Figure 4 shows four plus two generic features for designing distribution networks. In the x-axis, these are (a) *Demand volatility*, as defined in Sect. 3.1; (b) *Demand variety*: High demand variety means that customers demand many different products. For these products the demand volatility is mostly high as well; (c) *Value density*, as defined in Sect. 3.1; (d) *Customer tolerance time*, as defined in Sect. 3.1. In the case of global distribution, the delivery lead time also includes the time required by customs procedures, which can disadvantage centralized distribution.

In the y-axis, the two features are (a) *Need for efficient returns using the same network*: Is it important that the customer be able to return goods efficiently through the same distribution network and that the network be able to handle these returns efficiently (keyword: reverse logistics)? (b) *Degree of customer involvement in picking up*: To what extent are customers willing *and* able to picking up the product themselves?

For more detailed discussion of Fig. 4, as well as for industrial examples for the four sectors D1, D2, D3 and D4, see [6].

3.4   Retail Network Design

For decentralized distribution, in the first approach points of sale (POS) with a smaller volume of goods (i.e. items and/or quantity per item) available at the POS, can be distinguished from those with a larger volume. Copied from [6], Fig. 5 shows the resulting design options for retail networks.

Figure 5 shows three generic features for designing retail networks. In the x-axis, these are (a) *Demand variety*: as in Sect. 3.3; (b) *Available time for shopping and simultaneously capacity of an available means of transport of the customer*: For private consumers (B2C), a car has a high capacity. On foot or by bicycle, the capacity is, in contrast, low. If time is limited, or the car is unavailable at the appropriate time, then the purchase option is restricted to a local outlet and limited size and weight. For B2B purchasers – depending on the transaction – a lorry offers high capacity. A small car can then only be used to purchase items of limited size and weight.

In the y-axis, the feature is *the required geographical catchment area* for the product range on offer: This characteristic assesses the size of the catchment area in which a "sufficient" number of customers are based, for whom the offered product range represents a good fit in terms of product quality and price. This assessment is carried out in consideration of purchasing power, time available and the choice of means of transport. "Sufficient" means that the frequency of purchases multiplied by the average value of each sale corresponds to a minimum sale value per time unit that is required in order to make the operation of the POS a profitable venture.

For more detailed discussion of Fig. 5, as well as for industrial examples for the three sectors R2, R3 and R4, see [6]. If efficient returns using the same network are possible, the distribution network can be used for taking back products at the end of their use phase in a natural way.

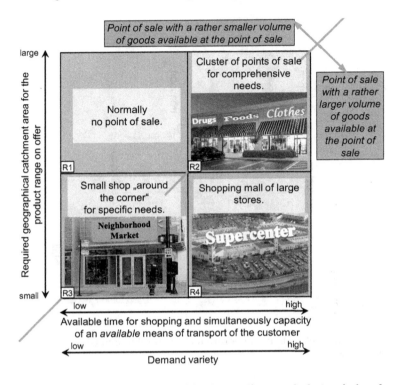

Fig. 5. Decentralized distribution: portfolio for retail network design (taken from [6]).

4 Integration of the Portfolios

An adequate design of the value-added network is decisive for customer satisfaction, given a sufficient quality of the delivered product or service. As Fig. 6 shows for the production and the delivery process, the production, distribution, retail (if needed), and various transport networks have to fit together in order to achieve the goal of a satisfied customer. There are dependencies between the design options of the different portfolios that should be considered for their integration. Here are some examples:

As the customer tolerance time is a feature for the design of both transport networks (see Fig. 3) as well as production and distribution networks (see Figs. 2 and 4), there are naturally close combinations when it comes to integrating the networks. This is the case when the customer tolerance time is low in both portfolios, or high in both portfolios. In the case of the distribution network, this means (1) *Decentralized distribution* is the preferred combination for direct transport, with the aim of reducing delivery lead time to a minimum; and (2) *Centralized distribution* is the preferred combination with indirect transport, since a short delivery lead time is not the priority and it is preferable to ensure that the means of transport is operating at better capacity utilization levels across the route to achieve lower transportation costs.

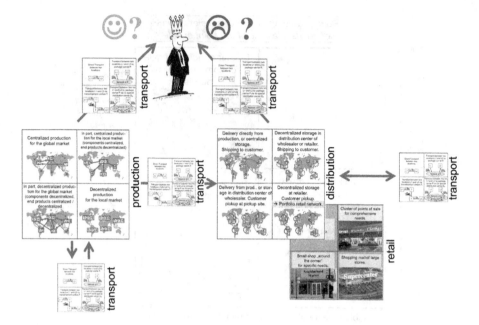

Fig. 6. Interrelation between and integration of the production, transport, distribution and retail network

However, the other combinations are also possible. (1) If the combination of centralized distribution and direct transport is advantageous, demand is highly varied and/or volatile. The reduced storage costs obtained from centralized warehousing thereby outweigh the disadvantage of a lengthier delivery lead time. Products with high value density allow anyway to select a means of transport that is fast enough. (2) If the combination of decentralized distribution with indirect transport is advantageous, the ability to reduce transportation costs or increase simplicity of a merged transport (the "in-transit merge" where the customer receives just one complete delivery) outweigh the disadvantages of a longer delivery lead time from the customer's perspective.

5   Conclusions and Outlook

In addition to existing methods and techniques that generally focus but on one kind of network design, there is a need for a method that allows an integrated determination of the design of the production, transport, distribution, and service network. This paper shows how a portfolio-based approach is a possible solution to this need. After a breakdown of the vendor's value-added network into its natural components, and using generic market and product or service features, potential design options for each area of the value-added network were established. The approach allows a subsequent integration: a combination of designs of the production, distribution, service and transport networks that suits both the product and the targeted customer segment, and that fits well together. At Bioforce (www.bioforce.ch or www.avogel.ca/en/) we used this approach when integrating the recently acquired Dutch partner company. FDA/GMP and economy-of-scale requirements lead to a centralized production of each product. Yet, decentralized finished-good storage at *both* production sites speeds up the delivery to the retail network of certain markets and allows continued delivery when issues of customs-clearance between an EU country and Switzerland (Non-EU) arise.

Once a fitting set of value-added networks has been determined, the next thing to do is to start, in each area, the location selection process. Here, factors like *political and economic business environment, market attractiveness, or cultural and infrastructure aspects* allow a systematic selection of locations. See here [4]. For evaluating potential business partners, techniques like *social network analysis* (SNA) can be helpful.

References

1. Abele, E., Meyer, T., Näher, U., Strube, G., Sykes, R. (eds.): Global Production. Springer, Berlin (2008)
2. Schönsleben, P.: Changeability of strategic and tactical production concepts. CIRP Ann. - Manuf. Technol. **58**(1), 383–386 (2009)
3. Váncza, J., Monostori, L., Lutters, D., Kumara, S., Tseng, M., Valckenaers, P., Van Brussel, H.: Cooperative and responsive manufacturing enterprises. CIRP Ann. - Manuf. Technol. **60**(2), 797–820 (2011)
4. Schönsleben, P.: Integral Logistics Management – Operations and Supply Chain Management Within and Across Companies, 5th edn. CRC Press, Boca Raton (2016)
5. Chopra, S.: Designing the distribution network in a supply chain. Transp. Res. Part E: Log. Transp. Rev. **39**(2), 123–140 (2003)
6. Schönsleben, P., Radke, A., Plehn, J., Finke, G., Hertz, P.: Toward the Integrated Determination of a Strategic Production Network Design, Distribution Network Design, Service Network Design, and Transport Network Design for Manufacturers of Physical Products. ETH e-collection (2015). http://dx.doi.org/10.3929/ethz-a-010423875
7. Blackstone, J.H., Jonah, J.: APICS Dictionary: The Essential Supply Chain Reference. APICS, Chicago (2013)

Selecting a Notation to Modeling Business Process: A Systematic Literature Review of Technics and Tools

Marcelo Bernardino Araújo[1,2]($\boxtimes$) and Rodrigo Franco Gonçalves[1]

[1] Paulista University, São Paulo, Brazil
mbernardinos@gmail.com, rofranco212@gmail.com
[2] Federal Institute of Education, Science and Technology, São Paulo, Brazil

Abstract. There are several different notations available in the market to business process modeling. An adequate business process model tool allows the understanding regarding the several operational flows inside an organization. This article has two objectives: first, to identify and to compare alternative business process modeling notations; second, to select an adequate notation to be applied in the modeling the business process of accounting system to higher education entities. Then, a literature review was carried out, including a rigorous research in indexed database. We also tested the available tools based on BPM model. Among the studied notations the BPMN was selected since it demonstrated to be the more adequate notation for complex processes once it contains a wide variety of symbols, which are easily comprehended.

Keywords: Layout · BPM · Costing systems · Modeling · Process

1 Introduction

Modeling and mapping a business helps the reduction of superfluous activities inside an organization. Both globalization and competitiveness in some sectors may lead companies to review their profit margins as well as their expenses. Optimization, i.e. the intense processes review, makes an organization more efficient, helping to increase both products and services quality and in some cases it also permits the reduction of the environmental impact [1].

Nowadays, there are several notations to represent a process, as for example: Business Process Management Notation (BPMN), Event-Driven Process Chain (EPC), Flowchart, Integrated Computer Aided Manufacturing DEFinition for Function Modeling (IDEF0), Unified Modeling Language – Activity (UML) and Value Stream Mapping (VSM). Choosing an notation contributes to the success of implementing an information system to manage the business [2]. But, among the diversity of available notations to represent and model a business, which one should we select?

© IFIP International Federation for Information Processing 2016
Published by Springer International Publishing AG 2016. All Rights Reserved
I. Nääs et al. (Eds.): APMS 2016, IFIP AICT 488, pp. 198–205, 2016.
DOI: 10.1007/978-3-319-51133-7_24

The present article aims to identify an adequate notation to model the necessary processes to develop an accounting system applied to higher education entities, since there is a global awareness regarding the expenditures of the universities [3].

In the following sections, we present a literature review of the main points to be addressed, detail the research performed, present observations regarding the response and the choice of a notation based on the literature and software tests to develop a costing system, and finally formulate the final observations that may be used to prepare a business model based on BPM.

2   Literature Review

Inside the organizations, several processes and procedures are created, reviewed and finalized every day. Process and procedure may be similar words, but they must be utilized correctly [4].

While a procedure describes how a task is performed in detail and how it fits in a process, regarding how and who execute the task, i.e. a procedure details the technical requirements of a task about a process [4], a process represents the aggregation of activities and behaviors executed by humans or machineries to achieve one or more results [5]. A process describes a sequence of activities carried out from the beginning until the end aiming to produce a result to the client, emphasizing the activity and its conduction [4].

The Fig. 1 represents the flow of a process and how its elements interact. Each process has its specific monitoring and measurement indicators necessary to its control. The formalization of a process is necessary to create either a product or a service, since it depends of inputs, several steps and procedures to fabricate a final product [5,6].

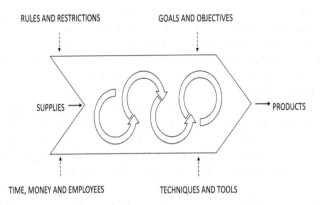

Fig. 1. Representation of the elements in a process

A notation is defined by a set of standard, symbols and rules that determine their meaning [5]. These representations support visually the understanding of a process, either simple or complex, and it can be understand more efficiently due to an adequate notation.

2.1 Mapping and Modeling Processes

A diagrammatic representation aims to simplify the understanding about several aspects of a process, since symbols can represent several contexts. In this sense, for a better comprehension of a process, standard notations constitute a set of knowledge due to their documentation [7,8].

The mapping process of an organization is the knowledge and the analysis of its processes and data interconnection, and it is structured in a top-down design (from the top of the organization to the base), to a level that allows a thorough comprehension of products, services and results [4].

It implies more precision when compared to a flow representation and it may aggregate more detail regarding, not only to the process, but also the relationship among several elements, such as stakeholders, events and results. A process map typically provides an overview about the main components of a process, but it may change from higher to lower levels of detail [5].

On the other hand, business process model is the set of activities regarding the representation of the current or a proposed process. It may provide a side-to-side perspective or a part of a primary process regarding to either support or management [5]. The process modeling is applied to represent graphically the current or a future process inside the organization [6].

While the mapping process regards to a current and non-documented process, and the modeling is applied to the development of new processes and procedures.

2.2 Business Process Management

The BPM is a management discipline that integrates strategies and objectives of an organization with customer expectations and needs, by focusing on processes, end to end. This methodology encompasses strategies, objectives, culture, organizational structures, roles, policies, methods and technologies to analyze, design, implement, manage performance, process and establish governance processes [5]. It is based on two pillars:

The first one regards on the studies [9,10] about statistical control of process that originates the current quality management represented by Six-Sigma.

The second one is related to business reengineering process [11,12] and it has interdependent positive and negative aspects. The reengineering was initially introduced not as a continuous improvement process, but as an occasional initiative.

The application of the BPM as a management method for business process, which involve several technologies such as online tools, cloud computing, is a competitive advantage and it also supports changes as: marketing, new technologies, IT infrastructure and both clients and suppliers necessities [7].

2.3 ISO, BPM CBOK and BABOK

The standardization of procedures has becoming usual mainly due to a globalized environmental [7]. There is three basic tools when applied together provide a support to build a process: ISO 9000, Business Process Management Common Body of Knowledge (BPM and CBOK) and Business Analysis Body of Knowledge (BABOK). A Body of Knowledge (BOK) is a practical guide for professionals that constitute the source of knowledge for most of professional curriculums. Its content represents the basic competences required for the professionals before their accreditation [7].

The International Organization for Standardization (ISO) was created in 1947 to promote normalization of products and services due to a continuous improvement ideology. Among several publications, the ISO 9000 series of standards concerns about quality management. The process approach [13] allows the management of the organization due to processes interaction. Several enterprises around the world search for the ISO certification [13], since the ISO 9000 conformity certification introduces credibility to the organization.

In order to avoid interference between the process and business analysts, they both have to understand the organization's necessities. The expertise of these professional can be attested by certification. The Association of Business Process Management Professionals (ABPMP) certifies the professionals due to the CBPP examination (Certified Business Process Professional) which demands a sound knowledge of the BPM CBOK procedures [5].

Moreover, two certifications are available by the International Institute of Business: CBAP (Certified Business Analysis Professional) for junior and CCBA (Certificate of Competency in Business Analysis) for senior level professionals. However, a thorough expertise of the BABOK is required [6].

3 Methodology

We carried out a systematic literature review to select the more appropriate modeling technic to develop an accounting system, once a peer review is a typical indicator for quality, since it is based on direct expertise of the reviewers and their knowledge [14]. A systematic literature review process has also been shown to be an appropriate tool to manage and organize the growing number of databases for articles, allowing the identification of relevant contributions.

The selected electronic databases where the searches were conducted from January to March 2016 are showed in Table 1. A 10-year time limit for sample studies was set in order to incorporate only recent studies. The searches were conducted using the following string: "business process modeling" AND ("costing system" OR "cost accounting").

After the systematic search in the databases, we selected the studies that only satisfy the objective of choosing a modeling process method. Additionally, we tested various free source modeling tools in order to verify which one would model precisely a complex processes as the ones in public sectors, since our goal is to develop a Time-Driven Activity Based Costing to the Federal Institution of Science and Technology of São Paulo. For the process modeling we used the software Yaoqiang BPMN Editor 4.0.42 [15], and Microsoft Visio 2010 to flowchart and UML – Activity [16]. These software allowed us to model using both BPMN, UML and flowchart concepts. Moreover, the flowcharts are tools constantly applied in patents [17]. In addition, we tested the open software named StarUML 5.0.2.1570.

Table 1. Electronic databases consulted

Name	Results
ASCE Library	4,074
DOAJ	2
EBSCO host	3
IEEE Xplore	109
ProQuest	1
ScienceDirect	155,94
Scopus	7
Web of Science	1
Wiley Online Library	176,06

The Based Knowledge Systems Incorporation (KBSI) maintains a paid version of the IDEF0 notation software, which is based on the Activity-Based Costing (ABC) method [18], however we did not tested the notation.

For EPC and VSM we applied the SmartDraw that can be used either in desktop or cloud version, which choice we based on expertise [19]. This software is a viable alternative for the Microsoft Visio once it is available freely and contemplates diverse notations as well as schemas, plots, flowcharts and BPMN.

4   Results and Discussion

The use of flowcharts is designed for users who use little information systems. The survey noted the recommendation to use BPMN in [2,16,20]. However, to perform the mapping and modeling processes properly, the business analyst to analyze the business requirements be careful when making the drawings, because the tasks are below the level of activities [4].

Among the notations on the market, the most known and used were analyzed in this research. The characteristics of each are shown in Table 2.

After the systematic process of reviewing the literature and consulted and analyzed nine studies, two professional guides and a book relevant to the process of choosing the appropriate notation for modeling business processes, we reached the result shown in Fig. 2.

After the analysis of the results, select the BPMN notation, because the advantages outweigh the disadvantages. Its main advantages are: ease of use,

Table 2. Notations for process modeling

Notation	Description	Developer
BPMN	It is useful to represent a model to different target audience	Object Management Group (OMG)
Flowchart	It facilitates the understanding of a process flow, however the symbols are not standardized	American National Standards Institute (ANSI)
EPC	It is useful to model complex sets of processes	Institut für Wirtschafts-informatik Universität des Saarlandes
IDEF0	It uses a systemic view highlighting inputs, outputs, control mechanisms, processes control and relation between lower and higher levels	United States Air Force (USAF)
UML activity	It is a diagramming technique oriented to describe the requirements of an information system	Object Management Group (OMG)
Value stream mapping	It shows the efficiency of processes mapping the use of resources and time variables	Toyota Motor

Features / Notations	BPMN	Flowchart	EPC	IDEF0	UML - Activity	VSM
Advantages						
Use and understanding spread	X		X		X	
Fast learning		X				X
Versatility in modeling	X		X			
Describes complex processes	X			X		
Supported by other tools	X	X			X	
Disadvantages						
It requires experience for using the symbology	X		X	X	X	
There are many variations on the symbology		X		X		X
Difficulty in viewing between levels	X		X	X	X	X
It does not describe complex procedures		X			X	X
May require different tools for use	X				X	

Fig. 2. Qualitative comparison of the notations

versatility, supported by other tools and mainly describe complex processes. The main drawback in using BPMN is a wide variety of symbols, therefore, the user requires a certain level of knowledge and proper use. In other notations, only IDEF0 is also capable of describing complex processes. This notation is recommended by [20].

5   Conclusions

The realized comparison of the business process notations allows the selection BPMN as the most adequate notation to map and model processes to the accounting system. This process requires a communication without noise from the Process Analyst and Business Analyst with a view to developing an IT solution. The main advantage of BPMN is that he is able to describe complex processes. However, it has the disadvantage of a great variety of symbols, but understandable.

A costing system will be developed to the Federal Institute of Education, Science and Technology of São Paulo – IFSP based on process modeling using a BPMN notation.

Acknowledgment. The authors would like to thank CAPES (Coordenação de Aperfeiçoamento de Pessoal de Nível Superior) and IFSP (Instituto Federal de Educação, Ciência e Tecnologia de São Paulo) for the financial support to develop this work.

References

1. Chompu-inwai, R., Jaimjit, B., Premsuriyanunt, P.: A combination of material flow cost accounting and design of experiments techniques in an SME: the case of a wood products manufacturing company in Northern Thailand. J. Clean. Prod. **108**, 1352–1364 (2015)
2. Thiemich, C., Puhlmann, F.: An agile BPM project methodology. In: Daniel, F., Wang, J., Weber, B. (eds.) BPM 2013. LNCS, vol. 8094, pp. 291–306. Springer, Heidelberg (2013). doi:10.1007/978-3-642-40176-3_25
3. Araújo, B.M., Gonçalves, R.: Costing systems for use in public universities: the Brazilian and international context. Int. J. Educ. Res. **2**(12), 1–12 (2014)
4. Stoneham, R.: Innovating Business Processes for Profit: How to Run a Process Program for Business Leaders. Balboa Press, Bloomington (2015)
5. ABPMP V3.0: Guide to Business Process Management Body of Knowledge – Common Body of Knowledge. Association of Business Process Management Professionals - ABPMP (2013)
6. IIBA: A Guide to the Business Analysis Body of Knowledge (BABOK Guide), Version 2.0. International Institute of Business Analysis (2009)
7. Bandara, W., Harmon, P., Rosemann, M.: Professionalizing business process management: towards a body of knowledge for BPM. In: Muehlen, M., Su, J. (eds.) BPM 2010. LNBIP, vol. 66, pp. 759–774. Springer, Heidelberg (2011). doi:10.1007/978-3-642-20511-8_68
8. Milani, F., Dumas, M., Ahmed, N., Matulevicius, R.: Modelling Families of business process variants: a decomposition driven method. Inf. Syst. **56**, 55–72 (2016)

9. Deming, W.E.: Elementary Principles of the Statistical Control of Quality: A Series of Lectures. Nippon Kagaku Gijutsu Remmei (1952)
10. Shewhart, W.A., Deming, W.E.: Statistical Method from the Viewpoint of Quality Control. Courier Corporation, New York (1939)
11. Hammer, M.: Reengineering work: don't automate, obliterate. Harv. Bus. Rev. **68**(4), 104–112 (1990)
12. Hammer, M., Champy, J.: Reengineering the Corporation: A Manifesto for Business Revolution. Harper Business, New York (1993)
13. Terziovski, M., Guerrero, J.L.: ISO 9000 quality system certification and its impact on product and process innovation performance. Int. J. Prod. Econ. **158**, 197–207 (2014)
14. Brinn, T., Jones, M.J., Pendlebury, M.: Measuring research quality: peer review 1, citation indices 0. Omega **28**(2), 237–239 (2000)
15. Geiger, M., Wirtz, G., Weberei, A.: BPMN 2.0 serialization - standard compliance issues and evaluation of modeling tools. In: EMISA, pp. 177–190 (2013)
16. Fu, L., Kara, L.B.: From engineering diagrams to engineering models: visual recognition and applications. Comput. Aided Des. **43**(3), 278–292 (2011)
17. Ramesh, A., Covert, P., Rhodes, S., Hunter, S., Vian, J., Wilmering, T.: Method and system for evaluating costs of various design and maintenance approaches. Google Patents (2006). uSPatent App. 10/972,916. https://www.google.com/patents/US20060089920
18. Tatsiopoulos, I., Panayiotou, N.: The integration of activity based costing and enterprise modeling for reengineering purposes. Int. J. Prod. Econ. **66**(1), 33–44 (2000)
19. Davies, I., Reeves, M.: BPM tool selection: the case of the Queensland court of justice. In: vom Brocke, J., Rosemann, M. (eds.) Handbook on Business Process Management 1: Introduction, Methods, and Information Systems. IHIS, pp. 371–392. Springer, Berlin (2015). doi:10.1007/978-3-642-45100-3_16
20. Trehan, V., Chapman, C., Raju, P.: Informal and formal modelling of engineering processes for design automation using knowledge based engineering. J. Zhejiang Univ. Sciencie A **16**(9), 706–723 (2015)

Workforce Planning Models for Distribution Center Operations

Athul Gopala Krishna$^{(\boxtimes)}$ and Vittaldas V. Prabhu

Pennsylvania State University, University Park, USA
aug276@psu.edu

Abstract. Customer order fulfillment at distribution centers (DC) is increasingly necessitated by innovative strategies to maximize operational performance that are primarily driven by cost and service level under supply chain variability. In order to better understand the trade-offs, in this paper, a generic computational model is developed to estimate forklift travel times for DCs with any arbitrary floor space and loading docks. In particular, travel times are modelled as random variables and the moments of the probability distribution of travel times are estimated and used as inputs to analytical queueing model and discrete event simulation model. Results show that the analytical and simulation models are within 3% under different demand scenarios. These models are used to determine the impact of work-force capacity on key performance measures such as Truck Processing Time (TPT) and Labor Hours Per Truck (LHPT). The workforce capacity for different demand scenarios is determined using three different approaches - Target Utilization Level, Square Root Staffing (SRS) rule (adapted from call center staffing) and Optimization. The result from these models indicate that adapting workforce capacity to match varying demand can reduce cost by 18% while maintaining desired service level.

Keywords: Distribution center · Workforce capacity · Simulation

1 Introduction

Supply chain variability can be caused by product seasonality, batch production and transportation, product consolidation or value added processing. DCs buffer the material flow in supply chains to accommodate this variability. Incoming items brought to the DC are unloaded at the receiving docks (receiving) and put into storage (storing). Outgoing items are retrieved from storage (order picking), processed and shipped to customers through the shipping docks (shipping). Resources such as space, labor, and equipment are allocated to different DC functions following organizational policies to achieve desired operational performance in terms of capacity, throughput and service at minimum cost. DCs can adapt to varying demand by adjusting workforce capacity to meet desired service level [1,2].

© IFIP International Federation for Information Processing 2016
Published by Springer International Publishing AG 2016. All Rights Reserved
I. Nääs et al. (Eds.): APMS 2016, IFIP AICT 488, pp. 206–213, 2016.
DOI: 10.1007/978-3-319-51133-7_25

Several authors had investigated the effects of warehouse design and control on operational performance and developed analytical and simulation models for performance analysis. Pandit and Palekar investigated the effects of warehouse design on response time and suggested a method for optimal design based on response time [3]. Chew and Tang presented a travel time model that evaluates performance of an order picking system with consideration to order batching and storage allocation strategies [4]. Graves et al. evaluated warehouse performance for several sequencing and class based storage policies using continuous analytical models and discrete evaluation procedures [5]. Bozer and White modelled the performance of an end-of-aisle order picking system by deriving analytical expressions and developed a design algorithm to determine the optimal configuration [6]. Koster proposed a modeling and approximate analysis method for a pick-to-belt order picking system based on Jackson network modeling and analysis [7]. Lee presented an analytical method for the stochastic analysis of a unit load AS/RS [8]. Hur et al. presented an analytical model for the stochastic analysis of a unit load AS/RS without assuming any specific distribution for the travel time of the S/R machine [9]. The existing literature has predominantly focused on warehouse design and control using travel time models and performance analysis in terms of throughput, resource utilization and storage strategy for order picking systems. As labor cost can be a significant component of variable cost in DCs, it is evident that there is a need for research to explore the impact of workforce capacity on DC performance by considering cost and service level trade-off for varying demand scenarios. This work has been motivated by paucity of models and tools that can be used by DC operations managers for workforce planning in practice. Hence, a decision model that integrates critical operational performance measures to evaluate DC performance and workforce capacity policies under varying demand scenarios is developed.

2   Model and Assumptions

A large scale, non-automated, rectangular DC is analyzed. A rectangular shape is the optimal geometrical shape for storing rectangular units such as pallets [10]. The storage locations are characterized by single-deep racks and drive-in racks. The racks are arranged back-to-back, to form a block, parallel to the dock of the DC, such that space between blocks form aisles. The blocks are arranged in a rectangular grid to form a network of aisles through which material handling devices such as forklifts travel as shown in Fig. 1(a) [3]. A generic computational model with length (L), width (W), aisle-width (A) and number of docks (N) as parameters is developed to estimate forklift travel times in DCs. The model is capable to evaluate DCs with a size between 60,000 sq.ft (small scale) and 500,000 sq.ft. (large scale) and up to 45 docks. A probability distribution is fit to the forklift travel times and moments of the distribution is provided as input to the analytical queueing model of DC. The skewness profile of forklift travel time distribution against distance from center dock and L and W of the DC is investigated. It is observed that for a given W, skewness profile is represented by a series of peaks and valleys with decreasing value as L increases and for a given L, skewness profile remains nearly constant as W increases as shown in Fig. 1(b). The skewness for forklift travel time distributions fluctuate significantly from dock 1 (end dock) and becomes negligible towards dock 23 (center dock) and remains negligible from the center dock to dock 45 (end dock) as shown in Fig. 2.

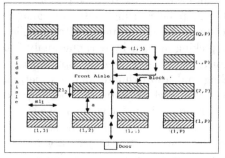

(a) DC Layout. Source:([3])

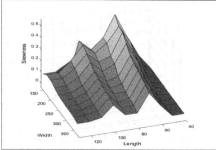

(b) Skewness of Travel Time Distribution against L and W of D

Fig. 1. DC layout and skewness of travel time distribution against L and W of DC

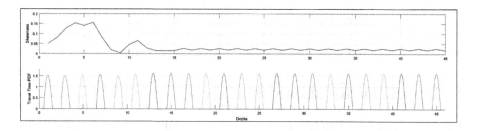

Fig. 2. Skewness for travel time distribution with distance from center dock

2.1   DC Queueing System

The outbound operations in the DC begins by "accumulation" of customer orders from storage area as pallet loads in the dock to form a truck load. The pallet loads then undergo a "wrapping" process to secure items in the pallet after accumulation. The pallet loads are then "inspected" to verify that items in the pallets have completed all processes before loading. Pallets are then "loaded" onto the truck for shipping. The process time associated with accumulation, wrapping, inspection and loading are denoted by Accumulation Time (AT) or Forklift Travel Time, Wrapping Time (WT), Inspection Time (IT) and Loading

Time (LT) respectively. The process time for a truck load, denoted by Truck Processing Time (TPT), is the sum of AT, WT, IT and LT. The operational productivity is expressed by a metric called Labor Hours Per Truck (LHPT). The movement of pallets are done using forklifts and pallet jacks. It is assumed that forklifts perform only accumulation operations and pallet jacks are used by wrapping team, inspection team and loading team for wrapping, inspection and loading respectively. The queueing model is shown in Fig. 3. The analytical queueing model facilitates development and evaluation of workforce capacity policies for the DC for several demand scenarios by providing a performance estimate for each policy-scenario combination.

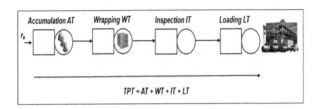

Fig. 3. DC queueing system

2.2 DC Analytical Queueing Model

This system can be modelled as an open network queueing system with a First Come First Serve (FCFS) queue discipline and an infinite queue space. The customer orders for accumulation arrive at a rate ra in the form of palletized truck loads. Forklifts, wrapping team, inspection team and loading team act as servers. The system is characterized by a series of G/G/m queues for accumulation, wrapping, inspection and loading with general interarrival and process time distributions. The following parameters are provided as input to the analytical queueing model: ra - rate of arrivals in truck load per unit time; u - Workforce Utilization; ta - Average time between arrivals (in minute); ca - Arrival CV; cd - Departure CV; te - Mean effective process time (in minute); ce - CV of effective process time. The performance of the queueing system is characterized by the following parameters and are considered as the output from the analytical queueing model: m - Workforce level in a process; CTq - Expected waiting time in queue for a process (in minute); CT - Expected time for a process (in minute); TPT - Truck Processing Time (in minute); WIP - Average work-in-process level at process (in truck load); WIPq - Expected WIP in queue (in truck load); ATL - Average Truck Load; LHPT - Labor Hours Per Truck [11].

3 Performance Analysis Using Analytical Models

The workforce capacity of the DC is analyzed for several demand scenarios that range from a low demand to a high demand for a given process time at 70% target workforce utilization for all the process using the analytical queueing model. It is concluded that TPT decreases steadily as workforce capacity increases and LHPT increases linearly with workforce capacity as shown in Fig. 4(a) and (b). This establishes that as more workforce is deployed to process a truck load, the time to process the truck load decreases (service level improves) but labor hour investment on a truck load increases (cost increases).

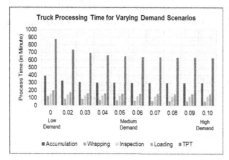
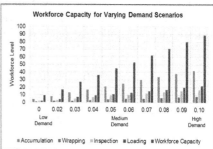

(a) Truck Processing Time for Varying De- (b) Workforce Capacity for Varying Demand Scenarios   mand Scenarios

Fig. 4. Truck processing time for varying demand scenarios and workforce capacity for varying demand scenarios

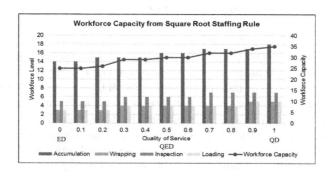

Fig. 5. Workforce capacity from SRS rule for ED, QED & QD operational regimes

The Square Root Staffing (SRS) rule is applied in call centers to determine the appropriate staffing levels for an offered load (R) and Quality of Service, (β) and is approximated as $R + \beta \sqrt{R}$, where, R is the amount of work that arrives in the system in unit time. The value of β signifies the operational regime of the system and can be a Quality Driven (QD) regime with emphasis on service level over efficiency, Efficiency Driven (ED) with emphasis on efficiency over service level or Quality Efficiency Driven (QED) regime with trade-off between service level and efficiency. Larger the β value, better the service level [12,13].

The workforce capacity the DC queueing system is computed by the application of SRS rule for ED ($\beta = 0$), QD ($\beta = 1$) and QED ($\beta = 0.5$) operational regimes. It is observed that workforce capacity increases steadily as DC operates from an ED regime towards a QD regime as shown in Fig. 5. This implies that as more workforce is deployed to process a truck load, the service level of DC improves.

4   Performance Analysis Using Simulation Model

The DC queueing system is modelled using Simio simulation software for a given interarrival and process time distribution and workforce capacity. The DC simulation model is run for 500 h with 30 replications after a warm-up period of 100 h. The results from simulation model is compared with that of the analytical queueing model. The analytical and simulation model results for cycle time and workforce utilization are highly comparable as shown in Fig. 6(a) and (b). The TPT and LHPT are determined with -3.13% and -6.49% error respectively from the simulation model with reference to the analytical queueing model.

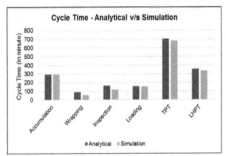

(a) DC Cycle Time Comparison: Anaytical   (b) DC Workforce Utilization Comparison:
v/s Simulation   Analytical v/s Simulation

Fig. 6. DC cycle time comparison: analytical v/s simulation and DC workforce utilization comparison: analytical v/s simulation

A simulation-based multi-objective optimization model is developed using OptQuest for Simio add-in. The optimal scenarios for workforce capacity that minimizes TPT and operating cost subject to constraints for a target workforce utilization policy is determined using pattern frontier optimization.

Minimize: TPT and Operating Cost subject to:

- $1 \leq$ Forklift ≥ 25
- $1 \leq$ Wrapping Team ≥ 6
- $1 \leq$ Inspection Team ≥ 8
- $1 \leq$ Loading Team ≥ 10
- $u \leq 0.70$

OptQuest optimizes across all responses and finds the set of scenarios that are optimal, rather than a single optimal solution based on weights, [15]. The model is run for 500 h after a warm-up period of 100 h with 30 replications for 100 scenarios. It is observed that there are six optimal scenarios with TPT, LHPT and operating cost that range between 628.24 min, 340 labor hours & 5915.95 and 689.66 min, 279 labor hours and 5000.07 respectively corresponding to a workforce capacity that range between 43 to 33 as shown in Fig. 7. It can be concluded from the optimal scenarios that the desired service level can be maintained by adapting workforce capacity to match demand and thereby reducing operating cost by up to 18%.

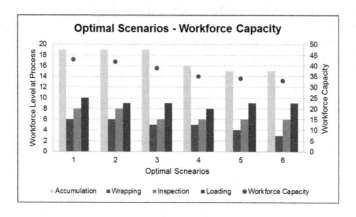

Fig. 7. Optimal scenarios - workforce capacity

5   Conclusions

A decision model is developed to evaluate the impact of workforce capacity on DC performance in terms of Truck Processing Time and Labor Hours Per Truck by considering cost and service level trade-off for varying demand scenarios. Industrial practitioners can use this model for tactical and operational decisions in DCs by application and integration of travel time computation model, analytical and/or simulation model based on the DC geometry considered. The desired service level can be maintained and opportunities to reduce operating cost can be identified by adapting workforce capacity to match demand. Delays in truck processing significantly impacts detention time, the time spent waiting for a truck to be loaded. Increased detention time implies lost revenue by paying late fees to the shipper or missing an opportunity to secure another load. The models can facilitate industrial practitioners to negotiate for better pricing and terms of contract by reducing detention time substantially. The models presented in this work can be extended to automated DC with conveyors and the resulting energy footprint can be estimated [14,15]. Ongoing work is focusing on implementing these models in a userfriendly spreadsheet tools for industrial practitioners.

References

1. Gu, J., Goetschalckx, M., McGinnis, L.F.: Research on warehouse operation: a comprehensive review. Eur. J. Oper. Res. **177**(1), 1–21 (2007)
2. Rouwenhorst, B., Reuter, B., Stockrahm, V., van Houtum, G.J., Mantel, R.J., Zijm, W.H.M.: Warehouse design and control: framework and literature review. Eur. J. Oper. Res. **122**(3), 515–533 (2000)
3. Pandit, R., Palekar, U.S.: Response time considerations for optimal warehouse layout design. J. Eng. Ind **115**(3), 322–328 (1993)
4. Chew, E.P., Tang, L.C.: Travel time analysis for general item location assignment in a rectangular warehouse. Eur. J. Oper. Res. **112**(3), 582–597 (1999)
5. Graves, S.C., Hausman, W.H., Schwarz, L.B.: Storage-retrieval interleaving in automatic warehousing systems. Manag. Sci. **23**(9), 935–945 (1977)
6. Bozer, Y.A., White, J.A.: Design and performance models for end-of-aisle order picking systems. Manag. Sci. **36**(7), 852–866 (1990)
7. Koster, R.: Performance approximation of pick-to-belt order picking systems. Eur. J. Oper. Res. **72**(3), 558–573 (1994)
8. Lee, H.F.: Performance analysis for automated storage and retrieval systems. IIE Trans. **29**(1), 15–28 (1997)
9. Hur, S., Lee, Y.H., Lim, S.Y., Lee, M.H.: A performance estimation model for AS/RS by M/G/1 queuing system. Comput. Ind. Eng. **46**(2), 233–241 (2004)
10. Berry, J.R.: Elements of warehouse layout. Int. J. Prod. Res. **7**(2), 105–121 (1968)
11. Hopp, W.J., Spearman, M.L.: Factory Physics, 3rd edn. Waveland Press Inc., Long Grove (2011)
12. Technion Israel Institute of Technology: http://ie.technion.ac.il/serveng/
13. Mandelbaum, A., Zeltyn, S.: Service engineering in action: the Palm/Erlang-A queue, with applications to call centers. In: Spath, D., Dipl.-Math, H., Fähnrich, K.P. (eds.) Advances in Services Innovations, pp. 17–45. Springer, Berlin (2007)
14. Krishna, A.G.: Workforce planning models for distribution center operations. Ph.D. thesis, State College, The Pennsylvania State University (2009)
15. Anand, V., Lee, S., Prabhu, V.V.: Energy-aware models for warehousing operations. In: Grabot, B., Vallespir, B., Gomes, S., Bouras, A., Kiritsis, D. (eds.) APMS 2014. IAICT, vol. 439, pp. 390–397. Springer, Heidelberg (2014). doi:10. 1007/978-3-662-44736-9_48

From English to RDF - A Meta-Modelling Approach for Predictive Maintenance Knowledge Base Design

Ana Milicic[1]([✉]), Dimitris Kiritsis[1], and Nesat Efendioglu[2]

[1] EPFL, Lausanne, Switzerland
ana.milicic@epfl.ch
[2] BOC Asset Management GmbH, Vienna, Austria

Abstract. Ever growing complexity of the information domains that are relevant for product life cycle management is pushing researchers to invest efforts into creating an abstract modelling techniques in order to structure the available knowledge. Ontology showed to be a convenient method for build such structures and number of domain specific ontologies has been developed in recent years. In this paper, we propose a meta-modelling approach that provides a guided, step-by-step solution for ontology design. Contribution is tested through an example of ontology for predictive maintenance.

Keywords: Meta-modelling · Ontology design · User story mapping

1 Introduction

In recent years, ontology for the Product Lifecycle Management (PLM) domain has raised a lot of interest in research communities, both academic and industrial. It has emerged as a convenient method for supporting the concept of closed life-cycle information loop [1], which is one of the most important issues of PLM. By modeling relevant aspects collected from all lifecycle stages of a product, within one ontology, a common knowledge structure is created accessible to all actors. Information availability within the company might seem like a trivial aspect but it is actually one of the most challenging issues. Large companies are divided into number of departments which have only limited communication protocols, employees change projects or leave company and information is generated over a long span of time and locations. In the same time, having the right information at the right moment when decisions about design, production or maintenance are made, is crucial for business success. The complexity of the information source domain translates directly into complexity of design of the ontology which will be mapping all relevant knowledge and the information sources, present in the

I. Nääs et al. (Eds.): APMS 2016, IFIP AICT 488, pp. 214–224, 2016.
DOI: 10.1007/978-3-319-51133-7_26

domain. There is number of different approaches and methodologies for ontology design addressing different problem setups and domain types, but that is out of scope for this work. In this paper, we address the User Story Mapping (USM) method [2] which is designed specifically for creation of ontologies in PLM domain where most of the actors and information sources are not experts in semantic technology.

A USM is an approach that creates a backlog along scenarios and users. It answers the question on how an employee in the company would like to use knowledge base that is being designed, what are the activities that he performs and which resources he uses. Defining usage by all relevant users, thus defines the domain knowledge, the existing one, needed one and produced one. A backlog consists of several structure blocks as shown in Fig. 1.

1. Usage dimension – It describes how a user would use the knowledge base, for which activities and with what purpose.
2. User dimension – This dimension defines the types of users that will use the knowledge base.
3. Backbone – This section describes the activities that a user performs within a usage step. This section is called backbone as it suits as a guideline for the definition of the user stories, which are actually a refinement of the backbone.
4. User stories as backlog items – This is the actual placeholder for the user stories. The user stories are ordered vertically under each activity and represent a refined version of an activity. It is recommended that user stories follow the pattern "As <user> I want to <feature> so that <value>".

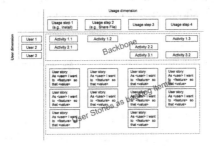

Fig. 1. USM backlog (Source: [2])

USM is the first step of gathering information regarding the domain of interest and the following step can be defined as translating functional needs into list of concepts. This is done manually, by taking into account the whole grasp of the domain, existing templates, resources and standards and by identifying a list of relevant concepts. The process is itterative and done in collaboration between semantic experts and the domain experts until every user story can be expressed though ontology concepts and ontology properties between concepts.

In this paper we present the contribution in form of meta-model of the entire ontology design process. As previously explained, ontology design is itterative and can be time consuming especially when performed manually. ADOxx meta model enables faster, more controlled design process as well as collaborative environment for distributed teams. Further on, the entire procedure is shown for the use case of predictive maintenance tasks.

2   Meta-Modelling

Conceptual modelling is a technique to "study" the real world – the so-called system under study – and provides concepts to abstract the complexity of the real world and establish a model environment that enables to knowledge processing on models (e.g. simulation, analysis, transformation etc.) of complex systems thanks to the conceptual abstraction.

Meta-modelling is an established approach to specify conceptual modelling languages and a proven technology to enable conceptual integration of information coming from different enterprise levels as well as from different domains. Moreover, meta-modelling makes information available for both machine computation and human interpretation to create value out of that information [3].

As above-mentioned the main objective of conceptual modelling is creation of value out of information stored in the models with applying appropriate knowledge processing algorithms. The ADOxx© is a meta-modelling platform, which enables realization of any kind of modelling method that consists of the conceptual modelling language, algorithms to process models of the modelling language and the procedure that defines the stepwise appropriate usage of the modelling language. Only prerequisite is, that the Generic Modelling Method Specification Framework – GMMSF (shown in Fig. 2) for conceptualization of the method is followed.

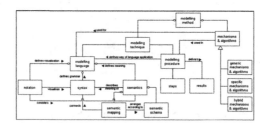

Fig. 2. Generic modelling method specification framework (Source: [4,5])

According to [4,5] the building blocks of a modelling method include: (1) the modelling language introducing modelling concepts pre-defined according their semantic, their syntax and their graphical notation, (2) the modelling procedure which defines the stepwise usage of the modelling language and may not be always available and (3) generic and domain specific mechanisms and algorithms enabling the computer-based processing of models. By applying this framework (and selecting ADOxx® as a realization platform) it can be guaranteed that defined modelling method can use all of the generic platform functionality (e.g. visualization, publishing, simulation, etc.) and can be amalgamated with other modelling methods based on the requirements of the stakeholders (e.g. adding Ontology Modelling to extend User Story Mapping Method) or extended with new concepts.

3   User Story Mapping Modelling Method Realized with Using ADOxx©

The User Story Mapping Modelling Method and its corresponding modelling environment aim to offer a model-based approach supporting User Story Mapping Method (USM Method) during capturing domain specific knowledge, virtualizing and transforming knowledge understandable by humans and machines.

The modelling method shall support all steps of the USM method and it count all steps as challenge to be targeted. Hence, the challenges are (C1) to enable creation of user story map, (C2) to enable gathering other source of information, (C3) enabling creation of unique list of concepts that covers entire domain, (C4) definitions of relations and dependencies among new concepts and concepts in initial knowledge base and (C5) creation of dynamic knowledge base covering domain expressed in standard format, which is machine interpretable.

3.1   Modelling Language

The modelling language of the USM Method consists of two model types; (1) User Story Mapping Model and (2) OWL Diagram. The Fig. 3 depicts the meta-models of both model types and the inheritance from ADOxx©Meta-model.

User Story Mapping Model targets challenge (C1) to enable creation of user story map, hence it consists of the concepts; "User", "User Story", "Activity", "Backlog" and "Group", which have been introduced in the section Fig. 3, and identifies relations among them.

Addition to User Story Mapping Model, we decided to enable modelling ontologies, hence to add so-called the OWL Diagram. The OWL Diagram is sub-set of the OWL Web Ontology Language (W3C, 2004) and we utilized it as it is implemented in (ADOxx.org, 2016). The OWL Diagram targets challenges; (C2) to enable gathering other source of information, (C3) enabling creation of unique list of concepts that covers entire domain, (C4) definitions of relations and dependencies among new concepts and concepts in initial knowledge base and (C5) creation of dynamic knowledge base covering domain expressed in standard format, which is machine interpretable.

The formalized overview of the meta-models defined in FDMM [6], where;

- A meta-model is a tuple $\mathbf{MM} = \langle \mathbf{MT}, \preceq, \text{domain, range, card} \rangle$ where MT is the set of the defined model types, i.e. for $i = 1, \ldots, m$ we have: $\mathbf{MT} = \{MT_1, MT_2, \ldots, MT_m\}$.

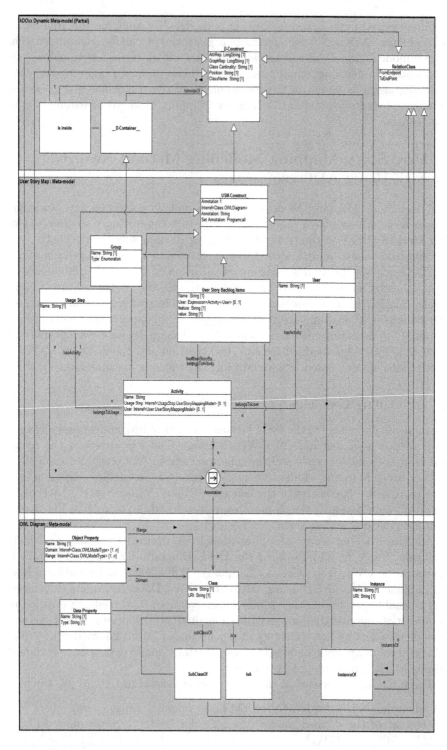

Fig. 3. Platform specific meta-model of USM modelling method

- The $\mathbf{MT_i}$'s $(i = 1, \ldots, m)$ are themselves tuples $\mathbf{MT_i} = \langle O_i^T, D_i^T, A_i \rangle$, where:
- O_i^T is the set of object types or classes,
- D_i^T is the set of data types, and
- A_i is the set of the attributes.
- The domain is a function with **domain**: $A \rightarrow P(O^T)$
- The range maps an attribute to the power set of all pairs of classes and model types, all data types, and all model types.
  range: $A \rightarrow P(\bigcup_j (O_j^T \times \{MT_j\}) \cup D^T \cup MT)$
- The cardinality function **card**: $O^T \times A \rightarrow P(\mathbb{N}_0^+ \times (\mathbb{N}_0^+ \cup \{\infty\}))$

The formalized overview of the meta-models defined in FDMM [6], where;
The Meta-model of USM Modelling Language is formalized in FDMM as following;

- User Story Map MT_{USM}
- OWL Diagram MT_{OWL}
- $MT_{USM} = \langle O_{USM}^T, D_{USM}^T, A_{USM} \rangle$
- $MT_{OWL} = \langle O_{OWL}^T, D_{OWL}^T, A_{OWL} \rangle$

Since we integrated already formalized and implemented OWL Diagram by [7], we describe just the model type User Story Map in details;

- $MT_{USM} = \langle O_{USM}^T, D_{USM}^T, A_{USM} \rangle$
- $O_{USM}^T = \{_USM_Construct, Group, Usage Step, User Story Backlog Items,
- Activity, User, Annotation$
- $D_{USM}^T = \{String, ProgramCall, Expression, Enum_{Group}, Interref_{Class},
- Interref_{UsageStep}, Interref_{User}\}$
- $A_{USM} = \{Annotation, Name, Type, User, Feature, Value, Usage Step,
  SetAnnotation\}$

Weaving is a modelling technique where different model types are linked with each other. For challenges (C2) and (C3) we utilize the so-called "Semantic Lifting Approach from [8]. As depicted in, we use weaving technique to enable Semantic Lifting by using Class object types defined in OWL models to annotate the objects modelled in User Story Map models.

Fig. 4. Weaving in order to use owl diagram into user story map.

The description of weaving depicted in Fig. 4 in FDMM is as following;

- **domain**(Annotation) =
  {_USM_Construct_}
- **range**(Annotation) = {Class}
- **card**(Annotation = $\langle m, n \rangle$) for m, n $\in$ N

3.2   Mechanisms and Algorithms

Using Mechanism and Algorithms capabilities of ADOxx modelling system, creation of list of ontological concepts is implemented by allowing ADOxx user to annotate Activities from Backbone with concepts from ontology. ADOxx user is enabled to define his own concepts and sub-concepts. For example, the Activity "Check Business Exploitation Results", needs to be annotated as "Data" → "Digital" → "Resource" → "User Feedback".

These new concepts Fig. 5 can be further used to annotate Activities. By annotating the entire Backbone of activities, list of concepts is created by merging all concepts that were used in annotation process, from those generic to more specific ones. ADOxx model will generate this list automatically and create a visualization.

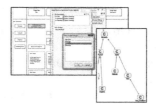

Fig. 5. Addition of new sub-concepts in ADOxx.

The next step in ontology design process is definition of relations between concepts. The challenge with definition of relations (or object properties, according to ontological terminology) is that some level of interaction can be usually found for every two concepts and only a small portion of them is relevant and useful for domain description. That is, it is not the issue of finding relation between two concepts, it is the issue of selecting the ones that are worth defining as object properties. Using ADOxx modelling tool, the recommendation system for this challenge was created, relaying again on Activity Backbone. The reasoning is that if one Activity, was annotated with two or more concepts, then it is reasonable to assume that those two concept should have object property connecting them. The tool is implemented as recommendation system, meaning that the ADOxx user is presented with an option to create object property which he can freely accept or decline Fig. 6.

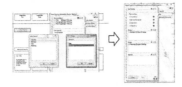

Fig. 6. Object property definition in ADOxx.

4 Application Scenario

Predictive maintenance is a field with ever-growing popularity. Compared to a standard, fixed period maintenance, it saves resources, cost and environment. The most relevant aspect of predictive maintenance is most certainly its reliability. Too wide confidence bounds will lead to non-optimal maintenance schedule while the too narrow confidence bounds might lead to costly down-time and repairs. The key of the solution to this problem is having all relevant information about machine usage conditions, usage patterns as well as machine lifecycle over all. This is especially true for machines which are large investments or when a long down time is not acceptable.

In this paper, we examine the real-life example of company X, which is a producer of healthcare equipment. They specialize in high-end machines such as MRI scanners which are highly complex, sensitive for calibration and usage modes. In the same time, the long or frequent down time is not acceptable since the hospital's patient treatment depends highly on availability of those machines. Today, company has two sources of information about machine usage and calibration that is log-files (stored in the machine and shared periodically) and help desk files (where workers are taking notes of all reported problems with integration with the rest of equipment and usage problems). In the same time, these information are requested by number of actors and with different summarization level requirements. Designers of future products will want to understand the most frequent issues that certain existing line of products exhibited, while the service team will want to understand the usage patterns and previous maintenance activities.

In order to aggregate this complex and wide domain, USM method as ADOxx application was applied. In Fig. 7 we show a sample of user activities defined (details of the work had to be omitted due to privacy constraints). Ontology generated based on given backlog is shown in Fig. 8 (again, only upper level concepts in parent-child hierarchy are displayed).

The ontology constitutes a knowledge base, where all the data are gathered and structured. It enables information retrieval using SPARQL semantic queries as well as integration to existing IT infrastructure of company X. It serves as ground layer for upper level applications preforming data analysis and serving as decision support system.

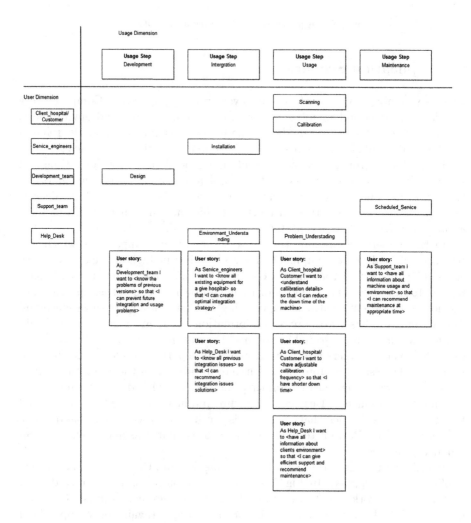

Fig. 7. Sample of user activities

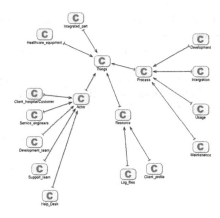

Fig. 8. Upper levels of predictive maintenance ontology

5   Conclusions and Outlook

By implementing USM methodology as ADOxx model the entire procedure is enhanced though automatization of deterministic steps and strategic procedure conduction. Each step can be performed independently and repeated if needed. Each step is documented and can be revisited or discussed in the future.

Having ADOxx model, opens a field of opportunities for future work that are out of scope of USM as ontology modelling methodology. ADOxx system allows export of models as RDF or XML structures making them available for other software tools. On the other hand, current export mechanism allow export of models while the procedures and algorithms defined on those models are not available outside ADOxx. One potential direction of future work is design of mechanism that will translate existing mechanisms into SWRL syntax. Using this approach, ontology in RDF could be enriched with ontological rules in SWRL giving more complete ADOxx model export and thus, interoperability.

References

1. Jun, H.B., Kiritsis, D., Xirouchakis, P.: Research issues on closed-loop PLM. Comput. Ind. **58**(8), 855–868 (2007)
2. Milicic, A., Perdikakis, A., El Kadiri, S., Kiritsis, D., Ivanov, P.: Towards the definition of domain concepts and knowledge through the application of the user story mapping method. In: Rivest, L., Bouras, A., Louhichi, B. (eds.) PLM 2012. IAICT, vol. 388, pp. 58–69. Springer, Heidelberg (2012). doi:10.1007/978-3-642-35758-9_6
3. Woitsch, R.: Hybrid Modeling: An Instrument for Conceptual Interoperability. Revolutionizing Enterprise Interoperability through Scientific Foundations (2014)
4. Karagiannis, D., Kühn, H.: Metamodelling platforms. In: Bauknecht, K., Tjoa, A.M., Quirchmayr, G. (eds.) EC-Web 2002. LNCS, vol. 2455, p. 182. Springer, Heidelberg (2002). doi:10.1007/3-540-45705-4_19
5. Kühn, H.: Method integration in business engineering. Ph.D. thesis, University of Vienna, Austria (2004)

6. Fill, H.G., Redmond, T., Karagiannis, D.: FDMM: a formalism for describing ADOxx meta models and models (2012)
7. ADOxx Realization Case: Web Ontology Language (OWL). https://www.adoxx. org/live/owl
8. Hrgovcic, V., Karagiannis, D., Woitsch, R.: Conceptual modeling of the organisational aspects for distributed applications: the semantic lifting approach. In: 37th Annual COMPSACW, pp. 145–150. IEEE (2013)

An Application of Operations Research for Reducing Fuel Costs

João Roberto Maiellaro[1,2(✉)], João Gilberto Mendes dos Reis[1],
Alexandre Formigoni[2], Robson dos Santos[2], Marcos A.M. de Oliveira[2],
and Celso Jacubavicius[2]

[1] Paulista University, São Paulo, Brazil
joao.maiellaro@fatec.sp.gov.br
[2] Faculdade de Tecnologia de Guarulhos, Guarulhos, Brazil

Abstract. The objective of this work is to identify gas stations out of the route predeter-mined by a transport company based both on refueling feasibility and on lower fuel costs. The work consists of a case study that collected data such as kilometers run, amount refueled, product transported, type of operation, and average diesel consumption during the trip. Through the Operations Research, we were able to evaluate the feasibility of deviating the vehicle from the current route (mainly highways) to stations in the surroundings. The aim was to check if the organization would obtain any significant fuel cost reduction from this deviation. Our findings suggested cost reduction for the route used in the model, as well as the need to apply the mathematical model whenever there was an intention to deviate from the route in order to refuel at stations with lower diesel prices.

Keywords: Fueling · Operations Research · Cost reduction · Gas stations

1 Introduction

Consistently searching for cost reduction in all stages of the logistic process is a goal to be reached. Freight movement absorbs between one-third and two-thirds of logistics costs, and that is exactly why improving efficiency using the most of the transport equipment and personnel is one of the greatest concerns of the segment [1].

In Brazil, the current scenario of inflation, economic stagnation, and poor economic growth has been causing increased fuel prices, and eventually impacting the transport companies' operating costs, as well as other services relying on fuel and oil derivatives.

Based on this scenario and on the high fuel costs observed, we attempted to strategically evaluate how to reduce these costs in order to achieve profitability without affecting the operation and customer service.

© IFIP International Federation for Information Processing 2016
Published by Springer International Publishing AG 2016. All Rights Reserved
I. Nääs et al. (Eds.): APMS 2016, IFIP AICT 488, pp. 225–231, 2016.
DOI: 10.1007/978-3-319-51133-7_27

To avoid any significant impact on the increased operating costs, it is necessary to get adapted and prepare a plan while seeking lower costs at the same time. To cut down operating costs, an organization has to adapt itself to the country's economic situation and prepare its operations aiming at the lowest costs possible. The Vehicle Routing and Scheduling (VRS) method is an important tool that many organizations that have been implementing this method through software applications in order to reduce the operating costs. The organization object of this study is engaged in transportation services and uses the VRS method to support the route planning process.

The objective of this work is to detect gas stations out of the route predetermined by a transport company based both on refueling feasibility and lower fuel costs.

2   Methodology

Stage one consisted of detecting the problem by observing transport related operations. To this end, we used reports extracted from an automated fueling control website, as well as dynamic spreadsheets and tables that are typically used to measure KPIs (Key Performance Indicators) used to assess a driver's award (prepared by the organization).

We also used reports extracted from the ERP system. Stage two consisted of collecting data from the organization regarding the management of financial costs with fuel, organizing such data into tables, and evaluating them. We used an online fuel management system that keeps record of the amount refueled and fuel price on a realtime basis, as well as of the location of each station on the route. For stage three, we assessed prices and refueling feasibility at stations where drivers are not authorized tore fuel their vehicles. To select these new stations, we used criteria such as local topography, infrastructure, and accessibility of the station. Stage four consisted of structuring the data into a mathematical model, taking into account the total kilometers of the route, tank capacity, average kilometers run per liter, and the location and prices of the selected stations.

3   Case Study

The organization object of this study has been present in the Brazilian market for 75 years providing road transportation services. Organizations must focus on providing its services with excellence, efficiency, and effectiveness and meeting their customers' requirements at low operating costs, for it sees both increased earnings and reduced costs as profit [2].

One of the operating costs comes from the fleet, that is the essence of a road transport organization, thus requiring full attention and dedication. The main fleet-related costs include tires, fuel, IPVA [Motor Vehicle Ownership Tax], driver's salary, lubricants, maintenance, tolling, and overheads. In this study, we focused on the fuel factor.

Transport sector is involved in a very competitive market and besides, it has been changing due the technological development e economic [3].

Among other factors, the amount of fuel to be consumed on a certain route depends on the distance, traffic, load weight, and km/l.

3.1 Defining the Problem

The problem consists of determining the best option to refuel the vehicle during the trip, taking into account the cost and distance variables and the feasibility of deviating from the route to refuel at a station where the price per liter is cheaper, due to the fact that, by failing to look at these factors, usually only the liter price alone is taken into account, while the kilometers run and respective consumption associated with the deviation are left aside.

Main aspects of a problem are the exact description of the study objectives, identification of possible decision alternatives, and confirmation of the system limitations, restrictions, and requirements [4].

Within these aspects, we have as exact description of the study objectives the cheaper fuel costs. The possible decision alternatives would be the methods to solve this problem, while the confirmation of the limitations would be the vehicle and its capacities.

Our findings suggested that there is a need to study the causes of the high prices left aside and to propose solutions to cut down these costs. We collected the following data: routes used, load weight, vehicle model and capacity, location of each station and diesel price per liter.

The organization currently uses an automated fueling control website to determine what stations their drivers are authorized to stop by and refuel. This authorization is granted on a real-time basis, and the diesel price can be negotiated through the system. As a consequence, only the agreed-upon prices can be carried out by the parties.

We identified that many stations that are close to the routes currently used offer diesel at a more affordable price, but drivers are not authorized to refuel at these stations.

We selected the route from Campinas/SP to Catalão/GO because it has the highest diesel consumption and worst consumption performance of liter per kilometer run. The route holds over 200 trips every month. With the help of Google Maps - Fig. 1 - we could see that the way to this route, through the BR-050 highway, is 601 Km long.

Based on Table 1, it is concluded that a truck with full tank can run at most 392.6 km. This means that it will need to refuel during the trip. To avoid any incidents, the organization requires drivers not to use a vehicle with less than 1/4 of the tank, thus making it necessary to scheduler fueling at intervals of approximately 300 km.

The load being carried consists of automotive parts, and we considered the vehicle operating at its maximum capacity. The customer from Catalão wanted the transportation to be carried out by a Mercedes-Benz truck Axor 2644 model.

Hence, it was possible to address the study as a function of the truck functional characteristics [5], as listed in Table 1.

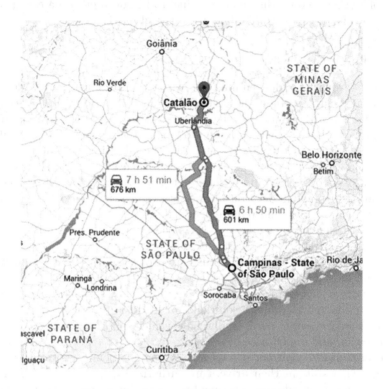

Fig. 1. Route from Campinas to Catalão

Table 1. Truck specification: Mercedes-Benz/Axor 2644

Load	Tank capacity (l)	Max. load (tons)	Tons × km/l
Empty	200	40	2.3
Full	200	40	1.963

The value of (t × km)/l was obtained by evaluating the fuel consumption history of this type of truck in February of 2015, where it showed a general average of t × km/liter = 1.963, according to Table 2.

Based on intervals of 300 km, with the help of Google Maps, we can see that on this route, the vehicle will pass through region of Guará and Ituverava—São Paulo's inland cities, and the organization has agreements with gas stations of both these cities located on the highway. The methods described in this work were applied to the city of Guará while trying to respect the most of the interval limits.

Table 2. (t × km)/liter

Manuf. year	Model	Branch	t × km/l	Fuel
2014	AXOR 2644	CATALÃO	1.99	Diesel
2014	AXOR 2644	CATALÃO	2.15	Diesel
2014	AXOR 2644	CATALÃO	1.75	Diesel
2014	AXOR 2644	CATALÃO	1.60	Diesel
2014	AXOR 2644	CATALÃO	1.97	Diesel
2014	AXOR 2644	CATALÃO	2.09	Diesel
2014	AXOR 2644	CATALÃO	1.86	Diesel
2014	AXOR 2644	CATALÃO	1.89	Diesel
2014	AXOR 2644	CATALÃO	1.95	Diesel
2014	AXOR 2644	CATALÃO	2.38	Diesel

3.2   Building the Model

To build the model, we needed details on the data used, an oriented graph, and mathematical modeling using linear programming principles.

We took infrastructure and accessibility into account to select the stations in a maximum distance of 4 Km from the road. Table 3 shows the data defining the actual price (AP) for each leg of the trip, i.e., the address of each station, its distance from the route (each way), and the fuel price per liter at each station. The Santo Expedito gas station is the one currently used, so there are no route deviations to get to it.

Table 3. Addresses, distances and prices

Trading name gas station	Address	Way In (km)	Way Out (km)	Diesel BRL/l
Santo Expedito	Anhanguera, km 395	0	0	2.869
Maranatha	Voluntários de Guará, 597	2.2	2	2.699
Guara	Duque de Caxias, 746	2.9	1.3	2.728
Avenida	Quinze de Setembro, 31	3.1	1	2.800

The branch of Campinas starts the trip after filling up at the Frango Assado gas station, at BRL 2.999 per liter. By applying these data to the formulas, the AP can be obtained, as listed in Table 4.

The linear programming model considered as the objective function the minimization of fuel cost, and constraints were related to origin and possible destinations. Constraints ensured that vehicle had only one origin for each destination

Table 4. AP structuring

	Trading name	Tank (l)	BRL per liter	Deviation to the station (km)	Liter price in the last refueling	AP1	Return to the highway (km)	AP2	total
P1	Santo Expedito	200	2.86	0	2.999	573.8	0	0.0	573.80
P2	Maranatha	200	2.69	2.2	2.999	543.1	2	2.75	545.91
P3	Guara	200	2.72	3.1	2.999	550.3	1.3	1.81	552.14
P4	Avenida	200	2.80	3.4	2.999	565.1	1	1.43	566.62
							$(t \times km)/l$		1963

and ensured that vehicle had not more than one destination for each origin on the route.

3.3   Results and Discussion

To solve the problem, it was used the software LINDO 6.1, due its nature, which consists of a minimum path problem. This group involves combinatory analysis problems, and the number of possible solutions is 5040 combinations and only one is optimal.

Station P2 showed a total cost of BRL 545.91 with fueling to the route/type of distribution being studied, road topography restrictions, bridges with height restrictions, narrow streets where big vehicles cannot running time, i.e., 4.86% less than the cost of the current station. This method had a positive impact on the decision of the best option to refuel.

In another application, the percentage reduction will subsequently vary according get past. As previously stated, this method serves to evaluate and support the decision, thus, occasionally a station with which the organization already has an agreement may lead to greater cost-effectiveness. However, we concluded that the proposed scenario, with routes from Campinas/SP to Catalão/GO, suggested a significant reduction, considering that this trip is repeated 200 times/month in average, i.e.:

$200 \times 573.80 = 114{,}760 - 4.86\% = 109{,}182.67$; a reduction of over BRL 5.5 thousand.

4   Conclusions

This study presents a study to identify new partner ships between the organization and its potential suppliers. Therefore, this study should be extended to other routes. The model will be subsequently adapted for Road Distribution operations, where the route goes from the city of Duque de Caxias, in Rio de Janeiro State, to the city of Campina Grande, in Paraíba State, in addition to several other routes that need to be evaluated.

The study shows that, with correct evaluation, a small deviation from the route to refuel at a lower price may have a big impact on the reduction of fuel costs. The proposed method is based in a traditional Operations Research' tools in the sense that it can be adapted to different situations, to longer or shorter distances, to any demographic region, and to any type of fuel and vehicle.

References

1. Ballou, R.H.: Business Logistics/Supply Chain Management: Planning, Organizing, and Controlling the Supply Chain. Pearson/Prentice Hall, Upper Saddle River (2004)
2. Slack, N., Chambers, S., Johnston, R.: Administração da Produção. Atlas, São Paulo (2002)
3. Novaes, A.G., Valente, A.M., Passaglia, E., Vieira, H.: Gerenciamento de Transporte e Frotas. Cengage Learning, São Paulo (2008)
4. Hillier, F.S., Lieberman, G.J.: Introdução à Pesquisa Operacional. AMGH, Porto Alegre (2013)
5. Mercedes-Benz do Brasil: https://www.mercedes-benz.com.br/caminhoes/axor/dados-tecnicos

The Profile of High-Tech Start-Ups: An Approach by the Prism of Graphical Analysis of Network Relations

Diego Rodrigues[(✉)], José Benedito Sacomano, Nilo Serpa, and Demesio Sousa

Paulista University, São Paulo, Brazil
2drodrigues@gmail.com, jbsacomano@gmail.com, niloserpa@gmail.com,
sousamtm@gmail.com

Abstract. This study applies two research methodologies, namely literature review and data survey, in order to analyze the behavioral context of contemporary society in its effects on individuals and organizations with regard to the uses of information technology. The behavioral conduct of contemporary society is different in several aspects from that presented in the past, so that new profiles are needed to undertake new business and enterprises. Bearing all this in mind, present paper discusses some important issues such as graphical analysis of the relationships in business networks, innovation, high-tech start-ups, public policies to encourage innovation, business models and their particularities, with a special emphasis in the subject of start-ups.

Keywords: High-tech start-ups · Social network analysis · Innovation processes · Local development

1 Theoretical Background

1.1 Start-Ups

For better understanding of the present study, it is necessary to differentiate the concepts of "start-up" and "spin-off", mainly because of the fact that the first has high level of informality, totally independent of the academic environment, although not necessarily created off this environment. Yet, spin-off is sometimes linked directly to educational institutions, applying in practice the theory learned in classroom or bibliographical research, mostly as proof of concept, with all cognitive tools which the academic environment can offer.

It is important to highlight that, in many situations, start-ups are initially self-employment options for young entrepreneurs, and it is not uncommon the presentation in the media of some cases in which these enterprises are consolidated and become to generate employment, which in general requires high technical knowledge standards.

© IFIP International Federation for Information Processing 2016
Published by Springer International Publishing AG 2016. All Rights Reserved
I. Nääs et al. (Eds.): APMS 2016, IFIP AICT 488, pp. 232–238, 2016.
DOI: 10.1007/978-3-319-51133-7_28

Nations, organizations and individuals are faced with multiple crises, a fact that aggravates the global climate change, the resource scarcity and the lack of decent employment for about two billion people over the next decade [1]. The environmental impacts caused by outdated models of economy are clear, which directly impacts the employment generation, taking into account the young people that shall get positions in the global labor market during the next 10 years. In addition, the extractive model has been the main driver of the current financial crises, alongside the energy and food crisis, causing the social disorders that we are facing with increasing frequency, pointing to the urgent need for a sustainable model [1].

1.2 Business Model

Two techniques of business models are widely used in Brazil, with the objective to better present the proposals for accelerators, investors and incubators: the first is the Business Plan, traditionally used by investment companies, banks and investors in rounds of more advanced investments; the second is the BMC (Business Model Canvas), with major representation in the planning of the start-ups; it tends to be the standard used for the selection of enterprisers projects by public policy programs, and instrument that guides the first meetings of entrepreneurs and investors on the most favorable cities to digital entrepreneurships [2].

The Business Model Canvas generation is the result of a creative and cooperative work of 470 entrepreneurs from 45 countries [3]. Maurya [4] proposes an adaptation of the so-called Lean Canvas. This model maintains the basic structure and proposal of the business model generation, but emphasizes specific questions of the niche, such as the main problems to be solved and the "features key" for further product development.

Chiavenato [5] exposes the Business Plan as a set of information that shows the concept of a new venture focusing on marketing, operational and financial perspectives. Its implementation sustains the future entrepreneur to avoid a declining path from enthusiasm to disappointment and failure. Still in accordance to the author, it is also considered as a tool that helps to attract investors, suppliers and partners.

In turn, the BMG was proposed by Osterwalder [6], which after analysis of the business models ontologies came to the conclusion that nine building blocks are enough to have a prior analysis as shown in Table 1.

1.3 Social Network Analysis

With regard to the topic "Social Network Analysis", a matter of substantial importance for the development of the work, [7] defines a network as a collection of individuals or organizations linked by various media relations, also points out that a network is composed of nodes and knots. Usually we call "nodes" the actors and they represent individuals or institutions; "knots" in turn represent the relationships between the actors.

Table 1. The nine building blocks of business model

Pillar	Building blocks	Description
Product	Value proposition	The value proposition is an overview of a company and product packages and services that add value to the customer
Client interface	Target customer	The target customer is a customer segment for those who wants to add value.
	Distribution channel	A distribution channel is a means of contact with the customer
	Relationship	The relationship describes the type of connection of a company establishes between itself and the client
Infrastructure management	Value creation	The value creation describes the arrangement of activities and resources that are needed to generate value for the customer
	Capability	The capability to perform a repetitive pattern of necessary actions in order to create value for the customer
	Partnership	The partnership is a cooperation agreement initiated voluntarily between two or more companies in order to create value for the customer
Aspect financial	Cost structure	The cost structure is the representation of money of all amounts used in the business model
	Revenue model	The revenue model describes how the company makes money through a variety of flows revenue

According to The Startup Ecosystem 2012 [2], a report of the most favorable environments for the implementation of start-ups based on a geographic indicator, the international ranking comprises the region of São Paulo (Brazil) with position number 13, preceded by Sydney (Australia) which occupies the position number 12; at the top of the list there are Silicon Valley (USA) and Tel Aviv (Israel) occupying the first and second positions respectively.

In addition to the data presented in the report, justifying the listing elaboration and the positioning of the Silicon Valley as a model to be followed, other authors confirm according to the subsequent statements.

- The current Australian public policy relative to the industry of information technology and communication has been strongly influenced by the ideas observed in Silicon Valley [8].
- One of the factors responsible for leading Israel to the top of the global scenario is the human capital [9]. Israel has a high proportion of scientists and

engineers as shown in CORDIS [10]. The positive aggressiveness in research and development is due to the fact that the country has 135 engineers and scientists to each 10,000 inhabitants, a significant advantage compared to the US which occupies the second position and has 81 per 10,000.

– Finally, Adams [11] reports the importance of the times when Silicon Valley got an infrastructure of risk capital, from other companies and law firms, not only from the academic movement of the 1980s and 1990s, exercising its role as an attractive environment for distant companies in order to win the development and acceleration of start-ups.

2   Methodology

For this study, there were applied two research methodologies: literature review and surveys. Specifically, regarding the literature review, this was extremely important to the recognition of the essential variables for the preparation of the questionnaire.

With respect to the format of the questionnaire, it was answered by two different profiles, but complementary to the development of the Brazilian ecosystem of start-ups. The first profile was defined by the experts and supporters of the ecosystem, as investors and professionals linked to supporting organizations to develop companies in Brazil, as well as consultants with experience in public and private policies related to the issue; the second profile are the entrepreneurs in their various skills, some with greater technical knowledge, others with management skills; they are those who had access to specific training or a strong theoretical basis concerning the entrepreneurship issue, as well as the entrepreneurs, who essentially taking decisions based on empirical findings, succeed to participate in a highly selective market in Brazil.

In short, there were two approaches, combining the two research methods: literature review (qualitative) and data survey (quantitative). The association features a mixed method, which was the research method applied [12].

3   Results and Discussion

After collecting the data obtained through the questionnaires, it was carried out a verification of data integrity, as well as an indexation, when there were assigned standard values aiming higher performance during the rendering and association among the nodes of the network.

Subsequently for development and better interpretation of the relationships between the actors, it was used the Gephi [13], an open source tool for the analysis and manipulation of representation in networks. In Gephi, the module of display and analysis of social networks and their interactions use a 3D rendering engine for real-time graphics. The same technique is used in the development of video games, where it is used the graphics board of computer providing that the CPU is available for other computer activities.

For clarity of the graphic result, different colors have been defined for each category of nodes; the categories presented are: (i) Start-ups—their names were not assigned from the questionnaires, so identified by S01 to S73; (ii) Type—identified the profile of the representative and the institution, if it was a Start-up in fact, or any organization of supporting or investment; There were filled 6 questionnaires with the supporter's profile, the others with the entrepreneurial profile; (iii) Gender—of the responsible of the enterprise, in which male entrepreneurs were prevalent, with 68 completed questionnaires; (iv) Representativeness—of the twenty-seven Brazilian Federative Units, from which twelve were registered in the questionnaire; (v) Formal education—of the stakeholders (also registered); (vi) Standard sectors—aligned with the public policy program Start-up Brazil, there were pre-established twelve of them, with an option to open response in the field "Others". Lastly, from the data obtained and used in the development of the work, it was presented category (vii), the current stage of the enterprises. All informed categories are displayed on the left side of the Fig. 1.

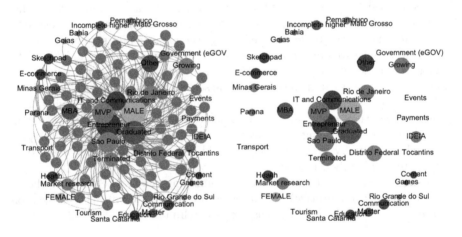

Fig. 1. Network generated with data from the research.

To better understand the representations, the nodes representing the Start-ups were removed of side b (Fig. 1).

It is possible to observe a pattern of spacing and appropriate distribution of network elements. It was applied the algorithm Fruchterman and Reingold [14], where the theoretical form is based on the spring forces (some of the concepts are equivalent to Hooke's law). In the aforementioned data structure there are not only repulsive forces between all nodes, but there are also attractive forces between the adjacent nodes.

In the above picture, it is possible to observe the concept of centrality regarding the categories that are more associated with start-ups in operation.

Even with regard to the centrality it is possible to see the segments with highest rate of associations, where the highlighted is the segment of Information and Communication Technologies.

The Federative Units that presented more projects are also positioned visibly in the network center, being that the Federative Unit of São Paulo is clearly the center of the Fig. 1, followed by the state of Rio de Janeiro and then by Distrito Federal. Although not displayed in the network center, the Federative Units Minas Gerais and Pernambuco are highlighted by the weight assigned to their respective nodes based on their dimensions.

Regarding the externality of the nodes, it is observed the nodes that represent the female gender, already mentioned, as well as the stages in research and idea representing the enterprises that are not available to their respective customers.

In contrast to previous statements, the following nodes are presented: the male gender, the stage Minimum Viable Product (MVP) and the degree of complete entrepreneur higher education. The respective centrality shows the predominance of the analyzed profiles. With this survey associated with the age and income of the enterprises, it is possible to propitiate new parameters to support strategic decision making.

4   Conclusions

Using the methodology proposed in the study, in addition to the contextualization of the issue addressed provided by literature review, it was possible to list the data that allowed a visual analysis of important features of some Start-ups basic network relations.

Objectively, it was demonstrated one of the distinct advantages from graphical analysis of networks, that is, the provision of results in visual form, which in turn provides greater clarity in the interpretation of data.

After the elaboration of the work, in addition to the variables presented, the questionnaire applied raised opinions about the Business Model Canvas blocks. By checking the answers, it was found a considerable level of subjectivity (this is the reason why the data were suppressed from the analysis). Therefore, it is possible to create a demand for the development of a tool to minimize or neutralize the subjectivity indices. Also it was identified, during the development of this article, the existence of sufficient inputs for the implementation of a model to support the modeling of new ventures and the analysis of feasibility of projects.

References

1. Almeida, F.: Experiências Empresariais em Sustentabilidade. Elsevier Science & Technology, Rio de Janeiro (2009)
2. Marmer, M., Herrmann, B., Dogrultan, E., Berman, R., Eesley, C., Blank, S.: The startup ecosystem report 2012. Technical report, Startup Genome (2012)
3. Osterwalder, A., Pigneur, Y.: Business Model Generation: A Handbook for Visionaries, Game Changers, and Challengers. Wiley, Hoboken (2013)

4. Maurya, A.: Running Lean: Iterate from Plan A to a Plan That Works. O'Reilly, Sebastopol (2012)
5. Chiavenato, I.: Empreendedorismo: Dando Asas ao Espírito Empreendedor, 3rd edn. Saraiva, São Paulo (2008)
6. Osterwalder, A.: the business model ontology - a proposition in a design science approach. Ph.D. thesis, University of Lausanne, Switzerland: 173 (2004)
7. Lazzarini, S.: Empresas em Rede. Cengage Learning, São Paulo (2008)
8. Mattar, Y.: Post-industrialism and Silicon Valley as models of industrial governance in Australian public policy. Telemat. Inform. 25(4), 246–261 (2008)
9. Chorev, S., Anderson, A.R.: Success in Israeli high-tech start-ups; critical factors and process. Technovation 26(2), 162–174 (2006)
10. CORDIS - Community Research and Development Information Service: Israel's R&D Capacity - A Promising Land (2014). http://cordis.europa.eu/israel/rd_en.html
11. Adams, S.B.: Growing where you are planted: exogenous firms and the seeding of Silicon Valley. Res. Policy 40(3), 368–379 (2011)
12. Miguel, P.A.C., Fleury, A., Mello, C., Nakano, D., Turrioni, J., Ho, L., Cauchick, P., Morabito, R., Martins, R., Pureza, V., Lima, E.: Metodologia de Pesquisa em Engenharia de Produção e Gestão de Operações, 2nd edn. Elsevier, São Paulo (2012)
13. Bastian, M., Heymann, S., Jacomy, M.: Gephi: an open source software for exploring and manipulating networks. In: International AAAI Conference on Weblogs and Social Media (2009)
14. Fruchterman, T.M., Reingold, E.M.: Graph drawing by force-directed placement. Softw.: Pract. Exp. 21(11), 1129–1164 (1991)

Business Modeling Toward Competitiveness and Ciborra's Criticism: Results from an IT-Business Strategic Alignment via an Action-Research

Nemer Alberto Zaguir$^{(\boxtimes)}$, Mauro de Mesquita Spinola,
and Fernando José Barbin Laurindo

University of São Paulo, São Paulo, Brazil
nemer.zaguir@gmail.com

Abstract. The IT-business strategic alignment (ITBSA) aims to promote greater IT effectiveness by making it active in the firms' competitiveness agenda. Despite the relevance of the theme, ITBSA is not free from criticism. Ciborra criticized how ITBSA research programs have been developed and its sufficiency for an effective strategic planning. This article shows how a business model in a small real estate firm was deployed for revenue generation through an Action-Research (AR) conducted to evaluate Ciborras' criticism. The results show ITBSA critics from the field and a new business model direction. The ITBSA was concluded to have structured the strategic discussion; however, Ciborra's inputs about the importance of bricolage, cyclical learning was conquered by an influence of the researcher as an agent of change applying AR under the critical theory paradigm. We suggest future research with more comprehensive literature review about our usual assumptions of economic rationality.

Keywords: Action research · Business modeling · Ciborra competitiveness · IT-business strategic alignment

1 Introduction

In recent years, the Brazilian real estate sector has experienced significant changes, whose reflections led companies to reassess their strategies, tactical actions and even their organizational structure [1]. For small and medium enterprises, abrupt changes in the external environment can pose threats that, if not properly managed, can compromise their performance, confirming the importance of competitiveness analysis. In this context, how can Information Technology (IT) contribute to the competitiveness of these companies?

© IFIP International Federation for Information Processing 2016
Published by Springer International Publishing AG 2016. All Rights Reserved
I. Nääs et al. (Eds.): APMS 2016, IFIP AICT 488, pp. 239–247, 2016.
DOI: 10.1007/978-3-319-51133-7_29

The literature on IT-Business strategic alignment (ITBSA) confirms that technological excellence, the pursuit of operational efficiency, optimization of implementation processes and development systems do not guarantee the effectiveness of IT and its contribution to competitiveness, thus requiring an analysis of the strategic impact of IT on the organization. To accomplish this, ITBSA models could be applied. One such model is the MAN/TI-2 [2] which includes company's structural factors, IT organizational factors and the recommendation to confront the analysis of two groups promoting adjustments for IT to be effective.

Although the ITBSA promotes the IT strategic role, it is not exempt from criticism. Ciborra [3] questioned how the ITBSA was developed, noting it is not enough for alignment in practice. Ciborra [4] also questioned the strategic planning process involving IT, stating that, to satisfy the condition to gain competitive advantage, it should seek innovation, which suggests a plan designed with greater freedom of experimentation, learning posture with flaws and opportunities.

This research was motivated by the need of a small real estate company, which required a new business model based on a peculiar opportunity identified after the sale of some internal business processes as a service to a real estate partner. The transformation of this opportunity into a new business, promises to be a source of revenue and competitive advantage empowered by IT. In order to address this issue, it was performed an ITBSA project to design and deploy this new business model, denominated "Business Process Outsourcing" (BPO).

This research aimed to assess four Ciborra's criticism during the ITBSA project. For this, the ITBSA project applied models from MAN/TI-2 using an action-research (AR), which results in practical and academic contributions. The practical one was the BPO deployment and alignment of business strategy, process, people and IT. The academic was the evaluation of Ciborra's criticism to this context.

The next section provides a brief review of the literature about ITBSA, the MAN/TI-2 model and Ciborra's criticism. The third topic discusses the methodology under the critical theory paradigm and the research model. The fourth topic shows some of the company's characteristics, the ITBSA project, the results and, the fifth, their discussion. The last topic, presents the findings with the limitations of the research and suggestions for future research.

2   Literature Review

This topic brings a brief description of MAN/TI-2 and four Ciborra's criticism about ITBSA.

2.1   MAN/TI-2 Model

According to Carvalho and Laurindo [5], the models that address the IT role in organizations can be classified into four groups: diagnostic, prescriptive, focused on actions, and integrative, which are those that add various elements of previous approaches. Laurindo [6] proposed the MAN/TI-2, an integrative model with two focus groups. The group of a company's structural factors and IT organizational factors. Table 1 represents the group of company's structural factors applied to this research.

Table 1. MAN/TI-2 structural factors (adapted from Laurindo [2])

Company's structural factors	Analysis models	Author
Business strategy decomposition in information needs	(a) Competitive forces	Porter (1979)
	(b) Generic competitive strategies	Porter (1996)
	(c) SWOT analysis	Porter (1979)
	(d) Critical success factors and prioritized applications	Rockart (1979), Torres (1989)
Actual and potential role of IT in the company	(a) Strategic GRID	Nolan and MacFarlan (2005)
	(b) Information intensity matrix	Porter and Millar (1985)
ITBSA perspective adopted	(a) Strategic alignment model	Henderson and Venkatraman (1993)
Network enterprise	(a) Evaluation of actual and potential role of internet in the company (evolutionary, revolutionary)	Porter (2001)
		Tappiscot (2001)
		Amitt and Zoot (2001)
		Anghern (1997)

2.2   Four Ciborra's Criticisms About ITBSA

Ciborra [3] disassembles the concept of ITBSA revisiting the history of publications criticizing the approach of Henderson and Venkatraman's model [7], highlighting the collapse of research programs and incentives to the subject sponsored by large firms. Four of the main Ciborra's criticisms follow below:

C1: The most careful consideration has been obtained from field observations and not from models, pointing out that strategic practices for alignment, such as "hospitality", "care", "culture" make more sense for management, suggesting that the human and social factors cannot be disregarded in this analysis;

C2: The strategic alignment process requires experimentation and is not observed or measured. Many information systems that supported the competitiveness emerged from this process and not from a structured approach. Phenomena, such as unexpected surprises, demand opportunities; adjustments arise from the field forcing managers to improvise. Ciborra [8] defined bricolage as adjustments by combining the resources available. "Let the world help you". Stahl [9] features that Ciborra was inspired by the notion of Weick [10] on improvisation and bricolage. The author of bricolage is someone who orders the chaos, using the local context and resources that have available;

C3: The graphical representation of abstracted alignment patterns can raise managers' awareness to align, but this is not enough to promote alignment in practice. The most detailed model of the concept remains confined in a world of idealized abstractions, with little impact on practice, considering them empty;

C4: Ciborra [4] discusses whether it is possible to achieve the goals promised by strategic planning processes, obtaining sustainable competitive advantages. He suggests that IT planning must be less formal, with greater freedom of experimentation and learning posture to take advantage of opportunities, besides being directed to innovation.

According to Stahl [9], Ciborra's works contributed to criticizing the heroic view of research on management and on IT, casting doubt on the objectivity of scientific statements derived from the natural sciences, which are useful in these areas.

3 Methodology

This section shows the action-research method under critical theory paradigm adopted, and the research model, with the propositions to be validated.

3.1 Action-Research (AR)

According to Thiollent [11], AR is a type of social research with an empirical basis designed and built in close association with an action or resolution of a problem in which the researcher and the participant's representative of the situation are involved collaboratively. AR goals may be defined with a practical goal and an academic goal. The practical one aims to contribute to the best possible solution to the problem centrally considered. The academic goal aims to obtain information that would be difficult to reach using other procedures, in order to increase the knowledge base of certain situations. For Coughlan and Brannick [12], AR is appropriate when the research question relates to describing the unfolding of a series of actions over time in a given group, to explain how and why the action of a member can change some aspects of the system. In this context, AR was the adequate approach for this research, once the ITBSA was required by the company and this project was an opportunity to observe the Ciborra's criticism. This research falls into the category of the critical theory paradigm. According to Coughlan and Coghlan [13], the ontological point of view of this theory, reality is considered "virtual", formed by social, economic, ethnic, political, cultural and gender; it is influenced by those trying to observable over there, and, from the epistemological point of view, the findings are mediated by these values. In this category, the researcher assumes the role of "transformative intellectual" amending the social world in which the participants live.

3.2 Research Model

This AR followed the three-stage route proposed by Coughlan and Coghlan [13]. First, the research context and purpose were established, defined by the adoption of Ciborra criticisms about ITBSA: (C1), (C2), (C3) and (C4) as four research proposition. Second, the main stage, performed in more than one cycle, consists of six steps: data collection, data feedback to participants, analysis, action planning, implementation, and evaluation. This stage was applied to each model of MAN/TI-2, with up to two cycles for the same model, promoting the technical results for the company. The last stage, monitoring, required the researcher's reflection over all the main stages and it was performed through active proposition observation. Figure 1 shows the Research Model.

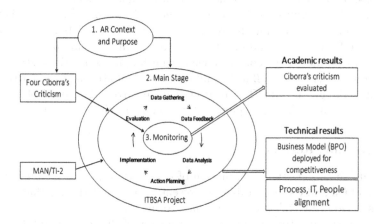

Fig. 1. ITBSA Project and AR (adapted from Coughlan and Coghlan [13])

4 Results

4.1 The Company and Its IT Environment

The company, at which this research was carried out, is a small developer and construction firm founded in 2007 with approximately fifty internal and external employees, PBPQ-level A certification (Brazilian Program for Productivity and Housing Quality) and ISO 9001 certified. The main products are incorporation, construction and sales of units in popular standard condominiums for the "Programa Minha Casa Minha Vida", a Brazilian government program, in five cities in Brazil. It has a strategic business unit, the traditional development and construction of its own works and services sold to real estate partners, which was used as an initial motivation to BPO modeling. Most business processes are operated centrally and are supported by an ERP system (Enterprise Resource Planning) specific to real estate industry. This ERP supports the parameterization of several companies separately, allowing remote access by users. IT is centralized with remote accesses by some areas, such as external sales offices and buildings operations.

4.2   The ITBSA Project and Practical Results

This AR was conducted by an ITBSA project sponsored by the board and led by the researcher. The ITBSA was facilitated by the company's culture and compromise with quality management and desire to improve its IT maturity. The two most important practical results successfully reached were the BPO deployed as a strategic business unit, focused on revenue generation. It was defined as a set of business process offerings, such as supplies, financials, quality management, sales operations, bank collection, customer relationship management and IT solutions as a service for qualified real estate partners. The second was the alignment of business processes, promoting reduction of departmental barriers, requiring involvement from people and effective support from IT. This project also has built and disseminated the company view regarding its competitive strategy, IT position on this view, as well as has influenced the attitudes of the participants regarding strategic agenda. The project team involved the board of directors, engineering team, architect, supply and finance supervisors and others.

4.3   Academic Results

The results show a partial confirmation of proposition C1 and C2 and full confirmation of C3 and C4. The Table 2 represents a sample of data gathered during the mais stage of ITBSA project and monitoring stage.

The strategic grid tool used brings a discussion of the actual and future views about IT. It conducts to some observation about the strategic alignment process like it was noticed by the management team; It was not "measured"; it was stimulated by a structured approach (grid framework) and also by improvisation posture, supporting partial confirmation of C2. On the other hand, the strategic alignment model, with a graphical representation of abstracted alignment patterns, have helped manager's awareness to align some business objectives and IT portfolio, but this model alone was not enough to promote alignment in practice, supporting confirmation of C3.

Table 2. Sample of observation registered during the AR

Model	Main stage: MAN/TI-2 deliverables AR cycles	Monitoring: research reflection
SWOT analysis	**Cycle 1:** **Data collection:** Five SWOT interviews	This analysis results in a partial confirmation of C1 and in an annotation of the research limitations
	Data feedback: SWOT statements confirmed	
	Data analysis: SWOT consolidation and review	
	Action planning: Planned meetings to discuss SWOT with four areas	
	Implementation: SWOT discussed with four areas and inputs for the company's IT strategy	
	Evaluation: Team awareness of the strategic agenda and of the importance of IT	C4 confirmed

5   Results Discussion

During the monitoring stage, the ITBSA project was observed to have stimulated the participants' reflections on competitiveness, on the role of IT, which had not been made earlier; promoted changes, and learning influenced by some strategic guidelines. Some considerations about each proposition are presented as follows:

C1: Partially confirmed. More attentive reflection on alignment was obtained from the field and not just from models. However, this research was limited, requiring a closer examination of the importance of strategic practices, such as "care", "hospitality" and "cultivation". We suggest covering this gap in future research;

C2: Partially confirmed. The BPO analysis and the identification of new potential opportunities for providing services to partners highlight the recognition that a business strategy can also arise from emerging and bricolage settings by combining the available resources towards innovation. However, is there no full agreement about Ciborra's consideration that the competitiveness agenda comes only from the "bricolage" process, and not from a "structured approach". This work confirmed that MAN/TI-2, a structured model in essence, also promoted and guided the strategic discussion. Due to its own limitation, the research could not provide any evidence of the C2 statement regarding the impossibility to measure the strategic alignment, which we suggest considering in a future research;

C3: Confirmed. It was showed that the gap of promoting alignment in practice came not from MAN/TI-2 models but was stimulated by the research approach based on the paradigm adopted and actions executed during the AR main stage;

C4: Confirmed. The actions proposed during the main stage cycles, influenced by the author and participants, gave freedom to experiment, promoting adequate plasticity, leading to a real business modeling driven by the competitive environment, learning along the way and actions, as suggested by Ciborra.

6   Conclusion

The purpose of the research wás to assess four Ciborra's criticism for ITBSA in a company of the Real Estate sector. It was considered partially satisfactory, given its limitation, to confirm the complete statements of two out of four propositions, but was considered satisfactory regarding the practical contribution to the company studied.

The MAN/TI-2 models promoted the collection of input for strategic business planning and IT using a structured approach. Research on the paradigm of critical theory held by the ITBSA project stimulated the researcher and participants to plan, execute and analyze actions, encouraging the bricolage process, cyclic learning, which according to Ciborra, are key elements for innovation to achieve sustainable competitive advantage aligned with the needs in the field. Then, a combination of an ITBSA model under an action-research positively contributed to new business modeling and knowledge generation.

In order to address the research limitations to validate the uncovered statements from the propositions studied, we recommend a more comprehensive literature review about the constructs such as "hospitality", "care", "culture" and its sense for management as future research, considering how human and social factors could be included in this analysis. Future research should also discuss the strategic alignment measurement issue and, finally, explore ontological and epistemological issues that underlie the different views on the debate related to rationality in the literature on information systems, as studied by Ciborra.

References

1. Camargo, C., Monetti, E., Alencar, C., Moraes, R.: A Inteligência Competitiva como Ferramenta de Apoio à Decisão em Empresas de Médio Porte: Estudo de Caso no Setor do Real Estate. In: 14th Conferência Internacional da LARES, Rio de Janeiro (2014)
2. Laurindo, F.: Tecnologia da Informação: Planejamento e Gestão de Estratégias. Atlas, São Paulo (2008)
3. Ciborra, C.: De profundis? Deconstructing the concept of strategic alignment. Scand. J. Inf. Syst. 9(2), 57–82 (1997)
4. Ciborra, C.: Digital Technologies and the Duality of Risk. Centre for Analysis of Risk and Regulation, London School of Economics and Political Science, London (2004)

5. Carvalho, M., Laurindo, F.: Estratégia Competitiva: Dos Conceitos à Implementação. Atlas, São Paulo (1997)
6. Laurindo, F.: Tecnologia da Informação como Suporte às Estratégias Empresariais. Redes entre Organizações Eficácia nas Organizações. Atlas, São Paulo (2005)
7. Henderson, J.C., Venkatraman, H.: Strategic alignment: leveraging information technology for transforming organizations. IBM Syst. J. **32**(1), 472–484 (1993)
8. Ciborra, C.: The Labyrinths of Information: Challenging the Wisdom of Systems. Oxford University Press, Oxford (2002)
9. Stahl, B.C.: The obituary as bricolage: the Mann Gulch disaster and the problem of heroic rationality. Eur. J. Inf. Syst. **14**(5), 487–491 (2005)
10. Weick, K.E.: The collapse of sensemaking in organizations: the Mann Gulch disaster. Adm. Sci. Q. **38**, 628–652 (1993)
11. Thiollent, M.: Metodologia da Pesquisa-ação. In: Metodologia da pesquisa-ação, Cortez (2011)
12. Coghlan, D., Brannick, T.: Doing Action Research in Your Own Organization. Sage, Thousand Oaks (2008)
13. Coughlan, P., Coghlan, D.: Action research for operations management. Int. J. Oper. Prod. Manag. **22**(2), 220–240 (2002)

AHP Modelling and Sensitivity Analysis for Evaluating the Criticality of Software Programs

André Felipe Henriques Librantz[1(✉)], Fábio Cosme Rodrigues dos Santos[1,2],
Cleber Gustavo Dias[1], Adriana Cristina Aipp da Cunha[1], Ivanir Costa[1],
and Mauro de Mesquita Spinola[3]

[1] Nove de Julho University - UNINOVE, São Paulo, Brazil
librantz@uninove.br
[2] Companhia de Saneamento Básico do Estado de São Paulo, São Paulo, Brazil
[3] Universidade de São Paulo – USP, São Paulo, Brazil

Abstract. In this paper the application of the analytic hierarchy process method (AHP) combined with the sensitivity analysis was proposed for evaluating the criticality of software programs and verify priority ranking stability. Results pointed that the proposed decision model could be implemented to help the decision-making process of classifying software programs, regarding their risk priority.

Keywords: Multicriteria decision-making · Risk assessment · Software

1 Introduction

In today's business and operational environments, multiple organizations routinely work collaboratively in pursuit of a common mission, creating a degree of programmatic complexity that is difficult to manage effectively. Success in these distributed environments demands collaborative management that effectively coordinates task execution and risk management activities among all participating groups [1]. In order to reduce errors caused by complex problems, mainly in distributed environment, Information Technology (IT) organizations require that the relevant activities risk management should be successful [1,2]. The management of risks is a central issue in the planning and management of any venture. In the field of software, Risk Management is a critical discipline. The process of risk management embodies the identification, analysis, planning, tracking, controlling, and communication of risk [3].

The strategy to be adopted for risk management of complex systems requires a comprehensive and full view, so that the uncertainties of these process can be managed with structured techniques and decision-making can be made in different areas in the organization, so that risks can be identified, prioritized and

© IFIP International Federation for Information Processing 2016
Published by Springer International Publishing AG 2016. All Rights Reserved
I. Nääs et al. (Eds.): APMS 2016, IFIP AICT 488, pp. 248–255, 2016.
DOI: 10.1007/978-3-319-51133-7_30

mitigated [4–6]. In this context, the analytic hierarchy process (AHP), a well-known multicriteria decision method has been used for risk assessment, forecasting benchmarking, resource allocation in several segments, such as manufacturing systems, financial systems, governmental, information technology, trying to reduce subjective judgement errors and increase the decision reliability [7–10]. AHP was also used for evaluating the risk in software projects [11].

Nevertheless, from your knowledge, this method was not used for evaluating the risk in software programs, in which management control is shared by multiple people from different organizations [1]. Therefore, the purpose of this article is to apply the AHP modelling combined to sensitivity analysis to the process of evaluating the risk priority of this complex system.

2   Risks Key Drivers

A systemic risk assessment is based on a small set of factors, called drivers, which strongly influence the eventual outcome or result. This set of drivers can be used to assess the program's current strengths and weaknesses, and forms the basis for the subsequent risk analysis. The Software Engineering Institute (SEI) risk management research that cataloged sources of risk in software development, system acquisition and operational security. The result of our analysis was the development of a common structure, or framework, for classifying a set of drivers that influence a program's outcome. As listed in Table 1, the driver framework comprises six categories:

Table 1. Risk key drivers categories [1]

Risk factor	Concept	Corroborating researches
Objectives	Related to items like product	[1,2,4,11]
Preparation	Cost and schedule focuses on the processes and plans required to achieve objectives	[1,2,4,11]
Execution	Focused on assembling, organizing, and overseeing the assets required to bring that plan to life	[1,2,4,11]
Environment	Involves items like enterprise, organizational, and political conditions to support the completion of program activities	[1,2,4]
Resilience	Involves capacity and capability to identify and manage potential events and changing circumstances	[1,4]
Result	Refers to the correctness and completeness of the software intensive system or system of systems that is being developed	[1,4]

3 Analytic Hierarchy Process (AHP)

AHP Saaty [12] is a multicriteria selection method that is applied to the solution of complex problems that can have multiple objectives that affect decision-making [10,13], making it possible to evaluate qualitative and quantitative criteria simultaneously according to the judgments and importance attributed to each criterion and alternative by the decision-makers, resulting in a classification of alternatives. Generally, the process can be divided into three steps.

1. Decompose the problem into a hierarchy structure. In this step, the problem is decomposed into criteria and subcriteria, defining a decision hierarchy, as depicted in Fig. 1.

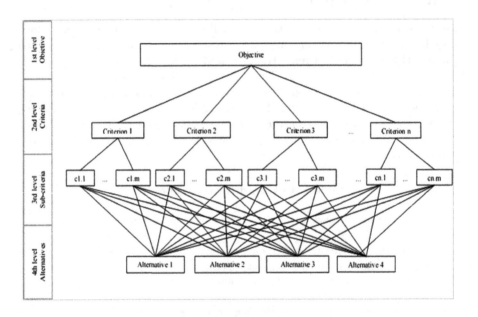

Fig. 1. Decision model scheme

2. Construct the pairwise comparison matrix using the Saaty scale importance [13].

The comparison between pairs is carried out by means of specific software or electronic spreadsheet programs. The process is done through decision matrix A, which calculates the partial results of weights of each criterion, as follows:

$$\nu_i(A_j), j = 1, \ldots, n \tag{1}$$

where A_j is the weight of an alternative relative to criterion i.

In order to interpret and give relative weights to each criterion, it is necessary to normalize the previous comparison matrix. To do so, the following expression is used:

$$\sum_{i=1} \nu_i(A_j) = 1, for\ j = 1, \ldots, n \tag{2}$$

where n is the criterion number, sub-criterion or alternative to be compared.

The judgments made by those involved in the judging process are evaluated by means of a consistency calculation. Firstly, it is necessary to obtain the maximum value of the eigenvector for each matrix through the following equation:

$$\lambda = (\Sigma_{i \in \kappa} C_{i\kappa}^{-1})/n \tag{3}$$

where n is the number of criteria. Index of consistency (CI) is calculated by:

$$CI = \frac{\lambda - n}{n - 1} \tag{4}$$

The consistency ratio (CR) is calculated by the following equation:

$$CR = \frac{CI}{RI(n)} \tag{5}$$

RI(n) is a fixed value based on the number of criteria, as presented in Saaty [12]. If CR $\leq$ 0.1, the degree of consistency is satisfactory, but if CR > 0.1, serious inconsistencies may exist, and the AHP may not yield meaningful results [12].

Next, the sums of partial results of each criterion are calculated by the following expression:

$$\nu_i(A_j) = \frac{a_{ij}}{\Sigma_{i=1}}, for\ j = 1, \ldots, n \tag{6}$$

3. Calculate the priority weights of alternatives according to the pairwise comparison matrix: For that, the priorities vectors of each alternative i relative to criterion Ck are calculated with the following expression:

$$\nu_k(A_i) = \frac{\Sigma_{i=1} \nu_i(A_j)}{n}, for\ j = 1, \ldots, n \tag{7}$$

After this, the weight of each criterion C_k and its impact on each of the alternatives is calculated using the following equation:

$$W_i(C_j) = \frac{C_{ij}}{\Sigma_{i=1} C_{ij}}, for\ j = 1, \ldots, m \tag{8}$$

where m is the value of criteria at the same level. The priority vector is obtained by:

$$w_i(C_i) = \frac{\Sigma_{i=1} w(C_j)}{m}, for\ i = 1, \ldots, m \tag{9}$$

Finally the evaluation of values of each alternative after normalization is obtained by Eq. 7:

$$f(A_i) = \Sigma_{i=1}\ w(C_j) * \nu_i(A), for\ j = 1, \ldots, n \tag{10}$$

where n is the number of alternatives.

4   Sensitivity Analysis

This approach involves changing the weight values and calculating the new solution. The method, also known as One-at-a-time (OAT), works by incrementally changing one parameter at a time, calculating the new solution and graphically presenting how the global ranking of alternatives changes. In this method, the global weights are a linear function depending on the local contributions [14]. Given this property, the global priorities of alternatives can be expressed as a linear function of the local weights. Furthermore, if only one weight wi is changed at a time, the priority Pi of alternative Ai can be expressed as a function of wi using the following formula:

$$Pi = \frac{Pi'' - Pi'}{w'' - w'} \left(wi - wi'\right) + Pi' \tag{11}$$

where Pi'' and Pi' are the priority values for wi'' and wi', respectively.

5   Numerical Application

In this section the proposed decision model was applied to evaluate the risk level of hypothetical software programs, as follows: the implementation of BI and CRM solutions (PROG 1); Solution Development and Embedded Systems Trading (PROG 2) and Computer Cloud Deployment in the organizations (PROG 3). Table 2 shows the normalized weights assigned to each risk driver obtained from the expert judgements. In this table one can see that the preparation (c2) is the more critical risk driver. Based on these results, the software programs were analyzed. Table 3 shows the decision matrix and the results obtained for the alternatives.

Table 2. Normalized pairwise comparison matrix

Risk drivers	Objectives	Preparation	Execution	Environment	Resilience	Result	Weights	Priority
Objectives	0.278	0.404	0.313	0.278	0.278	0.071	0.2702	2
Preparation	0.278	0.404	0.438	0.5	0.5	0.643	0.4603	1
Execution	0.056	0.058	0.063	0.056	0.056	0.071	0.0597	4
Environment	0.056	0.045	0.063	0.056	0.056	0.071	0.0576	5
Resilience	0.056	0.045	0.063	0.056	0.056	0.071	0.0576	6
Result	0,045	0.045	0.063	0.056	0.056	0.071	0.0576	3
CR = 0.075	$\Sigma = 1$	$\Sigma = 1$	$\Sigma = 1$	$\Sigma = 1$	$\Sigma = 1$	$\Sigma = 1$	$\Sigma = 1$	

Once obtained the decision matrix, it was possible to evaluate the score and classify the software programs according to their risk priority. The final classification is shown in Fig. 2, giving the following order, from first (more critical) to last: PROG 1 (0.4487), PROG 2 (0.29579) and PROG 3 (0.2721). The PROG 1 presents a higher risk level, when compared to the PROG 2 AND PROG 3, which have very close values. Alternatively, the weights for each risk driver assigned to the alternatives can be compared against each other graphically as shown in Fig. 3.

Table 3. Decision matrix

Alternative	Objectives	Preparation	Execution	Environment	Resilience	Result
PROG 1	0.09	0.15	0.04	0.04	0.05	0.07
PROG 2	0.09	0.15	0.01	0.01	0.01	0.02
PROG 3	0.09	0.15	0.01	0.01	0.01	0.01

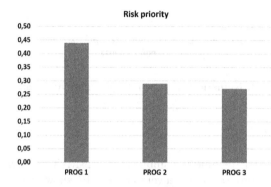

Fig. 2. Final evaluation of the alternatives.

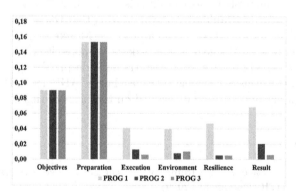

Fig. 3. Driver risks weights assigned to the alternatives.

5.1 Sensitivity Analysis

Figure 4 illustrates how the alternatives perform with respect to the risk driver "objectives". One can see that by shifting the current value (27%) to 100%, there is no change in ranking. Similarly, when shifting the value of this driver to zero, it does not result in any changes in the rank. This behavior can also observed for the other risk drivers. Overall, based on the sensitivity analysis, it can be concluded that the final decision is consistent and reliable.

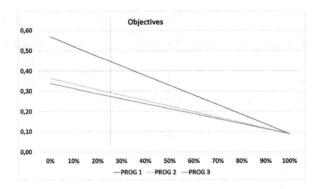

Fig. 4. Numerical incremental sensitivity analysis.

6   Conclusions

In this work, The AHP technique combined to sensitivity analysis was applied to evaluate software programs risk level. The results show that PROG 3 is less critical, as it presents lower values for the main risk drivers.

The sensitivity analysis performed in this study showed that changes in current values do not lead to ranking changes showing that the decision process was well-conducted, being useful for decision-makers. Moreover, as knowing which risk factors is more critical, the decision maker can more effectively focus his/her attention to that one in a given multicriteria decision problem.

Finally, hybrid decision models, such as Fuzzy AHP (F-AHP) and Fuzzy TOPSIS techniques may also be developed on the basis of this model.

References

1. Alberts, C.J., Dorofee, A.J.: A framework for categorizing key drivers of risk. Technical report, DTIC Document (2009)
2. dos Santos, L.R., et al.: Fatores de Risco nas Alianças em Projetos de TI: Estudo de Casos no Banco Central do Brasil. Revista de Administração **49**(1), 217 (2014)
3. Mead, N.R.: Requirements prioritization case study using AHP. Software Engineering Institute 2008 (2006)
4. Davies, A., Brady, T.: Organisational capabilities and learning in complex product systems: towards repeatable solutions. Res. Policy **29**(7), 931–953 (2000)
5. Benta, D., Podean, I.M., Mircean, C.: On best practices for risk management in complex projects. Inform. Econ. **15**(2), 142 (2011)
6. Corral-Quintana, S., Legna-de la Nuez, D., Verna, C.L., Hernández, J.H., de Lara, D.R.M.: How to improve strategic decision-making in complex systems when only qualitative information is available. Land Use Policy **50**, 83–101 (2016)
7. Ishizaka, A., Labib, A.: Review of the main developments in the analytic hierarchy process. Expert Syst. Appl. **38**(11), 14336–14345 (2011)
8. Syamsuddin, I.: Multicriteria evaluation and sensitivity analysis on information security (2013). arXiv preprint arXiv:1310.3312

9. Funo, K.A., Muniz Jr., J., Marins, F.A.S.: Risk factors in aerospace supply chain: qualitative and quantitative aspects. Prod. **23**(4), 832–845 (2013)
10. Göl, H., Çatay, B.: Third-party logistics provider selection: insights from a Turkish automotive company. Supply Chain Manag. Int. J. **12**(6), 379–384 (2007)
11. Rodríguez, A., Ortega, F., Concepción, R.: A method for the evaluation of risk in IT projects. Expert Syst. Appl. **45**, 273–285 (2016)
12. Saaty, T.L.: Decision making with the analytic hierarchy process. Int. J. Serv. Sci. **1**(1), 83–98 (2008)
13. Neves, R.B., Pereira, V., Costa, H.G.: Auxílio Multicritério à Decisão Aplicado ao Planejamento e Gestão na Indústria de Petróleo e Gás. SciELO Brasil (2013)
14. Chen, H., Kocaoglu, D.F.: A sensitivity analysis algorithm for hierarchical decision models. Eur. J. Oper. Res. **185**(1), 266–288 (2008)

A Comparative Analysis Between BPMN and ISO 19440 Modeling Language Constructs

Ângela Teresa Rochetti[✉] and Renato de Campos

São Paulo State University, Bauru, Brazil
angela.rochetti@yahoo.com, rcampos@feb.unesp.br

Abstract. Enterprise modeling is a tool that can be used for simple objectives, such as understanding how a part of the enterprise works, to more complex objectives, such as information flow for the computerized systems, or knowledge storage in an organization. There are several languages proposed for enterprise modeling, such as BPMN, CIMOSA and UML. They have different characteristics, advantages and disadvantages. This paper presents a comparison in relation to representation capacity between the ISO 19440 language constructs and the BPMN notation based on their constructors and icons. The analysis shows that BPMN has less representation capacity, showing differences between one language for modeling various aspects in an enterprise (ISO 19440) and a notation (BPMN) which focuses on process modeling and has few constructs for representing other aspects such as an enterprise's resources and organization.

Keywords: Process modeling · Enterprise · Modeling · BPMN · ISO 19440

1 Introduction

For business enterprise be understood and integrated, it is necessary for them to be systematically represented as models [1]. They differs in the number of details according to the perspective of the person, where each person will naturally have a slight difference in the point of view of enterprise objectives and visions [2,3]. Enterprise modeling languages define generic modeling constructors for enterprise modeling adapted to the needs of people who create and use enterprise models [4]. There are several languages and notations for enterprise modeling, such as BPMN, UML and CIMOSA, among others [5–7]. ISO 19440 defines a generic set of language constructs for enterprise modeling with common semantics, capable of unifying models developed by different people at various stages of development of business models, which support decision-making, monitoring and control. New proposals have emerged aimed at enterprise business modeling and management [8,9]. Business Process Management (BPM) is gaining force, which is normally supported by use of modeling tools based on Business Process Modeling Notation (BPMN) [10]. Since several alternative proposals exists, it

© IFIP International Federation for Information Processing 2016
Published by Springer International Publishing AG 2016. All Rights Reserved
I. Nääs et al. (Eds.): APMS 2016, IFIP AICT 488, pp. 256–263, 2016.
DOI: 10.1007/978-3-319-51133-7_31

becomes important to know the characteristics, advantages, disadvantages and representation capacities of each for appropriate use.

This paper presents a comparison between ISO 19440 language constructors and BPMN notation. Thus, below we give a brief description of ISO 19440 constructs and BPMN. Then, a comparative analysis is presented and final considerations.

2   ISO 19440 Modeling Constructs

The standard ISO 19440 supports enterprise modeling, and was created based on developments of modeling techniques as CIMOSA, GRAI, GERAM, among others [11]. His last update was in 2007, and was prepared by the European Committee for Normalization (CEN), Technical Committee CEN/TC 310, in collaboration with Technical Committee ISO/TC 184 (Integration and Industrial Automation Systems), Subcommittee SC 5 (Architecture and Structures Integration and Communication). They were also received contributions from members of the Task Force on Enterprise Integration IFAC/IFIP, the consortium CIMOSA, and the European project ATHENA [12]. ISO 19440 defines generic constructors to a modeling language based on enterprise business processes, described on templates. These constructs include generic attributes pre-defined in this standard, however, other attributes can be added for a particular need. They can be categorized according to their main views:

- Function and process-related: Domain, Business Process, Enterprise Activity, Event, Functional Operation, and Behavioral Rules;
- Information-related: Enterprise Object, Enterprise Object View, Order, Product;
- Resource-related: Capability, Operational Role, Resource, and Functional Entity;
- Organization-related: Person Profile, Organizational Role, Organization Unit, and Decision Centre.

These constructs are described below, based on the standard itself [12]:

- *Domain:* Represents the boundary and the content of an enterprise or a portion of an enterprise for which an enterprise model is to be created.
- *Business Process:* Represents all or part of the domain functionalities, its internal structure and its dynamic behavior. A Business Process construct shall describe the functionalities needed to produce a desired result that satisfies business objectives.
- *Behavioral Rules:* The purpose of the behavioral rules is to identify the start of the main Business Process, and describe the logical sequencing relationships of constituent Business Processes or Enterprise Activities, or both.
- *Enterprise Activity:* Represents the part of process functionality that is needed to realize a basic task within a Business Process. They are the lowest level constituents of a Business Process defined according to required user objectives for control.

- *Functional Operation:* Represents a part of the functionality of an Enterprise Activity, which has been decomposed into a number of transformation functions.
- *Event:* The purpose of the Event construct is to capture reason, origin and destination of an event. An Event shall represent the initiation of a state change in the enterprise or its environment, to be used to initiate the execution of one or more processes.
- *Enterprise Object:* Describe those characteristics (attributes and relational structure) and to provide for selection of relevant parts (Object Views) that are to be identified in the modeling process and used during the operational phase.
- *Enterprise Object View:* The purpose is to enable the identification of relevant attributes from a particular Enterprise Object as required by a Domain, a Business Process, or an Enterprise Activity for the definition of their inputs and outputs. It shall represent a subset of the descriptive attributes of an Enterprise Object.
- *Product:* This construct describes all intermediate stages of product life cycles with regard to both material and informational aspects. It is a very important construct because fabrication and sale of products are the aim of the enterprise.
- *Order:* Order construct describes what has to be done, which products are to be produced, which resources are to be used, and what purchases have to be made.
- *Resource:* The purpose of the Resource construct is to classify and describe in terms of capabilities all material and informational aids in an enterprise, such as machining equipment, tools and facilities, documents and files containing geometrical, material and informational characteristics, related the execution of Enterprise Activities.
- *Capability:* Represents the elements of both the capabilities required by an Enterprise Activity and those provided by a resource.
- *Functional Entity:* Describe the Operational Roles and Capabilities provided by the Functional Entity as well as the set of functional operations that can be assigned to it and which it can execute in a quasi-autonomous mode.
- *Person Profile:* Describe the human skill profiles available to serve the assigned organizational and operational tasks and to fulfill the responsibilities associated. Organizational Unit: This construct describes an identifiable entity together with its position relative to other such entities in the enterprise organizational structure.
- *Decision Centre:* The purpose of the Decision Centre construct is to describe its contents (in terms of classes of decisional functions) and its relations to other Decision Centers (the related decisional and information flow) and to Organizational Units.
- *Organizational Role:* Describes the skill profile required to serve organizational responsibilities and to fulfill those responsibilities. A skill profile shall be a list of predefined or user-defined human organizational skills, described in terms appropriate to the user of those skills and understandable by the person providing them.

– *Operational Role:* Skill profile required and provided to undertake the defined operational tasks. It shall be a list of predefined or user-defined human operational skills, described to the user of those skills and understandable to the person.

3 Business Process Management Notation (BPMN)

Business Process Management (BPM) gathers business management and information technology promoting the integration and improvement of the organizations' business processes using methods, techniques and tools to model, publish, control and analyze operational processes involving diverse people and systems. BPM's objectives are typically [6]: obtain knowledge about the enterprise's business processes; use this knowledge of business processes in the reengineering project of business processes to optimize the operation; facilitate enterprise decision making; support the interoperability of business processes. In the context of BPM, one of the main characteristics is the Business Process Management System (BPMS) modeling tools, which usually adopt Business Process Modeling Notation (BPMN). The latter refers to a series of standard icons for designing processes, which facilitates user understanding [13].

BPMN's main objectives are to standardize business process modeling, expand modeling resources and create a formal mapping between high-level modeling and execution languages. BPMN create a simple mechanism to develop business process models while also ensuring the inherent complexity of the processes. This notation was developed by the Business Process Management Initiative (BPMI) in May 2004, and in June 2005, BPMI merged with the Object Management Group (OMG). In February 2006, OMG adopted and officially published version 1.0 [14].

One of BPMN's major benefits is the reuse of code, because, according to the author, when enterprises construct models of components that represent a specific implementation, they can be stored in model libraries that can be used in the future by another similar application by just importing the model's code [6]. BPMN provides a basic set of diagrams to represent business processes in a simple manner, but that at the same time are capable of controlling the inherent complexity of the business processes. This basic set is divided into four categories [14]: Connection Objects (Fig. 1); Flow Objects (Fig. 2); Swimlanes (Fig. 3); Artifacts (Fig. 4).

Element	Description	Icon
Sequence Flow	Used to show the order (sequence) in which activities will be carried out in a process.	⟶
Message Flow	Used to show the message flow between two different participants who send and receive them.	┄┄┄⟶
Association	Used to associate data, text, and other artifacts with flow objects. Associations are used to show inputs and outputs of activities.	⋯⋯⋯⟶

Fig. 1. Connection Objects. (Source: Adapted from BPMI [14])

Element	Description	Icon
Event	Something that happens during a business process. These events affect the process flow and generally have a cause (trigger) or an impact (result). There are three types of events, based on how they affect flow: Start, Intermediate, and End.	○
Activity	This is a generic term for a job done. Activity types are: Tasks and sub-processes. A sub-process is distinguished by a small cross at the bottom center of the figure.	▢
Gateway	This is used to control the divergence and convergence of a flow's sequence. It will thus determine traditional decisions like joining or dividing routes.	◇

Fig. 2. Flow Objects. (Source: Adapted from BPMI [14])

Element	Description	Icon
Pool	A pool represents a participant in a process. It acts as a graphic container to divide a set of activities from other pools, generally in the context of Business to Business situations.	
Lane	A lane is a subdivision in a pool used to organize and categorize activities.	

Fig. 3. Swimlanes. (Source: Adapted from BPMI [14])

Element	Description	Icon
Data Objects	A data object is a mechanism to show how data is requested or produced by activities. They are connected to activities with the associations.	
Group	A group is represented by a rectangle and it can be used for documentation or analysis purposes.	
Annotations	Annotations are mechanisms for providing additional information to the reader of a BPMN diagram	

Fig. 4. Artifacts Objects. (Source: Adapted from BPMI [14])

4 Comparisons Between ISO 19440 and BPMN

4.1 Procedures for Analyses and Comparisons

After introducing the ISO 19440 language and BPMN notation, a comparative analysis is conducted. The analysis is conducted as per functional, information, resource and organization views. The synthesis of these comparisons is shown in Fig. 5, and the respective discussions and analyses are shown in sequence. It is understood that class objects in ISO 19440 and icons in BPMN are constructors of the respective languages. The classification used in the comparison between modeling language constructors (and their construction elements) was conducted in accordance with the 'correspondence' between constructors. The analysis is made in relation to how much a specific constructor conceptually representing an object or typical entity of an enterprise in a language corresponds to a constructor in the other language (or notation). These correspondences are classified as:

– **Strong,** for when constructors are conceptually **very similar**, corresponding to the representation of the same object or entity in a model, admitting a few minor and insignificant differences in this representation;

- **Average,** for when constructors are conceptually **similar**, corresponding to the representation of the same object or entity, however with significant differences in representation of the same concept, for example, in the case of constructors that have a large number of elements of different information (or attributes);
- **Weak,** for when constructors are conceptually **little similar**, not exactly representing the same object, but having aspects related to the objects being represented.

When a language **does not have** a constructor representing some aspect of a constructor of another language, the relative space in the box is kept blank.

4.2   Analyses and Comparisons

The framework of Fig. 5 shows the name of the languages being compared and the respective classifications of correspondences, followed by analyses and observations. For Business Process, Event, Enterprise Activity and Functional Operation, constructors of ISO 19440, it was identified strong correspondences (very similar) in BPMN.

The Business Process constructors in ISO 19440 can be represented in BPMN by the Sub-Process constructor, a specific case of Activity.

ISO 19440	BPMN	Classification of Correspondences
Function View		
Domain	Group	Weak
Business Process	Sub-Processes [Activity]	Strong
Event	Event	Strong
Behavior Rule	Gateway and Connections	Average
Enterprise Activity	Tasks [Activity]	Strong
Functional Operation	Atomic Task [Activity]	Strong
Information View		
Enterprise Object View	[Data Object]	Average
Enterprise Object	[Data Object]	Average
Product	[Data Object]	Average
Order	[Data Object]	Average
Resource View		
Capability	-	-
Operational Role	-	-
Resource	-	-
Functional Entity	-	-
Organization View		
Organization Unit	Pool [Lane]	Weak
Decision Centre	[Lane]	Weak
Person Profile	-	-
Organizational Role	-	-

Fig. 5. Comparison between ISO 19440 and BPMN constructors

The Domain construct in ISO 19440 could be represented in a weak similar manner with Group notation, grouping a certain number of processes from an enterprise's functional area in the model (which could be a department or not).

The Domain Relationship could be represented by a set of Events, Messages or Data Object. The ISO 19440 Behavior Rule construction element can be represented by the combination of Events and Flows in BPMN, being considered of average correspondence (similar). Although it is possible to conceptually represent the same object (behavior rules for processes) with these symbols, behavior rules in ISO 19440 have greater flexibility in representation in terms of logical expressions and are not restricted to BPMN's graphic representations.

Information view constructors in ISO 19440 has correspondence average (little similar) with Artifacts in BPMN, being more similar to Data Objects. In BPMN, an artifact represents a datum, however, without interfering in the flow.

Weak correspondences were also considered between ISO 19440's Organization unit constructors and Pool and Lane element (since it is a sub-division in BPMN), and between ISO 19440's Decision Centre and the Lane element (which be used as a container to separate a decision activities). Then, BPMN symbols represent few aspects related to organization.

In the comparisons between ISO 19440 and the BPMN language, a synthesis analysis show that four of six ISO 19440's constructors in the Function View have a strong correspondence in BPMN, and two have average correspondence. For the Information View, the constructors have average correspondence. The ISO 19440 constructors in the Resources View do not have any correspondence, and in the Organization View, two of its four constructors have a weak correspondence.

Since BPMN focuses on processes, it would be expected for this notation to be fitting for process modeling (functional and business related aspects). Thus, from the comparisons, it can be perceived that it minimally represents some aspects of the information and organization views, and that it does not explicitly represent aspects of the resources view.

5   Final Considerations

This paper presented a comparison in relation to representation capacity between the ISO 19440 language and the BPMN notation based on their constructors. The analysis shows that BPMN has less representation capacity, showing differences between one language for modeling various aspects in an enterprise (ISO 19440) and a notation (BPMN) which focuses on process modeling and has few constructs for representing other aspects such as an enterprise's resources and organization.

In BPMN notation, the basis for representing enterprise aspects is the graphic elements. Although BPMN has a significant number of graphic symbols, these constructors do not present detailed templates, like ISO 19440.

Although ISO 19440 defines a larger and much richer set of modeling constructors, on the other hand, a standard for the graphic representation of its main constructors is lacking. The graphic representation could provide a first understanding of the model, and then moving on to an understanding of details using templates that refer to its classes of objects and description elements (properties). The procedure used for analyses and comparisons employs a certain degree of subjectivity, and if more detailed comparisons are wanted, another technique must be used. However, the comparison and analysis in this paper will help users or analysts identify some gaps and correspondences that eventually permit discarding or classifying the languages in relation to some modeling objective, or for needs in terms of some specific view (functional, information, resources or organization), or a specific level of detail.

References

1. Kalpic, B., Bernus, P.: Business process modelling in industry—the powerful tool in enterprise management. Comput. Ind. **47**(3), 299–318 (2002)
2. Eriksson, H.E., Penker, M.: Business Modeling With UML: Business Patterns at Work. Wiley, Hoboken (2000)
3. Doebeli, G., Fisher, R., Gapp, R., Sanzogni, L.: Using BPM governance to align systems and practice. Bus. Process. Manag. J. **17**(2), 184–202 (2011)
4. IFIP-IFAC Task Force: GERAM: generalised enterprise reference architecture and methodology. IFIP-IFAC Task Force on Architectures Enterprise Integration March Version 1.6.3 (1999)
5. Mertins, K., Jochem, R.: Architectures, methods and tools for enterprise engineering. Int. J. Prod. Econ. **98**(2), 179–188 (2005)
6. Minoli, D.: Enterprise Architecture A to Z: Frameworks, Business Process Modeling, SOA, and Infrastructure Technology. Auerbach Publications, T&F Group, New York (2008)
7. Vernadat, F.: Enterprise Modeling and Integration: Principles and Applications. Chapman & Hall, London (1996)
8. McCormack, K., Willems, J., Van den Bergh, J., Deschoolmeester, D., Willaert, P., Indihar Stemberger, M., Škrinjar, R., Trkman, P., Bronzo Ladeira, M., Paulo Valadares de Oliveira, M., et al.: A global investigation of key turning points in business process maturity. Bus. Process. Manag. J. **15**(5), 792–815 (2009)
9. Palmberg, K.: Experiences of implementing process management: a multiple-case study. Bus. Process. Manag. J. **16**(1), 93–113 (2010)
10. Kohlbacher, M.: The effects of process orientation: a literature review. Bus. Process. Manag. J. **16**(1), 135–152 (2010)
11. Carnaghan, C.: Business process modeling approaches in the context of process level audit risk assessment: an analysis and comparison. Int. J. Account. Inf. Syst. **7**(2), 170–204 (2006)
12. International Organization for Standardization: ISO 19440: 2007 - Enterprise Integration (2007)
13. ABPMP: Guide to the Business Process Management Common Body of Knowledge (2013)
14. OMG: Business Process Model and Notation (BPMN). http://www.omg.org/spec/BPMN/2.0/PDF/

Adaptive Configuration of the Organization in Manufacturing Startup Companies

Christina Reuter, Bartholomäus Wolff, and Pia Walendzik(⊠)

Laboratory for Machine Tools and Production Engineering (WZL), RWTH Aachen
University, Aachen, Germany
{c.reuter,b.wolff,p.walendzik}@wzl.rwth-aachen.de

Abstract. This paper presents an approach for manufacturing startup companies to reconfigure their organization and processes as a consequence of changing preconditions. Startup companies can be agile and adapt their organization continuously towards their preconditions and given resources better than established companies. The presented approach comprises three main levers for the configuration: process standardization, form of organization and the strategy for growth. Within the three dimensions the configuration can be done between process effectiveness or efficiency, between organization with specialists or generalist and between fast growth or sustainability in the organization.

Keywords: Process management · Organization · Organizational change

1 Challenges in the Set-Up of Manufacturing Startup Companies

In recent years companies face the challenge of designing more innovative products in less time to stay competitive. The number of product or business innovations has increased and companies are trying to provide an environment which is favorable for innovation and flexibility. Nevertheless some of the organizational structures of the companies don't fit with the new products or business innovations. Especially the organization's values and organization's processes need to fit with the innovation. As shown in Fig. 1, there are different opportunities to handle those misfits. If a fit, both with the values and processes of an organization, isn't possible, the solution needs to be a separate team in a spin-off organization with new structures and processes [1]. The example of Audi AG proves this idea. In 2013 the Audi Business Innovation GmbH was established as a spin-off of the Audi AG. The objective of this spin-off is the implementation of interdisciplinary work and flexible working methods to develop products in the field of future mobility and digitisation complements. The highly interdisciplinary work to enable innovations in shorter cycles was not possible within the structures of an established company [2].

© IFIP International Federation for Information Processing 2016
Published by Springer International Publishing AG 2016. All Rights Reserved
I. Nääs et al. (Eds.): APMS 2016, IFIP AICT 488, pp. 264–271, 2016.
DOI: 10.1007/978-3-319-51133-7_32

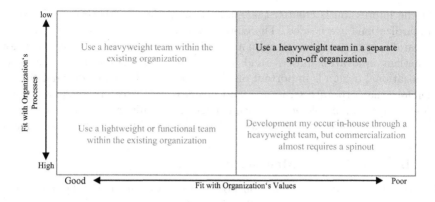

Fig. 1. Integration of innovative ideas in organization (Source: Adapted from [1])

Besides spin-off organizations there are more and more startup companies which focus on innovative product or business ideas. Spin-off and startup companies start without any given organizations. They need to build-up new organizational structures and processes. If the company focus is set on manufacturing processes compared to IT based innovation, the company needs more organizational structure directly from the beginning as there are usually more people involved. Manufacturing companies consist of different departments such as the production and manufacturing itself and several surrounding needed functions, e.g. purchasing, sales, material management, quality management, etc. Therefore structures and processes from startups developing software, where many examples can be found, can't be easily transferred. In 2011 IT based startup companies tried to focus on a new approach of developing software. Therefore software developers created a manifesto for agile software development. The Manifesto for Agile Software Development consists of four main principles [3]:

– Individuals and interactions over processes and tools
– Working software over comprehensive documentation
– Customer collaboration over contract negotiation
– Responding to change over following a plan.

Today besides software developing startup companies more and more manufacturing companies are trying to implement these principles within their product development processes to react more flexible towards changes. The challenge is to adapt the principles, such as interactions over processes and tools, as well in their organizations to be more agile within their organizational structures.

2 Deficiencies in the Set-Up of Organizational Structure and Processes

In the startup phase manufacturing companies are identifying which organization and process suits. After the initial phase of orientation, there is a risk that the impression is created that more organizational structures and process standardizations are needed. Therefore companies try to implement structures comparable to those of large companies which don't fit their needs and will slow down their innovation process and loose agility. On the one hand the initial organizational design is important on the other hand the organizational change. Therefore the corporate structures and business processes are explained in the following as the main elements which changes the configuration of the organization. The organization development explains in general the growth of a company.

2.1   Business Process Management

Business Process Management's purpose is to enable strategic alignment with the business goals and processes [4]. Within business process management there are several concepts and approaches towards that goal. The most relevant for this approach are the concepts of business process improvement, process innovation [5] or business process reengineering [6].

Business process reengineering, introduced in the 1990s by Hammer and Champy focusses on a radical strategic change in the organization. In contrast to incremental improvement in the optimization of single processes, business process reengineering considers a change in the holistic structure of a company: the business strategy, organization structure, culture and its processes. The different approaches towards business process reengineering have in common that they try to achieve a more efficient organization by running through the steps of mobilization, continued with the diagnosis, the redesign and ends with the transition [6]. The other named process management concepts are based on similar phases.

The concept of business process reengineering has been criticized as companies disregard the experience and expertise of their employees during the change process. Business process reengineering doesn't focus on people and their learning process but only on the process efficiency. In practical use many projects fail in the planning phase as the middle management is working against a structural change [7]. The concept of business process reengineering is lacking flexibility for startup companies. To be more agile, startup companies need to run through the phases several time in shorter cycles.

2.2   Corporate Structure

The corporate structure consists of several elements, such as the organizational structure and procedures, resources, the information system and communication management as well as the corporate culture. The organizational structure and information and communication system will be explained in the following as they are most relevant for the approach [8].

There are different types of organizational structures, such as functional, process or matrix organization. A functionally structured company is set-up with different department responsible for one task and competence each. Process oriented company focus on their business processes. A process organization focusses on the realization of process objectives and their optimization. The matrix organization tries to use economies of scale of the functional organization combined with the process focus on a special product or business unit. Employees in a matrix organization are working on two objectives from different leaders [9].

The information system deals with the supply of all needed information for the employees to fulfill their tasks. Information is usually connected between each other and can be linked between different systems [5].

The communication system is closely linked to the information system. It covers the infrastructure to share the information. This can be technical equipment, reporting lines or different boards. New ways of combining information and communication are interactive management systems. Interactive management systems combine the process of creating and sharing information, as each employee can access those systems easily and renew information in a defined workflow [10].

Each of the presented categories of the organization structure needs to be considered when designing new organizations. Especially the different types of organization structures do not fit the needs of startup companies. During the growth the requirements towards the organization are changing so that neither one nor the other approach fits the whole time. The challenge for startup companies is the transformation from one organizational structure to another.

2.3 Organization Development

Organization Development is the reaction of an organization towards external changes. It comprises the strategic planning and implementation of organizational changes including the behavior modification to improve the organization. The objective of organization development is to increase employees' level of satisfaction and commitment, increase cooperation and collaboration abilities among the employees and to increase the organization's problem solving [11].

The change process in the organizational development can be described in three phases by Lewin [12]. Organizational stability is maintained when there is a balance of two sets of forces acting upon the organization. The driving forces pushing on the organization to move in a new direction, whereas the restraining forces are hindering the movement. Therefore the first phase is about introducing a change by leaders to unfreeze the status quo. In the second phase leaders introduce the change by creating a possibility for movement towards the change vision. In the third phase the change gets stabilized by refreezing.

The approach by Lewin describes a process which should be done frequently in short cycles by startup companies to adapt to the given preconditions anytime.

In conclusion it can be said, that the business process management and organization development approaches explain how structures and processes can be adapted. The organization of manufacturing startup companies needs to be agile to adapt to the current situation on the one hand. On the other hand startup companies have different preconditions, such as limited resources. To handle the different preconditions the strategic organizational structures need to be changed. Therefore a guideline with the main levers for the organization configuration is needed.

3   Approach

The presented approach includes the main lever process management, the organization of corporate structures and the organizational development.

As shown in Fig. 2, there is an appropriate balance for process management within the organization. The value proposition of process control depends on the scope and detailing of the process control. During the growth of the company the appropriate balance of process control can be different, so that a continuous observation and adaption of the organization is needed.

The presented approaches of business process management can be placed on the right side of the graph in the context of Startup companies. As described above they represent important methods to reorganize business processes.

On the other hand approaches such as the Lean Startup theory are usually based on low scope of process control which can be placed on the left side of the graph in the context of Startup companies. These are useful methods for the product development which reach their limits in terms of business process management.

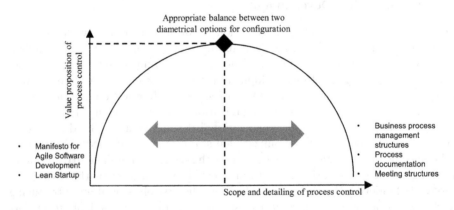

Fig. 2. Value proposition of process management (Source: Adapted from [4])

Turning points of the organization and its processes are so called business process instances [13]. In the original context business process instances are used to build business processes without any workflows. The aim of this paper is to put business process instances in a wider context to describe major changes in the organization, such as increase of employees or changing product requirements. At those turning points the existing organizational structures and the processes need to be reviewed if their value proposition is still at the appropriate balance.

If a change is needed the three levers of process, organization and the strategy for growth should be taken into consideration to reconfigure the existing set-up.

The first lever represents the process standardization. Processes, which are predominantly focusing on the Process effectiveness, are reflected by flexible and creative processes, such as an agile product development. Process effectiveness is needed when starting the development of a new product. On the other hand predominantly process efficiency is shown through process standardization and itemization. Efficiency in the organization is needed to structure recurring processes. The trade-off is between process standardization or individual coordination.

The second lever is the form of organization between specialists and generalists. Specialization is given in a rigid organization when employees can focus on a special task. On the other hand generalists are employees working on different tasks which can be enabled through a flexible organization. The trade-off is given between differentiation and integration.

The third lever is the difference between fast growth and sustainability in the organization. Quick growth can be enabled through flat hierarchy as small teams stay agile and can take decisions quickly. Sustainability in the organization is the establishment of standards. The trade-off is between the a decentralized organization with decision-making authority in each department and a centralized organization.

4   Case Study

The approach will be investigated with an ongoing case study with a startup company. The method used to conduct the case study are semi-structured interviews to get information about the development of the startup company in regard to the changes within the processes and the organization.

The company is a startup company developing products for electromobility. The company was founded with around 30 people working in different departments such as the product development, prototyping production or even the purchasing. At the beginning each employee worked on a special task, mostly development tasks in agile development processes. There was only one hierarchy level to enable fast decision taking and each team could organize their work on their own. Information was mainly spread on inquiry via face-to-face communication as the employees were located close to each other. The communication system was based on short weekly meetings to keep each other informed about the current status of the projects. Processes were implemented step by step according to the needs of the company. At that time the appropriate balance of process control was found.

The startup company grew quickly within its first year by acquiring new employees. During the growth of this startup company the number of employees increased fast so that it wasn't possible to spread all information needed only on inquiry as important information got lost. This was the first business process instance. As shown in Fig. 3, the value of the existing process configuration was not the appropriate balance anymore but more detailing was needed.

Therefore standard meetings and reporting structures for the different tasks in the organization were developed to keep each other informed. The processes were documented in a flexible interactive management system to be efficient in simple, reoccurring processes, such as the purchasing process.

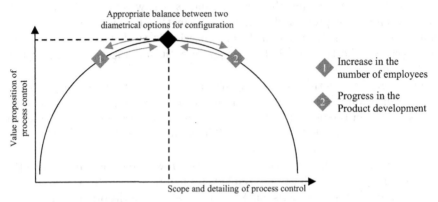

Fig. 3. Business process instances change value proposition of process management

Business Process Instance	Process standardization	Form of organization	Strategy for growth
0	Agile development process	Flat hierarchy, information on inquiry, shortly weekly meetings	Fast growth, less standardization
1	Process documentation to enable efficient reoccurring processes and agile development process	Flat hierarchy, but more standard meetings and reporting structures	More standardization to enable efficiency
2	Agile development process with small autonomous teams for specified tasks	Meetings in the autonomous teams, less meetings for all employees	Fast growth

The second business instance has been the progress in the product development. As the product was specified more and more the development speed slowed down with the existing organization structures. The value of process control was not at the appropriate balance any more as the existing structure of information meetings for the whole team was too much. Therefore the organization was transformed to small autonomous teams by using the portfolio work [12] approach. Each employee working in the purchase department was linked to one development team to do their purchasing tasks. Meetings were organized in smaller teams on special task and less meetings for all employees together.

The investigation will be continued to identify more business process instances and the needed changes for the processes, the organization and the strategy for growth.

5   Conclusion

In summary, there is a lack of finding the appropriate balance for the process and organization management of startup companies. Therefore the challenge is to create adaptive processes and organization structures. The presented approach is based on business process instances to identify needed changes within the organization and its processes. Further work needs to be done to detail and validate the presented approach. The main levers for the configuration can be detailed. In a second step the identified specific business process instances need to be transformed into generic business process instances. The third step is the description of the needed change configuration according to the business process instances. Overall a validation of the concept needs to be done to prove the presented approach. Therefore the method of semi-structured interviews will be conducted with more startup companies during their growths.

Acknowledgement. The authors would like to thank the German Research Foundation DFG for the kind support within the Cluster of Excellence "Integrative Production Technology for High-Wage Countries".

References

1. Christensen, C.M., Overdorf, M.: Meeting the challenge of disruptive change. Harv. Bus. Rev. **78**(2), 66–77 (2000)
2. Audi. http://www.audi.com/corporate/de/unternehmen/unternehmensstruktur/audi-beteiligungen/audi-business-innovation.html
3. Agile Manifesto. http://agilemanifesto.org/iso/en/
4. Bergsmann, S.: End-to-End-Geschäftsprozessmanagement. Springer, Heidelberg (2011)
5. Vom Brocke, J., Rosemann, M., et al.: Handbook on Business Process Management. Springer, Heidelberg (2015)
6. Harrington, H.J.: Business Process Improvement: The Breakthrough Strategy for Total Quality, Productivity, and Competitiveness. McGraw Hill, New York (1991)
7. Davenport, T.H.: Process Innovation: Reengineering Work Through Information Technology. Harvard Business Press, Boston (1993)
8. Hammer, M., Champy, J.: Reengineering the Corporation: Manifesto for Business Revolution. HarperBusiness, New York (1993)
9. Chandler, A., Hagstrom, P., Solvell, O.: The Dynamic Firm: The Role of Technology, Strategy, Organization, and Regions. Oxford University Press, Oxford (2003)
10. Behrens, C., Weßel, S.: Interaktive Prozessorientierte Managementsysteme. Dynamische und Stabile Prozesse im Unternehmen mit nachhaltiger Nutzung des Organisatorischen Wissens der Mitarbeiter. Ind. Manag. **30**, 2 (2014)
11. Lewin, K.: Field Theory in Social Science: Selected Theoretical Papers. Harpers Torchbooks, New York (1951)
12. Gross, P.: Jobholder-Value und Portfolio-Work: die Neuerfindung der Arbeit. Haupt, Bern (2000)
13. Rosa, M., Soffer, P.: Business Process Management Workshops. Springer, Berlin (2013)

Support Policies and Collective Efficiency in a Furniture Cluster

Elizangela Maria Menegassi de Lima[1]([⊠]), Walter C. Satyro[2],
José B. Sacomano[2], Esdras Jorge Santos Barboza[2], and Renato Telles[2]

[1] Paranaense University, Umuarama, Brazil
menegassi@unipar.br
[2] Paulista University, São Paulo, Brazil

Abstract. The aim of this research is to analyze the support policies and the collective efficiency in a furniture cluster in the South region of Brazil, subject of scarce studies despite its importance. Using quantitative methodology we made a survey with 20 companies of this furniture cluster. The results indicated that support policies and collective efficiency were statistically correlated. The contribution of this paper to the literature is to reinforce that the findings that support policies are a way to improve collective efficiency, and so provide competitiveness to all the companies that belong to the cluster. This research was made on a temporal transversal cut, a characteristic of studies in networks, so the result does not allow generalizations.

Keywords: Cluster · Human capital · Technology · Innovation · Qualitative

1 Introduction

Contemporary companies need to be competitive to manage their businesses in the face of the turbulence imposed by the globalized environment of the economy. In addition, the companies look for to adapt to the new patterns of competition, effects of technology on competitiveness, cultural influences and other environmental factors that affect the day-to-day of the companies [1].

The competitive environment forces the companies around the world to reduce costs to provide innovative products/services in a demand led by consumers and supply chains stimulated by the buyers [2,3]. In order to overcome this situation new organizational arrangement appeared, formed by groups of companies in strategic alliances, called interorganizational networks [4] that can be defined as a group of interdependent companies, involving the use of services and good, production and distribution [5].

Under the standpoint of the interorganizational network, a cluster can be seen as a group of companies that belongs to similar and/or complementary sector, located in a certain geographical region [6,7].

© IFIP International Federation for Information Processing 2016
Published by Springer International Publishing AG 2016. All Rights Reserved
I. Nääs et al. (Eds.): APMS 2016, IFIP AICT 488, pp. 272–279, 2016.
DOI: 10.1007/978-3-319-51133-7_33

Organizational theory is especially interested in networks, trying to understand the complemental system of interdependence, such as production, coordination, research and engineering, which is different from the analysis of a simple company [6,7].

The analysis of the competitiveness of clusters in relation to collective efficiency, government policy support, human capital, governance, logistics, technology, quality and productivity is essential to understand the factors that can provide competitiveness to a cluster in its stage of development [4].

The Brazilian furniture industry is made up of 13,500 companies, corresponding to 10,000 micro, 3,000 small and 500 medium companies approximately, situated mostly in the Central-South region of Brazil [8]. The state of Parana is among the largest producers of furniture in Brazil, and in the city of Umuarama is located the second largest furniture cluster of this state, with a consumption of 3,000 m^3 of wood per month [9].

Using quantitative methodology, the aim of this research is to analyze support policies and collective efficiency that can provide competitiveness to the furniture cluster of the city of Umuarama, subject of scarce studies despite of its importance.

2 Literature Review

2.1 Support Policies

The competitiveness of the companies can be determined by various factors, such as networks, human resources, customers and government support policies, among others [10]. Support policies are the policies that try to improve the efficiency and competitiveness of the companies [10]. Efficiency is associated to the ability of a policy measure to support growth without generating negative feedback effects [11,12].

Support policies can increase the competitiveness of the clusters and have a potential to support the recovery of development, contributing to the generation of income and employment, and so reducing the regional and social inequalities [13].

2.2 Industrial Clusters

The competition of the modern days forces the companies to have so many capacities and abilities to compete that it is no more possible to operate alone; to overcome these requirements, the companies form strategic alliances with other companies, including customers, suppliers, or even competitors to survive [14].

The complexity to compete is so great that it is possible to say that all companies operate in networks, from small to big enterprises, using or not connections with their partners [15]. The interorganizational network and the companies that belong to it share, exchange and also joint development technology, products or services among themselves [14].

A cluster can be defined as a sectoral and geographical concentration of companies that provide efficiency gains, which the companies that compete individually, can seldom achieve [16]. The cluster is formed by suppliers, competitors and complementary companies that in order to provide competitive advantage to these companies, exchange information, knowledge, expertise, and products/services [14].

In the cluster, the companies cooperate among themselves, but at the same time, they compete in the market [4,5]. The cluster can also provide geographical development to the area where it operates, and one example can be presented: the BioRegion of Catalonia, Spain that deals with bioscience and medical technology, formed by 481 companies, 80 research centers, 15 hospitals and 12 universities [17].

2.3   Collective Efficiency

Collective efficiency can be understood as the ability and capacity of a group to organize and execute actions needed to conduct to objectives that the companies, which belongs to this group, could not reach individually [18].

The cluster per se is a way to improve collective efficiency by the interrelationship of the many companies that form the cluster, enabling these companies to obtain positive results, improving competitiveness [19] to ensure the market or to reduce the competition [20]. Cooperation between these companies is important to lead to collective efficiency [21].

In the cluster the collective efficiency is gained by the competitive advantage that comes from joint actions and local external economies [16]. Collective efficiency is derived from the individual action and from the consciously chased joint action [18].

3   Methodology

We wanted to analyze a phenomenon (support policy and collective efficiency) in a certain population (furniture cluster), so we used a descriptive approach with a degree of exploratory research [22] and quantitative methodology of analysis [23], where the collected evidences and data can be measured in order to use statistic to investigate the results [24].

In the Furniture Union of the city of Umuarama we got the general information and main contact of the 56 companies that constitute this furniture cluster. By email we kept in touch with them explaining in general terms our research, and two days later, we sent the survey by email. After a week we sent an email to schedule a meeting to collect personally the questionnaires.

In total we gathered 20 answered questionnaires. These questionnaires were divided in two parts; in the first one we asked general questions and in the second one we introduced some assertions based on a Likert scale of five points [25]. We used the IBM SPSS Statistic v. 21 to test the Pearson correlation coefficient between the assertions.

4   Results

From these 20 companies, 55% were established for over 10 years, 30% from 5 years to 10 years and the left 15% from 2 to 4 years, as exhibited in Fig. 1.

The majority of these companies, 95%, hire people locally and just one uses to hire 60% of its workforce locally and 40% from surrounding cities. These companies were critic about the relationship between them and the institutions that could provide support policies: 65% did not trust in this relationship, 30% trusted partially and 5% trusted, as shown in Fig. 2.

This rate of distrust was attributed by 80% to the lack of cooperation between the institutions that could provide support policies and these companies; and the other 20% believed that this cooperation was partial, as presented in Fig. 3.

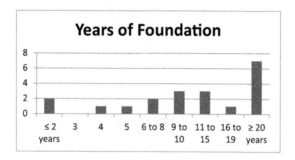

Fig. 1. Years of company foundation in the cluster studied

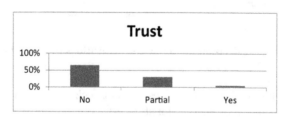

Fig. 2. Trust between these companies and the institutions that could provide support policies

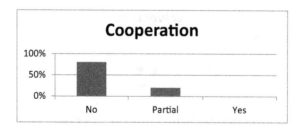

Fig. 3. Cooperation between the institutions that could provide support policies and these companies

The majority of these companies, 85%, did not agree that the support policies that these institutions could provide took into account the interests of the majority of the companies, and 15% agreed partially, as exhibited in Fig. 4.

The vast majority, 85% of these companies, did not agree that these institutions were democratic in their decision taking; and 15% agreed partially, as displayed in Fig. 5.

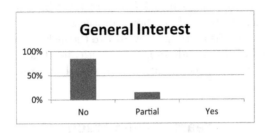

Fig. 4. Respect to the general interest of these companies

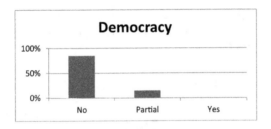

Fig. 5. Democracy in the decision taking by the institutions that could provide support policies

On the other hand, these companies did not seek to approach these institutions to improve this grade of relationship; 80% did not have any involvement with these institutions and 20% had a partial involvement, as exhibited in Fig. 6.

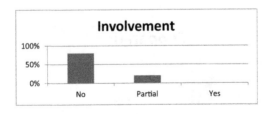

Fig. 6. Grade of involvement between the institutions that could provide support policies and these companies

In the questionnaires there were three assertions about support policies related to: trust, government support policies and competitiveness; and other three about collective efficiency related to: cooperation, general interest and competitiveness, in a Likert scale of five points. Using the data of the questionnaires we made the analysis of the Pearson correlation coefficient (r) between support policies and collective efficiency, using the statistical software IBM SPSS version 21, as shown in Table 1.

Table 1. Pearson correlation coefficient (r)

		Collective efficiency	Support policy
Collective efficiency	Pearson correlation Sig. (2 extremities)	1	.952* 0.048
Support policy	Pearson correlation Sig. (2 extremities)	*0.048	1

The Pearson correlation coefficient (r) equal to 0.952 at a level of significance p value for two tailed test of 4.8% suggested a strong correlation between support policies and collective efficiency. The assertions that got correlation were: (a) Support policies are important to bring competitiveness to our companies, and (b) Collective efficiency can improve competitiveness of our companies.

This result suggested that these companies valorized support policies to bring collective efficiency and so bring positive results, providing competitiveness to this furniture cluster [19], although these companies did not trust in the institutions that were supposed to support them, due to the lack of cooperation of these institutions to the companies.

5 Conclusion

This research investigated the support policies and the collective efficiency in the furniture cluster of the city of Umuarama, located in the State of Parana, Brazil. We analyzed 20 companies of this cluster, in a total of 56 that were registered in the Furniture Union of this city.

The prevailing part of these companies was established for over 10 years. These companies were critic about the relationship between themselves and the institutions that could provide support policies. The greater part did not trust in this relationship, and this rate of distrust was attributed by the majority of the interviewed to the lack of cooperation between themselves and these institutions. These companies did not agree that the support policies that these institutions could provide took into account the interests of the majority of the companies, or that these institutions were democratic in their decision taking. On the other hand, these companies did not seek to approach these institutions to improve the grade of relationship, what can keep the situation.

Using statistic we could correlate support policies and collective efficiency, suggesting that these companies valorized support policies [10] to bring collective efficiency to improve the competitiveness of this furniture cluster [4,5,14,19], although these companies did not trust in the institutions that were supposed to support them, due to the lack of cooperation of these institutions to the companies.

We suggest that the same research could be done in some other cluster to compare the results. As a characteristic of studies in networks, this study was based on a temporal transversal cut, so the results do not allow generalizations.

Acknowledgements. The authors acknowledge CAPES – Coordenacao de Aperfeicoamento de Pessoal de Nivel Superior of the Ministry of Education, Federal Government, Brazil, for the resources to make this research.

References

1. Tilahun, N., Fan, Y.: Transit and job accessibility: an empirical study of access to competitive clusters and regional growth strategies for enhancing transit accessibility. Transp. Policy **33**, 17–25 (2014)
2. Sun, Y., Shang, R.A.: The interplay between users' intraorganizational social media use and social capital. Comput. Hum. Behav. **37**, 334–341 (2014)
3. Hahn, M.H., Lee, K.C., Lee, D.S.: Network structure, organizational learning culture, and employee creativity in system integration companies: the mediating effects of exploitation and exploration. Comput. Hum. Behav. **42**, 167–175 (2015)
4. Neto, J.A.: Gestao de Sistemas Locais de Producao e Inovacao (Clusters/APLS): Um Modelo de Referência. Atlas, São Paulo (2009)
5. Reis, J.G.M., Neto, M.M., Vendrametto, O., Costa Neto, P.L.O.: Qualidade em Redes de Suprimentos: A Qualidade Aplicada ao Supply Chain Management. Atlas, São Paulo (2015)
6. Huggins, R., Izushi, H.: Competition, Competitive Advantage and Clusters: The Ideas of Michael Porter. Oxford University Press, Oxford (2011)
7. Menegassi Lima, E.M., Pona, J.G.A., Sacomano, J.B., Reis, J.G.M., Lobo, D.S.: Relationships and centrality in a cluster of the milk production network in the state of Parana/Brazil. In: Umeda, S., Nakano, M., Mizuyama, H., Hibino, H., Kiritsis, D., Cieminski, G. (eds.) APMS 2015. IAICT, vol. 459, pp. 11–19. Springer, Heidelberg (2015). doi:10.1007/978-3-319-22756-6_2
8. Brazilian Institute of Geography and Statistic. http://www.ibge.gov.br/home/estatistica/economia/demografiaempresa/2013/default.shtm
9. Unipar. http://www.tvup.org.br
10. Yoon, J., Lee, H.Y., Dinwoodie, J.: Competitiveness of container terminal operating companies in South Korea and the industry–university–government network. Transp. Res. Part A: Policy Pract. **80**, 1–14 (2015)
11. Papadelis, S., Stavrakas, V., Flamos, A.: What do capacity deployment rates tell us about the efficiency of electricity generation from renewable energy sources support measures in Greece? Energies **9**(1), 38 (2016)

12. Kulovesi, K.: International trade disputes on renewable energy: testing ground for the mutual supportiveness of WTO law and climate change law. Rev. Eur. Comp. Int. Environ. Law **23**(3), 342–353 (2014)
13. Ministry of Development, Industry and Foreign Trade: Technical report
14. Gulati, R.: Alliances and networks. Strateg. Manag. J. **19**, 293–317 (1998)
15. Nohria, N.: Is a network perspective a useful way of studying organizations? In: Nohria, N., Ecles, R. (eds.) Networks and Organizations: Structure, Form, and Action, pp. 287–301. Harvard Business School, Boston (1992)
16. Schmitz, H.: Collective efficiency and increasing returns. Camb. J. Econ. **23**(4), 465–483 (1999)
17. Ministry of Development and Foreign Trade: http://www.desenvolvimento.gov.br
18. Schmitz, H.: Collective efficiency: growth path for small scale industry. J. Dev. Stud. **31**(4), 529–566 (1995)
19. Callois, J.M.: The two sides of proximity in industrial clusters: the trade-off between process and product innovation. J. Urban Econ. **63**(1), 146–162 (2008)
20. Mintzberg, H., Ahlstrand, B., Lampel, J.: Safári da Estratégia. Bookman, Porto Alegre (2009)
21. Mulder, L.B., Van Dijk, E., Wilke, H.A., De Cremer, D.: The effect of feedback on support for a sanctioning system in a social dilemma: the difference between installing and maintaining the sanction. J. Econ. Psychol. **26**(3), 443–458 (2005)
22. Hair Jr., J.F., Babin, B., Money, A.H., Samouel, P.: Fundamentos de Métodos de Pesquisa em Administração. Bookman, Porto Alegre (2005)
23. Creswell, J.W.: Projeto de Pesquisa Métodos Qualitativo, Quantitativo e Misto. Artmed, Porto Alegre (2010)
24. Gil, A.C.: Como Elaborar Projetos de Pesquisa. Atlas, São Paulo (2002)
25. Theóphilo, C.R., Martins, G.D.A.: Metodologia da Investigacao Cientifica para Ciencias Sociais Aplicadas, vol. 2. Atlas, São Paulo (2009)

Applying the Paraconsistent Annotated Evidential Logic Eτ in a Solar Tracker for Photovoltaic Panels: An Analytical Approach

Álvaro A.C. Prado[1(✉)], Marcelo Nogueira[1,2], Jair Minoro Abe[1], and Ricardo J. Machado[2]

[1] Software Engineering Research Group,
Paulista University, UNIP, Campus Tatuapé, São Paulo, Brazil
py2alv@gmail.com, marcelo@noginfo.com.br,
jairabe@uol.com.br
[2] School of Engineering, ALGORITMI Centre,
University of Minho, Campus of Azurém, Guimarães, Portugal
rmac@dsi.uminho.pt

Abstract. There is an increasing contrast between large urban centers and rural areas, even nowadays, where the most basic resources can be scarce, leading an increasing development of technologies based upon self-sustainable solutions, where the electrical power is an important demand to be supplied. Through Bibliographic and Experimental research, plus a prototype using embedded and real-time software, and its testing, it was possible to develop a workable solution. This paper presents a self-oriented solar panel based on Paraconsistent Annotated Evidential Logic Eτ, its construction and practical tests, where total power of 3.19375 W was obtained against 2.427556 W from a fixed panel of same type, representing an increase of 31.56239% in the overall power.

Keywords: Solar energy · Photovoltaic · Power optimization · Energetic sustainability · Paraconsistent Annotated Evidential Logic Eτ

1 Introduction

Nowadays, despite development of new technologies being a constant activity, many cases of very scarce resources are not rare, particularly in locations far from urban centers [13].

One of the most important of these resources is the electricity, often unavailable because of large distances between distribution networks and the locations itself, or even because the great importance of local ecosystems [1].

The difficulties in bringing rural electrification to these places, and the need to limit the use of fossil fuels, replacing them with non-polluting and renewable energy alternatives, make urgent investments in research and development of improved alternative energy sources [2].

I. Nääs et al. (Eds.): APMS 2016, IFIP AICT 488, pp. 280–287, 2016.
DOI: 10.1007/978-3-319-51133-7_34

Fossil fuels are the main source of energy in the world and are at the center of the world's energy demands. However, its availability is limited, and its large-scale use is associated with environmental degradation. The negative effects known from use of these fuels include acid rain, depletion of the ozone layer and global climate changes [3].

Following this panorama, an important method for obtaining electricity without burning fossil fuels is through a photovoltaic solar panel. Supply only implies in the cost of equipment itself, with no carbon liberated during operation [4, 13].

However, an important problem is related to the positioning of the solar panel, which is often fixed and does not have the ability to follow the natural movement of the sun throughout the day, which is related to the question of Maximum Power Point (MPP) of the panel [5], as seen on Fig. 1.

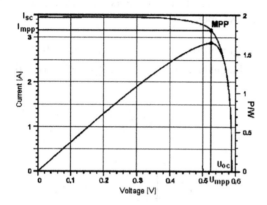

Fig. 1. Typical curve of a solar cell [5, 13].

Many systems are proposed to circumvent this problem, but without the ability to handle situations of inconsistency or contradiction in the collected data [6, 7].

By using embedded and real-time software, a controller board and a sample from the voltage provided by the photovoltaic panel, it is possible to obtain a correct positioning with a stepper motor mechanically attached to it [14].

Through Paraconsistent Annotated Evidential Logic Eτ, it is intended to reach an optimal performance by the decision-making process, being able to handle situations where the signals from the panel are not conclusive or contradictory [13].

2 Paraconsistent Logic

2.1 Historical Background

The Genesis of Paraconsistent Logic originated in 1910, by the work of logicians N.A. Vasil'év and J. Łukasiewicz. In 1948, Jaskowski, encouraged by his professor Łukasiewicz, discovered Discursive Logic. [8, 14]. Going beyond the work of Jaskowski, the Brazilian logician Newton C.A. Da Costa extended its systems for the treatment of inconsistencies, having been recognized for it as the introducer of

Paraconsistent Logic. Abe [8, 14], also a Brazilian logician, set several other applications of Annotated Systems, specially Logic Eτ, establishing the basic study of Model Theory and the Theory of Annotated Sets. Many previous publications have heterogeneous nomenclatures. This paper presents a new convention.

2.2   Certainty and Uncertainty Degrees

By using the properties of real numbers, it is possible to build a mathematical structure with the aim of materializing how to manipulate the mechanical concept of certainty, uncertainty, inconsistent and indeterminate, among others (Fig. 2) [18]. Such mechanism will embark the true and false states treated on classical logic, with all its consequences [14, 18]. Therefore, several concepts are introduced which are considered "intuitive" for the purpose above:

Perfectly defined segment AB: $(\mu - \lambda) = 0;\ 0 \leq \mu,\ \lambda \leq 1;$

Perfectly undefined segment CD: $[(\mu + \lambda) - 1] = 0;\ 0 \leq \mu,\ \lambda \leq 1;$

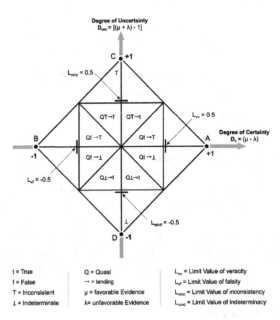

t = True   Q = Quasi L_{vv} = Limit Value of veracity
f = False   → = tending L_{vf} = Limit Value of falsity
T = Inconsistent   μ = favorable Evidence L_{vinc} = Limit Value of inconsistency
⊥ = Indeterminate   λ = unfavorable Evidence L_{vind} = Limit Value of indeterminacy

Fig. 2. τ reticulate [18].

Therefore, in the first case, the favorable evidence is the Boolean complement of unfavorable evidence and, second, the unfavorable evidence is the Boolean complement of favorable evidence, which shows that the evidence, both favorable and unfavorable 'behave' as if classic. It varies continuously from the false (0, 1) to the truth (1, 0) [14, 18].

The logical states can be defined by:

Inconsistency Degree:	$G_{inc}(\mu, \lambda) = \mu + \lambda - 1$, since $\mu + \lambda - 1 \geq 0$
Indeterminacy Degree:	$G_{ind}(\mu, \lambda) = \mu + \lambda - 1$, since $\mu + \lambda - 1 \leq 0$
Truth Degree:	$G_{tru}(\mu, \lambda) = \mu - \lambda$, since $\mu - \lambda \geq 0$
Falsehood Degree:	$G_{fal}(\mu, \lambda) = \mu - \lambda$, since $\mu - \lambda \leq 0$

It is seen that the Truth Degree "measures" how an annotation (μ, λ) "distances" from the perfectly defined segment and how it "approaches" of the state, and the degree of Falsehood "measures" how an annotation (μ, λ) "distances" from the segment perfectly defined, and how it "approaches" the false state [14, 18].

Similarly, the inconsistency degree "measures" how an annotation (μ, λ) "distances" from the undefined segment and how "close" it is from the inconsistent state, and the Indeterminacy degree "measures" how an annotation (μ, λ) "distances" of the undefined segment, and how "close" it is from the indeterminate state [14, 18].

Is called G_{unc} uncertainty degree (μ, λ) from an entry (μ, λ) to any of the degree of inconsistency or indeterminacy. For example, the maximum degree of uncertainty is in an inconsistent state, i.e. $G_{inc}(1, 1) = 1$. It is called the Certainty Degree $G_{cer}(\mu, \lambda)$ of an annotation (μ, λ) to any of the degrees of truth or falsity [14, 18].

2.3 Embedded and Real-Time Software

Embedded software can be defined as a combination of computer hardware and software, and perhaps additional mechanical or other parts, designed to perform a dedicated function. In some cases, embedded systems are part of a larger system or product [16].

Real-time systems can be any computer system, embedded or otherwise, that has timeliness requirements. The following question can be used to distinguish real-time systems from the rest: "Is a late answer as bad, or even worse, than a wrong answer?" In other words, what happens if the computation doesn't finish in time? If nothing bad happens, it's not a real-time system. If someone dies or the mission fails, it's generally considered "hard" real-time, which is meant to imply that the system has hard deadlines. Everything in between is "soft" real-time [17].

The principal role embedded software is not the transformation of data, but rather the interaction with the physical world. It executes on machines that are not, first and foremost, computers. There are cars, airplanes, competition cars, audio equipment, autonomous robots, toys, security systems, cell phones, heart monitors, weapons, Smart televisions, Laser printers, scanners, microwaves devices, traffic system, climate control systems, manufacturing systems, and so on. Software with a principal role of interacting with the physical world must, of necessity, acquire some properties of the physical world. It takes time. It consumes power. It does not terminate, unless it fails [17].

2.4 Paraconsistent Controller

The Para-analyzer controller was built in order to embark the paraconsistent logic by treating the values of favorable and unfavorable evidence, resulting in certainty and uncertainty degrees, plus a logical state [8, 13].

Both evidence values are obtained with an interval of 500 ms between them, which allows a proper distinction and the capture of the logic states Indeterminate ($\perp$) – with low intensity and uniform λ and μ, representing a dimly lit room – and Inconsistent ($\top$), with high-intensity and uniform μ and λ, representing an external environment with nuisances like shadows of trees, birds or other moving obstacles [14, 18].

3 Practical Implementation and Results

The prototype was built upon a wooden base support and a mobile holder for the photovoltaic panel, tractioned by a stepper motor and a belt system.

For sensing purposes, the voltage supplied by the panel itself was sampled, applied to the input of the controller board and subjected to an inverter, as part of the embedded software, to obtain the favorable (μ) and unfavorable evidence degrees (λ).

Tests were run under normal sunlight conditions during three days, being the prototype subject of any weather variations except rain. An increase of 34.84213% in average power could be achieved in the end of the first day, 38.62905% on the second and 22.51104% on third day, as seen on graphics of Figs. 3, 4 and 5, respectively.

Day 1					
Fixed - Panel			LPAEτ - Panel		
V	A	W	V	A	W
11,3	0,1	1,13	13,9	0,19	2,641
12,1	0,12	1,452	14,3	0,2	2,86
12,8	0,12	1,536	14,4	0,21	3,024
13,6	0,18	2,448	14,7	0,22	3,234
14	0,2	2,8	14,6	0,2	2,92
15,2	0,22	3,344	14,5	0,2	2,9
15	0,22	3,3	15,3	0,23	3,519
14,7	0,21	3,087	15,2	0,23	3,496
14	0,2	2,8	15,4	0,22	3,388
13,7	0,16	2,192	15	0,2	3
13	0,14	1,82	15	0,2	3
11,5	0,11	1,265	14	0,19	2,66
	P(AVG)	2,2645		P(AVG)	3,0535
				Result %	34,84213

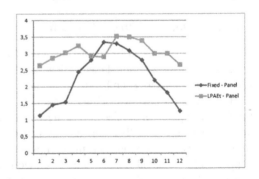

Fig. 3. Power output of Paraconsistent × Fixed panels – Day 1.

Day 2					
Fixed - Panel			LPAEτ - Panel		
V	A	W	V	A	W
10,7	0,14	1,498	13,4	0,19	2,546
12,7	0,15	1,905	14	0,2	2,8
12	0,15	1,8	13,9	0,19	2,641
12,3	0,17	2,091	15	0,23	3,45
14,4	0,17	2,448	15,7	0,24	3,768
15,6	0,24	3,744	16	0,27	4,32
15,4	0,23	3,542	15,8	0,24	3,792
15	0,21	3,15	15,7	0,24	3,768
14,3	0,2	2,86	15,2	0,22	3,344
13,7	0,16	2,192	14,8	0,22	3,256
12,8	0,14	1,792	14,5	0,21	3,045
11,5	0,11	1,265	13,8	0,18	2,484
	P(AVG)	2,35725		P(AVG)	3,267833
				Result %	38,62905

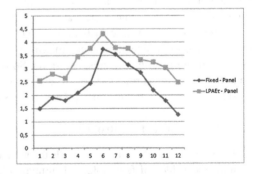

Fig. 4. Power output of Paraconsistent × Fixed panels – Day 2.

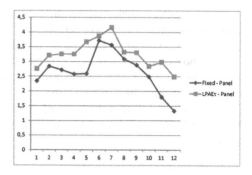

Day 3					
Fixed - Panel			LPAEτ - Panel		
V	A	W	V	A	W
13	0,18	2,34	13,8	0,2	2,76
14,2	0,2	2,84	14,6	0,22	3,212
14,3	0,19	2,717	14,8	0,22	3,256
14,3	0,18	2,574	14,8	0,22	3,256
14,4	0,18	2,592	15,3	0,24	3,672
15,5	0,24	3,72	15,5	0,25	3,875
15,5	0,23	3,565	16	0,26	4,16
14,7	0,21	3,087	15,1	0,22	3,322
14,4	0,2	2,88	15	0,22	3,3
13,8	0,18	2,484	14,2	0,2	2,84
12	0,15	1,8	14,2	0,21	2,982
11,1	0,12	1,332	13,8	0,18	2,484
	P(AVG)	2,660917		P(AVG)	3,259917
				Result %	22,51104

Fig. 5. Power output of Paraconsistent × Fixed panels – Day 3.

4 Final Results and Conclusions

This paper proposes a low-environmental impact alternative for places where electricity is not available, by using a self-oriented solar photovoltaic panel and Real-time embedded software.

The Paraconsistent Annotated Evidential Logic Eτ was used in order to make the decision process by the embedded software, allowing the panel to be more accurately positioned in situations of inconsistency or indeterminacy in the data collected. For each case, a reticulate chart can be created. In this work a general graph was presented, which may be the source for other studies.

By using the voltage supplied by the panel itself sampled and applied to the controller board it was possible to obtain favorable (μ) and unfavorable evidence degrees (λ) directly from the same source as the generated electricity, allowing a better tracking than using a separate sensor, as done in early projects.

After practical tests, the power generation of the prototype was enhanced by 31.56239% in an average value for the three days, as seen on graphic of Fig. 6.

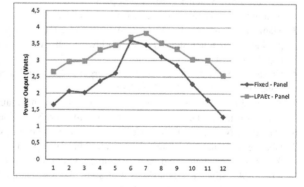

Final Results			
Fixed - Panel		LPAEτ - Panel	
id	W	id	W
1	1,656	1	2,649
2	2,065667	2	2,957333
3	2,017667	3	2,973667
4	2,371	4	3,313333
5	2,613333	5	3,453333
6	3,602667	6	3,698333
7	3,469	7	3,823667
8	3,108	8	3,528667
9	2,846667	9	3,344
10	2,289333	10	3,032
11	1,804	11	3,009
12	1,287333	12	2,542667
P(AVG)	2,427556	P(AVG)	3,19375
	Result %	31,56239	

Fig. 6. Power output of Paraconsistent × Fixed panels – final results.

With this new analytical approach, the data collected were presented with a greater number of decimal places, decimals floating point (DFP), besides being recalculated, providing greater accuracy and confiability in the final results.

This shows that the results are compatible with other similar systems [9, 10] and demonstrates that the actual implementation is capable of being implemented as a solution for manufactures of any type.

This result is similar to others found in the literature, as found in Huang et al. [11] (35.8%) and Salas et al. [12] (2.8%–18.5%), specially when compared with fixed panel systems.

5 Future Works

Both the embedded software and the experimental arrangement presented here allow deployments in larger systems with more solar panels, combining greater sophistication and power generation capacity.

With the revisiting of this study, it reinforces the importance of the topic addressed in this research observing that it is an area in truly expansion and frequent evolution. New technologies such as mobile applications and the Internet of Things (IoT) can be integrated.

Acknowledgements. This work has been supported by COMPETE: POCI-01-0145-FEDER-007043 and FCT – Fundação para a Ciência e Tecnologia within the Project Scope: UID/CEC/00319/2013 by Portugal and University Paulista - Software Engineering Research Group by Brazil.

References

1. Bursztyn, M.: A Difícil Sustentabilidade: Política Energética e Conflitos Ambeintais. Garamond, Rio de Janeiro (2001)
2. Dantas, J.M.: Sistema Fotovoltaico para Comunidades Isoladas utilizando ultracapacitores para armazenamento de energia. Univesity of Ceará, 2013
3. Manzano-Agugliaro, F., Alcayde, A., Montoya, F.G., Zapata-Sierra, A., Gil, C.: Scientific production of renewable energies worldwide: an overview. Renew. Sustain. Energy Rev. (2011). Elsevier
4. Cresesb, Centro de Referência para Energia Solar e Eólica Sérgio de Salvo Brito: Energia Solar: Princípios e Aplicações (2006)
5. Santos, J.L., Antunes, F., Chebab, A., Cruz, C.: A maximum power point tracker for PV systems using a high performance boost converter. Solar Energy (2005). Elsevier
6. Da Costa, N.C.A., et al.: Lógica Paraconsistente Aplicada. Atlas, São Paulo (1999)
7. Ishaque, K., Salam, Z.: A review of maximum power point tracking techniques of PV system for uniform insolation and partial shading condition. Renew. Sustain, Energy Rev (2012)
8. Abe, J.M., Silva, F., da João I., Celestino, U., de Araújo, H.C.: Lógica Paraconsistente Anotada Evidencial Eτ. Comunicar (2011)

9. Nogueira, M., Machado, R.J.: Importance of risk process in management software projects in small companies. In: Grabot, B., Vallespir, B., Gomes, S., Bouras, A., Kiritsis, D. (eds.) APMS 2014. IAICT, vol. 439, pp. 358–365. Springer, Heidelberg (2014). doi:10.1007/978-3-662-44736-9_44

10. Torres, C.R.: Sistema inteligente baseado na lógica paraconsistente anotada Eτ para controle e navegação de robôs móveis autônomos em um ambiente não estruturado. Doctoral thesis, University of Itajubá (2010)

11. Huang, B.J., Ding, W.L., Huang, Y.C.: Long-term field test of solar PV power generation using one-axis 3-position sun tracker. Solar Energy (2011)

12. Salas, V., Olias, E., Lásaro, A., Barrado, A.: Evaluation of a new maximum power point tracker (MPPT) applied to the photovoltaic stand-alone systems. Solar Energy Mater. Solar Cells. (2004). Elsevier

13. Prado, Á.A.C., Nogueira, M., Abe, J.M., Machado, R.J.: Improving photovoltaic applications through the paraconsistent annotated evidential logic Eτ. In: Gervasi, O., et al. (eds.) ICCSA 2016. LNCS, vol. 9788, pp. 345–355. Springer, Heidelberg (2016). doi:10.1007/978-3-319-42111-7_27

14. Prado, Á.A.C., Nogueira, M., Abe, J.M., Machado, Ricardo, J.: Power optimization in photovoltaic panels through the application of paraconsistent annotated evidential logic Eτ. In: Umeda, S., Nakano, M., Mizuyama, H., Hibino, H., Kiritsis, D., Cieminski, G. (eds.) APMS 2015. IAICT, vol. 459, pp. 655–661. Springer, Heidelberg (2015). doi:10.1007/978-3-319-22756-6_80

15. Prado, Á.A.C., Oliveira, C.C., Sakamoto, L.S., Abe, J.M., Nogueira, M.: Reaching energetic sustainability through a self-oriented battery charger, based on paraconsistent annotated evidential logic Eτ. In: Prabhu, V., Taisch, M., Kiritsis, D. (eds.) APMS 2013. IAICT, vol. 415, pp. 369–374. Springer, Heidelberg (2013). doi:10.1007/978-3-642-41263-9_46

16. Barr, M.: Embedded Systems Glossary. http://www.barrgroup.com/embedded-systems/glossary

17. Lee, E.A.: Embedded software. Adv. Comput. 56, 55–95 (2002)

18. Nogueira, M.: Engenharia de Software: Um Framework Para a Gestão de Riscos em Projetos de Software. Ed. Ciência Moderna, Rio de Janeiro (2009)

Virtual, Digital and Smart Factory

Virtual Factory Framework for Supporting Production Planning and Control

Deogratias Kibira[1]([⊠]) and Guodong Shao[2]

[1] Morgan State University, Baltimore, USA
deogratias.kibira@morgan.edu
[2] National Institute of Standards and Technology (NIST), Gaithersburg, USA
gshao@nist.gov

Abstract. Developing optimal production plans for smart manufacturing systems is challenging because shop floor events change dynamically. A virtual factory incorporating engineering tools, simulation, and optimization generates and communicates performance data to guide wise decision making for different control levels. This paper describes such a platform specifically for production planning. We also discuss verification and validation of the constituent models. A case study of a machine shop is used to demonstrate data generation for production planning in a virtual factory.

Keywords: Virtual factory · Simulation · Production planning and control

1 Introduction

Conventional simulation tools are generally limited in their ability to capture and analyze multiple decision levels and system configurations [1]. A virtual factory, on the other hand, creates an integrated model that reproduces scenarios of information flow and capable of generating multi-level metrics to guide users in decision-making. These decisions can among others increase agility and productivity by reducing product realization time [2]. Virtual factories have been constructed to aid manufacturing system design, implementation, and modification [3].

Besides designing production systems and products, Choi et al. [4] sees the potential of a virtual factory to predict, solve, and manage problems during production. It is our view that the virtual factory's ability to integrate engineering tools and models such as simulations, design data, and optimizations could improve production planning activities. As such, this paper focuses on operations and performance monitoring, particularly production planning.

The rest of the paper is organized as follows. Section 2 reviews literature on technology, application of virtual factories, and verification and validation (V&V) concepts for the virtual factory. Section 3 describes the roles of a virtual factory for production planning as per control levels defined in the ISA-95

© IFIP International Federation for Information Processing 2016
Published by Springer International Publishing AG 2016. All Rights Reserved
I. Nääs et al. (Eds.): APMS 2016, IFIP AICT 488, pp. 291–298, 2016.
DOI: 10.1007/978-3-319-51133-7_35

standard. Section 4 presents a demonstration case of a virtual factory. Section 5 presents final discussion and conclusion.

2   Related Work and Virtual Factory Validation

A virtual factory is composed of multi-level, multi-resolution models that are typically developed by different tools. This section overviews technologies employed for developing a virtual factory, various applications, and verification and validation issues.

– **Technology requirements for a virtual factory:** Virtual data management, automatic model generation, static and dynamic simulation, and integration and communication are paramount to realizing a virtual factory [4,5]. Most software tools are, in general, not supplied with these capabilities making developing a virtual factory challenging. The situation has, however, been recently improving with emergence of modeling, computation, communication, and integration technologies and standards [6]. Indeed, much related literature centers on technologies for enabling the virtual factory. A few of these technologies are overviewed next.
– **Overview of technologies and purpose of developing virtual factories:** To enhance conventional simulations for a virtual factory, Bal and Hashemipour [1] used the PROSA architecture for modeling controls while the Quest simulation tool models the physical elements. Hints et al. [7] developed a software tool named Design Synthesis Module to integrate models and enhance communication. Terkaj et al. [8] produced an ontology for a virtual factory to aid planning decisions. Ghani [9] developed an integrative tool to match low-level machine-component activities with targets set by aggregate planning.
– **Previous initial virtual factory models:** A virtual factory generates data at different levels of model resolution. Shao et al. [10] developed and validated a virtual model for generating energy usage data for machining operations. Furthering this research, Jain et al. [11] uses a two-tailed z-test to prove statistical concurrence of experimental results from a virtual factory at both the machine and manufacturing cell levels of detail.
– **Verification and validation of virtual factory models:** To ensure that a virtual factory is accurate for its intended purpose, V&V of constituent models and related data has to be carried out [12]. When developing and applying formal V&V methods, key features to distinguish about models are (1) deterministic or stochastic, (2) analytical or simulated, and (3) computationally efficient or computationally expensive.

When carrying out formal V&V, Uncertainty Quantification (UQ) needs to be considered for better correctness and appropriateness [13]. Uncertainties can be epistemic or aleatoric in nature. Epistemic uncertainties arise from ignorance of involved processes, such as invalid assumptions in modeling. Aleatory uncertainties arise from inherent variability in processes, such as physical properties of a system. Model fidelity and data availability typically vary greatly across different system levels of resolution. This issue complicates both the computation of metrics that describe process performance, and decision-making based upon those metrics. V&V of a virtual factory as well as UQ can be achieved through intermediation environment, such as one created by Hibino et al. [14] to synchronize collected data and virtual factory computed data.

3   A Virtual Factory Approach to Multi-level Production Planning

The virtual factory concept uses the ISA-95 standard (ANSI 2013) to specify decision levels that define functions supporting multi-level production planning. This standard was developed for all types of industries that represent different manufacturing processes, such batch, continuous, discrete, and repetitive processes. As such, the description of the virtual factory herein should likewise be universally applied.

- **Framework and role of models:** Fig. 1 shows the functional hierarchical levels of ISA-95 as well as virtual factory roles at each level. At level 4, an aggregate plan is developed over a long-term planning horizon after investigating for stability using system dynamics [15]. Level 3 covers short to mid-term plans to determine actual start and finish times of individual product batches. Level 2 covers decisions on activities such as resource allocations. Level 1 is the manipulation of production process (level 0) to achieve required output. Data is collected in real-time at level 0 to update various models.
- **Multi-level performance analysis and improvements using the virtual factory:** The objectives of production planning include minimize late orders, minimize inventory, or maximize resource utilization. Such objectives are basis for defining Key Performance Indicators (KPIs) which, along with metrics and constituent measures, are communicated and monitored. Decisions are then made to maintain them within a target performance envelop. The relationship between data, metrics and KPIs at different levels can be numerical, analytical, or heuristic influence. With heuristic influence, a KPI is expressed in terms of supporting data, parameters, metrics or other KPIs. The direction of change (increase or decrease) in the dependent KPI is investigated through the relationship equation. The *Supply Chain Operations Reference* (SCOR) model (SCC 2012) adopts this approach by taking KPIs and performs a metrics decomposition, performance diagnosis, or metrics root-cause analysis. SCOR then constructs a metrics dependency tree of multiple measures that would generally be generated by different models within the virtual factory.

Metrics decomposition establishes a diagnostic relationship showing how metrics serve as diagnostics for dependent KPIs. For example, overall equipment effectiveness (OEE) index, as defined by ISO 22400-2 [16], depends on availability, effectiveness, and quality rate. OEE belongs to level 3 of ISA-95 while its

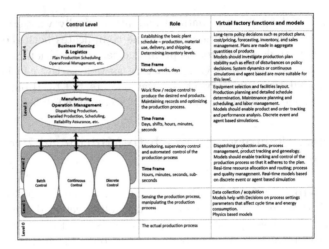

Fig. 1. Role of virtual factory models according to ISA-95 levels

constituent measures can be monitored at level 2. Availability is determined by the equipment model incorporating failure and repair time study data obtained from samples of equally-spaced discrete observations during operation. The availability model can be constructed with high resolution using a programming language. Effectiveness performance model may be of low resolution constituted of run time per unit produced, number of units made, and actual production time. The quality rate is products that meet specifications compared with total units made.

Once a diagnostic relationship has been established, attention may be directed to a higher resolution of the production line model or resource responsible for a measure needing improvement while other parts of the virtual factory may remain at a lower resolution. The data, resources, and workflow through this model may then be further analyzed to balance any competing objectives that may occur. The analyst may also validate diagnosis and decision made through high visualizations of the virtual factory.

4   Case Study

The study is a case of monitoring KPIs at multi-resolution levels in metal machining using a virtual factory concept. The enterprise level determines an aggregate plan of same size batches to be produced per period (week) over a 12 period timeline. Lower level management then distributes batches for production to each of the two available machine cells that are shown in model Fig. 2(b). Each machine cell has two processes: turning and milling. Machines undergo different states during production. As prototypical virtual factory is developed using AnyLogic simulation for three levels of decision control. Table 1 shows the functions and type of models employed at each level.

Table 1. Functions of multi-level models according to ISA-95 standard

ISA-Level	Physical system	Function	Virtual modeling method
4	Enterprise	Aggregate planning	System dynamics
3	Machine cell	Production scheduling	Discrete event simulation
2	Machine	Machine loading	Agent based modeling

- **Enterprise level model:** This model is shown in Fig. 2(a) and is built using System Dynamics (SD). The product batches for each period are input into the model to determine the production start rate at the routed shop. The production start rate is converted into inter-arrival times for the work cell model. In turn, the cycle time and work in progress levels are obtained from the machine cell model.
- **Machine cell model:** This is a model of the processing of a product on the shop floor. Discrete event simulation (DES) is employed, as shown in Fig. 2(b). Entities enter the system from the source and routed to the first available machine for both turning and milling. The machines undergo periodic failure and repair cycles.
- **Machine level model:** This is a model of states of a machine during normal operation. Machine failure and repair cycle are indicated in the statechart shown in Fig. 2(c). When a machine is "Up", default substate is idling to which a machine reverts after repair or after ejection of the previous batch. Other machine states are "Down" or "Under repair" and, in these states, incoming parts cannot be routed to them. The machines undergo this cycle independently.
- **Model interactions:** When these models are integrated, the SD model receives input data from DES for update to aggregate planning. In turn, DES is updated with agent based simulations of machine processes. Figure 3 shows the exchanged data. Figure 4 shows that there is enough visual concurrency in monitored generated data: work in progress levels and production quantity between models at different resolution levels.

Such data can be used, for example, to monitor and maintain planned throughput rate. According to ISO 22400-2 [16], throughput rate = quantity produced or order execution time. Maximizing throughput in a job-shop production environment requires deploying the "shortest remaining processing time" priority rule [17]. If throughput rate is reduced, the causes are investigated using the constituent measures monitored at level 2 of ISA-95. These are analyzed with the discrete event simulation model. The cause could be an increase in order execution time which in turn depends on manufacturing cycle time. The causes of increase in cycle time can further be analyzed using work cell model.

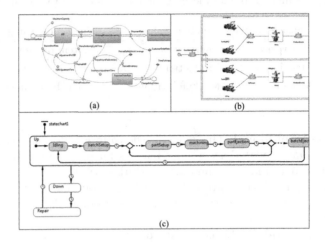

Fig. 2. Multi-resolution models of the virtual factory

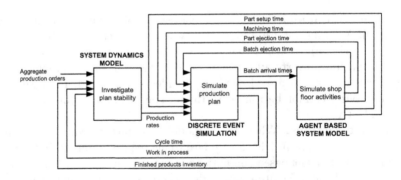

Fig. 3. Data generated and exchanged between models

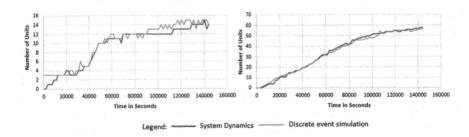

Fig. 4. Work in progress and cumulative production with time for system dynamics and discrete event simulations

5 Discussion and Conclusion

A virtual environment can be developed for generating and communicating production planning decisions from floor and optimize production, inventory, and cost objectives. Communicating performance of production plans and schedules in a virtual environment is beneficial to achievement of the smart manufacturing objectives. The industrial internet is one technology for connecting, collecting and communicating data. This framework is a first step in describing how the virtual factory can be used for developing and integrating models at different hierarchical levels. The example in this paper used a multi-method simulation software. To take advantage of strengths of different tools, a virtual factory would be developed using heterogeneous tools. Description of needed interfaces and review of existing standards will be the subject of future research work.

Acknowledgement. This effort has been sponsored in part under the cooperative agreement No. 70NANB13H153 between NIST and Morgan State University. The work described was funded by the United States Government and is not subject to copyright. The contribution of David Lechevalier of NIST in the simulation work is acknowledged.

Disclaimer

No approval or endorsement of any commercial product by the National Institute of Standards and Technology is intended or implied. Certain commercial software systems are identified in this paper to facilitate understanding. Such identification does not imply that these software systems are necessarily the best available for the purpose.

References

1. Bal, M., Hashemipour, M.: Virtual factory approach for implementation of holonic control in industrial applications: a case study in diecasting industry. Robot. Comput. Integr. Manuf. **25**(3), 570–581 (2009)
2. Colledani, M., Pedrielli, G., Terkaj, W., Urgo, M.: Integrated virtual platform for manufacturing systems design. Procedia CIRP **7**, 425–430 (2013)
3. Yang, X., Malak, R.C., Lauer, C., Weidig, C., Hagen, H., Hamann, B., Aurich, J.C., Kreylos, O.: Manufacturing system design with virtual factory tools. Int. J. Comput. Integr. Manuf. **28**(1), 25–40 (2015)
4. Choi, S., Kim, B.H., Do Noh, S.: A diagnosis and evaluation method for strategic planning and systematic design of a virtual factory in smart manufacturing systems. Int. J. Precis. Eng. Manuf. **16**(6), 1107–1115 (2015)
5. Zhai, W., Fan, X., Yan, J., Zhu, P.: An integrated simulation method to support virtual factory engineering. Int. J. CAD/CAM **2**(1), 39–44 (2009)
6. Jain, S., Shao, G.: Virtual factory revisited for manufacturing data analytics. In: Proceedings of the 2014 Winter Simulation Conference, pp. 887–898. IEEE (2014)
7. Hints, R., Vanca, M., Terkaj, W., Marra, E.D., Temperini, S., Banabic, D.: A virtual factory tool to enhance the integrated design of production lines. In: Proceedings of DET 2011 7th International Conference on Digital Enterprise Technology, Athens, Greece, pp. 28–30 (2011)
8. Terkaj, W., Tolio, T., Urgo, M.: A virtual factory approach for in situ simulation to support production and maintenance planning. CIRP Ann. Manuf. Technol. **64**(1), 451–454 (2015)

9. Ghani, U., Monfared, R., Harrison, R.: Integration approach to virtual-driven discrete event simulation for manufacturing systems. Int. J. Comput. Integr. Manuf. **28**(8), 844–860 (2015)

10. Shao, G., Shin, S.J., Jain, S.: Data analytics using simulation for smart manufacturing. In: Proceedings of the 2014 Winter Simulation Conference, pp. 2192–2203. IEEE (2014)

11. Jain, S., Lechevalier, D., Woo, J., Shin, S.J.: Towards a virtual factory prototype. In: 2015 Winter Simulation Conference, pp. 2207–2218. IEEE (2015)

12. Sargent, R.G.: Verification and validation of simulation models. In: Proceedings of the 37th Conference on Winter Conference Simulation, pp. 130–143 (2005)

13. Roy, C.J., Oberkampf, W.L.: A comprehensive framework for verification, validation, and uncertainty quantification in scientific computing. Comput. Methods Appl. Mech. Eng. **200**(25), 2131–2144 (2011)

14. Hibino, H., Inukai, T., Fukuda, Y.: Efficient manufacturing system implementation based on combination between real and virtual factory. Int. J. Prod. Res. **44**(18–19), 3897–3915 (2006)

15. Sterman, J.D.: Business Dynamics: Systems Thinking and Modeling for a Complex World. McGraw-Hill, New York (2000)

16. ISO 22400-2: Automation Systems and Integration – Key Performance Indicators (KPIs) for Manufacturing Operations Management – Part 2: Definitions and Descriptions of KPIs (2011)

17. Panwalkar, S.S., Iskander, W.: A survey of scheduling rules. Oper. Res. **25**(1), 45–61 (1977)

Reflections on Identity Management in Smart Industry: The Paradox of Theseus' Ship and Beyond

Hans Wortmann[1,2(✉)] and Wico Mulder[1,2]

[1] University of Groningen, Groningen, The Netherlands
j.c.wortmann@rug.nl
[2] KPN Consulting, Groningen, The Netherlands

Abstract. Sustainable digitization of factories (and especially IoT) requires all data related to "things" (products, equipment, but also informational objects) to be stored for later reference in a so-called *digital shadow*. This paper addresses an identity question: "which data should be stored as a so-called digital shadow of an object?" and identifies two opposing principles, Single Source of the Truth vs Local Autonomy. The first principle keeps data objects small and uses links to other data objects. It expands object's life time. The second principle advices to keep objects large, reduces linkages but limits object's life time. The paper analyses these two principles for physical objects as well as for related informational objects. Some guidelines for application are given.

Keywords: Smart factories · Sustainability · Object life cycle · Digital shadows

1 Introduction

The impact of data in the field of smart industry goes well beyond the level of optimizing production. Data is guiding the manufacturing processes. Whilst being designed, manufactured or shipped, the status of every product is kept in systems in the form of data. The same holds for related information that accompanies the product, such as the contracts, version information, ownership, user manuals or maintenance schedules. All of those are reflected by data. Once built, products leave the factory either serving as component of a different product, or starting to operate somewhere in our connected world. In a sustainable, circular economy, data that was collected during manufacturing of a product, will not only be used during the phase of manufacturing and operation, but also during refurbishment and reuse. Moreover, new data will be added. One can say that a modern data management platform[1] maintains information of objects during their full life cycle – from cradle to grave. However, such view is not straightforward. When using concepts such as cradle or grave in relation to the physical world of manufacturing, our language is metaphoric. Physical objects are not born in a cradle and do not end in a grave: these are anthropomorphic notions. For example, if a

---

[1] Data management platforms are computer infrastructures that provide the means for the storage, connectivity and analysis of data.

© IFIP International Federation for Information Processing 2016
Published by Springer International Publishing AG 2016. All Rights Reserved
I. Nääs et al. (Eds.): APMS 2016, IFIP AICT 488, pp. 299–306, 2016.
DOI: 10.1007/978-3-319-51133-7_36

component C disappears because it becomes part of an assembly A, should the life cycle of C be considered as ended ("grave")? In many cases, this question would be denied, because the usage of C may be monitored as part of the assembly A. Accordingly, does the life cycle of C end when the assembly A is discarded and scrapped? Not necessarily, the component C may be refurbished and reused elsewhere. So when does the life cycle of C end? Who responsible for the data? What is implicit in our usage of the term 'platform'? Maybe the lifecycle of C ends when C has no longer a necessity or purpose, although even this statement may be disputed.

Also, the notion of a connected world is problematic. Loosely speaking, it means that objects (representing e.g. things and humans) are ubiquitously connected to the internet. However, the implicit meaning is that objects have references to other objects' data and that these can always be retrieved when needed. For example, manufacturing orders refer to products, to operations, to machines, and many other objects. Still, the assumption that such references can always be retrieved, is problematic. Objects are owned by applications and these applications have a finite life cycle. More fundamentally, relations between objects are temporary and references should therefore be time stamped. If component C is manufactured by supplier S according to manufacturing instructions I, how can we be sure that the right version of these instructions I are retrieved? In many cases, we cannot be sure, unless these instructions are stored together in a data management platform in the form of a so-called digital shadow (which we will explain in the next section). Accordingly, related to concepts such as smart manufacturing and the associated developments such as the internet of things (IoT) and cyber-physical systems (CPS), there are two questions which seem fundamental to be elaborated: (i) What is the life cycle of an object? Or more precisely: what are the criteria to create a digital shadow of an object or delete it? (ii) What is the boundary of an object? Or more precisely: what are the criteria to include related objects and their data in the digital shadow of an object?

2   Terminology Background

Before discussing the above questions, it is worthwhile to present some working definitions. In the field of software development people use the word object to model elements from the real world into their design. We would like to use more conceptual but more precise notions, namely *digital shadows* and avatars. The Definition of *A digital shadow* is a digital representation of an object that manifests itself in the world around us.

A digital shadow refers to an entity inside a digital environment, e.g. in a database, that contains all the data of one particular object which exists in our real world. A digital shadow is tightly coupled to that physical object. In the context of internet of things, the digital shadow holds an ip-address, which allows for interaction with other objects during the phase of creation as well as during its operation.

As an example, one can think of any object, e.g. a bus, a plane or a cow, or one of their constituting components. Whenever we want to store or retrieve information from such an object, we do this via its digital shadow. Anyone who wants to have information about a particular thing or product X can do so via its digital shadow X'. This also holds for any object Y which needs to exchange (retrieve or store) data with object X. As depicted in figure one, there is one important constraint to take in mind; namely that Y cannot interact with X' directly, but only via its own digital shadow Y' (Fig. 1).

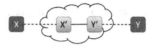

Fig. 1. Schematic picture of objects that exist in our physical world (denoted with X and Y). Together with their digital shadows (denoted with X' and Y'). The dashed lines show that X and Y are connected with their digital shadows. X and can Y communicate with each other via their digital shadows, as denoted with the solid line between X' and Y'.

Thus, there is an important design principle for digital shadows: it is not allowed to have a direct connection between an object Y and a digital shadow X'. As an example think of a bus B having a digital shadow B' and an organization O (owning the bus) that wants to have access to the maintenance schedule of this particular bus. Suppose also that a traveler T (taking that bus) is interested in information about the actual time schedule of that particular bus.

As we see in many contemporary IT architectures, B' will be accessed by both O and T. Such IT architectures require multiple interfaces and something like a role-based access system. But as the number of interactions increase (which will happen given the evolution of internet of things) maintenance and flexibility reasons imply to automate the management of those interfaces.

A possible way to do this is to make use of the concept of digital shadows and let the interaction with B' take place via two other digital shadows O' and T'. This allows for more flexibility from an IT maintenance perspective, and possibilities for time-dependent, automated managed interfaces.

An example in the area of smart factories could be the manufacturing of con-stituents of an airplane which are manufactured by multiple organizations. During the phase of creation a digital shadow of those constituents serves as a digital product dossier. Many vendors, customers, shipping companies can have access to this dossier. Also machines can access the products bill of materials via this digital dossier. Later on, when the plane is in operation, information about maintenance schedules may be used by various groups of users. E.g. flight carrier organizations or insurance com-panies, passengers that following that particular plane (Fig. 2).

It's a small step here to think of complete mimicked worlds of goods, plants and organizations that manifest themselves as a complete universe within a cloud envi-ronment. So far, we talk about a digital shadow as a passive set of data inside a platform that can provide access by means of a (web) interface. Now, if we extend this concept to an active entity, that is something that can be programmed to perform tasks we could use notion of avatar[2]. Avatars are quite similar to the concept of agents [3, 4],

---

[2] The concept of avatars is known in the field of computer gaming, but the name of the concept originates from ancient Hinduïsm beliefs in reincarnated bodies.

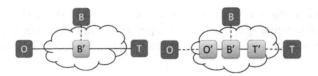

Fig. 2. Schematic picture stressing the design principle of digital shadows

but with one important restriction: they are uniquely connected to a (unique) object in our real world. The definition of an *avatar* is an active digital representation of an object that manifests itself in our physical world.

Avatars can be useful in situations where information about status and quality needs to be exchanged frequently or under certain restricted conditions. They play a role in local decision making and in the exchange of information with various stakeholders inside and across organizational boundaries, e.g. in production chains or when interacting in an Internet of Things context. Avatars can also be useful for simulation purposes and the analysis of what-if scenarios in situations where information is only locally available. A data management platform, as we mentioned in the previous section, can be regarded as a habitat for avatars.

3 Theseus' Ship and Beyond

3.1 Physical Objects

With these two concepts in mind, it is possible to elaborate on the questions mentioned in the introduction of this paper. The first question, related to the life cycle and identity of (physical) objects raised interest from philosophers in ancient times. In the form of Theseus Ship paradox, it was introduced by Plutarch in the 1st century, and it remained in philosophers interest until modern times. However, a related question was earlier posed by Heraclitus (6th century BC), who discussed the possibility to enter twice in the same river. Theseus Ship paradox goes as follows:

"The ship wherein Theseus and the youth of Athens returned from Crete had thirty oars, and was preserved by the Athenians down even to the time of Demetrius Phalereus. They took away the old planks as they decayed, putting in new and stronger timber in their places, in so much that this ship became a standing example among the philosophers, for the logical question of things that grow; one side holding that the ship remained the same, and the other contending that it was not the same [1]. Plutarch thus questions whether the ship would remain the same if it were entirely replaced, piece by piece" [2].

In modern times, the same issue emerges for our industrial society. Basically the same question emerges for many industrial products, viz. when to introduce a new identification for changing products. For reasons of conciseness, we describe here the solution adopted for standard assembled products, known as the form, fit, function rule. In many industries the so called Form-Fit-Function rule is applied to the problem at hand [5]. This rule states that companies will define a new item replacing an old one, if: (i) The item has a new form and/or; (ii) The item has a new fit (e.g. new tolerances) and/or, (iii) The item has a new function.

Therefore, new raw material to be used for an item, for example, is in itself not a reason for defining a new item. Also, if the item would get a new price, if it were stored in another warehouse, or if documentation of the item would be changed, this is not a reason for defining a new item or for issuing a new item code number.

But how can companies then keep track of significant changes that do not change the form, fit or function? For example, how can companies reflect the fact that the weight or the carbon footprint of a product has become much less due to the use of other materials? For these purposes, the notion of versions exist in manufacturing industries. The FFF-rule goes together with a versioning policy. This policy states, that items can have versions, and that a new version will be issued for all changes in the item documentation, which don't violate the FFF-conditions.

If something changes in the definition of an item O inside a product P, but there is no new form, fit, or function regarding P, then there is no reason to define an entirely new item of product P. In this case, a new version of O will be created.

3.2   Informational Objects

The notion of versions is crucial in the FFF-rule. However, what is a version? First of all, it should be acknowledged that the FFF-rule does not refer really to physical products, as we are tempted to believe, but to so-called informational objects. Informational objects are objects that describe physical objects. Versions are no exception. Versions do not refer to physical instances, but to the informational description of these instances.

The question, what a version really is, can now be answered. A version is a new (or updated) description of a standard physical product. What makes a version different from other informational objects? Obviously, the fact that a (new) version refers to a previous version, and carries forward some attribute values or other informational elements (e.g. methods) from the previous version. Because the FFF-rule stems from the pre-digital era, it is not exactly defined which informational elements are carried forward.

4   Single-Version-of-the-Truth vs Self-containedness

In practical discussions about smart manufacturing, there are two principles which can be encountered. These principles are also underlying much academic work, although these principles are (to our best knowledge) not elaborated in the context of smart manufacturing. These principles are: (i) The principle of *single version of the truth* which states that data should always be retrieved from their source. Data kept by the digital shadow is often a reference to other digital shadows; (ii) The principle of *autonomy* or *self-containedness*. This principle states that all data describing an object should reside in its digital shadow or under control of its avatar.

The principle of single-version-of-the-truth tries to avoid redundancy, because redundant data are difficult to maintain: there are always updates which get lost. Therefore, this principle states that copying data or documents should be avoided. Data in e.g. digital shadows of objects should refer to data in other objects whenever such sources exist. When applied to versions of physical products, the principle states that a new version should contain only information in which the new version differs from the old version and all other information should be retrieved from the older version. When applied to components that are part of assemblies, the principle states that digital shadows of assemblies should not contain the information about the components, but rather refer to the digital shadows of these components.

For versions of software products the principle of single-version-of-the-truth leads to software architectures based on Software-as-a-Service (SaaS) principles. Therefore, the principle assumes that ownership of data is well organized and remains available over a long period of time. Accordingly, informational objects should have a long life cycle in this view, and hardly ever be deleted, because there may always remain links which require information form these objects. Also, the platform on which avatars or digital shadows reside, are assumed to have a long life cycle.

The principle of autonomy aims at robustness. Physical objects should have digital counterparts which are self-contained and proactive. Physical objects as components, parcels, tools, or machines should be enabled to take initiative, communicate, negotiate and get decisions taken. Advocates of the principle of autonomy are not primarily interested in avoiding redundancy. They do not argue against copying of data. They acknowledge the fact that objects may need updates from other objects, but they claim that e.g. publish-and-subscribe protocols are sufficient means for this purpose. They also do not have SaaS architectures in mind. Rather, they see smart manufacturing as consisting of decision-making applications where avatars interact with each other. In addition, they see analytical applications, where digital shadows of objects of the same type are analyzed by human professionals or by artificial intelligence applications. These applications typically take a broad view on the objects analyzed, and therefore many data are taken into the digital shadow.

Because the necessary data are carried in the digital shadow of the object, there is less interest in the longer life time of objects. Digital shadows and other digital objects are seen as created for a certain purpose, and when the purpose vanishes, the digital object or the digital shadow may vanish as well.

5   Discussion

5.1   Digital Assemblies

It is interesting to note that advocates of both principles see information objects largely as being constructed from other information objects. The term digital assembly can be coined for this process. This leads to the question, if the Theseus ship paradox is also applicable for digital assemblies. The answer is yes, there is an issue with the identity of digital assemblies, but there is also an important difference: if a digital component is taken into a digital assembly, the original component does not disappear. It can either be copied into the new object, according to the principle of autonomy or it can be referenced in the new object, according to the principle of single-version-of-the-truth.

It is also interesting that advocates of both principles refer to earlier experience with integration problems. Advocates of the first principle are well aware of the difficulties of heterogeneous systems and the advantages of open standards, web services and common databases. They claim that redundancy should be avoided. Advocates of the second principle are also well aware of integration problems. They claim that integration should be avoided.

5.2 Ownership

It is obvious that the advocates of the first principle (single-source-of-the-truth) must assume that the smart manufacturing organization has implemented proper ownership of digital shadows and of other digital documents. If data are not properly maintained, or if there is no ownership of data management platforms, the smart factory will not survive. This is not only required for the own organization, but also for partner organizations in New Product Development, in Supply Chain, in Distribution, in the product use phase and in recycling or refurbishment.

However, also the advocates of the second principle (autonomy) must assume that their digital shadows are informed if related objects change. For example, if an assembly is dismantled, the components must re-appear. If new components failure modes are detected, the assembly digital shadow must become aware. As said, this will be implemented in autonomous systems by e.g. publish-and-subscribe protocols. However, these protocols also assume that ownership for platforms, applications and data is well established in the smart manufacturing organizations and with related stakeholders.

To be more precise, if a new digital object is made with its own life cycle, there should always be an owner. This owner either relies on references to existing data (e.g. for versions, following the first principle) or relies on copies (following the second principle), but ownership which guarantees the quality of the data cannot be avoided in smart manufacturing. In the end, the owner determines the solution chosen for the Theseus ship paradox in the case of digital documents.

Ownership means, that a party in the real world takes responsibility for the correctness of data [8, 9]. The difference between the two principles resides in the nature of this responsibility. With single-source-of-the-truth, updates and changes are carried forward. With local autonomy, the data are frozen at the moment of creation. It is interesting that here the notion of shared ownership of frozen data becomes possible due to block chain technology, a distributed public ledger of all transactions or digital events that have been executed and shared among participating parties [7].

5.3 Can Digital Objects Have Digital Shadows and Avatars?

Initially, our discussion has been primarily focusing on the situation where there is a digital shadow and/or avatar which represents a physical product. However, the example of the FFF rule showed, that there are important informational objects in the digital world which may claim a similar status as physical objects. For example, an invoice may take initiative to be paid, a contract may urge to be signed. There is no reason to restrict the notion of avatar to representatives of physical objects.

However, the digital shadow of a digital object may technically be realized in the same environment as the digital object itself. Conceptually, however, there is no reason to make a distinction between physical and informational objects in this respect.

6 Conclusion

In this paper, we posed two questions, related to sustainable smart manufacturing. As for the first question, we concluded that ownership of data objects is crucial in (smart) manufacturing. The life cycle of physical objects is ultimately related to a company's strategy in circular economy (including partnerships) but this can only be realized with properly assigned responsibility for data.

As for the life cycle of informational objects, our analysis revealed that informational objects are usually assemblies of other informational elements. The paper discussed two principles: (i) The principle of *single-source-of-the-truth*, which tends to keep longer life cycles and to keep distinct objects, leading to SaaS architectures; (ii) The principle of *autonomous objects*, which tends to have shorter object life cycles and allows overlapping objects, leading to Data Warehousing architectures.

These principles also provide conflicting guidelines for the second question. The first principle would create objects as small as possible with references to other objects, whereas the second principle would do the opposite. In practice, one sees combinations of these principles, still a guideline is to apply the first principle for objects which are used in applications that require real-time relational flexibility, whereas the second principle can be used for objects in applications that require robustness or historical compliancy.

References

1. Plutarch: Theseus. The Internet Classics Archive (2008)
2. Wikipedia. https://en.wikipedia.org/wiki/Ship_of_Theseus
3. Jennings, N.R., Bussmann, S.: Agent-based control systems: why are they suited to engineering complex systems? IEEE Control Syst. Mag. 23(3), 61–73 (1999)
4. Wooldridge, M.: MultiAgent Systems. Wiley, New York (2002)
5. Romero Rojo, F.J., Roy, R., Shehab, E.: Obsolescence management for long-life contracts. Int. J. Adv. Manuf. Technol. 49(9–12), 1235–1250 (2009)
6. Erkoyuncu, J., González Muño, R., Shehab, E., Weinitzke, M., Bence, R., Fowler, C., Tothill, S., Baguley, P.: Understanding the life cycle implications of manufacturing. Procedia CIRP 37, 24–29 (2015)
7. van Zuidam, R.: Whitepaper Government as a Service (Dutch). http://www.dutchchain.nl
8. Loshin, D.: Who owns information? In: Enterprise Knowledge Management: The Data Quality Approach. Morgan Kaufmann (2001)
9. Wende, K.: A model for data governance – organising accountabilities for data quality management. In: 18th Australasian Conference on Information Systems, pp. 417–425 (2007)

The Importance of Timely Feedback to Interactivity in Online Education

Esdras Jorge Santos Barboza$^{(\boxtimes)}$ and Márcia Terra da Silva

Paulista University, São Paulo, Brazil
esdrasjorge@yahoo.com.br

Abstract. This paper discusses the main factors that influence interactivity in online education. The literature points out that time to feedback in education is one of the factors which affect communication among people. Therefore, we did a survey in which participated 67 teachers and 105 students in all. As a result, it was noticed that the level of interactivity students perceived lessens as the time to feedback increases. Also, teachers who give fast feedback review the course as having excellent interactivity. Offering more creative/dynamic activities, giving faster feedback to students, and encouraging students to participate more often in the Virtual Learning Environment are crucial to improving interactivity in Distance Education.

Keywords: Feedback · Online Education · Interactivity · VLE

1 Introduction

Information technology is a resource of fundamental importance in Online Education. The development of C&IT favors cheaper and more efficient communication and Education Institutions take advantage of that to increase the offer of Online Education courses. This type of course makes access to education possible to a significative number of students interested in high-quality learning even if they live in remote areas and provide improvements in learning [1]. On the other hand, the experience of learning mediated by technology has been more and more common for students [2]. Therefore, the number of online students has been increasing all over the world [2–4]. DEMIRKAN [5], indicated that in 2007, the worldwide number of people taking distance courses had already reached 3.5 billion, with an annual projection of 21.5% growth. In 2014, in Brazil alone, the number of online students enrolled was above 3.8 millions [6].

Due to the spatial and temporal distance in online education which separates students from their peers and teacher, the learning is influenced by the various elements student/student, student/teacher and student/content. Interaction between the student and the various elements of the course is mediated by the virtual learning environment - VLE of the course and ignited by the teacher [7,8].

© IFIP International Federation for Information Processing 2016
Published by Springer International Publishing AG 2016. All Rights Reserved
I. Nääs et al. (Eds.): APMS 2016, IFIP AICT 488, pp. 307–314, 2016.
DOI: 10.1007/978-3-319-51133-7_37

The active role of the teacher is fundamental to the teaching-learning process. The time of feedback is stressed as a preponderant factor for student to feel listened to. Besides, the comments made shall be customized and show constructive criticism [9–11].

This paper goes on to identify teachers' and students' opinion about the time to feedback and how it influences their notion of the level of interactivity as well as the advantages and disadvantages of the main VLE communication tools.

2   Theoretical Base of Feedback

According to Mory [12], feedback can be described as any procedure or communication held to inform the student about the accuracy of their response, usually related to an instructional question. The feedback can allow the learner to compare their current performance with the standard or expected one, in distance education. Feedback is information presented to the learner after any input in order to shape their perceptions [9].

Feedback is an important element for the learner to regulate learning. The information that is addressed in the feedback interact with prior knowledge, promoting learning [10,13,14]. Through feedback participants learn how to behave, interact, speak, reason and do their tasks in the environment in order to be able to achieve the proposed objective [9].

In order to instruct the learner and gradually improve interactivity/learning in Online Education, the time to feedback is one of the factors which need to be analyzed [1]. Must important is the communication aiming the behavior changing or their frame of mind, aiming at an improvement in the learning [15].

2.1   Time of Feedback

Feedback is useful if it is received after the submissions of the students and before the next activity [16]. If the response time is great, the student may lose interest in the content or feel isolated in the course [17].

In the online environment, giving constant feedback to students is one of the tutors tasks [18]. In distance learning, students feel more isolated because, although there are communication tools in the Virtual Learning Environment they are smaller if compared to classroom learning. Hence, feedback becomes a vital element to consolidate the learning [19].

In order for the tutors to be able to organize their time of work and the consistency of their feedbacks, it is recommended that they access the Virtual Learning Environment (VLE) daily. It is also recommended a pace of response which will not make students wait for feedback for more than 24 h [9].

2.2   Concept of Interactivity

Despite the importance of interaction in distance education, the material studied does not present a single definition of the term. For purposes of this research, interactivity is understood as a process of communication between two or more individuals [20], which takes place in a circuit of separate coherent messages which should complete the cycle (to and from the student) [17].

According to the definition of these authors, interaction is an event that occurs between two or more subjects. It may occur synchronously or asynchronously using technology and provision of response or feedback as a result [7].

3   Method

This research compares the perceptions of interactivity between teachers and students, as well as elements which influence interactivity such as: time of response and communication media.

As for the technical procedures, the analysis was structured in a survey format, which proved to be more adequate for the achieving the goal of this work.

The data gathering was carried on in two steps with teachers and students. In the first step, students from college education institutions answered to the survey. The conclusion was that in order to improve students' perception of teacher-student interactivity, it is necessary that the response time be less than 24 h after submissions of doubts, activities or exercises. Above that period, the sensation of isolation increases. In order to improve students' participation in the environment, it was verified that teachers need to constantly motivate students to participate, and take part in forums and chats. Students resents the absence of practical exercises, videos and audiovisual animations for spreading the content in a more dynamic and interactive way [21]. This article continues the initial research band analyze the view of the tutor of Online courses.

In this step, the questionnaire aimed at the tutors of online courses. The tool used was Google Docs, and the form consisted of 21 questions, being 7 multiple choice questions, 9 closed questions and 5 aimed at identifying the teacher's general profile. The form was available at the link: http://goo.gl/forms/iXTF6ktDQp and the teachers responded to the survey from 03/08/2016 to 03/16/2016. To the students, we changed a few questions from the first survey and we provided students with a new form consisting of 20 questions, 6 were multiple choice questions, 5 were closed questions, and 5 were aimed at identifying students' general profile. The form was available in the link: http://goo.gl/forms/PTKKBw7MyU and students answered to the survey from 03/08/2016b to 03/16/2016.

The first step 95 students answered the survey. They were from 16 education institutes, 10 were private and six were public. 41 students come from private institutions, out of which 35 were graduation students and 6 were post graduation students; 44 students were from public institutions, out of which 25 were graduation students and 19 were from post graduation students; 10 of them did not inform the kind of institution they are from.

In the second step, the survey was answered by 67 teachers from 44 education institutes, 25 teachers were from private institution, 16 from public institutions and 3 did not state the kind of institution they are from. The form for students received 10 valid answers in 10 education institutions, out of which 4 were from private institutions and 6 from public ones.

The main analysis points were the interaction between teachers and students in order to learn the opinion of the respondents as for interaction in the online learning environment, establishing an axis for verification of the hypotheses raised in this work.

The results of this study were analyzed on the following criteria: interactivity as a factor of improvement of learning; effect of interaction between teachers and students in the tasks; and the analysis of the time of feedback teachers give on the tasks/doubts and the degree of interactivity perceived.

4   Data Analysis

The data analysis allowed us to evaluate the view of the teacher tutor as for the interactivity and main points to be improved on that matter in Online Courses as well as Online students' point of view.

The respondents were mainly professors from Administration, Graduation, Engineering and Technical Courses, with predominant experience ranging from 4 years.

Points presented as a differential for online students who did not have previous studies opportunity due to their work and time availability were flexibility and reliability, which allow students to get qualified with a better management of time and smaller costs.

The most used Virtual Learning Environment identified in the survey was Moodle (87.9%) which is the most popular teaching management system platform, it is open and free, created by Martin Gougiamas in 2001. Teachers and students stated that platforms provide communication tools and those tools are effective in the teaching/learning process, the main used tools being forums, e-mail and chat. The main difficulties addressed in the survey were the sluggishness of the communication tools 41.5% and the lack of training, besides the fact that the environment shows too much or confusingly displayed information.

It was found that the teacher's perception of interactivity increases along with experience background. Teachers with a 1-to-3-year experience perceive interactivity as below average or good and the more experience ones have a good perception of interactivity in Distance Education.

In the Figs. 1 and 2, it can be found that there was a disparity between the answers given by teachers and the students when it comes to the response time and the degree of perception of interactivity. The majority of the teachers stated that they give feedback to students in up to 24 h, however, students stated that they normally receive feedback from 24 h on. It was found that the degree of perception of interactivity lessens as the time of feedback increases. The teachers who give fast feedback to students evaluated interactivity as excellent.

On Fig. 3, which shows the perception of the degree of interactivity between teachers and students with the factors 1 meaning non-existent and 5 excellent, teachers on average evaluated 4.1, as good and students 3.6 as average nearly

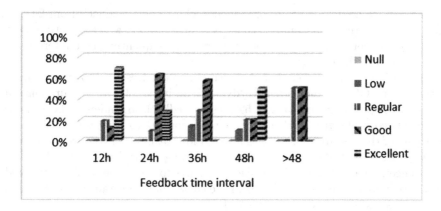

Fig. 1. Time of feedback vs. degree of perception of interactivity - teacher

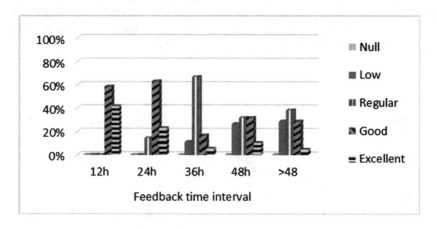

Fig. 2. Time of feedback vs. degree of perception of interactivity - students

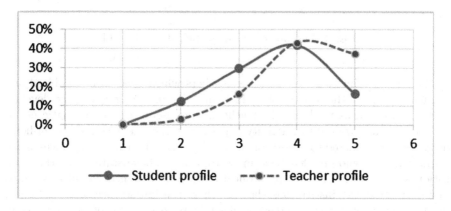

Fig. 3. Perception of the degree of interactivity

good when we analyze a group of students who receive feedback from 24 h on, the degree of perception of interactivity is reduced to 3.2, which directly reflects on students' perception of interactivity and, consequently, their interest and development in the course.

According to teachers' comments, the main points presented to improve interactivity were: Offering more creative/dynamic activities 60.9%; Encouraging students' participation in the VLE 56.5%; faster feedback to students 53.6%. These comments coincide with students' opinions, according to what was found in the first part of the research [21]. It was also found that in order to have more interactivity between students and teachers, according to students, there should be more encouragement from the teachers to participate in the VLE, faster feedback; previously scheduled meetings in the chats, more constant participation in the forums and easier access to the VLE.

Figure 4 is about teachers' encouragement for students to discuss their doubts among them aiming at a collaborative learning in the VLE. The variation between 1-never and 5-always shows that teachers usually tend to encourage students to participate in the VLE (4.4). On the other hand, students state that they are not usually encouraged by their teachers 3.9.

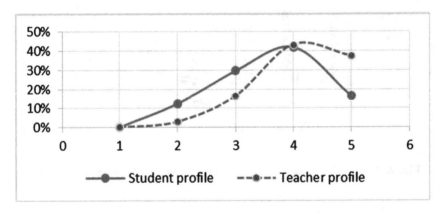

Fig. 4. Encouragement to participate in the VLE

The main points addressed by the teachers which need to be analyzed and commented on by the institutions which offer distance courses are the development of other tasks made by the teachers, the absence of an automatic notification when a new doubt or activity is posted by the students and the 24-hour, deadline be considered too short for the teachers. Besides those hindrances, some of the teachers who give feedback in up to 48 h or above stated that the institution sets that deadline or it is due to the time assigned to tutoring. It is important that the institutions show teachers the importance of the 24-hour-deadline feedback for the increasing of students' perception of interactivity in the course, which is a vital factor for these kind of courses.

Besides VLE tools, teachers use Whatsapp 59.1%, Facebook 59.1% and other social network as an alternative to communicate with students, such as Skype, LinkedIn, Instagram, Telephone among others. These tools are inserted in the teachers' and students' routine and allow communication to be more dynamic for online students and teachers.

5 Conclusions

This research allows us to evaluate the interactivity process between teachers/students, comparing teachers' and students' points of view.

In order to improve interactivity in Online Education it is necessary to have more creative/dynamic activities, faster feedback, more encouragement to participate in the VLE, more adequate communication tools and easier access to the environment. It was found that in order to improve students' interest in the course and their perception of interactivity it is necessary to lessen the time to feedback; previously schedule meetings in the chats; to offer practical exercises and to incentive constant participation in the forums.

It was also found that the degree of perception of interactivity by the students lessens as the time to feedback increases. Institutions could provide teachers with an e-mail automatic notification system or SMS whenever a new doubt or activity is submitted in the VLE, encourage teachers to access the platform on a daily basis, besides assess the time of feedback as a quality requirement for their job.

The main difficulties teachers and students alike have in accessing the VLE should be revised and improved in order to increase the interest and access of distance education students and teachers alike. The main purposes are: to improve the speed of access to communication tools, provide constant training to users, make information in the environment more pragmatic and clearer and make access to the platforms easier.

References

1. Blasco-Arcas, L., Buil, I., Hernández-Ortega, B., Sese, F.J.: Using clickers in class. The role of interactivity, active collaborative learning and engagement in learning performance. Comput. Educ. **62**, 102–110 (2013)
2. Henrie, C.R., Halverson, L.R., Graham, C.R.: Measuring student engagement in technology-mediated learning: a review. Comput. Educ. **90**, 36–53 (2015)
3. Garbin, M.C., Garcia, M.F., do Amaral, S.F., da Silva, D., de Abreu, R.R.: Teachers perception on collaborative learning processes: experiencing continuing teacher education in Brazil. Procedia Soc. Behav. Sci. **191**, 2231–2235 (2015)
4. Picciano, A.G., Seaman, J., Shea, P., Swan, K.: Examining the extent and nature of online learning in American K-12 education: the research initiatives of the Alfred P. Sloan Foundation. Internet High. Educ. **15**(2), 127–135 (2012)
5. Demirkan, H., Goul, M., Gros, M.: A reference model for sustainable e-learning service systems: experiences with the Joint University/Teradata Consortium. Decis. Sci. J. Innov. Educ. **8**(1), 151–189 (2010)

6. Associação Brasileira de Educação a Distância. http://www.abed.org.br/censoead 2014/CensoEAD2014_portugues.pdf
7. Joksimovic, S., Gavsevic, D., Loughin, T.M., Kovanovic, V., Hatala, M.: Learning at distance: effects of interaction traces on academic achievement. Comput. Educ. **87**, 204–217 (2015)
8. Tirri, K., Kuusisto, E.: Interaction in Educational Domains. Springer Science & Business Media, Heidelberg (2013)
9. Abreu, D.M., Alves, M.N., et al.: O Feedback e sua Importância no Processo de Tutoria a Distância. Posições **22**(2), 189–205 (2016)
10. Gandra, D.C.: A Importância do Feedback na Educação a Distância. Rev. Aprendiz. Em EAD (4) (2015)
11. Hattge, A., Ribas, C., Paulo, A.: A importância do feedback na educação a distância. Rev. Eletrônica Curso Pedag. Fac. OPET **16**, 1–16 (2014)
12. Mory, E.H.: Feedback research revisited. Handb. Res. Educ. Commun. Technol. **2**, 745–783 (2004)
13. Ausubel, D.P., Novak, J.D., Hanesian, H., et al.: Educational Psychology: A Cognitive View. Holt, Rinehart and Winston, New York (1968)
14. Bruner, J.S.: Acts of Meaning, vol. 3. Harvard University Press, Cambridge (1990)
15. Shute, V.J.: Focus on formative feedback. Rev. Educ. Res. **78**(1), 153–189 (2008)
16. Kerka, S., Wonacott, M.E.: Assessing learners online. Practitioner file (2000)
17. Yacci, M.: Interactivity demystified: a structural definition for distance education and intelligent CBT. Educ. Technol. **40**(4), 5–16 (2000)
18. Paiva, V.: Feedback em Ambiente Virtual. In: Interação na Aprendizagem das línguas, pp. 219–254. EDUCAT, Pelotas (2003)
19. Maia, C., Mattar, J.: ABC da EaD: A Educação a Distância Hoje. Pearson Prentice Hall, Upper Saddle River (2008)
20. Wagner, E.D.: In support of a functional definition of interaction. Am. J. Distance Educ. **8**(2), 6–29 (1994)
21. Barboza, E., Silva, M.: Technological development and the perception of interactivity for distance education (2016)

Flexible, Sustainable Supply Chains

Assessment of Structural Qualities of Production Systems

Ulf Bergmann and Matthias Heinicke[(⊠)]

Otto von Guericke University Magdeburg, Magdeburg, Germany
Matthias.heinicke@ovgu.de

Abstract. Turbulent changes of the production program challenge the suitability of the operating point of the production system. This can result in a lack of efficiency and productivity of a formerly mature configuration of a production system. In this case, the logistic positioning becomes obsolete. Therefore, a periodic monitoring of the system configuration is necessary to ensure a resilient production. To cope with those challenges, this paper introduces an approach which evaluates strategies in terms of adjusting the system configuration. On the one hand, this refers to control strategies influencing the temporal organization and thus the system's behavior. On the other hand, also a variation of the spatial organization in terms of the layout of the production system can be considered. For different production structures effects of changed production programs on the system configuration and its resilience is explained and adequate measures for adapting the temporal or spatial structure are appraisable.

Keywords: Temporal Structure · Spatial Structure · Operating point · Production system configuration · Resilience · Structural Quality

1 Introduction

The production industry – mainly due to the globalization of sales and purchase markets – is faced with new kinds of general conditions, resulting in decreasing quantities of similar products and, at the same time, increasing numbers of customer-specific variations. A clear change is noticeable, from multi-variant large-scale production towards customer-specific batch production, which comes as a result of this very individualization of the customers' demands. This often leads to short-cycle adjustments within the factory and production structure, since mastering these types of production largely depends on the implemented system structure. As for the operating routine, there is no objectively measurable parameter to verify the appropriateness of the installed system structure: The Structural Quality, the development of which is currently undertaken by several research activities at the Otto von Guericke University in Magdeburg.

© IFIP International Federation for Information Processing 2016
Published by Springer International Publishing AG 2016. All Rights Reserved
I. Nääs et al. (Eds.): APMS 2016, IFIP AICT 488, pp. 317–324, 2016.
DOI: 10.1007/978-3-319-51133-7_38

2 Scientific Background

A system is regarded as an entity of elements, the interrelations existing between these elements and the respective characteristics of these very elements and interrelations. Based on the production-technical approach, a factory can be defined as a production site providing an efficient manufacturing of goods. Production in this context is the system itself as the location where the actual manufacturing takes place [1]. In principle, production systems are socio-technical systems, since during the manufacturing process the elements of the technical subsystem (machines and plants) together with the elements of the social subsystem (people) enable the internal production process [2]. In order to simplify the structural approach for these kinds of production systems, the subcomponents of the technical and social system will be regarded as the smallest system units in form of work systems [3].

As a matter of fact, production systems exist – as any field of known matter – in space and time and are classified; thus, they do possess a structure in terms of a certain organization of the system (System Configuration). Based on the system-specific type and number of system elements (System Composition), a structure describes the basic order of a system (System Setup) depending on the existing system interrelations. As a result, it determines the function of the system (System Behavior). The System Setup is, therefore, determined by the existing System Composition, i.e. the type and number of all system elements, depending on the type, orientation and intensity of the system-inherent, physical interrelations between the system elements. This preferably economical arrangement of system elements for implementing the processing sequences is called Spatial Structure [4]. The System Behavior is characterized by the type, number and order of any kinds of processes that might be implemented through the functional linking of the system elements (processing sequences). The chronological structuring of the processes into segments and their timely interaction is called Temporal Structure [1]. In the context of manufacturing and assembly systems, resilience is the ability of the system to cope with changes of all sorts [5]. This concept refers to the System Behavior and the System Setup in terms of both, rapidly and flexibly reconfiguring the operating states of a production system or enduring to changes due to the preservation of a stable system configuration [6]. In particular, the property called robustness that allows a system to maintain its functions despite external and internal perturbations [7], is important due to an adequate response to turbulent market and customer changes.

Analytical approaches for checking or evaluating an installed system structure are contrasted by design approaches to pre-determine flexible system structures in the context of factory and production structure planning. Deficits in such structure configurations are mainly provoked by the mostly one-sided observation of the spatial aspects of structuring (before Start-of-production – SOP), since the temporal component will usually only be determined by the time sequence of the production processes (after the real SOP) [8,9]. Only the temporal dependency of type, number, linking and arrangement of the system elements is considered with the help of dynamic structuring approaches [10]. A fact often ignored is that, besides the arrangement of the system elements, it is also the manner of their interactions which defines an entire system structure. Therefore, an evaluation of the structure's appropriateness is necessary which considers both the spatial and the temporal aspects of production structures. Following the previous remarks, the evaluation of the Structural Quality should be based on the System Setup as well as the System Behavior.

3   Model for Structural Evaluation

3.1   System Setup – Basic Considerations

The setup of a production system mainly depends on the System Composition and is reflected in the plant layout as regards the Spatial Structure. Consequently, the System Setup should be understood as function of the System Composition and the concrete Spatial Structure (Eq. 1):

$$System\ Setup = f\ (System\ Composition;\ Spatial\ Structure) \qquad (1)$$

These determinations usually occur during the planning stage of a production system, starting with the definition of the type of operational means and the technologies on which they are based. In a next step, this will provide the system-specific level of concentration or the differentiation of the working steps, respectively, leading eventually to the level of task distribution that is possible during the system's operation. In order to guarantee the required capacitive performance of the system-specific means, its number will be determined at last. After this functional determination and dimensioning, the next step of structuring is to work out an ideal Spatial Structure. Existing procedures may optimize such a spatial arrangement, usually by minimizing the length of present transport routes between the individual operational systems (Eq. 2). Thus, the focus is mainly set on optimizing the material flow [8,9].

$$\sum_{i=1}^{m} \sum_{j=1}^{m} l_{ij} \cdot D_{ij} \Rightarrow min \qquad (2)$$

l_{ij} Intensity between object i and object j
D_{ij} Distance between object i and object j
m Number of objects.

3.2   System Behavior – Basic Considerations

The concrete behavior of a production system will only become transparent during operation. Therefore, the System Behavior is based on the System Setup defined before and causally influenced by the selection of the Temporal Structure. Accordingly, the System Behavior can be understood as function of the System Setup and the selected Temporal Structure (Eq. 3):

$$System\ Behavior = f\ (System\ Setup;\ Temporal\ Structure) \qquad (3)$$

Previous methods for evaluating the operational quality of a production structure mainly focus on three parameters in this respect: throughput time, output rate and the work in progress (WIP). Completing this by adherence to delivery dates, we will have all the figures for the so-called logistic performance indicators. These are usually visualized in form of operating curves, thus locating the current operating point of a production system multi-dimensionally [9]. Based on the operating curve, a theoretical optimum for running a production structure can be determined. In this context, the WIP features a double role as control variable and evaluating parameter and is used as an assessment tool. Accordingly, the WIP in the production system is the only parameter that is directly influenceable by the activities of production planning and production controlling - which during the operation of a production structure have a big impact on determining their System Behavior - and immediately affects the remaining logistic performance indicators. Therefore, the individual objectives must be weighed up against each other in order to achieve an adequate picture of the present operational target system. As for the strategic focus of an enterprise, hierarchic target systems are common practice and are also used when projecting production systems. However, when operating such elaborated production systems, the focus is mostly set on the logistic performance indicators. Here, the quality of the System Behavior, which is mainly determined by the System Setup, is evaluated and, in the next step, the quality of the system structure is assessed by using operating curves.

Moreover, specific versions of the characteristic curves depend on different conditions for the respective production system (e.g. the integration of operating systems into the material flow), i.e. the comparability of operating points depends on the respective aspects of the production structure [11]. Basically, the characteristic of a production program for a concrete production system influences the System Composition as well as the Spatial and Temporal Structure. Except for the production program, all factors can be directly influenced by the enterprise. While in case of an identical Spatial Structure, the operating points of a system might be compared for different Temporal Structures, e.g. with changed controlling processes, it is not easy to make a reverse assessment with the help of the logistic performance indicators. This is due to the fact that changing the Spatial Structure often induces a change in the resource basis as regards the System Composition. Only with unchanged type and number of system elements, a consistent basis for evaluation is guaranteed. Otherwise, the different dimensioning and/or a changed functional scope of individual resource elements distort the comparison's significance. In order to compensate for this deficit, it is required to normalize the parameters. Thus, a normalized presentation of the logistic performance indicators is required to be able to draw conclusions which are largely independent from the system-specific conditions [11].

3.3   Main Findings – The Structural Quality

In order to assess the quality of a present production structure it is necessary to determine adequate reference values for the normalization. For the output rate and the WIP it is advisable to relate these values to the ideal operating point, thus expressing them as relative values. If the maximum output rate is set on 100%, then the medium output rate can be directly converted and interpreted as medium utilization. For the WIP it is advisable to normalize with the ideal minimum WIP as reference point. The resulting relative WIP indicates to which degree the absolute WIP of a production system deviates from the ideal minimum WIP. If the ideal minimum WIP and the maximum utilization are set on 100% respectively, the normalized output rate operating curve will be the result. A relative measure for the throughput time or the range respectively is the flow rate. If the mean WIP is set in relation to the output rate, the weighted flow rate will be obtained as normalized value for the operating range [11].

As a result of this normalization, the calculation equations for the utilization, the relative WIP and the weighted flow rate do not include the specific order (production program) and direct capacity figures (system composition) any longer. Resulting normalized operating curves are therefore mainly system-independent, focusing exclusively on the Spatial and Temporal structure of the observed production system.

Accordingly, the Structural Quality of production systems can be seen as vector of the quality of the Spatial and Temporal structure (Eq. 4):

$$\overrightarrow{SQ} = \left(\frac{SQ_{spatial}}{SQ_{temporal}} \right) \tag{4}$$

where,

$\overrightarrow{SQ}$ Structural Quality
$SQ_{spatial}$ Spatial Structural Quality
$SQ_{temporal}$ Temporal Structural Quality.

4   Application Scenario

4.1   Use Case and Results

Basically, the Structural Quality provides the planner with a number to evaluate an implemented production structure. Moreover, the Structural Quality may also serve as a planning index when reconfiguring an observed production structure. Such a reconfiguration is based on changing general conditions (mainly the change of the production program) as well as on changes of system-inherent characteristics: this refers to the System's Composition, Setup and Behavior.

Figures 1 and 2 illustrate the way the Structural Quality is applied as key number by using a typical manufacturing system of the metal processing industry as an example. Produced are shaft, gearing and housing components with machine tools applying different operation sequences, respectively. The implemented production structure is arranged in an operation-oriented setup (workshop structure), with a levelled dispatching of the manufacturing orders being provided by a standardized production program. At first the characteristic curve was plotted by using a discrete variation of the production program in terms of an order load on a percentage basis in order to evaluate the temporal structure. Thus, the load of the production system as measured by the WIP was modified stepwise. As a result, a reasonable curve regarding the lead time and the output rate depending on the respective WIP arose. Moreover, the transport effort of the spatial structure was calculated according to Eq. 2. The optimal Spatial Structure relates to an ideal arrangement of machines. Due to layout constraints arising from the real circumstances of the building, the attained spatial quality amounts to 1,75 (percentage compared to the optimal material flow).

Subsequently, the numbers for normalization were computed. The ideal minimum WIP amount in a workload of about 2500 h. The maximum output rate considered the capacity of the entire system, i.e. the sum of the capacity of all particular work systems. It amounts 448 h per working day. The theoretical minimum throughput time is the sum of all net process times. In this ideally consideration absolutely no transition or waiting time occurs. The normalized values for each operation point (level of WIP) can be calculated on the basis of these numbers (minimum throughput time, ideal minimum WIP, maximum output rate). For this purpose, the percentage gap between achieved and ideal value are arithmetically averaged and yield the figure for the temporal quality. According to the definitions of Structural Quality, the spatial and temporal vector components for this workshop structure result in the values 1,75 (normalized transport effort) and 1,71 (normalized operating point), combined in the column vector Structural Quality (Fig. 1, Eq. 4). Thus, the Structural Quality enables to check a potential variation within the System Setup.

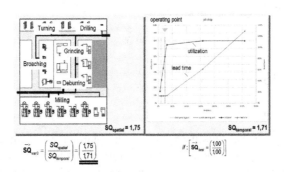

Fig. 1. Structural Quality of a manufacturing system (as-is state)

In the given example occurs an object-oriented reconfiguration of the spatial arrangement (line structure). Here, various products share a specific production line and in this context certain resources which are necessary to produce the respective products. All together the products are allocated to three different production lines. Neither the production program nor the System Composition (in type and number of the operating systems) are subjected to any changes in this respect and remain fixed. The System Behavior (in form of dispatching and controlling the manufacturing orders) is altered first into a reorder point procedure (variant 1) and subsequently into a Kanban principle (variant 2). Thus, this results in a variation of the Spatial and Temporal Structure. Again, characteristic curves for the new production structures were plotted. The numeric values for the normalization are equal to the first calculation. The numbers for the spatial and temporal vector components, now with the values 1,40 (normalized transport effort) and 4,60 (normalized operating point of the reorder point procedure) or 3,41 (Kanban principle), are combined again in the column vector Structural Quality (Fig. 2, Eq. 4).

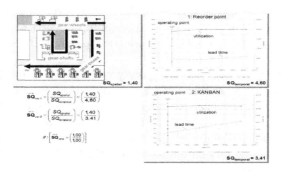

Fig. 2. Structural Quality of a manufacturing system (1: reorder point procedure, 2: kanban)

4.2 Discussion

The concrete Structural Quality of both variants depends on the aims of the company. A clear advantage of one of the variants is not assessable due to the fact that vectors for the spatial and the temporal reveal a different tendency. While the numerical value of the spatial vector is decreasing due to the change from a workshop to a line production, the value of the temporal vector is increasing simultaneously. On the contrary, the vector for the temporal quality of the structures reveals that all in all the workshop structure enables a better performance compared to the line structure with reorder point procedure or Kanban principle. However, the Kanban structure reveals a clear advantage compared to the reorder point procedure due to the fact that the inventory inherent in the systems is lower for the Kanban principle. Nevertheless, capacity utilization of the workshop structure is higher than the value of the production lines because of the multi-variant production program. Additionally, the actual operation point of the workshop production is closer to its optimal operation point than the respective operation points of the line production (Figs. 1 and 2).

5   Conclusion and Outlook

The Structural Quality shall be used to analyze the efficiency that is the temporal and cost-oriented input-output-relation with the idea of minimizing the factor input while keeping the output quantity. Under consideration of the company-specific objectives, the Structural Quality, therefore, provides the potential of an exogenously induced and/or endogenously enabled variation of the production structure. Thus, at this point the Structural Quality facilitates an assessment of a change of the Spatial and Temporal Structure.

As a result, the vectors for the spatial and the temporal Structural Quality changed. This highlights the insight that variations of one of the three system aspects (quantity of elements, interrelations between these elements or characteristics of these elements and interrelations) can lead to shifts regarding both the temporal and the spatial quality of the system structure. Accordingly, this measurable parameter enables verifying the appropriateness of the installed system structure concerning a specific production program in terms of a proper function of the production system.

On the contrary, the Structural Quality can serve as a mean to assess the resilience of a system regarding a changing production program and its impact of the system's configuration. This refers to both the Spatial and the Temporal Structure. The first one indicates the impact of a variation of the production program on the appropriateness of the disposal of resources (layout). The second one relates to attaining objectives (lead time, WIP, utilization) despite changes of the production program.

References

1. Costanzo, F., et al.: Enterprise organization and operation. In: Grote, K.-H., Antonsson, E.K. (eds.) Springer Handbook of Mechanical Engineering, pp. 1267–1359. Springer, Heidelberg (2009)
2. Ropohl, G.: Allgemeine Technologie: Eine Systemtheorie der Technik. KIT Scientific Publishing, Karlsruhe (2009)
3. Bokranz, R., Landau, K.: Handbuch Industrial Engineering-Produktivitätsmanagement mit MTM, Band 1 Konzept, 2. Überarbeitete und erweiterte Auflage, Schäffer-Poeschel Verlag, Stuttgart (2012)
4. Kühnle, H., Henn, G.: Strukturplanung. In: Eversheim, W., Schuh, G. (eds.) Hütte-Produktion und Management "Betriebshütte" 2.2. Springer, Heidelberg (1996)
5. Töyli, H.L., Lauri Ojala, J., Wieland, A., Marcus Wallenburg, C.: The influence of relational competencies on supply chain resilience: a relational view. Int. J. Phys. Distrib. Logist. Manag. **43**(4), 300–320 (2013)
6. Heinicke, M.: Influence of shifts in production programs on the resilience of production systems. Procedia CIRP **41**, 117–122 (2016)
7. Kitano, H.: Biological robustness. Nat. Rev. Genet. **5**(11), 826–837 (2004)
8. Francis, R.L., McGinnis, L.F., White, J.A.: Facility Layout and Location: an analytical approach. Prentice-Hall, Upper Saddle River (1992)
9. Tompkins, J.A.: Facilities Planning. Wiley, Hoboken (2010)
10. Hildebrand, T., Mäding, K., Günther, U.: Plug + Produce – Gestaltungsstrategien für die Wandlungsfähige Fabrik. IBF. Techn. Univ. Chemnitz (2005)
11. Nyhuis, P., Wiendahl, H.P.: Fundamentals of Production Logistics: Theory, Tools and Applications. Springer, Heidelberg (2014)

The Introduction Process of Low-Volume Products: Challenges and Potentials of Information Management

Siavash Javadi[1(✉)], Mads Bejlegaard[2], Ann-Louise Andersen[2], and Jessica Bruch[1]

[1] Mälardalen University, Eskilstuna, Sweden
{siavash.javadi,jessica.bruch}@mdh.se
[2] Aalborg University, Aalborg, Denmark

Abstract. The product introduction process plays an important role in development of new products and launching them to the market on-time with a high quality. The product introduction process has been studied primarily in high-volume manufacturing industries and therefore, the influences of the characteristics of low-volume manufacturing industries on the product introduction process has not been investigated. The aim of this paper is to study challenges and potentials of information management during the product introduction process in low-volume manufacturing industries by a multiple-case study in two Scandinavian low-volume manufacturing companies. The paper contributes in covering the knowledge gap about the information management during the product introduction process in low-volume manufacturing industries.

Keywords: Design-manufacturing interface · Product development · Production-design integration

1 Introduction

Manufacturing companies are forced to develop and launch new products to the market more frequently with a high quality because of different factors such as increased competition in the globalized market, introduction of new technologies and faster obsolescence of the products. The product introduction process as the final sub-process of the product development is of high importance to reduce the production disturbances during the early stages of the production of new products and to reach the intended quality, production goals and time to market/payback [1, 2]. An effective management of information in the product introduction process is central for the success of the product introduction process [3–6].

Although information management in the product introduction process has been studied in the context of product development [3, 7], production system development [5] and production ramp-up [6], the influences of the characteristics of low-volume manufacturing industries on it has remained unexplored. Therefore, the aim of this paper is to study challenges and potentials of information management during the product introduction process in low-volume manufacturing industries. To achieve this

© IFIP International Federation for Information Processing 2016
Published by Springer International Publishing AG 2016. All Rights Reserved
I. Nääs et al. (Eds.): APMS 2016, IFIP AICT 488, pp. 325–332, 2016.
DOI: 10.1007/978-3-319-51133-7_39

aim, a multiple-case study has been conducted in two Scandinavian low-volume manufacturing companies.

2 Frame of Reference

The product introduction process is the finishing process of product development projects which is also known as the industrialization process [8, 9]. The product introduction process influences critical outcomes of the product development projects such as time to market and product quality [4]. Bellgran and Säfsten [8] define the product introduction process as "transferring from engineering design to production including those activities required to make the product manufacturable and to prepare production". Fewer disturbances during production, a shorter time to market and higher quality of the products are some outcomes of a well-implemented product introduction process [6, 10].

The product introduction process goals are to develop a production system for production of a product [1, 8] and to adapt product and production system together to ensure the manufacturability of the product [1, 2]. Frishammar [3] summarizes the activities of the product introduction process as the mid-phase of new product development process. These activities include development of product and production system, test and refinement of the product functionality mainly by development of engineering prototypes, test and refinement of the production system and adapting the product and production system together by production of pre-series and reaching the production goals and training the production personnel during the production ramp-up [1, 3, 6, 11]. However, the phases of product introduction process in low-volume manufacturing industries are restricted to development of product and production system, testing and refinement of the functionality of the product and limited production of pre-series and no conventional ramp-up phase is feasible [11, 12]. This is primarily because of high costs, low production volume, and high variety of the products in low-volume manufacturing companies [11, 12] which lead to following a full make-to-order production policy [13].

However, the novelty of products and production systems in low-volume manufacturing industries are usually low [11] which can facilitate the product introduction process based on Almgren's [14] model of complexity of product introduction process. The products in low-volume manufacturing industries are usually modified versions of the existing products [11]. In addition, the production systems of low-volume manufacturing companies are usually flexible enough to produce several products and their variants and to accommodate new products to avoid high costs of developing dedicated production systems for each product [11, 12].

One of the main sources of disturbances during the product introduction process is lack of integration between design and production [14, 15]. The production-design integration can be achieved by 1. More formal and structured activities between the departments such as processes, routines and planned meetings and flow of documents. 2. Informal unstructured continuous relationships between departments which lead to developing common understanding, sharing resources and achieving shared objectives [9]. Information management i.e. acquisition, sharing and using the information [5, 7] plays an essential role in supporting the design-production integration and avoiding or mitigating disturbances during the product introduction process [6, 7] e.g. by reducing uncertainty and equivocality [16]. Therefore, this paper aims at investigating challenges and potentials of information management during the product introduction process in low-volume manufacturing industries, which has not been considered in the literature [15].

3 Research Method

Case study is a suitable method for in-depth study of a contemporary phenomenon when the knowledge is limited about the phenomenon [17] which was the case for the subject of this study. Two product development projects were selected as cases from two Scandinavian companies based on possession of the characteristics of low-volume manufacturing companies mentioned by Jina et al. [13]. The first case study, hereafter called Case A, was conducted from October 2012 to September 2013 in a company which develops and produces underground construction and mining equipment. The company is a large company with over 1300 employees. The products of the company were produced in five product families including several variants with numerous options to meet the requirements of different customers and markets. The production activities at the company included the final assembly of the products and sub-assembly of some of the product modules.

The second case, here referred to as Case B, was conducted in a company producing earth-moving equipment. The product series contain three main types of machines with a total of 30 variants, which can be further configured through an additional eight parameters with numerous different options to choose from. The vast majority of the products are customized from well-defined modular product architectures. The case study was conducted from August 2014 to June 2015. The company has approximately 150 employees and therefore, is considered as a small-medium enterprise. All of the products offered by the company are developed and produced in the same location, where production activities cover the manual final assembly, and a steel processing setup that includes manual handling of large components and automatic welding.

In both cases, different sources of data were used including the observation of project meetings and events, documents related to the disturbances during the product introduction process and interviews. Eight and three semi-structured interviews were conducted with the product development project team members of Case A and Case B, respectively. In addition, some follow up interviews were conducted with the production operators to validate and complete the findings of the case studies during 2015. The collected data from these interviews were primarily covered. Five and two final assembly operators were interviewed in Company A and Company B, respectively about information on new products received by assembly operators and production equipment for new product introduction. Initially, the gathered data from each case were recorded and analysed separately to understand how information management during the product introduction in low-volume manufacturing industries is influenced by the characteristics of such industries. Thereafter, a cross-case comparison was conducted to compare the similarities and differences of the cases.

4 Empirical Findings

4.1 Case A

The goal of the product development project was a general modification of one of the existing products. The product was planned to be produced in the existing production system. The assembly line was designed to produce different products with slight changes. Such flexibility was achieved mainly by manual operations, general-purpose tools and material handling equipment.

The product development project was managed according to a stage-gate model and the project team consisted of different functions such as product design, production, product introduction, purchasing, marketing and product support. The product introduction manager responsibility was basically facilitating the product introduction process by coordinating activities between design and production and considering the limitations and requirements of the production system for the production of the new product. This coordination was necessary because of inter-departmental barriers between design and production as well as their separate locations. Some of the main activities followed by the product introduction manager were collecting the requirements of the production and sharing them with the project team during the development phase, coordinating design reviews to update production personnel about new features of the products and the manufacturability implications of those features and developing assembly sequences and instructions during development of the prototypes.

After the product design phase, two prototypes were developed outside of the normal production facilities with very limited contribution of production personnel because of limited human resources and prioritizing involvement of production personnel in the ongoing production over the product development projects. The assembly sequences and instructions were developed during this phase. In addition to the prototypes, four first products were planned as pre-series to be produced in the production system. However, because of low and discontinuous demand for the product, only two of those pre-series were produced immediately after the prototypes. Production of the pre-series encountered many disturbances. These disturbances, their causes and solutions were registered in a database. The most frequent and considerable types of these disturbances were lack of information about the product details, lack of considering manufacturability of the products and late consideration of required changes and limitations of the production system. In addition, based on the follow-up interviews, the information received by production about the new products was incomplete, incorrect and/or ambiguous in many cases.

4.2 Case B

The product development project in Case B aimed at developing a completely new generation of a product. The product was planned to be produced in the existing production system with some necessary changes. The production system possessed the same characteristics as in Case A regarding its flexibility to produce different products and their variants.

Because of the small size of the company, the product development project was managed in a less formalized way and with more face-to-face communications which were facilitated by co-location of different functions. The product design phase was conducted with limited involvement from other functions than product development. However, the designers' knowledge about the production system was extensive because of their long experience at the company and continuous informal communication with the production. After the development phase, two prototypes were developed to test and refine the functionality of the product. No pre-series were produced. Instead, mutual adjustments by informal face-to-face communication between design and production and other functions continued after the start of the production to remove the remaining problems and adjust product and production system together.

Among the predominant disturbances during production start-up were difficulties in implementing and specifying an externally-supplied main component. In addition, necessary changes in the production system were implemented late because of limited resources for designing and implementing new tooling, and due to prioritising quick market introduction over an optimal production setup. The follow-up interviews justified that the information about parts were often in-complete or incorrect during production start-up. The respondents also mentioned that a direct communication with few intermediaries between design and production was a great advantage in handling the product introduction. The advantage of this was that the experience of the operators were used directly in development, which in addition increased the awareness of the operators and their perceived project responsibility.

5 Discussion

Managing information during the product introduction process was influenced by the characteristics of the studied low-volume manufacturing companies in different ways. Limited resources in both cases led to challenges regarding the production-design integration. In both cases, the early involvement of production in the product introduction process was limited because the production personnel had to prioritise the ongoing production activities over the product development projects. However, some processes such as collecting the requirements of production at the start of development phase, using the design reviews to inform production about the new features of the product and production of four pre-series product were foreseen in Case A. In Case B the integration was supported more by co-location of design and production and informal relations whereas these informal communications were limited in Case A because of inter-departmental barriers and separate locations of design and production.

The limited integration between design and production resulted also in difficulty of acquiring information from production personnel about the required changes in the production systems and the requirements and limitation of the production system. Furthermore, sharing the information about the new features of the product and their implications for production with the production personnel was challenging because of lack of integration which is in line with the propositions of Frishammar and Ylinenpää [3]. High number of problems caused by neglecting design for assembly guidelines and requirements and limitations of the production systems in Case A and late delivery and installation of the new production equipment in both cases indicate that the information about the requirements and limitations of the production system are not managed properly during the product introduction project in the low-volume manufacturing industries [6, 15]. This problem was intensified by extra focus of the designers as well as other project team members on the functionality of the products and under-prioritizing the manufacturability of the products because of the high customizability level and variety of the products. Especially in Case A, since the product was a modified version of an existing product, in many instances the effects of the modifications on the other parts and components were not considered and the information about them was not acquired and shared with production.

In addition, because of lack of integration, no formal process was planned for sharing and using the acquired information about the problems and disturbances. In Case A, a database was used for registering the information about product-related problems and their solutions. However, there was no foreseen mechanism for sharing the information with designers and using it in future products. In Case B, the information about problems and disturbances was not documented nor shared. Furthermore, the follow-up interviews showed that the lack of integration affects the characteristics of the information received by production about the new products. In both cases the information was not comprehensive, correct or/and clear in several instances. Incorrect/incomplete information about small connecting parts and incorrect/incomplete assembly instructions are some examples of such problems. Therefore, in many instances using the received information was impossible or difficult.

Beside the lack of integration, limited opportunities for test and refinement of the products and production system caused challenges for acquiring and sharing the information about the disturbances and critical events. Since there were limited opportunities for test and refinement, many of the problems and critical events surfaced late in the project, i.e. after the start of production. Therefore, acquisition of the information about them and eliminating them was not possible during the earlier phases. This lack of information about the disturbances and non-conformities increased the level of information uncertainty [16]. Another factor which affected the information management in the studied product introduction processes was introducing new products in the current production systems with slight modifications. Since the production system was considered primarily "as is" by the product development team, information on the required changes related to the production system development were acquired and shared late. Late consideration of the required changes in production system in Case A and late implementation of them in both cases was partially caused by this characteristic. However, this reduced novelty of production systems in product introduction process in low-volume manufacturing companies can potentially lead to reduced complexity of information management. The low newness level of the production system can provide the designers and production personnel with information about the introduction of previous products in that production system and help them to avoid similar disturbances during the introduction of new products. The complexity could be reduced even more when the product is a modified version of an existing product like Case A. However, a process should be established to acquire information from the introduction of new products, to share the information with the product development team members including the designers and production personnel and to

Table 1. The challenges and potentials of information management caused by the characteristics of product introduction process in low-volume manufacturing industries

Characteristics of the product introduction process in low-volume companies	Information management	
	Challenges	Potentials
Lack of resources	- Reduced integration between design and production - Difficulty of acquiring necessary information from production - Difficulty of sharing information about the new products with production	- Facilitating acquiring and sharing the information by encouraging face-to-face and informal relations by co-location of design and production
Lack of opportunities for test and refinement of products and production systems	- Fewer opportunities for acquiring information about problems and disturbances - Increased information uncertainties about the products	–
Using the similar production system for production of new products	- Late acquisition and sharing of information about required changes in production	- Sharing and using information from introduction of previous products to reduce the complexity
Modifying existing products instead of developing completely new products	- Uncertainties about the affected parts and components and the required information	- Sharing and using information from introduction of previous products to reduce the complexity

use it during the introduction of the future products. Table 1 summarizes the discussed challenges and potentials of information management during the product introduction process in low-volume manufacturing companies.

6 Conclusions

Regarding its aim, this paper achieved to identify a number of challenges and potentials of information management during the product introduction process in low-volume manufacturing industries. The characteristics of product introduction in low-volume manufacturing industries impose difficulties of timely and complete acquisition and sharing of information between production and design. However, those characteristics provide a potential to facilitate the product introduction process by reusing the information from introduction of previous similar products. In this regard, the paper contributes to covering the knowledge gap about the information management during the product introduction process in low-volume manufacturing industries. The paper also provides practitioners with insights about management of information during the product introduction process.

The paper provides the basis for future research about the further details of information management during the product introduction process in low-volume manufacturing companies and how to use the information management to facilitate and support the product introduction process in such industries.

References

1. Johansen, K.: Collaborative product introduction within extended enterprises. Department of Management and Engineering, Assembly Technology, Linköping University, Sweden (2005)
2. Ruffles, P.C.: Improving the new product introduction process in manufacturing companies. Int. J. Manuf. Technol. Manag. 1(1), 1–19 (2000)
3. Frishammar, J., Ylinenpää, H.: Managing information in new product development: a conceptual review, research propositions and tentative model. Int. J. Innov. Manag. 11(04), 441–467 (2007)
4. Adler, P.S.: Interdepartmental interdependence and coordination: the case of the design/manufacturing interface. Organ. Sci. 6(2), 147–167 (1995)
5. Bruch, J., Bellgran, M.: Characteristics affecting management of design information in the production system design process. Int. J. Prod. Res. 51(11), 3241–3251 (2013)
6. Fjällström, S., et al.: Information enabling production ramp-up. J. Manuf. Technol. Manag. 20(2), 178–196 (2009)
7. Frishammar, J.: Managing information in new product development: a literature review. Int. J. Innov. Technol. Manag. 2(03), 259–275 (2005)
8. Bellgran, M., Säfsten, K.: Production Development: Design and Operation of Production Systems. Springer, London (2010)
9. Berglund, M., Harlin, U., Gullander, P.: Challenges in a product introduction in a cross-cultural work system - a case study involving a Swedish and a Chinese company. In: The 5th International Swedish Production Symposium, Linköping, Sweden (2012)
10. Almgren, H.: Towards a framework for analyzing efficiency during start-up: an empirical investigation of a Swedish auto manufacturer. Int. J. Prod. Econ. 60, 79–86 (1999)
11. Javadi, S., Bruch, J., Bellgran, M.: Characteristics of product introduction process in low-volume manufacturing industries: a case study. J. Manuf. Technol. Manag. 27(4), 535–559 (2016)
12. Andersen, A.-L., Bejlegaard, M., Brunø, T.D., Nielsen, K.: Investigating the impact of product volume and variety on production ramp-up. In: Bellemare, J., Carrier, S., Nielsen, K., Piller, F.T. (eds.) Managing Complexity, pp. 421–434. Springer, Cham (2016)
13. Jina, J., Bhattacharya, A.K., Walton, A.D.: Applying lean principles for high product variety and low volumes: some issues and propositions. Logist. Inf. Manag. 10(1), 5–13 (1997)
14. Almgren, H.: Pilot Production and Manufacturing Start-up in the Automotive Industry. Principles for Improved Performance. Chalmers University of Technology, Gothenburg (1999)
15. Surbier, L., Alpan, G., Blanco, E.: A comparative study on production ramp-up: state-of-the-art and new challenges. Prod. Plan. Control 25(15), 1264–1286 (2014)
16. Frishammar, J., Florén, H., Wincent, J.: Beyond managing uncertainty: insights from studying equivocality in the fuzzy front end of product and process innovation projects. IEEE Trans. Eng. Manag. 58(3), 551–563 (2011)
17. Meredith, J.: Building operations management theory through case and field research. J. Oper. Manag. 16(4), 441–454 (1998)

Large-Scale Supply Chains

A Simulation Based Approach to Investigate the Procurement Process and Its Effect on the Performance of Supply Chains

Volker Stich, Daniel Pause$^{(\boxtimes)}$, Matthias Blum, and Nina Hinrichs

Institute for Industrial Management (FIR), Aachen, Germany
daniel.pause@fir.rwth-aachen.de

Abstract. Influenced by the high dynamic of the markets the optimization of supply chains gains more importance. However, analyzing different procurement strategies and the influence of various production parameters is difficult to achieve in industrial practice. Therefore, simulations of supply chains are used in order to improve the production process. The objective of this research is to evaluate different procurement strategies in a four-stage supply chain. Besides, this research aims to identify main influencing factors on the supply chain's performance. The performance of the supply chain is measured by means of back orders (backlog). A scenario analysis of different customer demands and a Design of Experiments analysis enhance the significance of the simulation results.

Keywords: Procurement · Supply chain · System Dynamics · Inventory management · Design of Experiments

1 Introduction

Today, manufacturing companies are confronted with the influences of a dynamic environment and the continuously increasing planning complexity [1]. Reduced time to markets, rising product diversity as well as complex multi-tier and world-spanning supply chains are faced with growing inter-connectivity of production machinery, enterprise resource planning systems and manufacturing execution systems. Due to globalization, the number of market participants rises resulting in a growing competition amongst the individual companies [2]. In particular, different wage levels in developed and developing countries induce enhanced price pressure on established companies in high-wage countries [3]. In order to remain profitable as a business, the industrial enterprises in high-wage countries must identify cost carrier of the production process in order to reduce unnecessary costs. This is why companies focus on the production steps with a high share of added value and reduce the depth of production [4]. A strong trend towards reduced inventory is sensed so that components are delivered "just-in-time" (JIT) for the production. Accordingly, the process of procurement must be designed in a way which ensures a smooth production. As part

I. Nääs et al. (Eds.): APMS 2016, IFIP AICT 488, pp. 335–342, 2016.
DOI: 10.1007/978-3-319-51133-7_40

of inter-company value chains the individual view of procurement is not adequate anymore. Rather, the analysis and optimization of the whole supply chain continues to gain importance [5]. This appears to be difficult in industrial practice due to unknown interactions of various parameters in the supply chain (e.g. interactions of the reorder level of the manufacturer on the backlog of the supplier are unknown). Considering these problems, companies lack on an efficient design of their procurement processes. In order to overcome the described issue, this paper presents an approach how to tackle the problem of inefficient procurement processes. Therefore, we designed a simulation model of a four-stage supply chain (sub-supplier, supplier, manufacturer and customer) covering all steps of the procurement process. The aim of simulating a supply chain is to display known interdependencies and phenomena and thus be able to improve the decision making process. In particular, different procurement strategies are investigated and evaluated in this paper. In order to further investigate the interactions of the parameters in the supply chain, a Design of Experiments approach was used. Hereby, the interactions of the parameters are investigated and principles how to design an efficient supply chain are derived.

2   State of the Art

Due to the close link between procurement, inventory management and production a separate analysis of these sections is not sufficient. Thus, the emphasis is put on the optimization of all companies involved in the value-added process (supply chain). To investigate the cooperation and acting of a supply chain various research approaches already exist. In the following these approaches are outlined. Moizer et al. examine the advantages of a close cooperation between the manufacturer and its suppliers of a retail supply chain and the influence of efficiency and performance. A simulation was used on the basis of a trial group consisting of 12 retailers in the US. It was shown that collaboration can cut costs, risks and inventory for both the retailer and their suppliers [6]. Langroodi and Amiri investigate the choice of the most appropriate region for order placements in a five stage multi-product supply chain, consisting of a customer, an incorporate retailer, manufacturer, material distributor and supplier, in four different regions using a System Dynamics model. A scenario analysis with varying costs and demands was conducted. The model aims to minimize the costs of orders between two stages consisting of transport, price for the product and order placement and thus choose the best supplier [7]. Hishamuddin et al. analyze disruptions of supply and transportation on the system's total recovery costs and other performance measures in a three stage supply chain with multiple suppliers. Thus, different scenarios of disruptions combined by kind and location of disruption were established to evaluate system costs and stock outs. It was shown that transportation disruptions have more damaging effects than supply disruptions due to the higher lost sales quantity. In addition, disruptions in the earlier stages have a higher negative impact to the supply chain compared to later disruptions [8]. Li et al. examine the dynamic risks effects in a chemical supply chain transportation system. Therefore, a System Dynamics model was built and risk scenarios were established regarding the probability and consequence severity in order to compare order fulfillment rate, transportation and inventory level to measure the performance. The major sources of risks transpired among other as breakdown in core operations, inappropriate choice of service provider and lack of inventory management. The researchers used only a questionnaire as the input for various risk scenarios which could be a source of bias. Thus, it would be necessary to use a more extensive data source [9]. This paper enables the user to evaluate different procurement strategies and interpret the influence of various parameters. The emphasis is put on the interplant relation instead of the internal production itself.

3   Methodology

System Dynamics is a methodology for modeling, simulating, analyzing and designing dynamic and complex issues in socio-economic systems. Simulation models based on System Dynamics contain four different types of elements [10]:

1. Levels represent state variables of the system
2. Flow variables symbolize temporal change of the state variables
3. Auxiliary variables are used for decision rules describing casual relations
4. Constants are parameters to be set for the simulation.

Supply chains mainly consist of inventory (information or material) as time based variables and flows as activities (transport of material and information). Decisions steer running activities and thus the state of the system [11]. A superior aspect to other simulation models is the possibility of feedback loops within the model. Thus, it is suitable for analyzing complex problems [12]. A common way to analyze a system's behavior using System Dynamics is a scenario analysis. This was done by using the tool Vensim.

4   Description of the Simulation Model

4.1   Model Structure

The model consists of a sub supplier, a supplier, a manufacturer and a customer (Fig. 1). Between the respective supply chain partners a material flow and an information flow is taking place. The sub supplier serves as an infinite source of order items and the customer is able to create different demand situations. The supplier and the manufacturer are modelled according to a simplified business structure, which is described in the following paragraph. The business structure both of the supplier and the manufacturer are composed of an arrival warehouse for incoming goods, a quality check (QC) for the incoming goods, a production and a shipping warehouse from which the products are delivered to the customer.

The parameters contained in the model are shown in Table 1. Conducting a scenario analysis target inventory, lead time, α service level and production rate were defined for both the supplier and the manufacturer.

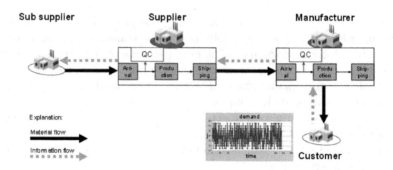

Fig. 1. Model structure

Table 1. Parameters in the simulation model for the supplier and the manufacturer

Code	Declaration	Setting range
HB	Target inventory supplier	500–2000 pieces
HB 0	Target inventory manufacturer	500–2000 pieces
L	Lead time supplier	2–14 days
L0	Lead time manufacturer	2–14 days
SG	α-Service level supplier	90–100%
SG 0	α-Service level manufacturer	90–100%
PL L	Production rate supplier	500–10,000 pieces/day
PL H	Production rate manufacturer	500–10,000 pieces/day

The customer demand is induced by an Excel based data generator. Thus, based on several parameters different demand situations can be applied to the simulation model. An expected demand and a standard variation need to be specified prior to the simulation as well as the initial situation with regard to a so-called trend, season or a constant demand.

4.2   Procurement Process

In the beginning of the simulation a certain stock is available in the shipping warehouse from which the demand is satisfied. As soon as the stock reaches the reorder level a new order is placed with the supplier. Between the time of ordering and the time of delivery the order quantity is put in the open purchase quantity. Before a new order is placed both the stock amount in the shipping warehouse and the amount in the open purchase quantity is checked if the stock moved below reorder level. The order quantity varies depending on the order policy investigated. This paper puts emphasis on a variable order point (s,S and s,Q order policy), because the order policies using a fix order point are mostly obsolete today [13]. The reorder level s, at which a new order is placed, establishes a link between the inventory level and the stochastic character of the demand. While the order quantity varies using a s,S strategy due to the stock replenishment up to a set target inventory a s,Q strategy purchases a fix quantity every time [14]. However, in this study the order quantity using a s,Q strategy can vary by the size of the backlog. In case the company is not able to meet the full demand in one period this amount is considered for the following order placed at the supplier. The reorder level is defined by the safety stock and the material which is used for the daily production. The daily production is determined by the moving average production of past periods in order to avoid a high volatility. The safety stock depends on the volatility of the demand. When the demand fluctuates substantially, a greater safety stock is necessary to ensure a smooth production. Depending on the delivery reliability towards the customer a greater safety stock has to be held. Another factor that influences the safety stock is the time it takes to restock the warehouse, defined as lead time.

5   Results of the Simulation

Different scenarios of demand situations have been investigated to identify the best order policy. The results were compared by evaluating the quantity of the backlog. This variable is linked to the service level which in turn has a direct influence on the customer's satisfaction and thus the supply chain's long-term success. In the following the scenario of a seasonal demand is exemplarily presented. Figure 2 illustrates the comparison of the ordered parts and delivered parts over time. Whereas the delivered parts do not vary between s,Q and s,S order policy, it is obvious that the backlog using the s,Q order policy is lower than the backlog of the s,S order policy. The s,Q order policy reorders the amount of backlog as well as the usual quantity and is thus able to better react on unstable

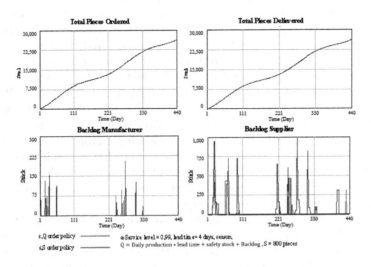

Fig. 2. Results of the scenario analysis on the basis of a seasonal demand structure

demand situations. Figure 2 also indicates that the backlog of the supplier occurs more often and in a higher quantity than the backlog of the manufacturer.

Based on the simulation results a Design of Experiments analysis was conducted to visualize and identify the factors that influence the backlog of delivered parts most. The main effects charts in Fig. 3 illustrate the examined factors (also see Table 1) and indicates if it has a positive or negative impact on the backlog when changing from a predefined minimum to a maximum value.

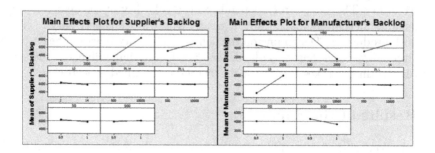

Fig. 3. Main effects charts for supplier's and manufacturer's backlog

A horizontal line implies that there is no effect on the backlog, the steeper the line the greater the influence on the backlog. It is obvious that the greatest influence on the backlog of the manufacturer and supplier are the lead time (L, L0) and the target inventory (HB, HB0). The backlog of the supplier increases with a greater lead time and a decreasing target inventory. The target inventory of the manufacturer and the lead time of the supplier have a positive influence on the backlog. A higher manufacturer's target inventory comes along with greater order quantities which leads to a higher backlog because the supplier is not prepared for these orders. The supplier can react by storing more inventories due to the negative effect as seen in the left graph (HB). Another fact which is seen in Fig. 3 is that the manufacturer's backlog is not much influenced by the actions of the supplier (lead time and target inventory). The line of the production rate between 500 and 10,000 pieces per day (PL L and PL H) as well as the α-service level (SG and SG0) in both plots are almost horizontal indicating a low influence on the backlog. After identifying the lead time and the target inventory (HB) as the major influencing factors, an analysis of the interaction between these parameters was conducted (Fig. 4). An interaction plot shows the interdependencies between particular factors when changing specific factor settings. Because an interaction can magnify or diminish main effects, evaluating interactions is extremely important.

The lines in Fig. 4 are indicating the strength of the interaction between the parameters. If the lines are parallel to each other, no interaction occurs. The more nonparallel the lines are, the greater the strength of interaction is. Evaluating the supplier's backlog it stands out that there is a great influence between the target inventories (HB) of the manufacturer and the supplier. Due to this fact it

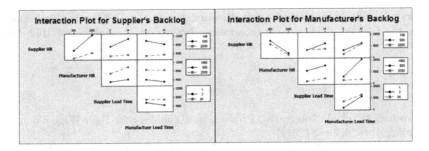

Fig. 4. Interaction between target inventory (HB) and lead time

would be advisable that the supplier and the manufacturer make arrangements on their target inventories for the purpose of a decreasing backlog. Apart from that only slight interactions are seen in the plot of the supplier's backlog. On the contrary the manufacturer's backlog shows almost no interaction between the target inventories (HB) of the manufacturer and the supplier. Even greater is the interaction between the manufacturer's target inventory (HB) and its lead time. It would therefore be advisable to choose the proper target inventory based on the lead time to the customer.

6   Conclusions and Outlook

In this paper, a simulation of a four-stage supply chain was presented and different order policies were compared. After introducing the basics of procurement and inventory as well as System Dynamics, the model structure was explained and two order policies were chosen for a comparison. It was shown that the lead time and target inventory are main causes for the supply chain's performance measured on the basis of the backlog. Due to the dependency of the backlog of the supplier by actions of the manufacturer, a close cooperation between all companies involved is advisable. The vendor managed inventory where the supplier manages the inventory and orders of the manufacturer is a method trying to decrease the backlog. In further investigations this method could be considered and implemented in the simulation model. Additionally, further parameter could be added to the model, which might influence the supply chain's performance. E.g. costs for inventory and procurement in order to further specify decision rules. Moreover, instead of using the backlog as a main measuring unit for the supply chain performance further objectives such as costs or average inventory level could be considered.

Acknowledgements. The presented research is a result of the Cluster of Excellence (CoE) on "Integrative Production Technology for High-Wage Countries" funded by Deutsche Forschungsgemeinschaft (DFG). Within the CoE "Integrative Production Technology for High-Wage Countries" several institutes at RWTH Aachen University are conducting research on fundamentals of a sustainable production strategy. The authors would like to thank the German Research Foundation DFG for the kind support within the Cluster of Excellence Integrative Production Technology for High-Wage Countries.

References

1. Brecher, C., et al.: Integrative Production Technology for High-Wage Countries. Springer, Heidelberg (2012)
2. Rushton, A., Croucher, P., Baker, P.: The Handbook of Logistics and Distribution Management: Understanding the Supply Chain. Kogan Page Publishers, London (2014)
3. Abele, E., Kluge, J., Näher, U.: Handbuch Globale Produktion. Hanser, Munich (2006)
4. Wannenwetsch, H.: Integrierte Materialwirtschaft, Logistik und Beschaffung. Springer, Heidelberg (2014)
5. Schuh, G.: Produktionsplanung und -Steuerung. Grundlagen, Gestaltung und Konzepte. Springer, Heidelberg (2006). (3., Völlig neu Bearb)
6. Elkady, G., Moizer, J., Liu, S.: A decision support framework to assess grocery retail supply chain collaboration: a system dynamics modelling approach. Innov. Manag. Technol. 5(4), 232 (2014)
7. Langroodi, R.R.P., Amiri, M.: A system dynamics modeling approach for a multi-level, multi-product, multi-region supply chain under demand uncertainty. Expert Syst. Appl. 51, 231–244 (2016)
8. Hishamuddin, H., Sarker, R., Essam, D.: A simulation model of a three echelon supply chain system with multiple suppliers subject to supply and transportation disruptions. IFAC-PapersOnLine 48(3), 2036–2040 (2015)
9. Li, C., Ren, J., Wang, H.: A system dynamics simulation model of chemical supply chain transportation risk management systems. Comput. Chem. Eng. 89, 71–83 (2016)
10. Coyle, R.G.: System Dynamics Modelling: A Practical Approach, vol. 1. CRC Press, Boca Raton (1996)
11. Aberle, E., Pfoh, H.C.: Management der Logistikkette. Kostensenkung - Leistungssteigerung - Erfolgspotential, vol. 9. Verlag (1994)
12. Wienholdt, H.: Dynamische Konfiguration der Ersatzteillogistik im Maschinen-und Anlagenbau. Verlag, Aachen (2011)
13. Gruen, O., Jammernegg, W., Kummer, S.: Grundzuege der Beschaffung, Produktion und Logistik, vol. 2. Aufl. Pearson (2010)
14. Kelle, P., Milne, A.: The effect of (s,S) ordering policy on the supply chain. Prod. Econ. 59, 113–122 (1999)

Sensor Triggered Replacement of Spare Parts: Customer Service Process Innovation

Muztoba Ahmad Khan[1], Gabriela Lais Rozati[1,2],
and Thorsten Wuest[1(✉)]

[1] West Virginia University, Morgantown, WV, USA
{mdkhan,garozati}@mix.wvu.edu, thwuest@mail.wvu.edu
[2] School of Engineering of Piracicaba, Piracicaba, Brazil

Abstract. Customer services hold an increasingly dynamic and crucial role in today's highly competitive world. It is also one of the important factors that enable companies to sustain their competitive advantage. The purpose of this study is to develop a basic model of customer service process automation, which will support the spare parts replacement procedure. The idea is to use sensors for identifying the condition of spare parts in real time and initiate an automated replacement process at the right time. A conceptual model of an integrated customer service process automation, derived from a case study, is illustrated, which emphasizes the significance of information exchange between business processes and communication between supply chain collaborators. The suggested changes for the model aim to improve the service level, machine and part life, design of the part and also to reduce human errors during ordering process, overall cost and inventory level.

Keywords: Supply chain · Sensor · Intelligent products · Service automation · Internet of things · Predictive maintenance · Spare parts replacement

1 Introduction

To thrive in today's highly competitive world, business organizations must constantly look for innovative strategies to improve their competitiveness. The advancement of Information and Communication Technology (ICT) and its creative use in business has compelled industries to revolutionize their business proposition and the way they operate [1]. Competition also has driven industries to transform into customer-focused, service-oriented organizations, irrespective of the products and services they offer. Even manufacturing firms need to be aware of the service aspects because the service component of the product-service mix, e.g. Industrial Product Service Systems, offers the best opportunity of achieving sustainable competitive advantage and revenue streams along the whole product and/or service lifecycle [2].

Among different processes in an organization, the customer service process, such as availability and supply of spare parts, after-sales service or repair service on products, affects customer satisfaction about products and purchases to a great extent [3]. The essence of today's business requires that firms interact with their customers and business partners using technology to provide these services instantaneously and

© IFIP International Federation for Information Processing 2016
Published by Springer International Publishing AG 2016. All Rights Reserved
I. Nääs et al. (Eds.): APMS 2016, IFIP AICT 488, pp. 343–350, 2016.
DOI: 10.1007/978-3-319-51133-7_41

globally. To do so, businesses can foster innovation to improve their service performance and efficiency that will ideally benefit both business and customer [4].

The aim of this paper is to (i) analyze the spare part replacement process within a company case study, (ii) identify the current shortcomings and issues and (iii) develop an innovative model of spare parts replacement process that will help to address the identified shortcomings and issues. The main idea is to use sensors to identify the current condition of spare parts and initiate an automated replacement process considering the lead time, inventory level, etc. The suggested changes for the model aim to improve the service level, machine and part life, design of the part and also to reduce human errors during ordering process, overall cost and inventory level.

This paper is organized as follows: Sect. 2 discusses the states of the art of sensor based predictive maintenance and business process reengineering. In Sect. 3, we first describe and then analyze the problems of the current spare parts replacement process within the boundary of our case study and then we propose our new customer service model. Section 4 discusses and concludes this paper.

2   State of the Art

In recent years, the utilization of sensors combined with condition monitoring is becoming more popular in many industries. Its application can be found in a variety of areas, e.g., on rotating equipment in order to measure vibration [10]; on military vehicles, mortar systems and other weapons to monitor wear-and-tear [8]; on bridges to record vibration, humidity, strain, inclination, load, cracks, etc. [7]; on diesel engines to verify the permittivity and viscosity of the fluids [9], on cars to measure tire pressure [6, 12], etc.

Sensor technology is rapidly improving and the availability of low-cost sensor is continuously growing. This enables applications and application scenarios that were not feasible until today. Condition-based monitoring, using sensors, algorithms and wireless communication, allows to identify when a part or equipment is in the process of failing and subsequently allows to take appropriate measures, e.g., repair, prior to the failure. This prevents machine downtime due to unexpected failure.

Commonly employed Preventive Maintenance (PM) schedules repairs, lubrication, adjustments, and machine rebuilds for all critical plant machinery at regular intervals, regardless of the performance of the equipment or machine. The main difference to Predictive Maintenance (PrM) is that the maintenance activities are performed at the time they are required. Based on findings from the US Department of Energy, the implementation of a functional predictive maintenance programs in the oil and gas industry has been shown, on average, 25 to 30% reduction in maintenance cost [5].

The application in the focus of this publication is the sensor based monitoring of spare parts to obtain information on current condition and identify potential issues and replacement needs at an early stage. Based on the sensor data, it is possible to predict the equipment's Residual Useful Life (RUL). The application of PrM can bring gains to all stakeholders of the supply chain, such as providing accurate lead time and preparing and executing the repair or the replacement of the part [11]. The focus of this research is not on the technical implementation of sensor-based monitoring but the combination of PrM with customer service processes and business process reengineering (BPR) of those to improve efficiency.

3   Case Study

In this section, a case study is presented to motivate the development of a new spare part replacement process. First, the case study and its background are illustrated before the current spare part replacement process, currently in use, is analyzed. Based on this analysis, existing issues of the process are identified and elaborated. Following, a new process is developed, aimed to address the previously identified issues.

3.1   Background of Case Study

The studied company is a manufacturer and service provider of construction equipment with a long history of manufacturing capital goods involving state of the art technology. This company will be referred to in the following as the Construction Equipment Manufacturer (CEM). The CEM operates globally with subsidiaries in all major markets while being headquartered in the United States. The CEM has been offering spare parts and technical field service for its equipment for a long time and has gradually added more services to its total offering. They pride themselves of superior customer service, making sure their customers will receive the best possible support to ensure their operations to run smoothly. This allowed them to build a reputation of high quality products and services, which in turn justifies their premium prices. CEM's customers include construction, agriculture, resource, energy and transportation industries. Thousands of small, medium and large organizations from these industries around the world utilize CEM's products and services.

The CEM currently offers thousands of spare parts for its equipment. In this study, the focus is on frequently replaceable parts that require minimal technical knowledge to replace (i.e. parts that can be easily diagnosed and replaced by end users). This is because a part that needs in depth technical knowledge to being serviced or repaired, will most likely require a different customer service process. Therefore, in order to being able to generalize the findings of the study, the scope is limited. Some of the most frequently replaced parts offered by CEM include, air filters, oil filters, batteries, radiators etc. Figure 1 presents the company's simplified spare parts distribution chain. We see that these subsystems are typical for a classic distribution chain and hence the case which is presented here can be understood as being generalizable to some extent.

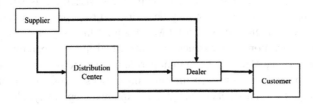

Fig. 1. CEM's simplified spare parts distribution chain.

3.2   Analyzing the Spare Part Replacement Process

In this sub-section, the current spare part replacement process employed by the CEM is analyzed in detail with the goal of identifying potential issues and potential for improvement. The current spare part replacement process is initiated by customer demand. It can be triggered in different ways; for example periodic replacement, sensor based recommendation, failure of the machine etc. Next, the customer communicates his/her order to the CEM authorized dealer (e.g., via email or phone). The placed order arrives at the dealer with the following attributes: customer information, part identity number, required quantity, due date of the order and customer tolerance for tardy job. The customer tolerance for tardy job translates into different priority levels defined by the CEM; for example, priority level 1 indicates that the due date must definitely be met with no room for delays. If the inventory level at the dealer is sufficient to fulfill the order, the parts are sent to the customer from the dealer's inventory. Otherwise, the dealer reorders the required parts from the distribution center (DC). Then the DC determines a shipping date based on the order attributes, inventory level and lead-time. The DC may ship the part from its own facility or may ask the supplier to send it to the dealer. Based on feasibility, the DC may decide to send the parts directly to the customer, avoiding shipping them to dealer's location first. Figure 2 illustrates the current spare part replacement process.

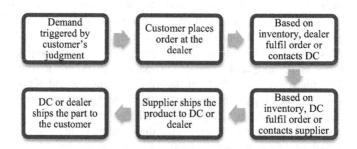

Fig. 2. Current spare part replacement process

3.3   Shortcomings and Issues of Existing Service Process

The current practice of the customer service process for frequently replaceable parts is successfully providing value to the customers. However, there is still potential for improvement and certain issues that may be addressed by a process redesign. Some of the challenges were indicated by the CEM personnel themselves as they previously emerged during operation. Other issues were identified in a comparative analysis. The identified issues are labeled as: suboptimal part and machine life, human errors during the process (especially critical was the ordering process), higher shipping cost and higher inventory level. Next, each category is explained separately, although some of them are interconnected.

Suboptimal Part and Machine Life: The replacement process starts with customer demand, which is often triggered by the customer's judgment of the condition of that part. For some parts they depend on periodic replacement. But here, any kind of misjudgment by the customer can result in too early or too late replacement of the part. For example, air filters can sustain more than its average lifespan if it works in a clean environment compared to a dusty environment. If the filter gets replaced earlier than it is supposed to, we lose the span of the RUL of the filter. Figure 3 illustrates this phenomenon. This is a waste of resources both environmentally and monetarily. If the part is overused (beyond its capability to fulfill its intended function), it may jeopardize the performance of the machine or even put other expensive parts or even the machine itself at risk.

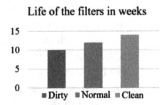

Fig. 3. Lifespan of air filters in different environments

Human Errors During Ordering Process: As most of the orders are communicated manually through emails or phone calls, there is always a risk of human errors involved. For example, the current ordering process requires the customer to provide a unique part number to the dealer. Any mistake by the customer or dealer in communicating this number correctly may result in a faulty shipment or even the production of a wrong part.

Higher Shipping Cost: Sometimes customers wait until the machine breaks down, before ordering a required spare part; this is because they do not have sufficient information about the current condition of the parts. As a consequence, to minimize the idle time of the machine, customers ask the dealer to provide the spare parts within the shortest possible time. This kind of rush translates often directly into higher shipping cost. Whether these higher shipping cost are covered by the supplier or the customer, they are still an unnecessary waste of resources.

Higher Inventory Cost: Currently the dealers need to maintain relatively high inventory levels in order to being able to react to the volatile customer demand. This is because they do not have any information about the current condition of machines used by their customers. Maintaining high inventory levels is very costly as it not only binds capital through the stored material but also as it increases the requirements towards the storage facility and workers. Besides, some of the parts may start degenerating if they are kept waiting on the shelf for a long period of time and/or under certain conditions.

Besides these four main issues presented, there are several other ones that can potentially benefit from a redesign of the process. Those include for example part design. With the implied access to real-life usage data within the new process, the part design can be improved based on a cross reference of the condition and cross-referenced environmental data. Leading to an improved design of parts for certain conditions, like application in desert (Hot, dry and dusty) environments.

3.4   Proposed Customer Service Model

In this sub-section, the previously identified issues are taken as a basis for a reengineering of the current business process. Creating an new customer service model is initiated by the need to address the issues and challenges presented in the previous section. Because the future model handles process innovation at a conceptual and theoretical level, it is called the basic model of customer service process innovation.

The main idea of the proposed model adaptations is to automate the spare parts ordering process by means of real-time, sensor-based condition monitoring of spare parts. Sensor data along with customer data, such as inventory level, location, preferred shipping method and reordering quantity etc., will be stored in the cloud. Any of the stakeholders with proper authority will have access to this data in real-time. In the new model, customer demands will be triggered automatically based on the integration of customer and sensor data stored in the cloud in the supplier specific ordering systems. Depending on predetermined individual customer preference, the system may ask the customer to approve the order before processing or may automatically start processing the order at the DC. Real-time customer and sensor data will allow the system to find best possible solution in terms of cost, accuracy, lead time, shipping, inventory and quality without the additional effort of the currently employed system. Figure 4 illustrates the new customer service process.

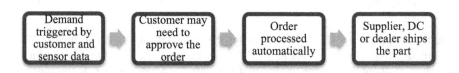

Fig. 4. New customer service process.

The proposed changes in the process will help customers to utilize the full RUL of a part. Additionally, it will prevent 'overuse' of a part beyond its RUL, which in turn will increase the overall machine life by avoiding failure during employment. The automated ordering process will also help to reduce potential human errors during the ordering and shipping process. The instantly available data will enable the system to plan a shipment before it will actually be needed at customer's inventory, which means that a slower but cheaper mode of transportation could be utilized while still meeting the customer demands on lead-time. When the CEM will have access to all of its customers' (relevant) data, it will be able to forecast demand more precisely, which in turn will help to reduce overall inventory across the whole supply chain (at both, the supplier and customer level). Better forecast will also allow to reduce the bullwhip effect.

The proposed model will be able to facilitate additional business-to-business (B2B) transactions such as invoicing and payment, reduction of procurement cost, and shortened lead-times better and more efficient than the traditional one. It may also have the potential to improve coordination and collaboration, both within and across companies due to the instantly available real-time data in the cloud. However, this has to be carefully assessed in further study and was not within the scope of this paper.

4 Discussion and Conclusion

After-sales customer services in manufacturing firms that are selling durable products have a strategic relevance in its potential contribution to a company's profitability, customer retention and product development [13]. Since customer service is a major source of competitive differentiation in today's business environment, many firms are trying to gain a competitive edge by innovating their customer service process. In this paper we have illustrated a case study of a leading Construction Equipment Manufacturer's spare part replacement process. We identified existing issues and scopes for improvement by analyzing the current process and proposed an improved conceptual model targeting these issues. The main idea of this proposed model is to automate the spare parts ordering process by means of real-time, sensor-based condition monitoring of spare parts making the data available in a cloud-based solution to all relevant stakeholders.

For small manufacturing firms this model may not be applicable because if the overall demand of spare parts remains relatively low, the proposed model might not be feasible from a financial perspective. However, some aspects, especially the direct connection to the customer's operation and access to use data might make it worthwhile.

The proposed model depends strongly on the reliability of the employed sensors. If a sensor fails to detect the current condition of spare parts with the required accuracy, then an incorrect order may be issued. However, this should not be an issue because sensor reliability is generally very high today.

Furthermore, the proposed model requires the customers to share information and data with the manufacturer. This might not be acceptable to some companies due to privacy issues. In this case it is important to ensure transparency of who has access and what data is exchanged for what application. Also there might be customers who may find this model too complicated for their operation and/or that want to remain in full control of their process and feel the automated variant is not providing that (felt) level of control.

In this paper we proposed a basic model of a customer service process innovation utilizing sensor technology and cloud infrastructure. The case study and the original spare part replacement process were analyzed and the process innovation was aimed to target the identified shortcomings. However, the proposed model only provides and outlook on the potential impact in full-scale industrial application. Further study needs to aim at operationalizing the proposed model and actually designing and implementing the technical solution, incl. sensors and cloud-connectivity to compliment the new business processes. Furthermore, additional use of the acquired data through the sensor-based condition monitoring is worthwhile to be explored. Potential areas are new services for Product Service Systems (PSS), innovations on the product design level and cross referenced analysis of the data for, e.g., environmental impact or worker safety solutions.

Acknowledgement. This work was partly funded by the Brazilian Coordination for the Improvement of Higher Education Personnel (CAPES) through the Science without Borders (CSF) fellowship program. The authors gratefully acknowledge the support of the CAPES. Finally, the authors would like to thank the reviewers for their helpful comments.

References

1. Rozendal, A., Lim, E.T., Tan, C.W.: A change for the better: realizing business-IT alignment through organizational change. In: 23rd European Conference on Information Systems (ECIS) (2015)
2. Gebauer, H., Kowalkowski, C.: Customer-focused and service-focused orientation in organizational structures. J. Bus. Ind. Mark. **27**(7), 527–537 (2012)
3. Paparoidamis, N.G., Chumpitaz, R., Ford, J.: Service quality, customer satisfaction, value and loyalty an empirical investigation in a service failure context. In: Robinson Jr., L. (ed.) Marketing Dynamism & Sustainability, p. 173. Springer, Heidelberg (2015)
4. Visnjic, I., Wiengarten, F., Neely, A.: Only the brave: product innovation, service business model innovation, and their impact on performance. J. Prod. Innov. Manag. **33**(1), 36–52 (2016)
5. Predictive maintenance: is the timing right for predictive maintenance in the manufacturing sector? Roland Berger, p. 5 (2014)
6. Pohl, A., Ostermayer, G., Reindl, L., Seifert, F.: Monitoring the tire pressure at cars using passive SAW sensors. IEEE Ultrason. Symp. **1**, 471–474 (1997)
7. Casas, J.R., Cruz, P.J.: Fiber optic sensors for bridge monitoring. J. Bridge Eng. **8**(6), 362–373 (2003)
8. U.S. Army Awards. http://www.thefreelibrary.com/U.S. Army Awards Augusta Systems $1. 18 Million Task Order to Monitor...-a0168777922
9. Scherer, M., Arndt, M., Bertrand, P., Jakoby, B.: Fluid condition monitoring sensors for diesel engine control. In: Sensors, pp. 459–462. IEEE (2004)
10. Hashemian, H.M.: Wireless sensors for predictive maintenance of rotating equipment in research reactors. Ann. Nucl. Energy **38**(2), 665–680 (2011)
11. Compare, M., Zio, E.: Predictive maintenance by risk sensitive particle filtering. IEEE Trans. Reliab. **63**(1), 134–143 (2014)
12. Brady, S., Van Order, D., Sharp, A.: Advanced sensors and applications: commercial motor vehicle tire pressure monitoring and maintenance. No. FMCSA-RRT-13-021 (2014)
13. Saccani, N., Johansson, P., Perona, M.: Configuring the after-sales service supply chain: a multiple case study. Int. J. Prod. Econ. **110**, 52–69 (2007)

Simulation and Optimization Models in a Business Game for Decision-Making in Logistics Processes

Marco Aurelio Butzke[1], Anete Alberton[2], Jeancarlo Visentainer[1],
Solimar Garcia[3(✉)], and Irenilza de Alencar Nääs[3]

[1] Unidavi, Rio do Sul, Brazil
{marco,jv}@unidavi.edu.br
[2] Univali, Itajaí, Brazil
anete@univali.br
[3] UNIP, São Paulo, Brazil
solimargarcia10@gmail.com, irenilza@gmail.com

Abstract. Business games using simulation and optimization models can help users to find out solutions to complex management problems and develop critical and strategic thinking skills. The main goal of this paper is to present the application of a business game provided with a simulation and optimization model for decision-making in logistics processes, including total cost, calculated results of costs and trade-offs involved in the logistics business operations. Furthermore, it is expected that the developed models can contribute to the use of business games in teaching and learning process with a focus on professional preparation of students for the labor market. In the end, it is observed that this tool may be useful for training professionals and students.

Keywords: Business games · Logistic processes · Optimization

1 Introduction

The importance of applying business games as a teaching strategy can help to evaluate students' results, and analyze the perceptions of a pedagogical tool in the teaching process, from the perspective of the knowledge, acquired and the content of learning with interaction and immediate feedback. Simulations and business games have produced a substantial impact on concepts and teaching applications and help overcome limitations of traditional methods [1].

In 2010, the cost of managing the global supply chain reached between 7.7% and 9.3% of GDP [2]. Therefore, any small improvement in the chain has the potential benefit to society, which is why the modeling and analysis of logistics systems stimulated worldwide interest [3].

M.A. Butzke—The authors wish to thank CAPES and CNPQ, and the Universitat Politècnica de València (UPV).

I. Nääs et al. (Eds.): APMS 2016, IFIP AICT 488, pp. 351–359, 2016.
DOI: 10.1007/978-3-319-51133-7_42

The simulation technologies have proven to be a great tool for modeling complex environments [4]. One kind of simulation for processes involving logistics and production is the business game [5]. The simulations can help analyzing the resulting events of logistical decisions and how they influence on the costs and their impact on organizational performance in a controlled environment to conduct experiments without risk or loss [6,7]. Business games blend skill, opportunity, and strategy to simulate aspects of reality [8].

Simulation softwares have high ability to replicate uncertainty, especially when it comes from discrete event simulation in which can handle the variability and uncertainties [9]. Despite these advantages, there are few examples of simulation games in supply chain education, whose main example is the Beer game that was introduced by MIT in 1960 as an industrial dynamic exercise [10]. The aim of this paper is to present the application of a simulation and optimization model in a business game for decision-making in logistics processes.

2   Theoretical Framework

Simulations challenge users to find out solutions for complex management problems, therefore they develop their critical and strategic thinking skills; if teachers aim to prepare students for the labor market, business games can contribute to improve students learning [11]. The simulation technologies have proven to be a competent way to analyze complex systems, allowing the changes and effects of processes and presenting predictions in a simpler way [4].

Deling et al. presented the analysis of logistics problems, considering the distribution and allocation of resources through a simulation model combined with optimization and showed the advantages of this method compared to simple mathematical analytic method to study the location of distribution centers [12]. As a kind of combination of modeling simulation and optimization methods to solve the problem of location regarding the distribution center was presented to Thiers and McGinnis [3]. According to the authors, this solution depends on the optimization of the system and there is no mathematical formula that can express the decision variables, and can be proved as an effective tool to solve such problems. The study of Feng and Ma, Arisha et al. [8,13] shows that the simulation method is closer to the real situation when applied to the location of distribution centers compared to the analytical method.

The optimization models applied to business games can help produce the best answers to the simulated problems in a given scenario [14]. The decision variables in the optimization model serve as ideal parameters to help in decision-making when using simulation softwares [11].

The construction of a simulation model must be based on answering important questions to provide fast and lower cost responses, resulting in a powerful and useful tool to improve the decision-making process. The impact analysis is a differential in the simulation process.

Business game as one of the types of simulation for processes involving logistics and production; therefore, managers can work in a simulated world interactively [5]. Simulations in logistics, especially in supply chain management have already been applied for a long time. The Beer Game, one of the most common in logistics, helps students to manage an efficient supply chain and to solve problems [15].

Davis et al. [16] shows the use of web application for games as a quality educational tool also for the supply chain, which encourages collaborative learning. The development of online technologies, particularly social networks, including improvements in the form of interaction between students that can be made into high-quality virtual environments [17], besides the advantage of being cheaper than simulation through softwares [14].

The application of online simulation games to teach supply chain management allows students to actively participate in the learning process, as well recognize the impact of their decisions on the execution of activities [8]. Modeling and simulation are the appropriate tools to measure cost reduction, increase gains between each step and measure the effects of these relationships predicting the possible outcomes before implementing a new process. Likewise, modeling and simulation identify points of improvement aiming to optimize them.

Optimization models can help to produce the best responses to simulated problems in a scenario [3]; decision variables in optimization model serve as optimum parameters to complement decision-making on applications for simulation use [12]. The optimization models when used in conjunction with simulated scenarios can contribute to the learning process of the participants of business games, which are proposed in modeled experimental environments in a simplified way [6,12]. However, business games must reflect the complexity of the reality of modern business, where decisions have to be taken in a systematic and integrated way.

3   Methodology

This descriptive and qualitative research analyzed the decision-making process in logistics processes and proposed a solution through a business game, addressed by simulation and optimization models developed in previous studies [4,18], which classifies itself as deductive research regarding outcomes that was applied in a business game called Entersim created to contribute to the teaching and learning process.

Regarding the logic, this research is classified as applied because it uses the findings to existing problems through the implementation of simulation and optimization models in a business game considering the decision-making scenario in logistics processes. In relation to the result, we can classify the research as deductive considering a model was developed from existing theories and concepts, and implemented in business games for contributing to the teaching and learning process.

The construction of a simulation model must be based on answering important questions to provide rapid and lower cost responses, resulting in a useful and appropriate tool. The optimization models, when used together with simulated scenarios can contribute to the learning of participants in a business game. In the proposed game metrics were defined for calculating the logistics costs of supply and distribution, product manufacturing, plant, and the acquisition value of raw materials. In addition, it was established efficiency levels and delivery times of raw materials and finished products, complemented by invoice delivered orders. Students could use the following options in decision-making toward logistics processes: manufacturing plant, production framework, supplier selection, transport modes for supply and distribution, freight, acquisition of lots, invoicing orders and stocks inventory.

The business game Entersim is developed on the Internet on a centralized server, Cloud Computing at Jelastic. The proposed simulation and optimization models intend to complement the use of business games to assist decision-making in an environment of complexity, with immediate feedback and the challenge of achieving the optimized proposed goal through a mathematical model.

4 Implementation of Simulation and Optimization Models in a Business Game

The business game Entersim was designed to be used as a simulator of environments in a company, which involves the company functions and organizational levels, whose business model used was a medium-sized company manufacturer of jeans, which manufactures six products, uses three categories of raw materials and receives orders from 27 Brazilian capitals such as business model. Based on simulated data, students choose the location of the plant installation and logistics related to the acquisition of raw materials and delivery of orders previously demanded, as well as the adjustments necessary in the production framework. Index and set of index represent the entities that set the model, such as products, cities, working days, production units, modes of transport and raw materials, which will be subject to the decision-making. The parameters are information that is fed into the process of simulation.

The results of the application of the formulas were produced from the decision variables that served as a basis for decision-making in the business game simulation process and the generation of the results of the optimization model performed to find out the better solution between the possibilities of the presented scenario.

The simulation model developed in business games allows experiments in a fictional situation, as well are used for training people to improve decision-making in complex and dynamic environments, in order to gain experience to perform in the labor market.

The determination of amounts related to logistics costs proposed in the business game simulator are the following ones: Gross revenue, Cost of raw material acquisition, Inbound cost, Raw material stock, Labor cost, Fixed cost, Leasing manufacturing plant, Outbound cost and Finished goods stock. Next, it will be presented the optimization model designed for parallel use to the business game. The model implemented in the business game to simulate decision-making in logistics processes is shown in Fig. 1.

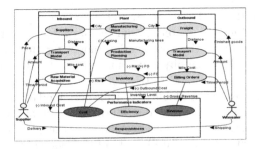

Fig. 1. Simulation model for business game

The construction of the optimization model was initiated by the logistic plant process, in which it was determined the quantity of product to be produced in the day and per unit of production. In the optimization process were considered the objective formula (1) and the demand of restrictions (2), orders (3), delivery (4), daily production by product (5) and unit (6), the amount of product per production unit (7), and the amount of production time in the shift (8).

$$CTPlnt_{pcdu} = Min \sum_{p} \sum_{c} \sum_{d} \sum_{u}$$
$$\left(Csmp_{p} + \left(\frac{Cmod_{u}}{Hrtr_{u}} * Qthr_{pu} \right) + \left(\frac{Cfix_{u}}{Hrtr_{u}} * Qthr_{pu} \right) \right) \tag{1}$$

$$\sum_{c} \sum_{d} \sum_{u} CTPlnt_{pcdu} \geq Dmnd_{p} \ \forall \ p \in Prod\,(p) \tag{2}$$

$$\sum_{d} \sum_{u} CTPlnt_{pcdu} \geq Qtpd_{cp} \ \forall \ p \in Prod\,(p)\,, \ c \in City\,(c) \tag{3}$$

$$\sum_{d} \sum_{u} CTPlnt_{pcdu} \geq Qtpd_{cp} \ \forall \ p \in Prod\,(p)\,, \ c \in City\,(c) \tag{4}$$

$$\sum_{c} \sum_{u} (CTPlnt)_{pcdu} \geq \sum_{p} (Qthr)_{pu} * (Hrtr_{u}) \forall \ p \ \epsilon \ Prod(p), d \ \epsilon \ Dias(d) \tag{5}$$

$$\sum_{c} \sum_{p} (CTPlnt)_{pcdu} \geq \sum_{p} (Qthr)_{pu} * (Hrtr_{u}) \forall \ u \ \epsilon \ Unid(u), d \ \epsilon \ Dias(d) \tag{6}$$

$$\sum_{c} (CTPlnt)_{pcdu} \geq (Qthr)_{pu} * (Hrtr_{u}) \forall p \ \epsilon \ Prod(p), d \ \epsilon \ Dias(d), u \ \epsilon \ Unid(u) \tag{7}$$

$$\sum_{c} \sum_{p} (CTPlnt)_{pcdu} x \left(\frac{1}{(Qthr)_{pu}} \right) \leq (Hrtr_{u}) \ \forall \ u \ \epsilon \ Unid(u), d \ \epsilon \ Dias(d) \tag{8}$$

At the end of the optimization routine from the logistical process plant resulted in the need for raw materials and the days that customer orders could be delivered. Accordingly, the optimization model for the logistics process of supply was developed by the objective function (9), by the variable inventory control of raw material (10) and restrictions need of raw material (11), by the security level (12), by the availability of transport modal (13) and the supply provider (14). The model of logistic distribution process was developed with the object-formula (15), with restrictions demand (16), the quantity of products per day and customer city (17) and availability of the mode of transport (18).

$$(CTAbst)_{tcdm} = Min \sum_t \sum_c \sum_d \sum_m (Vlun_{ct} + (Vlun_{ct} * Icms_c) +$$
$$\left(\frac{(Dist_{cm} * Cskm_m)}{Qlmp_t * Vlmp_t * Capc_m} \right) + \left(\frac{Txem_m}{Qlmp_t} * \frac{Vlmp_t}{Capc_m} \right) \tag{9}$$

$$Invt_{tcdm} = Efmp_{dt} + Abst_{tcd} - Cons_{dt} \tag{10}$$

$$\sum_c \sum_d \sum_m CTAbst_{tcdm} \geq Necs_t \ \forall \ t \ \epsilon \ Mtpr(t) \tag{11}$$

$$CTAbst_{tcdm} \leq Aces_{cm} * Abst_{tcd} \ \forall t \epsilon Mtpr(t), c \epsilon \ City(c), d \ \epsilon Dias(d), m \ \epsilon \ Mode(m) \tag{12}$$

$$Invt_{tcdm} \geq Nvmp_t \ \forall \ t \ \epsilon \ Mtpr(t), c \ \epsilon \ City(c), d \ \epsilon \ Dias(d), m \ \epsilon \ Mode(m) \tag{13}$$

$$\sum_m CTAbst_{tcdm} \leq Abst_{tcd} \ \forall \ t \ \epsilon \ Mtpr(t), c \ \epsilon \ City(c), d \ \epsilon \ Dias(d) \tag{14}$$

$$CTDstr_{pcdm} = Min \sum_p \sum_c \sum_d \sum_m \left(\left(\frac{Dstr_{pcd}}{Qlpr_p} * \frac{Vlpr_p}{Capc_m} \right) * \frac{Dist_{cm} * Cskm_m}{Qtpd_{cp}} \right) \tag{15}$$

$$\sum_c \sum_d \sum_m CTDstr_{pcdm} \geq Dmnd_p \ \forall \ p \ \epsilon \ Prod(p) \tag{16}$$

$$\sum_m CTDstr_{pcdm} \geq Dstr_{pcd} \ \forall \ p \ \epsilon \ Prod(p), c \ \epsilon \ City(c), d \ \epsilon \ Dias(d) \tag{17}$$

$$CTDstr_{pcdm} \leq Aces_{cm} * Dstr_{pcd} \ \forall p \epsilon Prod(p), c \epsilon \ City(c), d \epsilon Dias(d), m \epsilon Mode(m) \tag{18}$$

In spite of alternative combinations involving the transports and activities related to suppliers and customers were designed in a simplified simulated environment they provided students a large number of possibilities at the time of decision-making. Additionally, it is possible to use the simulation models to evaluate each step the influence of decisions in costs and indicators. Furthermore, the optimization model helped to indicate how close the student was from the optimized solution with the data previously informed.

In the application of business games, some aspects such as knowledge of the operations of a company and problem-solving were considered important in the teaching-learning process. There was also conformity and consciousness of some students on learning in the decision-making process: decisions can influence the results more than others, "it was observed that small details may generates different paths and outcomes".

The use of simulation and optimization models in this research allowed that the options for decision-making and the results produced were built from a scientific perspective and not empirically. The simulation models helps to improve the decision-making process with fictitious situations to represent the reality of the business environment and students can virtually view the company's daily routine and interact in the process. Moreover, the optimization model helps finding out the best decisions based on the simulated scenario and to indicate the goal to be achieved in the teaching process.

5   Final Remarks

The use of simulation and optimization models in business games helps in the decision-making process and enhances the perception of students in how to manage a business. These models define the goal that students should reach and also demonstrate applied sciences to decision model [12]. Through the application of these models in business games it is possible to predict performance accurately within a certain range than to implement one optimal solution based on a fixed decision model [5]. The ways of using current technology platforms for business games have allowed modifying the evolution of the interaction and immediate feedback on the decision-making results. Therefore, participants will have a good opportunity to apply their learning outcomes in terms of decision analysis of business situation [14].

In this research, students would like to play again and recognize the contribution of business simulation games in learning process about decision-making. Students enjoy to play games and when they use business games may see the impact of decision immediately [8]. Educators are constantly striving to bring management education to close to reality [11]. Thus, Students perceived that over the use of business simulation games is possible to increase the knowledge about how to solve problems in logistics and how to operate the inner workings. Moreover, they recognize benefits but consider that it is difficult for them to truly understand the challenges and find out solutions [15], mainly in aspects related to instructions and the time available to perform the teaching activity.

Finally, business games are used as a teaching strategy at universities and the discussion on the use of this active learning methodology, as well its impact and contribution to the teaching process, has produced studies that demonstrate the importance of their evolution and adaptation to the innovations of information technology and communication. Furthermore, as suggestions for continuing this research, new routines as the decision model of implementation and financial module, reverse logistics and sustainability could be carried out.

References

1. Ruben, B.D.: Simulations, games, and experience-based learning. Simul. Gaming **30**(4), 498–505 (1999)
2. Zhao, E.: Business Logistics Costs Dropped in 2009. The Wall Street Journal (2010)
3. Thiers, G., McGinnis, L.: Logistics systems modeling and simulation. In: Proceedings of Winter Simulation Conference (WSC), pp. 1531–1541. IEEE (2011)
4. Arisha, A., Young, P.: Intelligent simulation-based lot scheduling of photolithography toolsets in a wafer fabrication facility. In: Proceedings of Conference on Winter Simulation, pp. 1935–1942. IEEE (2004)
5. Tarokh, M.J., Golkar, M.: Supply chain simulation methods. In: 2006 IEEE International Conference on Service Operations and Logistics, and Informatics, pp. 448–454. IEEE (2006)
6. Keys, B., Wolfe, J.: The role of management games and simulations in education and research. J. Manag. **16**(2), 307–336 (1990)
7. Melnyk, S.A., Rodrigues, A., Ragatz, G.L.: Using simulation to investigate supply chain disruptions. In: Zsidisin, G.A., Ritchie, B. (eds.) Supply Chain Risk. International Series in Operations Research & Management Science, vol. 124, pp. 103–122. Springer, New York (2009). doi:10.1007/978-0-387-79934-6_7
8. Feng, K., Ma, G.: Evaluating two online simulation games in an undergraduate supply chain management course. Rev. Bus. Res. **2**(9), 67–75 (2009)
9. Mahfouz, A., Hassan, S.A., Arisha, A.: Practical simulation application: evaluation of process control parameters in twisted-pair cables manufacturing system. Simul. Model. Pract. Theory **18**(5), 471–482 (2010)
10. Iyer, A., Seshadri, S., Vasher, R.: Toyota Supply Chain Management: A Strategic Approach to Toyota's Renowned System, 1st edn. McGraw-Hill Education, New York (2009)
11. Doyle, D., Brown, F.W.: Using a business simulation to teach applied skills: the benefits and the challenges of using student teams from multiple countries. J. Eur. Ind. Train. **24**(6), 330–336 (2000)
12. Deling, L., Liping, H., Zhongwei, L., Xuping, W.: Logistics distribution center location decision-making model based on simulation optimization. In: Proceedings of International Conference on E-Business and E-Government, ICEE 2010, pp. 3384–3387. IEEE Computer Society, Washington, DC (2010)
13. Arisha, A., Abo-Hamad, W., Ismail, K.: Integrating balanced scorecard and simulation modelling to improve emergency department performance in Irish hospitals. In: Proceedings of Winter Simulation Conference. IEEE (2010)
14. Tobail, A., Crowe, J., Arisha, A.: Learning by gaming: supply chain application. In: Proceedings Winter Simulation Conference, pp. 3935–3946. IEEE (2011)
15. Sparling, D.: Simulations and supply chains: strategies for teaching supply chain management. Supply Chain Manag. **7**(5), 334–342 (2002)

16. Davis, D.M., Gottschalk, T.D., Davis, L.K.: High-performance computing enables simulations to transform education. In: Winter Simulation Conference. IEEE, Piscataway (2007)
17. Syrjakow, M., Berdux, J., Szczerbicka, H.: Interactive web-based animations for teaching and learning. In: Proceedings of Conference on Winter Simulation, vol. 2, pp. 1651–1659. IEEE (2000)
18. Alemany, M., Boj, J., Mula, J., Lario, F.C.: Mathematical programming model for centralised master planning in ceramic tile supply chains. Int. J. Prod. Res. **48**(17), 5053–5074 (2010)

Sustainable Manufacturing

Human-Centric Manufacturing Workplaces: Aiming at Increasing Attractiveness and User Experience

Paola Fantini[1(✉)], Marta Pinzone[1], Marco Taisch[1], and Jaume Altesa[2]

[1] Department of Management, Economics and Industrial Engineering,
Politecnico di Milano, Milan, Italy
{paola.fantini,marta.pinzone,marco.taisch}@polimi.it
[2] Alstom Transporte SA, Santa Perpetua de Mogada, Barcelona, Spain
jaume.altesa-cabanas@transport.alstom.com

Abstract. The pursuit of Human-Centric Manufacturing Workplaces is one of the strategic objectives of the industrial and academic research community, as a contribution to the creation of sustainable and attractive jobs in production. The concepts of User experience (UX), Interactive Virtual Prototyping (VP) and the connected scientific background can lead to new perspectives and methods for the design and evaluation of future workstations. The traditional focus on productivity and ergonomics, might be extended to encompass multisensory features and to consider the different usage stages in order to improve the experience of the workers and contribute to enhance the attractiveness of manufacturing workplaces. The application case of a train manufacturer's is taken to exemplify possible results of the application of this UX and VP-inspired approach to the design of Human-Centric Manufacturing Workplaces.

Keywords: Manufacturing · User experience · Workplaces

1 Manufacturing Jobs and Workplaces

The manufacturing industry plays an important role in the European economy in terms of GDP (16% of EU GDP) and employment (30 millions).

Although currently decreasing, unemployment is a major concern in Europe: Eurostat estimates that 23.887 million men and women in the EU-28 were unemployed in February 2015 of which 4.850 million young persons (under 25 [1]). Interestingly, in spite of the high level of unemployment, manufacturers find difficulties in filling jobs [2–5].

As a consequence, attracting skilled workers is becoming one of the top priorities for industrial companies and the creation of socially sustainable, safe and appealing workplaces is among the main objectives of the strategic multi-annual research roadmap produced by the European Factory of the Future Research Association [6].

© IFIP International Federation for Information Processing 2016
Published by Springer International Publishing AG 2016. All Rights Reserved
I. Nääs et al. (Eds.): APMS 2016, IFIP AICT 488, pp. 363–370, 2016.
DOI: 10.1007/978-3-319-51133-7_43

2 Motivation for Human-Centric Manufacturing Workplaces (HCMW)

The emphasis on Human-Centric Manufacturing Workplaces (HCMW) derives from different objectives and needs. The adaptation of work demands to the physical and cognitive capabilities of the workers, especially for older operators and disabled people [6] is required to increase manufacturing performances - flexibility, agility, and competitiveness - by leveraging the full potential and the experience of each individual. There is also an emerging value orientation towards considering workers' wellbeing in manufacturing settings, besides considering the pure execution of tasks [7] and towards motivating potential employees, especially young people, to even consider working in the factories. Furthermore, there is recognition that workplaces must evolve in relationship to technological and organizational changes and taking into account the needs of employees to balance privacy, collaboration and work objectives [8].

3 Design Concepts

Human-centric and personalized work design has been so far addressed mostly with the aim of adapting the geometry, the functional demand, the knowledge and skills requirements, besides the occupational health and safety aspects, failing to consider the complexity of the interaction between human beings and their environment. There is in fact a continuous and dynamic interaction between employees and their workspace, encompassing light, temperature, noise, vibrations, gases and particulates in the air, pressure, etc. which generates physiological and psychological effects on the workers [9].

Industrial firms, confronted with the challenge of filling the skills gaps by attracting young people to manufacturing jobs and improving the workers' wellbeing, should elaborate new approaches to the design of jobs and workstations aiming at improving the individual experience, taking into account inter-individual differences (gender, anthropometrics) and intra-individual differences (physiological and psycological states) [9], instead of statistic data referred to a population of employees.

Design of consumers goods might provide inspiration and lesson learnt transferable to the industrial design. If the aim is creating attractive workplaces, the workers should not be considered only as users, but should be equated to customers. Research on interactive products has mainly focused on functionalities, but an increasing attention has been recently given to the user experience (UX), as the notion of capturing the wide variety and emerging effects of technology in use, including emotional, affective and experiential factors [10]. The HCMW design should therefore focus on the user experience (UX) of the workers and on the perceived value, that encompasses different aspects, such as innovativeness, customization, usability, coolness and the emotional content.

Studies have referred to sensory modalities and to time as relevant dimension of analysis on user-product interaction (i.e. [12, 13]).

In fact, if consumers' experience with products is always multisensory [12], the concept can easily be extended to workers interaction with their workplace. To the knowledge of the authors, there are no studies on the experience of the workers with the workstation that take into account emotions, aesthetics, and symbolism. However, potentially, there seem to be similarities and differences between the interactions that workers experience with their equipment and tools, and those that the consumers live with certain types of goods. For instance, within the consumers' products analysed [12], some home appliances or even vehicles can be considered as tools to perform some tasks and therefore can be assimilated to industrial equipment and tools, at least to some extent. Home appliances such as coffee maker or washing machines or even vehicles, for example, have been analysed under the perspective of sensorial dominance and usage stage. Findings show that vision is the most important modality at the beginning, but after one week of usage other modalities gain increasing relevance [12], in particular touch and audition.

The design of user experience, and of multisensory user experience, is acquiring increasing recognition not only for computer-based systems but for any kind of system users interact with [14].

Among the different methods and tools available in order to integrate user experience concern in the design phase of products, VP appear as extremely valuable. Virtual prototypes, equipped to recreate all the senses actually involved in the real interaction, can in fact enable capturing the UX from the users during the system design, before building the physical system [14]. In some cases also complex simulations Human in the Loop can support the prediction of UX, but they require the existence and availability of human models incorporating interaction behaviour [15].

4   Pursuing Attractiveness and User Experience in HCMW

The stimuli and the concepts of the Interactive Virtual Prototyping lead to considering an extension of the perspective adopted to design HCMW with the aim of improving the attractiveness of manufacturing jobs. In particular, the traditional perspective of focusing on productivity and ergonomics could be enhanced by integrating two additional perspectives considering the time dimensions along the usage stages and the multisensory dimension of user experience.

4.1   Productivity and Ergonomics

Workspace design obviously needs to leverage all the pre-existing knowledge accumulated especially with reference to assembly lines, within manufacturing systems. Available frameworks and methodologies consider technological as well as environmental variables to design and optimize productivity and ergonomics (i.e. [17]).

In particular, workplace design include the definition of the geometrical disposition of the working area, the place were the parts are placed for picking with respect to the worker location and posture has to be defined. Furthermore the level of physical or cognitive automation provided through supporting devices such i.e. lifting or motorized wire carousel devices or such as displays, "wearables" etc.

This aspects have been extensively studied to pursue workers health, safety and wellbeing but without addressing more hedonistic and emotional characteristics that may influence workers experience and thus workplaces attractiveness.

4.2   Usage Stages

The literature on user experience with consumers' goods has identified significant stages on the time dimension that, depending on the specific goods, may be: the first encounter, the purchase, the first use, the use in the first week, etc.

Concerning workstations, the time dimension can be considered as characterized by the following stages:

- **acquaintance**. This corresponds to the "getting familiar" stage [13], in which the users get to know the workstation for the first time and receive the first impressions. The pre-purchase and buying stages are out of this scope as undertaken by organizational roles other than the workers;
- **configuration/personalization**. This stage, which is not always meaningful for consumers goods, is relevant for workstations with personalization features;
- **usage/operation**. This stage can be subdivided in periods to capture the different user-product interaction patterns that usually shift in time, as for sensorial dominance [12];
- **end-of-shift resetting**. This stage may be required for shared goods. In manufacturing systems, workers' assignment to the workstations changes according to the shifts, job rotation mechanisms and other issues. According to the degree of personalization implemented, it might be convenient to incorporate a resetting functionality. As an alternative, the configuration/personalization might directly overwrite any previous setting.

4.3   Sensorial Experience

The influence of the sensorial characteristics on user experience have been analysed with reference to consumers' goods and attributes that produce positive effects have been identified, however the overall feeling of pleasantness of a good seems to be quite difficult to predict and therefore to define guideline for design [16].

The difficulty seems due to the complex combinations of stimuli [18] and sensorial experiences and to situational variables, symbolic meanings, as well as the impact of cognitive beliefs and expectations [16].

Workplaces differ from consumers' goods under several perspectives, and are subject to several constraints related to productivity and ergonomics, different standards and norms. Furthermore they are permeated with meanings related to the work and social context.

Finally they imply a long term, recurring, regulated interaction with the users.

Research on HCMW might potentially highly benefit from the lesson learnt of consumers' goods to encompass the usage stage and multisensory dimensions.

IVP could support the design of workplaces and allow quick and affordable acquisition of the users' feedback, although the development of human model would be needed in order to predict the workers' interaction and experience along the different stages of usage.

5   HCMW Design Application Case

5.1   Productivity and Ergonomic

Research on human-centric workplaces [19] has addressed a case taken from the train manufacturing process: the vertical wiring mock-up, which consists in the preparation of the electrical wires prior to their installation in the trains. The preparation job requires several hours and is performed in the electrical department of the manufacturer. The current workplace is illustrated in the picture on the left in Fig. 1.

Fig. 1. Current workplace

The human-centric approach has led to the re-designing these workplaces with novel equipment adjustable according to the morphologic characteristics of each individual worker, as illustrated in the central and right pictures of the figure.

This result, developed in a FP7 funded research [20], represents a significant advancement with reference to the AS IS situation and to design ergonomics, as it allows taking into account individual characteristics of the workers.

5.2   Exploring Multi-sensorial and Lifecycle Oriented Re-design

Identification of Additional Features to Workplace Re-design. The human-centric re-design of the workplace described in Sect. 5.1 might be enhanced by leveraging the knowledge, methods and tools developed in the field of virtual prototyping and user experience for consumers' goods.

In particular, a proposal to extend the perspective to HCMW design by leveraging the multisensory and usage-phase related concepts stimulate design research to explore additional features for the workstation to be validated through VP.

As an example, through VP it would be possible to predict the interaction and acquire workers' feedback with reference to different design options addressing the configuration/personalization phase of the workstation: different types of vertical adjustment mechanisms with associated friction, visual, acoustic and/or haptic feedback to guide upward or downward the vertical movement and to signal the achievement of the correct position etc.

Similarly, through VP it would be possible to evaluate and validate alternative design solutions with reference to the usage/operation phase. Possible examples may include for example equipping the workstation with auxiliary devices to rule the local lighting (intensity, orientation, colour), the heating/cooling, or to create a pleasant sounds cape and - why not? - aromatic odour waves. Furthermore, multisensory stimuli could be possibly associated to the completion of individual tasks or work phases in order to provide feedback to the worker and underline the progress of his/her work.

Initial Validation of Concepts and Features. The concepts developed and the design features preliminary identified ground on the assumptions that making workplace more attractive is becoming a priority for industrial enterprises and that theories and techniques can be derived from the design of consumers' goods and applied in manufacturing environments in order to improve the user experience of the operators. Before going further in the development of these notions, it is therefore important to start a validation process with the relevant stakeholders. In the case of the train manufactures, three main roles were identified to this purpose: the Engineer in charge of the design, the Production Manager and the Operator. For each role, a representative, all involved in the design or management or operations of vertical mock-up, with more than five years experience in the role were selected to be confronted with a set of questions aiming at understanding the alignment of the goal of making the working experience more enjoyable with the objectives of their roles; the relevance of the identified concepts; the relative importance of the workplace lifecycle phases and of the multisensorial features; and finally, to what extent the results of the proposed approach are perceived as relevant in comparison with other possible interventions, such as social networks or smart devices to support the operators during their work.

Results. The orientation of the company, as perceived by the representatives of the different roles, seems to prioritize safety and ergonomics objectives overall; productivity, workers well being and flexibility appear to be important for all the roles, capital expenditure and operational expenditure only for the Production Manager, and work pleasantness important for the Operator, very important for the Production Manager and not important for the Engineer.

The human centric re-design is considered as more beneficial for the company and for the workers than the use of wearable equipment by the Engineer and Production Manager, but not at all by the Operator.

The importance of all the phases of the workplace lifecycle is equally important for the Production Manager, and for the Operator, but for the resetting, which is considered as not really important by the latter. The Engineer however has a clear ladder of decreasing significance from the initial phase of acquaintance, to the usage, to the configuration and finally to the resetting.

The appreciation of the multi-sensorial features proposed appears to favour the Lightening and HVAC personalization. Sound design appears to be considered important only by the Engineer, while the tactile features are disregarded. The evaluation of the Operator in particular sharply distinguishes between these two characteristics as very important and the others as not important at all.

Finally, the Human centric re-design of the workplace as a whole is considered more important than the availability of smart devices. However, the Operator would rather prefer the availability of social networks.

Overall these results appear to confirm the relevance of the human-centric re-design of the workplace, and of some multi- sensorial features. However, there is no clear indication about the significance of the different phases of the lifecycle and for sound and tactile design features, as shortly described.

6 Conclusions

The design of Human-Centric Manufacturing Workplaces may potentially benefit from the lesson learnt in the design of consumers' goods. In principle, the traditional perspective on the design of industrial goods might be extended to create attractive workplaces. A preliminary attempt to apply this comprehensive perspective to the application case of a vertical mock up wiring workstation for a train manufacturer seems to lead to interesting, unexplored possibilities. The preliminary results supports only the relevance of the matter and do not provide indications or confirm that enhancing the design methods with lifecycle consideration and tactile and sound characteristics is valuable. However these preliminary results suffer from the limitation of using short verbal descriptions to propose the different design alternatives to the stakeholders. An avenue for future research could stem from the use of VP to better capturing the feedback of the operators and other actors in the interaction with alternative design options, as suggested by the VP literature.

References

1. Eurostat Statistics: Explained - Unemployment statistics. http://ec.europa.eu/eurostat/statistics-explained/index.php/Unemployment_statistics
2. Accenture, Manufacturing Institute: Accenture 2014 Manufacturing Skills and Training Study - Out of Inventory Skills Shortage Threatens Growth for US Manufacturing (2014)
3. Deloitte, The Manufacturing Institute: The Skills Gap in U.S. Manufacturing (2015)
4. Deloitte, The Manufacturing Institute: Boiling Point? The Skills Gap in U.S. Manufacturing (2011)
5. World Economic Forum: Matching Skills and Labour Market Needs - Building Social Partnerships for Better Skills and Better Jobs (2014)
6. EFFRA: Factories of the Future PPP - FoF20220 Roadmap - Consultation document. Bruxelles (2012)
7. Profita, H., Lim, A., Brinkman, D., Smith, R.: Wall relief: a health-oriented interactive installation for the workplace environment. In: TEI, Standford, CA, USA (2015)

8. Lee, S.Y., Brand, J.: Effects of control over office workspace on perceptions of the work environment and work outcome. J. Env. Psychol. **25**, 323–333 (2005)

9. Parsons, K.: Environmental ergonomics: a review of principles, methods and models. Appl. Ergon. **31**, 581–594 (2000)

10. Goh, J.C.-L., Karimi, F.: Towards the development of a 'user-experience' technology adoption model for the interactive mobile technology. In: Nah, F.F.-H. (ed.) HCIB 2014. LNCS, vol. 8527, pp. 620–630. Springer, Heidelberg (2014). doi:10.1007/978-3-319-07293-7_60

11. Cugini, U.: Virtual prototypes and real products. In: Virtual Prototyping Summer School 2015 - PPT Presentation (2015)

12. Fenko, A., Schifferstein, H.N.: Shifts in sensory dominance between various stages of user-product interactions. Appl. Ergon. **41**, 34–40 (2009)

13. Chen, N.-F., Ho, C.-H., Ma, M.-Y.: Sensory importance and emotions at early stage of product experiences - a qualitative study of jiuce squeezer. In: Department of Industrial Design, National Cheng Kung University, Tainan City, Taiwan (2009)

14. Ferrise, F., Furtado, G., Graziosi, S., Bordegoni, M.: Digitalizing and capturing haptic feedback in virtual prototypes for user experience design. In: IEEE (2013)

15. Filippi, S., Barattin, D., Ferrise, F., Bordegoni, M., Cugini, U.: Human in the loop: a model to integrate interaction issues in complex simulations. In: Marcus, A. (ed.) DUXU 2013. LNCS, vol. 8012, pp. 242–251. Springer, Heidelberg (2013). doi:10.1007/978-3-642-39229-0_27

16. Fenko, A., Schifferstein, H.N.: The influence of sensory product properties on affective and symbolic product experience. In: Proceedings of 8th International Design and Emotion Conference, London (2012)

17. Battini, D., Faccio, M., Persona, A., Sgarbossa, F.: New methodological framework to improve productivity and ergonomics. Int. J. Ind. Ergon. **41**, 30–42 (2011)

18. Liberati, D., Bedarida, L., Brandazza, P., Cerutti, S.: A model for the cortico-cortical neural interaction in multisensory-evoked potentials. IEEE Trans. Biomed. Eng. **38**(9), 879–890 (1991)

19. MAN-MADE: D1.3 Validation Scenarios Definition. Manufacturing through Ergonomic Safe and Anthropocentric Adaptative Workplaces (2014)

20. MAN-MADE Project. http://www.man-made.eu/

Comparing Techniques for Selecting Automation Technology

Erlend Alfnes[1(✉)], Maria Kollberg Thomassen[2], and Marthe Bostad[1]

[1] Department of Production and Quality Engineering,
Norwegian University of Science and Technology, Trondheim, Norway
erlend.alfnes@ntnu.no
[2] Industrial Management, SINTEF Technology and Society, Oslo, Norway
maria.thomassen@sintef.no

Abstract. Automation of industrial processes is a necessary step towards the Industry 4.0 vision. There are several justification techniques available that can help to improve chances for success in automation projects. A literature review on justification techniques and their usefulness is carried out. Based on the review, a set of criteria for evaluating justification techniques are developed. A case study is carried out in a company with an ongoing manufacturing system development project that includes decisions regarding processes and technologies that require a systematic evaluation and justification. Two justification techniques were selected and tested in the development project. The tests show that both justification techniques provide good support for the technology acquisition process. Strengths and weaknesses of the tested techniques are highlighted. The study suggests that the choice of method should depend on the type of acquisition process of a company, especially with respect to technology strategy, competences, and supplier relations.

Keywords: Operations strategy · Automation · Technology acquisition · Justification techniques

1 Introduction

Manufacturing companies are forced to look for progressive automation technologies to keep their market share and maintain competitive [1, 2]. The capability of the companies competitiveness is essential for their survival [1, 3]. Automation technology has been the development key driver of processes in manufacturing plants since it entered the manufacturing industry [4, 5]. Implementing an automatic system can result in cost savings within production or increased efficiency, productivity and competitiveness [6, 7]. However, the introduction of automation technology will need time to achieve successive implementation [8, 9]. It is also important to be aware that automation can bring problems and failures and not necessarily immediate success [10]. Additionally, Frohm [8] states that increasing level of automation in unforeseen production situations can be related to production disturbances, while Duncheon [11] list challenging cases like innovative products or products with short life cycle because of the uncertainty related to such production.

I. Nääs et al. (Eds.): APMS 2016, IFIP AICT 488, pp. 371–378, 2016.
DOI: 10.1007/978-3-319-51133-7_44

The development of manufacturing systems entail large investments, which will require justification of the decisions that are to be made [2, 4, 12]. The literature consists of many justification techniques for the acquisition of automation technology, but the use of such techniques in industry is limited. The existing techniques are criticised for being too time consuming, or not user friendly, or for putting too much weight on the financial aspects, or for a lack of sufficient support to the decision maker in certain phases of the selection process [3, 13–15]. There is a need to verify the usefulness of such methods in the industry [16, 17].

The purpose of this paper is identify two justification techniques that support the main phases of an automation technology selection process, to test these techniques in a case, and evaluate their usefulness in practice. The main contribution is a set of criteria for evaluating justification techniques, and insights about the usefulness of two justification techniques in industry.

The paper is organised as follows. First, the methodological approach is discussed. Next, the most common justification techniques is reviewed. Two techniques are applied and evaluated in a case study. Finally, conclusions are presented together with suggestions for further work.

2 Methodological Considerations

This study is based upon a literature review and a case study of an automation selection and acquisition process. The purpose of the literature was to investigate the main criteria for evaluating and prioritising justification techniques. Based on the review, a set of criteria for evaluating justification techniques is developed. An single case study approach was chosen to ensure enough detail and in-depth insights about actual use of justification techniques in industry. The case company was selected because they have an ongoing manufacturing system development project that include decisions regarding several processes and technologies that require a systematic evaluation and justification. Case company data was collected in several iterations over a year. Most of the data were collected in workshops with case company representatives. Interviews and discussions with key personnel were carried out combined with plant visits.

3 Theoretical Discussion

Chan et al. [1] classifies justification techniques into the three groups; strategic, economic or analytic approach which can be used unaided or combined. The combination of strategic and economic approaches is a common combination since the strategic approach has direct tie to the goals of the firm, and the possibility of overlooking the economical and tactical impacts gets covered by the economic approach [1]. The economic approach is based on an evaluation of the economic aspects and can contribute to the final decision of choosing an automation technology [1]. The strategic approach involve analysis of competitive advantage, business objectives, research and development, and technical importance [1, 16].

3.1 Justification Techniques

The main phases that should be supported by a justification technique is technology strategy, analysis of operations competences and requirements, analysis of potential technologies, investments analysis, and implementation policy analysis [18]. The main justification techniques and their support for different phases are listed in Table 1.

Table 1. Justification techniques and the main phases they support.

References	Strategic	Operations	Technology	Investment	Implementation
Baines [13]	X	X	X		X
Chan et al. [1]	X	X	X	X	X
Chuang et al. [19]	X	X	X		
Durrani et al. [14]	X	X	X		
Efstathiades et al. [20]	X	X	X	X	X
Farooq and O'Brien [21]	X		X		
Iakymenko [22]	X		X	X	
Raafat [23]				X	
Sambasivarao and Deshmukh [2]		X		X	
Shehabuddeen et al. [17]		X	X		
Thomassen et al. [18]	X	X	X	X	X
Torkkeli and Tuominen [24]	X		X		X

3.2 Criteria for Selecting Justification Techniques

An utilisation of justification techniques can contribute to evaluate important areas when acquiring automation technology [1, 15, 25, 26]. The important areas can vary in the different techniques, which depends on their aim of support. However, it is essential that a technique contributes with enough support in the acquisition process [24], as well as evaluating the necessary area for the particular process [3, 13, 14, 24].

For a justification technique to be supportive in an acquisition of automation technology, it has to be applicable and well explained [13, 14, 18]. Such technique will be easy to follow and prevent unnecessary use of time or expertise. Effective techniques will reduce the time and work load for a practitioner. Additionally, production processes with special challenges will benefit justification techniques with the possibility of modifying evaluation areas [17, 24]. The most important criteria for evaluating the usefulness of justification techniques is listed in Table 2.

Table 2. Key criteria for evaluating the usefulness of justification techniques.

Category	Important elements	References
Ease of performance	Effective in execution	[2, 17, 18, 21, 24]
	Applicable	[13, 14, 18, 21]
	Well explained	[13, 14, 18, 21]
Covers necessary areas	Include the important areas	[1, 15, 25, 26]
	Ability to evaluate distinctive areas for the process	[3, 13, 14, 17, 24]
	Guides the selection part of the acquisition process	[2, 17]
	Guides multiple parts of the acquisition process	[13, 14, 18, 21]
	Exclude the practitioner's "gut" feeling	[1, 15, 17, 25, 26]
Type of approach	Combine strategic and economic approach	[1, 16]
	Prioritise technology alternatives	[2, 13, 14, 17, 18, 22, 24]
	Evaluate with a visualising model	[14, 15, 18]
	Evaluate with a scoring model	[15, 17, 22, 25]

4   Case Study

The case company is within the aerospace and defense industry. The company wants to automate a production line for medium and large caliber ammunition, where many operations currently are performed manually and several processes are very challenging to automate. Two justification methods were selected for testing. The APROS (Automation Project Selection) method [18] was chosen because it support all phases of a technology acquisition process. The technology selection framework [17] has a more limited scope, but were selected because it provides a set of scoring models that enables a thorough evaluation of a certain technology.

4.1   The Automation Project

The planned production line to be transformed into fully automated production line consists of stamping tracer and explosives (semi-automated), assembly (semi-automated), marking (fully automated) and packing (manual process). A mapping of the processes has shown that the assembly process seems to be the most challenging to automate, and a plan with milestones has been to automate the assembly process, Table 3.

4.2   The Evaluation of Technologies

The automation technology offers received from three different suppliers were evaluated with the two justification techniques in the case study. The first offer, technology

Table 3. Milestones in the automation project.

Date	Activity
12. 2015	Project start in the production department
01. 2016	Tender sent for the assembly process
02. 2016	Meetings held with potential suppliers for the assembly process
03. 2016	Offers received from suppliers on the assembly process
04. 2016	Supplier selected for an automation technology in the assembly process
06. 2016	Order is placed for the selected automation technology on the assembly process
05. 2017	Automation technology for the assembly process is implemented
07. 2019	The production line is fully automated in the manufacturing company

alternative 1, consists of robots processing and transferring one product at time between the stations. The second offer, technology alternative 2, consists of transporting pallets with multiple products. In addition, the input is handled by a robot and navigated with a camera solution. The last offer evaluated, technology alternative 3, consists of an input with a blister and transports multiple products with pallets. The practitioner picked out three parts of the assembly process for evaluation, which were the three most important parts in the assembly process to be supported by techniques. Three processes in assembly were selected for evaluation, (1) material handling between work station, (2) feeding components to a station, and (3) gluing and control (Table 4).

Table 4. Results of the technology evaluation.

Part of the process	Selected alternative in the first technique	Selected alternative in the second technique
Intern transport	Technology alternative 1	Technology alternative 3
Input	Technology alternative 2	Technology alternative 3
Glue applying and control	Technology alternative 1	Technology alternative 3

The more strategic evaluation performed by the APROS method suggested that the company should select technology 1. The second justification technique gave scores with very small deviations (technology 1: 6,1, technology 2: 5,7, and technology 3: 6,4). The final decision was therefore to go for technology 1, with robots processing and transferring one product at time between the stations.

5 Discussion

The two justification techniques point out different solutions, but the differences between the results of technologies are not so different with a closer look. The results are in close race in both of the techniques for each process, which make all results from the justification techniques valuable. The evaluation of the usefulness of the justification techniques is summarized in Table 5.

Table 5. Evaluation of the techniques based on evaluation criteria.

Category	Criteria	APROS	The tech. selection framework
Ease of performance	Effective in execution	X	X
	Applicable	X	X
	Well explained	X	
Covers necessary areas	Include the important areas	X	X
	Possibility to include additional areas		X
	Guides one part of the acquisition process		X
	Guides multiple parts of the acquisition process	X	
	Exclude the practitioner's "gut" feeling		X
Type of approach	Combination of strategic and economic approach	X	X
	Evaluate with a visualising model	X	
	Evaluate with a scoring model		X

Both justification techniques provides good support for a automation technology acquisition process. The APROS approach is suited to guide the complete acquisition process from establishing strategy to investment in technology. The APROS methodology supports multiple parts of the acquisition process, and this makes it possible to use the technique in different areas dependent on the practitioner's requirements. It is visual, highly effective, easy to understand, and evaluate important areas of the technologies. However, it should include earlier experience with the suppliers and their reputation, and does not explain the cost calculations well enough. The technology selection framework, only supports the core selection process in the acquisition of an automation technology. It is based on a detailed scoring model and is a more thorough justification technique. However, it is difficult to understand at first. It does not explain the meaning of the scores in the model, which made the practitioners insecure of how to understand the score scale. The cost calculations are not explained well enough. The choice of method therefore depends on the type of acquisition process a company is performing, and how well the technology strategy, competences, and supplier relations are established in the company.

6   Conclusion

This paper reviews justification techniques and test how such methods perform in practice. The main contribution is a set of criteria for evaluating justification techniques, and some insights about the usefulness of two justification techniques in industry. The application of two techniques in a case study showed that both techniques has strengths and weaknesses, and their applicability depend on the purpose and manufacturing environment for a technology acquisition process.

Further work should be done to test justification techniques and evaluate their usefulness in case companies that has different technology challenges and manufacturing environments.

Acknowledgements. This research is supported by the Research Council of Norway through the research projects EFFEKT and Manufacturing Network 4.0.

References

1. Chan, F.T.S., et al.: Investment appraisal techniques for advanced manufacturing technology (AMT): a literature review. Integr. Manuf. Syst. **12**(1), 35–47 (2001)
2. Sambasivarao, K.V., Deshmukh, S.G.: A decision support system for selection and justification of advanced manufacturing technologies. Prod. Plan. Control **8**(3), 270–284 (1997)
3. Säfsten, K., Winroth, M., Stahre, J.: The content and process of automation strategies. Int. J. Prod. Econ. **110**(1), 25–38 (2007)
4. Ordoobadi, S.M., Mulvaney, N.J.: Development of a justification tool for advanced manufacturing technologies: system-wide benefits value analysis. J. Eng. Technol. Manag. **18**(2), 157–184 (2001)
5. Jovane, F., Koren, Y., Boer, C.R.: Present and future of flexible automation: towards new paradigms. CIRP Ann. Manuf. Technol. **52**(2), 543–560 (2003)
6. Frohm, J., et al.: The industry's view on automation in manufacturing. In: Proceedings of the 9th Symposium IFAC on Automated Systems Based on Human Skills and Knowledge, France (2006)
7. Groover, M.P.: Automation, Production Systems, and Computer-Integrated Manufacturing. Prentice Hall Press, Upper Saddle River (2007)
8. Frohm, J.: Levels of automation in production systems. Chalmers University of Technology Gothenburg (2008)
9. Meredith, J.R.: Managing factory automation projects. J. Manuf. Syst. **6**(2), 75–91 (1987)
10. Lindström, V., Winroth, M.: Aligning manufacturing strategy and levels of automation: a case study. J. Eng. Technol. Manag. **27**(3), 148–159 (2010)
11. Duncheon, C.: Product miniaturization requires automation-but with a strategy. Assem. Autom. **22**(1), 16–20 (2002)
12. Parsaei, H.R., Wilhelm, M.R.: A justification methodology for automated manufacturing technologies. Comput. Ind. Eng. **16**(3), 363–373 (1989)
13. Baines, T.: An integrated process for forming manufacturing technology acquisition decisions. Int. J. Oper. Prod. Manag. **24**(5), 47–467 (2004)
14. Durrani, T.S., et al.: Managing the technology acquisition process. Technovation **18**(8), 523–587 (1998)
15. Granlund, A., Jackson, M.: Managing automation development projects: a comparison of industrial needs and existing theoretical support. In: Azevedo, A. (ed.) Advances in Sustainable and Competitive Manufacturing Systems, pp. 761–774. Springer, Heidelberg (2013). doi:10.1007/978-3-319-00557-7_63
16. Small, M.H., Chen, I.J.: Economic and strategic justification of AMT inferences from industrial practices. Int. J. Prod. Econ. **49**(1), 65–75 (1997)
17. Shehabuddeen, N., Probert, D., Phaal, R.: From theory to practice: challenges in operationalising a technology selection framework. Technovation **26**(3), 324–335 (2006)

18. Thomassen, M.K., Sjøbakk, B., Alfnes, E.: A strategic approach for automation technology initiatives selection. In: Grabot, B., Vallespir, B., Gomes, S., Bouras, A., Kiritsis, D. (eds.) APMS 2014. IAICT, vol. 440, pp. 288–295. Springer, Heidelberg (2014). doi:10.1007/978-3-662-44733-8_36

19. Chuang, M., Yang, Y.S., Lin, C.T.: Production technology selection: deploying market requirements, competitive and operational strategies, and manufacturing attributes. Int. J. Comput. Integr. Manuf. **22**(4), 345–355 (2009)

20. Efstathiades, A., Tassou, S., Antoniou, A.: Strategic planning, transfer and implementation of advanced manufacturing technologies (AMT). Development of an integrated process plan. Technovation **22**(4), 201–212 (2002)

21. Farooq, S., O'Brien, C.A.: Technology selection framework for integrating manufacturing within a supply chain. Int. J. Prod. Res. **50**(11), 2987–3010 (2002)

22. Iakymenko, N.: An approach for evaluating the appropriateness of automation in manufacturing processes with increasing product mix. Norwegian University of Science and Technology, Faculty of Engineering Science and Technology, Department of Production and Quality Engineering, 57 (2014)

23. Raafat, F.: A comprehensive bibliography on justification of advanced manufacturing systems. Int. J. Prod. Econ. **79**(3), 197–208 (2002)

24. Torkkeli, M., Tuominen, M.: The contribution of technology selection to core competencies. Int. J. Prod. Econ. **77**(3), 271–284 (2002)

25. Suresh, N.C., Meredith, J.R.: Justifying multimachine systems: an integrated strategic approach. J. Manuf. Syst. **4**(2), 117–134 (1985)

26. Gregory, M.: Technology management: a process approach. Proc. Inst. Mech. Eng. Part B: J. Eng. Manuf. **209**(5), 347–356 (1995)

Quality in Production Management

Customization Process of the Process for the Development of Embedded Components for the Aerospace Industry

Magda A.S. Miyashiro[1]($\boxtimes$), Maurício G.V. Ferreirao[1], Mauro M. Spínola[2],
Marcelo S.P. Pessoa[2], and Rodrigo Franco Gonçalves[2]

[1] National Institute for Space Research, São José dos Campos, Brazil
magda.silverio@globo.com
[2] University of São Paulo, São Paulo, Brazil

Abstract. In the aerospace industry, the number of products using embedded components is increasing. Nevertheless, there are still processes to ensure that the embedded components can be constructed without failure. Therefore it is necessary to identify and establish process of adaptation to achieve the product quality through the quality of its production process, preventing flaws the process rather than fixing them in the final product actions to be considered in the customization process. From a set of factors obtained from the literature, they were listed CMMI elements and embedded system characteristics for definition of the criteria used for Aerospace Industry. It was obtained a sequence of actions to be taken to adapt any process to meet the particularities of its component products. The use of a static process could not meet the characteristics of each component, but you can set an adaptive process from a default and thus meet their individualities.

Keywords: Adaptation · Aerospace · CMMI · Embedded components · Customization · Quality factors · Software process

1 Introduction

An embedded component is an installed device in a product, it is generally dedicated to performing a set of predefined tasks with specific requirements. They are formed by hardware and software that are closely related, where the hardware is the physical part and the software component is the computing part, namely, the logic of which is shown in Fig. 1.

With the development and evolution of technology, embedded systems have also become increasingly sophisticated and complex, which directly influences their development process, making it a costly and prone to errors activity [2].

Several accidents show that embedded components designed to perform critical systems often fail, as in the cases of rocket Ariane 5 [2], which exploded 37 seconds after launching, and Therac-25 [3], radiation therapy machine, which made six fatalities, among others.

© IFIP International Federation for Information Processing 2016
Published by Springer International Publishing AG 2016. All Rights Reserved
I. Nääs et al. (Eds.): APMS 2016, IFIP AICT 488, pp. 381–388, 2016.
DOI: 10.1007/978-3-319-51133-7_45

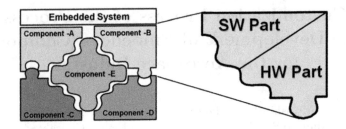

Fig. 1. Representation of parts of a system (Source: adapted [1])

A sad conclusion presented by researcher Lim Joanne on one of the most significant examples about software failure in embedded components, demonstrates the emergency of continuous in-depth studies to ensure the quality of these products: *"In many senses, a computer had killed their mother, father, son, daughter, or whoever was closest to their heart. It is hard to believe that through simple human error, an unnecessary loss of lives could take place. It has happened, and may happen again in the future. Therefore, it must be our goal to never let such a tragedy as Therac-25 take place again".*

The aerospace industry demands highly specialized and customized components. The increased use of these systems, their diversity and the number of functions that are being incorporated into a single embedded system multiplies the degree of criticality [4], especially on devices that perform critical functions in systems that directly affect people's lives. A software product is considered critical when, in case of failure, takes a system into a dangerous state, that is, when the software can cause disasters or fatalities [5].

The software quality theme, whether in academia or in companies, reports the various models and methodologies to be applied in the development process. However, when it comes to embedded component, which means developing software and hardware together, the question is: how to integrate these two realities ensuring quality? [6].

A study developed by Carnegie Mellon University's Software Engineering Institute (CMU/SEI) on industry trends in the use of software components pointed out, among other weaknesses, that software engineering lacks methods to produce quality systems [7]. Current researches show great need of processes, methods, techniques and tools to assess the quality of software components, even more specifically for embedded software [1,2].

CMMI V1.3 (Capability Maturity Model Integration) was developed by the Software Engineering Institute - SEI using total quality concepts introduced by Humphrey (2000) and his team. CMMI is based on the concept of maturity of software processes and is compatible with ISO/IEC 15505e ISO/IEC 12207 standards. It has five levels of maturity in a growing range of control and visibility that allows the classification of processes, technical results and software project managements [1].

For this study, we considered a number of factors obtained from the literature, elements of CMMI, ISO standards and quality factors, and characteristics of embedded systems in general were listed, in order to set a definition for the criteria used for aerospace industry based on a specific case, as Fig. 2. The following activities were carried out: problem identification to be searched, literature revision, definition of the scope of the search, study of quality models and proposal in line with the research model presented by Creswell [8].

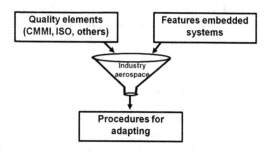

Fig. 2. Search methodology

This paper presents criteria for adaptation of a process for the development of embedded components following the CMMI (Capability Maturity Model Integrated), being part of a study being carried out to provide the adaptation criteria with different arguments. It is being held at the Postgraduate Course in Space Engineering and Te - National Institute for Space Research in continuing the research work in doctoral technology, specialization in Engineering and Space Systems Management at INPEld at the same institution [1].

2   Current Situation of Embedded Components

There are considerable references to embedded systems in literature. However, few of them direct their researches or activities considering only the software components independently. Therefore, it is necessary to use a software development approach that takes into account the characteristics and peculiarities of this context.

A survey conducted by Accenture shows that this increase in the embedded component usage proportionally increases the demand for solutions and services that meet such systems [9]. Most of the effort involved in producing components for embedded systems is directed to the development of software part of the component, being 62% of the budget for research and development and 67% of the cost [9]. It was also observed in this research that 33% of the produced devices do not meet the requirements of functionality or product performance, and that 80% of the development effort is spent on correcting unidentified errors during the earlier stages of production [9]. In addition, 80% of the reasons for failure in embedded systems come from problems in the software, not the hardware [10].

For being older and having more consolidated processes, the hardware industry (manufacturing) has had for a long time a higher level of maturity for the development of its products, while software production, despite its progress, is still at the beginning of development, and needs more studies and applications in order to accomplish this maturity [1]. This means that the stability of the hardware is not enough to ensure the quality of the system as a whole, since the development of software components of the product may present weaknesses that can cause execution failures.

The problems caused by the development of complex software show us that even with all the efforts made, the software can also be built with a few flaws that compromise their performance. This can be seen by the high number of defects presented by such programs [7].

3   Cyclic Process: A Model

The development of design of an embedded component system must follow a specialized life cycle, since these components perform specialized activities. For this, quality models were examined, especially the CMMI-DEV, and it was found out that the application of its recommendations in the preparation of a development process that suits the characteristics of the embedded system component can contribute to increase the quality of the product to be designed.

The "Cyclic Process" is being used in this study, and it was organized in phases where its activities are designed to be applied in an independent form and shared between the software and hardware parts of the embedded component. The process is called cyclic because each embedded system component to be developed according to their specifications must perform all phases and process activities, thus forming a complete cycle of development of components for embedded system. This operation is shown in Fig. 3.

Development cycle is the linear execution of all phases and activities of the life cycle, where each development cycle will result in a component and all documents are produced during its development. In general, an embedded system consists of several components, then for each component individually, it should perform different development cycles.

The phases of the "Cyclic Process" consist of activities and are implemented through actions directed by procedures and documents (models) that result in shared artifacts, which make up the embedded component (programs and their documentation), as follows: (a) Common activities, (b) Engineering, (c) Analysis of requirements, (d) Analysis and design, (e) Implementation and integration, (f) verification and validation of the system and (g) cycle assessment [1]. As an example, Fig. 4 shows the Analysis and Design phase.

Even the "Cyclic process" particularly designed for the development of embedded components, it should allow the adaptation of activities to be undertaken in the development of each developed component. The "Cyclic Process" induces the adjustment of its activities for each component to be produced, but does not provide criteria or guidelines to be followed while carrying out such adaptations.

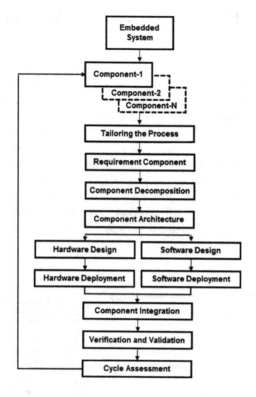

Fig. 3. Operation of the "Process Cyclic" (Source: [1])

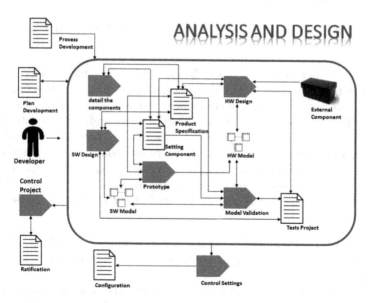

Fig. 4. Phase analysis and design (Source: [1])

4   Criteria to Be Considered in the Adaptation by CMMI-DEV

In general, the whole development process that meets the CMMI model, follows standards, procedures, tools and methods that should be employed in their preparation, and their adjustment is given as a set of standard processes of the organization, according to its guidelines for adaptation [1]. The area in the Organization Processes Focus (OPF) directs the development of the standard process following the organizational needs, while the process area Definition of the Organization's Processes (OPD) has fundamentals that must be followed during the process of adaptation, so that it maintains the basic requirements of CMMI model. Figure 5 shows the structure of adaptation where the standard process was drawn from the OPF process area and the requirements for each product to be produced it is defined an adapted process, following the process area of requirements OPD.

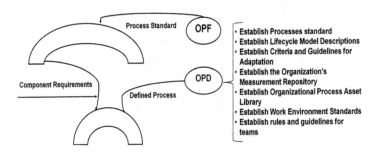

Fig. 5. Adaptation of "Cyclic process according to CMMI"

Every software component, especially embedded ones, require mechanisms to provide the monitoring service of their requirements during production. Therefore, it is necessary to know the component requirements and parameters that define its full service by performing identification and adjustments through inspection of the aspects of the process that might not meet the acceptable limits of the required result for the component to be produced. These mechanisms should be the result of an elaborate process, carefully adapted and documented. Generically, these activities are shown in Fig. 6. As a result of the implementation of the activities to the "Cyclic Process", the following adjustments were made:

- Abstraction of requirements - This activity requires the understanding and details of the component requirements, and must be registered in the "Development Plan" document.
- Identification of the factors of the requirements that must be observed - This activity should be performed based on the records held in the "Development

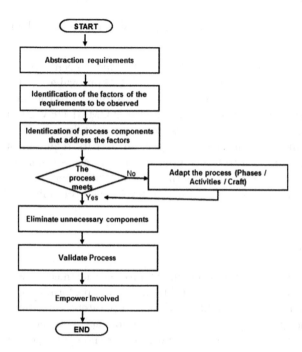

Fig. 6. Activities adaptation

Plan". Based on the characteristics and component requirements and on quality standards or models, it should specify which factors and care are the appropriate criteria for the component needs, and it must be registered in the "Development Plan".

– Identification of process components that address the factors - for this activity, it should identify items which should describe the actions that meet the component requirements in the activities of the lifecycle process and its artifacts.

– Adapt the process (Phases/Activities/Artifacts) - This activity should carry out the adjustments in the documents and artifacts of the process: "Development Plan", "Product Specification", "Component Specification", "Test Project" "Settings" and "Approval".

– Eliminate unnecessary components - this activity should be carried out to evaluate the life cycle and process artifacts, eliminating unnecessary items from the development of the component. As a result, it may cause adjustments in the documents and artifacts of the process, "Development Plan", "Product Specification", "Component Specification", "Test Project", "Settings" and "Approval".

– Validate process - this activity is necessary to evaluate the adapted process and to validate the compliance regarding the component to be produced. The result of this action must be registered in the artifact "approval".

– Training the involved ones - Every process must be known by those who use it. Then, any adjustment that might occur should be informed and the involved ones, be trained to use. The training plan, when necessary, should be recorded in the artifact "Development Plan".

The documents "Development Plan", "Product Specification", "Component Specification", "Test Project", "Settings" and "Approval are part of the "Cyclic process" and are published in the thesis "An approach to the process of embedded system development that meets the level 2 CMMI-DEV maturity" [1].

For the adaptation process, it is necessary to take into account the environment in which it is inserted (the system and its requirements) as part of requirement, in addition to the component requirements themselves.

As a result, this paper presents the basic activities and criteria to be considered for adaptation of a process for the development of embedded components with CMMI-DEV's vision.

5   Conclusions

It is clear that the use of a development process that meets the characteristics of each embedded component, in particular when performing the treatment of software and hardware parts differently and separately, contributes significantly to improve the quality of the produced component, as in the "Cyclic Process". However, the same process, in a static way, is not enough to meet the particularities of different components to be produced. This requires adaptations that meet their development and operation constraints and should also take into account the special features of the component to be developed.

References

1. Marwedel, P.: Uma Abordagem para o Processo de Desenvolvimento de Sistema Embarcado que Atende ao Nível 2 de Maturidade do CMMI-DEV. Ph.D. thesis, Instituto Nacional de Pesquisas Espaciais (2015)
2. Sommerville, I., Melnikoff, S.S.S., Arakaki, R., de Andrade Barbosa, E.: Engenharia de Software, vol. 6. Addison Wesley, São Paulo (2003)
3. Lim, J.: An Engineering Disaster: Therac-25. Technical report (1998)
4. Wehrmeister, M.A., Becker, L.B., Pereira, C.E.: Metodologia de Projeto Orientada a Objetos Baseada em Plataformas para Sistemas Tempo-Real Embarcados. In: 25° Simpósio Brasileiro de Redes de Computadores e Sistemas Distribuídos. Belém do Pará (2006)
5. Páscoa, J.: Fatores e Subfatores para Avaliação da Segurança em Software de Sistemas Críticos. Ph.D. thesis, Universidade de São Paulo (2002)
6. Barroso, M.: Um Processo de Desenvolvimento para Sistemas Computacionais Aderente ao MPS. Ph.D. thesis, Universidade de Fortaleza (2010)
7. Spinola, M.M.: Diretrizes para o Desenvolvimento de Software de Sistemas Embutidos. Ph.D. thesis, Universidade de São Paulo (1999)
8. Creswell, J.W.: Educational Research: Planning, Conducting, and Evaluating Quantitative. Prentice-Hall, Upper Saddle River (2002)
9. Accenture. www.accenture.com
10. Gomes, H.: Metodologia de Projeto de Software Embarcado Voltada ao Teste. Ph.D. thesis, Mestrado Universidade Federal do Rio Grande do Sul (2010)

Base and Extended One-Dimensional Warranties Analyses for Remanufactured Products

Ammar Y. Alqahtani[1(✉)] and Surendra M. Gupta[2]

[1] King Abdulaziz University, Jeddah, Saudi Arabia
aaylqahtani@kau.edu.sa
[2] Northeastern University, Boston, MA, USA
gupta@neu.edu

Abstract. Uncertainties in the quality and reliability of remanufactured products from the buyer's perspective might lead to a decision of not buying it. Remanufacturers must search for market mechanisms that provide assurance about the durability of remanufactured products. This paper considers a Remanufacturing-To-Order (RTO) system for sensor embedded products (SEPs). It presents an approach to determine how to predict base warranty (BW) and extended warranty (EW) periods for the remanufactured products using the sensor information about the age of each of the end-of-life (EOL) components on hand to meet the demand while minimizing the cost associated with warranty, maximizing manufacturer's profit and finding an attractive price for the extended warranty. An example is considered to illustrate the implementation of the model.

Keywords: Reverse supply chain · Simulation · Non-renewable warranty policies · Closed loop supply chain

1 Introduction

Management at the end-of-life (EOL) stage of products has been a topic of interest of many researchers. This is because of environmental factors, government regulations, public demands, and in recent years potential economic benefits that could be realized by implementing reverse logistics and product recycling policies. For this, companies need to remanufacture or come up with schemes to minimize the amount of waste sent to landfills by recovering materials and components from end-of-life products (EOLPs).

The quality of a remanufactured product is often a suspect for consumers. That is, the consumers are unsure if the remanufactured products will render the expected performance. This ambiguity about a remanufactured product could lead the consumer to decide against buying it. With such apprehension held by consumers, remanufacturers must seek market mechanisms that provide assurance about the durability of the products. One strategy that the remanufacturers could use is to offer warranties on their products [1].

© IFIP International Federation for Information Processing 2016
Published by Springer International Publishing AG 2016. All Rights Reserved
I. Nääs et al. (Eds.): APMS 2016, IFIP AICT 488, pp. 389–397, 2016.
DOI: 10.1007/978-3-319-51133-7_46

2 Literature Review

2.1 Environmentally Conscious Manufacturing and Product Recovery

Reviews of wide-ranging issues in environmentally conscious manufacturing and product recovery are offered by Gungor and Gupta [2] and Ilgin and Gupta [3]. Disassembly is the most common feature in remanufacturing research area. For different aspects of disassembly, see the book by Lambert and Gupta [4].

In recent years, many scholars have studied remanufacturing processes because traditional production planning methods fall short in product recovery settings. A review of 76 journal articles on remanufacturing was reported by Lage and Godinho Filho [5]. For additional aspects of remanufacturing, see the book by Ilgin and Gupta [6].

2.2 Warranty Analysis

Product warranties have three key roles. The first role is insurance and protection, allowing consumers to transfer the risk of product failure to sellers [7]. Next, product warranties can also signal product reliability to customers [8–11]. Lastly, the sellers use warranties to extract additional profitability [12]. There are several references that consider basic and extended warranty policies analysis for new products' supply chain management [13–15]. However, there are a few that consider the warranty for remanufactured products' reverse and closed-loop supply chain management [16–19]. Modeling and analyzing the warranty cost for used product is a new research field with a limited number of publications.

3 Remanufacturing-to-Order System Description

The Remanufacturing-To-Order (RTO) system considered in this study is a product recovery system. A sensor embedded air conditioner (AC) is considered here as an example product. Based on the condition of EOL AC, it will go through a series of recovery operations as shown in Fig. 1.

EOL ACs arrive at the RTO system for information retrieval using sensor reader. The information retrieved is stored in the facility's database. Then the ACs go through a six-station disassembly line. Complete disassembly is performed to extract every single component. There are nine components in an AC consisting of, evaporator, control box, blower, air guide, motor, condenser, fan, protector, and compressor as shown in Fig. 2. Exponential distributions are used to generate the disassembly times at each station, interracial times of each component's demand, and interarrival times of EOL AC. Two different types of disassembly operations, viz., destructive or nondestructive, are used depending on the component's condition. If the disassembled component is nonfunctional (broken, zero remaining life), then destructive disassembly is used such that the other components' functionalities are not damaged. Unit disassembly cost for a functional component is higher than nonfunctional component.

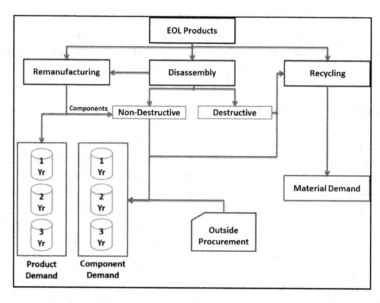

Fig. 1. RTO system's recovery processes

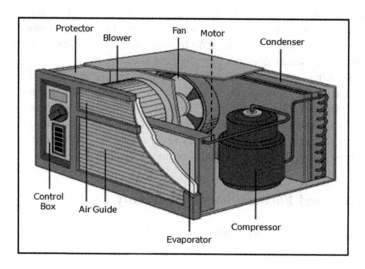

Fig. 2. Air conditioner (AC) components

Recovery operations differ for each SEP based on its condition and estimated remaining life. Recovered products and components are characterized based on their remaining life times and are placed in different life-bins (e.g. 1 year, 2 years, etc.) where they wait to be retrieved via a customer demand.

4 Warranty Cost Analysis

In the process of deciding to purchase a product, the buyers usually compare features of the product with other competing brands that are selling the same product. In some cases, the competing brands make similar products with similar features such as cost, special characteristics, quality and credibility of the product and even insurance from the provider. In such cases, the sale is influenced by such factors as discount, availability of parts, repairs and additional services. These factors may be very significant to the buyer and can be further enhanced by offering warranty to the buyer as it further assures the buyer of the reliability of the product.

A warranty is an agreement that requires the manufacturer to correct any product failures or compensates the buyer for any problems that occur with the product during the warranty period in relevance to its sale. A base warranty (BW) is typically associated with products. It is a predetermined agreement between a remanufacturer and a buyer at the time the product is bought. On the other hand, the extended warranty (EW) is purchased separately and the buyer may even have a choice of terms.

Nowadays, EWs are offered on a wide range of products, including automobiles, electronics and appliances. Usually, the buyer has to buy an EW at the same time as the product is purchased with extra amount separated from the product's price depending on the duration and the terms of the EW. In contrast, a BW is integral to the sale of a product and the customer does not pay anything extra for it.

There are different base and extended warranty types that most manufacturers offer to their buyers. The most popular policies are the Free Replacement Warranty (FRW) and Pro-Rata Warranty (PRW). The main expense of the extended warranty is the cost of the product plus the cost of servicing an item that fails during the extended warranty period. The warranty cost is the expense of servicing all warranty claims for a product during the overall period of the warranty (base and extended).

5 Notation and Formulation for Warranty Cost

The nomenclature used in this paper is given in Table 1.

5.1 Base Free Replacement Warrantee (FRW) Formulation

The expected warranty cost could be calculated using Blischke and Murthy [1] formula as follows:

Table 1. Parameters used in BW and EW

Parameters	Definition
L	Life cycle (remaining life)
X	Time to failure of an item
W_B	Length of base warranty period
W_E	Length of extended warranty period
Cs	Cost to the remanufacturer of supplying a remanufactured item
Cp	Sales price per unit
Cr	Average cost of each repair
$MTTF$	Mean time to failure
α	Weibull distribution shape parameter, $0 \le \alpha \le 1$ (where $\alpha = 1$, MTTF = 20 days, $\alpha = 2$, MTTF = 40 days and $\alpha = 3$, MTTF = 60 days)
$M(W_B)$	Average number of replacement during the base warranty period
$M(W_E)$	Average number of replacement during the extended warranty period
$M(W_B + W_E)$	Average number of replacement during the total warranty period
μ_W	Partial expectation of X
$f(x)$	Exponential distribution probability density function
K_W	Long-run average proportion of rebate
$C(W_B)$	Expected based warranty servicing cost
$C(W_B; W_E)$	Expected extended warranty servicing cost
$C_E(W_B; W_E)$	Expected extended warranty servicing cost per unit sale
$C(W_B + W_E)$	Expected total (based + extended) warranty period servicing cost

$$Expected\ warranty\ cost = Cs \, . \, [1 + M(W)] \tag{1}$$

5.2   Base Pro-Rata Warranty (PRW) Formulation

The PRW expected cost to remanufacturer is given by Blischke and Murthy [1] as follows:

$$Average\ cost\ per\ unit = C_s + C_p \, . \, [F(W) - \mu_W / W] \tag{2}$$

$$\mu_W = \int_0^W xf(x)dx \tag{3}$$

$$Expected\ cost\ to\ the\ remanufacturer\ of\ a\ warranty = C_s + K_w \, . \, C_p \tag{4}$$

$$Rebate = [(1 - \frac{X}{W})/C_p] \tag{5}$$

5.3   Extended Free Replacement Warrantee (FRW) Formulation

The expected EW servicing cost per unit sale is given by Murthy and Jack [20] as follows:

$$E[C_E(W_B; W_E)] = E[C(W_B + W_E)] - E[C(W_B)] \tag{6}$$

$$E[C(W_B)] = Cs \cdot [1 + M(W_B)] \tag{7}$$

$$E[C(W_B + W_E)] = Cs \cdot [M(W_B + W_E)] - M(W_B)] \tag{8}$$

6   Numerical Example

An AC with three different remaining lives (1 year, 2 years and 3 years) is sold with a base FRW or PRW policy. The relevant cost elements are the cost of providing the AC and the expected cost of servicing all warranty claims in case of FRW or the expected amount of the rebate in case of PRW. To examine the effect of fluctuating the warranty period, warranty lengths of W = 30, 60, and 90 days are considered.

Moreover, the example considers extended FRW policy for the remanufactured AC's components and products with three different remaining lives (1 year, 2 years and 3 years), 90 days base warranty period and three different extended warranty periods (1 year, 2 years and 3 years). The AC failure follows a Weibull distribution with a mean time to failure MTTF of the AC = 0.5 years. The other data used for the implementation of the model is shown in Table 2.

Table 2. Operation costs, sale price and repair cost for AC components

Product	C_s = Operation costs ($/unit)	C_p = Sale price ($/unit)			C_r = Repair costs ($/unit)
		L = 1 year	L = 2 years	L = 3 years	
AC	$55.00	$180	$240	$310	$85.00

7   Results

All results in this section were obtained using ARENA 14.0 program to compute the expected number of failures and expected cost to remanufacturer.

7.1   Case I: Base Free Replacement Warrantee (FRW)

In Table 3, expected number of failures represent the expected number of failed items per unit sale. In other words, it is the average number of free replacements that the remanufacturer would have to provide per unit sold during the warranty period. Expected cost to remanufacturer includes the cost of supplying the original item, Cs. Thus, the expected cost of warranty is calculated by subtracting Cs from the expected cost to remanufacturer.

Table 3. Expected number of failures and cost for remanufactured AC during BW

Product	W (days)	Expected number of failures			Expected cost to remanufacturer		
		$\alpha = 1$	$\alpha = 2$	$\alpha = 3$	$\alpha = 1$	$\alpha = 2$	$\alpha = 3$
AC	30	0.0120	0.0054	0.00046	$57.50	$55.16	$54.64
	60	0.1900	0.0218	0.00339	$60.00	$60.65	$57.20
	90	0.2490	0.0485	0.01102	$70.50	$69.45	$59.33

Although not showing in the table, the expected cost of warranty to the remanufacturer can easily be calculated for W = 30, 60, and 90 days. For example, for W = 30 and $\alpha = 1$, the warranty cost for AC is $57.50 − Cs = $57.50 − $55.50 = $2.50 which is ([$2.50/$55.00] × 100) = 4.5% of the cost of supplying the item, Cs, which is significantly less than that $55.00, Cs. This may be acceptable, but the corresponding values for longer warranties become excessive. For example, for 90 days and $\alpha = 1$, corresponding percentage is ([$70.50 − $55.00/$55.00] × 100) = 28.18%.

7.2   Case II: Base Pro-Rata Warranty (PRW)

The result of all ACs (1 year, 2 years and 3 years remaining life) K_W values for different mean times to failure represented by α and warranty periods are calculated in Table 4. For instance, from Table 4 a 1 year remaining life AC with a median time to failure of 20 days and a 30 days warranty has $K_W = 0.1346$, i.e., the cost of the warranty is $0.1346 \times Cp$. Therefore, if the total cost of the 1 year AC to the remanufacturer is $55 and it sells for $180, the cost to the remanufacturer, including warranty, is $55 + (0.1346) × 180 = $79.23.

Table 4. Factor K_W for calculating remanufacturer's cost of base PRW policy

AC remaining life	MTTF	K_W		
		W = 30	W = 60	W = 90
1 year AC	$\alpha = 1$	0.1346	0.1883	0.2335
	$\alpha = 2$	0.1183	0.1437	0.1793
	$\alpha = 3$	0.0851	0.1199	0.1457
2 years AC	$\alpha = 1$	0.2667	0.3390	0.4011
	$\alpha = 2$	0.2110	0.2620	0.3232
	$\alpha = 3$	0.1727	0.2245	0.2665
3 years AC	$\alpha = 1$	0.2878	0.3349	0.3870
	$\alpha = 2$	0.2101	0.2622	0.3244
	$\alpha = 3$	0.1740	0.2273	0.2628

7.3   Case III: Extended Free Replacement Warrantee (FRW)

Table 5 shows the expected EW cost of all AC's components and products for $W_E = 1$, 2, 3 years. Also, it shows the expected number of failures as the expected number of failed items per unit sale. In other words, it is the average number of free replacements that the remanufacturer would have to provide per unit sold during the warranty period. Note that, the expected cost to remanufacturer includes the cost of supplying the original item, C_s. Thus the expected cost of warranty alone is calculated by subtracting C_s from the expected cost to remanufacturer.

The results given in Table 5 are useful in order to choose the length of an extended FRW warranty. The cost of the warranty is dependent on the value of Weibull shape parameters α. For example, the EW for 3 years remaining life AC with $\alpha = 1$ will cost $104.44 − $55.00 = $49.44 which is 81% of Cs.

Table 5. Expected number of failures and cost for remanufactured AC during EW

Product	W (years)	Expected number of failures			Expected cost to remanufacturer		
		$\alpha = 1$	$\alpha = 2$	$\alpha = 3$	$\alpha = 1$	$\alpha = 2$	$\alpha = 3$
AC	1	0.0837	0.0517	0.0447	$62.11	$59.39	$58.80
	2	0.4608	0.2288	0.1135	$94.17	$74.45	$64.65
	3	0.5817	0.3497	0.1436	$104.44	$84.72	$67.21

8 Conclusion

The Base Warranty (BW) and Extended Warranty (EW) costs for remanufactured products and components were evaluated in this paper using the one-dimensional Free Replacement Warranty (FRW) policy and Pro-Rata Warranty (PRW) for different periods. The main objective was to introduce the idea of providing a base and an extended warranty for a remanufactured product and how to predict a warranty period for using the sensor information about the age of each and every EOL product on hand to meet product demand while minimizing the cost associated with warranty and maximizing manufacturer's profit.

References

1. Murthy, D.P., Blischke, W.R.: Warranty Management and Product Manufacture. Springer, London (2006)
2. Gungor, A., Gupta, S.M.: Issues in environmentally conscious manufacturing and product recovery: a survey. Comput. Ind. Eng. 36(4), 811–853 (1999)
3. Ilgin, M.A., Gupta, S.M.: Environmentally conscious manufacturing and product recovery (ECMPRO): a review of the state of the art. J. Environ. Manag. 91(3), 563–591 (2010)
4. Lambert, A.F., Gupta, S.M.: Disassembly Modeling for Assembly, Maintenance, Reuse and Recycling. CRC Press, Boca Raton (2004)
5. Lage Jr., M., Godinho-Filho, M.: Production planning and control for remanufacturing: literature review and analysis. Prod. Plan. Control 23(6), 419–435 (2012)
6. Ilgin, M.A., Gupta, S.M.: Remanufacturing Modeling and Analysis. CRC Press, Boca Raton (2012)

7. Heal, G.: Guarantees and risk-sharing. Rev. Econ. Stud. **44**, 549–560 (1977)
8. Balachander, S.: Warranty signalling and reputation. Manag. Sci. **47**(9), 1282–1289 (2001)
9. Gal-Or, E.: Warranties as a signal of quality. Can. J. Econ. **22**, 50–61 (1989)
10. Soberman, D.A.: Simultaneous signaling and screening with warranties. J. Mark. Res. **40**(2), 176–192 (2003)
11. Spence, M.: Consumer misperceptions, product failure and producer liability. Rev. Econ. Stud. **44**, 561–572 (1977)
12. Lutz, N.A., Padmanabhan, V.: Why do we observe minimal warranties? Mark. Sci. **14**(4), 417–441 (1995)
13. Blischke, W.R., Murthy, C.N.P.: Warranty Cost Analysis. Marcel Dekker, New York (1994)
14. Blischke, W.R., Murthy, C.N.P.: Product Warranty Handbook. Marcel Dekker, New York (1996)
15. Blischke, W.R., Karim, M.R., Murthy, D.P.: Warranty Data Collection and Analysis. Springer, London (2011)
16. Alqahtani, A.Y., Gupta, S.M.: End-of-life product warranty. In: Northeast Decision Sciences Institute (NEDSI) Conference, Cambridge (2015)
17. Alqahtani, A.Y., Gupta, S.M.: Warranty policy analysis for end-of-life product in reverse supply chain. In: 26th Production and Operations Management Society (POMS), Washington D.C. (2015)
18. Alqahtani, A.Y., Gupta, S.M.: Extended warranty analysis for remanufactured products. In: International Conference on Remanufacturing (ICoR), Amsterdam (2015)
19. Alqahtani, A.Y., Gupta, S.M.: Warranty cost analysis within sustainable supply chain. In: Akkucuk, U. (ed.) Ethics and Sustainability in Global Supply Chain Management, pp. 1–25. IGI Global, Hershey (2017)
20. Murthy, D.P., Jack, N.: Extended Warranties, Maintenance Service and Lease Contracts Modeling and Analysis for Decision-Making. Springer, London (2014)

Sustainable Economic Development and High Quality Engineering Education: Correlating Factors in Brazil's Macro Regions

Vitor Mendes Caldana[1,2](✉) and Márcia Terra da Silva[2]

[1] IFSP, Santana de Parnaíba, Brazil
vitor.caldana@ifsp.edu.br
[2] Paulista University, São Paulo, Brazil
marcia.terra@uol.com.br

Abstract. GDP development over time is one method of measuring the economic evolution of a country. According to the OECD, there are several factors that can influence GDP, one of which is Engineering Education. A possible way to determine the potential for economic development would be assessing the performance of high-level education, especially if the GDP-Engineering correlation is taken into account. Studies were overtaken to study the lack of engineering in Brazil as a structural problem. However, there is no analysis about the regional factor and the engineering education performance. The objective of this paper is to assess if there is a correlation between the regional GDP and good performance Engineering Education in Brazil. The study is based on official data provided by governmental organizations. A conclusion is reached were the regional disparity in GDP is similar to the disparity on High Quality Engineering Education.

Keywords: Economic development · Regional development · Engineering education

1 Introduction

Brazil is the seventh biggest economy in the world; however due to the continental dimensions of the country $(8,515,767 \, km^2)$ there is a great challenge to equally develop all the regions. Global Brazil's Gross Domestic Product (GDP) has had an increase of a 5.27% on average in the last 20 years. In this period, the annual increase has not been consistent. This shows that Brazil's GDP growth results are inconsistent facing big fluctuations when compared to the average growth [1].

The GDP results also showed that the regional disparity is still significant, as shown in Table 1.

The GDP percentage participation of the regions, aligned with the GDP and GDP per capita retraction scenario shows the challenge to equally develop regions.

© IFIP International Federation for Information Processing 2016
Published by Springer International Publishing AG 2016. All Rights Reserved
I. Nääs et al. (Eds.): APMS 2016, IFIP AICT 488, pp. 398–405, 2016.
DOI: 10.1007/978-3-319-51133-7_47

Table 1. Macro-regions GDP participation. Source: [2]

Macro region	GDP percentage
Central-West	9,60%
Northeast	13,40%
North	5,40%
Southeast	65,20%
South	16,20%

For that, according to Lins [3], there is a direct correlation observed by the Organization for Economic Co-operation and Development (OECD) in terms of Human Resources in Science and Technology (HRST) and GDP. The discussion of sustainable regional development is a pressing issue [4,5], and is met with similar concern on the development of expertise [5,6].

This study correlates the regional factor on the GDP percentage participation and the performance of reginal engineering education. The objective of this work is to compare the recent results in GDP with the current engineering education performance and try to verify if there is a correlation between both.

2   Methodology

This work is an analysis of bibliographical references and governmental data. It is a research to better understand the impact of Higher Education Institutions (HEIs) in engineering on regional GDP.

Recent studies conducted to analyze the lack of engineers were influenced by parameters suggested by Butz et al. [7]. Butz proposed five parameters to measure the shortage of products. This can be adapted to be understood as "production of high performance engineers" if necessary considerations are made. The parameters suggested by Butz are:

- Production is lower than in recent past.
- Leader's market share has been increasing over time.
- Production is lower than what expected by the suppliers.
- Production is lower than what expected by society.
- Production does not meet market needs, which can be demonstrated by ascending prices.

Another study made by Nascimento [8] included specific parameters for understanding the lack of engineers. He understood that the parameters suggested by Butz were not specific to deal with the issue of skill shortage and proposed the following adaptations:

- Low unemployment rates.
- Rising proportion of graduates taking typical occupations on the area.

- High job rotation between engineers, what suggests they receive job offers from the competition or different business with better employment conditions.
- New job positions are difficult to be filled.
- Increase in working hours.
- High competition between companies for the top professional.
- Reduction in hiring demands.

Based on both the parameters from Butz et al. [7] and Nascimento [8], Lins et al. [3] conducted a study of lack of engineers. The parameters selected by Lins et al. [3] for the study, properly adapted to the case study, were:

1. The number of engineering graduates is lower than in the past.
2. The number of engineering graduates is lower than expected.
3. The number of engineering graduates is lower than what would be needed by the market, which would reflect on an escalation of salary.
4. Low unemployment percentages among engineers than in the past.
5. Increase in number of engineers working among the typical professions from the past.
6. High job rotation between engineers, what suggests they receive job offers from the competition or different business with better employment conditions.

Using those parameters, the conclusion was that Brazil doesn't have a structural lack of engineers. Even though the consensus is that the lack of engineers is not a structural issue, there are variables on the analysis of the study that showed a positive indication towards it (parameters 3, 4 and 5). The studies also do not investigate the regional factor, in which different regions and different clusters may have a very specific need for technical background, as well as do not take into consideration the quality factor of the degrees – although mentioned - and the curriculum design. The studies also do not reach a conclusion as to why, according to Maciente and Araújo [9], only 38% of graduates remain with their main occupation as engineers.

This paper will focus on the discussion of better understanding if the results of regional GDP and HEI's point to a regional lack of engineers, if the regional GDP and HEI's results are similar and if Engineering Education can affect a sustainable development scenario.

To continue the discussion of this paper, we will take a closer look on the factors of high-level education engineering schools performance, curriculum design, the roles of academia in regional development and the development of expertise.

3 Data Analysis and Bibliographical Review

3.1 High Level Education Engineering Performance

Brazil has a performance exam of high education named ENADE (Nacional Exam of Student Performance). The result from ENADE evaluates graduation students on a grade from 1 to 5, with 5 being the highest score. There is also a SC concept that is given to HEIs that do not have at least two graduates taking the exam in that term, which is common on new approved universities. The exam is annual however, due to the number of different careers and HEIs, each one is evaluated every three years.

ENADE takes into consideration both specific and general performance. The general graduation curriculum represents 25% of the total grade and the specific represents 75%. After calculating the average grade and standard deviation for each particular HEIs, the method than calculates the average and standard deviation of all HEIs in that specific area that took the test to standardize the grade in all Brazil [10].

According to ENADE the number of engineer graduates who took the test rose from 25,657 in 2008 to 46,675 in 2011. Only 20% of the graduates received grades 4 and 5 in 2011, with a significant decrease from 2008 when the result was 29%. The increase of number of participants does not indicate necessarily an increase of number of graduates, as the exam has been gaining importance as the years pass.

Table 2. Number of engineering HEIs per region and ENADE results in 2011

Region	Engineering schools						
	1	2	3	4	5	SC	Total
Central-West	6	13	17	12	3	8	59
Northeast	11	41	50	34	4	21	161
North	5	19	19	4	0	25	72
Southeast	36	197	176	84	43	82	618
South	7	44	96	59	15	38	259

Good performance evaluation is considered on grades 4 and 5. With that parameter, we can see that southeast has the biggest amount of schools (127 or 49%). The values shows a decrease in HEIs with grade 1, that can be explained by both evolution of grade and also closure of some institutions, as consecutive 1 results will cause the HEI to close, according to ENADE policy. The evolution of quantity of HEIs with grade 2 (2.28%), 3 (25.61%) and 4 (33.10%) shows not only new institutions; a deeper look at the database shows an increase in institutions quality, with HEIs being able to increase their test scores over the three evaluations. The biggest warning comes from the significant reduction of 5 grade: 25.29%. This value can only be explained by the decrease in education performance [11].

The low percentage of high performance HEIs (22.07%) can be a determinant factor as to why engineer graduates can't keep jobs in their typical applications as they lack the necessary specific knowledge to perform properly.

3.2   Curriculum Design

The standard curriculum design is still not what the market expects according to Lansu. He proposes a method of developing the design based on an interactive workshop, divided in two rounds in which the key actors of each region would unite to formally discuss and reach a consensus on the necessary design for that region. The study is consistent with the idea that graduates must have the qualifications desired by their region. Bringing the industry as a consultant to properly design the curriculum of the career, especially on cases such as engineering, will bring a better understanding of the needs for development [12].

Another positive factor is the possibility of keeping the graduate in the region through local employment. This supports the regional scenario without the need of migration to seek job opportunities, allowing continuous and sustainable development. Through the continuous "upgrade" of the curriculum design and the necessary adaptation of the industries demands each region will get the necessary professionals to proper develop such region. That being said, it is important to notice that the needs from regions can be significantly different from each other, as described by the Central-west example of high participation of agroindustry or the Northeast tourism industry.

There are also other examples of adaptive curriculum, in cases as analyzed by Avard and Zenios in the case study of the Polytechnic of Namibia where core competences such as Networked Learning, Innovation and Problem solved based learning were introduced in the curriculum. Even though not utilizing the process proposed by Lansu, it generates a result from an established analysis of the market and the needs for specific graduation curriculum [13].

Curriculum Design is also a factor that would remove engineers from the typical applications jobs, as even though the student might even have a good performance on the course, the curriculum itself is not what is expected by the market and thus the candidate still is unable to develop properly in the profession due to an unmatched skill set.

3.3   Roles of Academia in Regional Development

Following the creation by OECD of the "Supporting the Contribution of High-Level Educational Institutions in Regional Development" program, studies were implemented to establish what roles and what contributions academia could give to regional development.

There are several roles that the academia can play according to the study made by Devine-Wright to support regional development [14]. According to Stephens et al., the main contribution is educational and training activities. Universities can also contribute in various forms to help the regional development [15].

According to the study made by Zilahy and Huisingh, some significant obstacles are present. The major obstacles are lack of understanding of concepts of Sustainable Development, lack of clear vision and objectives; lack of commitment; conflicting interests; lack of information about the regional activities; lack of leadership; high organizational costs and lack of sufficient funding. Those obstacles justify as to why the majority perception of academics, 70%, still believe that the participation of academia in regional sustainable initiatives is still not sufficient [16].

Oliveira also contributes to this idea, specially taking into consideration what he proposes as "learning region". It would be the role of academia to implement, with help from local and political actors, an environment that would allow research and development to evolve regions from an exploratory context to a development context. With an innovation scenario present, with help from academia to produce the necessary expertise, the region would enter in a potent development self-sufficient circle [4].

3.4   Development of Expertise

The development of expertise is fundamental as a method of training and continuous upgrading workforce capacity to deal with new and unseen difficulties. It is a corner stone for regional development as it allows regions to innovate to achieve goals [5].

Sgobbi and Cainarca demonstrated on their research, conducted by 1,800 interviews, that the high-performance work practices – HPWPs – are conducted by high-performance professional [17]. However, the growth in core wage is inconclusive unless other aspects are accounted for. Not only high performance but a series of other skills that are growing in importance in Engineering Education to supplement this finding, such as the factor described by Avard and Zenios [13].

Litzinger reached a conclusion that is fundamental to align the curriculum and the teaching skill/methods [6]. This can be done in several ways; however, the expected outcome will be the development of the necessary expertise to properly prepare the graduate to be able to produce in the region, raising his wage and thus the GDP per capita.

Ultimately, the generation of expertise will be responsible for several enhancements not only in better HEIs, but also in a networking standpoint between academia and industry. Through this enhanced expertise it is possible to introduce the "learning regions" proposed by de Oliveira [4] and achieve a solid and virtuous cycle of development.

4   Results

It is possible to notice in Fig. 1 that the difference in regional GDP is significant. It also shows a disparity that is consistent with the relation between economic development and quantity of graduates from HEIs with good performance, thus showing a challenging scenario to achieve a sustainable and constant growth of Brazil's regions. The conclusion by Litzinger also point to generation of expertise as a mutual process between HEIs and the industry that can profit both [6].

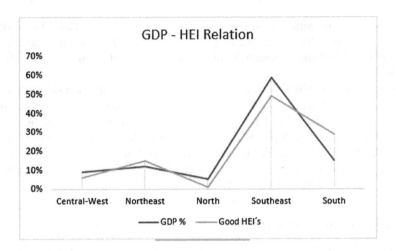

Fig. 1. GDP – HEI Performance

5   Conclusions and Outlook

Analyzing the difference in regional contribution of the national GDP, as shown in Table 1, it is clear that there is a significant disparity and the challenge is even bigger considering the difference between the industrialization level and the quantity and quality of the universities from the different regions as shown in Table 2.

Concerning the quantity of engineering degrees, there's been an increase in number of universities, which will lead to an increase in total number of graduates. The quality factor however has declined as shown especially at the 25.29% decrease of grade 5 ("State of the Art") Engineering Education Universities.

It is important to bring forth mechanisms to further include the academia in regional development. Several policies and actions can be taken by both sides (academia and regional actors) to enhance their participation and further increase the bond between them.

It is clear that the lack of engineers on the regions and the low occupation rate have a direct impact on the regions as shown by the proximity of the GDP percentage and the quantity of quality of degrees. It is also possible to asses from Fig. 1 that the High Quality Engineering HEI's and the GDP have very similar behavior between the macro regions.

To finalize, the sources quoted enforce the need for innovation and technical background as fundamental to regional development, especially if the cluster mode and academia fomented research is to be installed as an alternative for sustainable development.

References

1. do Brasil, B.C.: Time Series Management System. https://www3.bcb.gov.br/sgspub/localizarseries/localizarSeries.do?method=prepararTelaLocalizarSeries
2. IBGE: Contas Nacionais Trimestrais. ftp://ftp.ibge.gov.br/Contas_Nacionais/Contas_Nacionais_Trimestrais/Fasciculo_Indicadores_IBGE/pib-vol-val_201404caderno.pdf
3. Lins, L.M., Salerno, M.S., Araújo, B.C., Gomes, L.A.V., Nascimento, P.A.M.M., Toledo, D.: Escassez de Engenheiros no Brasil? Uma Proposta de Sistematização do Debate. Novos Estudos - CEBRAP **98**, 43–67 (2014)
4. Oliveira, G.B.: Regiões Inteligentes como Estratégia de Desenvolvimento Local. Revista Orbis Latina **1**(1), 35–39 (2011)
5. Quandt, C.O.: Inovação e Território: Elementos para a Formulação de Políticas de Capacitação Tecnológica e Desenvolvimento Regional. CMDE/UFPR, Curitiba
6. Litzinger, T., Lattuca, L.R., Hadgraft, R., Newstetter, W.: Engineering education and the development of expertise. J. Eng. Educ. **100**(1), 123–150 (2011)
7. Butz, W., Bloom, G., Gross, M., Kelly, K., Kofner, A., Rippen, H.: Is there a shortage of scientists and engineers? How would we know? (2003)
8. Nascimento, P.A.M.M.: Há Escassez Generalizada de Profissionais de Carreiras Técnico-Científicas no Brasil?: Uma Análise a Partir de Dados do CAGED. Mercado de Trabalho, pp. 19–28 (2011)
9. Maciente, A., Araújo, T.: A Demanda por Engenheiros e Profissionais Afins no Mercado de Trabalho Atual. Radar Brasília, pp. 43–54 (2011)
10. INEP: Relatório Síntese. http://portal.inep.gov.br/web/guest/enade/relatorio-sintese-2011
11. INEP: Enade. http://portal.inep.gov.br/enade
12. Lansu, A., Boon, J., Sloep, P.B., van Dam-Mieras, R.: Changing professional demands in sustainable regional development: a curriculum design process to meet transboundary competence. J. Clean. Prod. **49**, 123–133 (2013)
13. Avard, G., Zenios, M.: Curriculum framework considerations for introducing networked learning within a career-focused higher education institution. In: Proceedings of the 8th International Conference on Networked Learning, pp. 1–9. Maastricht School of Management, Maastricht (2012)
14. Devine-Wright, P., Fleming, P.D., Chadwick, H.: Role of social capital in advancing regional sustainable development. Impact Assess. Project Appraisal **19**(2), 161–167 (2001)
15. Stephens, J.C., Hernandez, M.E., Romàn, M., Graham, A.C., Scholz, R.W.: Higher education as a change agent for sustainability in different cultures and contexts. Int. J. Sustain. High. Educ. **9**(3), 317–338 (2008)
16. Zilahy, G., Huisingh, D.: The roles of academia in regional sustainability initiatives. J. Clean. Prod. **17**(12), 1057–1066 (2009)
17. Sgobbi, F., Cainarca, G.C.: High-performance work practices and core employee wages: evidence from italian manufacturing plants. ILR Rev. **68**(2), 426–456 (2015)

Evaluation of Additive Manufacturing Processes in Fabrication of Personalized Robot

Shushu Wang[(✉)], Rakshith Badarinath,
El-Amine Lehtihet, and Vittaldas Prabhu

Penn State University, University Park, PA, USA
sxw351@psu.edu

Abstract. Customers increasingly participate in the design stage of creating personalized products. Additive manufacturing (aka 3D printing) has become a popular enabler of personalization. In this paper we evaluate fabrication of an open source robot arm in terms of cost, build time, dimensional and locational accuracy, and mechanical properties. The mechanical components of the table-top robot were fabricated using two different AM processes: Fused deposition modelling (FDM) and Material Jetting (Polymer Jetting). Reducing the infill density to 50% in the FDM process resulted in a slight decrease in building time, material cost and tensile strength, and caused a 95% drop in yield strength. Simulation of the robot's mechanical assembly using its CAD model based on the expected tolerances of the components, resulted in estimation of the end-effector positioning accuracy to be 0.01 to 0.22 mm.

Keywords: Personalization · Fused deposition modelling · Material jetting · Infill density · Robot · Dimensional and locational accuracy · Tensile strength

1 Introduction

In recent decades, companies have tried a new strategy called mass production to provide broad provision of personalized products and services (Davis 1989), and the strategy is considered as an important competitive advantage (Fiore et al. 2003, Salvador et al. 2009). Kumar (2007) points out that personalization of products and services has been put forward as a business strategy to expand the market share for the past twenty years. 3D printing enables people to fabricate things as per their preferences and serves as an alternative to purchase mass-produced goods.

3D printing creates physical products from a computer generated design file by building up each layer on top of other to produce the final part. In this work, two 3D printing techniques were used: Fused Deposition Modeling (FDM) and PolyJet 3D printing. The FDM machine extrudes and deposits a semi-molten thermoplastic filament in a crisscross manner layer by layer from the bottom up. PolyJet 3D printing, being relatively new, jets UV curable liquid photopolymer onto the building platform (PolyJet Technology, Stratasys).

A number of studies on 3D printing process characteristics have been carried out. Generally, benchmark parts, instead of functional products, are tested in these studies. Mahesh et al. (2004) developed specific part design for benchmark tests and evaluated

© IFIP International Federation for Information Processing 2016
Published by Springer International Publishing AG 2016. All Rights Reserved
I. Nääs et al. (Eds.): APMS 2016, IFIP AICT 488, pp. 406–414, 2016.
DOI: 10.1007/978-3-319-51133-7_48

abilities of different AM processes based the test parts. Kim and Oh (2008) performed quantitative comparisons of mechanical properties, accuracy, roughness, speed, and material cost of several rapid prototyping processes, such as stereo lithography (SL), FDM, PolyJet, and selective laser sintering (SLS). Baich et al. (2015) investigated the relationship between infill density and the resulting mechanical properties, production cost and time of FDM process. 3D Matter website (2015) featured an article on influence of infill rate, layer height and infill pattern on mechanical performance for the FDM process involving PLA material.

The objective of this paper is to evaluate the characteristics of different 3D printing machines and processes in context to fabrication of a personalized robot. A personalization case study was conducted based on MeArm®, an open-source desktop robot arm. It is a 4-axis pick and place robot arm controlled by a joystick. The robot parts are laser cut from acrylic sheets and assembled with M3 self-tapping screws.

The paper is organized as follows. Section 2 provides insight on the linkage mechanism of the robot arm, 3D printing process parameters settings and finite element analysis (FEA) simulation constraints and results. Section 3 compares the parts printed from different 3D printing machines in terms of material cost, building time, dimensional accuracy, assembly accuracy, and part strength. Accuracy and strength of the original MeArm parts were calculated as well. Section 4 concludes the research and puts forth future research opportunities.

2 Case Study-3D Printing of a Desktop Robot Arm

Eight linkage parts from MeArm robot were 3D printed using three different machines that are available in Penn State: Makerbot Replicator (5th Generation), Fortus 250 mc, and Object30 Prime, and corresponding materials are Polylactic acid (PLA), Acrylonitrile butadiene styrene (ABS), and Rigid Opaque photopolymers (VeroBlue RGD 840). To evaluate the quality 3D printed parts: (1) building time and material cost was evaluated; (2) Hole diameter at each functional robot joint, distance between holes, and part thickness was measured; (3) Assembly tolerances were calculated; (4) Tensile tests were conducted to evaluate part strength. The evaluation results were compared with the results of tests conducted on original parts from MeArm Robotics.

2.1 Specimens Fabrication

A 3D CAD model of MeArm linkage was built using SolidWorks and 3D printed as shown in Fig. 1, and the parts highlighted in red are the driving links.

Various manufacturing parameters can be adjusted in build-preparation software. One set of linkage specimens are printed under each setting option listed in Table 1, while other parameters just following the machine default setting.

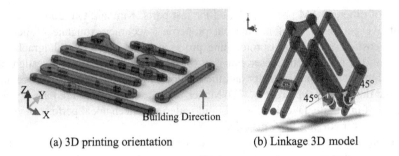

(a) 3D printing orientation   (b) Linkage 3D model

Fig. 1. Linkage parts (Color figure online)

Table 1. Manufacturing parameters

Specimen	Apparatus model	Material	Layer thickness (mm)	Interior density
1	MakerBot Replicator	MakerBot PLA Filament	0.150	100%
2				50%
3	Fortus 250 mc	ABSplus-P430	0.178	Solid
4				Sparse-low density
5	Object30 prime	VeroBlue RGD840	0.016	-

2.2 Test Procedures

To inspect dimensional accuracy of printed specimens, the diameter of holes on each link were measured precisely using SmartScope Flare from Optical Gaging Products; additionally, the average value of part thickness measured using a precision caliper at 3 different points of each part is considered as the thickness of that part.

With the above measurements, an assembly simulation was conducted in Solid-Works to evaluate the positional accuracy of the gripper location. In the static FEA simulation, the servo angles were set to 45° on the xz plane as shown in Fig. 1(b). The red dot represents the midpoint the gripper, and thus is considered as the gripper location. It is assumed that only the linkages have dimensional errors. The errors of all the other parts in the assembly such as screws, and the tolerance of servo angles was not considered in this study.

In order to have a more comprehensive comparison of the accuracy of gripper location of the three 3D printers, a simulation with more data is carried. First, the deviations of distance between holes are assumed to follow normal distributions, and the quality requirement of 3D printing parts is supposed at ±2σ level based on the expected tolerance. Second, for each machine type, 50 deviations were sampled from the normal distribution for every distance value. And the sampled deviations were added to the distance for every linkage. Finally, linkages with modified distance between holes were assembled in SolidWorks. For each machine type, 50 assembly were created and the corresponding gripper locations were recorded. Since MakerBot does not provide estimating dimensional accuracy, this paper assumes ±0.500 mm as the dimensional accuracy based on the work of Melenka *et al.* (2015). The stated dimensional accuracies of Fortus and Object 3D printers' is ±0.241 mm and ±0.100 mm respectively.

A finite element analysis (FEA) simulation is performed on the linkage mechanism in SolidWorks. The simulation is to evaluate the stress and strain of each link when robot arm is picking up a 1 N object (including gripper weight) with each servo produces a torque of 0.17 Nm according to specification of the micro servo. "Fixed Hinge" was applied to the revolute joints of the robot arm. To compare the mechanical performance of 3D printing specimens and MeArm robot's acrylic parts, tensile tests were done.

3   Results and Discussions

3.1   Specimens Fabrication Results

Based on the 3D printing settings in Sect. 2, 5 sets of specimens were fabricated and are shown in Fig. 2.

The building preparation software of 3D printers provided an estimated building time and raw material consumption. Figure 3 provides a comparison between printed specimens in terms of building time and material cost calculated from the consumption.

Obviously, the FDM process needs a longer building time than the PolyJet process. To build solid parts, MakerBot Replicator requires a building time of about 2 times longer than Object30 Prime. Additionally, the building time of MakerBot Replicator is about 15% longer than that of Fortus 250 mc. Moreover, the reduction in infill density only results in a slight decrease in building time for the FDM process.

The PolyJet process has a higher raw material cost than the FDM process. For solid parts, the Object30 Prime costs about 6 times more than the MakerBot Replicator, and 20% more than the Fortus 250 mc. Actually, ABS has a higher unit price than Object's material. However, Object still cost more for the same parts due to its higher density. In terms of material cost, the reduction of interior density resulted in an apparent decrease of 16% for MakerBot Replicator and 21% for Fortus 250 mc.

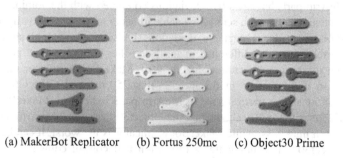

(a) MakerBot Replicator   (b) Fortus 250mc   (c) Object30 Prime

Fig. 2. Specimens fabricated by 3D printers

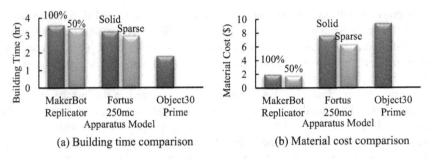

(a) Building time comparison   (b) Material cost comparison

Fig. 3. Comparison of apparatus models and processes

3.2   Dimensional Accuracy and Assembly Accuracy

To investigate dimensional accuracy, several functional dimensions were measured, including the diameter of circular holes at links, the relative location of these holes, and the thickness of parts. Figure 4 describes deviations in these measurements, observed in the 5 sets of printed specimens and original MeArm pats.

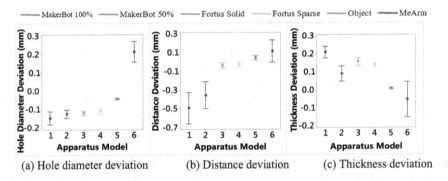

(a) Hole diameter deviation   (b) Distance deviation   (c) Thickness deviation

Fig. 4. Dimensional deviation

Figure 4(a) indicates that Object 30 Prime provides the best performance in hole size with the smallest deviation and variance, and MeArm parts are the worst. The holes of MeArm parts have positive deviations compared with the nominal size, which results in a clearance fits with screws to enable joints to rotate smoothly. In contrast, 3D printing process produces negative deviations because of material shrinkage after cooling. Furthermore, the difference in infill densities does not have any significant influence on dimensional accuracy. In Fig. 4(b), MakerBot Replicator makes the largest deviation and variance in distance. Fortus 250 mc and Object30 Prime have smaller deviations. The performance of MeArm parts is between MakerBot and other two 3D printers. Figure 4(c) shows that the Object30 Prime and MeArm have the best performance in thickness, while MakerBot Replicator is the worst. It can be concluded that the Object30 Prime has better z resolution and control compared to other two printers.

Table 2. Gripper location deviation

Apparatus model	Interior density	Deviation (XYZ) (mm)
MakerBot replicator	100%	(0.81, 0.16, −0.87)
	50%	(0.57, 0.07, −0.42)
Fortus 250 mc	Solid	(−0.10, 0.03, −0.61)
	Sparse	(−0.04, 0.02, −0.58)
Object30 prime	-	(0.10, 0.01, −0.03)
MeArm parts	-	(−0.22, 0.32, 0.03)

Based on the measurement of distance between screw holes and parts thickness, linkages are assembled in SolidWorks. Table 2 lists the deviation of gripper location of 3D printing specimens and the original MeArm parts.

Assembly of MeArm parts has more accurate gripper location than MakerBot parts assembly, but is worse than Fortus and Object. The assembly of Fortus parts has similar accuracy in XY plane with Object, but Object has much better Z axis accuracy. The reason is that Object parts have similar distance accuracy to Fortus parts but are more accurate in thickness. The MakerBot Replicator produced the largest deviation in gripper location.

Simulation result of gripper location deviations is shown in Fig. 5. MakerBot Replicator has the most scatter, thus larger deviations in gripper location, and is followed by Fortus 250 mc, while Object30 Prime has the smallest deviations.

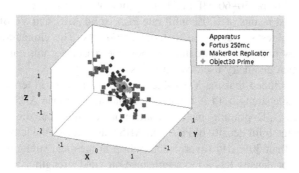

Fig. 5. Simulated XYZ deviations of gripper location

3.3   FEA Simulation and Tensile Tests

In the static FEA, the maximum stress and the maximum strain was observed at the driving links due to servo torque, and the simulation results of different materials are similar as shown in Table 3. Table 4 shows the tensile test results of the same part fabricated from different processes, and Fig. 6 is a comparison of stress-strain curves.

As stated in datasheet from MakerBot, the average tensile strength of PLA is 48 MPa. 3D Matter website concluded from several experiments that the elongation at break of PLA in 3D printing is 4–6%. Furthermore, according to the datasheet by Stratasys, for ABSplus-P430, the yield strength is 31 MPa; the tensile strength is

Table 3. FEA simulation results

Strength	Material			
	MakerBot PLA filament	ABSplus-P430	VeroBlue RGD840	Acrylic sheet
Maximum stress (MPa)	7.42	7.41	7.42	7.42
Maximum strain (%)	0.19	0.27	0.29	0.19

Table 4. Tensile test results comparison

Material	Density	Yield strength (MPa)	Tensile strength (MPa)	Break elongation (%)
MakerBot PLA filament	100%	22.55	45.31	4.0
	50%	1.65	39.14	3.4
ABSplus-P430	Solid	32.13	32.66	7.5
	Sparse	1.22	23.79	6.0
VeroBlue RGD840	-	52.66	54.52	6.9
Acrylic sheet	-	1.37	42.87	2.0

33 MPa; and elongation at break is 6%; while for VeroBlue RGD840, the tensile strength is stated to be 50–60 MPa and elongation at break is 6%.

The tensile test results of 100% infill rate PLA, solid ABS, and VeroBlue RGD840 are similar to values stated in the material datasheets. The elongation at break of VeroBlue is only half of official data. The possible reason for this can be attribute to different specimen geometry used by Stratasys.

It can be concluded that the VeroBlue material is the best in terms of both yield strength and tensile strength. PLA has larger tensile strength than ABS, but lower yield strength. Besides, 3D printing materials are more ductile than the MeArm acrylic material. When the infill density of PLA and ABS was reduced, the tensile strength was reduced by less than 30%. However, a sharp drop in the yield strength was observed. Therefore, interior density has a large influence on yield strength.

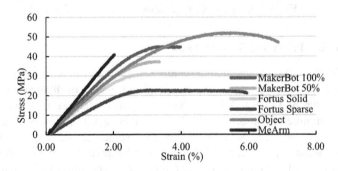

Fig. 6. Stress-strain curve comparison

According to the tensile test results and FEA simulation results, 3D printing parts were evaluated to be strong enough for the robot arm.

4 Conclusions and Future Work

In this paper, a case study of 3D print the linkage mechanism of a desktop robot arm was carried out. Among the three 3D printers applied in this paper, Object30 Prime had the best performance in terms of building time, dimensional accuracy, and end effect accuracy. MakerBot Replicator was the most material cost effective machine. Specimens of both Fortus and Object printers were better in dimensional accuracy and assembly accuracy than the original MeArm robot arm. All the hole diameters of 3D printing parts were smaller than the nominal size because of material shrinkage. Moreover, 3D printing parts were thicker than the nominal size in the z direction. The tensile test showed that VeroBlue had the largest yield strength and tensile strength. PLA part had larger tensile strength than ABS part and acrylic part, but it was not as ductile as ABS part. Acrylic part was the most brittle of the specimens. According to FEA simulation results, 3D printing specimens were able to meet the mechanical property requirements. For the FDM process, reducing interior density resulted in a slightly decrease in building time and material cost, but caused a significant decrease in yield strength.

Further research on devising an optimal way to adjust process parameters to meet a given set of requirements can be carried out.

References

Baich, L., Manogharan, G., Marie, H.: Study of infill print design on production cost-time of 3D printed ABS parts. Int. J. Rapid Manuf. 5(3–4), 308–319 (2015)

Davis, S.M.: From "future perfect": mass customizing. Plan. Rev. 17(2), 16–21 (1989)

Fiore, A.M., Seung-Eun, L., Kunz, G.: Psychographic variables affecting willingness to use body-scanning. J. Bus. Manag. 9(3), 271 (2003)

Kim, G.D., Oh, Y.T.: A benchmark study on rapid prototyping processes and machines: quantitative comparisons of mechanical properties, accuracy, roughness, speed, and material cost. Proc. Inst. Mech. Eng. Part B: J. Eng. Manuf. 222(2), 201–215 (2008)

Kumar, A.: Mass customization: manufacturing issues and taxonomic analyses. Int. J. Flex. Manuf. Syst. 19(4), 625–629 (2007)

Mahesh, M., Wong, Y.S., Fuh, J.Y.H., Loh, H.T.: Benchmarking for comparative evaluation of RP systems and processes. Rapid Prototyp. J. 10(2), 123–135 (2004)

Melenka, G.W., Schofield, J.S., Dawson, M.R., Carey, J.P.: Evaluation of dimensional accuracy and material properties of the MakerBot 3D desktop printer. Rapid Prototyp. J. 21(5), 618–627 (2015)

PolyJet Technology, Stratasys. http://www.stratasys.com/3d-printers/technologies/polyjet-technology

Salvador, F., De Holan, P.M., Piller, F.T.: Cracking the code of mass customization. MIT Sloan Manag. Rev. **50**(3), 71 (2009)

What is the influence of infill %, layer height and infill pattern on my 3D prints? (2015). http://my3dmatter.com/influence-infill-layer-height-pattern/

Retail Tactical Planning: An Aligned Process?

Heidi Dreyer[1(✉)], Iskra Dukovska-Popovska[2], Kasper Kiil[1],
and Riikka Kaipia[3]

[1] The Norwegian University of Science and Technology,
7491 Trondheim, Norway
Heidi.C.Dreyer@ntnu.no
[2] Aalborg University, Aalborg, Denmark
[3] Aalto University School of Science, Otaniementie, Finland

Abstract. This paper addresses tactical planning in retailing through a case study approach in one grocery retailing company. The issues are how tactical planning is conducted and how the different plans are connected. The study complements earlier retail planning studies by showing the sequence of planning phases and by studying the fragmented plans as a process. The master category planning is important and sets borders for the other planning phases. This stabilizes overall planning. However, the retailer loses responsiveness to demand. The study proposes better integration among planning phases.

Keywords: Grocery retailing · Planning processes · Tactical planning

1 Introduction

Efficient supply and demand planning is an appropriate solution to ensure product availability in stores at lower costs [4, 12]. Retailers fix some important variables, such as store product segmentation, category management, planograms and delivery patterns and replenishment lead times, at a tactical level and pass the decisions to the execution level as parameters [12]. How the different tactical planning issues affect the retail operations (stores, transportation and distribution) and responds to demand has been treated to a limited extent [4, 12]. Even though the basic structure of a coordinated planning framework in the grocery retail industry has been proposed [7], the interdependency of the planning decisions requires a good balance between individual planning processes and supply and demand management. The need for more integrative retail logistics and collaborative planning has been identified [7, 12].

This study addresses tactical planning processes in retailing. In particular, the purpose is to analyse the planning processes and their aim, and to what extent these are integrated to serve the need for alignment and demand responsiveness. Consequently, the research questions are: (1) How is tactical planning conducted at a retail company? (2) How are the different plans connected and interact?

© IFIP International Federation for Information Processing 2016
Published by Springer International Publishing AG 2016. All Rights Reserved
I. Nääs et al. (Eds.): APMS 2016, IFIP AICT 488, pp. 415–422, 2016.
DOI: 10.1007/978-3-319-51133-7_49

2   Literature on Retail Planning

The main objective of mid-term, aggregated supply chain (SC) planning is to build a plan that satisfies demand while maximizing profit [2] in a timely manner. Mid-term planning often covers multiple SC stages [6, 11] is based on aggregate demands for entire product families and covers a medium-term horizon. Creating such a collaborative plan could be challenging since different functions may achieve profitability in conflicting ways. Coordination between stages and functions becomes the core element in SC mid-term planning.

Retail operations and SC management in the retailing context have been largely studied [5]. Most studies focus on some aspect of planning, like delivery patterns [12], in-store operations [13], retail store replenishments or reducing waste in fresh food SCs [10]. An overall understanding or syntheses of retail planning are rarely presented, with an exception being the grocery retail planning framework by [7]. Mid-term planning comprises several planning phases conducted by and related to one or more functions. First, mid-term planning deals with category and product-related aspects that are grouped as product segmentation and allocation (covering issues related to procurement, warehousing and distribution) and master category planning, related to sales. Second, mid-term planning covers plans for managing the product flow (inbound planning, production planning and distribution planning) and in-store planning, including capacity and personnel planning (Fig. 1).

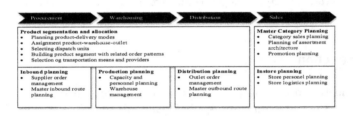

Fig. 1.   Grocery retail planning framework at the mid-term level [8] (modified).

Agrawal and Smith [1] describe a more process-oriented SC planning framework at a (furniture) retailer covering the planning steps, their succession and interrelation. Based on combining the two SC planning overviews, the different planning activities are discussed below. Following the planning process design [8], we identified, based on theory, design parameters (planning horizon and aggregation level), inputs, outputs, objectives and functions involved in each planning phase.

In grocery retail, selection of vendors is more a strategic decision [7]. For products that are carried over multiple seasons, contracts may allow for modifications in order quantities within certain ranges, depending on the observed demand for the product. In addition, retailers can evaluate vendors based on past performance and can be involved in the vendors' production planning more actively or by sharing forecasts and placing purchase orders [1].

The planning of product logistics deals with coordination of flow of products from suppliers to warehousing and to retail stores. These decisions are made on different planning objects, product-specific and product segment-specific decisions. For inbound logistics, the following planning issues are done at different levels of aggregation: supplier-specific level (related to product ordering) and supplier-segment level (related to transportation issues). Distribution planning deals with decisions to fulfill customer service targets at minimum costs as a trade-off between inventory management policies for each store and delivery policies from the central warehouse. As in inbound planning, the decisions are done at different aggregation levels, some are store (concept) related and others focus on delivery regions.

To summarize, master category planning and sourcing are driven more by the demand and product segmentation and allocation are aimed at balancing demand and supply (and are performed by including several functions); the other mid-term planning decisions are aimed at ensuring supply is driven by lowering costs.

3 Methodology

The aim of the study is to understand the tactical planning processes in grocery retailing. The methodology we chose is a single exploratory case study since this allowed us to gain the needed in-depth insight into the planning process and to enable us to study the planning process in its natural environment [3]. A single case was selected in the grocery sector because of the novel nature of the retail planning process and the wide product range and the mix of product types (fresh, frozen and dry food), which make it relevant from a planning perspective.

Data were collected in two steps. First, site visits and workshops focusing on describing processes and operations, and observations at warehouses and stores were the main means to understand the planning environment. Second, the data about the tactical planning process were collected in structured interviews following a case study protocol [14]. The protocol was designed to cover four topics: the objective and content of the tactical planning process, the structure of the planning processes, planning interconnectedness and performance.

The interviews took place at three levels: retail chain, procurement and suppliers and logistics and it involved key managers with responsibility for tactical planning. The field notes from the interviews were converted to a description of the tactical planning and structured according to the literature in Sect. 2. We asked the key interviewees to review the case description to ensure its validity [14].

4 Results

The case is a Nordic grocery retailer offering a full-range grocery assortment. The organization is structured into three main functions: retail chain (stores), procurement and assortment, and logistics. Altogether, the retailer runs hundreds of stores divided in different store concepts ranging from discount stores and supermarkets to premium stores. Centralised planning tasks include the development of the different store concepts, their assortments, marketing, sales and promotions and various purchasing and supplier network decisions. Managing the logistics consists of the inbound logistics from suppliers to the warehouses, warehouse operations and outbound logistics to the stores. The main physical operations are the pick-and-pack process at the warehouses together with inbound and outbound transport. All the stores are supplied from the central warehouse, regional warehouses or a combination of the two.

Figure 2 illustrates the tactical planning process, while Table 1 includes a more detailed description of each activity. The tactical planning process takes place at all three functions (Fig. 2), but contrary to what is illustrated in the framework presented by [7], the process begins at the retail chain. The tactical planning process can be described as follows: (1) The retail chain decides the main profile of the chain concept and the product categories (category, profile, depth, price, etc.) and promotions for each concept. The decisions are made at an aggregated level covering a time horizon of 12 months, with two main objectives: revenue and profit per chain concept. (2) This plan is afterwards disaggregated into specific products, volumes and time periods for the promotions. (3) Additionally, the specifications of each profile act as an input to the procurement and assortment function, which disaggregates the master category plan into specific products and suppliers while (4) negotiating and making the final contract with the suppliers. The suppliers' contracts regulate the terms and conditions for the purchase and deliveries (price and discounts, volume, frequency, promotions, packaging size) for a 12-month period, while the planograms for each store or store concept are updated every 4 months. Planograms define where specific products are placed on shelves and the stock level. (5) Based on the volumes specified in the contracts and the expected sales in each area (can be derived from the sizes of the shelf in the planograms), the inventory structure is decided upon. This may be adjusted during the year. Hereafter, (6) to ease inventory management decisions, all products are divided into different logistical product groups, which should share the same service level before (7) the final inventory policy and delivery plan is finalized. By grouping the suppliers into smaller regions, the inventory and delivery plan specifies when and how much to collect from each supplier. Lastly, the plan for outbound deliveries from warehouse to stores is made on two hierarchical levels, also with a varying time horizon. Based on the profile of each concept or the store revenue and the inventory structure, (8) guidelines are provided for the number of weekly deliveries for three high-level product groups: (a) frozen/dry/fresh food, (b) fruits and vegetables and (c) products from the central warehouse. Large stores get more frequent deliveries than smaller stores. Finally, (9) the individual routes from the warehouse to the stores are calculated by balancing the delivery plan with the utilization of each truck.

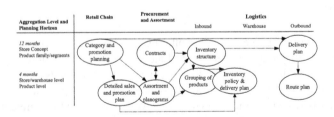

Fig. 2. The sequence of tactical planning phases in the case company.

Figure 2 shows that planning is top–down oriented by starting at an aggregated level and letting the aggregated decisions be the premises for lower level planning. We observed two layers in the tactical planning: one that focuses on a 12 months horizon and is aggregated (store concept and product category) and the second that focuses on product family and individual products and has a 4-month time horizon.

The planning is functional, and the output from one function acts as the input and sets the premises for the next function. Limited feedback loops and interaction between the planning steps are apparent. At the tactical level, there is no joint planning team that joins and coordinates the main planning areas to integrate and align between the functional plans. However, the company does apply different types of meetings to discuss cross-functional issues between the plans.

For each tactical plan there are objectives that serve the aim of the function. Revenue and profit are the objectives of the retail chain, and logistics is measured according to the cost and service level. At this level there do not appear to be any cross-functional objectives that align the SC.

Logistics planning is done under the constraints set in former planning steps, and the aim for logistics is to focus on cost and delivery service to stores given the assortment decided on. Similarly, the stores operate on decisions made by the retail chain and procurement and assortment.

5   Discussion

Content and Sequence in a Tactical Planning Process. Planning in the case company has several of the characteristics described in the literature. We observed the functional structure of the planning described by [7], but we also found the planning was process oriented, including different steps and sequences as [1] describe. The planning in the case company started in the retail chain, which decided the master plan for the chain and assortment concept, followed by the assortment and sourcing decisions before logistics decided how and when to move products. Additionally, decisions taken on a higher level is the input from lower planning levels, the planning follows a sequence and is repeated every 4 or 12 months.

The initial planning phases seem to be driven by demand management objectives [2], while the later phases are driven by supply management. The start of the planning process is the master category, store profile and sales and promotion decisions, which set important premises for the rest of the planning. The retailer obeys the practice presented by [12] as it fixes some important variables, such as store product segmentation, category management, space management and planograms and delivery patterns and replenishment lead times, on a tactical level and passes the decisions down to the execution level as parameters. The next planning step also focuses on demand management decisions as procurement and assortment decides on the products and suppliers. When logistics is brought into the planning process, then supply management aspects are brought into the planning, e.g. inbound and outbound logistics and transportation and warehouse capacity.

Table 1. Description of planning process

Activity	Aggr./Horizon	Input	Output	Objectives	Functions
(1) Category and promotion plan	Store concept, Product family	Limited restrictions	Profile of each concept, including price range and promotions	Profit, Revenue	Retail chain
(2) Detailed sales and promotion plan	4 months, Product level, Concept	Input from master category planning, Demand forecast or similar promotions	Specify products - Volume, time and period - Price/promotion per product/concept - Input to inbound logistics call-offs	Revenue, Profit, Waste	Retail chain
(3) Assortment and planograms	4 months, Product level, Store/concept level	Profile of the concept	- Specify products - Shelf allocation (planograms)		Procurement, Spacing
(4) Contracts	12 months, Product/family	Assortment	Supplier contract (yearly volumes, delivery frequency, discounts)		Procurement
(5) Inventory structure	12 months/Trigged by season/as needed, Product level	Warehouse capacity, Store demand, Seasons, Locations of suppliers	Storage/location plan (where to locate each product)	Warehouse capacity	Logistics
(6) Grouping of products	4–12 months, Product level	Planograms	Allocation of individual products into A, B, C, D, E categories for planning decisions–service level		Logistics, procurement
(7) Inventory policy and delivery plan	4–12 months, Product/category level	Product shelf life, Balancing transportation cost and inventory cost, Demand uncertainty, Discounts	Quantity, Time/frequency, Safety stock, Grouping suppliers into regions and delivery frequency	Service level, Warehouse waste, Tied-up capital	Logistics
(8) Delivery plan	12 months, High product family level	Profile of the concept/Store revenue, Inventory structure	Delivery structure for stores - Delivery frequency - Delivery time	Service level, Waste and cost, Dry, Inv. turnover max 12 days	Logistics
(9) Route plan	4–12 months, Store level	Delivery plan, Size of trucks	Routes for deliveries to stores		Logistics

The planning process makes the planning inert since the outcome of the higher level planning is fixed for a long time horizon (12 months) and it is top–down oriented. This makes the planning more predictive and less sensitive to disturbance and market changes and makes it easier to focus on resource utilization and efficiency. However, this makes the planning less dynamic and adjustable to the actual demand situation. Long-term assortment planning and promotion planning (12 months) actually stabilise the planning, and other plans are adjusted.

5Interplay between organizational functions. Constraints are decided by the objectives of the retail chain and procurement and assortment function, and the main role of logistics is to make a plan that optimizes cost and service level. The 'what' decisions are managed by the retail chain and assortment and procurement, leaving the 'when' and 'how much' decisions of warehouse, transport capacity and delivery frequency to the inbound and outbound logistics planning. The store profile and assortment planning constrains the following planning phases to an extent that the other plans keep the role of implementing the plan.

The overall tactical planning process is fragmented as it consists of a set of sequential plans that are only loosely integrated. First, coordination is done when needed and there is no common arena for integrating all the functions that are involved in the process in order to have consensus in the planning. When planning is done in quite separated loops that serve different demands, they can easily end up in sub-optimising. Second, the planning objectives are different in the main planning functions; some obey commercial objectives, revenue and profit, and others cost and service level. The planning is driven by several goals, but it remains unclear how the planning quality is defined and measured.

Some improvement proposals emerged. First, the different plans can be better coordinated and integrated in general. Second, there need to be efficient feedback loops from implementing the plan to tactical planning. This is essential for keeping the plan responsive to demand and achieving alignment. The company needs to have a practice to update the plan between planning rounds if needed. Third, the whole process, particularly the operational part, could benefit from adopting more formal practices. Instead of the reactive way of operating, with ad hoc meetings and fire fighting, the company could operate in a more proactive manner. Furthermore, we suggest that differentiated planning [9] can be realised to some extent.

6 Concluding Remarks

The operating environment of retail business increases competitive pressure because of multichannel operations, global sourcing and increasing number of product variants. To survive in this competitive environment, retailers need to ensure product availability at stores and at the same time operate efficiently. Our study examines how a retail company has implemented these challenges in its planning solution.

The case company uses a solution for defining retail store assortments for a long period of time and ensuring the supply of products by supplier agreements. This practice stabilises the planning and sets targets for the operations. The downside of the practice is the low level of demand responsiveness. In this paper we suggest that the company, if better demand responsiveness is desired, could realise formal feedback loops from operations to assortment planning. This would allow adjusting the assortment. This could be applied when planning the next 4-month assortment but also between the planning rounds. The company could also benefit from more formal planning practices and integration mechanisms in realising integrated planning.

This study reports initial results from an on-going research project concerning one retail company. The next steps are to collect more data, particularly on outbound logistics and store planning in order to look deeper into demand responsiveness.

References

1. Agrawal, N., Smith, S.A.: Supply chain planning processes for two major retailers. In: Agrawal, N., Smith, S.A. (eds.) Retail Supply Chain Management, pp. 11–23. Springer, New York (2009)
2. Chopra, S., Meindl, P.: Supply Chain Management: Strategy, Planning and Operation. Pearson Higher Education, London (2013)
3. Eisenhardt, K.M.: Building theories from case study research. Acad. Manag. Rev. **14**(4), 532–550 (1989)
4. Ettouzani, Y., Yates, N., Mena, C.: Examining retail on shelf availability. Int. J. Phys. Dist. Log. Manag. **42**(3), 213–243 (2012)
5. Fernie, J., Sparks, L., McKinnon, A.C.: Retail logistics in the UK: past, present and future. Int. J. Ret. Dist. Manag. **38**(11/12), 894–914 (2010)
6. Fleischmann, B., Meyr, H., Wagner, M.: Advanced planning. In: Stadler, H., Kilger, C. (eds.) Supply Chain Management and Advanced Planning, pp. 71–95. Springer, Berling (2008)
7. Hübner, A.H., Kuhn, H., Sternbeck, M.G.: Demand and supply chain planning in grocery retail. Int. J. Ret. Dist. Manag. **41**(7), 512–530 (2013)
8. Ivert, L.K., et al.: Contingency between S&OP design and planning environment. Int. J. Phys. Dist. Log. Manag. **45**(8), 747–773 (2015)
9. Kaipia, R., Holmström, J.: Selecting the right planning approach for a product. Supply Chain Manag.: Int. J. **12**(3), 3–13 (2007)
10. Kaipia, R., Dukovska-Popovska, I., Loikkanen, L.: Creating sustainable fresh food supply chains. Int. J. Phys. Dist. Log. Manag. **43**(3), 262–276 (2013)
11. Kreipl, S., Pinedo, M.: Planning and scheduling in supply chains: overview on issues in practice. Prod. Oper. Manag. **13**(1), 77–92 (1994)
12. Kuhn, H., Sternbeck, M.G.: Integrative retail logistics: an exploratory study. Oper. Manag. Res. **6**(1), 2–18 (2013)
13. van Donselaar, K.H., et al.: Ordering behavior in retail stores and implications for automated replenishment. Manag. Sci. **56**(5), 766–784 (2010)
14. Yin, R.K.: Case Study Research. Sage, Thousand Oaks (2014)

Influence of Quality and Productivity on Milk Production Sustainability: From an Anthropocentric to an Ecocentric View

Max W. Oliveira[1,2], Feni Agostinho[2(✉)], Cecília M.V.B. Almeida[2], and Biagio F. Giannetti[2]

[1] Federal Institute of Sul de Minas Gerais, Inconfidentes, Brazil
[2] Paulista University, São Paulo, Brazil
feni@unip.br

Abstract. Brazil ranks fourth worldwide position on milk production, and Minas Gerais State corresponds to 27% of national production. Eighty percent of the Brazilian milk producers are extensive-familiar, characterized by the absence of technicization and inefficient management that leads to low productivity and quality. Aiming to improve milk productivity and quality, the governmental program *"Minas Leite"* was launched. This work aims a regional sustainability multicriteria assessment of milk production in Minas Gerais. Social, economic, and environmental indexes are calculated before and after implementing *"Minas Leite"*. Results show that *"Minas Leite"* should be promoted because it leads to higher sustainability than current production (2.3 times more liters of milk per year, 8.9 times more annual net income, 52% more available jobs, and an increase of 13% on salaries paid). However, efforts are needed to reach a regional strong sustainability under an ecocentric perspective, because *"Minas Leite"* showed worst performance for environmental indicators.

Keywords: Milk production · *"Minas Leite"* program · Minas Gerais State · Sustainability

1 Introduction

Cow milk, a source of protein, vitamins, minerals and energy is amongst the most consumed food items worldwide. Brazil holds the fourth position in the world milk production ranking, accounting for 5.3% of the overall production, below to the United States (14.7%), India (8.6%) and China (6%) [1]. The milk production chain currently holds a social and economic importance in Brazil, because it employs nearly three million workers and produces annually 35 billion liters of milk; in 1990 this value was 19.5 billion and the goal is to reach 41 billion

M.W. Oliveira—Authors are grateful to CAPES-PROSUP and CNPq (proc. no. 307422/2015-1).

I. Nääs et al. (Eds.): APMS 2016, IFIP AICT 488, pp. 423–430, 2016.
DOI: 10.1007/978-3-319-51133-7_50

in 2023 [2]. The state of Minas Gerais is the number one milk producer in Brazil, accounting for 27% of the total national production [3].

Some characteristics of the dairy farming in Brazil are its distribution all over the country, the heterogeneousness among the productive systems, and a considerable participation of small family producers on the national yield. According to Carvalho [4], until the 90's there was a national interventionism on every stage of the milk productive chain, which caused a standardization on the dairy products. For the industry, this interventionism discouraged the willingness of the market to develop new products, bringing to the consumer a restricted range of dairy products. However, this government policy were considered as positive for the producers, as they would know in advance how much they would receive for the milk produced. After the trade opening occurred between 1990 and 1992, the prices were then ruled by the market law of supply and demand.

Aiming to modernize and increase the competitiveness of the milk productive chain, the Brazilian government approved the Normative Instruction no. 51 in 2002, which determined the minimum quality standards for the raw milk (in natura). This corresponded to a major pressure on the producers, as they were forced to fit in those new standards under penalty of being excluded of the market [5]. According to CEPEA [2], from these changes and considering the new food requirements for the consumers, a different business behavior for milk producers and for the entire milk chain agents were also required. All these changes led to another pressure on the producers, for higher specialization, adoption of new technologies, increase of production, decrease of seasonality, improvement of the product and increase on the production scale.

Brazil currently has highly technified productive systems (such as the Fazenda Colorado in the municipality of Araras that produces 62,000 L_{milk}/day [6]), but about 80% of the producers has low level of intensification and production (<200 L_{milk}/day; [7]). This majority, called as small family producers, faces many technical and economic difficulties to keep their production, which demands for governmental support as financing and technical assistance. CEPEA [2] shows, for example, that meanwhile the effective operational cost of the milk production in the state of Minas Gerais increased 1.86% between November 2014 and December 2015, the average price paid for the producer in 2015 was the lowest in the last five years, reaching only 0.95 BRZ. Another difficulty faced by the small producer is the increase of the volume and quality for the milk produced, because the dairy houses pay more for producers who provide higher volumes of milk with higher nutritional and better sanitary conditions.

On the effort to overcome these liabilities and avoid other potential socioeconomic problems that would raise if the small producers gave up producing milk (rural exodus, for example), the government of Minas Gerais launched in 2005 the Milk Productive Chain State Program, known as "Minas Leite". The goal of this program is to enable the small-family milk production by providing technical and management qualification focused on their productive systems, aiming the increase of productivity, quality of milk, and producer income. Although this program can be considered as positive on the short term politics, creating public policies such as the *"Minas Leite"* rarely consider a systemic view of the issue (i.e. in different scales), which may result in additional problems for a larger scale perspective. For example, what would be the impact on the sustainability of the regional milk production of implementing the *"Minas Leite"* program?

This work aims to use a multimetric approach to assess the regional sustainability of milk production in southern Minas Gerais. Environmental, social and economic indexes are analyzed to discuss on the regional sustainability of the current yearly milk production, as well as after the intensification of extensive systems as envisioned by the *"Minas Leite"* program.

2 Methods

2.1 Case Study Description and Raw Data Source

The environmental performance of the productive systems analyzed in this work were previously studied by Oliveira and Agostinho [8]. These authors considered 92 milk producers by obtaining raw data in situ (through personal interviews and local observations), and through cluster analysis that resulted in five representative systems – shown on Table 1. G1 and G2 are rated as semi-intensive, they have Dutch cattle created in good grazing quality, in addition to feeding supplemented with fodder and feed. G3 is an extensive system, it has cattle with not genuine genetics created in degraded grazing with forage supplement during winter. The G4 and G5 are intensive systems, they have Dutch cattle that are confined in sheds (free stall model) and are fed with feed and fodder during the year; the facilities have high technology (i.e. extraction and pre-processing of milk, as well as thermal comfort for animals). Greater details on the characteristics of the systems and on the criteria used for the cluster analysis are shown in Oliveira and Agostinho [8].

Table 1. Main characteristics of milk production systems existing at southern region of Minas Gerais State

System	Area (ha)	Production (Lmilk/day)	Productivity (Lmilk/cow/day)	Regional representativeness[a] (%)
G1 (semi-intensive)	182	4.400	21	1
G2 (semi-intensive)	19	360	12	17
G3 (extensive)	17	36	5.5	80
G4 (intensive)	21	1060	21	1
G5 (intensive)	99	3500	31	1

[a]Percentage of total regional area (600,000 ha) allocated to milk production

2.2   Indices on Milk Production Sustainability

The meaning of sustainability in this paper consider the traditional conceptual model in which the importance of social, economic and environmental aspects are acknowledged to ensure that the current society develops without negatively affecting the capacity of future generations to have their needs assisted. The indexes chosen and considered as representative of sustainability concept, for the purposes of this work, are shown on Table 2. The economic and social indexes were established after identifying those that are most used and accepted by the scientific community and governmental research agencies focused on milk production studies; additionally, experts on technical issues related to livestock were consulted to validate the chosen indexes. Concerning the environmental aspects, among a wide variety of tools and indexes available on the literature that assess the pressure on environment caused by productive systems, in this work we have used the environmental accounting based on emergy (spelled with "m"). This method was chosen due to its strong scientific background, it is based on the energy of biological systems, the general theory of systems, and the thermodynamics. Details regarding definitions, meanings and rules for the environmental accounting using emergy can be found mainly in Odum [9]. Among the indexes derived from this method, it were chosen those which expressed directly the environmental sustainability of the systems analyzed: emergy renewability index (%R) and environmental sustainability index (ESI).

Table 2. Social, economic and environmental indicators considered in this work to represent sustainability

Indicators	Meaning	Source
Social h_{labor}/yr	Hour of labor per year	a
BRZ/h_{labor}	Income received (in Brazilian currency) per labour hour	a
Economic L_{milk}/yr	Liters of milk produced per year	a
BRZ/L_{milk}	Net income per liter of produced milk	a
Environmental %R	Emergy renewability index (renewable emergy/total emergy)	b
ESI	Environmental sustainability index	b

[a]This work; [b]Oliveira and Agostinho [8]

The indexes on Table 2 were initially calculated for each individual group as presented in Table 1 (G1, G2, G3, G4 and G5), what allows a comparison among groups concerning their social, economic and environmental performance. Next, the indexes obtained for each group are expanded for all the southern Minas Gerais area; for this purpose, the regional representativeness (% in land use, Table 1) of each group is considered. This scenario is called as Scenario#0, which allows the discussion about the current sustainability of regional milk production. At the same time, the indexes obtained for each group are expanded again for the entire southern region of Minas Gerais, but now considering the complete replacement of the extensive systems G3 by the semi-intensive system G2 as envisioned by *"Minas Leite"* program. This scenario is called as Scenario #1, which allows a discussion about a potential sustainability "if" the *"Minas Leite"* program were implemented; the potential distribution of milk production groups in Scenario #1 becomes G1 (1%), G2 (97%), G3 (0%), G4 (1%) and G5 (1%). Exclusively for the indicator income received per hour of labor (BRZ/h_{labor}), the average value was considered for both Scenario #0 and #1 instead of an expansion using hectares as for all other indicators. This consideration was performed due to existing conceptual issues regarding the use of area units in expanding the BRZ/h_{labor} indicator in the entire region, which could mislead important information and result in non-precise numbers.

2.3   Graphical Representation for Sustainability Indicators

The indexes considered in this study to assess the sustainability of milk production in southern region of Minas Gerais State have different dimensions and scales, which hampers a direct assessment. According to Ulgiati et al. [10], this difficulty can be overcome by applying normalization techniques on indicators, which allows comparison among them. From other options, the normalization based on the total impact generated is used in this work as described: the value of each index is divided by the sum of the same indexes obtained by the two scenarios. Next, the normalized indexes are shown in a radar chart type for easier interpretation. Considering that every index (economic, social and environmental) have the same importance (or weight) in representing the sustainability concept, the biggest area shown on the graph indicates the scenario with the greatest sustainability.

3   Results and Discussion

3.1   Sustainability Study for the Assessed Milk Production Groups

Considering the indicators shown on Table 3, when comparing one another, G3 has the lowest production, lowest labor demand, lowest compensation for the employee, and a negative net income – the economic survival of this group is due to its other products and services traded, excluding milk production. These indexes corroborate with the results obtained by Oliveira et al. [11], Buainain [12], Rodrigues et al. [13] and Fassio et al. [14], which justify the low socioeconomic performance of group G3 due to the low efficiency on production management and the need for its intensification through better facilities, herds, technical and management knowledge. On the other hand, G3 shows the best results for environmental indexes, achieving a renewability of 24% and an environmental sustainability index of 0.66, even though the ESI values lower than 1 leads to low sustainability according to Brown and Ulgiati [15] criterion.

   Even though it is rated as an intensive management that usually means an economically powerful system, G4 shows to be economically inefficient with a

Table 3. Social, economic and environmental indicators obtained by the assessed milk production groups

Indicators	G1	G2	G3	G4	G5
Social h_{labor}/yr	19,36	5,06	2,64	9,68	14,52
BRZ/h_{labor}	6.18	3.01	2.47	5.39	5.99
Economic L_{milk}/yr	1,606,000	131,4	12,045	386,9	1,277,500
BRZ/L_{milk}	0.50	0.52	−0.51	−0.24	0.19
Environmental %R	8.79	12.36	24.64	3.07	3.47
ESI	0.11	0.17	0.66	0.03	0.04

net loss of 0.24 BRZ per liter of produced milk. This characteristic existing in some intensive systems was also noticed and discussed by Santos et al. [16], who argues that inefficient management of systems with high intensification (e.g. the waste of inputs and inadequate handling of herd) also lead to low economical indexes, which means that intensification should not be considered as synonymous with high economic performance. On the other hand, although G2 is classified as a semi-intensive system (i.e. less intensive than G4), it has an adequate technology and applies an efficient management on production, which results in higher net income than G4 and G5. This was also identified and discussed by Souza and Buainain [5] that relate economic performance with the synergy among different activities within system, public policies that enable the incorporation of technologies with technical assistance, as well as the access of producers to technology and information.

Table 3 stresses that the intensification of the productive system may lead to an increase on the productivity – and maybe on the quality [17] – of milk produced, which also reflects in better socio-economical indexes. However, the intensification of productive systems demands higher quantity of global resources (material and energy), that are usually comes from outside of system boundaries and are often fossil-based (i.e. non-renewable resources). Thus, the intensification may result on reducing the environmental performance because additional non-renewable global resources are necessary to maintain and/or increase the intensification of milk production systems.

3.2   Regional Sustainability of Milk Production

Figure 1 notices that scenario #0 shows better performance for the socio economical indexes. A decrease of 36% on the use of renewable resources was obtained on #1 compared to #0 because the intensification of the productive systems presupposes higher requirements of external resources, decreasing its resilience over the pressures from the market and its renewability; this is also the reason for the decrease of ESI value. The productivity increase is usually linked to the increase of demand for external resources, which results in a worse environmental performance.

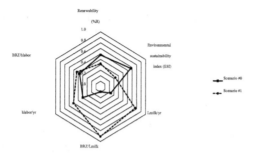

Fig. 1. Comparison among social, economic and environmental indicators

Concerning the socio-economical indexes, Fig. 1 shows: (i) higher regional milk production (2.3 times more L_{milk}/yr) for scenario #1 compared to scenario #0, which results in a net income 8.9 times higher; (ii) the higher quality and quantity of milk produced on scenario #1 leads to higher selling price for scenario #0, which is the reason why net profit increases in a proportion higher than the milk production. Even to a lesser extent, the same behavior occurs for the social indexes: (i) for scenario #1, the region would demand higher amount of labor-hours (i.e. it provides aproximately 52% more jobs); (ii) scenario #1 rewards better the employee (income 13% higher) which supports a stronger regional economic performance. These results are in accordance with those obtained by Tupy and Primavesi [18], in which the most intensified systems usually yield more milk, require more qualified employees, and are able to pay better salaries. Finally, an overview of all indicators present in Fig. 1 leads to a higher area obtained by #1, which means higher sustainability in accordance to methodological approaches considered in this work; in this sense, the "Minas Leite" program should be supported.

4   Conclusions

A local perspective analysis show that G3 (family-extensive) has the worst socio-economic performance, as it provides lower amount of jobs per year (2,640 h_{labor}/yr), pays lower salaries (2.47 BRZ/h_{labor}), has lower milk production (12,045 L_{milk}/yr), and has a negative net income (-0.51 BRZ/L_{milk}). On the other hand, G3 shows the best environmental indexes, achieving 24% of renewability and 0.66 for environmental sustainability index. A trade-off between socio-economic and environmental aspects is evident, which claims for efforts towards production systems intensification with reduced demand for non-renewable external resources.

A regional perspective analysis show that decision makers should support "Minas Leite" program because it represents higher regional sustainability for milk production. However, it still claims for further efforts in assessing the limits of the larger economy in providing all resources demanded for the milk production systems intensification. This ecocentrism perspective is important to reach the so-called strong sustainability, in which the biosphere acts as both energy supplier and waste sink.

References

1. Food and Agriculture Organization: http://www.fao.org
2. Cepea: http://www.cepea.esalq.usp.br
3. Ibge: http://www.ibge.gov.br
4. Carvalho, G.: A Indústria de Laticínios no Brasil: Passado, Presente e Futuro. Embrapa Gado de Leite, Juiz de Fora (2010)
5. Souza, R.P., Buainain, A.M.: A Competitividade da Produção de Leite da Agricultura Familiar: Os Limites da Exclusão. Estudos Sociedade e Agricultura 2, 308–331 (2013)
6. Milkpoint: http://www.milkpoint.com.br/top.100/2015/EBOOK-TOP100.pdf
7. Zoccal, R.: http://www.cileite.com.br/content/panorama-do-leite
8. Oliveira, M., Agostinho, F.: Assessing alternative developments for milk production in the Southern Region of Minas Gerais State, Brazil. In: 8th Biennal Emergy Research Conference, pp. 237–246. University of Florida, Gainesville (2015)
9. Odum, H.T.: Environmental Accounting. Wiley, Hoboken (1996)
10. Ulgiati, S., Ascione, M., Bargigli, S., Cherubini, F., Franzese, P., Raugei, M., Viglia, S., Zucaro, A.: Material, energy and environmental performance of technological and social systems under a life cycle assessment perspective. Ecol. Model. 222(1), 176–189 (2011)
11. Oliveira, N., Aleixo, A., Sato, S., Junkes, M., Habitzreuter, P.: Práticas Produtivas da Agricultura Familiar: Um Estudo no Município de Espigão D'Oeste, RO. In: X Congresso Internacional de Administração, Gestão Estratégica, Tecnologia do Impacto nas Organizações. Ponta Grossa (2015)
12. Buainain, A.M.: Alguns Condicionantes do Novo Padrão de Acumulação da Agricultura Brasileira. In: Buainain, A.M., Alves, E., Silveira, J.M., Navarro, Z. (eds.) O Mundo Rural no Brasil do século 21, pp. 213–240. Embrapa (2014)
13. Rodrigues, M.H.S., Souza, M.P., Rodríguez, T.D.M., Aguiar, I.S., de Souza Rodrigues, E.F.: Análise de Eficiência dos Produtores de Leite do Município de Rolim de Moura, no Estado de Rondônia. Gestão Regionalidade 27(79), 61–76 (2011)
14. Fassio, L.H., Reis, R.P., Geraldo, L.G.: Desempenho Técnico e Econômico da Atividade Leiteira em Minas Gerais. Ciência e Agrotecnologia 30(6), 1154–1161 (2006)
15. Brown, M.T., Ulgiati, S.: Emergy analysis and environmental accounting. Encycl. Energy 2, 329–354 (2004)
16. Santos, J.A., da Cruz Vieira, W., dos Santos Baptista, A.J.M.: Eficiência Técnica em Propriedades Leiteiras da Microrregião de Viçosa-MG: Uma Análise Não-Paramétrica. Organizações Rurais and Agroindustriais 7(2), 162–172 (2015)
17. Embrapa: https://sistemasdeproducao.cnptia.embrapa.br/FontesHTML/Leite/LeiteSudeste/introducao.html
18. Tupy, O., Primavesi, O.: Avaliação dos Impactos Econômicos, Sociais e Ambientais de Tecnologias da Embrapa Pecuária Sudeste. Embrapa Pecuária Sudeste, São Carlos (2006)

Innovation and Quality

Pedro Luiz de Oliveira Costa Neto$^{(\boxtimes)}$ and Marcos de Oliveira Morais

Paulista University, São Paulo, Brazil
politeleia@uol.com.br

Abstract. This is not a theoretical or applied paper, but with appropriate relevant discussion about the influence of progress in the fields of quality and innovation. These two important achievements of human intelligence can not certainly be fully accepted as wonders in service of humanity, as well as for the issue of sustainability. At the end of the discussion, it is placed by the authors the challenge of creating. The discussion is enriched writer the presentation of existence of case in where the presence of innovation may not lead to the dared results an indicator for quality of innovation.

Keywords: Sustainability · Quality of life · Quality of innovation · Pros and cons

1 Introduction

There is no question on the importance of quality of products, services and processes, as also is not in discussion the importance of innovation to improve the quality of life in society. However, the undeniable importance of these achievements of human intelligence can not be accepted without a minimum of discussion, for what a vast early observation of present reality gives abundant material.

Subsidy to this discussion is the purpose of this article which focuses not on technical issues, related to quality and innovation, but on those linked to their social and human surroundings.

In the text, are avoided existing discussions contributing on the concept and the achievement of quality, as, for example, the well known five approaches to quality: transcendental, based on the product, based on the user, based on the process, and based on the value, as proposed in [1].

These visions of quality, however, are eminently technical and do not consider ethical, social and human aspects. Another definition, of interest to this present discussion, dared in his master work by a graduate student at the Polytechnic School of São Paulo University named Fabio Cerquilho, under guidance by one of the authors of this article, is: Quality is the sum of all the characteristics and properties of the goods and services offered to meet the reasonable needs of customers, along with the set of situations involved in the obtenance and use of these products that promote a healthy and truly human existence to all that are affected [2].

© IFIP International Federation for Information Processing 2016
Published by Springer International Publishing AG 2016. All Rights Reserved
I. Nääs et al. (Eds.): APMS 2016, IFIP AICT 488, pp. 431–437, 2016.
DOI: 10.1007/978-3-319-51133-7_51

For innovation there are certainly, among others, the following definitions: Technological innovation is defined as the implementation of new or substantially improved products (goods or services) or processes. The implementation of innovation occurs when the product is accepted by the market or the process is operated by the company [3].

Technological Innovation in Products and Processes (TIPP) is understend by the implementations of technologically new products and processes and significant technological improvements in products and processes. A TIPP is considered implemented it has been introduced in the market (product innovation) or used in the production process (process innovation). A TIPP involves a series of scientific, technological, organizational, financial and commercial activities [4]. To [5], innovation is idea more action more results.

The first two definitions emphasize the use of technology, but this feature, while important, is not a necessary condition for the existence of innovation. The condition actually necessary is to add value to its use. Many inventions are not innovations for this reason.

Technological innovation is, as a rule, the result of an extensive process, as illustrated in Fig. 1.

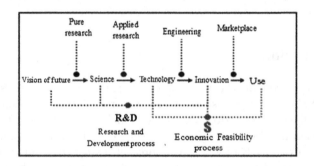

Fig. 1. The innovation process (Source: [6])

Pure research (or basic, or fundamental) is the research conducted with the aim of enhancing scientific knowledge, without looking for the possibility of practical applications.

Applied research is the search for new scientific knowledge or not, that offer solutions to objective problems, previously defined.

Science is the organized body of knowledge concerning the objective universe, involving its natural, environmental and behavioral-phenomena.

Technology is the ordered set of all scientific knowledge, empirical or intuitive, employees in the production and commerce of goods or services.

Innovations have undoubtedly brought great contribution to the progress of mankind, but can also bring undesirable consequences. Indeed:

Innovation can bring: Competitive advantage; More knowledge / technology; More recreational possibilities; More health and safety; Better use of time; and Better quality of life.

Innovation may bring: Isolation of people; Technological dependence; False illusion of status; Culture vulgarization; Excessive specialization; Worse quality of life.

These considerations suggest thinking innovation in its overall abrangence, as made Fabio Cerquinho with his definition of quality.

So does the Brazilian National Quality Foundation, which has innovation among the basements for excellence in management, but requiring for it the promotion of an environment of creativity, experimentation and implementation of new ideas capable of generating growing earnings of competitiveness with sustainable development [7].

By the way, according to Gro Harlem Brundtland, former prime minister of Norway, "Sustainable development is one that meets the needs of the present without compromising the ability of future generations to meet their own needs" [4].

2 Innovation Classifications

The main objective in seeking quality and innovation is to promote quality of live for people in the society. This truism is represented in Fig. 2. Given the precariousness of the world situation in the search for global sustainability, which will not be discussed in this work, this figure also serves as a background for those who aim a true and permanent quality of life in the world.

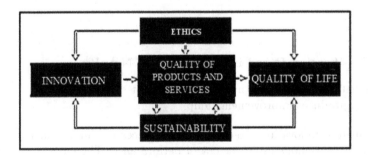

Fig. 2. Ingredients of quality of life

2.1 Classification Based in Knowledge

– Technological
– Organizational

Examples of organizational innovations:

– Use of appropriate technologies
– Cargo containers
– Urban transportation by buses in Curitiba and Bogota cities
– Restaurants per kilo
– In soccer, restriction to the goalkeeper in retracted balls.

2.2   Classification Based in Focus

– Generated inside (inward)
– Generated for the market (market - driven)

The intersection of these two classifications points to where innovations apply, as shown in Fig. 3.

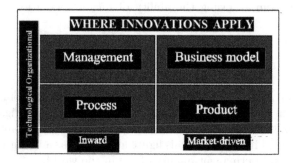

Fig. 3. Incidence of innovations (Source: Adapted from [5])

2.3   Classification Based in the Degree of Novelty

– Incremental: produces continuous improvement
– Radical: produces improvement jump

Incremental innovations consist of small successive improvements with the objective of continuous improvement of performance. The cumulative result of a continuous series of small ideas can in many cases be greater than that of a single radical innovation [8]. This statement suggests a new vision for the process of improvement, as shown in Figs. 4 and 5.

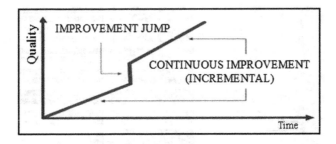

Fig. 4. The improvement process (Source: [6])

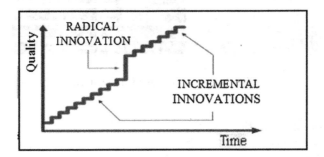

Fig. 5. Alternative view of the improvement process

3   Food for Thought

Innovation is the source of great opportunities in the twenty-first century. Right? Of course, but let's look at Fig. 6.

However, nothing against innovation. To paraphrase the words of the great Portuguese poet Fernando Pessoa ("Sailing is necessary"), to innovate is necessary!

But perhaps it is also necessary to work the concept of innovation quality, in a similar way of Fabio Cerquinho's definition of quality. Therefore, it is suggested the creation of an indicator called Innovation Quality - IQ, which:

- It is a measure of the benefits or harms that innovation brings to individuals and society;
- It is proposed for this measure a range between -1 and $+1$.

This leads to a new classification for innovation:

- With $IQ > 0$
- With $IQ \leq 0$

Theorem 1: The IQ value is a function of the time of use of the innovation.

Theorem 2: The time value of IQ depends on the long term planning of the use of the innovation.

Factors affecting IQ:

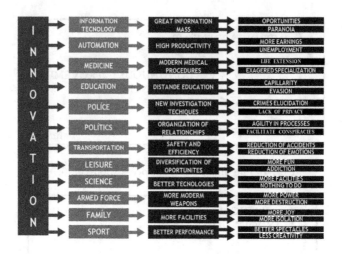

Fig. 6. Pros and cons of innovation

- Level of use of innovation
- Market amplitude
- User satisfaction
- Ethical aspects
- Contribution to sustainability
- Easy to use
- Real provided advantage

Exercise: Establish a IQ value for the following innovations:

- Car
- Zeppelin
- Atomic bomb
- Television
- Computer
- Telemarketing

It is launched the challenge to researchers!

4 Conclusion

The present article seeks to call attention to the negative aspects that may arise from the indiscriminate and widespread use of innovations without regard to their actual interest in improving quality of life of society.

The challenge of building an indicator for the real benefits or harms of innovation is placed. The authors are ready to discuss it with the interested parties.

References

1. Garvin, D.A.: Managing Quality: The Strategic and Competitive Edge. Simon and Schuster, New York (1988)
2. Cerquinho, F.: Ética e Qualidade nas Empresas. Dissertação de mestrado, Escola Politécnica da USP, Departamento de Engenharia de Produção. São Paulo (1994)
3. IBGE: http://www.ibge.gov.br
4. OECD: http://www.finep.gov.br
5. Vasconcellos, M.: Gestão da Inovação. FNQ, São Paulo (2015)
6. de Oliveira Costa Neto, P.L., Canuto, S.A.: Administração com Qualidade: Conhecimentos Necessários para a Gestão Moderna. Blucher, São Paulo (2010)
7. FNQ: http://www.fnq.org.br
8. Alvares, A.C.T.: Desmistificando a Inovação. FIESP, São Paulo (2010)

Health Tourism as an Inducer of Economic and Social Development in Teresina City

Átila Melo de Lira, Herbert Gonçalves Espuny,
Pedro Luiz de Oliveira Costa Neto, and Reinaldo de Araújo Lopes(✉)

Paulista University, São Paulo, Brazil
mestradoua@bol.com.br

Abstract. In recent years, the global growth of the economy contributed to the significant increase of tourism in the world, spreading its concepts in Brazil. There have also grown the related researches in the academic sector, as well as its concern with long life companies, growth in the Northeast region, globalization and other changes occurring in the short term. Thus, this work aims to present how a state among those with lower income per capita in the Federation, as Piaui, has a health care system in its capital which is a benchmark in Northeastern Brazil, influencing positively health tourism. The work deals with issues involving tourism as a product and service, having as a result the existence of a cluster of health in the city of Teresina with economic expression that justifies its importance as a generator of income, employment, science and technology and a promoter of sustainable development in that city.

Keywords: Tourism · Health pole · Sustainable development

1 Introduction

According to the World Tourism Organization [1], tourism receipts reach US$ 919 billion. There was a slowdown in the tourism sector due to the global economic crisis of 2008, which caused some instability in the confidence of agents for future events. However, despite the crisis, to make a comparative analysis of ten years prior to 2010, the foreign exchange earnings from tourism in 2008 (US$ 857.40 billion) was 92.67% higher than in 1999 (US$ 445,00 billion), demonstrating a significant growth in a decade. Also according to the UNWTO [1], between 1999 and 2010, the international flow of tourism in the world grew by 49%, beating the mark of 935 million trips in 2010, an estimated 1.6 billion in 2020. The Fig. 1 illustrates the growth of the sector during the period.

The UNWTO researches of 2010 also present important data of the tourism sector in Brazil, indicating that in the same period the foreign exchange earnings more than tripled from US$ 1.81 billion in 1999 to US$ 5.92 billion in 2010.

Contextualizing the city of Teresina, in this article, with about 850,000 inhabitants, Piaui state capital, Brazil, Northeast, one of the poorest in the country,

I. Nääs et al. (Eds.): APMS 2016, IFIP AICT 488, pp. 438–444, 2016.
DOI: 10.1007/978-3-319-51133-7_52

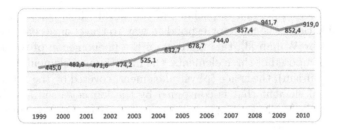

Fig. 1. Growth of the tourism sector (Source: [1])

but whose capital emerged as a respectable health pole with qualified service as a result of the entrepreneurial spirit of its main managers. The Health Pole of Teresina (PI) has shown strong growth in recent years, becoming a regional referral center. A first diagnosis made by Piaui Hospitals' Union shows that 30% of clients served come from six other states of the federation, generating jobs and income for the city [2].

The beginning of the development of a health cluster, with the formation of a supply chain and connected services, bringing benefits in terms of cost reduction, quality improvement, training of skilled labor, capital attraction and generation of employment and income. This benefit extends to the Health Private Network, increasing their participation in services to the population through an investment which reached US\$ 68 million reais in 2011, according to the Medical Union of Piaui.

The central objective of this article is to demonstrate the contribution of health tourism as an encouraging instrument for the beginning and the growth of companies as well as a mechanism that contributes to the company to assume more effectively its social function, contributing to improving the quality of life of a particular region and also as immediate growthinducing factor of Teresina.

2   Definition of Tourism and Its Classifications

Tourism can be focused as a phenomenon that refers to the movement of people within their own country (domestic tourism) or crossing national borders (international tourism). This movement reveals elements such as interactions and individual or team relationships, human understanding, feelings, perceptions, motivations, pressures, satisfaction, the concept of pleasure, etc. [3].

According to Castelli [4], the comprehension of the phenomenon of tourism current must necessarily pass through an analysis of the meaning of the trips in the course of history. These, frequently, were moved by economic political and military interests. Nowadays, travels with these same objectives continue to move people from one region to another.

Travelling is an action arising from a context which is inserted into the society at a specific moment in history. It has always been one of the elements of economic and social life and, especially, of the world which is inserted. To each type of civilization or society corresponds a way to travel or accept the traveler.

As stated by Wahab [3], the anatomy of the phenomenon of tourism would be basically composed of three elements: the man (human element as the author of the act of tourism), the space (physical element, covered by the act itself), and time (temporal element that is consumed by the journey itself and by staying at the destination). These elements are representative of the conditions of this phenomenon existence.

However, other factors distinguish tourism from the simple act of traveling. Such factors relate mainly to the goals, the temporary nature of displacement, the use of tourist services and equipment and, what would be the most important among them, the concept of pleasure and recreation as fundamental.

Olimpio [5] affirms that a revolution in the traditional concepts of trips was performed by the tourism phenomenon from the middle of the nineteenth century when the Protestant Pastor Thomas Cook inaugurated the first tourist agency in England.

Countries such as Italy, France and Spain, old military powers and colonialists, managed to stabilize their balances of payments in the postwar due to tourism, reaching to the point of this activity is to constitute real industry, with its own public body, specific legislation, which aims to regulate the various aspects of social, economic, commercial and cultural tourism, always aiming at better income and greater expansion of the tourist industry.

2.1   Factors that Influence Tourist Decisions

Every person is a tourist in potential, being necessary, however, the action of the tourist trip to characterize as so. For this reason there are some constraints as: the desire (animus) and the possibility [5]. The desire can originate from different causes such as: propaganda, the status, habit, physical convenience, moral or intellectual, seduction, commercial interest or of profit and health. The second constraint involves factors that are beyond the control of man, as: time vacant, money, means of transport, among others.

As the possibility was always easier to exist in the most privileged classes, the concept of tourism is usually bound by luxury. However, with paid vacations, social tourism became easier and popular.

In this way, there are various reasons that people become tourist: business, religious reasons, health, culture, education and pleasure are just a few examples.

According to Arrillaga [6], the needs that tourism satisfy can be very varied, since the subjective causes that determine the tourist trips are as diverse as the needs which the body or the human soul may experience.

The tourist motivations or subjective causes of tourism can be classified into primary and secondary; direct and indirect; proximate and remote; individual and social.

However, the tourist deciding to travel generally has more than one cause, as shown below.

- **Primary and secondary causes.** For example, a person who performs a pilgrimage has, as main cause, the obtaining of a grace of the spiritual order, however, also weighs in its decision the possibility to get to new places, visit the famous monuments, rest, among others.
- **Direct and indirect causes.** The achievement of a certain journey may occur due to an invitation or the desire to know some locality. However, it can involve indirect causes, such as the habit of travel or the socioeconomic level of the traveler.
- **Proximate and remote causes.** As an example of proximate cause of a trip, is the propaganda of a travel agent and as remote cause example, the remembrance of a previous trip.
- **Individual and social causes.** The Individual Causes act in the decision of a person to travel and the Social Causes influence by equal in sectors of the population. As an example of the first, we can mention the practice of a sport and of the second, the fashion or ideological affinities. The particular motivation for health tourism allows to consider it due to primary, direct, proximate and individual causes.

3 Tourism Classifications

According to a first general classification according to Andrade [7], the city of Teresina case and its health pole may be classified as a regional receptive nucleus of people for health treatment, and internal, because the temporary flow is typically regional in the country itself. The Table 1 exposes in objective way the more common tourism types.

Table 1. Tourism types classifications (Source: [7])

Classification	Description
Vacation	Vacation configures a guarantee of an intensive tourism, because the sequence of days available to leisure and rest. It is one of the highest points of the profitability of tourism
Cultural	Covers the activities for the satisfaction of artistic emotions, scientific, training and information in the various existing branches
Business	Is the set of activities of travel, accommodation, food and leisure activities practiced by travelers relating both to commercial and industrial activities
Active sports	Refer to all the activities of travel with an objective to participate in sporting events, in the country or abroad
Health	Also known as therapeutic tourism or treatment, refers to the set of tourist activities to acquire good physical and mental health
Religious	Set of activities that involve visits to the receptive that express mystics feelings or raise the faith, hope and charity to believers

For purpose of this work we will use the typology of health tourism, because that is what happens in some health poles regional throughout Brazil as, for example, the focus of this paper, the case of Teresina. Table 2 presents a tourism form classification.

Table 2. Tourism form classification (Source: [7])

Classification	Description
Individual	Also known as private tourism or self-financing, refers to the set of activities required for planning and travel implementing, without the intermediary of travel agencies or tourism entities
Organized	Is the set of tourist activities programed, administered and implemented by tourism agencies, associations, class entities, clubs or another organization involving a group of people
Social	A type of organized tourism for people of social layers whose rents, without the help of others, not would allow them to plan a travel. Generally, concerns the vacation colonies of associations, class entities, companies or hostels that work with governmental resources or special funds
Intensive	Refers to the set of tourism programs in which people remain hosted in a single location, even if they set tours and excursions to other places
Extensive	Refers to the hosting and the set of activities in a same core, with duration of at least three weeks. This method excludes the tours and excursions to other receptive
Itinerante	Involves a series of lodging in different places, consists of visits to the greatest possible number of receptive cores, on a single trip, with short stay in the visited places

According to the form, you can classify the people who migrate to Teresina for health treatment in individual, because most of the time travelers get to the city with its own resources by regional and interstate bus that cut the city through the various highways in the state.

4 Tourism Industry

The internal relationship that exists between tourism and the economic science is always expressed in terms of the contribution of tourism to economic development. Wahab [3] writes that:

"Tourism is a phenomenon that involves the transfer of capital from one country to another through the movement of tourists who go to certain touristic "product" and consume. They are potential consumers of complex goods and services that are offered with a specific goal. The tourism, through the aspects of consumption and investment, affects different sectors of the economic system of a country, and it is believed that its multiplier effect is higher than that observed in other sectors of the economy such as industry..."

Tourism is productive, accurate and determined with specific characteristics, joined to the field of development and commerce. So, depending on the stage of development of a country or a region, it can be considered the first force, ahead of industry and agriculture.

According to data from the Brazilian Tourism Company - Embratur [8], the tourist industry in recent decades has shown representative economic value. This fact is evidenced by the volume of transactions carried out as a result of increased demand for travel and tourism.

The following part of this paper, will discuss some economic concepts that are directly linked to the tourism industry of the real economy of a region.

4.1 Economic Concepts

Some economic concepts that influence the study of tourism as an industry are: economic good, utility, economic agents, tourist product, demand and supply of tourism.

As Lage [9] presents, all that is rare and exists in less quantity than needs is an economic good. Thus, because of this lack, something need to be produced, taking the form of goods (materials) or services.

As the consumers cannot get everything they want, they are forced to make choices. Therefore, they may have preference for a given good service but accept a minor amount of another. However, in any situation, consumers act rationally in order to obtain maximum satisfaction from their spending.

5   Economic and Social Implications of Tourism

As state by Baptista [10], tourism advantages for a country or a receiving state are:

- Increase of revenues in foreign currency from the sale of goods and services;
- Creation of new sources of revenue in various economic sectors;
- Low investment compared to the revenue stream that it promotes;
- The integration between people of regions, languages, habits and different tastes.

The economic impacts generated by tourism can be classified according to Gunn [9] as: direct impact, known as the total income generated in the tourist sector as a direct result of the variation in spending on these products; indirect impact, the total income generated by the spending of the tourism sectors in goods and services offered in the economy, and induced impact, a result of the direct and indirect impacts of tourism, income levels increase throughout the economy, and that part of this additional income will be spent on goods and services produced domestically.

5 The implication of health tourism at Teresina city As a result of these impacts related to health tourism in Piaui capital, it is possible to show in an objective way, that an integrated set of these impacts on the local economy, created 15,000 direct jobs and an annual average investment of 80 million reais (approximately US$ 22 million, values converted to the exchange of 04.05.2016) order of direct and indirectly related to sectors linked with the area in question. The tourism industry has the positive impact on the economy of a city, according to Andrade [7], by: (i) increased income of the visited place by foreign exchange inflows; (ii) stimulation of investments and creation of new jobs; (iii) the redistribution of wealth between the places of origin and destination.

As negative impacts are mentioned: inflationary pressure, being harmful to the population of the tourist regions, because the high prices in general also affect goods and essential services; high dependence on tourism, making the economy of the region vulnerable to seasonal fluctuations in demand for tourism products; and the social and environmental costs in the tourist areas and residents; So, with these definitions and characteristics of tourism, it is clear the importance and complexity of the tourism for sector in a particular country or region, since it can not only brings capital exchange, but also prosperity to a particular community with regard to professional qualifications, better quality of life with a better performance of the services offered to the population.

6 Conclusion

Tourism is an industry with multivariate interests. Bringing the tourist to a particular location has different motivations. A developing region, like the Brazilian Northeast, needs to use all possible ways to seek an economic and socially sustainable development that adds value to their economy. The pursuit of excellence in health services, as demonstrated by the Teresina case, is an economic and social way of doing this, especially in regions waiting for development.

References

1. Organização Mundial do Turismo: Conselho de Turismo e Negócios da Fecomercio. Technical report (2011)
2. Prefeitura de Teresina: Agenda 2015 da Prefeitura de Teresina. http://www.teresina.pi.gov.br/
3. Wahab, S.E.A.: Introdução à Administração do Turismo. Pioneira, São Paulo (2008)
4. Castelli, G.: Hospitalidade: A Inovação na Gestão nas Organizações Prestadoras de Serviços. Saraiva, Rio de Janeiro (2010)
5. Olimpio, B.N.: Introdução ao Estudo do Turismo. Atlas, São Paulo (1984)
6. Arrilaga, J.I.d.: Introdução ao Estudo do Turismo. Rio, Rio de Janeiro (2010)
7. Andrade, J.V.: Turismo: Fundamentos e Dimensões. Ática (2008)
8. Baptista, M.: Caderno temáticos da Embratur. Technical report (1991)
9. Lage, B.H.G., Milone, P.C.: Economia do Turismo. Papirus, Campinas (2010)
10. Baptista, M.: Turismo: Gestão Estratégica. Atlas, São Paulo (2004)

Mitigating Serialization and Traceability, a Study on the Strategies for the Implementation of the System and Adaptation to the TBR nº. 54 2013

André Gomes de Lira Muniz[✉], Debora Adriana Mões Correa,
Jair Minoro Abe, Fábio Vieira do Amaral, and Lauro H.C. Tomiatti

Paulista University, São Paulo, Brazil
a.gdelira@gmail.com

Abstract. Following a worldwide trend, Brazil is regulating control actions and traceability of medicines Through Board Resolution (TBR) nº. 54, which provides for the establishment of the national system drug control and the mechanisms and precedents for your tracking in the chain of pharmaceuticals. Depending on the responsibility to ensure, ensure the maintenance, enhance quality, promote the safety and efficacy of products to the final consumer and seeking to avoid the risks and adverse health effects, companies, factures or importers, have a responsibility to adopt mechanisms and procedures that address is resolution. This article presents an overview of the needs of serialization and traceability pharma-protection products, as well as value creation opportunities in the implementation of systems and their adequacy to rules for companies that make up the cahate pharmaceutical value.

Keywords: Paraconsistent Logic Annotated Evidential · Traceability · WHO

1 Introduction

The improvement program, of the regulatory process of The Brazillian Health Regulatory Agency (Anvisa), established by Decree nº. 422 of April 16, 2008, and also the provisions of Law nº. 11,903, of January 14, 2009, it provides for the implementation of the national system of drug control and the mechanisms and procedures for tracking drugs in the chain of pharmaceutical products; practice that determines the new guidelines and unique identification rules for drug being called UIR.

This resolution is based on the concept of serialization and traceability, Despite widely publicized by the media Brazilian society did not absorb all the concepts involved. Some questions have not been September permanently. When measured technological solutions to a subject, there are several options

I. Nääs et al. (Eds.): APMS 2016, IFIP AICT 488, pp. 445–451, 2016.
DOI: 10.1007/978-3-319-51133-7_53

in both the national and international market, however, there is great difficulty in understanding the new resolution in terms of understanding the standard, as well as the concepts of serialization and traceability which makes complex close the process to implement the solution throughout the chain so that the solution is unique and the data can bring all necessary information at all stages of the selection of raw materials, production, marketing to the end consumer.

This work seeks to demonstrate macro form the concept, methodology, and application with the technological solutions that have been used in Brazil. It is noteworthy that this study has as main objective the drug developers.

2   Theoretical Background

2.1   Information Technology

To Santos [1] using information technology when it comes to health is fundamental prioritize therefore can often be a fine line between over-experience of fatality. In the Industry of Health, there is always an attempt to cut public spending and demand greater efficiency in this industry, several companies associated with the health as the American Hospital Association, the Health Industry Business Communication Council, the National Wholesale Druggists Association, among others, invest in research called Efficient Healthcare Consumer Response. In this research, a strong recommendation is to implement information systems to automate the current processes of the supply chain [2].

The best way to promote the performance of the supply chain, while in parallel, control is the short-term costs, not to colortar budgets, expenses, but invest in process improvements, and technological resources, which will eliminate costs of supply chain [2].

To Taraboulsi [3] it is essential that health institutions have as a tool management systems provided by IT, because that enhance the processes of treatment, spread and transfer of information, add value to serve vices and make decision-making more agile, effective and consistent.

Holland and Nimno [4] report that hospital pharmacies were incorporating advanced technological resources with computerized prescription, automation system for distribution of drugs and computerization processes.

According to Gomes and Reis [5], computer automation as acts as an important tool for rationalization of use of time and agility of activities in the pharmacy.

2.2   Tecnologies Used for Product Traceabilitys

Bar codes to a use widely disseminated. Used in various industries was initially used in the retail market and therefore, widely disseminated in markets. Barcodes have a lot of information and graphs numeric and alphanumeric data. This encoding has intervals of diffuse reflectivity alternating, are represented by rectangles, however, no information, but certainly make typing easier [6]. The GS1 System is based on bar codes and is the global standard used, presenting the data layout to be followed:

- EAN/UPC Universal Product Code, that is widely used in point of sale (POS) and have an agility in capturing information;
- DataBar: This code family can be used in POS (point of sale), but has a smaller size and has the capacity to have more information than EAN/UPC.
- Code 128: Standard Code of GS1 keys. This pattern should not be used for identification at the POS;
- ITF-14 (Interleaved Two of Five): This standard should not be used for identification at the POS; It can be printed on cardboard;
- Data Matrix: It has a higher storage capacity being a symbol it with greater capacity than that linear codes.

Table 1 shows a comparison of the technologies used for product traceability, which highlights its main use factors. Through the table is possible to verify that the Radio-Frequency Identification Technology - RFID, the principle is the most suitable for traceability because medicines, among other factors, the minimum data manipulation, which gives security to the supervisory body and its wide range in the distance data capture, which increases safety and mapping process, being able to control not only their location in real time, but act quickly if the exit load predefined script and can avoid the theft of the same [7].

Table 1. Comparison of different traceability technologies (Source: [7])

	Bar code	QR code	RFID
Storage capacity	Low	High	High
Reading device diversity	Only infrared	Mobile camera application to read QR code	Mobile NFC and specific application and systems with antennas that have a software
Reading need to line of sight	Yes	Yes	Yes
Distance for information capture	Small	Small	Far
Safety data	High, there may be change image	High, there may be amendments image	Minimum, capture and send data without intervention

3   Understand Serialization and Traceability of Medicines

We can divide the process of serialization and traceability in two stages that are serialization and aggregation. In designing serialization, it happens in the coding phase, because at this time are entered the data that references all information as batch identification, expiration dates and the dates and the details of the label and the definition of data [8]. In other words, the serialization is the definition and implementation of a unique identifier, such as a serial number that identifies the individual packages of medicines, your application is through the code printing (2D) and production batch data.

It is important to keep the information in unit doses or rather the lower marketed dose. For this and crucial that printing equipment can print the information in the Data Matrix format, this standard is defined and regulated by ANVISA, such code have the serial number, product registration number, batch, manufacturing and expiry dates that have quality standard [8].

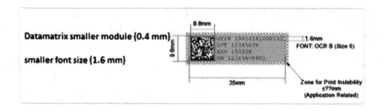

Fig. 1. Printer of datamatrix

In order to check the printed information, see the example in Fig. 1, the serialization equipment needs of visual inspection systems as well as waste efficient and analyzing the printed data evaluating and making sure they are within the minimum criteria set out in the DRC Standard n°. 54 2013 in order to be accepted. The requirements are [8]:

- Standard print size.
- Comparison and analysis of the data reported by the ERP system with the label.
- Quality Printing.
- Process analysis and in case of failure in print or evidence of divergence in the data printed a reject process should be established. Standard print size.

3.1   Aggregation

When measured aggregation of drugs, it occurs after the codification of the serialization information, medications that have been identified in photographic form containing the data of aggregates cartridges rows and the data to be easily identifiable to get information regarding the composition, origin and storage. It is important that a label is printed after closing the box when it is complete. The box must have a label that will be unit must be aggregated into a single shipment box so to have a single record doing the same family or group [8].

The shipping box should be inspected and it is important to have the printed record by the system and will have the information of the whole makeup box, and constitute a new code. This new label "father" must be fixed in the shipment box to identify the "children" [8] (Fig. 2).

Fig. 2. Label aggregation (Source: [8])

The TBR n°. 54 of 2013 does not have a mandatory requirement regarding the aggregation of shipping boxes on the pallet, however, to be effective control and traceability during all stages of the process is required data to be stored and sent to the server traceability of the manufacturer and stored in a database for later to take effect the transmission of information to ANVISA where there will also be storage in a database.

For this to happen in a way that facilitates the control of the physical location is important that shipping boxes have an identification number and can easily get the information inspected, and that the place of storage, to be easily identified. So that the process can be completed, after collecting boarding box data and validation of them will require a new label is printed with all units of parents and children and this information should be in a visible place, after "stretching" or "strecht wrap" (placement strectch film) to protect the packing boxes to be sent to the logistics operator.

3.2 Definition of the Production Line

In the consignment of production data step is defined to be included in Datamatrix, such as the data of separation of raw material, weighing the production of semifinished data, reconciliation, release, among other information related to production.

For this phase of the process it is necessary to define a unique serial number for each product unit and for this serial also used the registry number of the product at ANVISA, including batch number, expiry and manufacturing dates (Fig. 3).

Fig. 3. Example of a two-dimensional code (2D) of the DataMatrix [12]

4   Methodology

This paper can be considered an exploratory study to generate a structure that will subsequently be tested in future studies, through the development of hypotheses to be investigated; descriptive, by engaging the attempt to control and manipulation of variables; case study, to be returned to the depth, targeting a full contextual analysis of a few facts; and laboratory research, because it was not applied yet [9].

Initially, there was a survey of macro use of technology in the drug supply chain, using materials such as articles published in scientific journals and international very important events. Then we made a study of the methods and drug traceability technologies used in Brazil and the world, and its effectiveness in relation to the following requirements: guarantee information along the supply chain, decrease in counterfeit drugs, traceability lot quickly, with quality that reaches the end customer and information available on the medicine for it.

Based on this knowledge, it concluded the elaboration of cover the reader ways to mitigate serialization and traceability, through a study on strategies for system implementation and adaptation to the TBR n°. 54, 2013. An attempt to improve the existing process and identify future research possibilities.

5   Results and Discussion

The new tracking law until the end of 2016 the entire pharmaceutical industry should follow the new rules. The proposal is that the production stage to consumption registration is made, storage and transmission of data. To provide greater security is being adopted this global trend.

Clearly there will be the expansion of the security when the traceability process is being used for medicinal products. This is a good practice and is also a trend in other countries that are seeking to increase the safety of medicinal products. Avoiding not only fraud, robbery of cargo it, but also providing greater security and protection to the consumer.

In the productive sector, it is the measure will allow the greatest control of all costs of the stages of production and logistics. The process and all the production and distribution chain links are essential for any drug traceability process to work. The links found pharmacies are one of the distribution links that need to inform the reception of this, during the delivery, the submission processes and anomalous situations, such as loss and falsification, the manufacturer of the drug, and the previous link in the supply chain. All existing connection in the chain has responsibility with the pharmaceutical laboratory that all stages of the delivery process until the sale can provide the information to ANVISA the repository of records of the manufacturer's traceability of events.

To protect consumers may be noted that traceability enables more secure and reliable buyers in the product they are buying. There will also be a feature of industries and government to manage health care costs and be more easily and efficiently, and regulators can monitor more effectively.

6 Conclusions

Traceability of medicines has not been standardized in the world, and that we still have large amounts of counterfeit drugs, which pose a safety hazard to the final consumer, therefore this product without origin does not have the necessary quality.

Traceability of drugs is no longer a competitive factor, but a necessity to get the safety of the product to the end consumer. For the traceability process is accepted, it is necessary that the existing steps are met, the change is planned and the use of appropriate technologies enabling assurance and tracking of the drug to its ultimate destination, and thus its quality, reducing cases of counterfeit medicines and providing a response and faster action, if necessary to withdraw a circulating drug. In that it contributes to the reverse logistics of these products, enabling the sustainability of the process.

References

1. Santos, G.A.A.: Gestão de Farmácia Hospitalar. Senac, São Paulo (2009)
2. Ching, H.Y.: Gestão de Estoques na Cadeia de Logística Integrada Supply Chain. Editora Atlas, São Paulo (2007)
3. Taraboulsi, F.A.: Administração de Hotelaria Hospitalar. Editora Atlas, São Paulo (2009)
4. Holland, R.W., Nimmo, C.M.: Transitions part 1: beyond pharmaceutical care. Am. J. Health-Syst. Pharm. **56**, 1758–1764 (1999)
5. de Magalhães Gomes, M.J.V., Reis, A.M.M.: Ciências Farmacêuticas: Uma Abordagem em Farmácia Hospitalar. Atheneu, São Paulo (2006)
6. Swartz, J., Wang, Y.P.: Fundamentals of bar code information theory. Computer **23**(4), 74–86 (1990)
7. Metzner, V.C.V., da Silva, R.F., Cugnasca, C.E.: Modelo de Rastreabilidade de Medicamentos Utilizando Identificação por Radiofrequência, Redes de Sensores Sem Fio e o Conceito de Internet das Coisas. In: XXVIII Congresso Nacional de Pesquisa e Ensino em Transporte, pp. 1–12. ANTP (2014)
8. Farmaceuticas. http://www.farmaceuticas.com.br
9. Bowersox, D.J., Closs, D.J., Cooper, M.B.: Supply Chain Logistics Management, vol. 2. McGraw-Hill, New York (2002)

Theoretical Framework of Performance Indicators with BSC for the Private Higher Education Institution

Átila de Melo Lira$^{(\boxtimes)}$ and Irenilza de Alencar Nääs

Paulista University/UNIP, São Paulo, Brazil
atilalira@hotmail.com

Abstract. Analyzing the performance of an organization requires the use of indicators. In recent decades, an indicator in particular has highlighted, the balanced scorecard (BSC). Therefore, a type of company specific, private higher education institutions (HEI's), has received little attention in research in this area, especially in how is the process of applying these indicators. Thus, this study aims to understand how is the balanced score card application process on a private higher education institution. For this, this study drew on research built by authors who discuss this application, in order to develop a theoretical framework, demonstrating how this process occurs. So, theoretical contributions were generated by this study with the analysis of other theoretical contributions of more extensive research, in which they individually could not handle to fill this theoretical gap in the literature.

Keywords: Balanced scorecard · Performance indicators · Private higher education institution

1 Introduction

The administrative process goes through stages ranging from planning to control the activities that are developed within an organization. In this sense, with the control we seek to correct flaws and distortions that have occurred along the production and management operations of the company. Therefore, it is necessary that performance indicators are applied within the organization to measure whether it can achieve the proposed organizational goals initially [1].

There are several types of performance indicators. Among them, one has won a special mention in recent decades, the Balanced Scorecard (BSC). It is in a strategic management tool that seeks to measure organizational performance based on four perspectives: financial, learning and growth, internal processes and client [2–4].

The financial perspective is related to the long-term financial goals, involving measures profitability, contribution margin, breakeven, shareholder return, return on time investment, among others. This perspective has its own complexity to involve a number of dimensions and stakeholders. It will provide the necessary capital support for the development of other perspectives [2–4].

© IFIP International Federation for Information Processing 2016
Published by Springer International Publishing AG 2016. All Rights Reserved
I. Nääs et al. (Eds.): APMS 2016, IFIP AICT 488, pp. 452–458, 2016.
DOI: 10.1007/978-3-319-51133-7_54

With regard to the customer's perspective, it deals with issues involving the central agent of the business, the company's mission, that is, for whom it will seek to sell their products or services. It involves issues related to answer the most appropriate market segment and have a mix of: price, place, promotion and product to this market segment chosen through well-defined positioning strategies [2–4].

Regarding the internal process perspective, it represents the entire measurement of the production and management operations of the organization. Still, it involves the company's entire value chain, from the search for raw materials to after-sales. In addition, it has three steps: (a) the process of innovation, which is to always seek to create new products that meet the needs and desires of customers; (b) the operational process, which involves all the production and marketing of products or services to the customer; and (c) the process of after-sales service, which has to evaluate customer satisfaction and accompany you to identify potential failures during the previous steps and make appropriate changes [2–4].

The learning and growth perspective involves people in the organization, the development of an appropriate infrastructure so that they are able to well perform their duties, issues concerning the motivation of the employees so that they maintain their ongoing performance and also empowerment to they feel increasingly part of the company. In this perspective, it is also present aspects related to training and development of people working in the organization [2–4].

In addition, we see the importance of analyzing a type of organization in particular that has singularities given its level of complexity management, higher education institutions (HEIs). This business segment has specific data dilemmas that occur in the decision-making process involved two dimensions that go in opposite directions, financial efficiency and quality in education [5–9].

Thus, seeking to answer the question: how does the application of BSC in a private HEI? This study aims to understand how is the balanced scorecard application process on a private higher education institution.

To meet the objective of this study, it proposed a theoretical framework that has nine steps. From step 1 to step 4, presents a inter-functional model of the BSC implementation of a private institution. Step 5 shows the influence of the sustainability category of the BSC on the financial perspective. Step 6 shows the impact of the decision-making process in institutional management. And the steps 7, 8 and 9 show the implications of issues related to BSC adaptations during the feedback of the inter-functional model. Thus, following the proposal in detail.

2 Theoretical Framework

As the figure below, in the center of the proposed framework, it is shown the BSC application process in a private institution. Following the sustainability of BSC shall involve in matters concerning the financial management of the same. Then the decision-making process has implications for institutional management.

In addition, the end of the BSC implementation process in a private institution, it does not end, continuous-become something that feeds back. During this feedback, the BSC can be adapted to the HEI thereafter begin to arise difficulties and adaptation

454   Á. de Melo Lira and I.A. Nääs

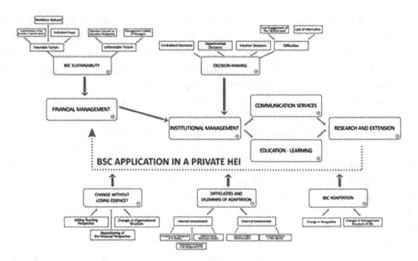

Fig. 1. Theoretical framework of performance indicators with balanced scorecard for the private Higher Education Institution

dilemmas, and finally make modifications without losing the gist of the BSC assumptions, to the BSC application process restarts (Fig. 1).

The first steps of the framework describe the application of BSC in a private HEI, by an inter-functional model performance. The proposed model supports the view that the starting point of the flow that involves activities and performance indicators starts from the financial management of the institution. The proposal is that effective financial management, characterized by solvency of finance, it is essential to ensure the development of a private educational institution. In turn, an appropriate institutional management, i.e. when coordinators and directors act effectively in carrying out its functions, and sectors such as library, laboratories and offices are directed to the needs of students the quality of teaching activities - learning and service communication emanate as a direct consequence [10] (Fig. 2).

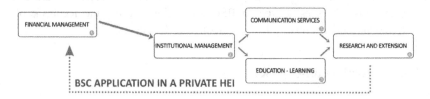

Fig. 2. Inter-functional model of BSC application in a private HEI

These two combined functions converge in research and extension activities, i.e., good internal communication tools, combined with educational incentives - learning are fundamental to foster the adoption of research and extension activities by universities. Because it is a private institution, the combination of all of these activities, developed satisfactorily provide profitable results financially, which leads back to the beginning of the model where these financial incomes will be managed in order to provide the continuity of the institution's activities. This feature justifies the flow of character given to the proposed model [10].

The later stage of the framework seeks to show that the financial management of inter-functional model is influenced by aspects of sustainability of the BSC. The analysis of institutional data (report of the committee for assessment, annual results records and financial statements of the institutions), allowed the identification of favorable and unfavorable factors to the sustainability of BSC in Brazilian HEI's. Among the favorable aspects are centralized power, reduced workforce and the implementation of key activities in specific sectors. But among the unfavorable aspects, present focused attention on the teaching perspective and the managerial inability of the managers [11] (Fig. 3).

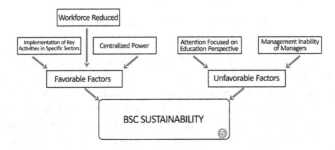

Fig. 3. BSC sustainability

Then he sought to demonstrate that the process of decision-making can influence the institutional management. This process is characterized by a centralization of decisions, decisions are taken departmental way, they get to be intuitive, at certain times, and have difficulties related to low engagement technical level and the lack of information [12] (Fig. 4).

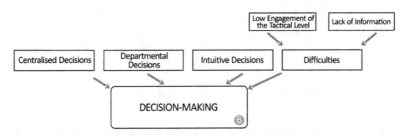

Fig. 4. The decision-making process in a private HEI

Already during the feedback phase of the inter-functional model, an adaptation of the BSC is important to note the difficulties and dilemmas of adaptation and change without losing the essence of the BSC. During the adjustment, may be changes in traditional perspectives (financial, customer, internal processes and learning and growth) to ensure the effectiveness of this strategic model. There may also be changes in the management structure of the IES to correct deficiencies that come true to the complexity of the method [13] (Fig. 5).

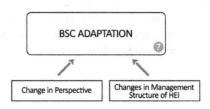

Fig. 5. BSC adaptation of a private HEI

With this, there are difficulties and dilemmas for adaptation, such as adapting the method to the institution or the institution of the method? These issues involve an analysis: (a) the internal environment due to complexity in the management of Brazilian HEI's, the ineffectiveness of existing performance indicators and the prevalence of educators in the management of HEI; and (b) the external environment due to expansion of the higher educational system and other successful experiences in other segments. Thus, the response indicates that the changes should be undertaken together [14] (Fig. 6).

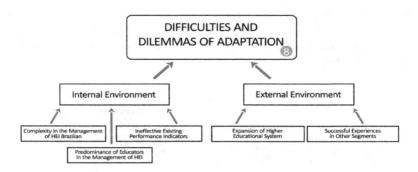

Fig. 6. Difficulties and dilemmas of BSC adaptation

Finally, during the implementation of these modifications should be changed without losing the gist of traditional BSC philosophy? The results indicate that for the HEI's successfully obtain the BSC is necessary that they modify this approach such that gets away from its traditional approach. Thus, within the context of HEI's analyzed, it is clear that these organizations gain greater successes in their activities when they leave the method as originally proposed and operationalize differently. Therefore, it is important to increase the education perspective, changes in organizational structure and repositioning of the financial perspective (given that the teaching perspective becomes the focus) [15] (Fig. 7).

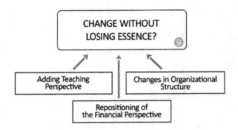

Fig. 7. Change without losing essence?

3 Conclusion

This study aims to understand how is the balanced score card application process on a private higher education institution. The first four steps can be carried out by means of a functional model performance. This model has as its starting point the financial management that supports the institutional management can carry out its tasks. The latter has a direct influence on teaching and learning operations and communication services, which together will result in research and extension activities of HEI.

Further, it is clear that to occur the sustainability of the process of the application, in the long run should be noted the favorable and unfavorable factors to it. This sustainability has direct implications on the financial management of the institution.

Another step corresponds to the decision-making that has features such as: centralized decisions, departmental decisions, intuitive decisions and difficulties of lack of information and low engagement tactical level. This step can directly influence the institutional management.

Finally, this internally-functional model needs to have a feedback loop which is made by the BSC adaptation step to correct possible distortions arising during application. Then we have the difficulties and dilemmas of adaptation and the last stage of modification by changing the traditional essence of the BSC, mainly due to the inclusion of the teaching perspective and changes in the management structure.

References

1. Miles, R.E., Snow, C.C., Meyer, A.D., Coleman, H.J.: Organizational strategy, structure, and process. Acad. Manag. Rev. **3**, 546–562 (1978)
2. Kaplan, R.S., Norton, D.P.: The Balanced Scorecard. Harvard Business School Press, Boston (1996)

3. Kaplan, R.S., Norton, D.P.: The balanced scorecard: measures that drive performance. Harv. Bus. Rev. **70**, 71–79 (1992)
4. Kaplan, R.S., Norton, D.P.: The Balanced Scorecard: Translating Strategy into Action. Harvard Business School Press, Boston (1997)
5. Beard, D.F.: Successful applications of the balanced scorecard in higher education. J. Educ. Bus. **84**, 275–282 (2009)
6. Chen, S.H., Yang, C.C., Shiau, J.Y.: The application of balanced scorecard in the performance evaluation of higher education. TQM Mag. **18**, 190–205 (2006)
7. Cullen, J., Joyce, J., Hassall, T., Broadbent, M.: Quality in higher education: from monitoring to management. Qual. Assur. Educ. **11**, 5–14 (2003)
8. Stewart, A.C., Carpenter-Hubin, J.: The balanced scorecard: beyond reports and rankings. Plan. High. Educ. **29**, 37–42 (2001)
9. Umashankar, V., Dutta, K.: Balanced scorecards in managing higher education institutions: an Indian perspective. Int. J. Educ. Manag. **21**, 54–67 (2007)
10. Lira, Á.M., Naas, I.A.: Performance indicators applied to Brazilian private educational institutions. Indep. J. Manag. Prod. **6**, 286–298 (2015)
11. Rodrigues, T.K.A., Lira, Á.M., Naas, I.A., Oliveira, D.M.S.: Sustainability of balanced scorecard: an analysis in the context of Brazilian Higher Education Institutions. In: POMS 2015, Washington (2015)
12. Rodrigues, T.K.A., Lira, Á.M., Naas, I.A.: The Balanced Scorecard (BSC) in Higher Education Institutions (HEI's): a management improvement strategy. In: POMS 2015 Proceedings CD, Washington (2015)
13. Rodrigues, T.K.A., Lira, Á.M., Naas, I.A.: Adaptation of the Balanced Scorecard (BSC) to the context of Higher Education Institutions (HEI's) Brazil. In: POMS 2015 Proceedings CD, Washington (2015)
14. Rodrigues, T.K.A., Lira, Á.M., Naas, I.A., Oliveira, D.M.S.: Difficulties and dilemmas of adaptation: the balanced scorecard in the context of Brazilian HEI's. In: POMS 2015 Proceedings CD, Washington (2015)
15. Rodrigues, T.K.A., Lira, Á.M., Naas, I.A.: Changing without losing the essence? A study of BSC adaptation at Brazilian Higher Education Institutions. In: POMS 2015 Proceedings CD, Washington (2015)

Collaborative Systems

System Thinking and Business Model Canvas for Collaborative Business Models Design

Sergio Gustavo Medina Pereira[✉], Franciele Alves dos Santos Medina,
Rodrigo Franco Gonçalves, and Márcia Terra da Silva

Paulista University, São Paulo, Brazil
medinasergiogustavo@gmail.com

Abstract. The purpose of this research is to reduce the existing gap between the abstraction of the real world and business modeling. For that, we combine two solutions: the soft systems methodology (SSM) and business model canvas (BMC). The first step is to introduce the theoretical concepts of both. The second step is the application of each methodology separately. Moreover, the final stage is to feed the BMC with the outputs of SSM. Was verified in the results what the concept of approximate the real world to systemic world (SSM) bring several benefits in the application of the BMC.

Keywords: Soft Systems Methodology · Body temperature · Mobile health

1 Introduction

The design of a new business model evolves the definition of business aspects or elements, like value proposition, cost structure, revenue structure, customer and suppliers relationship definition and so on, that can be integrate in a whole. In addition evolves a complex view of the reality and demands collaborative work. The Soft Systems Methodology (SSM) is a methodology of System Thinking Theory focused on structuring issues. The SSM is a comparison between the real world and some models of the world as it should be (world systems). With this comparison, there is the potential for expanding the real-world understanding to later be implemented to systems [1]. The SSM applications are growing in structuring decision problems of organizations, due to their usefulness in clarifying the problem and help decision makers to think about possible actions in feasible and desirable changes, before taking a decision [2]. A system is a representation of mental abstraction of reality according to the interpretation of the participating actors of this reality [3]. The Business Model Canvas (BMC) is a visual representation of how an organization creates, delivers and adds value [4]. The business model term has a large number of different settings. In general, a business model describes how an organization creates value [5]. There are also contributions that explicitly addresses business-modeling task. They aim to guide the process of modeling and design when it comes to developing a new

© IFIP International Federation for Information Processing 2016
Published by Springer International Publishing AG 2016. All Rights Reserved
I. Nääs et al. (Eds.): APMS 2016, IFIP AICT 488, pp. 461–468, 2016.
DOI: 10.1007/978-3-319-51133-7_55

business [5]. The steps have been designed by a multidisciplinary team involving the principles of Design Collaborative in system modeling and also addressed the business model. The aim of this study is to combine two methods. With the purpose to reduce the existing gap between the abstraction of the real world and business modeling through the application SSM at a high level and BMC as a tool to ensure the collaborative definition of the business elements.

2   Literature Review

This section aims to discuss issues related to Soft Systems Methodology (SSM) and Business Model Canvas (BMC).

2.1   Characteristics of Soft Systems Methodology (SSM)

Created by Peter Checkland in the early 70s, the Soft Systems Methodology (SSM), came about when the author and his colleagues searched a better approach to the resolution of bad structured problems that characterized human affairs [6, 7]. The crucial move in the research was to add to the 'natural' notions and systems "designed/drawn" the idea that a set of activities linked together could form a whole. Therefore, they realized that such systems could be clearly and adequately described only in relation to a particular problem, considering the view of the world individually [6, 8]. The SSM methodology goes on to consider the cultural and political aspects to better address the situations studied. For the development of the methodology, Checkland proposes that the situation studied is developed through seven stages as shown in Fig. 1, resulting in possible and desirable measures, according Fig. 1. The seven stages include the following features [1, 3, 6]. Stage 1: The first stage is to obtain information related to an unstructured problem. Project stakeholders explain their views on the problem. Stage 2: It aims to express the problem more formally in order to identify and record what changes slowly and which is constantly changing. A graphic

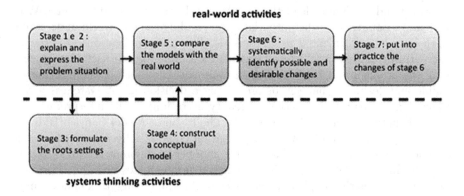

Fig. 1. Seven stages of SSM (Source: Adapted by [6])

called rich picture represents this step. Stage 3: After specifying the actual situation and their understanding, the definition of the causes is established. At the stage it is also elaborated the formulation of the problem root settings, the system ideal setting, who will be part and who will be affected. This stage follows the CATWOE structure: C - Costumer; A - Actors; T - Transformations; W - Weltanschauung (view of the world); O - Owner and E - Environmental constraints.

Stage 4: the construction of the conceptual model identifying intentional activities and a set of logical actions implicit by the root of definition. Stage 5: In this stage, a comparison is made of the conceptual model to the real world. A comparison may be represented by four different ways: informal discussion, formal interrogation scenarios description, creating a real world model in the same way that the conceptual model and then compare them [9]. Stage 6: This stage deals with the possible changes that may occur after the comparison made in the fifth stage, these changes should follow two criteria systematically desirable and culturally achievable [9]. Stage 7: The latter refers to the implementation of actions; here are elaborate plans of actions, which will only occur when any of the criteria mentioned in stage 6 is accepted.

2.2   BMC (Business Model Canvas) Features

A business model (BMC) can be considered as a tool to represent the core logic of an organization, and to communicate their strategic choices. It also describes how a company creates, delivers and adds value based on their strategic choices. The main contribution of a business model is due to fact that allows the creation of practices that enable and help organizations capture, understand, design, and analyze their logical business changes [10]. The business model is composed of nine building blocks that cover the four major areas a business: customers, supply, infrastructure and economic viability, and they are inter connected (Table 1).

Several studies have suggested elements that should make the business models. Among the studies, it was contacted that there are more than fifty four different elements [10]. These elements include value network, target market, value proposition, skills, cost elements, the company's strategy, processes and activities, considerations of income and prices, competitors, customer relationships, and many others. For to create different models, exists a variety of elements in the business model shows that different structures. This can be confusing to establish the related characteristics for each element and therefore can make it difficult the development of a complete business model.

2.3   Definitions of Collaborative Design

A define for collaborative design as a new methodological concept for developing the systems field [8]. It consists of a concept based on optimization of engineering processes. Its main objectives: to improve product quality, shorter time, promoting greater competitiveness and costs also focuses on increasing customer

Table 1. Elements of canvas business model

Functions		Definition
For who?	Customer segments:	The stakeholder the company aims to achieve and serve
	Customer relationships	Describes the types of relationships that a company establishes with specific customer segments
	Distribution channels	Explains how to the company communicates and reaches its customer segments to offer a value proposition
What?	Value propositions	Determines the value generated to a particular customer
	Key resources	Assets required offering and delivering the aforementioned elements
How?	Key activities	It presents the most important factors a company should do to model its business
	Key partners	Represent the network of partners and suppliers that support the execution of the business model
How much?	Revenue streams	Is the monetary values
	Cost structure	The costs incurred to operate a business model

satisfaction [11]. Products created by collective efforts this process is called collaborative design. The aims are to disseminate knowledge, ideas, resources or responsibilities [11].

3   Business Model Design

The system developed here called REmote MOnitoring System of body temperature (REMOS-BT), consists of a device (hardware) with the ability to perform remote sensing worker's body temperature. Figure 2 shows a system overview. Where a device, non-invasive, is coupled via a clamp to the worker. The device will perform measurements of their body temperature, relative humidity and temperature of the workplace. The generated data are sent to a Web Service, via a mobile device. The data shall be processed by software and presented in a form of graphical interface and/or tables, either on a personal computer, notebook or a mobile device, regardless of platform and operating system. The visualization of data is allowed by predetermined permissions to a health professional who can analyze and make a diagnosis.

The recorded data enable to create a user history, electronic medical record. These data can be used to predict an abnormal event by sending alerts to the health team and later for the users themselves, who can stop/slowing down the activity that carry on. This model integrates hardware, software and service as its differential. The service makes possible the monitoring happens in real time, with data sent over a dedicated server.

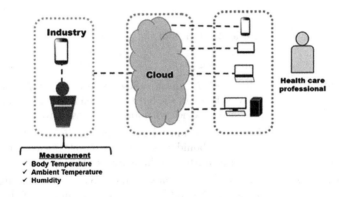

Fig. 2. Representation of system elements (Source The authors).

3.1   Implementation of the Seven Stages of SSM

Stage 1 (Explore the problematic situation): Survey of technical information about sensors, and low-cost components for the construction of the device (hardware). Check areas that have interest in adopting the device in its activities. Stage 2 (Expressing the problematic situation): After completion of step 1, It was decided to allocate the worker who operates in areas that have extreme temperatures. Stage 3 (succinct definitions): the CATWOE will be set after the extracted information of rich picture (Table 2).

Table 2. Situations modeled by CATWOE

Acronyms	Definition
C	Companies with focus on accident prevention/health worker
A	Professionals and workers responsible for monitoring. Also supervisors of workers and the health sector and responsible for production planning
T	Prevention that implies the reduction of factors that affect worker productivity, causing lower losses to the organization
W	Company performing on prevention
O	The persons responsible for organization that adopts the system
E	Acceptance of the monitoring by the employee which implies a cultural change in the organization

Considering the raised situations, the root definition is as follows: the proposed system aims to prevent accidents related to occupational health, and prevent future situations that injure the health of it, and consequently generate savings for the company. Stage 4: conceptual model (processes and sub-processes) represented in Table 3.

Table 3. Models of the processes

Processes	Sub processes
User registration	The system must allow access to users who are allowed through the authentication process. Each employee assigned a device with login and password
Device registration	Every device must have a unique identification number. The data should be sent to the mobile device of the worker and transmitted to the network via a server
Data transmitting and receiving alerts	The system will send the data to a central repository (web service). The system should receive an alert if there is any abnormal situation in the worker's health status
Accessibility	Message should be brief. Simple vocabulary
Portability usability	Responsive Website, accessible from any platform and/or mobile. Graphical representations for easy understanding

Stage 5: A comparison of models. They have related features; modelling the processes in both steps.

Stage 6: possible and desirable changes as shown in the representation of Table 4.

Table 4. Changes possible and desirable

Conceptual model	Desirable	Possible
The system must have an authentication system for each type of user	Yes	Yes
Each device has a unique identifier code	Yes	Yes
The system will allow the registration of new devices, users and healthcare professionals	Yes	Yes
Each device will perform three types of measurements: body temperature (BT), ambient temperature (AT) and humidity (HU)	Yes	Yes
The device should be low cost and less non-invasive as possible	Yes	Yes
The data transmission can be synchronous mode (online) and asynchronous mode (offline)	Yes	Yes
The health care professional can visualize in a chart the three measurements (BT, AT and HU) of the worker inside a set interval of time in minutes	Yes	Yes

Stage 7: Action to improve the situation Interface Prototyping developed for each step. Creating functional prototypes and cases of real tests with some users in a predefined environment, application submission for professionals, both those who use the devices as the health care professionals who carry out remote monitoring.

3.2 Results Obtained from BMC

All information acquired is organized according the nine dimensions of BMC approach. The potential customer segment is companies that want to prevent accidents and problems in occupational health. The value proposition defines the value of the service. Here, the system provides a service for the monitoring of real-time enterprise worker health, quickly and safely. Finally, the data of workers' body temperature can be collected through a low cost and non-invasive device. In the business model channels, the main element is the digital media, Internet, via Web, e-mail and disclosure companies. This connection is built on ads and other promotions. Additional services such as after-sales and interactions offered between the service and its customers. The business owner has the guarantee of an online service $(24 \times 7 \times 365)$. As well as the health professional is in direct contact, online mode, with the worker who can monitor their body temperature. Many different computing devices can perform access to the service. The main source of revenue is the sale of devices, usage rates, online service maintenance fees, support and system upgrade. Licenses, patents and trademarks are necessary to finalize these business resources. Elements of infrastructure, such as web services, applications for mobile devices and for systems with access via browser are needed to allow access the service. Moreover, it is necessary human resources to enable the different activities. The required activities include research and development (R & D), advertising and marketing and logistics/distribution. Some resources and activities need to be provided by partners such as component suppliers and web hosting service providers. An important detail is the technology and hardware infrastructure that the web service provider must have, thus offering a good service. The cost structure is mainly derived from the need of activities and resources. Costs occurs during the manufacturing process, R & D, marketing and logistics system. In addition, to be considered the cost of infrastructure, the operation of the service, advertising and promotion.

4 Final Discussion

Soft System Methodology aims to make a connection between the system of the world and the real world. This research studied a complete system, which covers the development of hardware and software. The goal is verify if the business is economically viable. The factors applied in the SSM were related to the first stage of the project, which is the idealization of business and their main features. The problematic of the business through a collaborative multidisciplinary environment with the application of SSM, the model proposed in this research, it has become quite effective as an aid to the business model of filling the canvas. Many aspects have already been studied during the seven stages of SSM, making the modeling easier and BMC closest real world because the questioning of some situations that were not included in BMC could be addressed in the SSM, which allowed a more comprehensive view of the business as a whole as a complete system. Using the SSM as a pre stage, we observe several benefits in the application of BMC. With results in a model canvas more complete and detailed.

References

1. Soares, V.M.S., Consenza, O.N., Gomes, C.F.S.: Técnicas Qualitativas e "Soft Systems Methodology" Aliadas ao Enfoque Sistêmico. Revista de Administração **36**(3), 100–107 (2001)
2. Curo, R.S.G., Belderrain, M.C.N.: Uma Aplicação de Soft Systems Methodology para Estruturar o Problema da Produção Científica de um Curso de Ensino Superior. In: XVIII Simpósio de Engenharia de Produção (2010)
3. Donaires, O.S.: A systemic approach to map and improve the software development process. FACEF Pesquisa **12**(2), 148–162 (2009)
4. Desai, H.P.: Business models for inclusiveness. Soc. Behav. Sci. **157**, 353–362 (2014)
5. Otto, B., Ebner, V., Baghi, E., Bittmann, R.M.: Toward a business model reference for interoperability services. Comput. Ind. **64**(8), 887–897 (2013)
6. Checkland, P.: Information systems and systems thinking: time to unite? Inf. Manag. **8**(4), 239–248 (1988)
7. Checkland, P., Holwell, S.: Information, Systems and Information Systems: Making Sense of the Field. Wiley, Hoboken (1997)
8. Alles, M.G., Kogan, A., Vasarhelyi, M.A.: Collaborative design research: lessons from continuous auditing. Acc. Inf. Syst. **14**(2), 104–112 (2013)
9. Checkland, P.: Systems Thinking, Systems Practice (1999)
10. Barquet, A.P.B., de Oliveira, M.G., Amigo, C.R., Cunha, V.P., Rozenfeld, H.: Employing the business model concept to support the adoption of product–service systems (PSS). Ind. Mark. Manag. **42**(5), 693–704 (2013)
11. Du, J., Jing, S., Liu, J.: Creating shared design thinking process for collaborative design. Netw. Comput. Appl. **35**(1), 111–120 (2012)

An Investigation to Manufacturing Analytical Services Composition Using the Analytical Target Cascading Method

Kai-wen Tien[1(✉)], Boonserm Kulvatunyou[2], Kiwook Jung[2], and Vittaldas Prabhu[1]

[1] Penn State University, State College, Harrisburg, USA
{kut147,vxp7}@engr.psu.edu
[2] National Institute of Standards and Technology, Gaithersburg, USA
{serm,kiwook.jung}@nist.gov

Abstract. As cloud computing is increasingly adopted, the trend is to offer software functions as modular services and compose them into larger, more meaningful ones. The trend is attractive to analytical problems in the manufacturing system design and performance improvement domain because (1) finding a global optimization for the system is a complex problem; and (2) sub-problems are typically compartmentalized by the organizational structure. However, solving sub-problems by independent services can result in a sub-optimal solution at the system level. This paper investigates the technique called Analytical Target Cascading (ATC) to coordinate the optimization of loosely-coupled sub-problems, each may be modularly formulated by differing departments and be solved by modular analytical services. The result demonstrates that ATC is a promising method in that it offers system-level optimal solutions that can scale up by exploiting distributed and modular executions while allowing easier management of the problem formulation.

Keywords: Factory Design and Improvement · Integration optimization · Analytical Target Cascading · Smart manufacturing · Services composition

1 Introduction

As cloud computing is increasingly adopted, the trend is to offer software functions, including analytical software functions, as modular services and compose them into larger, more meaningful ones [1,2]. The trend is attractive to analytical problems in the manufacturing system design and performance improvement domain because (1) finding a global optimization for the system is a complex problem; and (2) sub-problems are typically compartmentalized by the organizational structure. However, solving sub-problems independently can result in a sub-optimal solution at the system level. This paper investigates the technique called Analytical Target Cascading (ATC) to coordinate the optimization

© IFIP International Federation for Information Processing 2016
Published by Springer International Publishing AG 2016. All Rights Reserved
I. Nääs et al. (Eds.): APMS 2016, IFIP AICT 488, pp. 469–477, 2016.
DOI: 10.1007/978-3-319-51133-7_56

of loosely-coupled sub-problems. Each sub-problem may be independently formulated by each stake-holding organization and be solved by modular analytical software services.

This study is motivated by the Factory Design and Improvement reference activity model developed in [3]. The model decomposes major activities into subtasks and key decision-makings needed in a typical factory design and performance improvement project. It entails the needs for interactions across optimization problems at multiple control-levels.

For simplification of the illustration, this paper investigated the ability of ATC to coordinate three sub-problems at the manufacturing process control level including capacity design, lot sizing, and storage layout design. These three sub-problems are interlinked and typically dealt by different stakeholders. Their linkages are shown in Fig. 1.

Many analytical techniques have been developed to solve each of these three sub-problems. These techniques are often used in isolation, but these problems are not independent. A change in one formulation can influence the outcomes and feasibilities of the other two. Therefore, capturing those dependencies and using them to integrate these three sub-problems is crucial.

ATC has been used to solve multidisciplinary-design-optimization problems that comprise heterogeneous sub-problems. These sub-problems are solved separately; but, each of their interim solutions is communicated regularly. This not only speeds convergence, it also gives a better solution than the one that is generated with no communication or one-way communication (such as in the hierarchical model in Fig. 1). The algorithm that ATC uses has been studied extensively and its convergence properties have been established mathematically [4]. The primary application of ATC has been in designing complex products such as automobiles and aircrafts [5,6]. Nevertheless, it has also been used in integrating supply chains and integrating marketing and production (DFM) [7,8].

The result of this investigation indicates that ATC is a promising method in that it offers (1) easier management of the problem formulation of the overall system and (2) coherent, optimal solutions that can scale up to the size of the overall system by exploiting distributed and modular executions.

The rest of the paper is organized as follow. In Sect. 2, the analytical sub-problems are introduced; and it discusses drawbacks of the two traditional integration structures to compose these sub-problems: centralized and hierarchical. Then, the mathematical formulation of the proposed ATC-based collaborative structure illustrated in Fig. 1(c), is described in Sect. 3. In Sect. 4, we apply ATC to the sub-problems and analyze the results using data from a production project at Penn State [9]. Finally, the conclusion is presented in Sect. 5.

2   Composing Manufacturing Analytical Models

In this section, we introduce the three optimization sub-problems and their corresponding links. The exact links depend on the multi-criteria optimization of throughput (TH), inventory (INV), and work-in-process (WIP). Links can be seen as either common decision variables or input/output parameters, which are assumed to be non-negative.

Note: $\pi(\cdot)$ is a penalty function which is used in the collaborative model and will be explained in Sect. 3.1. In this section, we set it as a zero function.

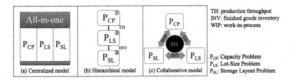

Fig. 1. Search methodology

2.1 Capacity Optimization

The important concern when optimizing capacity is that cycle times and WIP levels grow dramatically with increasing utilization [10]. Thus, the designers of this activity should decide on a reasonable throughput which minimizes the average WIP.

$$(P_{CP}) \quad \min \ z_1\,(\text{TH, WIP}) = \ c_w \cdot \text{WIP} + \pi\,(\text{TH, WIP})$$

$$s.t. \quad \text{CT}_q = \frac{c_a^2 + c_e^2}{2} \cdot \frac{u}{1-u} \cdot t_e \tag{1}$$

$$\text{WIP} = \text{TH} \cdot \text{CT}_q \tag{2}$$

$$u = \text{TH} \cdot t_e \tag{3}$$

$$TH \leq \text{TH}_{\text{limit}} \tag{4}$$

Where c_w is the unit cost for holding one unit of WIP during the planning period, and π represents any penalty functions. Equation (1) represents the approximation of the waiting time in queue, CTq, in a G/G/1 system. The formulation shows that CT_q is effected by the coefficient of variation (CV) of inter-arrival times c_a, the CV of effective processing times c_e, the utilization u, and the effective process time t_e. The formulation can be generalized to multi-machine, multi-station systems. (2) represents the Little's law formula. (3) shows the equation of utilization and (4) restricts TH.

2.2 Lot-Sizing Optimization

A wealth of models can be used for making lot-size decisions including EOQ (Economic Order Quantity) and EPL (Economic Production Lots) [10]. Here, we minimize the total inventory cost over T periods.

$$(P_{LS}) \quad \min \quad z_2 \, (\text{TH, INV}) = \sum_{t=1}^{T} p_t x_t + h_t i_t + \pi \, (\text{TH, INV})$$

$$s.t. \quad i_t = x_t + i_{t-1} - D_t, \quad \forall t = 1 \dots T \tag{5}$$

$$x_t \leq \text{TH} \cdot \text{WH}, \qquad \forall t = 1 \dots T \tag{6}$$

$$x_t + i_{t-1} \leq \text{INV}, \qquad \forall t = 1 \dots T \tag{7}$$

Where p_t is the unit production cost and h_t is the unit holding cost for period t. Equation (5) shows the inventory balance in each period, in which D_t is the demand and x_t is the production amount in period t. The constraint (6) indicates the production amount should be less than capacity limit, in which WH is the available working hours during the period. Equation (7) shows the inventory level should be less than INV.

2.3   Storage Layout Optimization

The storage layout sub-problem determines the optimal layout to minimize the material handling costs in terms of the distances (1) from WIP storage locations to locations of machines, and (2) between finished-goods inventory locations to the shipping docks. The storage layout problem is usually formulated as an assignment problem in which the storage floor is first subdivided into N grid squares and each item (WIP or INV) is assigned to a grid square.

$$(P_{SL}) \quad \min \quad z_3 \, (\text{INV, WIP}) = \sum_{k=1}^{N} [c_k^{(w)} y_k^{(w)} + c_k^{(f)} y_k^{(f)}] + \pi \, (\text{INV, WIP})$$

$$s.t. \sum_{k=1}^{N} y_k^{(w)} \geq \text{WIP} \tag{8}$$

$$\sum_{k=1}^{N} y_k^{(f)} \geq \text{INV} \tag{9}$$

$$y_j^{(w)} + y_j^{(f)} \leq 1, \qquad \forall \, j = 1, 2, \dots, N \tag{10}$$

$$y_k^{(w)}, \, y_k^{(f)} \in \{0, \, 1\} \tag{11}$$

Where $c_k^{(w)}$ and $c_k^{(f)}$ are the material handling cost for respectively storing one work-in-process and inventory in the grid square k. $y_k^{(w)}$ ($y_k^{(f)}$) is a binary decision variable, which value is 1 if one unit of WIP (INV) is assigned to the grid square k. (8) and (9) represent the storage spaces demanded for WIP and INV, respectively. (10) restricts that one grid square can store only one unit of the items.

2.4   Centralized vs. Hierarchical Integration Structures

The centralized-structure approach, shown as Fig. 1(a), is an intuitive and coherent way to think about integrating the sub-problems. It results from minimizing the three objective functions of the sub-problems subject to all constraints (1) to (9). So, in essence there is only one, multi-objective function and one set of constraints. There are, however, two serious drawbacks associated with this centralized approach. First, is the issue of poor scalability of the approach in terms of the increasing number of decision variables and constraints. The other drawback occurs when reformulation of the model is needed, e.g., when the factory changes: essentially you basically have to start over.

The hierarchical-structure approach, shown in Fig. 1(b), reduces, but does not eliminate, the difficulty in addressing these two challenges. The sub-problems are solved individually, so reformulation is easier. Additionally, the sub-problems are typically solved in a prescribed order. That order is P_{CP}, P_{LS}, then P_{SL}[4]. The links are directed links and are obtained as the outputs of the previously solved sub-problems. Clearly, this approach is not guaranteed to find a coherent, optimal solution. In addition, the quality of the final solution is highly dependent on the initial inputs to the initial process, P_{CP}. Therefore, in practice, it requires many experiments, by varying the input conditions until an optimal solution is found across all the sub-problems!

3   Proposed Collaborative Approach

Our collaborative approach achieves both the high solution quality of the centralized approach as well as the reconfigurability of the hierarchical approach. The ATC algorithm connects sub-problems as if they were building-blocks. First, sub-problems at two ends of a link are assigned two specific roles: sender or receiver. Then, the link value in each sub-problem is replaced by two variables: target t_i and response r_i. The sender solves the target t_i and the receiver solves the response variable r_i within its own local variables and constraints. The ATC algorithm seeks to minimize the discrepancies between targets and responses with respect to the links. In this paper, as we said above, P_{CP} is the sender of both WIP and TH; P_{LS} is the receiver of TH and the sender of INV; and P_{SL} is the receiver of both WIP and INV as Fig. 1(c).

3.1   The Collaboration Strategy

In order to achieve global consistency, each of the three sub-problems is assigned a different penalty function. It "punishes" a sub-problem, by adding high costs to its objective function, when its solution violates consistency constraints. Realizing this, we decided to use the augmented Lagrangian as our penalty function and the basis for our collaboration strategy [11]. The penalty function is shown in Eq.(12). Note that the notation "∘" means the elementwise product for arrays.

$$\pi(\cdot) = \sum_{i=1}^{n_t} \left(v_i t_i + \left\| w_i \circ (t_i - \overline{r_i}) \right\|_2^2 \right) + \sum_{j=1}^{n_r} \left(-v_j r_j + \left\| w_j \circ \left(\overline{t_j} - r_j \right) \right\|_2^2 \right) \tag{12}$$

The Lagrangian penalty function includes two new variables, Lagrangian multiplier v_i and quadratic penalty weight w_i. They are updated in the outer loop of ATC. The updating methods are expressed below, where l represents the iteration of the ATC algorithm.

$$v_i\,(l+1) = v_i\,(l) + w_i(l) \circ w_i(l) \circ (t_i(l) - r_i(l)) \tag{13}$$

$$w_i\,(l+1) = \beta \,\circ w_i(l) \tag{14}$$

The ATC algorithm has three main steps:

Step 1: Inner loop – solving sub-problems separately and updating the target and response variables.

Step 2: Outer loop – updating the Lagrangian multipliers and weights via expression (13) and (14).

Step 3: Termination – terminating the algorithm when the discrepancies of all target and response pairs are smaller than a given tolerance.

3.2   Reconfigurability and Discrepancy Visualization

As mentioned in the previous section, the ATC algorithm connects the sub-problems through target and response variables. It has the advantage of reusability. Suppose, for instance, a company wants to replace their current EOQ sub-problem with a (Q, r) sub-problem for lot-sizing design; the other two sub-problems are still reusable. Furthermore, since the overall system-problem has been partitioned into three sub-problems, the structural complexity of the overall system is reduced. Stakeholders of each sub-problem can also formulate their problems independently; therefore, the factory design and performance improve project can progress efficiently.

The ATC approach also allows feasibility issues across sub-problems to be conveniently resolved. It monitors the target/response values and showing the discrepancies between differing objectives in sub-models. For example, if there was a space reduction made in P_{SL} problem causing the responses r_{WIP} and r_{INV} not meeting the targets given by the other two sub-problems. The discrepancy can be shown in the results. This allows for the stakeholders to effectively collaborate and resolve the specific conflict.

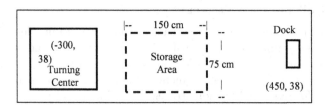

Fig. 2. Factory layout

4 Case Study

We use the IME Inc. project [9] to demonstrate the potential benefits of our collaborative approach over the other two. The aluminum chess set is the primary product in this case study. The associated process plan includes only one turning center and 240 labor hours. In addition, the product will be delivered to customers at the end of each quarter (March 31th, June 30th, etc.). Note, this knowledge could be used to determine the minimum value for storage size. That minimum value has to be large enough to store both WIPs and finished products during that time. Table 1 shows the parameters for the design sub-problems. c_a is approximated by the variance of the demand and c_e is significant because of the long set-up time of this product. t_e represents the effective processing time for the whole chess set. The production costs p_t changes because of the fluctuation of material costs. The holding cost for one set per one week is estimated by the typical interest rate per quarter (about 6.25%) times the production costs. The factory has 150×75 (cm^2) area for both WIP and the finished products (see Fig. 2). A finished product is wrapped into a $15 \times 7.5 \times 7.5$ (cm^3) box. Moreover, the boxes cannot be piled up because of the strength of the boxes. Hence, the storage area is divided into a grid of 100 squares, each of which can store only one box or one working-in-process. The material handling cost of a finished product at a certain location is calculated by multiplying the unit operation cost with the rectangular distance between the machine and the exit dock. With a technician's suggestion, we assume the unit costs of the material handling costs is $0.01/2.5$ cm.

Table 1. The parameters of sub-problems

P_{CP} Sub-problem		P_{LS} Sub-problem (Quarterly Plan)		P_{SL} Sub-problem	
c_a	0.685	p_t($/sets)	(20.0, 25.0, 18.0, 20.0)	Area (cm^2)	(150, 75)
c_e	0.942	h_t($/sets)	(1.25, 1.56, 1.13, 1.25)	Box (cm^2)	(15, 7.5)
t_e(hrs)	1.388	D_t(sets)	(100, 80, 130, 90)	Unit cost ($/cm)	0.01
c_w($)	4	WH(hrs)	240		

Table 2. The computational results

	Centralized model	Hierarchical model	Collaborative model
Comp time (sec)	4.9176	0.0742	132.7390
Total cost ($)	8290.5	8388.4	8290.5
(TH$_0$, WIP$_0$, INV$_0$)	(0.43, 0, 0)	(0.43, 0, 0)	(0.43, 0, 0)
(TH*, WIP*, INV*)	(0.67, 7.80, 80.01)	(0.43, 0.54, 62.5)	(0.67, 7.80, 80.01)

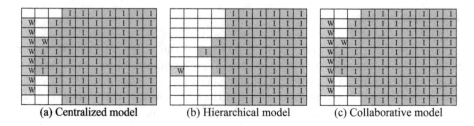

(a) Centralized model   (b) Hierarchical model   (c) Collaborative model

Fig. 3. The storage layouts

The desired throughput (initial value) is determined by the average demand rate 0.43 sets/h. The three models were constructed and run in MATLAB 2015a. The collaborative model was terminated after 96 iterations, resulting in a tolerance value of 10E-6 for the discrepancies between sub-problems. When terminated, $w = (1, 1, 1)$ and $v = (-3.75, 1.34, 1.76)$. The results show that the proposed collaborative approach can find the same solution as overall optimal solution generated by the centralized approach, but the hierarchical approach cannot. However, the computation time of the collaborative model is much larger than those of the other two (less than 5 s). This implies that the collaborative model is more suitable for solving problems in the factory "design stage," where the system complexity issue is much more critical than the computational time. Nevertheless, a parallel computing model could be explored to speed up the solver to provide a solution in a near real-time (Table 2).

5   Conclusion

In this paper, we proposed a collaborative approach, called Analytical Target Cascading (ATC), to composing analytical sub-problems and possibly associated software services to meet the overall objective. Our experiment shows a promising result. Sub-problems can be formulated and executed modularly and possibly under a distributed computing scheme. Even so, ATC connects these sub-problems and has the capability to achieve the coherent optimal as in the centralized model. Furthermore, unlike the centralized approach, our approach allows sub-problems to be changed or improved easily. Moreover, the discrepancies between targets and responses in each sub-problem are visible allowing for feasibility issues to be easily resolved. In the future work, we are planning to integrate control-level problems and design-level problems.

Acknowledgement. The work described in this paper was funded in part by NIST cooperative agreement with Penn State University No. 70NANB14H255.

Disclaimer. Any mention of commercial products is for information only; it does not imply recommendation or endorsement by NIST.

References

1. Kulvatunyou, B., Ivezic, N., Srinivasan, V.: On architecting and composing engineering information services to enable smart manufacturing. J. Comput. Inf. Sci. Eng. (2016)
2. IBM Watson Developer Cloud. Internet Web Site: https://www.ibm.com/smarterplanet/us/en/ibmwatson/developercloud/
3. Choi, S., Kim, B.H., Do Noh, S.: A diagnosis and evaluation method for strategic planning and systematic design of a virtual factory in smart manufacturing systems. Int. J. Precis. Engi. Manuf. 16(6), 1107–1115 (2015)
4. Michelena, N., Park, H., Papalambros, P.Y.: Convergence properties of analytical target cascading. AIAA J. 41(5), 897–905 (2003)
5. Kim, H.M., Rideout, D.G., Papalambros, P.Y., Stein, J.L.: Analytical target cascading in automotive vehicle design. J. Mech. Des. 125(3), 481–489 (2003)
6. Allison, J., Walsh, D., Kokkolaras, M., Papalambros, P.Y., Cartmell, M.: Analytical target cascading in aircraft design. In: 44th AIAA Aerospace Sciences Meeting and Exhibit, pp. 9–12 (2006)
7. Qu, T., Huang, G.Q., Cung, V.D., Mangione, F.: Optimal configuration of assembly supply chains using analytical target cascading. Int. J. Prod. Res. 48(23), 6883–6907 (2010)
8. Michalek, J.J., Ceryan, O., Papalambros, P.Y., Koren, Y.: Balancing marketing and manufacturing objectives in product line design. J. Mech. Des. 128(6), 1196–1204 (2006)
9. FAME LAB. http://www.engr.psu.edu/cim/FAME/CIMLAB/cim_p_2000.html
10. Hopp, W.J., Spearman, M.L.: Factory Physics. Waveland Press, Long Grove (2011)
11. Tosserams, S., Kokkolaras, M., Etman, L., Rooda, J.: A nonhierarchical formulation of analytical target cascading. J. Mech. Des. 132(5), 051002–051013 (2010)

ERP Systems and BSC in the Operations Management: An Analysis of Results by Companies

Celso Affonso Couto$^{(\boxtimes)}$, Oduvaldo Vendrametto,
Pedro Luiz Oliveira Costa Neto, Marcos de Oliveira Morais,
and Antonio Sérgio Brejão

Paulista University, São Paulo, Brazil
celsoacouto@hotmail.com

Abstract. This study objectives to verify, analyze and describe the difficulties and synergies between the strategic management methodology BSC (Balanced Scorecard) and integrated information system ERP (Enterprise Resource Planning) in the operations management. This is a multiple case study, which focuses on the relationship between these systems, contributing to a theoretical model that relates the characteristics of both management systems. Based on a broad theoretical framework that addresses several issues related to operations management, strategy, organizational system, ERP, performance indices and BSC, five companies were visited to questionnaires that enabled the identification of synergies, benefits, problems and difficulties between the BSC and ERP. In conclusion of this study, observations were made in relation to the BSC and ERP systems, especially regarding the difficulties identified and synergies between them in the operations management. Stood out in this work, the importance these two systems for planning, implementation and monitoring of strategy in organizations.

Keywords: Balanced Scorecard · Enterprise Resource Planning · Synergies and difficulties · Strategy

1 Introduction

Maximsing productivity, profitability and competitiveness in today's business context is required in a globalized and competitive world stage, with rapid advances in production and information technology, and other transformations. Companies need to be prepared for the intensification of disputing for customers, using effective management technologies and appropriate to their needs [1].

The production puts the strategy into practice and management of information is one of the most important issues in planning and control of the production [2].

© IFIP International Federation for Information Processing 2016
Published by Springer International Publishing AG 2016. All Rights Reserved
I. Nääs et al. (Eds.): APMS 2016, IFIP AICT 488, pp. 478–484, 2016.
DOI: 10.1007/978-3-319-51133-7_57

One of the applications advancement of these technologies is the development of Integrated Management Systems, that it allows the information's integrated automation that results in transactions made through the various processes of management and operation carried out within the company.

The German company called SAP (Systeme, Anwendungen, Produkt) with its software that enables the full connection between all functional areas of a company, as well as many industrial functions of the planning and production control [3].

Kaplan and Norton [4] developed the concept of the BSC, strategic management system initially used as monitoring tool performance and strategy control; it evolved into its potential, going to be treated as an important strategic management system in organizations.

To the BSC methodology dealing with excellence and effectiveness to the company's strategy, it must have the support of an "Integrated Management System" – ERP [5].

2   Formulation of the Problem/Main Issue Search

This study aimed to examine whether the ERP meets the BSC strategic management system requirements in accordance with the following specific objectives:

- Identify if there is integration between ERP and BSC in the operations;
- Identify benefits that ERP provides the BSC in the operations;
- Identify problems and difficulties of the ERP to meet the BSC; and
- Identify the consequences for the organization of the problems and difficulties generated by ERP to meet the BSC in the operations.

3   Literature Review

It presents a solid theory necessary to support the study of operations management, strategy, organizational systems, ERP systems, performance indicators and BSC strategic management system.

The topics were discussed as a theoretical basis for individual understanding of each theory, the relationship between themselves and the research objective, which is check the alignment (synergies/difficulties) between BSC and ERP in the operations management in implementing the strategy in organizations.

3.1   Operations Management

The operations management area develops planning, coordination and execution of all activities that create goods and provide services. Issues important as productivity, competitiveness and strategy relate to that area [1].

Information systems like MRP (Materials Requirements Planning), MRP II (Resources Planning), ERP (Enterprise Resource Planning) are tools that contribute directly to implementation of the strategy in the operations [6].

3.2 Strategy

The competition in several business segments, is very fierce, so that management systems as integrated BSC and ERP would create a competitive advantage, emerging unique opportunities, offering benefits to be realized by customers, expanding into new products and services.

It is seen as a corporate resource that supports strategies at the operational level, as the case of BSC methodology, or direct the strategies at a higher level, supporting the business in achieving competitive advantage [7].

3.3 Organizational System

The life cycle of an ERP-System extended phases of systems life cycle, as treated by Systems Theory.

The decision to adopt or not a technological trend would be outside the company's control when certain technology becomes a widespread use. Thus, companies have no alternative to adopt them or not, and are taken by majority decision, because if not come to adopt the new trend, compromise their competitiveness [8].

3.4 Systems ERP (Enterprise Resource Planning)

It sets up define an ERP system as a software package computes applications that support most business processes and information needs of an organization, such as production, supply chain, human resources, accounting, administration, sales, etc. The purpose of ERP is to integrate all areas and functions of the organization into a unified system for obtaining information in an efficient and timely manner [9].

3.5 Performance Indicators

Because the BSC use of performance indicators for analyzing the results in organizations, it is important to address some concepts of these indicators.

Indicators are quantifiable forms of representations of the characteristics of products and processes. They are used by the organization to control and improve the quality and performance of its products and processes over time [10].

Indicators help the organization to concentrate their efforts towards strategy and test the progress of the organization.

3.6 Balanced Scorecard - BSC

The term Balanced Scorecard was coined by Robert Kaplan and David Norton in a joint article in the Harvard Business Review in 1992 (HBR on Measuring Body-rate performance: Measuring performance in the Organization of the future) [4].

The BSC is a method of business management in which strategic objectives are established and monitored by defining performance indicators [11]. The BSC methodology is based on four perspectives around the mission, vision and strategy of the organization [12].

The Strengths of BSC. Outcome indicators of alignment with trend indicators; The BSC considers different interest groups in the analysis and implementation of strategy; Communication strategy; Promotes organizational synergy; The BSC is directed and focused on actions; translates the strategy into objectives and measures; Organization's alignment with the strategy; Constructs a strategic management system and links the strategy with planning and budget; Facilitates communication of strategic objectives, focusing on the employees in their implementation; The BSC helps reduce the amount of information used to set a minimum critical and vital indicates pain.

The Weaknesses of BSC. Does not separate cause and effect in time; Lack of mechanisms for validation; Link between strategy and operation is insufficient; Very internally focused.

4   Methodology

The method study of multiple cases is appropriate in this work because, in his empirical research, we sought to describe and analyze the integration and synergy between the BSC and ERP, taking into account the business environment in which they occur. Are part of that context the reasons for the need for integration between the BSC and ERP associated with implementing the company's strategy at all hierarchical levels. This is a descriptive and explanatory research.

It is reported that "the use of study cases specifically to the area of information systems is adequate for capturing the knowledge of professionals and build theories from this". Both in the case of the ERP system and in the BSC, it is interesting the experience obtained in practice by the professionals involved in the implementation and utilization of these management systems [13].

They were used in this study unstructured interviews made with the main participants of the implementation of processes and use of ERP systems and BSC, analysis of documents and records and direct observation.

Script's questions were based on the following issues:

- Why the surveyed companies have decided to use the ERP and BSC systems?
- How occurred the supplier selection processes in the sourced companies?
- As implementation processes occurred in the surveyed companies? What problems occurred during the implementation?
- What benefits have been or are being obtained with the use of ERP and BSC systems? How and why were obtained?
- What difficulties occurred or are occurring on the use of ERP systems and BSC in the surveyed companies? How and why that happened?

- What changes the ERP and the BSC system brought to the respondent department? And for the company?
- Is there synergy/integration between ERP and BSC system? Because yes? Why not?
- What are the improvements to meet synergy/integration between ERP systems and BSC?
- Can you list the ERP system and BSC system competitiveness gains in business?
- What are the next steps of the company in relation to information technology and business management methodology?

It was used in this work, for the presentation of cases, the analytical-linear model described by Yin [14].

Case reports were from the following points:

- If the context (type of business, size, description of the decision-making and choice of ERP, BSC, which used package and other factors considered relevant);
- Description of the implementation process of ERP and the BSC and its main problems;
- Benefits and problems encountered in the case.

The analysis of the cases was made considering the following points:

- Differences between the contexts of different companies;
- Similarities and differences between the results obtained in different companies;
- New ideas generated from the comparison of the cases;
- Analysis of the results against the initial proposals and the theoretical framework developed in the literature.

Some precautions to interpretation of the data were taken, some of them such as:

- Questionnaire used to guide the interviews;
- The researcher himself did the interviews, transcripts and writing cases;
- The use of multiple sources of evidence (triangulation) to confirm or supplement the information obtained in the interviews;
- Confirmation of case descriptions by the respondents.

5 Discussion of the Case Study Results

This multiple case study was conducted in five companies: power company, beverage company, steel industry, hospital and pharmaceutical industry. They all operate with ERP and BSC.

The research objectives were to identify whether there is integration between ERP and BSC in the operations, identify the benefits that ERP can offer the BSC in the operations, identify the problems and difficulties of the ERP to meet the BSC and identify the consequences for the operations problems and difficulties generated by ERP to meet the BSC.

The main considerations are presented, according to understanding of the comparative analysis between the companies surveyed. They are:

- In all businesses was implemented and first deployed ERP, for over ten years; and when it occurred, it was not thought to implementing the BSC;
- In all companies, the implementation of ERP occurred because the existing systems did not meet the needs of businesses;
- In all businesses and in all ERP modules were necessary customizations and improvements to meet the operations and business enterprises;
- In all companies, the planned cost for ERP implementation was not enough;
- In all companies, training for key users of ERP and more users was not enough;
- Despite all the difficulties and high costs in implementation and even in the initial phase of ERP implementation, all companies recognize the importance of ERP;
- In all companies implemented the BSC for more than seven years;
- The company decided to implement the BSC to improve the strategy, taking the strategy paper and turning it into actions in all areas;
- Companies expected the BSC communication strategy, synergies between the areas of strategy and translation into objectives and concrete actions;
- Companies have focused on four perspectives addressed by the BSC, namely: financial perspective, customer, internal processes and learning and growth;
- All companies reported that the BSC has improved the understanding of the strategy of the company, also improving its competitive edge, market share and especially its profitability and relationships with stakeholders;
- In all companies it was essential to have customizations and improvements in the ERP to attend the BSC;
- The main synergies between the BSC and ERP are planning, estimating, monitoring and reporting of performance indicators, speed, quality and confiability of information;
- Some benefits generated by the integration and synergy between the BSC and ERP: monitoring of the objectives and goals of the company; correction in a timely manner in decisionmaking, management reports available anytime and improvements in processes and cost rationalization;
- In every business synergy and integration of ERP and BSC brought productivity gains, increasing market participation, transparency and quality of information provided to stakeholders, competitive advantages and increased of profitability.

6   Considerations and Recommendations

In summary, for managers of enterprises, ERP information is generated in real time, systematized with clarity and transparency, in short summary, sequential and projected, numerical, narrative or graphic, easy understanding, and that support the needs of each area, and provide financial and management reports that attend the BSC and decision-making, through the planning, implementation and monitoring of the company's strategy.

In the surveyed companies show that the ERP brings the possibility of real gains in business efficiency, control and which provides synchronization of activities that require your best planning. Its integration with the BSC provides efficiency gains for the company. The answers of respondents indicated efficiency improvements and gains in competitiveness, through the integration between the ERP and the BSC or extension of its functionality.

However, in addition to the BSC, there are other systems and strategic management tools that could be studied with the use of ERP and enterprise management system that supports the management of information aimed at processing efficiently, transparent, principled and reliable to describe, implement and manage the strategy at all levels of the company, linking objectives, initiatives and measures with the overall strategy of the company.

References

1. Neumann, C.: Gestão de Sistemas de Produção e Operações. Rio de Janeiro (2013)
2. Slack, N., Chambers, S., Johnston, R.: Administração da Produção. Atlas, Rio de Janeiro (2009)
3. Stevenson, W.J.: Administration of Production Operations. LTC, Rio de Janeiro (2001)
4. Kaplan, R.S., Norton, D.P.: Having trouble with your strategy? then map it. Focusing Your Organization on Strategy-with the Balanced Scorecard, p. 49 (2000)
5. Emlio Filho, H.: Balanced Scorecard e a Gestão Estratégica: Uma Abordagem Práitica. Editora Campus (2005)
6. Laugeni, F.P., Martins, P.G.: Administração da Produção. Saraiva, São Paulo (2006)
7. Canépa, P.C.V., Rigoni, E.H., Brodbeck, Â.F: Práticas de Alinhamento Estratégico: Um Estudo Exploratório em Organizaçães Industriais e de Serviços. Revista de Administração Mackenzie 9(1) (2008)
8. Brodbeck, A.F., Henrique Rigoni, E., Hoppen, N.: Strategic alignment maturity between business and information technology in Southern Brazil. J. Glob. Inf. Technol. Manag. 12(2), 5–32 (2009)
9. Souza, C., Zwicker, R.: Sistemas ERP: Estudo de Múltiplos Casos em Empresas Brasileiras. In: Souza, C., Saccol, A. (eds.) Sistemas ERP no Brasil: Teoria e Casos. Atlas, São Paulo (2003)
10. Takashina, N.T.F., X., M.C.: Indicators of Quality and Performance. Qualitymark, Rio de Janeiro (1997)
11. Cesar, R.: http://computerworld.com.br/tecnologia/2003/03/28/idgnoticia. 2006-05-15.5335549649
12. Kaplan, R.S., Norton, D.P.: The Balanced Scorecard: Translating by Luiz Euclydes T. F. Filho. Elsevier, Rio de Janeiro (1997)
13. de Souza, C.A., Zwicker, R.: Sistemas Integrados de Gestão Empresarial: Estudos de Casos de Implementação de Sistemas ERP. Faculdade de Economia, Administração e Contabilidade (2000)
14. Yin, R.K.: Case Study Research: Design and Methods. Bookman, Porto Alegre (2010)

Toward a Matching Approach to Support CBM (Collaborative Business Model) Processes Between Regional Entrepreneurs Within the RIS3 Policy

Jérémie Faham[1(✉)], Maxime Daniel[1], and Jérémy Legardeur[1,2]

[1] ESTIA, Bidart, France
{j.faham,m.daniel,j.legardeur}@estia.fr
[2] IMS, Talence, France

Abstract. One of the objectives of the European Commission for 2014–2020 is to establish "Research and Innovation Strategies for the Smart Specialization" (RIS3). The originality of RIS3 is the "bottom-up" identification of regional priorities especially through the "Entrepreneurial Discovery" (ED) process. The Collaborative Business Models (CBM) approach has probably a role to play within this process as a suitable strategic tool to set up regional "value networks". However, the preparatory stage of CBM and especially the identification and the matching processes among potential RE partners is often not addressed. This work is based on the need to support the discovering and the matching processes between "regional entrepreneurs" (companies, research, consulting, association, public authorities...) in order to improve the efficacy of CBM and RIS3. In this paper, we propose a review of the state of the art concerning the different dimensions linked to the matching processes.

Keywords: Matching · RIS3 · Entrepreneurial Discovery · CBM · Profile comprehension

1 Introduction

The "Entrepreneurial Discovery" process of RIS3 is an attempt to support the proactive participation of all the regional "entrepreneurs" (RE) (enterprises, universities, research institutes, consulting organizations, institutional authorities etc.) in the strategic orientations of their region. However there is a lack of operational propositions (tool, methodology...) to instrument the implementation of the ED process [1]. Thus, this ED engenders the same limitations of past policies: the usual regional "leaders" (big companies, high-tech start-up, big laboratories etc.) are often solicited during the launch of RIS3 policies whereas the smaller actors (SMEs, individuals, association, laypersons etc.) are rarely taken into consideration and feel unable to contribute to the definition of the economic orientations of their regions.

© IFIP International Federation for Information Processing 2016
Published by Springer International Publishing AG 2016. All Rights Reserved
I. Nääs et al. (Eds.): APMS 2016, IFIP AICT 488, pp. 485–492, 2016.
DOI: 10.1007/978-3-319-51133-7_58

Therefore, one of the major challenge for the RIS3 is to find new ways to foster the collaboration between all the RE in order to facilitate the active involvement of a broader set of regional stakeholders into an open and more inclusive ED process. Previously, we developed the WeKeyInnovation (WKI) [2] which is an open and collaborative wikiplatform to share information about existing innovation supports and to stimulate the identification of all the RE. As a complementary approach, we analyzed how the Collaborative Business Model (CBM) processes [3] could be used for the design of innovative copropositions leaded by RE at the territorial level [4]. However, the literature doesn't address the question of the preparatory stage of CBM processes but some works emphasize on the potential to gather the right partners before to start any CBM processes [5]. Indeed, it is difficult to find mechanisms to help RE to identify the appropriate partners to achieve a successful collaboration. Thus, this paper is focused (Sect. 2) on the need to improve the "Matching" efficiency between RE as a necessary pre-step of CBM processes. Then, we present in Sect. 3 a deep characterization of RE profiles directed to support the comprehension of their respective expectations. In Sect. 4 we propose a conclusion and some perspectives toward visual representations of RE profiles to support their potential of "Matching".

2   Enhancing the Matching Potential of RE to Increase CBM Efficiency

2.1   A More Comprehensive Profile Characterization to Enhance the "Matching" Potential of RE

Our main assumption is that achieving a better characterization of RE profiles before their participation to any networking or collaborative event increases the probability of matching among them. During this preparatory phase of CBM, it is a critical issue to enhance their mutual understanding and maximize their chances of collaboration. Moreover, getting a more comprehensive knowledge about the different aspects of each RE profile and their expectations when they meet during specific events is also strategic:

– for organizers of networking events (business meeting, seminar, workshop, conference...) to better prepare their affair with a more efficient consortium of participants;
– for RE participants that better explicit and specify their true needs concerning the event. They can also decide to attend or not to the different proposed events and identify, "filter" and match with more appropriate profiles of potential partners.

Indeed, we will face a plurality of RE profiles attending to the same event depending on:

– each RE individual socio-demographic characteristics (age, gender, education etc.), personality traits (need for achievement, risk predisposition etc.), values orientation (continuity, openness to change, self-enhancement) [6,7];

– and according to its affiliated organization features (size, sector, structure etc.), its organizational culture (hierarchical, results-oriented, group-oriented etc.) [8,9], its environmental confines (stability, uncertainty, hostility...), the hierarchical structure of its motivations or success criteria and its instantaneous strategic expectations in a specific context or regarding to the topic of one meeting [10,11].

Previous works have been considered only unidirectional influencing factors that led to an increasing number of entrepreneurs' typologies or taxonomies [12,13] which were strongly criticized because they were inappropriate to grasp entirely such a complex and multidimensional phenomenon [14]. Moreover, this set of heterogeneous entrepreneur's typologies and taxonomies led to the multiplication of contradictory results, classification or prescriptions which are impossible to compare [15] and casting doubt on the existence of homogeneous entrepreneurs' profiles. The limits are even stronger if we study this phenomenon through the perspective of RIS3 "entrepreneurs" i.e. the RE because it implies to consider a broader set of unusual socio-economic actors than in others entrepreneurship researches.

We present in the next section a methodology proposition to support a more detailed characterization of RE profiles in order to facilitate their matching and enhance their potential of collaboration.

3   Toward a More Comprehensive Characterization of RE Profile: A Configurational and Multidimensional Approach to Support Their Potential of Collaboration

3.1   From Entrepreneur to RIS3 "Regional Entrepreneur" Characterisation

The characterization of ED is an increasing challenge because the two founding concepts of RIS3, the RE and the ED process broadens the scope of the fields and the range of socio-economic stakeholders to consider. RIS3 is open to all individuals and all types of organizations embedded in the society at regional level. In this context, studies which focused on specific aspects of the entrepreneurial dynamics are too narrow to grasp the full dimensions of the heterogeneous set of RE potentially affected by the ED process of RIS3.

Based on others studies which encompassed the use of classifications and quantitative analysis [16], our goal is to support RE during the process of identification-selection of potential partners. It requires to foster the matching efficiency which occurs between RE as a pre-step of any CBM attempt. The objective is only to bring them more information regarding to each RE characteristics and contextual expectations. Our purpose is to facilitate their mutual understanding in order to offer them an increased range of choices and possibilities of collaboration with unexpected regional actors. However, the challenges are multiple and it implies therefore to define which information to get, the adequate ways to collect it, and to choose the proper supports to use to make it accessible to all RE.

3.2   Embracing a Configurational Approach

We need to think in terms of crossed variables because the characteristics of RE profiles form a unique combinations of interconnected dimensions. We embrace a configurational approach [17–19] to overcome the shortcomings of past studies that restricted their analysis to one dimension of the entrepreneur's profiles or to precise aspects of entrepreneurship. The configurational approach enables to grasp much of the multiple areas interacting in the characterization of RE profiles. The definition of unique configurations of variables copes with the aim of this study because:

- It brings a more comprehensive understanding of the interrelated dimensions embedded into each unique RE profile and its specific expectations,
- It lets at the same time the possibility for further analysis of separated sets of different aspects (e.g. personality traits, organizational features, resources, environment etc.).

A strong literature review had been made to settle this configurational analysis of RE profiles. We selected the areas that correspond to the most often cited dimensions which influence their decisions and their behaviors. We gathered in (Fig. 1) the most complete set of items that have demonstrated constant significance in the relevant research or that were the most often cited in the literature review.

3.3   The Combination of Generic and Contextual Dimensions of RE Profiles

We suggest to use both generic and contextualized information as an interesting alternative to get a more comprehensive understanding of each specific RE profile. Hence, all the items and RE profiles aspects that we gathered in the literature review were grouped into two distinct but complementary sets of "Generic" and "Contextual" dimensions (Fig. 1). The "generic dimensions" are RE characteristics which remain stable or that evolve very slowly in the long-term whereas the "contextual" ones are more inclined to change depending on each particular context [20].

To cope with this challenge, the "context-dependent" dimensions are listed as a set of possible dialogical (i.e. antagonistic but complementary) orientations [21]. RE will have to precise their expectations regarding to those dialogical orientations before to participate to any specific event. It is precisely the arbitration between pertinent and rival values which is guiding their attitudes and their behaviors in different acts, at different moments and in different contexts [22].

This consideration of each RE positioning can help them to clarify their oppositions but it also facilitates the identification of common or complementary interests. This effort toward a better mutual understanding between RE makes it easier to match and start a dialogue or a collaboration with a broader set of potential unexpected partners.

Dimension and aspects of RE profile	Items precisions	Sources
	GENERIC DIMENSIONS	
Personal characteristics	*(Examples of Socio-demographic characteristics)*	
Age	• Less than 25 years, 25 o 29, 30 to 39, 40 to 49, • 50 years and more	(Espiritu-Olmos et al., 2015) (Robert et al., 2009) (Gartner, 1985)
Education level	No diploma, Professional ability certificate, professional diploma, Bachelor, Bachelor +3 years education or more	(Korunka 2003) (Robert et al., 2009)
Experience	Former work, Industry, Entrepreneurship, Family business precedents	(Robert et al., 2009) (Korunka 2003)
Entrepreneurial Position	Business-Owner, Non-Owner Manager, Auto entrepreneur, Latent, Student, Other	(Gorgievski et al., 2011) (Avenier, 1997)
Organization features	*(examples)*	
Age	Latent, pre-birth, nascent, post-natal, mature	(Vamvaka, 2014) (Jayawarma, 2013) (Zahra, 2009)
Entrepreneurial Stage		(Miner, 997)
Size	Very small enterprises, SMEs, MNT...	(Robert et al., 2009)
Type	Craft, Promotion, Admin	(Filley et Aldag, 1978) (Marmuse, 1992)
Activity-Skills	Sector, Expertise	(Jaouen 2008)
Area of development	Big city, small city, geographic area	(Espiritu-Olmos et al., 2015)
Family embeddedness	"family-in" vs "family-out"	(Espiritu-Olmos et al., 2015) (Crant, 1996) (Collins and Moore, 1970) (Shapero, 1972)
Culture	Hierarchical, Entrepreneurial, Market-driven, Group-oriented	(Randerson et al., 2011) (Quinn & Rohrbaugh, 1983) (Cameron & Quinn, 2006) (Cherchem, 2009) (Zahra, 1993) (Ireland et al., 2009)
Structure	Degree of flexibility allowing to catch-up opportunities (Bureaucratic vs. Organic structures)	(Randerson, Fayolle, 2011) (Fayolle, 2008) (Covin et Slevin 1990, 91) (Lumpkin et Dess 1996) (Miller et Friesen, 1983)
Entrepreneurial Orientation	Innovation, pro-activity and risk-taking (Conservative vs. Entrepreneurial orientation)	(Randerson et Fayolle, 2011) (Stevenson et Gumpert, 1985) (Davies, 2010)
Organizational priority	• LT Viability-Efficiency, Stability • ST Gain-Growth • Flexibility • Balance	(Jaouen et Lasch, 2015) (Marchesnay, 1992) (Marchesnay et Julien, 1996) (Laufer, 1975) (Miles and Snow, 1978)
Personality traits		
Entrepreneurial Sensitivity	Rational-Cautious vs. Sentimental-Emotional	(Jaouen, 2008)
Need for achievement	Perception of your capacity to take-up challenges to reach a personal achievement	(Randerson, Fayolle, 2011) (Stefanovic and al. 2010) (Filley and Aldag, 1978)
Locus of control	Perception of your capacity to control your behavior and your destiny believing that success depends more on your actions than on the influence of external factors.	(Randerson, Fayolle, 2011) (Korunka 2003) (Frese et al., 1997) (Krampen 1991)
Self-efficacy	Perception of your capacity to succeed in achieving specific tasks and take-up challenges instead of seeking the *statu quo*	(Poon et al. 2006) (Wood and Bandura 1989) (Boyd et Vozikis 1994)
Risk taking	Aversion vs. propensity to take risks	(Espiritu-Olmos et al., 2015) (Jaouen et Lasch, 2015)
Tolerance for ambiguity	Find ambiguous situations challenging	(Teoh and Foo, 1997)
Neuroticism	Normal, Calm, Relaxed, Anxious	(Zhao and Seibert, 2006)
Kindness (socialization skills)	Tendency to be cooperative, attentive, friendly, modest and ability to build collaborative relationships	(Schneck, 2014) (Vamvaka et Botsaris, 2014) (Pearce and Doh, 2005)
Emotional intelligence	Appraisal and expression of emotions, regulations of emotions (self & others), utilization of emotions	(Cross and Travaglione, 2003) (Goleman, 1998) (Mayer, Caruso et al., 1990)
Entrepreneurial intention	Quality that leads an individual to pursue a career in self-employment or establish his own business	(Espiritu-Olmos et al., 2015) (Vamvaka et Botsaris, 2014) (Fayolle & Liñan, 2014) (Cherchem & Fayolle, 2010) (Thompson 2009) (McGee et al., 2009)
Positive Role model	• Family tradition influence • Admiration-idolatry	(Jayawarma et al., 2013) (Robert et al., 2009)
Psycho-technic characteristics	Personal achiever, Empathic super sales, Real manager, Expert idea generator.	(Miner, 1997)
Personal values orientation		
Refined version of Basic HUV	(19) *Universal Human Values*	(Cieciuch et al., 2014) (Knoppen, 2009) (Schwartz, 1992)
Organization culture		
Organization Culture Profile	(54) *OCP-Items*	(Borg et al., 2011) (Bilsky 2002) (O'Reilly, Chatman, Caldwell, 1991)
Success Criteria	(10) *Success-Items*	(Gorgievski, 2011)
Motivations criteria	Profitability, Public recognition, Growth, Firm survival/continuity, Contributing to society, Satisfied Stakeholders, Utility – Usefulness, Innovation, Personal Satisfaction, Work-life balance	(Jayawarna et al., 2013)
	(6) *Motivations-Items*	
	Materialism-money, Status-power-control, Necessity, Community, Achievement-challenge, Flexibility	
	CONTEXTUAL DIMENSIONS	
Instantaneous Expectations & environmental confines	*(capacity-strategy needs and goals related to a specific context/topic)*	
View of the future	Prediction	Creation	(Sarasvathy, 2001; 2005) (Silberzahn, 2014)
Basis to take action and acquire Stakeholders	Goals	Means	-
Predisposition toward Risk	Expected Return	Affordable loss	-
Planning	Commitment	Contingency	-
Basis for Commitment	Should	Can	-
Attitude toward outside Firms	Competition	Partnership	-
Decision for action if	Desirable	Possible	(Bruyat, 1993)
-	Coherence	Contingence	-
Desired Strategy	Global Vision	Local Action	(Avenier, 1997)
Hierarchical level	Global	Local	-
Goals orientation	LT Goals	ST Objectives	(Marshall, 2013) (Collins et Porras, 1996)
Position Seeking	Rules-Security	Risk	(Borg et al., 2011)
-	Results	Relations	-
Value Seeking	Self-enhancement	Self-transcendence	(Schwartz, 2006)
	Conservation	Openness to change	-
Decision Drives	Acquire	Connect	(Schwartz, 2006) (Lawrence & Nohria, 2002)

Fig. 1. Generic and contextual dimensions of Regional Entrepreneurs profiles

The combination of such a complementary set of characteristics and the hybridization of the generic and the contextual dimensions of RE profiles in a configurational approach is a promising path to facilitate their interaction and to increase their possibilities of collaboration at regional level. However, this list is not exhaustive and it is still adjustable by and for all organizers-facilitators regarding to the topic and the goals of each event. It also requires to be completed to further improvements, reductions or extensions directed by complementary researches and empirical testing.

4   Conclusions and Further Perspectives

As a conclusion, the goal of our study is to get a better profile characterization of each RE to facilitate their mutual comprehension and increase their probability of "Matching" successfully. The aim is to enhance the "collaboration" between RE at regional level and to support a broader participation of smaller actors in the flow of the "bottom up" propositions of the ED process of RIS3. This work is also opening a research perspective for the design of new tools to support the recognition and the comprehension of each personalized RE profile or expectations in order to facilitate their "matching" (Fig. 2). This paper highlighted several shortcomings in different levels and areas of regional innovation strategy. We underlined first the limits of the actual ED process and the need for its instrumentation within heterogeneous European regions. Secondly we presented the use of the CBM approach as a suitable strategic tool to support the collective participation of a broader set of RE within the RIS3. However we pointed out the necessity to focus on the preparatory stage of those CBM processes in order to increase their efficiency. Third, we emphasized on the necessity to get a comprehensive characterization of RE profiles. We presented a table embracing a

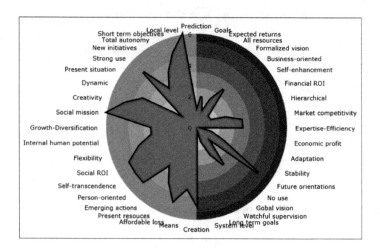

Fig. 2. An example of radar-charts to give a visual representation of RE profile

configurational approach which combine both generic and contextual dimensions of RE profiles.

This contribution aims to grasp much of the multiple dimensions which characterize each single and unique RE profile. The main objective is to:

- Include a broader set of unexpected RE which have not previously been consulted about the RIS3 initiative;
- Reach a more comprehensive view of their respective and instantaneous expectations;
- Facilitate their mutual understanding and their interactions;
- Support the identification of potential partners and foster their probability of "matching";
- Enhance the potential of collaboration between all RE in the long term to feed a continuous dynamic of co-constructed propositions within the ED process of RIS3.

Acknowledgements. Authors would like to acknowledge our partner AGEFA PME for its support concerning the Chair on SMEs 3.0 and the NEPTUNE project that has received funding from the European Union's Horizon 2020 research and innovation programme.

References

1. Foray, D., David, P.A., Hall, B.H.: Smart specialisation from academic idea to political instrument, the surprising career of a concept and the difficulties involved in its implementation. Technical report, EPFL (2011)
2. Faham, J., Takouachet, N., Legardeur, J.: WeKeyInnovation, a Wiki based on crowdsourcing to share information about innovation support. In: Grabot, B., Vallespir, B., Gomes, S., Bouras, A., Kiritsis, D. (eds.) APMS 2014. IAICT, vol. 438, pp. 289–297. Springer, Heidelberg (2014). doi:10.1007/978-3-662-44739-0_36
3. Konnertz, L., Rohrbeck, R., Knab, S.: How collaborative business modeling can be used to jointly explore sustainability innovations. In: ISPIM Annual Conference, Hamburg, Germany (2011)
4. Faham, J., Lizarralde, I., Legardeur, J.: WeKeyInnovation et Business Model Collaboratif: Une proposition pour faire Participer les PME dans le Cadre des RIS3. In: 14e'me Colloque Nationale AIP Primeca (2015)
5. Breuer, H., Lüdeke-Freund, F.: Values-based innovation framework-innovating by what we care about. In: XXVI ISPIM Conference (2015)
6. Schwartz, S.H.: Universals in the content and structure of values: theoretical advances and empirical tests in 20 countries. Adv. Exp. Soc. Psychol. **25**(1), 1–65 (1992)
7. Cieciuch, J., Davidov, E., Vecchione, M., Schwartz, S.H.: A hierarchical structure of basic human values in a third-order confirmatory factor analysis. Swiss J. Psychol. **73**, 177–182 (2014)
8. O'Reilly, C.A., Chatman, J., Caldwell, D.F.: People and organizational culture: a profile comparison approach to assessing person-organization fit. Acad. Manag. J. **34**(3), 487–516 (1991)

9. Borg, I., Groenen, P.J., Jehn, K.A., Bilsky, W., Schwartz, S.H.: Embedding the organizational culture profile into Schwartz's theory of universals in values. J. Pers. Psychol. **10**(1), 1 (2011)
10. Jayawarna, D., Rouse, J., Kitching, J.: Entrepreneur motivations and life course. Int. Small Bus. J. **31**(1), 34–56 (2013)
11. Gorgievski, M.J., Ascalon, M.E., Stephan, U.: Small business owners' success criteria, a values approach to personal differences. J. Small Bus. Manag. **49**(2), 207–232 (2011)
12. Robert, F., Marques, P., Lasch, F., Le Roy, F.: Entrepreneurship in emerging high-tech industries: ICT entrepreneurs between experts and kamikazes. Int. J. Entrep. Small Bus. **7**(3), 258–283 (2009)
13. Zahra, S.A., Gedajlovic, E., Neubaum, D.O., Shulman, J.M.: A typology of social entrepreneurs: motives, search processes and ethical challenges. J. Bus. Ventur. **24**(5), 519–532 (2009)
14. Gartner, W.B.: A conceptual framework for describing the phenomenon of new venture creation. Acad. Manag. Rev. **10**(4), 696–706 (1985)
15. Rauch, A., Wiklund, J., Lumpkin, G.T., Frese, M.: Entrepreneurial orientation and business performance: an assessment of past research and suggestions for the future. Entrep. Theory Pract. **33**(3), 761–787 (2009)
16. Jaouen, A., Lasch, F.: A new typology of micro-firm owner-managers. Int. Small Bus. J. **33**(4), 397–421 (2015)
17. Espiritu-Olmos, R., Sastre-Castillo, M.A.: Personality traits versus work values: comparing psychological theories on entrepreneurial intention. J. Bus. Res. **68**(7), 1595–1598 (2015)
18. Korunka, C., Frank, H., Lueger, M., Mugler, J.: The entrepreneurial personality in the context of resources, environment, and the startup process: a configurational approach. Entrep. Theory Pract. **28**(1), 23–42 (2003)
19. Fayolle, A.: Entrepreneurship and New Value Creation: The Dynamic of the Entrepreneurial Process. Cambridge University Press, Cambridge (2007)
20. Sarasvathy, S.D.: Causation and effectuation: toward a theoretical shift from economic inevitability to entrepreneurial contingency. Acad. Manag. Rev. **26**(2), 243–263 (2001)
21. Morin, E.: Restricted Complexity, General Complexity, pp. 5–29. World Science, Singapore (2007)
22. Schwartz, S.H.: Les Valeurs de Base de la Personne: Théorie, Mesures et Applications. Revue Fr. Sociol. **47**(4), 929–968 (2006)

Office Location, A Strategy for Legal Logistics

Cícero Tadeu Tavares Duarte[1(✉)], José Benedito Sacomano[1],
Jorge Luiz de Macêdo[2], Élissa Tavares Duarte Cavalcante[3],
and Layse Andreza de Sousa Carvalho[3]

[1] University Paulista, São Paulo, Brazil
tadeu@tdca.com.br, jbsacomano@gmail.com
[2] Uninovafapi, Teresina, Brazil
jorge@uninovafapi.edu.br
[3] Piauí Federal University - UFPI, Teresina, Brazil
elissatd@yahoo.com.br, lay.carvalho@gmail.com

Abstract. Center of gravity is a geographical location method widely used in industrial management. Apply for legal logistics were a challenge to find possible locations to settle future law firms in other locations. Brazil is a continental country with different population densities that make the use of technologies and methodologies necessary to become more assertive geographical location. Using the problem-solving method and the creation of an electronic simulator was possible to find the optimum location to minimize both costs and results.

Keywords: Office location · Localization strategy · Logistics legal · Gravity center · Location businesses

1 Introduction

The present work aims to expose the case study results conducted at law firm Araújo HIDD & Melo, which was calculated the location of the best city for the settlement of a new subsidiary, aiming to reduce corresponding costs, increase operating area as well as the company's profits. To achieve these results, the Logistics Center of Gravity model was applied.

The center of gravity is a quantitative data model used to determine the location of a facility based on weighted weights determined, the results of this method are the Cartesian coordinates X and Y so that the weight "cost" is minimized.

For the study used data from the acts performed in Brazilian cities of Piauí and Maranhão (Brazilian states), by law firms Araújo HIDD & Melo from Teresina, São Luís, as well as their corresponding (lawyers/Supervisor of support) in the period from January to June 2015.

The acts referred in this paper should be understood as the Hearings and Diligences made in the above period, of the active customers in September 2015.

The software used for the study was the Microsoft Office Excel 2013 version that is very usefull for those who domine the formulas that can automate various stages of the calculation of the Centre of Gravity process. The company provided the entire cost of database and receipt by city in spreadsheets. Also in format spreadsheets, they were

I. Nääs et al. (Eds.): APMS 2016, IFIP AICT 488, pp. 493–500, 2016.
DOI: 10.1007/978-3-319-51133-7_59

willing to location of cities in the state of Piauí and Maranhão. These data(s) are available at database of the IBGE initials for Brazilian Institute of Geographic and Statistics (Instituto Brasileiro de Geografia e Estatística).

2 Lower's Office in Brazil

Brazil has a projection for 2018 that will have 1 million lawyers. Increasingly increases competitiveness among professionals of law. In 2014, Brazil had more than 835,000 lawyers [1]. Brazil has 357 lawyers for every 100,000 inhabitant, those numbers put the country in the second place in world ranking after the USA - United States of America [2] (Fig. 1).

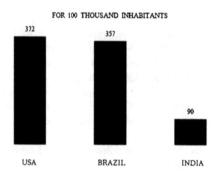

Fig. 1. World ranking lawyers amount

Appear in the middle of this competitive Lawyer's market a new term called Legal Logistics or lawyerly logistics. They are basically two activities: Diligence and audience. Diligences are copies, distribution, protocols, removal of documents and charters, emission of certificates and guides, loads, diligences in Procon (an institute that works in Brazil for Consumer Protection and Defense Foundation - Fundação de Proteção e Defesa do Consumidor), real estate records and government agencies, as well as every effort involving electronic processes, including transfer of subpoenas. Audiences are designations of lawyers and agents for all judicial and administrative spheres [3].

The legal logistics basically works by hiring a company that operates throughout the country and hire a law firms to take care of all legal demands, usually dealing with final costumer. This office performs contracting with the company and outsourcing services in the Brazilian states, each one in each state of the federation that stay one outsourced. In each state there is a third one who needs a fourth to share the service. Usually in this agreement there is a severe penalty clause if the service is not due in a timely manner which causes the office the need for improved efficiency and effectiveness in the general services.

2.1   The Law Office

The Office Araújo HIDD & Melo located in Teresina – PI owns a subsidiary at the city São Luís capital of Maranhão State located at 450 kms (279,617 miles) from Teresina. Basically it is an outsourced service for the major offices working sorely with the legal logistics making over 1000 acts of investigations and hearings, working in both states Piauí and Maranhão.

In order to find, the best geographic location for a new office, the research used a mathematical model to help the shareholders to make the decisions.

3   Methodology

The company location can directly affect logistics costs. The company's location is a fundamental issue, thinking in retail can be decisive for the success or failure of it. It impacts directly in operations costs, prices and service capacity. According to Krajewski et al. [9] one of the companies localization best method for logistics tools is the Center of gravity to find the optimum point based on the criteria of each location. In this research for legal logistics it has one more aggravating point because of the large numbers of activities (hearing and occurrences) and a fine of not running at the time set by law.

According to Martins one of the goals of the study for logistics is the movement of materials. The location of the company or its deposits will directly interfere in this matter. The service also works similar to other branches. The author reports that there are quantitative factors and goals and also no quantitative and subjective factors. In the current study the two cases was used: the first was the aim of the location through the center of gravity method with electronic simulator (http://zip.net/bgsBLm) and the second with the approach using subjective criteria as access road in good condition, suitable internet to work, city Forum and facility rental. This simulator can be used by anyone with other data from another company.

Initially used the problem solving method to identify and analyze the root causes and elect a key element to be treated [5] as related in Falconi's book. Once identified the main problem made a detailed study to find the best location solution for the law office under study.

Archimedes (287 BC-212 BC) was the one who systematized the center of gravity in his study identifies the center of gravity of geometric figures in Archimedes book [6], center of gravity and leverage is a classic mechanics and subsequently used this principle to other areas of science.

Define the location of installations is a study that has been conducted since the nineteenth century, created several methods and theories in various areas of logistics. This work in particular was based on the method proposed by Weber.

Alfred Weber [7] initiated the study Factories location in 1909 aiming to minimize the distance among the facility and the points of supply and demand. Initially in his calculations were considered only two-dimensional space variables assuming the absence of constraints and path as a straight-line shortest distance between two points. As deepened in his studies, it became clear that both the production and the location was affected by raw materials and other factors, were then inserted some variables that ponder the calculation, contributing to increase or decrease the weight given point.

With this method, it is possible to find a center point P that minimizes the sum of pondered distances.

For this study, the Weber's method was adapted considering each point as the set of coordinating for a city that will be called city "i" (Dxi, Dyi), inclused a weighted by the sum of Amount Received by acts performed in this city "I" (Ri) and also the Value payed per Correspondents also in the city "i". Upon sum calculation described above and dividing by the sum of the weights, the coordinates (Px, Py) of the Center of Gravity is found (Eqs. 1 and 2).

$$Px = \frac{\sum (Dxi \times Ri \times Ci)}{\sum (Ri \times Ci)} \tag{1}$$

$$Py = \frac{\sum (Dyi \times Ri \times Ci)}{\sum (Ri \times Ci)} \tag{2}$$

In this paper, was used the electronic simulator engine with Microsoft Office Excel 2013 version. In the simulator enters with the data of cities and their corresponding latitude and longitude, then adds the weights of the criteria chosen, in our case the criterions were: the amount received and the amount paid. The simulator returns the geographic coordinates of the center of gravity; this result puts up on Google Maps and identifies the nearest place found in such cities. In Brazil, you can find the geographical coordinate of the cities in the IBGE. The simulator is available for download by the author.

In the simulator, you should only fill the cells in yellow as shown in Fig. 2, the simulator, according to the criterion or weights established in the cells F7, G7 and H7 address in each city, returns the center of gravity in D3 address. From now on, it is necessary to copy in the Google Maps and the system returns the location of the point indicated.

	A	B	C	D	E	F	G	H
1		Coordinates Found						
2		LATITUDE	LONGITUDE	Copy these data on Google Maps				
3		-5°47'22"	-42°22'42"	-5°47'22",-42°22'42"			COPY THESE DATA	
4								
5						Weighting		
6	CITY	CITY LATITUDE	CITY LONGITUDE	X	Y	Weighting - I	Weighting - II	Weighting - III
7	Teresina	05° 05' 21" S	42° 48' 07" W	5,09	42,80	38.000,00	14.000,00	1
8	Picos	07° 04' 37" S	41° 28' 01" W	7,08	41,47	43.000,00	12.000,00	1
9	Parnaíba	02° 54' 17" S	41° 46' 36" W	2,90	41,78	26.000,00	14.000,00	1
10	Floriano	06° 46' 01" S	43° 01' 21" W	6,77	43,02	44.000,00	4.000,00	1
11	Corrente	10° 26' 36" S	45° 09' 44" W	10,44	45,16	18.000,00	7.000,00	1

Fig. 2. Electronic simulator (Color figure online)

The center of gravity method is a mathematical model of location, after finding that point took into consideration other variables finding the nearest city from the point found that has the best structure to host a law firm of this magnitude such as: easy access, internet available, affordable rent, competent professional, Proximity regional Forum.

4 Results and Discussion

Once defined the working method, collected the data and treated on an electronic simulator as the EXCEL spreadsheet was reached the following results. The study was based on the latitude and longitude of Piauí and Maranhão cities where the offices acts, making various analyzes according to the classification.

The calculation was classified as follows:

- North Piauí: Between Teresina and Piauí's Coast (Luís Correia City 02°52'45"S 41°40'01"W) – Fig. 3 – Yellow Part;
- South Piauí: Between Teresina and Extreme South of Piauí (Corrente City 10°26' 36"S 45°09'44"W) Fig. 3 – Blue Part;
- Piauí without the city of Teresina and nearby cities (radius ilustred at Fig. 3) it is called High Teresina or metropolitan region of Teresina;
- Maranhão without the city São Luís and nearby cities (radiuesilustred at Fig. 3) it is called High São Luiz or metropolitan region of São Luiz;
- Entire Maranhão;
- Entire Piauí and Maranhão (General result);

The following Fig. 3 illustrate the division of the studied areas.

The results of the study, showed a sort of cities concentrate on the central location at the above regions, considering the criterion of the amount of costs and receipts. The analyze of quantitative data resulted in the Cities demonstrated in Column 3 (City

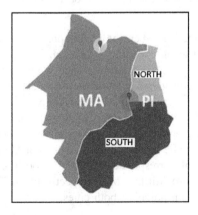

Fig. 3. Map according to the classification (Color figure online)

Table 1. Results found in the simulation Center of Gravity.

	Latitude	Longitude	Correspondent city	Near city
PI - North	04° 01′30″S	42° 04′30″W	Batalha	Batalha
PI - South	07° 21′18″S	40° 54′16″W	Padre Marcos	Picos
PI - Teresina	04° 49′40″S	42° 10′07″W	Campo Maior	Teresina
Ma - São Luis	04° 40′00″S	44° 51′00″W	Poção de Pedras	Bacabal
MA	04° 06′53″S	45° 08′23″W	Olho D'agua das Cunhãs	Bacabal
General	04° 07′48″S	44° 07′27″W	Coroatá	Bacabal

Correspondent) of Table 1. According to the processes results, were analyzed qualitative data that approached the result for larger cities.

The cities found in the present study are show in Fig. 4, and emphasized the best locations by region. Wine color is located in the best cities according to qualitative data.

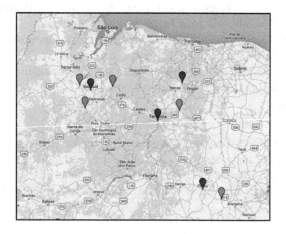

Fig. 4. Map with the results obtained in the study

It is often a discrepancy between the results presented by the Center of Gravity method and common sense on choosing a location. The Center of Gravity is based purely on logic, the input data to determine what would be the most advantageous choice, through it are not considered external factors such as difficulty of travel, cost of new facilities, etc. These criterions are called qualitative data.

This part of the work will expose some qualitative data on the city with the best location according to the quantitative data, and the city proposed by the shareholders of the law firm, they believe to be an open door to regions of Maranhão that difficulties in commuting and absence of correspondents is still a poorly explored area. They are, Bacabal - MA and Itapecuru Mirim - MA, respectively. In Table 2 follow the comparative data listing the main points of both cities.

Table 2. Comparative data between two cities.

Data	Itapecuru Mirim	Bacabal
Human Development Index	0.599	0.651
Population	62.110	100.014
Area of territorial unit	1.471,438km²	1.682,963 km²
	568,12538796mi²	649,79564705 mi²
Gross Domestic Product (GDP)	R$ 4.357,26	R$ 5.221,41
Received Value	R$ 8.775,00	R$ 17.865,00
Pay Value	R$ 3.506,66	R$ 6.235,00
Profit	R$ 5.268,34	R$ 11.630,00

5 Conclusion

The main objective was to expose the results obtained from the Logistics Center of Gravity Calculation. According to the results, the city of Bacabal - MA presents the best location. With the installation of a new subsidiary in this city, according to the data, the amount received should be maximized and the cost corresponding minimized.

According to qualitative data, characteristics of location, this presents an excellent structure to attend the acts carried out in the town and nearby.

As a suggestion for future studies can use the same simulator to find the best residence location of the possible agents or forth party services of Araújo HIDD & Melo office.

The simple and objective way that had created the simulator can be used for other companies in various lines of business to find the best geographical location for minimize the commuting costs and consequently maximize results.

References

1. Blog Portal Exame de Ordem. http://blog.portalexamedeordem.com.br/blog/2012/09/segundo-oab-brasil-tem-750-mil-advogados-e-mais-de-1-5-milhao-de-bachareis-em-direito/
2. IG Colunistas, Leis & Negócios. http://leisenegocios.ig.com.br/index.php/2010/10/23/brasil-e-o-segundo-pais-com-mais-advogados-por-habitante/
3. Gazeta do Advogado. http://gazetadoadvogado.adv.br/2015/12/17/a-logistica-juridica-na-gestao-legal/
4. Vivaldini, M.: Terceirização, Quarteirização e Primarização Logística. Revista GEPROS 10(4) (2015)
5. Campos, V.F.: Gerenciamento da Rotina do Trabalho do Dia-a-Dia. INDG Tecnologia e Serviços (2004)
6. Assis, A.K.T.: Arquimedes, o Centro de Gravidade e a Lei da Alavanca. Montréal, Apeiron (2008)

7. Etzold, D., Plotzki, R.: Industriestandorttheorie von Alfred Weber. GRIN Verlag (2002)
8. Electronic simulator. http://zip.net/bgsBLm
9. Krajeewski, L., Ritzman, L., Malhotra, M.: Administração de Produção e Operações: Lee. São Paulo, Pearson (2009)

RFID Integration for Material Management Considering Engineering Changes in ETO Industry

Quan Yu$^{(\boxtimes)}$, Pavan Kumar Sriram, Erlend Alfnes,
and Jan Ola Strandhagen

Norwegian University of Science and Technology, Trondheim, Norway
{Quan.yu, pavan.sriram, erlend.alfnes, ola.strandhagen}
@ntnu.no

Abstract. Radio Frequency Identification (RFID) is a type of auto-identification technique developed in 1950s. However, its wide applications in manufacturing industries does not start until early 2000s. Discussions about applications of RFID in Engineer to Order (ETO) industry have been raised since mid-2000s. Over a decade's technical development, it is becoming a common view that RFID is an important part of Cyber Physical Systems, Internet of Things, or Industry 4.0. Although researchers have started discussion about RFID applications in ETO industry, it is not well addressed that how RFID can be applied for the material management with respect to engineering changes (ECs), which has strong impacts on an ETO company. This paper reviews RFID applications in ETO industry and gives suggestions on how an RFID system can be integrated in an ETO company? How has RFID been utilized for material management under engineering changes? And what is the general framework of RFID in material management in ETO industry?

Keywords: RFID · ETO · Engineering changes · Material management

1 Introduction

Radio Frequency Identification (RFID) is one of auto-identification techniques developed in 1950s, which has increasing applications in manufacturing industries as a decisive data collection approach since 2000s [1]. Discussions about applications of RFID in Engineer to Order (ETO) industry have been raised since later-2000s [2], and still continue [3] partially because the benefits of applying RFID in ETO industry are obscured regarding higher initial investment than general barcode systems. Discussions on benefits of RFID application in supply chain started from mid 2000s [4–6]. As barcode technology is a well-accepted identification approach in manufacturing companies for quite a long time, it is not a one-step process to use RFID as a substitution. Concurrent operation for RFID and barcode has been systematically studied [7].

Furthermore, an RFID system is a front-end system for data accessing rather than an alternative of an ICT system for resource management. Thereby, RFID is often discussed with ICT system together [1, 8, 9]. It will not be economical and even

I. Nääs et al. (Eds.): APMS 2016, IFIP AICT 488, pp. 501–508, 2016.
DOI: 10.1007/978-3-319-51133-7_60

feasible solution to use RFID without the integration with an ICT system. Additionally, it is quite often for an ETO company to have engineering changes due to high probability of design and production changes; while efficient material management can provide an opportunity to increase competitiveness because materials account for 50–60 percent of total project costs [10]. This paper reviews applications of RFID in ETO industry, mainly focusing on material management and gives suggestions of utilizing RFID for material management under engineering changes, which provides a reference for ETO industry to implement RFID technique.

1.1   RFID Technique and Characteristics

RFID uses a wireless non-contact radio system to transfer data from a tag attached to an object, for the purposes of identification and tracking. In such a system, RFID tags are attached to physical objects, which are wirelessly interrogated by antennas powered by RFID readers. Tags respond with some identifying information that may be associated with arbitrary data records, which makes an RFID system as a type of auto-identification system. Multiple readers and antennas are commonly used to build an RFID system as shown in Fig. 1.

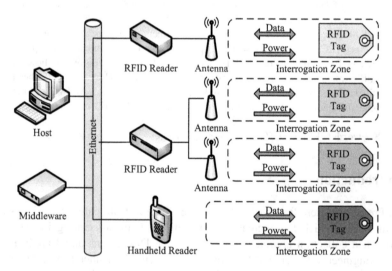

Fig. 1. A general RFID system

Main characteristics of RFID include non-line-of-sight data access and rewriteable on-chip data, which enable functionalities of remote and batch accessing, real-time accessing on-chip memory such as data retrieving, appending, erasing and protecting. In an RFID system, it is the RFID tag that is utilized as the data carrier, while other devices are used for accessing, transferring and managing the on-chip data. The working distance and the cost of an RFID tag depends on the working frequency and

Table 1. Characteristics of passive RFID systems working at different frequencies

Characteristics	Working frequency		
	Low	High	Ultra-high
Frequency	30–300 kHz	3–30 MHz	300–3000 MHz
Reading distance	0.1 m	1 m	12 m
Applications	Access control livestock tracking	eTicket payment	Inventory management many others
Standards	ISO14223 ISO/IEC 18000-2	ISO 15693 ISO/IEC 18902 etc.	EPCglobal Gen2 (ISO 18000-6c)
Cost	High	Medium	Low
Sensitivity	Low	Medium	High

the additional power supply with the RFID tag. Characteristics can be compared as shown in Table 1.

Potential applications at different decision levels based on these two characteristics are shown in Table 2.

Table 2. Applicability of RFID

Decision level	Applicability
Strategic level	Information sharing Increasing visibility
Tactical level	Tracing and tracking Decentralized data storage Life-cycle management Lead time reduction
Operational level	Far/near field identification Real-time locating system (RTLS) Processing history recording Automated item registration BOM recording Maintenance history recording

1.2 Material Management Under Engineering Changes in ETO

ETO is a strategy for manufacturing one-of-a-kind products (OKP) [11]. ETO companies are faced with the increasing complexity of products, production structures and processes [12]. ETO environment is characterized mostly by large and complex products which are designed and produced by customers' requirements. Products in this type of supply chain are required in low quantities and sometimes in medium volumes, but generally they contain a diversity of components in a complex combination. Each component should be assigned to specific operation in the production.

Engineering changes are considered as a major obstacle to the delivery of the product in ETO environment. Four main factors effecting engineering change are identified, including unidentified change propagation, knowledge management, distributed environment and capacity and congestion [10].

Material planning which also named as material management concerns balancing supply and demand by initiating, controlling and monitoring of production and purchasing orders to allow the efficient material flow going without interruptions through-out the production. Overall task of material planning process is to ensure material availability at the right stage of production and at the right time. To do so material planning uses bill of materials, inventory data, and data from master production schedule in order to determine time-phased plans for all components and raw materials required for production. Material planning process includes broad set of tasks and activities like planning required materials, sup-plier selection, purchasing, inventory management and forecasting. Therefore, this process is not only simple computer calculations but also it includes an effective communication mechanisms, education activities and training programs. The material planning process starts when the order is received, materials specifications and materials coding systems are established and bill of materials is created. In order to link bill of materials with process structure, each component in the bill of materials should be assigned to specific operations in the production.

Having a supply chain with large number of suppliers creates even greater need for an effective and efficient management of material flow, as it is required to take into account deliveries of numerous components from different suppliers [13]. The material management starts when the order is received, materials specifications and materials coding systems are established and bill of materials is created. Material management uses bill of materials, inventory data, and data from master production schedule in order to determine time-phased plans for all components and raw materials required for production, including broad set of tasks and activities like planning required materials, supplier selection, purchasing, inventory management and forecasting.

2   Applications of RFID in ETO Industry

The earliest application of RFID in ETO industry was component tracking, similar as in other industries. RFID was tested in construction industry for tracking components from a precast storage yard to a construction site [14] and providing a reference for maintenance service [2]. In addition, researchers used RFID for managing life-cycle data of ETO construction components [15]. Based on component tracking, main RFID applications occurred in ETO fields including item management [16], lead time estimation [17], and operation times estimation [18]. Shop floor monitoring was another commonly used in for manufacturing industries [19–21].

As mentioned above, processes integration has considerable potential to improve performance of an ETO company [9, 22]. An ICT system is vital to implement RFID in material management. Regarding this point, ubiquitous work systems [23] and current ERP system adaption [24] are studied by researchers to improve ETO production from the ICT perspective.

RFID is a decisive technique to enhance the performance of an MES/ERP. Regarding the integration of RFID with an MES/ERP, applications can generally cover identifying objects, realization of online interfaces, intra-enterprise logistics, quality management, access and attendance control and shop floor control [1, 9, 25]. ERP system has developed interface for RFID data transmission [8].

Ship building is another section where RFID is used for material management [16], ship block positioning during the assembly [26, 27] and safety management [28]. Besides implementation studies, researchers also focused on factor analysis in adoption process of vertical supply chains [29]. RFID also contributes in information sharing between different actors i.e. clients and suppliers within the supply chain [3].

3   RFID Integration Framework

To successfully implement RFID in an ETO environment, it is the first and foremost thing that integrating the RFID with the management system. Although standards are being established and interfaces are provided by commercial software, e.g. the Auto-ID infrastructure of SAP and BizTalk server for Microsoft Dynamics AX, they are relatively focused on business processes. Regarding complex requirements under high engineering changes probability, it is more important to embed the engineering related information in the RFID tag from the management system, other than the identification of the tracked item. However, this step is always performed by the RFID system provider without knowing well about the ETO process, which produces a large gap between a local test and the global feasibility. Performance indicators for Materials Management were proposed under engineering change [13] as shown in Fig. 2, providing a reference for the intervention of an RFID system.

According to performance indicators in Fig. 2, five RFID modules are expected especially for material management considering ECs as described in Table 3.

Among five modules above, data synchronizing needs more attention because it ensures the timely and accurate information before any decision is made. As distributed

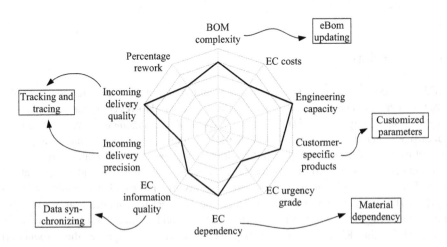

Fig. 2. Performance indicators for materials management under ECs (based on [13]) and relevant RFID modules

Table 3. RFID modules for material managment

Module	Description
eBOM updating	Designed for eBOM tag, which keeps detailed BOM and revision history
Customized parameters	Aim at special orders, which stores order specified engineering parameters, suppliers, customers, etc.
Material dependency	To record dependencies between orders/materials, for a quick lookup if ECs happen
Data synchronizing	To setup an error-free data updating mechanism, and ensure all confirmed changes are synchronized both in tag and database
Tracking and tracing (delivery reporting)	Especially for real-time delivery reporting, giving a clear picture of current state to decision makers

environment is one of the most important factors effecting EC [10], local ECs must be reported and updated in time for all relevant processes, so that misoperations can be avoided.

Hereby, RFID integration principles are proposed as a reference for designing an RFID system regarding engineering changes in ETO environment.

1. Evaluate components with high engineering changes probability.
2. Select suitable RFID devices according to characteristics of monitored components.
3. Main parameters related to engineering changes, suppliers and clients must be defined and pre-allocated in RFID tags referring performance indicators for Materials Management.
4. RFID data must be accessible both online and offline. Synchronization mechanism should be designed considering the network availability.
5. Authorize shared information in accordance with role of partners, i.e. suppliers and clients. On-chip data should be segmented so that they are visible to relevant partners.

4   Conclusions

RFID is becoming a promising technology and draws increasing attention with the improvement of technical performance and reliability. However, regarding complex engineering changes in ETO industry, material management always needs a tailor-made technical solution, so that RFID technique needs to be adapted and integrated to the ICT system to achieve the efficient management and maximum benefits. Current researches are still mainly focusing on components tracking and locating at the shop floor level. To be noticed, it is a trend to involve information sharing via RFID system. However, it cannot be ignored that the engineering changes connect component monitoring and information sharing process, and related information must be reflected in the RFID tag via management system to improve the production performance.

References

1. Günther, O.P., Kletti, W., Kubach, U.: The role of manufacturing execution systems. In: Günther, O.P., Kletti, W., Kubach, U. (eds.) RFID in Manufacturing, pp. 35–59. Springer, Heidelberg (2008)
2. Ergen, E., Akinci, B., Sacks, R.: Life-cycle data management of engineered-to-order components using radio frequency identification. Adv. Eng. Inform. **21**, 356–366 (2007)
3. Pero, M., Rossi, T.: RFID technology for increasing visibility in ETO supply chains: a case study. Prod. Plan. Control **25**, 892–901 (2014)
4. Uckelmann, D., Hamann, T., Mansfeld, J.: Strategic benefit potentials of RFID application in supply chains. In: 5th European Workshop on RFID Systems and Technologies, pp. 1–9 (2009)
5. Vance, A.: An empirical investigation of the potential of RFID technology to enhance supply chain agility. In: Baskerville, R.L., Mathiassen, L., Pries-Heje, J., DeGross, J.I. (eds.) TDIT 2005. IIFIP, vol. 180, pp. 147–156. Springer, Heidelberg (2005). doi:10.1007/0-387-25590-7_9
6. Chen, J.C., Cheng, C.-H., Huang, P.B.: Supply chain management with lean production and RFID application. Expert Syst. Appl. **40**, 3389–3397 (2013)
7. Schmidt, M., Thoroe, L., Schumann, M.: RFID and barcode in manufacturing logistics: interface concept for concurrent operation. Inf. Syst. Manag. **30**, 100–115 (2013)
8. Knolmayer, G.F., Mertens, P., Zeier, A., Dickersbach, J.T.: SAP systems for supply chain management. In: Knolmayer, G.F., Mertens, P., Zeier, A., Dickersbach, J.T. (eds.) Supply Chain Management Based on SAP Systems, pp. 73–159. Springer, Heidelberg (2009)
9. Canetta, L., Salvadè, A., Schnegg, P.A., Müller, E., Lanini, M.: RFID–ERP key data integration challenges. In: Canetta, L., Redaelli, C., Flores, M. (eds.) Digital Factory for Human-oriented Production Systems, pp. 73–95. Springer, London (2011)
10. Sriram, P.K., Dreyer, H.C., Alfnes, E.: Understanding key engineering changes for materials management in ETO environment. In: Umeda, S., Nakano, M., Mizuyama, H., Hibino, H., Kiritsis, D., Cieminski, G. (eds.) APMS 2015. IAICT, vol. 460, pp. 256–262. Springer, Heidelberg (2015). doi:10.1007/978-3-319-22759-7_30
11. Adrodegari, F., Bacchetti, A., Pinto, R., Pirola, F., Zanardini, M.: Engineer-to-Order (ETO) production planning and control: an empirical framework for machinery-building companies. Prod. Plan. Control **26**, 910–932 (2015)
12. Váncza, J., Monostori, L., Lutters, D., Kumara, S.R., Tseng, M., Valckenaers, P., Van Brussel, H.: Cooperative and responsive manufacturing enterprises. CIRP Ann. Manuf. Technol. **60**, 797–820 (2011)
13. Sriram, P.K., Andersen, B., Alfnes, E.: Designing a performance measurement system for materials management under engineering change situations in ETO environment. In: Umeda, S., Nakano, M., Mizuyama, H., Hibino, H., Kiritsis, D., Cieminski, G. (eds.) APMS 2015. IAICT, vol. 460, pp. 263–270. Springer, Heidelberg (2015). doi:10.1007/978-3-319-22759-7_31
14. Ergen, E., Akinci, B., Sacks, R.: Tracking and locating components in a precast storage yard utilizing radio frequency identification technology and GPS. Autom. Constr. **16**, 354–367 (2007)
15. Yin, S.Y.L., Tserng, H.P., Wang, J.C., Tsai, S.C.: Developing a precast production management system using RFID technology. Autom. Constr. **18**, 677–691 (2009)
16. Desselles, L., Sarder, M.D.: RFID enabled material management at US ship building industry. In: IIE Annual Conference and Expo 2010. Institute of Industrial Engineers

17. Zhong, R., Huang, G., Dai, Q.-Y., Zhang, T.: Estimation of lead time in the RFID-enabled real-time shopfloor production with a data mining model. In: Qi, E., Shen, J., Dou, R. (eds.) The 19th International Conference on Industrial Engineering and Engineering Management, pp. 321–331. Springer, Heidelberg (2013)

18. Zhong, R., Huang, G., Dai, Q.Y., Zhang, T.: Mining SOTs and dispatching rules from RFID-enabled real-time shopfloor production data. J. Intell. Manuf. **25**, 825–843 (2014)

19. Leung, Y.K., Choy, K.L., Kwong, C.K.: Development of a real-time collaborative process planning management system for the mould industry. In: Portland International Conference on Management of Engineering & Technology, PICMET 2008, pp. 266–275

20. Leung, Y.K., Choy, K.L., Kwong, C.K.: A Real-time hybrid information-sharing and decision support system for the mould industry. J. High Technol. Manag. Res. **21**, 64–77 (2010)

21. Poon, T.C., Choy, K.L., Lau, H.C.W.: An efficient production material demand order management system for a mould manufacturing company. Prod. Plan. Control **22**, 754–766 (2011)

22. Hicks, C., McGovern, T., Earl, C.F.: Supply chain management: a strategic issue in engineer to order manufacturing. Int. J. Prod. Econ. **65**, 179–190 (2000)

23. Husejnagić, D., Sluga, A.: A conceptual framework for a ubiquitous autonomous work system in the engineer-to-order environment. Int. J. Adv. Manuf. Technol. **78**, 1971–1988 (2015)

24. Nakayama, R.S., de Mesquita Spinola, M.: Production planning and control in small engineer-to-order companies: understanding difficulties and pragmatic approach. In: 2015 Portland International Conference on Management of Engineering and Technology (PICMET), pp. 1449–1460

25. Wang, M.L., Qu, T., Zhong, R.Y., Dai, Q.Y., Zhang, X.W., He, J.B.: A radio frequency identification-enabled real-time manufacturing execution system for one-of-a-kind production manufacturing: a case study in mould industry. Int. J. Comput. Integr. Manuf. **25**, 20–34 (2012)

26. Lee, S., Eun, S., Jung, J.J., Song, H.: Application of sensor technology for the efficient positioningand assembling of ship blocks. Int. J. Nav. Archit. Ocean Eng. **2**, 171–176 (2010)

27. Jeong, S.H., Son, H.W.: UHF RFID tag antenna for embedded use in a concrete floor. IEEE Antennas Wirel. Propag. Lett. **10**, 1158–1161 (2011)

28. Yun, J.M., Park, P.: Development of industrial safety management system for shipbuilding industry using RFID/USN. In: 9th IEEE International Conference on Ubiquitous Intelligence and Computing, pp. 285–291 (2012)

29. Quetti, C., Pigni, F., Clerici, A.: Factors affecting RFId adoption in a vertical supply chain: the case of the silk industry in Italy. Prod. Plan. Control **23**, 315–331 (2012)

Innovation and Collaborative Networks

Improving the Sustainability of SOA Providers' Networks via a Collaborative Process Innovation Model

João F. Santanna-Filho[1]([envelope]), Ricardo J. Rabelo[2], Peter Bernus[3],
and Alexandra A. Pereira-Klen[2]

[1] Federal Rural University of Amazon, Belem, Brazil
joao.santanna@ufra.edu.br
[2] Federal University of Santa Catarina, Florianópolis, Brazil
[3] Griffith University, Brisbane, Australia

Abstract. Companies from the software sector have been seeking new, sustainable business models. A key strategy to achieve is innovation. Being a sector largely formed by SMEs, a general problem is to keep innovation a sustainable practice. Many companies have been shifting their systems' architectures to SOA, but despite its potentials, SOA projects are often costly, complex and risky. One approach to mitigate this is endowing companies with means to innovate collaboratively. Current innovation models are mostly devoted to the manufacturing sector, without supporting the many software and SOA specificities. We present a collaborative innovation process model as a contribution to fill this gap. The model combines open and network innovation approaches and allowing the tailoring of process composition to accommodate the uniqueness of innovation projects. The proposed model was evaluated by industry.

Keywords: Collaborative networks · Innovation · Software services

1 Introduction

The software sector plays a significant role in the world economy [1]. Advances in Internet technologies and the rise of the services oriented economy challenge the industry to develop new, competitive and sustainable business models [2]. One key strategy to achieve this is innovation [3]. A general problem is that the industry mostly consists of SMEs, which have limited capacity to keep innovation as an ongoing sustainable practice, aligned to their strategies in an environment of permanent change [4].

One of these technological changes is the gradual shift towards implementing systems using the SOA (Service Oriented Architecture) paradigm [5]. In SOA, a software system is formed by a composition of a set of modules – called software services – which are decoupled, distributed, heterogeneous and of several natures, forming a single logical unit to create products and processes [6].

© IFIP International Federation for Information Processing 2016
Published by Springer International Publishing AG 2016. All Rights Reserved
I. Nääs et al. (Eds.): APMS 2016, IFIP AICT 488, pp. 511–519, 2016.
DOI: 10.1007/978-3-319-51133-7_61

Despite its technological and commercial potentials, SOA projects can be complex and costly, difficult to manage, and hence risky [7]. Existing innovation models are basically devoted to manufacturing, without considering the software specificities [8]. This paper exploits the premise that the innovation initiative's risk can be mitigated if the SMEs involved in a given SOA development can jointly innovate, within wider and open networks, sharing risks, investments, resources (human and software/services assets), knowledge and benefits, while keeping their autonomy and independence.

Within this general goal, this paper focuses on the process perspective. It presents the final results of an innovation process model – called SIGMA – directed to networks of SOA providers to innovate collaboratively and openly towards generating a valuable outcome in a flexible and non-linear flow considering the particular requirements of every SOA project and its network governance model. Such outcome can be a software prototype, a proof of concepts, a set of ideas for new business models and products, among others. As a value proposition, this model intends to be used as a "guide" that systematizes the innovation process itself. This enables better innovation management, provides a basis for the introduction of good innovation practices, and leverages the continuous maturity improvement of processes, people and the involved organizations.

2   Basic Concepts and State-of-the-Art Reviews

Collaborative Networks are strategic alliances focused on intense and fluid collaboration among autonomous organizations [9]. In order to support the dynamics of an innovation network, the Virtual Organization (VO) concept is of particular importance. A VO is a temporary and dynamic entity formed out of select autonomous network members that join their complementary core-competencies and general resources to attend to a demand [9].

Innovation Models covering the phases and processes of innovation, via the so-called funnel, namely: selection and/or generation of ideas, concept development, concept evaluation/selection, concept design/specification, implementation and exploitation (adapted from [10]). Innovation models evolved from linear to open and network models [11,12]. Gates are added between steps to constrain the continuation of the process. Processes may be executed in sequence or in parallel, and can go back and forth during the innovation processes. Different types of actors and roles may be involved, including member companies and external supporting partners [13]. A collaborative innovation network is a temporary or long-term alliance of disparate autonomous organizations with the willingness to jointly develop or exploit an innovative business vision by sharing of ideas, knowledge, capacity, resources and services, costs, risks and benefits, supported by the intense use of ICT, and grounded by principles of trust, preparedness, governance and intellectual property rights [8].

A Systematic Literature Review was conducted to oversee the state-of-the-art. Journal papers and conference proceedings from 2002 and 2015 were searched in IEE-Explore, ACM, Web of science and ScienceDirect, complemented by the search in the EU CORDIS projects database [14]. The essential search terms used were innovation, collaborative networks, SMEs, SOA & services. No work has been found that dealt with the envisaged open and flexible innovation model based on a network of autonomous SMEs that can participate in all phases of the innovation process, regarding the particular nature of software and SOA. On the other hand, 8 papers [3,10,11,15–20] and 7 projects (BIVEE, ComVantage, IMAGINE, CoVES, Laboranova, PLENT and GloNet [14] provided some useful insights for our proposed model. In summary: (i) most works are directed to manufacturing, with some of them also covering related services (but not software services); (ii) most works presents linear models, where the innovation process seems to follow the same mandatory steps, starting with a business plan, and some aspects that do not fit at all the reality of the software/SOA development process; (iii) many models are incomplete in the sense that they support only some phases of innovation; (iv) none supports collaboration along the entire innovation process; (v) few models cover open innovation; (vi) no work gives methodological support to aid companies regarding methods, techniques, etc. recommended to be used in each process.

3   Proposed Innovation Model

The model is based on two premises: the innovation process may be serendipitous and unique [21], involves creativity and therefore some unpredictability [22]. Considering this, the model was generally inspired by the Design Thinking method [22] and in particular its notion of innovation "spaces" and evolution stages. This was complemented and adapted taking the six classical innovation processes proposed in [10] into account.

Other requirements are: (i) companies may participate in the whole or part of the entire innovation process and related software development cycle, depending on their agreed roles, rights and duties; (ii) companies and supporting organizations may join, operate in, and leave the innovation network at different points in time and possibly do so a number of times, during normal network operation or when problems or changes occur; (iii) there is no single, predefined or linear progression for the innovation "path".

Our model, called 'SIGMA', supports collaborative innovation from initial exchange of ideas to final delivery/deployment (Fig. 1). The three model spaces represent different moments a typical innovation initiative may go through: (i) *Ideas development space*: includes processes supporting the management of ideas and their preliminary evaluation/selection. This space is open for all members of the long-term collaborative alliance (e.g. the federation); (ii) *Solution development space*: includes processes supporting the development of the selected ideas by a VO; i.e. the companies selected considering the required expertise and financial, commercial, technological and software skills; (iii) *Solution delivery space*: includes processes supporting the delivery of the innovation's outcomes in the case of its commercialization.

The innovation process sequence in these spaces is determined on-the-fly based on the needs of the innovation initiative, i.e. processes may be revisited

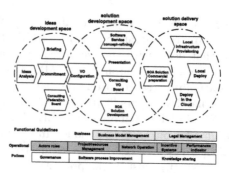

Fig. 1. The SIGMA innovation model

and some of them (or even an entire space) may not be performed (e.g. the third space in case the innovation is not yet ready to be transformed into products). Yet, an initiative does not necessarily have to start from the first space and the ideas analysis process. The innovation can progress in decoupled cycles of evolution between the spaces, where new ideas, prototype versions, goals, etc., can be generated and refined along the time. In order to support such flexibility, and inspired by the SOA paradigm, the model's processes are seen as a set of decoupled building blocks. They act as reference processes that should be selected based on needs and be further instantiated by the VO team.

An innovation initiative can be interrupted, radically changed or shelved (for later use) anytime. The model also uses the classical gate concept for that, although in a slightly different way: a formal evaluation of process outcomes may act as a filter to continue the initiative (decided by the VO) but this is not a mandatory decision.

- **Ideas Development Space.** *Idea Analysis*: a company from the alliance can propose a joint innovation to the federation's committee, which will evaluate the initial idea's potential; *Briefing*: the idea is presented in detail, describing the necessary technologies, potential partnerships, eventual estimated ROI, foreseen market, etc.; *Commitment*: the company that had the original idea may want to protect it using confidentiality contracts before presenting the idea to the other VO members; *VO configuration*: formation of the VO that will carry out the innovation. This involves partner search and selection, negotiations, setting up VO governance and revenue mode, and contract signature, as well as the definition of performance indicators to be applied upon partners and the innovation process; *Consulting federation board*: triggered in the case the VO needs advisory about some issues. Although it can depend on how the governance model had been set up, the board usually does not have the power to kill an idea. This board can be formed by some alliance members and may also involve external experts. The main goal here is trying to anticipate problems and propose possible solutions.
- **Solution Development Space.** *Presentation*: a more complete project plan and ICT analysis are produced and the eventual business model is refined.

It also includes issues of IPR and ownership, accounting, and knowledge gaps in the VO and in the federation; *Software-service conceptualization*: concept development of the SOA solution, the software architecture, the required services to be developed and their functional and non-functional requirements, etc.; *SOA solution development*: it is similar to the previous one, but at a very detailed level. It includes services coding and composition, their integration and final verification. It covers the SOA/services life cycle development [7,23], but respecting the par ticularities when the project is to be performed by a group of companies [24]; *Consulting VO Board*: process triggered in the case the innovation team needs advisory about some issues, for example, the need for new members; *SOA solution commercial preparation*: this process ends the SOA solution development space, making the planned outcomes available for whomever has the rights. VO members make agreements and sign contracts, comprising commercial support for the product/service, IPR, commercialization model, price policy, etc.

- **Solution Delivery Space.** *Local infrastructure provisioning*: depending on the agreed business model, contracts and QoS requirements, it is necessary to prepare the required infrastructure for the SOA solution deployment at the customer's infrastructure, third party provider, a specific member's site, or the alliance's site; *Local deployment*: process triggered to make the physical deployment of the SOA solution/product once the infrastructure is ready; *Deployment in the cloud*: deployment of the SOA solution/product in a third party or alliance's cloud(s).

- **Functional Guidelines (FG).** Network members are basically SMEs, and their managers may not be fully aware of the issues to consider in each of the processes. FGs correspond to supporting methods, techniques and tools that may be considered by the VO team during collaborative innovation. Ten FGs have been identified after a compilation of several papers on innovation (e.g. [25,26]). FGs are grouped into business, operational and policies levels: (i) *Business level*: FGs related to commercialization of innovation. Involves the issues of Business Model management and Legal aspects management; (ii) *Operational level*: FGs to support the daily operation of the innovation development. Involves the issues of Actors' roles, Project/Resources management, VO Network operation, Incentive systems, and Performance indicators; (iii) *Policies level*: FGs related to relations within the VO, the VO with other actors (internal or external), and with customers. Involves the issues of Governance, Software process improvement, and Knowledge sharing and management. The proposed model does not offer such methods, tools, etc. Instead, adopting the vision of reference models, they have to be instantiated regarding existing practices, available financial resources, prepared people, etc.

4 Model Validation

The SIGMA model was evaluated by a group of SOA experts from a cluster of ICT/SOA provider companies located in two cities in the South of Brazil. A total of 29 professionals from 17 companies were involved in three small workshops. The selected companies had some level of experience on innovation.

The model was presented and doubts clarified. Hypothetical but representative business cases were proposed by them so as to simulate near-real innovation scenarios. The professionals were split into groups in order to also simulate autonomous companies. The authors of this research acted as "moderators", sometimes representing members of the Network or the VO Board.

A survey composed of 18 questions was prepared adopting the GQM method [27] and applied to the companies after the group dynamics. Twelve objective questions were answered using the Likert scale and there were 6 open questions.

In summary: (i) 90% agreed about the separation of the process model into 3 spaces; (ii) 80% fully agreed that the process systematization has the potential to decrease costs, time and/or risks of SOA innovation projects; (iii) 100% agreed that the model properly supports the required flexibility of innovation in software and SOA; (iv) all devised processes and FGs were considered as pertinent, although with different levels of importance; (v) 100% agreed that SMEs of software providers will need to adopt more formal innovation practices and will be involved in wider value chains in the next 5 years; (vi) although more directed to SMEs, 50% pointed out a sort of technical and cultural obstacles as well as organization impacts to adopt the model.

Some initiatives were mentioned by the companies as enablers for the model adoption, like the creation of common training courses on the several related issues; the strengthening of the collaboration culture and trust among companies; and adequate legal frameworks also considering intellectual property rights. On the other hand, some barriers to adopt the model were also identified, like the lack of governance culture at the network level; the lack of systematic collaboration culture by SMEs; and lack of ICT tools to support the distributed innovation and project/innovation management.

5   Conclusions

This paper presented the final results of a novel innovation process model devoted to support collaborative innovation among software services provider SMEs. The model has been developed with the view of Collaborative Networks providing the foundation for supporting SMEs to work as a network, sharing costs, risks and benefits, where an innovation initiative is operated as a Virtual Organization (VO).

The most relevant supporting constituents to be taken into account in the innovation process were identified and briefly described. They are called 'functional guidelines' and aim at helping companies to be aware of the issues to be managed in the collaborative innovation life cycle.

The model presents a number of new contributions compared to related works, namely: it is directed to software and SOA; it introduces the concept of 'functional guidelines'; the model allows flexibility, non-linearity and on-the-fly composability of the innovation process for every innovation initiative; it introduces the concept of 'building block' as a reference process to be instantiated according to existing cultural or other general conditions; it adapts the SOA development process to cope with the requirements of collaborative innovation among disparate companies.

From the business standpoint, the adoption of the proposed model has the potential to provide a number of benefits, such as: the sharing of risks among partners, which decreases their losses in the case if unsuccessful innovation initiatives; faster response to innovation demands; greater synergy and networking among companies so generating a wider scope of complementary skills that can be used in future businesses in other value chains; higher ROI as companies' services can be reused by other companies; newer business models derived from the networked business architecture; and the breeding of more intense culture of innovation in the companies, reinforcing the ecosystem's strength.

Working collaboratively is a learning process. Companies are heterogeneous (culture, working methods, human resources' qualification, core competences, etc.) and autonomous, meaning that their different strategies must be accommodated and interoperate regarding their different priorities, exploitation plans, and trade-offs in terms of acceptable risks, trust and benefits. Although presented in its final version, the model cannot be seen as fixed. New processes and FGs can be added and existing one may evolve.

The innovation process model is not an end in itself. It is part of a much wider framework instead. Complementary issues, like having an innovation model, fostering and reinforcing leadership and innovation culture, having appropriate legal and funding mechanisms, among many other conditions, should be developed and supported for a successful and healthy innovation environment. The next main step of this research refers to validate the model in real cases and to test it close to a greater number of companies.

References

1. Kramer, W.J., Jenkins, B., Katz, R.S.: The Role of the Information and Communications Technology Sector in Expanding Economic Opportunity. Harvard University, Cambridge (2007)
2. Nie, Z.: Credibility evaluation of SaaS tenants. In: International Conference on Advanced Computer Theory and Engineering, vol. 4, pp. 488–491. IEEE (2010)
3. Li, Y., Shen, J., Shi, J., Shen, W., Huang, Y., Xu, Y.: Multi-model driven collaborative development platform for service-oriented e-business systems. Adv. Eng. Inform. **22**, 328–339 (2008)
4. Westphal, I., Thoben, K.D., Seifert, M.: Managing collaboration performance to govern virtual organizations. J. Int. Manuf. **21**(3), 311–320 (2010)
5. PRWEB. http://www.prweb.com
6. Papazoglou, M.: Web Services: Principles and Technology. Pearson Education, Upper Saddle River (2008)
7. O'Brien, L., Merson, P., Bass, L.: Quality attributes for service-oriented architectures. In: Proceedings of the International Workshop on Systems Development in SOA Environments, p. 3. IEEE (2007)

8. Santanna-Filho, J.F., Rabelo, R.J., Pereira-Klen, A.A.: An innovation model for collaborative networks of SOA-based software providers. In: Camarinha-Matos, L.M., Afsarmanesh, H. (eds.) PRO-VE 2014. IAICT, vol. 434, pp. 169–181. Springer, Heidelberg (2014). doi:10.1007/978-3-662-44745-1_17

9. Afsarmanesh, H., Camarinha-Matos, L., Ollus, M.: Methods and Tools for Collaborative Networked Organizations. Springer Science Business Media, Heidelberg (2008)

10. du Preez, N.D., Louw, L.: A framework for managing the innovation process. In: 2008 Portland International Conference on Management of Engineering Technology, PICMET 2008, pp. 546–558, July 2008

11. Rycroft, R., Kash, D.: Self-organizing innovation networks: implications for globalization. Technovation 24, 187–197 (2010)

12. Chesbrough, H.W.: Open Innovation: The New Imperative for Creating and Profiting from Technology. Harvard Press, Brighton (2006)

13. Tidd, J., Bessant, J., Pavitt, K.: Innovation Management. Wiley, Hoboken (2001)

14. CORDIS. http://cordis.europa.eu/projects/home_en.html

15. Janner, T., Schroth, C., Schmid, B.: Modelling service systems for collaborative innovation in the enterprise software industry-the st. gallen media reference model applied. In: IEEE SCC, vol. 2, pp. 145–152. IEEE (2008)

16. Berre, A.J., Lew, Y., Elvesæter, B., de Man, H.: Service innovation and service realisation with VDML and ServiceML. In: 17th IEEE International Enterprise Distributed Object Computing Conference Workshops, pp. 104–113. IEEE (2013)

17. Kourtesis, D., Bratanis, K., Bibikas, D., Paraskakis, I.: Software co-development in the era of cloud application platforms and ecosystems: the case of CAST. In: Camarinha-Matos, L.M., Xu, L., Afsarmanesh, H. (eds.) PRO-VE 2012. IAICT, vol. 380, pp. 196–204. Springer, Heidelberg (2012). doi:10.1007/978-3-642-32775-9_20

18. Hoyer, V., Christ, O.: Collaborative e-business process modelling: a holistic analysis framework focused on small and medium-sized enterprises. In: Abramowicz, W. (ed.) BIS 2007. LNCS, vol. 4439, pp. 41–53. Springer, Heidelberg (2007). doi:10.1007/978-3-540-72035-5_4

19. Belussi, F., Arcangeli, F.: A typology of networks: flexible and evolutionary firms. Res. Policy 27(4), 415–428 (1998)

20. Camarinha-Matos, L.M., Afsarmanesh, H., Oliveira, A.I., Ferrada, F.: Cloud-based collaborative business services provision. In: Hammoudi, S., Cordeiro, J., Maciaszek, L.A., Filipe, J. (eds.) ICEIS 2013. LNBIP, vol. 190, pp. 366–384. Springer, Heidelberg (2014). doi:10.1007/978-3-319-09492-2_22

21. Hwang, V.W., Horowitt, G.: The Rainforest: The Secret to Building the Next Silicon Valley. Regenwald, Los Altos Hills (2012)

22. Mootee, I.: Design Thinking for Strategic Innovation: What They Can't Tteach you at Business or Design School. Wiley, Hoboken (2013)

23. Kontogiannis, K., Lewis, G.A., Smith, D.B.: A research agenda for service-oriented architecture. In: Proceedings of the 2nd International Workshop on Systems Development in SOA Environments, pp. 1–6. ACM (2008)

24. Cancian, M.H., Rabelo, R.J., Wangenheim, C.G.: Supporting processes for collaborative SaaS. In: Camarinha-Matos, L.M., Scherer, R.J. (eds.) PRO-VE 2013. IAICT, vol. 408, pp. 183–190. Springer, Heidelberg (2013). doi:10.1007/978-3-642-40543-3_20

25. Munkongsujarit, S., Srivannaboon, S.: Key success factors for open innovation intermediaries for SMEs: a case study of ITAP in Thailand. In: 2011 Proceedings of PICMET 2011, pp. 1–8. IEEE (2011)
26. Van Zyl, J.: Process innovation imperative [software product development organisation]. In: Proceedings of the Change Management and the New Industrial Revolution, IEMC 2001, pp. 454–459. IEEE (2001)
27. Basili, V.R., Caldiera, G., Rombach, H.D.: The goal question metric approach. In: Encyclopedia of Software Engineering. Wiley (1994)

Theoretical Models to Classify the Type of Interorganizational Networks in Productive Systems

Marcelo T. Okano[1]([⊠]), Oduvaldo Vendrametto[2], Marcelo Eloy Fernandes[3],
Osmildo S. Dos Santos[4], and Marcos Antonio Maia de Oliveira[5]

[1] CPS/EAESP-FGV, São Paulo, Brazil
marcelo.okano@fatec.sp.gov.br
[2] Paulista University/Uninove, São Paulo, Brazil
oduvaldov@uol.com.br
[3] Fatec Barueri/Uninove, São Paulo, Brazil
marcelo.fernandes3@fatec.sp.gov.br
[4] Universidade Potiguar, São Paulo, Brazil
osmildosobral@yahoo.com.br
[5] Fatec Guarulhos, São Paulo, Brazil
marcos.maia@fatec.sp.gov.br

Abstract. The purpose of this article is to research the theoretical models to analyze Interorganizational systems and networks in a production chain. To achieve the objective of this study a bibliographic research was conducted to study and selection of indicators of theoretical models found. With the defined indicators was conducted a pilot with five large companies that provide for industrial manufacturers to test and evaluate the research process. In this pilot had the chance to prove the search results to the theory, the chosen production system was the automotive industry and their first-tier suppliers. It is a chain known and established for over 30 years. The IOS type can be classified sequential interdependence, the pattern of use is the exploitation, the type of network is a cluster and the main goal is to improve operational efficiency.

Keywords: IOS · Indicators · Productive systems

1 Introduction

Businesses increasingly are allying other companies to obtain some kind of value in the production chain, be it financial, social, and productive or any other value. These types of partnerships are becoming common in various areas, creating a network level, the great difficulty we have today is how to classify them and verify the benefits of these associations.

According to Mariano et al. [1], collaborative interorganizational networks have become increasingly common; the companies have continuously realized the competitive advantages gained by establishing alliances. Thus, it is important to note that a network can be defined as a set of nodes that bind each other and a

© IFIP International Federation for Information Processing 2016
Published by Springer International Publishing AG 2016. All Rights Reserved
I. Nääs et al. (Eds.): APMS 2016, IFIP AICT 488, pp. 520–527, 2016.
DOI: 10.1007/978-3-319-51133-7_62

collaborative network level can be defined as a set of three or more organizations that are united by means of an alliance in around some purpose.

Several authors define what an Interorganizational System. From simple shapes to more elaborate, the IOS feature essential characteristics, both techno- logical and organizational [2]. The use of IOS differs from a traditional informa- tion system, as it involves communication networks that push the boundaries of companies.

The purpose of this article is to research the theoretical models to analyze Interorganizational systems and networks in a production chain and apply them in one productive system.

2   Literature Review

2.1   Interorganizational Networks

According to Puffal and Puffal [3], "consider based on research conducted on the evolution of interorganizational networks studies field that the past 30 years the interest on interorganizational networks has grown significantly, and pro- duced several studies and publications on the subject and the theme networks interorganizational is a fragmented field, multidisciplinary and his studies being conducted from various theories, from various points of view it is necessary to periodically analyze this field of study and to identify the most discussed topics and the light which theories it is being analyzed".

According to Pereira [4], "both in practical and theoretical context, the issue of interorganizational relationships is applied to a wide variety of relationships between organizations, for example, joint ventures, strategic alliances, clusters, franchising, supply chains, groups export, interorganizational networks, among others". Interorganizational networks are important in economic life, because facilitate the complex transactional and cooperative interdependence between organizations. Its importance is recognized from the point of theoretical saw, because it can be, and indeed are studied from different theoretical approaches. Thus, studies on networks provide a valuable basis of common interests and potential dialogue between the various branches of social science [5].

According to Baum and Ingram [6], "interorganizational networks can be divided into two classes' analysis: horizontal and vertical networks". The "verti- cal networks" involve the coordination of activities of suppliers and distributors by a coordinating company, exerting considerable influence on the actions of other actors in the production chain. The "horizontal networks" through similar organizations that combine their activities to achieve collective goals. Figure 1 reflects the main divisions of studies on interorganizational networks [4].

2.2   Interorganizational Systems

Several authors define what an Interorganizational System. From simple shapes to more elaborate, the IOS feature essential characteristics, both technological and

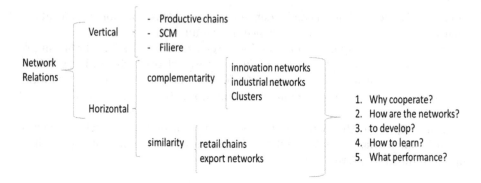

Fig. 1. Divisions of interorganizational networks. Source: [4].

organizational [2]. The use of IOS differs from a traditional information system, as it involves communication networks that push the boundaries of companies.

Cash and Konsynski [7] present a simple definition of Interorganizational System: "(...) an automated information system shared by two or more companies." Interorganizational systems are built using IT - computers and communication technology, to facilitate the creation, storage, processing and transmission of information. Johnston and Vitale [2] define the IOS:

"As systems, interorganizational systems allow the movement of information across organizational boundaries."

For Tsui et al. [9], in the broadest sense, an IOS consists of computer and communications infrastructure to manage the interdependence between companies. Companies need to manage carefully the interorganizational processes in order to access external resources, mitigate strategic uncertainties, and gain competitive advantage [10].

Recent studies have considered the supply chain management (SCM) of an inter ability digitally enabled and seen the IOS as modern systems typical supply chain management [11,12].

2.3   Type for IOS

Kumar and Van Dissel [13] classify the IOS based on a typology of interorganizational interdependencies, highlighting the role of IOS in managing inter-firm dependency and force building trust, by reducing potential conflicts aimed at sustained cooperation. The types of interdependencies presented by the authors are:

– Interdependence of set (pooled) - companies share and use common character resources (e.g., the use of a common data center for a number of companies).
– Interdependence Sequential - refers to the situation where companies are connected by a chain, targeted and well-defined relationships where the outputs of a task processor turn into inputs to others (e.g., the customer-supplier relationship over a source current) (Fig. 3).

- Interdependence Reciprocal - describes a relationship in which each company outputs are transformed into inputs for other (for example, a team of concurrent engineering with the participation of customers, suppliers, distributors, etc.) (Fig. 3).

Characteristics	Agglomerate	Cluster	Local Productive Arrangement	Social networks
Types of actors involved	Private and public organizations.	Private and public organizations	Private, public, educational institutions, non-governmental organizations, associations, unions and the community in general.	Private, public, educational institutions, non-governmental organizations, associations, unions and the community in general
Form of actors	Organizations	Organizations	Organizations	Organizations and individuals.
Typology	Market	Market and communications	Market, communications and support	Support
Models	Vertical and horizontal	Vertical and horizontal	Vertical and horizontal	Horizontal
Organizations in a given geographical area	concentrated	concentrated	concentrated	concentrated
Types of organizations	Various sectors	A sector or activity	A sector or activity	One or more sectors or activities
Strategy level	organizational	Organizational	Among all the local agents	Among all the local agents
Actions	competitive	Competitive-cooperative	Competitive-cooperative	Cooperatives
Interaction Form	Formal and informal	Formal	Formal	Informal
Essential factors of strengthening	Geographical proximity, similarity of market and regional competences.	Geographical proximity, similarity of market, regional expertise and strong competition.	Close geographic, similar market, regional expertise, strong competition and social cooperation.	Trust, reputation and cooperation
Goal setting	Does not exist	Common goals between partners	Common objectives with all local actors	Common objectives with all local actors
Types of Goals	Economics	Economics	Economics and Socials	Economics and Socials

Fig. 2. Characteristics of the types of networks. Source: [8].

2.4   Usage Patterns of IOS

Figure 4 shows that according to the standard adopted by the company, for the use of IT, exploration or exploitation, are obtained as primary outcome, operational or strategic benefits and benefits as second order, competitive performance. Considering the relationship represented by the arrows, the research

Type of Interdependence	Set of Interdependence	interdependence Sequential	Reciprocal interdependence
Configuration			
Coordinating Mechanisms	Standards & Rules	Standards, Rules, Schedules & Plans	Standards, Rules, Schedules, Plans & Mutual Adjustment
technologies	Mediator *(mediating)*	On along the chain *(Long-linked)*	Intensive *(Intensive)*
Structure	High	Average	Low
Potential for Conflict	Low	Medium	High
Type of IOS	IOS with Information Resources Together	IOS *Value / supply-chain*	IOS networks

Fig. 3. Characteristics of the types of networks. Source: [8].

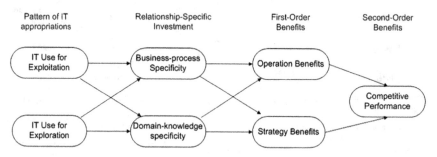

Fig. 4. IT use, specific investments in relationships and supplier benefits. Source:[14].

conducted by Subramani [14], confirmed not only the connection between operational benefits and performance competitive. Subramani [14] presents two types of specific intangible assets:

– Business Process Specificity - is the degree to which key business processes from a supplier, and operational processes (administrative and quality control) are particular to the requirement of the focal company in the relationship. The author believes that the business process of specificity is an important factor in performance linked to inter-firm relationship.
– Domain Specificity of knowledge - is the degree that the critical expertise of a supplier, such as the formulation of competitive analysis and strategy and the development of a new product are particular to the requirement of local firm in the relationship. Specificity of domain knowledge is seen in the examples of firms that rely on suppliers for innovation and critical decisions.

3   Research Methodology

To achieve the objective of this study a bibliographic research was conducted to study and selection of indicators of theoretical models found. With the defined indicators was conducted a pilot with five large companies that provide for industrial manufacturers to test and evaluate the research process.

To collect the information needed for the analysis, exploratory research, qualitative was used. Gil [15], the exploratory research aims to provide greater familiarity with the problem, in order to make it more explicit.

Zikmund et al. [16] considers that exploratory studies are conducted to clarify ambiguous issues; research is needed to better understand the dimensions of the problems. The qualitative approach presents a reality that cannot be quantified or measured and involves subjective items of reality research. You can work with data without specific statistical analysis, seeking the understanding of reality [17].

4   Analyses of Results

The several visits and interviews in businesses say that interorganizational relationships are small and largely are limited between the leader of the network and suppliers. These relationships refer only to trade relations. The only application that companies use is EDI.

The characteristics of this network, according to Fig. 2 of the literature, lies in Fig. 5. The theoretical framework of verifies the existence of characteristics of "cluster".

The IOS type can be classified sequential interdependence as the data analyzed according to Kumar and Van Dissel [13], refers to the situation where companies are connected by a chain, directed relations and well defined, where the outputs a task processor turn into inputs to others (e.g., the customer-supplier relationship along a current source). These theoretical characteristics could be confirmed in the surveyed companies, because the chain is used for Value/supply-chain.

This group is characterized as an organizational network and second inter Balestrin and Vargs [5]. Interorganizational networks are increasingly important in economic life, because facilitate the complex transactional and cooperative interdependence between organizations.

Subramani [14] proposes a way to categorize EDI ownership patterns in organizations considering that there are two main standards: "Exploitation" or "Exploration". We asked the managers of the companies about which standards the company fits and how the pattern interferes with the company's plans. The result was that 100% of the cases are categorized as exploitation, that is, the goal is to improve operational efficiency.

The Alfa company manager commented: The EDI is being used only for data transfer, its implementation improved processes and streamlined procedures for programming, deliveries and invoices. Once deployed, there are few changes in EDI. Respondents were unanimous in considering that as benefits of the first order have the operational benefits.

	Characteristics	Companies				
		Alfa	Beta	Gama	Delta	Épslon
	Types of actors involved	Private organization	Private organization	Private organization	Private organization	Private organization
	Form of actors	organization	organization	organization	organization	organization
	Typology	Market	Market	Market	Market	Market
	Models	Vertical	Vertical	Vertical	Vertical	Vertical
N e t w o r k s	Organizations in a given geographical area	concentrated	concentrated	concentrated	concentrated	concentrated
	Types of organizations	Various sectors	Various sectors	Various sectors	Various sectors	Various sectors
	Strategy level	organizational	organizational	organizational	organizational	organizational
	Actions	competitive	competitive	competitive	competitive	competitive
	Interaction Form	Formal	Formal	Formal	Formal	Formal
	Essential factors of strengthening	Geographical proximity and regional competences	Geographical proximity	Geographical proximity, similarity of market and regional competences	Geographical proximity, similarity of market	Geographical proximity, similarity of market and regional competences
	Goal setting	by automaker - Network leader	by automaker - Network leader	by automaker - Network leader	by automaker - Network leader	by automaker - Network leader
	Types of Goals	Economics	Economics	Economics	Economics	Economics
	Type of IOS	Alfa	Beta	Gama	Delta	Épslon
	Configuration	sequential	sequential	sequential	sequential	sequential
	Coordinating Mechanisms	Standards, Rules, Schedules & Plans	Standards, Rules, Schedules & Plans	Standards, Rules, Schedules & Plans	Standards, Rules, Schedules & Plans	Standards, Rules, Schedules & Plans
	technologies	On along the chain (Long-linked)	On along the chain (Long-linked)	On along the chain (Long-linked)	On along the chain (Long-linked)	On along the chain (Long-linked)
	Structure	Average	Average	Average	Average	Average
I O S	Potential for Conflict	Average	low	Average	low	Average
	Examples of Implementation and Application Technologies	EDI	EDI	EDI	EDI	EDI
	Type of IOS	Value or Supply Chain	Value or Supply Chain	Value or Supply Chain	Value or Supply Chain	Value or Supply Chain
	IOS standard	Alfa	Beta	Gama	Delta	Épslon
	Exploitation	x	x	x	x	x
	Exploration					

Fig. 5. Summary of responses.

5   Conclusion

Theoretical models presented in the conceptual framework allowed to establish indicators to analyze the type of IOS, IOS use pattern and network Features to set the type. As secondary outcomes were able to identify the benefits, used standards and objectives.

In this pilot had the chance to prove the search results to the theory, the chosen production system was the automotive industry and their first-tier suppliers. It is a chain known and established for over 30 years. The IOS type can be classified sequential interdependence, the pattern of use is the exploitation, the type of network is a cluster and the main goal is to improve operational efficiency. These indicators should be tested with other production systems and more players to check their efficiency. As a future project, we can incorporate the analysis of social networks to verify the structural characteristics of the network as centrality, grouping etc.

References

1. Mariano, E.B., Guerrini, F.M., Rebelatto, D.A.D.N., et al.: Análise da Relação entre Estrutura e Desempenho de Redes Interorganizacionais Colaborativas. Gestão Produção **19**(3), 471–479 (2012)
2. Johnston, H.R., Vitale, M.R.: Creating competitive advantage with interorganizational information systems. MIS Q. **12**, 153–165 (1988)
3. Puffal, D.D.P., Puffal, C.W.: A Evolução do Campo de Estudos de Redes Interorganizacionais: Uma Análise de Publicações Internacionais das Relações entre Empresas. Revista Brasileira de Gestão e Inovação (Braz. J. Manag. Innov.) **1**(3), 63–86 (2014)
4. Pereira, B.: Estrutura de Relacionamentos Horizontais. Tese (Doutorado em Administração)-UFRGS, Porto Alegre (2005)
5. Balestrin, A., Vargas, L.M.: Evidências Teóricas para a Compreensão das Redes Interorganizacionais. In: Encontro de Estudos Organizacionais 2 (2002)
6. Baum, J.A., Ingram, P.: Interorganizational learning and network organization: toward a behavioral theory of the interfirm. In: The Economics of Choice, Change, and Organization, pp. 191–218 (2002)
7. Cash, J.I., Konsynski, B.R.: IS redraws competitive boundaries. Harv. Bus. Rev. **63**(2), 134–142 (1985)
8. Cruz, J.A.W., Martins, T.S., Augusto, P.O.M.: Redes Sociais e Organizacionais em Administração. Juruá, Curitiba (2009)
9. Tsui, E., Chi, L., Holsapple, C.W.: Understanding computer-mediated interorganizational collaboration: a model and framework. J. Knowl. Manag. **9**(1), 53–75 (2005)
10. Zhao, K., Xia, M.: Forming interoperability through interorganizational systems standards. J. Manag. Inf. Syst. **30**(4), 269–298 (2014)
11. Rai, A., Patnayakuni, R., Seth, N.: Firm performance impacts of digitally enabled supply chain integration capabilities. MIS Q. **30**, 225–246 (2006)
12. Zhang, C., Xue, L., Dhaliwal, J.: Alignments between the depth and breadth of inter-organizational systems deployment and their impact on firm performance. Inf. Manag. **53**(1), 79–90 (2016)
13. Kumar, K., Van Dissel, H.G.: Sustainable collaboration: managing conflict and cooperation in interorganizational systems. Mis Q. **20**, 279–300 (1996)
14. Subramani, M.: How do suppliers benefit from information technology use in supply chain relationships? Mis Q. **28**, 45–73 (2004)
15. Gil, A.C.: Como Elaborar Projetos de Pesquisa, vol. 5. Atlas, São Paulo (2002)
16. Zikmund, W., Babin, B., Carr, J., Griffin, M.: Business Research Methods. Cengage Learning, São Paulo (2012). H4 B
17. da Costa, M.A.F., da Costa, M.D.F.B.: Metodologia da Pesquisa: Conceitos e Técnicas. Interciência, Caracas (2009)

Business Model Innovation in State-Owned and Private-Owned Enterprises in China

Yan Li$^{(\boxtimes)}$, Maria Holgado, and Steve Evans

University of Cambridge, Cambridge, UK
{yl483,mh769,se321}@cam.ac.uk

Abstract. The aim of the paper is to identify the complexity of policy execution, investment and financial support between state-owned and private-owned enterprises in China. Based on the literature review of business model innovation, and current situation of private-owned and state-owned enterprises in China, there is a lack of evidence and case analysis in the power of policy execution and the version of future development between two kinds of industries. The authors conducted qualitative research in four typical industries. Two of them are private-owned and the others are state-owned. The research aims to make a specific comparison between two kinds of industries in China.

Keywords: Business model · Business model innovation · Private-owned enterprise · State-owned enterprise · China

1 Introduction

Over the past decade, market competition has become fiercer, especially at a global scale, with an enormous percentage of large-scale enterprises facing a great challenge for surviving, let alone small and medium companies. High market competition together with sustainability-related social, legal, political and economic requirements has increased the importance of corporate sustainability strategies [1]. Ultimately, business model innovation emerges as a significant concept for supporting value creation and improving the core competitiveness for companies. It is especially relevant in current moments of economic distress [2].

Business model innovation, however, may not represent something easy or straightforward to be realized as often implies a remarkable change to get the innovated "revolution" adopted in the enterprise. Additionally, the possibilities and capacity to perform the business model innovation may differ for different types of companies. Organizational culture and structure would influence the process and outcomes of innovations targeting companies; business model [3]. In this regard, small and medium companies may lack the necessary resources already in place to perform the innovation but, on the contrary, may be more agile to reach rather than large companies. An unexplored potential difference on the approach towards business model innovations is also present when considering different types of ownership, i.e. state-owned versus private owned enterprises. This study focuses on China due to its particular region that offers the

© IFIP International Federation for Information Processing 2016
Published by Springer International Publishing AG 2016. All Rights Reserved
I. Nääs et al. (Eds.): APMS 2016, IFIP AICT 488, pp. 528–535, 2016.
DOI: 10.1007/978-3-319-51133-7_63

possibility to understand whether these two types of ownership influence the barriers and opportunities for business model innovations. Concretely, the aim of this article is to explore what are the explicit differences between state-owned enterprise and private-owned enterprises in nurturing a business model. Reviewing the existing literature and conducting empirical research based on case studies carried out this exploratory study. The contribution of this paper is to perform a comparison on current business innovation initiatives in Chinese companies, with a focus on the complexity of policy execution, the investment and the leader's contribution in business model innovation and the external financial support.

2   Background

2.1   Business Model Innovation

The emergence of the business model concept is associated with the advent of internet and initially used in corporate practice [2,4]. Since then, there are many suggested definitions of business models [2], most of them sharing a common focus on value creation and the close connection with the concept of value.

The business model has three core components: the value proposition, the value creation and delivery system, and the value capture [5]. Identifying these core components would help industry to build a successful business model. An effective business model would lead to a successful company, as referring to the business model analysis, executives identify all of the constituent parts and understand how the model fulfills a potent value proposition in a profitable way [6]. The economic value of a technology will not be fully generated until it's commercialized with a business model [7].

The key of most successful business models is to develop of a 'powerful, focused customer value proposition'. In turn, this requires 'a comprehensive understanding' of your target customer's 'job-to-be-done' [8]. A strength of business model as a planning tool is that it focuses on how the elements fit into a whole system [9]. In Chesbrough's [10] research, business model performs two important functions: value creation and value capture. It defines a series of activities, from procuring raw materials to satisfying the final consumer, which generates a new product or service. In such a way, net value will be created throughout the various activities [10].

The main reasons for innovating a business model are related to create and acquire more value as well as to address new customers or societal requirements. Every new product development should be joined with the development of a business model, which is defined as 'going to market' and 'capturing value' strategies [11]. The business model innovation refers to creating or reinventing something new or different in doing business [12]. In other words, at least one constitution element of current business model is changed [13]. At this stage, Velu and Jacob [14] explained business model innovation can "redefine what a product or service is, how it is provided to the customer, and how it is monetized". Therefore, business model innovation can change the mode of competition through altering the performance metrics [15].

Business model seems easy to imitate in a superficial level. Nevertheless, in practical, implementing a business model may need systems, processes and assets, which is difficult to replicate. Furthermore, a level of opacity may exist that makes it difficult to understand how a business model works in detail. Thirdly, incumbents in the industry may be reluctant to cannibalize existing profits or upset other necessary business relationships [11].

2.2   State-Owned and Private-Owned Enterprise

Since the late 1970s, China's economy has undergone reforms. The market- oriented reforms are placed instead of a more planned economy; the private sectors are expanded in China afterwards. Since 1990s, urban areas are selected to restructuring the state-owned enterprise, which is privatization. Since then, the "modern enterprise system" is started [16].

After two and a half decades of reforms, state-owned enterprise ownership is no longer dominated Chinese business [17]. But the state-owned factor is still plays a significant role in China. The government has the ambitious to build a national team in several pillar enterprises, such as automotive, pharmaceutical, electronics, and petrochemical [18]. This makes China the most adequate scenario for this exploratory study.

Most of the pillar enterprises are still owned by the state in China, such as those in the energy, telecommunication and finance industries. It is relatively easy for them to get support (i.e. financial, policy-related) from the government. Nevertheless, the execution of innovation may be more challenging, due to the large number of employees and the dispersion of the different departments. Moreover, the internal and external challenges for these enterprises are also sever. The competitions from both internal (i.e. restructure, private-owned enterprise) and external (i.e. domestic private sector, foreign-controlled business sector) are compelling state-owned enterprise innovate business model.

The Chinese definition of the private sector is: "it includes private limited liability corporations, private share-holding corporations, private partnership enterprises and private sole investment enterprises" [17]. Due to the mentioned "open to door" policy, the private sector expanded greatly in China since the late 1970s. Innovations in this type of companies would emerge and evolve in a different manner. In contrast to state-owned enterprises, the private-owned enterprises need to discover a suitable business model and try to survive by themselves as the Chinese government to them may give scares support. At this stage, the leader of the private-owned enterprise has to consider a long future version of the enterprise to make a sustainable profit. Thus, the private-owned enterprise would more likely make efforts to invest more money in innovating their business model.

3 Methodology and Data Collection

This research uses a qualitative case study to explore and analyze uncultivated knowledge (Eisehardt [22]). There are two main activities in the theory development, which are "the formulation of propositions" and "testing whether they can be supported" [19]. Therefore, this research is based on exploration for theory to discover the current gaps and suggest research propositions. Case study and observation methods help to formulate new propositions, which will be verified in future work.

There are three justifications to select case study as our main research method. Firstly, case study is perhaps the most flexible methods, which could provide a plenty of detailed description of a particular phenomenon [20]. Secondly, this research focuses on the contemporary event, which is identical to the conditions of case study method [21]. Thirdly, both single-case and multiple-case study will be used in this research. According to Eisenhardt [22] and Hagg et al. [23], many single-case are criticized, as they cannot provide any basis for generalization, while multi-case construct a stronger basis for knowledge building.

4 Empirical Case Study

4.1 Overview of State-Owned Company A&B

Company A: Has approximate 40 years history in China and around 4000 employees. It is convened to provide blower for either state-owned or private-owned manufacturing industries and serves to diverse fields, such as Petroleum, Metallurgy, Chemical, Electricity, Fertilizer and Pharmacy. In the year 2007, they increased funding and attracted several strategic partners. In the year 2010, this company was listed.

The traditional business model of Company A was based on direct product sales. Currently, this company not only sells products but also provides services to its consumers. Moreover, they have innovated their business model in the following three aspects: (i) The main source of business profit has changed its focus from equipment, physical power and technical ability to brand value, knowledge and human capital; (ii) A previous technical-oriented approach was modified to extend business boundaries and adopt a more customer-oriented approach; (iii) Improvements in the integration of resource capability from a self-owned resource based to a integration external resource.

As the competition from both internal and external are getting fierce, company A tried to make a sustainable profit to survive. As a state-owned enterprise, company A could get continues financial support from the state. Thus, they could have a better policy execution. For example, Company A constructed an eco-system factory. It's difficult to execute for private-owned enterprise because of the lack of profit stimulation. Companies need to invest a huge amount of money to build the system and the profit would mostly need to be expected after several years. Apparently, it's a burden for most of small to medium private owned companies. However, it's much easier for state-owned company to get the Land Use Right and the local government would support for their construction.

Company B: Is a state-owned numerical machine tool industry. It was founded in the year 1965 and the current employees are around 3500 people. In the year 1995, company B upgraded from numerical machine tool factory to numerical machine tool company. In the year 1998, company B experienced shareholding reform and went to the public. In the year 2007, company B upgraded by means of merger and acquisition other small numerical machine tool company. During the merger and acquisition, the government offered enormous supporting. Specifically, the government let the company reorganizing their core product and abandons their deficit product. It is worth to mention that the government paid for their deficit product and invests huge money to their core product.

The current operating performance of Company B is barely satisfactory. For one thing, most of the numerical system needs to be imported from abroad, as the technology in the local market cannot satisfy the high requirements in precision yet. Besides, some high precision machine tool parts are also need to be imported from abroad as well. Thus, the profit margin is very low. For another, most of the senior employees in this state-owned company have life-long position. Even if they don't work that hard, the company normally will not layoff them until they get formally retired. The system makes the senior employee doesn't have a passion to make innovation. In contract, although most of the joiner employees are signed short-term renewable contract, they don't have a protection of the position. In addition, as the working condition of numerical machine tool industry is terrible, fewer striplings are willing to choose this job. For the current striplings work as apprentice, they mostly would like to change a job afterwards.

4.2   Overview of Private-Owned Company C&D

Company C: Is a large-scale equipment manufacturing enterprises, which was founded in the year 1966. They mainly produce numerical machine tool part; energy equipment; miner equipment; engine; compressor; wind turbine; track and so on. Company C was a state-owned enterprise until the year 2004. After that, Company C reformed to a private-owned enterprise and attracted several strategic partner. Currently, Company C owns dozens of subsidiary company.

As a leading casting enterprise in China, Company C has a deep understanding of their advantage and insisted in their core competitiveness continuously. They do expand their business to new areas such as chemical and biomedical engineering, but casting still takes the largest market share of their products.

During the qualitative research, the author identified that there exist two reasons to make Company C successful. Firstly, the leader has a powerful ability to judge the development direction of the industry. For instance, in the year 2012, the leader decided to build their company as an innovation enterprise. They explored their technology to digitization and intellectualization. In the year 2015, the Chinese state issued a policy - building the Chinese industry digitization and intellectualization by 2025. This new policy for manufacturing companies is exactly accordance to the policy company C issued three years ago. Secondly, the efficient to execute a new policy of Company C is remarkable.

For example, in November 2015, the leader decided to change their management pattern. Formerly, their management mode is a traditional way that the supervisors set a profit target and the employees follow their instruction to fulfill the task. However, the new business model is to divide one department into several teams, each team includes 3 to 4 people. The team would find their customers by themselves. They changed their working pattern from passive to initiative. The more contract they signed, the higher deduction wage they will get. This management mode motivates every employee to make profit, but this innovation put the people waiting for others instruction into a difficult situation. Surprised, Company C only use three month to execute this new policy.

Company D: Is a traditional private-owned family firm. Their business is mainly to produce numerical machine tool part, as well as the numerical system. The main capital resource is from the profit of traditional manufacturing product (i.e. industrial robot, hydraulic system equipment, sensor etc.). They also produce customized product. This company was founded in 1993, it used be a family industry, with a single ownership structure. From 2015, their subsidiary company is preparing for IPO. In the future, Company D will keep working as single ownership structure but their subsidiary company will work as board of directors and operated by CEO.

The main customer of this company is aerospace and military industry. Company D has ambitious to replace the market share of import product from Japan and German. Family enterprise has widespread characteristics that their leader has absolute authority to decide the future development of the enterprise. That situation leads a risk that the leader may make a wrong decision. For instance, the leader in Company D decided to produce numerical control system. However, this is an advance technique that difficulties are not fully overcome yet. This company spends more than ten years in this technique, but the profit is unsatisfactory. Moreover, comparing with state-owned enterprise. It is more difficult for private-owned companies to get funding from the government. Mostly, Company D needs to survive all on them own.

4.3   Findings and Discussion

Leader's Perspective in Business Model Innovation. There exist a policy for state-owned company that the state or the local government nominates the leader. In this qualitative research, we explored another reason makes Company A succeed, which is the future perspective and the execution status of the leader's idea. Comparing the leader between Company A and Company B. There exist a significant difference. Company A doesn't change their leader for 14 years, which makes this leader's strategy and target carried out in a most effective way. In contract, Company B changes their leader every four to five years. This phenomenon makes each leader only consider the company performance during his term of office.

Both of the two private-owned enterprises have the common characteristics: the leader has the absolute authority to decide the enterprise's development direction. Company C has a board of directors to decide their innovated policy. Therefore, the leader would have an opportunity to hear different voice and make a proper decision. In contract, Company D is a family industry; it is difficult to make the leader change the decision, especially when it is a wrong one.

Complexity of Policy Execution in Business Model Innovation. In empirical study, the authors discovered that private-owned enterprise has a significant high efficient in execution innovated policy. For instance, Company A needs to take several years to implement an innovated idea. Because the authority is more divided comparing with the private-owned company. Thus, it takes a longer time to get the idea approved by the leader, let along to implement the idea. Nonetheless, it only takes several months for Company C to change their management mode. One of the possible reasons is the employees in state-owned enterprise are mostly have the life-long position. They lack a sense of crisis for the position.

Investment and the Financial Support. Through the case study, we discovered that private-owned enterprises are very difficult to get financial support from the state. Therefore, to make a sustainable profit, private-owned enterprises have a stronger eager to innovate their ideas and business model. In contract, state-owned enterprise could get funding much easier from the government. This would lead two situations: the advantage is companies would be much easier to realize innovation, as they would get support from local government and could get benefit from preferential policies. The disadvantage is that employees' working attitude might be passive. Because of their life-long position would make them have a financial guarantee from the government no matter what are their work efficiency is.

5 Concluding Remarks

Through the empirical study, the authors identified that the private-owned company has higher innovation ability. It is very difficult for private-owned enterprise to get large amount of funding support from the state. Therefore, they have much stronger eager to innovate new technology as well as their business model to make a sustainable profit. Moreover, private-owned enterprise has a significant high efficient in execution innovated policy. Because most of employees signed short-term renewable contract, they have a sense of crisis for their position. Additionally, the authority in state-owned enterprise is more divided than the private-owned company. That result in a longer period to execute a policy. Furthermore, the leader's perspective of the innovation not only depends on the leader's personal ability, but also depends on their nomination duration. This phenomenon is more general in state-owned enterprise.

In this research, the case study is mainly focus on the company's current situation. In future works, we plan to conduct further research in government policy and legalization. Finally, we will design a tool to instruct both kind of enterprise to carry forward their advantages, especially how to maximize their resources.

References

1. Schaltegger, S., Lüdeke-Freund, F., Hansen, E.G.: Business cases for sustainability: the role of business model innovation for corporate sustainability. Int. J. Innov. Sustain. Dev. **6**(2), 95–119 (2012)
2. Zott, C., Amit, R., Massa, L.: The business model: recent developments and future research. J. Manag. **37**(4), 1019–1042 (2011)
3. Bock, A.J., Opsahl, T., George, G., Gann, D.M.: The effects of culture and structure on strategic flexibility during business model innovation. J. Manag. Stud. **49**(2), 279–305 (2012)
4. George, G., Bock, A.J.: The business model in practice and its implications for entrepreneurship research. Entrep. Theory Pract. **35**(1), 83–111 (2011)
5. Richardson, J.: The business model: an integrative framework for strategy execution. Strateg. Change **17**(5–6), 133–144 (2008)
6. Johnson, M.W., Christensen, C.M., Kagermann, H.: Reinventing your business model. Harv. Bus. Rev. **86**(12), 57–68 (2008)
7. Chesbrough, H.: Business model innovation: opportunities and barriers. Long Range Plan. **43**(2), 354–363 (2010)
8. Leavy, B.: A system for innovating business models for breakaway growth. Strateg. Leadersh. **38**(6), 5–15 (2010)
9. Magretta, J.: Why business models matter. Harv. Bus. Rev. **80**, 86–92 (2002)
10. Chesbrough, H.: Business model innovation: it's not just about technology anymore. Strateg. Leadersh. **35**(6), 12–17 (2007)
11. Teece, D.J.: Business models, business strategy and innovation. Long Range Plan. **43**(2), 172–194 (2010)
12. Björkdahl, J., Holmén, M.: Business model innovation: the challenges ahead. Int. J. Prod. Dev. **18**(3/4), 213–225 (2013)
13. Eurich, M., Weiblen, T., Breitenmoser, P.: A six-step approach to business model innovation. Int. J. Entrep. Innov. Manag. **18**(4), 330–348 (2014)
14. Velu, C., Jacob, A.: Business model innovation and owner-managers: the moderating role of competition. R&D Manag. **46**, 451–463 (2014)
15. Danneels, E.: Disruptive technology reconsidered: a critique and research agenda. J. Prod. Innov. Manag. **21**(4), 246–258 (2004)
16. Nolan, P., Xiaoqiang, W.: Beyond privatization: institutional innovation and growth in China's large state-owned enterprises. World Dev. **27**(1), 169–200 (1999)
17. Ralston, D.A., Terpstra-Tong, J., Terpstra, R.H., Wang, X., Egri, C.: Today's state-owned enterprises of China: are they dying dinosaurs or dynamic dynamos? Strateg. Manag. J. **27**(9), 825–843 (2006)
18. Nolan, P.: China and the Global Economy. Palgrave, New York (2001)
19. Dul, J., Hak, T.: Case Study Methodology in Business Research. Routledge, London (2007)
20. Hakim, C.: Research Design. Routledge, London (2000)
21. Yin, R.K.: Case Study Research: Design and Methods. Sage Publications, Thousand Oaks (2013)
22. Eisenhardt, K.M.: Building theories from case study research. Acad. Manag. Rev. **14**(4), 532–550 (1989)
23. Hagg, I., Hedlund, G., et al.: Case studies in accounting research. Acc. Organ. Soc. **4**(1–2), 135–143 (1979)

Analysis of Inter-firm Co-operation in Joint Research and Development Projects

Matti Majuri[✉], Hasse Nylund, and Minna Lanz

Tampere University of Technology, Tampere, Finland
{matti.majuri,hasse.nylund,minna.lanz}@tut.fi

Abstract. Companies need to renew themselves to be able to compete in the dynamic global markets. Especially for the SMEs this is often challenging due to their weaker risk tolerance and fewer resources. Co-operation is often considered to be effective way to tackle these challenges and considerable amount of public funding has been directed to stimulate this co-operation. Still, deep research and development (R&D) co-operation between companies exists rarely. The paper presents qualitative analysis on co-operation in two joint R&D projects. The level of inter-firm co-creation in studied cases was low. This was explained by lack of resources, differences of R&D goals and changes in project consortium. Finally, we present two possible solutions to increase the level of inter-firm co-creation in joint R&D projects.

Keywords: Networks · Renewal · Innovation · R&D

1 Introduction

Rapid changing markets and increasing competition have led to a situation where ability for renewal has become one of the dominant capabilities in the pursuit of competitive advantage [1]. The renewal may focus on processes, offering or business concepts and can be radical or incremental by nature. Challenges related to renewal are somewhat different between large companies and SMEs. SMEs have typically less bureaucracy and more concentrated ownership, which in general support agility. Additionally, with fewer resources, the personnel of SMEs' are used to work in wider scope of processes, which in turn supports flexibility. On the other hand, compared to the large companies, SMEs' have typically weaker risk tolerance, smaller knowledge base, fewer sales channels and narrower offering. All of these factors can be considered essential for successful renewal, development and innovation. Inter-firm co-operation creates a major opportunity to tackle these challenges and altogether enables firms to achieve stronger position than they could alone [2].

In general, deep inter-firm R&D co-operation between SMEs in the Finnish technology industry is rare [3]. On the other hand, several public funding instruments require this co-operation and multiple organizations have been established to support the co-operation. Focus of the paper is on collaborative R&D projects that received funding from Tekes, Finnish Funding Agency for Innovation. The paper increases understanding on the challenges and opportunities the companies are facing in their

I. Nääs et al. (Eds.): APMS 2016, IFIP AICT 488, pp. 536–543, 2016.
DOI: 10.1007/978-3-319-51133-7_64

co-operation attempts during these projects. Research data was collected with eight semi-structured company interviews in two separate R&D projects.

2   Joint Research and Development Projects

The research concerning inter-firm R&D co-operation is fragmented. Several frameworks and concepts from multiple fields of science have been presented to model the dynamics of inter-firm co-operation. Majority of the studies concerning inter-firm co-operation seem to be quantitative by their nature, although this was not systematically studied. In recent years concept of open innovation has got a lot of attention. Open innovation processes includes outbound, inbound and coupled processes [4] from which coupled processes are closest to the topic of this study. However, the research focusing on coupled processes does not seem to include inter-firm joint R&D projects in which the companies are from different value chains.

Hagerdoorn [5] has created classification for co-operative agreements based on the amount of the organizational interdependence, which can be considered to be a central dimension defining the mode of co-operation. The classification has four main modes: (1) Joint R&D ventures, (2) Joint R&D and technology exchange agreements, (3) Equity investments and (4) Customer-supplier relationships and one-directional technology flows. The second mode is divided into three categories: joint research pacts, joint development agreements and technology sharing agreements. Study presented in this paper contributes to the areas of joint research pacts and joint development agreements.

Barnes et al. [6] have identified 40 success factors for inter-firm co-operation which they have divided into six categories: choice of partner, project management, universal success factors, ensuring equality, monitoring environmental influences, project manager and choice of partner. Lee et. al. [7] have summarized intermediary's role in SME innovation networks based on literature review into framework that consists of five. Categories: Network Database, Network Construction, Network Management, Culture of co-operation and Facilitation of co-operation. Frameworks that illustrate the characteristics and dynamics of R&D inter-firm network are presented by e.g. Kirkels [8], Esterhuizen et al. [9], Möller et al. [10], and Dasgupta and Gupta [11].

The frameworks have plenty of similarities but they are still different. A conclusion can be made, that the inter-firm co-operation as a phenomenon is heavily case dependent. None of studies dealt with the same situation as ours. Therefore it is justified to increase the understanding on inter-firm R&D co-operation from perspective of this paper. At least the following features can be considered to be defining in our study: public funding, significant role of research institute, project-centeredness, formality, non-equity, non-value chain and technological orientation of R&D topics. Considering the high volume of joint R&D projects receiving public support they are surprisingly rarely in the focus of the qualitative studies, which could provide in depth knowledge on the phenomenon.

3 Method

Priority of our research was to deepen the understanding on actual experiences that companies had on inter-firm co-operation in publically funded join R&D projects. Research approach was qualitative and inductive. This approach was chosen due to fragmentation of the previous research and case dependence of the phenomenon dynamics.

The data was collected by interviewing eight persons from eight companies that had been participants in collaborative R&D projects funded by Tekes. Interviews were semi-structured and they lasted 75 min on average. Central answers concerning project phases, quantity and quality of co-operation, goal achievement and co-operation characteristics were collected into an excel sheet that was visible for the interviewee during the interview. The interviewees were asked to define the project phases freely according to project goals they found relevant. Illustration of the excel sheet is presented on Table 1. There was also data collected concerning the co-operation with research institutes, but it is not in the focus of this paper.

Table 1. Excel sheet base filled with the interviewee

	1	...	n
Number of the project phase			
Goal of the project phase			
The amount of the collaboration with research institutes 0 = none, 1 = little, 2 = moderately, 3 = plenty			
The quality of the collaboration with research institutes 0 = poor, 1 = moderate 2 = high			
The amount of the collaboration with other companies in the project			
The quality of the collaboration with other companies in the project			
Goal achievement 0 = not achieved, 1 = achieved partially, 2 = achieved well			

All interviewees were the major participants in the projects from their companies. Introduction for the interviewee about research objectives was kept short to avoid inducement. All interviews were recorded and transcribed. Atlas TI computer program was used for qualitative coding.

Aim of the paper is to answer the following research questions:

1. What characteristics companies associate with high and low quality inter-firm co-operation?
2. What reasons explain the realized amount of co-operation?

Additionally, the paper gives suggestions for new project structures that would increase the quality and quantity of inter-firm co-operation in R&D projects. There is also data presented on the amount of co-operation between companies and also between companies and research institutes. However, this data cannot be generalized due to small sample size, but it can be considered to be useful for planning future research and also to stimulate the public discussion on the matter.

The research presented in this paper is part of the ongoing research project called Renaissance of the Regions (ReRe) – Challenging the Status Quo of Innovation Policy Implementation in Regional Manufacturing Networks. Project goal is to create improved methods and means for public or private network coordinators to support and develop the innovation process in SME networks. To be able to work efficiently it is necessary that the coordinator has an understanding on what characteristics high quality co-operation consists of. Understanding on the mechanisms how to influence those characteristics and on the mechanisms how those characteristics influence the co-operation is also needed. Additionally, this understanding is valuable also for the companies. With deeper understanding they are able to manage their co-operation activities and capabilities more coherently to support their innovation co-operation with other companies.

Tampere University of Technology's research goal in the ReRe project is to create generic model for evaluating the status of prioritized co-operation characteristics in DIR network (Development, Innovation, Renewal). Table 2 explains the research phases. The results and analysis presented in this paper contributes to the current state analysis. They also create valuable information for planning a web survey on phase 2.

Table 2. Research phases.

Phase no.	Phase	Methodology
1.	Current state analysis	Literature review and qualitative study (interviews)
2.	Generalization	Quantitative study (web survey)
3.	Deepening the understanding	Qualitative study (interviews)
4.	Synthesis	Combining and evaluation of the knowledge from phases 1 to 3 (expert workshops)
5.	Verification	Testing the model by using it to analyze 3 to 5 DIR networks

4   Interview Outcomes

Table 3 presents the amount of co-operation the interviewed company had with other companies and with the research institutes during the different phases of the project. It also presents the quality of the co-operation in each phase and how well the goals were achieved.

Although the study sample is small and as such not generalizable, it was still surprising to notify how little inter-firm co-operation existed. With further analysis on the transcribed interviews we formed Table 4, which includes explanations the companies gave for the low amount of inter-firm co-operation.

Due to small amount of inter-firm co-operation it was natural that the data did not offer much information on the co-operation characteristics. Since all inter-firm co-operation was considered by the interviewees' to be of high-quality (Table 2.) only

Table 3. Amount and quality of cooperation.

	C1			C2			C3			C4		C5		C6		C7			C8	
The amount of the collaboration with research institutes 0=none, 1=little, 2=moderately, 3=plenty	0 3 3 0	0 2 3 1 1	0 3 1 0 1 3	0 2 0 3 0	2 1 2 2	2 2 2 1	1 0 3 2 1 2	0 3 0 1 0													
The quality of the collaboration with research institutes 0=poor, 1=moderate 2=high	2 2	2 2 2 2	2 2	0 1	2	2	2 2 2 2 2 2 3 1 1	2 1 0 2	1	1											
The amount of the collaboration with other companies in the project 0=none, 1=little, 2=moderately, 3=plenty	0 0 1 0	0 0 0 0 0 0	3 1 0 1 3 0	0 0 0 0	2 0 0	0 0 0 0	0 0 0 0 0 0 0	0 0 0 0													
The quality of the collaboration with other companies in the project 0=poor, 1=moderate 2=high	2		2 2	2 2		2															
Goal achievement 0=not achieved, 1=achieved partially, 2= achieved well	2 1 1 2	0 1 2 2 2 1	2 2 2 0 0 1	2 0 0 2 0	2 2 2 2	2 2 1 1	1 2 1 2 2 2 2 1	2 1 2 2													

Table 4. Explanations for the lack of inter-firm co-operation.

C1	Company with synergetic business interests left the project in early stage. This was possibly due to financial challenges
	Other companies were distant
C2	Other companies had different focusses in their R&D
	Company, that was considered as a potential partner, focused on different technology
C3	Big customer, that encouraged C3 to participate, did not participate the "group project". The customer was not able to reach an agreement with other participating companies
	Other companies were already in their own networks, and P3 was not able to fit into them
C4	Other companies were interested in C4 part, but did not want to allocate resources to collaboration. From business perspective the times were difficult and this affected the resourcing
	One potentian company to do collaboration with left out just before project started
C5	Project topic in C5 was different. Other companies focused on product development when C5's aim was to develop their risk management processes
	Insufficient resources in C5
C6	R&D subjects were close, but not close enough to do collaborative development
C7	Lack of resourcing in C7. Collaboration would have required human resources from wide range of functions in C7)
	Scope of R&D was such that it did not lead to collaboration
C8	Desired results were delivered with very little collaboration. Knowledge exchange between companies happened through research organization

characteristics describing high-quality can be listed. Characteristics describing high-quality inter-firm co-operation are: (i) Common vision; (ii) Partner was showing trust; (iii) Encouragement by the partner; (iv) Desire to help; (v) Honest and straight dialogue; (vi) Good relations; (vii) Openness Experienced appreciation; (viii) Similar commercial goals.

5 Conclusions and Discussion

In this paper the characteristics of inter-firm R&D co-operation in the Finnish technology industry was discussed. The explanations for the lack of inter-firm co-operation in a joint research project, presented in Table 4, can be summarized with the following three categories:

1. Own R&D goal was different from the ones other companies had
2. The project consortium changed into less synergetic
3. Qualitative of quantitative lack of resources.

The projects that we studied were put together mainly by research institutes which had their own research projects going alongside the companies' R&D projects. The construction phase of the projects, including putting the consortium together, is usually carried out fast. This means, that not much resources are allocated into finding companies with similar or synergetic R&D goals.

Sherer [12] divides the critical success factors for manufacturing networks into trust, commitment, selection choice, information technology, and intermediary. The role of an intermediary, which in our study was a research institute, is important at the construction phase of a project. An intermediary can facilitate networking both by selecting potential participants and aiding companies interested in participating in a R&D project. Barriers, such as conflicting goals and expectations can be eliminated by an efficient facilitation [13].

One challenge in the forming of the R&D project is, in addition to the putting the consortium together is a short time, is the small amount of potential companies that can be contacted. Research institutes typically rely on their existing contacts, which narrows down the selection choice of companies. Thorgren et al. [14] state that larger number of companies relates to a greater innovation. The greater number of companies increases the selection choice, which can lead to more synergetic R&D projects. In the forming phase, trust and commitment is mainly focused on the intermediate in that the potential companies are confident with the intermediate and are more willing to participate in a R&D project. Potential companies should have clear vision of the R&D project to invest into it [15].

Trust and commitment is essential in both forming and during a R&D project. During a R&D project the role of an intermediate changes more on supporting the participating companies in the trust and commitment issues between the participating companies [16]. The trust and commitment issues between the participating companies emphasizes during a R&D project. A company should have clear image of the benefits it can gain from the project. In the inter-firm co-operation an important issue is how the co-operation with other companies enhances their own objectives [17]. This requires open sharing of information and resources in that opportunities are clear, which is an evident benefit of a functional network [18].

The lack of resources can be explained with both lack of needed skills and lack of time dedicated to the project even when personnel with required skills exist. This can be explained with the short time of construction of a project. It is important that the participating companies are devoted to the ongoing R&D project. In addition to the role of the intermediate, top management of the companies should recognize the importance of the co-operation [19]. Two relatively different solutions can be identified to tackle these challenges.

The first solution we propose is that there should be knowledge available on the R&D goals of large amount of companies for the person who is coordinating the project planning, e.g. in some kind of database solution. This would allow contacting widely potential participants that have similar or synergic R&D interests. When companies with similar genuine R&D needs would be identified in early stages of the project planning, commitment inside the consortium would rise and fewer changes in the consortium would occur. It should also be noted, that in the studied cases the company participants did not interact together in planning phase and the first face to face meetings were organized after the projects had already started. It is quite likely, that the presented solution would also increase pre-project co-operation, besides increased co-operation during the projects.

In projects with public funding involved, the companies tend to define their R&D goals with narrow scopes and have often very little resources allocated into free innovative renewal. This is partly because the public funding system requires coherent narrowly defined plans and partly because of small R&D resources due to hard competition situation in many business fields.

The second solution we suggest would be a kind of hybrid model for the project plan. There would still be straightforward plans with narrow scopes but the project plan would also include resources for loosely defined collaborative R&D and interaction, e.g. topical workshops. This would create opportunities and space for new ideas that were not possible to be identified in the planning phase of the project. In the current model the project participants become sort of prisoners of the project plan. This leads often to minimal or zero slack and weak co-operation. This is problematic, because slack and co-operation can be considered to be cornerstones of innovativeness [20].

Acknowledgements. The research presented in this paper is co-financed by Tekes, the Finnish Funding Agency for Technology and Innovation, and Tredea Oy, the Tampere Region Economic Development Agency.

References

1. Jovane, F.: The ManuFuture road towards competitive and sustainable HAV manufacturing. In: Tampere Manufacturing Summit, Tampere, Finland (2009)
2. Boddy, D., Macbeth, D., Wagner, B.: Implementing co-operation between organizations: an empirical study of supply chain partnering. J. Manag. Stud. **37**(7), 1003–1018 (2000)
3. Parhaat, T.: Valmistavan teknologiateollisuuden tutkimusagenda 2020. Edita Prima Oy, Helsinki (2011). (in Finnish)
4. Enkel, E., Gassman, O., Chesbrough, H.: Open R&D and open innovation: exploring the phenomenon. R&D Manag. **39**(4), 311–316 (2009)
5. Hagedoorn, J.: Organizational modes of inter-firm co-operation and technology transfer. Technocation **10**(1), 17–30 (1990)

6. Barnes, T.A., Pashby, I.R., Gibbons, A.M.: Managing collaborative R&D projects development of a practical management tool. Int. J. Proj. Manag. **24**, 395–404 (2006)

7. Lee, S., Park, G., Yoon, B., Jinwoo, P.: Open innovation in SMEs – an intermediated network model. Res. Policy **39**, 290–300 (2010)

8. Kirkels, Y.: Brokerage in SME Networks. Eindhoven University Press, Eindhoven (2010)

9. Esterhuizen, D., Schutte, C., du Toit, A.: Knowledge creation processes as critical enablers for innovation. Int. J. Inf. Manag. **32**, 354–364 (2012)

10. Möller, K., Rajala, A., Svahn, S.: Strategic business nets – their type and management. J. Bus. Res. **58**, 1274–1284 (2005)

11. Dasgupta, M., Gupta, R.: Innovation organizations: a review of the role of organizational learning and knowledge management. Glob. Bus. Rev. **10**(2), 203–224 (2009)

12. Sherer, S.: Critical success factors for manufacturing networks as perceived by network coordinators. J. Small Bus. Manag. **41**(4), 325–345 (2003)

13. Halme, M., Fadeeva, Z.: Small and medium-sized tourism enterprises in sustainable development networks. Greener Manag. Int. **30**, 97–113 (2001)

14. Thorgren, S., Wincent, J., Örtqvist, D.: Designing interorganizational networks for innovation: an empirical examination of network configuration, formation and governance. J. Eng. Technol. Manag. **26**(3), 148–166 (2009)

15. Ahlström-Söderling, R.: SME strategic business networks seen as learning organizations. J. Small Bus. Enterp. Dev. **10**(4), 444–454 (2003)

16. Hanna, V., Walsh, K.: Small firm networks: a successful approach to innovation? R&D Manag. **32**(3), 201–207 (2002)

17. Wincent, J.: An exchange approach on firm cooperative orientation and outcomes of strategic multilateral network participants. Group Organ. Manag. **33**(3), 303–329 (2008)

18. Fuller-Love, N., Thomas, E.: Networks in small manufacturing firms. J. Small Bus. Enterp. Dev. **11**(2), 244–253 (2004)

19. Huggins, R.: The success and failure of policy-implemented inter-firm network initiatives: motivations, processes and structure. Entrep. Reg. Dev. **12**, 111–135 (2000)

20. Facó, J.F.B., Csillag, J.M.: Innovativeness of industry considering organizational slack and co-operation 109. J. Oper. Supply Chain Manag. **3**(2), 108–120 (2010)

The Identification of the Professional Profile that Uses Canvas Approach

Irapuan Glória Júnior[1,2(✉)] and Rodrigo Franco Gonçalves[1]

[1] Paulista University, São Paulo, Brazil
ijunior@nsdgn.com.br
[2] Centro Paula Souza, São Paulo, Brazil

Abstract. This paper shows the study of the canvas approach to the profiles of team members. It has a qualitative character. The objective is to identification the professional profile that uses the canvas approach. The results relate 12 Canvas Models and its interaction with 6 consulted professional profiles. The main contribution is the identification of relations between the use of the tools and professional profiles. However, the sequence of use idealized by the Canvas creators is not followed by the professional in practice.

Keywords: Canvas · Business model canvas · Profile · Project model canvas

1 Introduction

The large number of projects that fail is great, often caused by the lack of an adequate approach to development [1]. There are several frameworks available in the market, but have many stages in its development cycle and the creation of various documents [2].

Some professional choose to use a faster alternative with graphical approaches and the use of post-it, called Canvas approach. This concept can help to speed up the process of creation by the development team of a new business [3], a new project [4] or until the creation of a digital game [5].

There are a considerable number of types of Canvas and the initial use in design applications has grown systematically, with several examples in the market and in academy [6]. It is possible to find applications in various types of projects, such as helping of SME [7].

The objective of this paper is to identification the professional profile that uses the "Canvas approach". Thus, can contribution to the evaluation of the companies if the adopt is possible an Canvas approach, can decrease the time learning and to show criterious for to hire members to form the "Canvas Model Team".

I. Nääs et al. (Eds.): APMS 2016, IFIP AICT 488, pp. 544–551, 2016.
DOI: 10.1007/978-3-319-51133-7_65

2   Theoretical Background

2.1   Model Canvas

Canvas has graphical approach, used annotations or post-its and containers to receive the informations [3]. It is used as process register instrument and create the reuse of information from one project to another [6].

The nomenclature of this technique can be found as "Canvas Approach", "Canvas Model", "Canvas" or "tool" that, without questioning the origin of the word and per simplification, will be used of the term "Canvas".

In this paper presented the main existing approaches Canvas, based answers for respondents, as shown in Table 1. In literature is possible can "Canvas" which can be grouped according to their functions:

– **Project Management.** The models are according to management of business practices of project and their strategies. Its main containers: project scope [3,4,8], stakeholders [4,8,9], risks [4,8,9], costs [3,4,10], strategies [10], value aggregate [11], proposed value [12], customer relationships [3] and process [4,9,12];
– **Innovation.** The models found are directed to innovation products or services. Have containers: alternate solutions [13], costumer relationship [14], costs [13], strategies [14] and customer segmentation [13];
– **Carrier.** The model addresses the development of professional items. Its based in "Business Model Canvas" [3], but with focus in persons. Your containers are: "who will help", costs and "what I win"[15];
– **Games.** The models have objective to development digital games. It has containers: gamer actions, sceneries, target public, behaviours of personages, costs [5,16] and game mechanics [16].

Thus, the various Canvas can help professionals to prepare their projects, careers and new products or services.

2.2   Profile of Team Members

The characteristics of a staff member are called "profile" [18], which can be divided into [2]: (1) hard skill, corresponding to technical aspects; and (2) soft skill, referring to interpersonal and intrapersonal behavior. Another aspects may be considered as temperament, gender [19], expansiveness [19], team spirit and cooperation among team member [18].

The Profile must be directly linked to role played by each professional in the project that will actuate and can impact the performance of the team and the success of the project [2,18].

3   Methodology

The definition of the ontological and epistemological guidelines helps to understand the assumptions and analysis of the items that make up the search [20].

Table 1. Canvas Model

Canvas	Description	Authors
Business Model Canvas (BMC)	It is the creation of a business model	Osterwalder and Pigneur [3]
Project Model Canvas (PMC)	Prioritize planning and control of project execution, based on the Project Management Body of Knowledge	Finocchio Jr. [4]
Value Proposition Canvas (VPC)	Value creation and submission pf the proposal to the client. It is an extension of BMC	Osterwalder et al. [11]
Kickoff Canvas (KC)	Presents the information for the project opening meeting	Kalbach [8]
Business Model You (BMY)	It is directed to professional career. Based on BMC	Osterwalder [15]
Game Model Canvas (GMC)	Aspects of the development of digital games	DRECON [5]
Startup Canvas (SC)	It is similar to a business plan and has the main items to business creation and customer acquisition	MethodKit [14]
Lean Canvas (LC)	It has focus to the startups which combines product concepts and market to generate innovation. The author suggests using the BMC after completing this Canvas	LeanStack [13]
Process Model Canvas (PrMC)	The key activities within a project and presents the link between strategic management and operational	Bijl and Ruting [12]
Program Model Canvas (ProgMC)	Designed to project managers and project management offices (PMO) to assist the development phase of definitions and planning of the project sets. There is compliance with the BMC and PMC	Sales et al. [9]
The Customer Journey Canvas (CJC)	It has aimed to map the different actions of consumers of services	Stickdorn and Schneider [17]
Portfólio Model Canvas (PtMC)	Allows to inventory the organization's projects, create their prioritizations according to the strategic objectives and resource constraints. There are adherence to PMC	Finocchio Jr. [10]

Ontology was objective, where reality exists independent of the researcher's knowledge [21]. The epistemology is interpretativist when it assumes that the data collected by the researcher can be used to test hypothesis or theories earlier. It has qualitative approach [22].

The flow of processes performed in this study follows the following order:

(1) **Sending electronic survey.** Have been sent a semi-structured electronic questionnaire [23] in Google Forms environment (drive.google.com) to groups of IT managers of Yahoo Groups (www.yahoogroups.com) and to social networks like Facebook (www.facebook.com) and LinkedIn (www.linkedin.com);

(2) **Filtering the replies.** It was only considered the respondents who mentioned that already using a Canvas;

(3) **Standardization of answers.** The role mentioned were standardized according the their functions;

(4) **Analysis of profiles.** It conducted a qualitative analysis of the collected items, without the study of frequencies [24].

3.1 Collect

The electronic questionnaire was sent to the group of IT managers of Yahoo Groups (7,917 contacts), for Facebook (666 contacts) and LikedIn (1,415 contacts) with profiles different, totaling 9,998 contacts.

There were 65 respondents. When removing the blank responses resulted in 63 valid. In this paper we considered the respondents indicated that they worked or work with some Canvas resulting 43 responses.

Regarding the respondents roles was identified: Project Manager, Professors, Researchers, IT Students, Software Developer and IT Analyst. In this research were those who acted as project managers, even taking office as "Project Manager", "Administrator Department", "Engineer", "Process Analyst", "Business Analyst" or "Senior Systems Analyst", labeled "Project Manager". Another functions ware maintained.

3.2 Propositions

This research considered the following propositions and justifications:

– **Proposition 1: There are a pattern between function exercised a team member and the use of Canvas.** The Canvas are targeted to specific types of professionals, as managers [3,4,8], innovator [14] and others;

– **Proposition 2: Professionals use in their activities the Canvas following suggested by the creators.** There are Canvas to be applied on sequence, such as BMC and VPM [3] or the PMC and PtMC [4].

4   Analysis of the Result

Considering the information from the questionnaires were collected by function showed: 67% of Project Managements, 12% of IT Analyst, 7% Professor, 7% IT Student, Software Developer 5% and 2% Researcher. The profile and analysis of the collected data, as shown in Table 2, are:

- **Project Manager.** Was identified that the PMC is used by 62% of respondents and 58% using the BMC. Only 38% use BMC and PMC together. Those who use only the BMC correspond to 21%. All those using the PMC also use another tool. When used the BMC not used GMC, PrMC, PgMC and CJC. None of the respondents in this group use GMC;
- **IT Analyst.** 80% used BMC. Those who used BMC also applies LC (40%) and GMC (20%). Respondents who used VPC and PrMC not used BMC. None used the PMC, KC, BMY, SC, PgMC, CJC e PtMC;
- **Professor.** All use the BMG. All use the BMG. It was possible to identify a group that used only the BMC (67%) and another group (33%) using various tools together as VPC and PMC. Professors belong to different educational institutions;
- **IT Student.** All Student IT used BMC and no other tool. The students are from different educational institutions.
- **Software Developer.** It was possible to identify that 50% used the GMC. The other 50% was used BMC. In all cases only a Canvas was used;
- **Researchers.** All said they use only BMG. There was no use of any other Canvas.

Table 2. Profiles and Canvas

Profile	Identifications
Project manager	- 62% use the PMC
	- 58% used BMC
	- 38% used BMC+PMC
	- 21% used PMC e outro Canvas
	- The BMC was not used with GMC, PrMC, PgMC and CJC
	- 0% used GMC
Analyst IT	- 80% use BMC
	- 40% used BMC and LC
	- 20% used BMC and GMC
	- 0% used PMC, KC, BMY, SC, PgMC, CJC and PtMC.
Professor	- 100% use BMC
	- 33% used in conjunction other tool
IT student	- 100% used only BMC
Software developer	- Just one Canvas used at a time
	- Canvas used BMC or GMC
Research	- 100% used only BMC

4.1 Discussion

In relation a behavior of use with Canvas of Project Managers, the BMC conceptualizes the rules and business details to be created and the PMC has plans to implement the project. Is possible that the BMC and PMC are presents as the project management tools, but this union was explicit in only a small percentage (38%). Despite the great use PMC (62%) of managers, the number should be higher, because the PMC is directed to project management. The fact not use GMC may indicate that they do not know or that the project is not to development a digital game.

IT Analyst e Software Developer mentioned apply the BMC, but unaware the PMC. The BMC is related to management and not with the program creating or codification. This point the PMC was expected for these profiles, but which was not presented as fact. The GMC was mentioned by the Software Developer which could indicate that one game has been developed.

Professors have experience in BMC and some other Canvas. This may be the reason of Students have only applied the BMC in their daily lives.

Another point that was expected several types of Canvas was used by Researchers, but was mentioned only the BMC. Due to the role of seekers of knowledge, was expected a large number of tools used. In this way they could get the most out of this type of approach.

Propositions created were compared with the results obtained during the research:

- **Proposition 1: There are a pattern between function exercised a team member and the use of Canvas.** It was possible to identify certain profiles determined using Canvas, such as Research, Professor and IT Student using BMC. Other profiles, as Project Manager, using more than two types;
- **Proposition 2: Professionals use in their activities the Canvas following suggested by the creators.** The research has shown the use of the Canvas did not follow the determination of creators. Is possible verify that the Project Manager uses the BMC and PMC that are of different authors and do not suggest a sequence in the application. Regarding IT Analyst were identified 10 types with different creators.

Regarding Proposition 1 research has shown that it is true, because it was possible to identify the Canvas according to the profile. Proposition 2 is false, because professionals do not follow the suggested sequence by the creators of the Canvas.

5 Conclusion

The canvas approach is a graphical alternative to the realization of planning. There are several types designed according to your goal as design, innovation, process or professional career. The profile of a member of team meets the technical and behavioral characteristics of the individual.

This paper presented 12 Canvas used by respondents, as the Business Model Canvas (BMC) and Project Model Canvas (PMC), the analysis of the type used by Project Manager, IT Analyst, Professors, Students, Software Developer and Researchers and showed interactions of profiles with Canvas.

The contribution to the academy is to present that there are relations between the use of the tools and professional profiles. However, the sequence of use idealized by the Canvas creators is not used by the professionals in practice. Regarding the practice, the results obtained can assist managers to choose the adequate Canvas Model, based on the profile of their team, indicating which tools are most popular and which can help to reduce the learning curve of the team members. The suggestion for future works is to study the barriers and challenges to the use of Canvas approach.

Acknowledgements. The authors thank CAPES for their support for the development of this research.

References

1. Sauser, B., Reilly, R., Shenhar, A.: Why projects fail? How contingency theory can provide new insights–a comparative analysis of NASA's Mars climate orbiter loss. Int. J. Proj. Manag. **27**(7), 665–679 (2009)
2. PMI: Project Management Body of Knowledge Guide. Four Campus Boulevard, Pensilvânia (2012)
3. Osterwalder, A., Pigneur, Y.: Business Model Generation (2009). http://businessmodelgeneration.com/canvas/bmc
4. Finocchio Jr., J.: Project Model Canvas: Gerenciamento de Projetos sem Burocracia. Elsevier, Brasil (2014)
5. DRECON: Game Model Canvas (2015). www.drecon.com.br/GMC/Game_Model_Canvas_1_0_0.pdf
6. Neves, A.: Design Thinking Canvas (2014). www.designthinkingcanvas.com.br
7. Frick, J., Ali, M.M.: Business model canvas as tool for SME. In: Prabhu, V., Taisch, M., Kiritsis, D. (eds.) APMS 2013. IAICT, vol. 415, pp. 142–149. Springer, Heidelberg (2013). doi:10.1007/978-3-642-41263-9_18
8. Wideman, M.: Project Kick-off Canvas (2012). http://calleam.com/?p=1209
9. Sales, L., Arrivabene, A., Prudencio, A.: Program Model Canvas (2015). www.programmodelcanvas.com.br
10. Finocchio Jr., J.: Portfólio Model Canvas (2015). http://www.pmcanvas.com.br
11. Osterwalder, A., Pigneur, Y., Bernarda, G., Smith, A.: Value Proposition Design (2014). https://strategyzer.com/value-proposition-design
12. Bijl, M., Ruting, D.: Process Model Canvas (2015). www.processmodelcanvas.net. Visited 02 Apr 2015
13. LeanStack: Lean Canvas (2015). www.leanstack.com
14. MethodKit: Startup Canvas (2015). www.methodkit.com
15. Osterwalder, A.: Business Model You (2012). www.businessmodelyou.com
16. Jimémez, S.: Gamification Model Canvas (2015). www.gameonlab.com/canvas
17. Stickdorn, M., Schneider, J.: The Customer Journey Canvas (2015). http://filesthisisservicedesignthinKING.com/tisdt_cujoca_portugese.pdf

18. IPMA: ICB-IPMA Competence Baseline, 3rd Version edn. International Project Management Association (2006)
19. Stawnicza, O.: Information and communication technologies–creating oneness in globally distributed IT project teams. Procedia Technol. **16**, 1057–1064 (2014)
20. Sarker, S., Xiao, X., Beaulieu, T.: Toward an anatomy of "successful" qualitative research manuscripts in IS: a critical review and some recommendations (2012)
21. Saccol, A.Z.: Um Retorno ao Básico: Compreendendo os Paradigmas de Pesquisa e sua Aplicação na Pesquisa em Administração. Revista de Administração da UFSM **2**(2), 250–269 (2009)
22. Walsham, G.: Doing interpretive research. Eur. J. Inf. Syst. **15**(3), 320–330 (2006)
23. Singh, K.: Quantitative Social Research Methods. Sage, Thousand Oaks (2007)
24. Yin, R.K.: Case Study Research: Design and Methods. Sage Publications, Thousand Oaks (2013)

Sustainable Development Within Enterprise Architecture

Daniel F.R. Alves, Renato de Campos$^{(\boxtimes)}$, and Fernando B. Souza

São Paulo State University, São Paulo, Brazil
danielfrancora@gmail.com, {rcampos,fbernardi}@feb.unesp.br

Abstract. Enterprises are looking for improvements in their processes, products and services, causing them to become more complex mainly due to the amount of information and requirements involved. At same time, governments and costumers are more conscious about Sustainable Development requirements. Enterprise Architectures supports the analysis, simulation, automated systems projects, distribution of responsibilities and authorities, aimed at reengineering or improvement of companies processes. However, they do not seem to contemplate the requirements related to Sustainable Development in a systemic and integrated way. This paper discusses the derivation and incorporation of Sustainable Development requirements into Enterprise Architecture Frameworks (EAF). Then, this works presents some initial guidelines to extend components of GERAM with ISO standards and frameworks related to sustainability.

Keywords: Sustainable development · Enterprise architecture · ISO · GERAM

1 Introduction

One way to better analyze, design and integrate enterprise process activities as well as provide support for decision making during production management is to use enterprise models. In other words, enterprise modeling can provide support to the entire life cycle in developing company systems from the definition of enterprise strategies and requirements to design and implementation of the systems [1]. There are several Enterprise Architecture Frameworks (EAF) for Enterprise Engineering, such as PERA (Purdue enterprise architecture framework), CIMOSA (Open system architecture for computer integrated manufacturing), ARIS (Architecture for information system), and TOGAF (The open group enterprise architecture framework). Although neither of them explicitly and systematically consider in a systemic and integrated way the requirements Sustainable Development (SD).

Enterprises use some methods to reach the SD using standards and systems, such as ISO 9001, ISO 14001, and ISO 26000 to achieve the economic, environmental and social requirements of SD. Nevertheless, it seems to be necessary

© IFIP International Federation for Information Processing 2016
Published by Springer International Publishing AG 2016. All Rights Reserved
I. Nääs et al. (Eds.): APMS 2016, IFIP AICT 488, pp. 552–559, 2016.
DOI: 10.1007/978-3-319-51133-7_66

consider the SD requirements into an EAF in a more explicit and systematic way, helping the companies to build their sustainable model.

Thus, this article aims to investigate the support of SD requirements by an EAF and its components. It is discussed the derivation and incorporation of Sustainable Development (SD) requirements into Enterprise Architecture Frameworks (EAF), and is presented some initial guidelines to extend components of GERAM (as GERA) with ISO standards and frameworks related to sustainability.

To accomplish these proposal, this research made a literature review of all important topics, creating through that a conceptual framework with connections between multiple bodies of literature and knowledge bases to make our proposal [2,3].

In that sense, searches were carried out at scientific databases such as Web of Science, Scopus, Springer Link, John Wiley & Sons, Google Scholar, Web of Knowledge and IEEE Xplore, using as keywords the terms: Enterprise Integration, Enterprise Engineering, GERAM, Enterprise Architecture, Sustainable Development, Enterprise Architecture Frameworks, ISO 9001, ISO 14001, ISO 26000 and GRI (Global Reporting Initiative). All of them performed using the default search engine for each data-base without any customization on the search engines, selecting the results through the reading of their abstracts.

Section 2 of this paper presents a literature review of standards and frameworks related to Sustainability, followed by Sect. 3 with a review about Enterprise Architecture Frameworks. In Sect. 4 it is developed a cross analysis of standards and frameworks with components of an enterprise architecture and requirements for sustainable development. Then, guidelines are described to extend components of GERAM with ISO standards and frameworks related to sustainability. Section 5 concludes this paper, by presenting the main results of this research and by discussing topics for future study.

2   Standards and Frameworks for Sustainability

The standards ISO 9001, ISO 14001 and ISO 26000 have been proposed to adopt SD and they became important for enterprises seeking Sustainable Development (SD) commitment [4–6]. ISO Standards such as ISO 9001, ISO 14001 and ISO 26000 became a source of technological knowledge in the economic, environmental and social dimensions, respectively [7].

ISO 9001:2000 covers quality, customer satisfaction, reduction of waste and customer complaints, standardization of work processes and communication improvement as well as an increase in market share. ISO 9001:2000 is based on a review of the twenty clauses of ISO 9001:1994, resulting in five key management requirements [8]. ISO 14000 include aspects of quality and the environment, mitigating the emission of effluents, reducing the environmental impact by improving customer satisfaction [7]. ISO 14000 consists of seventeen clauses divided into five categories. Each clause was written to suit a wide variety of enterprises [5,9]. ISO 26000, unlike ISO 14001 and ISO 9001, this standard provides guidelines rather than requirements, so it cannot be certified [4,10].

The standard considers that the enterprise has responsibility for the impacts of its decisions and activities on society and the environment. Thus it must be transparent and ethical, in order to contribute to the SD, health and well-being of society. The structure of ISO 26000 consists of seven clauses [11].

Following these efforts, the GRI framework emerges with guidelines that consist of recommendations, principles, and a standardized report helping enterprises in how to report their commitment with SD [12]. It was created as a common reporting framework covering the entire organization. The GRI specifies directives in which organizations report their performance based on SD indicators related to economic, social and environmental aspects [12,13]. The GRI Reporting Framework contains general and sector-specific content that has been agreed upon by a wide range of stakeholders around the world to be generally applicable for reporting an enterprise's SD performance [12].

Actually EAF do not fully support the implementation of ISO Standards and GRI, and it is the responsibility of the enterprise itself to create the full scope and controls to deal with it.

3   Enterprise Engineering with GERAM

Enterprise modeling is considered the principal item of Enterprise Engineering, because the modeling process creates a model that represents all (or part of) enterprise operations. This model allows simulations and evaluations that conducts the enterprise operation to an optimized structure, behavior, and content [14,15]. Reference Architectures for modeling and engineering enterprises aim to provide a 'map' with which is possible to design business processes and other systems of a company [16,17].

Enterprise Architecture Frameworks (EAF) are intellectual paradigms which facilitate the analysis, discussion and specification of a given area, providing a base and a way to understand, design, and discuss a matter [18]. The main goal of an EAF is to define and implement enterprise strategies, being a guide to its evolution, balancing all needs and limitations to achieve an acceptable and feasible project [19,20]. Several EAF were proposed such as CIMOSA, ARIS, TOGAF, PERA and GERAM.

GERAM (Generalized Enterprise Reference Architecture and Methodology) uses the best parts of GRAI-GIM (Graphs with results and activities interrelated), PERA and CIMOSA architectures to provide a reference to the enterprise integration area. GERAM provides a description of all components recommended for an Enterprise Engineering and a collection of tools and methods to perform enterprise design and changes with success. It also considers enterprise models as an essential approach to support EE and integration [21–24].

GERAM has nine main components. The most important component is the Generic Reference Architecture – GERA, which defines a set of concepts to be used in Enterprise Engineering, as enterprise entities, life cycle, life histories of enterprise entities, and others (see Fig. 1 adapted of IFIP/IFAC [21] with a new view proposed in this work).

GERAM defines again as components the Enterprise Engineering Methodologies (EEM), and distinguishes them from Enterprise Modeling Languages (EML) used by the methodology to describe aspects of the enterprise, like the structure, content, and behavior of the entities to be modeled. The modeling language semantics may be defined by anthologies, meta-models and glossaries that are collectively called Generic Enterprise Modeling Concepts (GEMC). Partial Enterprise Models (PEM), which are reusable models of human roles, processes and technologies, are used to facilitate modeling. Enterprise Engineering Tools (EET) supports the methodologies and languages used for enterprise modeling. The modeling process results in particular Enterprise Models (EM) that represent all or part of the enterprise's operations (manufacturing or services tasks), its organization and management, and its control and information systems. These models can be transformed into an Enterprise Operational System (EOS), or be used to perform simulations, and to promote changes in the enterprise. The EOS is a set of enterprise modules (EMO) that support the operational use of enterprise models. EMO provide prefabricated products like human skills, common business procedures or IT infrastructure services, used as components in implementation of the EOS [21].

Users of other reference architectures can use GERAM as a benchmark, and identify what to expect from the particular architecture chosen, when their features are compared [22, 25].

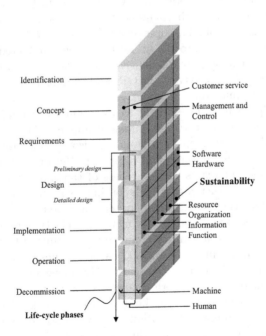

Fig. 1. Proposal for extending GERA with a sustainability view. (Source: adapted of [21]).

The component GERA recommends the modeling of the enterprise according to four basic and complementary viewpoints (other views can be defined) (see GERA adapted in Fig. 1):

- Function view, which represents the functionality and behavior of the company (i.e., events, activities and processes) including temporal and management of exception aspects;
- Information view, which represents the objects of the enterprise and its information elements;
- Resources view, which represents the means of the enterprise, its capabilities and management;
- Organization view, which represents organizational levels, authorities and responsibilities.

Despite its comprehensive support to enterprise common aspects, a few requirements related to SD are explicitly supported by GERA originally.

4   Analysis and Discussion

With the objective of analysis and integrate sustainability requirements into Enterprise Architectures, based on literature review done in Sects. 2 and 3, it was possible evaluate intersections of covered concepts by a cross analysis of standards and frameworks with components of an enterprise architecture and requirements for sustainable development (Table 1). It was built and structured with a Likert scale according to the literature review conducted by the authors to demonstrate the existing comprehensive relationships between the concepts presented by the ISO standards and the GRI and its agreements with the requirements needed by SD and components of a EAF.

ISO 9001 helps companies seeking to maintain their image while serving customers concerned about the environmental impacts the production of their products causes the environment. The standard also provides guidelines on developing, implementing, maintaining and improving the quality of organizational processes. ISO 14001 increases the awareness of the enterprise and its involvement in environmental practices through continuous improvement processes and programs related to the management system provided by the standard. ISO 14001 has been used as an important factor in selecting potential suppliers, because it requires the entire supply chain to be committed to SD by acquiring and producing green products. ISO 26000 has guidelines to implemented social requirements, then, the enterprise can reach a given level of social responsibility.

GRI report, one of the main performance indicators for evaluating the enterprise's SD commitment today can be used to create guidelines within the GERAM structure, helping the creation and evaluation of SD indicators during the enterprise's operation. With this, a SD perspective can easily analyze all the enterprise process and products involved. Furthermore, reporting all the efforts done to achieve the SD commitment to costumers, governments and stakeholders.

GERAM was proposed for analyzing and developing the extensions to integrate SD requirements due the fact that all Enterprise Architecture can be assessed and broken down according to GERAM structure [21,23,24].

The cross analysis of the Table 1 shows gaps and opportunities to incorporate sustainability into components of an enterprise architecture.

GERAM components touch various aspects of SD requirements with different perceptions and abstractions. The economic aspect is addressed by GERAM [21]; however it focuses on investment, different from SD, which encompasses society as part of the economic dimension. As for the social aspect, the architecture considers only workers' care while conducting their technical work, which covers their skills to perform the function and show the result of that work (i.e. the product or service they transform). The environmental aspect is minimally addressed by GERAM architecture. Nonetheless, it is possible to complement GERAM economic, social and environmental aspects in order to reconcile with the requirements of SD.

Table 1. Analysis of intersections of covered concepts.

Techniques, Systems, Tools	Sustainable Development			Components of an Enterprise Architecture Framework			
	Economic	Environ-mental	Social	Enterprise Architectures	Metho-dologies	Partial Models	Modeling Languages
ISO 9001	5	2	1	3	4	5	2
ISO 14001	3	5	2	3	4	5	2
ISO 26000	2	2	5	3	4	5	2
GRI	5	5	5	2	5	3	2
Legend:	0 – No relation encountered; 1 – Minimal relation; 2 – Weak relation; 3 – Medium relation; 4 – Strong relation; 5 – Very strong relation						

Analyzing Table 1, it is possible to propose improvements in the ability of a EAF (as GERAM) to design enterprises, supporting the goals and requirements of SD based on presented ISO Standards and GRI. Some guidelines are proposed:

- Enterprise Architectures (as GERA) could include a new view of Sustainability in its structure (Fig. 1);
- Enterprise Engineering Methodologies (EEM) could integrate in its phases or steps techniques, practices and tools systems related to ISO standards and frameworks as GRI;
- Some Partial Enterprise Models (PEM) related to sustainability already exists and can be identified in the literature. Thus, these, ISO standards and sustainability
- frameworks could be merged in partial models and be available in Enterprise Engineering Tools (EET) to facilitating particular sustainable Enterprise Models (EM);

– To describing partial or particular model, Enterprise Modeling Languages (EML) need to be extend to express the related sustainability aspects and requirements.

In this work, GERAM is presented as the basis and reference for developing academic or corporate works for extending SD requirements to enterprise modeling and engineering, because these efforts may be mapped in other framework architectures later.

For example, a possible proposal is shown in Fig. 1, with the creation of a new view in GERA named Sustainability, that highlight the need to include concepts of SD, as ISO standards and GRI.

5   Final Considerations

Enterprise architectures, methodologies and tools for Enterprise Engineering must support the integration of various issues to be addressed in an organization, such as its information system, factory layout, logistics systems, quality system, cost, as well as describe human and organizational aspects. However, the available EAFs do not address accordingly all SD requirements adequately in a systemic and integrated way.

This works presents some guidelines to extend components of GERAM with ISO standards and frameworks related to sustainability.

A new modeling view was proposed in GERA. In this sense, when the requirements of ISO Standards are transported to GERA it is possible to align the requirements of SD (i.e., economic, environment and social) with the other components of GERAM.

Maybe, it is not necessary a new view in GERA, but, sustainability aspects should be considered in the others components as EM, PEM, and EML, as discussed. Details of how to integrate these techniques, systems and tools are challenges for future work.

References

1. Vernadat, F.: Enterprise Modeling and Integration: Principles and Applications. Chapman & Hall, London (1996)
2. Callahan, J.L.: Constructing a manuscript: distinguishing integrative literature reviews and conceptual and theory articles. Hum. Resour. Dev. Rev. 9, 300–304 (2010)
3. Yadav, M.S.: The decline of conceptual articles and implications for knowledge development. J. Mark. 74(1), 1–19 (2010)
4. International Organization for Standardization: ISO 26000 - Social Responsibility. http://www.iso.org/iso/home/standards/iso26000.htm
5. MacDonald, J.P.: Strategic sustainable development using the ISO 14001 standard. J. Clean. Prod. 13(6), 631–643 (2005)
6. Oskarsson, K., Von Malmborg, F.: Integrated management systems as a corporate response to sustainable development. Corp. Soc. Responsib. Environ. Manag. 12(3), 121–128 (2005)

7. Steele, R.: Rethinking Rio+ 20 - How ISO Contributes to Sustainable Action. http://www.iso.org/iso/home/news_index/news_archive/news.htm?refid=Ref1519

8. Zeng, S., Tian, P., Tam, C.: Overcoming barriers to sustainable implementation of the ISO 9001 system. Manag. Audit. J. **22**(3), 244–254 (2007)

9. International Organization for Standardization: ISO 14001–1996 - Environmental Management Systems - Specification with Guidance for Use. Distributed through American National Standards Institute (2007)

10. Hahn, R.: ISO 26000 and the standardization of strategic management processes for sustainability and corporate social responsibility. Bus. Strateg. Environ. **22**(7), 442–455 (2013)

11. International Organization for Standardization: ISO 26000–2010 Guidance on Social Responsibility. International Organization for Standardization (2010)

12. Initiative, G.R.: Sustainability Reporting Guidelines. Global Reporting Initiative, Amsterdam (2011)

13. Brown, H.S., de Jong, M., Levy, D.L.: Building institutions based on information disclosure: lessons from GRI's sustainability reporting. J. Clean. Prod. **17**(6), 571–580 (2009)

14. Vernadat, F.B.: Enterprise modeling and integration (EMI): current status and research perspectives. Annu. Rev. Control **26**(1), 15–25 (2002)

15. He, D., Lobov, A., Moctezumas, L.E.G., Lastra, J.L.M.: An approach to use PERA in enterprise modeling for industrial systems. In: IECON 2012–38th Annual Conference on IEEE Industrial Electronics Society, pp. 4196–4203. IEEE (2012)

16. Mertins, K., Jochem, R.: Architectures, methods and tools for enterprise engineering. Int. J. Prod. Econ. **98**(2), 179–188 (2005)

17. Minoli, D.: Enterprise Architecture A to Z: Frameworks, Business Process Modeling, SOA, and Infrastructure Technology. CRC Press, Boca Raton (2008)

18. Vernadat, F.: Interoperable enterprise systems: architectures and methods. IFAC Proc. Vol. **39**(3), 13–20 (2006)

19. Lankhorst, M., Iacob, M.E., Jonkers, H., van der Torre, L., Proper, H., Arbab, F.: Enterprise Architecture at Work: Modeling, Communication, and Analysis. Springer, Berlin (2009)

20. Wegmann, A.: On the systemic enterprise architecture methodology (SEAM). In: Proceedings of 5th International Conference on Enterprise Information Systems, pp. 179–188, no. 483–490. ICEIS (2003)

21. IFIP-IFAC Task Force: GERAM: generalised enterprise reference architecture and methodology. IFIP-IFAC Task Force on Architectures for Enterprise Integration March Version 1.6.3 (1999)

22. Noran, O.: A systematic evaluation of the C4ISR AF using ISO15704 Annex A (GERAM). Comput. Ind. **56**(5), 407–427 (2005)

23. Noran, O.: Building a support framework for enterprise integration. Comput. Ind. **64**(1), 29–40 (2013)

24. Vallejo, C., Romero, D., Molina, A.: Enterprise integration engineering reference framework and toolbox. Int. J. Prod. Res. **50**(6), 1489–1511 (2012)

25. Chaharsooghi, K., Achachlouei, M.A.: Developing life-cycle phases for the DoDAF using ISO15704 Annex A (GERAM). Comput. Ind. **62**(3), 253–259 (2011)

Agrifood Supply Chains

Effects of Price and Transportation Costs in Soybean Trade

João Gilberto Mendes dos Reis[1(✉)], Pedro Amorim[2],
and José António S. Cabral[2]

[1] Postgraduate Studies Program in Production Engineering,
Paulista University, Dr. Bacelar St. 1212, São Paulo, Brazil
betomendesreis@msn.com
[2] Department of Engineering and Industrial Management,
University of Porto, R. Dr. Roberto Frias s/n, Porto, Portugal
{pamorim,jacabral}@fe.up.pt

Abstract. The United States, Brazil, and Argentina are responsible for 83% of world's soybean production. Together, they respond to more than 80% of soybean grains and soybean meal exported and for more than 60% of soybean oil exportation. This paper studies the soybean trade of these three major exporters with the top ten commercial partners of each one in order to examine the main factors that influence this relationship. We follow a network analysis approach to evaluate the level of inter-dependence between exporters and importers. Our research studies the three main soybean products: grain, meal, and oil. The findings seem to indicate that countries prefer importing soybean grains to process inside their borders due to commodity prices and logistics costs.

Keywords: Soybean production · Competitiveness · Logistics impacts · Network relationship

1 Introduction

The major players of soybean production in the world are the United States, Brazil and Argentina. During 2014/15 crop year, they were responsible for 83% of world's production and for 88.9% soybean grain exports [1]. Soybean is traded as whole soybean and through its two derivative products, soybean oil and soybean meal, result from pressing and separating soybeans, a process known as crushing [2]. Around 85% of soybean production is crushed, where soybean meal is processed into animal feed, soy flour and proteins, and soybean oil is refined as edible oil, fat acids, and biodiesel [3]. This market is of large significance as the soybean grain exported by the United States represented in 2014 around US$ 23.8 billion, while in Brazil, in the same year, the value was US$ 23.3 billion [4,5]. Despite these numbers, there are still many issues to be faced by the soybean supply chain to ensure animal and human supply around the world.

© IFIP International Federation for Information Processing 2016
Published by Springer International Publishing AG 2016. All Rights Reserved
I. Nääs et al. (Eds.): APMS 2016, IFIP AICT 488, pp. 563–570, 2016.
DOI: 10.1007/978-3-319-51133-7_67

These issues are related to the agricultural inputs, production, logistics, environment and relationship among players. Cavalett and Ortega, for instance, argue that soybean production uses high amount of resources and for this reason the managers should adopt sustainable production for the long term environmental sustainability of this chain [6]. Denicoff et al. point out that transportation is an essential part of the soybean supply chain and the soybean growers depend on an efficient transportation system to move their crops and bring inputs such as fertilizer and seeds [7].

Several studies have realized the complexity of soybean supply chains to indicate ways of to improve seed characteristics, production, and marketing, and logistics costs [8–12]. However, these studies fail to understand the complexity of the partners relations in this network and its influence in decision making.

The aims of this paper are to analyze the soybean trade flows of the three major exporters with the top ten commercial partners of each one and to examine the main factors that influence this relationship. To that end, we studied the volume of transactions of soybean grain, soybean meal and soybean oil among them using network analysis, with the assistance of UCINET ©software.

The paper is organized as follows. After this introduction, the second section presents the methodology. In the third section, we address the results and discussion, and in the final section, the conclusion and outlook of this study are presented.

2 Methodology

To examine the trade flows of the three major exports we use the following methodology, which is divided into five steps:

1. **First:** We mapped the soybean supply chain to understand the process, products and foreign markets using knowledge available in the literature.
2. **Second:** We identified the main products commercialized by soybean trade companies and processing industries in the international market. These products are grains, soybean meal, and soybean oil.
3. **Third:** We use the report "Oilseeds: World Market and Trade" of the United States Agriculture Department [1] to identify the major countries exporters of grains, soybean meal and oil and we selected the three major as individual countries. The reference was the 2014/15 crop year.
4. **Four:** We collected data about the exportations for these countries using as reference 2014, last year with real data of exportations available. The data were collected by the Foreign Agriculture Service of United States Department of Agriculture [4], the System of Analysis of the Foreign Trade Information of Ministry of Development, Industry and Foreign Trade of Brazil (MDIC) [13], and Statistical Annuary 2014 of the Rosario Board of Trade in Argentina [14]. We focus on our study on the ten major destinations of exports from Argentina, Brazil and United States.
5. **Fifth:** We organized the data of soybean trade between countries in groups of trade: Soybean total, Soybean grain, Soybean meal and Soybean oil. To perform the analysis, we use the software UCINET 6.0. According to

Kim et al. [15] "UCINET is a comprehensive software for analysis of social network data, which is the most widely accept as social network analysis (SNA) tool for conducting a structural analysis of inter-organizational networks". In this case, we adopt the countries as organizations, and quantity of exportation as a relation between exporters and importers. Furthermore, the UCINET program was chosen because it contains several networks analysis methods, such as centrality measures, subgroup identification, elementary graph analysis [15].

3   Results and Discussion

The major products of the soybean supply chain are grains, soybean meal, and oil. It is important to reiterate that, the United States, Brazil, and Argentina divide the first three places as major exporters for these kinds of products. Considering data provided by the United States Department of Agriculture [1] to the 2014/15 crop year, they have responded to 88.3% of soybean grains exportation, 68% of soybean meal exportation, and 85.9% of soybean oil exportation. Brazil and the United States compete for the first place in soybean grain exports, in this case, Brazil exported 50,612 million metric tons (MT) face of the United States who exported 50,169 million metric tons, while Argentina is the major export of soybean meal and oil. According to Schnepf et al. [16] this situation occurs due to the decision of the Argentine government, in the 1990s, of aggregating value to the soybean supply chain exportations, selling processed soybean, once it could not compete with Brazil and the United States in the soybean grain market. Note that the major top importers from Argentina, except China, all those are peripheral markets neither served by Brazil and nor the United States.

3.1   Soybean Trade

First of all, our work analyzed the soybean supply chain market as a whole. To that end, we sum the exportations of soybean grains, soybean meal and soybean oil of the top ten major destinations from the United States, Brazil, and Argentina. We plotted a network using Netdraw module of UCINET software and the results can be seen in Fig. 1.

The blue nodes represent the three major exporter countries, green nodes American countries, red nodes European countries, gray nodes Asian countries, yellow nodes African and Middle East countries. The major importer of these three countries is China that imports 53% of these total soybean products sent from the United States, Brazil, and Argentina. The network highlights the intensity of this relation through the line strength. China is the main actor in the network creating the hypothesis that it possesses a high centrality in this network. This hypothesis will be verified in further study.

We could identify that Argentina responds for secondary markets, such as Colombia, Peru, Poland, and Venezuela, except China. While Brazil is responsible for several important markets such as Germany, Japan, Netherlands, Spain,

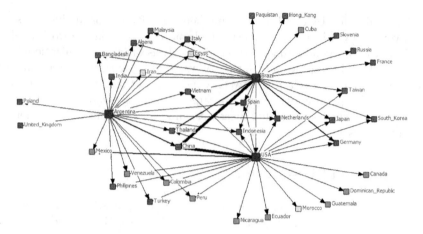

Fig. 1. Soybean supply chain export market to the three major players (Color figure online)

Taiwan, and the United States competes with Brazil in these markets and attend secondary markets in America, such as Canada, Guatemala, Mexico, and Nicaragua.

Our study allows concluding that after China, the secondary important relations of Argentina, Brazil, and the United States are: Germany, Netherlands and Thailand. Therefore, further analysis will need to understand how the network reacts considering these markets together with China.

3.2   Soybean Trade by Product

In order to further understand the market of the soybean supply chain, we divide our analysis by product as it can be seen on the following networks (Figs. 2, 3, 4).

When we analyze Fig. 2 is possible to conclude that China alone is the major importer of soybean grain. When we compare in numbers the three major export players sent to China in 2014 around 73.6% of its grains exported to the top ten major importers. About 75% of Chinese soybean demand is supplied by these countries [2]. This situation probably will not change, once China's arable lands and water supply in the main soybean production zone are rapidly diminishing [2]. China's increasing dependence on imported soybean is not only a result of its reduced capacity to produce soybeans, but also its increasing demand. The country is the most populous and the rising population purchasing power include more soy products in their diet, such as edible oil and demand for meat that is fed with soybean meal [2]. The graphic analyzed allow also conclude that Brazil exports to European countries and the Asian market, the United States competes with Brazil and export grains to South Korea, while Argentina, beyond the China, sell to peripheral markets, such as Bangladesh, Colombia, and Venezuela.

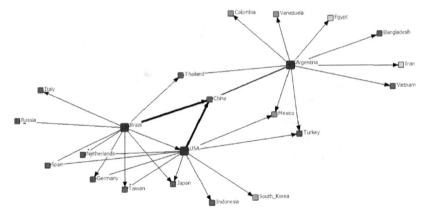

Fig. 2. Soybean grains export market to the three major players

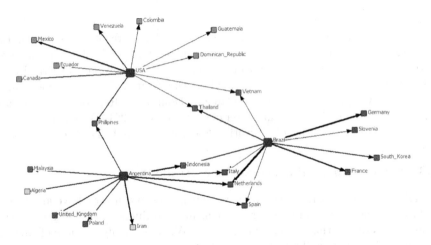

Fig. 3. Soybean meal export market of the three major players

When we analyze Fig. 3 is possible to observe that in soybean meal China does not appear as a top importer. The country prefers buying grains and aggregate value in Chinese soil because it has a developed industry in this area. The Chinese issue is the demand that is huge due to its population. We can observe that Thailand and Vietnam are a common market between Brazil and the United States, while Italy, the Netherlands, and Spain are common between Brazil and Argentina. The United States, in general, attends the near markets in Latin America, and Canada. Argentina appears with more strength in this case selling its soybean meal to Malaysia, Poland, the United Kingdom, for example. Brazil exports the soybean meal most to Europe.

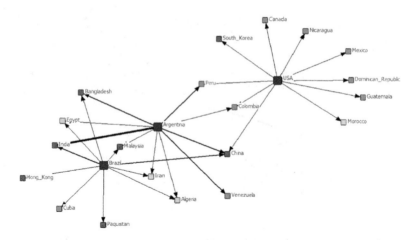

Fig. 4. Soybean oil export market of the three major players

Finally, when we analyze Fig. 4 is clear that Argentina is the major exporter. In numbers, the country is responsible for 63.6% of what the three major exporters send for ten top major importers. Argentina and Brazil compete directly for the same market, while the United States commercializes in secondary markets that include Canada, Dominican Republic, Mexico, and Nicaragua. India is the major importer of soybean oil, in 2014 the country was the major commercial partner of Argentina and Brazil with 43.4% of exportations.

3.3   Factors That Influence Soybean Trade

Countries are searching for competitive advantages and if they have an efficient industry to aggregate value to the agricultural products, they will go buy soybean grains rather than processed products. When we analyze prices of soybean products there is a striking difference. In 2014, for example, the average price of soybean grain FOB according to Chicago Trade Board was US\$ 492.50 to soybean grain ton, US\$ 482.24 to soybean meal ton and US\$ 833.6 to soybean oil ton [14]. Furthermore, the transportation costs influence directly the volume of soybean grains moved around the world. The transportation systems are controlled by trading companies and the high volume ensures transportation cost reduction. Ocean rates from Brazil to Shangai in China reduced from US\$ 42.12 in 2013 to US\$ 37.57 in 2014 [10]. Table 1 compares the transportation costs among the United States, Brazil and Argentina to Shangai in August 2014 [17].

As can be seen in Table 1, Brazil has a slight advantage of the freight rate when to compare Argentina and the United States, however, its internal transportation cost is higher. If we compare the soybean oil with soybean grain and soybean meal, we realize that seen more interesting to buy grain and not soybean oil for the importer countries. Note that soybean meal is a residue of soybean oil extraction, therefore its price is almost the same of grain. Table 2, summarize the

Table 1. Transport costs

	Argentina	Brazil	United States
Cargo mean quantity (ton)	60,000	66,000	56,000
Nautical miles	11,186	11,031	9,977
Total voyage (days)	66.5	65	60
Freight rate per tonnes (US$)	55.06	45.68	56.67

comparison of transportation and commodity cost for the United States (more expensive) to show the difference between soybean grain and oil [14,17].

Table 2. Comparison between soybean grain and soybean oil

	Grain	Oil	Difference
Price (US$)	492.54	833.66	69%
Freight rate per tonnes and m^3 (US$)	56.67	111.58	96%
Total (US$)	549.21	945.24	72%

4   Conclusions and Outlook

In this paper, we used UCINET software to produce the supply network for soybean trade. Our analysis considers the volume of exportation between three major exporters and its top ten major importers. In this research, we focus on analyzing the relationships in the networks considering the size of the player and the strength of relationships through the size of the link between countries. The tools are based on social network analysis and can be pretty useful in the study of enterprises or organization's relationship. As the work is exploratory, we only focus on the graphic network relationship, leaving SNA social network analysis measures for further studies.

Through this analysis, we conclude that commodities and transportation prices are the main factors in soybean trade. The countries prefer to pay less for raw material and afterward process it in own country. The major reasons for that are the low transportation cost between origin port and destinations, and the difference between the price of soybean grain and of soybean oil. However, this work represents only a preliminary attempt to establish such a link.

Soybean is the main product to animal nutrition and has a huge market for the grains and sub products like edible oil for human consumption. Therefore, study the characteristics of this market, process and logistics are essential to creating a supply chain that is more efficient, and without losses and wastes. Furthermore, the next steps of this research will be to conduct a study evaluating the impact of logistics on the competitiveness of the soybean supply chain analyzing the countries involved.

References

1. U.S. Department of Agriculture, Foreign Agriculture Service: Oilseed: world market and trade. Technical report, FAS/USDA (2015)
2. Brown-Lima, C., Cooney, M., Cleary, D.: An overview of the Brazil-China soybean trade and its strategic implications for conservation. Technical report, The Nature Conservancy (2012)
3. Murphy, S., Burch, D., Clapp, J.: Cereal secrets: the world's largest grain traders and global agriculture. Technical report, OXFAM (2012)
4. U.S. Department of Agriculture, Foreign Agriculture Service. http://apps.fas.usda.gov/gats/default.aspx
5. Brazilian Agricultural Research Corporation. https://www.embrapa.br/soja/cultivos/soja1/dados-economicos
6. Cavalett, O., Ortega, E.: Emergy and fair trade assessment of soybean production and processing in Brazil. Manag. Environ. Qual. Int. J. **18**, 657–668 (2007)
7. Denicoff, M., Prater, M.E., Bahizi, P.: Soybean transportation profile. Technical report, U.S. Department of Agriculture, Foreign Agriculture Service (2014)
8. Hossain, Z., Mustafa, G., Sakata, K., Komatsu, S.: Insights into the proteomic response of soybean towards Al2O3, ZnO, and Ag nanoparticles stress. J. Hazard. Mater. **304**, 291–305 (2016)
9. Hasan, N., Suryani, E., Hendrawan, R.: Analysis of soybean production and demand to develop strategic policy of food self sufficiency: a system dynamics framework. In: The Third Information System International Conference, vol. 72, pp. 605–612 (2015)
10. Salin, D.: Soybean transportation guide: Brazil 2014. Technical report, U.S. Department of Agriculture, Foreign Agriculture Service (2015)
11. Zhang, L., Feike, T., Holst, J., Hoffmann, C., Doluschitz, R.: Comparison of energy consumption and economic performance of organic and conventional soybean production: a case study from Jilin Province China. J. Integr. Agric. **14**, 1561–1572 (2015)
12. Chen, W., Marchant, M.A., Muhammad, A.: China's soybean product imports: an analysis of price effects using a production system approach. China Agric. Econ. Rev. **4**, 499–513 (2012)
13. Brazilian Ministry of Development and Foreign Trade. http://aliceweb.desenvolvimento.gov.br/
14. Bolsa de Comercio de Rosario: Statistical annuary. Technical report, Bolsa de Comercio de Rosario (2014)
15. Kim, Y., Choi, T.Y., Yan, T., Dooley, K.: Structural investigation of supply networks: a social network analysis approach. J. Oper. Manag. **29**(3), 194–211 (2011)
16. Schnepf, R.D., Dohlman, E., Bolling, C.: Agriculture in Brazil and Argentina: developments and prospects for major field crops. Technical report, U.S. Department of Agriculture, Economic Research Service (2001)
17. O'Neil, J.: U.S. - South America ocean grain freight spreads. IGP Technical report (2015)

Effects of the Logistics in the Volume of Soybean by Export Corridor of Mato Grosso

Rodrigo Carlo Toloi[1,2(✉)], João Gilberto Mendes dos Reis[1],
Oduvaldo Vendrametto[1], Sivanilza Teixeira Machado[1,3], and Valdir Morales[1]

[1] Paulista University, São Paulo, Brazil
[2] Federal Institute of Mato Grosso Campus Rondonópolis, Rondonópolis, Brazil
rodrigo.toloi@roo.ifmt.edu.br
[3] Federal Institute of São Paulo Campus Suzano, Suzano, Brazil

Abstract. Brazil is one of the biggest producer and exporter of soybean. Its production is basically divided among six main players which Mato Grosso alone responds for 29,3% of total production of the country. The aim of this paper is to investigate the relation between logistics factors and the volume of soybean transported by corridors of exportation. To this end, we develop a multi-linear regression model and tested using data of Mato Grosso state. The results show that low transportation costs per ton, port capacity and increase soybean volume in the corridor of exportation.

Keywords: Transportation cost · Soybean exportation · Multi-linear regression model · SPSS · Brazil

1 Introduction

Brazil is responsible for approximately 40% of the world soybean production [1]. Its production is divided into six main states: Mato Grosso (29,3%), Paraná (18%), Rio Grande do Sul (15,4%), Goiás (9,2), Mato Grosso do Sul (7,4%), and Bahia (4,5%). Mato Grosso is located in the midwest region and it is responsible itself for 27,87 millions of tons of soybean grain [2]. However, despite the excellent productivity of the State and the huge market for Brazil's soybean, the logistics can be considered a challenge for whole supply chain due to their costs [3].

The country has demonstrated logistical shortcomings in its handling of soybean trade, marketing fragility to ensure the efficiency of this export system [4]. Brazil's infrastructure is creaking under the country's rapid economic growth, presenting difficulties for importers and exporters [5]. Transport soybeans overland in Brazil may be up to three times more expensive than in the United States [5,6].

Soybean is a commodity and has its price established internationally, therefore, the producers don't have its price control. Thus, to become competitive, the soybean supply chains needs to be capable of manage effectively the move costs [7].

© IFIP International Federation for Information Processing 2016
Published by Springer International Publishing AG 2016. All Rights Reserved
I. Nääs et al. (Eds.): APMS 2016, IFIP AICT 488, pp. 571–578, 2016.
DOI: 10.1007/978-3-319-51133-7_68

In this context, the aim of this paper is to investigate how logistics factors such as time travel, transportation costs, and port capacity can influence in the volume of soybean exportations by route. To this end, a multi-linear regression was performed using exportation data and costs of the Mato Grosso state.

The paper is organized as follows. After this Introduction, the section two shows the methodology, section three the results, section four the discussion, and finally section five the main conclusions of the work.

2 Methodology

To understand the influence of the logistics in soybean exportations, we choose Mato Grosso state in Brazil for three reasons: (i) Brazil is top three in production and exportation of soybean; (ii) Mato Grosso state is the major producer and exporter of the country; (iii) The large availability of data to conduct the study.

Mato Grosso export soybean for the follow ports: Aracaju (Sergipe), Bacarena (Pará), Ilhéus (Bahia), Imbituba (Santa Catarina), Manaus(Amazon), Paranaguá (Paraná), Rio Grande (Rio Grande do Sul), Salvador (Bahia), Santarém (Pará), Santos (São Paulo), São Francisco do Sul (Santa Catarina), São Luiz(Maranhão), and Vitòria (Espirito Santo). In a previous study, we could analyse the volume to route and use to operational research to propose improvements in soybean exportation corridors of Mato Grosso state [8]. Now, we are trying to comprehend why these current routes are used to move Mato Grosso soybean to exportation.

In this analysis, we opted to use logistics factors related to soybean movement in the transport corridors of Mato Grosso. Therefore, we choose transportation costs per ton, transportation costs by total volume, port capacity to move soybean, and time travel.

This is an exploratory study and by now we used some variables with data available. However, we believe that does not affect the final conclusions because is a preliminary study and other kinds of variables will be used in the future such as modal of transportations available, storage systems, road quality and so on.

To test the hypothesis that the logistics have effect in the volume of soybean per route in Mato Grosso, we used the multi-linear regression analysis [9]. The model was created considering the variables showed in the Eq. (1).

$$X_{ijt} = \alpha + \beta_1 TT_{ij} + \beta_2 CUT_{ij} + \beta_3 CAP_j + \beta_4 CTT_{ijt} \tag{1}$$

Where,

- X_{ijt} is the dependent variable that represents volume of soybean transported between Mato Grosso (i) and a specific port (j) per year (t) between 2005 and 2015;
- TT_{ij} is the independent variable that corresponds to time travel between Mato Grosso (i) and specific Brazilian port among the indicate above (j);
- CUT_{ij} is the independent variable that corresponds to cost of transport per ton in Brazilian monetary;

- CAP_j is the independent variable that corresponds to port capacity;
- CTT_{ijt} is the independent variable that corresponds to the total cost of transportation to move soybean grain between Mato Grosso (i) and a specific port (j) in a year (t).

2.1   Sample

The sample considered in this study were 129 movements of soybean grains between Mato Grosso state and its main ports of exportation during the period from 2005 to 2015.

In our study, we exclude 57 moves because of volume was under 5.000 tons. However, the other 72 transactions corresponding to 99,98% of soybean volume. The source of data can be seen in Table 1

Table 1. Data source

Data	Source
Volume of transportation between Mato Grosso state and Brazilian ports during 2005–2015 period (Xijt)	Aliceweb (Brazilian Government Information System of trades) http://aliceweb.desenvolvimento.gov.br/
Time Travel between Mato Grosso and Brazilian ports (TT)	Mapeia (the site for calculation of distances and time spent on routes) http://www.mapeia.com.br
Unit Cost Transportation in Brazilian reais per ton between Mato Grosso state and Brazilian ports (CUT)	Research applied with logistic carriers in city Rondonopolis, MT Brazil
Port capacity in ton for soybean grain (CAPj)	Aliceweb (Brazilian Government Information System of trades) http://aliceweb.desenvolvimento.gov.br/
Cost total of transport between Mato Grosso and Brazilian ports (CTTijt)	Volume versus CUTij

2.2   Regression Analysis

The regression analysis it is a statistic technique to model and investigate the relation between some variables. One of the regression analysis is to establish a relation that allows predicting one or more variables in terms of others. The study data were processed using the IBM® SPSS® version 22 Software. The SPSS – Statistical Package for the Social Science is a statistic and data software that analyze and offer advanced techniques easily and intuitively to help and get a better efficiency minimizing the risks concerned to statistic and handling from the data.

3   Results

In order to verify the relation between the variables studied we start summarizing the descriptive statistics (Table 2).

Table 2. Descriptive statistics.

V	N	Minimum	Maximum	Average	Std. dev.
TT	72	26.01 h	34.03 h	30.02 h	2.67 h
CUT	72	$ 61.58 ton	$ 77.03 ton	$ 69.30 ton	$ 5.15 ton
X	72	9,681 ton	7,199,622 ton	3,599,815 ton	2,399,871 ton
CAP	72	9,754 ton	384,583 ton	197,168 ton	124,943 ton
CTT	72	$ 0.74*	$ 443.32*	$ 222.03*	$ 147.53*

*Million dollars

In relation to the transport time (TT), they have spent an average to the transport of soybean, 30,02 h [7]. The transport cost per ton (CUT), was defined a medium amount of US$ 69.30 per ton. As the transport time as well as the transport costs per ton can be considered high when compared with the main Brazilian competitor which is the United States that has a cost over 43% less on internal transport and three days less in travel time [6,10].

The port capacity showed a striking difference between the minimum values (9.754 ton) and a maximum of (384.583 ton). It may indicate that there is filler concentration in some ports. The port capacity (CAP) was 197.168 ton. The variable cost total transport (CTT) it has a standard deviation cost of US$ 147.53 million with a media value of US$ 222.03 million, that confirms that the value movement transport in different volumes between ports. Santos and Paranguá ports are responsible together for to transport 45,3% of Brazil's soybean exportation and 66,22% of Mato Grosso soybean [11].

The variables were inserted in the multi-linear regression model using the Stepwise method, to verify which variables could be considered important. The importance of all variables to the Study Model it is resumed on Table 3.

Table 3. Model result

Model	Estimate	Std. error	t	Sig.
(Constant)	708,302.90	135,509.440	5.23	0,000
CTT	0.004	0.000	88.71	0.000
CTU (US$/metric ton)	832.30	139.20	-5.98	0.000
CAP	0.468	0.170	2.83	0.006

a. Variable Dependent: Volume (metric ton)

Observing the significance, it is shown that the volume of soybean transported per route can be explained by the behavior of the variables, Transport Cost per ton and Port Capacity ($p < 0,05$). We conclude that the initial model can be adjusted Eq. (2).

$$X_{ijt} = \alpha - \beta_1 CUT_{ij} + \beta_2 CAP_j + \beta_3 CTT_{ijt} \qquad (2)$$

That replaces the coefficient values has the following relation (Eq. 3).

$$X_{ijt} = 708,302.9 - 832.30CUT + 0.468CAP + 0.004CTT \qquad (3)$$

The independent variables CAP and CTT show a positive coefficient, in other words, they influence positively the transport volume. When the capacity of port increase, it can provokes effect in load flow in the route. However, the CTT presented low influence (0.004), therefore, is not possible conclude its effect in corridor use. Note that has a higher difference between volume per route and this may affect the result (Table 2).

The most important independent variable in our study was CUT. This variable confirms the operational practice from routes with major load volume, where the low price of transportation per ton increase volume (negative signal).

However, it is important to realize that the inverse may occur, where the high volume reduce the freight prices, but this situation needs to confirm statistically in further studies.

The validation of this model and their results can be estimated based on values measure R, that can be visualized on Table 4.

Table 4. Model summary

Model	R	R square	Adj. R square	Std. error	Durbin-Watson
1	0,999a	0,999	0,999	65.939,23	0,448

a. Predictors: (Constant), Total Cost of Transportation, Transport Unit Cost (US/ton), Port Capacity.
b. Dependent Variable: Volume (ton).

Note that R represented the positive value 0,999, thus, the adjustment got close to 1, therefore, the difference is justify through the estimated mistake. In this dependente model the transport and all the variables, independent it was the transport total cost, unitary transport cost, unitary total transport cost, unitary total transport cost from the Port. The proposed R model explains the dependent variables volume (ton) around 99,9% from all the cases as shown the value R^2 (0,999). Lastly, to observe if the equation is right (2), Fig. 1 describes the relation between independent and dependente as the linear multi-linear regression model.

Note that R represented the positive value 0,999. The proposed R model explains the dependent variables volume (ton) around 99,9% from all the cases as shown the value R^2 (0,999). Lastly, to observe that Eq. 2 can be confirmed (2).

Figure 1 describes the relation between independent and dependent in the multi-linear regression model.

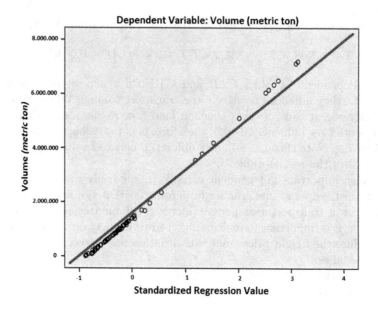

Fig. 1. Scatter chart

4   Discussion

Considering these results, some discussion can be made to understand the Brazilian reality:

- **Logistical Deficit:** Brazil needs improve logistical infrastructure such as storage, rivers infrastructure, modal with higher capacity of transportation. The Agricultural Department of United States suggests the logistical deficit in Brazil is the obstacle to the development of Brazilian agroindustrial sector [12].
- **Transporte Cost:** The soybean transport costs can achieve around 25% from the product value [12]. The obstacle is the excess of roadways with less load capacity and major costs of transportation per ton versus kilometers. The roadway model still shows a big amount of obstacles that goes such the low capacity and fleet density, bad conservation in high levels of accidents frequently lost os grains during transport [12,13]. The Transport Cost in the United States is average 30 dollars while in Brazil is about 70, mainly Because of use of railroad and Waterway transports [10].
- **Port Capacity:** Brazil has only two ports with a major capacity to the grains flow. They are Paranaguá and Santos. These two ports have main routes to flow the major quantity of freight which makes have been used intensively. It raises a bottleneck in loading and unloading and retention value. Thus, can be defined as bottlenecks and less availability to storage [14]. Besides a great

traffic such as on the ground and in the sea: truck rows that stay in ports to upload and the time that the big ships. The results of this problem are long rows, delays, shipments, and losses. The demand is about 30% major than the offer. The greatest demand should the rent ships increase, which increase the freight costs [15]. Lastly, The Brazilian Port system floodgate two realities: the private terminal and the public dock. The private terminal has gains of productiveness, consequently in a better management, which made possible make equipment modernization and movimentation process from the loads. The situation on the public dock is really the opposite with obsolescence and bad use of facilities and equipment, which commits the competitiveness in the soybean chain [16].

5 Conclusions

The soybean is responsible for a large movement and foreign exchange for the country. However, as soybean is low value added product is necessary to optimize process and reduce costs. Considering that the growth of the soybean culture is migrating into the country is essential improved logistics infrastructure, given that the distance between the growers and ports can exceed easily two thousand kilometers.

This study used a multi-linear regression model to analyze the behavior soybean volume in relation to logistics variables. We could confirm that low transportation costs and port capacity can increase of soybean volume by route and vice versa.

References

1. United States Department of Agriculture: Oilseed: World Market and Trade. Technical report, United States Department of Agriculture, EUA (2016)
2. Ministry of Agriculture, Livestock and Food Supply: Projections of Agribusiness: Brazil 2014/15 to 2024/25: Long Term Projections. MAPA, Brasília (2015)
3. Bustos, P., Garber, G., Ponticelli, J.: Capital allocation across sectors: evidence from boom in agriculture. Working paper series, Banco Central do Brasil, Brasília (2016)
4. Reis, S.A., Leal, J.E.: A deterministic mathematical model to support temporal and spatial decisions of the soybean supply chain. J. Transp. Geogr. **43**, 48–58 (2015)
5. Pearson, S.: Infrastructure: poor logistics present a problem for partnership. Financial Times (2011)
6. Salin, D.: Soybean transportation guide: Brazil 2014. FAS/USDA (2015)
7. Gonçalves, D.N.S., de Morais Gonçalves, C., de Assis, T.F., da Silva, M.A.: Analysis of the difference between the Euclidean distance and the actual road distance in Brazil. Transp. Res. Procedia **3**, 876–885 (2014)
8. Toloi, R.C., Reis, J., Vendrametto, O., Machado, S., Rodrigues, E.: How to improve the logistics issues during crop soybean in Mato Grosso State Brazil?. In: ILS 2016: Building a Resilient Future, vol. 1, pp. 1–7. ILS, Bordeaux (2016)

9. Asadi, S., Amiri, S.S., Mottahedi, M.: On the development of multi-linear regression analysis to assess energy consumption in the early stages of building design. Energy Build. **85**, 246–255 (2014)

10. Reis, J.G.M., Vendrametto, O., Naas, I.D.A., Costabile, L.T., Machado, S.T.: Avaliação das Estratégias de Comercialização do Milho em MS Aplicando o Analytic Hierarchy Process (AHP). Rev. Econ. Sociol. Rural **54**(01), 131–146 (2016)

11. Ministério Desenvolvimento Indústria e Comércio (2016). http://aliceweb.mdic. gov.br//consulta-ncm/consultar

12. United States Department of Agriculture: World Agricultural Supply and Demand Estimates, vol. 550. United States Department of Agriculture, Washington (2016)

13. Kussano, M.R., Batalha, M.O.: Custos Logísticos Agroindustriais: Avaliação do Escoamento da Soja em Grão do Mato Grosso para o Mercado Externo. Gest ão Produção **19**, 619–632 (2012)

14. Instituto Mato-grossense de Economia Agropecuária: Entendendo o Mercado da Soja. Technical report, Instituto Mato-grossense de Economia Agropecuária, CuiabáMT (2015)

15. Pontes, H.L.J., Carmo, B.B.T., Porto, A.J.V.: Problemas Logí-sticos na Exportação Brasileira da Soja em Grão. Rev. Eletrôn. Sist. Gestão **4**(2), 155–181 (2009)

16. Filardo, M.L.R., Ilario, A.A., da Silva, G.D., de Carvalho, M.A.: A Logística da Exportação de Soja do Estado de Mato Grosso para o Porto de Santos. Rev. Econ. Mackenzie **3**(3), 35–52 (2005)

Does the VHP Sugar Price Influence in the Ethanol Volume Production?

Edison Sotolani Claudino[1], João Gilberto Mendes dos Reis[1,2(✉)],
Pedro L.O. Costa Neto[2], Antônio C.V. Lopes[1], and Alessandra Q. Silva[1]

[1] Federal University of Grande Dourados, Dourados, Brazil
edisonclaudino@ufgd.edu.br
[2] Paulista University, São Paulo, Brazil
betomendesreis@msn.com

Abstract. Brazil has become one of the major producers of sugar and
ethanol. However, as both products share the same production process,
the volume of production of sugar or ethanol is influenced by government
policies and marketing prices. The purpose of this research is to analyze
the influence of the international prices of VHP sugar in the mix of
production of hydrous ethanol and sugar. A multiple linear regression
studies with statistical software R was conducted using as reference data
of Mato Grosso do Sul state, Brazil between 2002/03 and 2014/15. The
results indicated that the sugar and ethanol production in this state was
bonded to the prices variance of VHP sugar on the international market.

Keywords: Sugarcane-ethanol production · Marketing price ·
Producion responsiveness

1 Introduction

The agro-industrial production of sugarcane-ethanol has emerged as one of the
most important sectors in developing countries due to its capability to produce
food and clean energy. Brazil, for instance, has become the greatest producer and
exporter of sugar worldwide. Since the 1970 s the country has responded to an
average of 45% of the world's exportations [1]. Moreover is a pioneer on ethanol
production as a vehicular fuel [2] using a blender with gasoline (25% ethanol
anhydrous and 75% gasoline) and pure (hydrous ethanol) [3]. Thus, the internal
demand of the product makes the fuel sector represents 1.5% of the Brazilian
GDP [4]. However, despite these numbers, the production of different products
at the same agriculture process has occasioned price floating and uncertainty
related to the supply of both sugar and ethanol, which are the most produced
items of the sugarcane supply chains [4].

This integrated production system was chosen because during the 1970s, with
the world oil crisis and with the creation of the "Proalcool" program, and the
urgency of ethanol production expansion, it made sense to annex to the existent

© IFIP International Federation for Information Processing 2016
Published by Springer International Publishing AG 2016. All Rights Reserved
I. Nääs et al. (Eds.): APMS 2016, IFIP AICT 488, pp. 579–586, 2016.
DOI: 10.1007/978-3-319-51133-7_69

sugarcane mills [5]. However, 40 years later, this decision has still affected the responsiveness of the supply chain in meeting the demands of both markets.

When the Proalcool program started the National Petroleum Council, a Brazilian government agency created in 1938, ensured parity prices between anhydrous ethanol (blended with gasoline), hydrous ethanol and sugar [6]. Moreover, consumers were stimulated to use hydrous ethanol by setting the price at 64,5% of gasoline [7]. During the middle of the 1980s, 90% of light duty vehicles were moved by ethanol fuel [8]. However, the decline in oil prices and the end of military government reduce drastically the production and use of ethanol as fuel [9]. Only in 2003, the ethanol started to be used as fuel largely again due to flex-fuel technology that allows cars to run with any blend combination of ethanol and gasoline [7].

Nowadays, the production of such commodities not always is bonded to the prices, once factors with previous contracts and the level of sugars present in the harvested canes are relevant aspects taken into consideration by the plants' directors. Such recoverable sugar (also known as Total Recoverable Sugar/TRS) is measured during the deliverance of sugarcane to the plants. This TRS measure has basically two purposes: (i) to estimate the amount of sugar that can be produced and (ii) to establish the value to be paid by the supplier.

In an overall view, the existence of this system makes that Brazil sugarcane agro-industry preferably concentrates its production on sugar (more profitable), what makes the ethanol a secondary product in this process. Nonetheless, the increase of the flex fuel cars and the current eco-friend pressures for the clean energy creation has resulted in an increase in ethanol demand and forced mills to reconfigure its priorities [1,5].

The aim of this paper is to find empirical evidence if the variable of sugar price in the international market really contributes to explain the formation of the production mix (sugar and ethanol) and Brazilian sugarcane-ethanol Agro-industry. With this regard, we opted by a multiple linear regression analysis, which comprised three variables: (i) sugar production, (ii) hydrous ethanol production and (iii) price of VHP sugar for exportation/crop. The data were collected between 2002 and 2014 and Mato Grosso do Sul (MS) state was chosen as referential. We tested statically the hypothesis that VHP sugar price affects the mix of production in sugar-ethanol complex.

2 Methodology

To understand the responsiveness of Brazilian sugarcane-ethanol agro-industry this research focused on which factors have influenced throughout the last 13 crops the MS production of sugar, in relation to the destination of the sugarcane syrup for ethanol production. It is about a long and important period in which it is possible to measure the process of sugarcane production expansion after 2006 when a strong regional expansion of this sector was registered.

All data were analyzed using multiple linear regression technique [10] and calculated with statistical R software. According to Guo et al. the multiple linear regression model can be expressed in matrix notation by [10]:

$$\gamma = \chi\beta + \xi \qquad (1)$$

Where, $\gamma =$ is the vector which contains the dependent variables (sugar production); $\chi =$ is a matrix which contains both k variable values either regressor or independent (fixed value); $\beta =$ is the vector which corresponds to the regression coefficients bonded to the independent variables; $\xi =$ is the vector of order of random non-correlated errors with multi-varied normal distribution with zero average vector and common variance (homogeneous variances).

The multiple linear regression technique comprises the dependent and independent variables. In this study, the dependent variable was the sugar production in tons (t) and the hydrous alcohol production (m^3), both obtained from the BIOSUL (Association of bioenergy producers from Mato Grosso do Sul state). The independent variable consisted on the series of prices of Very High Polarized (VHP) sugar for exportation furnished by CEPEA/ESALQ (Center of Advanced Studies in Applied Economy/Superior School of Agriculture Luiz de Queiroz). To obtain the VHP sugar price, we used the month average between May to March (official date of center/south region crops) that comprises nearly the whole crops harvests and processing from MS state. The values were estimated in US dollars.

3 Results

In our study, we proposed a multiple regression to better establish the presented evidence that the sugar production (variant γ) may be explained by the prices of the VHP sugar on the international market and the hydrous ethanol production. We normalized the experimental errors from the result of the Shapiro-Wilk ($W = 0.9276$ e ρ-value $= 0.3172$) test. However, the Durbin-Watson test for the original data seemed to be significant for indicating the correlation among the residuals. In order to solve this problem, we applied the logarithmic transformation, proportioned by the exponential model ($Ln(\gamma)$) and, posteriorly, the test confirmed the independence of the errors ($DW = 1.7583$ and ρ-value $= 0.163$). Table 1 presents the analysis of variance of the regression.

Table 1. Analysis of variance of the regression

Source of variation	GL	SQ	QM	F	ρ-value
Regression	2	4.578905084	2.289452542	121.4182048	9.67836×10^{-8}
Residual (error)	10	0.188559248	0.018855925		
Total	12	4.767464332			

As we can see, test F showed a significant multiple linear regression, in other words, the sugar production may be explained by the price of sugar in the international market either for the hydrous ethanol production or for both productions. Table 2 shows the averages of regression parameters through the method of least squares.

Table 2. Estimation of the regression parameters

Variables	Parameters	Std error	T statistic	p-value
Intercept	12.34000	0.09815	125,747	$<2 \times 10^{-16}$
Sugar price (x_1)	0.04068	0.01047	43.885	0.003036
Ethanol production (x_2)	6.989×10^{-7}	1.153×10^{-7}	6.062	0.000122

We observe by the p-value that both coefficients are not null to the significant level of 1%. Thus, based on the variance of prices, the proposed model is able to attract the reality of the local sugar production ($R^2 = 0.9604$). We conclude that the sugar production from the last 13 crops is strongly influenced by the variation of price of the VHP sugar in the international market and by the increase of the hydrous ethanol production. The model that better fits into the data may be described by the following equation:

$$ln(\gamma) = 12.3400 + 0.04068x_1 + 6.989 \times 10^{-7}x_2 \tag{2}$$

Where γ corresponds to sugar production (t); x_1 price of VHP sugar (US dollars); x_2 hydrous ethanol production (m^3). It worth mentioning that Eq. 2 refers to the $ln(\gamma)$, not to the original variant itself. Thus, when we analyze the results, under the perspective of the problem, we must apply the inverse operation, we mean, reuse the unities of the original values from the model $\gamma k e^{k' x_1} e^{k'' x_2}$ (k, k' and k'' are constant estimated by least squares or maximum likelihood).

Our results allowed to observe that the behavior of the regional production of sugar is elastic to the positive variation of the international quotation of the VHP sugar. This result expresses that the regional sugar plants direct their production mix and the destination of the TRS based on the international prices, even if the production flows seem to be unfavorable, once there is no appropriated logistic infrastructure and the distance to the ports is very long.

There are evidenced of a good capacity of response of the sugarcane chain on the destination of the TRS to more profitable markets, even if the decision of production mix being taken differently every crop. Another factor that corroborated for the strategy of productive chain's responsiveness is that the plants have the option of working with the future deliverance of sugar. This mechanism enables the plants to stock the product throughout the crop and to execute their contracts only when the market is favorable, thus, they capture the value in the spot market of ethanol (anhydrous or hydrous), in other words, there is available commercialization throughout the crop.

4   Discussion

4.1   TRS and the Location of Production

The sugar and ethanol productions' trade-off from the Total Recoverable Sugar values requires the verification of plants both technical and economic possibilities for the determination of which commodity will be more/less concomitantly produced.

The plants often have previously defined both the total volume of sugarcane to be processed during crop period (around six or seven months) and a daily capacity of sugar and ethanol, thus, it is not feasible to concentrate the production in a single commodity, because they run the risk of having extra mature cane to be cut. For this reason, the operational conditions force the mixed plants owners to produce simultaneously sugar and ethanol [11].

Mato Grosso do Sul state presents the lowest yield when compared to other states of the region, but if we analyze the local production, the new agricultural enterprises also brought some innovations and other varieties of cane (which are already in process of adaptation) consolidated in other Brazilian regions for a long period.

Salgado Jr., assures that the plants' efficiency also depends on the variable "localization". For example, São Paulo state presents the edaphoclimatic conditions more favorable to the extraction of a cane with a higher tenor of saccharose, which, consequently, may influence the operational efficiency of sugarcane plants [12]. In Fig. 1, we compare the variance of TRS yields of the crops from 2002/03 to 2014/15 by state.

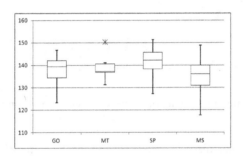

Fig. 1. Box plot graphic of the average TRS between SP and the states of Goiás (GO), Mato Grosso (MT) and Mato Grosso do Sul (MS).

The important combination for the development of the cane in São Paulo region resulted from the good soil conditions, better infrastructure of energy and transportation, proximity to bigger markets and, above all this, a regional system of innovation that comprises producers, capital goods industries, research institutes and universities [13].

The expansion process of sugarcane is a result from the new expansion routes, especially from the advance of new agricultural frontiers, like the Midwest states and Minas Gerais. This movement results from the great availability of farmable lands, with adequate topographic conditions to the mechanization and edaphoclimatic characteristics favorable to sugarcane cultivation [14].

This way, it is possible to infer that even TRS is an important factor that determines the production mix, the sugarcane-ethanol agro-industries have opted for regions with low prices of lands and high fiscal incentives, despite the low TRS yields [14].

4.2   Ethanol and Sugar Responsiveness

The factor that directs the ethanol production is bonded to the price policies for fossil fuel adopted in Brazil. Hydrous ethanol presents 70% of price limit for consumers in relation to gasoline and cannot be readjusted due to the increase in prices over the last years. The increase in costs is due mainly to factors like the high tax burden, strong valorization of the current currency, precarious infrastructure of the production flow, inter alia [15].

Considering the financial ceiling's limit of 70% of the gasoline at the pump, Fig. 2 presents ethanol how ethanol has lost competitiveness over the years in comparison with the gasoline in Brazil, even in São Paulo state, which is the biggest national consumer.

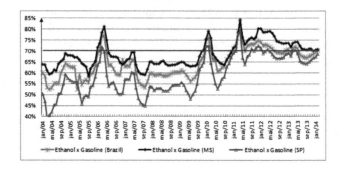

Fig. 2. Comparison chart of parity between gasoline and ethanol

São Paulo state has historically shown the most competitive biofuel taxes of the country with respect to gasoline, especially due to its privileged geographic position close to consumers from urban centers and due to the fact that there have been for a long time good operational and logistic conditions favorable to production and distribution of ethanol [16].

In Mato Grosso do Sul state, the parity ethanol versus gasoline is less competitive when compared to São Paulo state, which follows the national average. Thus, we observe the normal market variations (seasonality), although is evident the strong political influence over the fuel prices.

In relation to sugar responsiveness a good alternative for compensating the low prices of ethanol is to direct part of the TRS production mix to sugar. Through this option, the plants have higher flexibility and capacity of market response in order to maximize their profitability and to reduce the market risks. Figure 3 compares the production of ethanol and sugar in Mato Grosso do Sul state during the crops of 2002/03 to 2014/15.

The evolution of crop series used in this study showed a slight increase in the sugar prices in US dollar, whose peak was reached during the crop 2011/2012. Right after the peak, we observe a decrease due to the world production increase. This scenario is in accordance with the international market [1,5].

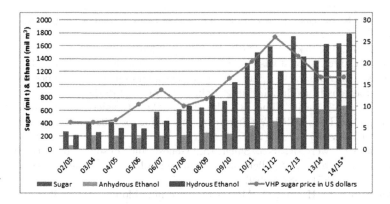

Fig. 3. Evolution of the ethanol and sugar productions in MS state and sugar prices

The sugar and hydrous ethanol production in Mato Grosso do Sul state increased after the 2008/09 crop, mainly influenced by the expansion of the activity in the state. Thus, it is possible to verify that the anhydrous ethanol production, in spite of a progressive increase in the last crops, still can be considered as residual in the regional plants. This reflects the challenge of the market in establishing to ethanol a competitive price along the year, by evidencing the influence of sugar in ethanol productivity and competitiveness [2]. Finally, we can conclude that sugar plays a predominant role in the decision of the production mix.

5   Conclusions

The data analysis enabled us to identify the evidence related to external factors, which interfere the decision makers during the process of directing the production. We verified that the regional sugar production during the crops of 2002/03 to 2014/15 was bonded to the price variance of VHP sugar in the international market.

The analysis of responsiveness of TRS, using the multiple regression model, indicated that the sugarcane supply chain in Mato Grosso do Sul state change its production mix to the more profitable markets, although the decisions are taken every 12 months, what corresponds to each crop.

In Further studies we intent analysis the responsiveness of sugarcane supply chain in Brazil to confirm the influence of VHP price in ethanol volume production showed in Mato Grosso do Sul state.

References

1. Pop, L.N., Rovinaru, M., Rovinaru, F.: The challenges of sugar market: an assessment from the price volatility perspective and its implications for Romania. Procedia Econ. Financ. **5**, 605–614 (2013)

2. Hira, A.: Sugar rush: prospects for a global ethanol market. Energ. Policy **39**(11), 6925–6935 (2011)
3. Cavalcanti, M., Szklo, A., Machado, G.: Do ethanol prices in Brazil follow Brent price and international gasoline price parity? Renew. Energ. **43**, 423–433 (2012)
4. Du, X., Carriquiry, M.A.: Flex-fuel vehicle adoption and dynamics of ethanol prices: lessons from Brazil. Energ. Policy **59**, 507–512 (2013)
5. Dias, M.O.S., Maciel Filho, R., Mantelatto, P.E., Cavalett, O., Rossell, C.E.V., Bonomi, A., Leal, M.R.L.V.: Sugarcane processing for ethanol and sugar in Brazil. Environ. Dev. **15**, 35–51 (2015)
6. Rico, J.A.P., Mercedes, S.S., Sauer, I.L.: Genesis and consolidation of the Brazilian bioethanol: a review of policies and incentive mechanisms. Renew. Sustain. Energ. Rev. **14**(7), 1874–1887 (2010)
7. Stattman, S.L., Hospes, O., Mol, A.P.: Governing biofuels in Brazil: a comparison of ethanol and biodiesel policies. Energ. Policy **61**, 22–30 (2013)
8. de Oliveira, J.P.: The policymaking process for creating competitive assets for the use of biomass energy: the Brazilian alcohol programme. Renew. Sustain. Energ. Rev. **6**(1–2), 129–140 (2002)
9. Lehtonen, M.: Social sustainability of the Brazilian bioethanol: power relations in a centre-periphery perspective. Model. Environ. Econ. Soc. Asp. Assess. Biofuels **35**(6), 2425–2434 (2011)
10. Guo, G., You, W., Qian, G., Shao, W.: Parallel maximum likelihood estimator for multiple linear regression models. J. Comput. Appl. Math. **273**, 251–263 (2015)
11. Valente, M.S., Nyko, D., Reis, B.L.S.F.S., Milanez, A.Y.: Bens de Capital para o Setor Sucroenergético: A Indústria está Preparada para Atender Adequadamente a Novo Ciclo de Investimentos em Usinas de Cana-de-açúcar? BNDES Setorial **1**(13), 119–178 (2012)
12. Salgado Jr., A.P., Carlucci, F.V., Novi, J.C.: Aplicação da Análise Envoltória de Dados (AED) na Avaliação da Eficiência Operacional Relativa entre Usinas de Cana-de-açúcar no Território Brasileiro. Eng. Agríc. **34**(5), 826–843 (2014)
13. Furtado, A.T., Scandiffio, M.I.G., Cortez, L.A.B.: The Brazilian sugarcane innovation system. Energ. Policy **39**(1), 156–166 (2011)
14. Milanez, A.Y., Nyko, D., Garcia, J.L.F., Xavier, C.E.O.: Logística para o Etanol: Situação Atual e Desafios Futuros. BNDES Setorial **1**, 49–98 (2010)
15. Regazzini, L.C., Bacha, C.J.C.: A tributação no Setor Sucroenergético do Estado de São Paulo: Anos de 2000 e 2008. Rev. Econ. e Sociol. Rural **50**(4), 801–818 (2012)
16. Costa, C.C., Guilhoto, J.J.M.: O Papel da Tributação Diferenciada dos Combustíveis no Desenvolvimento Econômico do Estado de São Paulo. Econ. Apl. **15**(3), 369–390 (2011)

Performance Assessment for a Sustainable Supply Chain at Local Level

Leticia Prevez[(✉)], Biagio F. Giannetti, Cecilia M.V.B. Almeida,
and Feni Agostinho

Paulista University, São Paulo, Brazil
lprevez50@gmail.com, feniagostinho@gmail.com

Abstract. This article aims to provide a tool to diagnose the supply chain management from a performance reference model allowing evaluating the links individually and the supply chain as a whole, taking as case study the mango pulp supply chain at local level in Santiago de Cuba in Cuba. The reference model considers a territorial approach to rural development that do not have a specialized logistics system. The identification and better understanding of the obstacles that limit the supply chain is the great importance both for the definition of public policies and for awareness and making sustainable decisions of companies operating in the sector.

Keywords: Supply chain at local level · Sustainable · Performance reference model · Agroindustry · Mango

1 Introduction

The Agriculture is ceasing to be an area isolated by force of industrialization and close relationships between several production units when concentrated in a specific territory. It increase and retain value added farmer production in rural areas [1–3] due to the use of local culture, valuing women's work and recognition of local knowledge through selection, washing, sorting, storage, preservation, processing, packaging, transport and marketing fruits [4]. Correa and Gomez [5] raised that the supply chain has become a key concept because consider business processes, people, organization, technology and physical infrastructure for enterprises.

The Management Supply Chain is a systemic approach that aims integrating the various direct and indirect actor in a chain, in order to gain competitive advantages, through cooperation with other companies that are part of the same competitive environment [6]. However, it could be defined "as a methodology developed to align all production activities in a synchronized manner in order to reduce costs, minimize cycles and maximize the value perceived by the end customer through the breaking of barriers between departments and areas" [7]. With the expansion of the concept of management, demand was raised for the development of models as a reference guide to assess performance, integrating concepts into a unified instrument, forming a systemic structure of management [8, 9]. Acevedo et al. [10] add that the reference models can

© IFIP International Federation for Information Processing 2016
Published by Springer International Publishing AG 2016. All Rights Reserved
I. Nääs et al. (Eds.): APMS 2016, IFIP AICT 488, pp. 587–597, 2016.
DOI: 10.1007/978-3-319-51133-7_70

identify strengths and weaknesses, barriers and opportunities offered by the environment in order to develop and implement a strategic plan for development. However, the other barriers to define a reference model are the internal strategy of each company that is not necessarily linked to the interests of the whole chain, the influence of the stronger actors' strategy upon the rests and the involvement of various members in various chains, difficulty implementation a single strategy [11].

Some authors attribute the lack of academic publications on real cases due to the diversity of companies, indirect stakeholders in the chain and the complexity observed in logistics processes given by interactions numbers, strategic alliances and contracts [2, 11, 12]. Already, Seuring [13] and [3] attribute this to the complexity that arises when different actors establish a business with shared objectives, conflict between participants, lack of appropriate measures that reduce customer expectations and chain optimization.

This article aims to provide a tool to diagnose the supply chain management from a performance reference model for evaluating the links individually and the supply chain as a whole, taking as case study the mango pulp supply chain at local level in Santiago de Cuba in Cuba.

2   Method

2.1   Supply Chain Case Study

The supply chain at local level, under study, was selected in the Santiago de Cuba province during 2012 mango season. The area designated for pulp mango production in monoculture regimen is the 130 ha with about 13 years old, an annual production of 1300 t. Nine associated producers compose the primary producers with 71 workers where 70% live on the property. The pulp industry processes daily 2 t of mango pulp hot filled into 3 L cans. The 38 workers support this activity. The main input suppliers are the same that provide the provincial level, so this study does not take into account the focal company. The chain receives support from government organizations such as research institutes, Ministry of Agriculture, Logistics Group, among others. The logistics system consists in transportation of the fresh fruit to the pulp industry and the pulp distribution in the local markets (4 points of sales, and 10 mobile sellers), by two independent companies. According with [3], this is a common situation in local supply chains, where a partnership between producers and transporters prevails, ensuring inputs and services. The price of the mango pulp can of 210 Cuban pesos is high in comparison with the 300 pesos of national population average wage. The chain begins with the fruit sale price of 2,180 Cuban Pesos per tons in the primary sector and ends on the market with 40,000 Cuban pesos per ton of pulp. Figure 1 shows the map of supply chain at local level. Each actors work as an independent company, connected by material, financial and information flow. The inter-business cooperation is developed in the framework of commodity-money relations between actors, and lack of other types of collaboration.

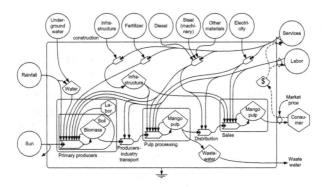

Fig. 1. Energy system diagram of the mango supply chain.

2.2   Performance Reference Model

The bases of reference model proposed for the assessment of supply chain at local level was adapted from the Model of Value Networks. The proposed model took into account the local conditions with small family farms that do not have a focal firm or a specialized logistics system. With this model is possible to assess each actors of the chain independently and inter-related, identifying those key points where could be improve competitiveness [9, 14].

The modules were selected from meetings, applying a participatory methodology, with direct and indirect actors of supply chain where were identified: infrastructure, technology, logistics, economics, environmental management and support programs and not only focusing on the logistics issues. The criteria for defining aspect was the relationship of technical and economic performance variables most relevant and which were common for companies into the chain [9]. The tool is a flexible questionnaire, which could be applied in all actors of the supply chain. Table 1.

Table 1. Reference model for performance evaluation

Modulo	Indicators	Descriptor	
1. Infrastructure	Location	*1.1*	It is located in a place where there is a productive organization
		1.2	Accessibility
	Installation	*1.3*	Water and electricity supply facilities
		1.4	Site requirements
		1.5	Sanitary conditions
		1.6	Lighting conditions
		1.7	Licenses
2. Human capital	Gender	*2.1*	Female, Male
	Educational level	*2.2*	Elemental, medium, university
	Social security	*2.3*	Accessibility to social security (low 2 points, high 5 points)

(continued)

Table 1. (*continued*)

Modulo	Indicators	Descriptor	
		2.4	Accessibility to public services
	Exude	*2.5*	Low: 5 points High: 2 points
	Attention to HR	*2.6*	Good: 5 points Bad: 0 points
	Salary	*2.7*	High: 5 points Low: 0 points
3. Technology	State	*3.1*	Regimen automatic/semi automatic/Manual
		3.2	Equipment (adequate 5)
		3.3	Consumption of resource (High 2, Medium 3 low 5)
		3.4	Maintenance (Adequate 5)
		3.5	Innovation
4. Logistic	Logistic service	*4.1*	Service quality
		4.2	Price (Adequate 5)
		4.3	Costs (Low 5)
		4.4	Availability of raw materials and supplies locally from national sources (Over 50%, 5)
		4.5	Delivery cycle (Adequate 5)
		4.6	Reliability
		4.7	Flexibility
		4.8	Contract
	Information system and communication	*4.9*	Exchange of information
		4.10	Frequency
		4.11	Reliability
		4.12	Technology
5. Economy	Economic indicators	*5.1*	Costs
		5.2	Price
		5.3	Yield
		5.4	Income
		5.5	Efficiency
		5.6	Productivity
6. Environmental management		*6.1*	Environmental action plan
		6.2	Waste treatment
		6.3	Reuse of resorce
		6.4	Use of renewable resources
7. Supporting programme		*7.1*	Training
		7.2	Management systems implemented QSM, ESM, SSSM and others
		7.3	Cleaner production management, Integrated programme, GMP, GMM green logistic, others
		7.4	Linking with national and international projects
		7.5	Credit support programs
		7.6	Certifications

2.3   Data Processing

The questionnaire was applied for each direct actors but the quantity of interviewed was statistically representative at the 95,0% confidence level. The Likert scale was used to numerically evaluate the responses of excellent = 5; good = 4, regular = 3, bad = 2 or very bad = 1 [15]. It was calculated the average for each indicators and respective module. The quantitative evaluation of each actor's performance is the average of all modules. The results was showed at matrix to visualize the behavior of each direct actors of the supply chain and also gives a rating of the behavior of each indicator involved in the performance of the supply chain as a whole system. The average of performance of the actors and the average of the modules of the supply chain have the same result and it represent the qualification of the chain as a system.

The weakness of actors were considered the aspects evaluated with 1 and up 3 points, and strengths of system with 4 and 5 points [10, 15]. The results with values between 3 and 5 was considered as the fulfillment of the basic indicators.

3   Result and Discussion

3.1   Analysis of Direct Actors of Supply Chain

Table 2 shows the results obtained by tabulating the questionnaires from actors of supply chain. The matrix allows viewing that the supply chain has problem with technology (2.8), logistics aspects (2.8), environmental management (2.5) and supporting program (1.9) for a general qualification of 2.9 points. These results indicate the need for an internal strategy for performance improvement of each direct actors, and public policy to establish a local development program.

Table 2. Evaluation matrix of supply chain at the local level

Module	Primary producer	Fruit transport	Pulp processing	Pulp transport	Market	Supply chain
Infrastructure	3,6	2,2	3,6	2,2	4,0	3,4
Human capital	4,1	3,0	4,4	3,0	4,1	3,9
Technology	2,5	2,8	2,3	2,8	3,8	2,9
Economy	3,2	3,0	3,0	3,0	3,2	3,1
Logistic	2,0	2,8	3,4	2,8	3,0	2,7
Environmental management	2,3	2,0	3,2	2,0	2,0	2,4
Supporting program	2,3	2,0	2,3	2,0	1,0	1,9
Average	2,9	2,4	3,4	2,4	3,0	**2,9**

Primary Producers. The results show that the primary producer needs deep internal improvements to increase performance in technology (2.5), logistics (2.0) and support program (2.5). Figure 2. The level of mechanization for pruning, fertilizing and harvesting is low due to using obsolete equipment and there is not local company that provides spare parts or perform equipment maintenance. The aspect of innovation was assessed as bad because it have not technology to add value to production as selection and washing fruit. The economic indicators was evaluated as regular due to low yield of 10t/ha compared with similar system of 20 t/ha, and high cost which shows that the current model of agricultural economy is characterized by little use of natural resources, the use of chemical fertilizers and great presence of labor. The assessment for this actor show that 41.3% of the aspect were evaluated as reasonable, 32.6% as bad, 10.9% as good, 8,7% as excellent and 6.5% as very bad which compliance of 57.4% of the basic indicators. The general assessment was 3 points. The most critical modules were technology, environment management, supporting programs and logistics system affected by the delivery planning, centralization, instability, low availability of inputs and unappropriated information communication, as well as high prices of service delivery and problems with hiring companies.

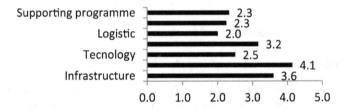

Fig. 2. Results of performance evaluation of primary producers

Pulp Processing. The pulp-processing actor needs to improve the production technology (2.3 points) and support programs (2.0 points). Figure 3. The obsolete technology, lack of automation in the process, high energy and water consumption influences in the number of hired workers. It is reflected in economic indicators such as production costs, efficiency and low yield. The infrastructure conditions were evaluated with 3.6 points due to the situation of roads, lack of space and lighting. The support programs was evaluated with 2.5 points and only the aspect of training received regular evaluation. The precariousness of technology and infrastructure, as well as difficulty in acquiring credits and financing limits the ability of management systems certification, which depend on these resources. The overall evaluation was 3.2 point with 64.4% of

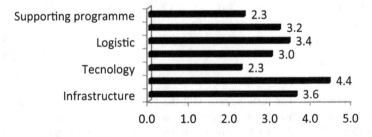

Fig. 3. Results of performance evaluation of pulp processing

compliance of the basic indicators. 45.7% of the aspects were assessed as regular,19.6% as bad, 21.8% as good, 10.9% as excellent and 2.2% as very bad. The supporting programs and the technology were the most critical modules.

Distributors and Transporters. The infrastructure module was evaluates inappropriate for both the road conditions (mountain) makes it difficult to access collection points of fruits and pulps and trucks are not suitable increasing the risk of production loss and quality of fruit. Compared with the previous links, the human resources module was evaluated with 3.0 points because employees are not paid for production; it has a fixed salary, and working conditions that are not appropriate. This factor causes instability, increases the exodus of workers, and affects the logistical costs of the rest of the actors. According to Bourlakis [3] and Grimm et al. [4], the link between small producers and consumers are complex chains of collection and distribution which producers have been traditionally submitted, and contributed to the decline profitability. The rating for each module was as follows: 41.3% of the descriptors were assessed as regular, 47.8% as bad, 2.17% was evaluated as good, 6.5% as excellent and 2.2% as very bad for an overall assessment of 2.8 point. The most critical modules were the technology, infrastructure, logistics, environment and supporting programs. Indicating a compliance of 56.8% of the basic indicators. Figure 4 shows the evaluation of this actor.

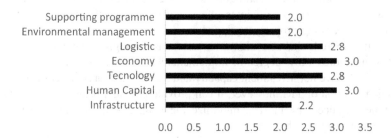

Fig. 4. Results of performance evaluation of distributing and transporting actors

Market. This actor bases its operation on mobile outlets appropriated to the local environment because do not require refrigeration to preserve the pulp of mango. One factor that affects product sales is an informal market that can set prices for products according to the quality levels, the season and demand. The critical aspects for this actor are the information and communication system. This actor evaluated as very bad the module of supporting programs because it is not offered programs or funding to develop marketing.

The 32.6% of the descriptors were assessed as regular, 10.86% as bad, 23.9% as good, 15 21% as excellent and 17.4% as very bad. Most critical modules were the supporting programs and systems of information and communication. The overall assessment was of 3 point indicating a compliance of 60% of basic indicators. Figure 5 shows results of performance evaluation of sales actors.

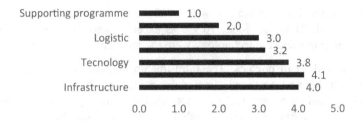

Fig. 5. Results of performance evaluation of sales actors

3.2   Analysis the Supply Chain as a Whole System

One of the strengths of this supply chain is the infrastructure and humans resource because is located in an area where there is a production base, with experience in mango cultivation, with favorable climatic conditions and organizational structures such as cooperatives to help manage the primary producer. The inclusion of women to labor, free access to medical and educational services and laws that guarantee the social security of members of the chains it was also appointed however, the exodus is indicating that the concrete measures to ensure the stability of labor actions could be done.

The technology module is a weakness in all actors and the whole supply chain. All actors have problem to introduce innovation in the production process where only processing actor adds value but still quite limited. It confirms that supply chains at local level lose opportunities to participate effectively in global value chains or other premises due to not being properly equipped.

The other module that is evaluated as ruin was the logistic. De Oliveira et al. [9] identified in studies a low degree of implementation in small and medium enterprises (SMEs) which have not investment capacity and an organizational structure to facilitate the implementation of TIC, however, it can provide potential benefits such as reduced cycle times, reduced inventories, minimize the whip effect, and improve the effectiveness of distribution channels.

In the national context in addition to the elements of macroeconomic policy there are other factors such as institutional aspects, given the fragility of both public and private organizations and sectorial vision limiting and difficult coordination. Producers tend to organize themselves into cooperatives but they could not capitalize to invest in processing. It have not appropriated mechanism for institutional support allowing access to financing channels. The main obstacles to access to credit by the direct chain actors is the disinterest from financial agents due to small value transactions, required guarantees and necessary documentation cost.

The other problem is the absence of environmental action plan and supporting programme in all actors. Van Hoof et al. [6] showed that companies arising from small economies scale with improved environmental performance and cost reduction are those with higher levels of collaboration capabilities and involves the assimilation and transfer of knowledge and changes organizational. In the other hand, according to Bourlakis [3] practices and implementation of development programs and audits are slow and expensive for these companies. However, better management will improve the economic, environmental and social performance of local supply chains supported by Quality Management System, Hazard Analysis and Critical Control Point Systems, Health and safety, environmental management systems, among others.

However, this scenario could be different if some cleaner production practices were implemented. To improve the performance of primary producers, 25% of chemical fertilizers were replaced by compost made from agricultural waste and solid waste from the small industry; new ones built from pruning residues replaced fruit containers; improvements in harvest organization allowed 50% reduction in labor force and 25% in fuels consumption. The use of animal traction when the efficient use of vehicles is limited and the poor state of the roads is also a viable option besides keeping animals on the property. The replacement of 50% of transportation by animal traction was considered to both producers-industry and distribution transportation. This action allows reducing in the same proportion the transportation machinery, labor and fuel consumption. New routes were organized prioritizing the most distant selling points and allowing direct purchase by the mobile sellers at the processing industry.

The application of good management practices, such as reorganization of production and technological flows, allowed to rise up the 75% processing installed capacity and to reduce the processing period from 5 to 3 months without any investment. An extra payment to primary producers supplying fruit directly to industry increased the production yield from 2.3 to 1.9 t of fruit/t of pulp. Additionally, the use of rain water for pulp cans cooling, its reuse in cleaning activities, the recirculation of water in the fruit washing machine were performed to reduce water consumption. The cleaner production and management training programs allowed increasing knowledge and motivation in finding sustainable solutions. The measures allowed savings of 50% water, 25% electricity and 40% wood. The labor force was reduced by 25% but was relocated to support services to the mango crop. Two points of sale were built with more simple structures, suitable for rural areas, because the mango pulp could be preserved without refrigeration.

4 Conclusion

The model to evaluate the sustainable performance of supply chain allowed to measure scope of the supply chain. The identification and better understanding of the obstacles that limit the development of the supply chain have a great importance for both the refinement of public policies and for awareness and decision-making of companies operating in the sector. In this case, the supply chain studied should be designed to increase the autonomy of producers; restructure the existing system; modify the storage and distribution system, incentives for technological innovation and added value, adopt new and sound environmental technologies; proper management of resources; reducing input costs, and reducing the intermediation between actors. This study also confirm the critical factors identified by [2, 4, 16, 17] among others authors about performance of supply chain at local level. However, other studies should be made and analysis other supply chains to validate the proposed model for performance evaluation of supply chain at local level. The advantage to use this model is it allowed the comparison between the actors, identify their strengths and weaknesses as well as enables them to connect in an integrated system in order to accompany the indicators and changes in strategy at local level into a single matrix for decision-making from vision and perception of the actors.

Note that three pillars of sustainability also were addressed in the analysis and it was considering social aspects absent in the most article as multiculturalism, gender, ability, exodus, access to services public and social security as well as institutional and organizational environment to support these local economies.

Acknowledgment. We would like to thank the financial support from Foundation of the State of Sao Paulo (Fundação de Amparo á Pesquisa do Estado de São Paolo. FAPESP), process no 2012/25492-0 and Pos graduation Programme of University Paulista (UNIP), Brazil. We also thank the all actors of local supply chain at local level for supplying the production data and the Laboratory of Logistics and Production Management (LOGESPRO) by support in this investigation.

References

1. Van der Heyden, D., Camacho, P.: http://www.ruralter.org/index.php?option=com_content&task=view&id=38&I
2. Briz, J., de Felipe, I.: La Cadena de Valor Agroalimentaria. Análisis Internacional de Casos Reales. Editorial Agrícola Española, S.A, Madrid, España (2011)
3. Bourlakis, M.: Firm size and sustainable performance in food supply chains: insights from greek SMEs. Int. J. Prod. Econ. **152**, 112–130 (2014)
4. Grimm, J.H., Joerg, S.H., Joseph, S.: Critical factors for sub-supplier management: a sustainable food supply chains perspective. Int. J. Prod. Econ. **152**, 159–173 (2013)
5. Correa, A., Gómez, R.A: Tecnologías de la Información en la Cadena de Suministro (2008)
6. van Hoof, B., Thiell, M.: Collaboration capacity for sustainable supply chain management: small and medium-sized enterprises in Mexico. J. Clean. Prod. **67**, 239–248 (2014)
7. Seuring, S., Gold, S.: Conducting content-analysis based literature reviews in supply chain management. Supply Chain Manag. Int. J. **17**(5), 544–555 (2012)
8. Lambert, D., Pohlen, T.: Supply chain metrics. Int. J. Logistics Manag. **12**(1), 1–19 (2001)
9. De Oliveira, J., Alexander, L.: Modelo Analítico De Suporte a Configuração e Integração da Cadeia de Suprimentos. Gest. Prod. **17**(3), 447–463 (2010)
10. Acevedo, J., Gómez, M., López, T., Acevedo, A.J., Pardillo, Y.: Reference model value networks for sustainable development. Revista de Investigación Agraria y Ambiental, UNAD, Colombia **2**, 29–50 (2010)
11. Sellitto, M.A., Mendes, L.W.: Avaliação Comparativa do Desempenho de Três Cadeias de Suprimentos em Manufatura. Produção **16**(3), 552–568 (2006)
12. Gomes, C., Yasim, M., Lisboa, J.: An examination of manufacturing organizations's performance evaluation: analysis, implications and a framework for future research. Int. J. Oper. Prod. Manag. **24**(5), 488–513 (2012)
13. Seuring, S.: A review of modeling approaches for sustainable supply chain management. Decis. Support Syst. **54**, 1513–1520 (2013)
14. Chan, F., QI, H.: Feasibility of performance measurement system for supply chain: a process-based approach and measures. Integr. Manuf. Syst. **14**(3), 179–190 (2003)
15. Torres L.: Diseño de un Modelo de Referencia para la Evaluación de Microindustrias. La Habana (2012)

16. Min, H., Kim, I.: Green supply chain research: past, present, and future. Logistics Res. **4**, 39–47 (2012)
17. López, T., Acevedo, J., Gómez, M.: Cadena de Suministro Agroalimentaria Municipio Marianao Nueva Empresa. Revista Cubana de Gestion Empresarial **7**(3), 20–30 (2012)

Food Supply Chain - Sustainability in Small Milk Industry

Simone Beux[1](✉), Arcione Viagi[2], Roberto Panizzolo[3], Martino Cassandro[3], and Nina Waszczynskyj[1]

[1] Federal University of Paraná, Curitiba, Paraná, Brazil
beuxsimone@gmail.com
[2] University of Taubaté, Taubaté, São Paulo, Brazil
[3] University of Padova, Padua, Veneto, Italy

Abstract. Farming is very important for the development of a country economy and, in Brazil, cattle (meat and milk) is one of the most important sectors of this segment. This paper aims to develop a conceptual framework to identify the key characteristics of the Short Food Supply Chain and, moreover, propose a model for the implementation of sustainability in the sector of small milk producers and dairy products. The research presents data from small producers located in Paraná, Brazil and utilizes the better condition of Italian producers in the Veneto region as a benchmarking to identify opportunities for improvement by adopting the concept of Short Food Supply Chain. The conclusion of the analysis showed that there are significant gains for small farmers with the adoption of the proposed model because it solves several issues that currently hinder the development of the sector.

Keywords: Sustainability · Production · Milk · Supply chain

1 Introduction

Brazil is among the largest producers of milk in the world, ranks sixth, according to data from the United States Department of Agriculture in the year 2014. It produced 35.2 billion liters, increased by 2.7% compared to 2013 [1]. Milk production in the country is growing, but the challenge will be hard in the coming years in relation to: adequate food for the herds in terms of quantity and quality, improving product quality indicators, business management for efficient use of resources and improving competitiveness for the world market competition. Another major challenge is to resolve issues such as low professionalization of the sector; it is characterized by many small and medium producers in a state of insolvency.

According to data from the last Census of Agriculture in 2006, it was observed that most producers have low production and they are responsible for the majority of national production (80% of farmers produce up to 50 liters/day and account for 26% of Brazil's milk production). In Paraná, 55.3% of farmers produce up to 50 liters/day, representing 14.7% of total production of the state,

I. Nääs et al. (Eds.): APMS 2016, IFIP AICT 488, pp. 598–605, 2016.
DOI: 10.1007/978-3-319-51133-7_71

about 60% of Paraná's production comes from small family farms. For these reasons, the Federal University of Technology-Paraná (Brazil) and University of Padova (Italy), has ongoing projects to technology transfer to improve the performance of producers of milk and dairy products.

The objective of this work is to propose a management model for the supply chain of small farmers and assess their applicability in Brazil. The work has exploratory approach, using case study and benchmarking, with data obtained from available literature and collected through qualitative research with small farmers in the state of Paraná.

This paper is organized into four sections: Sect. 2 presents the theoretical framework, Sect. 3 analyze State of Paraná situation and describe the proposed model, and Sect. 4 draws the conclusions followed by the references.

2   Theoretical Framework

2.1   Sustainability in Food Industry

The concern with sustainability is recent (1980) and defines which companies are part of a whole and their activities generate impacts throughout society, so they should get reasonable economic results without destroying nature or creates problems for society today and in the future [2]. In the 1990s, the proposed balance received the designation of triple bottom line (Fig. 1) and advocated that sustainability is achieved when there is a balance between value creation, environmental responsibility and social responsibility [2–4].

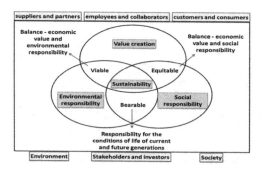

Fig. 1. Triple bottom line [2]

The approach for this paper in terms of sustainability is to develop actions that improve the management of small producer of milk and dairy products and increase their profitability.

2.2   Supply Chain Management in Food Industry

Growing competition and higher consumer expectations have forced companies to seek alternative forms of management in order to reduce costs and increase the quality and availability of products. As a result of this trend, Supply Chain Management (SCM) has been adopted in order to improve the efficiency of operations through increased collaboration between trading partners and greater proximity to customers [5,6]. For the adoption of SCM two major problems have been arisen: the first concerns the need for traceability (Fig. 2) of products due to increased consumer attention for safe and animal-friendly production methods, such as the origin and production techniques used. The second is related to the aspect of providing more speed to the process, reducing losses due to food and agricultural products shelf life constraints, therefore alternatives are: to reduce product crossing time in the agrifood chain or to use preserving agent in order to increase products life. This solution has been questioned and rejected by the most demanding consumers [7]. The SCM enables the production and the delivery of food products at competitive prices in all parts of the planet. In a Food Supply Chain (FSC) several companies collaborate strategically in more than one area without losing their own identity and autonomy. In general, the quality assurance of products in the agrifood chain depends on integration, awareness and collaboration of participants in the supply chain because misconduct can compromise the result of all the others [5]. The focus has been produce with sustainable methods and processes, quality products and offers them in the consumption places, at the right time to meet consumer expectations. However, this represents a problem for small producers who not have production volume or financial capacity to be representative in this new competitive regional, national and global market.

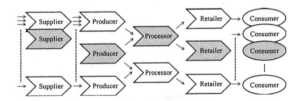

Fig. 2. Supply chain network and specific [6]

Because of the difficulties faced by small producers and their importance in the overall context of the economy, there are a number of actions in several countries, aimed to provide viable alternatives for strengthening the small farmers. One of them is the Short Food Supply Chain (SFSC) (Fig. 3), initially created for the purpose of achieving goals of "sustainable agriculture" by reducing transport costs and, hence, CO_2 emissions and promoting biodiversity by strengthening periurban agriculture.

Currently, interest in this alternative has grown and has been incorporated into the Europe Union (EU) scope and has encouraged states members to use this concept in the local markets to strengthen them. Moreover, the EU has considered the key role of small farmers in the food supply chain and provides a credit line to finance projects aimed at the participation of farmers to a "structured" short food supply chain, where quality products are linked to territory [8]. The SFSC can be structured in two basic ways always focusing on marketing in the local market or region, ensuring the reduction of transport costs. The first is the vertical integration of a producer and the second is the integration of various agricultural producers, located within walking distance that can process the products and distribute them in the local market or region.

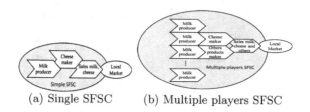

(a) Single SFSC   (b) Multiple players SFSC

Fig. 3. Single and multiple players SFSC

2.3 Food Supply Chain in Italy

Italy has a great tradition in the production of dairy products and, therefore, this activity receives great attention from public and private agencies: largest usage of milk is to cheese making [9]. Cheeses have one of the greatest values in milk chain, which contributes to the strengthening of the sector in the country. Even with the strong dairy chain with several positive points, between the small Italian producers, the operating current form is the vertical integration (multifunctional diversification), the milk processing is performed by the producer and marketing through direct sale, in a process known as "short-chain"; it has a direct influence on many weaknesses listed because it strengthens local production and supply chain management (Fig. 4).

The economic crisis and the growing desire of consumers for fresh and healthy products had boosted the interest and adoption of the concept of "short chains" in Italy and in the European Union as a whole. In fact, the need to support producer organizations and direct sales, to strengthen the activity, led to one of the objectives of the new Common Agricultural Policy (CAP) [10].

The creation and ongoing operation of SFSC proved to be a highly effective model because farmers or distributors can add value to rural activity by encouraging the production and consumption in the local market. Also, in order to promote local agriculture, the European Union (EU) approved a rule which provides farmers can make the labeling of products for direct sale [8]. The young farmers with higher education have better understanding of this market trend, and they recognize that the consumers prefer to buy regional products due to growing concerns about safety and nutrition of food. Another important initiative is the denomination Small Local Production (SLP) by the "Regional Veneto Council" for the recognition of traditions value [11].

	STRONG POINT	WEAK POINT
Farming	Strong economic importance of production	management difficulties at the national level of the quota system
	high level of know-how (management, technology, genetics) of farms	presence of restrictive legislative constraints (animal welfare, management of spills and the question nitrates, hygiene package, the security package, etc.) with a negative impact on costs
	livestock strategic role for the activation of induced upstream (feed industry) and downstream (dairy industry)	presence of structural constraints (nature of the territory, fragmentation of ownership, etc.) that impact on production costs
	presence of extensive husbandry with attitude to the exploitation of marginal areas	conflictual inter-relationships and unbalanced to the detriment of the agricultural part
Industry	high diversification of production dairy linked to a strong typicality and continuous product innovation	high fragmentation of the production system and strong regional and territorial disparities between the types of business
Product and Supply Chain	high incidence of PDO and PGI recognitions	fragmentation of the rendering system, characterized by the presence of numerous companies with plants modest technical and economic dimension
	good level of vertical integration that It produces at certain production plants especially cooperative	logistical problems related to the difficulty of concentration of supply in certain disadvantaged areas
	responsiveness of most milk products to new food consumption patterns oriented nutritional and health aspects, of freshness and lightness, quality and typicality	marketing deficit in terms of market strategies, product positioning, brand
		high bargaining power of large retailers

Fig. 4. Strong and weak points of the phase [7]

3   Analysis of Milk Production in the State of Paraná and SFSC Management Model for Small Producers

The Brazilian reality is different; the small producers are struggling to maintain activity, because they have no bargaining power with dairies and distributors. In the recent years, public policies stimulate an increasing of milk production and influence the improvement of milk quality, ensuring the standardization of products according to the demand, especially in the dairy industry. But many farmers cannot meet the required standards [12], the worst consequence of this situation is that many farmers become bankrupt or they cannot influence the descendants to continue the activity, creating a rural exodus. One of the strong points in Italy is that farmers have high knowledge of management, technology and genetics while in Brazil, mainly in small properties, there is a deficiency in these areas, resulting in low productivity of herd.

In Brazil, the average production is 950 kg/cow/year versus 5.579 kg/cow/year in Italy and in state of Paraná, in 2013 milk, production was 2.533 kg/cow/year [13,14]. The strengthening of the Italian chain is also associated with typical products, as well as high supply of products with Protected Geographical Identification (PGI) and Protected Designation of Origin (PDO). A survey in Europe showed that more than 50% of consumers recognize the certifications and willing to pay between 10% and 30% more [15], in Brazil it is necessary to consolidate and enhance product with these concepts.

Other problems are these collection system due to the distance of the property and aggravated due to the precariousness of the roads [16,17] and small number of laboratories accredited in Paraná, about 18 laboratories [18]. In Italy, considering only the region of Veneto, which has less than 10% of Paraná size, there are 61 laboratories. Regarding the hygienic-sanitary quality, the Brazilian normative requires quality standard, but without presenting alternatives to solve the problems, it results in a greater impact on small producers. An alternative to the small farmer is the agribusiness with production of cheeses, yoghurts and others dairy products, adding value to raw materials and providing relative autonomy, however, these several factors hinder this initiative. In this context, after reviewing the data on the current conditions of small farmers agricultural and compare with data considered as benchmark in the industry, it became clear that the evolution of the recent years does not eliminate the gaps between policies and effective practices to ensure the sustainability of Brazilian agribusiness. Figure 5 shows the strengths and weaknesses identified in the exploratory survey answered by farmers in the southwestern state of Paraná region in conjunction with information obtained from related industry literature review. As can be seen, it is already evident big difference in terms of strengths and weaknesses, demonstrating that a few factors have been crucial in maintaining the sector's competitiveness. However, according to Cassandro [19] the add value (AV) for cheese in the southwest of Paraná is satisfying, the production cost (per liter) of milk is around \$0.207 and the value of cheese produced is \$0.443, with these values AV generated is positive, \$0.235, this demonstrates a good opportunity for producers.

	STRONG POINT	WEAK POINT
Farming	Availability of land with variety of efficient production systems: extensive livestock / confinement and creating pasture / feed	Low level of knowledge about management and technologies on farms, particularly in small properties
	Use of the property for different applications (livestock with other crops): increasing profitability	Low investment in bovine genetics, health management, herd productivity, sanitary conditions
	Increasing economic importance	Sprayed activity, generating dependence on producers in relation to dairy products
	Favorable climate	Credit access difficulties
	Several possibilities of pastures	Difficulty to suit the herd to the standard set out in legislation
		High cost of shipping due to distance and quality of roads
		Lack of incentives to strengthen the cooperative of small-scale system
		Low level of vertical integration of small producers
		Small number of accredited laboratories or accredited to meet the demand
Industry	Wide acceptance of dairy products in the basic diet of families	Diversity of milk production without classification and control (genuine products)
	Unified System for the Agricultural Health (USAH - SUASA)	Low adherence to USAH – SUASA
		Fragmentation of the production system and large regional differences in the types of business
		Difficult to adapt production to the rules of law
		Lack financial incentives for the purchase of machinery and equipment
		Low capacity for small-scale production linked to agribusinesses
		Small number of accredited laboratories
Product and Supply Chain	Dairy products appropriate quality standards regarding the nutritional aspect	Fragmentation of the processing system (small operations, low-tech, technical and economic problems)
	Possibility of developing and adding new products to the current portfolio	Low level of integration of the supply chain
		Low recognition and adherence to IO and DO certification
		Low quality logistics (collection and distribution of products)
		High cost of products with nutritional appeal
		Concentrated bargaining power in large distributors
		Lack marketing strategy in terms of market, product positioning and brand
		Low valuation of regional products

Fig. 5. Strong and weak points: agriculture, industry and product/supply chain

Figure 6 shows the steps to implementation SFSC in the approved and promoted manner by the EU and observed operating in Italy. The proposed change is not easy and requires the assessment of priorities before you start it, because the distrust of the entrepreneur disturbs the identification of potential business partners. In Italy, the economic crisis and the lack of jobs for young people have generated the return of many to the agricultural activities of the family. They return with training and willingness to take an innovative approach and this has been a success factor and facilitator for the implementation of some public policies to encourage the creation of local SFSC.

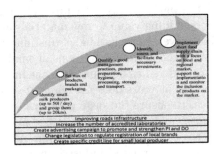

Fig. 6. Main steps to implement SFSC

The activities to structure a SFSC are: Choosing the right business partners; Make a logistic map, role of each player and the flow of market information; Define the capacity and bottlenecks; Define service model (push or pull); Define the joint logistics to support the process; Implement an information system and Define how the profits will be shared. As in Italy it is possible applied this systems for small producers in Paraná, and create a structured of the milk SFSC as a sustainable alternative for them.

4   Conclusions and Outlook

This work confirmed the problems identified in the literature review as the situation of the Brazilian milk production and the State of Paraná and identified other factors that have contributed negatively to the development of rural family farms in milk production and dairy products sector. It was found that there were significant structural problems whose solution will not be achieved in the short term; in this sense the SFSC for dairy chain can represent a viable alternative for sustainability of small and medium milk producers.

The growing concern about the future of small farmers and the alternatives to become more competitive are considered important to motivate them to accept the proposal. To enable the pilot deployment, the team should be composed of universities (researchers), rural service, trade associations, and industry regulators to give agility, support and structuring. Since this work is just an early effort in the pursuit of competitive advantages for small farmers, new scientific studies could open new opportunities of application of the model through process simulations and case studies.

References

1. IBGE: Projeção da População do Brasil por Sexo e Idade para o Período 2000/2060. Technical report (2015)
2. Azapagic, A., Perdan, S.: Indicators of sustainable development for industry. Process Saf. Environ. Prot. **78**(4), 243–261 (2000)
3. Foran, B., Lenzen, M., Dey, C., Bilek, M.: Integrating sustainable chain management with triple bottom line accounting. Ecol. Econ. **52**(2), 143–157 (2005)
4. Gimenez, C., Sierra, V., Rodon, J.: Sustainable operations: their impact on the triple bottom line. Int. J. Prod. Econ. **140**(1), 149–159 (2012)
5. Rong, A., Akkerman, R., Grunow, M.: An optimization approach for managing fresh food quality throughout the supply chain. Int. J. Prod. Econ. **131**(1), 421–429 (2011)
6. Van der Vorst, J.G.A.J., Da Silva, C.A., Trienekens, J.H.: Agro-Industrial Supply Chain Management: Concepts and Applications. FAO, Rome (2007)
7. D'Alessio, M.: Filiera Latiero-casearia: Caratteri Strutturali e Andamenti Congiunturali. Economia della produzione **17**, 15–24 (2014)
8. Canfora, I.: Is the short food supply chain an efficient solution for sustainability in food market? Agric. Agric. Sci. Procedia **8**, 402–407 (2016)
9. Cassandro, M.: Comparing local and cosmopolitan cattle breeds on added values for milk and cheese production and their predicted methane emissions. Anim. Genet. Resour. **53**, 129–134 (2013)
10. De Fazio, M.: Agriculture and sustainability of the welfare: the role of the short supply chain. Agric. Agric. Sci. Procedia **8**, 461–466 (2016)
11. Morgan, K., Marsden, T., Murdoch, J.: Worlds of food: place, power, and provenance in the food chain. In: Oxford Geographical and Environmental Studies. Oxford University Press, Oxford (2006)
12. Schmitz, A.M., Santos, R.A.: A Produção de Leite na Agricultura Familiar do Sudoeste do Paraná e a Participação das Mulheres no Processo Produtivo. Terra Plural **7**(2), 339–356 (2014)
13. DERAL - Departamento de Economia Rural: Analise da Conjuntura Agropecuária. Technical report, Departamento de Economia Rural, Curitiba (2013). http://www.agricultura.pr.gov.br
14. Júnior, G., Santos, E.B.: Evolução da Produção de Leite no Brasil. Revista Veterinária e Zootecnia 20 (2013)
15. Kakuta, S.M., Souza, A., Schwanke, F.H., Giesbrecht, H.O.: Indicações Geográficas: Guia de Respostas. Porto Alegre: Sebrae/RS, p. 38 (2006)
16. Paixão, M.G., Domingo, E.C., Gajo, A.A., Torres, L.M., Abreu, L.R., Pinto, S.M.: Carretagem de Leite a Granel: Um Estudo de Caso. Revista do Instituto de Laticínios Cândido Tostes **66**(382), 42–47 (2011)
17. Zoccal, R., Dusi, G.A.: Modelo Ideal para Produção de Leite no Brasil. Technical report Animal Business-Brasil, Sociedade Nacional da Agricultura, Passo Fundo (2013)
18. Inmetro - Instituto Nacional de Metrologia, Qualidade e Tecnologia: Inmetro - Consulta ao Catálogo da RBLE (2016). http://www.inmetro.gov.br/laboratorios/rble/
19. Cassandro, M.: Sustainable milk production in different dairy cattle systems and valorisation of environmental chain on the basis of added value. Poljoprivreda **21**(1), 22–27 (2015)

Post-Harvest Soybean Loss During Truck Transport: A Case Study of Piaui State, Brazil

Paola Medeiros, Irenilza de Alencar Nääs[(✉)], Oduvaldo Vendrametto,
and Mathilde Soares

Paulista University, São Paulo, Brazil
paola.o.medeiros@gmail.com, irenilza.naas@unip.br

Abstract. Reducing post-harvest losses in the grain production system are of great interest to Brazilian agricultural production. Truck transport is commonly used world wide for the distribution of goods for trade. In Brazil, truck transportation is usually the most economical way to distribute goods in places where inexpensive or natural means of transport alternatives are not available. Truck transport plays a significant role in moving raw materials and processed products from the agricultural production. This study aimed to evaluate the post-harvest loss in transportation in soybean in the state of Piaui. The route of trucks loaded with soybean was analyzed from two regions. The trucks were weighted when leaving the farm and again weighted when arriving at the processing plant. Results indicate that there was a difference in weight between the farm and final destination indicating possible losses during the road transport.

Keywords: Distribution networks · Logistics · Transportation plan

1 Introduction

Post-harvest losses in food grains at different stages of their handling would help assess the extent and magnitude of losses and propose mitigation actions to reduce the losses. Amongst the cereals post-harvest losses the truck transportation represents nearly 1% of losses [1,2].

Truck transport is commonly used worldwide for the distribution of goods for trade. In Brazil, truck transport is usually the most economical way to provide an allocation of goods in places where inexpensive (railways) or natural (rivers) transport alternatives are not available. Truck transport plays a significant role in moving raw materials and processed products from the agricultural rich North and Midwestern region of Brazil to the port cities of the South. Current estimates of grain loss during truck transport are reported to be between 1–5% of a typical load of cereals (27,000 kg), and losses stem from inadequately drying the grain before transport and the use of non-grain trucks to haul grain for distances upwards of 2,500 to 3,000 km. For soybeans, these long hauls may take up to 2–3 days during the rainy season and the grain loses quality when it reaches the

I. Nääs et al. (Eds.): APMS 2016, IFIP AICT 488, pp. 606–611, 2016.
DOI: 10.1007/978-3-319-51133-7_72

port [3]. Brazil has large proportions and distances and the costs for transport of materials and products over long geographical distances are high. These increases cost and consequently the price of the final product. This scenario continues to bring investment losses, and the decline in the quality of the Brazilian modal transport infrastructure increases the loss of international competitiveness [4]. Worldwide, Brazil stands in the 48th position Global Competitiveness Index, and in the 107th place in infrastructure [5]. The adoption of freight transportation adopted in Brazil is shown in Fig. 1.

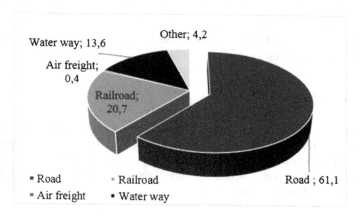

Fig. 1. Freight transportation forms in Brazil. Adapted from [6]

Brazilian soybean production is distributed in 25 million hectares with a harvest of 73.3 million metric tons during the 2011/2012 harvest. Peak production occurred in the Midwest and South regions (states of Mato Grosso, Parana, and the Rio Grande do Sul with yields of 20.83, 14.37, and 10.05 million metric tons respectively. Current production costs for soybeans in the central regions of Brazil are estimated at $1,156 U.S. per hectare [7]. The occupation of Piauí savanna began between the 1970s and 1980s with live-stock projects and cashew cultivation incentivized by the government credit lines, which encouraged people from other states to migrate to Piaui. From 1990, it intensified the implementation of large scale soybean production in the state, which currently represents 24% of the area planted in the Northeast and 2% of Brazil's area. According to [8] in the last soybean harvests the state of Piaui had an increase of 76% of the planted area. This value was higher than the whole Northeastern region development (46%), and the Brazilian increase in soybean production (32%) in the same period. This scenario characterizes the state as a new agriculture frontier mainly the Mapitoba compound, which represents 18% of the state planted area. Soybean production is located in high and flat agricultural lands with appropriate rain index; however, the newly developed areas lack in logistic infrastructure. According to [9] 65% of the soybean produced in Brazil is transported by roads to processing plants and ports. The bad conditions of the roads increase the operational costs by 30%. In the Piaui state, 100% of produced and harvested soybean is transported by two ways routes, and some of them are dusty roads. The truck is not appropriate as well implicating in the additional cost of freight [10]. The cargo composition refers to the distance of transport, season, and the product [11]. The proper transportation of grains is an important issue in reducing the losses [12]. Perishable materials such as cereals require specific environmental conditions (such as air temperature and relative humidity) to maintain quality. The excess of moisture in the truck loads might induce the product fermentation reducing final quality [13]. Although worldwide the grain loss limit in transportation is around 1% [1], in Brazil it is acceptable values near 3% of bulk grain transportation [10]. This study aimed to analyze the soybean post-harvest loss by loads transported in trucks from two different regions to the processing plant.

2   Methodology

The case-study designed to verifying the amount of soybean loss that occurred during truck transportation from the producing area to the central point from where the grain is directed to the industrial processing plant in the county of Uruçui Table 1. Data were recorded from March to May 2014 from four farms located in two different regions.

Table 1. The data are recorded and the dataset organization.

Region	Farm	Data recorded	Truckloads (n)
1 (Nova Santa Rosa)	a	Distance from the farm to	222
	b	destination; truck load weight	
2 (Baixa Grande do Ribeiro)	c	(t) at farm and destination;	273
	d	type of road	

Information was recorded from 495 truckloads of soybean from the farm to the processing plant (crushing operation) located in Uruçuí in the interior of Piauí State, Northeastern of Brazil. From the total of loads 222 where originated from two farms in region 1 (Nova Santa Rosa), and 273 from two farms in region 2 (Baixa Grande do Ribeiro). For each load, the weight in the farm and the weight at the final destination was compared and the eventual loss calculated. Several trucks were used in the soybean transportation; therefore, the specificity of the vehicle was not considered in this study. The distance from the farms in region 1 (a, b) to the final destination was 166 km. In this scenario, 60% (110 km) of the distance the road was covered with asphalt and 34% (56 km) was a dusty road. The distance from the farms in region 2 (c, d) to the processing plant was 296 Km with approximately 85% (246 km) of asphalt road and 15% (50 km) of the dusty road. Descriptive analysis was applied to data using the calculations

of the mean trend such as the median, dispersion, and the standard deviation
for each distance and weight.

3   Results and Discussion

Truckloads (222 from farms a and b) from region 1 (Nova Santa Rosa) presented
an absolute difference in weight of 25.56 t (0.28%), as shown in Table 2. The 273
loads from region 2 (Baixa Grande do Ribeiro) traveled 346 Km to reach the
processing plant. The total volume transported was 10,968 t, from that 10,952 t
reached the final destination. The amount of bulk load of 15.59 t (0.14%) was
lost along the way Table 3.

Table 2. Data on the truckloads of soybean transported from the farms in region 1
(Nova Santa Rosa)

	Load (n)	Weight at farm (t)	Weight at destination (t)	Loss (t)	Average	Median	SD
Farm 1	106	4344	4336	8.52	0.08	0.06	0.15
Farm2	116	4562	4545	17.04	0.15	0.09	0.13
Total	222	8906	8880	25.56	0.12	0.07	0.14

n = number of loads; SD = standard deviation.

Table 3. Data on the truckloads of soybean transported from the farms in region 2
(Baixa Grande do Ribeiro)

	Load	Weight at farm (t)	Weight at destination (t)	Loss (t)	Average	Median	SD
Farm 1	230	9210	9197	13.50	0.06	0.05	0.03
Farm2	43	1758	1756	2.10	0.05	0.05	0.01
Total	273	10968	10952	15.59	0.06	0.05	0.03

n=number of loads; SD=standard deviation.

According to [2], in a study of two communities in Bangladesh, it was found
that the losses in the transport of rice and wheat, amounted respectively to
13.90% and 5.53% of total losses in post-harvest. The authors [14] described a
case study in India found transport losses for rice and 9.63% to 11.81% wheat,
reaffirming that the losses transportation are also present in other grain crops.
The route from region 1 to the processing plant (Nova Santa Rosa - Uruçuí)
was done using the road PI 391 and BR 324, totaling 166 km, of which 56 km
(34%) consists of the unpaved (dusty) road. However, the route from region 2
to the processing plant (Baixa Grande do Ribeiro – Uruçuí) was held using the
road BR 342/IP 392, that has 15% (50 km) of its entire route of the unpaved
(dusty) road. Relating the amount of losses in the total volume transported the

loads Nova Santa Rosa were moved longer distances on the unpaved road and had more volume of lost grain. Therefore, in this case, it can be inferred that the larger the unpaved road route, the higher the volume loss, possibly due to greater load trepidation on this kind of road. According to [15] in developing countries, the transport losses occur due to accidents, poorly maintained roads, lack of infrastructure and vehicles. This fact is confirmed by the value of the average losses found in charges in the region 1 showed higher average, almost double compared to loads of region 2. About the median, the discrepancy is smaller because a region has median loss of 0.07 t and another a loss of 0.05 t. In a report of the World Bank [16], in the Logistic Performance Index (LPI) that evaluates the quality of domestic trade and transport infrastructure, Brazil is ranked in 55th place, with a long wait in ports for international trade. Therefore, investment in improving transportation of cereals of crucial for the country, especially that the economy is highly based on the grain/commodity trade.

4   Conclusions and Outlook

In both areas studied and considering all considered loads, there was a difference in weight between the source and destination indicating possible losses during the road transport. The international standards find 0.25 of losses acceptable within the players along the supply chains. As the losses in this study are 0.14%, there should not be a problem when considering of supply chains point of view. However, when the scale of business in applied the total loss was nearly 25 tons, and this amount is certainly not a slight loss. Regarding the type of road, the path that has the longest section without pavement showed a higher degree of grain loss.

Acknowledgment. The authors wish to thank CAPES - Minter.

References

1. Bala, B., Haque, M., Hossain, A., Majumdar, S.: Post harvest loss and technical efficiency of rice. assessment and measures for strengthening food security. Technical report, Wheat and Maize Production System (2010)
2. Begum, E.A.: Economic analysis of post-harvest losses in food grains for strengthening food security in Northern Regions of Bangladesh. Int. J. Appl. Res. Bus. Adm. Econ. **1**(3) (2012)
3. Olsen, J.W., Wilhelmi, C.R., Zandonadi, R.S., Danao, M.G.C., Gates, R.S.: Monitoring grain bed conditions during truck transport of soybeans in brazil. In: 2013 Kansas City, Missouri, July 21-July 24, 2013. p. 1. American Society of Agricultural and Biological Engineers (2013)
4. Garcia, S., Vicens-Salort, E., Nääs, I.: Investment in Intermodal Transportation in Brazil could Benefit the Country's Agribusiness GDP Growth. Revista Brasileira de Engenharia de Biossistemas **9**(1), 90–98 (2015)
5. Schwab, K., Sala-i Martín, X., Brende, B.: World economic forum: the global competitiveness report 2012–2013. Technical report (2012)

6. CNT: Pesquisa CNT de Rodovias 2012. Technical report (2012)

7. IMEA: Custo Médio Efetivo de Produçã de Soja Safra 2013/2014 - Centro-Sul (2013). http://www.imea.com.br

8. CONAB: Série Histórica de Produção de Soja das Safras 1976/77 a 2014/15 (2015). www.conab.gov.br

9. CNT: Entraves Logísticos ao Escoamento de Soja e Milho. Technical report (2015)

10. Soares, M.G., Caixeta Filho, J.V.: Caracterização do Mercado de Fretes Rodoviários para Produtos Agrícolas. Gestão Produção **4**(2), 186–203 (1997)

11. Martins, R.S.: Estudo da Formação do Frete Rodoviário e Potencial de Conflitos em Negociações em Cadeias do Agronegócio Brasileiro. Organizações Rurais Agroindustriais **10**(1) (2011)

12. D'Arce, M., Regitano, A.B.: Pós Colheita e Armazenamento de Grãos. Technical report (2011). http://www.esalq.usp.br/departamentos/lan/pdf/Armazenamentodegraos.pdf

13. Jedermann, R., Nicometo, M., Uysal, I., Lang, W.: Reducing food losses by intelligent food logistics. Philos. Trans. R. Soc. Lond. A: Math. Phys. Eng. Sci. **372**(2017), 20130302 (2014)

14. Basavaraja, H., Mahajanashetti, S., Udagatti, N.C., et al.: Economic analysis of post-harvest losses in food grains in india: a case study of Karnataka. Agric. Econ. Res. Rev. **20**(1), 117–126 (2007)

15. Redlingshöfer, B., Soyeux, A., et al.: Food losses and wastage as a sustainability indicator of food and farming systems. In: Producing and reproducing farming systems. New modes of organisation for sustainable food systems of tomorrow. 10th European IFSA Symposium, Aarhus, Denmark, 1–4. International Farming Systems Association (2012), July 2012

16. Arvis, J.F., Saslavsky, D., Ojala, L., Shepherd, B., Busch, C., Raj, A., Naula, T.: Connecting to compete 2016. Trade Logistics in the Global Economy. Technical report (2016)

Production Economics

Cost Modelling Approach for the Source Specific Evaluation of Alternative Manufacturing Networks

Christina Reuter, Jan-Philipp Prote[(✉)], and Torben Schmitz

RWTH Aachen University, Aachen, Germany
{c.reuter,j.prote,t.schmitz}@wzl.rwth-aachen.de

Abstract. In order to seize the full potential of production on a global scale, companies need to constantly evolve their production networks and reconsider the number of sites. Decision making in this context forces corporations to process a substantial amount of information and complexity. Prominent examples of German companies (e.g. Stihl or Steiff) prove the present struggle of decision makers. Existing approaches are either too complex and effortful or they do not consider all decision relevant cost factors in a cause-fair way. This paper presents a pragmatic cost modelling approach which focuses on the identification and projection of decision relevant cost factors as well as their source specific allocation in terms of the impact on existing sites in the network.

Keywords: Global supply networks · Manufacturing networks · Location decisions · Cost modelling · Source specific cost allocation

1 Challenges Within the Evaluation of Alternative Global Manufacturing Networks

Producing companies nowadays mostly operate in global manufacturing networks consisting of globally spread production sites. These networks are mainly determined by the quantity and the geographical distribution of its production sites. Evaluating alternative network scenarios in terms of adjusted number of sites is therefore one important mean to elaborate a manufacturing network. However, as recent research studies of the Fraunhofer ISI show, companies struggle with designing global manufacturing networks and location decision making in particular: 25% of locations decisions made by German companies needed to be revoked [1]. Four major challenges within location decisions can be identified: The first challenge is the missing transparency about decision relevant (cost) information. In a production network each site is under the influence of a variety of internal and external interdependencies (e.g. cross-linkages to other sites and suppliers as well as the development of markets and economical or political conditions). Many managers, especially in SME, are overwhelmed by the complexity of the decision situation [2]. Therefore it is necessary to establish

© IFIP International Federation for Information Processing 2016
Published by Springer International Publishing AG 2016. All Rights Reserved
I. Nääs et al. (Eds.): APMS 2016, IFIP AICT 488, pp. 615–623, 2016.
DOI: 10.1007/978-3-319-51133-7_73

transparency by understanding the cause-effect relationship between costs and cost drivers. Another shortcoming is the availability and validity of decision relevant cost data. The required accounting information might not be available or only in the local location controlling which decision makers might not want to incorporate in the process for confidentiality reasons. Moreover local controlling divisions are still given an ample scope so that it takes high efforts to ensure the comparability of cost information.

Studies showed that misvalued cost advantages were the main reason for companies to revoke their location decision. On the one hand cost savings, flexibility and quality are overvalued while on the other hand, time and investment efforts are often underestimated [3]. Especially during the startup phase a potential new location needs to be supported and coordinated. In many cases the resulting overhead costs are not allocated to the causing new location but to the existing locations. Moreover the impact on existing sites in the network is often neglected. A new site might cause a structural cost impact on existing locations if for example complete product lines or only production volumes are relocated. Fixed costs for staff, production area or equipment cannot fully be adapted to the declining production volumes. This phenomenon is known as cost stickiness [4]. It leads to a lower productivity and ability to bear overhead costs in the existing sites. In general, the shift of fixed costs across the network is not duly taken into account.

To contribute to solving these deficits this paper pursues the following objectives:

- Systematical and comprehensible cost modelling using cost drivers
- Allocation of relevant costs in a source-specific way (in terms of the decision situation) to depict impact on existing sites
- Pragmatical approach to ensure applicability in industrial practice

2   Deficiencies of Existing Approaches

In the following state of the art section a cross selection of contemporary research on cost modelling and decision support in the field of evaluating alternative global production networks is presented.

Vahdani and Mohammadi present a bi-objective optimization model for supply chains aiming at the minimization of total costs and waiting times in services. Their cost model includes fixed costs, transportation costs, manufacturing costs as well as distribution costs. The cost model is combined with a priority queuing system and enriched by a uncertainty approach. To verify the results of the model various theoretical experiments are performed, no actual cost data however is utilized. The cost model does not depict costs in detail which change within a location decision. The modeling effort for costs is high since a closed loop supply chain is considered [5].

Schuh et al. developed the software tool OptiWo for the optimization of manufacturing networks. By the use of an optimization algorithm and a total landed cost function complete networks are modeled and evaluated. As the method focuses on a balanced state of a production network not all relevant costs are presented detailed enough to support single location decisions [6].

A mixed integer programming model for integrated production and distribution planning is introduced by Yuan et al. They utilize a branch-and-bound algorithm to assign multiple products to a certain numbers of sites and warehouses which distribute to the customers. The approach implicates a low modelling effort, while the focus however is mostly on costs for opening up and operating warehouses [7].

Wagner and Nyhuis deliver an approach for a global manufacturing system for product variants. Especially the needs of SME which often produce a variety of products with high demands on quality are taken into account. Production systems are designed and evaluated by a cost based system for relocation decisions. As a first step, the actual state is analyzed based on the total cost of ownership. Afterwards various scenarios are created to enable an evaluation of different locations [8].

Christodoulou et al. provide an approach with 4 phases for the continuous configuration and improvement of production networks. The first step is to understand the need for change and to define a network strategy. Afterwards a Make-or-Buy analysis is made to find the products that should be considered. A multi-stage approach is used to determine the suitable manufacturing location of each product. Finally the relocation process is planned. The decision making process is rather in focus than a profound cost modelling [9].

To support location decisions Yang uses the AHP decision model which allows comparing decision-makers preferences with location characteristics. The cost modeling however is not very profound. By evaluating alternative sites under both quantitative and qualitative factors it is possible to take managerial experience and judgement into account [10].

All in all it can be stated that several approaches in this field exist. Especially the cost modeling approaches are quite effortful and time-consuming. Most approaches do not consider all required cost elements, which are affected by a location decision, in a source specific way. Neither do they offer the possibility to calibrate the cost model using (aggregated) actual costs. Thereby an opportunity to improve the methods validity is missed.

3 Cost Modelling Approach for the Source Specific Evaluation

In this paper we present a new cost modelling approach which enables a pragmatic cost modelling of decision relevant cost types based on cost drivers and the consumption of resources. Special attention is paid to source specific evaluation of the impact on existing sites in the network. The model consists of four phases. In the preparation phase the decision situation is specified (e.g. concrete objectives, data availabilities and implications) and the level of aggregation as well as the decision relevant cost types are derived based on the specifics of the decision situation. In the second step the operational cost model is built in a combined top down/bottom up approach to use the modeled and calibrated actual costs as basis for prediction of costs in the decision scenarios. An extended evaluation model is used in the next step to evaluate the additional costs associated with the decision (e.g. investments, transaction costs) and to include the structural impact on existing sites (e.g. sticky costs) in the assessment. Lastly a decision support is built to efficiently evaluate alternative network scenarios by a profitability calculation and a source specific unit cost comparison. The overall approach is outlined in a comprehensive overview in Fig. 1.

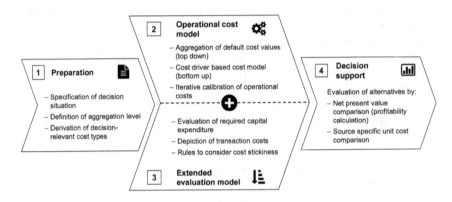

Fig. 1. Source specific cost modelling approach

The operational cost model and the source specific evaluation model (steps two and three) as the core of this paper are depicted in more detail in the following. Further information on the preparation phase, especially the derivation of decision relevant cost types, can be found in Reuter et al. [11].

4   Operational Cost Model and Calibration

The objective of the operational cost model is to depict all decision relevant costs of one product group in a pragmatic way and allow decision makers to track the costs back to their causing source. For this purpose, the resource-based cost modeling approach for product variants of Schuh is adapted to the specifics of a location decision process [12]. The detailed operational cost modeling approach is shown in Fig. 2.

The model consists of a twofold top down/bottom up approach to derive the required data and parameters. The bottom up stream defines the basic set of cost types, resources and cost drivers which represent the cost consumption. The top down part prepares and aggregates actual costs from standardized sources like the external accounting for example in order to assign these cost information to the defined cost types. Both streams are merged in the next step and the

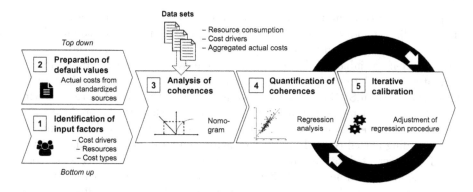

Fig. 2. Operational cost modelling approach

coherences between cost drivers, resources and resulting costs are analyzed and quantified. The approach is based on the idea, that a cost driver is responsible for a certain resource consumption (e.g. produced quantity of a product group). This correlation can be formalized in a consumption function. The resource consumption (e.g. weight of raw materials) in turn causes costs (e.g. raw material costs). The correlation might be formalized in a cost function. The coherence of both functions can best be visualized by the use of a simplified nomogram shown in the following Fig. 3.

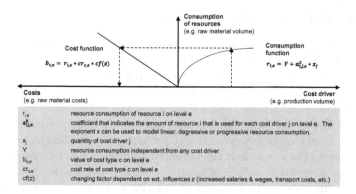

Fig. 3. Example of a nomogram and equations

4.1 Work Guideline

The effect of each cost driver on the consumption of its corresponding resource and ultimately on the related cost type is modeled individually but can be depicted by one mathematical equation that integrates both functions. In order to quantify the consumption function as well as the cost function, a regression analysis will be conducted. In a first step a standard ordinary least square (OLS) regression is used to predict the corresponding cost value (e.g. material costs) as the dependent variable. OLS is a standardized, easy to use statistical method for estimating the relationships among variables. Stock & Watson provide detailed information on OLS [13]. In order to conduct the OLS, actual data sets with several points in time (e.g. years 2013–2015) are needed which should provide information on the resource consumption, the value of the cost drivers and the corresponding actual costs. In order to ensure comparability, the numerical values of each set of data has to be prepared: inflation induced effects on costs as well as any one time special effects which do not correlate with the regular serial production need to be eliminated. Once the OLS delivers a first quantification of the coherences, the consumption and cost function can be validated by predicting the actual costs of the latest data set. Hereto only values for the cost drivers of the corresponding data set are needed. If the predicted costs are not sufficiently close to the actual costs (e.g. measured with the mean square error or root mean square error), the cost model can be calibrated iteratively by trying out different regression models. These procedures include generalized least squares analysis (GLS) or nonlinear regression.

The procedure of cost modelling is done for all cost types (per product group) and for all focused product groups. A complete overview of all relevant cost types, resources and cost drivers can be found in another paper presented by the authors [14].

4.2   Extended Cost Evaluation Model

The extended evaluation model is used to evaluate the additional costs associated with the decision (e.g. investments, transaction costs) and to include the structural impact on existing sites through cost stickiness in the assessment. Investments as well as transaction costs (e.g. costs for coordination and control, travel expenses, trainings and educations, etc.) are well known concepts which do not need further detailing, since several approaches illustrate their consideration. [e.g. 3] Sticky costs however are not yet integrated in the location decision making process. They represent the potential negative impact a new site has on existing ones since their ability of bearing overhead costs is weakened. This is particularly the case for building costs, salaries and partly for machinery and equipment costs. If production volumes or complete products are relocated to a new location, idle capacities in terms of production and office area, management capacities and machinery and equipment are left at the original site. These idle capacities cannot be reduced immediately. A factory manager for example cannot be paid 80% of his salary if 20% of "his" products are relocated. The value of these idle capacities (fixed costs) can be interpreted as sticky costs.

The operational model (c.f. Chap. 3.1) can be used to determine the level of cost stickiness per product group in the three cost types by using the corresponding cost drivers.

4.3   Decision Support

The decision support incorporates the data from the cost models and combines a standard profitability calculation using the net present value (NPV) with a source specific unit cost comparison. The NPV focuses on the purely cash-based effects of the potential new site while the unit cost comparison includes implicit costs such as sticky costs in order to ensure a source-specific evaluation for the specific decision situation. A source-specific unit cost comparison provides transparency about the structural impact of the decision for the complete production network and helps to reduce the weight of allegedly short term cost advantages which lower wage levels might offer. Sticky costs however might easily overcompensate the wage level advantage. The following industrial case study illustrates the source specific unit cost comparison using a concrete example of one product group.

5   First Case Study and Basic Validation

The approach is provisionally validated with an industrial partner in the metal working industry. Objective of the bilateral project was the preparation of a decision paper for a potential new location in Eastern Europe. The management wanted to know whether the partly relocation of production capacities would make sense in order to utilize lower factor costs as a typical profitability calculation (NPV based) indicated. The results of the source-specific cost modelling approach are shown in Fig. 4 exemplarily for one product group as a unit cost comparison. By explicitly considering the sticky costs associated with the decision situation it becomes obvious that the savings in purchase and labour are overcompensated by the cost stickiness of building costs and salaries of the remaining management functions.

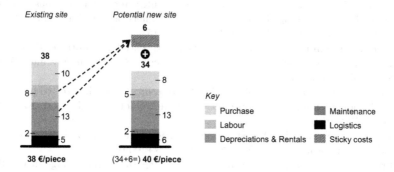

Fig. 4. Exemplary unit cost comparison for one product group

All in all, this first case study proved the general applicability of the source specific cost modelling approach. Transparency regarding the decision specific cause-fair shift of fixed costs could be established.

6   Conclusions

The approach presented in this paper offers a pragmatic cost modelling method to improve location decisions by evaluating alternative manufacturing in a more source specific way through explicitly considering the impact on exiting sites. The cost model enables decision makers to gain more transparency on the cause and effect relationships between drivers, resource consumption and resulting costs. The impact on existing locations in terms of a weaker ability to bear fixed costs can be evaluated and integrated in the decision. The approach was validated with an SME. Further research needs to be done on how to handle special effects (e.g. productivity growth, periodic variations) and on how to include a degradation rate for cost stickiness. More validation needs to be done to further detail the approach and to ensure applicability in various fields/sectors.

Acknowledgement. The authors would like to thank the German Research Foundation DFG for the kind support within the Cluster of Excellence "Integrative Production Technology for High-Wage Countries".

References

1. Zanker, C., Kinkel, S., Maloca, S.: Globale Produktion von einer starken Heimatbasis aus. Mitteilungen aus der ISI-Erhebung zur Modernisierung der Produktion. Fraunhofer ISI, Karlsruhe (2013)
2. Abele, E., Kluge, J.: How to Go Global-Designing and Implementing Global Production Networks. McKinsey & Company, Inc., NewYork (2005)
3. Abele, E., Meyer, T., Näher, U., Strube, G., Sykes, R. (eds.): Global Production. Springer, Heidelberg (2008)
4. Dalla Via, N., Perego, P.: Sticky cost behaviour: evidence from small and medium sized companies. Acc. Finance **54**(3), 753–778 (2014)
5. Vahdani, B., Mohammadi, M.: A bi-objective interval-stochastic robust optimization model for designing closed loop supply chain network with multi-priority queuing system. Int. J. Prod. Econ. **170**, 67–87 (2015)
6. Schuh, G., Potente, T., Varandani, R., Schmitz, T.: Global footprint design based on genetic algorithms-an "Industry 4.0" perspective. CIRP Annal-Manuf. Technol. **63**(1), 433–436 (2014)
7. Yuan, X.M., Low, J.M., Yeo, W.M.: A network prototype for integrated production-distribution planning with non-multi-functional plants. Int. J. Prod. Res. **50**(4), 1097–1113 (2012)
8. Wagner, C., Nyhuis, P.: A systematic approach to analysis and design of global production networks. Prod. Eng. **3**(3), 295–303 (2009)
9. Christodoulou, P., Fleet, D., Hanson, P.: Making the Right Things in the Right Places. University of Cambridge, IfM Publication, Cambridge (2007)
10. Yang, J., Lee, H.: An AHP decision model for facility location selection. Facilities **15**(9/10), 241–254 (1997)
11. Reuter, C., Prote, J.P., Pohlig, D.: Approach for the cause-fair allocation of costs in location decisions in global production networks. In: Proceedings of Abstract and Papers of ICPR23. Manilla (2015)

12. Schuh, G.: Produktkomplexität Managen: Strategien-Methoden-Tools. Carl Hanser Verlag GmbH Co KG, Munich (2014)
13. Stock, J.H., Watson, M.W.: Introduction to Econometrics, vol. 104. Addison Wesley, Boston (2003)
14. Reuter, C., Prote, J., Schmitz, T.: A top-down/bottom-up approach for modeling costs of a manufacturing network. In: Proceedings of the 23rd EurOMA Conference, Trondheim (2016)

Measuring the Economic Impact
of Metrological Frauds in Trade Metrology
Using an Input-Output Model

Bruno A. Rodrigues Filho[1,2(✉)] and Rodrigo Franco Gonçalves[2]

[1] National Institute of Metrology, Quality and Technology – INMETRO,
Duque de Caxias, Brazil
bafilho@inmetro.gov.br
[2] Paulista University, São Paulo, Brazil

Abstract. The present study aims to evaluate the economic distortion in trade metrology due to metrological frauds in measuring instruments used in the commerce and industry. The economic distortion represents the economic losses due to measurement deviations in trade. An Input-Output Model approach is carried out in order to determine the economic distortion whenever an output in a process represents the input to another one and it considers the aggregation of values of products traded in the economy. A case test is also conducted using empirical data of measurement errors and metrological frauds in the fuel sector in Brazil in order to determine their economic impact. The results show that the impact of metrological frauds increase the distortion uncertainty from US\$ 54,910,307.13 to US\$ 303,734,309.35 toward consumers' losses creating a great asymmetry in the market.

Keywords: Legal metrology · Economic distortion · Market asymmetry · Leontief

1 Introduction

The commerce has always been present in the human history and it is not possible to imagine our society separately from it. Specifically, the commerce involving goods which values are based on weights and measures has always been present in people's everyday life. Initially, weights and measures were initially introduced to control food in trade [1] and the origins of the weighing instruments which are a symbol of parity, truth and justice date back to the oldest cultures 10,000 years ago [2].

The necessity for protection regards on the economic distortion or market asymmetry that is describe as the monetary value associated to a measurement deviation due to the inaccuracies intrinsic to the measuring processes as a consequence of errors, uncertainties, operator's inaccuracy, environmental conditions and others.

This economic distortion impacts both economy and society since deviations between buyers and sellers cause economic losses and unfair competition. Moreover consumer's protections aspects are also related to this market asymmetry that may be an indicator of the economic impact of legal metrology [3]. Several researchers have

© IFIP International Federation for Information Processing 2016
Published by Springer International Publishing AG 2016. All Rights Reserved
I. Nääs et al. (Eds.): APMS 2016, IFIP AICT 488, pp. 624–632, 2016.
DOI: 10.1007/978-3-319-51133-7_74

also presented the importance of legal metrology and its social and economical impact to the society, trade, industry and governments [4–8]. The initiative regarding using empirical data do evaluate the economic impact of inaccuracy of measuring instruments was initially proposed during the decade of 1970 [4] and several formulations using proxy variables have also been proposed, such as [5]: number of measurement related patents in comparison to the total; cost of certification as an indicator of industries willingness to pay for reliability; the sum of all industry equipment.

Despite the deviations of the measuring instruments regards to the measurement error theory, an intentional error or a metrological fraud caused by the operator in order to prejudice a buyer in a commercial transaction creates a great distortion in the economy. An example is the energy market in Germany, where the global competition has led to tighter profit margins increasing the risk for metrological frauds [6]. Recently, the global market has also been overflowed by metrological frauds in the fuel market occasioning severe losses to the buyers and competitors [7].

Regardless of the obvious aspect that a metrological fraud is prejudicial to the consumers and consequently the economy, its economic impact is not well known. The Input-Output Model allows to compute how a change in a product demand impacts its production contemplating the interconnections of productive processes since it considers that an output of a process can be an input to another one [8].

Consequently, the Input-Output Model, hereinafter called I-O for simplicity, permits to evaluate the economic impact a measurement deviation in a product to the economy, introducing a factor representing these deviations to the traditional Leontief's formulation, identifying how the deviations spreads across every sector on the economy.

Then, based on the I-O theory, the present study aims to evaluate the economical uncertainties cause by metrological frauds in trade. The measurement errors report for fuel disperses in the field in Brazil is used to provide an empirical case. In order to understand the impact of metrological frauds, we replaced a percentage of the empirical deviations by values based on known metrological frauds to evaluate the behavior of these frauds to the economy.

2 Methodology

2.1 Formulation to Compute the Economic Distortion

The I-O formulation is based on the assumption that the productive processes are connected since an input of a process is the output of another process [8]. This interconnection is represented in a matrix system where the lines represent the outputs and columns the inputs. The basic conception is given by the product output q, which is represented by the final demand of products F plus the intermediate consumption of industries U, as seen in (1).

$$q = U + F \tag{1}$$

Due to linear algebra, the basic formulation of the I-O is given by (2), where g represents aggregation of q in industry sectors, I the identity, and D and B are coefficient matrices.

$$g = (I - D.B)^{-1}.D.F \tag{2}$$

Consequently, the total national production of the n aggregate products g is given by the sum of the vector g, as shown in (2), where g is given in monetary units.

$$g = \sum_{i=1}^{n} g_i \tag{3}$$

To compute the impact of measurement deviation, a multiplier factor δ representing a percentage of deviation due to measurement errors is introduced in both intermediate consumption of industries and the final demand, as seen in (4).

$$q' = \delta.U + \delta.F \tag{4}$$

Finally, the influence of the distortion due to measurement deviations, i.e. the economic distortion ED, is given by the difference of total production including δ, g' less the total production of the n aggregate products g, as shown in (3).

$$ED = \sum_{i=1}^{n} (g_i' - g_i) \tag{5}$$

2.2   Evaluating the Impact of Metrological Frauds

A metrological fraud can be understood as an intentional deviation introduced in a measuring instrument to promote financial gains to the seller over the buyer. The definition of measurement error is given in (6), where the error e is equal to the instrument value e_i less the value of the standard used for comparison e_s.

$$e = e_i - e_s \tag{6}$$

Consequently, positive values of e represent buyer' losses and negative values seller's losses. For example, in the fuel market, for a petro pump displaying 20.10 l and the standard displaying 20.00 l, and for 1 l = \$1.00, it would represent a loss of \$0.10 for the buyer.

Since the measurement deviations of instruments can be represented by an average and measurement uncertainty regarding a statistical distribution, the economy distortion must also contain an uncertainty. For the present study it is reasonable to assume that measurement errors of the instruments used in the market and industry follow a gauss distribution. We also assumed the standard deviation to represent the measurement uncertainty in the present study.

However, the set of illegal devices would follow a different statistical distribution once they are intentionally regulated to provide higher positive measurement errors. Thus, the contributions of fraudulent devices contribute only to positive values of deviations. So in order to analyze the contributions of errors to the economic distortion uncertainty, we considered the mutual distribution uncertainty to positive values (buyer's losses) and the regular devices distribution to negative values (seller's losses), as seen in Fig. 1.

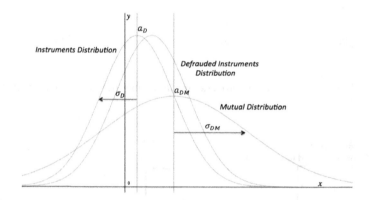

Fig. 1. Uncertainty evaluation for the economic distortion.

A mutual distribution uncertainty σ_{DM} is obtained combining deviations of both fraudulent and regular measurement instruments distributions. The measurement uncertainty is represented in (7), where a_{DM} represents the average of the mutual distribution, a_D the average and σ_D the standard deviation of the instruments distribution.

$$\sigma_D - a_D \leq measurement\ uncertainty \leq a_{DM} + \sigma_{DM} \qquad (7)$$

2.3   Simulating a Metrological Fraud

In order to evaluate the economic impact of metrological fraud we used an empirical database of measurement errors for automotive ethanol dispensers in Brazil [9]. And, the metrological frauds for the fuel market usually varies from 6% to 12% [7].

To analyze how the economic distortion behaves when fraudulent instruments are used in the commerce, we have established two variables: the percentage of fraudulent devices and the measurement error due to the fraud. Then, a Scilab 5.5.2 algorithm replaces randomly a percentage of instruments in the database by fraudulent values, as follow:

```
Sheets=readxls('Ethanol_Error.xls') // Reading empirical data
  typeof(Sheets) Error=Sheets(1)
  typeof(Error)   Error.value()
  percentage=0.05//% Defining percentage to be replaced
  total=fix(37719*percentage/100)+1
  fraudError=Error.value()
  VolumeFraud=2000 //ml
  for i=1:total //Replacing values
        fraudError((fix(37719*rand())+1))=VolumeFraud
  end
write_csv(fraudError,"Fraud_Error.xls") //new dataset//End
```

Figure 2 also illustrates the process of simulating fraudulent instruments in the market.

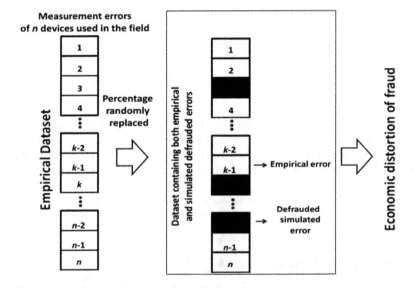

Fig. 2. Process for replacing empirical measurement errors for simulated defrauded values.

The empirical data of measurement errors of automotive ethanol dispersers where the average (a_D) and the standard deviation (σ_D) comprising 37,719 ethanol dispensers verified in 2014 are represented in ml units by: $a_D = 4.22$; $\sigma_D = 40.83$. The great divergence of these dispensers is mainly caused by the imprecisions of the measurement of fuel, such as environmental conditions, humidity, user's proficiency and others [10].

Finally, to compute the economic distortion according to 5, we used the latest published Brazilian Input-Output matrices representing the economy in 2005 [11] as well as the dollar exchange rate [12]: US$ 1.0000 = R$ 2.3407.

3   Results

For a bigger percentage of fraudulent devices used in trade, the economic distortion associated to the measurement errors is consequently bigger. Table 1 shows the results of economic distortion from a range of 0.01% to 1% of fraudulent measuring instruments introduced in the commerce comparing to a scenario where no frauds are used. A fraud value of 10% is applied to the results presented in Table 1, representing a deviation of 2 l for each 20 l traded.

The measurement uncertainty regarding seller's losses remains constant once a fraud affects only the buyers. The average representing the economic distortion is linear dependent of the percentage of fraudulent devices (R^2 = 0.9998).

Table 1. The variation of the measurement uncertainty according to the percentage of fraudulent devices for a 10% volume deviation.

% of fraudulent instruments in the market	Economic distortion average (US$)	Measurement uncertainty		Range (Buyer + Seller)
		Buyer loss	Seller loss	
0	$ 5,673,853.89	$ 54,910,307.13	$ 49,236,453.24	$ 104,146,760.38
0.01	$5,969,647.42	$ 67,441,271.42		$ 116,677,724.66
0.05	$7,018,370.10	$ 88,496,693.13		$ 137,733,146.37
0.1	$7,018,370.10	$ 109,686,654.24		$ 158,923,107.49
0.5	$19,119,034.64	$ 216,363,722.30		$ 265,600,175.55
1	$32,295,351.86	$ 303,734,309.35		$ 352,970,762.60

Figure 3 shows the economic distortion variation due to metrological frauds, displaying the measurement uncertainty. It is also possible to observe the great divergence between consumer and seller's losses.

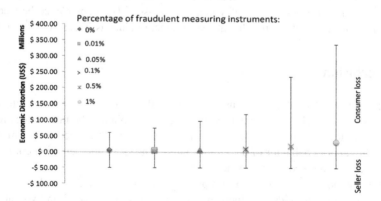

Fig. 3. Effect of metrological frauds on the economy according to the percentage of fraudulent instruments.

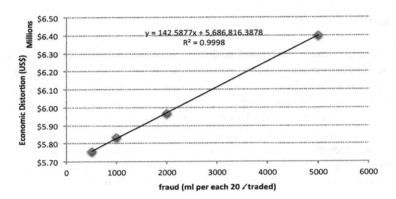

Fig. 4. Economic distortion for a constant number of fraudulent devices and volume variation.

The economic distortion for bigger percentage values of fraudulent instruments in the market introduces bigger consumers' losses differently when comparing to the sellers' losses, which remains constant. As a direct consequence, the probability of consumers' losses is bigger than sellers' and it indicates a component of unfair competition caused by the asymmetry of information. The range of US$ 352,970,762.60 uncertainty caused by 1% of irregular instruments in the commerce is more than three times bigger than the range of uncertainty if no fraudulent instruments were used and the uncertainty toward consumer's losses is six times bigger than the initial uncertainty, where no fraud is applied to the market.

In order to identify the behavior of the economic distortion due to the volume fraud dispensed to the consumers, we simulated the economic distortion for a constant number of fraudulent instruments and ranged the value of fraud, from 500 ml to 5000 ml for each 20 l traded. Figure 4 shows the behavior of the economic distortion for different values of fraud when keeping the percentage of 0.01% fraudulent instruments in the market constant.

The economic distortion introduced in the economy increases the consumers' losses in the trade due to bigger errors of volume dispensed. The dependence between the economic distortion and the fraudulent measurement values is linear, for $R^2 = 0.9998$.

4 Conclusion

The Input-Output Model allowed us to compute the economic distortion due to the measurement errors of instruments used in trade contemplating the interconnections of the sector on the economy. Since a fraud is intentionally introduced in the market it changes the random behavior of deviations and add a systematic deviation component, which reflects in the economic impact to the economy.

The methodology proposed to compute the impact of fraudulent devices in the market also permitted to identify their impact on the economy based on two variables: the percentage error of measurement traded and percentage of fraudulent instruments.

Empirical information of the fuel market in Brazil also enable to evaluate the impact of metrological frauds showed to be expressive and it increases the range of uncertainty of the economic distortion from US$ 104,146,760.38 to US$ 352,970,762.60 toward consumers' losses, for 1% of fraudulent devices for a 10% deviation. The uncertainty representing buyer's losses increases from US$ 54,910,307.13 to $ 303,734,309.35 creating a big asymmetry between buyers and sellers in the market. Moreover, we identified that the economic loss is linearly dependent of the volume deviation introduced in the instrument, for a constant number of fraudulent devices.

The big impact of metrological frauds in the commerce may affect the relation between buyer and seller due to the great asymmetry of information caused by the intentional deviation in the measurements, creating unfair competition that may also impact honest sellers leading the economy to a failure.

Additionally, the proposed model can also be applied to any industry's quality management system in order to evaluate the losses due to the measurement processes since the I-O analysis is a consolidate model in economy.

Acknowledgement. The authors acknowledge the support of INMETRO, which enabled us to carry out this research.

References

1. Birch, J.: The expanding scope of legal metrology and the changing role of the state in a globalised world. OIML Bull. **XLV**, 23–24 (2004)
2. Euler, W.: History of scales part 15: automatic gravimetric filling instruments (AGFIs) - weighing and bag filling machines for loose bulk products. OIML Bull. 4, 8–9 (2015)
3. Rodrigues Filho, B.A., Gonçalves, R.F.: Legal metrology, the economy and society: a systematic literature review. Measurement **69**, 155–163 (2015)
4. Stiefel, S.W.: Management assistance for weights and measures progress, measuring inaccuracy's economic distortion. Presented at the 58th National Conference on Weights an Measures (1973)
5. Birch, J.: Benefit of Legal Metrology for the Economy and Society - A Study for the International Committee of Legal Metrology. International Organization of Legal Metrology - OIML, Paris (2003)
6. Kochsiek, M., Schulz, W.: Modernization of legal metrology in Germany. OIML Bull. **XLV**, 27–31 (2004)
7. Leitão, F.O., Vasconcellos, M.T., Brandão, P.C.R.: Contramedidas De Hardware Y Software Sobre El Fraude De Alta Tecnología Al Surtidor De Combustible Bajo El Alcance De Metrología Legal. In: 9th International Symposium "Metrologia 2014" Proceedings, Havana, Cuba, p. 8 (2014)
8. Leontief, W.: Structure of the world economy: outline of a simple input-output formulation. Proc. IEEE **63**, 345–351 (1975)

9. Rodrigues Filho, B.A., Soratto, A.N., Gonçalves, R.F.: Information systems as a tool to improve legal metrology activities. In: 8th Brazilian Congress on Metrology Proceedings, Bento Gonçalves, RS, Brazil (2015)
10. Batista, E., Almeida, A., Almeida, N., Reis, C., Filipe, E.: Comparison on the verification of fuel dispensers. OIML Bull. **LIV**, 19–24 (2013)
11. IBGE, Rio de Janeiro, Brazil (2008)
12. Brazilian Central Bank. http://www4.bcb.gov.br/pec/taxas/port/ptaxnpesq.asp?id=txcotacao

Effects of Transport Infrastructure in the Economic Development

José Alberto Alencar Luz[1,2], João Gilberto Mendes dos Reis[1(✉)], Fábio de Araújo Leite[1,2], Karmem Weruska Fortes de Araújo[1,2], and Gorthon Moritz[1,2]

[1] Paulista University, São Paulo, Brazil
josealberto@socimol.com.br, betomendesreis@msn.com
[2] Faculdade Santo Agostinho, Teresina, Brazil

Abstract. This paper investigates the relationship between transport infrastructure and economic development. The analysis considers a sample of the ten countries with the highest Gross Domestic Product (GDP) among to 2010 to 2014. The GDP is correlated to the Logistic Performance Index of the World Bank (LPI) using linear regression. The results showed that there is not a relationship between the two variables, but suggest that this relationship is positive when considering the GDP per capita of the ten countries surveyed.

Keywords: Logistics infrastructure · LPI · GDP · Linear regression

1 Introduction

Previous work has mentioned a relationship between transport infrastructure and economic development of a country or region [1]. Transportation is economically and socially vital for the countries and the result of their investments has impacts in the following decades [2]. In addition, transportation is a critical ingredient in the economic development supporting this growth and also important for the well-being of the population [3]. However, it is necessary to understand the extent of this relationship and what economic development factors are associated with transport infrastructure.

There are several factors that can discuss of economic development, among which the Gross Domestic Product (GDP), the Human Development Index, and the Distribution of Income. It is important to mention that, transport infrastructure is associated with the extent of various types of network, its usability, and quality.

Morais Aragon was the first one that pointed that the investments in the urban transport sector in Brazil generate economic growth, but he did not make a quantitative approach, which makes it impossible to a study to confirm the empirical analysis [4]. Bertussi and Ellery Junior investigated the results of public spending on transport in Brazil between 1986 and 2007. The results showed

© IFIP International Federation for Information Processing 2016
Published by Springer International Publishing AG 2016. All Rights Reserved
I. Nääs et al. (Eds.): APMS 2016, IFIP AICT 488, pp. 633–640, 2016.
DOI: 10.1007/978-3-319-51133-7_75

that public investment in transport causes positive effect and it is statistically significant on the economic performance of the Brazilian states [5].

Despite this evidence, it wonders whether countries and regions that have better transportation infrastructure are related to a higher gross domestic product. Generally, the GDP has been used to establish the percentage of investments in the country's transport. Thus, the percentage that countries have invested in transport between 1995 and 2009 has been an average of 1% per year [2]. Whereas GDP varies depending on the country's wealth, it can be assumed that the economically richest countries invest more in transport and therefore have a better infrastructure that influences in trade. This creates a circle that shows the gap between rich and poor countries.

This work seeks to answer this research gap, in other words, if there is a direct influence of the transportation infrastructure and the country's GDP. Thus, the purpose of this article is to assess the importance of transport infrastructure in relation to GDP for the ten largest economies and position Brazil in this scope. To conduct this study it was established a comparison of transport infrastructure in relation to GDP using a linear regression model.

2   Theorethical Background

The GDP is the value of all production of goods and services occurred in a particular place and it can be measured within the country's borders, in a state, county or region, in certain period [6]. It is considered by most researchers of the economy as the main indicator of the wealth of a country and covers three main groups of activities: agriculture, industry and services. The importance of GDP is based on the fact that there are standards it should be calculated, allowing comparisons between study sites. It is an indicator widespread and applied in various analyzes, being one of the main ways to measure the level of development and economy of certain locations.

It is important to highlight that the infrastructure of a region promotes quality of life for residents, as it induces physical interaction of locations, enabling a good performance of the flow of people, goods, and conveyances. Rostow et al. in his theory of stages of development, advocated that any growth impulse "has been preceded, almost without exception, by a substantial accumulation of investments in transport and other public works" [7].

In this reasoning, the authors go on to assert that "the most important functions of these investments have been, therefore, reduce transport costs, enable an efficient combination of resources, expand the domestic market and make possible an effective conduct of international trade" [7].

Rozas and Sánche's work provides an excellent summary of the main empirical studies in this respect of possible economic development relationship with the infrastructure [8]. According to the authors, the first measurements date back to Aschauer's study in the 90s, which measured the impact on the product at the national level in the United States, investment in public works and improvement of related services during the period of 1945–1985. Overall, the author found an elasticity of investment to the growth of 0.39, meaning an increase of 10% in infrastructure investments would allow an increase of 3.9% in the domestic product [8,9]. These estimates seem quite high, resulting in a broad debate about them, especially in the econometric field, since apparently, there were problems of definition and omitted variable and endogeneity. However, numerous studies with different methods and specifications found the positive relationship between infrastructure and growth.

More recent studies, such as Liu Yu ones, made for a Chinese economy, corroborate this positive relationship between infrastructure investment and economic growth [10]. In effect, the author found that for the period of 1978–2009, investment in public infrastructure was a "long-term unidirectional positive impact, in the aggregate product" [10]. The elasticity found by Liu Yu, for the case of China, was 0.24, meaning that a 10% increase in investment in infrastructure would leverage the product in 2.4% [10].

For the specific case of Brazil, the work of Araujo Junior found that infrastructure investments are positively related to economic growth, especially in the long term [1]. In the short term there is also a positive influence, by means of aggregate demand, but to a lesser extent than that achieved in the long run. In their latest work Bertussi and Ellery measured the impact of public spending in transportation in the Brazilian states of the growth rate for the period of 1986–2007, finding a positive and statistically significant effect, realizing a positive contribution to reducing income inequalities between them [5].

Regarding the economic aspect Mallon [11] states that the existence of a transport system is one of the essential differences of subsistence system to a market economy, as it provides an economic integration at various levels. That is, without an adequate transportation system, you cannot have a market economy, hence the importance of studying and understanding the content.

Already Aschauer considered the pioneer in the study of the effect of transport infrastructure on economic growth, says that although there was always consensus among economists that a well-developed transportation infrastructure benefits from economic growth, so far, there are no studies that prove this premise in practice [9].

In this sense, Banister and Berechman [12] emphasize that investments in transport infrastructure provide long-term economic development and states that, while necessary to generate economic growth, it is not enough.

3 Methodology

This article aims to investigate the possible relationship between transport infrastructure and economic development, in this case, linked to GDP. For GDP we used the values for the ten largest economies in the period between 2010-2014, according to Table 1. This research develops simulation considering two situations. The first relating the conventional GDP with LPI and the second GDP per capita with the same LPI.

For transport infrastructure reference was chosen the logistics performance index (LPI) established by research conducted by The Word Bank, the reference

Table 1. GDP growth of the ten largest economies in the years 2010–2014

Country	GDP (billion dollars)				
	2010	2011	2012	2013	2014
USA	15,060	15,060	16,163	16,768	17,416
China	5,815	6,989	8,461	9,469	10,355
Japan	5,458	5,855	5,954	4,898	4,769
Germany	3,391	3,629	3,539	3,635	3,820
France	2,671	2,808	2,681	2,807	2,902
RU	2,137	2,481	2,630	2,523	2,847
Brazil	2,350	2,518	2,413	2,246	2,244
Italy	2,060	2,246	2,074	2,071	2,129
Rússia	1,479	1,791	2,016	2,096	2,057
India	1,727	1,843	1,831	1,876	2,047

year 2014 [13]. This survey refers to an international score using six key dimensions for logistics performance of countries. The scorecard allows comparisons with the world (with the option to display the best performance of the world) on the six indicators and the overall index LPI. The logistics performance is the weighted average of the scores of countries on six dimensions. The used index of the six indicators is only the transport infrastructure. The data used in the ranking comes from a survey of logistics professionals, where questions are asked about the foreign countries in which they operate. The LPI represents respectively each country as Table 2.

Table 2. Indicator of transport infrastructure performance

Countries	LPI
USA	4.18
China	3.67
Japan	4.16
Germany	4.32
France	3.98
UK	4.16
Brazil	2.93
Italy	3.78
Russia	2.59
India	2.88

The sources used to collect data were from The Word Factbook [14], Word Economic Outlook Database [15], National Transport Confederation (CNT) [16], Brazilian Institute of Geography and Statistics (IBGE) [17], and Logistics Performance Index [13].

Data were analyzed using Microsoft Excel software ©v. 13. A linear regression was used to verify the correlation between GDP and LPI variables, the first considered the dependent variable and the second variable the self-contained.

4   Results

To understand the research question in the first place we developed an average of the conventional GDPs between 2010 and 2014. From the result of this average, we related it to the LPI index for each country as can be seen in Fig. 1.

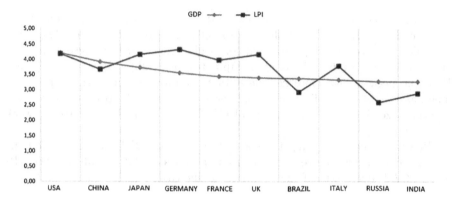

Fig. 1. GDP versus LPI

We conclude that although the LPI is different among the ten largest economies in the world, the GDP value of countries remained largely stable over this period, suggesting no influence of the performance of economic countries, which somehow contrasts the results presented by World Bank [13].

Using data collected from the survey, we seek to validate or not the highlighted conclusions and it was considered the following equation.

$$Ln(GDP) = \alpha - \beta LPI \tag{1}$$

Where $Ln(GDP)$ we take the logarithms of GDP and LPI refers to Logistics Performance Index of the World Bank.

It was chosen to extract the logarithm of GDP to achieve a normal linear equation and to use Ordinary Linear Squares (OLS) for verification of the hypothesis. This is a technique used in Econometrics to reduce the size of the number and Facilitate comparison in the ordinary linear squares [18,19]. The regression results are presented in Table 3.

According to Crespo the analysis of colinearity correlation is in the trial of R - SQUARE where if $0.3 \geq r < 0.6$, there is a relatively weak correlation between variables and $0 > r < 0.3$, the relationship is very weak so, it was not possible to conclude many things about the relationship between the variables under study [20].

Table 3. Regression result

Statistical regression	
R MULTIPLE	**63.91%**
R-SQUARE	**40.85%**
R-SQUARE SET	0.383
ERROR STANDARD	0.47653
SAMPLE NUMBER	50

A confidence level of 95% was used, after the regression calculation, it can empirically demonstrate that there is a relatively weak correlation between the variables, because the regression explains only 40.85% of the cases. Thus, this study failed to establish the relationship between variables. However, there has been the need to use more sample data to confirm or reject the hypothesis. The data analyzed are limited to the years of 2010–2014, so it is not possible to generalize that in a wider range of GDP continues to be a relatively weak correlation.

However, when analyzing the correlation between GDP per capita and the LPI, it shows a high correlation between variables (0.722). Analyzing the LPI and $LnGDP$ per capita of the countries, as shown in Fig. 2.

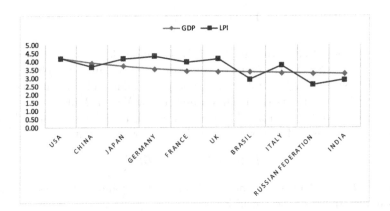

Fig. 2. LPI versus GDP per capita

With the exception of India, the countries with higher GDP per capita have a higher index of the average LPI, which considers the World Bank surveys in 2007, 2010, 2012 and 2014.

To check whether there would be significant change in the regression model, it was remade linear regression considering the GDP per capita and the result is shown in Table 4.

Table 4. Regression result

Statistical regression	
R MULTIPLE	**72.22%**
R-SQUARE	**52.10%**
R-SQUARE SET	0.461
ERROR STANDARD	0.83369
SAMPLE NUMBER	10

The model fits better with R Multiple value above 0.7 and regression explaining 52.1% of cases. Of course it is necessary to considerer the smaller sample size, and although there is more adhesion, it would not be possible to conclude that the LPI directly influences GDP.

5   Conclusions

This paper aims to highlight the relationship between logistics performance index of the ten largest economies in the world in relation to GDP. After the development of a linear regression model it is concluded that there is no relationship between the LPI and GDP for countries in the selected sample. However, a second analysis suggests that this relationship exists between LPI and the GDP per capita, with a strong correlation between the following variables (0.722).

The next step of this research would be searching for more data to confirm or refute the hypothesis that the LPI is related to GDP per capita. In addition, it intends to verify whether this relationship can be assigned regionally, in the specific case considering the Brazilian states by developing an equivalent regional index to LPI.

References

1. de Araújo Júnior, I.T.: Investimentos em Infra-estrutura e Crescimento Econômico no Brasil. Revista Economia e Desenvolvimento **5**(2), 161–188 (2006)
2. OECD/ITF: Spending on transport infrastructure 1995–2011. Technical report (2013)
3. OECD/ITF: Understanding the value of transport infrastructure. Technical report (2013)
4. Morais, A., Aragão, J.: Gasto Público em Infraestrutura de Transporte é Produtivo. In: XVI Congresso Brasileiro de Transporte e Trânsito. ANTP, Maceio (2007)
5. Bertussi, G.L., Ellery Jr., R.: Infraestrutura de Transporte e Crescimento Econômico no Brasil. J. Transp. Lit. **6**(4), 101–132 (2012)
6. Gay, A.L., Kohler, R.: Projeto de Teste de Correlação entre o Vab Serviços e o Vab Total de Municípios do Rio Grande do Sul no Periodo 1999–2012. Salão do Conhecimento **1**(1), 1–5 (2015)

7. Rostow, W., Baker, R., Rex, G.: The Economics of Take-Off into Sustained Growth. Palgrave Macmillan, London (1963)
8. Rozas, P., Sánchez, R.: Desarrollo de Infraestructura y Crecimiento Económico: Revisión Conceptual. Naciones Unidas, CEPAL, División de Recursos Naturales e Infraestructura, Santiago (2004)
9. Aschauer, D.: Is public expenditure productive? J. Monet. Econo. **23**(2), 177–200 (1989)
10. Liu, Y.: Public infrastructure investment and economic growth in China: an empirical analysis using VAR. Tese Economy, University of Ottawa, Ontario (2011)
11. Mallon, R.: Transport and economic development. Econ. Dig. Summer **1**, 8–13 (1960)
12. Banister, D., Berechman, J.: Transport and Economic Development. UCL, Santiago (2000)
13. Arvis, J.F., Saslavsky, D., Ojala, L., Shepherd, B., Busch, C., Raj, A.: Trade logistics in the global economy: the logistics performance index and its indicators. The World Bank, Washington (2014)
14. CIA: The World Factbook (2016). https://www.cia.gov/library/publications/the-world-factbook/
15. International Monetary Fund: World Economic Outlook Database. https://www.imf.org/external/pubs/ft/weo/2015/02/weodata/index.aspx
16. Confederação Nacional do Transporte. http://www.cnt.org.br/
17. Instituto Brasileiro de Geografia e Estatística. http://www.ibge.gov.br/home/
18. Head, K., Mayer, T.: Gravity equations: workhorse, toolkit, and cookbook (Chap. 3). In: Gita Gopinath, E.H., Rogoff, K. (eds.) Handbook of International Economics, vol. 4, pp. 131–195. Elsevier, Amsterdam (2014)
19. Bensassi, S., Márquez-Ramos, L., Martínez-Zarzoso, I., Suárez-Burguet, C.: Relationship between logistics infrastructure and trade: evidence from Spanish regional exports. Transp. Res. Part A: Policy Pract. **72**, 47–61 (2015)
20. Crespo, A.: Estatística Fácil. Saraiva, São Paulo (2009)

Contributions of the Program Inovar-Auto to the Automotive Manufacturers in Brazil

Nivaldo Luiz Palmeri[1,2(✉)], Oduvaldo Vendrametto[1],
João Gilberto Mendes dos Reis[1], and Rosangela Kronig[3]

[1] Paulista University, São Paulo, Brazil
nivaldoluiz@uol.com.br
[2] Centro Universitário Fundação Santo André – FSA, Santo André, Brazil
[3] Faculdade de Tecnologia do Estado de São Paulo – FATEC, São Bernardo, Brazil

Abstract. The Brazilian government intents to stimulate and modernize the national automotive industry. The Inovar-Auto program propose to improve the international competitiveness of automobile auto parts industry and to reduce the importations. This paper aims to verify the influence of the Inovar-Auto program in competitiveness of Brazilian automotive industry. To this end, we carried out a search regarding the investments to the following years of the program, the participation of international enterprises as stakeholders of the national industry and its next goals. The results showed that the major investments came from international companies.

Keywords: Competitiveness · Automotive industry in Brazil · Developing countries · Globalization

1 Introduction

Since the 90s the Brazilian automotive sector has being part of an international transformation. The opened market for a free trade and economy growth made the Brazilian market more attractive to the transnational automotive companies. Thus, the manufactures initiated a remodeling process, including the relationship with the local suppliers, incorporating hierarchical strategies, global sourcing, follow sourcing and its variations [1,2]. However, in the last five years, a trade balance deficit and a decrease of the automotive parts produced in Brazil jeopardize the future of the national supply chain [3].

The Brazilian government, as an attempt to change this scenario, issued the Acts 12.715 and 7.819 that created the Program to Incentive Technological Innovation and Aggregate the National Automotive Supply Chain (Inovar-Auto) [4,5]. The program aims to support the technological development, innovation, environmental protection, energetic efficiency and quality of both vehicles and

© IFIP International Federation for Information Processing 2016
Published by Springer International Publishing AG 2016. All Rights Reserved
I. Nääs et al. (Eds.): APMS 2016, IFIP AICT 488, pp. 641–648, 2016.
DOI: 10.1007/978-3-319-51133-7_76

auto parts. The Inovar-Auto has been build by a working group with participation of the Brazilian government, automotive enterprises, universities, associations, working unions and consultants [6]. The working group aim to evaluate if the program is robust enough to promote the national technological development to include Brazil in the international scenario.

The present study aims to evaluate the contributions of the Inovar-Auto program to the national automotive competitiveness. Thus, we analyzed the current legislation regarding the program, the investments proposed by the automotive sector in Brazil, and the nationality of the companies working in Brazil as well as the targets and requirements proposed by the national government. However, the initial proposal for the program has changed, since the financial resources, i.e. the incentive of the Inovar-Auto Program, has been applied not to either technological development or its transference, but to support new manufacturer plants, capacitation and marketing.

2   Methodology

We conducted an exploratory study based on a literature review. The information about to the Inovar-Auto program was obtained from the current legislation regarding it. In addition data were also collected from: specific publications of ANFAVEA (National Association of Manufactures of Automotive Vehicles); MDIC (Ministry of Development, Industry and International Trade); MCTI (Ministry of Science, Technology and Innovation); journals and specialized websites regarding the automotive sector as Automotive Business, Exame and others.

In order to evidence the divergences from the initial proposal of the program we analyzed the current legislation that supports it. Seventeen different legal acts have amended the program since the initial issued Act 12.715 in 20.112, until the Decree 8.544 in 2015.

These amendments represent requirements and procedures to capacitation of suppliers, expenses of strategic inputs, traceability, habilitations of companies and other factors that evidence the constant evolution the Inovar-Auto. We obtained the proposed investments of the manufacturers by the statistical report that was published in the website Automotive Business – Special Reports: Investments of Manufacturers 2011–2020, updated in August 2014 where the exchange rate is US\$ 1 = R\$ 2,40 e Euro 1 = R\$ 3,30 [7].

The information about the majority control of the enterprises was collected either in the Exame magazine [8] or in the Internet. The main goals and the achieved targets are available in the MDIC website [9].

The present research provides information to analyze the proposed budged by the manufacturers in Brazil, the goals of the program and the expected results initially proposed. This dataset constitutes the base to the conclusion of the present study.

3   Literature Review

Brazil has one of the biggest markets for production and commercialization of vehicles. The national supply chain is vast and it includes basic inputs production, auto parts suppliers, the productive process and the distribution chain [3]. The country needs to improve the production, search and expand the commerce to new markets as well as to support the national market, and stimulate the competition, efficiency and increase the productivity in the automotive chain from the production to the commercialization [9].

The program Inovar-Auto stimulates the competitiveness, the search for efficiency systemic gains due to the productivity increase in the automotive supply chain, the stages of production as well as the technological and commerce network. It also encourages investments due to taxes reduction, consequently it increases the technological standards of the vehicles, parts, components, and vehicular safety. To the enterprises that fulfill the requirements in order to be licensed to the program may be applied an IPI reduction up to 30%. Fifty-five enterprises have the license regarding the program, comprehending 23 manufacturers, 15 importers and 17 project investors [9], and it must be renewed annually. In 2015, 25 enterprises applied to renew their licenses and were approved by the MDCI [9].

It is possible to correlate the stage of development level of the automotive sector and the economic development of a country. Countries with a developed automotive industry such as USA, Germany, Japan, South Korea, have competitive factors in common such as: majority part of the manufacturers and their main suppliers, knowledge and comprehension of developed technology, innovation, connections in the international market and success regarding the technological development [10]. On the other hand, in most of the developing countries as Mexico and Brazil, the industrial park depends on both foreign capital and technology. Some characteristics are familiar between these countries as geographical latitude, cultural aspects and dependence of international technology for the automotive segment. The foreign manufacturers working on developing countries are connected to their supplier, mostly working also on the country, for market reasons in order to maximize their profits [2]. The local suppliers represent the 2nd or 3rd level in the supply chain. Their products are limited to supply the local market and they are represented by small and medium companies that are focused on operation activities [1]. These national small companies do not have conditions to fulfill the formal requirements to attend the Inovar-Auto Program. They are still part of the peripheral supply chain, producing exclusively technological obsolete components that are still being in use in national vehicles.

4   Evolution of the Program Inovar-Auto

The program Inovar-Auto represents an alternative to develop technology in vehicles produced in Brazil. Its main focuses are: safety; fuel consumption reduction; technological development; supply chain capacitation. However, it is still necessary additional efforts [11]. Laws, decrees and acts represent the legislation Table 1 [6,12].

Table 1. Relevant legislation to Inovar-Auto

Legislation	Relevant
Law n° 12.715/2012	It releases the program to incentive the technological innovation and aggregation of the automotive supply chain
Law n° 12.996/2014	It alters the Law n° 12.715/2012
Decree n° 7.819/2012	It regulates the Law n° 12.715/2012
Decree n° 8.015/2013	It alters the Decree n° 7.819/2012
Decree n° 8.294/2014	It alters the Decree n° 7.819/2012
Act 106/2013	It postpones the special licenses up to May 31, 2013
Act 113/2013	It establishes the complementary regulation
Act 280/2013	It alters the Act 113/2013
Act 296/2013	It regulates the program Inovar-Auto
Act 297/2013	It establishes the complementary regulation to the Decree n° 7.819/2012
Act 772/2013	It establishes the complementary regulation to the Decree n° 7.819/2012
Act 257/2014	It establishes the complementary regulation to the Decree n° 7.819/2012
Act 290/2014	It alters the Act 113/2013
Act 318/2014	It alters the Inter-Ministerial Act n° 772
Act 74/2015	It establishes the complementary regulation to the Decree n° 7.819/2012
Decree n° 8.544/2015	It alters the Decree n° 7.819

The program is currently: renewing the licenses; studying the availability of applying the surplus credit to next term of the licenses; conducting follow up auditing in the licensed enterprises to the continuation of the program during its term end in 2017 [6].

5 Planned Investments

The vehicles manufacturers have announced investments of US$ 22.3 billions in Brazil for the next years, where US$ 2.3 billions comprehends new manufacturers not yet producing in Brazil as Audi, BMW, Jaguar Land Rover, Chery, Foton, JAC Motors e Sinotruk. The remaining amount of US$ 20.0 billions investments are related to manufacturers already install in Brazil that plans to implement new assembly lines to increase their production capacity, modernization of facilities, production of engines and components, new vehicles projects, nationalization and development of new product and R&D and others. The planned investments and the period, as well as the majority participation of the enterprises. Only US$ 500 millions out of US$ 22.3 billions initially announced, representing 2%, are originated from Brazilian companies, as follow: Agrale, Volare e MMC Automotores do Brasil (Table 2) [7].

Table 2. Investments of the automotive manufacturers working in Brazil (Source: [7])

Manufacturers	Majority participation	US$ Billions	Period
Agrale	Brazilian	0.017	2014/2015
FCA - Fiat Chrysler	Italian	4.167	2011/2014
Ford	American	1.994	2011/2015
General Motors	American	2.708	2014/2018
Honda	Japanese	0.417	2013/2015
Iveco	Italian	0.481	2012/2014
MAN	German	0.417	2012/2016
Mercedes-Benz	German	0.625	2014/2016
MMC Automotores do Brasil	Brazilian	0.417	2011/2015
Nissan	Japanese	1.083	2011/2014
PSA Peugeot Citroën	French	1.542	2012/2015
Renault	French	0.308	2014/2019
Scania	German	0.417	2014/2024
Toyota	Japanese	0.417	2012/2015
Volare	Brazilian	0.015	2014/2015
Volkswagen	German	4.167	2014/2018
Volvo	Sweden	0.820	2013/2015
Audi	German	0.183	2013/2015
BMW	German	0.275	2012/2014
BYD (Build Your Dreams)	Chinese	0.083	2014/2015
Chery	Chinese	0.530	2012/2014
Foton Aumark do Brasil	Chinese	0.142	2012/2016
JAC Motors	Chinese	0.417	2011/2014
Jaguar Land Rover	English	0.313	2013/2020
Metro-Shacman	Chinese	0.167	2012/2014
Sinotruk	Chinese	0.125	2014/2016
Yunlihong Motors do Brasil	Chinese	0.075	2012/2015

6 Targets of the Program Inovar-Auto

The program Inovar-Auto program provides that's the qualified companies could take advantages of taxes (IPI). On the other hand, assumed commitments under the current targets of the goals [13].

6.1 New Investments

Investments must be implemented to install new facilities and vehicle production plants or new projects to improve vehicle assembly lines already working in Brazil. The licensed enterprises must present their projects and after approval they must implement it. The enterprises may import similar vehicles to the ones that will be produced by the new facility during its construction and apply the IPI reduction, introducing the product to the market with similar conditions comparing to a future stage when the plant start the production locally. The enterprises must also present the information regarding the investment projects evolution. The legal acts issued after the initial proposal for the program have altered the targets of the program due to pressure of the selected enterprises, stripping the proposals of its original characteristics. Basically, it was influenced to become a public funding to finance private interests as tax relief. These resources are including in the companies budgets as investments. A diversity of scopes with no relevance to technological development were also aggregated in the program. In the following items are described the topics of the program if implemented it would enhance the national competitiveness for exportation, and it would also provide national research and development centers of expertize.

6.2   Energy Efficiency

Energy efficiency, for the present study, is understand as the autonomy of a vehicle in kilometer per liter units, or energy consumption represented in mega joules per kilometer (MJ/km) and these measures are made according to the methodology established by the legislation of the program. The licensed enterprises must reach the minimum target of 12.08% reduction according to the Federal Decree no 7819/2012. The current results are evaluated in specific periods during the license (Nov/16–Oct/17).

6.3   Research and Development

The investments may be applied to basic research, applied research, experimental developments and technical support services. The enterprises must invest a percentage of their revenue in R&D, increasing from 0.15% in 2013 to 0.50% in 2017. This investment aims to improve technology and innovation of new products and processes in the country.

6.4   Engineering and Basic Industrial Technology

The enterprises licensed as manufacturer or importer may also invest their capital in engineering, basic industrial technology and suppliers' capacitation. These investments may be applied in engineering development, basic industrial technology, employees' capacitation, new products development, creation of new projects for laboratories and research, test tracks, development of machinery and suppliers' capacitation.

The minimum percentage of investments in engineering increases progressively from 0.50% in 2013 to 1.00% in 2017 of the revenue of the licensed enterprise.

This requirement aims to develop the technology and innovation of new products and productive processes. Complementary regulation to the program Inovar-Auto introduces concepts, orientations, models, requirements and methodologies to follow up the accordance of the enterprises to the requirements.

6.5   Manufacturing Stages

The licensed manufacturer must fulfill the minimum manufacturing stages, direct or indirect, regarding infrastructure and engineering. The manufacturing stages that must be conducted are: upholstery, welding, anti corrosive treatment and painting, plastic modeling, manufacture, gearbox manufacture, steering system and suspensions assemblage, electrical system assemblage, brake system and axis assemblage, chassis production or assemblage, assemblage, final checking, compatible tests and self infrastructure of laboratories to develop product tests, and others. At least 80% of the vehicles must fulfill the manufacturing stages, promoting the development of the national industry regarding productive capacity, fomenting the development of new suppliers to the manufacturing stages. The minimum amount o manufacturing stages rises from 8 in 2013 to 10 in 2017.

6.6   Labeling and Standard Vehicle

One of the specific objectives of the program is to increase the participation in the Labeling and Standard Vehicle Program (PBEV) conducted by INMETRO that aim to provide information regarding energetic performance of products contributing to consumer's decision.

6.7   Industry Sustainability

The suppliers of strategic inputs and machinery must inform in the Inovar-Auto Program Monitoring System the products provided to the licensed enterprises, including values and other characteristics. This information will provide knowledge about the automotive supply chain allowing the governmental institutions implementing policies to support the sector. The strategic inputs are: raw material, parts and components used to manufacture and aggregate in the vehicles; machinery and aggregate parts; upholstery and injection machinery and their parts. This objective is divided in two different targets:

Target 1 – The minimum of 700 suppliers registered in the Inovar-Auto Program Monitoring System until March/2015. This target considers the automotive supply chain in general (basic inputs, auto parts, tires, painting, etc.) and enterprises that are associated to the National Industry Union of Components to Automotive Vehicles (Sindipeças). It represents 85% of total sales to the Inovar-Auto licensed enterprises. Target 2 – Accordance of 95% of the supplier inputs and machinery.

7   Discussion and Conclusions

The program Inovar-Auto is contributing to the sustainable development of the automotive industry in Brazil. It has stimulating new plants as well as the modernization of the ones already producing, production of more modern vehicles, energy efficiency increase, investments in R&D and engineering, nationalization of industrial processes and more participation in the Labeling and Standard Vehicle Program (PEBV).

When comparing the Brazilian initiative to developed countries automotive industry it is possible to notice that these countries have the majority participation of the enterprises the mains suppliers. In Brazil, however, the industrial plants are exogenous and international dependent regarding both technology and investments.

The investments provided by the program Inovar-Auto are 98% from international majority participation, influencing the technology transfer to the automotive sector and limiting the sustainable development in Brazil. The technology is introduced and licensed and do not incorporate the learning process of the research and development, keeping the industries in a position of dependent buyer.

The program Inovar-Auto has financed international enterprises using public resources investing in their production. These resources should come from the enterprises as a plan to become more competitive maintaining their markets. The enterprises in a capitalism society must compete for profits and as a consequence assume the risks.

The innovation and implementation of the segments that bring technology and competitiveness to boost the national automotive industry is no longer contemplated in scope of program Inovar-Auto.

This research aimed to evaluate using indicator the progress of the Inovar-Auto Program. However, we identified several distortions between the initial proposal and the current program. Consequently, politics and enterprises are being investigated for frauds.

References

1. Costa, I., Queiroz, S.R.: Autopeças no Brasil: Mudanças e Competitividade na Década de Noventa. Revista de Administração **35**, 27–37 (2000)
2. Furtado, J.: La Transformation des Conditions d'insertion des Économies á Industrialisation Tardive dans L'économie Mondiale: Un Examen des Facteurs Généraux Suivi de leur Particularisation dans Cinq Secteurs Industriels. Université de Paris-Nord, France, Thése de doctorat (1997)
3. ANFAVEA. http://www.anfavea.com.br/anuario.html
4. Brazil: Lei 12.715/2012. http://inovarauto.mdic.gov.br
5. Brazil: Decreto 7819/2012. http://www2.camara.leg.br
6. Garcia, C.L.C., Laignier, G.: Inovar-Auto na Prática. The World Bank, São Paulo (2015)
7. Automotive Bussiness. http://automotivebusiness.anankecdn.net.br
8. Exame. http://exame.abril.com.br/topicos/melhores-e-maiores-2015
9. MDCI. http://www.desenvolvimento.gov.br
10. Ruff, F.: The advanced role of corporate foresight in innovation and strategic management. Technol. Forecast. Soc. Change **101**, 37–48 (2014)
11. SIMEIA. http://www.simea.org.br/2015/pt/um-balanco-do-inovar-auto
12. MDCI. http://www.simea.org.br/2015/pt/um-balanco-do-inovar-auto
13. ABDI. http://inovarauto.mdic.gov.br

Lean Manufacturing

Supermarkets vs. FIFO Lanes: A Comparison of Work-in-Process Inventories and Delivery Performance

Denis Wiesse[1] and Christoph Roser[2]($\boxtimes$)

[1] Robert Bosch GmbH, Rutesheim, Germany
denis.wiesse@gmail.com
[2] Karlsruhe University of Applied Sciences, Karlsruhe, Germany
christoph.roser@hochschule-karlsruhe.de

Abstract. Pull production is a key element for a lean manufacturing system. In pull production, buffer inventories between two processes can be implemented either through a FIFO lane as part of a kanban loop, or through a supermarket, in which case the value stream is split into two different kanban loops. This paper compares the usage of FIFO lanes and supermarkets with respect to the work-in-process inventory needed to achieve a similar delivery performance. The results clearly show that there is only a minor difference in inventory between the usage of FIFO lanes and supermarkets.

Keywords: Inventory reduction · FIFO · Supermarket · Pull · Delivery performance · WIP

1 Introduction

Pull production is a key element for a lean manufacturing system. Kanban systems are commonly used to implement pull production. A pull system can consist of multiple kanban loops, each of which can include multiple processes along the value stream. The buffer inventory between two processes can be implemented either through a FIFO lane as part of a kanban loop, or through a supermarket, in which case the value stream is split into two different kanban loops.

Buffer inventories are necessary to decouple fluctuations between processes, which may stem from technical problems, cycle-time variations, unsteady material delivery, and many other reasons. The larger the buffer, the better the decoupling of fluctuations.

Yet, buffer inventories also cause significant costs. Industry usually calculates the cost due to the bound capital, sometimes also including storage and handling cost. What is usually not included is the delay of information through the material flow (e.g., detecting flawed parts too late), obsolescence cost, deterioration over time, etc. [1]. One of the key insights in lean manufacturing is to realize the significance of these inventory related costs and to pursue inventory reduction as part of the continuous improvement process.

© IFIP International Federation for Information Processing 2016
Published by Springer International Publishing AG 2016. All Rights Reserved
I. Nääs et al. (Eds.): APMS 2016, IFIP AICT 488, pp. 651–658, 2016.
DOI: 10.1007/978-3-319-51133-7_77

When establishing a pull production, between each pair of sequential processes the designers have the option to add a FIFO lane as part of a bigger kanban loop, or to add a supermarket and split the flow into two kanban loops (see Fig. 1 below for the example used within this analysis). There are no fixed rules on when to use a FIFO and when to use a supermarket, although there are recommended guidelines [2]. In general, it is recommended to use a FIFO lane, which is much easier to manage, unless there are compelling reasons to go for a supermarket.

This paper compares the usage of FIFO and supermarket with respect to both work-in-process and delivery performance. The goal is to determine if a supermarket or a FIFO requires less work-in-process inventory for the same delivery performance. Is it better for inventory to have a supermarket or a FIFO between processes? This paper is based on a master thesis by one of the authors, supervised by the other author [3]. To the best of our knowledge such a comparison has not yet been undertaken before. However, before we go into the details of the analysis, we first need to define the terms as used within this paper.

1.1   Definition of Push and Pull

While the term pull is used almost everywhere in lean manufacturing, the definition of pull is often quite different. It is only agreed that pull is the opposite of push. Powell and Arica recently surveyed the literature and found around 30 definitions in production management, supply chain management, and project management [4]. Within this paper we follow the, in our view, most compelling definition by Hopp and Spearman "A pull production system is one that explicitly limits the amount of work in process that can be in the system. By default, this implies that a push production system is one that has no explicit limit on the amount of work in process that can be in the system" [5].

1.2   Definition of FIFO Lanes

A FIFO lane stands for First-In, First-Out. This automatically gives the first part of a definition, which requires that the parts leave in the same sequence as they arrive [6]. However, since the FIFO lane is part of a pull system, it needs to incorporate the definition of pull from above and needs to have an upper limit on inventory. This brings us to our own definition of a FIFO lane: "A FIFO lane is an inventory where the parts leave in the same sequence as they arrive. There is a limit to the maximum inventory. If the FIFO lane is full, the receding process stops".

1.3   Definition of Supermarkets

A supermarket differs from a FIFO lane in that the material flow and the information flow splits. In a FIFO lane, the material automatically includes the information on what the material is. If material is removed from a supermarket, the information on the part goes back to the beginning of the kanban loop to replenish the part. This information is the kanban. A supermarket consists of multiple parallel FIFO lanes, one for each material type that is handled by the supermarket. As with the FIFO lane, the supermarket has an upper limit on the number of parts, although this is usually maintained through the number of kanban in circulation and not implemented separately. This leads us to our definition of supermarket "A supermarket is an inventory where the parts are stored separately by type. The parts by type leave in the same sequence as they arrive. When a part leaves, information is sent back along the value stream to replenish the part".

1.4 Definition of Work-in-Process Inventory

The definition of work in process is rather straightforward. "Work in process (WIP) is the amount of material – measured in pieces, or by weight, volume, or value – for one part type or for multiple part types combined for a certain section of the value stream".

Depending on the situation, this may or may not include the supermarket inventory. For our purposes, we do include the supermarket inventory to get a reasonable comparison between a system with a FIFO and a system with a supermarket. For pull systems, this quantity has to be limited. In kanban systems, it is limited through the number of kanban [7].

1.5 Definition of Delivery Performance

Delivery performance aims to measure the reliability of satisfying customer orders, both quantity-wise and timewise (i.e., in full on time) [8]. Disagreement exists in industry if a too-early delivery is counted as good or not, which tolerances are allowed around the scheduled delivery date, and if the scheduled delivery date is the first date requested by the customer or the date agreed on between customer and supplier. For our purposes, we define delivery performance as follows: "Percentage of the customer orders that can be fulfilled on time and in full".

2 Analysis

For the analysis, a simulation environment was used. This allows for an easy gathering of data and comparison of different systems.

2.1 Analyzed System

For a stringent comparison, we analyzed a simple system consisting only of two processes, P1 and P2, and a single product variant. Two different systems were compared, where either a single kanban loop includes both processes with a FIFO in between, or the system is split into two different kanban loops. This is shown

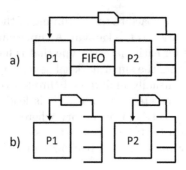

Fig. 1. Two processes connected through FIFO within one kanban loop (a) or split into two different kanban loops using a supermarket (b)

in Fig. 1 below as (a) and (b) respectively. For the diagrams, we used standard value stream mapping notation as introduced by Rother and Shook [9].

Intuitively, a supermarket has more inventory than a FIFO lane. However, having a longer replenishment time in (a) requires one large supermarket at the end, whereas the two separate loops in (b) each have a shorter replenishment time and hence both supermarkets require less material for a similar delivery performance. In the following, we will call (a) a single-loop system, and (b) a double-loop system.

2.2   System Settings

The systems in Fig. 1 have been compared using different settings of cycle times and customer demand to represent a variety of different situations that may be expected in industry. Since the durations are all relative to each other, no time units are required, although for simulation purposes, minutes were used. Table 1 gives an overview of the tested systems. We examined systems that had both equal cycle times and unequal cycle times. Additional systems were tested in the original master thesis with similar results [3]. The systems have been simulated using the commercial Simul8 software package.

Table 1. Overview of the mean time between parts of the simulated systems. All times were exponentially distributed

System	Cycle time P1	Cycle time P2	Customer takt
1	10	10	12
2	10	9	12

All times were exponentially distributed. The duration of each simulation exceeded 8,000 parts, excluding a warm-up period of 300 parts. Each simulation was repeated at least 51 times to verify the accuracy of the results using confidence intervals.

All systems have been simulated using a wide range for the number of kanban both for a single-loop and a double-loop system to determine the relation between the WIP and the delivery performance. For example, the single-loop system 1 has been simulated with any number of kanban cards between 1 and 40 in combination with any number of FIFO capacity between 1 and 40. In total, 1,600 simulations have been repeated 51 times, each merely for the single-loop system with equal cycle times and a slow customer takt. The double-loop system 1 has been simulated with any number of kanban cards between 1 and 30 for each loop (i.e., a total of 900 simulations, all of them repeated 51 times for accuracy).

Similar simulations were performed for system 2 both for the single-loop and double-loop system. Simulations of additional systems can be found in [3]. In all cases, the best combination of WIP and delivery performance were determined, as well as the expected results, using a standard kanban formula. Overall, in excess of 300,000 simulations using weeks of computation time were used to derive the data below.

3 Analysis Results

3.1 System 1 – Equal Cycle Time

All combinations of kanban cards between 1 and 40, and FIFO capacity between 1 and 40, for the single loop as well as all combinations of number of kanban cards for both loops between 1 and 30 have been simulated. Both the delivery performance and the WIP have been measured for each simulation. Figure 2 shows the best combination with minimal WIP for any delivery performance between 0 and 100% for both the single-loop and the double-loop system.

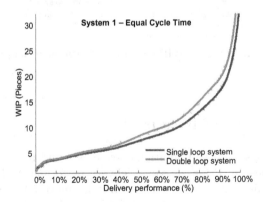

Fig. 2. Delivery performance vs. WIP for system 1 with equal cycle times

As expected, a higher WIP through a higher number of kanban and FIFO capacity improves the delivery performance. The relation is not linear, and a disproportionally larger inventory is needed to achieve a near-perfect delivery performance. The optimal combination of WIP and delivery performance for both the single-loop and the double-loop system looks very similar. Additional statistical analysis, however, confirms that the two curves are indeed statistically significant different for delivery performances in excess of 30% [3]. This analysis shows that the single-loop system (a) in Fig. 1 requires less WIP to achieve the same delivery performance as the alternative double-loop system (b).

3.2   System 2 – Unequal Cycle Time

The second system is similar to system 1, except that the second process P2 now has a faster mean cycle time of nine time units instead of ten time units. Figure 3 shows again the best combination of WIP and delivery performance for the single-loop and double-loop system. Again, the single-loop system requires statistically significant less WIP for the same delivery performance compared to the double-loop system.

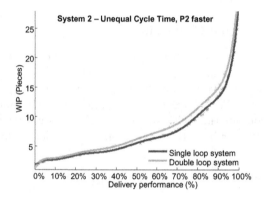

Fig. 3. Delivery performance vs. WIP for system 2 with unequal cycle time, P2 faster

4   Interpretation of Results

In all simulated systems (and additional systems found in [3]), the single-loop system requires less WIP for the same delivery performance. These results are statistically significant for delivery performances above 50%. This means that since most companies have a delivery performance above 40%, these results are statistically significant.

The single-loop system is able to "work ahead" more during times of low demand. Figure 4 shows the material distribution for times with low or no demand. In the single-loop systems, all kanban would eventually end up with

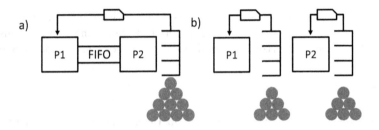

Fig. 4. WIP locations during low demand

material in the supermarket, and all WIP would be concentrated in the supermarket. If demand would pick up again, the single-loop system would be theoretically able to deliver products equivalent to all kanban cards immediately.

A double-loop system, however, would have only part of the material in the final supermarket, and part of the material in the intermediate supermarket. The exact allocation of the WIP depends on the number of kanban cards in each loop. Hence, the double-loop system would theoretically be able to deliver only the material equivalent to the last kanban loop. If the demand would be higher, material from the intermediate supermarket would first have to pass through process P2.

Since delivery performance is a benefit but WIP is a cost, a system that has better delivery performance for the same WIP (or the same delivery performance for less WIP) performs better. In all tested systems, the single-loop system was statistically significant better than a double-loop system.

However, statistically significant does not necessarily mean practically significant! The single-loop system would come at a cost of potentially quite uneven material distribution as shown in Fig. 4 part (a) above. Besides reduction in WIP, however, lean manufacturing also emphasizes a level production. The idea of having a pile of material at one point but none at the other goes against lean thinking. It is difficult to quantify, but it is definitely one reason against using a single-loop system despite lower WIP.

For a delivery performance of around 95%, the single-loop system required about 20% less WIP in both cases. Hence, there would be a small benefit in WIP. Yet, these results were achieved only after exhaustive testing of all possible combinations of number of kanban and FIFO capacities. In reality, such an exhaustive test is usually not possible. Instead, the number of kanban cards are estimated using either gut feeling or a kanban formula – which by itself is also nothing but a rough estimation with a significant margin of error. For the FIFO capacity, an expert estimate is the most common way in industry, which is also quite uncertain. Overall, it is unlikely that a real line will get the "just right" number of kanban cards and FIFO capacity to benefit from these optimal conditions.

As a conclusion, using a single-loop has a small advantage in respect to WIP and delivery performance. However, in practice there are many other considerations that can easily overrule the small WIP benefit of a single-loop system.

References

1. Richardson, H.: Control your costs then cut them. Transp. Distrib. **36**(12), 94–96 (1995)
2. Roser, C., Nakano, M.: Guidelines for the selection of FIFO lanes and supermarkets for Kanban-based pull systems – when to use a FIFO and when to use a supermarket. In: Umeda, S., Nakano, M., Mizuyama, H., Hibino, H., Kiritsis, D., Cieminski, G. (eds.) APMS 2015. IAICT, vol. 460, pp. 282–289. Springer, Heidelberg (2015). doi:10.1007/978-3-319-22759-7_33
3. Wiesse, D.: Analyse des Umlaufbestandes von Verbrauchssteuerungen in Abhängigkeit von der Nutzung von Supermärkten und FiFo-Strecken. Ph.D. thesis, Karlsruhe University of Applied Sciences, Karlsruhe (2015)
4. Powell, D., Arica, E.: To pull or not to pull: a concept lost in translation? Am. J. Manag. **15**(2), 64 (2015)
5. Hopp, W.J., Spearman, M.L.: To pull or not to pull: what is the question? Manuf. Serv. Oper. Manag. **6**(2), 133–148 (2004)
6. Marchwinski, C., Shook, J.: Lean Lexicon: A Graphical Glossary for Lean Thinkers. Lean Enterprise Institute, Cambridge (2003)
7. Karmarkar, U.S.: Kanban Systems. Technical report, University of Rochester, Rochester (1986)
8. Rao, M.C., Rao, P.K., Muniswamy, V.V.: Delivery performance measurement in an integrated supply chain management: case study in batteries manufacturing firm. Serbian J. Manag. **6**(2), 205–220 (2011)
9. Rother, M., Shook, J.: Learning to See: Value Stream Mapping to Add Value and Eliminate Muda. Lean Enterprise Institute, Cambridge (2003)

Lean Manufacturing and Sustainability: An Integrated View

Barbara Resta$^{(\boxtimes)}$, Stefano Dotti, Paolo Gaiardelli, and Albachiara Boffelli

Università degli Studi di Bergamo, Bergamo, Italy
barbara.resta@unibg.it

Abstract. Lean Manufacturing has always been seen as a mean to improve efficiency by reducing operations costs, but the recent focus on sustainability and its three pillar (economic, environmental and social) brought new issues to be addressed. In this paper, a new framework that links lean manufacturing with sustainability is proposed and then refined through a cross-sectoral multiple case study. The results highlight the need to align the lean implementation process with the sustainability strategy in order to avoid the negative impacts that lean production could have on the environmental and social components of sustainability.

Keywords: Lean manufacturing · Environmental sustainability · Social sustainability · Economic sustainability · Corporate social responsibility (CSR)

1 Introduction

Since its introduction at Toyota Motor Corporation in 1950's, Lean Manufacturing (LM) has evolved over time. Such a process of evolution has maintained the adherence to Operations Management evolving eras [1], and may be summarised as a focus on quality up to the early 1990s, through quality, cost and delivery (late 1990s), to customer value from 2000 onwards [2]. As sustainability (or Corporate Social Responsibility) began to be an increasingly essential element of Operations Management in the early 2000's [3], scholars started to explore how a traditional LM operations system could be aligned with environmental goals and practices [4], identifying synergies and trade-offs. However, this focus on the environment, while clearly significant, has overshadowed a broader range of sustainability issues [5], which also include the integration of both social and economic aspects, in a systemic and interconnected perspective [6]. In light of the shortcomings of existing literature on the relationship between LM and sustainability, this paper aims to address this gap by shading light on the following research question: *How does LM implementation affect corporate sustainability across its multiple dimensions (economic, environmental and social)?*

In the following section, extant literature on LM and its relation with economic, environmental and social sustainability aspects is presented. Then, Sect. 3 describes the adopted methodology. Results are presented and discussed in Sect. 4, which precedes the final conclusion, as well as the limitations of the study and future research directions.

© IFIP International Federation for Information Processing 2016
Published by Springer International Publishing AG 2016. All Rights Reserved
I. Nääs et al. (Eds.): APMS 2016, IFIP AICT 488, pp. 659–666, 2016.
DOI: 10.1007/978-3-319-51133-7_78

2   Theoretical Background

Sustainability. Over the last thirty years, the idea of sustainability has become associated with the integration of economic, social and environmental aspects. In this context, the Global Reporting Initiative (GRI) has developed a hierarchical framework [7] consisting of 14 categories, divided into the three pillar of sustainability (as included in Fig. 1), to help companies make their operations sustainable.

Lean Manufacturing. As argued by Shah and Ward [8], LM is "an integrated socio-technical system whose main objective is to eliminate waste by concurrently reducing or minimizing supplier, customer, and internal variability". It is a multi-dimensional approach that encompasses a wide variety of management practices, working synergistically and mutually reinforcing, which have been grouped into four complementary bundles [9]: Just-in-Time (JIT), Total Quality Management (TQM), Total Preventive Maintenance (TPM), and Human Resource Management (HRM).

Lean Manufacturing and Economic Sustainability. As extensively reviewed by [10], extant literature attributes a wide range of operational benefits to the implementation of LM philosophy and practices, including production cost reduction and speed, quality, dependability and flexibility improvement. Although most of the existing studies suggest that synergies exist among lean practice bundles, only a few scholars translate the operational benefits into economic and financial indicators (as reviewed in [11]), with mixed results. Moreover, when analyzing the relationship between LM and financial performance, the conceptualization of LM is typically narrowly focused on JIT (e.g., [12]), which is part of but not synonymous with LM.

Lean Manufacturing and Environmental Sustainability. Many authors suggest that companies can use LM as a catalyst to improve environmental practices [13], describing green as the "good public spillover of lean" [4] and a natural extension or stepping stone [14]. Carvalho and Cruz-Machado [15] empower this connection and describe lean and green practices as a synergistic connection of environmental and operations management. However, despite the positive relationships of lean practices and environmental results have been found to exist [16,17], several scholars identify areas where the two approaches cannot be combined and potential conflicts and trade-offs exist [18]. In order to avoid contradictory results and non-conclusive results, it is thus fundamental analyzing the relationship between LM and environmental impacts in a systemic and integrated way, avoiding to focus the attention on a specific lean bundle or on a few environmental aspects.

Lean Manufacturing and Social Sustainability. As for the environmental pillar, literature on the relationships between LM and social sustainability does not provide definite results [19]. On the one hand, lean has been argued to have a positive effect on workers' attitudes due to a more varied work, an increased responsible autonomy and a rise in intrinsic motivation [20]. On the other hand, several authors point out the fact that the work is more intense, monotonous and standardized, there is more stress and a loss of autonomy and freedom, with an excessive pressure on people [2]. On the contrary, there seems to be consensus on the positive effects of LM on health and safety in the work environment due to the design of workstations in accordance with ergonomic standards [21], which improves workers' work conditions.

As described in the previous paragraphs, lean operations, when properly defined, have the potential to address a wide range of sustainability issues, included in the conceptual model underlying this research (Fig. 1). More empirical research is needed to fully address the benefits of LM for sustainability, which while previously suggested, have never been fully explored across a range of industrial sectors and case studies [22].

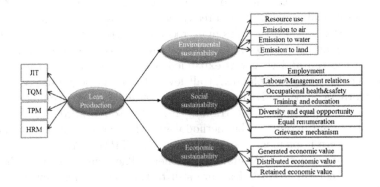

Fig. 1. The conceptual model

3   Research Methodology

To ground theoretical insights, an inductive case study methodology was employed. The aim of the empirical investigation is to further refine the conceptual model, as well as to shape and develop hypotheses from the collected data [23], regarding the relationship existing between LM and sustainability. In particular, five case studies were theoretically selected, characterised by different level of sustainability and LM implementation. The selected companies were also different in terms of industries and firm sizes. The main information about the sample is reported in Table 1.

For each case, multiple respondents were interviewed. Data were collected through semi-structured interviews as defined in the research protocol, developed around the previously explained conceptual model to guide the research and strengthen reliability [24]. Moreover, direct observations and the analysis of secondary sources, such as company documentation and corporate website, have been used for triangulation to check the internal consistency of data. Data analysis had two main components: within and across case analysis.

Table 1. Sample companies

Company	Industry	N° Employees	Revenues (mio.€,2014)
A	Electric and Automation	140K	32,806
B	Glass fiber insulation	182K	41,054
C	Hi-tech navigation systems	7,5	1,834
D	Textile	385	55
E	Automotive	4,3	1,21

4   Results and Discussion

Company A was the first firm to make the change towards LM in 2006 and several operational benefits have already been observed. The other companies begun to approach lean principles more recently, so they are characterized by a lower lean implementation level. In all the companies the requirement to change came from the top and then was expanded towards the bottom: some companies started to engage employees of all levels from the beginning (case B, C, D) while others (case A, E) involved them gradually after training managers first, with an expansion of the training from the top towards the bottom of the organizational pyramid. The methodologies that constitute the backbone of LM and that are implemented more often are 5S, TPM, polyvalence and polycompetence principles and Visual Management. The firms that are still in the process of transition towards lean are still testing and making evaluations on "pilot" production or assembly lines so the Yamazumi (organization based on takt-time) and Kamishibai (standard work) principles are not so common in the analyzed sample. Kanban and Heijunka are tools that are worthwhile to be used only if a set of conditions are fulfilled (level of product standardization; type of production system). On the other hand, when the product portfolio is wide, SMED techniques are likely to be implemented. Regardless of the industry, most of the companies are investing in Idea Suggestion tools and Stand Up Meetings, in order to foster cooperation and alignment of efforts and operations, not only amongst colleagues but also with managers from various levels or from other departments/functions. All the companies involved in this study have clearly designed their sustainability goals and they have already implemented social or environmental actions. All the companies have clear idea about what their impact is on the surrounding environment and on the social community they operate in.

Lean Manufacturing and Economic Sustainability. With a LM system, all the analyzed companies were able to increase the level of output with a less than proportional increase in inputs, meaning that LM is effective in increasing operational efficiency. Moreover, four out of the five analyzed companies implemented LM after the great recession that stroke the world, as a new production paradigm to help them survive in the global competition. On the side of economic results, they were not immediate in most cases: the interviewed companies that have most recently applied the principles have not experienced such benefits yet. The ones that have been able to see this effect present an increase in profits and a fall in working capital mostly thanks to inventory reduction. In the sample there was also a company that had abandoned the path towards lean a few times in the past, due to excessive investment and a poor cost-benefit analysis. Excessive investments are not part of the lean philosophy, so this is a case of misinterpretation of lean principles that leads to failure. Another economic benefit that emerges from the studied cases is the fall in non-quality management costs, which is due to the TQM principle of lean. Overall, despite LM seems to entail a positive economic return for a company, these benefits may not always be immediately measurable and visible. If benefits do not seem to emerge, a firm must first understand whether it is implementing them correctly and coherently to its context. For the sample companies, the main causes of this lack of success are related to problems that arose in the human element during the changeover to lean.

Lean Manufacturing and Environmental Sustainability. No explicit correlation between these two dimensions was found, except some socalled "green spillovers", meaning the general trend of reducing waste, energy use and resources need. Some environmentally friendly ideas can also be indirectly induced by lean tools; the idea suggestion system has proven to be effective not only for production efficiency matters, which is the purpose for which it is usually implemented, but also for environmental actions. The reason may be that lean and green actions do not ever collide; lean and green seem to be running on two parallel lines that go in the same direction, without being necessarily integrated into a single vision. The main reason for which they do not collide is that they both aim to reduce wastes, even if sometimes they are of different nature. As time goes by and green and lean activities become more deeply-rooted in the company, it may be possible that the two parallel lines they run on become gradually closer, until they eventually become a sole and integrated effort. About the possibility of an increase in transportation due to batch reduction, companies seem to be aware of it, probably also due to the cost, so they tend to prevent it from happening, therefore this risk seems to not be a hazard.

Lean Manufacturing and Social Sustainability. LM leads to increased personal skills and individual competencies through training programs oriented to all employees, provided in order to achieve poly competence, polyvalence and job rotation. In all cases workers became an important and key asset to the companies. Workers also seemed to react positively to this increased task significance and skill variety, becoming more proactive and not feeling as mere task executors. Despite the positive reaction in the long term, in all cases workers showed some initial fear and also opposition to the change. This initial resistance was caused by the need for communication of the principles and underlying reasons of change by the managers. The involvement of professional psychologists was a successful solution to drive the mind-set change. Workers' conditions seem to be improved also on the safety side, especially thanks to methodologies like 5S, Jidoka, TPM and idea suggestion systems. The resulting improvements in ergonomics also entail better working conditions. About the increase in stress level predicted by some scholars, it was found to be mainly related to the workers' personality; in any case, companies seem to be well aware of such risk, and, for this reason, it is kept monitored and addressed when it seems to rise. Not only the condition for workers seems to be improved, but also the one of the managers; thanks to lean principles, they can rely on various and well-rounded opinions, leading to more robust and conscious decision making processes. Such positive impacts were confirmed by the fact that the cases unions did not stand against the change towards a lean system. For example, none of the companies reduced the number of employees. However, the positive impact can occur only if the implementation is correct, well balanced and shared among all the employees. In cases where LM is not implemented properly it may turn out to be extremely harmful. For example, if only kanban and time regulating systems were to be applied with no other precautions, the increase in workers' stress would probably lead to negative social returns. A summary of the discussion of results is presented in Fig. 2, where the dimension of the conceptual model have been included.

		IMPACTS		
		ECONOMIC	ENVIRONMENTAL	SOCIAL
LEAN BUNDLE	JIT	Lower costs due to lower WIP, stock, lead times, occupied spaces.	Lower waste and more efficient use of resources.	Higher workplace safety and ergonomics, lower accidents and muscular disorders, higher stress level for most of the workers.
	TQM	Higher quality (lower non-quality costs and higher turnover).	Lower waste, increased energy consumption.	Reduced risks for workers, higher employee satisfaction.
	TPM	Higher efficiency (lower costs) and higher quality (lower costs and higher turnover).	Lower waste and lower resource consumption.	Lower risks for employees, reduced stress level.
	HRM	Long-term results.	No evidence found.	Higher commitment, satisfaction and lower stress level.

Fig. 2. The Effects of LM bundles on the Three Pillars of Sustainability

5 Conclusion

The overall aim of this research was to analyze how the introduction of a LM system in an organization may affect people, environment and corporate profitability.

The scientific contribution of this paper is related to the development of an innovative research model that describes and explains in an integrated and systemic way how the introduction of LM principles and tools contribute to achieve sustainability goals. Managers may use such findings to understand the possibilities given by the integration of lean and sustainable principles, but also that the potential positive return that the implementation of a LM system may bring is not the merely economic, for which such transformation is usually undertaken, but it has also environmental and social impacts. Particularly, the results confirm the strictly positive impact of lean on the economic component. Interestingly, HRM practices are considered as a leverage for maintaining the positive results in the long term because they contribute to build a lean culture in the organization. On the contrary, the effect on the other two components in some cases is found to be negative. This is due to the lack of alignment between the lean implementation process and the sustainability strategy, or worse to the lack of a sustainability strategy in the first place. In particular, lean and social activities may seem different concepts with different objectives, but by taking a closer look to their components and the results they bring to the production system, they do not seem to be that different. LM also focuses on the reduction of wastes LM gives great value to people and to their ideas and well-being, which recalls social sustainabilityand scrap items that leads to greatly environmentally friendly benefits. For all these reasons, the concept of the parallel lines that become increasingly closer with time, eventually merging in one single effort, may be generalized for the concept of sustainability as a whole.

The qualitative nature of the investigation is coherent with the state of the art, which is still in an initial phase. In the future, a quantitative survey on a large amount of companies with different levels of lean and sustainability implementation, from "beginners" to extremely advanced systems, should be carried out to test the hypothesize relationships between lean and sustainability.

References

1. Kleindorfer, P.R., Singhal, K., Van Wassenhove, L.N.: Sustainable operations management. Prod. Oper. Manage. **14**(4), 482–492 (2005)
2. Hines, P., Holweg, M., Rich, N.: Learning to evolve: a review of contemporary lean thinking. Int. J. Oper. Prod. Manage. **24**(10), 994–1011 (2004)
3. Angell, L.: Integrating environmental issues into the mainstream: an agenda for research in operations management. J. Oper. Manage. **17**(5), 575–598 (1999)
4. King, A.A., Lenox, M.J.: Lean and green? An empirical examination of the relationship between lean production and environmental performance. Prod. Oper. Manage. **10**(3), 244–256 (2001)
5. Fliedner, G., Majeske, K.: Sustainability: the new lean frontier. Prod. Inventory Manage. J. **46**(1), 6–13 (2010)
6. Adams, W.M.: The Future of Sustainability: Re-thinking Environment and Development in the Twenty-First Century. World Conservation Union, Gland (2006)
7. Sustainability Reporting Guidelines on Economic, Environmental, and Social Performance. Boston
8. Shah, R., Ward, P.T.: Defining and developing measures of lean production. J. Oper. Manage. **25**(4), 785–805 (2007)
9. Shah, R., Ward, P.T.: Lean manufacturing: context, practice bundles, and performance. J. Oper. Manage. **21**(2), 129–149 (2003)

10. Belekoukias, I., Garza-Reyes, J.A., Kumar, V.: The impact of lean methods and tools on the operational performance of manufacturing organisations. Int. J. Prod. Res. **52**(18), 5346–5366 (2014)
11. Hofer, C., Eroglu, C., Hofer, A.R.: The effect of lean production on financial performance: the mediating role of inventory leanness. Int. J. Prod. Econ. **138**(2), 242–253 (2012)
12. An examination of the relationships between JIT and financial performance
13. Dües, C.M., Tan, K.H., Lim, M.: Green as the new lean: how to use lean practices as a catalyst to greening your supply chain. J. Cleaner Prod. **40**, 93–100 (2013)
14. Franchetti, M., Bedal, K., Ulloa, J., Grodek, S.: Lean and green: industrial engineering methods are natural stepping stones to green engineering. Ind. Eng. **41**(9), 24–30 (2009)
15. Carvalho, H., Cruz-Machado, V.: Integrating lean, agile, resilience and green paradigms in supply chain management. In: Proceedings of the Third International Conference on Management Science and Engineering Management (2009)
16. Moreira, F., Alves, A.C., Sousa, R.M.: Towards eco-efficient lean production systems. In: Ortiz, Á., Franco, R.D., Gasquet, P.G. (eds.) BASYS 2010. IAICT, vol. 322, pp. 100–108. Springer, Heidelberg (2010). doi:10.1007/978-3-642-14341-0_12
17. Vinodh, S., Arvind, K.R., Somanaathan, M.: Tools and techniques for enabling sustainability through lean initiatives. Clean Technol. Environ. Policy **13**(3), 469–479 (2011)
18. Rothenberg, S., Pil, F.K., Maxwell, J.: Lean, green, and the quest for superior enviromental performance. Prod. Oper. Manage. **10**(3), 228–243 (2001)
19. Martínez-Jurado, P.J., Moyano-Fuentes, J.: Lean management, supply chain management and sustainability: a literature review. J. Cleaner Prod. **85**, 134–150 (2014)
20. Treville, S., Antonakis, J.: Could lean production job design be intrinsically motivating? Contextual, configurational, and levels of analysis issues. J. Oper. Manage. **24**(2), 99–123 (2006)
21. Taubitz, M.A.: Lean, green & safe: integrating safety into the lean, green and sustainability movement. Prof. Saf. **55**(5), 39 (2010)
22. Piercy, N., Rich, N.: The relationship between lean operations and sustainable operations. Int. J. Oper. Prod. Manage. **35**(2), 282–315 (2015)
23. Voss, C., Tsikriktsis, N., Frohlich, M.: Case research in operations management. Int. J. Oper. Prod. Manage. **22**(2), 195–219 (2002)
24. Yin, R.: Case Study Research: Design and Methods. Sage publishing, Beverly Hills (1994)

Direction of the Bottleneck in Dependence on Inventory Levels

Carolin Romeser[1] and Christoph Roser[2(⊠)]

[1] Fahrion Engineering GmbH & Co. KG, Kornwestheim, Germany
carolin.romeser@gmail.com
[2] Karlsruhe University of Applied Sciences, Karlsruhe, Germany
christoph.roser@hochschule-karlsruhe.de

Abstract. Buffers decouple fluctuations in the material flow. It is common wisdom in industry that a full buffer indicates a downstream bottleneck and an empty buffer indicates an upstream bottleneck. Numerous different bottleneck detection methods use this approach to detect the bottlenecks. However, so far this common wisdom on the shop floor has not yet been verified academically. The authors tested this hypothesis using a bottleneck detection method that was able to detect the bottleneck in a system at any given time. The bottleneck direction can reasonably be determined based on the inventory levels of the buffer only for symmetrical systems. In asymmetrical systems, the likelihood of the bottleneck direction is biased toward the bottleneck.

Keywords: Inventory · FiFo · Bottleneck direction · Bottleneck detection

1 Introduction

Bottleneck detection is the key to improving capacity in any production system. Only the improvement of the throughput of a bottleneck process will lead to an improvement of the throughput of the overall system. This is complicated by the tendency of bottlenecks in industry to shift between different processes. We define the bottleneck as follows: "Bottlenecks are processes that influence the throughput of the entire system. The larger the influence, the more significant the bottleneck" [1].

In many bottleneck detection methods, both in academic publications as well as in industrial practice, the buffer inventory between two processes is investigated. The hypothesis is usually not explicitly stated but is often implicitly indicated to be as follows: "If the buffer between two processes is full or rather full, the bottleneck is probably downstream [...]. If the buffer is empty or rather empty, the bottleneck is probably upstream [...]. If the inventory is half full, the bottleneck may be in either direction" [1].

However, while in compliance with conventional wisdom and logical deduction, to the best of our knowledge this assumption has never before been analyzed

I. Nääs et al. (Eds.): APMS 2016, IFIP AICT 488, pp. 667–674, 2016.
DOI: 10.1007/978-3-319-51133-7_79

in detail even though it is the basis of several bottleneck detection methods. This is probably due to the fact that until recently there was no reliable method available to follow the shifting of bottlenecks.

2 Literature Review

Despite this, there are many different bottleneck detection methods that use inventory levels or the closely related waiting times as an integral part of their method. Law and Kelton base their method on the average waiting time or queue length [2]. Elmasry and Hon measure the average waiting time and average queue length [3]. Roser et al. use the inventory level to determine the bottleneck direction [1,4]. Li et al. use the largest inventory to detect the bottleneck [5]. Lawrence and Buss look at the greatest number of waiting jobs in the queue [6]. Also in industry, the inventory size is commonly used to determine bottleneck locations. Most of the above methods also include the flaw to use averages in bottleneck detection, and hence they are unable to follow shifting bottlenecks.

3 Logical Deduction

Using logical reasoning, it can be deduced that the commonly used hypothesis is approximately correct. Figure 1 shows an example material flow with four processes and five inventories. If the situation shown remains stable, it can be assumed that process P3 is the bottleneck, as material is accumulating upstream of P3 and there is a lack of material downstream of P3.

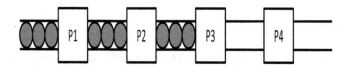

Fig. 1. Example of stable material flow with four processes and five inventories

Yet, this is valid only for a stable system. It becomes more complex for an unstable system. Figure 2 shows an example of an unstable system, where it is much less clear how the inventories influence the bottleneck. For easier understanding, we narrow it down to an example of two processes with a buffer

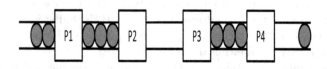

Fig. 2. Example of unstable material flow with four processes and five inventories

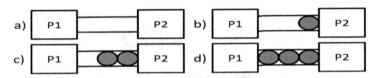

Fig. 3. All combinations of two processes with a buffer inventory capacity of three parts

inventory with a maximum capacity of three parts. All possible inventory levels are shown in Fig. 3. It is commonly assumed that with a completely empty buffer as in (a), the bottleneck must be upstream, and with a completely full buffer as in (d), the bottleneck must be downstream. However, this is not certain. Assume in Fig. 3(a) that process P2 would normally be the bottleneck. Due to a breakdown in process P1, the buffer between P1 and P2 has emptied. Process P2 is currently still processing its last part. Despite the buffer being empty, process P2 has yet to wait on process P1. Only if P2 finishes its part, process P2 would have to wait on process P1, and P1 would definitely be the bottleneck. If the problem in P1 is fixed and P1 supplies a part before P2 needs it, P1 was not the bottleneck, despite the empty buffer.

Similar is true for Fig. 3(d) if P1 is still working on a part, and the buffer opens up one space before the part in P1 is completed and has to be added to the buffer. In both cases it cannot be said for certain if the bottleneck is upstream for (a) or downstream for (d) until process P2 and P1 respectively have to wait for the other process. Hence, for a completely empty buffer as in (a), there is still a small chance that the bottleneck is NOT upstream. Similarly, for a completely full buffer as in (d), there is still a small chance that the bottleneck is NOT downstream.

The situation becomes even more complicated for Fig. 3(b) and (c). As the inventory levels are only the result of the past behavior of P1 and P2, however, it can reasonably be assumed that these inventory levels have a likely bottleneck direction between the situations (a) and (d). Hence, the more material an inventory contains, the more likely the bottleneck is downstream. The less material an inventory contains, the more likely the bottleneck is upstream.

Manufacturing is usually seen as handing parts downstream. However, it is equally valid to see it as handing free slots upstream. Hence, we have a symmetric behavior, and for this reason of symmetry, it can be expected that the influence by the preceding process and the succeeding process be of similar magnitude. Therefore, for an inventory level of 50%, it is equally likely that the bottleneck is upstream or downstream.

Hence, the likelihood of the bottleneck direction can be deduced as shown in Fig. 4, with the caveat that a momentary observation of a completely full inventory is not a 100% likelihood of the bottleneck being downstream, and a completely empty buffer is not a 100% likelihood of the bottleneck being upstream.

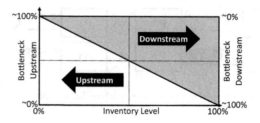

Fig. 4. Theoretical likelihood of bottleneck direction based on inventory levels

4   Simulated System

For the experimental analysis, a simple system with two processes and one buffer inventory, as shown in Fig. 5, has been analyzed. These two processes can also stand for several processes in a system. The system has been analyzed for a buffer capacity of 10 pieces. The reason for choosing an even amount of pieces as buffer was that the filling level can be precisely 50% by having a filling level of 5 pieces. The random distribution of the cycle times has been varied both in distribution type and width to understand the bottleneck behavior for different situations. An Exponential Distribution was tested as well as two Erlang Distributions with the Standard Deviations of 10% and 100%. The benefit of all of these distributions is that at no time will they be negative. This is important for the simulated system because cycle times can never be negative. Finally, the mean cycle times have been changed so that the mean cycle time of P1 was 80% of the mean cycle time of P2. Additional simulations can be found in the underlying master's thesis [7]. The systems have been simulated using the commercial Simul8 software package.

Fig. 5. Experimental system

5   The Active Period Method

The challenge is to verify the above assumptions through experiments. While the inventory level can easily be measured, the bottleneck direction is more complex, especially since we cannot use the inventory levels to avoid circular reasoning. However, the active period bottleneck detection method is able to determine the location of the bottleneck at any given time based solely on the duration a process was active without interruption [8,9]. This method is highly accurate and can determine the influence of a process on the entire system with a very high degree of accuracy [10]. The method was also verified by independent researchers who compared this method to other bottleneck detection methods and found it to be superior [11].

The active period method looks at the durations a process is active without interruptions by being blocked or starved. This is called the *active period*. At any given time, the process with the longest active period is the bottleneck. If the longest active periods of the processes overlap, the bottleneck is shifting between the two processes as shown in Fig. 6. If there is no overlap, then the process is the sole bottleneck.

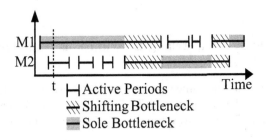

Fig. 6. Experimental system

This method has been used in the simulated system to determine the bottleneck for any given time. At any given time, there are three possible outcomes: The bottleneck is in the first process (P1); the bottleneck is in the second process (P2); or the bottleneck is unknown (shifting).

6   Simulation Results

6.1   Symmetric System, Exponential Distributions

The first experiment analyzed a system with a buffer capacity of 10 pieces and exponentially distributed cycle times, where the cycle times of process P1 and P2 had identical distribution. Figure 7 shows the results of these simulations, including the confidence intervals based on multiple repetitions of the simulation and the theoretically expected perfect result as a dashed line.

Due to the occurrence of shifting bottlenecks, there is a gap between the two bottleneck directions where the direction of the bottleneck is not known because of shifting bottlenecks. Yet, these curves are symmetrical within the limits of the confidence intervals. Neither a completely empty nor a completely full buffer had certainty with its respective bottleneck direction. For example, a completely full buffer had an 86.4% likelihood of the downstream process being the bottleneck but also a slim but real 0.32% likelihood of the upstream process being the bottleneck. Similarly, a completely empty buffer had an 88.7% chance of an upstream bottleneck but also a 0.35% chance of a downstream bottleneck.

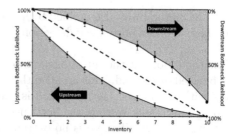

Fig. 7. Bottleneck location for a system with identical exponential distributed cycle times

6.2 Symmetric System, Erlang Distributions, Standard Deviation 10%

In another experiment, the same system was tested using an Erlang distribution, where the standard deviation was 10% of the cycle time for each process. The results are shown in Fig. 8. The system behaved very symmetrically and similarly to Fig. 7.

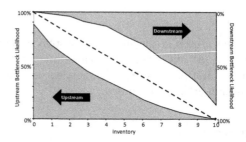

Fig. 8. Bottleneck location for Erlang distributions with 10% standard deviation

6.3 Symmetric System, Erlang Distributions, Standard Deviation 100%

This experiment was repeated with a much higher standard deviation equal to 100% of the cycle time as shown in Fig. 9. Again, there was no practical difference from the previous results.

6.4 Asymmetric System with P1 at 80% of the Cycle Time

Finally, the average cycle time of process P1 has been reduced to 80% of the previous value, and hence to 80% of P2. In effect, P1 is now much faster than

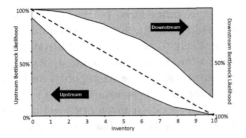

Fig. 9. Bottleneck location for Erlang distributions with 100% standard deviation

P2, and P2 is much more likely to be the bottleneck. Both cycle times are still exponentially distributed.

The result of this experiment is shown in Fig. 10. Now the bottleneck locations are no longer symmetrical to the inventory levels. For example, for an inventory level of three, the bottleneck is still with a 40.0% likelihood of being downstream, and with only a 17.1% likelihood of being upstream. The theoretical ideal value is expected to be only around 30%. For any inventory level, it is much more likely that the bottleneck is in P2 than expected theoretically (Fig. 4) or analyzed for symmetrical systems experimentally (Figs. 7, 8, and 9).

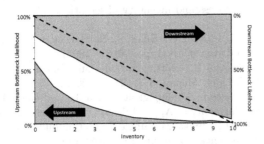

Fig. 10. Bottleneck location for unequal cycle times with P1 at 80% of P2

7   Conclusion

We experimentally analyzed the direction of the bottleneck based on the inventory levels and compared it to the theoretically expected results. The type of distribution and the width of the standard deviation made no difference to the outcomes. For systems with (near) identical cycle times, it is valid to assume that the buffer inventory is a good indicator of the bottleneck direction.

However, if the cycle times are different, this assumption no longer holds true. As the differences between the cycle times increase, so does the likelihood of the bottleneck direction getting skewed toward the slower processes.

Naturally, having a more pronounced bottleneck downstream creates inventory levels that are more often full. If, due to random fluctuations, the inventory empties, it is much more likely to recover to its full state due to a strong downstream bottleneck than to turn empty due to a temporary upstream bottleneck. This explains the skewedness toward the strong bottleneck. Similar but symmetrical behavior occurs in case of an upstream bottleneck [7].

Overall, a linear relation between inventory level and bottleneck direction can be assumed only for systems with similar cycle times. The more pronounced the difference in cycle times, the less valid is this assumption. Further research is needed to analyze the relation between inventory levels and the bottleneck direction for asymmetric systems.

References

1. Roser, C., Lorentzen, K., Deuse, J.: Reliable shop floor bottleneck detection for flow lines through process and inventory observations: the bottleneck walk. Logist. Res. **8**(1) (2015)
2. Law, A.M., Kelton, W.D.: Simulation Modeling and Analysis, 2nd edn. McGraw-Hill, New York (1991)
3. Elmasry, G., McCann, C.: Bottleneck discovery in large-scale networks based on the expected value of per-hop delay, vol. 1, pp. 405–410 (2003)
4. Roser, C., Lorentzen, K., Deuse, J.: Reliable shop floor bottleneck detection for flow lines through process and inventory observations. Procedia CIRP **19**, 63–68 (2014)
5. Li, L., Chang, Q., Ni, J., Xiao, G., Biller, S.: Bottleneck detection of manufacturing systems using data driven method, pp. 76–81 (2007)
6. Lawrence, S.R., Buss, A.H.: Shifting production bottlenecks: causes, cures, and conundrums. Prod. Oper. Manag. **3**(1), 21–37 (2009)
7. Richtung des Engpasses in Abhängigkeit vom Füllstand eines Bestandes. Masters thesis, Karlsruhe University of Applied Sciences, Germany (2015)
8. Roser, C., Nakano, M., Tanaka, M.: Single simulation buffer optimization. In: Winter Simulation Conference, vol. 4, pp. 1079–1086 (2002)
9. Roser, C., Nakano, M., Tanaka, M.: Tracking shifting bottlenecks. In: Japan-USA Symposium on Flexible Automation, pp. 745–750 (2002)
10. Roser, C., Nakano, M.: A quantitative comparison of bottleneck detection methods in manufacturing systems with particular consideration for shifting bottlenecks. In: Umeda, S., Nakano, M., Mizuyama, H., Hibino, H., Kiritsis, D., von Cieminski, G. (eds.) Advances in Production Management Systems: Innovative Production Management Towards Sustainable Growth, pp. 273–281. Springer, Heidelberg (2015)
11. Lima, E., Chwif, L., Ribeiro, M., Barreto, P.: Metodology for selecting the best suitable bottleneck detection method, pp. 1746–1751 (2008)

Cyber-Physical (IIoT) Technology Deployments in Smart Manufacturing Systems, an SM & CPPS SIG Workshop Session

The Operator 4.0: Human Cyber-Physical Systems & Adaptive Automation Towards Human-Automation Symbiosis Work Systems

David Romero[1,2(✉)], Peter Bernus[2], Ovidiu Noran[2], Johan Stahre[3], and Åsa Fast-Berglund[3]

[1] Tecnológico de Monterrey, Monterrey, Mexico
david.romero.diaz@gmail.com
[2] Griffith University, Nathan, Australia
{P.Bernus,O.Noran}@griffith.edu.au
[3] Chalmers University of Technology, Gothenburg, Sweden
{johan.stahre,asa.fasth}@chalmers.se

Abstract. A vision for the Operator 4.0 is presented in this paper in the context of human cyber-physical systems and adaptive automation towards human-automation symbiosis work systems for a socially sustainable manufacturing workforce. Discussions include base concepts and enabling technologies for the development of human-automation symbiosis work systems in Industry 4.0.

Keywords: Operator 4.0 · Human cyber-physical systems · Adaptive automation · Human-automation symbiosis · Socially sustainable manufacturing

1 Introduction

Industry 4.0 enables new types of interactions between operators and machines [1], interactions that will transform the industrial workforce and will have significant implications for the nature of work, in order to accommodate the ever-increasing variability of production. An important part of this transformation is the emphasis on *human-centricity* of the Factories of the Future [2], allowing for a paradigm shift from independent automated and human activities towards a *human-automation symbiosis* (or 'human cyber-physical systems') characterised by the cooperation of machines with humans in work systems and designed not to replace the skills and abilities of humans, but rather to co-exist with and assist humans in being more efficient and effective [3].

In this sense, the history of the interaction of operators with various industrial and digital production technologies can be summarised as a generational evolution. Thus, *Operator 1.0* generation is defined as humans conducting 'manual and dextrous work' with some support from mechanical tools and manually operated machine tools. *Operator 2.0* generation represents a human entity who performs 'assisted work' with the support of computer tools, ranging from CAx tools to NC operating systems (e.g. CNC machine tools), as well as enterprise information systems. The *Operator 3.0* generation embodies a human entity involved in 'cooperative work' with robots and other machines and computer tools, also known as - human-robot collaboration. The

© IFIP International Federation for Information Processing 2016
Published by Springer International Publishing AG 2016. All Rights Reserved
I. Nääs et al. (Eds.): APMS 2016, IFIP AICT 488, pp. 677–686, 2016.
DOI: 10.1007/978-3-319-51133-7_80

Operator 4.0 generation represents the 'operator of the future', a *smart and skilled operator* who performs 'work aided' by machines if and as needed. It represents a new design and engineering philosophy for adaptive production systems where the focus is on treating automation as a further enhancement of the human's physical, sensorial and cognitive capabilities by means of *human cyber-physical system* integration (see Fig. 1).

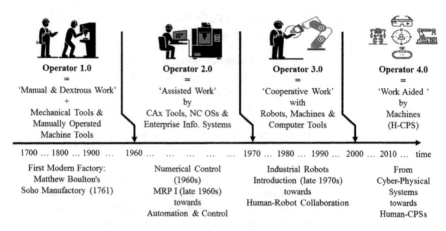

Operator 1.0	Operator 2.0	Operator 3.0	Operator 4.0
=	=	=	=
'Manual & Dextrous Work' + Mechanical Tools & Manually Operated Machine Tools	'Assisted Work' by CAx Tools, NC OSs & Enterprise Info. Systems	'Cooperative Work' with Robots, Machines & Computer Tools	'Work Aided' by Machines (H-CPS)

1700 ... 1800 ... 1900 ...	1960	1970 ... 1980 ... 1990 ... 2000 ...	2010 ... time
First Modern Factory: Matthew Boulton's Soho Manufactory (1761)	Numerical Control (1960s) MRP I (late 1960s) towards Automation & Control	Industrial Robots Introduction (late 1970s) towards Human-Robot Collaboration	From Cyber-Physical Systems towards Human-CPSs

Fig. 1. Operator generations (R) evolution

This paper explores a vision for the *Operator 4.0* in the context of *human cyber-physical systems* and *adaptive automation* towards *human-automation symbiosis work systems* for a socially sustainable manufacturing workforce. The discussions within the following sections include base concepts and enabling technologies for the development of the proposed human-automation symbiosis work systems in Industry 4.0.

2 Base Concepts

The concept of *Balanced Automation Systems (BAS)* [4] was introduced in the early 90's as an attempt to achieve the right combination of automation and manual operations (*cf.* Operator 2.0 & 3.0) in production systems, taking into account economic and socio-organisational aspects for the (re-)engineering of competitive and socially sustainable production systems. BAS implementations have mainly been based on the principles of 'anthropocentric production systems' [5] and the advantages offered by flexible automation as an extension of programmable automation in manufacturing systems. In [6], it has been previously defined a *Next Generation BAS* concept with the aim of stepping beyond the 'right balance' between automated and manual tasks in production systems, so as to the achieve 'human-automation symbiosis' for enhancing workforce capabilities (*cf.* Operator 4.0) and increasing manufacturing flexibility (*cf.* Factory 4.0) of production systems. The vision of Next Generation BASs is that while they will still rely on the guidelines of 'anthropocentric production systems' [5], they will moreover feature 'adaptive automation' [7–9] for the dynamic allocation of control over manufacturing and assembly tasks to a human operator and/or a machine for the purpose of optimising overall production system performance. This will be done considering [10, 11]: (a) sustainable technical and economic benefits for the manufacturing enterprise (e.g. improved quality, increased responsiveness, shorter throughput times, easier planning and control of production processes, increased capacity for innovation and continual improvement) and (b) social-human benefits for the workforce (e.g. increasing quality of working life, higher job satisfaction through meaningful tasks, greater personal flexibility and adaptation, improved ability and skills of shop-floor personnel).

Based on the previous context, we define *Human Cyber-Physical Systems (H-CPS)* as systems engineered to: (a) improve human abilities to dynamically interact with machines in the cyber- and physical- worlds by means of 'intelligent' human-machine interfaces, using human-computer interaction techniques designed to fit the operators' cognitive and physical needs, and (b) improve human physical-, sensing- and cognitive-capabilities, by means of various enriched and enhanced technologies (e.g. using wearable devices). Both H-CPS aims are to be achieved through computational and communication techniques, akin to adaptive control systems with the human-in-the-loop.

The *Adaptive Automation (AA)* movement [7, 8, 12, 13] aims at optimising human-machine cooperation to efficiently allocate labour (cognitive & physical) and distribute tasks between the automated part and the humans in the workstations of an adaptive production system [13]. AA allows the human and/or the machine to modify the level of automation by shifting the control of specific functions whenever predefined conditions (e.g. critical-event, measure-based and/or modelling-based) are met [14]. The ultimate AA goal is the achievement of human-automation symbiosis by means of adaptation of automation & control across all workstations of a human-centred and adaptive production system in order to allow a dynamic and seamless transition of functions (tasks) allocation between humans and machines that optimally leverages human skills to provide inclusiveness and job satisfaction while also achieving production objectives.

Human-in-the-loop (HITL) feedback control systems are defined as systems that require human interaction [15]. HITL control models offer interesting opportunities to a broad range of H-CPS applications, such as the 'Operator 4.0'. HITL control models can help to supervise an operator's performance in a human-machine interaction, and (a) let the operator directly control the operation under supervisory control, (b) let automation monitor the operator and take appropriate actions, or (c) an hybrid of 'a' and 'b', where automation monitors the operator, takes human inputs for the control, and takes appropriate actions [15]. HITL control models, although being challenging due to the complex physiological, sensorial and cognitive nature of human beings, are an important enabler for 'human-automation symbiosis' achievement.

3   Human-Automation Symbiosis: Intelligent Hybrid Agents

In this section, the strategy to attain *human-automation symbiosis* in manufacturing work systems is explored through a discourse of 'adaptive automation' and 'intelligent multi-agent systems' as the bases for a sharing and trading of control strategy [14].

An *intelligent agent* is an entity (human, artificial or hybrid) with the following characteristics [16]: (a) *purposeful* - displays goal-seeking behaviour, (b) *perceptive* - can observe information about the surrounding world and filter it according to relevance for orientation, (c) *aware* - can develop situational awareness that is relevant for the agent's purpose, (d) *autonomous* - can decide a course of action (plan) to achieve the goal, (e) *able to act* - can mobilise its resources to act on its plan; these resources may include parts of the self or tools at the autonomous disposal of the agent, and resources for physical action or information gathering/processing, (f) *reflective* - can represent and reason about the abilities and goals of self and those of other agents, (g) *adaptable* and *learning* - can recognise inadequacy of its plan and modify it, or change its goal, and (h) *conversational* and *cooperative* - can negotiate with other agents to enhance perception, develop common orientation, decide on joint goals, plans, and action; essentially participate in maintaining the 'emergent agent' created through joint actions of agents. Note that this classification of agent functions may be interpreted as the ability to perform the Observe, Orient, Decide and Act (OODA) Loop of Boyd [17, 18], developed as a theory to explain the conditions and functions of successful operation, and therefore this classification may be used to direct the engineering and development of intelligent agents [16], which, as we shall see below, are expected to be 'adaptive' and 'hybrid' in nature.

Human agents, under certain circumstances, and in defined domains of activity, are able to act as intelligent agents (e.g. able to perform complex assembly sequences and operations in a flexible production line). However, once the assumptions are no longer true (e.g. due to a heavy physical, sensorial and/or cognitive workload), the quality of *agenthood* deteriorates; thus the human does no longer have the ability to perform one or several functions that are normally attributed to an intelligent agent. Consequently, the question is: how to restitute human agenthood by extending human capabilities (physical, sensorial and/or cognitive) through automation-aided means?

Similarly, *artificial (machine) agents,* under certain circumstances and in defined domains of activity can act as intelligent agents (e.g. they are able to perform repetitive and routine tasks in a high volume production line, make decisions based on learnt patterns, etc.). Nevertheless, once the assumptions are no longer true (e.g. the need (ability) to improvise and use flexible processes to reduce production downtime due to an error), the quality of *agenthood* deteriorates; thus the machine does no longer have the ability to perform one or several functions that are normally attributed to an intelligent agent. Therefore, the question is: how to restore machine agenthood by extending the machine's capabilities through human-aided means?

Hybrid agents are intelligent agents established as a symbiotic relationship (human-automation symbiosis) between the human and the machine, so that in situations where neither would display agenthood in isolation, the symbiotic hybrid agent does. In this research, the vision is that at any time a human (the 'Operator 4.0') lacks some of these *agenthood* abilities, such as due to heavy physical, sensorial and/or cognitive workload, automation will extend the human's abilities as much as necessary to help the operator to perform the tasks at hand, according to the expected quality of performance criteria. Thus, it is proposed to implement *hybrid agents,* as a form of 'adaptive automation', in order to sustain *agenthood* by determining whenever and wherever the operator requires augmentation (e.g. using *advanced trained classifiers* to recognise this need [19]), and prompting the appropriate type and level of automation to facilitate optimal operator performance. An important objective is that the level of this extension need not be a 'design time' decision, but should be able to be dynamically configured as needed. Furthermore, the 'hybrid agents' view of the Operator 4.0 is a component of the solution to preserve the operator's *situation awareness* [20], as the status, experience and information processing capability of the operator can cause loss of agenthood and consequent decision-making errors, thus the need for 'symbiotic technical support'. Work on *affective computing* [21] showed that the task allocation and adaptation between humans and machines/computers supporting them is not a trivial task and should involve sensory assessments of humans' physical and cognitive states in order to be efficient.

For the purpose of comparison, in the case of an Operator 3.0 (*cf.* human-robot collaboration), the design time decision would be determined by the required capability of the manufacturing or assembly operation (e.g. speed, accuracy, capacity, reliability, etc.), which then would decide (based on technical, economic, social and human benefits) the level of automation of the process, as well as the accompanying skills and abilities required by the human role. In contrast, in the case of an Operator 4.0, automation level would be determined in less detail at design time, allowing an initial detailed procedure and much automated support (e.g. in case of a novice or new-to-the-task operator), while providing 'on the fly' solutions that develop together with the individual operator's skills. Apart from achieving job satisfaction and a variety of desired process 'ilities' [22], such dynamic allocation of different levels/extent of automation fosters the use of human skills and abilities. This includes the creation of favourable conditions for workforce development and learning, the improvement of human-robot collaboration and tacit knowledge development, as it is well known that in many (although not all) tasks acting based on tacit knowledge are much more efficient and effective than following predetermined procedures.

Emergent agents are virtual entities, who exist as a cooperative and negotiated arrangement between multiple agents of either kind above (sometimes on multiple levels of static or dynamic aggregation), whereupon two human agents, or a human and a machine/robot, or two machine/robot agents, or more than two agents of any of these types, form a 'join entity agent' that from the external observer's viewpoint acts as a single intelligent agent. It is expected that an Operator 4.0 will have the ability to be part of an intelligent group of agents with appropriate functionality for the formation, operation, transformation and dissolution of these groups. Note that it is not necessary for every agent to have the same level of contribution to such self-organising ability; agents may specialise in certain tasks and assume different roles in the lifecycle of the emergent agent.

4 The Operator 4.0: Aiding for Enhanced Workers Capabilities

A *capability* is the "measure of the ability of an entity (e.g. department, organisation, person, system) to achieve its objectives, especially in relation to its overall mission" [23]. In the case of human beings, this involves having the resources and the ability to deploy their capabilities for a purpose.

4.1   Automation Aiding for Enhanced Physical Capabilities

A *physical activity* is any bodily movement produced by skeletal muscles that requires energy expenditure. We define *physical capability* as the operator's capacity and ability to undertake physical activities needed for daily work, and can be characterised by multiple attributes, including the description of the physical function (e.g. ability to lift, walk, manipulate and assemble) together with its non-functional properties (e.g. speed, strength, precision and dexterity), as well as the description of the ability in terms of maturity- and expertise-level. The agent's activity supported is that of (physically) acting, i.e. the 'A' in the OODA loop.

For example, the operator may be: (a) 'procedure following - novice' with no autonomy over the details of the operation and under supervision along the whole procedure, (b) 'procedure following - advanced' with limited operational autonomy and less supervision across the procedure, or (c) 'expert' - featuring internalised tacit knowledge (know-how) and autonomy towards improving the operation, where only the operation's outcome is supervised. The vision of Operator 4.0 acknowledges that capabilities are not static, but they evolve over time, as well as change depending on context (e.g. the operator may be tired or rested, new- or accustomed- to-the-task), therefore physically aiding an Operator 4.0 assumes that one can assess the physical capabilities in a dynamic and timely fashion, preferably in real-time. Some assessment tools for testing an operator's physical capabilities may include: (a) *Physical Abilities Tests (PATs)* [24, 25] capable of matching the physical abilities of an operator with the physical demands of a job (or operation) up-front to its allocation (e.g. such methods are getting increased attention in the defence community); and (b) *Advanced Trained Classifiers (ATCs)* [26], based on a variety of machine learning techniques, to measure (test) in real-time the operator's physical performance and dynamically identify when an assisted/enhanced operation is necessary in an unobtrusive manner, relying on physiological measures (*cf.* ergonomics [27]). This is done in order to actively determine when an operator actually requires assistance and subsequently prompt the appropriate type and level of physical (aided) capability to facilitate optimal physical performance by the operator. Moreover, PATs may be useful for job role allocation and/or for determining training needs (e.g. how to handle lifting, posture correction, etc.), while ATCs may be advantageous for reducing the chances of accidents due to tiredness or of injuries due to repetitive strain, or to improve product quality by reducing errors and re-work.

4.2   Automation Aiding for Enhanced Sensing Capabilities

A *sensorial* capability is the operator's capacity and ability to acquire data from the environment, as a first step towards creating information necessary for orientation and decision-making in the operator's daily work [28]. There are two components to sensing: (a) the physical ability to collect data from the environment (by vision, smell, sound, touch, vibration), and (b) the ability to selectively perceive it (as we know that a very low percentage of the data generated by the physical sense of an operator enters the short-term memory and is made available for processing). It is known that an operator is selectively filtering out what he/she does not consider important: "of the entire amount of new information generated by our environment, our senses filter out >99% of signals before they reach our consciousness" [29]. It is also known that this filtering is not a conscious process. Therefore, OODA is not a simple loop; there is information that flows to make an operator perceive selectively what his/her brain considers important (i.e. what data are useful for analysis and decision-making). This selectivity is acquired by the operator through learning. As a consequence, there are two points where the operator's sensing abilities are subject to assessment and where these abilities may need improvement, as further described.

The first potential sensory improvement is the creation of new- or augmentation- of existing senses (e.g. by way of using sensor devices to collect, convert, aggregate signals that would not be accessible for the operator, either due to physical accessibility of the data source, general human limitations, or due to individual personal limitations). Also, due to the different levels of sensitivity of humans across senses, transforming one signal to another form may increase the ability of the human to identify information within the data (e.g. transforming temperature to visible colour, vibration to audible spectrum sound, or using data aggregation, can enable the human to make use of otherwise inaccessible data). The second type of sensory limitation is more difficult to overcome if it is to be done exclusively at sensor level. This is because information feedback produced by analysis (orientation) and decision-making must be used to filter out unwanted data (i.e. containing irrelevant information) and to sensitise selective perception to smaller signals, which may carry relevant information.

Some assessment tools for testing an operator's sensorial capabilities may include: (a) *Sensorial Abilities Tests (SATs)* [30] capable of matching the sensorial abilities of an operator with the sensorial demands of a job (or operation) up-front to its allocation. This is not a trivial tasks, because even though the sensorial abilities of an operator can be tested (such as by using simple vision and hearing tests), sensing successfully in the situation (i.e. registering/perceiving signals necessary for analysis and orientation) is also dependent on the nature and level of prior experience of the operator as previously explained.

It is therefore expected that the solution to selective perception deficits is not simply providing operators with 'bionic ears and eyes' (even though in some situations that may be sufficient), but in using the 'emergent agent' model, where the machine agent has its own intelligence in terms of analysis and orientation, and the ability to reason about the human agent's needs and decision what data to present for the human's needs and when.

The traditional limitation for decision-making has been scarcity of information, requiring human (and machine) agents to make decisions in light of insufficient data about the operations. With the proliferation of sensor devices (the so-called 'Internet of Things') this situation could change, but only if sensor agents are made intelligent in terms of what data to register and transmit to other agents.

New algorithms are needed for cooperative and collaborative learning of situations for collective sense-making and decision-making by sensor agents (including agent networks). This is so that the situational knowledge base of participating agents can be utilised to adaptively filter unwanted data and to 'zoom-in' to enhance faint but relevant signals, as well as negotiate signal bandwidth for priority communication. Part of this

situation recognition may be implemented by machine learning techniques, such as
(b) *Advanced Trained Classifiers (ATCs)* [26], where part of an intelligent sensor agent
may use machine learning to support human-automation symbiosis and to learn about
the individual operator and that operator's behaviour in action, to actively determine
when an operator actually requires assistance, and to subsequently prompt the appropriate type and level of sensing (aided) capabilities to facilitate optimal sensing performance by the operator.

4.3   Automation Aiding for Enhanced Cognitive Capabilities

A *cognitive capability* is the operator's capacity and ability to undertake the mental
tasks (e.g. perception, memory, reasoning, decision, motor response, etc.) needed for
the job and under certain operational settings [31]. In the OODA model, these cognitive
tasks are to 'Orient' and to 'Decide', together amounting to a mental workload,
decision-making, skilled performance, human-computer interaction, maintaining reliability in performance, dealing with work stress whether in training or in the job.

As the Factories of the Future become increasingly dynamic working environments
(*cf.* Industry 4.0) due to the upsurge in the need for flexibility and adaptability of
production systems, the upgraded shop-floors (*cf.* Factory 4.0) call for *cognitive aids*
that help the operator perform these mental tasks, such as those provided by augmented
reality (AR) technologies or 'intelligent' Human-Machine Interfaces (HMI) to support
the new/increased cognitive workload (e.g. diagnosis, situational awareness,
decision-making, planning, etc.) of the *Operator 4.0*. It can be expected that this aid
would increase human reliability in the job, considering both the operator's well-being
and the production system's performance.

Some assessment tools for testing an operator's cognitive capabilities may include:
(a) *Cognitive Abilities Tests (CATs)* [32] capable of matching the cognitive abilities of
an operator with the mental demands and cognitive skills needed for performing a job
(or operation) up-front to its allocation; and (b) *Advanced Trained Classifiers (ATCs)*
[26] based on various machine learning techniques, to measure (test) in real-time the
operator's cognitive performance and dynamically identify when an assisted/enhanced
action is necessary, and do so in an unobtrusive manner, relying on cognitive load
measurements (*cf.* cognitive ergonomics [33]).

5   Conclusions and Further Work

Industry 4.0 would be inconceivable without human beings. Hence, human-automation
symbiosis by means of H-CPS and AA aims to take into account established principles
of the design of operator-friendly working conditions [34] for aiding the workforce
[35], such as: (a) *practicability,* considering compliance with 'anthropometric' and
physical, sensorial and cognitive norms in the design of a work system; (b) *safety,*
bearing in mind in the design of work systems embedded security and safety measures
to avoid accidents; (c) *freedom from impairment,* by providing automation-aided means
to compensate various individual (human) limitations and thus keep with the physical,

sensorial and cognitive quality performance of the job; and (d) *individualisation and personalisation of the working environment* thanks to adaptive systems (*cf.* AA) that support the operator as an individual and promote learning (e.g. by means of sharing and trading of control strategy [14]).

The development of 'human-automation symbiosis' in work systems [6, 36] offers advantages for the social sustainability of the manufacturing workforce in *Industry 4.0*, in terms of improving operational excellence, safety and health, satisfaction and motivation, inclusiveness, and continuous learning. Hence, the purpose of H-CPS and AA in this research is to support the *Operator 4.0* to excel in the job by means of automation-aided systems that aim to provide a sustainable relief of physical and mental stress and contribute to the development of workforce creativity, innovation and improvisational skills, without compromising production objectives.

Further work aims to explore 'intelligent' human-machine interfaces and interaction technologies, and adaptive and human-in-the-loop (HITL) control systems to support the development of 'human-automation symbiosis' work systems for the *Operator 4.0* in the Factory of the Future.

References

1. BCG Group: Report on Man and Machine in Industry 4.0 (2015)
2. European Factories of the Future Research Association (EFFRA) Roadmap 2020
3. Tzafestas, S.: Concerning human-automation symbiosis in the society and the nature. Int. J. Fact. Autom. Robot. Soft Comput. **1**(3), 6–24 (2006)
4. Camarinha-Matos, L.M., Rabelo, R., Ósorio, L.: Balanced automation. In: Tzafestas, S.G. (ed.) Computer-Assisted Management and Control of Manufacturing Systems, pp. 376–413. Springer, London (1996)
5. Kovács, I., Brandão-Moniz, A.: Issues on the anthropocentric production systems. In: Camarinha-Matos, L.M., Afsarmanesh, H. (eds.) Balanced Automation Systems: Architectures and Design Methods, pp. 131–140. Springer, New York (1995)
6. Romero, D., Noran, O., Stahre, J., Bernus, P., Fast-Berglund, Å.: Towards a human-centred reference architecture for next generation balanced automation systems: human-automation symbiosis. Adv. Prod. Manag. Syst. **460**, 556–566 (2015)
7. Hancock, P.A., Chignell, M.H.: Adaptive control in human-machine systems. In: Hancock, P.A. (ed.) Human Factors Psychology, pp. 305–345. Elsevier Science Publishers, North Holland (1987)
8. Hancock, P.A., Jagacinski, R.J., Parasuraman, R., et al.: Human-automation interaction research: past present and future. Ergon. Des. **21**(2), 9–14 (2013)
9. Sheridan, T., Parasuraman, R.: Human-automation interaction. Hum. Factors Ergon. **1**(1), 89–129 (2006)
10. Kidd, P.: Organisation People and Technology in European Manufacturing. CEC, FAST, Brussels (1992)
11. Lehner, F.: Anthropocentric Production Systems: The European Response to Advanced Manufacturing and Globalization. CEC, Brussels (1992)
12. Kay, M.: Adaptive automation accelerates process development. Bioprocess Int. **4**(4), 70–78 (2006)

13. Calefato, C., Montanari, R., Tesauri, F.: The adaptive automation design. In: Asai, K. (ed.) Human Computer Interaction: New Developments, pp. 141–154. InTech, Rijeka (2008)
14. Inagaki, T.: Adaptive automation: sharing and trading of control. In: Handbook of Cognitive Task Design, pp. 147–169 (2003). Chapter 8
15. Munir, S., Stankovic, J.A., Liang, C-J.M., Lin, S.: Cyber-physical system challenges for human-in-the-loop control. In: Feedback Computing (2013)
16. Kasabov, N.: Introduction: hybrid intelligent adaptive systems. Int. J. Intell. Syst. **6**, 453–454 (1998)
17. Boyd, J.R.: The Essence of Winning and Losing (1996). www.dnipogo.org
18. Osinga, F.P.B.: Science, Strategy and War: The Strategic Theory of John Boyd. Eburon Academic Publishers, Delft (2005)
19. Willson, G.F., Russel, C.A.: Performance enhancement in a UAV task using psycho-physiologically determined adaptive aiding. Hum. Factors **49**(6), 1005–1019 (2007)
20. Endsley, M.R.: Towards a theory of situation awareness in dynamic systems. Hum. Factors **37**(1), 32–64 (1995)
21. Picard, R.W.: Affective Computing. MIT Press, Cambridge (1997)
22. Ricci, N., Fitzgerald, M., Ross, A.M., Rhodes, D.H.: Architecting systems of systems with Ilities: an overview of the SAI method. In: Conference on Systems Engineering Research (2014)
23. Capability (General) Business Dictionary. http://www.businessdictionary.com (2016)
24. Committee on Measuring Human Capabilities: Measuring Human Capabilities: An Agenda for Basic Research on the Assessment of Individual and Group Performance Potential for Military Accession (2015)
25. Campion, M.A.: Personnel selection for physically demanding jobs: review and recommendations. Pers. Psychol. **36**, 527–550 (1983)
26. Woźniak, M., Graña, M., Corchado, E.: A survey of multiple classifier systems as hybrid systems. Inf. Fusion **16**, 3–17 (2014)
27. Lee, J.D., Seppelt, B.D.: Human factors and ergonomics in automation design. In: Salvendy, G. (ed.) Handbook of Human factors and Ergonomics, pp. 1615–1642. Wiley, Hoboken (2012). Sensory activity
28. Attwood, D., Deeb, J., Danz-Reece, M.: Personal actors. In: Tooley, M. (ed.) Design Engineering Manual, pp. 234–247. Elsevier, New York (2010). Chapter 6.1
29. Simon, H.: Artificial intelligence as a framework for understanding intuition. J. Econ. Psychol. **24**, 265–277 (2003)
30. Stone, H., Bleibaum, R., Thomas, H.A.: Sensory Evaluation Practices, 4th edn. Elsevier, Amsterdam (2012)
31. Carrol, J.B.: Human Cognitive Abilities. Cambridge University Press, Cambridge (1993)
32. Hutton, R.J.B., Militello, L.G.: Applied cognitive task analysis (ACTA): a practitioner's toolkit for understanding cognitive task demands. Ergonomics **41**(11), 1618–1641 (1998)
33. Falzon, P., Gaines, B.R., Monk, A.F.: Cognitive Ergonomics: Understanding, Learning, and Designing Human-Computer Interaction. Academic Press, Cambridge (1990)
34. Hacker, W.: Allgemeine Arbeitspsychologie: Psychische Regulation von Wissens Denk und körperlicher Arbeit, 2nd edn. Verlag Hans Huber, Bern (2005)
35. Bailey, R.W.: Human Performance Engineering, 2nd edn. International Prentice-Hall, London (1996)
36. Kaber, D.B., Riley, J.M., Tan, K., Endsley, M.R.: On the design of adaptive automation for complex systems. Int. J. Cogn. Ergon. **5**(1), 37–57 (2001)

Supporting the Requirements Elicitation Process for Cyber-Physical Product-Service Systems Through a Gamified Approach

Stefan Wiesner[1(✉)], Jannicke Baalsrud Hauge[1,2], Florian Haase[1],
and Klaus-Dieter Thoben[1,3]

[1] BIBA – Bremer Institut für Produktion und Logistik GmbH, Bremen, Germany
{wie,baa,has,tho}@biba.uni-bremen.de
[2] KTH – Royal Institute of Technology, Stockholm, Sweden
[3] University of Bremen, Bremen, Germany

Abstract. Solutions are offered more and more in the form of Product-Service Systems (PSS), which combine tangible and intangible components into a comprehensive package for the customer. The rise of Internet of Things technology enables new ways of integrating products and services. So-called Cyber-Physical Systems (CPS) include the necessary sensors, actuators and software to provide reconfigurable functionalities for changing demands. However, engineering complexity is increased by the evolutionary aspect, as well as the increased number of stakeholders and system components involved over the whole life cycle. Understanding the underlying requirements is fundamental to establish a common perception of the targeted system among the manufacturer, service providers and the other stakeholders. This paper presents a gamified approach to elicit stakeholder requirements for the development of these complex systems. Four industrial users will use the gamified environment for refining their existing requirements.

Keywords: Requirements elicitation · Product-service systems · Cyber-physical systems · Serious games

1 Introduction

Customers are looking for solutions and benefits, forcing the manufacturer to give increasing attention to understand and answer their problems over the whole life cycle. Product-Service Systems (PSS) emerge as a result through the integrated development, realization and application of tangible and intangible components for a common objective. Additionally, new levels of human-machine interaction have become possible and more widespread, paving the way for reliable, sustainable, technology-driven ecosystems [1]. As a result, Cyber-Physical Systems (CPS) integrate embedded systems, application systems, and infrastructure in

© IFIP International Federation for Information Processing 2016
Published by Springer International Publishing AG 2016. All Rights Reserved
I. Nääs et al. (Eds.): APMS 2016, IFIP AICT 488, pp. 687–694, 2016.
DOI: 10.1007/978-3-319-51133-7_81

complex networks [2]. They follow a holistic system approach, requiring the collaboration of different disciplines such as mechanical engineering, electrical engineering, and computer science for their realization [1]. The collaboration with stakeholders from different disciplines as partners during Requirements Engineering (RE) becomes more and more important. The high number of components involved in the system and its evolution along the life cycle require the RE approach to adapt to a volatile set of user requirements, evolving over the life cycle as the technical development continues and the needs of the different customers and stakeholders change over time.

Consequently, for CPS based PSS the need for continuous interaction between the development process and the requirement elicitation process is inevitable for ensuring a consistent and traceable elicitation and management of requirements [3]. This requires new elicitation approaches and tools, being more flexible, dynamic and considering future needs even before they have appeared, in order to reduce the costs and the quality challenges arising from this dynamic environment, i.e. there is a need for a collaborative approach of all stakeholders involved in the entire product life cycle. This article present the first results of a gamified approach for the requirements elicitation for CPS based PSS that can be applied in such dynamic environments. The work is based on a RE framework that enables a symbiotic specification of dynamic systems in a collaborative way along the whole value chain.

2   Methodology

For the development of the gamified approach, we combine literature review and action research. In a first step, the relevant characteristics of CPS based PSS and the RE process are identified. Secondly, several existing approaches that might serve as a good basis for the gamification will be assessed for their suitability. The main assessment criteria are to what extent the existing approaches and methodologies are transferable to CPS based PSS, as well as to what extent it appears likely that their re-use or adaption will contribute to improved quality of requirements elicitation. Thirdly, based upon this analysis, existing gamification approaches can be further developed or changed in order to address these points.

For the literature review, scientific papers were accessed through suitable portals (Scopus, Elsevier, Google Scholar etc.) searching for key words (serious games + requirement elicitation, product-service systems, cyber-physical systems, Requirements Engineering, dynamic systems) [4]. The relevance of the identified papers for this article was based on assessing the abstract, as well as by searching for the combination of elicitation, PSS and CPS in the full papers, considered being the most challenging, and that there is a need of tools supporting the process.

The work with four industrial use cases had a different methodical approach. The researchers have been involved in the specifications and development of the CPS/PSS scenarios. Design Science was the overall scientific approach in this work. More specific, action research was applied. The game has been developed using an agile software development approach.

3 Requirements Engineering Approaches for CPS Based PSS

From the PSS definitions, the main components to be covered in an integrated approach are tangible product and intangible service shares jointly fulfilling a users need [5,6]. Additionally, IT components, such as software, are becoming more and more a distinct part of PSS [7], ultimately leading to the provision of services through CPS [8]. In order to derive the challenges for requirements elicitation for CPS based PSS, the specific characteristics of the separate components and their development processes are described below.

For **product** development, RE approaches have already been implemented with a high degree of formalization. Structured fundamental models exist that provide a general development procedure including RE. However, they focus almost exclusively on requirements development as the main process, which is only conducted at the beginning of the development approach, e.g. by specifying the product requirements document [9]. Sometimes, also aspects of requirements management are adopted, but without explicit instructions for implementation [10]. For requirements elicitation, first, the stakeholders are identified; however, procedures for the elicitation of requirements for product-related services are not described. Moreover, there are weaknesses in the derivation of requirements from the customers value chain processes, and cross-domain knowledge is not considered [11].

Models for the systematic development of **services** have been created [12]. However, no systematic procedures for the implementation of RE have been established, because the characteristics of a service, e.g. its complexity, pose greater challenges. Thus, service engineering procedures do not integrate a holistic RE until now, but focus more on methods like "trial and error" [13]. The elicitation process in service engineering comprises the tasks of identifying essential information – e.g. service ideas, possible customers and their expectations, and the sources of the requirements – and determining the goals, chances and risks. The procedures are service-domain specific; cross-domain knowledge is not considered. Furthermore, no precise methods for the elicitation are provided. Procedures for the requirements elicitation are described on a relatively general level [10].

In the **IT** sector, RE is widely recognized as a special discipline; RE "has begun to evolve from its traditional role, as a mere front-end in the software development lifecycle, towards becoming a key focus in the software development process" [14]. In direct comparison with product and service development, RE is integrated deeper and more comprehensive into software development [10]. Customer-integration is emphasized in the software engineering approaches, but the focus is laid upon the software domain – interdisciplinary requirements are not considered. The procedures provided for the identification of conflicts focuses solely on the software domain; interdisciplinary conflicts are not discovered. Negotiation with stakeholders is suggested to resolve conflicts and find a compromise [11].

4   Gap Analysis

According to [11], the literature about PSS development and design discusses the process of development only abstractly without going into detail. Firstly, the "organizational conditions are created in order to enable an integrated development of services and hardware/software". The stakeholder needs – regarding products and services – are identified. Concrete techniques or methods are not mentioned. Current RE approaches are not able to handle the large number of different and conflicting requirements without exponentially increasing time and cost, as contradictions and interdependencies have to be assessed for a large number of requirements in various domains [15].

Based on this gap analysis, requirements elicitation for CPS based PSS has to be formal enough to describe the targeted system unambiguously and in a verifiable way, but has to have the flexibility to include non-formal inputs. The different stakeholder needs and changing requirements must be managed. As the functionalities of a PSS emerge from the cumulative interactions of the product, service and IT components, elicitation methods and tools have to be able to integrate the mechanical, service and IT domain for capturing requirements. These requirements have to be mapped subsequently to the different PSS elements, to be either fulfilled by a physical functionality or a cyber-service execution. Berkovich et al. [16] propose to apply the Domain-Mapping-Matrix (DMM) to relate the requirements with the PSS functions. This implies communication between stakeholders from different disciplines and that the following aspects have to be observed:

- Complexity: Elicitation has to be able to handle a large number of interrelated product, service and IT requirements.
- Distributed stakeholders: Elicitation has to be applicable for a large number of stakeholders that are typically separated spatially and organizationally. This involves the user, who defines the scope and purpose of the PSS, as well as specialized partners with distinct processes, which develop the individual system components.
- Different disciplines: The elicitation approach has to be usable in multiple disciplines. Requirements exchange has to be supported in order to create a common view of the targeted system.

The following sections will describe how a gamified approach could support requirements elicitation to fulfill the preconditions above.

5   Gamification

A gamification of RE activities does not imply turning PSS development into a game. It means using game-based elements and mechanisms in this non-game environment with the purpose of employing the motivational properties of games [17]. Thus, the gamification components and elements need to be designed and adapted to the context of RE for cyber-physical Product-Service Systems. To do so, it is necessary to establish clear goals and rewards, mechanisms of progression, intermediary and final statuses, challenges, as well as avoiding to manipulate users into following certain patterns that are unlikely to take otherwise, relying too much on extrinsic motivational factors [18].

The objective of a gamified requirements elicitation would be to make the work routine of need identification more effective. The outcome of the game could be initial ideas, but also imply "options", e.g. solutions for specific problems. One advantage of this approach compared to other current techniques is the motivating aspect, which could reduce the frustration in an idea generation process. The game can easily contain multiple and contradictory knowledge structures and promote discussion and reframing of ideas. At the same time, gamification provides incentives to change existing culture, routines and behaviour. Additionally, the game can develop explicit routines for team-based ideation work, together with a technological infrastructure that allows for communication about, and experimentation with more or less finished ideas, early stage innovations and concepts not yet implemented. The objective for the elicitation process would therefore be to play with different options in a virtual environment for discovering the limitation of the defined requirements as well as to use the virtual environment to support the ideation of new possible services. The final criteria for why incorporating gamification in elicitation is the possibility to provide the user with immediate feedback on how the decision or a change in a variable will influence the system configuration for validation.

We decided to use "Unity" as game engine [19], so that the player can get an individually adapted end user scenario without having the need of reprogramming. The game is as much as possible adapted to the known business environment of the industrial cases, with a direct and participatory involvement of stakeholders. Based on these considerations, the gamified environment needs to:

- Involve all stakeholders independent from location or organization, which could be done using internet-based games.
- Mirror the working environment for each role sufficiently, which requires an analysis of each stakeholders work processes.
- Support the users possibility to contribute to a disruptive innovation, e.g. by providing support for out-of-the-box thinking without limiting ideas.
- Visualize the consequences of the defined requirement, e.g. for other requirements and the resulting solution.

The above-mentioned boundaries lead to the following consideration on how to prepare a gamified environment. In the engine, we mapped the existing to-be scenarios and the preliminary user requirements. These requirements are included as functions, where the player can change the variables. We use narrative story telling for leading the player through the game play. It is facilitated and the roles are similar to those in their own companies.

6   Use Case

The gamification approach has been successfully applied in three industrial PSS use cases and is currently being prepared for an additional cyber-physical Product-Service System scenario. The company is a vendor for the aviation sector, which offers fully integrated solutions for surveillance systems, certified according to aviation standards. Customers are airlines, which retrofit their aircraft with the buyer furnished surveillance solutions from the vendor. It generates video streams, which are stored on a memory cartridge within the Central Video Unit (CVU/DVR). The idea is to use this product and extend it with different services. The scenario is depicted in Fig. 1 below.

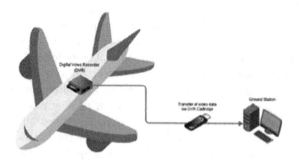

Fig. 1. Cabin Video Surveillance System (CVSS) scenario

Based on a to-be analysis and a first specification of the end user needs, the following restrictions for service development have been identified:

- The product in the aircraft (CVU/DVR) must not be modified.
- The product outside of the aircraft - as for instance the Ground Station (where the data are viewed) – can be modified. For the service-based Aircraft Surveillance System modifications of the hardware (e.g. internal hard drive to copy the data to) as well as software are required.
- In addition, processes within the company has to be re-viewed and re-organized, thus resulting in several as well as radical changes.

Thus, the requirements need to be defined for a fuzzy area, since it is expected that the service the aircraft vendor would like to offer will be customized and in addition, since nothing similar exists, be adaptable to still uncovered needs. The game play starts with a screen that allows the players to enter their name and role (e.g. production, sales etc.) according to their position in the company. Through storytelling, they get the task to develop a cyber-physical Product-Service System, e.g. for an airline that wants a specific service. The players are then able to specify requirements for support in this process from the perspective of their role. They have the possibility to look into an existing repository for similar already existing ideas and requirements or write their own. The different players look at the challenge from different perspectives and provide ideas for the other roles requirements. The results are then displayed by the game and can be rated by all players. Based on the ratings, the players discuss the best ideas to create an integrated solution. This ends the game and it can be restarted iteratively to discuss more requirements and ideas.

The game scenario has been implemented as described above. Additional game mechanics related to KPIs (costs, time, quality, and possible market price), interaction and collaboration could be added. Letting the player first play around with the system and the data that can be collected will make him aware of the CPS environment and its limitations. Furthermore, in order to foster the creativity and to think out of the box, different events may trigger the game play in future releases, and the players are obliged to use tools (like a modelling tool for products or services) in the phase where they are normally not used – e.g. in the test phase. The idea is here to support the critical thinking and to let the player verify that the tool is flexible enough to react on future needs.

7 Conclusion

This paper first outlines the challenges that are related to the requirements elicitation process of CPS based PSS. It discusses the challenges that arise from the fact that the requirements for such complex systems being applied in a dynamic environment need to involve distributed stakeholders from different disciplines. The second part of the article presents a gamified approach for PSS. The approach has been applied in three industrial use cases with good results.

It is able to meet the needs defined in Sect. 5, with regards to the gaps identified in Sect. 4. Gamification is able to involve all stakeholders in a servitization scenario. While the approach currently only includes company roles, it is no problem to extend it to third party suppliers, service providers and the customer. As it is playable over the internet, also distributed partners can be involved. The role model also allows the game to sufficiently mimic the working environment of the players from different disciplines by simulating specific tools, office spaces and work processes. Disruptive innovation is supported by giving the player the freedom to enter ideas independently from existing solutions and share them beyond domain borders. Finally, the ideas are discussed collaboratively by all stakeholders, thus taking into account their needs to define a suitable solutions despite the inherent complexity.

Future research and development needs to strengthen simulation as game component, to give the players a more realistic environment and prediction of results. This would strengthen the feedback to the players and contribute to more dynamic and detailed requirements as an outcome.

Acknowledgements. This work has been funded by the European Commission through the Projects PSYMBIOSYS: Product-Service sYMBIOtic SYStems (No. 636804) and BEACONING (No. 687676). The authors wish to acknowledge the Commission and all the project partners for their contribution.

References

1. Follett, J.: Designing for Emerging Technologies: UX for Genomics, Robotics, and the Internet of Things. O'Reilly Media Inc., Sebastopol (2014)
2. Baheti, R., Gill, H.: Cyber-physical systems. Impact Control Technol. **12**, 161–166 (2011)
3. Hull, E., Jackson, K., Dick, J.: Requirements Engineering. Springer, London (2005)
4. Kitchenham, B., Brereton, O.P., Budgen, D., Turner, M., Bailey, J., Linkman, S.: Systematic literature reviews in software engineering – a systematic literature review. Inf. Softw. Technol. **51**(1), 7–15 (2009)
5. Baines, T.S., Lightfoot, H.W., Evans, S., Neely, A., Greenough, R., Peppard, J., Roy, R., Shehab, E., Braganza, A., Tiwari, A., et al.: State-of-the-art in product-service systems. J. Eng. Manuf. **221**(10), 1543–1552 (2007). Proceedings of the Institution of Mechanical Engineers, Part B
6. Goedkoop, M., Van Halen, C.J., Te Riele, H., Rommens, P.J. et al.: Product service systems, ecological and economic basics. Rep. Dutch Ministries Env. (VROM) Econ. Aff. (EZ) **36**(1), 1–122 (1999)
7. Meier, H., Roy, R., Seliger, G.: Industrial Product-service Systems-IPS 2. CIRP Ann. Manuf. Technol. **59**(2), 607–627 (2010)
8. Geisberger, E., Broy, M., Agenda, C.: Integrierte Forschungsagenda Cyber-Physical Systems, Acatech Studie. März (2012)
9. Pahl, G., Beitz, W., Feldhusen, J., Grote, K.: Konstruktionslehre: Grundlagen Erfolgreicher Produktentwicklung; Methoden und Anwendung 7. Auflage. Aufl. Springer, Heidelberg (2007)
10. Husen, C.V.: Anforderungsanalyse für Produktbegleitende Dienstleistungen (2007)
11. Berkovich, D.I.M., Leimeister, J.M., Krcmar, H.: Requirements engineering fur product service systems. Wirtschaftsinformatik **53**(6), 357–370 (2011)
12. Bullinger, H.J., Scheer, A.W.: Service Engineering—Entwicklung und Gestaltung Innovativer Dienstleistungen. In: Service Engineering, pp. 3–18. Springer, Heidelberg (2006)
13. Spath, D., Demuß, L. : Entwicklung hybrider Produkte—Gestaltung Materieller und Immaterieller Leistungsbundel. In: Service Engineering, pp. 463–502. Springer, Heidelberg (2006)
14. Aurum, A., Wohlin, C.: Engineering and Managing Software Requirements. Springer, Heidelberg (2005)
15. Jarke, M., Loucopoulos, P., Lyytinen, K., Mylopoulos, J., Robinson, W.: The brave new world of design requirements. Inf. Syst. **36**(7), 992–1008 (2011)
16. Berkovich, M., Leimeister, J.M., Hoffmann, A., Krcmar, H.: A requirements data model for product service systems. Req. Eng. **19**(2), 161–186 (2014)
17. Wood, L., Reiners, T.: Gamification. In: Khosrow-Pour, M. (ed.) Encyclopedia of Information Science and Technology, 3rd edn, pp. 3039–3047. IGI Global, Hershey (2015)
18. Kapp, K.M., Blair, L., Mesch, R.: The Gamification of Learning and Instruction Fieldbook: Ideas into Practice. Wiley, New York (2014)
19. Unity - Game Engine (2016)

Smart Manufacturing System Characterization, an SM & CPPS SIG Workshop Session

Applications of the Factory Design and Improvement Reference Activity Model

Sangsu Choi[1][(✉)], Gyhun Kang[1], Kiwook Jung[2], Boonserm Kulvatunyou[2], and KC Morris[2]

[1] IGI, Clarksburg, USA
{sangsu.choi,gyhun.kang}@igiamerica.com
[2] National Institute of Standards and Technology, Gaithersburg, USA
{kiwook.jung,boonserm.kulvatunyou,kcm}@nist.gov

Abstract. Developed countries and global manufacturing enterprises are leading the way for developing smart manufacturing systems (SMS) to improve competitiveness and possibly make technological breakthroughs. SMS is based upon the integration of information and communication technology with manufacturing technology; and all the heterogeneous technologies must be seamlessly connected. However, there is a lack of guidance in what technologies should be deployed and how they may be used. This paper introduces a reference activity model and describes various ways in which it can be used as guidance for deploying smart manufacturing technology.

Keywords: Smart manufacturing systems design and analysis · Cyberphysical systems · Factory design and improvement · Manufacturing enterprise integration

1 Introduction

The world is now going through another industrial revolution where manufacturing enterprises will reach a new level of interconnectivity both within their production environments and throughout their business value chains. Examples of work towards this vision are seen world-wide including Industry 4.0 in Germany, Industrial Internet Consortium in the United States, Robot Strategy in Japan, and Manufacturing 2025 in China [1]. The core of the current industrial revolution is the development of smart manufacturing systems (SMS). SMS emphasize the integration of core technologies, such as, sensors, cyber-physical systems (CPS) [2], additive manufacturing, sustainable manufacturing, Information and Communication Technologies (ICT), cloud computing, big data, hologram, and cyber security with infrastructure components (such as, standards, regulations, organizations, and trainings) [1]. This paper introduces a Factory Design and Improvement (FDI) model as a reference activity model and describes how it

The rights of this work are transferred to the extent transferable according to title 17 § 105 U.S.C.

I. Nääs et al. (Eds.): APMS 2016, IFIP AICT 488, pp. 697–704, 2016.
DOI: 10.1007/978-3-319-51133-7_82

can be used as a guide to develop a SMS. The activity model provides a high-level view that helps to integrate the core technologies of SMS with components in a manufacturing enterprise.

2   Smart Manufacturing Systems

Figure 1 shows a SMS concept [3] where all manufacturing enterprise functions including materials management, productions, logistics, services, and products are connected on a network as a unified system and the production is controlled through a CPS. A CPS consists of virtual factory models that are connected with the real world and are continually exchanging information with enterprise software through distributed software services (a.k.a. the Internet of Services or IoS) and with distributed devices and equipment (a.k.a. the Internet of Things or IoT or more specifically Industrial Internet of Things - IIoT). Analyses from the CPS can produce dynamic plans for optimally controlling the entire production process.

Standards are important to enable such a CPS-based SMS [4,5] and new standards are needed to connect various IoT and IoS technologies. In the IoT sector, ISO/IEC 30141 [6] was proposed by China to define a reference structure for IoT. IEEE 802.24 [7] is also a representative standard activity. The 'IEC SG8 Industry 4.0 – Smart Manufacturing' [8] strategic group, comprised of members mainly from Europe and United States, is working on IEEE P2413 – Standard for an Architectural Framework for the Internet of Things (IoT). The group is leading the way for the first international standard for an IoT architectural framework. OneM2M [9] was established to improve Machine-to-Machine (M2M) communication standards that are inconsistent globally due to variances in different regions. In the IoS sector, standards are being enhanced based on representative functional systems under use in manufacturing enterprises. The maturity of standards in this sector are relatively high. For product life-cycle management (PLM), STEP 242 [10] is the representative standard, while for supply chain management (SCM) and

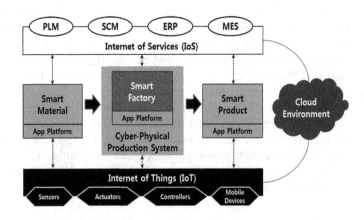

Fig. 1. The concept of SMS (Source: [3])

enterprise resource planning (ERP), OAGIS [11] is used as a standard. For MES, ISA-95 [12] are used. On the other hand, IEC 62264 Enterprise-Control Integration [13] is used for integration across these functional systems.

3 Factory Design and Improvement Model

FDI, developed by the National Institute of Standards and Technology (NIST), formalizes activities, enterprise software functions, and information relevant to operation design and management tasks in a SMS, such as that shown in Fig. 1. FDI is based upon the work processes [14,15] common to global manufacturing enterprises in the areas of factory, manufacturing line, process, and equipment operations. It currently consists of four activities and twenty-eight tasks. The top-level activities are illustrated in Fig. 2. Details of the FDI can be found in [16].

FDI is modelled using IDEF0, where tasks are represented and related via Inputs (data), Outputs (products and performance measures), Controls (organization), and Mechanisms (tools/systems), collectively called ICOMs as is shown in Fig. 2. Information inter-connectivity between tasks is expressed through these ICOMs. FDI tasks encompass both factory design and improvement tasks. Factors related to both cyber and physical systems of a SMS can be reflected in this model. FDI encompasses all control levels as described in the ISA-88 reference control architecture [17] from the equipment level up to the enterprise level. Thus, the FDI model is suitable for identifying information requirements for standard-based integration between software tools across control levels [18].

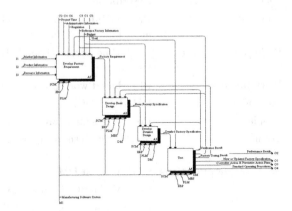

Fig. 2. IDEF0 model of the 'Develop/Update a Factory' activity (Source: [16])

4 Applications of FDI

FDI can be used in different ways to facilitate the deployment of smart manufacturing technologies. This section introduces three uses for the FDI model—as a

- Guideline for planning for new factory designs and improvements to existing factories
- Tool for assessing current capabilities of a manufacturing enterprise in terms of digital information flows for operations planning
- Basis for guiding the development of interoperability and integration technology within the operational environment.

4.1   Work Guideline

As previously mentioned, the FDI model provides an overview of the operational processes in a global manufacturing enterprise involving the factory, manufacturing line, manufacturing processes, and equipment. The model can be used to guide the analysis of performance measures, organizations, tools, systems and related data. As such, the FDI model can be used as a work guideline when designing or operating factories. For example, the FDI model breaks down the design activity into basic and detailed design tasks. A factory development project following this break down resulted in a better delivery time because plant engineering and construction could start earlier without having to wait for all the design details to be completed [14,19]. The FDI model can also be used when adopting systems and tools to a specific workplace. A case of work guideline is described in Table 1.

Table 1. A case: 'verify process throughput'

ICOM	Factors	Description
INPUT	Information	Product Info., production schedule, equipment info., labor info.
OUTPUT	Performance indexes	Lead time, cycle time, WIP, production output
CONTORL	Work process	PLM-based work process
	Methodology	DMAIC, PDCA
	People	Process designer, process manager
	Technology	Stochastic method, discrete event simulation
MECHANISM	Tools/System functions	Simulation in DM
		E-BOM, M-BOM management in PLM
		Production planning in ERP

4.2   SMS Assessment

The ICOMs identified in FDI enable assessment of SMS readiness levels (SMSRL).

SMSRL evaluate a factory in four dimensions: organization, ICT, performance management, and information connectivity as shown in Fig. 3. Consolidating these four dimensions into a single measure creates a maturity index

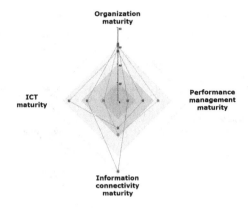

Fig. 3. SMSRL' four categories

Table 2. High-level recommendation

SMSRL range	Performance category	Improvement focus
0–0.33	Financial	IT
	Operational	Information connectivity
0.33–0.78	Financial	Organization
	Operational	Inconclusive
0.78–1	Financial	IT
	Operational	Information connectivity

reflecting a manufacturer's readiness to deploy smart manufacturing solutions or to participate in a network of smart manufacturers.

The output of the SMSRL model can be used in two different ways. The first is to identify and prioritize which smart manufacturing initiatives a manufacturer should undertake to have the greatest impact on operational performance. For example, based on a classification study Table 2 shows the recommendation for the area of improvement focus given the SMSRL value. The second use of the output is to provide criteria for selecting a supplier to be included in a supply chain. When designing and assembling a supply chain, understanding each supplier's smart manufacturing readiness level can better inform sourcing decisions, resulting in overall improved performance.

4.3   Data Interoperability and Integration for SMS

Schemas for enabling information interoperability between the FDI-defined tasks are under development. These schemas take into account not only the FDI tasks and data, but also relevant performance indicators and information connectivity. Based on these schemas, cases have been published where various heterogeneous software were seamlessly integrated in a SMS's cyber system [20].

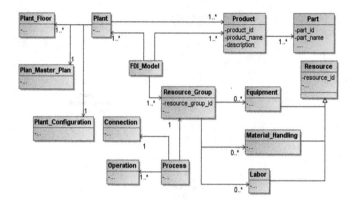

Fig. 4. Conceptual model of the interoperable schema

As shown in Fig. 4, the schemas consist of four major components related to product, process, resource, and plant data. The product data component represents information about the products and components produced by a plant. The resource data component represents information about the manufacturing equipment, manpower, and material handling system(s) (MHS). The process data component represents information on each process and the relationship between processes. The plant data component represents factory operation information and information on the factory's construction, such as the relations among the products, processes, and resources, and the facility configuration and master plan. The schemas are being refined to expand the scope of factory's physical and cyber systems connectivity.

The adoption of the FDI as a work guide line (as described in Sect. 4.1) along with the deployment of the integrated system based on the illustrated schema resulted in significant reductions in times required for a new factory development/improvement projects as well as operational performance improvements. In particular, the deployment in the electromechanical component factory resulted

Table 3. Effectiveness of FDI application to factory performance (Source: [14,20])

	Improvement of factory performance		
	Cost index	Productivity index	Capacity index
New factory development	25%	25%	12%
Existing factory improvement	20%	20%	9.20%
	Reduction in project time		
	Layout design	Material flow analysis	Capacity analysis
New factory development	55%	50%	35%
Existing factory improvement	40%	45%	-

in the reduction in the combined time to complete critical project activities, which included layout design, capacity analysis and material flow analysis, from 6 weeks to 1.5 weeks in the new factory development case and from 4 weeks to 1 week in the factory improvement case [14]. A breakdown of how these improvements affected factory performance is summarized in Table 3.

5 Conclusions

This paper introduced FDI as reference activity model for enabling a SMS. Three applications of the FDI were described including as a work guideline, as a basis for maturity assessment of SMS, and as a specification for information requirements of a CPS-based SMS integration schema. While FDI tasks were designed as an abstract representation of the work involved in factory design and improvement, they may be further decomposed to reflect the more specific tasks within a particular factory. Validation of this approach is ongoing. The model is also being improved based on the development of the SMS maturity assessment by considering other assessment models, such as, MESA Manufacturing Operation Management Maturity Model [21] and the Supply Chain Readiness Level [22]. Currently, a Web system to enable the SMSRL self-assessment is under development. Also, research on artificial intelligence (AI) is being conducted in order to extract the optimized recommendations from the model.

Disclaimer: Any mention of commercial products is for information only; it does not imply recommendation or endorsement by NIST.

References

1. Kang, H.S., Lee, J.Y., Choi, S., Kim, H., Park, J.H., Son, J.Y., Kim, B.H., Do Noh, S.: Smart manufacturing: past research, present findings, and future directions. Int. J. Precis. Eng. Manuf. Green Technol. **3**(1), 111–128 (2016)
2. Lee, J., Bagheri, B., Kao, H.A.: A cyber-physical systems architecture for industry 4.0-based manufacturing systems. Manufact. Lett. **3**, 18–23 (2015)
3. LG CNS. http://www.lgcnsblog.com
4. Kibira, D., Choi, S.-S., Jung, K., Bardhan, T.: Analysis of standards towards simulation-based integrated production planning. In: Umeda, S., Nakano, M., Mizuyama, H., Hibino, H., Kiritsis, D., Cieminski, G. (eds.) APMS 2015. IAICT, vol. 460, pp. 39–48. Springer, Heidelberg (2015). doi:10.1007/978-3-319-22759-7_5
5. Lu, Y., Morris, K., Frechette, S.: Current standards landscape for smart manufacturing systems. Technical report, National Institute of Standards and Technology (2016)
6. ISO/IEC CD 30141. http://www.iso.org/iso/home/store/catalogue_tc/catalogue_detail.htm?csnumber=65695
7. IEEE. http://www.ieee802.org/24/
8. IEC SG8. http://www.iec.ch/dyn/www/
9. Coskun, H., Pfeifer, T., Elmangosh, A., Al-Hezmi, A.: Open M2M data-position paper. In: IEEE 38th Conference on Local Computer Networks Workshops, pp. 904–911. IEEE (2013)

10. Feeney, A.B., Frechette, S.P., Srinivasan, V.: A portrait of an ISO STEP toleranc-
    ing standard as an enabler of smart manufacturing systems. J. Comput. Inf. Sci.
    Eng. 15(2), 021001 (2015)
11. Open Applications Group. http://www.oagi.org/dnn2/
12. International Society of Automation. https://www.isa.org/isa95/
13. ISO/IEC   62264–1:2013.   http://www.iso.org/iso/catalogue_detail.htm?
    csnumber=57308
14. Choi, S., Lee, B., Shin, Y., Park, Y., Kang, H., Jun, C., Jung, J., Noh, S.: The inte-
    grated design and analysis of manufacturing line (I)-digital virtual manufacturing
    based on automated modeling & simulation system. Trans. Soc. CAD/CAM Eng.
    19(2), 138–147 (2014)
15. Choi, S., Sung, N., Shin, Y., Noh, S.: The integrated design and analysis of man-
    ufacturing lines (II)-continuous design, analysis and optimization through digital
    virtual manufacturing. Trans. Soc. CAD/CAM Eng. 19(2), 148–156 (2014)
16. Jung, K., Choi, S., Kulvatunyou, B., Cho, H., Morris, K.C.: A reference activity
    model for smart factory design and improvement. Prod. Plan. Control 28(2), 108–
    122 (2017)
17. Instrument Society of America: Batch control. Part 1, ISA, Research Triangle Park,
    N.C (1995). oCLC: 36500861
18. Choi, S., Jung, K., Kulvatunyou, B., Morris, K.C.: An analysis of technologies and
    standards for designing smart manufacturing systems. J Res Natl Inst Stan 121
    (2016)
19. Choi, S., Kim, B.H., Do Noh, S.: A diagnosis and evaluation method for strate-
    gic planning and systematic design of a virtual factory in smart manufacturing
    systems. Int. J. Precis. Eng. Manuf. 16(6), 1107–1115 (2015)
20. Choi, S.S., Jun, C., Zhao, W.B., Noh, S.: Digital manufacturing in smart man-
    ufacturing systems: contribution, barriers, and future directions. In: Umeda, S.,
    Nakano, M., Mizuyama, H., Hibino, H., Kiritsis, D., Cieminski, G. (eds.) APMS
    2015. IAICT, vol. 460, pp. 21–29. Springer, Heidelberg (2015). doi:10.1007/
    978-3-319-22759-7_3
21. MESA International. https://services.mesa.org/ResourceLibrary/ShowResource/
    a4fcb3cc-bc28-4f87-84cb-3da7432cc3b2
22. Tucker, B., Paxton, J.: SCRL-model for human space flight operations enterprise
    supply chain. In: Aerospace Conference, pp. 1–9. IEEE (2010)

An Overview of a Smart Manufacturing System Readiness Assessment

Kiwook Jung[1], Boonserm Kulvatunyou[1(✉)],
Sangsu Choi[2], and Michael P. Brundage[1]

[1] National Institute of Standards and Technology (NIST),
Gaithersburg, MD, USA
{kiwook.jung, serm, mpbl}@nist.gov
[2] IGI, LLC, Clarksburg, MD, USA

Abstract. Smart manufacturing, today, is the ability to continuously maintain and improve performance, with intensive use of information, in response to the changing environments. Technologies for creating smart manufacturing systems or factories are becoming increasingly abundant. Consequently, manufacturers, large and small, need to correctly select and prioritize these technologies correctly. In addition, other improvements may be necessary to receive the greatest benefit from the selected technology. This paper proposes a method for assessing a factory for its readiness to implement those technologies. The proposed readiness levels provide users with an indication of their current factory state when compared against a reference model. Knowing this state, users can develop a plan to increase their readiness. Through validation analysis, we show that the assessment has a positive correlation with the operational performance.

Keywords: Smart manufacturing readiness · Smart factory · Maturity model

1 Introduction

Manufacturers lack a concrete methodology to choose and prioritize emerging technologies that aid in the creation of smart manufacturing systems and factories. On top of this, manufacturers may need to implement organizational and process improvements to realize the full benefits from these technologies. A survey indicate that most manufacturers have trouble making such improvements [1]. While larger companies can bring in consultants to assist with such issues, small and medium size manufacturers typically do not have the funds to do the same.

Existing methods such as the Supply Chain Readiness Level [2] and MESA Manufacturing Transformation Strategy [3] exist, but they largely ignore the use of information and communication technologies (ICT) as a primary foundation for making those improvements. There are existing works, which study the impact of Information Technology (IT) adoption to businesses (also known as business & IT alignment). However, each study typically focuses on evaluating a single technology

© IFIP International Federation for Information Processing 2016 (outside the US)
Published by Springer International Publishing AG 2016. All Rights Reserved
I. Nääs et al. (Eds.): APMS 2016, IFIP AICT 488, pp. 705–712, 2016.
DOI: 10.1007/978-3-319-51133-7_83

such as the Enterprise Resource Planning (ERP) system or Manufacturing Execution System (MES). These studies have not taken into account other aspects of the organization that can affect the impact of the respective technology adoption.

This paper describes our initial work to develop a method for assessing a factory's readiness for incorporate emerging ICT technologies to become a smart factory. In our view, a smart factory uses ICT to maintain and improve its operational performance in response to its changing environment. Consequently, the method breaks down the assessment into four maturity components including the IT, the information connectivity, organization, performance management program maturities. Our method then combines these assessments into a single Smart Manufacturing System Readiness Level (SMSRL) index, which can be used for benchmarking individual factories or as criteria for selecting a supplier among several factories. In addition to describing our method, we discuss a correlation analysis that we performed. That analysis shows that the SMSRL index has a positive correlation with the operational performance.

Next we discuss related work in more detail before describing the SMSRL assessment method. Then, the result from the validation study is presented and a conclusion and remarks are given.

2   Related Work

Several types of readiness levels are used within the manufacturing sector. **Technology** Readiness Level (TRL) indicates the maturity of a technology for commercial adoption [4]. Similarly, **Manufacturing** Readiness Level (MRL) indicates the maturity of a manufacturing process technology [5]. An organization can use the same scale to indicate the maturity/capability of its respective technology as well. These methods do not evaluate a particular company for its readiness to adopt a particular technology.

Supply Chain Readiness Level (SCRL) [2] provides a method to assess the ability of the supply chain to operate and to achieve specific operational performance targets. The readiness levels are associated with characteristics within fifteen (15) categories that discretely provide an improvement roadmap for a supply chain design and the operation. Similar to the TRL and MRL, SCRL does not provide a methodology for a particular organization to assess its readiness to adopt a particular technology, which may correspond to some categories of the characteristics.

The MESA manufacturing transformation strategy (MTS) provides a framework based on the ISA-95 standard [3] to prepare an organization for Manufacturing-Operation Management (MOM) technologies adoption in four (4) business domains including Business Processes, Organization Structure, Personnel Skill Sets, and Manufacturing System Technology.

The SMSRL assessment objective is similar to that of the MESA-MTS albeit with the scope going beyond MOM technologies. Technically, the SMSRL index provides an indication of the current state with respect to a reference model. Both the SMSRL and the MESA-MTS allow the reference model to evolve as new technologies emerge and become available. Because of this, the assessment piece of the method, by design, is kept independent of the reference model.

3 Method

Figure 1 provides an overall architecture of the readiness level assessment. It summarizes the steps, the inputs, and the outputs involved in the assessment followed by improvement plan development. The process is iterated after the plan has been implemented. The primary purpose of the proposed assessment based on the SMSRL index is to (1) help manufacturers determine their current level and (2) develop a customized improvement plan.

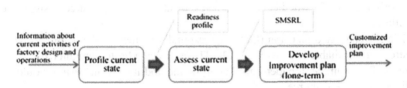

Fig. 1. Overall assessment framework

3.1 Profiling the Current State

The SMSRL proposed in this paper is based on the Factory Design and Improvement (FDI) reference-activity model defined in [6]. That model provides a set of reference activities; information entities for input, output, and constraints on each activity; and relevant software functions using the IDEF0 functional requirement modeling method [7]. On the basis of this model, we developed a questionnaire for profiling [8]. It is to be answered by relevant factory personnel. The questionnaire is organized into four measurement dimensions (C1 to C4) each of which consists of measurement items (process, designated personnel, etc.) as shown in Fig. 2. See the citations in Table 1. for the sources of these dimensions. Next we discuss each dimension in more detail.

The Organizational maturity dimension (C1) is conceptually defined as the comprehensiveness of the activities in the reference activity model performed by the manufacturers. It is measured by (1) whether there is a process that formally manages

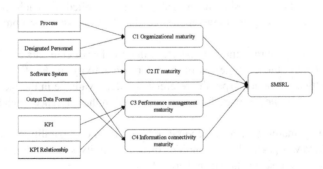

Fig. 2. SMSRL measurements

Table 1. Computation Methods for SMSRL

SMSRL construct	Computation method
C1: Organizational maturity [10]	Counting measure, Activity maturity scoring scheme
C2: IT maturity [11]	Counting measure
C3: Performance management maturity [12]	Counting measure
C4: Information connectivity maturity [13]	Incidence matrix-based similarity measure, Incidence scoring scheme

each activity; and (2) whether there is a responsible human resource assigned to the activities.

The IT maturity dimension (C2) is conceptually defined as the degree to which IT resources are available and working. The IT resources refer to computerized tools and methods. For example, a paper-based analysis method for layout design would not be qualified as an IT resource.

The Performance Management maturity dimension (C3) is conceptually defined as the degree to which the performance measures are used and monitored. This dimension also takes into account the connectivity between different operational performance measures where appropriate.

Lastly, the Information connectivity maturity dimension (C4) is conceptually defined as the maturity of the method to exchange the required information and the degree to which the information is shared/exchanged.

Profiling the current state consists of three operations: scope determination, information collection and consolidation. The scope is represented by relevant activities and stakeholders. The FDI model also indicates stakeholders relevant to each activity based on the ISA-88 manufacturing control architecture [9]. Information collection and consolidation are performed collaboratively among the group of stakeholders that are relevant to the scope.

3.2   Evaluate Current State

The evaluation of the current state compares the profile to the reference activity model. Computation methods, as shown in Table 1, are applied to each measurement dimension resulting in quantitative measures that can be used for comparison and benchmark.

The counting measure is the ratio between the number of elements employed in the current practice and those suggested in the reference activity model. For example, the number of software functions (per the reference model) available in the factory divided by the number of all the software functions identified in the reference model gives a C2 measure.

The Activity maturity scoring scheme is based on the Capability Maturity Model Integration (CMMI) [14]. The stakeholder of each activity scores the maturity of the activity based on the scale shown in Table 2.

Table 2. Activity maturing scoring scale

Linguistic scale	Task score	Characteristics
Not performed	0	–
Initial	1	Processes established, but unpredictable
Managed	3	Processes characterized for projects
Defined	5	Process characterized for the organization
Qualitative	7	Processes measured and controlled
Optimizing	9	Focus process improvement

The incidence matrix is commonly used to represent and analyze interactions between entities in a complex system. Here, an incidence matrix is used to represent the information entities connected between activities; and as such can be used to quantify the information connectivity maturity (C4). It is an n x n matrix where n is the number of activities under evaluation, the row is the activity that provides the information entity (from-activity or sender activity), and the column is the activity taking the information entity as an input (to-activity or receiver activity). The cell, the incidence, indicates the maturity of the information flow from the row to the column. Table 3 shows a schematic view of an incidence matrix. The maturity of the information flow is marked by the scoring scheme shown in Table 4 with the highest score (1) being connected by a

Table 3. Activity incidence matrix

From/To	To Act_1	...	To Act_j
From Act_1	inc_{11}	...	inc_{1j}
...	...	...	...
From Act_i	inc_{i1}	...	inc_{ij}

Table 4. Incidence scoring scheme

Score	Scoring rule	Definition
1	if $a \in (S_j \cap B_m)$ then, $c = 1xRef$	Standard data formats for activity j (and) compatible data formats for software system m
0.7	if $a \in B_m$ then, $c = 0.7xRef$	Compatible data formats for software system m
0.3	if $a \notin B_m$ then, $c = 0.3xRef$	Manual transformation required from output data a to compatible data formats for software system m
0	if $Ref = 0$ then, $c = 0xRef$	No exchange required
0	If i or $j = \emptyset$ then, $c = 0xRef$	The current state does not perform the activity i or j. to be performed
0	If $i = j$ then, $c = 0xRef$	Recursive

Where i is the sender activity; a is the output data format of the activity i; S_j is a set of standard data formats associated with the receiver activity j; B_m is a set of compatible data formats for the receiver software system m; and c is the incidence score.

standard data exchange. All reference incidence matrices assume the highest score where there is the information connectivity between the from- and to-activity. A score of 0.7 represents that software capability for data exchange among activities exists, but information is not currently exchanged. When the data is exchanged manually between activities, the score is 0.3. A score of zero indicates that there is no data exchange between the activities.

The evaluation result can be visualized as shown in Fig. 3. Each indicator can be used individually or combined into a single SMSRL index. For simplicity, a single SMSRL index was computed using an average of C1, C2, C3 and C4. The overall index and/or individual construct can be used to prioritize the factory improvements or to evaluate potential suppliers.

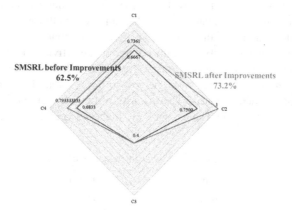

Fig. 3. An exemplary assessment result

3.3   Develop Improvement Plan

In the last step, the evaluation result is used to develop and prioritize an improvement plan. A classification analysis shown in the next section provides a high-level improvement recommendation. Our future work lies in developing a method to provide a more detailed recommendation.

4   Validation Study

This section investigates the validity of the proposed assessment using a similar approach to [13]. First, data about the relationships between the SMSRL and operational performance was collected. Then, hypothesis tests for the statistical significance of the relationships were performed. Lastly, we analyzed patterns of the SMSRL that can guide an improvement plan development. These activities are explained below.

Data Used for the Validation. Existing studies in the domain of business and IT alignment were used for the validation. A detailed analysis on the existing studies can be found in [8]. Different alignment constructs (i.e., measurement items) from these studies were mapped to performance categories (e.g., operational, financial) and were statistically correlated using empirical data.

Validation Method. To establish the relationship between the SMSRL assessment and the performance categories, the measurement items of the SMSRL assessment are mapped to those considered in the studies (operational, financial, value-based, and overall). A similarity value between the SMSRL assessment and the target study is then calculated using the n-gram measure (intersection divided by union). This gives the basis for the correlation analysis shown in the next subsection.

Hypothesis Test. Four hypothesis tests were performed. Statistically significant, positive-correlations with the SMSRL index were found on the operational performance, overall performance, and value-based performance as shown in Table 5. The financial performance was not found (hence not shown) to have a statistically significant positive-correlation.

High-level Recommendation. A k-means-clustering analysis on the simulated

Table 5. Hypothesis test results

Hypothesis	p-value	Sig
H1: the higher the similarity value, the higher the operational performance attributable to alignment	0.713	Yes ($p < 0.05$)
H2: the higher the similarity value, the higher the overall performance attributable to alignment	0.404	Yes ($p < 0.05$)
H3: the higher the similarity value, the higher the value-based performance attributable to alignment	0.529	Yes ($p < 0.05$)

SMSRL results has been performed ($k = 3$). Based on its result shown in Table 5, a high-level recommendation can be made for each SMSRL cluster. The cells with bold-font values show the category of improvement a factory should focus on to have the largest impact on a respective performance category. For example, the first row indicates that improvements in the information connectivity (C4) is likely to have the best impact on the operational performance (Table 6).

Table 6. High-level recommendation

SMSRL centroid (mean score)	Performance category	Standardized coefficient of independent variables			
		C1	C2	C3	C4
Low (0.1957)	Financial	−0.0276	**0.1169**	−0.0035	−0.0048
	Operational	−0.0996	0.0511	−0.0471	**0.0753**
Med (0.4608)	Financial	**0.0179**	0.004	−0.0021	−0.0278
	Operational	−0.065	−0.0013	−0.1052	−0.0139
High (0.6453)	Financial	−0.0250	**0.0439**	−0.0074	−0.1083
	Operational	−0.0270	0.0327	−0.0109	**0.0672**

5   Conclusion and Remark

We introduced a new, smart manufacturing system readiness assessment (SMSRL). SMSRL measures the readiness using maturity scoring of four dimensions: Organizational, IT, Performance management, and Information connectivity maturities. The core of the smart manufacturing concept is the ability to use information effectively. The SMSRL assessment provides a quantitative measure of this ability. Such measure, which is in the form of an index, can be used for benchmarking. The statistical analysis shows that the index has a positive correlation with three types of performance: operational, overall, and value-based.

The SMSRL index provides a real number as its readiness measure. The SCRL, on the other hand, provides discrete readiness levels. Each type of measure has its advantages. Discrete measures lend themselves readily to definitional levels. Real-numbered levels do not; however, they can be used in other quantitative analysis – such as the ones shown in Sect. 4. Discrete measures cannot

In our future work, we will (1) develop a method to provide more detailed improvement recommendations (2) extending and/or experimenting with other models used as a reference for the assessment.

References

1. Manufacture Innovation. http://nistmep.blogs.govdelivery.com
2. Tucker, B.: SCRL-model for Human Space Flight Operations enterprise supply chain (2010)
3. MESA: Transforming Manufacturing Maturity with ISA-95 Methods (2011)
4. Mankins, J.C.: Technology readiness levels. White Paper, 6 April 1995
5. Wheeler, D.J., Ulsh, M.: Manufacturing Readiness Assessment for Fuel Cell Stacks and Systems for the Back-Up Power and Material Handling Equipment Emerging Markets. National Renewable Energy Laboratory (2009)
6. Jung, K., et al.: An Activity Model for Smart Factory Design and Improvement. Production Planning and Control
7. IEEE 1320.1 IEEE Functional Modeling Language – Syntax and Semantics for IDEF0. International Society of Electrical and Electronics Engineers, New York (1998)
8. Jung, K.: Reference Activity Model-based Factory Design and Operations Evaluation Framework. Pohang University of Science and Technology
9. ANSI/ISA-88.00.01-2010 Batch Control Part 1: Models and Terminology
10. Raymond, L., Paré, G.: Measurement of information technology sophistication in small manufacturing businesses. Inf. Resour. Manage. J. 5(2), 4–16 (1992)
11. Powell, D., et al.: Lean production and ERP systems in small- and medium-sized enterprises: ERP support for pull production. Intl. J. Prod. Res. 51(2), 395–409 (2013)
12. Maasouman, M. A., Demirli, K.: Development of a lean maturity model for operational level planning. Intl. J. Adv. Manuf. Technol., 1–18 (2016)
13. Chung, S.H., et al.: The impact of information technology infrastructure flexibility on strategic alignment and application implementations. Commun. Assoc. Inf. Syst. 11(1), 44 (2003)
14. CMMI Product Team. CMMI for Development, Version 1.3 (2010)

Applying Gamification for Developing Formal Knowledge Models: Challenges and Requirements

Jannicke Baalsrud Hauge[1,2(✉)], Stefan Wiesner[1], Ioana A. Stefan[3],
Antoniu Stefan[3], and Klaus-Dieter Thoben[1,4]

[1] BIBA – Bremer Institut für Produktion und Logistik GmbH at the University
of Bremen, Hochschulring 20, 28359 Bremen, Germany
{baa,wie,tho}@biba.uni-bremen.de
[2] KTH Royal Insitute of Technology, Mariekällgatan 3,
15181 Södertälje, Sweden
[3] Advanced Technology Systems, Tineretului 1, 130029 Targoviste, Romania
{ioana.stanescu,antoniu.stefan}@ats.com.ro
[4] Faculty of Production Engineering, University of Bremen,
Badgasteiner Straße 1, 28359 Bremen, Germany

Abstract. A main challenge in developing formal knowledge models is to efficiently elicit knowledge from various resources and form a coherent body of knowledge that can be validated and extended by user communities. The higher the complexity of a system, the more challenging it is to establish these models, specifically if there are several stakeholders involved, with various level of knowledge and needs. The usage of participatory design approaches in combination with Serious Games (SG) could ensure that all stakeholders are active, as well as that each perspective can be considered. So far manufacturing concepts have not reached their full potential due to the fact that gamification efforts are costly, time consuming to develop, and require the constant involvement of developers even for small changes. The authors discuss the use of a gamification tool to support knowledge processes, respectively knowledge experiencing, conceptualizing, analyzing and applying in engineering environments. To support this approach, especially in terms of costs, the paper presents an approach that makes customization accessible for non-SG professionals.

Keywords: Gamification · Knowledge capturing · Product service system

1 Introduction

Nowadays, the field of systems engineering is influenced by rapid technological change and ever growing competition. In order to be the first to react on market trends, methodologies like concurrent engineering (CE) are introduced to shorten development cycles and reduce "time to market" [1, 2]. However, just being fast is not sufficient; additionally, the system has to be both appropriate and cost effective [3]. Customers

© IFIP International Federation for Information Processing 2016
Published by Springer International Publishing AG 2016. All Rights Reserved
I. Nääs et al. (Eds.): APMS 2016, IFIP AICT 488, pp. 713–720, 2016.
DOI: 10.1007/978-3-319-51133-7_84

demand integrated solutions and services, covering the whole system life cycle, from ideation to decommission, thus more and more companies are evolving their business activities to form product-service-systems. These systems are complex and dynamic and their requirements evolve in time. The already existing knowledge (either on existing products, and services or just related to the ideas never brought to the market) is often distributed among employees, and different departments in an organization do often have different requirements.

Requirements define the needs of organizations, groups, or people along with their surroundings, and describe what a solution must offer in order to satisfy those needs. Their formulation, documentation and maintenance are the main objectives of requirements engineering (RE). It describes "a process, in which the needs of one or many stakeholders and their environment are determined to find the solution for a specific problem" [8]. Inadequate RE is one of the main sources for the failure of development projects and culminates in exceeding budgets, missing functionalities or even the abortion of the project [9, 10]. For complex systems this requires that the knowledge within the organisation can be captured and transferred. Within complex systems, as well as for product development, participatory or co-creative design approaches are often used in order to involve stakeholders in the decision-making process at early stage in order to ensure that the developed system is in line with their needs. The same approaches can also be used in order to capture the knowledge existing in the organisation, but it requires that there is a tool that is able to capture the knowledge, as well as involving the right people. This might also lead to a better usage of resources. From a technical point of view this integration can be realized today focusing on reusability of components [9] as well as through better collaboration across different process steps [10].

The required competencies for system development and support in other life cycle phases are included through collaboration with partners from different domains [4]. This increases both the number of stakeholders involved in systems engineering and the complexity of the system itself. Consequently, understanding what the customer and the other affected stakeholders expect from the system, i.e. their underlying needs, and linking information from all phases of the life cycle to the development process is a prerequisite for successful systems engineering [5–7]. This represents however a challenge, since much of the knowledge is not formalized and unstructured, thus difficult to retrieve and process.

Previous work [11, 12] has highlighted that sustainable adaptation and integration of game design elements into engineering systems can be a good approach for both increasing the process innovation as well as to help collecting information from complex processes [13]. However, [11] also show that further analysis of the enabling mechanisms as well as on how to capture the knowledge are needed [13]. A more detailed analysis of the challenges shows that accommodation of gamification concepts, mechanics and components into engineering systems implies substantial modifications of these systems. A key is here the development of the knowledge models. One of the main challenges in developing formal knowledge models is to efficiently elicit knowledge from distributed resources and form a coherent body of knowledge that can be validated and extended by user communities.

This paper builds upon the perspective where gamification supports knowledge processes using a participatory and gamified approach for complex engineering processes like the requirement engineering of PSS.

2 Methodology

The methodological approach is based on combination of research methods. A literature review was carried out targeting gamification, knowledge processes, and information on engineering applications like PSS and supporting technologies. Scientific papers were accessed through Scopus searching for associated key words [13, 14]. The relevance of the downloaded papers for this article was based on assessing the abstract, as well as by searching for the combination of gamification and mechanisms in the full papers [13]. The first search based on abstracts followed by a refined search. As several expressions are used in literature to describe the PSS concept, we applied TITLE-ABS-KEY ("product-service" OR PSS OR IPS OR "Extended Product") as the first search term, combined with AND TITLE-ABS-KEY ("knowledge management" OR "knowledge sharing") as the second term. This resulted in 214 identified abstract and the refine search identified 40 articles. The search related to gamification of engineering applications was carried out using the ("ENGINEERING APPLICATION" AND ("GAMIFICATION" OR "SERIOUS GAMES" OR "SIMULATION".)). This resulted in 369 abstracts. Adding the same key words as in the definition search resulted in only identifying 15 articles that could be considered of being relevant.

The work with the specific engineering applications and the gamification had a different methodical approach. The researchers have been involved in the specifications and development of the scenarios. Design Science was the overall scientific approach in this work [13, 15, 16], so action research was applied [17].

3 Characteristics of a PSS

In order to capture the knowledge needed for a RE approach for PSS, it is necessary to identify the specific characteristics of such systems. In the following, some widely used definitions of PSS found in the literature are analyzed for these characteristics.

*"A Product Service system (PS system) is a **marketable set of products and services** capable of jointly fulfilling a user's need. The PS system is **provided by either a single company or by an alliance of companies**. It can enclose products (or just one) plus additional services. It can enclose a service plus an additional product. And **product and service can be equally important for the function fulfilment**. The researcher's need and aim determine the level of hierarchy, system boundaries and the system element's relations."* [18]

*"A PSS is an **integrated product and service offering** that delivers **value in use**. A PSS offers the opportunity to **decouple economic success from material consumption** and hence reduce the environmental impact of economic activity. The PSS logic is premised on utilizing the knowledge of the designer-manufacturer to both increase value as an output and decrease material and other costs as an input to a system."* [19]

*"'An Industrial Product-Service System is characterized by the **integrated and mutually determined planning, development, provision and use of product and service shares** including its immanent **software components** in Business-to-Business applications and represents a **knowledge-intensive socio-technical system'**....*

*IPS^2 enable **innovative function-, availability- or result-oriented business models**."* [20]

The analysis of the above definitions reveals some characteristics that seem to be specific for PSS in general. These characteristics are listed below:

- Integration of product and service shares, including software components;
- Mutual planning, development, provision and use of product and service shares;
- Fulfilling an end user need by delivering value in use;
- Provided by either a single company or by an alliance of companies;
- Dynamic adoption of changing customer demands and provider abilities;
- Enabling innovative function-, availability- or result-oriented business models.

The characteristics shows the complexity of PSS, thus defining the requirements and the system specification are challenging. The next section therefore looks at how a participatory design approach can be used for supporting the challenging task.

4   Participatory Design Approach

Knowledge capturing remains a compelling case for organizations, especially because knowledge is a dynamic asset that continually must be updated, revised, and built on to maintain a valid base [21] and value [13]. Furthermore, it is a challenge that a lot of the information is not formalized, and thus it is difficult to capture with current tools. To address this challenge, the authors have considered key knowledge-centric drivers that apply to organizations, regardless of their industry [13, 22–24].

- The failure of organizations to know what they already know;
- The emergent need for smart knowledge distribution;
- Knowledge velocity.
- The issue of knowledge walkouts and high dependence on tacit knowledge.
- The need to deal with knowledge-hoarding propensity among employees.
- A need for systemic unlearning.

Highly interconnected systems like smart manufacturing systems need to be explained and managed across many layers - technological, social, data, human and institutional [25]. Further, in the absence of suitable analytical and formal tools, institutions within complex systems take decision based on heuristics. Such heuristics contain significant knowledge both about the stakeholders' perspectives on the systems and on their management strategies. These heuristics needs to be collected in some form to overcome limitations and embed local institutional knowledge in formal tools. This implies that the development of these models and tools should be done in a participatory manner, to ensure all stakeholders collectively develop and reach an understanding of the model. Such participatory methods, in conjunction with these complex models and tools also support model validation. Simulation Gaming provides ways to collectively decide on the problem formulation, system boundaries and on the dynamics of the system that will be addressed.

By implementing adaptable and customizable gamified SMEs that support knowledge management, the organization will be able to plan and implement activities that stimulate employee interest and participation [21, 25], and that enables them to benefit of a wide range of opportunities. The challenge in the knowledge capturing part of PSS and manufacturing application is that much of the information is not formalized and not structured. The next section discusses under which circumstances gamification of an application can support the knowledge gathering and improve the knowledge model.

5   Gamification of Manufacturing Environments: Requirements on Concept and Challenges

Gamification consists of using game-based elements and mechanisms in non-game environments with the purpose of employing the motivational properties of games [13, 27]. Gamification as a method has be criticized, and there are some drawbacks like the manipulation aspect [13, 28]. A simple addition of gamifying elements does not automatically translate into the desired outcomes, so gamification components and elements need to be designed and adapted to the context they are applied to. To do so, it is necessary to establish clear goals, incremental goals and rewards, mechanisms of progression, intermediary and final statuses, etc. [13].

Another key challenge concerns the actual incorporation of gamification processes into existing application, which is a complex task even for experienced developers. Integration of gamification mechanisms carried out by manufacturing environments' developers can answer to some of the above-mentioned issues [13]. However, these environments do not fully benefit of the potential of gamification mechanisms, as identified by Wood and Reiners [27], if such systems do not allow tutors/users customize their working environments. Users are not actively involved in the SMEs architecture and this limits their capabilities and abilities to perform better. Moreover, the emergence of new technologies requires new approaches and more flexible solutions for integration, empowering users to customize [13].

Based on the consideration above, a gamified manufacturing environment that aims at capturing, process and feed a formal model need to have the following characteristics [13]:

- Recognition and reward systems for outstanding individual contributions at a project or the organization level.
- Examples and best practices can be extracted from tracked gameplay.
- Recurring challenges that employees are experiencing can be identified and addressed.
- Contextual knowledge reuse is automatically supported, and knowledge transfer can potentially impact all PSS users.
- Exploit the added value of social knowledge through a gamified approach that enables people to discover and share knowledge.
- Access to personalized working environments is enabled.

We are currently working on the gamification of engineering process for knowledge capturing. The gamification is realized in Unity. It mirrors the main processes for future PSS system. It is designed as a gamification of the requirements elicitation process. Even though it uses role playing mechanisms, each player plays they normal position in the company. The example below explains one of three case studies where we have carried out the beta testing, so still in progress.

In the given example, the task is to decide which requirements future PSS need to fulfil within the manufacturing of office furniture. In this example the 3D model of the office of the service providers was important into the Unity engine directly. In a second step a narrative story line, describing the main steps of the requirements elicitation process was added and game elements like time restriction and rewards were applied. The gamification is facilitated and uses creativity methods like adapted versions of six thinking hats etc.

The beta test was carried out Mid-June 2016 with 6 different participants covering all the involved stakeholders' groups. It was set up as a workshop of 2 × 2 h. The first initial results showed that the gamification of the environment helped in analyzing the existing requirements (collected using a traditional method) from different perspectives and to refine these. These first set of stakeholder requirements were related to

- Support for collaboration between the stakeholder
- Business models for servitisation
- Measurement and assessment of brand value and sales bids
- Integration of technologies like sensor and
- Feedback integration either via data analytics or customer/employee
- Interface design

For the more concrete applications (i.e. how to integrate sensors and how to use data for a new service), the gamification supported the process sufficiently according to the participants, and the collected outcome regarding capturing more details of the system was achieved. However, the current gamification showed some weaknesses related to the support on more abstract requirements like future business models. The gamification clearly showed some limitations here, so that it we did not capture much of the participants' knowledge here in one of the group. In the second group, this worked better. Why this problem occurred needs further investigation.

6   Conclusion

The paper describes the challenges of generating a formal modal and capture knowledge in a simulation game built using previously developed tools. The authors discuss the characteristics of PSSs and the participatory design approach, with the purpose of supporting the implementation of gamification mechanisms in manufacturing environments.

Technology reshapes the world we learn, work, and live in. New levels of interaction between men and machine have become possible and more widespread, opening the way towards reliable, sustainable, technology-driven ecosystems.

The growth, maturation, and widespread adoption of technologies have the potential to disrupt and innovate, and offers new opportunities for data collection and retrieval. This paper discusses the current challenges of PSS and the potential of gamification to enhance knowledge processes and user interface in PSS. Present and future scenarios are presented to reflect how gamification can impact current and future systems of systems. The concept of a gamification tool is introduced as a mean to streamline knowledge processes and enable PSS tutors/users to directly adapt and personalize PSS to better answer their needs [13].

Future work will explore the integration of digital gams into PSS, exploring key challenges in terms of standardization and interoperability, as well as advances in hardware and software to discover new opportunities for enhancing user experiences and outcomes [13].

Acknowledgements. This work has been funded by the European Commission through the Projects PSYMBIOSYS: Product-Service sYMBIOtic SYStems (No. 636804) and BEACONING (No. 687676). The authors wish to acknowledge the Commission and all the project partners for their contribution.

References

1. Corsetti, A., Ribeiro, E.A., Garbi, G.P., Zanta, K., Medeiros, M., Loureiro, G.: Complex systems developed with system concurrent engineering. In: Stjepandić, J., Rock, G., Bil, C. (eds.) Concurrent Engineering Approaches for Sustainable Product Development in a Multi-disciplinary Environment, pp. 1057–1068. Springer, London (2013)
2. Chang, W., Yan, W., Chen, C.H.: Customer requirements elicitation and management for product conceptualization. In: Stjepandić, J., Rock, G., Bil, C. (eds.) Concurrent Engineering Approaches for Sustainable Product Development in a Multi-disciplinary Environment, pp. 957–968. Springer, London (2013)
3. Kossiakoff, A., Sweet, W.N., Seymour, S., Biemer, S.M.: Systems Engineering Principles and Practice, vol. 83. Wiley, Hoboken (2011)
4. Blanchard, B.S.: System Engineering Management, vol. 64. Wiley, Hoboken (2012)
5. Sage, A.P., Rouse, W.B.: Handbook of Systems Engineering and Management. Wiley, Hoboken (2011)
6. Elgh, F.: Modelling and management of manufacturing requirements in design automation systems. In: Loureiro, G., Curran, R. (eds.) Complex Systems Concurrent Engineering, pp. 321–328. Springer, London (2007)
7. Nilsson, P., Fagerström, B.: Managing stakeholder requirements in a product modelling system. Comput. Ind. **57**(2), 167–177 (2006)
8. Nuseibeh, B., Easterbrook, S.: Requirements engineering: a roadmap. In: Proceedings of the Conference on the Future of Software Engineering, Limerick (2000)
9. Hauksdóttir, D., Mortensen, N.H., Nielsen, P.E.: Identification of a reusable requirements structure for embedded products in a dynamic market environment. Comput. Ind. **64**(4), 351–362 (2013)
10. Boehm, B., Basili, B.: Software defect reduction top 10 list. In: IEEE Computer, vol. 34, no. 1, pp. 135–137. IEEE Computer Society, Los Alamitos (2001)
11. Kosmadoudi, Z., et al.: Harmonizing interoperability – emergent serious gaming in playful stochastic CAD environments. In: Gloria, A. (ed.) GALA 2013. LNCS, vol. 8605, pp. 390–399. Springer, Heidelberg (2014). doi:10.1007/978-3-319-12157-4_34
12. Hesmer, A., Hribernik, K., Baalsrud Hauge, J., Thoben, K.-D.: Supporting the ideation processes by a collaborative online based toolset. Int. J. Technol. Manage. **55**(3/4), 218–225 (2011)

13. Baalsrud Hauge, J., et al.: Integrating gamification in mechanical engineering systems to support knowledge processes. In: 35th Computers and Information in Engineering Conference, Boston, MA USA, August 2015 (2016). doi:10.1115/DETC2015-47695
14. Kitchenham, B., et al.: Systematic literature reviews in software engineering, a systematic literature review. Inf. Softw. Technol. **51**(1), 7–15 (2009)
15. Kuechler, B., Vaishnavi, V.: Promoting relevance in IS research an informing system for design science research. Inf. Sci. Int. J. Emerg. Transdiscipline **14**(1), 125–138 (2011)
16. Pries-Heje, J., Baskerville, R., Venable, J.R.: Strategies for design science research evaluation. In: ECIS 2008 Proceedings, vol. 87 (2008). http://aisel.aisnet.org/ecis2008/87
17. Sein, M.K., et al.: Action design research. MIS Q. **35**(1), 37–56 (2011)
18. Goedkoop, M.J.: Product service systems, ecological and economic basics. [The Hague], Zoetermeer: [Ministry of Housing, Spatial Planning and the Environment, Communications Directorate]; Distributiecentrum VROM [distr.] (1999)
19. Baines, T.S., Lightfoot, H.W., Evans, S., Neely, A., Greenough, R., Peppard, J., et al.: State-of-the-art in product-service systems. Proc. Inst. Mech. Eng. Part B: J. Eng. Manuf. **221**(10), 1543–1552 (2007). doi:10.1243/09544054JEM858
20. Meier, H., Roy, R., Seliger, G.: Industrial product-service systems—IPS2. CIRP Ann. Manuf. Technol. **59**(2), 607–627 (2010). doi:10.1016/j.cirp.2010.05.004
21. Atwood, C.G.: Knowledge Management Basics. American Society for Training & Development, Danvers (2009)
22. Tiwana, A.: Knowledge Management Toolkit. Pretince Hall, Upper Saddle River (2000)
23. Uden, L., Eardley, A.: Innovative Knowledge Management. IGI Global, Hershey (2010)
24. Loh, A.E., Lim, L.K., Ahmed, P.K.: Learning Through Knowledge Management. Routledge, Abingdon (2013)
25. Palfrey, J.G., Gasser, U.: Interop: The Promise and Perils of Highly Interconnected Systems. Basic Books, New York (2012)
26. Girard, J., Girard, J.P.: Social Knowledge. IGI Global, Hershey (2010)
27. Wood, L.C., Reiners, T.: Gamification. In: Khosrow-Pour, M. (ed.) Encyclopedia of Information Science and Technology, 3rd edn. IGI Global, Hershey (2014)
28. Kapp, K.M.: The Gamification of Learning and Instruction Fieldbook: Ideas into Practice. Pfeiffer, San Francisco (2013)

Knowledge Management in Production Systems

Workers' Perspective About Organizational Climate in Knowledge Management: Automotive Assembly-Line Case

Indira A. Rodriguez[1(✉)], Aline Garcia[1], Suelen C.F. Morais[1],
Jorge Muniz Jr.[1], and Timothy P. Munyon[2]

[1] Universidade Estadual Paulista, São Paulo, Brazil
indiraarias1986@gmail.com
[2] University of Tennessee, Knoxville, USA
tmunyon@utk.edu

Abstract. The purpose of this paper is to analyze the relation between Organizational Climate and Knowledge Management in the shop floor. The study is conducted in an auto part plant inserted in a Truck Factory with 7 partners. 44 blue collar workers were interviewed. The results show a relationship between Organizational Climate and Knowledge Management in the automotive sector, evidenced by the significant correlations between the variables analyzed. The unemployment situation can negatively influence the climate of organizations. The positive social interaction can preserve knowledge sharing even when there are weaknesses in the organizational climate. Future research can compare the results of this study with another sample in the same environment in stable employment situation. Other research may replicate this study with a larger number of participants.

Keywords: Organization climate · Knowledge management · Shop floor workers

1   Introduction

This paper, analyses the relation between Organizational Climate and Knowledge Management in the industry shop floor. The Organizational Climate (OC) is the way in which members of the organization perceive or characterize their working environment [1]. OC encompasses the organizational structure and processes, interpersonal relationship, management compensation, employee behavior, performance expectations and growth opportunities. It is the result of interaction among the organizational components: structure, systems, culture, leader behavior, and the psychological needs of workers.

Organizational Climate refers to common practices, shared ideas and value systems that an organization follows [2]. For members of the organization, climate takes the form of a set of attributes and expectations that describe the general

© IFIP International Federation for Information Processing 2016
Published by Springer International Publishing AG 2016. All Rights Reserved
I. Nääs et al. (Eds.): APMS 2016, IFIP AICT 488, pp. 723–730, 2016.
DOI: 10.1007/978-3-319-51133-7_85

pattern of organizational activities [3] playing a key role in shaping employees, behaviors and influences their perception of Knowledge Management - KM [4].

The study of OC is multidisciplinary and encompasses criteria that are related to the KM, but studies indicate lack of consensus on evaluating this influence [5–11]. Highlighted the importance of provoking beliefs, commitments, situations and appropriate interactions in organizations, elements connected with the OC, and to provide the information that is converted into knowledge and can move by organizations, positively influencing judgments, behaviors and attitudes [12].

The KM is the systematic, formal and deliberate acting in order to capture, preserve, share, and (re) use the tacit and explicit knowledge, created and used by persons during routine tasks and improvement of production processes in order to generate results measurable for the organization and for the people [13]. The theme relevance is related to its impact on the organization's performance improvements. KM benefits focusing on organizational problems solving, which will connect KM with the company's performance and demonstrate financial impacts and non-financial [14, 15].

Competitive advantage for organizations is relating the continuously innovative environment in its internal processes, procedures and resources [16]. Enterprises can encourage employees to collaboration, information exchange, open communication, and to explore non-routine alternatives through formulation of innovative climate [17]. Cooperation among individuals plays a critical role on development interesting and innovative ideas occur [3].

Research indicates the importance of creating a favorable psychological environment within the company as the facilitator of knowledge sharing in sectors as banking [9], educational, hospital [17], steel making, computer and telecommunications. The research results discussion are grouped in (a) positive impact raised by the OC in KM, (b) negative impact of unfavorable OC in KM and (c) best practices of Organizational Climate to favor the Knowledge Management.

Moreover, literature analyzed shows a consensus to point out that the favorable OC can promote benefits of the KM as higher degree of sharing and application of knowledge through social interaction and favorable cooperation, open communication, socialization among employees, coordination behavior, increased confidence and integration with work [6–9].

There is a necessity to create a OC to support organization members to develop a positive attitude towards the work, followed by subjective norms, extrinsic motivation [9, 10], promoting an open climate that encourages risk-taking, trust and open interaction, collecting and describing individual knowledge, intellectual capital and organizing your organization's information [11]. Innovative organizations need a OC that stimulates an open mind, committed and involved relationships of trust and mutual support [6], to develop new ideas and respond to new opportunities, must involve a cultural change, by dedicating time of transformation of knowledge into innovation activities, providing reinforced KM levels [8].

Examples are the positive impact and in turn best practices of organizational climate to favor the knowledge management, but Organizations with a lot of formalization and centralization hinder integration among members of the organization and social interaction which ends up promoting the organizational climate barriers that compromise the good performance of knowledge management levels [5].

New information technologies and innovation also have a cause-effect relationship between organizational climate and knowledge management. The use of information can help the application of knowledge management technology, so it should prevail a grip of climate to the system, which must be practical and dynamic, otherwise the positive impact can be reversed and seen as an obstacle in organizations [5].

2 Method

The research is a quali-quanti study conducted in one assembly line working in Modular Consortium [18]. The Modular Consortium is designed as a radical case of outsourcing among an automaker and the small number of direct suppliers, in which: suppliers assume that the pre-assembly of the module is under its responsibility and its subsequent mounting is directly on the production line for the assembly plant, investments in equipments and tools and supply chain the management module; the assembler provides the plant and the final assembly line to execute the coordination of the same and the final test of vehicles [18].

Literature Review is based on Web of Science and Scopus, using descriptors "organizational climate" and "Knowledge Management".

The research instrument use Likert scale (5 points). The analysis of results were performed using SPSS version 21.0. 44 blue collar workers were interviewed. The participants were of the male sex with average experience time in 9 years industry with standard deviation 4.49 and the average time in the company of 7.64, standard deviation of 4.19. All participants were immersed in the production process and distributed as follows: assembly (n = 20), brake systems (pipe) (n = 7), manufacturing (n = 7), quality inspectors (n = 2), others (n = 8).

3 Results and Discussion

The descriptive analysis of the variables (Table 1) showed that the organization are conspicuous personal interests above the collective and organizational interests (OC1, OC2, OC4), there is a widespread perception in the sample of the company's workers that spent time cajoling theirs superiors (OC3). The majority of the sample preferred not to comment about the OC5 item concerns -Some co-workers try to manipulate the groups which they belong, the most frequent response of the participants was: neutral. Participants agree to point out that within the organization people speak ill of the other to be well valued (OC6).

Respect to Knowledge Management, participants indicated that seek talking to people who help them with their work problems (KM1), or to keep them updated with important information about the organization (KM2). The use of e-mail in this sample is not a tool for the sharing of knowledge, 43.2% declined to comment on this item (KM3), expressing neutrality and 21.5% fully disagreed. Most also expressed agreement to point out that there is sharing environmental knowledge within the organization (KM4; KM5; KM6; KM7).

The correlation analysis (Table 2) assesses the relationship among the variables related to Organizational Climate and Knowledge Management in the working environment of the organization and relevant results were found and are set out in the Table 2. Significant correlations were shown between the questions studying the Organizational Climate ($p < 0.001$) and it was similarly as looking to the interior of the questions concerning the Knowledge Management ($0.01 < p < 0.05$), but the level of significance was less strong when compared with the organizational climate.

The KM2 item relating to the use of personal conversation to keep others updated with important information about the organization, showed significant correlation with all the Organizational Climate questions. KM3 and KM7 items of Knowledge Management have not shown correlations with any item on the organizational climate.

The participants have the general view of the existence of an unfavorable organizational climate, OC seen as the way in which members of the organization perceive or characterize their working environment [1]. This can be explained by the availability situation experienced in the organization prior to the questionnaire, in which were sent away a group of workers, according [19], the unemployment situation ends up influencing the climate of organizations because of the constant need to meet targets, to be updated, be versatile, teamwork, form great pressure on employees who feel powerless against this context.

Knowledge Management showed a significant relationship to the organizational climate, but the KM doesn't show the weaknesses observed in the OC. One explanation could be that the unemployment situation is recent and may the Organizational Climate has not influenced negatively on the development of knowledge tab. Another explanation may be given by the fact that, despite the employees of the view that colleagues interpose personal interests above the collective and organizational interests, there is still a good communication among them and the prevailing social interaction; as point out by [6]. Positive social interaction results in a higher degree of knowledge sharing and knowledge application, being a mediator in the relationship between organizational structure and Knowledge Management.

However, it was found the correlation between Organizational Climate and Knowledge Management in the plant researched, evidenced by the significant correlations among variables in the analysis, the results are consistent with research in banking [9], educational, hospital [17], among others.

Table 1. Descriptive data evaluating the responses of participants for each variable.

	Mean (SD) Moda	Strongy agree %	Agree %	Neutral %	Disagree %	Fully disagree %
There is a lot of self-serving behavior going on here. (OC1)	4.09 (1.14) 5	45.5	34.1	9.1	9.1	0
People do what's best for them, not what's best for the organization. (OC2)	3.55 (1.19) 4	20.5	40.9	18.2	15.9	2.3
People spend too much time cajoling to those who can help them. (OC3)	3.73 (1.23) 4	29.5	36.4	20.5	6.8	4.5
People work behind the scenes to make things for themselves. (OC4)	3.48 (1.17) 4	18.2	36.4	29.5	9.1	4.5
Many employees are trying to maneuver their way into the in group. (OC5)	3.11 (1.15) 3	13.6	20.5	36.4	25.0	2.3
People speak ill of the other to be well valued. (OC6)	3.68 (1.12) 4	22.7	40.9	25.0	6.8	2.3
I talk to the others seeking help them with their work problems (KM1)	3.30 (1.19) 4	13.6	34.1	31.8	11.4	6.8
I use personal conversation to keep others updated with information I have about the organization (KM2)	3.52 (1.11) 4	15.9	43.2	25.0	11.4	2.3
I use email to communicate and help colleagues with problems work (KM3)	2.59 (1.11) 3	0	19.5	43.2	13.6	21.5
I share my experiences so others can improve their own work (KM4)	4.11 (0.92) 4	34.1	50.0	13.6	0	0
My co-workers share their knowledge and experiences while working (KM5)	3.64 (1.04) 4	15.9	50.0	20.5	11.4	0
Most people in my organization are willing to share what they know (KM6)	3.80 (1.15) 4	25.0	47.7	18.2	4.5	0
My co-workers volunteer sharing their knowledge and experiences even without being asked (KM7)	3.75 (1.01) 4	20.5	47.7	22.7	6.8	0

Table 2. Analysis of correlations among variables Organizational Climate and Knowledge Management

		OC1	OC2	OC3	OC4	OC5	OC6	KM1	KM2	KM3	KM4	KM5	KM6	KM7
OC1	r	1	0.72*	0.84*	0.70*	0.60*	0.76*	0.13	0.46*	0.09	0.43*	0.21	0.26	0.20
	P		0.00	0.00	0.00	0.00	0.00	0.45	0.00	0.58	0.003	0.18	0.09	0.19
OC2	r	0.72*	1	0.74*	0.71*	0.64*	0.73*	0.23	0.31*	0.03	0.41*	0.11	0.17	0.15
	p	0.00		0.00	0.00	0.00	0.00	0.07	0.04	0.84	0.01	0.49	0.28	0.32
OC3	r	0.84*	0.74*	1	0.77*	0.68*	0.77*	0.25	0.42*	0.02	0.42*	0.23	0.17	0.19
	P	0.00	0.00		0.00	0.00	0.00	0.11	0.01	0.90	0.01	0.13	0.26	0.23
OC4	r	0.70*	0.71*	0.77*	1	0.74*	0.76*	0.33*	0.56*	0.12	0.40*	0.19	0.14	0.10
	p	0.00	0.00	0.00		0.00	0.00	0.03	0.00	0.44	0.01	0.23	0.36	0.51
OC5	r	0.60*	0.64*	0.68*	0.7*	1	0.72*	0.32*	0.57*	0.07	0.45*	0.15	0.27	0.23
	P	0.00	0.00	0.00	0.00		0.00	0.04	0.00	0.63	0.00	0.32	0.08	0.14
OC6	r	0.76*	0.73*	0.77*	0.76*	0.72*	1	0.28	0.53*	0.04	0.51*	0.34*	0.36*	0.24
	P	0.00	0.00	0.00	0.00	0.00		0.06	0.00	0.78	0.00	0.02	0.02	0.12
KM1	r	0.12	0.28	0.25	0.33*	0.32*	0.28	1	0.65*	0.45*	0.44*	0.62*	0.52*	0.45*
	P	0.45	0.07	0.11	0.03	0.04	0.06		0.00	0.002	0.003	0.00	0.00	0.002
KM2	r	0.46*	0.31*	0.42*	0.56*	0.57*	0.53*	0.65*	1	0.37*	0.58*	0.51*	0.52*	0.41*
	P	0.00	0.04	0.01	0.00	0.00	0.00	0.00		0.01	0.00	0.00	0.00	0.01
KM3	r	0.09	0.03	0.02	0.12	0.07	0.04	0.46*	0.37*	1	0.02	0.25	0.15	0.09
	P	0.58	0.84	0.90	0.44	0.63	0.78	0.002	0.01		0.88	0.10	0.33	0.55
KM4	r	0.43*	0.41*	0.42*	0.40*	0.45*	0.51*	0.44*	0.58*	0.02	1	0.56*	0.53*	0.65*
	P	0.00	0.01	0.01	0.01	0.00	0.00	0.003	0.00	0.88		0.00	0.00	0.00
KM5	r	0.21	0.11	0.23	0.19	0.15	0.34*	0.62*	0.51*	0.25	0.56*	1	0.56*	0.73*
	P	0.18	0.49	0.13	0.23	0.32	0.02	0.00	0.00	0.10	0.00		0.00	0.00
KM6	r	0.26	0.17	0.17	0.14	0.27	0.36*	0.52*	0.52*	0.15	0.53*	0.56*	1	0.59*
	P	0.09	0.28	0.26	0.36	0.08	0.02	0.00	0.00	0.33	0.00	0.00		0.00
KM7	r	0.20	0.15	0.19	0.10	0.23	0.24	0.45*	0.41*	0.09	0.65*	0.73*	0.59*	1
	P	0.19	0.32	0.23	0.51	0.14	0.12	0.002	0.01	0.55	0.00	0.00	0.00	

Legend: r: correlation coefficient of Pearson, p: significance.
* The correlation is significant at the 0.05 significance level.

4 Conclusions

Through theoretical research and the collection of field data, which were treated with descriptive statistics, we could come to some considerations about the relationship between Organizational Climate and Knowledge Management and the existing process influences among these variables in environment workers in the researched automotive industry. The results show a relationship between Organizational Climate and Knowledge Management in the automotive sector, evidenced by the significant correlations between the variables analyzed. The unemployment situation can negatively influence the climate of organizations. Participants agree to point that in the organization: personal interests are above the collective and organizational interests and people speak ill of the other to be well valued. Respect to Knowledge Management, participants indicated that seek talking to people and help them with their work problems or keep them updated with important information about the organization. The above suggests that positive social interaction can preserve knowledge sharing, even when there are deficiencies in the organizational climate. Future studies can compare the results of this study with another sample in the same environment in the stable employment situation. Other research may replicate this study with a larger number of participants.

References

1. Bamel, U.K., Rangnekar, S., Stokes, P., Rastogi, R.: Organizational climate and managerial effectiveness: an indian perspective. Int. J. Organ. Anal. **21**(2), 198–218 (2013)
2. Janz, B.D., Colquitt, J.A., Noe, R.A.: Knowledge worker team effectiveness: the role of autonomy, interdependence, team development, and contextual support variables. Pers. Psychol. **50**(4), 877–904 (1997)
3. Jaw, B.S., Liu, W.: Promoting organizational learning and self-renewal in taiwanese companies: the role of HRM. Hum. Resour. Manage. **42**(3), 223–241 (2003)
4. Chen, C.J., Lin, B.W.: The effects of environment, knowledge attribute, organizational climate, and firm characteristics on knowledge sourcing decisions. R&D Manage. **34**(2), 137–146 (2004)
5. Chen, C., Huang, J., Hsiao, Y.: Knowledge management and innovativeness: the role of organizational climate and structure. Int. J. Manpower **31**(8), 848–870 (2010)
6. Chen, C.J., Huang, J.W.: How organizational climate and structure affect knowledge management-the social interaction perspective. Int. J. Inf. Manage. **27**(2), 104–118 (2007)
7. Lin, H., Lee, G.: Effects of socio-technical factors on organizational intention to encourage knowledge sharing. Manag. Decis. **44**(1), 74–88 (2006)
8. Chen, S.S., Chuang, Y.W., Chen, P.Y.: Behavioral intention formation in knowledge sharing: examining the roles of KMS quality, KMS self-efficacy, and organizational climate. Knowl. Based Syst. **31**, 106–118 (2012)
9. Chatzoglou, P.D., Vraimaki, E.: Knowledge-sharing behaviour of bank employees in Greece. Bus. Process Manage. J. **15**(2), 245–266 (2009)

10. Llopis, O., Foss, N.J.: Understanding the climate: knowledge sharing relation: the moderating roles of intrinsic motivation and job autonomy. Eur. Manag. J. **34**(2), 135–144 (2016)
11. Radaelli, G., Mura, M., Spiller, N., Lettieri, E.: Intellectual capital and knowledge sharing: the mediating role of organisational knowledge-sharing climate. Knowl. Manage. Res. Pract. **9**(5), 342–352 (2011)
12. Nonaka, I., Takeuchi, H.: Criação de Conhecimento na Empresa: Como as Empresas Japonesas Geram a Dinâmica da novação. Campus, Rio de Janeiro (1997)
13. Muniz, J., Trzesniak, P., Batista Jr., E.: Um Enunciado Definitivo para o Conceito de Gestão do Conhecimento: Necessidade para o Avanço da Ciência e para a Aplicação Eficaz. Tópicos Emergentes e Desafios Metodológicos em Engenharia de Produção: Casos, Experiências e Proposições 2 (2009)
14. Agarwal, N.K., Islam, M.A.: Knowledge retention and transfer: how libraries manage employees leaving and joining. VINE **45**(2), 150–171 (2015)
15. Massingham, P.: An evaluation of knowledge management tools: part 1 - managing knowledge resources. J. Knowl. Manage. **18**(6), 1075–1100 (2014)
16. Merrifield, D.B.: Changing nature of competitive advantage. Res. Technol. Manage. **43**(1), 41–45 (2000)
17. Rees, G.H.: Lean Thinking in New Zealand Emergency Departments. Thesis Doctoral, University of Otago, New Zealand (2011)
18. Pires, S.R.I.: Gestão da Cadeia de Suprimentos e o Modelo de Consórcio Modular. Revista de Administração da Universidade de São Paulo **33**(3) (1998)
19. Zamberlan, C.O., Sonaglio, C.M., Ghiliardi, W.J., Dias, E.P.: Influência do Desemprego no Clima Organizacional: Um Estudo de Caso nas Concessionárias de Automóveis de Santa Maria–RS. Jovens Pesquisadores–Mackenzie **9**(1) (2012)

ERP Software Quality Using Paraconsistent Logic

Priscila F. Tavaves$^{(\boxtimes)}$, Jair M. Abe, Genivaldo Carlos Silva, and Avelino P. Pimenta Jr.

Paulista University, São Paulo, Brazil
pri1979@gmail.com

Abstract. This study shows the perception of users regarding the ERP software (Enterprise Resource Planning). We used ISO/IEC 9126-1 for the evaluation of quality questions. As a decision-making tool, we used the Paraconsistent Annotated Evidential Logic Eτ, assisting software factories in which quality item to invest in ERP order to improve the production process and consequently their final product.

Keywords: Software quality · ISO 9126-1 · ERP · Paraconsistent logic

1 Introduction

In the decade of the 90s of last century, the implementation of ERP software (Enterprise Resource Planning) was presented as a major focus of investments related to the use of information technology in enterprises [1], which sought to gain competitive advantage through cost reduction and product differentiation by using these systems.

Thus, it was necessary to integrate business processes of companies with ERP was originally built. As the use of the ERP among companies gets more popular, the concern about the quality arises [2], as there are in the market several software development centers of this segment.

The question of this research is: how can IT users assess existing quality aspects in ERPs?

This research proposes to evaluate the perception of the user regarding the quality of ERP, based on ISO/IEC 9126 [3] and apply Paraconsistent Annotated Evidential Logic Eτ, with the focus on helping you software factory in which quality characteristic should invest to improve production process of ERP software and user satisfaction.

The research is relevant because it is motivated by the difficulties encountered by small and medium-sized software companies with limited financial resources O'Brien and Marakas [4] to implement international standards. It helps to verify that the ERP meets the quality standards established by the standard ISO/IEC 9126 through Paraconsistent Logic, which analyzes the responses of IT experts that are often inaccurate or contradictory and that, if verified by other methods, will not have adequate accuracy for decision making. Thus, this work demonstrates that there are reasonable solutions for this niche of software market to work with quality in its products.

© IFIP International Federation for Information Processing 2016
Published by Springer International Publishing AG 2016. All Rights Reserved
I. Nääs et al. (Eds.): APMS 2016, IFIP AICT 488, pp. 731–738, 2016.
DOI: 10.1007/978-3-319-51133-7_86

2   Literature Review

2.1   Software Quality

Some thoughts on quality: for Deming [5], product quality has a purpose: satisfying the customer. Crosby [6] states that "quality is the accordance to requirements".

There are many international norms and frameworks on software quality. We present them briefly:

ISO 12207 was created in order to standardize the quality of various types of life cycle of existing softwares in Software Engineering (Pressman 2014). It is divided into: Primary Processes, Organizational Support and additional information on ISO/IEC 12207.

CMMI (Capability Maturity Model Integration) is an approach of process improvement that helps in the development of products, services and procurement. It has five levels of maturity: 1 - Initial, 2 - Managed, 3 - Defined, 4 - Quantitatively Managed and 5 - Optimized, details at: www.cmmiinstitute.com.

ISO/IEC 15504 or SPICE, includes a reference model in two dimensions: the Process Dimension, divided into five big categories: Customer - Supplier, Engineering, Support, Management and Organization and Capacity Dimension, divided into six levels: Incomplete, Realized, Managed, Established, Predictable or Optimized.

Both of the norms above mentioned, including ISO 9126, have some points to note:

- Years are necessary for process improvement, organizational changes, employees training and putting the standards cited in practice completely;
- Significant investment in specific training for human resources;
- Greater investment in consulting for internal audits aimed at validation of requirements specified in each ISO;
- Revalidation of certification constantly achieved in software factories, which also generate investments.

Observing the aspects shown above, the small and medium-sized software factories don't have financial resources for implementation of norms in software quality, which makes their competition in the global market in which they are impossible. To attenuate this problem, the use of Paraconsistent Logic along with ISO 9126 is suggested, which doesn't replace the international standards mentioned, but contributes to the study, requiring significant financial investment to assess in which aspects the ERP needs to adapt, assisting companies in this decision making.

2.2   ISO/IEC 9126-1

It is divided into four regulations, but for this study we used only Part 1: Quality model. The ISO/IEC 9126-1 presents six groups that assess quality to the software, as shown in Table 1 below [3]:

Table 1. Characteristics of software quality according to ISO/IEC 9126-1

Characteristics	Description
F1-Functionality	Functions that meet the explicit and implicit needs for the purpose to which the product is intended
F2-Reliability	Performance is maintained under prescribed conditions over time
F3-Usability	It highlights the ease of using the software
F4-Efficiency	The resources and time involved are compatible with the level of performance required for the product
F5-Maintainability	It points out if there's ease for corrections and updates
F6-Portability	It uses multi-platforms and little effort to adapt

2.3   ERP - Enterprise Resource Planning

The ERP arose from the confluence of factors such as: integration of transnational companies requiring a unique and real-time treatment of information; tendency towards substitution of functional structures by structures anchored in processes; and integration of various information systems into a single system.

It maintains a unique and consistent flow of information across the enterprise in a single database and it shows transactions made by the company, designing scenarios of its business processes [4].

It offers a set of programs that connect and incorporate the administrative procedures or data generated by other applications [7].

Also, ERP integrates the company's management, improving decision making and allowing real-time monitoring [1].

2.4   Paraconsistent Annotated Evidential Logic Eτ (Logic Eτ)

Roughly speaking, Paraconsistent logics are logics that can serve as underlying logic of theories in which there are formulas A and A (the negation of A) both true without being trivial [8]. There are infinitely many paraconsistent systems. In this work we consider the Paraconsistent Annotated Evidential Logic Eτ.

The atomic formulas of the language of the Logic Eτ are of the type $p_{?\mu???\lambda?}$, in which p is a proposition and e $(\mu, \lambda) \in [0, 1]$ is the real unitary closed interval.

$p_{(\mu,\lambda)}$ can be intuitively read as: "The favorable evidence of p is μ and the contrary evidence is λ" [9]. For instance, $p(1.0, 0.0)$ can be read as a true proposition, $p(0.0, 1.0)$ as false, p(1.0, 1.0) as inconsistent, $p(0.0, 0.0)$ as paracomplete, and $p(0.5, 0.5)$ as an indefinite proposition [10]. Also we introduce the following concepts: Uncertainty degree: $G_{un}(\mu, \lambda) = \mu + \lambda - 1$ $(0 \leq \mu, \lambda \leq 1)$ and Certainty degree: $G_{ce}(\mu, \lambda) = \mu - \lambda$ $(0 \leq \mu, \lambda \leq 1)$ [11].

An order relation is defined on [0, 1]: $(\mu_1, \lambda_1) \leq (\mu_2, \lambda_2) \Leftrightarrow \mu_1 \leq \mu_2$ and $\lambda_2 \leq \lambda_1$, constituting a lattice that will be symbolized by τ.

With the uncertainty and certainty degrees we can get the following 12 output states Table 2 extreme states, and non-extreme states. It is worth observed that this division can be modified according to each application [12].

Table 2. Extreme and non-extreme states

Extreme states	Symbol	Non-extreme states	Symbol
True	V	Quasi-true tending to inconsistent	QV→T
False	F	Quasi-true tending to paracomplete	QV→⊥
Inconsistent	T	Quasi-false tending to inconsistent	QF→ T
Paracomplete	⊥	Quasi-false tending to paracomplete	QF→⊥
		Quasi-inconsistent tending to true	QT→V
		Quasi-inconsistent tending to false	QT→F
		Quasi-paracomplete tending to true	Q⊥→V
		Quasi-paracomplete tending to false	Q⊥→F

Some additional control values are:
V_{scct} = maximum value of uncertainty control = Ft_{un}
V_{scc} = maximum value of certainty control = Ft_{ce}
V_{icct} = minimum value of uncertainty control = $-Ft_{un}$
V_{icc} = minimum value of certainty control = $-Ft_{ce}$
All states are represented in the next figure (Fig. 1).

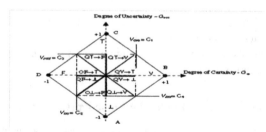

Fig. 1. Extreme and non-extreme states

From data standardization experts and the same being submitted - Aces rules Para-consistent Logic, the graph of Fig. 1 is generated and from the ordered pairs indicated in the graph, the analysis can be performed using the Table 2.

3   Methodology

We forwarded an online questionnaire to thirty IT users of the ERP in daily operations, where we dealt with questions about the perception of users regarding the six charac-teristics of ISO 9126-1 shown in Table 1.

Answers from all requested users were obtained and the results were grouped by expert teams (Final Users, System Analysts and IT managers) where we obtained quan-titative data.

From these data, we used the Logic Eτ to support the Software Factories in deciding in which quality feature related to the ISO 9126-1 to invest efforts in correcting problems in order to, consequently, improve the product and get satisfaction of ERP customers.

Below, procedures for the application of Logic Eτ:

(a) Definition of Proposition: To start the study, we went to the following statement: There were problems in the quality of ERP software.
(b) Factors for expert analysis: The factors used for the analysis of respondents were the same as listed in Table 1, from the ISO / IEC 9126.
(c) Sections for expert analysis: The sections, asked in accordance to each factor, are related as shown in Table 3:
(d) Definition of expert groups: The questionnaire was sent to 3 groups of IT specialists: Final Users, System Analysts and IT managers, (thus following assessment standard ISO/IEC 9126-1), where each group had ten replies, totaling thirty ERP users interviewed.
(e) User responses: Each quality factor was evaluated by ERP users about the positive and negative aspects (μ, λ) ranging from 0 to 1.
(f) Assigning weights to the responses of experts: a weight "2" was assigned to the answers of the final user group, as this is the central axis of the research.
(g) Database construction: From Table 3, the responses of experts were grouped according to their group and the data were normalized by arithmetic average and distributed among each type of specialty, as shown in Table 3:

Table 3. Factors and sections used in structuring the database

Factors		Sections
F1	Functionality	S1 - Do the functions that the ERP contemplate meet the current needs?
F2	Reliability	S1 - Does the ERP maintain its performance level (does not freeze) even in critical situations?
F3	Efficiency	S1 - Is the performance level vs response time of the ERP balanced?
F4	Usability	S1 - Is the effort required for the use of the ERP irrelevant, is the software easy to learn and operate?
F5	Maintainability	S1 - It is necessary to make great effort to upgrade or to perform maintenance on the ERP?
F6	Portability	S1 - Does the ERP work in multiplatforms like: Windows, Linux, Os2, SQL, Oracle, DB2, etc?

With data from Table 4, we drew the favorable and contrary evidence from experts on the factors (F1 to F6). The rules of Maximum and Minimum have been applied.

(h) Maximization and Minimization rules: We used the rules of Max and Min to the evidence of experts for each factor and section identified.

Table 4. Data collection from experts

FACTOR	SECTIONS	G1: Users												G2: System analysts						G3: IT managers					
		E1		E2		E3		E4		E5		E6		E7		E8		E	
		μ	λ	μ	λ	μ	λ	μ	λ	μ	λ	μ	λ	μ	λ	μ	λ	μ	λ
F1	S1	0.8	0.2	0.7	0.3	0.7	0.3	0.9	0.1	0.7	0.3	0.8	0.2	0.4	0.4	0.6	0.8	0.6	0.3
F2	S1	0.9	0.1	0.6	0.4	0.5	0.7	0.5	0.1	0.8	0.2	0.8	0.2	0.5	0.5	0.5	0.6	0.5	0.7
F3	S1	0.9	0.1	0.5	0.5	0.6	0.3	0.6	0.1	0.4	0.3	0.8	0.2	0.6	0.6	0.7	0.3	0.7	0.3
F4	S1	0.8	0.2	0.5	0.5	0.6	0.4	0.4	0.7	0.5	0.1	0.8	0.2	0.7	0.3	0.5	0.5	0.5	0.4
F5	S1	0.3	0.7	0.3	0.7	1	0	0.5	0.5	0.6	0.3	0.9	0.1	0.5	0.3	0.9	0	0.9	0
F6	S1	0.8	0.2	0.5	0.5	0.8	0.2	0.7	0.2	0	0	0.9	0.1	0.5	0.7	0.1	0.9	0.1	0.2

4 Analysis and Discussion

We have favorable or contrary evidence relating to software quality characteristics, if there is a certainty degree equal or greater than 0,6. The certainty degree is defined as: $G_{ce} = \mu - \lambda$

The division criterion adopted was:

$G_{ce} \geq 0,6 \rightarrow$ Truth (T), the valued software can be considered of good quality;

$G_{ce} \leq -0,6 \rightarrow$ False (F), the valued software has no good quality; and $-0.6 < G_{ce} < 0.6$. Region between Truth and False is called DOUBT, where the amount of data presented was inconclusive to determine whether the software factor has good quality or not.

We applied the Max and Min rules to the data of Table 4, below on Table 5.

Observing the degree of favorable and contrary evidence resulting from the application of MAX (OR) and MIN (AND) rules to the evidence of the experts, it is noted that the degree of certainty (G_{ce}) to F1 (functionality) is G_{ce} 0.6 experts say ERP meets the quality questions herein. When analyzing the F2 factor (reliability) the G_{ce} showed 0.0, which means experts have not reached a conclusion.

For the F3 factor (efficiency), the presented G_{ce} 0.4, i.e., experts report that the ERP does not offer good response times and uses many computational resources.

Table 5. Evidence degrees resulting from the application of Max and Min rules

Factors	Sections	Number of lines: 6		control value: ≥ 0.6		
		Max and Min between groups		Conclusions		
		μ_{1R}	λ_{2R}	Gce	G_{contr}	Decision
F1	S1	0.9	0.3	0.6	0.2	True
F2	S1	0.5	0.2	0.0	−0.3	Paracomplete
F3	S1	0.7	0.3	0.4	0.0	False
F4	S1	0	0	0.0	−1	Paracomplete
F5	S1	0.2	0.9	−0.7	0.1	False
F6	S1	0.8	0	0.8	−0.2	True

Regarding the F4 factor (usability), the G_{ce} = 0.0, that is, the experts have not reached a conclusion.

Regarding the F5 factor (Maintainability) the G_{ce} presented −0.7, meaning the maintenance of ERP is for bug fixes, product enhancements or version migration which are complex to run.

Finally, for the F6 factor (Portability), the G_{ce} showed 0.8, in which experts agree that ERP can work in computer multi-platform, showing no significant problems.

On the Unit Square in the Cartesian Plane, adapted from Abe [10], we are presented the coordinates and abscissas from Table 5 (Fig. 2).

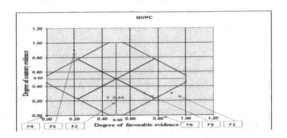

Fig. 2. Unit square in the cartesian plane (USPC)

For factors F2 and F4 there were doubts among the experts; in order to clarify them, stricter criteria for evaluation is needed, i.e., for a safer and more reliable decision, it may be necessary to increase the Requirement Level or to use a larger number of experts in the search, or to even consider the given evidence in terms of each expert's weight.

5   Conclusion

After applying the Logic Eτ, it was noted that the Factors F3 (Efficiency) and F5 (Maintainability) require significant improvements related to quality of ERP software, according to ERP users questioned.

With this research, it was possible to identify and assess the user perception, supported by ISO/IEC 9126, as ERP softwares are characterized in the aspect of quality.

It was from the Logic Eτ that it was assessed that among the six quality traits studied, two of them - Efficiency and Maintainability - must be reviewed and better structured by software factories.

Software Factories, knowing their vulnerability among the groups studied by ISO 9126, will benefit from the results, reducing rework and domestic spending on their projects, and their potential customers will not be affected by unscheduled stoppages caused by defects in the ERP, avoiding financial losses of this type of incident and consequently increasing satisfaction with the services provided.

In resume, the Logic Eτ was essential to eliminate the contradictions, assisting the management of software factories in which quality characteristics to invest, thus improving its processes and therefore its ERP software products, reaching then the goals at the beginning this study.

References

1. Laudon, K.C., Laudon, J.P.: Management Information Systems, vol. 8. Prentice Hall, Upper Saddle River (2011)
2. Pressman, R., Maxim, B.: Engenharia de Software. McGraw Hill, Sao Paulo (2016)
3. International Organization for Standardization: ISO/IEC: 9126 information technology-software product evaluation-quality characteristics and guidelines for their use. Technical report, ISO (1991)
4. O'Brien, J.A., Marakas, G.M.: Administração de Sistemas de Informação. Grupo A-AMGH (2013)
5. Deming, W.E.: Qualidade: A Revolução da Administração. Marques Saraiva, Sao Paulo (1990)
6. Crosby, P.B.: Quality is Free: The Art of Making Quality Certain. Mentor Books, Dublin (1992)
7. Cherene, L.P., da Silva, L.S., Silva, S.V.: Dificuldades e Benefcios na Implementao de um Sistema de Gesto Empresarial (Sap R/3). Perspectivas OnLine 2007–2010 4(16) (2014).
8. Abe, J.M., Akama, S., Nakamatsu, K.: Introduction to Annotated Logics: Foundations for Paracomplete and Paraconsistent Reasoning, vol. 88. Springer, Heidelberg (2015)
9. Carvalho, F.R., Abe, J.M.: Tomadas de Decisão com Ferramentas da Lógica Paraconsistente Anotada: Método Paraconsistente de Decisão. Edgard Blucher, São Paulo (2012)
10. Abe, J., Silva, F., João, I., Celestino, U., Araújo, H.: Lógica Paraconsistente Anotada Evidencial Eτ (2011)
11. Carvalho, F., Brunstein, I., Abe, J.: Paraconsistent annotated logic in analysis of viability: an approach to product launching. In: Sixth International Conference on Computing Anticipatory Systems (CASYS-2003), vol. 718, pp. 282–291 (1997)
12. de Carvalho, F.R., Brunstein, I., Abe, J.M.: Decision making based on paraconsistent annotated logic. In: Proceedings of the 2005 Conference on Advances in Logic Based Intelligent Systems: Selected Papers of LAPTEC 2005, pp. 55–62. IOS Press (2005)

A Structured Outsourcing Procedure

Maria Flavia Mogos[1(✉)], Børge Sjøbakk[2], and Erlend Alfnes[1]

[1] Norwegian University of Science and Technology (NTNU), Trondheim, Norway
{maria.f.mogos,erlend.alfnes}@ntnu.no
[2] SINTEF Technology and Society, Trondheim, Norway
borge.sjobakk@sintef.no

Abstract. Outsourcing of production entails a vast amount of activities and decisions. Although it has many acknowledged benefits, it is associated with substantial risk, and may lead to increased costs and loss of business if it is not carried out carefully and in a systematic manner. The identified outsourcing literature mainly focuses on specific parts of the outsourcing process and often provides limited practical guidance. Therefore, the purpose of this paper is to synthesize existing research on outsourcing processes into one structured outsourcing procedure. This can guide companies in carrying out outsourcing activities in a systematic manner. The suggested procedure is discussed in light of a case study of two production transfers between a Norwegian supplier of advanced maritime monitoring systems and one of its strategic suppliers.

Keywords: Outsourcing · Production transfer · Operations strategy

1 Introduction

Many Western companies choose to transfer parts of their production to other actors in their supply chains. Such transfers are often denoted outsourcing or offshoring processes, depending on the ownership structure (internal or external) and target location (domestic or foreign) of the transfer [1]. Outsourcing generally refers to the handover of responsibility for certain activities across organizational borders, whereas offshoring indicates that the responsibility is transferred to a subsidiary or supplier in a foreign location. Due to its many stated benefits, such as lower factors costs, access to new materials, distribution channels and technologies, as well as increased capacity to focus on core competences, outsourcing has been a very popular strategy in many industries [2]. Still, it is associated with substantial risk and may lead to increased costs and loss of business if it is not carried out carefully and in a systematic manner – reflecting the high complexity of such transfer processes [2].

Outsourcing of production entails a vast amount of decisions to be taken. Although several outsourcing frameworks and guidelines exist, only a few (e.g. [3,4]) describe all stages of the outsourcing process. These are typically rather general in their description of the activities that need to be carried out at the different stages. More detailed frameworks typically focus on the make-or-buy

© IFIP International Federation for Information Processing 2016
Published by Springer International Publishing AG 2016. All Rights Reserved
I. Nääs et al. (Eds.): APMS 2016, IFIP AICT 488, pp. 739–747, 2016.
DOI: 10.1007/978-3-319-51133-7_87

phase of the process, by e.g. discussing possible benefits and risks when outsourcing [5], or they end before the physical transfer [6]. Frameworks that address the production transfer (PT), i.e. the actual relocation of manufacturing of products or components between two production facilities (Sender and Receiver), either focus on specific parts of the PT [6], or provide only a general overview of interdependent activities important for supply performance [3,7,8]. No comprehensive frameworks integrating all these aspects have been identified. Therefore, the purpose of this paper is to synthesize existing research on outsourcing processes into one structured outsourcing procedure. This can guide companies in carrying out outsourcing activities in a systematic manner. The procedure is discussed in light of an instrumental case study of two PTs between a Norwegian supplier of advanced maritime monitoring systems and one of its strategic suppliers within electronic manufacturing services (EMS).

2   Research Method

The structured outsourcing procedure is proposed on the basis of a thorough study of literature on production-, knowledge-, and technology-transfers, as well as more general literature on outsourcing, production start-up and ramp-up. When structuring the literature, the most comprehensive identified models and methods [3–5] were taken as a starting point. During the structuring of the literature a need to add, rearrange and adjust phases emerged – more or less resulting in the proposed procedure. However, an instrumental case study approach [9] has been selected to test and accomplish it. This was designed as a single case study as the access to adequate empirical data was limited to one supplier-buyer relation; however, two PTs were followed to increase the research quality. The empirical data was collected through workshops and semi-structured interviews with key representatives from both case companies, e.g. quality managers, product developers, key account managers and process engineers.

3   Structuring Outsourcing

In broad terms the production outsourcing process can be divided into three parts: (1) deciding what (if any) to outsource, (2) selecting and committing a supplier, and (3) transferring the production. Each of these contains a number of activities that a company needs to go through during an outsourcing process. These are briefly described and summarized below. IDs are assigned to the activities, in order to link them to the suggested outsourcing procedure at the end of the section.

3.1   The Outsourcing Decision

In describing the outsourcing decision, a framework by Kremic et al. [5] is adopted. This depicts typical elements of the outsourcing decision, and shows where motivators, benefits, risks and other factors are typically encountered. The first step is to consider outsourcing in the first place. Here, the sender's motivation for outsourcing is weighed against general risks and benefits. According to [5] (a combination of) three major categories of motivation drives outsourcing: cost, strategy, and politics. The sender should have a conscious attitude towards these (A1). For instance, the outcome of outsourcing is often more successful if the decision is based on strategic considerations rather than solely on financial problems [10]. Further, the sender should analyze whether common benefits and risks of outsourcing either strengthen or weaken the decision (A2). Although it is not explicitly stated in the literature, we suggest documenting (A3) and communicating (A4) the resulting outsourcing policy internally. Next, the sender should identify (A5), evaluate (A6) and select (A7) what, if any, to outsource based on strategic-, financial-, functional- and environmental factors of each candidate and on the outsourcing policy [5]. When production is outsourced, Semini et al. [11] suggest careful attention to aspects such as logistics, equipment utilization, proximity to product development and intellectual property.

3.2 Supplier Selection

When the company has selected which functions, products or processes it should outsource, the next stage is to select a target supplier and location for the transfer. Here, a fourstage supplier selection process by Cousins et al. [12] is adopted. First, suppliers are prequalified (A8). Prequalification criteria will vary between companies and industries; however, suppliers' manufacturing capabilities and financial viability will usually be assessed. Often, companies keep a record of prequalified suppliers, enabling them to skip this phase. Otherwise, information about suppliers needs to be collected and evaluated. Next, the company should agree on measurement criteria (A9) that are specific to the product under consideration (e.g. unit price, lead time, supplier flexibility). Third, relevant information about suppliers should be gathered (A10), for example through requests for proposal or quotation. This information is used to make a selection in the fourth phase (A11). Danilovic and Winroth [13] argue that no matter how hard management strives to have a high level of integration in collaborative networks, the integration must be supported by legal agreements (A12). Draft agreements would often need to be designed for each case. Examples of issues that need to be included are forms of decision making, risk allocation, security issues and renegotiation/termination rules [13]. As will be evident in the next section, the contract may need to specify responsibilities before, during and after the transfer.

3.3 Production Transfer

Finally, when the receiving supplier has been selected the PT can commence. Based on [7], a PT process consists of four phases: the preparation for transfer, the physical transfer of equipment and inventories, the production start-up at Receiver, and the steady state. The Steady State starts after there has been reached a full-scale and stable production, at targeted levels of cost and quality [14]. Each of the PT related activities identified in the literature has been assigned to one of these four phases (Table 1).

Table 1. Overview of the studied production transfers and their main activities

Outsourcing policy: **A1.** Identify the amount of cost-driven, strategy-driven and politically-driven outsourcing [5,10] **A2.** Analyze whether benefits and risks will strengthen or weaken the decision to outsource [5] **A3.** Establish policy document **A4.** Communicate the company's outsourcing policy to employees **Outsourcing candidate selection:** **A5.** Identify possible candidates for outsourcing (functions, products or processes) [5] **A6.** Evaluate identified candidates [5, 11] **A7.** Select candidate(s) [5] **Supplier selection:** **A8.** Prequalify suppliers [12] **A9.** Agree on measurement criteria [12] **A10.** Obtain relevant information [12] **A11.** Make selection [12] **A12.** Contract negotiation [13] **Transfer preparation:** **A13.** Establish Project team [4,7] **A14.** Kick-off meeting [15] **A15.** Establish other teams [4,14] **A16.** Sign formal agreement [13,16] **A17.** Plan as Stepwise Transfer during low demand season (if possible) [17] **A18.** Ensure interaction with Receiver. Higher uncertainty, higher requirements [18] **A19.** Develop training plan [19] **A20.** Create transfer register. Include Transfer plans and checklist, Change Control procedure, etc. [4] **A21.** Evaluate Receiver's preparedness (premises, equipment., support services) [4] **A22.** Perform Transfer Risk Assessment. Implement measures [17] **A23.** Problem solving upgrading recalibration test of production system [7, 14]	**A24.** Define Engineering Change process [14] **A25.** Train Receiver's personnel [14,19] **A26.** Update/create documentation with Receiver [14,17,19] **A27.** Improve Receiver's performance [20] **A28.** Update Planning & Control system [17] **A29.** Develop Communication plan [4] **A30.** Transfer information [4] **A31.** Receiver reviews info. and finds gaps [4] **A32.** Ensure joint info. sharing platform [14] **A33.** Establish relations to sub-suppliers [21] **A34.** Verify preparations [17] **Physical Transfer:** **A35.** Transfer production equipment [7] **A36.** Send personnel to Receiver [14] **A37.** Install and test production equipment [7] **Production Start-up:** **A38.** Sender temporary transfers personnel [14] **A39.** Set up experimental line [14] **A40.** Involve all affected personnel [7] **A41.** Qualify component vendors [14] **A42.** Decide when to transfer responsibility to order raw material to Receiver [17] **A43.** Adapt processes to a new environment [22] **A44.** Problem solving on parts/materials [7] **A45.** Verify production [23] **A46.** Continuously monitor performance. Consider shutdown when lower than targets to solve problems [14]. Implement measures [17,24] **A47.** Adapt docs and Plan. & Control system [17] **A48.** Conduct post-transfer audit. Evaluate transfer [16,23] **A49.** Generate summary report (lessons learned, etc.) [4] **Production Steady State:** **A50.** Continuously monitor and improve production [7]. Consider maintaining experimental line [14]

Apart from the Physical Transfer, a PT consists of three additional types of transfers: knowledge transfer (KT) (of tacit knowledge), administrative transfer (AT) (of explicit/codified knowledge), and supply chain transfer (SCT) (by establishing relations to vendors of materials) [25]. It is important to ensure all these types of transfers during a PT. In addition, transfer parties will have to perform certain project administrative activities, such as establishing a PT organization and manage the PT project [4].

The transfer preparation phase includes the most identified activities. Here, KT activities are mainly related to the training (A25) and involvement of Receiver personnel in the preparation of documentation, the systems, and of the production equipment and processes (A26). In addition, it might be necessary to implement KT activities for performance improvement at Receiver, such as six sigma or lean [20] (A27). AT activities are related to e.g. updating of planning and control systems with data based on the estimated lead times and other performance indicators for the PT [17] (A28), and the transfer of the updated information to Receiver (drawings, materials planning method, packaging procedures, etc.) (A30). SCT primarily concerns a possible transfer of suppliers to the Receiver (A33). Examples of project management (PM) activities are kick-off meeting (A14), signing of formal agreements (A16), and generating a transfer register with plans, flow diagrams, instructions and control procedures (accessible to both parties and up-to-date) (A20). The physical transfer mainly involves transfer of production equipment (A35), installation and testing of equipment (A36), but also certain KT by temporary transferring personnel from Sender to Receiver (A36) to provide support and report back to Sender [14]. Such a transfer can also take place during start-up (A38). Other KT activities during start-up imply setting up an experimental line for learning and for testing of performance improvement solutions at the Receiver (A39), and involving all the affected personnel along the process (A40). An AT task for the Receiver is to adapt documentation and systems to their own planning environment (A47). SCT activities during start-up are mainly related to qualification of component vendors (A41) and the decision about when to transfer the responsibility to order raw material to the Receiver (A42). As a PM activity, a summary report (A50) should be generated and stored in the transfer register.

4   Discussion and Conclusions

The empirical data collected during the case research is summarized in Table 2.

As seen in Table 2, Sender and Receiver had a series of challenges with the two PTs that might have been reduced by some of the actions from Table 1. For instance, communicating the company's outsourcing policy internally (A4) and organizing a kick-off meeting where the reason for the PT is clarified (A14), could have increased the Product Team's motivation to share essential information with the Receiver in Case A [15]. The PT parties should have constituted a project team (A14), with PT managers and other members from all the affected disciplines and with clear roles [14]. Moreover, as stated by [4], PTs should be

Table 2. Overview of the studied production transfers and their main activities

Completed transfer: Case A	Ongoing transfer: Case B
Transfer object: Acoustic sensor. Mature product. High volumes. Not too complex. Little IP	**Transfer object:** Signal converter. New version of existing product. More complex than Product A
Original location: Sender's production facility in Norway. Before, Sender had been producing the sensors and assembled them with housings and electronics from two different suppliers	**Original location:** The same as in Case A. For previous version, Sender installed PCBs from Receiver in cabinets from one supplier, and power supply and wiring from another supplier. Sender tested the final products
New location: After transfer, Receiver assembles, tests and delivers final products to Sender. Receiver is expected to reduce unit cost over time	**New location:** Same Receiver as in Case A. After transfer, Receiver installs electronics including own PCBs in cabinets. Sender still tests final products
Outsourcing policy: Combination of cost and strategy. Need to reduce cost; aim to be a 'technology company' rather than manufacturing company	**Outsourcing policy:** Same as in Case A
Outsourcing candidate selection: High volume product that requires higher efficiency and less competence than the Sender has	**Outsourcing candidate selection:** Product was selected due to the upcoming new version, 'now was the time'. Key components were already outsourced
Supplier selection: The Receiver was prequalified and used to deliver electronics for the product	**Supplier selection:** Same as in Case A. Their experience with product A was partly decisive
Preparations: Parties had no kick-off meeting. Key personnel in the Product Team, Sales, and Test were little involved in the preparations. Product Team was little informed about the reason for the transfer and their motivation to support Receiver was low. It had been unclear who was responsible for what at Sender and a transfer plan and risk assessment had not been prepared and conducted before transfer. Initially, it was decided that all test equipment would be moved from Sender to Receiver. When Product Team found this out, they realized that the Sender would not be able to run spot-checks, losing the control over the quality of their deliveries. Moreover, initially, Sender was to manufacture the product until Easter and Receiver everything after that (clean-cut). This turned out to be unrealistic. [*KT:*] Receiver participated in VSM at Sender and sent 3 operators to learn the process at Sender. [*SCT:*] Sender's original suppliers of housings and electronics were transferred to Receiver	**Preparations:** The transfer started in Sept. '14, with a kick-off. Sender asked Receiver to secure material from sub-suppliers without any formal agreement. A significant amount of this material became obsolete because of BOM changes, and the financial consequences were unsettled for a long time. The transfer was planned with partially overlapped product development at Sender and process development at Receiver. Often, BOM and other product design changes came too late (e.g. during continuous production instead of the Pilot phase). 4 BOM changes were sent after Receiver had ordered material. Moreover, Sender had problems with own change control system that did not allow purchasing materials for prototypes before design-freeze. Thus, many changes were unrecorded until Product Developer started to collect them in a common excel-file. [*KT:*] No personnel from Receiver were transferred for training at Sender. Receiver appreciated having one contact person at Sender (Product Developer) whereas Sender's Prod. Developer felt that it had been challenging to know whom to contact at Receiver. She had also experienced that two contacts at the Receiver had different BOM revisions. [*SCT:*] Sender's original supplier of cabinets was transferred to Receiver. Later on, Sender may replace them by its own subsidiary in a low-cost country
Physical Transfer: Sender copied their test equipment and transferred the copy to Receiver	**Physical Transfer:** None
Start-up: Receiver experienced that several of their process improvement suggestions were rejected without a clear justification and the latest ones even turned out to be futile. During a workshop (April '15), the Product Team revealed, to the Receiver's surprise, their plans to update the product to a new version. Finally, Sender was unaware if the transfer had been profitable or not, but they said that the start-up was long with high scrap rates and stock levels	**Start-up:** At the time of the workshop in April '15, the production had been transferred from Receiver's Development department to Manufacturing

managed by help of a PM plan based on risk management principles (A20). Hence, all the activities with potentially negative consequences (e.g. transferring the test equipment to Receiver) should have been identified together with experienced personnel and measures should have been implemented (i.e. risk management) (A22). Further, some authors state that PTs, to the extent possible, should be planned as 'stepwise' transfers (A17) instead of 'clear-cut', as in Case A. Production at Sender should be gradually decreased as volumes increase at Receiver. Thus, in case of unexpected demand or major production disruptions during Start-up, one would have a secondary source of supply at the Sender [17]. Further, parties had several communication issues in both Case A and B. Thus, by preparing a communication plan (with e.g. points of contact and their roles) (A29), they could have minimized these challenges. This plan should be included in the PT register along with the PT plan and other tools, such as activities checklists, a change control system, and a flow diagram [4, 14]. Moreover, the register should be continuously updated and easily accessible to both parties (A20). Finally, at the end of the Start-up in Case A, Sender could have conducted a post-transfer audit, comparing the pre- and post-outsourcing costs [16] and evaluating whether the Steady-state had been achieved and whether the production should be relocated to other manufacturer or not (A48). In addition, Receiver's performance should be monitored along the entire PT and measures should be implemented (A50) [4]. With respect to Case B, several authors stress the importance of a formal agreement (A12, A16) between parties, signed as early as possible during Preparations. The agreement should include each party's responsibilities along the process (e.g. who bears the cost of obsolete material), and desired performance targets (e.g. yield) [14]. Further, to effectively manage engineering changes, parties could also define the change control process (A24) during Preparations, and they could create a flow diagram of the PT with necessary decisions gates [4]. For instance, before starting with the continuous manufacturing, the production should have passed a verification gate (A45). Finally, with higher uncertainty of the PT (i.e. novelty, complexity, and tacit knowledge) there are higher requirements of interaction between parties (A18). For Case B, the assembly of product B was novel for the Receiver; the product version was an innovation, and it had a high amount of uncodified knowledge. Thus, parties could have invested more in information management systems (e.g. a common IT platform) and could have drawn advantage from the domestic proximity by having regular and more frequent meetings with the Receiver [23].

In this study, existing research on outsourcing processes is synthesized into one structured outsourcing procedure, comprising the outsourcing decision, the supplier selection, and the PT stage. We argue that one of the strengths of this procedure is providing a detailed overview of the PT specific activities, which are often overseen in earlier outsourcing procedures despite their impact on final performance results. The proposed procedure can guide practitioners in conducting production outsourcing processes in a systematic manner. Nevertheless, it should be validated in different manufacturing contexts and adapted to different types of production outsourcing. The authors' objective for the future is to configure and validate a phase model comprising activities from the current procedure, decision gates, suggested disciplines for each activity, as well as appropriate methods and tools.

Acknowledgements. This research has been conducted with support from the research project SoundChain funded by The Research Council of Norway. The authors would like to thank the project participants for providing valuable empirical data.

References

1. CAPS Research Organization: Outsourcing Strategically for Sustainable Competitive Advantage. Tempe (2005)
2. Kinkel, S., Maloca, S.: Drivers and antecedents of manufacturing offshoring and backshoring: a german perspective. J. Purch. Supply Manage. **15**(3), 154–165 (2009)
3. Momme, J., Hvolby, H.: An outsourcing framework: action research in the heavy industry sector. Eur. J. Purch. Supply Manage. **8**(4), 185–196 (2002)
4. World Health Organization: Expert Committee on Specifications for Pharmaceutical Preparations, Who Good Manufacturing Practices: Main Principles for Pharmaceutical Products. World Health Organization, Technical report (2011)
5. Kremic, T., Icmeli, T., Rom, W.: Outsourcing decision support: a survey of benefits, risks, and decision factors. Supply Chain Manage. **11**(6), 467–482 (2002)
6. Fredriksson, A.: Materials Supply and Production Outsourcing. Chalmers University of Technology (2011)
7. Madsen, E.S.: Knowledge Transfer in Global Production. Aalborg Universitet (2009)
8. Zeng, A.: Global sourcing: process and design for efficient management. Supply Chain Manage. **8**(4), 367–379 (2003)
9. Baxter, P., Jack, S.: Qualitative case study methodology: study design and implementation for novice researchers. Qual. Rep. **13**(4), 544–559 (2008)
10. Brandes, H., Lilliecreutz, J., Brege, S.: Outsourcing-success or failure? Findings from five case studies. Eur. J. Purch. Supply Manage. **3**(2), 63–75 (1997)
11. Semini, M., Sjøbakk, B., Alfnes, E.: What to offshore, what to produce at home? a methodology. In: Emmanouilidis, C., Taisch, M., Kiritsis, D. (eds.) APMS 2012. IAICT, vol. 398, pp. 479–486. Springer, Heidelberg (2013). doi:10.1007/978-3-642-40361-3_61
12. Cousins, P., Lamming, R., Lawson, B., Squire, B.: Strategic Supply Management. Principles, Theories and Practice. Pearson Education, Upper Saddle River (2008)
13. Danilovic, M., Winroth, M.: A tentative framework for analyzing integration in collaborative manufacturing network settings: a case study. J. Eng. Tech. Manage. **22**(1), 141–158 (2005)
14. Terwiesch, C., Bohn, R., Chea, K.: International product transfer and production ramp-up: a case study from the data storage industry. R. Manage. **31**(4), 435–451 (2001)
15. Dudley, J.: Successful technology transfer requires more than technical know-how. Biopharm. Int. **19**(10), 70–74 (2006)
16. Zhu, Z., Hsu, K., Lillie, J., Zhu, Z.: Outsourcing: a strategic move: the process and the ingredients for success. Manage. Decis. **39**(5), 373–378 (2001)

17. Fredriksson, A., Wänström, C., Johansson, M., Medbo, L.: A structured procedure for materials planning during production transfer. Prod. Plann. Contr. **26**(9), 738–752 (2015)

18. Stock, G., Tatikonda, M.: A typology of project-level technology transfer processes. J. Oper. Manage. **18**(6), 719–737 (2000)

19. Andre, M., Peter, B.: Towards a framework for transferring technology knowledge between facilities. Strateg. Outsourcing Int. J. **5**(3), 213–231 (2012)

20. Modi, S.B., Mabert, V.A.: Supplier development: improving supplier performance through knowledge transfer. J. Oper. Manage. **25**(1), 42–64 (2007)

21. Aaboen, L., Fredriksson, A.: The relationship development aspect of production transfer. J. Purch. Supply. Manage. **22**(1), 53–65 (2015)

22. Grant, E., Gregory, M.: Adapting manufacturing processes for international transfer. Int. J. Oper. Prod. Manage. **17**(9–10), 994–1005 (1997)

23. Hilletofth, P., Wlazlak, P., Johansson, G., Säfsten, K.: Challenges with industralization in a supply chain network: a supplier perspective. In: MakeLearn and TIIM Joint International Conference, pp. 309–318 (2015)

24. McCormack, K., Wilkerson, T., Marrow, D., Davey, M., Shah, M., Yee, D.: Managing risk in your organization with the SCOR methodology. The Supply Chain Council Risk Research Team, pp. 1–32 (2008)

25. Fredriksson, A., Wänström, C.: Manufacturing and supply chain flexibility towards a tool to analyse production network coordination at operational level. Strateg. Outsourcing: Int. J. **7**(2), 173–194 (2014)

The Need for Knowledge Management When Backsourcing is Embraced

Bella B. Nujen[1](✉) and Rickard Damm[2]

[1] Molde University College, Molde, Norway
Bella.B.Nujen@himolde.no
[2] TeliaSonera, Stockholm, Sweden

Abstract. This paper focuses on a relatively new sourcing strategy referred to as backsourcing, where we emphasize the importance of knowledge reintegration and how it can be managed. Our reference for this approach is built upon Knowledge Management theory and contribution from different academics that have discussed and highlighted the reversal of global manufacturing strategies. This is illustrated through an interview study with three members within the maritime industry at a high-cost location, which have already embraced a backsourcing strategy, or are preparing to embark on one. Findings in this paper contribute toward providing strategic choices that should be considered when reintegrating globally fragmented knowledge.

Keywords: Knowledge Management · Manufacturing · Backsourcing · Backshoring

1 Introduction

The reversal of global outsourcing strategies through e.g. backsourcing or backshoring has led to the rethinking of core competence within businesses and has highlighted the importance of how to retain or revive knowledge platforms within manufacturing sectors [1]. Earlier, work within manufacturing was usually assumed to consist of simpler assembly work. However, much of the work conducted within manufacturing consists of complex work sequences which require hands-on knowledge which sometimes, because of its tacitness and contextual embeddedness, does not lend itself to be easily articulated or codified. Hence, according to knowledge- and innovation theories these types of dimensions and capabilities are of fundamental importance since they underpin the further development of extant and new knowledge which are crucial elements for innovation to occur [2,3]. According to [4] manufacturing strategies should not be restricted to, "...*only cover quantifiable aspects such as how much-, how- and where- to produce. Stakeholder's relations, knowledge and innovativeness, and organizational culture are examples of intangible aspects that are increasingly important in manufactur-ing strategies*" (p.1) [4]. The current discussion indicates that businesses of today have to manage their work within manufacturing differently

© IFIP International Federation for Information Processing 2016
Published by Springer International Publishing AG 2016. All Rights Reserved
I. Nääs et al. (Eds.): APMS 2016, IFIP AICT 488, pp. 748–755, 2016.
DOI: 10.1007/978-3-319-51133-7_88

and apply it beyond traditional logistics measurements. Hence, manufacturing organizations are no longer limited to assembling and improvements, instead they consist of more intangible resources and capabilities that are both contextual and individual bounded. A wider exploration of how to manage these capabilities might therefore be necessary in today's competitive environment. Especially since there is a shift towards a more advanced manufacturing industry which not only incorporates new technology but also needs to revive important knowledge within an organizations own boundaries. Empirical research shows that important knowledge especially of the tacit dimension is about to erode within different industries like e.g. the US auto industry discussed by [5] and the Norwegian shipbuilding industry discussed by [1] and co-authors. In theoretical and empirical terms, there is a need to combine the interest in Knowledge Management (KM) and development when re-evaluating capabilities in relation to a successful sourcing- and manufacturing strategy.

In this paper we focus on a relatively new sourcing strategy referred to as backsourcing, where we emphasize the importance of knowledge re-integration within manufacturing. Our reference for this approach is built upon KM theory and contribution from different academics that have discussed and highlighted the reversal of global sourcing strategies. This is illustrated through an interview study with three members within the maritime industry at a high-cost location which have already embraced a backsourcing strategy, or are preparing to embark on one. Data was collected through in-depth semi-structured individual interviews with seven leaders on strategic levels. All interviews, except for one, were conducted on site, recorded and later transcribed verbatim. Additional data was obtained from published company documents regarding their new choice of sourcing strategy.

The composition of the paper is as follows: First, we give a brief introduction to the field of reversed global sourcing strategies, concluding with the need of a greater use of KM principles. Section 2 highlights potential challenges which may come of re-transferring and re-integrating a once outsourced activity or competence. Section 3 gives a presentation of the case, which also represents the frame of reference for the discussion and conclusion in Sect. 4.

2 Theoretical Background

2.1 The Reversal of Global Outsourcing Strategies

Global outsourcing, also referred to as offshoring, is part of the disaggregation of the value chain, and represents a critical interface between assets and geography where organizations try to achieve a competitive edge, by combining comparative advantages, usually at different low-cost locations with in-house resources [6]. The leading arguments for the strategy is to understand which part of the operational setup that are not core, to enable other companies to create the organizational scale and leverage needed to run a specific production or service process. Thus, theory shows that cost considerations are highly emphasized in favor of core competence [7]. According to [8] and co-authors, we are now rethinking global outsourcing strategies, which has been the dominating choice of strategy within manufacturing for almost 50-years. Today, a growing attention is being paid to global contracting failures and increased labour costs at traditionally low-cost locations among manufacturing businesses, which has led to different choices of where and how to produce in addition to where to source from. Consequentially, organizations not only source in the direction from internal- to external environments, but also from external back to internal. The latter phenomenon can be seen as a trend of global outsourcing fade-out, or simply as a sign that outsourcing as part of a manufacturing strategy continues to be transformed adapted and developed in parallel with the inherent global environment.

Hence, as a consequence of the aforementioned issues, together with the increas-ingly knowledge intensive corporate climate, a new trend has emerged called backsourcing. Backsourcing can be defined as the process of recalling operations "back in-house" after they have been (globally) outsourced [9].

Others define it as the process of bringing once outsourced activities back into the organization, with the goal of rebuilding internal capabilities [10]. The latter definition of the phenomenon describes backsourcing as a strategy and includes a perception of *rebuilding* which is a significant aspect to consider when one decides whether to bring back an activity (including personnel) or not, which is the definition this paper supports. Thus, this is only one of several relocation strategies which have emerged during the last decade or so.

Others are referred to in similar terms such as backshoring, reshoring, home-sourcing, inshoring and nearshoring [7,9,11] which all include a recall of value creation processes back to the original manufacturing-location or to a neighboring country. What's interesting though is that these strategies have a greater emphasizes with regards to location aspects [8] compared to the overall backsourcing strategy, where the activity that is being brought back, is more dependent on the ownership structures. This important feature of the backsourcing definition is worth noting, since there seems to be a confusion regarding the more traditional definition when activates are being performed in-house, referred to as insourcing. Here, one is usually buying-in external resources to work under in-house management, where the activity that is being bought has not previously been developed or owned by the buyer [10] which is a significant difference from the backsourcing definition, but also from the above mentioned ones, since they all imply a re-integration of an activity or process, either back in-house, or relocated from a foreign location back to the home location or a neighboring one. Furthermore, the current discussion and academic field of reversed global outsourcing strategies, show that some of the circumstances fall under the heading of correcting prior (poor) decisions, whereas others fall under the course of responding to changes in the environment, technologies and competitiveness of the foreign and home location [7].

However, despite the aforementioned research, there is still a conspicuous absence as far as substantial elaboration, regarding the knowledge re-integration process, especially in relation to the management part of it.

2.2 Incorporating Knowledge Management

Knowledge is a complex phenomenon with several different dimensions, where the most commonly referred is provided by [12] where he makes a distinction between a tacit and an explicit one. Tacit knowledge can be characterized as personal, abstract and difficult to communicate by verbal articulation, in contrast to explicit knowledge, which is codified knowledge, easy to communicate and transform since it in theory has a universal way of interpretation. Furthermore, tacit knowledge is embedded in organizational structures through common knowledge platforms, culture, mind-sets and competences that are shared through interaction between members, which gives it a context specific dimension [3,12,13].

When organizations are going global with their resources they are letting go of capabilities and skills, which involves transformation of embodied knowledge. After all, capabilities are to a large extent carried out, in one way or another, by the members of the organization using their individual competencies and skills involving the tacit knowledge dimension, which may cause potential problems of retention and accumulation within the organizational boundaries. As earlier mentioned, manufacturing work of today consists of more intangible resources and capabilities, which require hands-on tacit knowledge. Distinctive core capabilities, which usually are unique because of their tacitness, can be strengthened if the organization focuses on knowledge building [3,14]. However, to achieve this one needs to identify and nurture activities that are built upon extant knowledge. A change in the employee base and the related tacit knowledge might be lost as a result of outsourcing. Nevertheless, this does not mean that organizations are not acquiring knowledge at foreign location, they are, but global outsourcing disrupts and might hamper informal social networks, structures and processes that play a critical role in an organization's system of creating, integrating and sharing knowledge [2,6].

Knowledge challenges will however often differ between strategies, which imply that the enablers for a successful knowledge transfer also may differ. A redefinition of the importance of specific knowledge, which is necessary within the organizational context, is therefore crucial [9]. Re-integration and the reviving of potentially lost competence might therefore be more easily facilitated through relocation, either in-house, nearby or to a more controlled structure.

Hence, even though it may look like it, we are not proposing that backsourcing is the best or right solution for all manufacturing organizations. However, when choosing to embark on one or another reversal form of global sourcing strategy, businesses need to incorporate a KM perspective, especially when a product or activity has been modified or changed dramatically at the outsourced organization. The success of re-integrating an outsourced activity will to a large extent depend on the presence of an in-house organizational knowledge platform [1] and the ability to capture and understand what types of knowledge that needs to be re-integrated, as well as making sure that the "right" knowledge dimension fits its organizational origin [9,13,14]. Nevertheless, outsourcing operations are challenging and costly to reverse. For example, if the contract has not ended, and the firm chooses to backsource because of e.g. quality, trust or lead-time dissatisfaction, one should carefully consider possible termination penalties, duties and responsibility agreements. Especially if the recall-activity involves confidential information or product protection, which might lead to expensive legal processes, in addition to hampering the chances of a successful knowledge-reintegration.

Consequentially, one of the most challenging obstacles when embarking on a backsourcing strategy relate to re-integrating or reviving knowledge. Organizations generally put too much focus on the aspects of knowledge itself, and neglect other important aspects such as the management part of it which is equally important when knowledge is transferred from one environment to another [3,14].

3   Three Members from the Maritime Industry

This case is illustrated through in-depth interviews with three members (A, B, C) from the maritime industry at a high-cost location in Scandinavia, were we describe their decisions concerning their choice of knowledge-operations and activities, through a backsourcing process. Company A and B are both part of a unique offshore cluster, where A is the largest family-owned shipbuilding organization in its country, and delivers complex and specialized vessels to demanding ship owners worldwide. Company B is a sub-supplier offering large winches and fairleads, mainly to yards, ship-owners and oil companies. Company C, offers innovative products and processes for the offshore sector, as well as for marine, furniture and aquaculture industries. All of the companies announced that they embarked on outsourcing during the 1990s; which first and foremost where based on, cost consideration in production processes, but also because of an so called "herd mentality".

The consequences of outsourced activities for all three companies have been described as partial erosion of their core competencies, and to some extent also for the nation. *"25 years ago we built in this country, however because of the search for cheaper manufacturing workers, we lost some of our competitiveness which forced us out of our regions..."* and *"...the steel competence is about to erode, which is not only a problem for the yards, but also for the entire value chain..."* Company A and C have both carried out a backsourcing strategy, while B is actively preparing to embark on one. However the reasons behind the decision are different for each one of the firms.

For company A it was not a deliberate strategic decision that led to their backsourcing journey, instead it was a lead-time aspect which was important for enabling them to win a contract, behind their action. Nevertheless, over time it developed into a decision of significant strategic importance for how they choose to continue with their future manufacturing activities.

Instead of constructing complete hulls through a third-party, using traditional assembling processes, they brought back critical parts and started to modularize these through automation and robotics in-house, which resulted in operational advantages such as increased flexibility. However, it was the awareness around their in-house knowledge base and their access to their employees tacit knowledge and important know-how, which led to a stronger desire to start with a wider backsourcing strategy. Thus, they also saw the need to develop new capabilities which led to hiring people with technology know-how and strategically encourage knowledge sharing within the organization through learning by doing and programmes supporting experience-based collective action with their existing workforce which was the same as the one before their outsourcing process.

The underlying message from these managers is that the company started to direct more attention to knowledge as a key strategic resource, since they saw that *"...the re-integration process depended on it as well as our future competitiveness"*.

Similar to company A, C's decision to backsource also started as a coincidence. The company participated in an international innovation project where they developed and invested in a machine which at the time was considered a failure, accumulating a loss of about 25 MNOK (Million Norwegian Kronor). However, when an opportunity appeared in the market for molding of large parts, it turned out they had just the machine needed. Previously these parts where mostly molded with the help of simpler automation processes and manual work, however when it came to large parts it was extremely labour intensive. This experience made the company realize that competitors in the international market were not necessarily more competitive than themselves, leading towards a higher desire and understanding that they could produce these large products in-house because of the enabling technology being a differentiator in combination with their employees knowledge about it *"...sometimes we have a tendency to worship international competitors for more than they are worth..."* Nevertheless, what this event led to was a realization that if there existed high enough knowledge in-house, and the activity in question is demanding enough and at the same time the direct labour costs are low enough, then accordingly the possibility for automation is profitable, which enables production at high cost locations.

Hence, just like company A, C had almost the same workforce as before they outsourced. Today, they have carved out a profitable niche in this market and 30% of their turnover last year came as a result of backsourcing activities from China. It should be mentioned though that the organization always has been innovation and technology driven, likewise when it comes to knowledge development.

Company C has a systematic process of storing employees (explicit) knowledge in different IT systems compared to company A, which is more traditional when it comes to internal knowledge seeking and technology use. And moreover, when trying to develop and integrate tacit knowledge, company C has a policy that at least one engineer in every innovation- or research project is involved, which is a requirement for participation. *"...if the person who develops the product does not possess production expertise, then he produces bad products or products that are difficult to produce, which in turn also makes it difficult to achieve good quality, which makes it challenging to commercialize"*.

In contrast to both A and C, company B has been working deliberately towards a backsourcing strategy for some years now. Learning from other organizations within their cluster as well as other industries at high cost locations, they have made heavy investments in technology. The technological approach perspective is what underpins their entire make or buy decisions today, and are analyzed on a scale described as, "technically too simple, too complex or technically proper". The goal is to backsource production activities and design processes, but only those that fit their available technology *"...technology controls which activity we should produce in-house, not the production- or knowledge base..."*. Their strategy is that the company should always invest in the best compatible technology (maximum technology/feature) and not by optimal technology. Obtaining this reasoning and combining it with the economic situation, they have discovered that in-house production has more benefits than was predicted. What is interesting though is that all of their employees have steel/welding or machinery certifications (which is obligatorily), and not a technological education in e.g. Computer Science. Consequently, their organizational knowledge platform is primarily based on hands-on knowledge developed through social interaction and experience (tacit) which also is the basis of their historical development. Nevertheless it is technology that decides how to produce or where to source from, not their core common platform.

That being said, the company desires a new knowledge platform which incorporates a higher technological dimension, however, still demanding a steel/welding certification from their employees *"...our knowledge platform is not always common, but in constant renewal"*. Nevertheless, they have not yet managed to bring back outsourced activities in-house. And top management still have a strong aspiration to continue preparing for implementing a backsourcing strategy through knowledge renewal, focusing on technological developments.

4   Discussion and Conclusion

This interview study illustrates that when embarking on reversed outsourcing strategies, organizations need to be capable of renewing capabilities to cover additional types of knowledge and reconfigure existing knowledge into new types of competencies. However, to be able to renew knowledge, you need to know what you know, and therefore also create an ability to revive previous knowledge. Implementing KM strategies when relocating recourses back to the organization's own boundaries is therefore of fundamental importance. Furthermore, the need to retain staff even after the organization has outsourced is a defining feature for knowledge accumulation, creating a strong organizational knowledge platform, which in turn can become an enabler for innovation and knowledge development.

This highlights the importance of identifying and addressing both tacit and explicit knowledge and the need to encourage a knowledge-sharing environment, through informal interaction or socialization so that tacit knowledge does not leave with its carrier, if outsourcing occurs. The respondents in the study also emphasized that knowledge needs to be managed in a structured way, both with the help of IT tools but also to be included when conducting the manufacturing strategy, since it has a huge impact on both how (and if) an organization can produce and where to produce from. Another very important aspect is illustrated through the high degree of technology use. However, it is too early to understand the wider impact of what advancement in manufacturing technologies represents or how it will develop. Nevertheless, what we can see is that it will radically redefine the competitive landscape within many industries worldwide, since advanced technologies will enable organizations to bring back manufacturing activities to high cost locations.

Though, one of the key insights of this study shows that knowledge re-integration work might be equally important for a successful backsourcing strategy, implying that heavy investments in robotics and automation alone, is not enough. On the limitation side it should be mentioned that the study only represents one side of the table when terminating outsourcing contracts or relationships, missing potential barriers that might hinder the knowledge re-integration process or enablers smoothening the process. The small sample of interviews which might restrict the validity of the findings should also be mentioned.

References

1. Nujen, B.B., Halse, L.L., Solli-Sæther, H.: Backsourcing and knowledge re-integration: a case study. In: Umeda, S., Nakano, M., Mizuyama, H., Hibino, H., Kiritsis, D., Cieminski, G. (eds.) APMS 2015. IAICT, vol. 460, pp. 191–198. Springer, Heidelberg (2015). doi:10.1007/978-3-319-22759-7_22
2. March, J.G.: Exploration and exploitation in organizational learning. Organ. Sci. **2**(1), 71–87 (1991)
3. Nonaka, I., Takeuchi, H.: The Knowledge-creating Company: How Japanese Companies Create the Dynamics of Innovation. Oxford University Press, Oxford (1995)
4. Henriksen, B., Onsøyen, L.E.: Measuring the intangible aspects of the manufacturing strategy – a case study from the automotive industry. In: Vallespir, B., Alix, T. (eds.) APMS 2009. IAICT, vol. 338, pp. 383–391. Springer, Heidelberg (2010). doi:10.1007/978-3-642-16358-6_48
5. Roos, G., Roos, G., Kennedy, N.: Manufacturing in a high cost environment-basis for success on the firm level. Chapter **13**, 393–480 (2014)
6. Mudambi, R.: Location, control and innovation in knowledge-intensive industries. J. Econ. Geogr. **8**(5), 699–725 (2008)
7. Ellram, L.M., Tate, W.L., Petersen, K.J.: Offshoring and reshoring. J. Supply Chain Manag. **49**(2), 14–22 (2013)
8. Bals, L., Daum, A., Tate, W.: From offshoring to rightshoring: focus on the backshoring phenomenon. AIB Insights **15**(4), 3 (2015)
9. Bhagwatwar, A., Hackney, R., Desouza, K.C.: Considerations for information systems "backsourcing". Inf. Syst. Manag. **28**(2), 165–173 (2011)
10. Lacity, M.C., Willcocks, L.P., Rottman, J.W.: Global outsourcing of back office services. Strateg. Outsourcing Int. J. **1**(1), 13–34 (2008)
11. Fratocchi, L., Di Mauro, C., Barbieri, P., Nassimbeni, G., Zanoni, A.: When manufacturing moves back: concepts and questions. J. Purchasing Supply Manag. **20**(1), 54–59 (2014)
12. Polanyi, M.: The Tacit Dimension. Garden City, New York (1967)
13. Lam, A.: Tacit knowledge, organizational learning and societal institutions: an integrated framework. Organ. Stud. **21**(3), 487–513 (2000)
14. Grant, R.M.: Prospering in dynamically-competitive environments. Organ. Sci. **7**(4), 375–387 (1996)

Service-Oriented Architecture for Smart Manufacturing System, an SM & CPPS SIG Workshop Session

Industrial IoT Gateway with Machine Learning for Smart Manufacturing

Tomáš Lojka$^{(\boxtimes)}$, Martin Miškuf, and Iveta Zolotová

FEI TU of Košice, Košice, Slovak Republic
{tomas.lojka,martin.miskuf,iveta.zolotova}@tuke.sk

Abstract. Working together is important aspect of future industry. Therefore, technologies like Internet of Things (IoT), cloud computing, SOA give rise to another industrial revolution. We propose here a concept definition, which focuses on data acquisition, integration and predictive control in the industry. The concept consists of industrial IoT gateway, cloud services and machine learning services. We used machine learning to verify our data acquisition solution and we implemented prediction control as a cloud service. Finally, proposed solution will exceed boundaries inside ICS (Information and Control System), improve flexibility, interoperability and test plant prediction control in smart manufacturing.

Keywords: Cloud service · Cyber-physical system · Gateway · Internet of things · Machine learning · Smart manufacturing

1 Introduction

IT is one of the fastest emerging field in the world and it influences a lot of revolution approaches in industry. The well-known industrial approach is Industrial revolution 4.0. The president and chief operating officer in Rockwell, Don H. Davis, Jr. describes industrial revolution principle in the meaning that the driving force behind productivity today isn't working faster, or cheaper, but working together.

Every industry is a heterogeneous system, which consists of many subsystems. Each subsystem consumes and produces data. Data, information and knowledge are the most important attribute in the ICS (Information and Control System). Therefore, working together between subsystems is very important in industry. There are lot of solutions, which solve cooperation in industry. The new approaches improve cooperation with using the newest IT trends. One of the most popular IT trends is IoT that deals with term working together [1–3]. IoT is named like IIoT in the industrial field.

Industrial IoT (IIoT) cares about low level devices. These devices produce a lot of data about processes in the ICS floor level. IIoT collects data and improves physical world digital representation of plant floor processes, machines. This representation of physical world is important to monitor, control and plan ICS floor

© IFIP International Federation for Information Processing 2016
Published by Springer International Publishing AG 2016. All Rights Reserved
I. Nääs et al. (Eds.): APMS 2016, IFIP AICT 488, pp. 759–766, 2016.
DOI: 10.1007/978-3-319-51133-7_89

processes. IIoT plays a key role in fast data acquisition and data processing, what changed the machine-to-machine (M2M) and machine-to-human (M2H) communication in the industry. The artificial intelligence is used in process description and control [3–5].

The IIoT data has be transferred into higher layers of heretical ICT system. Plant is wide distributed heterogeneous system. It consists of many different devices with network communication interfaces, which are distributed across a whole plant. The data acquisition is problematic due the different distributed devices and their communication protocols. SCADA (Supervisory Control and Data Acquisition) uses M2M protocols, which are focusing on reliability and speed. The Service Oriented Architecture (SOA) improves the SCADA. The interoperability and flexibility is increased and some parts of ICS can be hosted in cloud, too. Nowadays, data from devices can be easily acquired into cloud system. Then we can use many cloud services for data storing, analytics, remote monitoring, management or control process [4–7]. As a result, the data acquisition, monitoring and control can be improved with the new IT approaches like IIOT, M2M communication, SOA and cloud. Where the flexibility, interoperability, modularity can improve whole ICS. We focus on data acquisition and better monitoring, control of plant floor processes. We propose data acquisition IoT gateway, which is based on M2M communication, SOA and cloud. We use machine learning to create a prediction model, which is published as a cloud service. This service is consumed by a control service, which uses IoT gateway to collect data from plant floor devices and send control commands to the plant floor devices. Finally, proposed solution will exceed boundaries inside ICS, improve flexibility, interoperability and test plant prediction control.

Paper consists of concept definition, which describes industrial IoT gateway, machine learning services, experimental application of our concept and final conclusion.

2   Industrial IoT and Cloud Services

CPS, IIoT, SOA and cloud are the key to the factory of the future. These technologies open plant floor data to every part of ICS system and help to make system "working together". CPS and workers are connected together with IIoT and cloud services into one big network [8,9]. Position of CPS, IIoT and cloud services is presented in the Fig. 1.

Plant can be divided into Operational technologies (OT) and Informational technologies (IT). The OT consists of various devices or CPSs, which produce data and connect physical world with its virtual (digital) representation. The IT consists of systems, which consume data, process data and are hosted in cloud. Integration between OT and IT is realized with IIoT [11,12] (Fig. 2).

The IT is implemented like services in cloud. Services represent data acquisition with device connectivity (buses and queues), analytics (data analytics) and presentation & Business services (mobile and web services, storage, machine learning services, business services (ERP) and third party services).

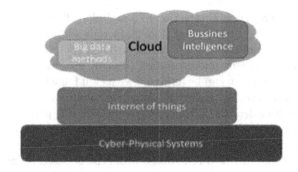

Fig. 1. Industrial connection with IoT, CPS, cloud, and Big data (Source: [10])

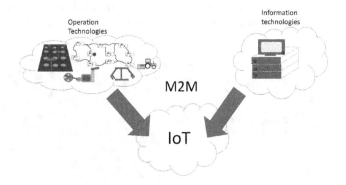

Fig. 2. IT and OT integration

Cloud services help to integrate data and create a digital representation of real processes. With such data acquisition based on IIoT, data can be centralized and processed very fast in the cloud. However, the data acquisition has big influence on service output quality [10]. For example, data analytics results might be evaluated wrong, because data are inconsistent or inappropriately sampled. Therefore, connection to the plant floor devices can be crucial. A lot of devices have specialized communication protocols, what makes data acquisition even more problematic and so exists a lot of field gateways and protocol adaptation solution to overcome this "working together" problem. Aim of this paper is to focus on data acquisition and data preprocessing due better data processing in analytics and presentation & business services.

3   Concept Definition of IIoT Gateway and Predictive Control

We designed data acquisition and control concept to our problem. Our concept is presented like an architecture, which consists of OT technology represented by plant floor devices and field gateway. This gateway plays a role of mediator.

Gateway helps to create an abstraction of a real plant floor device network. The abstraction is used for better plant floor data representation without knowing the real network topology. The abstraction helps to implement better M2M communication and better understanding of plant processes. We focus on idea that data from abstraction can be analyzed with cloud machine learning services. This will help us to create predictive control. IoT hub service, stream analytics service and machine learning service represents the IT part. The result from machine learning is a cloud service, which cooperate with control service. This control service represents an adaptive regulator, which is using cloud gateway to control the agents in the OT. Proposed concept is based on SOA, cloud and CPS. We used these technologies to monitor and control of plant floor processes. We used IoT gateway and machine learning to collect data, integrate, monitor, process, analyze, predict, and future control. We divided our concept into two main subchapter IoT Cloud/Field Gateway and machine learning (Fig. 3).

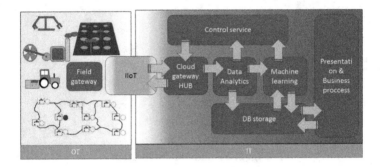

Fig. 3. Proposed architecture of IoT Gateway and Predictive Control

3.1 IIoT Cloud/Field Gateway

It already exists many devices and technologies, which connect individual subsystems to work together. They are called like a gateway or mediator. Industrial router, which is IoT field gateway. This router encapsulates industrial protocols and forwards data through the Ethernet interface. Such devices enable better interactivity with cloud services using M2M communication [10]. This type of gateway is a field gateway. On other hand, it exists software for IoT Cloud Software. The software enables to integrate production machines and processes with cloud service. It has a running instance in the cloud. This type of gateway is a cloud gateway. We focus on the interoperability with cloud services and low plant floor devices, which is based on services. The service interoperability is one of the SOA feature, which reflex the "working together" idea. Cloud services interoperates with relation, nonrelation databases, blob storages, third party services, web services and remote monitoring services. Therefore, the gateway is important in OT and IT integration. The proposed gateway can be implemented like a field gateway or like a cloud service gateway. The gateway concept definition and some results are published in [10]. Our concept helps to integrate network devices and data. It creates consistent and interoperable monitoring and control service between cloud and plant floor devices. The flexibility, interoperability, modularity is inherited from SOA [13]. The machine learning and predictive control are used to predict and control simple and predictable plant process. In our experiment, we selected a slow process due the cloud response time, which we had less than 1.1 s. The key role in monitoring and predictive control. Our next step is to improve plant floor device integrity and verified designed IoT gateway.

Today, the cloud system and some services has own graphical interface, which does not require a programming skills. What decreases implementation time and reliability [14]. Therefore, we would like to implement graphical configuration interface in our gateway in the future.

3.2   Machine Learning and Experiment Conditions

Enterprises want to increase performance and work efficiently, which is depending on machine learning and IIoT. Therefore, the data acquisition and integration are important for the enterprise. The machine learning predicts, prescribes and automates process in the plant. The prediction tries to describe behavior of the process in the future while nothing unforeseen will influence the processes. The prescription tries to offer better decisions, which are based on monitoring and recommendations. The automation tries control a monitored process in finding the best solution for each situation in real time. In this publication, we are focusing on the adaptive control with a prediction of the monitored process.

This part of concept receives data from data storage, IoT gateway or databases. The data are spited into train and evaluation set. Then we train model, which is used to predict process. After training and evaluation, we used this prediction model as cloud service. This allows better interoperability with other services in the cloud. The control service is a consumer of machine learning service, which offer process prediction. This prediction is used in adaptive control. The adaptive control is part of control service and its behavior depends on the prediction. The control service is used to control plant floor processes. The service sends control commands to plant floor devices thru the IoT gateway.

4   The Implemented Solution and Evaluation

We used the designed concept and applied it on the plant process. We focused on coke ovens that are one of the first production units in the steelmaking process. Blast-furnace coke or metallurgical coke is produced using the process of dry distillation of black coal in the ovens. For transport, coke needs to be cooled down with right amount of water. It is important to measure humidity in coke. We were not able to measure humidity of coke directly, because the coal is hot and moving. Therefore, we created model where we considered influence of atmospheric temperature on water evaporation from coal. Our experiment was realized in laboratory conditions. This use case is used as a proof of concept and it is not realized in all detail yet (Fig. 4).

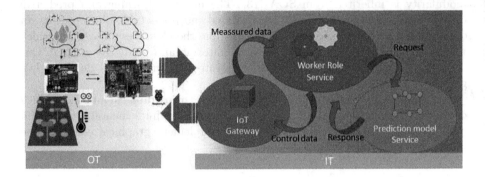

Fig. 4. Real-time representation of the predictive control solution

We have collected temperature data, integrate with our industry IoT field gateway. The gateway communicates with cloud gateway. The cloud gateway transfers the data to the listeners (cloud service listener). In our experiment, the worker role service is the listener. The worker role service represents a control service in the concept. This service contains an adaptive regulator that control the irrigation systems.

We used nearest weather station which is collecting atmospheric temperatures. We took data from past 3 years and we have built a prediction model. Example of predictions from semi-skilled model is presented on the graph in the Fig. 5. The prediction model was deployed like a service in the Azure. This service is consumed by the Worker role service. Worker service has own adaptive

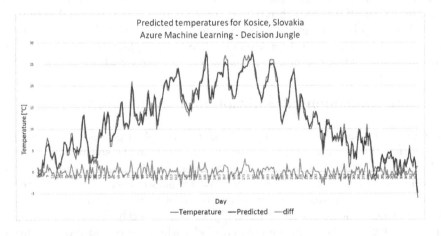

Fig. 5. Real-time representation of the predictive control solution

regulator, which adapts according the temperature and humidity prediction. The adaptation changes a behavior of the regulator. The regulator can better react on the predicated changes. Temperature and humidity changes can be better handle with regulator adaptation. Robustness and precision of the regulation is based on the prediction. Finally, the control from Worker role service is sent thru the IoT Gateway to the field gateway. This gateway communicates with the irrigation system and control the irrigation.

This proof of concept is more focusing on the architecture. We want to show a cooperation between services, which influences plant floor processes. As a final result, the direct control OT is better to place closer to OT. Our controlled system had a slower dynamics. Measured 1.1 s delay does not have a notable influence in control. Therefore, we could use cloud control service, which represents a plant floor controller.

5   Conclusions and Future Work

The CPS, IIoT, SOA, machine learning and cloud computing are technologies, which improve data acquisition, data integration and changing data into information and then into wisdom [10–13,15]. We focused on concept, which will improve data acquisition and control for smart manufacturing. We collect data into cloud - Microsoft Azure. We used our industrial IoT gateway, which collects and integrates data. After that, we used weather station data to build a prediction model for atmospheric temperatures. This prediction model was deployed as cloud service. This service is consumed by control service, which contains an adaptive regulator. This regulator adapts according data from service. On the other hand, control service controls plant floor process.

We want to increased industrial modularity, flexibility, efficiency, robustness and realize "working together" idea. Therefore, we have designed an IoT gateway and cloud services. The future work includes artificial intelligence methods and bigger amounts of data acquisition to better predicate and control processes. Our goal is to improve communication between services, machines and plant processes.

Acknowledgements. This publication is the result of the Project implementation: University Science Park TECHNICOM for Innovation Applications Supported by Knowledge Technology - II. phase, supported by the Research & Development Operational Programme funded by the ERDF (49%), Grants FEI 2015 FEI-2015-10 (1%) and by grant KEGA - 001TUKE-4/2015 (50%).

References

1. Atzori, L., Iera, A., Morabito, G.: The internet of things: a survey. Comput. Netw. **54**(15), 2787–2805 (2010)
2. Li, J., Biennier, F., Ghedira, C.: An agile governance method for multi-tier industrial architecture. In: Frick, J., Laugen, B.T. (eds.) APMS 2011. IAICT, vol. 384, pp. 506–513. Springer, Heidelberg (2012). doi:10.1007/978-3-642-33980-6_55

3. Kaihara, T., Kokuryo, D., Kuik, S.: A proposal of value co-creative production with IoT-based thinking factory concept for Tailor-made rubber products. In: Umeda, S., Nakano, M., Mizuyama, H., Hibino, H., Kiritsis, D., Cieminski, G. (eds.) APMS 2015. IAICT, vol. 460, pp. 67–73. Springer, Heidelberg (2015). doi:10. 1007/978-3-319-22759-7_8

4. Zuehlke, D.: SmartFactory-towards a factory-of-things. Ann. Rev. Control **34**(1), 129–138 (2010)

5. Brizzi, P., Conzon, D., Khaleel, H., Tomasi, R., Pastrone, C., Spirito, A., Knechtel, M., Pramudianto, F., Cultrona, P.: Bringing the internet of things along the manufacturing line: a case study in controlling industrial robot and monitoring energy consumption remotely. In: 2013 IEEE 18th Conference on Emerging Technologies and Factory Automation (ETFA), pp. 1–8. IEEE (2013)

6. Spiess, P., Karnouskos, S., Guinard, D., Savio, D., Baecker, O., De Souza, L.M.S., Trifa, V.: SOA-based integration of the internet of things in enterprise services. In: International Conference on Web Services, pp. 968–975. IEEE (2009)

7. Kulvatunyou, B.S., Cho, H., Son, Y.J.: A semantic web service framework to support intelligent distributed manufacturing. Int. J. Knowl. Based Intell. Eng. Syst. **9**(2), 107–127 (2005)

8. Lojka, T., Bundzel, M., Zolotová, I.: Industrial gateway for data acquisition and remote control. Acta Electrotechnica et Informatica **15**(2), 43–48 (2015)

9. Schuh, G., Potente, T., Thomas, C., Hauptvogel, A.: Cyber-physical production management. In: Prabhu, V., Taisch, M., Kiritsis, D. (eds.) APMS 2013. IAICT, vol. 415, pp. 477–484. Springer, Heidelberg (2013). doi:10.1007/ 978-3-642-41263-9_59

10. Zolotová, I., Bundzel, M., Lojka, T.: Industry IoT gateway for cloud connectivity. In: Umeda, S., Nakano, M., Mizuyama, H., Hibino, H., Kiritsis, D., Cieminski, G. (eds.) APMS 2015. IAICT, vol. 460, pp. 59–66. Springer, Heidelberg (2015). doi:10. 1007/978-3-319-22759-7_7

11. Tarkoma, S., Ailisto, H.: The internet of things program: the finnish perspective. IEEE Commun. Mag. **51**(3), 10–11 (2013)

12. Bloem, J., van Doorn, M., Duivestein, S., Excoffier, D., Maas, R., van Ommeren, E.: The Fourth Industrial Revolution. Things to Tighten the Link Between IT and OT (2014)

13. Lee, J., Bagheri, B., Kao, H.A.: A cyber-physical systems architecture for industry 4.0-based manufacturing systems. Manuf. Lett. **3**, 18–23 (2015)

14. Lojka, T., Zolotová, I.: Improvement of human-plant interactivity via industrial cloud-based supervisory control and data acquisition system. In: Grabot, B., Vallespir, B., Gomes, S., Bouras, A., Kiritsis, D. (eds.) APMS 2014. IAICT, vol. 440, pp. 83–90. Springer, Heidelberg (2014). doi:10.1007/978-3-662-44733-8_11

15. Jammes, F., Smit, H.: Service-oriented paradigms in industrial automation. IEEE Trans. Industr. Inf. **1**(1), 62–70 (2005)

The Paradigm Shift in Smart Manufacturing System Architecture

Yan Lu$^{(\boxtimes)}$, Frank Riddick, and Nenad Ivezic

Systems Integration Division, NIST, Gaithersburg, USA
{yan.lu,frank.riddick,nenad.ivezic}@nist.gov

Abstract. Smart Manufacturing seeks to integrate advanced manufacturing methods, operational technologies (OT), and information and communication technologies (ICT) to drive the creation of manufacturing systems with greater capabilities in cost control and performance. A crucial differentiation of smart manufacturing systems (SMS) lies in their architectures, which are organized as networks of cooperating manufacturing components specialized for different functions as opposed to the previous organization characterized by rigid, hierarchically-integrated layers of application components. This "ecosystem" of manufacturing components enables SMS that can provide heretofore unattainable levels of performance for manufacturers with respect to agility, productivity, and quality. This paper provides a study of the architectural impact of individual ICT technologies on the emerging manufacturing ecosystem that potentially eliminates the need to design manufacturing systems based on the hierarchical levels of the legacy ISA 95 model. Additionally, we propose a service-oriented SMS architecture that leverages the benefits of ICT and the safety and security requirements from the OT domain. Key challenges of implementing such architectures are also presented.

Keywords: System architecture · Smart manufacturing · Cyber physical production system · Service oriented architecture

1 Introduction

In the current market, customers call for products tailored to their particular needs. Manufacturers seek to meet the demand for these products, but many current manufacturing systems cannot meet the increased requirements for product customization at mass production rates that are profitable. Yet, advanced manufacturing methods, such as 3D printing and flexible production, are emerging with the promise to make highly-personalized production at scales both possible and affordable. Simultaneously, rapid advances in information and communications technologies (ICT) are being applied to manufacturing systems, driving a shift from traditional labor-intensive processes to advanced-technology-based processes [1]. This on-going integration of advanced manufacturing methods, operation technologies (OT), and the ICT technologies, is fueling the current Smart Manufacturing (SM) trend to enable systems that

---

© IFIP International Federation for Information Processing 2016 (outside the US)
Published by Springer International Publishing AG 2016. All Rights Reserved
I. Nääs et al. (Eds.): APMS 2016, IFIP AICT 488, pp. 767–776, 2016.
DOI: 10.1007/978-3-319-51133-7_90

can respond in real time to meet changing demands and conditions in the factory, in the supply network, and in customer needs [2].

Historically, manufacturing systems have been designed to follow the Purdue Reference Model for Computer Integrated Manufacturing [3], which was standardized in ISA95 [4]. The ISA 95 model includes 5 levels of manufacturing functions that are often implemented as logically separated layers of applications or systems. Specifically, lower level systems (0, 1 and 2) and higher levels applications (3 and 4) are separated into the OT[1] and information technology (IT) domains. The legacy architecture has been widely adopted and implemented in last 30 years accompanied by hierarchical, diverse and domain specific communication structure [8]. However, under the legacy architecture, not only is integration between IT and OT difficult, but skip-level function integration is not supported, which makes it too rigid to adapt rapidly to evolving opportunities from ICT technology integration. For example, in the Internet of Things (IoT) world, every part of a manufacturing enterprise is designed to be connected on the internet so that communication, integration and automation can be achieved without constraints. In addition, cloud and mobile computing enable manufacturing functions once implemented at different levels of the hierarchy to now be available without even knowing where they are hosted. Smart components and smarter systems on the shop floor can run advanced analytics and simulations, and make decisions beyond the lower functions defined in ISA 95.

This suggests that a new, information-centric architecture is needed in order to realize ICT's full potential for SMS and facilitate transformation of closed or proprietary manufacturing system architectures into networks of cooperating manufacturing components so as to attain higher degrees of flexibility and integration. This paper provides a study of the architectural impact of ICT on a manufacturing ecosystem and proposes a service oriented architecture that leverages the benefits of ICT and safety and security requirements from the manufacturing OT domain.

The rest of the paper is structured as follows. Section 2 defines a manufacturing ecosystem to scope our research followed by a description of the legacy architectural model based on ISA 95. Section 3 describes the key ICT technologies identified that contribute most to the SMS architecture paradigm shift and presents their architectural impacts on SMS. In Sect. 4 we propose a new SMS reference architecture. Key challenges of implementing such an architecture are presented. Section 5 concludes the paper with future research direction.

2 SMS and the Legacy Architecture

Smart manufacturing encompasses a broad scope of systems in a manufacturing business including production, management, design, and engineering functions. The collection of hardware components, their related software components, and the support applications that make up a manufacturing enterprise are what we term the smart

---

[1] Operational technology (OT) is hardware and software that detects or causes a change through the direct monitoring and/or control of physical devices, processes and events in the enterprise. http://www.gartner.com/it-glossary/operational-technology-ot/.

manufacturing ecosystem [5, 6]. Figure 1 illustrates three dimensions of concern that are manifest in the smart manufacturing ecosystem. Each dimension — product, production system, and business — is shown within its own lifecycle. Each of these dimensions comes into play in the vertical integration of machines, plants, and enterprise systems in what we call the Manufacturing Pyramid.

The Manufacturing Pyramid, in the center of Fig. 1, is often referred to as the manufacturing system and implemented based on the ISA 95 model. The ISA 95 standard defines a 5-level model for activities in the manufacturing enterprise. Each level provides specialized functions and has characteristic response times [7]. Level 0 and Level 1 define field-level activities including the actual physical production process and the sensing and manipulating of the process. Level 2 defines the functions of monitoring, automated control, and supervisory control of the production process, which usually are performed by programmable logic controllers (PLC), distributed control systems (DCS) and/or supervisory control and data acquisition systems (SCADA). Level 1 and Level 2 communicate within time frames on the order of hours, minutes, seconds, and sub-seconds. Level 3 defines the Manufacturing Operation Management (MoM) activities of work flow and stepping the process through states to produce the desired end products. It deals with maintaining records and optimizing the production process. Level 3 deals with time frames of days, shifts, hours, minutes, and seconds. Level 4 defines the Enterprise Resource Planning (ERP) activities to establish the production (master) schedule (i.e., what to produce, which materials to use, where to deliver the product, and how to ship it there). It deals with determining inventory levels and making sure that materials are delivered on time to the right place for production. Level 4 deals with time frames of months, weeks, days, and shifts.

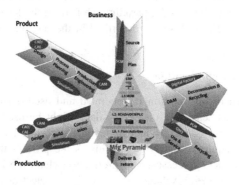

Fig. 1. Manufacturing ecosystem (Source: [2, 5, 6])

While the ISA 95 model is used widely to support the definition of architectures for manufacturing systems, recently some drawbacks with its use have emerged [8]. These drawbacks include:

(1) Integrating systems across level boundaries is difficult due in part to the use of different network technologies on different levels.

(2) Integrating between Supply Chain Management (SCM), Customer Relation Management (CRM), and Product Lifecycle Management (PLM) activities on different ecosystem dimensions is not supported.

Various methods have attempted to deal with the drawbacks of systems architected based on the ISA95 model. Some software vendors and system integrators have provided solutions focused on the vertical integration of manufacturing components in the manufacturing pyramid to enable advanced controls at the shop floor and optimal decision making at the plant and enterprise. Efforts have also been observed that focus on exchanging information between manufacturing ecosystem dimensions, such as continuous process improvement (CPI) programs, flexible manufacturing systems (FMS), and design for manufacturing and assembly (DFMA) approaches. Some lean enterprise efforts connect SCM with ERP to reduce inventory and enable demand-based manufacturing [6]. However, these individual efforts fall short in providing widely applicable methods for integration within and across the three ecosystem dimensions required for SMS. The combination of these perspectives requires a new reference architecture.

3   Architectural Impacts of ICT Technologies

For our study, ICT technologies are classified in three clusters: (1) digital technology including digital thread, product/production/process modeling and simulation, knowledge management, and visualization; (2) infrastructure technology including IoT, big data and advanced computing; and (3) Smart systems technology involving Cyber Physical Production System (CPPS) and service-oriented architecture. All technology of the three clusters contribute to the paradigm shift from the legacy architectures to a new SMS architecture. Each cluster is described in the sections below.

3.1   The Impact of Digitalization

An enormous amount of information is generated and used during the product, production system and business lifecycles. This data might be used to ensure customer requirements are met, to assess product and process performance, or to meet environmental reporting requirements. Digitalization is the process through which information about the product, processes, and production chain are rendered in a digital form that can be archived, exchanged, or analyzed electronically. Digitalization capabilities help manufacturing companies create virtual representations of their products, assets and processes, exchange large amounts of data rapidly, store data efficiently, enrich processes with digital expert knowledge, generate valuable insights from analyzing "big data", and facilitate communication and collaboration through digital channels within their value chain [9].

The pervasive adoption of digital technology will have two dominant impacts on SMS and their architecture.

(1) There will be an increase in the availability of collaborative environments for product development. Their architectures will exhibit a tighter integration of PLM, ERP, MES, SCM, CRM and asset management functions. These platforms will enable customers and suppliers to directly participate in product design and manufacturing. In this way, high-quality customized products can be manufactured and increased traceability can be achieved. Direct feedback from manufacturing and product use to product development will shorten product innovation cycles.

(2) Digital representations of products, physical assets, production operations, and business processes will enable the creation of a digital "twin" of the factory—a comprehensive virtual representation of a real factory and its processes that can be made to run in parallel to the real factory [20]. Models and simulations can be instantiated with product and production system data and used in the real factory decision making processes to optimize business, manufacturing, and supply chain operations and to improve product development processes. At the same time, the data coming from the real factory can be fed back to the digital factory to improve the models, knowledge bases, and simulations (Fig. 2).

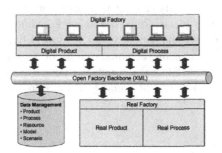

Fig. 2. Digital twin for manufacturing (Source: [9])

3.2 The Impact of IoT

The development and adoption of the Internet of Things (IoT) is a critical element of Smart Manufacturing [10]. The technologies that will become pervasive because of the IoT—network-addressable physical and application components and standard communication protocols through which those components can communicate—will enable enterprise architectures, in general, and industrial system architectures, in particular, to move on from their traditional hierarchically and domain-specific network structure to a unified and IP-based structure [11], as shown in Fig. 3. This shift will enable enterprise services, such as data analytics and edge computing services, that today are typically only available at the highest levels of an enterprise to be available to serve system components in all areas of the industrial enterprise.

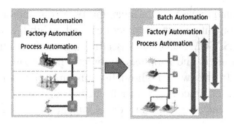

Fig. 3. Ubiquitously connected manufacturing systems (Source: adapted from [11])

The transition to more open network architectures, combined with Big Data and Cloud computing, will bring profound opportunities to SMS. At the same time, new security challenges are presented with billions of new smart devices being interconnected in the world of the IoT [12]. The biggest security concern comes from connecting IoT devices, sensors, actuators and edge-computing units, with existing controllers, automation and manufacturing information networks, and applications. Existing OT and IT security approaches and policies will need to be adapted to embrace these new IoT security challenges. Most automation and information suppliers have established industry security services to assist clients to assess security risks and harden their manufacturing plants. Reference network architectures are available from both network equipment and automation system vendors [13]. Additional challenges of integrating IoT include unreliable communications of sensors and actuators on IP networks, how to leverage IoT to boost computing power for advanced manufacturing analytics, and accessibility issues of gaining accesses to the legacy manufacturing assets.

3.3   The Impact of CPPS

While the IoT deals with unique, identifiable, and internet-connected physical objects, cyber-physical systems efforts are concerned with the nature of cyber-physical coupling and the system of systems characteristics of networked and software-controlled systems. CPPS is considered the core component for German Industrie 4.0 program, where they are also referred to as I4.0 Components [14]. SMS are essentially composed of CPPS, which can respond intelligently to changing tasks and conditions and reconfigure themselves. CPPSs partly break the traditional automation pyramid and potentially turn the manufacturing ecosystem into a service-oriented architecture (SOA) [15, 16]. To leverage the safety and security requirements from the OT domain, real-time and safety critical functions in legacy automation systems will remain organized in a hierarchy, and only level 2 components will be allowed to connect as services. IoT devices connected in the IT world will naturally be part of the service-oriented architecture. Figure 4 shows how the legacy hierarchical functional architecture will be transformed to a SOA-based manufacturing system architecture.

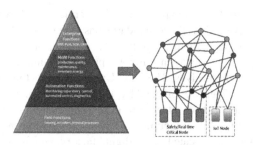

Fig. 4. CPPS impact on manufacturing system function architecture (Source: adopted from [19])

4   Smart Manufacturing Architecture

With the architectural impacts from ICT technologies in mind, we propose a SOA for Smart Manufacturing systems.

As shown in Fig. 5, the proposed architecture provides a completely integrated manufacturing ecosystem on a single manufacturing service bus, including both OT domain systems and IT domain systems and applications. Interactions with suppliers, customers, and logistics systems are enabled through a collaborative Business intelligence (BI) service.

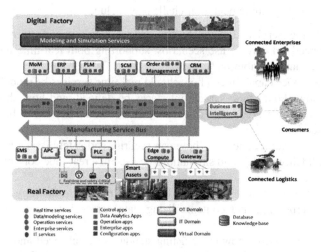

Fig. 5. A service oriented and model based SMS architecture

In the new architecture, services are classified as being one of four types: IT domain services, OT domain services, virtual domain services and management/common services. IT domain services include IoT services (e.g., smart devices, edge computing, fog computing, cloud computing, etc.), MoM services, ERP services, PLM services, and other enterprise services such as Asset Management, Energy Management, SCM, Order Management and CRM. The integration approach that will be used for IT domain services is similar to today's enterprise service bus (ESB) based approach, which is built using event-driven and standards-based message-oriented middleware in combination with message queues. In the OT domain, services involve functions provided by machines, workstations, robots, production lines, complete production cells or even products themselves. The OPC Unified Architecture (OPC UA) provides interoperability at level 2 and beyond and has the potential to provide a service-oriented architecture for OT application integration [14]. Data analytics services are provided through edge computing, fog computing and cloud computing in the IoT world [18]. Virtual domain services are located in the digital factory, which stores the data models, function models, behavior models, and process models of a manufacturing enterprise and provides query and simulation functions for manufacturing applications. Management/common services sit at the core of the SOA architecture. They help manage the lifecycle of the SMS services, map client requests with service providers, and ensure quality of service levels met. Device management, network configuration, data management, knowledge management, and security management are provided by services in this cluster.

Based on the architecture described above, SMS can be developed and deployed that provide efficient and flexible solutions for the problems faced by the modern manufacturing enterprise. Supporting more streamlined processes, the SOA-based architecture enables customized production at mass production rates.

However, implementing the proposed architecture to create new SMS is neither simple, quick, nor cheap. It will take many years to fully realize the strength of the new architecture. The key implementation challenges include:

- Manufacturing Service Bus capabilities - can a single manufacturing service bus meet the needs of diverse use scenarios, supporting both real-time messaging and big volume data distribution?
- Real-time service capabilities - how should real-time services be modeled in the OT domain, how should their service interfaces be defined, and how should resource constraints be managed, i.e., when and where should resources be available to provide services?
- IT – OT integration concerns - how can security and safety issues be handled?
- Can high fidelity models and simulations be used in a real-time control environment without re-engineering?
- Knowledge management concerns – how can we close technology gaps in conditioning, interpreting, and contextualizing data across heterogeneous systems or situations?
- Integration standards - how can existing standards be enhanced and new standards be developed to enable more information flow among more stakeholders.

5   Conclusion

In a new era of smart manufacturing, every part of a manufacturing enterprise will be digitized and connected. With the introduction of smart devices accessible as services on a network, more embedded intelligence at every level, predictive analytics, and cloud technology, the next generation of manufacturing systems will indeed get smarter. In order to realize the vision of smart manufacturing where systems respond in real time to changing demands and conditions in the factory, in the supply network, and in customer needs, the classical manufacturing system architectural paradigm based on a hierarchical control model will no longer dominate. A new paradigm based on distributed manufacturing services is starting to be adopted.

This paper described a smart manufacturing ecosystem that enabled systems integration within and across three manufacturing lifecycle dimensions – product lifecycle, production system lifecycle, and business lifecycle. We examined how the introduction of ICT is going to impact the SMS architecture. Adoption of IoT, CPPS and cloud computing technology potentially will drive the transformation of the existing rigid hierarchical architecture style. Digital thread and digital factory technology will enable the enterprise to be fully integrated with its value chain. Based on the study of the ICT architectural impact, we propose an SOA-based and model-enabled Smart Manufacturing reference architecture. The proposed reference architecture will integrate both ICT and OT systems on a single manufacturing service bus. We discussed implementation challenges that include standards for communication protocols, data model, knowledge representation, and CPPS characterization that are necessary to facilitate the adoption of Smart Manufacturing technology and the proposed architecture.

Disclaimer. Any mention of commercial products is for information only; it does not imply recommendation or endorsement by NIST.

References

1. Institute for Defense Analyses. https://www.wilsoncenter.org/sites/default/files/Emerging_Global_Trends_in_Advanced_Manufacturing.pdf
2. Frechette, S., Morris, K.C., Lu, Y.: Smart Manufacturing Isn't So Smart Without Standards. http://blog.mesa.org/2016/03/smart-manufacturing-isnt-so-smart.html
3. Williams, T.J.: The Purdue Enterprise Reference Architecture: A Technical Guide for CIM Planning and Implementation. Instrument Society of America (1992)
4. ANSI/ISA-95.00.01-2010 (IEC 62264-1 Mod): Enterprise-Control System Integration - Part 1: Models and Terminology (2010)
5. Lu, Y., Morris, K.C., Frechette, S.P.: Standards landscape and directions for smart manufacturing systems. In: IEEE Conference on Automation Science and Engineering, Gothensburg (2015)
6. Lu, Y., Morris, K.C., Frechette, S.P.: Current Standards Landscape for Smart Manufacturing Systems, NISTIR 8107 (2016)
7. Brandl, D.: The IT Implications of ISA 95 and ISA 99. http://www.brlconsulting.com/Files/The%20IT%20Implications%20S95%20and%20S99.pdf
8. LNS Research: Agile MES and IIoT: How the Traditional Hierarchies in Manufacturing Operations Management Are Being Dissolved, Webinar, 29 February 2016
9. Wolfgang, K.: Digital factory-integration of simulation enhancing the product and production process towards operative control and optimisation. Int. J. Simul.: Syst. Sci. Technol. **7**(7), 27–39 (2006)
10. Lopez Research. https://www.iotwf.com/resources/6

11. Guido, S.: Internet of Thing and Services, Siemens Future Forum@ Hanover Messe 2014. https://w3.siemens.com/topics/global/en/events/hannover-messe/program/Documents/pdf/Internet-of-Things-and-Services-Guido-Stephan.pdf

12. Davidson, M.: IoT in Manufacturing Hurdle #2: New Security Challenges, July 2014. http://blog.lnsresearch.com/blog/bid/199506/IoT-in-Manufacturing-Hurdle-2-New-Security-Challenges

13. GE's Intelligent Platforms Business & CISCO. http://www.cisco.com/c/dam/en_us/solutions/industries/docs/manufacturing/architecting-robust.pdf

14. VDI/VDE Society Measurement and Automatic Control (GMA), Reference Architecture Model Industrie 4.0 (RAMI4.0) (2015)

15. Boyd, A., Noller, D., Peters, P., Salkeld, D., Thomasma, T., Gifford, C., Pike, S., Smith, A.: SOA in Manufacturing—guidebook. MESA International, IBM Corporation and Capgemini Co-Branded White Paper (2008)

16. IBM: SOA Approach to Enterprise Integration for Product Lifecycle Management. IBM, International Technical Support Organization (2008)

17. Monostori, L.: Cyber-physical production systems: roots, expectations and R&D challenges. CIRP **17**, 9–13 (2014)

18. Abdelshkour, M.: IoT, from Cloud to Fog Computing. http://blogs.cisco.com/perspectives/iot-from-cloud-to-fog-computing

19. Vogel-Heuser, G., Kegel, G., Bender, K., Wucherer, K.: Global information architecture for industrial automation. In: Automatisierungstechnische Praxis (atp). Oldenbourg-Verlag, Muenchen (2009)

20. Michael Grieves. http://innovate.fit.edu/plm/documents/doc_mgr/912/1411.0_Digital_Twin_White_Paper_Dr_Grieves.pdf

A Hybrid Method for Manufacturing Text Mining Based on Document Clustering and Topic Modeling Techniques

Peyman Yazdizadeh Shotorbani[1], Farhad Ameri[1(✉)],
Boonserm Kulvatunyou[2], and Nenad Ivezic[2]

[1] Engineering Informatics Group, Texas State University, San Marcos, USA
`ameri@txstate.edu`
[2] National Institute of Standards and Technology (NIST), Gaithersburg, USA
`{boonserm.kulvatunyou,nenad.ivezic}@nist.gov`

Abstract. As the volume of online manufacturing information grows steadily, the need for developing dedicated computational tools for information organization and mining becomes more pronounced. This paper proposes a novel approach for facilitating search and organization of textual documents and also extraction of thematic patterns in manufacturing corpora using document clustering and topic modeling techniques. The proposed method adopts K-means and Latent Dirichlet Allocation (LDA) algorithms for document clustering and topic modeling, respectively. Through experimental validation, it is shown that topic modeling, in conjunction with document clustering, facilitates automated annotation and classification of manufacturing webpages as well as extraction of useful patterns, thus improving the intelligence of supplier discovery and knowledge acquisition tools.

Keywords: Text mining · Topic modeling · Document clustering · Supplier discovery · Manufacturing service · Knowledge acquisition

1 Introduction

Manufacturing companies are increasingly enhancing their web presence in order to improve their visibility in the global market and generate high quality leads. Besides using conventional webpages, manufacturing companies publish online white papers, case studies, newsletters, blogs, info-graphics, and webinars to advertise their capabilities and expertise. This has resulted in rapid growth in the volume of online manufacturing information in an unprecedented rate. The online manufacturing information is typically presented in an unstructured format using natural language text.

The growth in the size and variety of unstructured information poses both challenges and opportunities. The challenge is related to efficient information search and retrieval when dealing with a large volume of heterogeneous and unstructured information. Traditional search methods, such as keyword search, with their limited semantic capabilities, can no longer meet the information retrieval and organization needs of the cyber manufacturing era. More advanced computational tools and

© IFIP International Federation for Information Processing 2016
Published by Springer International Publishing AG 2016. All Rights Reserved
I. Nääs et al. (Eds.): APMS 2016, IFIP AICT 488, pp. 777–786, 2016.
DOI: 10.1007/978-3-319-51133-7_91

techniques are needed that can facilitate search, organization, and summarization of large bodies of text more effectively. At the same time, the unstructured text available on the Internet contains valuable information that can be extracted and transformed into business intelligence to support knowledge-based systems.

In this paper, a hybrid text mining technique is proposed for processing and categorizing plain-language manufacturing narratives and extracting useful patterns and unseen connections from them. Text mining is the process of deriving new, previously unknown, information from textual resources [5]. There exist multiple text mining techniques, such as summarization, classification, clustering, topic modeling, and association rule mining that can be applied to the manufacturing documents. Text mining techniques are either supervised or unsupervised. In supervised (also known as predictive) techniques, fully labeled data is used for training machine learning algorithms, whereas in unsupervised (also known as descriptive) techniques, no training dataset is required. Supplier classification using supervised text mining technique was previously proposed and implemented [1].

In this research, two unsupervised text mining techniques, namely, clustering based on k-means algorithm and topic modeling based on LDA algorithm, are adopted. Clustering is the process of grouping documents into clusters based on their content similarity, while topic modeling is a method for finding recurring patterns of co-occurring words in large bodies of texts [7]. Clustering and toping modeling can be regarded as complementary techniques since the unlabeled clusters, as the output of clustering process, can be characterized and described by their core theme using topic modeling technique. The primary objective of this research is to use document clustering to build clusters of manufacturing suppliers and to use topic modeling to identify the core concepts that form the underlying theme of each cluster. Organization of manufacturing capability narratives into various clusters with known properties will improve the efficiency of the supplier discovery process. Furthermore, extraction of hidden patterns from the capability narratives could lead to generation of useful information and insights about new trends and developments in manufacturing technology.

This paper is organized as follows. The next section discusses the relevant literature in text analytics. The proposed hybrid method is presented in Sect. 3. This section also provides information about a proof-of-concept experimentation and validation. The paper ends with concluding remarks.

2 Background and Related Works

Text mining has already been applied in areas ranging from pharmaceutical drug discovery to spam filtering and summarizing and monitoring customer reviews [9]. In the manufacturing domain, however, it is a relatively new undertaking.

Kung et al. [2] used text classification techniques for identifying quality-related problems in semiconductor manufacturing based on the unstructured data available in hold records. Dong and Liu [3] proposed a tool for manufacturing website classification in based on determined genres for the websites [3]. Their proposed website classifier works based on a hybrid Support Vector Machine (SVM) algorithm. However, SVM is a supervised technique that requires high quality training data. Therefore, in absence of well-prepared training data, the proposed approach will not yield the expected outcome. To address this issue, researchers have adopted unsupervised approaches that eliminated the need for preparation of pre-labeled data. Topic modeling [4] and Clustering [5] are two prominent unsupervised methods for text classification and mining. While Clustering is a long existing technique, topic modeling is considered to be a relatively new method. Topic modeling techniques are used to discover the underlying patterns of textual data. Probabilistic Latent Semantic Analysis (PLSA) is one of the first topic modeling techniques introduced by Hofmann [6]. PLSA is a statistical technique that discovers the underlying semantic structure of data [7]. PLSA assumes a document is a combination of various topics. Therefore, by having a small set of latent topics or variables, the model can generate the related words of particular topics in a document. One successful application of PLSA is in the bioinformatics context where it is being applied for prediction of Gene Ontology annotations [8]. However, PLSA can suffer from over-fitting problems [9]. Latent Dirichlet Allocation (LDA) [10] extends the PLSA generative model. In LDA method, every document is seen as a mixture of different topics. This is similar to the PLSA, except that topic distribution in LDA has a Dirichlet prior which results in having more practical mixtures of topics in a document. LDA, as a method for topic modeling, has been used in different applications. For instance, [11] discusses a LDA-based topic modeling technique that automatically finds the thematic patterns on Reuters dataset. The main distinctive feature of their proposed method is that it incrementally builds and updates a model of emerging topics from text streams as opposed to static text corpora. Some researchers have applied LDA method to public sentiments and opinion mining in product reviews [12, 13]. Application of LDA-based topic modeling for exploring offline historical corpora is discussed in [14, 15].

Most of the existing methods use either clustering or topic modeling techniques to help users categorize existing data and infer new information from unstructured data. This paper proposes a hybrid model based on clustering and topic modeling methods to facilitate online search and organization of manufacturing capability narratives and also extraction of thematic patterns in manufacturing corpora.

3   Proposed Methodology for Text Mining

The standard method for web-based information search and retrieval is the keyword-based method. For example, in a supplier search scenario, a customer from the medical industry who is looking for precision machining services can simply use precision machining and medical equipment as the search keywords in a generic search engine. Nevertheless, the sheer size of the returned set would undermine the usefulness of the search result. One way to make the results more useful is to present them to the user as chunks or clusters of similar documents and then characterize each cluster using a set of features or themes. In the precision machining example, a cluster characterized by features such as precision machining, medical industry, inspection, and assembly would be of interest for the user if inspection and assembly were the secondary services that the user is looking for. This work proposes a hybrid text mining technique, which facilitates automatic clustering and characterization of the documents available in a large manufacturing corpus. The overall structure of the proposed approach is demonstrated in Fig. 1. As can be seen in this figure, the proposed approach is composed of four major steps as described below.

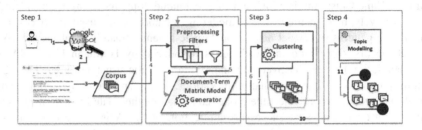

Fig. 1. The proposed hybrid classifier

3.1   Step 1: Building the Corpus

The first step is to create a corpus of manufacturing documents to be used as the test data. The scope of this work was limited to the suppliers of CNC machining and metal casting services. Therefore, to collect relevant websites, a generic web search based on a few keywords such as machining service, contract manufacturing, casting service, milling, turning, and sand casting were used. This keyword-based search is intended to return a set of webpages related to providers of contract manufacturing services. The keywords are selected subjectively based on the requirements of the search scenario and no particular protocol or guideline is used for keyword selection in this work. Each document (i.e., webpages) in the returned set was converted into a text-only document with the XML format. The XML format, due to its generality and simplicity, can be used across different platforms and applications. Figure 2 illustrates an example of a

```
<?xml version="1.0" encoding="UTF-8"?>
<Info>
    <Type>Casting</Type>
    <text> ISO 9001:2008 certified manufacturer
        of castings including machined finished
        castings. Capabilities include precision
        manufacturing, designing, building,
        repairing, milling, lathe work, assembly,
        grinding, metal stamping, EDM, welding,
        turning, reverse engineering, injection
        molding, CAD, custom labeling, pad
        printing silk screening. Kan Ban vendor
        managed inventory programs available.
        On-time delivery. Custom manufacturer
        of castings in alloys including
        continuously cast gray ductile iron, 6061
        T6 aluminum, SAE 660 bronze , chrome
        1045, 5041, 1018 1117 steel. Capabilities
        include finished machining of parts from
        0.5 in. to 8.0 in. dia., centerless grinding,
        boring, rough turning, cut-to-length plate
        cutting . Mid to high-volume production
        capabilities from 100 to 100,000 piece
        runs. Rods, bars, bearings, bushings,
        forgings, plates sheets are also available.
        </text>
    </Info>
```

Fig. 2. XML-based representation of a document in the corpus

website that is converted to the XML format with only two tags, namely, type and text. A corpus containing 100 XML documents with 13544 terms was created for experimental validation of the proposed approach.

3.2 Step 2: Customized Preprocessing of the Corpus

Corpus documents need to be noise-free before they can be analyzed and mined efficiently. Corpus preprocessing entails removing the redundant and less informative terms in order to create a clean corpus. The first preprocessing step is to remove numbers, punctuations, and symbols. The next step is to remove the stop words that do not contain significant manufacturing information. The words such as "quote", "inquire", "call", "type", "request", "contact", and "address" that frequently appear in manufacturing websites, but has marginal information about the manufacturing capability, belong to this category. After the removal of numbers, punctuations, symbols, and stop words, the number of words in the corpus is reduced to 10357. Word stemming is the next step in preprocessing which deals with reducing the derived words into their word stem. For example, terms such as "casted" and "casting" are stemmed to "cast". This step is necessary for reducing the dimensionality of data and improving the computational efficiency of the text analytics algorithms. Stemming reduces the number of words to 7470.

The last preprocessing step is to generate the Document-Term Matrix (DTM) for the manufacturing corpus. DTM is a matrix containing the frequency of the terms in the manufacturing documents. In the DTM, documents are denoted by rows and the terms are represented by columns. If a term is repeated n times in a specific document, the value of its corresponding cell in the matrix is n. The DTM represents the vector model of the corpus and is used as the input to the next step, document clustering.

3.3 Step 3: Document Clustering

This step involves creating groups of similar documents in the corpus. In this work, a K-Means clustering algorithm is implemented which automatically clusters the documents of the corpus such that documents in a cluster are more similar to each other than the documents in other clusters. In K-Means clustering technique, the user needs to specify the number of clusters (K) in advance [16]. Then the algorithm defines K centroids, one for each cluster. The next step is to assign each document to the nearest centroid. The distance from a document to the centroids of the clusters is calculated based on the projection of multidimensional DTM on Euclidean planes. The objective function of the k-means algorithms is to minimize the sum of square of distances from the data points (i.e., documents) to the clusters. Therefore, multiple iterations are required until the convergence condition is met. The main steps of the clustering algorithm are listed below: 1. Randomly distribute the documents among the K predefined clusters; 2. Calculate the position of the centroid of each cluster; 3. Calculate the distance between each document and each centroid; 4. Assign each document to the closets centroid; 5. Iterate over steps 1 to 4 until each document is assigned to at least one cluster, no document is relocated to a new cluster, and the convergence condition is met.

To estimate the proper number of clusters in the dataset, the Sum of Squared Error (SSE) method is used in this work. SSE refers to the sum of the squared distance between each document of a cluster and the centroid of the cluster. The corpus holds 100 documents. Therefore, the value of K ranges from 2 to 99. The challenge is to select the proper number of clusters through investigating the SSE corresponding to each cluster. Generally, as it is depicted in Fig. 3, when the number of clusters increases from 2 to 99, the SSE decreases since the clusters become smaller in size.

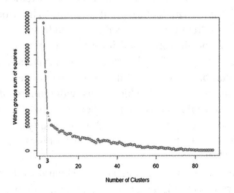

Fig. 3. SSE curve for different values of k

Based on the SSE plot, the suggested number of clusters is determined by the point where the sharp drop in SSE ends [16]. This points is referred to as the elbow point. As can be seen in Fig. 4, the elbow point occurs where the number of clusters is equal to 3. Therefore, three clusters were generated for this particular dataset. These three clusters with their assigned manufacturing documents are illustrated in Fig. 4.

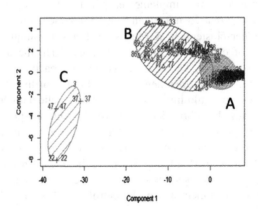

Fig. 4. Result of clustering

The plot of clustering result, shown in Fig. 4, is obtained based on a dimension reduction technique called Principle Component Analysis (PCA). The proposed clustering algorithm is based on the number of words in the corpus (7470 words or dimensions) which makes it impossible to visualize the documents of the clusters. To overcome this problem, PCA is used to enable the projection all data points (i.e., documents) on a 2D plane.

As it can be seen in the plot, the two upper right clusters (clusters A and B) have partial overlap, while the third cluster (Cluster C) in the lower left corner is clearly distinct from the other two. After inspecting the clusters, it was revealed that the members of the over-lapped clusters (A and B) were the websites of contract manufacturers who offer machining and casting services. The distinctive feature of the overlapping clusters is the depth of information provided by the member websites. The websites in cluster A contain general and high-level information about the type of process and services the suppliers offer while the websites in cluster B provide more detailed information about the type of processes, sub-processes, secondary services, and materials offered by the company. Cluster C mainly contained trade websites, blogs, or technical white papers. This experiment demonstrated that the clustering algorithm can successfully build meaningful clusters based on the type and nature of documents and also the level of detail incorporated in them. However, the clustering algorithm did not make a distinction between machining and casting websites. Also, it is not possible to learn about the characteristics of each cluster without exploring each cluster and investigating its contents. To further analyze and explore each cluster automatically, topic modeling technique is used in the next step. Cluster B, which contains 50 documents, is selected as the input to the topic modeling process.

3.4   Step 4: Topic Modeling

Document clustering results in partitioning a heterogeneous dataset into multiple clusters with more similar members. However, it doesn't provide any description or characterization for the generated clusters. Topic Modeling is a text mining technique for analyzing large volumes of unlabeled text. Latent Dirichlet Allocation (LDA) is used as the underlying algorithm for topic modeling. LDA technique can be used for automatically discovering abstract topics in a group of unlabeled documents. A topic is a recurring pattern of words that frequently appear together. For example, in a collection of documents that are related to banking, the terms such as interest, credit, saving, checking, statement, and APR define a topic as they co-occur frequently in the documents. LDA technique assumes that each document in the dataset is randomly composed of a combination of all available topics with different probabilities for each. The basic steps of the LDA technique are listed below. The reader is referred to [4] for more detailed discussion of the LDA technique:

1. For each document d, randomly allocate each word in the document to one of the t topics. This random allocation provides topic representations of all the documents and also distributions of words of all the topics.
2. For each document d, calculate two values.

a. p (topic t | document d), which is the proportion of words in document d which are currently assigned to topic t.

b. p (word w | topic t), which is the proportion of allocations to topic t over all available documents that are using word w.

3. Reassign the word w to a new topic.

4. Repeat the steps 1 through 3 until a steady state is achieved where the word-to-topic assignments sound meaningful.

As the last stage of the experiment, the application is run to find a predetermined number of topics in the dataset. The number of topics depends on the diversity of the documents in the dataset. More diverse documents discuss more topics, whereas more focused documents are centered around only a few themes. In this experiment, the desirable number of topics was set to four after studying the documents and their themes. Table 1 shows these four topics and their 10 most frequent words.

Table 1. Top 10 stemmed terms in Topic 1 through Topic 4

	Topic 1	Topic 2	Topic 3	Topic 4
1	Turn	Cast	CNC	Machine
2	Service	Die	Turn	Custom
3	Steel	Mold	Part	Process
4	Industry	Aluminum	Tool	Product
5	Component	Sand	Equip	Quality
6	Alloy	Housing	Mill	Manufacture
7	Format	Iron	Material	High
8	Stainless	Rang	Product	Engine
9	Standard	Test	Chuck	Grind
10	Aerospace	System	Precision	Provide

From Table 1, it can be inferred that Topic 2 is mainly about casting processes while Topic 3 corresponds to the turning and milling processes. However, as mentioned earlier, each document can address more than one topic. The LDA addresses this issue by returning topic probabilities associated with each document. Table 2 lists these probabilities for five example documents in the dataset.

From Table 2, it can be concluded that the first document belongs to topic 3 which is mainly about CNC machining services. Also, the calculated probabilities suggest that the fourth document belongs to topic 2, which corresponds to the casting process and

Table 2. Documents and their topic probabilities

Document	Topic 1	Topic 2	Topic 3	Topic 4
1.xml	0.091	**0.166**	**0.554**	**0.187**
2.xml	**0.609**	0.053	0.223	0.113
4.xml	0.149	**0.659**	0.085	0.105
5.xml	**0.215**	**0.203**	**0.226**	**0.354**

services. Furthermore, document 5 equally discusses topics 1 through 5 which implies that the supplier pertaining to this document is not specialized in only one manufacturing process. The performance of the proposed technique can be improved in time by adding more terms to the list of stop words that will be filtered out at the preprocessing stage. For example, the terms component and format under topic 1 are not as informative as the other terms in the group and can be eliminated from the vector model.

4 Conclusions

This paper presents a hybrid text mining method based on document clustering and topic modeling techniques. The objective of the proposed method is to build clusters of manufacturing websites and discover the hidden patterns and themes in the identified clusters. Furthermore, it harvests the key manufacturing concepts that can be imported into manufacturing thesauri and ontologies. Given the unsupervised nature of the algorithms used in this work, there is no need to prepare training data. This significantly reduces the initial setup cost and time. The results provided in this paper are only based on a single run of the mining process. The performance of the proposed method can be further improved through multiple iterations and subsequent elimination of less informative words under each topic. When highly informative terms are clustered together under a topic, the likelihood of discovering useful patterns in data increases. The corpus used in this proof-of-concept implementation contains only 100 documents. To reap the true benefits of text mining in manufacturing, the size of the corpus has to be significantly larger.

There are multiple areas that can be further explored in the future. One future task is to evaluate the performance of different topic modeling algorithms that can be used in the proposed framework. In the current implementation, the number of topics is determined upfront by the user, but there is a need for calculating the optimum number of topics in the corpus automatically.

Acknowledgement. The work described in this paper was funded in part by NIST cooperative agreement with Texas State University No. 70NANB14H255.

References

1. Yazdizadeh, P., Ameri, F.: A text mining technique for manufacturing supplier classification. In: 35th Computers and Information in Engineering (CIE) Conference, ASME IDETC 2015 (2015)
2. Liu, Y., Kung, J, James, L., Hsu, Y.B.: Using text mining to handle unstructured data in semiconductor manufacturing. In: Joint e-Manufacturing and Design Collaboration Symposium (eMDC), International Symposium on Semiconductor Manufacturing (ISSM), pp. 1–3. IEEE, Piscataway (2015)
3. Dong, B., Liu, H.: Enterprise website topic modeling and web resource search. In: Sixth International Conference on Intelligent Systems Design and Applications (2006)
4. Blei, D.: Probabilistic topic models. Commun. ACM **55**(4), 77–84 (2012)

5. Manning, C., Raghavan, P., Schütze, H.: Introduction to Information Retrieval. Cambridge University Press, New York (2008)
6. Hofmann, T.: Probabilistic latent semantic indexing. In: Proceedings of the 15th Conference on Uncertainty in Artificial Intelligence (1999)
7. Steyvers, M., Griffiths, T.L.: Probabilistic topic models. In: Landauer, T., McNamara, D., Dennis, S., Kintsch, W. (eds.) Latent Semantic Analysis: A Road to Meaning. Laurence Erlbaum (2005)
8. Masseroli, M., Chicco, D., Pinoli, P.: Probabilistic latent semantic analysis for prediction of gene ontology annotations. In: The 2012 International Joint Conference on Neural Networks (2012)
9. Alghamdi, R., Alfalqi, K.: A survey of topic modeling in text mining. Int. J. Adv. Comput. Sci. Appl. **6**(1) (2015)
10. Blei, D.M., Ng, A.Y., Jordan, M.I.: Latent dirichlet allocation. J. Mach. Learn. Res. **3**, 993–1022 (2003)
11. AlSumait, L., Barbará, D., Domeniconi, C.: On-line LDA: adaptive topic models for mining text streams with applications to topic detection and tracking. In: 2008 Eighth IEEE International Conference on Data Mining (2008)
12. Shulong, T., Yang, L., Huan, S., Ziyu, G., Xifeng, Y., Jiajun, B., Chun, C., Xiaofei, H.: Interpreting the public sentiment variations on Twitter. IEEE Trans. Knowl. Data Eng. **26**(5), 1158–1170 (2014)
13. Zhai, Z., Liu, B., Xu, H., Jia, P.: Constrained LDA for grouping product features in opinion mining. In: Huang, J.Z., Cao, L., Srivastava, J. (eds.) PAKDD 2011. LNCS (LNAI), vol. 6634, pp. 448–459. Springer, Heidelberg (2011). doi:10.1007/978-3-642-20841-6_37
14. Hu, Y., Boyd-Graber, J., Satinoff, B., Smith, A.: Interactive topic modeling. Mach. Learn. **95**(3), 423–469 (2013)
15. Yang, T.I., Torget, A.J., Mihalcea, R.: Topic modeling on historical newspapers. In: Proceedings of the 5th ACL-HLT Workshop on Language Technology for Cultural Heritage, Social Sciences, and Humanities, pp. 96–104 (2011)
16. Kodinariya, T.M., Makwana, P.R.: Review on determining number of cluster in k-means clustering. Int. J. Adv. Res. Comput. Sci. Manage. Stud. **1**(6), 90–95 (2013)

Advances in Cleaner Production

A Thermal System Based on Controlled Entropy for Treatment of Medical Waste by Solar Energy

Nilo Serpa[1(✉)], Ivanir Costa[2], and Rodrigo Franco Gonçalves[3]

[1] GAUGE-F Scientific Researches, Brasília, Brazil
niloserpa@gmail.com
[2] UNINOVE, São Paulo, Brazil
[3] Paulista University, São Paulo, Brazil

Abstract. This article discusses the implementation of a large scale way of urban waste management in terms of its non-aggressive and productive destination, at low energy costs and with high reuse of byproducts. Aiming at the processing of medical waste, but not excluding other types of residues, present work is primarily focused on the so-called infectious waste, because they have greater virulence, infectivity and concentration, and wastes of type "skin-scissoring-piercing", which are objects and instruments containing corners, edges or rigid and acute protuberances capable of cutting or drilling. In this paper, it is proposed an industrial solar system to recycling medical waste based on pyrolysis induced by plasma and controlled entropy.

Keywords: Medical waste · Thermodynamics · Solar energy

1 Introduction

One of the most discussed topics at the tables of environmentalists and ecologists is the solid waste management (SWM). The SWM consists of a set of control procedures, planned and implemented from scientific, technical, regulatory and legal principles to minimize the production of waste and the risks involved in its disposal, and protecting workers and preserving public health, natural resources and the environment in general, at low cost [1]. The implementation of a solid waste management system requires skilled professionals, being essential for the preservation of life quality [2]. It should be noted here the urgency to banning land common in Latin America and other regions of the Third World [1,3]. This article proposes a possible thermodynamic engineering system for large-scale solid waste eradication based on solar pyrolysis. In present work, the adopted definition of solid waste is provided by the Ministry of Health Brazil [1,4].

© IFIP International Federation for Information Processing 2016
Published by Springer International Publishing AG 2016. All Rights Reserved
I. Nääs et al. (Eds.): APMS 2016, IFIP AICT 488, pp. 789–797, 2016.
DOI: 10.1007/978-3-319-51133-7_92

2   Current Situation and the State of the Art

2.1   Hygiene and Sanitation: Weaknesses of the Global World

The dangers of exposure to medical waste are known from very early, although little is heard of it. Current literature indicates that direct and indirect exposure to hazardous waste includes, among many others, carcinogenic and reproductive system damage [4–6]. In Brazil, the indifference of the governmental authorities is high. Only in 2000, it was estimated that 76% of the Brazilian cities disposed of domestic and medical wastes together in public landfills. Despite the federal resolutions from ANVISA-2004 (Brazilian Sanitary Surveillance National Agency) and CONAMA-2005 (Brazilian Environmental National Council), requiring the management of waste generated by all healthcare units, medical waste is still being carried on landfills without treatment [1]. Brazilian law is mandatory when it claims the implementation of a medical waste management plan (MWMP), a subset of SWM, to be applied in all medical establishments, but they recognize that such plan is far from the real practice [1,2].

2.2   The Risks of Conventional Incineration of Medical Waste

Incineration and disposal of its ash scraps by land filling are the most important available procedures to treat and transport medical waste and solid waste in general [7]. The conventional incineration leads to polluting the environment when not treated properly, with molecules that accumulate in the food chain such as dioxins, furans and coplanar polychlorinated biphenyls [3]. Many attempts have been made to perform locally medical waste treatment [3,4] but failed regarding safety in the process of waste loading and the treatment of emissions. The only valid form to optimize the process and to reduce the formation of these substances is to apply temperatures far above 800 °C, preventing the formation of effluent gases at temperatures within the range of 200 °C to 400 °C that occurs in combustion [3]. Only by atomic disruption we could control the ultimate condition of such materials, recombine atoms in ways that make inert substances.

When a gas is heated to high temperatures, there are significant changes in its properties. At about 2,000 °C, the gas molecules begin to dissociate in atomic level. At 3,000 °C, the atoms are ionized by the loss of electrons. This ionized gas is called plasma. In certain conditions, the plasma may induce a pyrolysis. Pyrolysis has been getting attention for many years because of its potential to produce biofuels from organic waste [8]. For our purposes, pyrolysis can be broadly defined as the chemical decomposition of the matter by heat in the absence of oxygen. The idea is to develop an engine dedicated to the disruption of waste, which associates the high temperatures of the plasma with the pyrolysis of the waste.

Pyrolysis applied to medical waste is not new [8,9]. The rest format of pyrolytic gasification introduced commercially in the early 1970's was the so-called batch-by-batch system which got a certain success to hospital process waste until the early 1980's. Some problems arose, and one of them was how to maintain continuously throughout the waste. Finally, from a 50 ton-per-day pilot plant, the Balboa Pacific Co. settled an advanced pyrolytic thermal conversion system with a proprietary thermal waste conversion equipment to eliminate organic wastes [10]. What is new in present work is the application in large scale of pyrolysis induced by plasma for nosocomial solid and liquid, organic or not, waste elimination based on the use of solar energy and not electricity. Even though the overall process is cleaner in comparison to conventional burning, there are evolved products which require special controls [9]. Figure 1 shows the fundamental proposed framework from which we shall discuss how we can minimize the problem of the generation of undesirable substances.

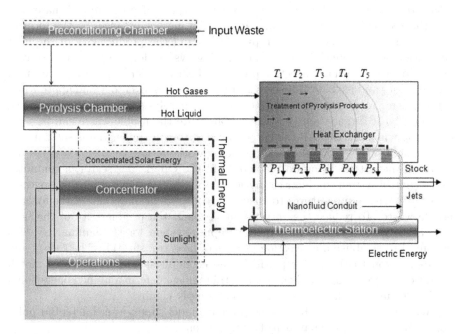

Fig. 1. The complete scheme of the proposed thermodynamic engine. Note the cicle of energy with a thermoelectric station feeding continually the usine as well as it is powered by solar energy (from Serpa's Ph.D. thesis in French [11]).

3   The Methods

Solar concentrators have become a reality in the day-to-day response to sanitary, and environmental preservation needs. Our proposed plant unifies fundamental issues in a comprehensive approach to thermal systems engineering. Virtually any material can be carried to the pyrolysis chamber. It is assumed that the preconditioning chamber gets material properly handled and encapsulated. Also, it is reasonable to believe that rubber, plastic, gauze, paper and cotton average out 90% of total medical waste [3, 12]. The waste fills (preconditioning chamber) is connected to a cylindrical graphite chamber. From the preconditioning chamber, we feed the graphite chamber in which pyrolysis shall take place. Internally subjected to a vacuum, this last receives the concentrated sunlight rays from a concave array of mirrors on a quartz window placed at one of the circular bases of the chamber. At high temperatures atomic disruptions produce gasses and liquids that go into the recycling device, inside which the gradient of temperatures $T_1, T_2, T_3, T_4, ..., T_n$ allows to a recovery of products $P_1, P_2, P_3, P_4, ..., P_n$ from the hottest layers to the cooler. In the Operations sector, a computational control system conducts catalytic agents, whose actions enter the processes associated with temperatures to ensure the outputs of programmed materials, and the recombination of remnant atoms into inert substances in the form of usable waste. To reduce the entropy and expand the productivity of the heat generation we introduced an auxiliary piping system for the laminar flow of a nanofluid to establish a convection process of heat transfer [11]. Lastly, products, final residues and usable waste are sent respectively to inventory and appropriate containment, remembering that the so called "pyrolysis ashes" – similar to the dust and blast furnace sludge – which constitute the usable waste can be used in the cement industry. All the energy needed to run the engine is solar, being the possible surplus routed to the public network.

From the hottest layers to the cooler. In the Operations sector, a computational control system conducts catalytic agents, whose actions enter the processes associated with temperatures to ensure the outputs of materials in the form of usable waste. To reduce the entropy and expand the productivity of the heat generation we introduced an auxiliary piping system for the laminar ow of a nanofluid to establish a convection process of heat transfer [11]. The theory and its application to the power platform the econophysics foundations to match operations management and environmental management in a unified operational level [8] to include the waste management supply chain.

Accordingly classical theory, the present model supposes a differential polynomial in ξ, the Lagrangian density $\mathcal{L}(\xi)$, given by

$$\mathcal{L} = (\partial_q \xi)^* (\partial^q \xi) - |\xi|^2 + 2\gamma^2 |\xi|^2 \ln |\xi|, \tag{1}$$

whose action over a certain region $\mathcal{D}$ in space and time is

$$\mathcal{S}(\xi) = \int_{\mathcal{D}} \left[(\partial_q \xi)^* (\partial^q \xi) - |\xi|^2 + 2\gamma^2 |\xi|^2 \ln |\xi| \right] d\mathcal{V} dt. \tag{2}$$

Here, from Serpa's first proposal, ξ represents a scalar complex massless caloric field, $d\mathcal{V}$ an infinitesimal volumn of space, dt an infinitesimal time interval, and γ a real scalar to be defined later which depends on the system's environment in question [11]. The caloric field obeys the field equation

$$\partial_q \partial^q \xi + \left(1 - \gamma^2\right) \xi - 2\gamma^2 \xi \ln |\xi| = 0, \tag{3}$$

being the field entropy in generalized coordinates q given by

$$S = \int -2\gamma^2 |\xi|^2 \ln |\xi| dq. \tag{4}$$

Thus, field equation includes an entropy term $-2\gamma^2 \xi \ln |\xi|$ in the dynamics of the field and expression (4) is just a straightforward generalization of Gibbs entropy. It is worth noting that for $|\xi|^2 < 1$ it follows that $2\ln |\xi| < 0$; thus, $S > 0$ for every non-trivial system state. The factor $(1 - \gamma^2)$ in the second term of Eq. (3), the so-called "luminothermic capacity", reflects the potential power offered by the natural surroundings. Its action under the field shows how field is influenced by the external conditions. Thus, caloric field equation governs the evolution of the thermal energy field and the corresponding entropy produced.

Regarding the efficiency of te engine the logical way to establish an asymptotic relation between the proposed heat engine efficiency and the Carnot machine efficiency is to introduce the irreversible coefficient φ, due to the irreversible events during the industry processes. So efficiency can be written as

$$\eta_t \leq \frac{1}{\varphi} \left(1 - \frac{T_{II}}{T_I} \right), \tag{5}$$

where T_I is the temperature associated with the initial state of the system (at which the waste enters the pyrolysis chamber) and T_{II} is the temperature associated with the final state of the system (time at which the recycling loop is completed). The heat engine efficiency may be compared to luminothermic capacity in order to measure the relation between the contribution of the environment and the technology of reduction of irreversible outputs. However, this comparison requires empirical results to be recorded and analyzed. Anyway, even if the plant operated very close to a Carnot machine, the efficiency would be limited by the maximum luminothermic capacity allowed by the Earth environments. In addition, while all the actual industry processes are irreversible, φ can only asymptotically approach unit with the minimization of irreversible events. Thereby, the more φ is closer to 1, the less is the number of irreversible processes and the entropy variation ΔS; the production becomes cleaner [10].

4   The Plant in Process and the Expected Results

The chosen area for the plant, with eight hectares, is about two km from the large dumpsite of Brasilia, Brazil. The design of the facility, solar concentrator uses linear Fresnel reflectors, that is, individually designed mirrors mounted on two-axis tracking devices, with very similar features in arrangement and operation to the conventional parabolic collectors. It is placed fifteen meters underground (beneath the soil level).

TFirst computational simulations of the concentrator proved capacity to achieve temperatures close to $1588\,^{\circ}C$ inside the pyrolysis chamber, on the contrary of the great majority of most industrial heating processes which run below $300\,^{\circ}C$. Also, these simulations pointed to an efficiency of the plant between

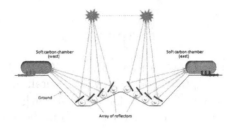

Fig. 2. Implementation scheme of the reflector device

68,44% and 72,82%. These outcomes are very encouraging in the sense that several persistent pollutants shall be avoided since the achieved temperature is far above 800 °C and much higher than the temperatures of formation of effluent gases, typically at 200–400 °C. The pyrolysis chamber (the receiver) is a hollow soft carbon cylindrical container —- with initial capacity for 1/2 ton of wastes — - placed east on the ground (soil level). Sunbeam is reflected and concentrated on the back of the chamber (quartz window), and the temperature gradient of the inner caloric field is controlled by thermal exchangers along the chamber. In fact, some improvements in the heat exchanger effectiveness for setting the temperature gradient were attained in simulations using vanes, whose positive influence on heat exchange in industrial air heaters was demonstrated by Atkins et al. for the range of air-side Reynolds numbers [13]. In addition, the heat transfer nanofluid circulates through the pyrolysis chamber, collecting and transporting thermal energy to storage units and power production for the Operations sector in a continuous process of feedback. Indeed, the complete plant shall include another identical soft carbon pyrolysis chamber placed west also on the ground (Fig. 2), so that we shall have one array of mirrors for each chamber. Since the receivers are separate units, the tracking is simple and efficient. As explained previously, caloric field inside the chambers is governed by field Eq. (3), where the constant γ in the second term and in the term of entropy defines the degree of obfuscation of the environment; we call it "blurring" or "opacity". Opacity depends on some environmental conditions such as the amount of dust in the air, industrial pollution and the local propensity to cloud accumulation. We defined five levels of blurring to be considered: very low, low, moderate, high and very high (Table 1). Braslia was classified having moderate blurring ($\gamma = 0.6882$) despite the high annual insolation because of the frequent wind dust spreading in Brazilian Central Plateau from August to October and the intermittent formation of clouds from December to March. The values found in Table 1 were established after observations conducted on the environmental luminosity in different seasons and times at distinct Brazilian localities. Also, the investigation was made considering the estimated daily average density of dust accumulated on the set of reflectors from the expression

$$\bar{\delta}_M = \frac{1}{92} \sum_{j=1}^{92} \left(\sum_{i=1}^{n} \left(\frac{\delta_M}{A} \right)_i \right)_j , \tag{6}$$

where δ_M is the total mass of dust deposition on the surface of the reflector, A is the reflector surface area, i is a counter of reflectors, and j is a counter of days (in present case, from August to October, the period considered as the peak interval of the wind regime during dry season). Measurements were made on site using common mirrors placed at positions provided for reflectors. For each daily measurement, mirrors were well cleaned to remove the mass of dust. Anyway, the shading caused by dust deposits shall also be counteracted with a minimum inclination of mirrors around $12°$ [7].

Table 1. Blurring (or opacity) of the environment and refractive index of the quartz window

Blurring level	γ	ϑ
Very high	0.8412	1.7935
High	0.7224	1.5419
Moderate	0.6882	1.4444
Low	0.6204	1.2010
Very low	0.5416	0.7953

In the chambers of pyrolysis and recycling, it is necessary that there is a polytropic process, i.e., an intermediate process between an isothermal process and an adiabatic process. In this case, the polytropic index n is equal to 2 for reasons of analytical symmetry and thermodynamical optimization [11]. Suppose a caloric field described by

$$\xi = e^{in\gamma q - \vartheta}, \tag{7}$$

where the quantity ϑ is the theoretical refractive index of the quartz window. One can easily demonstrate that field Eq. (3) gives

$$n = \frac{\sqrt{1 + (2\vartheta - 1)\gamma^2}}{\gamma}. \tag{8}$$

From this result, we can establish the values shown in Table 1, where the quartz refractive index is achieved with good approximation to the levels of high and moderate opacity.

5 Conclusion

The system was conceived and prepared to operate at high precision to minimize entropy production, so that an accurate physical analysis was performed.

Nevertheless, it would be impossible to make extensive mathematical deductions in this paper, reason why we restrict ourselves to report that all the physical process is summarized in three fundamental equations as follows:

1. About the diffusion model: the combined equation Lane-Emden/Langmuir for $n = 2$ [11],

$$-\frac{1}{x^2}\left(2x\frac{d}{dx}y\left(x\right)+x^2\frac{d^2}{dx^2}y\left(x\right)\right)+3y\left(x\right)\frac{d^2}{dx^2}y\left(x\right)+\left(\frac{d}{dx}y\left(x\right)\right)^2 \quad (9)$$

$$+\,4y\left(x\right)\frac{d}{dx}y\left(x\right)-1=0; \quad (10)$$

   this equation describes the evolution of the dimensionless caloric density y on a conductive cylindrical symmetry, keeping the density relatively stable over a longer radius measured by x; it serves to establish a curve which defines a useful level of energy balance.

2. About the relationship between the thermodynamic variables S, $\mathcal{P}$, T and V (entropy, pressure, temperature and volume): Serpa's equation in partial derivatives [11],

$$\tilde{c}\frac{\partial^2 V}{\partial S \partial P}=-\frac{1}{P}\frac{\partial T}{\partial P}; \quad (11)$$

   this second-order equation, with the parameter $\tilde{c} > 0$ corresponding to the polytropic index (n), describes the variation in volume due to entropy and pressure (assuming $\mathcal{P}$ parameterized with respect to S).

3. About the control of system's entropy: Serpa's caloric field Eq. [11],

$$\partial_q \partial^q \xi + \left(1-\gamma^2\right)\xi-\gamma^2\xi\ln\left|\xi\right|^2=0; \quad (12)$$

   that is, by definition, the equation that governs the field inside the pyrolysis reactor.

These three equations are crucial to the construction of the production control algorithm to run up in the sector "Operations". The reader should note that these equations have in common the polytropic index (Table 1) was constructed from this base) because it is always possible to give field ξ parameterized by n. It is also important to note that all we can do is to work on systems with a good approximation for $n = 2$.

References

1. Ministry of Health: Technical Guidelines for Preparation of the Program of Health Education and Social Mobilization. ASCOM/FUNASA, Brasília, Brazil (2004)
2. ICRC: Medical Waste Management. Geneva, Switzerland (2011)
3. Ananth, P., Prashanthini, V., Visvanathan, C.: Healthcare waste management in Asia. Waste Manag. **30**, 154–161 (2010)
4. Moreira, A., Günther, W.: Assessment of medical waste management at a primary health-care center in São Paulo - Brazil. Waste Manag. **33**, 162–167 (2013)

5. Tsakona, M., Anagnostopoulou, E., Gidarakos, E.: Hospital waste management and toxicity evaluation: a case study. Waste Manag. **27**, 912–920 (2007)
6. Franka, E., El-Zoka, A., Hussein, A., Elbakosh, M., Arafa, A., Ghenghesh, K.: Hepatitis B virus and hepatitis C virus in medical waste handlers in Tripoli - Libya. J. Hosp. Infect. **72**, 258–261 (2009)
7. El-Shobokshy, M., Hussein, F.: Degradation of photovoltaic cell performance due to dust deposition on to its surface. Renew. Energy **3**(6/7), 585–590 (1993)
8. Deng, N., Zhang, Y., Wang, Y.: Thermogravimetric analysis and kinetic study on pyrolysis of representative medical waste composition. Waste Manag. **28**, 1572–1580 (2008)
9. Zhu, H., Yan, J., Jiang, X., Lai, Y., Cen, K.: Study on pyrolysis of typical medical waste materials by using TG-FTIR analysis. J. Hazard. Mater. **153**, 670–676 (2008)
10. Balboa Pacic Corporation: From Waste to Electricity — A Pyrolysis Technology. Advanced Thermal Conversion Technologies, San Diego, California (2014)
11. Serpa, N.: Sur l'entropie contrôlée des systèmes – le traitement des déchets médicaux et hospitaliers ou une nouvelle approche de la production plus nette basée. Ph.D. thesis, L'Universit Libre des Sciences de L'Homme de Paris, Sorbonne (2014)
12. Xiea, R., Li, W., Li, J., Wu, B., Yi, J.: Emissions investigation for a novel medical waste incinerator. J. Hazard. Mater. **166**, 365–371 (2009)
13. Atkins, M., Neale, J., Walmsley, M., Walmsley, T., de Leon, G.: Flow maldistribution in industrial air heaters and its effect on heat transfer. Chem. Eng. Trans. **39**, 295–300 (2014)

Analysis of the Polyethylene Terephthalate Production Chain: An Approach Based on the Emergy Synthesis

Gustavo Bustamante$^{(\boxtimes)}$, Biagio F. Giannetti, Feni Agostinho, and Cecília M.V.B. Almeida

Paulista University, São Paulo, Brazil
gustamante1000@hotmail.com

Abstract. The petrochemical industry is characterized by the intense use of non-renewable resources, such as crude oil, associated to a high environmental load derived from efforts from nature and human systems to produce these products. These efforts may be accounted for by emergy synthesis, which is a tool that determines the amount of energy, directly or indirectly, necessary to obtain a product or service by means of a common unit (solar equivalent Joules seJ). In this work, emergy synthesis is applied to the polyethylene terephthalate (PET) production chain in the European petrochemical sector. The unit emergy values (UEV) of the system products are estimated, enabling comparative interpretations among the quality of energy usage and processes' efficiency.

Keywords: Emergy · Specific emergy · Environmental accounting · Petrochemical industry · PET

1 Introduction

The importance of the petrochemical industry lies in being a source of large amounts of intermediate products, which are the main raw materials for many other industries like plastic, automotive, transportation, textile and agriculture. However, the production processes with intensive usage of non-renewable natural resources are often associated with high environmental costs, especially in regard to the risk of resource depletion. Therefore, there is an increasing awareness concerning the environmental problems that may arise in the future due to the misuse of strategic non-renewable resources, such as crude oil. In the recent decades, different methods, techniques and research were developed providing knowledge about the specific environmental problems caused by the oil-based production systems. The emergy synthesis, developed by Odum [1], is an environmental accounting method, based on the laws of thermodynamics and systems ecology, to determine the amount of energy, directly or indirectly, required to

© IFIP International Federation for Information Processing 2016
Published by Springer International Publishing AG 2016. All Rights Reserved
I. Nääs et al. (Eds.): APMS 2016, IFIP AICT 488, pp. 798–804, 2016.
DOI: 10.1007/978-3-319-51133-7_93

produce a good or service. Since the emergy is measured in units of solar equivalent joules (seJ), coefficients called transformities, which represent the emergy intensity through the ratio of emergy (required by the process) to energy (embodied in the product) are used as conversion factors allowing accounting flows are not directly solar origin. The unit emergy values (UEV) refer to the relationship between the quantity of emergy per unit of mass, volume, area, etc., and include the transformities (seJ/J). The UEVs are a measure of energy quality and process efficiency, since the same amount of invested emergy can derive in different types of energy, with different capabilities to produce work and, therefore, different qualities.

Oil-based production systems have been evaluated using the emergy synthesis. Bastianoni et al. [2] determined the UEVs of oil and natural gas, according to the geological production process and proposed the use of average transformities between the new values and those calculated by Odum [1]. Later, these results were complemented with the estimation of the transformity of liquid petroleum products [3]. This transformity was used as the emergy contribution of naphtha in a study where different ethylene production processes were evaluated and compared using the emergy synthesis [4].

Another method widely used to evaluate the environmental burdens of products and process in petrochemical industry is the Life Cycle Assessment (LCA) [5,6]. This method allows estimations of environmental impacts related to different categories, such as global warming, energy use, ozone depletion and abiotic resource use. The complementarity of LCA and emergy synthesis [7] was proposed as an alternative approach, through the application of transformities to the data reported in life cycle inventories (LCI). In spite of the inconsistency issues addressed by Bakshi [8] to integrate both approaches, highlighting the differences of the analysis boundaries, the integration of both methods may provide a more comprehensive analysis, including not only the economic and environmental resources required by the production, but also the impact of their emissions [8]. LCIs are not conventional data sources for emergy synthesis, but some authors highlighted the accuracy and consistency of results based on this type of information [9]. Obstacles, limitations, restrictions and critical points of complementarity or integration of LCA and emergy methods are discussed in [9,10].

Almeida et al. [11] applied the emergy accounting based on data from a previous Brazilian LCA study of the PET and aluminum packaging production chains for beverage, including the recycling stages. This analysis contributed for the selection of the materials and processes during the product design stage. In this case, the inventory data was based on the information reported by group of Brazilian companies, collected through questionnaires, including data on raw materials use and consumption, energy, semimanufactured and auxiliary materials and fuels for transport, considering only the Brazilian domestic production. The use of LCIs for calculating emergy was performed taking into account aspects about coherence of emergy algebra rules, the structure of the inventory data and the boundaries of the considered systems. In this work, similarly to Almeida et al. [11], the production of PET resin as preform for beverage packages is also analyzed. However, a more comprehensive analysis is sought regarding the specific emergies of eleven intermediates products that make up this petrochemical chain, considering each of its processes separately based on a different inventory for each intermediate product. The data structure used in this study has a higher level of detail since the eleven intermediate products are tracked back, considering the cumulative amounts of all the elementary flows throughout the life cycle of each one. More details about data sources and methods will be described in the following sections.

The objective of this study is to apply an LCI-based emergy synthesis to determine the UEVs of the products for and within the polyethylene terephthalate production chain (PET), based on the information about the European petrochemical production. These UEVs are compared with those obtained by Bastianoni et al. [3] and Sha et al. [4], calculated in the traditional way.

2   Method

2.1   PET Production System

Figure 1 shows the stages of the PET production chain. The first stage is the extraction and processing of crude oil and natural gas. These resources are a mixture of hydrocarbons which can be derived into chemical compounds that are used as raw material of other products along the production chain. The main fraction of crude oil used in the petrochemical industry is naphtha. The production route includes several unitary processes, each with an important contribution in the total balance of resources. At the end of the production chain, the thermoplastic resin in solid state (bottle-grade) is obtained, and used as raw material for the production of bottle packaging, via injection or blown.

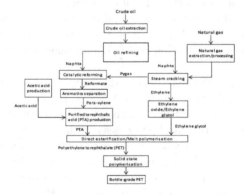

Fig. 1. Production route of polyethylene terephthalate (PET) bottle-grade (Source: adapted from [12])

2.2   Emergy Method

Emergy is a measure in solar equivalent joules (seJ) of all contributions received by any system including the production ones. These contributions come in the form of material and energy flows, fuels, metals money, and labor. The result is a scientific measure of the energy previously used, directly or indirectly to obtain each flow. Emergy tracks all things to their source in the biosphere, the supplier, recognizing the environmental effort needed for the production of a good or service, in which lies the value of a resource, ensuring the use optimization [13].

The emergy results are presented in a common unit, called solar equivalent joules, seJ, and unit emergy values (UEV) are used for the conversion of one type of energy to another. The UEVs can be expressed as seJ/unit (e.g. grams, liters, currency) and the term transformity is used when the UEVs are expressed in seJ/J. As a measure of energy conversion and process efficiency, the UEVs refer to one unit of product that can be obtained from the lowest emergy investment.

The emergy tables are built based on the recorded information about the input and output flows of the system analyzed. The amount of each input is multiplied by its respective UEV, giving as a result the emergy of each input, which can be summed to determine the total emergy of the process and, thus, of the product. It should be noted that flows related to the plant construction phase, infrastructure and maintenance, were not taken into consideration in this work, since their influence in the total emergy required is around 4%, and considered negligible [3,4]. Similarly, since this study intends to evaluate only the technological efficiency of each process, labor and services inputs are not included. These flows depend, to a large extent, on the local social and economic structures, and consequently, limit the assessment to a given region and the overall scope of the analysis restricted. As the results refer to technological aspects, they can be used for comparison with other production systems of the same products, and assist strategic decision making.

2.3   LCI Databases

The databases comprise flows that are the result of tracking back each product along the production chain, including upstream processes as many as needed to identify the environmental source. Hence, the only economic or transformed output in the resulting data is the functional unit: 1 kg of product ("at gate" representing the average of European industrial production). All other values correspond to cumulative totals of all operations traced back to the extraction of raw materials from nature [14]. Such information is contained in documents known as Eco-profiles, which include all streams belonging to the processes from the extraction of natural resources to obtaining 1 kg of each product, ready for transport or transfer to the consumer. The Eco-profiles are established following the ISO 14040-44 standards and the International Reference Life Cycle Data

System (ILCD)[1]. The databases used in this work are part of the Eco-profile Program and Environmental Product Declaration (EPD) of the Association of Plastics Manufacturers, PlasticsEurope.

3 Results and Discussion

Table 1 shows the UEVs calculated for PET and for 10 of its precursors. The calculation was performed using emergy tables to quantify the emergy contributions of input flows to the production system for 1 kg of each product. The different UEVs determined represent the emergy intensities per gram of product (seJ/g). Table 1 also shows the UEVs previously calculated by other authors [2,4,5]. Differences may be attributed to assumptions for the calculation and to the processes intrinsic characteristics. In the case of ethylene, Sha et al. [4] assumes a yield of 31% of ethylene based on naphtha and considers other co-products of the steam cracking process. Differently, the UEVs of this work are result of tracking back the inflows that belong to production route of 1 kg of ethylene (the same for all other products). Therefore, instead of yield conversion of the raw material, it is taken into account the elementary feedstock content in the product, i.e. crude oil through naphtha, tracked back to the first stage of the production chain (crude oil extraction). In this regard, it is worth noting that naphtha and other petroleum derivatives are not considered as co-products, but as splits of crude oil with different densities [3].

Regarding to the specific emergy of PET, the differences observed correspond to dissimilar levels of efficiency in the use of resources for production. However, there is some uncertainty by evaluating and comparing production systems from different countries or regions, since the emergy results do not directly reflect differences between systems for reasons other than technological, e.g., political or socio-economic aspects. Therefore, lower UEVs are the outcome of the highest efficiencies in the use of resources in highly industrialized countries or regions with advanced production technology. In this way, the emergy results can contribute in selecting production technologies with lower environmental costs, ensuring a more appropriate technological configuration for the use of resources. In parallel, these results can be interpreted as measures of quality of energy by defining ratios between amounts of emergy required per joule of product, i.e., transformities (seJ/J). Thus, an estimate of the process efficiency, in terms of emergy, is obtained (Fig. 2). The transformity increases linearly along the production chain, as more inputs (energy and materials) are incorporated into the chain to obtain the next derivative.

This result also establishes an expected range for UEVs of the petrochemical industry. From crude oil to the final product, the transformity approximately doubles its value, and all UEV's estimated lie within a range between 3.99×10^9 seJ/g, from ethylene glycol, and, 6.40×10^9 seJ/g, from ethylene, which is the

---

[1] Details about the Eco-profiles methodology, interpretation and data collection can be found at: http://www.plasticseurope.org/plastics-sustainability-14017/life-cycle-thinking-1746/eco-profiles-programme.aspx.

Table 1. Calculated unit emergy values (UEV) by product of the PET production chain and literature values.

	UEVs*/x10^9 (seJ/g)*	UEVs**from literature (seJ/g)*	Reference
Crude oil	4.47	3.90×10^9	[2]
Natural gas	4.14	3.69×10^9	[2]
Naphtha	4.75	5.02×10^9	[4]
Py gas	5.77		
Xylene	5.24		
P-Xylene	6.15		
Ethylene	6.40	1.69×10^{10}	[4]
Ethylene oxide	5.40		
Ethylene glycol	3.99		
PTA	5.00		
PET	5.94	6.32×10^{10}	[4]

* All the emergy measures in this work are related to baseline 15.83×10^{24} seJ/year [15].
** Calorific values between mass and energy in [2]: 4.19×10^4 J/g for oil, and 5.13×10^4 J/g for natural gas.

Fig. 2. Transformity values for derivatives of the PET production chain

derivative with the largest emergy required per gram of the products of the chain. The tendency line also establishes the rate in which petrochemical transformations occur in the PET production chain. The expected range reduces the level of uncertainty in the UEVs selection for emergy estimations in the petrochemical industry, offering a possible alternative for future research to facilitate scientific and operative work on data collection to calculate UEVs in this sector.

4   Conclusions

In current scientific publications, emergy synthesis has been sparsely applied to the downstream production processes of extraction and refining of fossil fuels. In this article, the PET production chain was analyzed, from the perspective of resources and energy usage comprising a variety of intermediate products.

The UEVs for petrochemical products were calculated and compared with the already existing in the literature; some of them are novel information (pyrolysis gas, xylene, para-xylene, ethylene oxide, ethylene glycol and purified terephthalic acid). Thus, this work contributes to the consolidation of the emergy databases and proposes an expectance range for the petrochemical industry as an approach that can be useful by applying the emergy method.

According to this study, it is considered that the use of LCIs in accounting emergy is a feasible and practical way to obtain reliable results. Additionally, it offers important contributions for integration and/or complementarity of both LCA and emergy methods.

References

1. Odum, H.T.: Environmental Accounting: Emergy and Environmental Decision Making. Wiley, New York (1996)
2. Bastianoni, S., Campbell, D., Susani, L., Tiezzi, E.: The solar transformity of oil and petroleum natural gas. Ecol. Model. **186**(2), 212–220 (2005)
3. Bastianoni, S., Campbell, D., Ridolfi, R., Pulselli, F.: The solar transformity of petroleum fuels. Ecol. Model. **220**(1), 40–50 (2009)
4. Sha, S., Melin, K., de Kokkonen, D.V., Hurme, M.: Solar energy footprint of ethylene processes. Ecol. Eng. **82**, 15–25 (2015)
5. Morales, M., Gonzalez-García, S., Aroca, G., Moreira, M.T.: Life cycle assessment of gasoline production and use in chile. Sci. Total Environ. **505**, 833–843 (2015)
6. Portha, J.F., Louret, S., Pons, M.N., Jaubert, J.N.: Estimation of the environmental impact of a petrochemical process using coupled LCA and exergy analysis. Resour. Conserv. Recycl. **54**(5), 291–298 (2010)
7. Raugei, M., Bargigli, M., Ulgiati, S.: Nested emergy analyses: moving ahead from the spreadsheet platform. In: Proceedings from the Fourth Biennial Emergy Conference, Gainesville, Florida (2007)
8. Bakshi, B.R.: A thermodynamic framework for ecologically conscious process systems engineering. Comput. Chem. Eng. **26**(2), 269–282 (2002)
9. Rugani, B., Benetto, E.: Improvements to emergy evaluations by using life cycle assessment. Environ. Sci. Technol. **46**(9), 4701–4712 (2012)
10. Raugei, M., Rugani, B., Benetto, E., Ingwersen, W.W.: Integrating emergy into LCA: potential added value and lingering obstacles. Ecol. Model. **271**, 4–9 (2014)
11. Almeida, C., Rodrigues, A., Bonilla, S., Giannetti, B.: Emergy as a tool for ecodesign: evaluating materials selection for beverage packages in Brazil. J. Clean. Prod. **18**(1), 32–43 (2010)
12. PlasticsEurope: Eco-Profiles and Environmental Product Declarations of the European Plastics Manufacturers - Polyethylene Terephthalate (PET) Bottle-Grade. Technical report (2012)
13. Ulgiati, S., Zucaro, A., Franzese, P.P.: Shared wealth or nobody's land? The worth of natural capital and ecosystem services. Ecol. Econ. **70**(4), 778–787 (2011)
14. Association of European Plastics Manufacturers, PlasticsEurope. http://www.plasticseurope.org/
15. Odum, H.T.: Folio #2: emergy of global processes. In: Handbook of Emergy Evaluation. Center for Environmental Policy, Florida (2000)

Urban Solid Waste: An Analysis of Energy Recovery Efficiency Three Different Treatment Systems in Brazil

Geslaine Frimaio[1,3](✉), Adrielle Frimaio[1], Cezar Augusto Frimaio[2], and Cecília M.V.B. Almeida[1]

[1] UNIP, São Paulo, Brazil
gfrimaio@gmail.com
[2] UFABC, São Paulo, Brazil
[3] IFSULDEMINAS, São Paulo, Brazil

Abstract. The final disposal of urban solid waste has become a major concern in a world where urbanization is a trend. In this study three different systems were analyzed by accounting renewable, non-renewable and paid resources in a common basis, with the emergy accounting methodology, so it is possible to obtain ratios and indices that aid the comprehension, management and enable the comparison among the three system: landfill, pyrolysis and plasma arc. The systems are now operating, except for the arc plasma, which is under implementation in the municipality of Hortolândia-SP. The indices show that the landfill with electricity production is the system with better performance for 5 out of 6 indexes. For every gram of USW treated, the landfill can produce 1.78 × 1016 joules of electricity, which means that this system is 5 times more efficient than the pyrolisis and the plasma arc systems in this scope.

Keywords: Urban solid waste · Emergy · Landfill

1 Introduction

During the Agenda 21 meeting of the United Nations [1], the majority of the countries committed on adopting policies that would lower the environmental impacts caused by the Urban Solid Waste (USW), based on the principles of sustainable development.

In Brazil Law 12.305/10 was sanctioned, which says about the Solid Waste National Policy [2] and stablishes the recovery of materials and the decrease on waste generation. Concerning to the treatment, Law 12.305 enforces that waste must be either treated thermally or disposed in landfills. Considering that USW is a heterogeneous fuel, this energy could be recovered either as biogas on landfills or gas from synthesis on thermal treatments.

The generation of electricity in one of the landfills has been occurring since the 1070's [3]. The organic matter is decomposed by methanogenic bacteria,

© IFIP International Federation for Information Processing 2016
Published by Springer International Publishing AG 2016. All Rights Reserved
I. Nääs et al. (Eds.): APMS 2016, IFIP AICT 488, pp. 805–811, 2016.
DOI: 10.1007/978-3-319-51133-7_94

which release biogas that will be converted into electricity on combustion engines. Plasma torch as a technology for USW treatment started to be used in the 1980's on the United States, Europe and Japan [4]. The organic share of waste is converted into synthesis gas (syngas) in a reactor where the temperature may reach up to 10,000 °C. Afterwards, syngas goes through a cooling and cleaning process and is used for producing electricity on turbines [4].

On the pyrolysis process the waste is decomposed on the pyrolytic reactor, where the chemical decomposition occurs due to the heat of waste, without oxygen and in temperatures ranging from 400 °C 1000 °C [5]. The CUW (Carbonized Urban Waste) from this process goes through a process of briquetting and pressing that will feed the pyrolytic reactor [6].

Researches using Life Cycle Assessment (LCA) stress that pyrolysis, gasification and plasma torch are more efficient for energy recovery, if compared to the incineration process [5,7], and the landfill should be the last option to be considered (PNRS, 2010).

Several studies employ the emergy synthesis to assess the possibilities, limitations, potentialities and the sustainability of USW treatment technologies, for example: [8–12].

2   Methodology

2.1   System Description

Landfill São João occupies 80 hectares in the municipality of São Paulo and has received 29 million tons of USW during the 17 years it has worked. In 2008, one year after it was closed, São João Energia Ambiental was implemented and started producing electricity capable of fulfilling the demand of a city with 400,000 inhabitants.

Projeto Natureza Limpa is located in the municipality of Unaí-MG. It started operating in 2014 and uses pyrolisys technology to treat 17,500 ton/year of USW. It occupies 18,000 m^2 and has daily treatment capacity of 70 tons of USW, operating 16 hours per day, 365 days per year. The coal obtained (CUW) is used as a feedback to the pyrolytic reactor and the exceeding production is sold on the market.

The plasma torch technology is under studies for implantation in a project designed for the municipality of Hortolândia-SP. The design aims to treat 94,900 ton/year in 30,000 m^2 – 200 ton/day of USW and 60 ton/day of waste from industry, hospitals and sewage sludge, operating 22 hours per day and 256 days per year.

2.2   Methodology

Emergy synthesis is a methodology developed by Odum in the early 80's. Emergy (spelled with M) is defined as the energy demanded, direct or indirectly, to obtain a good or service, and it s unit is the sej (joules of solar emergy). All the inputs for implementing and operating the system, characterized as energy flows, are converted into a common basis, called joules of solar emergy (sej), for which calculation we use the transformity (sej/J) if the flows are expressed in joules or the UEV (Unit Emergy Value) if the flows are expressed in other measures (sej/unit). This conversion enables to include on the global accounting of the system all the work performed by the men, as well as that performed by nature to obtain each flow of the system.

The emergy accounting table enables to determine the transformity and/or UEV of the good or service under study. The UEV may be used as an indicator of efficiency: a high value would say that the system has made a great effort to obtain one unit of the good or service.

The emergy synthesis, according to [13], is performed in four stages: designing the diagram of energy flows, building the environmental accounting table, calculating the indicators (Table 1) and discussion of the results.

Table 1. Indicators used on the USW systems assessment

Indicator	Description	Observation
Recovered energy	Energy of product(J)/mass of treated USW (g)	Indicates the efficiency of the system, able to provide the amount of recovered joules from one gram of USW
Recovered emergy	Recovered energy (J) x transformity (sej/J)	Allows estimating the quantity of emergy that the system can recover from 1 g of USW
Net emergy	Recovered emergy (sej/g) – emergy per gram of USW(sej/g)	Indicates how much emergy the system recovers. The higher the index, the better the system
Emergy investment recovery	Recovered emergy (sej/year)/used emergy (sej/year)	Indicates the cost-benefit, measures the advantage, in emergy, that the system may get compared to all the emergy used for the treatment. The higher the value, the greater will be the benefit obtained by the system – in emergy
Emergy balance	Total emergy of system (sej/year) - recovered emergy (sej/year)	Indicates how much emergy the system spends. The lower the index, the better for the system

3   Results and Discussion

Every interaction within the treatment systems during the processes, as well as with the landscape may be observed on the diagrams. The energy diagram for the landfill is showed on Fig. 1, the plasma torch system on Fig. 2 and the pyrolysis on Fig. 3.

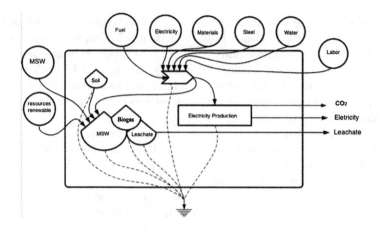

Fig. 1. Landfill energy diagram

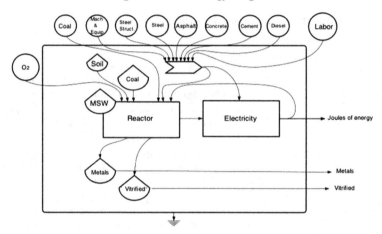

Fig. 2. Plasma torch energy diagram

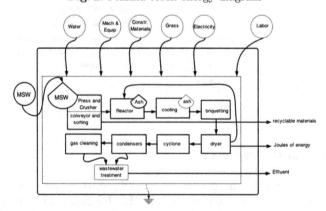

Fig. 3. Pyrolysis treatment system energy diagram

On Table 2 the results of the emergy accounting for each system, as well as the yearly amount of USW treated in each system.

Table 2. Emergia total dos sistemas

	Landfill	Plasma arc	Pyrolysis
TOTAL EMERGY (sej)	1.93×1020	4.35×1018	2.32×1018
Treated USW (g)	5.72×1011	9.49×1010	1.75×1016

The electricity on the operation stage is the most significant flow for the systems of thermal treatment, representing 52% of the total for the pyrolysis and 34.5% for the plasma torch system, due to the reactors of both. On the landfill the most significant flow is the Oxygen (O_2), responding for 63.1% of the flows and used to burn methane on the motogenerators (Table 3).

Table 3. UEV(s) of systems

Indicators	Landfill	Plasma arc	Pyrolysis
UEV (sej/g)	3.37×108	4.58×107	1.33×108

UEV is an indicator that may be used to compare the efficiency of the waste treatment system. It comprehends the ratio between the emergy used by the system and the total emergy of the treated USW for this indicator the plasma arc is three times more efficient than the pyrolysis system to treat 1 g of USW and about 2.5 times more efficient if compared to the landfill. Table 4 shows two indicators: Net Emergy and Recovered Emergy. The latter highlights that the landfill recovers 4.59×109 sej per gram of treated USW. The landfill is about 30 times more efficient on emergy recovery when it is compared to the pyrolysis system and about 26 times more efficient compared to the plasma arc. For the Net Emergy indicator the landfill has also shown the best performance: it is 30 times more efficient than the plasma arc system and 198 times more efficient than the pyrolysis.

Table 4. Results for net emergy and recovered emergy

Indicators	Landfill	Plasma arc	Pyrolysis
NET EMERGY (sej/g)	4.61×109	1.45×108	2.32×107
RECOVERED EMERGY (sej/g)	4.95×109	1.91×108	1.56×108

The results for Recovered Energy, Emergy Investment Recovery (EIR) and Emergy Balance are shown. The landfill is the system which recovers the greatest amount in joules of energy per gram of USW – about 8.5 times more than the other systems. Recovered emergy is the ratio between the recovered emergy and that one used to treat one gram of USW. This indicator stresses that the plasma arc system is 3.5 times more profitable in terms of emergy than the pyrolysis system, as it is able to recover more of the invested emergy due to the greater production of energy per gram of treated USW. For the indicator Emergy Recovery Index, the landfill showed to be 12.5 times more efficient that the pyrolysis system and this relations is 3.5 times greater compared to the plasma arc system (Table 5).

Table 5. Results of indicators for recovered energy, emergy investment recovery and emergy balance

	Landfill	Plasma arc	Pyrolysis
RECOVERED ENERGY	3.11×104	3.64×103	3.11×105
EIR (sej/sej)	14.66	4.16	1.19
EMERGY BALANCE	1.93×1020	4.35×1018	2.32×1019

For the Emergy Balance, the system that obtained the best index was the pyrolysis, 2 times more efficient than the plasma arc system and 8 times more efficient when compared to the landfill with electricity generation. Regarding that the landfill is the waste treatment system that obtains the greatest amount of energy joules per gram of treated waste, it means, that recovers more energy on its product and which recovered energy is considered a component for calculating most of the indicators, it is possible to say that the landfill with electricity production is the most effective option to recover or generate energy from USW. It is also the treatment system that has the greatest share of renewable resources (about 60% of O2).

Acnowledgement. CAPES, UNIP and IFSULDEMINAS, RGT International, Projeto Natureza Limpa as well as Alexandre Citvaras (Fox Ambiental).

References

1. CNUMAD. http://www.mma.gov.br/estruturas/agenda21/_arquivos/cap01.pdf
2. Brazil: Política Nacional de Resíduos Sólidos: Lei 12.305 de 02 de agosto de (2010). www.planalto.gov.br/ccivil_03/_Ato9.2007--2010/2010/Lei/L12305.htm
3. Tammemagi, H.Y.: The Waste Crisis: Landfills, Incinerators, and the Search for a Sustainable Future. Oxford University Press, New York (1999)
4. Ducharme, C.: Technical and economic analysis of plasma-assisted waste-to-energy processes. Ph.D. thesis, Columbia University, Columbia (2010)
5. Zaman, A.U.: Life cycle assessment of pyrolysis-gasification as an emerging municipal solid waste treatment technology. Int. J. Environ. Sci. Technol. **10**(5), 1029–1038 (2013)

6. Tôrres Filho, A.: Aplicação do Processo de Pirólise para Valoração, Cogeração de Energia e Tratamento de Resíduos. Ph.D. thesis, Federal de Minas Gerais, Belo Horizonte (2014)

7. Chakraborty, M., Sharma, C., Pandey, J., Gupta, P.K.: Assessment of energy generation potentials of MSW in Delhi under different technological options. Energy Convers. Manag. **75**, 249–255 (2013)

8. Tiezzi, E.: Analisi di Sostenibilitá Ambientale del Trattamento dei Rifiuti nel Comune di Modena (1998)

9. Luchi, F., Ulgiati, S.: Energy and emergy assessment of municipal waste collection: a case study. In: Proceedings of the 1st Biennial Emergy Analysis Research Conference, pp. 303–316. University of Florida, Gainesville (2000)

10. Bastianonil, S., Porcelli, M., Pulsellil, M.F.: Emergy evaluation of comporting municipal solid waste. WIT Trans. Ecol. Environ. **56**, 243–252 (2002)

11. Rugani, B., Pulselli, R.M., Niccolucci, V., Bastianoni, S.: Environmental performance of a XIV century water management system: an emergy evaluation of cultural heritage. Resour. Conserv. Recycl. **56**(1), 117–125 (2011)

12. Zhang, X.H., Deng, S., Jiang, W., Zhang, Y., Peng, H., Li, L., Yang, G., Li, Y.: Emergy evaluation of the sustainability of two industrial systems based on wastes exchanges. Resour. Conserv. Recycl. **55**(2), 182–195 (2010)

13. Odum, H.T.: Emergy and Environmental Decision Making. Wiley, Hoboken (2005). http://www.wiley.com/WileyCDA/WileyTitle/productCd-0471114421.html

Naphtha Production Assessment
from the Perspective of the Emergy Accounting

G. Bustamante$^{(\boxtimes)}$, B.F. Giannetti, F. Agostinho, Márcia Terra da Silva,
and C.M.V.B. Almeida

Paulista University, São Paulo, Brazil
gustamante1000@hotmail.com, cmvbag@unip.br

Abstract. Naphtha is the main petroleum derivative used as a feedstock
for the steam cracking of olefins and aromatic petrochemical products.
The environmental performance of the production of 1 kg of naphtha is
evaluated using a Life Cycle Inventory-based emergy accounting, considering the environmental load of labor and services. The biophysical
flows, which reflect the work of nature in the creation of the resources
required for the production and the monetary systems, are evaluated in
terms of emergy. The information recorded in a life cycle inventory (LCI)
is used for the estimation of the specific emergy of naphtha. The results
show that labor and services flows correspond to 10.54% and 12.93% of
the total system emergy, respectively. The LCI-based emergy accounting, although being an unconventional measurement method, was found
feasible bringing additional information that may help decision making.

Keywords: Emergy · Specific emergy · Environmental accounting ·
Petroleum fuels · Oil refining · Naphtha

1 Introduction

When production systems are analyzed by conventional methods for decision
making, the monetary flows related to the purchase of goods and services (materials, energy, labor, infrastructure) are often the only components taken into
account. The economy bestows values upon these resources, in monetary terms,
such as prices, which only correspond to the payments made for services in production, extraction, processing and delivering of these products in the global
market. However, money does not pay for the resources provided by nature and
prices are just the value that different market participants directly or indirectly
grant to human services required by the production processes [1].

Currently, different methods and measurement tools are used to assess the
environmental burdens caused by the intensive extraction and use of renewable and non-renewable resources by the production systems. Still, only few
tools, such as emergy accounting, can reflect in a common unit (solar equivalent
joules, seJ) the value of the biophysical and monetary flows of a production system. This measurement tool includes into formal accounting the contribution of

© IFIP International Federation for Information Processing 2016
Published by Springer International Publishing AG 2016. All Rights Reserved
I. Nääs et al. (Eds.): APMS 2016, IFIP AICT 488, pp. 812–817, 2016.
DOI: 10.1007/978-3-319-51133-7_95

natural ecosystems for producing the raw materials used up by human systems, quantifying all production costs in comparable physical units [2].

Campbell and Tilley [3] determined the value of the goods and services provided by nature based on emergy flows. They estimated the economic values for the ecological work, and called these values "eco-prices", which were defined as the emergy flow of an ecosystem service for the estimated amount of money flowing in countercurrent. Given the importance of the petroleum-based production systems, which use massive amounts of non-renewable resources, Bastianoni et al. [4] determined the specific emergies (seJ/g) of oil and natural gas, according to their geological production process. Later, in [5], these authors determined the emergy per joule (transformity) for liquid petroleum several derivatives, and quantified the cost structure of two refineries in emergy terms.

This article assesses the emergy flows of naphtha production, including those related to labor and services, using data obtained from the life cycle inventory (LCI) of naphtha production chain. The emergy of labor and services reflects the support required by the human labor directly and indirectly involved in the production processes. The results that combine environmental and economic information may help decision making [6, 7].

2   Method

Odum [8] defined emergy as the amount of available energy of a kind required, directly or indirectly, to obtain a product (good or service) or of an energy flow required by a process. Emergy is expressed in solar energy joule (seJ), which is the common basis of all energy flows within the biosphere. The higher the total emergy, the greater the amount of solar energy previously contained, processed and consumed by an input flow. The emergy intensity coefficients, known as transformities (seJ/J), can be calculated as the ratio of solar energy, directly or indirectly required to produce a joule (J) of another type of energy.

The emergy accounting method [8] is applied to assess the energy inflows that make up the transformation process required to produce naphtha, and to determine the unit emergy value (UEV, seJ/g) of the product (Eq. 1). Transformities and UEVs can be considered as a measure of the process efficiency.

$$EM = \sum_{k=1}^{n} EM_k = \sum_{t=1}^{n} Tr_k \times En_k \qquad (1)$$

Where EM is the total emergy of the system; EMk is the emergy of the input k; Trk is the transformity or UEV of the same input flow and; Enk, the energy used to obtain a specific flow.

The appropriate way of accounting for labor and services linked to the production processes by applying emergy is related to that described by Ulgiati and Brown [1], in detail. These authors proposed alternatives to calculate the emergy flows when there is no local information about the different levels of training and education. Thus, the emergy values of labor are determined by means of payments in the form of salary, multiplied by the UEV of money or the emergy to money ratio (EMR, seJ/GDP), in a year and a specific economy. An average of the European's EMR (seJ/€) in 2008 was used to determine both the emergy of labor and services (indirect labor inputs). In this case, it was assumed that wages represent education levels, training or experience of employees [1], and, as mentioned earlier, the price of the goods only reflects the value of human activities related to extracting and producing and not to the good or resource by itself.

The EMR is the emergy value of money for a country or region. It corresponds to the total emergy required to generate the Gross Domestic Product (GDP), and is measured in seJ/currency.

2.1 Data Source

Inputs data were taken from Eco-profiles documents, which are part of the Eco-profile Program and Environmental Product Declaration (EPD) of the European Association of Plastics Manufacturers, PlasticsEurope[1]. These documents are LCIs that take into account the life cycle of the product from "cradle to gate", i.e. from the extraction of raw materials, to the product ready for transport or transfer to the consumer. The inventories contain the mass and energy flows that enter the system, regarding the functional unit: 1 kg of product "at gate", and represent the average European production. The input flows have been tracked back throughout the system to its source in nature, including upstream processes as needed. The result of this tracking is the accounting of all elementary flows, so that the only economic or transformed flow is the output: 1 kg of naphtha [9].

3 Results and Discussion

The input-output flow diagram of the naphtha production (Fig. 1) shows all elementary flows that enter the system, according to the LCI (Table 1). Direct labor and services, are also included, and, their emergy measures are estimated by salaries and input prices, respectively.

The emergy analysis allowed determining the UEV of naphtha and the representativeness of each emergy inflow contributing to the total emergy, with and without labor and services. The results without services assess technological aspects and can be used for comparison with other naphtha production systems. The results, including labor and services, are site-specific and, therefore, should not be compared with systems outside the European region. The contribution of labor and services is equivalent to 10.54% and 12.93%, respectively. Services refer to the "background" processes or those out of operational control that contribute to the total emergy of the analyzed system.

The LCI-based specific emergy of naphtha without labor and services $(4.75 \times 10^9$ seJ/g) is similar to the value of 5.02×10^9 seJ/g determined by

---

[1] Details about the Eco-profiles methodology, interpretation and data collection can be found at: http://www.plasticseurope.org/plastics-sustainability-14017/life-cycle-thinking-1746/eco-profiles-programme.aspx.

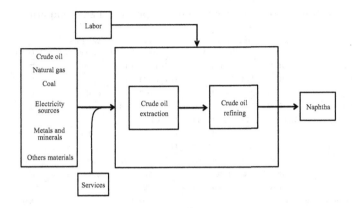

Fig. 1. Input-output flows of the naphtha production system

Sha et al. [10], who took as reference the transformity estimated by Bastianoni et al. [5] for petroleum liquid fuels (1.12×10^5 seJ/J) and multiplied by the calorific value of naphtha (44.5 kJ/g). Therefore, the specific emergy estimated in this study can be applied in the evaluation of downstream processes of the production chain, such as production of petrochemicals, resins and plastics.

Figure 2 shows the emergy contribution of the main inputs required for the production of naphtha. As shown in Table 1, crude oil, which is the main feedstock and energy source to the system, has the largest emergy contribution (with or without labor and services).

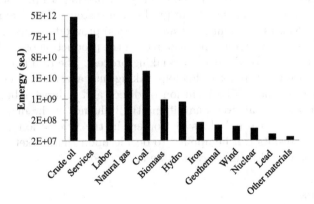

Fig. 2. Emergy contribution of the main inputs required for the production of naphtha

Table 1. Solar emergy required to produce 1 kg of naphtha.

Inputs		Quantity	Unit	Transformity or UEV*	Solar emergy (seJ)	% of emergy (without L&S)	% of emergy (with L&S)
1	Crude oil	4.80E+01	MJ	9.45E+04 seJ/J	4.54E+12	95.62	73.18
2	Natural gas	1.62E+00	MJ	6.83E+04 seJ/J	1.11E+11	2.33	1.79
3	Coal	3.57E-01	MJ	5.71E+04 seJ/J	2.04E+10	0.43	0.33
4	Hydro	7.16E-03	MJ	1.35E+05 seJ/J	9.65E+08	0.02	0.02
5	Nuclear	2.36E-01	MJ	1.60E+11 seJ/g	67300000	0.00	0.00
6	Biomass	1.77E-02	MJ	6.75E+04 seJ/J	1.20E+09	0.03	0.02
7	Geothermal	2.07E-04	MJ	4.52E+05 seJ/J	9.36E+07	0.00	0.00
8	Wind	8.28E-04	MJ	9.90E+04 seJ/J	8.19E+07	0.00	0.00
9	Iron	1.03E+01	mg	1.20E+10 seJ/g	1.23E+08	0.00	0.00
10	Lead	7.90E-02	mg	4.80E+11 seJ/g	3.79E+07	0.00	0.00
11	Other materials				2.89E+07	≈0	≈0
12	Labor	1.32E-01	€	4.97E+12 seJ/€	6.54E+11		10.54
13	Services	1.61E-01	€	4.97E+12 seJ/€	8.02E+11		12.93
Output							
14	Naphtha	1.00E+03	g	6.21E+09 seJ/g	6.21E+12		

*Transformities used for calculating the emergy of inflows, except for labor and services, were obtained from the literature and related to the baseline 15.83×10^{25} seJ/year [11]. The EMR corresponds to the weighted average of these countries by 2008.
Lines 4–8: sources of electricity used along the production chain.
Line 11: other materials corresponding to 43 elementary flows recorded in the LCI.
Line 12: the average salary of 10 European countries with highest naphtha production in 2008.

4   Conclusions

The use of LCI databases in this research has led to reliable UEV results for naphtha, according to the comparison with previous literature studies. The results show that Life Cycle Inventory-based emergy accounting is a practical and feasible way to account for the emergy of production systems. The evaluation of the technological aspects (without labor and services) proved to be useful to account for the contribution of energy and resources in the production of naphtha, and to provide reliable data for the decision making process. The results can be applied to decide for a given type of technology taking into account the environmental cost of each input flow. The inclusion of direct and indirect labor (labor and services, respectively) allowed quantifying the influence of the market, the level of training, experience and skills of workers in the production of naphtha in Europe. These results can be applied to decide upon the market (or region) in which a given type of technology may be implanted.

References

1. Ulgiati, S., Brown, M.T.: Labor and services as information carriers in emergy-LCA accounting. J. Environ. Account. Manag. 2(2), 163–170 (2014)
2. Almeida, C., Carvalho, N., Agostinho, F., Giannetti, B.F.: Using emergy to assess the business plan of a small auto-parts manufacturer in Brazil. J. Environ. Account. Manag. 3(4), 371–384 (2015)
3. Campbell, E.T., Tilley, D.R.: The eco-price: how environmental emergy equates to currency. Ecosyst. Serv. 7, 128–140 (2014)

4. Bastianoni, S., Campbell, D., Susani, L., Tiezzi, E.: The solar transformity of oil and petroleum natural gas. Ecol. Model. **186**(2), 212–220 (2005)
5. Bastianoni, S., Campbell, D., Ridolfi, R., Pulselli, F.: The solar transformity of petroleum fuels. Ecol. Model. **220**(1), 40–50 (2009)
6. Rugani, B., Benetto, E.: Improvements to emergy evaluations by using life cycle assessment. Environ. Sci. Technol. **46**(9), 4701–4712 (2012)
7. Bakshi, B.R.: A thermodynamic framework for ecologically conscious process systems engineering. Comput. Chem. Eng. **26**(2), 269–282 (2002)
8. Odum, H.T.: Environmental Accounting: Emergy and Environmental Decision Making. Wiley, New York (1996)
9. Association of European Plastics Manufacturers, PlasticsEurope. http://www.plasticseurope.org/
10. Sha, S., Melin, K., Kokkonen, D.V., Hurme, M.: Solar energy footprint of ethylene processes. Ecol. Eng. **82**, 15–25 (2015)
11. Odum, H.T.: Folio #2: emergy of global processes. In: Handbook of Emergy Evaluation. Center for Environmental Policy, Florida (2000)

Economic and Environmental Advantages of Rubber Recycling

Geraldo Cardoso de Oliveira Neto, Henrricco Nieves Pujol Tucci$^{(\boxtimes)}$,
Luiz Fernando Rodrigues Pinto, Ivanir Costa, and Roberto Rodrigues Leite

Nove de Julho University, São Paulo, Brazil
geraldo.prod@gmail.com, henrricco@gmail.com

Abstract. This research aims to evaluate the economic and environmental advantages of the adoption of Cleaner Production practices in a rubber products manufacturer. The inappropriate waste disposal of rubber was an issue to be solved, so recycle this material was the way to mitigate environmental impact. The economic gain was evaluated by calculating the return over investment and the environmental benefits through the methodology of mass intensity factor. The results showed a return over investment in 17 months, however the most expressive advantage was at the environmental perspective.

Keywords: Rubber recycling · Cleaner production · Mass intensity factor methodology

1 Introduction

Most of the companies are oriented to generate profit, but this management style can blind them to the sustainability trends. As a consequence those companies can't keep up for a long time. Their operations have to be sustainable with initiatives such as reducing resources consumption and the reuse or recycle of materials waste, in order to get economical and environmental benefits [1]. Actions focused on the reduction of the generation of waste and the consumption of energy and raw material contribute to increase productivity, efficiency and profit. Those initiatives are aligned with the Cleaner Production (CP) concept [2].

The Brazilian government has established a Solid Waste Policy that aims to promote the adoption of the CP practices by the companies. This policy covers actions such as reduce, reuse and recycle, as well the solid waste treatment, final waste disposal, environmental education and other guidelines [3]. The CP intends to link the environmental impact reduction and the cost saving, in order to improve human health, safety and increase the process efficiency [4].

Environmental initiatives are not adopted by most of the companies due their old mindset, that believe that environmental practices are too complex, few efficient and don't return their investments [5].

© IFIP International Federation for Information Processing 2016
Published by Springer International Publishing AG 2016. All Rights Reserved
I. Nääs et al. (Eds.): APMS 2016, IFIP AICT 488, pp. 818–824, 2016.
DOI: 10.1007/978-3-319-51133-7_96

The literature review about rubber and the CP showed three alternatives about waste: (i) mix rubber and concrete to improve durability [6]; (ii) mix rubber with a compound of glass and plastic [7]; and (iii) mix rubber and asphalt [8]. The CP practices results in economical and environmental benefits and improves the image of the company [5]. In China, half of the generated rubber waste is forwarded to automotive industry, as an alternative to recycle this material [9].

Manufacturing rubber products requires additional substances to achieve the optimal point in terms of manufacturability and composition. In order to mitigate environmental impacts, Brazilian government created laws to the companies incorporate good practices like recycling and the correct disposal of lubricants. Thus, companies have been acting to contribute on the environmental performance improvement [10,11]. Despite that, many companies consider that investments on those initiatives are a barrier on the CP practices implementation [12].

There are many papers related to the CP initiatives, however as a quantitative assessment, none measured the economic and environmental benefits. This indicates the gap to be explored in this research. Then, how to evaluate economic and environmental advantages with the adoption of the CP practices in the rubber recycling? Thus, this research aims to evaluate economic gain by calculating the Return Over Investment (ROI) and the environmental gain through the Mass Intensity Factor (MIF) methodology in a rubber products manufacturer.

2   Methodology

This case study was performed in a rubber products manufacturer. It has an exploratory purpose with both qualitative and quantitative approaches, and is a research strategy focused in comprehending the scenery to be analyzed. Evidences were gathered by interview, questionnaires and observations, in order to create the adequate conditions to understand the studied object of this research [13]. The data collected were obtained through interview with experts and through observation.

To evaluate the economic and environmental advantages with adoption of the CP practices, four steps were realised: (i) data collect; (ii) economic assessment; (iii) environmental assessment; (iv) comparison between economic and environmental gains.

In the first step, it was possible to measure the total waste and the emissions generated by the process, in order to estimate the mass balance. It was focused on the recycling of the rubber waste from the internal process and external sources through reverse logistics. In addition, it was analysed the total of saved raw material (MTE) due to the rubber recycled.

The second step is related to the economic assessment. It was calculated the Economic Gain (GE) and the period to Return On Investment (ROI), as seen in the Eq. 1.

$$ROI = \frac{Investiment}{Profit\ in\ the\ period} \tag{1}$$

In the third step, environmental impact was measured in abiotic, biotic, water and air compartments through the Mass Intensity Factor (MIF) methodology, that considers Mass (M) and Intensity Factor (IF), as seen in the Eq. 2.

$$MIF = M \times IF \qquad (2)$$

After that, it was calculated the Mass Intensity per Compartment (MIC), to measure theenvironmental impactreduction per compartments: abiotic (w), biotic (x), water (y), air (z) and other (n). In the Eq. 3 is shown how calculate MIC for (w), the same way for othercompartments.

$$MIC = IFWasteA_{(W)} + IFWasteB_{(W)} + IFWasteC_{(W)} + ... \qquad (3)$$

Then, it is possible to calculate the Mass Intensity Total (MIT), as seen in the Eq. 4.

$$MIT = MIC_{(w)} + MIC_{(y)} + MIC_{(z)} + MIC_{(n)} \qquad (4)$$

In the fourth step, it was compared both economic and environmental gains to get the Economic Gain Index (IGE) and the Environmental GainIndex (IGA), as seen in the Eqs. 5 and 6 respectively:

$$IGE = \frac{MTE}{GE} \qquad (5)$$

$$IGA = \frac{MIT}{GE} \qquad (6)$$

Now it's possible to compare whichgain is more representative, economic or environmental [14].

Values in the Table 1 refers to the Material Intensity Factors (MIF) of rubber.

Table 1. Material intensity factors

Substance	Specification	Abiotic	Biotic	Water	Air
Rubber	SBR	5.70	-	146.00	1.65

3   Results and Discussion

In the oldest process, all rubber waste was forwarded to the final disposal without any treatment. After process improvements, all rubber waste are now grinded and returns to the process where it is mixed with virgin raw material. It works in a closed cycle to preserve the same chemical composition and physical properties. This result is aligned with the Solid Waste Policy that aims the recycling in a closed cycle, in according to [3].

Further important aspect observed in this study is recycling and reuse of rubber waste that is provided as a filler charge in the rubber products manufacturing system. Thus, it can be used for production of vehicles components, in according to [9]. This finding also contributes to the literature, because cases researched addressed the use of rubber waste in other applications instead of reuse in the internal process of the company. For example, use the recycled rubber in asphalt [8], use the recycled rubber on concrete [6] and add the recycled rubber on the glass and plastic mixture [7].

Results showed that the adoption of the CP practices contributed to save costs with waste disposal and at raw material acquisition. This evidence is in according to [2] that aims to maximize the reuse of waste through recycling in the production system.

In the first step, it was collected the production data, as shown at Table 2. The average output of this company are 580 ton per month. Recycling station demands 4 operators, 2 on the first shift and 2 on the second shift. The recycling station capacity are 55 ton per month. In addition, the company acquires monthly 52 ton of virgin raw material. This finding indicates similar characteristics with other recycling and reuse processes in a production system, in according to [5–9].

Table 2. Data collection

Description	Amount
Average output per month	580,000 kg
Recycling station capacity per month	55,000 kg
Employees	4 (two shifts)
Rubber consumption per month	52,000 kg

This company spent around USD 13,650 per month with virgin raw material acquisition. In addition, there were costs in order to dispose the generated waste, around USD 1,444 per month. So, the total costs in previous scenery were USD 15,094 per month. Recycling came up as an alternative, the operational costs to recycle the waste were around USD 7,150 per month, meaning USD 7,944 of saving per month.

Investments in equipments acquisition, infrastructure, and other expenses to build the recycling station were USD 128,750, resulting in a ROI in 17 months, as seen in Table 3. This result contributes to the literature since it demonstrates by quantitative calculations the opportunities of economic gains with the recycling and reuse of rubber in a production system. The qualitative approach is usually adopted in the researches without maths methods as cost saving, investment calculation and return on investments. This evidence is reinforced when analyzed studies of [5, 10–12].

The process generates 52 ton of rubber waste per month. The inappropriate disposal results in 296,400 kg in the abiotic compartment, 7,592,000 kg in the

Table 3. Economic assessment

	Description	Costs (USD)
Monthly cost	Monthly raw material acquisition (52 ton)	13,650.00
	Monthly waste disposal	1,444.00
	Virgin raw material + waste disposal	15,094.00
	Monthly rubber recycling (52 ton)	7,150.00
	Monthly economic gain with recycling	7,944.00
Investment	Cylinder 1500 × 500 mm	45,000.00
	Rubber mill 1100 × 800	55,000.00
	Vibration equipment for 30 mash	21,250.00
	Transport and other expenses	7,500.00
	Total investment	128,750.00
	Return On Investment (ROI)	17 months

water compartment and 85,800 kg in the air compartment. Then, it was identified environmental benefits with the CP practices implementation, as seen at Table 4. Thus, the total reduction of environmental impact was 7,974,200 kg. This result contributes to advance the current literature due to demonstrate the reduction of environmental impact in the abiotic, biotic, water and air compartments through the adoption of environmental assessment methodology, in according to [14]. The qualitative approach is usually employed in researches to show the potential environmental gain or demonstrated by the percentage of mass balance, as verified in studies of [5,10–12].

Table 4. Environmental assessment

Rubber	Abiotic	Biotic	Water	Air
IF	5.70	-	146.00	1.65
Mass	52	-	52	52
MIC	296,4	-	7,592,000	85,8
MIT	7,974,200 kg			

The Economic Gain Index (IGE) and the Environmental Gain Index (IGA) were compared, as seen at Table 5. It was demonstrated by calculating IGE that corresponds to 6.54 kg/USD of goods saved.

When considered the Mass Intensity Total (MIT) by each USD, there is a benefit of 1,003.80 kg of goods that are not modified nor taken from the ecosystems. So, this case study has demonstrated that it's possible to get economic and environmental gains through adoption of the CP practices. Finally, the comparision of the economic and environmental gains also contributes to the science.

Table 5. Comparison between economic and environmental gains

	IGE	IGA
Mass	52,000 kg	7,974,200 kg
GE	USD 7,944.00	USD 7,944.00
	6.54 kg/USD	1,003.80 kg/USD

4 Conclusions

The present research demonstrated that the adoption of the CP practices in a rubber products manufacturer, resulted in economic and environmental gains, that was this research objective. The environmental gain was very expressive, 153 higher than the economic gain, justifying the adoption of the rubber recycling. In addition, it was verified an economic gain with the return over investments in 17 months. This results contribute to increase the knowledge about this subject, as well to encourage other companies to the preservation of the natural resources.

The environmental impact due the inappropriate waste disposal was known by the company, however the costs saving and comply with the ISO 14000 requirements were the main reasons to implement the rubber recycling.

This research limitation consists in the application of a unique case, so it's not possible to generalize the results. It's suggested to perform new researches to allow comparisons.

References

1. Jabbour, C.J.C.: Non-linear pathways of corporate environmental management: a survey of ISO 14001-certified companies in Brazil. J. Clean. Prod. **18**(12), 1222–1225 (2010)
2. Almeida, C., Giannetti, B.F.: Ecologia Industrial: Conceitos, Ferramentas e Aplicações. Edgard Blucher, São Paulo (2006)
3. Joinhas, L.A., S.A.S.J.S.R.: Logística Reversa, Sustentabilidade e Educaçõ. Todas as Musas, São Paulo (2013)
4. Limpas, C.C.N.D.T.: http://www.pha.poli.usp.br/LeArq.aspx?id_arq=7985
5. Gombault, M., Versteege, S.: Cleaner production in SMEs through a partnership with (local) authorities: successes from the Netherlands. J. Clean. Prod. **7**(4), 249–261 (1999)
6. Richardson, A.E., Coventry, K.A., Ward, G.: Freeze/thaw protection of concrete with optimum rubber crumb content. J. Clean. Prod. **23**(1), 96–103 (2012)
7. Osmani, M.: Innovation in cleaner production through waste recycling in composites. Manage. Environ. Qual. Int. J. **24**(1), 6–15 (2012)
8. Oliveira, J.R., Silva, H.M., Abreu, L.P., Fernandes, S.R.: Use of a warm mix asphalt additive to reduce the production temperatures and to improve the performance of asphalt rubber mixtures. J. Clean. Prod. **41**, 15–22 (2013)
9. Liu, Y., Liu, Y., Chen, J.: The impact of the Chinese automotive industry: scenarios based on the national environmental goals. J. Clean. Prod. **96**, 102–109 (2015)

10. Ghosh, A., Rajeev, R., Bhattacharya, A., Bhowmick, A., De, S.: Recycling of silicone rubber waste: effect of ground silicone rubber vulcanizate powder on the properties of silicone rubber. Polym. Eng. Sci. **43**(2), 279–296 (2003)
11. Nabil, H., Ismail, H.: Fatigue life, thermal analysis and morphology of recycled poly (ethylene terephthalate)/commercial fillers hybrid filled natural rubber composites. Prog. Rubber Plast. Recycl. Technol. **30**(2), 115 (2014)
12. Van Berkel, R., Willems, E., Lafleur, M.: Development of an industrial ecology toolbox for the introduction of industrial ecology in enterprises–I. J. Clean. Prod. **5**(1), 11–25 (1997)
13. Yin, R.K.: Case Study Research: Design and Methods. Sage Publications, Thousand Oaks (2015)
14. Neto, G.C.O., Souza, S.M., Baptista, E.A.: Cleaner production associated with financial and environmental benefits: a case study on automotive industry. In: Advanced Materials Research, vol. 845, pp. 873–877. Trans Tech Publications (2014)

Energy Efficiency and Global Warming Potential of a Wind-Energy Complex at Brazilian Piauí State

Márcio Costa, Feni Agostinho$^{(\boxtimes)}$, Cecília M.V.B. Almeida, and Biagio F. Giannetti

Paulista University (UNIP), São Paulo, Brazil
feni@unip.br

Abstract. The human addiction to fossil fuel and global warming leads to the search for alternative energy sources. The Brazilian government intends to increase its dependence on renewable energy sources, including hydropower, biomass, and wind. Many political and economic efforts have been directed to wind-energy, however, there is a lack of case-specific information regarding its performance for CO_2 emissions and dependence on fossil fuels. The aim of this work is to assess the global warming potential (GWP) and the fossil energy embodied in an important wind-energy complex located at Piauí State, Brazil. Results show that evaluated wind-complex demands lower amount of fossil energy (0.0404 MJ) and has lower GWP (4.13 $gCO_{2-eq.}$) per kWh of electricity generated when compared to landmark studies. Wind-electricity showed better performance than hydroelectricity (0.1516 MJ/kWh and 11.84 $gCO_{2-eq.}$/kWh), which supports wind-electricity as an important alternative towards an economy decarbonization.

Keywords: Embodied energy · Global warming · Wind-electricity

1 Introduction

According to Wind Energy Brazilian Association (www.portalabeeolica.org.br), Brazil has the world's first position in the generation of clean and renewable electricity – i.e. it releases low amount of fossil carbon – mainly derived from hydro energy resources. Forty-five percent of Brazil's energy matrix comes from these so-called clean energy sources, which can be considered as a positive aspect when considering the global average of twenty percent. In addition, Brazil has several options to expand its clean and competitive electricity generation, including more hydropower, cogeneration, biomass, and wind energy.

The current worldwide concerns about climate change and the consequent efforts to reduce greenhouse gas emissions (GHG) led to the search for alternative systems of power generation that could reach high economic performance and, at the same time, generate less environmental impacts. Among others, an important political attitude comes as the growing economical investments in renewable energy sources such as wind energy. According to the Intergovernmental Panel on Climate Change [1], this

© IFIP International Federation for Information Processing 2016
Published by Springer International Publishing AG 2016. All Rights Reserved
I. Nääs et al. (Eds.): APMS 2016, IFIP AICT 488, pp. 825–834, 2016.
DOI: 10.1007/978-3-319-51133-7_97

energy source offers great potential for reducing GHG emissions. Although distributed unevenly among countries, wind-energy potential is greater than the current total world electricity generation. Taking into account the political, economic and technological barriers, it is estimated that wind-energy could supply up to 20% of global electricity demand by 2050 [1]. In Brazil, the development of renewable energy sources is supported by the Incentive Program for Alternative Sources of Electric Energy (PROINFA), created by the Ministry of Mines and Energy (MME) by law no. 10438/2002. The aim is to boost economies of scale, allow technological learning, increase the industrial competitiveness in domestic and foreign markets, and especially in assisting decision-making for future projects of electricity generation using cleaner and sustainable sources.

PROINFA aims to reach up to 2030 an amount of 3,300 MW installed capacity to be incorporated into the national integrated electricity system. Of this amount, 1,100 MW are planned to come from wind, 1,100 MW from small hydropower plants, and 1,100 MW from biomass projects. From this strategic planning, it is expected an amount of avoided emissions of 2.5 million tCO_2/yr, which could generate an environmental carbon emission certification under the Kyoto Protocol [2].

In addition to greenhouse gases, the reduction on fossil energy dependence also plays an important role in scientific and political discussions. The long term goals is to allow a societal development independent (or at least to a lesser extent) of fossil resources, which are considered non-renewable because their availability at low energy cost is being reduced over years [3]. According to the Brazilian Energy Plan for 2030 [2], the strategic planning is focused on energy efficiency increasing that could lead to a lower load on environment by demanding a reduced amount of resources, increase jobs opportunities, and increase market competitiveness. Energy efficiency addresses the energy consumption reduction, but also the opportunities for energy sources replacement towards a systemic efficiency gains.

In this scenario with reduced CO_2 emissions and fossil energy dependence, wind energy has been considered as a potential alternative towards a cleaner Brazilian energy matrix. Although cleaner, wind energy necessarily generates environmental impacts. For example, although the wind farms do not use fossil energy sources to generate electricity and do not releases fossil carbon to atmosphere during functioning phase, they require a lot of energy resources and materials for construction, operation and maintenance phases that could cause even greater impact on the environment. Thus, before labeling an energy source as "clean", "green", "renewable" or other adjective related to sustainability, a quantitative diagnosis must be performed to support such label; careful attention must be driven to the entropic trap (term used by Ulgiati et al. [4]), i.e. the whole life cycle of the good or service must be considered in the evaluation. Thus, before claim that wind-electricity is a clean or green energy source, what is its global warming potential and fossil energy demand?

This work aims to calculate the global warming potential and the fossil embodied energy in generating electricity from wind-energy at "Chapada do Araripe" wind-energy complex located at Piauí state, Brazil.

2   Method

2.1   Case Study Description and Data Source

This work evaluates the wind-energy complex called *"Chapada do Araripe"*, located at Piaui state, Brazil (Fig. 1). It was chosen as case study due to its socio-economic importance in generating wind-energy at Piauí state, as well as due to availability and updated data. This region is identified as the most appropriated place to install wind farms in Piaui state, due to landscape (accessibility and availability) and wind conditions. Within this complex, seven wind farms are being implemented and will generate about 500 GWh/yr of wind electricity (Table 1).

This work considers the processes of wind-turbines manufacturing, transportation, installation, operation and maintenance. Decommissioning was not included at this time due to lack of trustable available information. Regarding temporal analysis, it is considered 20-years of lifespan for wind-turbines (as considered by [5, 6]), thus all resources needed in operating and maintaining the wind-turbines during this period are accounted for. Raw data on energy and materials comes mainly from Yang et al. [7], while raw data on labor and services were obtained *in loco* through direct interview with experts in the field. All raw data were carefully verified together with specialists who are currently in charge of several wind-farms projects being installed at Piauí state; including the wind energy complex assessed in this work. Detailed calculations on primary data are provided by Costa and Agostinho [8]. All energy intensity and CO_2 equivalent factors were obtained from Ecoinvent Database v.3.1-2014 (the life cycle assessment database available at www.ecoinvent.ch) and available in Appendix Table 3. Uncertainty analysis was not addressed in this work because single values of raw data for each system's input were considered, which implies that findings can be exclusively used to discuss about the analyzed system, and focusing on the previously established primary objectives of this study. For a future work it is intended to obtain raw data from other different wind-energy complexes and then run the Monte Carlo simulation for uncertainty analysis.

Fig. 1. Localization of *"Chapada do Araripe"* wind-energy complex in the Piaui State, Brazil.

Table 1. Main characteristics of the "*Chapada do Araripe*" wind-energy complex evaluated (195 MW).

Wind farms	Land use (ha)	Wind-turbines[a] (units)	Electricity generated[b] (GWh/yr)
Ventos de Santa Joana IX	278	16	70.08
Ventos de Santa Joana X	353	16	70.08
Ventos de Santa Joana XI	187	16	70.08
Ventos de Santa Joana XII	593	17	74.46
Ventos de Santa Joana XIII	245	16	70.08
Ventos de Santa Joana XV	489	17	74.46
Ventos de Santa Joana XVI	443	17	74.46
Total:	2,588	115	503.70

[a]Model GE 1.7-100 MW hh80 m with 1.7 MW of nominal power.
[b]Average of generated electricity per each wind-turbine = 1 MWh/h or 8.76 GWh/yr. Considering 50% for conversion efficiency, each turbine provides about 4.38 GWh/yr of electricity.

2.2   Energy Efficiency and Global Warming Potential

Sustainability is the goal for societal development – and maybe for its survival – by considering all potential problems related to overconsumption of energy and materials, as well as the increase amount of waste disposal. Based on a well-recognized sustainability indicator of ecological footprint, the Ecological Footprint Network (www.footprintnetwork.org) states that current society is living beyond the Earth's biocapacity. This claim for efforts towards a reduction of pressure that human is causing on nature. Among several indicators available on scientific literature that can subsidize decisions to achieve sustainability, the embodied energy demand and global warming potential are currently receiving special attention by society and worldwide scientific community. Due to this, and also because the evaluated system is an energy plant, the energy efficiency and global warming potential are considered as sustainability indicators in this work.

The load on environment affecting sustainability can, in general, be divided in "upstream" and "downstream"; deeper information regarding this approach can be found mainly in Ulgiati et al. [4]. "Upstream" load are related to all impacts caused far away from where the wind-farm is located, i.e. all emissions and fossil-energy demanded to make available all components existing in the wind turbines are considered. These loads are not caused by wind-farm locally, but they are caused in somewhere within the Earth and result in a load under a global perspective. For instance, Fig. 2 shows that CO_2 emissions are caused by the upstream process rather than the wind-farm itself. Differently, the "downstream" loads are those ones caused locally, during system installation, operation and maintenance. In this work, as the evaluated system is a wind-energy complex that converts wind energy into electricity, the local load on environment can be considered as insignificant compared to "upstream" loads and thus it was disregarded. The methodological approaches in calculating energy efficiency and global warming potential under the "upstream" approach are following described.

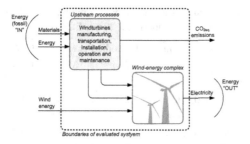

Fig. 2. Macro view of the evaluated system (dashed line) including two internal processes, the demand for materials and energy, and the outputs generated.

Embodied Energy Analysis [9]: This method aims to evaluate the direct and indirect gross energy requirement by the system. It offers a useful indicator about the energy efficiency of the produced good or service under a large scale view, i.e. it considers all "commercial" energy embodied. Commercial energy here is related to fossil energy. Energy intensity factors representing all fossil energy previously demanded to make available a good or service (usually in units of MJ/product) are used to convert all the systems input of matter and energy into fossil equivalent energy. In this work, the energy intensity factors provided by Ecoinvent Dataset v.3.1-2014 (www.ecoinvent.ch) are used. By adding the fossil energy equivalent of all system inputs will result in the gross energy required to generate wind-electricity, in units of MJ/kWh.

Global Warming Potential: Considering that evaluated wind-energy complex do not use fossil fuel or even burn any carbon-based energy resource locally to generate electricity, its emissions are located far away from where the wind-farms are installed. This "upstream" approach take into account all the indirect emissions released to make available all materials and energy used for components manufacturing, transportation, installation, operation and maintenance. For this, appropriated intensity factors provided by Ecoinvent Dataset v.3.1-2014 (www.ecoinvent.ch) that reflects the amount of CO_2 equivalent released to atmosphere were used and are available in Appendix Table 3; those intensity factors represents all emissions that can contribute to global warming potential. Additionally, all emissions due to diesel burned during transportation phase are also accounted by considering the emission factors provided by Sheehan et al. [10] as available in Appendix Table 4. For this, the following CO_2 equivalent factors published by Jensen et al. [11] are used: $CO_2 = 1$; $CH_4 = 62$; $N_2O = 290$; $CO = 1.6$; Hydrocarbons $= 3.1$. Both emission sources (indirect and direct, that occurred during transportation phase) when added provides the global warming potential in generating wind-electricity, in units of $kgCO_{2eq.}/kWh$.

3   Results and Discussion

Table 2 shows the results of embodied energy and CO_2 emissions for the evaluated wind-energy complex as a whole, and to generate 1kWh of electricity as functional unit. Focusing on energy demand, fiber glass corresponds to 23% of total embodied

Table 2. Fossil fuel energy requirement and global warming potential (GWP) for the "*Chapada do Araripe*" wind-energy complex considering a 20 yrs lifespam.

Item	Amount[a]	Unit/yr	Embodied energy		GWP	
			MJ/yr	MJ (%)	kgCO$_{2eq}$./yr	kgCO$_{2eq}$. (%)
Components manufacturing						
Steel	1.05E + 03	ton	4.25E + 06	20.88	3.61E + 05	17.32
Fiber glass	1.29E + 02	ton	4.73E + 06	23.24	4.03E + 05	19.36
Epoxy	1.50E + 01	ton	1.83E + 06	9.01	1.25E + 05	6.00
Copper	4.97E + 01	ton	2.21E + 06	10.87	2.29E + 05	11.01
Aluminum	2.88E + 00	ton	2.54E + 04	0.12	2.42E + 03	0.12
Glass	2.01E + 00	ton	2.43E + 04	0.12	2.22E + 03	0.11
Polyester	1.73E + 00	ton	1.63E + 05	0.80	1.24E + 04	0.60
Labor & services	1.22E + 07	USD	–	–	–	–
Components transportation						
Diesel (production)[b]	4.37E + 11	J	6.25E + 05	3.07	4.29E + 04	2.06
Diesel (usage)[b]	4.37E + 11	J	–	–	4.52E + 04	2.17
Steel	3.67E-02	ton	1.49E + 02	<0.00	1.26E + 01	<0.00
Labor & services	1.24E + 06	USD	–	–	–	–
Wind-turbine installation, operation & maintenance						
Wind	7.55E + 15	J	–	–	–	–
Concrete	5.98E + 03	ton	3.87E + 06	19.01	6.29E + 05	30.21
Steel	2.19E + 02	ton	8.86E + 05	4.35	7.52E + 04	3.61
Diesel (production)[b]	3.32E + 11	J	4.75E + 05	2.33	3.26E + 04	1.56
Diesel (usage)[b]	3.32E + 11	J	–	–	3.44E + 04	1.65
Water	1.74E + 03	ton	–	–	–	–
Electricity	1.04E + 12	J	1.67E + 04	0.08	7.32E + 04	3.52
Gasoline	1.01E + 12	J	1.24E + 06	6.10	1.45E + 04	0.70
Labor & services	1.24E + 05	USD	–	–	–	–
Output electricity	5.03E + 08	kWh				
Total			2.04E + 07		2.08E + 06	

[a]Most of raw data were obtained from Yang et al. [7], then complemented and verified by Brazilian experts which work on the wind-energy complex evaluated.
[b]Diesel (production) represents the energy demand and emissions related to diesel production, while diesel (usage) represents the emissions due to diesel burning during transportation phase. Emissions from diesel burning were estimated based on the emission factors available at Appendix Table 4 and the CO$_2$ equivalent factors of Sect. 2.2.

energy, closer followed by steel (20%) and concrete (19%). While fiber glass and steel are mainly used during components manufacturing, concrete are used for wind-turbines installation. Copper and epoxy used during components manufacturing also reached a moderated importance on energy demand with 10 and 9% respectively. This indicates that aiming a reduction on fossil energy demand for the evaluated wind-energy complex, efforts should be directed to reduce the usage of fiber glass, steel and concrete mainly. The total energy embodied by the evaluated wind-energy complex is 2.04E7 MJ/yr or 0.0404 MJ/kWh.

Focusing on CO_2 emissions, a different figure was obtained. Concrete is the first emitter reaching 30% of total CO_2 released to atmosphere by the evaluated wind-energy complex, followed by fiber glass (19%), steel (17%) and copper (11%). Thus, in a scenario in which CO_2 emission deserves higher attention than fossil energy demand, efforts should be done in reducing these materials. The total global warming potential for the evaluated wind-energy complex is 2.08E6 $kgCO_{2-eq}$/yr or 4.13 gCO_{2-eq}/kWh. Interesting to note that, although more than 2,500 km of covered distance by components transportation (e.g. rotor and tower are produced in the southeast region of Brazil) which demands high amount of diesel and steel for trucks, this phase can be considered as insignificant compared to components manufacturing and installation phases.

Figure 3 shows the results obtained in this work compared to others obtained from scientific literature. For both indicators, embodied energy and global warming potential, the values obtained in this work are lower than referenced values, i.e. they represent better performance. The highest value obtained from literature for energy demand was 0.4680 MJ/kWh [12], a value about 11 times higher than obtained in this work (0.0404 MJ/kWh). Similar behavior can be seen by the GWP, in which the highest value found in literature (41.2 gCO_{2-eq}/kWh; Ecoinvent Database) correspond to about 10 times higher the GWP of 4.13 gCO_{2-eq}/kWh obtained in this work. These comparisons are an attempt to visualize, under a macroscopic view, an order of hierarchy among the assessed wind-energy systems. However, it must be emphasized that for a deeper comparison some changes should be done to standardize the coefficient factors used and scale considered for all referenced values. For instance, most works analyzed by Lenzen and Munksgaard [13] and Ecoinvent Database have considered the equipment's decommissioning phase while the present work disregarded this phase. Anyhow, the numbers obtained in this work could be considered as promising because they show better performance than those obtained by Yang and Chen [5] and Riposo [14] who have evaluated similar systems to this present work.

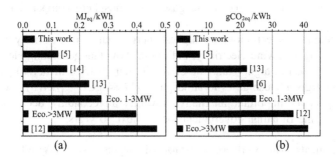

Fig. 3. Comparison of fossil embodied energy (a) and global warming potential (b) for different wind-electricity generation systems. Observations: for reference [13] a median value from 69 (embodied energy) and 29 (global warming) case studies was used; 1–3 MW and >3 MW indicates the installed power of systems – data Ecoinvent Database.

After calculating the GWP and embodied energy for each kWh of electricity generated by the wind-energy complex evaluated, it is important a comparison of these indicators against the largest energy source for electricity produced and used in Brazil: hydropower (reaching 71% of total). According to Brown and Ulgiati [12], hydropower releases 11.84 $gCO_{2\text{-eq}}$. per kWh of generated electricity, a value about three times higher than for wind-electricity obtained in this work (4.13 $gCO_{2\text{-eq}}$/kWh). Regarding the embodied energy, the same authors provides a value of 0.1516 MJ/kWh, which corresponds to about 3.7 times higher than the 0.0404 MJ/kWh obtained in this work. In short, both indicators show better performance for the wind-electricity than hydro-electricity.

It is recognized that a political decision on such important issue for the Brazilian society (energy) should consider several other indicators than exclusively GWP and energy demand. For instance, differently from hydropower, wind is a seasonal energy source that varies along year, it is impossible to storage this energy source for better management, the proper functioning of wind turbines depends on weather conditions, storms can damage wind turbines and electricity generation can become interrupted, economical aspects, social aspects, etc. Anyhow, this work presents that, considering the evaluated wind energy complex, generating electricity from wind energy results in lower global warming potential, (i.e. it releases lower amount of fossil carbon to atmosphere) and it demands lower amount of fossil energy than hydroelectricity.

4   Conclusions

The embodied energy and global warming potential for the *"Chapada do Araripe"* wind-energy complex evaluated are 2.04E7 MJ/yr and 2.08E6 $kgCO_{2\text{-eq}}$/yr respectively. Considering the functional unit of electricity generated, values obtained were 0.0404 MJ/kWh and 4.13 $gCO_{2\text{-eq}}$/kWh. Both numbers are lower (i.e. higher performance) than other found in scientific literature, which implies that generating electricity from wind-energy by the evaluated system demands lower amount of fossil energy and releases lower amount of greenhouse gases to atmosphere compared to referenced systems.

Comparing hydroelectricity – the highest energy source for electricity generation in Brazil, 71% – against wind-electricity, indicators show that generating electricity from hydropower demands higher amount of fossil fuel (0.1516 MJ/kWh) and releases higher amount greenhouse gases to atmosphere (11.84 $gCO_{2\text{-eq}}$/kWh), indicating that wind-energy is an important alternative towards an economy decarbonization as envisioned by the Brazilian government for the next 30 years.

Acknowledgements. This work received financial support from the Vice-Reitoria de Pós-Graduação e Pesquisa of Universidade Paulista (UNIP). Thanks also to CNPq Brazil (proc. no. 307422/2015-1) for the fellowship provided to second author.

Appendix

See Tables 3 and 4.

Table 3. Intensity factors used in this work.

Item	Unit	Intensity factors[a]		Observation
		MJ_{eq}/Unit	$kgCO_{2eq}$/ Unit	
Wind	b	b	b	b
Steel	kg	4.05E + 00	3.44E−01	Market for hot rolling, steel, GLO
Fiber glass	kg	3.67E + 01	3.12E + 00	Market for glass fibre, GLO
Epoxy	kg	1.22E + 02	8.33E + 00	Market for epoxy resin, liquid, GLO
Copper	kg	4.45E + 01	4.61E + 00	Market for copper, GLO
Aluminum	kg	8.82E + 00	8.42E−01	Market for sheet rolling, aluminum, GLO
Glass	kg	1.21E + 01	1.11E + 00	Market for flat glass, uncoated, GLO
Polyester	kg	9.43E + 01	7.19E + 00	Market for polyester resin, unsaturated, GLO
Diesel	J	1.43E−06	9.81E−08	Diesel, burned in building machine, GLO
Concrete	kg	6.47E−01	1.05E−01	Market for concrete, 50 MPa, GLO (density of 3800 kg/m^3)
Water	b	b	b	b
Electricity	kWh	5.79E−02	2.53E−01	Electricity production, hydro, reservoir, tropical region, BR
Gasoline	kg	5.53E + 01	6.48E−01	Market for light fuel oil, CH (HHV of 45 MJ/kg)
L&S	b	b	b	b

[a]All intensity factors were obtained from Ecoinvent Database v.3.1-2014 (www.ecoinvent.ch);
[b]Wind, Water and L&S (Labor & Services) are not accounted for both methodologies considered in this work (energy analysis and emission inventory).

Table 4. Emission factors (in kg/MJ) affecting global warming potential from diesel oil combustion in an industrial boiler.

CO_2	CH_4	N_2O	CO	Hydrocarbons
0.0762	8.3E-8	3.7E-7	0.017	6.7E-7

Source: Sheehan et al. [10]

References

1. Intergovernmental Panel on Climate Changes. http://www.ipcc.ch.pt.mk.gd/activities/activities.shtml
2. Brazilian Energy Plan. http://www.mme.gov.br/web/guest/publicacoes-e-indicadores/matriz-energetica-nacional-2030
3. Odum, H.T., Odum, E.: A Prosperous Way Down: Principles and Policies. University Press of Colorado, Boulder (2001)
4. Ulgiati, S., Raugei, M., Bargigli, S.: Overcoming the inadequacy of single-criterion approaches to life cycle assessment. Eco. Mod. 190, 432–442 (2006)
5. Yang, J., Chen, B.: Integrated evaluation of embodied energy, greenhouse gas emission and economic performance of a typical wind farm in China. Ren. Sus. Ener. Rev. 27, 559–568 (2013)
6. Dolan, S.: Life cycle assessment and emergy synthesis of a theoretical offshore wind farm for Jacksonville, Florida. M.Sc. thesis, University of Florida (2007)
7. Yang, Q., Chen, G.Q., Liao, S., Zhao, Y.H., Peng, H.W., Chen, H.P.: Environmental sustainability of wind power: an emergy analysis of a Chinese wind farm. Ren. Sus. Ener. Rev. 25, 229–239 (2013)
8. Costa, M., Agostinho, F.: Net emergy assessment of wind-electricity generation in the Brazilian northeast region. In: Brown, M.T. et al. (eds.) Proceedings of the 9th Biennial Emergy Conference, University of Florida, Gainesville (2016)
9. Slesser, M. (ed.): Energy Analysis Workshop on Methodology and Conventions, 89 p. IFIAS, Stockholm (1974)
10. Sheehan, J., Camobreco, V., Duffield, J., Graboski, M., Shapouri, H.: Life cycle inventory of biodiesel and petroleum diesel for use in an urban bus. Final Report, National Renewable Energy Laboratory, USA (1998)
11. Jensen, A.A., Hoffman, L., Moller, B.T., Schmidt, A., Christiansen, K., Elkington, J., van Dijk, F. (eds.): Life Cycle Assessment: A Guide to Approaches, Experiences and Information Sources. European Environmental Agency (1997)
12. Brown, M.T., Ulgiati, S.: Emergy analysis and environmental accounting. Enc. Ener. 2, 329–353 (2004)
13. Lenzen, M., Munksgaard, J.: Energy and CO2 life-cycle analysis of wind turbines – review and applications. Ren. Ener. 26, 339–362 (2002)
14. Riposo, D.: Integrated energy and environmental analysis of utility-scale wind power production. M.Sc. thesis, University of Maryland (2008)

Sustainable Production Management - Which Approaches Work in Practice?

Climate Change and the Brazilian Broiler Meat Production Chain

Robert A. Waker$^{(\boxtimes)}$ and Irenilza de Alencar Nääs

Paulista University, São Paulo, Brazil
bobwaker@gmail.com

Abstract. Brazil is one of the world largest exporters of broiler meat, and this sector is highly vulnerable to the estimate of climate change. The objective of this theoretical research is to present the importance of climate change, considering the effect of global warming, in the broiler meat supply chain, as well as the main guidelines for the analysis of the variables related to the production cost of the poultry farms. The theoretical concepts of the broiler chicken production process chain and the dynamics of climate change have been studied. Moreover, by mapping the productive network with their respective inputs and outputs, applying the cause/effect diagram it was possible to display the primary variables that might contribute to the operational performance of the chain. The result of the study pointed out the most important components that contribute to cost generation in the broiler meat production chain, considering the global temperature variations.

Keywords: Meat market · Climate change · Broiler meat supply chain

1 Introduction

A vast increase in demand for animal production is expected in the next decades, due to the world population growth. It is estimated that the human population by 2050 will reach 9.6 billion, with most of the increase expected to take place in developing countries. It is estimated that 85% of world population will live in regions of developing countries [1]. Chicken meat is one of the most important meat in the global market since it is easy to produce and it does not require much use of land. Global production is expected to increase by 2% to a record 89.3 million tons by all key international players. After overcoming China and becoming the second largest producer in 2015, Brazil will continue to expand due to the stable feed costs and an increase in exports [2]. Considering the meat production in Brazil, chicken meat is the first in production, followed by beef and pork, in this order [3].

A global climate change will cause changes in the local climate and will impact on agricultural and livestock production, in the two levels respectively. The main conclusions of the Intergovernmental Panel on Climate Change (IPCC), the Fifth Assessment Report (AR5) were [4]:

© IFIP International Federation for Information Processing 2016
Published by Springer International Publishing AG 2016. All Rights Reserved
I. Nääs et al. (Eds.): APMS 2016, IFIP AICT 488, pp. 837–843, 2016.
DOI: 10.1007/978-3-319-51133-7_98

- The warming of the climate system is unequivocal;
- Anthropogenic warming is likely to continue for centuries due to the timescales associated with climate processes;
- The heating of the air at the surface in the 21st Century, at the best estimate, will vary from 1.1 °C to 2.9 °C for an "optimistic scenario" and 2.4 °C to 6.4 °C for a "worst case scenario".

Authors believe [5] that animal production systems based on grazing and mixed farming systems will be most affected by global warming, when compared to industrial systems, such as poultry farms. This is due to the negative effect of lower rainfall generating more droughts and affecting crops and pasture growth, besides the direct effects of high temperatures and direct solar radiation on animals.

The challenge is how to achieve a better balance, increased production or productivity per unit, and at the same time improving the sustainability of the poultry industry. The broiler meat supply chain typically has the following configuration: breeder – poultry farm - slaughterhouse - end consumer [6]. Figure 1 shows the supply chain in the present study, where the actors were identified, as well as its roles, and the flow of products within the chain [7,8]. The flow of product/capital/information starts from the producer of broiler matrices at the beginning of the chain and flows to the consumer market at the end of the chain. This flow is bidirectional, and in one direction we have the products of each actor and in the opposite direction, we have feedback with information plus the capital payback of its operations. Each player can generate sub-products, such as raw material for fertilizers or materials for disposal. The animal production facilities are large generators of ammonia, nitrous oxide, methane and carbon dioxide in the atmosphere and contribute to the acidification of soil and global warming [9].

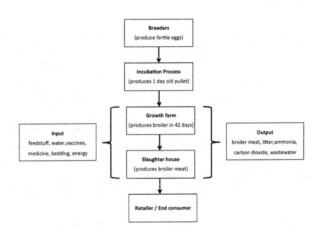

Fig. 1. Broiler meat production chain flow. Source: Adapted from [7].

The dynamic of broiler activity is directly related to the technology employed which generates substantial benefits in productivity, through improved feed conversion rates, increased nutritional gains, genetic research, and especially by automation of farms and slaughterhouses, and better production management [7]. Brazilian chicken meat is sold both in the domestic and international markets, as carcass and/or parts with aggregated value [8]. The poultry production chain is considered an industrial system. These industrial systems through the processing plants are the most important source of pig and poultry meat. Today this meat industry provide to the world' consumers nearly 70% of chicken, 60% of eggs and 55% of pork [5].

In the present scenario, the organizations that compose the meat supply chain have considerable challenges to manage their business units. There are goals and results to be achieved in a high competitive market. For these administrations, there are several factors to being known and mastered to obtain the expected results.

The objective of this research is to describe the possible effects of climate change in the evolution of broiler meat production chain. This paper presents the main system components that will be affected by climate change derived from global warming.

2 Methodology

Initially, secondary data were obtained with the objective of increase the necessary knowledge of issues such as climate change; chicken production chain and production processes. Many different reference sources were used, such as books and scientific articles, which provided the theoretical basis for the current study. In sequence, we used the cause/effect diagram, which is an analysis tool, to compile a list of components that may vary due to climate change.

The main issues on the influence of climate change on rearing broilers are: how this production system is dependent on the weather, which components of this system will be affected, and what can we do to deal with these effects. The weather dependency level acts directly on the animal (performance; health; well-being; nutrition and reproduction), and it can be affected by the weather conditions in a short or medium period [10].

Data were organized, and the productive chain was studied considering only two actors: (1) the farms that produce broilers, and (2) the slaughterhouses that produce carcasses and other cuts. The inputs and outputs of this subsystem were considered as (1) inputs to produce broilers (goods and capital), and (2) the output of the meat production destined for the domestic market and exports (goods and capital) [8]. Figure 2 shows the studied actors with their respective inputs and outputs. The cause/effect diagram is an analysis tool used to display the relationship between a result of a process (effect) and factors (causes) that may have caused the considered result. For the current study, the variables were identified through literature review. The brainstorming technique was used to determine the possible accountable factors for the performance of the production cost.

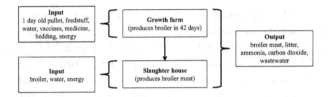

Fig. 2. Analyzed actors of the broiler meat production chain with their inputs and outputs

Due to a large number of variables involved, both in direct or indirect climatic effects that configure the productive system, the variables affected were simplified. An accurate study would require much knowledge and data in many disciplines, and it would be time-consuming. Therefore, the present study provides an overview of some relevant effects of global warming on the production of poultry and the dynamic components involved.

3 Results and Discussion

Climate change through global warming can dramatically affect the performance of the broilers production system, impacting the worldwide production [5]. The input components that undergo variations due to climate changes in the evaluated production system are shown in Fig. 3 through the cause/effect diagram. A high-temperature environment can compromise the reproductive efficiency of livestock production in both sexes and thus adversely affect the milk, meat and egg production. Exposure to high ambient temperature decreases fertility in broilers, rabbits and horses [5]. Temperatures greater than 30 °C are sufficient to generate heat stress to poultry. Especially in hot regions, heat stress is a great concern for the poultry industry due to the poor growth and performance and high mortality rates [11]. High ambient temperatures in the rearing area may lead to high mortality in broilers. Other effects are the reduction in feed intake, low body and carcass weight, low protein content in the carcass, and a little caloric muscle content [5]. It is important that the environment is maintained at 32 °C for the one-day-old pullet, and is reduced by one degree Celsius every life day until chicks reach ambient temperature [12].

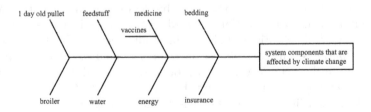

Fig. 3. Cause/effect diagram

Under global warming, water will be the main common weak point in livestock production systems. The water consumption by the birds is higher at higher temperatures [12]. The animals exposed to hot environments drink an amount of water 2 to 3 times more than those in thermally neutral conditions [5]. A study on the management of water use in a poultry slaughterhouse showed a more intelligent use should be applied in poultry production and processing [11]. The study refers to the procedures for dry cleaning, control over the amount of water utilized in a sector by sector basis, better disposal of blood residues, water automation and changes in the configuration system of the treatment wastewater plant.

Agriculture is the most vulnerable economic sector considering climate change, especially in developing countries. The two most important crops in the broiler feedstuff composition are corn and soybeans, respectively [12]. The feedstuff can be considered as a primary variable responsible for the cost of the broiler production system. Three variables must be evaluated to estimate the relationship between the production of corn and soybeans and climatic variations, which are the temperature, precipitation, and solar radiation [13]. In theory, the standard broiler producer, which is a rational farmer, take the production decisions based on, among other factors, the prices set by the market, to maximize net returns of crop production. The farmer can also make adaptations to climate change, adjusting cropping systems and using irrigation water in warmer seasons [13].

Manipulation of animal diet can be a practical way to limit the impact of the production on the environment by controlling the amount and composition of the produced manure and greenhouse gas emissions associated with this, as well as redefine the diet for a change in cost and availability of feed. Variations in the animal diet can affect the level of nitrogen, phosphorus and amount of excreta without penalizing animal health, welfare or performance [9]. The reduction in crude protein content in the poultry diet is also possible. It is important that the most suitable standard amino acid for each species of poultry is achieved by the addition of supplements. Ammonia reductions have been reported up to 50% when the crude protein content of the diets was reduced this way. For example, the decrease in crude protein content in laying rations of 30 g/kg at constant lysine content will increase feed costs by about 16% [14].

The effects of climate change on the health of livestock have not been studied in depth. The acclimatization of the animals to face the thermal challenges results in reduced feed intake and changes in many physiological functions that are linked to decreased health and the change of productive and reproductive efficiency have been studied [5]. As an indirect impact on the animals, there is the influence of climate on microbial populations, distribution of vector-borne diseases, small host resistance to infectious agents, shortages of food and water, and food-borne diseases. At first, some used vaccines should not be changed, but according to [6], several studies have evaluated the relationship between thermal stress and immune responses in cattle, chickens and pigs. That is, with a lower immune response the probability to use a larger amount of medicine is inevitable.

The air purification systems of the facilities are used to reduce NH_3 emissions, especially from pigs and broilers. The houses are mostly closed with forced ventilation. Forced ventilation also aims to control the room temperature to a more suitable thermal comfort for the birds [9]. Depending on the latitude of which the farm is located, there are different levels of electricity consumption for cooling or heating the place where the birds are. The air treatment can also remove fine dust and odor. For fattening livestock farms (chicken, turkey, duck) the main techniques for better production performance are (1) reducing loss of water from the system of the poultry using nozzles instead of bell drinkers, (2) treating the exhaust air, and (3) drying the manure by using forced air in order to reduce the emission of NH_3 around 40% to 60%. For farms that use bedding, waste management is as important as keeping the surface as dry as possible [9,11].

The use of techniques to adjust the air temperature of poultry farms for a thermal neutral comfort for the animals, causes higher power consumption and thus aggravates global warming and increases the overall costs of animal production [5]. Research should continue to develop new techniques for cooling systems, such as thermal insulation; focusing more, in techniques that require less energy expenditure. The cost of the energy used is one of the crucial factors in the financial performance of farms and slaughterhouses.

Risk management requires using insurance to minimize potential losses regarding a particular event. A variety of different instruments exist, including protections directly attached to weather (the insured are paid in response to "trigger events" such as abnormal rainfall, for example) [10].

Inevitably, the reasons to resist implementing technology to protect specifically the environment of animal production activity will vary greatly depending on the local situation in which the actors are. The cost is an obvious problem, and it would be fair to say that few producers will invest in additional technologies that bring little benefit to them in the absence of regulatory pressure from the government [9].

4   Conclusions

Probably the effects of global warming on water availability may force the broilers production sector to establish a new priority in producing animal products that need less water (for feeding, cleaning, etc.).

Determine whether a particular farm or slaughterhouse meets environmental standards, or require investment in one or more areas is more a regulatory issue than a scientific question. The production response to meet food demand has to take place, not only in facing climate change, but should also consider the increase in world population as an additional challenge. Scientific research can help the broiler production chain in the battle against climate change. All scientists who work with animals should seek collaboration with colleagues from other disciplines (agronomists, meteorologists, engineers, economists, among others) to optimize the operating performance of the chain.

The raised components will have an enormous impact on small or large production systems. A better understanding of these probable impacts will be vital to determine and select strategic alternatives that may help the actors of the production chain to increase its financial performance, improve food security and sustain its natural resource base in the future.

References

1. UNDP (ed.): No. 2015 in Human development report, United Nations Development Programme, New York (2015)
2. USDA: Livestock and poultry: world markets and trade. Technical report, United States Department of Agriculture, Office of Global Analysis (2015)
3. ABPA.: Relatório Anual UBABEF 2015. Technical report, Associação Brasileira de Proteína Animal, São Paulo (2015)
4. Intergovernmental Panel on Climate Change (ed.): Climate Change 2014: Synthesis Report. Intergovernmental Panel on Climate Change, Geneva, Switzerland (2015)
5. Nardone, A., Ronchi, B., Lacetera, N., Ranieri, M., Bernabucci, U.: Effects of climate changes on animal production and sustainability of livestock systems. Livestock Sci. **130**(1–3), 57–69 (2010)
6. Bukhori, I.B., Widodo, K.H., Ismoyowati, D.: Evaluation of poultry supply chain performance in XYZ slaughtering house yogyakarta using SCOR and AHP method. Agric. Agric. Sci. Procedia **3**, 221–225 (2015)
7. Oliveira, D., Nääs, I.D.A., Mollo Neto, M., Canuto, S., Waker, R., Vendrametto, O.: Issues of sustainability on the Brazilian broiler meat production chain. In: Conference Proceedings of the International Conference on Advances in Production Management Systems (2012)
8. Nääs, I., Mollo Neto, M., Canuto, S., Waker, R., Oliveira, D., Vendrametto, O.: Brazilian chicken meat production chain: a 10-year overview. Revista Brasileira de Ciência Avícola **17**(1), 87–94 (2015)
9. Loyon, L., Burton, C., Misselbrook, T., Webb, J., Philippe, F., Aguilar, M., Doreau, M., Hassouna, M., Veldkamp, T., Dourmad, J., Bonmati, A., Grimm, E., Sommer, S.: Best available technology for European livestock farms: availability, effectiveness and uptake. J. Environ. Manage. **166**, 1–11 (2016)
10. Thornton, P.K., Herrero, M.: Climate change adaptation in mixed crop-livestock systems in developing countries. Glob. Food Secur. **3**(2), 99–107 (2014)
11. Skunca, D., Tomasevic, I., Djekic, I.: Environmental performance of the poultry meat chain - LCA approach. Procedia Food Sci. **5**, 258–261 (2015)
12. Figueiredo, E.A.P.D., Schmidt, G.S., Avila, V.S.D., Jaenisch, A.R.F., Paiva, D.P.D.: Recomendações Técnicas para a Produção, Abate, Processamento e Comercialização de Frangos de Corte Coloniais. Sistemas de Produção **3**, 1678–8850 (2007)
13. Chen, S., Chen, X., Xu, J.: Impacts of climate change on agriculture: evidence from China. J. Environ. Econ. Manage. **76**, 105–124 (2016)
14. Veldkamp, T., Star, L., Van Der Klis, J., Van Harn, J.: Reduction of ammonia emission from poultry houses by nutrition. Technical report, Wageningen UR Livestock Research, Netherlands (2012)

Production Planning and Control: The Dissemination Tool of the Operation Strategy

Walter C. Satyro$^{(\boxtimes)}$, Jose B. Sacomano, and Jose Celso Contador

Paulista University, São Paulo, Brazil
satyro.walter@gmail.com, jbsacomano@gmail.com

Abstract. The objective of this research is to analyze the Production Planning and Control (PPC) as a dissemination tool of the operation strategy in industries that compete in environmental sustainability. We used a qualitative methodology supported by cases studies, based on interviews with managers responsible for the production planning and control of four big Brazilian industries. The results indicated that PPC can be an efficient tool to dissiminate the operation strategy for its power of integration with the many key areas involved in an industry, what can bring pratical implications to the ones responsible for the formulation and implementation of the operation strategy. The result is of value because PPC can be used as an ally of the operation/production managers to promote and lead the implementation of the operation strategy on the shop floor.

Keywords: Production planning · Production control · Sustainability · Advantage · Qualitative

1 Introduction

The manufacturing industry is in a challenge to supply a number of human beings that increases each time more, from 7.4 million in 2016 [1] to 8 million by 2024 [2]; and to meet the need of operating under the conditions of legislation on environmental control that is each time more tight, supplying products and services for the human welfare [3].

The operations strategies models, such as: mass manufacturing, lean manufacturing, responsive manufacturing, mass customization, agile manufacturing [4], and quality models, such as Six Sigma [5], etc. have focused on achieving cost efficiency, high quality standards, continuous improvement of product/service, and other factors to be more competitive.

These operations strategies models do not focus properly on the sustainability of the planet. The just-in-time (JIT) system aims to reduce waste and keep stock low, but it does not care about the traffic caused by the many trucks on the roads to supply the industries, or the pollution associated to them, and even

© IFIP International Federation for Information Processing 2016
Published by Springer International Publishing AG 2016. All Rights Reserved
I. Nääs et al. (Eds.): APMS 2016, IFIP AICT 488, pp. 844–851, 2016.
DOI: 10.1007/978-3-319-51133-7_99

the waste reduction is more linked to cost reduction than to any environmental sustainability politic.

The aim of these operation strategies is mainly with the industry, to keep the operations running at profitable margins, but the industries depend upon raw materials and natural resources to transform them in useful products and services.

The Factories of the Future Report [6] mentions megatrends that can cause impact and generate changes in nearly all manufacturing sectors, such as:

- demographic changes (increasing urbanization, world population growing, ageing societies, and now refugees);
- resources scarcity (water, energy and other commodities);
- climate change challenge (global warming, CO_2 increasing, ecosystem at risk);
- global responsibility sharing (growing power of the NGOs – Non Governmental Organizations, philanthropy increasing and shifting to global cooperation).

Conscious of these trends, the clean production strategy appeared. These sustainable or green industries [7] are concerned with the environmental sustainability of the planet and try not to prejudice the environment.

These clean production industries have challenges: they have to invest in new technologies/processes to follow efficient usage of resources, keeping emissions low, and at the same time, they need to try to be competitive in their markets, contending with their competitors that do not invest like them nor care about a sustainable world.

The clean production industries need business strategies that can give them competitive advantage to survive, but not only this, they also need an operational strategy aligned with the business strategy that can be implemented on the shop floor, to produce competitive advantage [8, 9].

All these changes, increased competition, and the development of new technologies and production processes lead to new conceptions of the Production Planning and Control (PPC) of the industries [4].

The objective of this research is to analyze PPC and study if it can be considered a dissemination tool of operation strategy in industries that compete in environmental sustainability.

2   Literature Review

2.1   Sustainability and Sustainable Development

Sustainability can be defined as the use of resources in a rate that allows them to regenerate and fulfill the supply of future generations [10]. Elkington created the term triple bottom line, considering that sustainability is interrelated to three points of view: environmental, economic and social (or sociocultural) [11].

Sustainable development is defined as "development which meets the needs of the present without compromising the ability of future generations to meet their own needs" [12]. The sustainable development is a route, a process to reach the objective, which is sustainability [13].

2.2   Operation Strategy

The aim of the operation strategy is to assist the productive areas to implement on the shop floor the business strategy, increasing competitiveness [9], to achieve the specific objectives of the industries, and support the competitive priorities of the organization [14].

The top executives often overlook the potential of operation/production not paying attention to this; they should be more involved with operations strategies to enhance the competitive ability of their industries [15–17], and to guarantee that business and operation strategies are aligned [8,9].

Skinner [18] points out that in 95% of the American industries analyzed there is a conflict between business and operation strategy, what can cause lack of competitiveness.

This misalignment causes adverse effects. The importance of the alignment is that business strategy affects operation strategy, and operation strategy affects business strategy [8,9,15,16]; and in the day to day of the operations on the shop floor, under pressure, when many decisions need to be done to keep operations running, it is easy to lose the focus and deviate operation strategy from business strategy.

2.3   Production Planning and Control (PPC)

In an uncertain world with the necessity of adapting to a dynamic market that demands competitive price, short delivery time, high quality standards, increased number of variants of products and ecologically friendly products (products that do not harm the environment, either in their production, use or disposal [19]), the production planning and control (PPC) plays an important role in the operational environment [20].

PPC is responsible for the planning, programming and control of the operational production processes, related to schedules, capacities, quality and quantities, and so is responsible for obtaining logistic and economic objectives [21,22], being an important link between the needs of the customers and the operational processes [20].

The general functions of PPC include: scheduling and sequencing (when to plan?), loading (how much to plan?) and controlling (to follow the plans) [22]; but it is also responsible for the identification of any possible causes of deviations that can arise, managing to counter deviations, identifying potential for streamlining [21] as well as reconfigurations of the manufacturing systems [20] to attain orders.

To help in such important actions, software were developed: MRP - Material Requirements Planning, to control the necessity of components/raw materials; MRP II - Manufacturing Resources Planning, that besides the control of the materials, manages the industry resources, and the ERP - Enterprise Resources Planning, that integrates all industrial processes to the entire enterprise [23].

Policies and strategies shall be used by PPC to reduce possible negative impacts in the production area when disturbances occur [22], particularly in green industries that face the challenge of integrating renewable energy sources to efficient technologies, producing with a minimum emission of greenhouse gases, low consumption of energy and water, reduced waste generated [24], and also keeping competitiveness.

3   Methodology

We used qualitative evaluation or methodology of analysis, as our intention was to discover and understand the interaction and complexity that represent PPC as a dissemination tool of the operation strategy on the shop floor of the industries that compete in environmental sustainability [25].

As strategy of research we used multiple cases studies supported by interviews [25] with operation/production managers in their own plants in a two phase interview: one with structured questions, and at the end, the interviewees were stimulated to talk more freely about the subject of the questions and also talk critically about our questionnaire. The interviews took about 1 1/2 h.

We selected industrial companies that had the ISO 14000 certification, reported in their websites their concerns for the environmental sustainability, and that were of relevance in the industrial community.

ETHOS Institute [26] helped us indicating companies to perform this research, and in FIESP - Industries Federation of the State of São Paulo, Brazil - we kept in touch with two companies recognized by this Federation for their excellency in environmental sustainability, but just one accepted to participate of this research.

Specialists indicated four other companies, but just two of them agreed to participate (Table 1).

Table 1. Some data of the companies selected

Industry	Sector	No. of employees
A	Auto parts	700
B	Auto parts	2000
C	Chemical	420
D	Auto parts	180

The three auto parts industries supplied directly the Brazilian automotive industries (tier 1), and the chemical industry was a public company with shares negotiated at the BM&FBOVESPA – Sao Paulo Stock Exchange.

4   Results

All the industries informed that PPC collected and centralized data that helped the responsible for the business strategy formulation (top managers) to elaborate

Table 2. Ways to send data to the top managers

Industry	Ways to send data to the top managers
A, C	PPC sent directly by daily report, via IT (Information Technology)
B	PPC informed the logistics that gathered other data and sent them
D	PPC sent data to the operation manager that resent them

them; these data were sent to the top managers in different ways, as can be seen in Table 2.

Although all these industries had business strategy, the grade of its disclosure to the production team and to the public in general was varied, as shown in Table 3.

Table 3. Grade of business strategy disclosure

Industry	Business strategy
A and D	Explicit – it was openly disclosed
B and C	Implicit – only the top managers knew it

All these industries had operation strategy and its grade of disclosure is presented in Table 4.

Table 4. Grade of operation strategy disclosure

Industry	Operation strategy
A, C and D	Explicit – opened to operation team and interested areas
B	Implicit

The operation strategy in industry B was kept with the operation manager; the interviewee said that their main objective was to supply their customers the best possible, with cost and stocks low at the quality required by the projects, but there was not an explicit operation strategy for doing so. "It was indirectly made explicit by the great goals formulated by the operation manager to the operation staff", said the manager of industry B.

PPC was called to participate in the operation strategy formulation, but in different degrees, as shown in Table 5. In industry A, PPC was so participative that it was responsible for suggesting an operation strategy to the accountable for that, which was free to accept, reject or reformulate it. The role of PPC in disseminating the operation strategy on the shop floor was presented in Table 6.

In industries A and D, PPC used planning and control to disseminate the operation strategy, taking into account the main goals of such strategy, "but it

Table 5. PPC: participation in the operation strategy formulation

Industry	PPC participation
A and C	Participative
B	Only when required
D	Only supplying data to the responsible for the operation strategy

Table 6. PPC: dissemination of the operation strategy on the shop floor

Industry	PPC: dissemination of the operation strategy
A and D	Through planning and control
B	Restricted to programming and reprogramming when required
C	PPC in group with the operation areas involved

also depends on the skills of the operation managers to reinforce this orientation almost daily", said manager of industry A.

"... It is a participative meeting, when I can also guide my team to the operation strategy, or be guided by them when we get away of our own strategy... PPC has a big role in this, for its capacity of contact with the many key areas of the company. I constantly emphasize to follow the operation strategy, and sometimes it happens that under the stress of our activities when we are at the point of missing the operation strategy, PPC remembers that we are missing the route and put us on the way again", told manager of industry C.

In industry B, PPC only interacted with production to keep production running. In industries A, C and D, PPC also tried to disseminate the operation strategy into other areas/departments, as presented in Table 7.

Table 7. PPC: areas involved in the operation strategy dissemination

Industry	Areas/departments involved
A, C and D	Sales, supply, operations, stock, logistics
A, D	Additionally: finance (budget) and quality
D	Additionally: human resources

PPC in these sustainable industries not only helped to follow and disseminate the operation strategy, but also helped to keep the environmental sustainability of these industries. For example, PPC in industry D suggested the use of returned packages, reducing waste and costs.

5   Discussion and Conclusions

PPC can be considered strategic to alert about any deviation from the operation strategy, because when under pressure to answer the demands and claims of the customers, the operation strategy can be lost. Additionally, PPC can improve waste reduction, through ideas to implement the environmental sustainability, contributing to the welfare of the planet [10].

The efficiency of PPC as a tool to disseminate the operation strategy can be improved when PPC is guided to work more interactively with other areas/departments involved, what can provide the guidance for the operations to do their work [15].

This research indicated that the ability of the operation managers is also important to remain focused on the operation strategy and emphasize it almost daily to the production team, what contribute to achieve the specific objectives of the industries, and support the competitive priorities of the organization [14].

The results pointed that, by the power of contact and integration with chain areas/departments of the industries when well guided, PPC can be a useful tool to disseminate the operation strategy through the shop floor and also in the interrelated areas, leading the implementation of the operation strategy, what can contribute to the increase of competitiveness [9].

As a practical implication, the managers involved in the operation strategy can use PPC to disseminate the operation strategy more effectively. This result is of value because PPC can be used as an important ally of the operation/production managers to promote and lead the implementation of the operations strategy on the shop floor.

As a limitation, the reduced number of industries here studied does not permit generalizations. We encourage the same research in other industries that compete in other areas than environmental sustainability to confirm or not the results here presented.

Acknowledgements. The authors acknowledge CAPES – Coordenacao de Aperfeicoamento de Pessoal de Nivel Superior of the Ministry of Education, Federal Government, Brazil, for the resources to make this research.

References

1. Worldometers (2016). http://www.worldometers.info/world-population/
2. United Nations (2015). http://esa.un.org/unpd/wpp/DataQuery/
3. Garetti, M., Fumagalli, L.: Industrial production type of processes, current needs and emerging challenges. In: Strzelczak, S., Balda, P., Garetti, M. (eds.) Open Knowledge-Driven Manufacturing and Logistics: The Escop Approach, p. 3. Warsaw University of Technology Publishing House (2015)
4. Andreatini, C.M.: Manufacturing and strategic management planning and production control from the perspective of managers of industries of auto parts. Ph.D. thesis, UNIP, São Paulo (2015)

5. Drohomeretski, E., Gouvea da Costa, S.E., Pinheiro de Lima, E., Garbuio, P.A.D.R.: Lean, six sigma and lean six sigma: an analysis based on operations strategy. Int. J. Prod. Res. **52**(3), 804–824 (2014)
6. EFFRA (2013). http://www.effra.eu/attachments/article/129/Factories%20of%20 the%20Future%202020%20Roadmap.pdf
7. United Nations Industrial Development Organization (2015). http://www.unido. org/greenindustry.html
8. Satyro, W.C., C.J.F.A.: Afinal, o que é Alinhamento Estratégico? In: SIMPOI - XVII Administration Symposium of Production, Logistics and International Operations (2014)
9. Contador, J.C.: Campos e armas da competição. Saint Paul, São Paulo (2008)
10. Bansal, T., Desjardine, M.: http://iveybusinessjournal.com/dont-confuse-sustaina bility-with-csr/
11. Elkington, J.: Enter the triple bottom line. In: Henriques, A., Richardson, J. (eds.) The Triple Bottom Line: Does it All Add Up. Routledge (2004)
12. WCED (1987). http://www.un-documents.net/our-common-future.pdf
13. Korhonen, J.: Special issue of the journal of cleaner production', from material flow analysis to material flow management': strategic sustainability management on a principle level. J. Clean. Prod. **15**(17), 1585–1595 (2007)
14. Kim, Y.H., Sting, F.J., Loch, C.H.: Top-down, bottom-up, or both? Toward an integrative perspective on operations strategy formation. J. Oper. Manag. **32**(7), 462–474 (2014)
15. Skinner, W.: Manufacturing-Missing Link in Corporate Strategy (1969)
16. Wheelwright, S.C., Hayes, R.H.: Competing through manufacturing. Harvard Bus. Rev. **63**(1), 99–109 (1985)
17. Krause, D., Youngdahl, W., Ramaswamy, K.: Manufacturing-still a missing link? J. Oper. Manag. **32**(7), 399–402 (2014)
18. Skinner, W.: Manufacturing strategy: the story of its evolution. J. Oper. Manag. **25**(2), 328–335 (2007)
19. Eco Friendly Products (2014). http://www.all-recycling-facts.com/eco-friendly-products.html
20. Hees, A., Reinhartat, G.: Approach for production planning in reconfigurable manufacturing systems. In: 9th CIRP Conference on Intelligent Computation in Manufacturing Engineering - CIRP ICME 2014, pp. 70–75 (2015)
21. Seitza, K.-F., Nyhuis, P.: Cyber-physical production systems combined with logistic models - a learning factory concept for an improved production planning and control. In: 5th Conference on Learning Factories, pp. 92–97 (2015)
22. Duffie, N., Chehade, A., Athavale, A.: Control theoretical modeling of transient behavior of production planning and control: a review. In: 47th CIRP Conference on Manufacturing Systems, pp. 20–25 (2014)
23. Mourtzis, D., Doukas, M., Lalas, C., Papakostas, N.: Cloud-based integrated shop-floor planning and control of manufacturing operations for mass customization. In: 9th CIRP Conference on Intelligent Computation in Manufacturing Engineering, pp. 09–16 (2015)
24. Putza, M., Stoldta, J., Fanghänel, C., Bierer, A., Schlegela, A.: Making sustainability paradigms a part of PPC. In: 22nd CIRP Conference on Life Cycle Engineering, pp. 209–214 (2015)
25. Martins, G.A., Theophilo, C.R.: Metodologia da Investigacão Cientifica para Ciências Sociais Aplicadas. Atlas (2009)
26. Ethos Institute (2016). http://www3.ethos.org.br/conteudo/sobre-o-instituto/ missao/

Solar Water Heating: Possibilities of Use in Industrial Processes in Brazil

Etevaldo Francisco Carreira Junior, Walter C. Satyro$^{(\boxtimes)}$, José B. Sacomano, and José Celso Contador

Paulista University, São Paulo, Brazil
fit.representacoes@uol.com.br, satyro.walter@gmail.com

Abstract. The increase of the global energy consumption generated the search for alternative sources of energy, including solar. This study aims to identify the current stage and the possibilities of the application of solar water heating for industrial processes and to characterize the current state of the solar sector in Brazil. This study is based on bibliographic review and secondary data. The findings indicate that the use of solar water heating is a viable alternative for industrial processes in Brazil, mainly in the sectors of food, beverages, textiles and chemicals. The industrial sector is big and one of the largest final consumer of electricity; although, the Brazilian development programs for the use of solar energy stimulate residential applications, a contradiction. The research also indicates that there is a lack of professionals specialized in renewable energies to work with solar heating systems in Brazil.

Keywords: Water heating · Solar heating · Alternative energy · Renewable energy · Industrial processes

1 Introduction

The technological advances and the economic and social development have demanded an increase of energy consumption; although, the alternative energy sources have a low share in the total volume of energy production around the world. The energy consumption for industrial purposes represents 29% of the total world consumption, and the use of alternative energy sources, including geothermal, solar, wind, heat etc. has a share of 1.2% [1].

The world industrial consumption of renewable energy accounts for 9%, and 8% from this comes from biomass with low participation of other alternative sources, including solar energy [2].

In 2014 the Brazilian industry consumed 32.9% of the total energy generated, but only 4.1% of this came from alternative renewable energy. The industries in Brazil are the largest consumer of electricity, followed by the sectors of transport, public use, residential, agricultural and commerce [3].

Almost all industrial processes require heat; 15% of the total energy consumed by industry is for heating, 13% of the thermal industrial applications require temperatures up to 100 °C and 27% up to 200 °C [4].

© IFIP International Federation for Information Processing 2016
Published by Springer International Publishing AG 2016. All Rights Reserved
I. Nääs et al. (Eds.): APMS 2016, IFIP AICT 488, pp. 852–859, 2016.
DOI: 10.1007/978-3-319-51133-7_100

Although in Brazil the industry is the largest consumer of electricity and the country is among the five with the largest area of solar collectors installed in the world, in 2014 water solar heating predominated in homes installations with 51%, while in industries it represented 17% of the total [5].

The research question is: Why the Brazilian industries have not yet awakened to the use of solar energy for water heating supply for industrial processes? This study aims to identify the current stage and the possibilities of the application of solar water heating for industrial processes, potential barriers, more favorable industrial sectors and characterize the current state of the solar sector in Brazil.

2 Methodology

As a strategy of search to collect data we used bibliographic research [6,7], in international and national articles of relevant scientific publications to build the theoretical framework, in a qualitative approach [6].

The exploratory research guided the collection of secondary data from the Brazilian market of solar water heating. For this, we tried to get the most up-to-date information available in the Brazilian Government websites and at FIESP – Federation of the Industries of the State of Sao Paulo, which comprises 131 associated unions, divided into 23 productive sectors that represent 150,000 companies of various sizes of the production chain in the state of Sao Paulo, Brazil [8].

3 Literature Review

3.1 The Solar Water Heating in Industrial Processes

Not all temperature levels required for industrial processes can be supplied by renewable energy sources, but the solar energy is adequate for low temperature applications (up to 100 °C) [2]. The industries search for efficient and cost-effective methods to capture, store and convert solar energy into useful energy to obtain hot water and steam.

The industrial applications more compatible with the integration of solar energy systems are pre-heating, pasteurization, sterilization, washing, cleaning, chemical reactions, food preparation and textile processes. Due to the fact that solar energy is intermittent, the heated water should be accumulated to controlled consumption, and when necessary, receive additional heat from another source [9].

The main component of a solar power system is the collector. Solar thermal collectors can be: (1) stationary (without mechanisms to track the sun, installed oriented to the north with a horizontal tilt angle approximately equal to the local latitude), (2) mobile (with tracking of a single axis to follow the sun or with two systems axes perpendicular to each other following the sun in the East-West and North-South directions), and (3) the most common, the flat plate collector, suitable for temperatures up to 80 °C, and evacuated tubes for temperatures up to 130 °C [10].

The selection of the heating system depends on the temperature required for the process. The most efficient systems and better cost/benefit are those for pre-heating, with flat plate collectors [4]. The solar heating for industrial processes is still in its early stages of development, but there would be great possibilities for applications with plan collectors and with evacuated tubes for temperatures up to 250 °C, such as in the food industry, textiles and beverages [10].

The potential use of solar heat for industrial processes are the ones that require temperatures up to 100 °C, mainly in the sectors of food and beverages, textiles and chemicals [11]. In the European region it is possible to find solar water heaters used in industrial processes [12–14].

3.2 Overview of the Brazilian Industrial Sector

We present some data of the Brazilian industry, represented by the manufacturing industry, the mining industry and the industrial services of public utility (composed by water, electricity etc.) in Table 1.

Table 1. Size of the Brazilian industrial sector (Source: adapted [15])

	GDP (%)	Formal employment (%)	Industrial plants (%)
Manufacturing industry	10.9	15.7	8.9
Mining industry	4.0	0,5	0.2
Industrial services of public utility	2.0	1	0.3
Total (Brazilian industry)	16.9	17.2 (8.5 million people)	9.4 (376,035 plants)

The industrial Brazilian sectors more relevant to the GDP were in this order: food products (15.2% of added value of the Manufacturing Industry), coke, oil products and biofuels (10.5%) and motor vehicles, vehicle body and auto parts (9.5%) [15].

The industrial sectors of: food, beverages, textiles (including clothing and leather) and chemicals (including pharmaceuticals), that possess the greater potential for application of solar water heating systems, have their important data in the Brazilian industry shown in Table 2, where the formal employment and industrial plants percentages are in relation to the total manufacturing industry.

3.3 The Solar Water Heating Sector in Brazil

In Brazil the solar heating sector is officially presented by DASOL - National Department of Solar Heating [5], founded in 1992, which had as members 14% of the 200 companies in the Brazilian industry that dealt with solar energy. The

Table 2. Potential industrial sectors for thermal solar energy in Brazil (Source: adapted [15])

Sectors	GDP (%)	Formal employment (%)	Employment (No. of people)	Industrial plants (%)	Industrial plants (No.)
Food	1.8	19.7	1,531,732	12.9	45,393
Beverage	0.4	1.8	138,25	0.7	2,436
Textiles	0.2	3.8	296,028	3.2	11,307
Chemicals	0.9	3.6	282,389	2.6	9,196
Total	**3.3**	**28.9**	**2,248,399**	**19.4**	**68,332**

national producers associated to DASOL produced plain solar collectors, that warmed the water from 30 °C up to 80 °C, and also solar collectors of vacuum tubes that had a market share of only 1.1%.

Austria, Brazil, China, India and Germany represented together more than 82% of the installed capacity in operation, and China was the largest user of solar thermal collectors in operation [16].

Brazil was the fifth country of accumulated area of installed solar collectors around the world, behind China, USA, Germany and Turkey, and in front of Australia, India, Austria, Greece and Israel, that formed the top 10 countries [16].

In 2014 the Brazilian solar thermal park produced 7,354 GWh, enough to supply with energy a city of about 3.7 million houses for a year, a city slightly smaller than Sao Paulo city. In this year, the accumulated area of installed solar collectors in Brazil was of 11.24 million m^2, when 1.44 million m^2 of solar collectors were produced.

Fig. 1. Solar heaters purchases by regions of Brazil (Source: adapted [5])

Among the Brazilian regions, the Southeast was the largest consumer of solar water heaters, representing 61.94% of the market, followed by the South (21.81%) and by the Midwest region (10.05%). The regions with smaller market shares in 2014 were the Northeast (4.51%) and the North (1.69%) [5], as shown in Fig. 1.

DASOL also develops programs to increase the use of solar water heaters in towns, called "Solar Towns", but this initiative is based on the use of solar plain collectors for houses, not industrial processes [5].

3.4   Aspects of the Viability of Solar Water Heating Systems

The efficiency and viability of solar water heating systems depend first on the solar radiation intensity, so Brazil is a privileged territory, by abundant intensity of annual average insolation, and by the average number of daily hours of insolation. The Direct Normal Irradiation (DNI) in Brazil varied from 1200 to 2400 kWh/m^2, as an average annual sum, in the period of 1999–2013 [17].

Industrial applications of solar technology require higher temperatures and larger volumes than residential and commercial applications, and should consider: (1) where and when the high temperature is used, (2) the variable nature of the supply of solar energy as the process heat demand, and (3) the supply profile (including storage, cold water replacement and controls), investments and variables which make it problematic and difficult to integrate solar thermal processes and determine the savings generated by the solar system in relation to the consumption of conventional energy [18].

The viability of solar heating systems depends, beyond its initial cost, on the price of fuel and electricity used to produce heat that the solar system replaces, being more viable when the solar panels become cheaper and when the subsidy of fuel and electricity are removed [4,13].

The barriers to the use of solar thermal technology are: the simplistic financial view of return on investment, not considering conventional energy saving in the long run; ignorance of politicians, managers and decisions makers on solar energy uses; lack of documentation and specific technical literature, tools, training and professional qualification to design typical solar thermal systems for industries [10].

It is worth mention the lack of education on renewable energy and the reduced global efforts to introduce training in renewable energies in traditional training programs, as well as the need to include disciplines in this area in engineering courses, specific undergraduate courses and short courses to meet more immediately the industry demands, and the intensification of courses and workshops taught by industries of this sectors, as well as lectures, seminars, and the exchange of experiences between institutions etc. [10].

4   Results and Discussion

Solar is one of the most promising source of energy to supply the industry among the alternative renewable energies, although it still has a very low share in the energy matrix [2,4,9,10,19]. The most favorable applications are in the industrial sectors of food, beverages, textiles and chemicals, at low temperature process (up to 100 °C), for which the most suitable collectors are flat plate and evacuated tube [10,13,14,20].

Brazilian industries have high potential for use of solar water heating systems, since the industrial park is large and diverse, having industries in all sectors considered as promising for the use of solar systems [8].

The Brazilian industry of food, beverage, textiles and chemicals represented together almost 30% of the added value of the Manufacturing Industry, and 3.3% of the Brazilian GDP; and are responsible for 2,248,399 formal employments, having 68,332 industrial plants [8], as shown in Table 2.

If we considered that only 10% of all plants of these four industrial sectors could invest in solar water systems, we could have a potential area of 683,320 m² of installed solar collectors (considering systems of 100 m²) to use in their processes. In addition, if 20% of the employees of the 2,248,399 total people could take hot shower before going home, an additional potential area of 224,838 m² would be required (considering 1 m² collectors for every 100 liters of water and 50 liters of water per bath). So, adding those two areas, we could reach a potential area of almost 1 million m² of solar water heaters, which would demand almost an additional 260 working days of the solar industry and would represent 8.9% of the already installed solar collectors in Brazil until 2014 [5].

Among the barriers identified to expand the use of solar thermal systems are: high costs considered of the systems, the low technological diffusion of solar heating to politicians, entrepreneurs, decision makers and potential users, the shortage of professionals with knowledge and experience in this area to design typical systems for industries, and even the lack of education and training in solar thermal engineering and in all professional levels: designers, installers, operators and maintainers, among others [21].

The use of electric shower for water heating is widespread in Brazil than nowhere else; as a result, electric showers are produced in large quantities at low price, representing an obstacle to the introduction of solar water heaters [21]. The use of solar water heaters could provide savings of up to 50% on electricity bill, with the return on investment varying from 1 to 24 months [5]. Due to the service life of 15 to 20 years on average, their use is advantageous [5].

On the other hand, the use of solar water heaters in industries had a growth from 3% in 2013 to 17% in 2014, although its main use is to substitute the electric showers in the dressing rooms of the workers.

The National Energy Efficiency Plan [21] tries to provide efficient energy programs in solar water heaters, to stimulate and regulate the expansion of the use of these systems, that are: NORMASOL (to revise and elaborate standards), QUALISOL BRAZIL (to qualify suppliers), PROCEL - Brazilian Labeling Program (to establish comparison criteria of efficiency and quality of the models available in the market), SOLAR TOWNS (to promote primarily the use of solar water heaters) and LEGISLATION (federal, state and local laws, on obligation or incentive).

5   Conclusions

The use of solar water heating systems in industrial processes, especially those using hot water at low temperature (up to approximately 100 °C) for direct use or for pre-heating processes of higher temperature, is an alternative viable for the Brazilian industry, especially in the food, beverage, textile and chemical sectors [9].

The use of solar water heaters could provide savings of up to 50% on electricity bill, with the return on investment varying from 1 to 24 months [5]. Due to the service life of 15 to 20 years on average, their use is advantageous [5].

The size of the Brazilian industrial market and the potential segments to the use of solar water heating systems makes it attractive from a marketing point of view, but only 17% of the industries use it, and in its majority, to substitute the electric showers in the dressing rooms of the workers, not for their processes [5].

Although Brazil is the fifth country of accumulated area of installed solar collectors around the world [16], there is much to do to increase the use of solar water heating systems in industrial processes, and the main difficulties are: the lack of culture and dissemination of knowledge and training to use these systems in the industrial environment, and the lack of incentives by the Brazilian development programs for the use of solar energy in industrial processes, stimulating the residential application, not the industrial application, which is one of the largest final consumers of electricity, a contradiction.

This research hopes to contribute to industrial companies and educational institutions as an indicator of the opportunities for the use and for professional training in renewable energy applications, particularly solar, in Brazil.

Acknowledgements. The authors acknowledge CAPES – Coordenacao de Aperfeicoamento de Pessoal de Nivel Superior, Ministry of Education, Brazil, for the resources to make this research.

References

1. International Energy Agency. https://www.iea.org/publications/freepublications/publication/key-world-energy-statistics-2015.html
2. Taibi, E., Gielen, D., Bazilian, M.: The potential for renewable energy in industrial applications. Renew. Sustain. Energ. Rev. **16**(1), 735–744 (2012)
3. Ministry of Mines and Energy. https://ben.epe.gov.br/downloads/Relatorio_Final_BEN_2015.pdf
4. Kalogirou, S.: The potential of solar industrial process heat applications. Appl. Energ. **76**(4), 337–361 (2003)
5. Nacional Department of Thermal Solar Energy. http://www.dasolabrava.org.br/informacoes/dados-de-mercado/
6. Martins, G.A., Theóphilo, C.R.: Metodologia da Investigação Cientifica Para Ciências Sociais Aplicadas. Atlas, São Paulo (2009)
7. Creswell, J.W.: Projeto de Pesquisa: Metodos Qualitativo, Quantitativo e Misto. Artmed, Porto Alegre (2010)

8. Federation of the Industries of the State of Sao Paulo. http://www.fiesp.com.br/sindicatos/

9. Mekhilef, S., Saidur, R., Safari, A.: A review on solar energy use in industries. Renew. Sustain. Energ. Rev. **15**(4), 1777–1790 (2011)

10. Cottret, N., Menichetti, E.: http://www.solarthermalworld.org/sites/gstec/files/story/2015-10-14/solar_heat_for_industrital_process_technical_report._state_of_the_art_in_the_mediterranean_region.pdf

11. Vannoni, C., Battisti, R., Drigo, S.: http://www.aee-intec.at/0uploads/dateien561.pdf

12. Quijera, J.A., Alriols, M.G., Labidi, J.: Integration of a solar thermal system in a dairy process. Renew. Energ. **36**(6), 1843–1853 (2011)

13. Calderoni, M., Aprile, M., Moretta, S., Aidonis, A., Motta, M.: Solar thermal plants for industrial process heat in Tunisia: economic feasibility analysis and ideas for a new policy. Energ. Procedia **30**, 1390–1400 (2012)

14. Karagiorgas, M., Botzios, A., Tsoutsos, T.: Industrial solar thermal applications in Greece: economic evaluation, quality requirements and case studies. Renew. Sustain. Energ. Rev. **5**(2), 157–173 (2001)

15. DEPECON. http://www.fiesp.com.br/

16. Mauthner, F., Weiss, W. Spörk-Dür, M.: https://www.iea-shc.org/data/sites/1/publications/Solar-Heat-Worldwide-2015.pdf

17. SOLARGIS. http://solargis.info/doc/_pics/freemaps/1000px/dni/SolarGIS-Solar-map-DNI-Brazil-en.png

18. Atkins, M.J., Walmsley, M.R., Morrison, A.S.: Integration of solar thermal for improved energy efficiency in low-temperature-pinch industrial processes. Energy **35**(5), 1867–1873 (2010)

19. Lauterbach, C., Schmitt, B., Jordan, U., Vajen, K.: The potential of solar heat for industrial processes in Germany. Renew. Sustain. Energ. Rev. **16**(7), 5121–5130 (2012)

20. Beath, A.C.: Industrial energy usage in Australia and the potential for implementation of solar thermal heat and power. Energy **43**(1), 261–272 (2012)

21. Ministry of Mines and Energy. http://www.mme.gov.br/mme/galerias/arquivos/noticias/2010/PNEf_-_Premissas_e_Dir._Basicas.pdf

Strategic Factors to Obtain Competitive Advantage in Industries that Compete in Environmental Sustainability

Walter C. Satyro[✉], José B. Sacomano, and José Celso Contador

Paulista University, São Paulo, Brazil
satyro.walter@gmail.com, jbsacomano@gmail.com

Abstract. The objective of this paper is to present factors that can impact the strategy, responsible for the understanding of the competitive context, so that a business and operation strategy can be formulated to reach competitive advantage. These factors were identified in CAC – Campos e Armas da Competicao (in Portuguese), Fields and Weapons of the Competition model of strategy formulation, and in the literature review. Using qualitative methodology supported on documentary research, we analyzed 10 industries listed in the BM&FBOVESPA Stock Exchange, Sao Paulo, Brazil, that composes the ISE Index (Enterprise Sustainability Index), with an estimated total market value of US$ 116 Billion based on October 2015. The results showed that the factors presented were used by these industries to formulate their strategies, but none used all of them. This research is designed for industries that compete in environmental sustainability.

Keywords: Strategy · Formulation · Sustainability · Advantage · Qualitative

1 Introduction

The industries are under pressure not only by the government policymakers, but also by the public, to be in line with the environmental politics [1–3]. In order to reduce their impact on the environment, the sustainable industries appeared, proposing to keep the production running with reduced environmental impact, that is, with lower consumption of energy, water, raw material, use of recycled material and minimum waste generated [4], using the cleaner production.

It is not easy for the sustainable industries to keep the competitiveness [5], since they need to invest to provide or buy technological innovation, new operation process and/or control, and at the same time maintain low costs to be competitive to remain in the market. Therefore, it is important that these sustainable industries can direct their strategies [6,7] to reach competitive advantage.

To formulate a business and operation strategy that can reach competitive advantage it is necessary to understand the competitive context by analyzing

© IFIP International Federation for Information Processing 2016
Published by Springer International Publishing AG 2016. All Rights Reserved
I. Nääs et al. (Eds.): APMS 2016, IFIP AICT 488, pp. 860–867, 2016.
DOI: 10.1007/978-3-319-51133-7_101

the factors that can impact the strategy. Based on qualitative methodology supported on documental research, the objective of this study is to provide the factors responsible for the understanding of the competitive context, so that the executives, leaders, entrepreneurs, and the responsible for the management of the industries that compete in environmental sustainability can understand the competitive context, and so, more effectively, formulate a strategy that can bring competitive advantage.

2 Literature Review

2.1 Sustainability and Sustainable Development

It is complex to define sustainability [8,9] and some authors use sustainability as a synonym for sustainable development. The term triple bottom line was created by Elkington to show that sustainability must be analyzed under three spheres: environmental, social (or socio-cultural) and economic [10], as shown in Fig. 1.

Fig. 1. The triple bottom line (Source: Adapted [10])

Sustainability is related to any human interaction with its environment [8], fostering business activities to fulfil the environmental, social, and economic requirement of the enterprise and its stakeholder for a longer period of time [11]. Other authors define sustainability as ways of making something sustainable [9], the use of resources in a way that allows them to regenerate and supply future generations [12], the ability of creating, testing and maintaining adaptive capacity, guided to the requirements of the ecosystem integrity and species diversity, also considering the social goals [13].

The term sustainable development was popularized in the report Our Common Future published in 1987 by the World Commission on Environment and Development, also known as the Brundtland Report, in which sustainable development is defined as "development which meets the needs of the present without compromising the ability of future generations to meet their own needs" [14]. The sustainable development is a way, a process to reach the target that is sustainability [15].

2.2   CAC - Campos e Armas da Competicao Model (Fields and Weapons of the Competition)

Designed by Contador [16], CAC - Campos e Armas da Competicao (in Portuguese), Fields and Weapons of the Competition model was based on quantitative and qualitative extensive research to understand why some companies are more competitive than others.

The central point of the CAC model is that, for a company to gain competitiveness, it is necessary to have high performance only in the few weapons of the competition that can give to this company some competitive advantage in the competition field selected for each pair product/market [16].

- Field of the competition is the imaginary locus, where products or companies dispute the preference of the customer, in which the companies seek to maintain or reach competitive advantage, such as short delivery time or innovative products [16];
- Weapons of the competition are the resources and capacities held by the company to maintain/achieve competitive advantage, such as technological control of the production processes and information system [16];
- Competitive advantage is a position of superiority recognized and valued by the customer, that leads a company to have a better competitiveness than itself in the past, or than its competitors; it is reached by a conjunction of some fields of the competition [16].

It is also important to present two other constructs of CAC: (1) Intensity of the weapons is the ability of the use of the weapon, or the power of a weapon, assessed at five levels, and (2) Relevant weapons of a company are the subset of the weapons that can furnish high competitive advantage to compete in a selected field, that must have a high level of intensity and, if necessary, investment shall be made to reach competence [16].

The formulation of competitive business strategy by CAC is to divide the market in segments, to establish the right product to the right segment and to select one or two fields of the competition, as well as one or two adjuvant fields of the competition for each pair product/market [16].

3   Methodology

We used a literature review and documentary research for analysis to find the factors that can impact the strategy, responsible for the understanding of the competitive context so that business and operation strategy can be formulated to reach competitive advantage.

The literature review started with the analysis of 54 papers published in the Journal of Cleaner Production number 96, 2015, that presented the best papers submitted to the 4th International Workshop Advances in Cleaner Production, held in Sao Paulo, Brazil, 2013, with the theme "Integrating cleaner production

Fig. 2. Initial literature review (Source: Authors)

into sustainability strategies"; we selected 8 papers that presented some of these factors in their researches, as shown in Fig. 2.

In these papers we could notice that the authors analyzed the strategy formulation under many aspects, but none of them gave a guidance that could help the responsible for the strategy formulation to understand the competitive context and so formulate a strategy that could lead to a competitive advantage, what is a gap.

We continued the literature review to find the factors responsible for the understanding of the competitive context, using EBSCO, ScienceDirect, Web of Science, and with the study of environmental standard ISO/NBR 14000:2015. We analyzed a total of 101 papers and selected 55 of them, where these factors were presented. Identified these factors, we made a research to analyze empirically if these factors were used to formulate a strategy possible to reach competitive advantage.

The selected group of research was constituted by 10 industries, listed and classified as industry by BM&FBOVESPA Stock Exchange, Sao Paulo, Brazil that composes the ISE Index (Enterprise Sustainability Index). The ISE was the 4th sustainability index released worldwide, which comprises 51 stocks from 40 Brazilian companies, publicly traded, listed on BM&FBOVESPA, among the issuing stocks of the 200 most liquid shares on the BM&FBOVESPA Stock Exchange [17].

Their names and sector of activities are presented in Table 1. The abbreviation "S.A." means publicly traded companies in Portuguese. We evaluated these 10 industries by their 2015 Sustainability Report, studying if the factors identified in the literature review were present and were used for the understanding of the competitive context.

4 Results

The factors identified in this research are presented below.

4.1 The Strategic Factors of the Business Strategy

The factors necessary for understanding the competitive context of the business strategy identified in the CAC model of strategy formulation and in the literature review were: Customers; Shareholders; Competitors/Newcomers; Board, Intensity of the Relevant Weapons; Interorganizational Networks; Labor

Table 1. The public companies under research and estimated total market value. Source: Adapted [18]

	Public companies	Sectors of activities	No. of pages analyzed
1	BRF S.A.	Processed food	117
2	BRASKEM S.A.	Chemicals	182
3	DURATEX S.A.	Wood and paper	172
4	EMBRAER S.A.	Transport material	88
5	FIBRIA S.A.	Wood and paper	152
6	GERDAU S.A.	Steel/metallurgy	49
7	KLABIN S.A.	Wood and paper	63
8	NATURA S.A.	Personal and cleaning products	128
9	VALE S.A.	Mining	119
10	WEG S.A.	Machines and equipment	162
	Estimated total market value (Oct., 2015): US$ 116 Billion		Total: 1,232 pages

Unions; Economy; Special Interests Group; Media; Supply Chain; Government/Regulatory Agencies; Climatic, Geographic and/or Geological Conditions; Natural Resources/Raw Material; Internationalization; Sustainable Development/Environmental Protection; Substitute Products; New Technologies; Research, Development and Innovation; Quality of Products; Values; Organizational Culture; Competencies/Know-how; Power and Logistics.

4.2   The Strategic Factors of the Operation Strategy

These ten industries focused on operation strategy identified with a cleaner production, and at the same time they needed to control their costs and other internal factors to keep the competitiveness in a market each time more globalized and competitive. The factors identified were: Reduction of Water and Energy Consumption; Occupational Safety and Health Management; Process Safety; Efficiency of Material and Resources; Eco-efficiency; Renewable Raw Material; Waste and Liquid Effluent Reduction; Greenhouse Gases Reduction; Reverse Logistics; and Recycling.

4.3   Competitive Context of the Business Strategy

Despite all these ten industries have emphasized in their Sustainability Report, which they have to issue yearly, their concern for the customer, only 30% put them as a central point to reach competitive strategy. Shareholders and board are important factors for 100% of these industries, but none of them analyzed potential competitors or newcomers, and 10% of these industries not even mentioned the competitors as an important factor of analysis.

All these industries took into account the following factors: Intensity of the Relevant Weapons (resources managed by the company); Interorganizational Networks (various associations to which the company belongs); Labor Unions (representing the interests of the workers); and Interest Groups that might affect or be affected by the company. The Economic and Financial factors were used by 60% of these public companies issuing an additional financial report to supplement the Sustainability Report. The term "company sustainability" was used by 20%, instead of sustainable company, expressing more concern with their companies per se than with environmental sustainability.

Despite 100% of the industries in analysis have emphasized the Media factor, none of them formally reported the use of social networks. Supply Chain; Government Regulatory Agencies; Natural Resources/Raw Material; and Sustainable Development/Environmental Protection were factors considered by all of them. Climatic conditions that take into account the rain standard, or other climatic changes as well as Geographic and/or Geological conditions that can provide more stable and fertile soil with reduced probability of floods or landslip were factors considered by 100% of these industries.

The Internationalization factor was subject of interest by 100% of them that have factories, branches or offices overseas, as well as the importance of the logistic factor to conduct all these operations closer to a harmony. Only 10% took into account the Substitute Products factor that can cause impact in the competitiveness of their products; in contrast to this, 100% of these industries reported their emphasis on Innovation, New Technologies, Research and Development as a competitive differential. All these public companies took into account the Quality of their products, as well as their Internal Values, Organizational Culture, Know-How and Skills. Only 10% of these industries took into account the Power factor, and the remaining 90% did not even mention Power as an important factor of analyzes.

4.4   Competitive Context of the Operation Strategy

These ten public companies showed that all of them had in their operation strategy the emphasis in the Reduction of Water Consumption and Energy factor. In Brazil the hydroelectric plants are responsible for 65% of the energy matrix of the country [19,20]; and in 2015 Brazil was in the middle of a hydric crisis [21] affecting the supply of water and energy at the same time.

Occupational Safety and Health Management were also factors taken into account in operation strategy for all these industries surveyed, however, only 30% of the industries mentioned concern for the Safety of the Production Process. Efficiency of Materials and Resources, understood as efficient use of raw materials and resources were mentioned by 60% of these industries; considering that these industries compete on environmental sustainability, it would be expected a higher percentage of industries adopting this operation strategy factor.

Only 10% of the industries investigated did not care about Eco-efficiency - an initiative that stimulates business to seek economic benefits using environmental improvements [22] - in its sustainability report. The use of Renewable Raw

Material factor was an operational strategy used by 60% of the industries in the research. Waste (solid, liquid and pasty) and the Liquid Effluent Reduction were operational strategies used by 90% of these industries; the Greenhouse Gases Reduction was not mentioned by 10%. Reverse Logistics was used only by 30% and Recycling was present in 70% of the operational strategies.

5   Conclusions

The objective of this research was to present factors that are important to take into account to understand the competitive context of the business and operation strategy for industries that compete in environmental sustainability. These factors were identified in CAC – Campos e Armas da Competicao (in Portuguese), Fields and Weapons of the Competition model of strategy formulation, and in literature review. These factors were analyzed in 10 industries listed in the BM&FBOVESPA Stock Exchange, Sao Paulo, Brazil that composed the ISE Index (Enterprise Sustainability Index), by their 2015 Sustainability Report [17]. The research showed that the factors proposed were used by these industries, but none used all of them.

These industries took into account Climatic, Geographical and Geological Factors, and also tried to promote the Sustainable Development, investing in New Technologies, Innovation, Research and Development, as well as Quality, but also considering their individual Values, Organizational Culture, Know-How and Skills. Just 10% of these industries took into account the Substitute Products factor that can impact the competitiveness of their products, and 90% did not consider Power as a factor of strategic analysis.

These industries were trying to reduce Waste (solid, liquid and pasty) and the Liquid Effluent, as well as seeking to reduce Waste generation, Water and Energy consumption, to reach the eco-efficiency [22]; however, only 30% of these industries emphasized the Safety of the Production Process and practiced Reverse Logistic, and just 10% did not even mention Greenhouse Gases Reduction [12,13] in their operation strategy in their Sustainability Report. The relevance of this research was to provide guidance for strategy formulation that can bring competitive advantage for industries [16]; as a limitation of this research the factors presented here were designed for industries that compete in environmental sustainability, so we suggest the use of these factors to analyze industries that compete in other fields to compare the results.

Acknowledgment. We thank the Coordenação de Aperfeicoamento de Pessoal de Nivel Superior (CAPES), Ministry of Education, Brazil, for the research grant.

References

1. Climateaction. http://www.climateactionprogramme.org/news/cop21_kicks_off_in_paris

2. Climateaction. http://www.climateactionprogramme.org/news/un_chief_hails_opening_week_of_cop21?utm_source=Feeds&utm_campaign=News&utm_medium=rss

3. Wang, Z., Subramanian, N., Gunasekaran, A., Abdulrahman, M.D., Liu, C.: Composite sustainable manufacturing practice and performance framework: Chinese auto-parts suppliers perspective. Int. J. Prod. Econ. **170**, 219–233 (2015)

4. Council, N.R.D.: http://www.nrdc.org/health/climate/airpollution.asp

5. Taisch, M., Stahl, B., May, G.: Sustainability in manufacturing strategy deployment. Procedia CIRP **26**, 635–640 (2015)

6. Robert, K.H., Schmidt-Bleek, B., De Larderel, J.A., Basile, G., Jansen, J.L., Kuehr, R., Thomas, P.P., Suzuki, M., Hawken, P., Wackernagel, M.: Strategic sustainable development—selection, design and synergies of applied tools. J. Clean. Prod. **10**(3), 197–214 (2002)

7. Almeida, C., Agostinho, F., Giannetti, B., Huisingh, D.: Integrating cleaner production into sustainability strategies: an introduction to this special volume. J. Clean. Prod. **96**, 1–9 (2015)

8. Marcelino-Sádaba, S., González-Jaen, L.F., Pérez-Ezcurdia, A.: Using project management as a way to sustainability. From a comprehensive review to a framework definition. J. Clean. Prod. **99**, 1–16 (2015)

9. Mishra, S.P., Mohanty, A.K., Mohanty, B.: Are there dominant approaches to strategy making? Vilakshan: XIMB J. Manag. **12**(1) (2015)

10. Elkington, J.: Enter the triple bottom line. In: Henriques, A., Richardson, J. (eds.) The Triple Bottom Line: Does it All Add Up. Routledge (2004)

11. Anåker, A., Elf, M.: Sustainability in nursing: a concept analysis. Scand. J. Caring Sci. **28**(2), 381–389 (2014)

12. Bansal, T., Desjardine, M.: http://iveybusinessjournal.com/dont-confuse-sustainability-with-csr/

13. Harris, J.M.: Sustainability and sustainable development. Int. Soc. Ecol. Econ. **1**(1), 1–12 (2003)

14. WCED (1987). http://www.un-documents.net/our-common-future.pdf

15. Korhonen, J.: From material flow analysis to material flow management: strategic sustainability management on a principle level. J. Clean. Prod. **15**(17), 1585–1595 (2007)

16. Contador, J.C.: Campos e Armas da Competicao. Saint Paul, São Paulo (2008)

17. BMF&FBOVESPA. http://www.bmfbovespa.com.br/indices/ResumoIndice.aspx?Indice=ISE&Opcao=0&idioma=pt-br

18. BMF&FBOVESPA: http://www.bmfbovespa.com.br/indices/ResumoCarteiraTeorica.aspx?Indice=ISE&idioma=pt-br

19. National Agency of Electric Energy of Brazil. http://www.aneel.gov.br/aplicacoes/capacidadebrasil/capacidadebrasil.cfm

20. TERMOPE Neoenergia Group. http://www.termope.com.br/Pages/O%20Setor%20Eltrico/matriz-energetica.aspx

21. National Agency of Water of Brazil. http://www2.ana.gov.br/Paginas/imprensa/noticia.aspx?List=ccb75a86-bd5a-4853-8c76-cc46b7dc89a1&ID=12684

22. World Business Council for Sustainable Development. http://www.wbcsd.org/pages/EDocument/EDocumentDetails.aspx?ID=13593

Approaches for the Integration of the Social and Environmental Dimensions of Sustainability in Manufacturing Companies

Paul Schönsleben$^{(\boxtimes)}$, Felix Friemann, and Manuel Rippel

ETH Zurich, BWI Center for Industrial Management, Zurich, Switzerland
pschoensleben@ethz.ch

Abstract. Social, environmental and economic challenges such as poverty, sub-standard working conditions, climate change, resource scarcity or environmental depletion lead to a rising importance of a multi-dimensional consideration of sustainability in manufacturing companies. The strong impact of manufacturing on humans and the environment necessitates the integration of social and environmental aspects in addition to the currently predominant focus on economic results. This paper exploits the potential of approaches with a cost, result and life-time perspective in order to obtain a well-balanced and measurable view on sustainability of manufacturing companies in industrial practice.

Keywords: Total cost of ownership · Triple bottom line · Life-cycle

1 Introduction

The effective and efficient manufacturing of goods has contributed significantly to rising living standards by meeting needs of society, advancing the development of infrastructure and education as well as offering employment and income. While the main focus of decision makers in manufacturing companies was on economic and technological issues, rising environmental pollution, scarcity of resources as well as the impact of globalization on local prosperity and working conditions started to change society and business values [1]. Sutherland et al. examine the activities of manufacturing companies and its effects on individuals and stakeholder groups with regard to social issues, such as corporate social responsibility (CSR), extended producer responsibility (EPR), outsourcing/reshoring [2]. The challenge for companies is to tackle the assumed dichotomy between competitive, environmentally friendly and socially responsible operations. This paper aims to highlight approaches that address the integration of the social dimension with the economic and environmental dimensions of sustainability. Thus, approaches with three different perspectives are presented in the following. Examples from industrial practice are provided in the third section in order to illustrate how manufacturing companies implement the integration of social and environmental dimensions on sustainability in varying degrees of detail and at different levels. The fourth section concludes this paper and presents an outlook.

© IFIP International Federation for Information Processing 2016
Published by Springer International Publishing AG 2016. All Rights Reserved
I. Nääs et al. (Eds.): APMS 2016, IFIP AICT 488, pp. 868–875, 2016.
DOI: 10.1007/978-3-319-51133-7_102

2 Approaches that Integrate Sustainability Dimensions

Regarding integrating the social and environmental dimensions of sustainability into manufacturing, this section reveals three approaches of varying degrees of detail with a cost, result or life-time perspective. The first approach, named "Total cost of ownership (TCO)", is widely used, but the extent to which it takes comprehensive ways of thinking and acting in terms of sustainability into account is minimal. The second approach, labeled as "Triple Bottom Line", goes much further, but also involves considerably more integration of sustainability concepts into corporate acting. The third approach, known as "Life-Cycle Sustainability Assessment (LCSA)", shows developments and future directions of measuring the social dimension of sustainability.

2.1 Cost Perspective: Total Cost of Ownership (TCO)

When taking decisions in a company, the cost perspective is an important driver for decisions. The favored alternative can vary depending on the temporal preference of the decision maker, e.g., whether they have a preference for a short-term or a long-term payback. The practical approach for decision support, the "Total cost of ownership (TCO)", converts relevant (both monetary and nonmonetary) considerations, criteria and factors for decision making into costs. Different cost elements and its categories (I-IV) are depicted in Fig. 1. The TCO approach supports globally active manufacturing companies to decide on make-or-buy alternatives (including in-house, outsourcing, offshoring) or to choose between different potential suppliers [3].

Fig. 1. Elements and categories of costs within total cost of ownership (Source: [4])

2.2 Result Perspective: Triple Bottom Line (TBL)

Nowadays, consumer awareness around sustainable consumption is increasing [5]. "Triple bottom line (TBL)" mindset (or three Ps: people, planet, prosperity) holistically takes into account the implications on environment, society, and economy of a product and its manufacturing [2,5]. An approach to address sustainability is full cost accounting. In a review of 4381 papers, ten full cost accounting methods with a diverse level of development and consistency in application were identified [6]. Investment and return should not be a tradeoff "between social and financial interest, but rather the pursuit of an embedded value proposition composed of both" [7].

2.3   Life-Time Perspective: Comprehensive Life Cycle Assessment (LCA)

Besides the previously introduced approaches, there is an active community in academia developing alternatives for assessing sustainability in a detailed and comprehensive way. This already has an impact on the thinking of scientists and practitioners of globally active manufacturing companies. Several authors dealt with the topic of merging life-cycle assessments (LCA) with other assessments combining all three sustainability pillars (environmental, economic and social) results in a "life-cycle sustainability assessment (LCSA)". Finkbeiner et al. conclude that LCSA "has to deal with the trade-off between validity and applicability" [8]. They propose a way to present LCSA results more effectively and efficiently to real world decision-makers in public and private organizations [8,9].

3   Social and Environmental Dimensions in Industrial Practice

The above introduced approaches of varying degrees of detail are explored here at the micro (company) level or at the macro (economy) level. Applications from industrial practice are presented related to TCO in a cost perspective, to TBL in a result perspective and to LCSA in a life-time perspective.

3.1   Examples for the Cost Perspective in Industrial Practice

The TCO approach is rather straightforward and was particularly developed for practical usability. It can be easily adapted to the managerial targets of a specific manufacturing company related to social and environmental business priorities by changing or extending cost elements and categories. Bremen et al. identified the importance of different TCO elements (Fig. 2) by conducting a survey with 178 Swiss companies from the machinery, electrical and metal industries in 2010 [3,4].

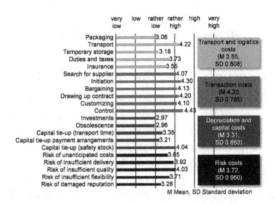

Fig. 2. Importance of the elements of the TCO (Source: [3,4])

The survey revealed related to the social dimension of sustainability that the risk of damaged reputation (lowest bar in Fig. 2) was still only of average importance compared to direct economic factors at this point of time. Basically, the TCO approach shows the limitations when trying to include the environmental and social aspects into the decisions of a short-term motivated manager.

3.2 Examples for the Result Perspective in Industrial Practice

In the following a small subset of frameworks, standards and indices is presented, showing examples of how sustainability (reporting) is done in practice today. To better understand environmental and social indicators, examples are shown in Table 1. The awareness from various stakeholders for TBL thinking and acting becomes evident when looking at the increasing effort of multinational corporations related to Corporate Social Responsibility (CSR). Sustainable behavior by corporates should be communicated and positively recognized. In Germany, for example, politics started to recognize the importance of these efforts recently and started to award a CSR award in 2013 [10]. In a survey conducted by Ernst &Young, the groups with the most influence on the organization's sustainability strategy were customers and employees, while the most important principal objectives of a sustainability strategy were adding value, identifying and mitigating risks and obtaining competitive advantages [11].

Table 1. Example indicator set for sustainability assessment according to [8]

Life cycle costing indicators	Environmental indicators	Social indicators
Extraction costs	Embodied energy	Salary per employee
Manufacturing costs	Global warming potential	% of female workers
Finishing costs	Human toxicity potential	% of females at the administration level
Waste disposal costs	Photochemical oxidation	% of employees with limited contracts
Electricity costs	Acidification	% of workers with yearly check up
Equipment costs	Eutrophication	Number of accidents
Revenues	Abiotic depletion	Percentage of child labor
Fuel costs	Ozone layer depletion	Number of discrimination cases
Raw material costs	Terrestrial eco toxicity	Social benefits per employee

The Global Reporting Initiative (GRI) is "the best-known framework for voluntary reporting of environmental and social performance by business worldwide" [12]. The extent of sustainability efforts is limited by company size. Most of the companies that report according to the GRI are large multinational corporations, while small and medium size companies (SMEs) are barely represented [12]. Also, the previously mentioned CSR award in Germany is differentiated by size of the company (1–49 employees, 50–499 employees, 500–4,999 employees, > 5,000 employees), recognizing that small and medium companies often do not have the knowledge and resources to work on CSR reporting as thoroughly as bigger corporations. Literature accordingly notes: "the sucess of widespread adoption of sustainability management tools rests upon two key factors: raising awareness of tools with SME managers and promoting the relative benefits from the implementation tools" [13].

An example, which is currently applied in industrial practice, for the above mentioned full cost accounting method is the integrated profit and loss statement (IPL) of LafargeHolcim Ltd. [14], the global leader in the building materials industry (cement, concrete, aggregates, and asphalt). LafargeHolcim has been included in the Dow Jones Sustainability Index for more than 10 consecutive years. The goal of this index is to track financial performance of best-in-class companies worldwide assessing economic, environmental and social criteria with a focus on long-term shareholder value [15]. The IPL of LafargeHolcim was introduced in 2014 for the first time in an effort to quantitatively measure the TBL [14]. Figure 3 shows the IPL as a waterfall chart, which represents the different indicators that have an impact on the TBL. Lafarge-Holcim indicate that the "Triple bottom line can be used to assess opportunities beyond compliance", whereby the corporate mentions "Compliance with governance, social and environmental requirements and standards" [14]. Basically, the IPL emphasizes the company's objective in measuring its sustainability aspirations in a consistent way and to measure its progress over time. Furthermore, it can already be used "to identify where 1 US dollar invested would bring the highest societal return" [14].

Sustainability reporting can be misused to "greenwash" the image of a company. To prevent this, there is a "need for reporting transparency, inclusiveness, completeness, relevance, and auditability" [16]. Accordingly, more than 80% of respondents from the aforementioned survey answered that assurance will add credibility to a sustainability report and reporting in a "relevant, comparable and meaningful way" is a key for a high credibility [11]. Still, we are far from measuring and communicating sustainability efforts in a comparable way: different frameworks and standards exist for corporate sustainability reporting, as well as a variety of different ratings and indices. The examples show advanced efforts from multinational corporations that still encounter problems in identifying and aggregating the right measurement variables.

3.3   Examples for the Life-Time Perspective in Industrial Practice

Rametsteiner et al. [16] analyze the following three science-led and two intergovernmental-led processes and ascertain that "a number of sustainability indicator development processes have been initiated within large research projects

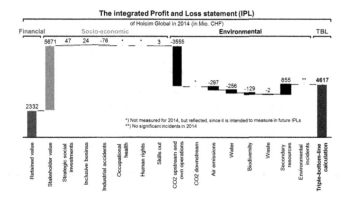

Fig. 3. The integrated profit and loss statement (IPL) of holcim global (Source: [14])

that aim to design tools for sustainability assessments, funded by the European Union" [16]: (i) EFORWOOD (Sustainability Impact Assessment of the Forestry-Wood Chain); (ii) SENSOR (Sustainability Impact Assessment: Tools for Environmental, Social and Economic Effects of Multifunctional Land Use in European Regions; (iii) SEAMLESS (System for Environmental and Agricultural Modelling, Linking European Science and Society); (iv) MCPFE C&I (Ministerial Conference on the Protection of Forests in Europe Criteria and Indicators); and the EUROSTAT (Sustainable Development Indicators SDI). However, except for the EUROSTAT SDI, these are mainly sector-specific and even the EUROSTAT SDI has to be extended to apply it for a specific sector (as has been done by EFORWOOD, which uses it as a basis [16]).

Within the life cycle sustainability assessment (LCSA) Sutherland et at. present a number of tools (and its associated principles and methods) related to life cycle assessment (LCA) and life cycle costing (LCC) across the three dimensions of sustainability [2]. An overview of these tools and the links are shown in Fig. 4. While there are well-established tools like LCA available for the environmental dimension, there is "still need for consistent and robust indicators and methods" for the economic and social dimension [7]. Efforts have been undertaken for deter-mining a functional unit to measure environmental performance in manufacturing systems (e.g., [19]) and integrating Life Cycle Assessment with common economic evaluations in order to increase the eco-efficiency (e.g., [20]). Still, especially the social life cycle assessment (sLCA) is considered to be in its infancy [21]. Like there has been a vast amount of research with regards to eco-efficiency in the last decades, there are still a variety of unsolved problems when explicitly considering the social dimension. In future, "focus needs to be placed on methods to quantitatively capture the social impacts of manufacturing" and also continue improving economic and environmental performance measures in this context [22] Overall, only a few of the international efforts on measuring sustainability "have an integral approach taking into account environmental, economic and social aspects" [23]. In addition, many of these efforts

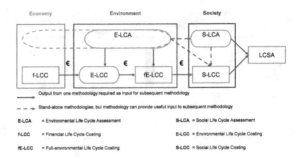

Fig. 4. Links of different sustainability assessment tools   (Source: adapted from [2,17,18])

currently still remain at the conceptual level and comprehensive, standardized approaches applicable to globally acting companies in different sectors still need to be developed.

4   Conclusions and Outlook

In order to address the integration of the social dimension with the economic and environmental dimensions of sustainability, the three perspectives "cost", "result" and "life-cycle" are presented. For each perspective associated approaches are introduced, namely total cost of ownership (TCO), triple bottom line (TBL) and life-cycle assessment (LCA). Examples from industrial practice are provided in order to illustrate how manufacturing companies implement the integration of social and environmental dimensions on sustainability in varying degrees of detail and at different system levels. Still, practical challenges with regard to indicator selection and weighting issues remain unsolved. The need for future research activities consists in e.g. collecting data or selecting impact categories/stakeholder groups. In order to raise a higher awareness of the full spectrum and importance of sustainability, it is of utmost importance to create comparable and standardized performance measurement systems. This will increase the transparency and will therefore help managers as well as customers to make better (i.e. more sustainable) decisions.

References

1. Rippel, M., Willner, O., Plehn, J., Schönsleben, P.: Bridging the gap between energy management systems and machine tools – embedded energy efficiency in production planning and control. In: Emmanouilidis, C., Taisch, M., Kiritsis, D. (eds.) APMS 2012. IAICT, vol. 397, pp. 80–87. Springer, Heidelberg (2013). doi:10.1007/978-3-642-40352-1_11
2. Sutherland, J.W., Richter, J.S., Hutchins, M.J., Dornfeld, D., Dzombak, R., Mangold, J., Robinson, S., Hauschild, M.Z., Bonou, A., Schönsleben, P., et al.: The role of manufacturing in affecting the social dimension of sustainability. CIRP Ann.-Manuf. Technol. **65**(2), 689–712 (2016)

3. Bremen, P.M.: Total Cost of Ownership: Kostenanalyse bei der Globalen Beschaffung Direkter Güter in Produzierenden Unternehmen. Diss. ETH (2010)
4. Schönsleben, P.: Integral Logistics Management: Operations and Supply Chain Management Within and Across Companies. CRC Press, Boca Raton (2016)
5. Bilharz, M., Schmitt, K.: Going big with big matters. The key points approach to sustainable consumption. GAIA-Ecol. Perspect. Sci. Soc. **20**(4), 232–235 (2011)
6. Jasinski, D., Meredith, J., Kirwan, K.: A comprehensive review of full cost accounting methods and their applicability to the automotive industry. J. Clean. Prod. **108**, 1123–1139 (2015)
7. Emerson, J.: The blended value proposition: integrating social and financial returns. Calif. Manag. Rev. **45**(4), 35–51 (2003)
8. Finkbeiner, M., Schau, E.M., Lehmann, A., Traverso, M.: Towards life cycle sustainability assessment. Sustainability **2**(10), 3309–3322 (2010)
9. Traverso, M., Finkbeiner, M., Jørgensen, A., Schneider, L.: Life cycle sustainability dashboard. J. Ind. Ecol. **16**(5), 680–688 (2012)
10. Bundesministerium für Arbeit und Soziales. http://www.csr-preis-bund.de/english-summary.html
11. Ernst & Young, Sustainability reporting (2015). http://www.ey.com/Publication/vwLUAssets/EY-Sustainability-reporting-the-time-is-now/$FILE/EY-Sustainability-reporting-the-time-is-now.pdf
12. Brown, H.S., de Jong, M., Levy, D.L.: Building institutions based on information disclosure: lessons from GRI's sustainability reporting. J. Clean. Prod. **17**(6), 571–580 (2009)
13. Johnson, M.P.: Sustainability management and small and medium-sized enterprises: managers' awareness and implementation of innovative tools. Corp. Soc. Responsib. Environ. Manag. **22**(5), 271–285 (2015)
14. Holcim Integrated Profit & Loss Statement. http://www.holcim.com
15. Laufer, W.S.: Social accountability and corporate greenwashing. J. Bus. Ethics **43**(3), 253–261 (2003)
16. Rametsteiner, E., Pülzl, H., Alkan-Olsson, J., Frederiksen, P.: Sustainability indicator development-science or political negotiation? Ecol. Ind. **11**(1), 61–70 (2011)
17. Kloepffer, W.: Life cycle sustainability assessment of products. Int. J. Life Cycle Assess. **13**(2), 89–95 (2008)
18. Hoogmartens, R., Van Passel, S., Van Acker, K., Dubois, M.: Bridging the GAP between LCA, LCC and CBA as sustainability assessment tools. Environ. Impact Assess. Rev. **48**, 27–33 (2014)
19. Plehn, J., Züst, R., Kimura, F., Sproedt, A., Schönsleben, P.: A method for determining a functional unit to measure environmental performance in manufacturing systems. CIRP Ann.-Manuf. Technol. **61**(1), 415–418 (2012)
20. Sproedt, A., Plehn, J., Schönsleben, P., Herrmann, C.: A simulation-based decision support for eco-efficiency improvements in production systems. J. Clean. Prod. **105**, 389–405 (2015)
21. Hunkeler, D.: Societal LCA methodology and case study (12 pp). Int. J. Life Cycle Assess. **11**(6), 371–382 (2006)
22. Haapala, K.R., Zhao, F., Camelio, J., Sutherland, J.W., Skerlos, S.J., Dornfeld, D.A., Jawahir, I., Clarens, A.F., Rickli, J.L.: A review of engineering research in sustainable manufacturing. J. Manuf. Sci. Eng. **135**(4), 041013 (2013)
23. Singh, R.K., Murty, H., Gupta, S., Dikshit, A.: An overview of sustainability assessment methodologies. Ecol. Ind. **15**(1), 281–299 (2012)

An Emergy Environmental Accounting-Based Study of Different Biofuel Production Systems

Maria de Fátima de Freitas Bueno[1,2]([✉]), Cecília Maria Villas Bôas Almeida[2], Feni Agostinho[2], Sérgio Ulgiati[3], and Biagio Fernando Giannetti[2]

[1] Federal Institute of South of Minas Gerais, Inconfidentes, Brazil
fatima.bueno@ifsuldeminas.edu.br
[2] Paulista University, São Paulo, Brazil
[3] University of Naples, Naples, Italy

Abstract. At the same time that the expectations grow around sustainable energy generation, biofuels emerge as an alternative to fossil fuels. This study evaluates the use of resources in the different biofuel production systems based on the emergy ternary diagram. A set of indicators was incorporated to the evaluation, aiming to display the environmental performance of each system. Results indicated that most of the analyzed systems are highly dependent on economy-sourced resources, evidencing that in a long term, there is no sustainable system. However, one of the public managers' aims is to search for a means to indicate which policies and patterns are sustainable for humanity and nature. Since economic development is dependent of the resources it uses, emergy accounting may be used as a tool in the process of selecting plans for sustainable development.

Keywords: Emergy · Biofuels · Indicators · Ternary diagram

1 Introduction

This paper reproduces part of a Ph.D. thesis under construction, and it is related to the emergy methodology robustness [1], and uses the ternary diagram [2] as a main tool in the biofuels evaluation.

Biofuels have emerged as a promising alternative to fossil fuels, they can be produced from a widely varied range of inputs. The most used are those from agricultural crops and their demand have been increased considerably. Nevertheless, their sustainability have been the object of many discussions [3,4]. In this sense, a large number of studies have been carried out in search for the most sustainable crop for biofuel production. Takahashi and Ortega [5] have presented the emergy analyses of five crops perceived as feasible feedstocks for biodiesel production. Ren et al. [6] have developed a capable mathematical model of evaluating the sustainability of bio-diesel supply chains produced from multiple-inputs and helping decision-makers choose the most sustainable model. Dong et al. [7] have performed an emergy and energy analysis of a typical distillery system. Ren et al. [8] have analyzed the sustain-ability of five different biodiesel production systems under a life-cycle perspective. Triana [9] has reviewed four studies by different authors with different approaches, and compared the results of

© IFIP International Federation for Information Processing 2016
Published by Springer International Publishing AG 2016. All Rights Reserved
I. Nääs et al. (Eds.): APMS 2016, IFIP AICT 488, pp. 876–883, 2016.
DOI: 10.1007/978-3-319-51133-7_103

bioethanol produced from sugarcane. Agostinho and Ortega [10] have performed a multicriteria evaluation of environmental and energy aspects of an integrated food, energy, and environmental services production system on a small-scale. Lu et al. [11] have carried out an integrated evaluation between economic and emergy cost-benefit of ethanol production from rice. Pereira and Ortega [12] have assessed large-scale production of ethanol from sugarcane. Seghetta et al. [13] have investigated potential production of bioethanol from macroalgae, compared to conventional system. Goh and Lee [14] have studied the possibility to create a renewable and sustainable energy source, using emergy evaluation methodology and energy from palm oil. Bastianoni et al. [15] have evaluated the use of two types of renewable inputs to produce biodiesel. Cruz and Nascimento [16] have performed an emergy analysis of oil production from microalgae. Yang et al. [17] have evaluated ethanol production from cassava. Cavalett and Ortega [18] have assessed the environmental impact of biodiesel production from soybeans. Felix and Tilley [19] have studied ethanol production from cellulose sources. Liu et al. [20] have compared petroleum production sustainability and two scenarios of ethanol production from rice. Emergy accounting has been used in the production systems assessment on all studies mentioned above.

Emergy is a real wealth measure, in terms of calculating the energy required for the production system. Odum [21] has defined emergy as the available solar energy used directly and indirectly to make a product or service. Its unit is the solar emjoule (sej).

The emergy methodology helps to identify and measure all inflows into a system, and it considers energy use aspects that are not considered in other methodologies, for instance natural resources, labor, and ecosystem services [22,23].

The ratio of the total emergy used by product energy results in a transformation coefficient, named transformity, whose dimensions are sej/J [24] and it is used to convert items from different scales into a common base. Consequently, different systems can be compared.

Albeit several biofuel production systems assessments are available in literature, none of those exhibit a wider discussion comparing fully different systems and presenting results in the form of graphs. Especially in the ternary diagram case, in which presents itself as a powerful tool that allows for a prompt and efficient interpretation of results, providing very important information to researchers and decision-makers [1]. Consequently, the aim of this study is to use the emergy ternary diagram to assess different biofuel production systems, mainly as for use of resources.

2 Methodology

This study was organized using an emergy databank, developed as part of a Doctorate project. The following actions were accomplished: data collection, calculation of emergy indicators, and application of collected data into the ternary diagram.

2.1 Data Collection

Data used in this study are from biofuels production systems assessments using emergy environmental accounting, and were organized to facilitate their interpretation. The feedstock for biofuel production, study site, baseline, unit, the product energy, transformity, emergy, and input flows were the used data in this study. However, emergy and transformity values may vary according to the analyst's choices, and also vary with the adopted baseline. Therefore, all emergy and input flows values herein have been adjusted to a common baseline (15.83×10^{24} sej/yr [25, 26] to allow comparisons.

2.2 Emergy Indicators Calculation

Collected data were tabulated and adjusted, and then the emergy indicators were calculated, based on input flows.

The input flows that are necessary to maintain the system are divided into three resources categories: renewable (R), non-renewable (N) and economy feedback (F). The R and N resources are provided by the environment and are economically free; however, the R flows have temporal and spatial renovation cycle capacity faster than its consumption cycle. Examples of R flows include the sun, the wind, the rain and so forth. The consumption cycle of N flows supersedes its renovation cycle. Examples of N flows include the soil, timber, mining resources and so forth. The F flows are associated with services and goods provided by economic system, or resources from other regions outside the system boundaries [2, 27]. Examples of F flows include fuels, fertilizers, services and so forth.

Resources flows allow for the calculation of different indicators that may help to analyze or to oversee a production system. Information on indicators based on emergy can be found on [21]. The indicators that were used herein are presented below:

EYR (Emergy Yield Ratio) is the ratio between the total emergy of a product ($Y = R + N + F$) by the emergy of F flows (Eq. 1) and represents the emergy return on the economic investment. Therefore, it reflects the ability of the process to explore local resources [2, 28], nevertheless it does not differentiate R and N resources.

$$EYR = \frac{Y}{F} = \frac{R + N + F}{F} \qquad (1)$$

ELR (Environmental Load Ratio) is the ratio between the emergy of F and N inputs by the emergy R inputs (Eq. 2). ELR is an indicator of the process pressure on the local ecosystem due to production activities [2]. An elevated ELR ratio may indicate a stress on the utilization of R flows [28].

$$ELR = \frac{N + F}{R} \qquad (2)$$

ESI (Emergy Sustainability Index) is the ratio between emergy yield by the environmental load index (Eq. 3). The concept of sustainability is linked to the EYR maximization and the ELR minimization, i.e. maximum use of the investment with minimum stress on local resources [2,27]. This index may be used to value the N investments in order to maximize the system effectiveness.

$$ESI = \frac{EYR}{ELR} = \frac{Y/F}{(N+F)/R} \tag{3}$$

2.3   Ternary Diagram

The emergy ternary diagram has been used in this study, aiming at a clearer presentation of the results.

The ternary diagram consists in an equilateral triangle with three variables associated with percentages. Each one of the vertices relates to a flow (R, N or F), and the sides represent binary combinations in the form of dots within the triangle internal boundaries. Full information on this tool are available on [2,27].

Using equilateral triangle properties provides further information on the studied system dependence on a given type of flow (either R, N or F), over the system's (eco) efficiency as for usage of reserves, and efficiency in supporting the environment, necessary to the system operation [2]. It also presents emergy indicators calculations and corroborates the emergy methodology robustness [1].

3   Results and Discussion

Table 1 shows the production systems evaluated in this study. The flows that were used in biofuel production, in conjunction with the three calculated emergy indicators are displayed. Labor and services resources were not considered in the calculations. Value interval for every indicator assessed herein was as suggested by [24].

As shown in the Table 1, a large part of the systems have EYR lower than 5, indicating an expressive use of F flows; furthermore, systems with EYR lower than 2 do not contribute enough to be considered energy sources, consequently acting more as consumers. In biofuels case, only the four systems with EYR higher than 5 are considered as primary energy sources, as those groups are capable of advantageously using environmental resources.

Most systems have ELR higher than 10. This means that those systems impact on the environment, are relatively concentrated, resulting from large investments, probably of N inputs, in a restricted area. Systems with ELR between 2 and 10 are considered moderate and those with ELR lower than 2 have low environmental load.

From the presented systems, only the bioethanol production system from macroalgae, in Denmark, has EYR and ELR adjusted for better use of R resources. The EYR is high, followed by a low ELR, indicating low environmental strain. On the other hand, around 40% of the systems have a low EYR, combined with a high ELR, consequently suggesting the occurrence of environmental stress.

Finally, it is noticeable that most systems (about 70%) features sustainability indexes lower than 1. The ESI of the bioethanol production system from

Table 1. Biofuel production systems and their respective indicators

Biofuel	EYR	ELR	ESI	Ref.
Ethanol from sugarcane – South Florida	5.84	3.93	1.49	[29]
Ethanol from grape – Italy	5.10	5.16	0.99	[29]
Oil from sunflower – Italy	1.43	2.51	0.57	[15]
Oil from macroalgae – Italy	2.71	1.99	1.36	[15]
Bioethanol from sugarcane – Brazil	2.00	7.66	0.26	[28]
Ethanol from sugarcane – South Florida Ref: [21]	5.33	10.26	0.52	[30]
Biodiesel from soybean – Brazil	1.94	1.57	1.23	[18]
Oil from microalgae – Texas	1.12	8.63	0.13	[16]
Ethanol from corn – Italy	1.25	6.11	0.20	[7]
Ethanol from wheat – China	1.47	5.36	0.27	[7]
Ethanol from switchgrass – Iowa	1.43	2.69	0.53	[19]
Oil from palm – Malaysia	1.24	4.55	0.27	[14]
Bioethanol rice + straw + chaff – Japan Ref: [20]	1.06	17.00	0.06	[11]
Bioethanol from rice – Japan Ref: [20]	1.07	15.15	0.07	[11]
Ethanol from rice – Japan	1.10	20.99	0.05	[11]
Oil from palm – Thailand	2.96	1.38	2.14	[31]
Oil from jatropha – Thailand	2.29	1.80	1.28	[31]
Ethanol from sugarcane – Brazil	1.99	1.36	1.46	[12]
Bioethanol from macroalgae – Italy	1.67	1.49	1.12	[13]
Bioethanol from macroalgae – Denmark	8.25	0.14	59.75	[13]
Biodiesel from palm – China	1.03	58.65	0.02	[8]
Biodiesel from sunflower – China	1.07	24.71	0.04	[8]
Biodiesel from soybean – China	1.09	17.05	0.06	[8]
Biodiesel from rapeseed – China	1.04	40.85	0.03	[8]
Biodiesel from jatropha – China	1.01	223.59	0.00	[8]
Fuel from cassava – China	1.07	15.11	0.07	[17]
Biodiesel from soybean – China	1.11	13.41	0.08	[6]
Biodiesel from rapeseed – China	1.05	29.99	0.03	[6]
Biodiesel from sunflower – China	0.08	20.04	0.05	[6]

macroalgae, in Denmark, deserves special attention, as it is the only long term sustainable system, among all. That system presents sustainability level of 59.75, probably due to the use of R resources in algae transportation, which, in this case is the energy from the sea waves, consequently avoiding use of fossil fuels, which is the resource used for that purpose in other systems.

These results, based on the values of flows R, N, and F are better visualized from ternary diagram, which also allows us for a comparison among the various configurations shown on the biofuels production systems (Fig. 1).

The Fig. 1 exhibits two sustainability lines that divide the graph into three parts. The area below the index equal to 1 (ESI<1) indicates the long term non-sustainable systems. The area between indices 1 and 5 (1<ESI<5) characterizes mid term sustainability. The area above the index equal to 5 (ESI<5) means long term sustainability. Three groups of biofuel production systems were identified in Fig. 1, considering sustainability and resource inflows.

The group 1 shows the systems that have a strong dependence on F resources, mainly of products derived from fossil fuels, such as fertilizers. These systems are not considered sustainable in the long term.

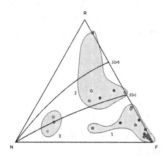

Fig. 1. Emergy ternary diagram of the biofuels production systems: (1) soybean, sunflower, rapeseed, rice, corn, wheat, switchgrass, cassava, microalgae, palm, jatropha, sugarcane, (2) macroalgae, jatropha, palm, sugarcane, (3) sugarcane, grape.

However, systems with low or no dependence on such resources are sought after, and that explains the presence, on the Fig. 1, of dots related to studies that involve sustainability assessments of non-conventional inputs for more sustainable biofuels production, such as macroalgae, jatropha and palm (group 2). These systems are considered as mid and long term sustainable.

Biofuels produced from grapes, and, in some cases, from sugarcane, are also characterized as mid-term sustainable, despite presenting high consumption of N resources (group 3).

Therefore, the dots in Fig. 1 show that biofuels produced from food crops, mainly, can not be considered long term sustainable (group 1 and group 3). Consequently, production systems that use non-conventional flows present themselves as more sustainable (group 2).

4 Conclusion

It is clear enough that dependence on N and F resources enhances environmental degradation, rendering the system relatively less sustainable. Consequently, the search for inputs for biofuels production that can replace fossil fuels remains a challenge, since it is necessary that they provide a net energy gain, that be sustainable, that feature a higher environmental benefit than the fossil fuel that they are intended to replace, that be economically competitive, and that be able to be produced in large quantities.

Such set of information can be obtained from an emergy analysis. However, graphic presentations are most convenient when it comes to visualize results. The interpretation of results and comparisons between systems is easier and faster with the application from the emergy ternary diagram (Fig. 1). Moreover, the emergy ternary diagram corroborates the robustness of the emergy accounting methodology by displaying the dots of studied systems in well-defined regions, with some plainly justifiable exceptions.

Acknowledgements. We are greatful for Universidade Paulista (UNIP) for the financial support, and for the Instituto Federal de Educação, Ciência e Tecnologia do Sul de Minas Gerais. We also want to thank to the CAPES-PROSUP for the scholarship provided to the first author.

References

1. Giannetti, B., Almeida, C., Agostinho, F., Bonilla, S., Ulgiati, S.: Primary evidences on the robustness of environmental accounting from emergy. J. Environ. Acc. Manag. **1**(2), 203–212 (2013)
2. Giannetti, B., Barrella, F., Almeida, C.: A combined tool for environmental scientists and decision makers: ternary diagrams and emergy accounting. J. Clean. Prod. **14**(2), 201–210 (2006)
3. Liao, W., Heijungs, R., Huppes, G.: Is bioethanol a sustainable energy source? An energy-, exergy-, and emergy-based thermodynamic system analysis. Renew. Energy **36**(12), 3479–3487 (2011)
4. Milazzo, M., Spina, F., Primerano, P., Bart, J.: Soy biodiesel pathways: global prospects. Renew. Sustain. Energy Rev. **26**, 579–624 (2013)
5. Takahashi, F., Ortega, E.: Assessing the sustainability of Brazilian oleaginous crops-possible raw material to produce biodiesel. Energy Policy **38**(5), 2446–2454 (2010)
6. Ren, J., Tan, S., Yang, L., Goodsite, M.E., Pang, C., Dong, L.: Optimization of emergy sustainability index for biodiesel supply network design. Energy Convers. Manag. **92**, 312–321 (2015)
7. Dong, X., Ulgiati, S., Yan, M., Zhang, X., Gao, W.: Energy and eMergy evaluation of bioethanol production from wheat in Henan province, China. Energy Policy **36**(10), 3882–3892 (2008)
8. Ren, J., Manzardo, A., Mazzi, A., Fedele, A., Scipioni, A.: Emergy analysis and sustainability efficiency analysis of different crop-based biodiesel in life cycle perspective. Sci. World J. **2013**, 1–12 (2013)
9. Triana, C.A.R.: Energetics of Brazilian ethanol: comparison between assessment approaches. Energy Policy **39**(8), 4605–4613 (2011)
10. Agostinho, F., Ortega, E.: Integrated food, energy and environmental services production as an alternative for small rural properties in Brazil. Energy **37**(1), 103–114 (2012)
11. Lu, H., Lin, B.L., Campbell, D.E., Sagisaka, M., Ren, H.: Biofuel vs. biodiversity? Integrated emergy and economic cost-benefit evaluation of rice-ethanol production in Japan. Energy **46**(1), 442–450 (2012)

12. Pereira, C.L., Ortega, E.: Sustainability assessment of large-scale ethanol production from sugarcane. J. Clean. Prod. **18**(1), 77–82 (2010)
13. Seghetta, M., Østergård, H., Bastianoni, S.: Energy analysis of using macroalgae from eutrophic waters as a bioethanol feedstock. Ecol. Modell. **288**, 25–37 (2014)
14. Goh, C.S., Lee, K.T.: Palm-based biofuel refinery (PBR) to substitute petroleum refinery: an energy and emergy assessment. Renew. Sustain. Energy Rev. **14**(9), 2986–2995 (2010)
15. Bastianoni, S., Coppola, F., Tiezzi, E., Colacevich, A., Borghini, F., Focardi, S.: Biofuel potential production from the orbetello lagoon macroalgae: a comparison with sunflower feedstock. Biomass Bioenergy **32**(7), 619–628 (2008)
16. da Cruz, R.V.A., do Nascimento, C.A.O.: Emergy analysis of oil production from microalgae. Biomass Bioenergy **47**, 418–425 (2012)
17. Yang, H., Chen, L., Yan, Z., Wang, H.: Emergy analysis of cassava-based fuel ethanol in China. Biomass Bioenergy **35**(1), 581–589 (2011)
18. Cavalett, O., Ortega, E.: Integrated environmental assessment of biodiesel production from soybean in Brazil. J. Clean. Prod. **18**(1), 55–70 (2010)
19. Felix, E., Tilley, D.R.: Integrated energy, environmental and financial analysis of ethanol production from cellulosic switchgrass. Energy **34**(4), 410–436 (2009)
20. Liu, J., Lin, B.L., Sagisaka, M.: Sustainability assessment of bioethanol and petroleum fuel production in Japan based on emergy analysis. Energy Policy **44**, 23–33 (2012)
21. Odum, H.T.: Environmental Accounting. Wiley, Hoboken (1996)
22. Patrizi, N., Pulselli, F.M., Morandi, F., Bastianoni, S.: Evaluation of the emergy investment needed for bioethanol production in a biorefinery using residual resources and energy. J. Clean. Prod. **96**, 549–556 (2015)
23. Wang, X., Chen, Y., Sui, P., Gao, W., Qin, F., Zhang, J., Wu, X.: Emergy analysis of grain production systems on large-scale farms in the North China plain based on LCA. Agric. Syst. **128**, 66–78 (2014)
24. Brown, M., Ulgiati, S.: Emergy evaluations and environmental loading of electricity production systems. J. Clean. Prod. **10**(4), 321–334 (2002)
25. Odum, H.T., Brown, M., Williams, S.: Handbook of Emergy Evaluation. A Compendium of Data for Emergy Computation. Introduction and Global Budget. University of Florida, Gainesville (2000)
26. Odum, H.T.: Handbook of Emergy Evaluation. A Compendium of Data for Emergy Computation. Emergy of Global Processes. University of Florida, Gainesville (2000)
27. Almeida, C., Barrella, F., Giannetti, B.: Emergetic ternary diagrams: five examples for application in environmental accounting for decision-making. J. Clean. Prod. **15**(1), 63–74 (2007)
28. Brown, M., Ulgiati, S.: Emergy-based indices and ratios to evaluate sustainability: monitoring economies and technology toward environmentally sound innovation. Ecol. Eng. **9**(1), 51–69 (1997)
29. Bastianoni, S., Marchettini, N.: Ethanol production from biomass: analysis of process efficiency and sustainability. Biomass Bioenergy **11**(5), 411–418 (1996)
30. Ulgiati, S., Brown, M., Bastianoni, S., Marchettini, N.: Emergy-based indices and ratios to evaluate the sustainable use of resources. Ecol. Eng. **5**(4), 519–531 (1995)
31. Nimmanterdwong, P., Chalermsinsuwan, B., Piumsomboon, P.: Emergy evaluation of biofuels production in thailand from different feedstocks. Ecol. Eng. **74**, 423–437 (2015)

Managing the Socially Sustainable Global Manufacturing Network

Paul Schönsleben$^{(\boxtimes)}$, Felix Friemann, and Manuel Rippel

BWI Center for Industrial Management, ETH Zurich, Zurich, Switzerland
pschoensleben@ethz.ch

Abstract. Footprint decisions in global manufacturing networks have an impact on local society, environment and economy. However, the reverse influence can also be detected: the globally increasing awareness of customers and politics related to socially sustainable manufacturing is driving the design of footprint decisions. This paper exploits the effects of offshoring and reshoring in global manufacturing networks from the social and economic dimensions of sustainability. It presents and examines examples from industrial practice.

Keywords: Production networks · Sustainability · Offshoring · Re-shoring

1 Introduction

Globalization is leading companies to revise their strategies related to their manufacturing footprint for several reasons [1]: Firstly, globalization of the targeted market segment requires the local presence of production and distribution facilities, due to official regulations, for example, or because the customer demands it. Secondly, for the entry into new market segments, the creation of new production facilities or a distribution center for finished products and/or service items is necessary. Thirdly, the increasing strategic importance of short delivery times demands to speed up all business and supply chain processes (e.g. development, order processing, service); one solution can be decentralized adaptation of products and services by completing them locally. Fourthly, the market competition and price sensitivity of customers and management attention to focus on core competencies force manufacturing networks to significantly reduce costs and accordingly to exploit associated options to relocate individual steps in value added to locations with specific know-how or lower costs.

These reasons call for offshoring of processes of the value chain to the country or area close to the customers. By means of industrial examples, this paper exploits the effects of offshoring and re-shoring in global manufacturing networks from the social and economic dimensions of sustainability The customers are part of the society in which the remote location is integrated, and sometimes even part of the local community. This makes the question of the potential for

I. Nääs et al. (Eds.): APMS 2016, IFIP AICT 488, pp. 884–891, 2016.
DOI: 10.1007/978-3-319-51133-7_104

manufacturing to be a bridge towards mutual benefits important [2]. In particular the fourth reason demands to offshore activities to low-wage countries. The social dimension of sustainability then becomes important related to potential reputation problems in the sales markets [2].

2   Offshoring from Industrialized to Developing Countries

The above presented factors for designing the manufacturing footprint are mainly motivated from an economic perspective. First and foremost, these reasons lead to a strategic decision about centralized or decentralized production. Only then can a profound decision be taken about offshoring. Figure 1 shows more centralized or decentralized design options between two (conflicting) dimensions, taking the example of a product with four operations (or production levels) and subsequent distribution (for detailed discussion and examples from industrial practice see [3]). The integrated approach is particularly advantageous by including the distribution, service and transport network within the strategic redesign of the production network [4].

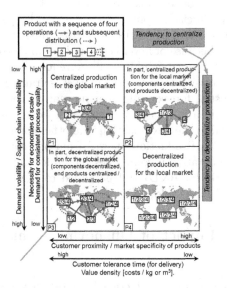

Fig. 1. Concepts for production networks, slightly modified from [2,3,5]

In short, the figure actually systematizes the following eight (or two times four) generic features for designing production networks:

– Demand volatility (Items have continuous demand if it is approximately the same in every observation period. Items have discontinuous demand if many periods with no or very little demand are interrupted by few periods with large demand, for example ten times higher, without recognizable regularity),

- Supply chain vulnerability (Disruptions can arise from either the supply chain partners or the macro-economic environment.),
- Necessity for economies of scale (Are the manufacturing costs of the product low enough?),
- Demand for consistent process quality (Can customer needs be satisfied despite differing process quality?),
- Customer proximity (To sell a product it can be necessary to locate the value-adding processes close to the customers),
- Market specificity of products (Adapting to the market is necessary for functional requirements or for appearance),
- Customer tolerance time (According to [1], this is the time span the customer will (or can) tolerate from the order release to delivery of the product),
- Value density (This variable is defined as item costs per kilogram or cubic meter. Transport costs are of greater consequence if value density is low than if value density is high.)

Where at least part of the production is decentralized, strategic consideration must lead to activities being offshored to the country or region where the potential customers are located (see sectors P2 and P4 in Fig. 1). Even in the case of centralized production, some operations can be performed offshore, as shown in sectors P1 or P3 of Fig. 1. In such cases, offshoring can occur for cost reasons, in particular because of lower costs in developing countries. Sometimes, offshoring of a part of the value-added will be required by a country's national legislation before permission to access the market is granted. In the chemical and pharmaceutical industry, for example, it is normal for certain operations to be carried out centrally in a particular country, and for the intermediate product then to be transported to the next location in another country. These are referred to as pipeline products: Production "flows" from one country to another. The location for the last operation is sometimes chosen for tax reasons, as significant overheads (particularly for R&D) will be added to the production cost of the product here (cost of goods sold, COGS).

3   Ambivalent Impact of Offshoring from a Social Perspective

Systematic location planning is of crucial importance due to the ambivalent nature of footprint decisions. Stakeholders have varying needs with regards to social indicators and much work has to be done in identifying representative social indicators throughout the upstream and downstream supply chains [2]. In the following the impact of offshoring decisions on both the original production location and the destination location is investigated from a social perspective on sustainability.

The impact on the society of the offshoring "home" location is multifold [2]: The location is mostly losing professional know-how in the long-term, since the manufacturing processes and associated expertise is transferred to the new location. There are different approaches how to conduct the knowledge transfer such as training the staff of the destination location for some time at the original location or sending experienced employees of the home location temporarily as trainers to the destination location. The workforce at the home location is reduced e.g. by early retirement arrangements, by lay-off, by retraining or by not replacing open job positions. Local communities are affected for instance by a higher unemployment rate and associated expenses or by migration of citizens. Another implication is that the company's reputation in its home location may suffer as a trustworthy employer, which could hamper recruiting of skilled staff in the long-term. In addition, regulations and requirements with regard to working conditions and emissions, which are introduced with the purpose to protect the environment and the staff, may be one part of the motivation to relocate manufacturing.

Likewise, the social impact on the destination location is multifold [2]: Local communities benefit from a large number of jobs that provide an income and thus a certain amount of prosperity for its local citizens. Thus, they have an interest in manufacturing companies being located in their area. Generally, the interests of society itself may vary (see [6]). For society, it is also a case of "social peace" being brought about by the social well-being of its citizens. That offers considerable potential for manufacturing to be a bridge towards mutual benefits. This regional political stabilization comes about through a stable income and local supplier contracts, and also through improved practical further education for its citizens, which has a positive impact on employability. Therefore, for local communities, the key issue is not the amount of tax that a company will pay in that location. Actually, the opposite is true: Local communities attract multinational companies to invest in their area by offering substantial subsidies [6]. One example is German-based car manufacturer Volkswagen in the USA (see [7]), where local communities made available 1400 acres (5.67 km^2) of land and some infrastructure. In return, Volkswagen made investments of over 1 billion US\$ (of which "\$379 million local and Tennessean construction contracts awarded, \$397 million local and Tennessean car supply contracts awarded annually"), creating employment for "more than 3,200 Volkswagen employees, and more than 9,500 indirect supplier employees" [7]. The economic effect for the local community and for society encompasses"\$12 billion expected in income growth in Tennessee, \$1.4 billion expected in total tax revenues in Tennessee" [7]. As the website data shows, the economic effect for society is considered by Volkswagen to be part of its double bottom line. The same can be said of Volkswagen's other locations, of other car manufacturers, of their globally active system suppliers, and also of other large companies in other sectors that offshore large amount of their production.

4   Managing Socially Sustainable Offshoring

When offshoring manufacturing from industrialized to developing nations, there are some managerial challenges to consider. These include, firstly, the need to put the right people in place in leadership roles to ensure that the subsidiary maintains the company's global standards. Initially, the senior management positions are given to people from the company's own home country. They are called "expats". This term highlights the fact that this status involves cultural, language and other social challenges that need to be handled carefully. Secondly, there may be a high level of local staff turnover, which sometimes also involves a loss of intellectual property.

Other managerial challenges associated with offshoring include partnerships with local suppliers or with representatives of local communities or society. Win-win think-ing, an underlying principle of close partnerships (see, for example, [1]) is not always perceived in the same way as it is at home. Oehmen et al. examined the duration of collaboration between Chinese suppliers and Swiss companies [8]. Even with goodwill on both sides, it often lasts for much less time than would be needed to compensate the expense of developing the supplier.

For socially sustainable offshoring, cooperation between a company's corporate social responsibility (CSR) department and national development organizations can lead to an acceleration of the company's CSR learning curve, because the company can gain insights from the governmental organizations in conceptual and operational areas. Furthermore, companies are defining and implementing a "code of conduct" (CoC), which constitute the company's policy and behavioral rules at a normative level towards the sustainability dimensions such as labor standards, health and safety, environment, ethics, and compliance [2]. They normally publish this information on their website. Within the supplier management, companies define and implement a specific "supplier code of conduct" (SCoC). Oehmen et al. conducted a survey (see Table 1) in order to examine the state-of-the-art of SCoCs in the electronics industry related to addressing issues and concerns in a social dimension of sustainability [9].

Table 1. SCoCs - issues addressed and frequency of occurrence (excerpt, acc. to [9]).

No.	SCoC element and frequency of occurrence (n=24)	
1	*Labor standards*	
1.01	Forced labor	83 %
1.02	Child labor	88 %
1.03	Juvenile workers	33 %
1.04	Non-discrimination	79 %
1.05	Harassment, inhum ane treatment	50 %
1.06	Respect and dignity	42 %
1.07	Freedon of association	50 %
1.08	Working hours, rest periods and breaks	54 %
1.09	Minimum wages and benefits	42 %
1.10	Overtime compensation	25 %
1.11	Recorded terms of employment	17 %

An example of industrial practice is the Code of (Business) Conduct of Lafarge-Holcim, a global leader in the building materials industry (cement, concrete, aggregates, and asphalt) [5]. With the aim of creating trust, protecting its reputation, lowering costs of doing business and enhancing shareholder value, LafargeHolcim defines the following three areas of integrity in its CoC [5]:

1. Integrity in the workplace focusing on e.g. health and safety, diversity, respect,
2. Integrity in business practices including e.g. anti-bribery, anti-corruption,
3. Integrity in the community addressing e.g. environment, human rights.

The company defined aspirations and targets in three focus areas "climate", "resources" and "communities" (see Fig. 2) within its "Sustainable Development Ambition 2030" [10]. To support working with local communities, community advisory panels (CAP) and CSR plans have been set up at country level.

Fig. 2. Sustainable development ambition 2030 of Holcim (according to [10]).

5   Effects of Re-shoring

The dynamics of the global environment can cause a change of a company's strategic priorities with the consequence that previously offshored manufacturing activities are re-shored to its original location. Surveys of the Fraunhofer ISI among medium-sized companies in the mechanical and electrical industry (M&E) in Germany (see Fig. 3) reveal companies' reasons for both offshoring and re-shoring production activities (mostly from Eastern Europe or Asia). Figure 3 shows the number of companies that re-shored their activities to their home country during the year in question. The other numbers in the chart show the percentage of this number that can be attributed to the specified reasons (multiple reasons were permitted). The two dominant reasons across the full time period covered by the study were quality (product quality at the offshore location was not good enough) and flexibility (mainly problems with the delivery time). When re-shoring the manufacturing activities, the following effects for the local communities are reported: In a specific instance in China the reshoring has had no negative consequences for the local community [8]. Chinese suppliers that had experienced substantial growth were a cause of the problems mentioned in [8], without actively wishing to be.

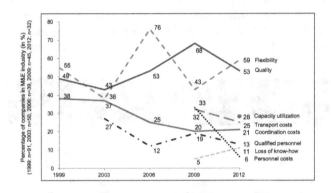

Fig. 3. Reasons for re-shoring (according to [1], data according to [11]).

However, a contrary effect is reported by Lynch et al., which examined social consequences for the local community in countries with a generally declining industrial sector [12]. In the described instance, the car manufacturers Ford, Holden and Toyota intend to stop producing cars in Australia in 2016 and 2017. Local suppliers will therefore lose most of their customers, which will have major consequences for the employment market and for research and development, including for university institutions. The German engineering and electronics company, Bosch, is worth mentioning in this context. Bosch closed their diode production facilities in Germany, and concentrated them in Australia. This off-shoring strategy was based on financial incentives provided by the Australian government. These were supposed to run until 2021, but may now end in 2017. For the multinational company, decisions about investments in its Australian subsidiaries have become much harder to make. The policies used by local communities to offer substantial incentives in order to make their area attractive to major companies have a downside here.

6   Conclusions

Globalization results in mainly economic motivated factors to constantly revise a company's manufacturing footprint. In order to achieve holistically economic and social sustainability in a company's manufacturing, the whole, globally connected network of suppliers, producers, and consumers should be addressed. There are eight generic features for designing production networks. These features lead to a strategic decision about centralized or decentralized production. Offshoring has an ambivalent impact on the original and destination location in a social dimension of sustainability. Thereby, the paper depicted effects and examples from industry practice about managing socially sustainable offshoring and re-shoring of manufacturing.

References

1. Schönsleben, P.: Integral Logistics Management: Operations and Supply Chain Management Within and Across Companies. CRC Press, Boca Raton (2016)
2. Sutherland, J.W., Richter, J.S., Hutchins, M.J., Dornfeld, D., Dzombak, R., Mangold, J., Robinson, S., Hauschild, M.Z., Bonou, A., Schönsleben, P., et al.: The role of manufacturing in affecting the social dimension of sustainability. CIRP Ann. Manufact. Technol. 65(2), 689–712 (2016)
3. Schönsleben, P.: Changeability of strategic and tactical production concepts. CIRP Ann. Manufact. Technol. 58(1), 383–386 (2009)
4. Schönsleben, P., Radke, A.M., Plehn, J., Finke, G., Hertz, P.: Toward the Integrated Determination of a Strategic Production Network Design, Distribution Network Design, Service Network Design, and Transport Network Design for Manufacturers of Physical Products (2015)
5. LafargeHolcim. http://www.lafargeholcim.com
6. Ciroth, A., Finkbeiner, M., Hildenbrand, J., Klöpffer, W., Mazijn, B., Prakash, S., Sonnemann, G., Traverso, M., Ugaya, C.M.L., Valdivia, S., et al.: Towards a Life Cycle Sustainability Assessment: Making Informed Choices on Products (2011)
7. Volkswagen: Chattanooga Facts. http://www.volkswagengroupamerica.com/facts.html
8. Oehmen, J., Schönsleben, P., von Bredow, M., Gruber, P., Reinhart, G.: Strategische Machtfaktoren in Kunden-Lieferanten-Verhältnissen. Industrie Management 25, 29–33 (2009)
9. Oehmen, J., De Nardo, M., Schönsleben, P., Boutellier, R.: Supplier code of conduct-state-of-the-art and customisation in the electronics industry. Prod. Plann. Control 21(7), 664–679 (2010)
10. Holcim Integrated Profit & Loss Statement. http://www.holcim.com
11. Kinkel, S.: Trends in production relocation and backshoring activities: changing patterns in the course of the global economic crisis. Int. J. Oper. Prod. Manage. 32(6), 696–720 (2012)
12. Lynch, J., Hawthorne, M.: Australia's Car Industry one year from Closing its Doors. Sydney Morning Herald, July 2015

Mapping a Value Stream with the Perspective of Sustainability

Veronica Lindström[1(✉)] and Niklas Ingesson[2]

[1] Department of Management and Engineering,
Linköping University, Linköping, Sweden
Veronica.lindstrom@liu.se
[2] TitanX Engine Cooling AB, Linköping, Sweden
Niklas.Ingesson@titanx.com

Abstract. Companies align lean production and sustainability differently depending on organization model. Lean provides social foundation for sustainability and makes it possible to implement sustainability, and integrate lean and sustainability. The work presented here maps a current value stream with measures from different methodologies presented in the literature. The objective of this paper is to integrate sustainability measures with a traditional value stream mapping. Economic, environmental, and societal metrics are presented. The result indicates that the interest of the different metrics depends on the role within the organization.

Keywords: Lean production · Manufacturing · Production operations · Value stream mapping

1 Introduction

Industrial companies that compete on a global market can choose to differentiate their manufacturing strategy depending on product family and its niche consumer. If industrial companies choose to differentiate their products towards a more narrow competitive scope and thus apply a differentiation strategy [1], sustainability as a competitive priority may be an order winner for a niche market [2] and may improve international competitiveness [3]. The competitive priority sustainability is thus adding a higher value to those niche markets and its customers. However, industrial companies within the car and truck industry compete today with products that are mature and thus need to find ways to add value besides continuous total cost reductions. Companies within the car and truck industry have applied Lean production for some decades with the purpose to eliminate waste in their value streams to add value. One common used tool is Value Stream Mapping (VSM). VSM is a tool to find and eliminate waste in a value stream. The original value stream is defined as the value stream for the end customer, or consumer. Lean thinking provides a way to specify value [4]. The basis for lean production development is to eliminate waste. According to the theory of lean thinking, one can learn to see the waste by mapping a value stream [5]. Recent research on the application of value stream mapping adds sustainability measures and integrates thus additional measures to evaluate environmental impact and societal well-being [6, 7].

© IFIP International Federation for Information Processing 2016
Published by Springer International Publishing AG 2016. All Rights Reserved
I. Nääs et al. (Eds.): APMS 2016, IFIP AICT 488, pp. 892–899, 2016.
DOI: 10.1007/978-3-319-51133-7_105

The work presented in this paper focuses on the integration of sustainability measures in a traditional VSM. Environmental measurements have been applied similar to the work of Sus-VSM [6, 7]. The ergonomic measurements have been applied according to the study presented as the method ErgoVSM [8].

2 Frame of Reference

2.1 Sustainability in Production Operations

Sustainability at the company level concerns the development of products, processes, and business models [2]. Therefore, product and process innovations will be needed to achieve sustainable production [10]. It also requires a holistic view and improved product performance models and optimization of individual manufacturing processes, to give some examples [10]. Several articles in the literature describe sustainable production. Issues within this area include managing processes with an input such as energy, people, equipment and machines with the objective of reducing waste, carbon footprint, rework, inventory and delays [11]. Sustainable production operations should lead to improvements in competitive priorities such as flexibility, customization, responsiveness, dependability, cost reduction and high quality of products and services [11]. To promote sustainability-driven decision-making, a so-called value creating framework could be applied in organizations where five factors are considered; product, process, equipment, organization, and human [12].

Companies applying lean manufacturing and its concepts align sustainability differently in their respective organizations depending on organizational model in the company [13]. Companies with a traditional organizational model tend to lack executive involvement and worker commitment that leads to that sustainability is underdeveloped. On the other extreme, companies with advanced organizational model tend to involve workers, and those companies have also a high cross-functional executive involvement [13]. To achieve sustainability in production operations, managers are suggested to apply methods and programs like just-in-time production, lean, total quality management, Kanban etc. [11]. According to Piercy and Rich [14], lean provides social foundation for sustainability and pairs it with technical system, which makes it possible to implement sustainability and thus integrate lean and sustainability [14].

2.2 Sustainability and Value Streams

Lean production principles start with defining "value" [4]. A value stream is the "set of all the specific actions required to bring a specific product through the three critical management tasks of any business: the *problem-solving task* running from concept through detailed design and engineering to production launch, the *information management task* running from order-taking through detailed scheduling to delivery, and the *physical transformation task* proceeding from raw materials to a finished product in the hands of the customer." (Womack and Jones, page 19) [4].

Sustainability is defined as taking into consideration the triple bottom line, i.e. economic, environmental, and societal goals [2, 15].

2.3   Different Types and Metrics of Sustainable Value Stream Mappings

Applying Lean production means to get the knowledge, leadership and it starts to identify the value streams [4]. Once you have identified a value stream, one can start to map it. Value Stream Mapping, VSM, is a lean tool that aims to reduce waste [4]. VSM can be a communication tool or a business planning tool, and a tool for managing the change processes of the company [5]. The mapping begins at "a door-to-door level" and includes the mapping of material- and information flows of operations. The measurements of the original VSM are mainly *time* and *inventory* (quantity) [5].

Sustainable value stream mapping (Sus-VSM) is a VSM that, in addition to lead time, includes environmental and societal metrics [6, 7]. The metrics types are thus economic, environmental, and societal metrics [7]. The environmental metrics consist of energy consumption, raw material usage, and process water usage. The societal metrics consist of the metrics of physical load and work environment metrics such as noise, risks for electrical systems, hazardous chemical/materials used, pressurized systems, and high-speed components [6].

Product Sustainability Index (ProdSI) is an assessment of the overall product sustainability throughout its product life cycle [16]. ProdSI is the overall aggregated product sustainability performance index, which consists of three subindex; economic, environmental, and societal. The ProdSI methodology suggests that individual metrics should be used and customized for each specific case [16].

ErgoVSM is a lean tool for integration of ergonomics in manufacturing in a value stream mapping activity [8]. ErgoVSM considers physical exposure. It assesses physical exposure and is structured by tasks, value streams, and job level. Similar to Sus-VSM, ErgoVSM is embedded in the original VSM tool by Rother and Shook [5].

3   Methodology

The methodology used in this study is the case methodology. For the application of sustainability metrics in a value stream, a single case is used. The reason for choosing a single case was for the purpose of a pilot study [17]. The choice of the specific case was chosen for its location, accessibility, and its application of JIT and lean principles, which, according to theory, has relationship to sustainability [13, 14]. The advantage of a single case is that it can provide greater depth, and the limits of a single case is whether one can make any generalizations or conclusions [18]. The study presented here was conducted from January through March 2016, and has included observations, interviews, and empirical data collection. To increase reliability and validity of this case, the principle informant in the case company was active during the whole process of setting up the research, data collection, and analyzing data. The approach presented here follows a typical deductive research, i.e. applying or revising an existing framework or hypothesis [19]. Following suggested approach for deductive case studies, the unit of analysis should be articulated and the case justified [19].

3.1   The Case Company and the Product of the Value Stream

TitanX is a dedicated supplier of engine and oil cooling products to the Commercial Vehicle industry. The company TitanX Engine Cooling AB in Linköping, Sweden, had a turnover of 329 million SEK in year 2015. Their main customers are Volvo Trucks and Scania. The factory has been situated in Linköping since 1895. Since year 2008 the factory is owned by TitanX, which is a global manufacturer of powertrain cooling solutions to the commercial vehicle industry. The factory in Linköping, as well as the other manufacturing sites at TitanX, applies lean manufacturing principles. TitanX has their own production system called "TIPS" (TitanX Production System). The factory in Linköping strives towards operational excellence and World Class capabilities.

The product chosen for the application of the value stream mapping is a SFI cooler, see Fig. 1. The production system of the SFI cooler has developed from a batch flow to a JIT production system, using Kanban and sequencing pull.

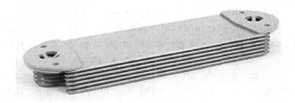

Fig. 1. Example of an SFI cooler

The reason for choosing this product for mapping purposes is that this cooler represents a modern manufacturing process and is thus interesting to map depending on possibility of future improvements. The product chosen consists of 9 turbulators of carbon steel, 18 plates of stainless steel plus on top plate, 8 foils of copper, two connections of stainless steel, and some rivets.

3.2   Data Collection

The data collection of this case study followed three different methodologies for the respective sustainability factor, see 3.2.1 to 3.2.3 below.

3.2.1   Economic Measures

The data collection of economic measures follows the VSM methodology by Rother and Shook [5]. First, a product family was chosen. A team of three people were mapping the value stream from "door-to-door" in the factory. Both material and information flows were mapped. Working times, cycle times, set-up times, OEE, scrap rates, and inventory levels were collected by either clocking the times or capturing the data from machine data that is stored. Inventory levels were counted manually on the shop-floor. The lead time from door-to-door was calculated, as well as the value-added time.

3.2.2   Environmental Measures

The data collection of environmental measures follows the Sus-VSM methodology by Faulkner and Badurdeen [7]. Process water consumption was measured per product and is captured as used water consumption, i.e. required and net water consumption was not captured. It is only one process that uses water; the brazing operation, see Fig. 2. Raw material was captured via data of raw material in the business system AS/400. After the stamping operation, the product was weighted. In this way, the lost material by the stamping process could be measured. Additional components in the pre-assembly station 2 and assembly station were weighted. Energy consumption was measured as direct energy consumption per manufacturing process by using the power rating per machine and using cycle time per product. This data was retrieved from the MPS-system. Transportation power rates were not captured in this study as well as indirect energy usage such as lightning, heating and so on.

3.2.3   Societal Measures

The data collection of societal measures follows the ErgoVSM methodology by Jarebrant et al. [8]. Ratings for five ergonomics issues are considered in this methodology; postures, forces, physical variation, and porosity on the value stream level. A fifth ergonomic issue is the physical variation in the job of the operators in the value stream [8]. By rating task category per work station, the potential of variation of the job is rated. If there is a wide range of task categories per workstation, the potential is higher than if the tasks are monotonous [8]. The lower the rating, the better potential. The impact on performance is measured via the working time and its potential of reducing it. On the other hand, ergonomic assessments have an impact on working environment and should be managed as an individual assessment of the production system.

4   Result and Application of Sustainability of a Value Stream

The current state map for the value stream with the perspective of sustainability is shown in Fig. 2. As in a traditional VSM, information flow is shown in the upper part of the figure, the material flow is shown in the middle, and measurements in the bottom part of the figure. Key performance indicators for the value stream is shown in Table 1.

Results of the ergonomics assessment at the value stream level is shown in Table 2 and results of the ergonomics assessment at the task level is shown in Table 3.

The data collection of environmental and societal measures took longer time to understand and collect than the economic measures, which are known before by the company.

Especially the ergonomics assessment was hard to understand as no one in the data collection team had any expertise in ergonomics knowledge.

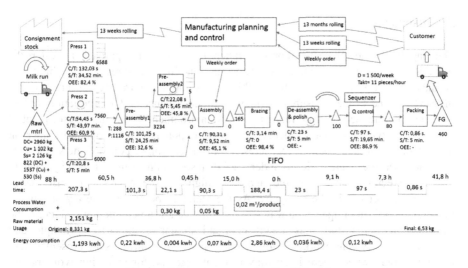

Fig. 2. Value stream map for the SFI cooler

Table 1. Key performance indicators for value stream of the SFI cooler

KPI	Value
Total lead time	1.75 weeks
Value-added time	0.203 h
Percentage value-added time	7.8%
Process water consumption	0.02 m³/product
Raw material usage	8.3 kg/product
Material utilization rate	78%
Energy consumption	4.5 kWh/product

Table 2. Ergonomics assessment at the value stream level of the SFI cooler

Ergonomics potential	5
Variation in jobs	5

Table 3. Ergonomics assessment at the task level in the value stream of the SFI cooler

ErgoVSM				
Task	Manual working time (s)	Posture rating	Force rating	Task category
Press 1	8.9	3	4	C
Press 2	31.6	3	8	C
Press 3	1.2	3	4	C
Pre-assembly 1	32.4	3	3	E
Pre-assembly 2	22.1	3	3	E
Assembly	90.3	5	3	E
Brazing	3.9	2	2	C and A
De-assembly & polish	23	6	3	E
Q control	5,5	3	3	E
Packing	0,9	7	3	A and C

5   Discussion

The mapping of the value stream presented here is holistic in its approach and offers the possibility of process innovations regarding sustainability measures. Sustainability can be measured in a value stream by combining economic, environmental, and societal measures. Some of the measures are related to performance of the production system while ergonomic measures are related to work environment. From an operator point of view, the ergonomics measurements were seen as positive. Thus, operators have an interest in developing societal measures. From an executive point of view, the performance measures were easier to understand than societal measures. This may relate to the way executives are measured and how higher, more aggregated performance measures are set within the company. As the literature points out, the organizational model of a company impacts the way sustainability is developed internally. TitanX, the case company in this study, has already an organization that follows lean principles and thus both executive and worker involvement in place. The current state presented here is a pilot study where there is an improvement potential for involving workers and executives further for developing sustainability and integrate the measures on operational level. The result also indicates that there is a conflict of interests between economic, environmental, and societal measures.

References

1. Porter, M.: Competitive Advantage: Creating and Sustaining Superior Performance. The Free Press, New York (1985)
2. Jovane, F., Yoshikawa, H., Alting, L., Böer, C.R., Westkamper, E., Williams, D., Tseng, M., Seliger, G., Paci, A.M.: The incoming global technological and industrial revolution towards competitive sustainable manufacturing. CIRP Annals – Manuf. Technol. 57(2), 641–659 (2008)
3. Epstein, M.J., Buhovac, A.R.: Making Sustainability Work: Best practices in Managing and Measuring Corporate Social, Environmental, and Economic Impacts, 2nd edn. Greenleaf Publishing Limited, Yorkshire (2014)
4. Womack, J.P., Jones, D.T.: Lean Thinking: Banish Waste and Create Wealth in Your Corporation. Free Press, New York (2003)
5. Rother, M., Shook, J.: Learning to See: Values-Stream Mapping to Create Value and Eliminate Muda. The Lean Enterprise Institute, Cambridge (2009). Version 1.3
6. Brown, A., Amundson, J., Badurdeen, F.: Sustainable value stream mapping (Sus-VSM) in different manufacturing system configuartions: application case studies. J. Cleaner Prod. 85, 164–179 (2014)
7. Faulkner, W., Badurdeen, F.: Sustainable Value Stream Mapping (Sus-VSM): methodology to visualize and assess manufacturing sustainability performance. J. Cleaner Prod. 85, 8–18 (2014)
8. Jarebrant, C., Winkel, J., Hanse, J.J., Mathiassen, S.E., Öjmertz, B.: ErgoVSM: a tool for integrating value stream mapping and ergonomics in manufacturing. Human Factors Ergonomics Manuf. Serv. Ind. 26(2), 191–204 (2016)
9. Wikinson, A., Hill, M., Gollan, P.: The sustainability debate. Int. J. Oper. Prod. Manage. 21 (12), 1492–1502 (2001)

10. Jayal, A.D., Badurdeen, F., Dillon Jr., O.W., Jawahir, I.S.: Sustainable manufacturing: modeling and optimization challenges at the product, process and system levels. CIRP J. Manufact. Sci. Technol. **2**, 144–152 (2010)

11. Gunasekaran, A., Spalanzani, A.: Sustainability of manufacturing and services: Manufacturing investigations for research and applications. Int. J. Prod. Econ. **140**, 35–47 (2012)

12. Bilge, P., Badurdeen, F., Seliger, G., Jawahir, I.S.: Model-based approach for assessing value creation to enhance sustainability in manufacturing. In: Proceedings of the 47th CIRP Conference on Manufacturing Systems, vol. 17, pp. 106–111 (2014)

13. Longoni, A., Cagliano, R.: Cross-functional executive involvement and worker involvement in lean manufacturing and sustainability alignment. Int. J. Oper. Prod. Manage. **35**(9), 1332–1358 (2015)

14. Piercy, N., Rich, N.: The relationship between lean operations and sustainable operations. Int. J. Oper. Prod. Manage. **35**(2), 282–315 (2015)

15. Elkington, J.: Cannibals with Forks: The Triple Bottom Line of 21st Century Business. Capstone Publishing Limited, Mankato (1999)

16. Shuaib, M., Seevers, D., Zhang, X., Badurdeen, F., Rouch, K.E., Jawahir, I.S.: Product Sustainability Index (ProdSI): a metrics-based framework to evaluate the total life cycle sustainability of manufactured products. J. Ind. Ecol. **18**(4), 491–507 (2014)

17. Yin, R.K.: Case Study Research: Design and Methods, 4th edn. Sage Publications, Thousand Oaks (2009). Applied Social Research Methods Series, 5

18. Voss, C., Tsikriktsis, N., Frohlich, M.: Case research in operations management. Int. J. Oper. Prod. Manage. **22**(2), 195–219 (2002)

19. Barratt, M., Choi, T.Y., Li, M.: Qualitative case studies in operations management: trends, research outcomes, and future research implications. J. Oper. Manage. **29**, 329–342 (2011)

Operations Management in
Engineer-to-Order Manufacturing

Buyer–Supplier Information Sharing in ETO

Espen Rød[1(✉)], Mikhail Shlopak[1], Gabriele Hofinger Junge[1],
and Erlend Alfnes[2]

[1] Møreforsking Molde AS, Molde, Norway
{espen.rod,mikhail.shlopak,gabriele.h.junge}@himolde.no
[2] NTNU, Trondheim, Norway
erlend.alfnes@ntnu.no

Abstract. This paper presents a case study of the information sharing practices in a buyer–supplier relationship of companies that deliver
products to the global maritime industry. The main research question
is whether improving the quality of shared information between buyer
and supplier will enhance information utilization by the supplier and
improve the operational efficiency of both companies. The case study
describes the process of analyzing the information flows between the
buyer and the supplier and the utilization of the shared information by
the supplier. Our main focus was on analyzing information quality and
information utilization, and finding solutions to improve the information
sharing practices between the two companies.

Keywords: SCM · Information sharing · Buyer–supplier relationship

1 Introduction

The many different manufacturing environments are commonly distinguished
using the following categories: make-to-stock (MTS), assemble-to-order (ATO),
make-to-order (MTO), and engineer-to-order (ETO). All of these manufacturing
strategies relate to the point at which a particular product is linked to a specific
customer [1]. The ETO-supply chain is generally regarded as a supply chain
where the 'decoupling point' is located at the design stage, while in MTO the
'decoupling point' is at the fabrication and procurement stage. ETO companies
can be categorized by supplying high value, customized products with a deep
and complex structure [2].

The case companies are a Norwegian ETO company (hereinafter, Company
A), and one of its suppliers which can be characterized as MTO (hereinafter,
Company B). Company A delivers capital-intensive, advanced products in low
volumes to customers in the global maritime industry, and the production can
be regarded as ETO. Company B supplies company A with components and can
be considered as an MTO company. The relationship between the two companies
is affected by uncertainties with regard to demand, which increases the need for
collaborative planning and information sharing throughout the supply chain.

© IFIP International Federation for Information Processing 2016
Published by Springer International Publishing AG 2016. All Rights Reserved
I. Nääs et al. (Eds.): APMS 2016, IFIP AICT 488, pp. 903–910, 2016.
DOI: 10.1007/978-3-319-51133-7_106

The case companies goals were to reduce the time between Company A ordering the components from Company B and the delivery to Company A, and to reduce inventory levels at both companies. The project's participants decided to approach these problems by analyzing information-sharing practices between the two companies.

The research question in the present paper is whether improvement of the quality of shared information will increase its utilization and hence affect operational efficiency in buyer–supplier relationships.

The purpose of this paper is to illustrate a method of analyzing and improving information flows in a buyer–supplier relationship in an MTO–ETO environment.

2 Theoretical Background

The literature presents several areas related to supply chain management, with an emphasis on information sharing, particularly topics such as information quality (IQ) and information utilization (IU). Literature focusing on information sharing in the automotive industry has also been reviewed.

Information sharing is often mentioned as an important factor in the successful creation of supply chains. According to [3], both information and material flow integration are important for supply chain integration, and have significant effects on performance. According to [4], large investments in IT could fail to produce expected benefits if they are not supported by a willingness to share required information. The two main reasons why information is not utilized are the ability and the willingness to utilize the information. The utilization of information is influenced by IQ and inter- and intra-organizational factors [5].

Information shared between customers and suppliers is used to facilitate manufacturing, planning, and control activities at the companies; according to [6], companies cannot expect high returns from their collaborative initiatives in terms of improved operational performance unless the exchanged information is of high quality.

There are four facets to information sharing: content, frequency, direction, and modality. The facets describe the actual information, while information utilization refers to what the shared information is used for (production scheduling, resource planning, etc.) [5,7].

[8] defined IQ as the "ability to satisfy stated and implied needs of the information consumer", and considered that the stated IQ requirements are according to planning restrictions, policies and procedures, and the implied needs of the staff. In this relation, an IQ deficiency is defined as "deviation between stated and implied needs and perceived information quality" [8]. IQ dimensions are well defined in the literature, although different notions are used to refer to them. [9] used "in time," "accurate," "convenient to access," and "reliable," while [8] used "complete," "concise," "reliable," "timely," "valid," "accessible," "appropriate amount," "credible," "relevant," and "understandable." According to [5] reliability and credibility are related to the accuracy of information; relevance and

validity are related to the value of information; conciseness, understandability, and appropriate amount are related to the format of information; and completeness, accessibility, and timeliness are related to the availability of information.

[5] also identified different levels of information utilization: (1) utilization as potential usage (potential to use the information in the receivers processes); (2) utilization as intended usage (intention and ability to use the received information); (3) utilization as actual usage (the information is actually being used in the process); and (4) utilization as efficient and effective usage (the information has a positive impact on the receiver's planning process performances).

Jonsson and Myrelid's [5] analysis of information sharing, quality and utilization in the automotive industry showed that the producer had five different information entities shared with the supplier. The supplier mainly utilized one of these entities – the delivery schedule – which contained three periods of orders: forecasts, planned orders and frozen orders. The supplier, in turn, developed a production plan consisting of one preliminary planning period and frozen planning period. Similar examples of planning and supply chain management in the automotive industry have been reviewed; see [10,11].

3   Research Methodology

This paper presents a case study of two companies: a Norwegian producer of advanced capital-intensive products to customers in the global maritime industry, and a major supplier. The literature on information sharing was reviewed, with primary focus on information quality and information utilization. We have especially emphasized an article by Jonsson and Myrelid [5], which used cases from the automotive industry, to develop the steps for improving information sharing practices. Based on an initial literature study, the authors conducted several workshops with participants from the companies and these workshops have been the main source of data collection. The workshops were the arena for discussions, which facilitated the introduction of changes in practices in the two companies.

4   Analysis

Keeping in mind the identified goals in the improvement of the relationship between the two companies, we started by mapping all of the information flows between them. We then categorized all information flows with regard to the facets of information sharing. The next step was to identify what the information that Company B receives is used for, and what processes the company performs based on the received information. The fourth step was to identify information quality deficiencies that hinder Company B in performing its processes. The last step was to suggest improvements in information flows and information quality adapted to Company B's processes.

4.1   Steps 1 and 2: Mapping and Categorization of Information Flows

We identified five different information flows related to production and delivery of components from Company B to Company A (Table 1).

Table 1. Information flows (AS-IS)

Shared information	Facets of information sharing			
	Content	Frequency	Direction	Format
Main production plan	# of components each week in the year	Approx. 1 per month	To supplier	E-mail – MS Excel
Purchase orders	PO, including delivery date	2 months before delivery date	To supplier	E-mail – PDF
List of changed orders	List of components with new date	Every two weeks	To supplier	E-mail – MS Excel
Meeting	Wrecks, deviations, general situation	Once a month	Two-way	Meeting
Spontaneous	Miscellaneous	Spontaneous	Two-way	Telephone, E-mail, meetings

4.2   Step 3: Information Utilization

Having identified all of the information flows between Company A and Company B, the next step was to identify what processes Company B performed based on the shared information. [5] distinguished among four levels of information utilization. Given that the main point of this step was to identify the actual usage of information, we focused on Levels 3 (information as actual usage) and 4 (information as efficient an effective usage).

In the workshops we identified that Company B conducted two planning processes: one was long-term capacity and resource planning and the other was production planning. To execute the long-term capacity and resource planning, Company B used the main production plan it received from Company A. To execute production planning, Company B used the purchase orders and a list of components with changed delivery dates. The planning activities were done in separate computer systems.

4.3   Step 4: Identify Information Quality Deficiencies

We used Gustavsson and Wänström's [8] definition of information quality deficiency ("deviation between stated and implied needs and perceived information quality") to analyze the quality of the shared information.

From the previous steps, all information flows were mapped and the actual usage of these flows was identified. In Step 4, the information flows should be evaluated from an IQ perspective. We have chosen all 10 of the dimensions presented by [8]. By using these, the analysis covers the accuracy, value, format and availability of information [5]. The IQ dimension was evaluated based on the definitions of each of the dimensions by [8], which are presented in Table 2.

Table 2. Definitions of IQ dimensions [8]

IQ dimension	Definition
Complete	The extent to which the information is comprehensive for the planning tasks
Concise	The information can be used directly, without needing to be reworked before use, in terms of format, content and/or structure
Reliable	The extent to which the information provided to the planning staff is accurate
Timely	The extent to which the information is delivered on time and at correct intervals; that is, not too often or too seldom for the planning process
Valid	The extent to which the information measures what it should measure
Accessible	The extent to which the information is easy to access when required
Appropriate amount	The extent to which filtration of the information is necessary
Credible	The extent to which information is accepted or regarded as true, real, and believable
Relevant	The extent to which the information is appropriate for the tasks and applications
Understandable	The extent to which information is easy to use, but also easy to learn and easy to manipulate, aggregate, and combine with other information

In our case the IQ was analyzed on three of the information entities. The two entities – "meetings" and "spontaneous" – were excluded as these would vary and are not directly connected to the planning tasks. The IQ dimensions 'valid', 'accessible', 'credible', 'relevant' and 'understandable' were all regarded as having good enough quality on all three information entities for the supplier to perform its processes.

In summary, five IQ dimensions did not fulfil the stated and implied needs and perceived information quality on all or some of the information entities: complete, concise, reliable, timely, and appropriate amount. An overview of the analysis of IQ deficiencies is presented in Table 3.

Table 3. Information quality deficiencies

Shared Information	Main production plan	Purchase order	List of changes
IQ dimension			
Complete	No, not rolling horizon	Yes	Yes
Concise	No, rework needed	No, must be typed into system	No, must be typed into system
Reliable	No, frequent changes	No, frequent changes of dates	No, frequent changes of dates
Timely	No, too few updates, and different times	No, non-specific times	No, not at reliable intervals
Valid	Yes	Yes	Yes
Accessible	Yes	Yes	Yes
Appropriate amount	No, much rework	Yes	Yes
Credible	Yes	Yes	Yes
Relevant	Yes	Yes	Yes
Understandable	Yes	Yes	Yes

4.4   Step 5: Improving Information Flows and Information Utilization

In order to maximize utilization of the shared information, we addressed the current processes at Company B. The long-term capacity and resource planning that Company B performed was based on the main production plan received from Company A. The production planning was done using information from the purchase orders and the list of changed dates.

The five identified IQ deficiencies were all preventing Company B from performing its processes in the best possible way. In order to increase IU, the IQ in the dimensions concise, reliable, timely, and appropriate amount needed to be improved.

The companies were positive about changing their routines, including both information sharing practices and the connected planning activities. Even though the case companies produce in much smaller volumes than car manufacturers, similarities between them were found, and best practice from the automotive industry was a basis for changing the information sharing practices and connected planning tasks. In the example from the automotive industry, the shared delivery schedule contained three periods of order: forecasts, planned orders, and frozen orders. The supplier then developed a production plan consisting of a preliminary planning period and a frozen planning period. Through several workshops involving company representatives and researchers, improvements were made to the current information sharing processes. Consideration was given to improving the IQ dimensions that were considered to be lacking quality and how this would affect the information utilization by Company B.

The main production plan that was previously shared was developed into containing three periods. One category comprised all forecasts and planned orders up to a certain point before delivery. Then there was an extended period of orders that could be considered slushy orders, which at a certain point before delivery date would be called off by a purchase order. The last period was frozen orders confirmed by a purchase order.

The list of forecasts and planned orders replaced the previous main production plan. Because of increased IQ, Company B was able to replace the previously used long-term capacity and resource plan by incorporating the information it contained in its current production planning tool. By doing this, the information sharing entities have been reduced from three to two, and the processes at Company B have been reduced from two to one (Table 4).

Table 4. Improved information quality dimensions

Shared information	List of forecast and planned orders	Purchase Order
IQ dimension		
Complete	Yes, rolling horizon	Yes
Concise	No, still need to be typed in, but more tailored to planning process	No, still need to be typed into system
Reliable	No, dynamic environment causes changes	Yes, closer to delivery date, fewer changes
Timely	Yes, every 14th day	Yes, once a week
Valid	Yes	Yes
Accessible	Yes	Yes
Appropriate amount	Yes, only relevant information	Yes
Credible	Yes	Yes
Relevant	Yes	Yes
Understandable	Yes	Yes

An analysis of the information quality showed an increase in the quality in several of the dimensions. The IQ dimensions complete, timely, and appropriate amount were improved. Two IQ dimension were not able to satisfy the stated and implied needs and perceived information quality. Although it had been improved, the concise dimension was not regarded well enough because the supplier still needed to type in all the information into its planning system. Since these companies operate in a dynamic environment, and changes in product specifications and delivery dates are very likely to occur in the planning phase on longer terms, the reliable dimension also had deficiencies which are difficult to eliminate as flexibility is considered a competitive advantage.

5 Conclusions

This paper presents an analysis of the information sharing practices between a Norwegian ETO and MTO company. For this purpose, a step-by-step procedure to analyze and improve information sharing practices in buyer–supplier relationships was used. The procedure was as follows: (1) map information flows; (2) categorize the information; (3) identify information utilization; (4) identify information quality deficiencies; and (5) improve information flows and information quality adapted to the supplier's processes. By using this procedure the companies were able to improve the information quality of the shared information, and by adjusting connected planning processes, they also increased the information utilization of the information at the supplier.

References

1. Olhager, J.: Strategic positioning of the order penetration point. Int. J. Prod. Econ. **85**(3), 319–329 (2003)
2. Hicks, C., McGovern, T., Earl, C.F.: Supply chain management: a strategic issue in engineer to order manufacturing. Int. J. Prod. Econ. **65**(2), 179–190 (2000)
3. Prajogo, D., Olhager, J.: Supply chain integration and performance: the effects of long-term relationships, information technology and sharing, and logistics integration. Int. J. Prod. Econ. **135**(1), 514–522 (2012)
4. Croom, S., Fawcett, S.E., Osterhaus, P., Magnan, G.M., Brau, J.C., McCarter, M.W.: Information sharing and supply chain performance. Supply Chain Manage. Int. J. **12**(5), 358–368 (2007)
5. Jonsson, P., Myrelid, P.: Supply chain information utilization conceptualization and antecedents. In: Proceedings of the Annual EurOMA Conference 2014 (2014)
6. Wiengarten, F., Humphreys, P., Cao, G., Fynes, B., McKittrick, A.: Collaborative supply chain practices and performance. Supply Chain Manage. Int. J. **15**(6), 463–473 (2010)
7. Mohr, J., Nevin, J.R.: Communication strategies in marketing channels: a theoretical perspective. J. Mark. **54**(4), 36–51 (1990)
8. Gustavsson, M., Wanstrom, C.: Assessing information quality in manufacturing planning and control processes. Int. J. Qual. Reliab. Manage. **26**(4), 325–340 (2009)
9. Forslund, H.: Measuring information quality in the order fulfilment process. Int. J. Qual. Reliab. Manage. **24**(5), 515–524 (2007)
10. Staeblein, T., Aoki, K.: Planning and scheduling in the automotive industry: a comparison of industrial practice at german and japanese makers. Int. J. Prod. Econ. **162**, 258–272 (2015)
11. Meyr, H.: Supply chain planning in the german automotive industry. In: Günther, H.O., Meyr, H. (eds.) Supply Chain Planning, pp. 1–23. Springer, Heidelberg (2009)

Developing Supplier Strategies for ETO Companies: A Case Study

Mikhail Shlopak$^{(\boxtimes)}$, Espen Rød, and Oddmund Oterhals

Møreforsking Molde AS, Molde, Norway
{mikhail.shlopak,espen.rod,oddmund.oterhals}@himolde.no

Abstract. The purpose of this paper is to present results of applying the Kraljic purchasing portfolio model at three Norwegian engineer-to-order (ETO) companies. The case companies operate in different markets, deliver products of different levels of complexity, and apply different organizational strategies, and differ in several other ways. The paper discusses the ways in which the case companies can develop their supplier strategies based on the executed Kraljic analysis, while emphasizing the importance of taking the companies' distinctive features into consideration.

Keywords: SCM · Inter-organizational management · Buyer-supplier relationship · Supplier strategies

1 Introduction

Supply chain management is a central topic for ETO companies. Some of them stick to own production, while others have outsourced manufacturing to lower-cost countries. The ETO companies vary in size, production volumes, product complexity, the markets they operate in, and in the ways their procurement, production, and project management are organized. However, establishing effective strategies for different suppliers remains highly relevant for all of them. In this paper we look at the three Norwegian ETO companies: two maritime lifting equipment suppliers and one aluminum casting equipment supplier. All three companies are participants in a research project supported by Norwegian Research Council through the MAROFF program. Each case company has categorized its suppliers using the Kraljic purchasing portfolio model. This paper presents the results of this work and discusses the ways in which the case companies can develop their supplier strategies based on the executed analysis.

2 Theoretical Background

There are several different classes of manufacturing. It is common to separate between make-to-stock (MTS), assemble-to-order (ATO), make-to-order (MTO), and engineer-to-order (ETO) [1]. According to [2], the commonalities with ETO supply chains are that they operate in a project environment and that each product is different.

I. Nääs et al. (Eds.): APMS 2016, IFIP AICT 488, pp. 911–918, 2016.
DOI: 10.1007/978-3-319-51133-7_107

Many of the frameworks for matching supply chains to the marketplace have been organized around the concept of the "decoupling point". The customer order decoupling point is a stock holding point that separates the part of the supply chain that responds directly to the customer from the part that uses forecast planning. In ETO supply chains, the customer order decoupling point is located at the design stage [2]. Another common feature of the ETO production situation comes in the form of change orders, which change a feature that was decided upon at contract execution. The capability to respond to these kinds of orders is often a prerequisite for success for ETO companies [3]. An analysis of 20 construction projects by [4] shows that 27% of non-conformities were related to the work of suppliers and sub-contractors. This indicates a high need to establish good relationships with suppliers. According to [5], there has been an increase in outsourcing by ETO companies, which makes supply chain management strategically important because of the reliance upon suppliers. According to [6], the most critical element of supply strategy is the company's capacity to handle various types of supplier relationships.

Several portfolio models have been developed for purchasing management, including those of [7,8]. According to [9], portfolio models can be a tool for management in organizing information and can be used to classify resources and suppliers. If a portfolio model is regarded as an indicator of how to deal with different suppliers, and as an eye-opener for a number of possible action plans, it can provide useful inputs for supply chain decision makers. The matrix by [7] was developed to find strategies regarding products and suppliers based on two dimensions – *profit impact and supply risk*. The profit impact of a given supply item can be defined in terms of the volume purchased, the percentage of total purchase cost, or the impact on product quality or business growth. Supply risk is assessed in terms of availability of the supply item, the number of suppliers, competitive demand, make-or-buy opportunities, storage risks, and substitution possibilities [7]. [8] used the same matrix, but different dimensions, namely "difficulty of managing the purchasing situation" and "the strategic importance of the purchase." Based on these dimensions, the sup-pliers or components are placed in one of the following categories: "non-critical," "bottleneck," "leverage," or "strategic." The portfolios are visualized in Fig. 1.

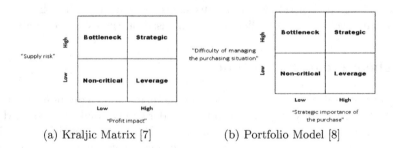

(a) Kraljic Matrix [7]   (b) Portfolio Model [8]

Fig. 1. Portfolios according [7,8]

3   Research Methodology

The research methodology is a multiple case study research [10]. The data was primarily collected through semi-structured interviews with the case companies' representatives and analysis of secondary sources, such as information from the companies' ERP systems, their steering documents, etc. The methodology suggested by Kraljic [7] was adjusted slightly, as described in paragraph 4.1 below, and was used as a tool for performing supplier evaluation at the case companies.

4   Analysis

4.1   Supplier Evaluation Procedure

Prior to the start of the supplier analysis at the case companies, separate meetings of the researchers with representatives of each of the three case companies were organized. At these meetings the researchers presented the Kraljic framework [7] and a step-by-step procedure for performing the analysis. As originally suggested by [7], two dimensions – 'supply risk' and 'profit impact' – were selected as the matrix's horizontal and vertical axes, respectively. A set of evaluation criteria (with weights) was suggested for each of the dimensions (Table 1).

Table 1. Evaluation criteria with weights

Supply risk	Profit impact
Product availability (20%)	Economic impact (50%)
Number of potential suppliers (20%)	Impact on end product quality (50%)
Switch costs (20%)	
Consequence of delay (20%)	
Competitive structure (20%)	

The product availability criterion is related to the delivery lead time of an item. Whether a product can be purchased in store or if it needs to be engineered and produced will affect the supply risk of the particular item. Number of potential suppliers is related to the number of suppliers that can supply the particular item; whether there is an abundant amount of suppliers or only one will affect the supply risk. The switch cost criterion is the cost of changing from one supplier to another. Consequence of delay is related to whether a delay in delivery of the item will affect the delivery of the final product. The competitive structure criterion has been used to describe the supplier's competitive position in the supply market ("Is it a solid supplier that will survive in the market in the future?"). The evaluation criteria that were selected for the dimension *profit impact are economic impact and impact on end product quality. Economic impact* refers to the economic value of the purchase, while *impact on end product quality* indicates the impact that the item has on the end product quality. The impact can range from negligible to significant (influencing the quality and safety of the final product).

The first step in the supplier evaluation was for each of the case companies to create lists of their suppliers and supplied items. The companies were given a choice between analyzing suppliers from a specific project or specific product segment, or analyzing all of their suppliers.

The second step was to set a score for each item and/or supplier on each evaluation criterion. The values of criteria could vary between 0 and 10. The companies were given some freedom in the score setting, regarding what scale to use, and how to assign specific scores to items and/or suppliers.

4.2   The Case Companies

Company A is a Norwegian producer of heavy lifting systems for the oil and gas industry. It specializes in producing one-of-a-kind highly technical and complex products. The products are usually engineered from scratch. Procurement is usually handled by the engineers attached to the project. Production takes place at various workshops around the world, usually the ones that are close to the final customer.

Company B is another Norwegian producer of lifting maritime equipment for the offshore oil and gas industry. It primarily produces cranes, in various sizes and applications. The degree of engineering complexity varies over the product line, but they mainly perform engineering based on already designed products. The company has a purchasing department, which is responsible for the procurement of components and fabrication for all projects. Company B produces its products at a small number of workshops, with which it seeks to establish close and long-lasting relationships.

Company C is a Norwegian producer of cast house solutions for the global aluminium industry. The degree of engineering complexity varies, but the engineering is usually performed based on the company's existing product portfolio. The company has a purchasing department that handles all procurement for the projects. The company produces at several locations globally, but assembly and testing are carried out at its facility in Norway.

4.3   Supplier Analysis – Company A

Company A chose to perform the analysis based on one particular project. In the analysis, the company used the evaluation criteria with their respective weights as provided in Table 1, except for one criterion, competitive structure, which was substituted with criterion cooperativeness, referring to service availability for the specific item and the response time from the supplier(s) of the item. The results of the categorization of the procured items in the project selected by Company A are presented in Fig. 2.

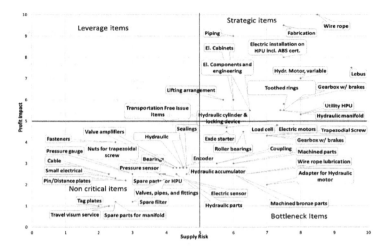

Fig. 2. Kraljic matrix – Company A

4.4   Supplier Analysis – Company B

Company B chose to perform the analysis on a segment of products. It initially created a list of the suppliers it used for this product segment. It chose to perform the analysis based on suppliers and not items or product groups. The scoring of the suppliers (for each supplier, for each criterion) was done by representatives from the purchasing department. The scores were based on the purchasing department representatives' experience and knowledge about the suppliers. These representatives sometimes went back and changed the scores of some suppliers after comparing with the scores of other suppliers. The results of the categorization of the suppliers for a selected segment of Company B's products are presented in Fig. 3 (note that, according to confidentiality requirements, the suppliers' names were substituted with the names of items they supply, so some of the items may appear several times on the matrix).

4.5   Supplier Analysis – Company C

Company C chose to execute the supplier analysis based on the entire database of its suppliers. The analysis was executed both on the item groups' level and on the supplier level. Like Company A, Company C used criterion cooperativeness instead of competitive structure when evaluating supply risk. The results of the categorization of Company B's groups of purchased items on the Kraljic matrix are presented in Fig. 4.

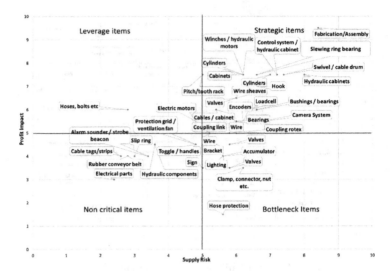

Fig. 3. Kraljic matrix – Company B

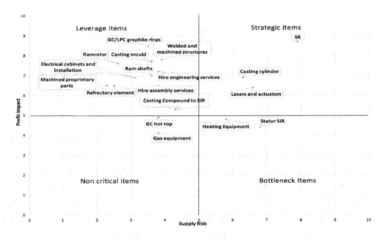

Fig. 4. Kraljic matrix – Company C

5 Towards New Supplier Strategies – Discussion

After completing the mapping of the procured item groups and/or suppliers on the Kraljic matrix, the natural next step is to try to define strategies for the supplies of the items categorized into the four groups: non-critical, leverage, bottleneck, and strategic.

According to [8], the key term for products in the non-critical category is standardization, which implies having a supplier relationship that basically manages itself. The focus must be on reducing administrative costs. For the products in the bottleneck category, some sort of relationship with supplier should be established, and cooperation in value analysis should be done in order to lower the cost of operations. For the products in the leverage category, it is important to identify the value added of the purchase and leverage volume across product lines and suppliers in order to lower the material costs. The goal is to create mutual respect in the supplier relationship and communicate requirements further into the future. For the products in the strategic category, it is important to establish a close relationship with the supplier and to focus on early supplier involvement and joint developments of products and services.

[11] suggested another way to establish new supplier strategies. They argued that for each item group, two kinds of strategic directions could be distinguished: (1) actions to hold the same positions in the matrix, and (2) actions to pursue other positions in the matrix. A total of nine strategic directions were proposed: (1) "Decomplex the product, find a new supplier" or (2) "Accept the dependence on a supplier, assurance of supply" (bottleneck items); (3) "Pooling of requirements" or (4) "Individual ordering, efficient processing" (non-critical items); (5) "Exploit buying power, maintain a partnership of convenience" or (6) "Develop a strategic partnership" (leverage items); (7) "Maintain a strategic partnership"; (8) "Accept a locked-in partnership" or (9) "Terminate a partnership, find a new supplier" (strategic items) [11].

In the ETO setting, it is common not only for the end product to be customized, but also for some of the components delivered by suppliers to be tailored to the customers' needs. In this respect, the level of detail of the component specifications sent to the supplier is important. [9] distinguished between how specifications should be developed for each item category in the Kraljic matrix. In the non-critical category, specifications of products should follow an industry standard. For leverage components, rough specifications should be developed with parameters such as function, quality, cost, and system fit. The supplier should be given the freedom to undertake further development and ultimate sealing of these components. In the case of bottleneck components, the reduced number of capable suppliers makes it necessary to have collaborative agreements with them. Because of low strategic importance, the supplier can gain responsibility for developing the components' specifications. The buyer should then help the supplier to standardize these components in order to reduce the costs in the entire supply chain. In the case of strategic products, there is need for close relationships with the suppliers and early or even continuous involvement.

The case companies are currently in the process of development of their supplier strategies. In this process, the approach suggested by [11] was taken as the starting point. However, it is clear that there is no one-size-fits-all approach for ETO companies with regard to managing suppliers of the items categorized into the four groups in the Kraljic matrix. Company A works mainly in the "temporary supply chain" environment because their customers are spread all over the world, and it is the company's strategy to fabricate and assemble its products close to the customers. This implies that a long-term strategy to build relationships with suppliers is difficult. Companies B and C, on the other hand, seek to build long-term relationships with their strategic suppliers, particularly with their fabrication suppliers.

6 Conclusion

This paper has presented an application of the Kraljic Matrix at three Norwegian ETO companies. We have described the process of conducting the analysis and presented the results of the analysis, and discussed possible methods to develop strategic directions towards the supplier base. We can conclude that there is no one-size-fits-all approach towards supplier strategies in the ETO setting, and the companies' distinctive features should always be taken into consideration. The feedback received from the case companies points to the effectiveness of the Kraljic approach as a tool for generation or development of supplier strategies.

References

1. Olhager, J.: Strategic positioning of the order penetration point. Int. J. Prod. Econ. **85**(3), 319–329 (2003)
2. Gosling, J., Naim, M.M.: Engineer-to-order supply chain management: a literature review and research agenda. Int. J. Prod. Econ. **122**(2), 741–754 (2009)
3. Sjøbakk, B., Thomassen, M.K., Alfnes, E.: Automation in the ETO production situation: the case of a norwegian supplier of ship equipment. In: International Workshop of Advanced Manufacturing and Automation. Akademika Forlag (2013)
4. Zavadskas, E., Vilutienė, T., Turskis, Z., Šaparauskas, J.: Multi-criteria analysis of projects' performance in construction. Arch. Civil Mech. Eng. **14**(1), 114–121 (2014)
5. Hicks, C., McGovern, T., Earl, C.F.: Supply chain management: a strategic issue in engineer to order manufacturing. Int. J. Prod. Econ. **65**(2), 179–190 (2000)
6. Gadde, L.E., Snehota, I.: Making the Most of supplier relationships. Ind. Mark. Manage. **29**(4), 305–316 (2000)
7. Kraljic, P.: Purchasing must become supply management. Harvard Bus. Rev. **61**(5), 109–117 (1983)
8. Olsen, R.F., Ellram, L.M.: A portfolio approach to supplier relationships. Ind. Mark. Manage. **26**(2), 101–113 (1997)
9. Nellore, R., Söderquist, K.: Portfolio approaches to procurement: analysing the missing link to specifications. Long Range Plan. **33**(2), 245–267 (2000)
10. Yin, R.K.: Case Study Research. Design and Methods. Sage Publications, Thousand Oaks (2009)
11. Gelderman, C.J., Van Weele, A.J.: Handling measurement issues and strategic directions in Kraljic's purchasing portfolio model. J. Purchasing Supply Manage. **9**(5), 207–216 (2003)

Categorizing Engineer-to-Order Companies Through Their Project Execution Strategy

Kristina Kjersem[1(✉)] and Gabriele H. Jünge[2]

[1] Møreforsking Molde AS, Molde, Norway
kristina.kjersem@himolde.no
[2] Norwegian University of Science and Technology, Trondheim, Norway
gabriele.junge@ntnu.no

Abstract. One of the main characteristics of engineer-to-order (ETO) manufacturing companies is that they are project organized and, by definition, each project is a unique endeavor [1]. The implication of this characteristic reflects in that most of the ETO companies apply own execution strategies to their projects. However, these strategies do not always fit the complexity of ETO projects that usually are phase-based managed and involve several participants in each of the phases. This research paper proposes a new categorization of ETO companies based on the project execution strategy applied by our case companies. The scope of such categorization is to support practitioners in defining their strategies for managing ETO projects.

Keywords: ETO categorization · Project execution strategy · Manufacturing companies

1 Introduction and Background

Engineer-To-Order (ETO) is a manufacturing approach where each artifact is customized (from the early design phase throughout the production and delivery phases) according to buyer's preferences. Main characteristics of ETO manufacturing approach are: low-volumes, high degree of customization and project-based environment [2]. In a comprehensive literature review presented by [3], the authors outline the commonalities and differences between different types of ETO supply chain. The first commonality is that ETO operates in a project-based environment while the second one is that it results in unique artifacts. Among the differences between ETO approaches can be the reusage of the same design versus creating a new one for each product. Another difference is sector specific like for example in construction, where the team complete the project on a new site each time, whereas in shipbuilding the product is manufactured at the same site [3]. One implication of the first commonality is that each ETO company must apply an own project execution strategy to manufacturing their products. However, in [4,5] the authors state that traditional project management approaches do not take into consideration the challenges of ETO environment.

© IFIP International Federation for Information Processing 2016
Published by Springer International Publishing AG 2016. All Rights Reserved
I. Nääs et al. (Eds.): APMS 2016, IFIP AICT 488, pp. 919–926, 2016.
DOI: 10.1007/978-3-319-51133-7_108

Among these challenges, [4] name the network organized projects, iteration of design/engineering activities and concurrent engineering. A network-organized project involves a large number of project participants who do not necessary belong to the company responsible for managing the whole project. Most of the ETO projects involve a large number of participants since more than 75% of the product's value is built with help from suppliers and subcontractors. Consequently, the company that manages the entire project executes only a small part of the project with own employees and at own facilities [6], which makes difficult to control all activities during the project. However, according to our empirical data, several case companies seem interested in developing project execution strategies that can give them better control over most of the project phases. We define project execution strategy (PES) as the management approaches applied by ETO organizations in order to plan, control and complete a project according to customer's requests. PES is influenced by the company's decision about who performs each activity and where each phase of the project is scheduled for completion.

Based on earlier research projects conducted by Møreforsking Molde AS (a Norwegian research institute), as well as on its long-term analysis of the Norwegian maritime cluster, this paper brings to discussion a new categorization of the ETO type of manufacturing. The background for this study comes from projects where our customers were interested in improving their PES for managing ETO projects. These companies were using traditional project management approaches that needed to be adapted to the challenges of the ETO environment and we learned that any PES must contain both standardized elements as well as customized features. Thus, we attempted to find a categorization of ETO companies by the strategies used during their project execution. The closest categorization we found is the one presented by Hicks et al. [7] where the authors use a similar line of thought. Nevertheless, their categorization is from a high-level management perspective and do not address the project management approached by their case companies. To our knowledge, there is no other studies categorizing ETO companies by their project execution strategies.

From our portfolio of companies, we selected ten cases manufacturing different ETO products and studied the similarities and differences between their PESs. Consequently, we identified different levels of integration between project phases as well as different strategies for managing these and that point toward a new categorization of ETO companies from the perspective of PES. In this paper, we first describe the models of PESs identified from our empirical data and based on these we group ETO companies in three categories that are relevant from the proposed perspective. The scope of this categorization is to highlight the need for integrated PES that fit different ETO challenges. A second scope of the categorization is to serve as a decision support for project managers when planning the strategy for delivering new ETO products. This is an important aspect when it comes to optimizing the project execution as a whole and not only some of its phases. In the following, we present a short review of the literature we found on ETO categorization.

2   Literature Review

Willner et al. [8] present a relevant literature review on categorization of ETO companies and according to their findings each classification contains a different ETO perspective like: type of modularization, point of customer involvement, engineer dimension referring to the number of standardized versus customized parts, etc. The same authors propose a categorization based on the complexity of the ETO product where they considered the following two factors: (1) the number of units sold annually and (2) the number of engineering hours used for producing the artifact. Their categorization resulted in a matrix of four groups: (1) Complex ETO, (2) Basic ETO, (3) Repeatable ETO and (4) Non-Competitive ETO [8]. This categorization is suitable at a high-level management when deciding strategies at the company level. Nevertheless, this matrix contributes to better understanding of the diversity of ETO products and the authors propose appropriate strategies for improving the outcome of such projects.

Cigolini et al. [9], categorizes ETO companies based on how the product design affects the timing for sourcing decisions. They identified three types of innovativeness: (1) pure incremental innovation, (2) only technology innovation, (3) technology and marketing innovation, which affect the timing of decision for sourcing activities. Suppliers in the third category are earlier involved in the project.

Another relevant categorization is presented by Hicks et al. [7], who use physical processes and the depth of the product structure for identifying four types of ETO companies specific to UK business environment. These are: (1) vertically integrated, (2) design and assembly, (3) design and contract, and (4) project management. However, these ideal types are quite general, especially when describing their project management approach. We have not identified these types of company among our case companies or other previous projects. To our knowledge, there is no ETO categorization that takes into consideration both the typical phase-based project environment as well as who performs each of the project phases. The categorization presented here is based on the processes defined by our case companies for managing each phase of their projects.

3   Methodology

The case companies have all had different research projects together with our institute. Through these projects, we performed both value and supply chain analysis, which means that our database is quite extensive. The selected companies manufacture different ETO products like offshore and fishing vessels, cranes, winches and alike. The criteria for selecting these cases was mainly their interest in research projects aiming to improve their project management strategies. We have sent the figures to several of the companies and receive feedback on the phases used for defining the project execution strategy. Moreover, the authors work closely through their Ph.D. studies with several of the case companies. The scope of this study is to explore the factors that contribute to the complexity of project execution strategy in ETO environment. Exploratory case studies as defined by [10,11] are reckoned as particularly suitable for this type of research. Case studies are suited for capturing knowledge from practitioners and use these to develop new theories [11,12].

4   ETO Project Phases

In order to grasp the intricacy of the ETO projects, we decided to map the most significant phases that influence the strategy applied to manage these projects. Several internal and external suppliers must deliver information, technical documentation - on specific systems and equipment - during each of the project phases described here. We illustrates each project phase in Fig. 1, and describe them next.

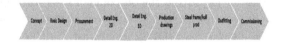

Fig. 1. Project phases

During the concept phase, a company develop a new product either by own internal projects or by collaborating with customers interested in improving their own business quality. Basic Design is an activity performed by the project responsible company in collaboration with the customer who is interested to decide and approve the main features of the product. This phase contains both 2D drawings and 3D models and some of the case companies chose to outsource partly or entire 3D modelling activities. The company who is responsible for managing the project performs usually the procurement activities. However, in some of the cases, the procurement responsibility is divided between two or three project participants (e.g., one company procures the steel and some of the systems, while the leading company buys all major equipment). The company in charge for the whole project performs and delivers 2D drawings. These types of drawings are considered an important core capability of the company and are very rarely outsourced. Among our cases, there is only one company who does not produce 2D drawings in-house, but collaborate closely with the one producing these drawings.

After completing 2D drawings, these are introduced in a 3D model. The majority of our case-companies perform this phase in-house with own people or people from own subsidiaries. Three of the case companies outsource big parts of 3D modeling activities to other project partners. The reason is that performing such activities necessitates considerable amount of time and resources.

Production drawings represent the drawings used during the production phase. These drawings contain many small details necessary to produce each piece of the product. In some cases, these drawings are produced by the steel frame/hull producing companies, while in other cases, these drawings are produced by the company delivering the basic design and detail engineering. Steel frame/hull production phase is in most of the cases outsourced both internal (the main company owns facilities outside Norway) or external (find new collaborating partners in Norway or other countries).

Outfitting and commissioning phases are most of the time performed by the companies managing the whole project. These phases are considered important core capabilities within the company. However, in one of the cases, the company performing these phases is not the one producing the basic design and detail engineering.

5   Mapping Project Execution Strategy

The table under is a visual presentation of how our case companies have chosen to execute their ETO projects. The colored boxes represent phases performed by partially owned or completely external companies with the symbol "out" as a shortcut for outsourcing. The "x" symbol confirms in-house execution of the respective phase. The last three columns denote producing equipment (Prod. equip.), procurement (Proc.) and final user. These columns represent an interesting trend among our case companies where at least two of them (A and D) started to produce specialized equipment that was previously supplied by external suppliers (Fig. 2).

Company	Concept	Basic Design	Detail 2D	3D	Prod. Draw.	Hull/Frame Prod.	Outfitting	Com.	Prod. equip.	Proc.	Final user
A	x	x	x	x	x	x	x	x	x	x	
B	x	x	x	x	Out	Out	x	x	Out	x	
C	Out	Out	Out	Out	x	x	x	x	Out	x	
D	x	x	x	x	Out	Out	Out	Out	x	x	
E	x	x	x	x	Out	Out	Out	x	x	Out	x
F	x	x	x	x	Out	Out	x	x	Out	x	x
G	x	x	x	x	x	Out	Out	x	x	Out	Out
H	x	x	x	x	x	x	x	x	Out	x	
I	x	x	x	Out	x	x	x	x	Out	x	
J	x	x	x	Out	x	x	x	x	Out	x	

Fig. 2. Map of the project execution strategy phases

The results show a certain similarity in that most of the companies choose to keep in-house the concept, basic design and some parts of the detail engineering phases. However, company C decided to approach a different strategy and outsourced most of the design, engineering and procurement phases keeping a minimum of engineering hours in-house while producing the steel frame, outfitting and commissioning (the column Com in the table) the final product before delivery. An interesting observation here is that this company seems to achieve quite good results during the present economic crisis. Engineers at company C work together with the company that deliver the design and engineering phases and give them the production perspective for the solutions applied to the product features. Companies C and D seem to complete each other's project phases in a feasible way. Company A is the one with a vertically integrated supply chain executing all the project phases in-house. The term in-house refers here to ownership of the process performed in each phase even when the companies performing these activities are not located in Norway, but are completely owned by a case company.

Company G, decided to outsource a big part of their procurement activities while company F decided to outsource the production of steel frame, keeps the outfitting and the commissioning in-house, but they invested in the final phase of the supply chain, namely using the final product in an own subsidiary. Another observation we made during our mapping process is that two of the companies have started to create departments or new subsidiaries that research and develop complex equipment. That means more vertical integration of their supply chains and more risk to be taken when the market is on a down turn. This evolution seem to contrast the trend towards vertical disintegration identified by Hicks et al. [13] several years ago. Analyzing the similarities and differences between our case companies, we identified a common need for dynamic and more integrative PES that would fit the challenges of ETO complex projects.

6   Categorization

From the mapping process presented above, we can identify three relevant categories of ETO companies: (1) a vertically integrated type (2) design and engineering type (3) production and testing type.

The vertically integrated companies own most of the processes in each project phase. They acquired smaller local or global companies that deliver services or products able to increase companies' competitive advantage. As a result, the project execution strategy seem more integrated and gives better possibilities for control and improvement. Other advantages are more flexibility for the management of customer change orders and transparency of the practices between project participants. An integrated project execution strategy is also an advantage when ETO companies plan to implement design for manufacturability (DFM) approaches, which is the case for one of the case companies in this study. In order to achieve a better level of DFM, vertically integrated companies consider to start producing own equipment. Among the disadvantages of such approach is that it requires a big organization that is more sensitive to economic downturns. Another disadvantage is that in order to utilize the capacity in a sustainable way, such organizations need a certain number of orders per year [7].

The second category identified in our study is design and engineering type. Companies embracing this strategy own only concept, design and detail engineering in both 2D drawings and 3D modeling. In many of the cases, they outsource also the production drawings to the company producing the steel frame. One advantages of this approach is that the organization is smaller and easy to readjust in times of crisis, which is the case for one of the case companies. Such organizations can also achieve a great deal of flexibility during the design and engineering phases, and less during the production period. Among the disadvantages is the separation from the production facility, which results in less accessibility to lessons learned from this process. Hicks et al. [7] mention also the disadvantage of being dependent upon concurrent procurement, which means viable partnership with the suppliers. One case company in this category decided to reduce such dependency and started to produce some of the strategic equipment.

The third category is production and testing (commissioning) where companies decided to focus on core competencies that were outsourced by other companies. The ETO aspect of these companies lays in their ability to find engineering solutions coming from practical experience. These companies reveal a good understanding and translation of customer requirements into practice. The advantages of such approach seem to be a more effective production process and the ability to implement automation on the appropriate processes. One disadvantage is the difficulty to achieve an effective design for manufacturability approach due to a separate ownership between design engineering and production phases. Another disadvantage could be a high dependency on the design company for modifications that require their permissions and participation. However, according to our study, this type of ETO companies seem to be able readjust quite fast during the economic crises.

7 Discussion and Limitations

ETO projects need a better management of the involved processes [14] and in order to achieve that we argue that project managers need to apply project execution strategies that take into consideration the complexity of their ETO supply chain. The three categories identified through our study can be useful when managers need to establish the strategy for the execution phase of their projects. The competition within the ETO environment challenges the practitioners to continually improve their manufacturing process so that projects can be deliver in a shorter time, at a lower price while maintaining high quality of the final product [15,16]. An efficient and well-adjusted project execution strategy can help ETO companies to achieve such targets. The empirical data suggest that using traditional project management approach is not enough and among the reasons is the number and differences between project participants as well as the iterative nature of design and engineering activities. Our categorization draws attention to the importance of understanding the configuration of the project phases and the necessity to adapt the management strategy to it. A future paper will discuss types of strategies recommended to each of the categories identified in this paper.

The limitations of this research lays in the small number of selected case studies and the fact that most of them are typical Norwegian ETO companies. Similar mapping in other countries might show different results and that would be an interesting research topic. The number of ETO companies grows at a rate of 20% per year due to an increasing demand for customized products [17] and so the need for categorization that help us understand which strategies to apply in order to achieve continuous improvement.

References

1. PMBOK: A Guide to the Project Management Body of Knowledge (2013)
2. Haartveit, D.E.G., Semini, M., Alfnes, E.: Integration alternatives for ship designers and shipyards. In: Frick, J., Laugen, B.T. (eds.) APMS 2011. IAICT, vol. 384, pp. 309–316. Springer, Heidelberg (2012). doi:10.1007/978-3-642-33980-6_35
3. Gosling, J., Naim, M.M.: Engineer-to-order supply chain management: a literature review and research agenda. Int. J. Produc. Econ. **122**(2), 741–754 (2009)
4. Kjersem, K., Emblemsvåg, J.: Literature review on planning design and engineering activities in shipbuilding. In: 22nd Annual Conference of the International Group for Lean Construction, pp. 677–688 (2014)
5. Koskela, L., Howell, G.: Reforming project management: the role of planning, execution and controlling. In: Proceedings of 9th International Group for Lean Construction Conference, pp. 185–198 (2001)
6. Dubois, A., Gadde, L.E.: Supply strategy and network effects—purchasing behaviour in the construction industry. Europ. J. Purchas. Supply Manage. **6**(3), 207–215 (2000)
7. Hicks, C., McGovern, T., Earl, C.F.: A typology of UK engineer-to-order companies. Int. J. Logistics **4**(1), 43–56 (2001)
8. Willner, O., Powell, D., Gerschberger, M., Schönsleben, P.: Exploring the arche types of engineer-to-order: an empirical analysis. Int. J. Oper. Prod. Manage. **36**(3), 242–264 (2016)
9. Cigolini, R., Pero, M., Sianesi, A.: When ETO companies design the supply chain during new product development process. Int. J. Eng., Sci. Technol. **6**(3), 30–41 (2014)
10. Voss, C., Tsikriktsis, N., Frohlich, M.: Case research in operations management. Int. J. Oper. Produc. Manage. **22**(2), 195–219 (2002)
11. Case Study Research: Design and Methods
12. Van Aken, J.E., Romme, G.: Reinventing the future. Organ. Manage. J. **6**(1), 5–12 (2009)
13. Hicks, C., McGovern, T., Earl, C.F.: Supply chain management: a strategic issue in engineer to order manufacturing. Int. J. Prod. Econ. **65**(2), 179–190 (2000)
14. Mello, M.H., Strandhagen, J.O.: Supply chain management in the shipbuilding industry: challenges and perspectives. Proc. Inst. Mech. Eng. **225**(3), 261–270 (2011)
15. Kjersem, K., Halse, L.L., Kiekebos, P., Emblemsvåg, J.: Implementing lean in engineer-to-order industry: a case study. In: Umeda, S., Nakano, M., Mizuyama, H., Hibino, H., Kiritsis, D., Cieminski, G. (eds.) APMS 2015. IAICT, vol. 460, pp. 248–255. Springer, Heidelberg (2015). doi:10.1007/978-3-319-22759-7_29
16. Semini, M., Haartveit, D.E.G., Alfnes, E., Arica, E., Brett, P.O., Strandhagen, J.O.: Strategies for customized shipbuilding with different customer order decoupling points. Proc. Inst. Mech. Eng. **228**(4), 362–372 (2014)
17. Grabenstetter, D.H., Usher, J.M.: Developing due dates in an engineer-to-order engineering environment. Int. J. of Produc. Res. **52**(21), 6349–6361 (2014)

Improving Planning Process for ETO-Projects: A Case Study

Kristina Kjersem[1]([✉]) and Gabriele H. Jünge[2]

[1] Møreforsking Molde AS, Molde, Norway
kristina.kjersem@himolde.no
[2] Norwegian University, Trondheim, Norway
gabriele.junge@ntnu.no

Abstract. This research paper builds on a case study performed at a Norwegian company that deals with a large number of small Engineer-To-Order (ETO) projects. Recently, the company started an improvement process pursuing lean principles. One of the initiatives taken by the company is to improve the present planning process, which lacks a whole-project view that can give managers a better decision ground. Two important departments, engineering and production, develop project plans that are based on their own specific approaches and with little collaboration between the departments. This paper presents the preliminary results of implementation of Lean Project Planning (LPP), a planning tool developed within shipbuilding industry, a typical ETO environment.

Keywords: Last planner system · ETO · Project planning · Earned value

1 Introduction

Increasing competition on product quality, cost, rapid project delivery while maintaining a certain flexibility during the design, engineering and production phases of a project are a few of the challenges many Norwegian ETO organizations encounter nowadays. In [1], the authors state that this type of industry is "characterized by low-volumes, high degree of customization and project-based processes" which means that the customer is involved from the design phase of a project and can decide specific features of the product all the way to the delivery phase. The case company subject of our research is an ETO organization producing pressurized storage tanks used within industries like shipbuilding, offshore platforms and other similar environments that require such products. The company is located in Norway and it has a good reputation on delivery of highly customized products by offering market design, engineering, manufacturing and testing of the final products. However, the competition on this specific market is increasing and the company focuses now on improving its working

© IFIP International Federation for Information Processing 2016
Published by Springer International Publishing AG 2016. All Rights Reserved
I. Nääs et al. (Eds.): APMS 2016, IFIP AICT 488, pp. 927–934, 2016.
DOI: 10.1007/978-3-319-51133-7_109

processes at every level within the company. The leaders and the employees are all committed to the improvement program and one of the proposed actions is to implement lean ideas that will help them to define a way of working smarter for achieving their goals: Shorter lead-time, lower production costs and better control over their projects. Another focus of the improvement program is on creating a proactive planning process that integrates all disciplines in a common project plan.

However, in traditional project management, the planning activity is often seen only as a technical process neglecting its human aspect and the need for collaboration [2]. In our paper, we argue for implementing a planning tool that combines both technical and human aspects of the planning process in a novel way: Lean Project Planning (LPP). The empirical data suggest that using traditional project management approach is not enough for ETO projects and among the reasons is the number and differences between project participants as well as the iterative nature of design and engineering activities.

The aim of this paper is: (1) to present the case and the challenges experienced by the company before implementing LPP; and (2) to present the preliminary results of implementing LPP. As a planning tool successfully implemented in other complex projects, LPP aims at improving the planning process by creating a project environment that inspires commitment and where open communication and a proactive planning attitude is the norm, not the exception. LPP combines Last Planner System and Earned Value Management concepts in a way that complete each other and give project team a good foundation for the decision process at the management level [3,4] as well at the project level.

2   Lean Project Planning

Lean Project Planning (LPP) is a management model that has been successfully implemented at Vard, a shipbuilding group in Norway [4,5]. LPP is based on several components : (1) Lean thinking ideas like the PDCA circle; (2) elements from Last Planner System (LPS) [6] used within Lean Construction environment; and (3) Earned Value Management (EVM) [7] used within project management practice.

LPP as it was implemented since 2009 at Vard Group [3,4]. LPP as a planning method distinguishes the system part and the planning process part within the project planning as a whole. For the system part, an IT tool (Primavera, Microsoft Project, etc.) is used as a planning and reporting structure. The planning process part is based on LPS, EVM elements and lean ideas.

The planning process focuses on collaboration, open communication and involvement from the people allocated to the project. The Project Plan is in fact the project's database as recorded in the IT system and only the planner manages the data in this plan. The plan that is first prepared and is a part of the contract signing is the Milestones Plan. This plan contains key events of the entire project from the contract signing to the delivery of the final product. The next plan is the Discipline Plan, which is created in collaboration among all disciplines (including relevant subcontractors) to be involved in the project. Together, Milestones Plan and Disciplines Plans generate the Master Plan that shows the whole project execution horizon. Activities within these plans are quite general and have a long duration. A more detailed plan is created at the Period Plan level that contains activities with duration between five to eight weeks: A look-ahead plan per discipline.

Due to high number of activities and the need for flexibility at weekly plan level, EVM is applied at the Period Plan level that is a suitable level of detail, consequently making the EVM reporting process quite reliable. By focusing five to eight weeks ahead, the Period Plan gives project organization the possibility to avoid deviations from the plan by removing any constraints before the activity supposed to start. The Period Plan contains work packages that are defined so that they can be used within the EVM planning and reporting procedures. Each supervisor reports on a weekly basis the status of their work packages: Percent physical complete on each activity, remaining hours and, if necessary, a new finish date in case of delays from the plan. During the reporting process the seven preconditions or constraints (Preceding work; Resources; Information; Materials; Space; Tools; External conditions) [8] for an executable activity are analyzed, making people aware of eventual problems that can cause delays. After the reporting process is completed, the project planner creates project reports and sends them to the whole project team and to high-level management.

The Period Plan is further developed into a more detailed plan that is called Week Plan. This is a detailed and dynamic plan created and followed by each supervisor who reports the completion of planned activities during the weekly lean meeting. These lean meetings are steered by the technical or production coordinators and have the purpose of enhancing communication and commitment among project participants. Each lean meeting takes less than one and a half hour and follows a standard procedure so that people involved in more projects know what to relate to. Some general rules for these meetings are: (1) Attendance is not voluntary (all invited people must participate). (2) People must come prepared to the meeting; (3) Line management join the meetings from time to time (supervisors are evaluated on the way they are prepared for the meetings). (4) People have to explain to the rest of the team the status of their own activities, causes for deviations and measures for recovery of deviations (this is important for other disciplines that might need to replan some of their activities) as well as which activities are planned for execution for the next week or two. (5) People must follow the rules of the meeting and are invited to come with suggestions for improvement [3].

The system part of LPP as represented in the triangle shows the cost breakdown structure (CBS) and different levels of work packages as implemented in the IT systems: one used for project planning purpose and the other one used for the financial purpose.

The idea behind LPP is according to [3], that EVM is good at handling issues at a high level of project management, but fails to handle issues concerning improving project performances relevant to supervisors. Among the critics to

EVM within lean construction literature, some authors argue that EVM treat project activities as independent when in fact they are interrelated [9], and that EVM does not provide indicators on the quality of the construction or the quality of the process [10]. On the other hand, [11], present an analysis showing that there is a statistic significant correlation between EVM and LPS and recommend to train project managers in the use of both methods in their work. The combination of these two methodologies add value to project planning and control involving and motivating the project team. The strength of LPS is that it systematically handles issues regarding project performance at supervisor level, but do not deal with high-level management issues as well as EVM does [3]. An important rule when using LPP is to find the right level of detail for each of the plans. Emblemsvåg [3], considering the level of uncertainty in an ETO project, recommends to *"train the organization to live with this uncertainty and then rely on the expertise of supervisors and coordinators to maneuver to find the best solution for given circumstances"* (p. 6). The focus here is on planning as a communication process among all project participants from the lowest to the highest level of decision-making pyramid.

3 Research Methodology

We apply case study methodology to this research. Yin [12], states that a case study investigates a contemporary phenomenon in its natural setting and the outcome is on relevant theories generated from understanding gained through observing actual practice. The focus of our research project is on how to improve the planning processes at the case company by using LPP as a method that can help them achieve the desired results: integrated plans. The data is mainly qualitative and we collected it through observations, discussions and interviews as well as frequent participation in day-to-day organizational processes related to some of the projects. In addition, one of the authors worked directly with LPP at the shipyard and later with the implementation at the case company. The scope of this paper is to bring to discussion the need for better planning tools for ETO projects as well as presenting preliminary results from implementation of LPP, a planning tool tested only in shipbuilding industry until now. We argue this research contributes to developing a more scientific approach to planning process as a management tool that integrates engineering and production activities performed in complex ETO projects.

4 Case Company

The case company is an ETO manufacturer offering market design, engineering, project management and manufacturing of pressure vessels, process vessels and storage tanks to the oil and gas market. Products are highly customized and are manufactured at the company location, which can accommodate over 35 projects at a time. Based on the size and complexity of each project it can take from 7–8 months to 12–15 months from the contract to the delivery of a new product. This long project duration include long lead items (e.g. special forged parts that can take up to several months to be delivered). However, based on market demands, the company is interested in shortening this lead-time by improving its working process.

We started the project by carrying out a mapping process that identified the working processes that were most beneficial to improve first. Together with company representatives, we decided to investigate a method for improving the project planning process. Currently, their project planning process is mainly divided in two sections: one performed by the technical manager and one performed by the production manager. There is very little integration between these two plans and the company is interested to achieve a total project overview that can give them a better control over their projects (even though the two departments disagree on the ownership of the total plan).

The organization model applied by the company is mostly line-organization (department leaders are part of the project team and allocate task to own people on a daily/weekly basis) type with only a few people allocated specifically per project. Such type of organization is not usually associated with ETO environment which, according to Gosling and Naim [13] is "primarily associated with large, complex project environments such as construction and capital projects" (p. 741). However, the case company specifically designs, engineers and manufactures every product according to each customer specifications, which is an important characteristic of an ETO organization. The final products are quite complex and must conform to high quality requirements due to their purpose on offshore platforms, vessels and other specific environments. In addition, an important customer requirement is the possibility to introduce last minute changes to the product while under production.

Shortly before the sale is completed, the sale manager transfers projects to a Project Manager (PM) and, considering that the planning process starts often during the negotiation phase, the results is that the PM has, at the taking-over point, a prearranged milestones plan that is difficult to change.

Resource allocation per project is performed at department manager levels where Technical Manager and Production Manager distribute tasks to people in their departments on a weekly basis by taking into consideration priorities from a project portfolio perspective. That is not always in accordance with each PM own plan for execution of the project. In order to follow their own project plans, each PM applies a certain stress on the engineering and production teams to produce what PM acknowledge as important from own project perspective. When PM comes with some urgent activities for one project, people will delay other activities committed to other projects, and this leads to a constant firefighting working environment. Another important aspect is that having allocated tasks on a weekly basis, employees do not have the possibility to plan and prepare activities so that these will be executed on time. The process of preparing activities is about all the actions and procedures that identify and remove constraints for future work [14].

The reporting process is performed on a weekly basis and employees report physical percent complete on the allocated activities to the Technical Manager and Production Manager who report further to each PM and other company leaders.

Technical department plans the design and detail engineering activities, which are performed both in Norway and in a foreign European subsidiary. The drawings are produced through an iterative process, as many of them need comments and approval from the customer and from classification societies. The drawing process is also dependent on the footprints from some of the suppliers of valves, pumps and other equipment to be installed inside and outside the tanks. The planning process for the entire engineering department is prepared by the Technical Manager in Norway who plans and allocates activities to all the engineers within the company on a weekly basis. There are no links between the engineering plan and the production plan prepared by the Production Manager for all the projects under execution. Planning of the procurement activities is mainly based on information from the production department and experience from previous project.

5   Discussion

The first step on the LPP implementation process at the case company started with hiring a planner who mapped the current planning processes and systems existing within the company. The result shows different thinking approaches as well as different IT systems between departments. We identify how different aspects of LPP can handle challenges in the planning process at the case company.

The next step of implementing LPP was to train some of the employees in using the different parts of LPP. However, the training was at a superficial level and did not get into significant details due to a high product order at the time of implementation.

The first department implementing some features of LPP was the production department where they introduced a constraint analysis for their planned activities and the result was a significant improvement in the number of activities completed as planned. According to the project planner, the percent of activities completed as planned before starting the new approach, was between forty five to fifty percent. After starting to use lean meetings and activity constrains analysis, the percent of completed activities increased to over sixty percent and the production department is now working for implementing the EVM reporting per project. However, there are some challenges due to the IT planning system that limits some of the EVM feature (the difficulty to report physical progress). The managers of the company are interested in this methodology and work for defining the best solution.

Another relevant result was an improved communication from people on the production department about which constraints might affect their activities on the near future. The supervisors' involvement and commitment resulted in a requirement for a white board containing weekly-actualized plans to be placed at the production department. These plans are created in collaboration with the production manager, the planner and relevant subcontractors.

The technical department remained reluctant to implementing LPP and one of the reasons is their difficulty and time-consuming planning activities with their iterative nature specific engineering activities. However, the planning process from the production department, showing constraints coming from the technical department, challenged the technical coordinator to take measures for eliminating these.

Overall, the preliminary results of implementing LPP show a significant improvement in the project planning process at our case company especially at the production department. The next step of the implementation is the technical department where we are in the process of defining what their typical constraints are when planning iterative engineering activities. Another aspect we are looking into is how to motivate engineers to plan the completion of their activities in close collaboration with the suppliers of technical documentation.

An important remark here is that the success of LPP implementation on the shipbuilding company was sustained by a dedicated training from the yard management. Without this type of training, the implementation of LPP is slower and the results might come after several projects. The preliminary results on our case company confirm this statement.

The preliminary results endorse also the idea that LPP is an appropriate tool for planning ETO projects and we are looking forward for the next phase of this implementation.

6   Conclusion and Limitations

In this study, we have investigated the planning process in the manufacturing company who organize and carry out projects in an ETO environment. The current processes have been analyzed and challenges and areas of improvement have been identified. Furthermore, the study demonstrates that LPP as a management model is able to meet these challenges and suggests specific measures to improve the planning process in this company.

By applying LPP principles, the company can first develop a good planning process that motivates people to participate and to make promises they want to keep. Then, in order to complete their activities as promised, people must communicate to each other, find out what can affect their plans and how would they avoid big deviations. However, a good reporting process showing the project status is an important issue both for the project team and for the leaders at the case company. Good routines on estimating budgets and durations must be developed for projects teams and managers.

Moreover, LPP gives leaders the possibility to make decisions based on right information from the people executing the work. Project reports obtained through the EVM elements can also support the managerial decisions by presenting a possible outcome of the project when no recovery measures are taken.

LPP is most of all about facilitating a dynamic communication process that enhance the project team capabilities to deal with variation and rapid changes during the project execution. However, implementation of LPP is dependent on the way people understand it and translate it to their working procedures.

References

1. Haartveit, D.E.G., Semini, M., Alfnes, E.: Integration alternatives for ship designers and shipyards. In: Frick, J., Laugen, B.T. (eds.) APMS 2011. IAICT, vol. 384, pp. 309–316. Springer, Heidelberg (2012). doi:10.1007/978-3-642-33980-6_35
2. Ballard, G.: If you can't say "no", you can't make a promise. In: Seminario Internacional de Confiabilidade da Petrobras. Brasília (2014)
3. Emblemsvåg, J.: Lean Project Planning: Using Lean Principles in Project Planning. International Journal of Construction Project Management (2014). (Accepted for publication)
4. Emblemsvåg, J.: Lean project planning in shipbuilding. J. Ship Prod. Des. **30**(2), 79–88 (2014)
5. Halse, L.L., Kjersem, K., Emblemsvåg, J.: Implementation of lean project planning: a knowledge transfer perspective. In: Grabot, B., Vallespir, B., Gomes, S., Bouras, A., Kiritsis, D. (eds.) APMS 2014. IAICT, vol. 440, pp. 248–255. Springer, Heidelberg (2014). doi:10.1007/978-3-662-44733-8_31
6. Ballard, H.G.: The last planner system of production control. Ph.D. thesis, The University of Birmingham (2000)
7. Sumara, J., Goodpasture, J.: Earned value-the next generation: a practical application for commercial projects. In: Proceedings Project Management Institute, pp. 839–843 (1996)
8. Hamzeh, F.R., Ballard, G., Tommelein, I.D.: Improving construction workflow the connective role of lookahead planning. In: Proceedings for the 16th Annual Conference of the International Group for Lean Construction, pp. 635–646 (2008)
9. Kim, Y.W., Ballard, G.: Is the earned-value method an enemy of work flow. In: Proceedings Eighth Annual Conference of the International Group for Lean Construction, IGLC, vol. 6 (2000)
10. Cândido, L.F., Heineck, L.F.M., Neto, J.d.P.B.: Critical analysis on earned value management (EVM) technique in building construction. In: 22nd Annual Conference of the International Group for Lean Construction, pp. 159–170 (2014)
11. Olano, R.M., Alarcón, L.F., Rázuri, C.: Understanding the relationship between planning reliability and schedule performance: a case study. In: Proceedings of 17th Annual Conference of the International Group for Lean Construction (IGLC-17) (2009)
12. Yin, R.K.: Case Study Research: Design and Methods, 5th edn. Sage Publications, Thousand Oaks (2014)
13. Gosling, J., Naim, M.M.: Engineer-to-order supply chain management: a literature review and research agenda. Int. J. Prod. Econ. **122**, 741–754 (2009)
14. Ballard, G.: Lookahead planning: the missing link in production control. In: Proceedings 5th Annual Conference of the International Group for Lean Construction (1997)

A Framework for Lean Flow in Turbulent High-Variety Low-Volume Manufacturing Environments

Erlend Alfnes[1(✉)], Maria Kollberg Thomassen[2], and Erik Gran[2]

[1] Norwegian University of Science and Technology,
Department of Production and Quality Engineering, Trondheim, Norway
erlend.alfnes@ntnu.no
[2] SINTEF Technology and Society,
Industrial Management, Trondheim, Norway
{maria.thomassen,erik.gran}@sintef.no

Abstract. Value stream mapping (VSM) is a widely applied method for manufacturing systems design in repetitive and stable industries. A literature review of challenges and modified solutions for lean flow in high-variety low-volume (HV/LV) value streams is carried out. The solutions are categorized according to manufacturing turbulence level. The review shows that existing VSM solutions take their starting point in the original VSM principles and incorporate other relevant works only to a limited extent. Based upon the review, a coherent framework with revised VSM principles that that can be used to develop lean flow in HV/LV environments with medium and high turbulence levels is proposed.

Keywords: Lean manufacturing · Value stream mapping · Manufacturing turbulence

1 Introduction

There is a need for research on extending the applicability of leanness into high variety low volume (HV/LV) environments [1]. A literature review of empirical case studies is carried out to investigate solutions of applying VSM in HV/LV environments. Many of the case studies propose modified VSM solutions to achieve a future state with lean flow in HV/LV settings, but the studies are mainly based upon the traditional VSM guidelines. They do not sufficiently build on each other to provide a more coherent set of solutions for this type of environment. The study confirms what authors such as Jina et al. [2] have observed, namely that it becomes more challenging to apply VSM as the turbulence in terms of schedule changes, mix variations, volume fluctuations, and design changes increases.

The purpose of this research is to identify principles for designing lean flows at different turbulence levels by reviewing modified VSM solutions for HV/LV in literature. The main contribution is a framework with revised VSM principles that that can be used to develop lean flow in HV/LV environments.

I. Nääs et al. (Eds.): APMS 2016, IFIP AICT 488, pp. 935–942, 2016.
DOI: 10.1007/978-3-319-51133-7_110

The paper is organised as follows. First, the methodological approach is discussed. Next, a review of challenges and modified solutions for VSM at different turbulence levels in HV/LV case studies is carried out. The review is used to develop a VSM framework for designing lean flow at medium and high turbulence levels. Finally, conclusions are presented together with suggestions for further work.

2   Methodological Considerations

The objective of the literature review is to identify relevant lean principles for designing a future state map in HV/LV manufacturing environments. The reason for this choice is that VSM is a well-known and widely used lean methodology often serving as a starting point for lean implementation as it offers a way to learning to see the process or value streams [3]. A review of relevant empirical cases in literature was carried out. The cases were identified through searches in relevant databases such as Scopus and Google Scholar. We identified 14 empirical cases that met the selection criteria; the majority of the cases (10) include a current or future state value stream map, while the additional cases (4) were selected because they propose useful solutions for how to improve value streams in an HV/LV manufacturing environment. All cases propose modified lean solutions for how to map or improve manufacturing flow.

The cases are classified into low, medium and high turbulence environments based on the turbulence factors proposed by Jina et al. [2]. The VSM design principles proposed by Rother and Shook [4] are used as a reference framework to structure the case studies. The modified VSM principles that proposed to meet major challenges are classified according to turbulence level.

3   Literature Review

The frame of reference is presented in this section. It includes general VSM design principles for flow manufacturing, HV/LV manufacturing and turbulence levels and a categorization of modified solutions for low, medium and high turbulence environments.

3.1   General VSM Design Principles for Flow Manufacturing

As part of the VSM methodology, Rother and Shook [4] defines a set of general design principles for creating flow. The principles represent rules that are to be followed and essential characteristics of a lean flow system;

- VSM is carried out for a specific product family. A family is a group of products that passes through similar processing steps and over common equipment in down stream processes.
- The production pace should be synchronized to match the pace of sales, i.e. to produce to takt time, where takt time refers to the "available production time "/" customer demand".

- Continuous flow should be developed where it is possible, i.e. producing one piece at the time, with each item passed immediately from one process step to the next without stagnation.
- A pull system should be used to control production where continuous flow is not possible. In supermarket pull systems, Kanban trigger replenishment of what is used. If it is not practical to keep all parts in a supermarket, FIFO lanes, CONWIP, or sequenced pull might be an alternative.
- The customer schedule should be sent to a single production process. The pacemaker is the only scheduling point, and sets the pace for all upstream processes. Flow (no pull) is required downstream of the pacemaker, and it is frequently the most downstream process in the value stream. With custom products and job shops, the pacemaker often needs to be further upstream.
- The production mix and volume should be levelled. This means that the production of different products should be distributed evenly over time at the pacemaker process. Hereby a daily production rate is established that is equal to the average expected demand and to release and withdraw small consistent increments of work (pitch) at the pacemaker process.

3.2   HV/LV and Turbulence

HV/LV manufacturing environments include one-of-a-kind as well as small batch manufacturing environments. Manufacturing is usually make-to-order or engineer-to-order, and is normally performed in job shops [5]. A main challenge for lean implementation in HV/LV is that they are experiencing more variability [6]. High levels of unpredictability and instability in dynamic environments make it difficult for lean operations to synchronise production processes and reduce inventory, and undermines the effectiveness of lean operations. Jina et al. [2] proposes four turbulence factors that create unpredictable and sub-optimal behaviour in manufacturing systems:

- Changes in schedule – irregular demand creates many schedule changes close to delivery due date.
- Changes in product mix – marked differences in product mix between one period and the next creates variations in workloads, especially when there is significantly different cycle time for each item.
- Volume changes – aggregate volume changes between periods over time.
- Design changes – the degree of design changes and amount of engineering work involved, and the frequency of design changes creates uncertainty and rework in manufacturing.

According to Jina et al. [2] these four types of turbulence will have a far greater impact on companies with lower manufacturing volumes than the typical lean manufacturers because the aggregated volumes in typical lean manufacturers have a beneficial dampening effect. The turbulence in HV/LV manufacturing will vary from medium to high levels. Many HV/LV manufacturers have a dominant flow in their job shops [5], and might experience less turbulence compared to the most volatile cases.

Most HV/LV manufacturing systems do not only include jobbing, but also batch and flow manufacturing processes for components with higher volumes [7]. HV/LV manufacturers with a share of flow manufacturing processes will probably experience reduced levels of turbulence. Product features will have a large impact on turbulence. HV/LV products will vary in innovativeness and complexity [8], and can range from purely customised designs to standard designs that are kept "in stock" [9]. Standard MTO designs, with moderate complexity and innovation, can reduce turbulence to a medium level.

3.3   Modified VSM Design Solutions

The review of relevant case studies highlights several challenges of applying general VSM principles related to level of turbulence. In low turbulence environments, most principles seem to be easily applicable, including product family, takt time, continuous flow, pacemaker and levelling due to low variability. More challenges occur in the higher levels of turbulence.

For instance, determining a product family is a major challenge when products are produced in low volumes, high mix, are combined with customization, include multiple branches that merges and there are limited similarities between products or projects [10–13]. Due to high variety and low volumes and constantly changing projects, the traditional definition of product families may not be applicable [14, 15]. Moreover, the production of a high mix of custom and standard products, that require a lot of different parts and materials, may impose major challenges for synchronizing flows [13, 16]. Also, in situations where customer influences products that are in production, there is limited applicability of Kanban and supermarkets [15].

In order to deal with major challenges and design a lean future state, several of the investigated case studies propose modified VSM solutions. These are listed in Table 1.

The few VSM case studies that propose future state maps in high turbulence environments seem to select "sheltered islands" in the manufacturing system that are separated from more unstable and varying value streams. Such units are typically producing components (such as motors or valves) that are used across many projects, and have sufficient volumes to utilise more flow-oriented manufacturing processes. They tend to have a dominant flow and a turbulence levels that make VSM more applicable. In high turbulence environments where no dominant flow or less turbulent production units can be identified, the applicability of VSM is limited.

VSM design principles, either in a standard or modified form, becomes more applicable as turbulence in schedule, mix, volume, and design decreases. The level of turbulence is partly determined by the product features that are offered. Product features is a strategic decisions, and there can be very good reasons, such as high margins, to position the offerings in the purely customised segment. In such situations, the manufacturer will experience high turbulence and VSM becomes less applicable. The level of turbulence is also determined by the ways the order fulfilment process has been arranged and managed. By predefining the product solution space and automate some of the engineering design processes associated with the specification of a product, turbulence is reduced.

Table 1. Modified solutions of investigated cases for low, medium and high turbulence levels

Principle	Turb. level	Proposed solutions
Product family	Low	Identify and map critical path including insertion points for other branches and shared resources [17]
	Medium	Make families of several products that have moderate differences in routings and cycle times [10, 11, 13, 16, 18, 19]
	High	Make families of similar projects [14] Separate repetitive and handicraft projects in two families [15]
Takt time	Medium	Use takt rate (pcs/day) when variation is high [10] Establish a set of takt modes to meet demand fluctuations [11] Apply the takt time concept to the production unit as a whole and not to each individual operation [19]
	High	A takt time is possible to implement for runners parts with high, stable demand [15]
Continuous flow	Low	Synchronisation between critical path and other branches through supermarkets and pull [17]
	Medium	Customised and standard products are produced in the same value stream [10, 11, 13] Customised products are only released for production when all material and engineering information is available [13] Connect resources that are shared by several families into the flow through sequenced FIFO [11]
	High	Flow runners parts in focused cells with processes that are temporarily dedicated for a given duration, produce repeaters and strangers in less frequent batches within cells, in flexible job shops, or contract out to suppliers [2] Assemble runners in lots and intersperse them with repeaters and strangers [2]
Pull system	Medium	Customised products are produced by customer order (directly to shipping) and standard products are produced to a finished goods super market [13] CONWIP is applied on the production unit as a whole [13, 19] Runners and medium volume repeaters are pulled by Kanban, low volume repeaters and strangers are controlled by sequential FIFO [16]
	High	Fast MRP with ability to monitor schedule changes and their impact on lower level demand [2] Use Kanban for parts with reasonably stable demand [2, 15] A central supermarket and picking zone are established to provide parts to the assembly department [15]
Pacemaker	Low	A pacemaker is implemented at the bottleneck in the value stream [20]
	Medium	The whole production unit is considered as a pacemaker [10] A pacemaker is located after the CODP [13] or at the bottleneck [12]
Levelling	Low	Work load and product mix is determined by the capacity and minimum lot size at the bottleneck [20]
	Medium	Daily production target defined by takt rate; mix levelling at family level only; buffering of runners as finished goods to deal with demand variability; variable lead-times quoted to customers provides additional buffering [10]
	High	Order sequencing with lead time and work content smoothing objectives [2] Outsource to external suppliers if needed. Split customer orders into smaller production orders, release equal time increments of work [14] Customer orders are split into smaller production orders (pitches) and scheduled to satisfy just-in-time delivery to the building site [15]

Table 2. A flow design framework for HV/LV environments

Category	Design principles
Product family	Make a family of several products with similar routings and cycle times. Map the critical path in the product structure, but also include insertion points for other branches and for shared resources
	If turbulence is high, routings and cycle time can vary wildly. Make broad families of projects with some similarities in demand, geometry, level of customisation etc.
Takt time	Apply takt time as = effective working time/sum of demand of all products in the family during that time. Establish a set of takt modes to meet demand fluctuations
	If turbulence is high, takt time does not make sense to control pace in daily production. Use a takt rate (pcs/day or pcs/week) that is revised monthly
Continuous flow	Produce customised and standard products in the same value stream and control the flow through FIFO lanes. Only release customised products for production when all material and engineering information is available. Connect shared resources and other branches into the flow through sequenced FIFO
	If turbulence is high, schedule changes and design changes happens, and numerous routings and cycle times are possible. Keep all products in the same value stream, or establish value streams based on broad project families in order create a "quasi-continuous" flow and a reduction of disturbances. If no takt is feasible, control the flow through CONWIP
Pull system	Produce customised products to customer order (directly to shipping) and pull standard products to a finished goods supermarket. Parts that are runners and medium volume repeaters are pulled into the main flow by Kanban, control low volume repeaters and strangers by sequential FIFO lanes
	If turbulence is high, the applicability of Kanban and supermarkets is limited to some standard runners parts
Pacemaker	The pacemaker has a backlog of productions orders, and release them in a takt to control the pace of the value stream. With custom products and job shops, the pacemaker often needs to be upstream. Locate a pacemaker after the CODP and/or at the bottleneck
	If turbulence is high, no single pacemaker can be identified. Use the whole value stream as a pacemaker
Levelling	Define daily production target by takt time, level mix at family level only, and use buffer of runners as finished goods to deal with demand variability. Use variable lead-times quoted to customers provides additional buffering.
	If turbulence is high, try to cope with schedule changes, design changes, and demand fluctuations trough order sequencing with lead time and work content smoothing objectives. Ramp up capacity if needed. Extreme load peaks are outsourced to external suppliers

4 A Flow Design Framework for HV/LV Manufacturing

Based upon the review of modified VSM solutions identified in literature, a framework for HV/LV manufacturing settings is proposed, see Table 2. The review reveals that higher level of turbulence in HV/LV manufacturing makes the general lean principles more difficult to apply.

The framework includes suggestions for both high and medium turbulence settings, since HV/LV manufacturing companies may represent both turbulence levels.

5 Conclusion

This paper analyses cases where VSM is applied in manufacturing environments that are relevant for HV/LV. The cases are classified according to turbulence level. A framework for flow design in HV/LV manufacturing is proposed. The review shows that the standard VSM design principles are easily applicable in low turbulence settings, and that modified versions of VSM are less problematic in medium turbulence environments compared to high turbulence environments.

The major contribution includes an overview of existing modified VSM design principles for HV/LV settings. Detailed insights to modified solutions for different turbulence levels are provided. The framework of modified VSM design principles may serve as a starting point for the development of practical guidelines in HV/LV environments. Manufacturers, especially with medium turbulence, may use the framework to establish flow. Manufacturers in highly turbulent environments should seek to reduce the level of turbulence to ensure efficient application of the modified VSM design principles.

The framework should be further refined by testing modified design principles in one or several case companies representing environments of different turbulence levels.

Acknowledgements. This research is supported by the Research Council of Norway through the research projects EFFEKT and Manufacturing Network 4.0.

References

1. Papadopoulou, T., Özbayrak, M.: Leanness: experiences from the journey to date. J. Manufact. Technol. Manag. **16**(7), 784–807 (2005)
2. Jina, J., Bhattacharya, A.K., Walton, A.D.: Applying lean principles for high product variety and low volumes: some issues and propositions. Logistics Inf. Manag. **10**(1), 5–13 (1997)
3. Rivera, L., Chen, F.F.: Measuring the impact of lean tools on the cost-time investment of a product using cost-time profiles. Robot. Comput.-Integr. Manufact. **23**(6), 684–689 (2007)
4. Rother, M., Shook, J.: Learning to See: Value Stream Mapping to Add Value and Eliminate Muda. Lean Enterprise Institute (2003)
5. Portioli-Staudacher, A., Tantardini, M.: A lean-based ORR system for non-repetitive manufacturing. Int. J. Prod. Res. **50**(12), 3257–3273 (2012)

6. Hines, P., Holweg, M., Rich, N.: Learning to evolve: a review of contemporary lean thinking. Int. J. Oper. Prod. Manag. **24**(10), 994–1011 (2004)
7. Hicks, C., McGovern, T., Earl, C.F.: A typology of UK engineer-to-order companies. Int. J. Logistics **4**(1), 43–56 (2001)
8. Cigolini, R., Pero, M., Sianesi, A.: When ETO companies design the supply chain during new product development process. Int. J. Eng. Sci. Technol. **6**(3), 30–41 (2014)
9. Wikner, J., Rudberg, M.: Integrating production and engineering perspectives on the customer order decoupling point. Int. J. Oper. Prod. Manag. **25**(7), 623–641 (2005)
10. Lander, E., Liker, J.K.: The Toyota production system and art: making highly customized and creative products the Toyota way. Int. J. Prod. Res. **45**(16), 3681–3698 (2007)
11. Duggan, K.J.: Creating Mixed Model Value Streams: Practical Lean Techniques for Building to Demand. Taylor & Francis, Boca Raton (2013). XX, 238 s. 12
12. Stamm, M., Neitzert, T.: Value Stream Mapping (VSM) in a Manufacture-To-Order Small and Medium Enterprise (2008)
13. McDonald, T., Van Aken, E.M., Rentes, A.F.: Utilising simulation to enhance value stream mapping: a manufacturing case application. Int. J. Logistics **5**(2), 213–232 (2002)
14. Matt, D.: Adaptation of the value stream mapping approach to the design of lean engineer-to-order production systems: a case study. J. Manufact. Technol. Manag. **25**(3), 334–350 (2014)
15. Matt, D.T., Rauch, E.: Implementing lean in engineer-to-order manufacturing: experiences from. In: Handbook of Research on Design and Management of Lean Production Systems (2014)
16. Horbal, R., Kagan, R., Koch, T.: Implementing lean manufacturing in high-mix production environment. In: Koch, T. (ed.) APMS 2006. ITIFIP, vol. 257, pp. 257–267. Springer, Heidelberg (2008). doi:10.1007/978-0-387-77249-3_27
17. Braglia, M., Carmignani, G., Zammori, F.: A new value stream mapping approach for complex production systems. Int. J. Prod. Res. **44**(18–19), 3929–3952 (2006)
18. Bertolini, M., Romagnoli, G.: Lean manufacturing in the valve pre-assembly area of a bottling lines production plant: an Italian case study. In: Proceedings of 2013 International Conference in Industrial Engineering and Systems Management (2013)
19. Bokhorst, J.A., Slomp, J.: Lean production control at a high-variety. Low-Volume Parts Manufacturer. Interfaces **40**(4), 303–312 (2010)
20. Serrano, I., Castro, R., Goienetxea, A.: Pacemaker, bottleneck and order decoupling point in lean production systems. Int. J. Ind. Eng. Theor. Appl. Pract. **16**(4), 293–304 (2009)

Prescriptive Cost Management for Lean Supply Chains:

Extending Inter-Organizational Cost Management Through Ratio Project Planning

Paulo Afonso[1(✉)] and João Leite[2]

[1] University of Minho, Guimarães, Portugal
psafonso@dps.uminho.pt
[2] Bosch Automotive Products (Suzhou), Suzhou, China
joao.leite@cn.bosch.com

Abstract. Nowadays, companies belonging to global supply chains should rely on the co-operation from suppliers to achieve their business objectives and the required profit levels. Inter-organizational Cost Management (IOCM) means coordinated activities to control and reduce global supply chain costs, which are promoted by buyers, suppliers or both. Ratio Project Planning (RPP) is closely related to IOCM and to Kaizen Costing (KC) and it can be viewed as an extension and a complement of these practices which have a prescriptive nature being focused on "what should we do?" instead on "what has happened?" or "what could have happen?". This research project was developed in Bosch Car Multimedia located at Braga, Portugal, a world-class manufacturer of electronic products, car radios and car navigation systems. This enterprise has many years of experience on reduction costs, particularly, using RPP.

Keywords: Target costing · Kaizen costing · Inter-Organizational Cost Management · Ratio planning project · Cutting-costs

1 Introduction

Nowadays, production and business strategies oriented only to the optimization of internal resources are inadequate, making it necessary to create links between internal processes, suppliers and customers in a (global) value chain perspective [1]. The pressure created by global competition forces companies to reduce costs from the design phase until the end of the product life cycle [2]. Thus, organizations have sought to improve their skills regarding a better management of supply chain overall costs or to understand the cost-to-serve in different contexts (e.g. business channels, specific clients). Simultaneously, there has been a concern and a real need to involve business partners earlier and more deeply in these processes.

The Japanese automotive industry has been improving and refining such cost management processes for several decades in the second half of the twentieth century [3]. Namely, through Target Costing (TC), Kaizen Costing (KC) and Inter-Organizational Cost Management (IOCM). On one hand, TC is applied in the development phase of a

© IFIP International Federation for Information Processing 2016
Published by Springer International Publishing AG 2016. All Rights Reserved
I. Nääs et al. (Eds.): APMS 2016, IFIP AICT 488, pp. 943–951, 2016.
DOI: 10.1007/978-3-319-51133-7_111

new product and Kaizen Costing (KC) in the production phase. On the other hand, IOCM is the extension of cost reduction systems and respective tools to the supply chain, i.e. involving suppliers [4].

Furthermore, in markets characterized by a high demand of quality, usability and functionality for their products along with the fierce competition, cost control and cost reduction practices need to evolve from the traditional descriptive approach, which uses business intelligence and data mining to ask: "What has happened?" or predictive, which uses statistical models and forecasts to ask: "What could happen?" to a more prescriptive logic, which uses optimization and simulation to ask: "What should we do?".

This research focused on cost reduction systems applied by companies in a lean supply chain context where companies are challenged to improve continuously the way they design, develop, produce and deliver their products and services. More specifically, it analyses and discusses a cost reduction approach developed and applied worldwide in Bosch plants. The research field is an important Bosch Car Multimedia plant located at Braga, Portugal, where car radios, electronic products and sophisticated car navigation systems are manufactured. This enterprise has many years of experience on reduction costs and particularly, using the Ratio Project Planning (RPP) methodology. Inter-Organizational Kaizen Costing activities are those that most closely match the RPP methodology. Often, an RPP involves suppliers and it is implemented only after the approval of the client because it must be a joint decision of Bosch and its clients. Therefore, the RPP is a cost management methodology that goes through the entire supply chain.

Through the analysis of this case, this work aimed to study and discuss the feasibility an importance of RPP in the context of IOCM and KC practices which contribute decisively to sustainable lean supply chains. The context, the reasons and the implications of the various aspects that separate and approximate theory and practice on supply chain cost management can be highlighted through this case. A particular importance to RPP benefits and limitations as well as challenges is given in this paper.

2   Inter-Organizational Cost Management (IOCM)

In global supply chain, companies need to involve business partners to explore properly cost reduction opportunities [5]. The increasing complexity of products, the reduction of the life cycle of products, the increasing complexity of the business and production processes, the greater (need for) interconnection between buyers and suppliers, make the success of each company be strongly dependent on efficient relationship with suppliers [5]. That is, it is necessary to have implemented successfully, in some degree, any kind of Inter-Organizational Cost Management Practices (IOCM). Furthermore, for these practices be effective and sustainable, each company must act in order to also benefit the other companies involved (i.e., clients and suppliers) namely, sharing the benefits achieved through cost reduction initiatives, i.e. building true win-win strategies [4].

IOCM should be included into the broader concept of Total Cost Management (TCM) which is characterized by the application of cost management practices to all stages of a product's life cycle, asking for the collaboration of all company employees and departments as well as business partners in the upstream (i.e. suppliers) and downstream (i.e. customers) supply chain. The TCM includes Target Costing (TC), Kaizen Costing (KC) and Inter-Organizational Cost Management (IOCM) [6, 7].

Target Costing (TC) is applied to the development phase of a new product and is focused on not exceed the maximum allowable cost which is computed considering the product's target price that the market accepts and the margin that the company intends to achieve for that product which should be aligned with the long term strategic planning of the company [8, 9]. Furthermore, Kaizen Costing (KC) is applied later in the production phase, being an extension to the production of the cost management activities performed using TC in the development phase. The Japanese term "kaizen" refers to cumulative improvements that result from repetitive activities rather than by improving by innovation. Improvements based on technological innovations are usually made in the development phase of a product's life cycle. Nevertheless, being applied to the production process, KC can result in cost reductions that affect multiple products over several years. The impact of KC will be leveraged if all supply chain elements participate in such projects of cost reduction. In fact, due to the outsourcing of many activities and processes through the supply chain (i.e. to the upstream or suppliers), the knowledge on the process and the materials is, nowadays, increasingly concentrated in the suppliers.

The Value Engineering (VE) and Value Analysis (VA) tools are characteristics of TC and KC, respectively. They are used to find ways to reduce the cost of the product in order to not exceed the target cost previously defined accordingly to the conditions of the market (i.e. target price) and of the business plan (i.e. target margin). This process involves the supplier to confirm the cost of purchased components and the production and assembling costs of the buyer [2]. Companies use several tools to attain the maximum allowable cost or target cost [9–11]. For example, Design for Manufacturing and Assembly (DFMA) that is focused on reducing costs by turn products easier to manufacture or assemble, maintaining its quality and functionality - i.e., lowering costs during the production and assembling stages in the buyer's plant. On the other hand, quality function deployment (QFD) proportionate a structured approach aimed at ensuring that the development process does not compromise customer requirements.

Inter-Organizational Cost Management (IOCM) is the extension of the cost reduction activities and respective tools to the supply chain [4]. The IOCM is described as a structured approach to coordinate cost management activities which can be generated or lead by buyers or suppliers or even jointly [4]. To put IOCM fully in practice, all companies in the network have to adopt lean buyer-supplier relationships dedicated to produce low-cost products with a high level of functionality and good quality that can meet the needs of the clients or the market. The use of IOCM to coordinate cost reduction projects in supply chains may be useful in three different ways. Firstly, it can contribute to reduce production costs. Secondly, it can help to find new and different ways to develop products at lower costs. And finally, it may be useful to identify ways to increase the efficiency of the customer-supplier interface.

3 Research Methodology and Case Study

The adopted research methodology was the case study. It is a research strategy whose results can be transferable to theory (not generalized to a population). In a case study, findings can be used to formulate theoretical propositions [12]. According to [12], the construction of a case study has to ensure a logical sequence and connection among the empirical data, the initial questions of the research work and the findings. In this work, several sources of data were used namely, company documentation, records of implemented RPP and direct observation of the methodology and its application.

The unit of study is the Purchasing department of a Bosch's plant located in Braga, Portugal. This plant has more than 2,000 employees and reached a turnover of 700 million USD. In 2017 it will have more than 3,000 employees and a turnover exceeding 1 billion USD. Among other products (for example, sophisticated car navigation systems) this plant produces printed circuit boards (PCB) which are applied in various products. One of the main objectives of the purchasing department is the definition of cost reduction activities. Indeed, the plant of Braga is very sensitive to the importance of reducing costs continuously. Its strategic challenges include: be cost competitive, have quality excellence, be efficient in all processes, optimize the plant, have excellent customer service and manage the supply chain efficiently.

4 Findings and Discussion

In this case study the application of the Ratio Project Planning (RPP) methodology was studied and analyzed. The findings were analyzed in the light of what is presented in the literature on IOCM and KC in order to connect theory and practice and also to extend both. The analysis of this case resulted in interesting findings considering that several similarities but also differences between the literature and the case were found.

4.1 Ratio Project Planning (RPP)

The Ratio Project Planning (RPP) is a cost reduction initiative or project aimed at making a product that is already in the production phase more profitable. Each RPP is reported in order to be achieved an aggregated view of all company's RPP. Such RPP tracking list is constantly updated and the results are entered in the quarterly business plan and contribute to the annual business plan of the company.

The RPP projects are usually justified by changes in product requirements/product design, changes in the product bill of materials, changes related to suppliers (e.g. inclusion of a new or a second supplier, change of locations), outsourcing, etc. Moreover, an RPP may also result from the application of ideas from other business units; results of market research; the introduction of a new supplier; changes in pricing strategies; updating suppliers for Request for Quotation (RFQ) and Comparison of Quotation (CoQ); existence of alternative manufacturing processes or improvement proposals/innovation; results or ideas produced in technical workshops; value analysis; benchmarking exercises; optimization of processes in the plant or in suppliers. The

Total Cost of Ownership (TCO) and Activity-Based Costing (ABC) are two important tools in RPP projects. The involvement of suppliers is of great importance. The RPP Process is presented in Fig. 1.

Figure 1 illustrates all stages of the RPP methodology from its creation to the implementation, and considering the necessary inclusion of the results into the business plan of the company. Thus, an idea that may reduce costs can be promoted externally or internally and it goes through three generic stages: (1) launching and planning, in which cost reduction opportunities that can result in a RPP are identified; (2) evaluation and approval, in which the RPP coordinator defines implementation priorities taking into account several aspects namely, the cost ratio (benefit) estimated, planning effort, requirements for the implementation, implementation date, volume planned in the context of the business unit and responsibility of the project, among others; and (3) implementation and monitoring, in which the RPP are implemented and evaluated. All changes need to be approved using an engineering change request (ECR). Engineering changes are allowed only if there is evidence of an improvement in customer satisfaction or competitiveness and/or the quality of the product.

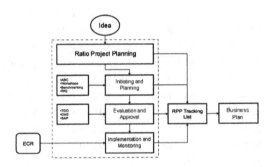

Fig. 1. The RPP process

4.2 Findings

In recent years, the Braga's plant has been diversifying its business portfolio, which led to the emergence of the Electronic Manufacturing Services (EMS) business unit. This product diversification has brought new customers who had "build-to-print" projects, in which the client is completely responsible for the product development and the manufacturing company is only responsible for producing the product just like it was designed. This situation resulted in potential new suppliers to other products.

Thus a RPP project was developed to test the possibility of inclusion of one of those new suppliers. A set of conditions were defined to determine which products would be targeted for the RPP project namely the following two, PCB with high planned purchase value (in order to magnify the impact of the RPP) and PCB that have been provided solely by one supplier. Having identified the PCB that would be the targeted for the RPP project, a series of requests for quotation were started initially with 6 PCB and 3 suppliers. The offers received showed that a supplier, hereinafter designated NewSupplier was the most competitive, with prices about 20% lower than the other competitors. Therefore, it was decided that the RPP activities would be focused on NewSupplier. It is important to notice that, for internal clients, i.e. companies belonging to the Bosch Group, there is not a fixed price for a product thus, the internal client will benefit of having a product that can be bought at lower cost. On the other hand, in the case of external clients, Bosch receives all the gains made by RPP projects. However, it is important to communicate to the customer the advantages of the changes implemented in order to get its agreement and its active participation in the implementation of the RPP. Table 1 summarizes the savings associated to the implementation of this RPP.

Table 1. Savings in USD by PCB and client of the RPP.

PCB	Client	Previous price	Price new supplier	Potential savings	Obtained savings	Total savings
0000001	Client 1	$4.262	$3.390	$0.872 (20%)	$0.062 (16%)	$174,320
0000003	Client 1	$4.189	$3.600	$0.588 (14%)	$0.749 (11%)	$61,230
0000004	Client 1	$4.058	$3.390	$0.537 (14%)	$0.118 (14%)	$448,656
0000006	Client 1	$3.577	$3.100	$0.477 (13%)	$0.019 (11%)	$42,140
0000007	Client 1	$3.294	$2.800	$0.494 (15%)	$0.043 (12%)	$31,616
0000009	Client 1	$2.025	$1.600	$0.401 (20%)	$0.401 (17%)	$87,995
0000012	Client 1	$2.219	$1.650	$0.569 (26%)	$0.569 (21%)	$66,459
0000013	Client 1	$4.210	$3.390	$0.798 (19%)	$0.798 (16%)	$32,995
0000021	Client 1	$1.475	$1.100	$0.375 (25%)	$0.375 (20%)	$33,044
0000005	Client 2	$0.487	$0.410	$0.077 (16%)	$0.062 (13%)	$61,600
0000010	Client 2	$3.893	$2.957	$0.936 (24%)	$0.749 (19%)	$74,880
0000014	Client 2	$0.606	$0.460	$0.140 (23%)	$0.118 (19%)	$51,920
0000015	Client 2	$0.194	$0.170	$0.024 (12%)	$0.019 (10%)	$25,728
0000027	Client 2	$0.404	$0.350	$0.054 (13%)	$0.043 (11%)	$12,163
0000037	Client 2	$0.214	$0.230	-$0.016 (-7%)	-$0.013 (-6%)	-$3,816
0000045	Client 2	$0.178	$0.182	-$0.004 (-2%)	-$0.003 (-2%)	-$605

This RPP allowed to find immediate opportunities to reduce costs which reached around 1.2 million USD as a result of the introduction of NewSupplier. Gains were achieved with two clients and different products (PCB) - Client 1: 978,456 USD and Client 2: 221,870 USD. In some products the savings exceeded 20% of the previous price but the final earnings were lower because the company chose to keep a second supplier which accounts for 20% of the total production volume. This potential loss can be considered as an investment to reduce supplying risk. On the other hand, in the case of Client 2, the company accepted higher prices in two products because the overall cost associated are significantly lower than in the past.

However, this RPP project and particularly the inclusion of this new supplier took a long time to be implemented. In the planning it was determined that this RPP would be completed in 25 weeks but it took 50 weeks. In other words, this project had a 25 weeks delay. This resulted in an opportunity cost and a loss of profitability for the company and for its customers. To estimate the value of the losses in this period of time, it was considered the estimated annual volume and the correspondent weekly production which was multiplied by the amount saved by PCB. The opportunity costs or cost savings that have been not achieved are presented in Table 2.

Table 2. Opportunity costs.

PCB	Annual volume	Volume for 25 weeks	Unitary savings (PCB)	Losses due to 25 weeks of delay
0000001	150,000	72,115	$0.697	$50,264
0000003	80,000	38,462	$0.471	$18,115
0000004	400,000	192,308	$0.561	$107,885
0000005	500,000	240,385	$0.062	$14,904
0000006	65,000	31,250	$0.381	$11,906
0000007	40,000	19,231	$0.395	$7,596
0000009	90,000	43,269	$0.345	$14,928
0000010	50,000	24,038	$2.930	$70,433
0000012	76,000	36,538	$0.455	$16,625
0000013	30,000	14,423	$0.660	$9,519
0000014	220,000	105,769	$0.118	$12,481
0000015	670,000	322,115	$0.019	$6,120
0000021	65,000	31,250	$0.300	$9,375
0000027	140,000	67,308	$0.043	$2,894
0000037	150,000	72,115	-$0.013	-$938
0000045	90,000	43,269	-$0.003	-$130

In this case the opportunity costs reached 351,978 USD what is a significant amount. Indeed, beyond savings obtained there are also hidden savings or opportunity costs which should also be taken into account. These lost opportunities appear frequently when many collaborators from different departments are involved in RPP projects. There is a lack of leadership in these projects what affects the good development and the effectiveness of the RPP. The inexistence of a department or specific collaborators to manage RPP projects is a relevant weakness of this methodology that deserves attention. The Bosch's plant located at Braga has a long experience with these cost reduction projects and those who are responsible for them indicated that delays are recurrent, typically when the RPP is launched internally.

5 Conclusions

Bosch has many years of experience on reduction costs and particularly, using Ratio Project Planning. Through this case study, this work aimed to study and discuss the relevance of RPP on the literature and practice. This methodology aims to achieve reduction costs in the production phase. Inter-Organizational Kaizen Costing activities are those that most closely match the RPP methodology. The case study presented here showed that the principles, concepts and cost reduction tools presented in the literature are already in some way internalized by the company and applied through the company's daily practices. However, there are important aspects that deserve to be highlighted.

Although some limitations, the methodology adopted by Bosch has been contributing to significant and substantial cost reductions. In the case presented here, the inclusion of a new supplier, they were obtained savings of more than 1.2 million USD. However, it was also clear that (recurrent) delays with the implementation of such kind of projects entail opportunity costs or lost savings; in this case, estimated in 350,000 USD. These delays are not only justified by internal operations. The fact that, generally, these activities of cost reduction ask for the involvement of both clients and suppliers imply long waiting times between the necessary iterations.

As a follow up of this work there are some research opportunities that can be suggested. On one hand, they can be developed studies to understand better other RPP projects in the company. On the other hand, the conceptualization and application of the RPP methodology can be improved. It applicability to other companies and industries can be also tested and validated. Furthermore, the comparison with other approaches and methodologies for cost reduction in supply chains is still requiring study and discussion. Particularly, KC literature needs contributions for both theory and practice. Finally, the collaboration and interaction between buyers and suppliers in supply chain cost management during the production stage also needs to be better conceptualized. In this case, the RPP methodology can be used to complement or extend IOCM-KC as it is discussed in this paper.

Acknowledgements. This work has been supported by COMPETE: POCI-01-0145-FEDER-007043 and FCT – Fundação para a Ciência e Tecnologia within the Project Scope: UID/CEC/00319/2013.

References

1. Christopher, M., Gattornab, J.: Supply chain cost management and value-based pricing. Ind. Mark. Manag. **34**, 115–121 (2005)
2. Bragg, S.M.: Cost Reduction Analysis: Tools and Strategies. Wiley, Hoboken (2010)
3. Monden, Y.: Cost Reduction Systems: Target Costing and Kaizen Costing. Productivity Press, New York (1995)
4. Cooper, R.A., Slagmulder, R.A.: Supply Chain Development for the Lean Enterprise: Interorganizational Cost Management. Productivity Press, New York (1999)
5. Micheli, G.J.L., Cagno, E., Di Giulio, A.: Reducing the total cost of supply through risk-efficiency-based supplier selection in the EPC industry. J. Purchasing Supply Manag. **15**(3), 166–177 (2009)
6. Cooper, R.A., Slagmulder, R.: Target Costing and Value Engineering. Productivity Press Inc., New York (1997)
7. Carr, C., Ng, J.: Total cost control: Nissan and its U.K. supplier partnerships. Manag. Acc. Res. **6**(4), 347–365 (1995)

8. Kato, Y.: Target costing support systems: lessons from leading Japanese companies. Manag. Acc. Res. **4**(1), 33–47 (1993)

9. Iii, A.L., Smith, W.I.: Target costing for supply chain management: criteria and selection. Ind. Manag. Data Syst. **100**(5), 210–218 (2000)

10. Weil, R.L., Maher, M.W.: Handbook of Cost Management. Wiley, Hoboken (2005)

11. Yoshikawa, T., Innes, J., Mitchell, F.: Applying functional cost analysis in a manufacturing environment. Int. J. Prod. Econ. **36**(1), 53–64 (1994)

12. Yin, R.K.: Case Study Research: Design and Methods. SAGE Publications, Thousand Oaks (2003)

Commercial Vehicle Production Flexibility Factors

Luis de Oliveira Nascimento[1], Jorge Muniz Jr.[1(✉)],
and Henrique Martins Rocha[2]

[1] Paulista State University, Guaratinguetá, Brazil
jorge86056@gmail.com
[2] Rio de Janeiro State University, Resende, Brazil
prof.henrique_rocha@yahoo.com.br

Abstract. In the competitive commercial vehicles market, new products are developed continuously in order to attend specific demands and surplus complexity is incorporated gradually to the manufacturing assembly plants. In this context, it is mandatory that the manufacturers enable a high flexibility production level to attend specific demands with low costs and agility. This paper aims to analyze factors that influence the flexibility of commercial vehicles production and to propose a prioritization model for industrial productivity enablement projects, in order to improve the production flexibility in a trucks and buses assembly plant. Managers and technical staff of a commercial vehicles production plant (88 professionals) were interviewed and data analyzed by Incomplete Pairwise Comparison (IPC), a multicriteria decision method. Results lead the company to implement lean office projects, which created the condition to reduce 30% in the firm horizon of order placement, reducing the time-to-market and leading customer to have a higher product value-added perception, levering company's service level and competitiveness.

Keywords: Flexibility · Lean · Agility · Decision making

1 Introduction

This work aims to analyze factors influencing the flexibility of the production of commercial vehicles and propose a prioritization model for industrial productivity enablement projects. The research was performed in a truck & bus manufacturing plant located in Brazil, which produces vehicles in high-volume/high variety operation under a production concept model in which the suppliers interact directly on the final product assembly line, sharing physical space, responsibilities, and standard control [1].

According to Sheffi [2], organizations are threatened by short product cycles and subglobal supply chains, putting them under pressure to develop a greater capacity to confront risk with some resilience.

© IFIP International Federation for Information Processing 2016
Published by Springer International Publishing AG 2016. All Rights Reserved
I. Nääs et al. (Eds.): APMS 2016, IFIP AICT 488, pp. 952–958, 2016.
DOI: 10.1007/978-3-319-51133-7_112

In this context, the automotive industry is offering wide range of products, but new models generally require new parts, which in turn, are incorporated and managed in the supply chain, along with parts of vehicles already underway.

In the commercial vehicle sector, i.e.: trucks and buses, the scenario is even more challenging: such market is characterized by high-volume production and high variety, delivering vehicles customized for specific applications, levering the manufacturing operation complexity up to uncontrollable levels.

Naga and Kodali [3] state that the complexity of automotive industry models corresponds to the variety in which the production system is based on the quantity of different platforms, bodies and models produced in their assembly lines. By the other side, complexity of components is caused by the existence of optional features offered to customers, but mainly the impact of product development and supply chain boundary conditions, i.e., one of the factor that causes complexity in carmakers' manufacturing and supply chain systems is the number of pieces combinations and its management.

Modrak et al. [4] correlate the growth of complexity with performance decrease. Their study indicates that larger variety of products in an automotive plant, higher the effort to deliver high-quality products at the desired time and at low cost.

Slack [5] suggests flexibility as solution for demands of quick responses and product variety in a fierce competition scenario, allowing high-performance manufacturing, with reliability, speed, and low costs. Flexibility results in better design and products developed in competitive contexts with high levels of uncertainty [6].

For those involved on tight schedules, consumer preference constant changes, and high uncertainty, manufacturing flexibility is not only desirable, but also a requirement for organizational survival [7–10].

Therefore, a question that emerges in this context is: How to evaluate the choice of relevant projects to improve flexibility in the production of commercial vehicles? How to prioritize these improvement projects forward the interests of different areas? There is a need for development of a model to rank and prioritize productivity improvement projects, considering lean thinking, agility, and mass customization, to support company's managerial decisions.

The next paper sections are as follows: Section "Theoretical Background" comprises the fundamentals of Lean production & Lean administration, Agility, Flexibility, and Mass Customization; Section "Procedures and Techniques" presents the research methodology; Section "Results and discussion" highlights the research results and findings. Finally, at the Section "Conclusions and Remarks", findings are assessed and discussed, while proposals for additional researches are made.

2 Theoretical Background

The concepts of Lean Thinking, Flexibility, Agility, and Mass Customization are discussed in this topic, while some related literature is also referenced.

Holweg [11] states that the Lean Thinking changed the paradigms of mass production, helped to change the relationship between the automobile industry productivity and quality and created a new way of thinking about operations, focused on waste source detection and elimination.

Intriguingly, Baines et al. [12] claim that Toyota's Lean manufacturing system is actually an extension of their product development philosophy and not the reverse, but most western manufacturers are focusing their Lean initiatives at operations with few attempts to adopt Lean in design-related activities, what could explain why all too often lean projects add little or no value, even though similar methods work very well at Toyota. Qudrat-Ullah et al. [13] stated that the Lean product development process can successfully be applied to improve the operations of a high variable-low volume product mix business.

Gupta and Buzacott [14] define flexibility as the property to be capable of responding or conforming to changing or new situations. Needs that lead to flexibility are, as per Kara and Kayis [15], related to the market (demand variability, short life cycle of products and technologies, great product variety, increased customization, and reduced delivery times) and/or related to the manufacture process (uncertainties in relation to machines and material in processes shortfalls, change in the delivery time of raw materials, and manpower variations).

Agarwal et al. [16] define agility as the ability of companies to cope with the uncertainties of the market and deliver goods and services with high level of service, concept which is directly related to flexibility and process speed.

Boyton et al. [17] define Mass Customization (MC) as the capacity to produce product variety rapidly and inexpensively, in direct contradiction of the assumption that cost and variety are tradeoffs. MC refers to fast, low cost, and varied production companies, fulfilling a large proportion of consumers through a large variety of products and innovations. As a result, organizations increase process efficiencies in clearly conditions of stable process change.

The concept of mass customization can be approached as a development strategy and production boosted primarily by sales teams and marketing that are in contact with the demands of customized products, bringing and discussing the information for development teams and production enterprises. MC goal is to create individually customized products, with mass production volumes, costs and competitive efficiencies [18].

3   Procedures and Techniques

The methodology used to carry out the present research went through the steps listed below, along an eight-month period (Jul/2015-Mar/2016):

1. Literature analysis, encompassing the conceptual basis of Lean Thinking, Lean Manufacturing, Lean Administration/Lean Office, Flexibility, Agility, and Mass Customization;
2. Research planning and managerial granting, i.e., data collection processes; identification of people to be interviewed, questionnaire development, research proposal submission, negotiation and approval; data analysis and results screening, etc.

3. Semistructured interviews with selected executive managers/directors involved to Operations (Production & Logistics, Quality, Finance, Information Technology, and Sales, Marketing & After-sales), having the following open-ended questions as an interview basis (C1 questionnaire): How does the company materials' planning process work?: Is a reduction in production planning horizon feasible? Which are the opportunities and impacts? Would it impact flexibility? Would it cause any impact on costs?: Is a reduction in purchase order planning horizon feasible? Which are the opportunities and impacts? Would it impact flexibility? Would it cause any impact on costs?: What would be the impact to reduce waste and make the supply chain lean?.

4. Interview content compilation, through a content analysis process, in order to get the understanding about the complexity/flexibility managerial perceptions and decisions, and also to identify elements that affect vehicles production flexibility, which were, then, classified as "dimensions" or "factors";

5. Those elements and their classification were used to develop a closed-ended questionnaire (C2 questionnaire), purposed to validate such elements and to identify correlations among them. This step aims to get a project prioritization matrix to be used by the studied company to establish an implementation plan for production flexibility improvement high-impact projects.

The questions were base on level of importance pair comparisons between elements: each element was compared with each other and respondents would rate them in a 1–9 scale, being: (1) same importance; (3) low importance; (5) mid importance; (7) high importance; and (9) extreme importance;

1. The electronic questionnaire/spreadsheet was presented to the senior executives and, after that, deployed to their staff members, a total of 158 people. 88 responses (55.7%) were received: one VP, six executive managers, ten managers, 20 supervisors, one specialist, one coordinator, and 49 technical staff/engineers;

2. Data was analyzed to rank elements based on respondent perception through Incomplete Pairwise Comparison (IPC), a variation of the Analytic Hierarchy Process (AHP), multicriteria decision method, which allows the comparison of pairs of factors and sort them by relevance, allowing decision-making based on responses that keep the accuracy of the results [19]; and

3. Results from the IPC step were used to define the scope of planning and execution of the suggested projects for flexibility alternatives as a pilot project. The execution of such project would provide a feedback in regards to production flexibility variance through lean thinking.

4 Results and Discussion

Out of the C1 questionnaire, the following elements that affect vehicles production flexibility were identified (Fig. 1):

- Factors: Lean Manufacturing (32.6%), Agility (27.2%), Mass Customization (25.3%), and Lean Office (14.8%).

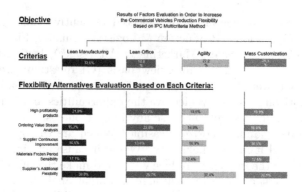

Fig. 1. Out of the C1 questionnaire

- Manufacturing flexibility: supplier's additional flexibility (FAS), materials frozen sensitivity analysis (ASF) and supplier continuous improvement (MCF).
- Materials ordering flexibility: ordering value stream analysis (VSM) and high-profitability products (PAL).

Those elements were used to feed the C2 questionnaire and, then, applied, as described in the previous section. For further detailing, Nascimentos's [20] dissertation shall be accessed.

From such analysis, the following elements were selected/validated: FAS (31.4%), PAL (20.2%), VSM (16.5%), MCF (16.2%), and ASF (15.7%). However, in regards to project prioritization, the sequence and level of agreement were different: MCF (29%), VSM (27%), FAS (23%), ASF (20%), and PAL (1%). Breaking them down, the following lean thinking projects were proposed and submitted for appraisal: (1) Make Product Development Faster; (2) Reduce Ordering Lead Time; and (3) Increase Administrative Service Level.

As it can be seen, project implementation priority is related to administrative/managerial activities, therefore, related to lean office (a.k.a. lean administration). Upon discussion, it was detected that even though the lean office factor had lower priority when compared with lean manufacturing, agility, and mass customization, such response conflicts with proposed projects' prioritization. Lean office low priority can be understood by the fact that the major focus has, so far, been given to increase value-added value in production environment.

Based on that assumption, the choice to pursue an implementation based on the research's results was the lean office application project, contained in the analysis of alternative applications of value stream. The rationale to such choice was: (1) several lean production projects were/are developed in the studied company since 2008: therefore, it is a known subject and results have proved their effectiveness. Besides that, the principles of agility are also present in the organization by focusing service tailored to customer needs, the pursuit of satisfaction in specific niches, resulting in time reduction activities, mainly in its supply chain. The mass customization was recently implemented in product development; and (2) the studied company had never tried to analyze/implement lean office techniques.

Implementation counted with the support of Shingijutsu Global Consulting (SGC), a global company specializing in performance increase efficiency in manufacturing, logistics and processes. SGC consultants attended to three kaizen events focused on logistics, production, and administrative processes, in which former performance jeopardizing the company competitiveness.

The results obtained with the implementation of the mapped improvements, discussed with the team and moderated by SGC consultants created the conditions to reduce 30% the firm horizon of order placement, reducing the time-to-market and leading customer to have a higher product value-added perception, levering company's service level and competitiveness.

5 Final Considerations

The research highlighted the importance of lean manufacturing factors, speed, mass customization, and lean office to improve the flexibility. It also established a model for productivity enablement projects ratting and prioritization, based on managers and technical staff perception.

Even though the company started lean implementation in 2008, it was, since then, focused on manufacturing activities. The initiation of lean office approach has proven to be able to unveil hidden waste-avoidance opportunities, uplifting performance in time-to-market, reducing overall manufacturing throughput time and planning horizon, which levered production flexibility.

Even though results are preliminary (complete implementation is still ongoing), favorable impacts are already perceived by senior managers. Future researches are to monitor results from now on and, upon adhering to actual trend, should be applied to other products and plants.

Acknowledgement. The authors thank for efforts referees during the revision process and comments. Also, we thanks the Brazilian National Research Council (CNPq), which supported this study with the Productivity Grants (Proc. 309028/2015-9).

References

1. Maitan Filho, P.L., Simoes, J.M.: Estruturas Organizacionais e Indústria Automobilística: Os Desafios e Contradições de um Setor em Transformações. Revista Uniabeu **8**(18), 114–128 (2015)
2. Sheffi, Y.: Building a Resilient Supply Chain. Harvard Bus. Rev. 1–4 (2005)
3. Jasti, N.V.K., Kodali, R.: An empirical study for implementation of lean principles in Indian manufacturing industry. Benchmarking: Int. J. **23**(1), 183–207 (2016)
4. Modrak, V., Marton, D., Bednar, S.: The influence of mass customization strategy on configuration complexity of assembly systems. Procedia CIRP **33**, 539–544 (2015)

5. Slack, N.: The flexibility of manufacturing systems. Int. J. Oper. Prod. Manag. **25**(12), 1190–1200 (2005)

6. MacCormack, A., Verganti, R., Iansiti, M.: Developing products on internet time: the anatomy of a flexible development process. Manag. Sci. **47**(1), 133–150 (2001)

7. Baykasoglu, A., Ozbakir, L.: Analysing the effect of flexibility on manufacturing systems performance. J. Manuf. Technol. Manag. **19**(2), 172–193 (2008)

8. Boyle, T.A.: Towards best management practices for implementing manufacturing flexibility. J. Manuf. Technol. Manag. **17**(1), 6–21 (2006)

9. Chang, S.C., Lin, R.J., Chang, F.J., Chen, R.H.: Achieving manufacturing flexibility through entrepreneurial orientation. Industr. Manag. Data Syst. **107**(7), 997–1017 (2007)

10. Wahab, M., Wu, D., Lee, C.G.: A generic approach to measuring the machine flexibility of manufacturing systems. Eur. J. Oper. Res. **186**(1), 137–149 (2008)

11. Holweg, M.: The genealogy of lean production. J. Oper. Manag. **25**(2), 420–437 (2007)

12. Baines, T., Lightfoot, H., Williams, G.M., Greenough, R.: State-of-the-art in lean design engineering: a literature review on white collar lean. Proc. Inst. Mech. Eng., Part B: J. Eng. Manuf. **220**(9), 1539–1547 (2006)

13. Qudrat-Ullah, H., Seong, B.S., Mills, B.L.: Improving high variable-low volume operations: an exploration into the lean product development. Int. J. Technol. Manag. **57**(1/2/3), 49–70 (2012)

14. Gupta, D., Buzacott, J.A.: A framework for understanding flexibility of manufacturing systems. J. Manuf. Syst. **8**(2), 89–97 (1989)

15. Kara, S., Kayis, B.: Manufacturing flexibility and variability: an overview. J. Manuf. Technol. Manag. **15**(6), 466–478 (2004)

16. Agarwal, A., Shankar, R., Tiwari, M.: Modeling the metrics of lean, agile and leagile supply chain: an ANP-based approach. Eur. J. Oper. Res. **173**(1), 211–225 (2006)

17. Boynton, A.C., Victor, B., Pine II, B.J.: New competitive strategies: challenges to organizations and information technology. IBM Syst. J. **32**(1), 40 (1993)

18. Smith, S., Smith, G.C., Jiao, R., Chu, C.H.: Mass customization in the product life cycle. J. Intell. Manuf. **24**(5), 877–885 (2013)

19. Harker, P.T.: Incomplete pairwise comparisons in the analytic hierarchy process. Math. Model. **9**(11), 837–848 (1987)

20. Nascimento, L.O.: Fatores que Influenciam a Flexibilidade da Produção de Veículos Comerciais (2016)

Author Index

Printed in the United States
By Bookmasters